LECTURES
on the
PHILOSOPHY
of
RELIGION

HEGEL LECTURES: SELECTED TEXTS
English Editor: Peter C. Hodgson

Lectures on Natural Law and Political Science
Edited by the staff of the Hegel Archives, Bochum, with an introduction by Otto Pöggeler. Translated by Z. A. Pelczynski and J. M. Stewart.

Lectures on the Philosophy of Art
Edited by A. Gethmann-Siefert. Translated by Martin Donougho.

Lectures on the Philosophy of Religion
Edited by Walter Jaeschke. English edition edited by Peter C. Hodgson; translated by R. F. Brown, P. C. Hodgson, and J. M. Stewart.

   Volume 1. *Introduction* and *The Concept of Religion*
   Volume 2. *Determinate Religion*
   Volume 3. *The Consummate Religion*

Lectures on the History of Philosophy
Edited by P. Garniron and W. Jaeschke. Translated by Robert F. Brown and J. M. Stewart.

   Volume 1. *Introduction* and *Oriental Philosophy*
   Volume 2. *Greek Philosophy I: Thales to the Cynics*
   Volume 3. *Greek Philosophy II: Plato to Proclus*
   Volume 4. *Medieval and Modern Philosophy*

Lectures on Logic
Edited by H.-C. Lucas and U. Rameil. Translated by Theodore Geraets and H. S. Harris.

GEORG WILHELM FRIEDRICH HEGEL

LECTURES ON THE PHILOSOPHY OF RELIGION

VOLUME II

DETERMINATE RELIGION

Edited by
PETER C. HODGSON

Translated by
R. F. BROWN, P. C. HODGSON, and J. M. STEWART
with the assistance of
H. S. HARRIS

UNIVERSITY OF CALIFORNIA PRESS
Berkeley, Los Angeles, London

University of California Press
Berkeley and Los Angeles, California

University of California Press, Ltd.
London, England

This edition is the result of collaborative work on the part of Ricardo
Ferrara (Conicet, Argentina), Peter C. Hodgson (Vanderbilt University,
Nashville, Tennessee), and Walter Jaeschke (Ruhr-Universität, Bochum),
who have shared equally in the preparation of the text. The German
text on which this translation is based is copyrighted © 1985 by Felix
Meiner Verlag GmbH, Hamburg. A German edition, edited by Walter
Jaeschke, and a Spanish edition, edited by Ricardo Ferrara, are appearing
concurrently with the English edition.

The English edition has been prepared with financial support from the
Program for Translations of the National Endowment for the
Humanities, the Fritz Thyssen Stiftung of Cologne, and the Vanderbilt
University Research Council. Appreciation is gratefully expressed for
the generosity of these sources.

Library of Congress Cataloging in Publication Data

Hegel, Georg Wilhelm Friedrich, 1770–1831.
   Lectures on the philosophy of religion.
   Translation of: Vorlesungen über die Philosophie der Religion.
   Includes bibliographies and indexes.
   Contents: v. 1. The concept of religion.
v. 2. Determinate religion.
v. 3. The consummate religion.
   1. Religion—Philosophy—Addresses, essays, lectures.
I. Hodgson, Peter Crafts, 1934–.   I. Title.
B2939.E5B76 1984 200'.1 83–9132
ISBN 0-520-04676-5

Printed in the United States of America
1 2 3 4 5 6 7 8 9

55,812

CONTENTS

v

CONTENTS

APPENDIXES

ABBREVIATIONS, SIGNS, AND SYMBOLS

SIGNS AND SYMBOLS

[. . .]   = Editorial insertions in the text.

⟨ . . . ⟩   = Passages in the margins of the *Ms.,* including both passages integrated into the main text and unintegrated passages that are footnoted.

~ . . . ~   = Passages in the main text that correspond to footnoted variant readings. These symbols are used only in the case of textual variants, which offer a different version of the designated passage, usually from a different source, not textual additions, which occur at the point marked by the note number in the main text. Normally the variant is placed in the notes at the end of the parallel in the main text; exceptions are noted.

–   = Freestanding en dash indicating a grammatical break between sentence fragments in footnoted *Ms.* marginal materials.

¹ ² ³ etc.   = Footnotes containing (a) unintegrated marginal materials from the *Ms.;* (b) textual variants, additions, and deletions; (c) special materials from *W* and *L,* both variant readings and additions; (d) editorial annotations. The type of note is designated by an initial italicized editorial phrase in each instance. Notes are at the bottoms of the pages and are numbered consecutively through each text unit.

[*Ed.*] = Editorial annotations in the footnotes; materials following this symbol are editorial.

34 | = Page numbers of the German edition, on the outer margins with page breaks marked by vertical slash in text. The German edition is *Vorlesungen: Ausgewählte Nachschriften und Manuskripte*, Vol. 4, *Vorlesungen über die Philosophie der Religion, II: Die bestimmte Religion*. Edited by Walter Jaeschke. Hamburg, 1985.

[31a] = Sheet numbers of the *Ms.*, in the text at the point of occurrence; "a" and "b" refer to the recto and verso sides of the sheets.

PUBLISHED SOURCES

W W$_1$ W$_2$ = *Werke*. Complete edition edited by an Association of Friends. Vols. 11–12 contain *Vorlesungen über die Philosophie der Religion*. 1st ed., edited by Philipp Marheineke (Berlin, 1832) (W$_1$); 2d ed., edited by Philipp Marheineke and Bruno Bauer (Berlin, 1840) (W$_2$). When no subscript is used, the reference is to both editions. Part II is contained in vols. 11–12 of both editions under the title *Die bestimmte Religion*.

L = *Vorlesungen über die Philosophie der Religion*. Edited by Georg Lasson. 2 vols. in 4 parts. Leipzig, 1925–1929 (reprint, Hamburg, 1966). Part II is contained in vols. 1/2 and 2/1 under the titles *Die Naturreligion* and *Die Religionen der geistigen Individualität*.

UNPUBLISHED SOURCES

Ms. = Hegel's lecture manuscript of 1821
D = Deiters transcript of the 1824 lectures
G = Griesheim transcript of the 1824 lectures
Ho = Hotho transcript of the 1824 lectures

K	=	Kehler transcript of the 1824 lectures
P	=	Pastenaci transcript of the 1824 lectures
An	=	Anonymous transcript of the 1827 lectures
B	=	Boerner transcript of the 1827 lectures
Hu	=	Hube transcript of the 1827 lectures
S	=	Strauss excerpts from a transcript of the 1831 lectures

SPECIAL MATERIALS IN W AND L

These are given in parentheses and identify the no-longer-extant sources of the variant readings and additions making up the special materials found in *W* and *L*. Since the source of special materials in *W* relating to the *Ms.* cannot be identified with certainty in each instance, the source designation is omitted from these passages, although the probability in most cases is that it is from *Hn*.

(Hn)	=	Henning transcript of the 1821 lectures
(MiscP)	=	Miscellaneous papers in Hegel's own hand
(1827?)	=	Unverified transcripts of the 1827 lectures
(1831)	=	Transcripts of the 1831 lectures
(HgG)	=	Notes by Hegel in the copy of G used by W_1 and W_2
(Ed)	=	Editorial passages in W_1 and W_2
(Var)	=	Variant readings in *W* or *L*

FREQUENTLY CITED WORKS BY HEGEL

Werke = *Werke.* Complete edition edited by an Association of Friends. 18 vols. Berlin, 1832 ff. Some volumes issued in second editions.

GW = *Gesammelte Werke.* Edited by the Academy of Sciences of Rhineland–Westphalia in association with the Deutsche Forschungsgemeinschaft. 40 vols. projected. Hamburg, 1968 ff.

Vorlesungen = *Vorlesungen: Ausgewählte Nachschriften und Manuskripte.* 10 vols. Hamburg, 1983 ff. Vols. 3–5 contain *Vorlesungen über die Philosophie der Religion,* edited by Walter Jaeschke.

Berliner Schriften = *Berliner Schriften 1818–1831.* Edited by J. Hoffmeister. Hamburg, 1956.

Early Theological Writings = *Early Theological Writings.* Partial translation of H. Nohl, *Hegels theologische Jugendschriften,* by T. M. Knox and R. Kroner. Chicago, 1948.

Encyclopedia (1817, 1830) = *Encyclopedia of the Philosophical Sciences.* Translated from the 3d German ed., with additions based on student transcripts and lecture manuscripts, by W. Wallace and

A. V. Miller. 3 vols. Oxford, 1892 (reprint 1975), 1970, 1971. *Enzyklopädie der philosophischen Wissenschaften im Grundrisse.* 1st ed. Heidelberg, 1817; forthcoming in *GW,* vol. 13. 3d ed., Berlin, 1830: *Werke,* vols. 6–7 (containing additions based on student transcripts and lecture manuscripts); forthcoming in *GW,* vol. 19. 6th ed., based on the 3d ed. without additions, edited by F. Nicolin and O. Pöggeler, Hamburg, 1959. Citations given by section numbers in the 1817 and 1830 editions.

Faith and = *Faith and Knowledge.* Translated by
Knowledge W. Cerf and H. S. Harris. Albany, 1977. *Glauben und Wissen, oder die Reflexionsphilosophie der Subjectivität in der Vollständigkeit ihrer Formen, als Kantische, Jacobische, und Fichtesche Philosophie.* Tübingen, 1802. *GW,* vol. 4 (edited by H. Buchner and O. Pöggeler).

History of = *Lectures on the History of Philosophy.*
Philosophy Translated from the 2d German ed. (1840) by E. S. Haldane and F. H. Simson. 3 vols. London, 1892. *Vorlesungen über die Geschichte der Philosophie.* Edited by C. L. Michelet. 1st ed., Berlin, 1833: *Werke,* vols. 13–15. Because of variations between the two German editions, the English translation often does not correspond exactly to the cited German texts. A new German edition is being prepared by P. Garniron and W. Jaeschke: *Vorlesungen,* vols. 6–9.

Phenomenology = *Phenomenology of Spirit.* Translated by
of Spirit A. V. Miller. Oxford, 1977. *Phänomenologie des Geistes.* Bamberg and Würzburg,

1807. *GW,* vol. 9 (edited by W. Bonsiepen and R. Heede).

Philosophy of World History = *Lectures on the Philosophy of World History*

Sibree ed. = *The Philosophy of History.* Translated from the 2d German ed. (1840) by J. Sibree. Revised edition. New York, 1900.

Nisbet ed. = *Lectures on the Philosophy of World History. Introduction: Reason in History.* Translated from Vol. 1 of *Vorlesungen über die Philosophie der Weltgeschichte* (ed. Hoffmeister) by H. B. Nisbet, with an Introduction by Duncan Forbes. Cambridge, 1975.

Vorlesungen über die Philosophie der Weltgeschichte.

Hoffmeister ed. = Vol. 1, *Die Vernunft in der Geschichte.* Edited by Johannes Hoffmeister. Hamburg, 1955.

Lasson ed. = Vol. 2, *Die orientalische Welt.* Vol. 3, *Die griechische und die römische Welt.* Vol. 4, *Die germanische Welt.* Edited by Georg Lasson. 2d ed. Hamburg, 1923. Vols. 1–4 are paginated cumulatively. Since Vols. 2–4 have not been translated, corresponding references from the Sibree translation of the 1840 ed. are cited when possible.

Science of Logic = *Science of Logic.* Translated by A. V. Miller. London, 1969. *Wissenschaft der Logik.* Vol. 1, *Die objektive Logik.* Nuremberg, 1812–13. *GW,* vol. 11 (edited by F. Hogemann and W. Jaeschke). Vol. 2, *Die subjektive Logik.* Nuremberg, 1816. *GW,* vol. 12 (edited by F. Hogemann and W. Jaeschke). 2d ed. of vol. 1, Book 1, *Die Lehre vom Sein.* Berlin, 1832. Forthcoming in *GW*, vol. 20 (edited by F. Hogemann and W. Jaeschke). The English translation uses the 2d ed. of vol. 1, Book 1, hence there is not an exact correspondence between it and *GW*, vol. 11, Book 1.

(Frequently cited works by other authors are included in the Bibliography of Sources at the back of the volume.)

INTRODUCTION

1. Text and Translation

Determinate Religion, Part II of Hegel's *Lectures on the Philosophy of Religion,* nearly equals in size Parts I and III together, *The Concept of Religion* and *The Consummate Religion.* Hegel would scarcely have devoted so much attention to a philosophical interpretation of the history of religions had he not been persuaded that this was a topic of special importance. Yet Part II of the lectures has generally been neglected, regarded as a mere appendix to the concept of religion or prolegomenon to the Christian religion.

This neglect is attributable in part both to the length and difficulty of the material and to the unsatisfactory character of the older editions, which amalgamated quite distinct lectures into an editorially constructed scheme. The present edition for the first time separates Hegel's four series of lectures on the philosophy of religion—1821, 1824, 1827, and (in the excerpted form provided by D. F. Strauss) 1831—publishing them as independent units on the basis of a complete reediting of the available sources.[1] When the lectures are read in sequence as originally delivered, it is possible to trace Hegel's unrelenting efforts to work out an adequate philosophical conceptualization of the history of religions. As Walter Jaeschke points out in the Preface to the German edition of this volume, when the materials are studied in this way it is unmistakably clear that "nothing

---

1. The reasons for doing so, the sources of the lectures, and the method of editing the texts are explained in detail in the Editorial Introduction to Vol. 1 of this edition, esp. pp. 8–20, 33–52. See also Vol. 3:1–2.

is more alien to Hegel's procedure than the customary picture of the pontificating philosopher who sets out to reduce the colorful array of historical actuality to pallid reason through a prefabricated net of abstract categories."

The detailed attention that Hegel devoted to precisely this part of his lectures is evidenced by the abundance of primary sources and literature he utilized. These sources are documented by the editorial annotations to this edition as well as the Bibliography of Sources for Hegel's Philosophy of Religion printed at the back of the volume. In Sec. 2 of the Introduction we provide a brief summary of the sources as they relate to specific religions. Sec. 3 offers a fairly detailed comparative analysis of the structure and development of Hegel's treatment of "Determinate Religion" in each of the lecture series. This kind of analysis is the first step in arriving at a valid critical assessment of Hegel's work. Such assessments of Part II are virtually nonexistent, and for good reason: a critical text has not been available.[2]

The primary translation work for this volume has been done by J. Michael Stewart, who assumed responsibility for all of the texts except the 1827 lectures, which were translated by Robert F. Brown. All translation drafts were thoroughly checked and revised by H. S. Harris and put into final form by the editor, who also prepared the English version of the annotations (with valuable assistance from Stewart) and wrote the Introduction. Walter Jaeschke contributed to the English edition in a variety of ways, and the editor continues to be deeply grateful for his colleagueship. The glossary that has guided the work of the translators is printed at the back of Vol. 3, and translation principles are detailed in the Introduction to

---

2. An important exception is the recent essay by Walter Jaeschke, "Zur Logik der Bestimmten Religion," which is discussed at the end of this Introduction (see below, n. 45). Also noteworthy is Reinhard Heede's 1972 inaugural dissertation at the University of Münster, *Die göttliche Idee und ihre Erscheinung in der Religion: Untersuchungen zum Verhältniss von Logik und Religionsphilosophie bei Hegel*. Heede was familiar to some extent with the structural and substantive differences between the several lecture series, and his section "Zur Komposition der 'Bestimmten Religion'" (pp. 147–181) is of particular interest; but unfortunately his work is not easily accessible.

Vol. 1.[3] The only word that needs to be added about the translation at this point is that the title of Part II, *Die bestimmte Religion,* is translated as "Determinate Religion" rather than as "Definite Religion," which was used by Speirs-Sanderson in their translation of the second edition of the *Werke.*

2. The Sources of "Determinate Religion"

What follows is not a critical analysis of the primary sources and secondary literature used by Hegel, either in the context of his own time or in the light of the enormous progress in the history and phenomenology of religions during the past century and a half. Rather what is provided is information that will be of value to such studies when they are undertaken by those with the necessary expertise. It is primarily a classification of data from the textual annotations and bibliography of sources—data that were gathered through the extraordinary diligence and knowledgeability of the German editor, Walter Jaeschke. Very few recent critical studies are available on this subject. The major work is by Reinhard Leuze, *Die ausserchristlichen Religionen bei Hegel* (Göttingen, 1975). While giving a valuable survey of Hegel's treatment of all the religions except primitive religion, the study is limited by the necessity of working with Lasson's edition, as well as by certain lacunae in the author's knowledge of the history of religions. Leuze cites a number of earlier studies, but they have been mostly superseded by his own work, which itself is now out of date. In preparing his annotations, Jaeschke found helpful not only Leuze's work but also the recent specialized study by Ignatius Viyagappa, S.J., *G. W. F. Hegel's Concept of Indian Philosophy* (Rome, 1980), which has not been available to the English editor.

Our Bibliography of Sources lists some 240 works upon which Hegel drew for his lectures on the philosophy of religion. This count includes only a single standard edition for each of the many classical authors upon whom he relied, so if individual classical works were included the number would increase substantially. A reasonable

3. See Vol. 1:52–58; also Vol. 3:8–9 for certain refinements.

estimate is that about two-thirds of these works were used primarily or exclusively for *Determinate Religion*; the remaining authors, mainly modern philosophers and theologians, were utilized for Parts I and III of the lectures.

Hegel knew more about the history of world religions than most of his contemporaries, but we do not know to what extent he had mastered all the available literature. Islam represented an obvious lacuna; it appears briefly in Part III as a contemporary rival to Christianity (and there are occasional references to it in Part II as well). Hegel focused his attention on the original or classical expressions of the religions, for the most part not attending to their subsequent histories or contemporary living expressions, if any. He viewed the history of religion as primarily a matter of the past, with the exception of Christianity. Much of the information he acquired was also put to good use in other lectures, such as the philosophy of world history, the philosophy of art, and the history of philosophy. More often than not he did not directly identify sources but rather alluded to them, frequently quoting from memory. Our list of identifiable sources demonstrates that he read and studied carefully works written in Latin, Greek, English, and French, as well as German.

In what follows we simply identify the major sources relating to Hegel's treatment of each of the determinate religions; complete information is provided in the Bibliography.

1. The Religion of Magic (Primitive Religion). This topic was addressed for the first time in the 1824 lectures, and Hegel's information remained quite limited. For his discussion of the Eskimos he relied on John Ross's *A Voyage of Discovery . . . for the Purpose of Exploring Baffin's Bay, and Enquiring into the Probability of a North-West Passage* (2d ed., 1819), although he also alluded to another report of a subsequent voyage by W. E. Parry. His treatment of African religion drew heavily upon Giovanni Antonio Cavazzi's *Istorica descrizione de' tre regni Congo, Matamba, et Angola situati nell'Etiopia inferiore occidentale* (1687, German translation 1694), a work which Hegel himself acknowledged to be quite out of date. It was supplemented by J. K. Tuckey's *Narrative of an Expedition to Explore the River Zaire* (1818), as well as James

4

Bruce's *Travels to Discover the Source of the Nile* (1790, German translation 1791).

In the 1827 lectures Hegel added a reference to T. E. Bowdich's *Mission from Cape Coast Castle to Ashantee* (1819), and in both 1824 and 1827 he derived some information about ancient Africa from Herodotus's *Histories*. Another general travel source was George Forster's account of travels around the world with his father, Johann Reinhold Forster, and Captain Cook (1778). There are a few allusions to Mongols, Chinese, and American Indians in the sections on the religion of magic; the sources for the first two were probably the same as for Chinese religion, but we have no information on the third.

2. Chinese Religion. The literature available at the time on Chinese life, history, and culture was quite limited, but Hegel's lectures on the philosophy of world history show that he was familiar with much of it.[4] In the 1824 philosophy-of-religion lectures, his discussion of Chinese religion was quite brief and limited to the ancient religion of the Zhou dynasty.[5] His sole source was the *Mémoires concernant l'histoire, les sciences, les moeurs, les usages, etc. des Chinois,* published by the Jesuit missionaries of Beijing in sixteen volumes, 1776–1814. In 1827 he supplemented the *Mémoires* with reports from the *Allgemeine Historie der Reisen* (1750), and he introduced a discussion of Daoism, which evolved from the old religion, for the first time. Information on the latter was provided by Gaubil's French translation, *Le Chou-king, un des livres sacrés des Chinois* (1770), and Abel-Rémusat's *Mémoires sur la vie et les opinions de Lao-Tseu* (1823). The 1831 lectures gave a more detailed account of Daoism and also included references to Confucianism, the latter based on *Confucius Sinarum philosophus; sive, Scientia Sinensis,* edited by P. Couplet and others (1687), and Joshua Marshman's *The Works of Confucius* (1809).

---

4. See Leuze, *Die ausserchristlichen Religionen bei Hegel,* pp. 17–22.
5. In accord with contemporary scholarly practice, we use the Pinyin system of romanization of Chinese characters. Hegel and his auditors employed a variety of forms, some quite fanciful, which have been standardized to the Pinyin system.

3. Buddhism. Buddhist research was just beginning in Hegel's time, and his knowledge of Buddhism was of necessity quite limited and often inaccurate.[6] He relied heavily on reports of English travelers to the Far East, notably Francis Buchanan's essay "On the Religion and Literature of the Burmas" in volume 6 of *Asiatic Researches,* but also William Jones and Samuel Turner. These were supplemented by additional reports in the *Allgemeine Historie der Reisen* (1750) and Wilhelm Harnisch's edition of *Die wichtigsten neuern Land- und Seereisen* (16 parts, 1821–1832), as well as Moyriac de Mailla's thirteen-volume *Histoire générale de la Chine* (1777–1785). In the 1827 lectures, Hegel attended more fully to the Buddhist doctrine of nirvana, basing his interpretation on information provided by volume 6 of the *Allgemeine Historie* (oriented to the Mahāyāna version). He also drew more heavily on accounts of the Tibetan lamas provided by volume 7 of the *Allgemeine Historie* and especially by Samuel Turner in *Asiatic Researches* and *Die wichtigsten Reisen.*

4. Hinduism. Systematic research on Indian history and religion was just beginning during Hegel's time. Earlier investigations had not been primarily by scholars but rather by officials associated with the Civil Service of the East India Company, who were not concerned with the ancient religious texts of Hinduism. The East India Company had a political interest in representing Indian culture and society as corrupt in order to justify its economic policies to Parliament. Hegel seemed to accept their description of conditions in India during the latter part of the eighteenth century as valid for the whole of its history. Moreover, he was suspicious of the longing of German Romanticism for a past golden age which was believed to have had its origins in India, a view expounded with great conviction by Friedrich Schlegel in his *Über die Sprache und Weisheit der Indier* (1808). These factors combined to produce an unusually negative assessment of Hinduism on Hegel's part.[7]

---

6. See our discussion of some of his misconceptions at the beginning of our analysis of the 1824 treatment of Buddhism in Sec. 3 below.

7. See Leuze, *Die ausserchristlichen Religionen,* pp. 77–81. On our translation of *die indische Religion* as "Hinduism," see 1824 lectures, n. 222.

More sources, however, were utilized by Hegel for his treatment of Hinduism than for any other Oriental religion. First there were the religious texts of Hinduism. He cited the *Institutes of Hindu Law* (the Code of Manu) in an edition published in 1794 in all of his lectures. He cited a well-known episode from the Rāmāyāna—the story of Vishvamitra—in two editions, one by William Carey and Joshua Marshman in 1806, the other by Franz Bopp (the founder of the comparative grammar of the Indo-Germanic languages) in 1816. He also made use of Bopp's translations of several episodes from the Mahābhārata, as well as Bopp's *Ueber das Conjugationssystem der Sanskritsprache* (1816). He referred to the Oupnek'hat, a collection of Upanishads in Persian translation, quoted by James Mill; and in 1827 he drew upon A. W. Schlegel's 1823 edition of the Bhagavad-Gītā, as well as Schlegel's *Indische Bibliothek* (1827). In the last two lectures, he utilized materials from his lengthy review of Wilhelm von Humboldt's paper, *Über die unter dem Namen Bhagavad-Gītā bekannte Episode des Mahā-Bhārata* (1825–1826), a review published in the *Jahrbücher für wissenschaftliche Kritik* (1827).

In the second place, Hegel relied on mostly unfavorable materials related to the East India Company. These included especially James Mill's *The History of British India* (1817), but also W. Ward's *History of the Hindus* (1817). J. A. Dubois's views concerning the irreformability of the Indian social system, as expressed in his *Moeurs, institutions et cérémonies des peuples de l'Inde* (1825), were referred to in the 1827 and 1831 lectures. In addition, however, Hegel had access to articles contained in *Asiatic Researches,* which had as its editorial policy the task of correcting English prejudice against India; these included materials by J. D. Paterson, Francis Wilford, William Jones, and especially H. T. Colebrooke, "On the Philosophy of the Hindus" (1824). Finally it should be noted that the first significant, comprehensive study of Indian culture by a German scholar did not appear until 1830, namely, P. von Bohlen's *Das alte Indien.* Given the current state of the sources, we cannot determine to what extent Bohlen's study may have influenced Hegel's portrayal of India in the last lectures.

5. Persian Religion (Zoroastrianism). Anquetil du Perron published the text of the Zend-Avesta in French translation in 1769–1771, and J. F. Kleuker translated this version into German in 1776–1783, adding in an appendix several treatises on different aspects of Parseeism. While the translation of a translation left much to be desired, this was Hegel's primary source for the treatment of Persian religion. He also made use of Joseph Görres's translation into German of the *Shāh-nāma,* the epic work by the medieval Muslim poet Firdawsi (1820). His major secondary sources were two works by J. G. Rhode: *Die heilige Sage und das gesammte Religionssystem der alten Baktrer, Meder und Perser oder des Zendvolks* (1820), and *Über Alter und Werth einiger morgenländischen Urkunden* (1817); he may also have relied upon A. H. L. Heeren's *Ideen über die Politik, den Verkehr und den Handel der vornehmsten Völker der alten Welt* (1804–1805). He supplemented these with reports by the ancient historians Herodotus and Plutarch, and in 1831 with Carsten Niebuhr's *Voyage . . . en Arabie et en d'autres pays de l'orient* (1780).

6. Egyptian Religion. Egyptology as a science began with archaeological expeditions following Napoleon's excursions up the Nile, and with the chance discovery of the Rosetta stone by a French officer, on the basis of which J. F. Champollion succeeded in deciphering the hieroglyphic system in 1824.[8] These discoveries, which were just being assimilated in Hegel's time, had little impact on his interpretation of Egyptian religion, which was based above all on the reports of several ancient historians: Herodotus, *Histories,* book 2; Plutarch, *De Iside et Osiride;* and Diodorus Siculus, *Bibliotheca historica.* He also made use of secondary studies that interpreted the ancient sources: J. D. Guigniaut's commentary on Tacitus, *Serapis et son origine* (1828); Creuzer's *Symbolik und Mythologie;* C. F. Dupuis's *Origine de tous les cultes, ou religion universelle* (1795); and A. H. L. Heeren's *Ideen über die Politik, den Verkehr und den Handel der vornehmsten Völker der alten Welt* (1804–1805). Finally, a few sources provided information based on the recent discoveries: Giovanni Belzoni's *Narrative of the Opera-*

8. Ibid., pp. 128–130.

tions and Recent Discoveries within the Pyramids, Temples, Tombs, and Excavations, in Egypt and Nubia (1822) (of limited value scientifically); Aloys Hirt's *Ueber die Bildung der aegyptischen Gottheiten* (1821); Brown's *Aperçu sur les hiéroglyphes d'Égypte* (1827); and the collection of the Egyptologist von Minutoli, which Hegel saw in Berlin and which was catalogued by J. Passalacqua in 1826. Most of these except for Belzoni were alluded to only in the last lectures.

7. Judaism. Hegel's interpretation of Jewish religion was based almost entirely on his own reading of the Hebrew scriptures, which in the first three lectures was limited to the "Books of Moses" (the Pentateuch), Job, and the Psalms. He had long been attracted to Job as the "philosopher of Mosaic antiquity" through the influence of his teachers in the Tübingen seminary as well as J. G. Herder's *The Spirit of Hebrew Poetry* (1787). The 1824 discussion of Job may have reflected the impact of F. W. C. Umbreit's recently published *Das Buch Hiob: Uebersetzung und Auslegung* (1824).[9] In 1831 Hegel alluded specifically to the universalism of the "later prophets," that is, Second and Third Isaiah and Haggai, as well as to certain passages in the Psalms, although references to the implicit universalism of Israelite faith were already found in 1824. The interest in Isaiah may have reflected the view of Wilhelm Gesenius's *Commentar über den Jesaja* (1821), to which Hegel's attention was called by the so-called Halle controversy of 1830.[10] The last lectures also indicated familiarity with G. P. W. Gramberg's *Kritische Geschichte der Religionsideen des alten Testaments* (1829–1830). Hegel did not engage in critical exegesis of texts, and he relied almost entirely on the translation of the Luther Bible, but he had a keen sense for fundamental themes and meanings. His own interpretation of the Old Testament evolved significantly during the eleven-year period of the lectures, as our subsequent analysis makes clear.

8. Greek Religion. Hegel had more resources at his disposal for the study of Greek religion than of any other. Not only was more known about Greece than about other ancient cultures at the beginning of the nineteenth century, but also Hegel had immersed

9. Ibid., pp. 171–173.
10. Ibid., p. 178.

himself in Greek philosophy, religion, art, and literature as a young man. He entered into the Greek world with great empathy and depth, but gradually was able to distance himself from it, recognizing both its strengths and its limits, and he was familiar with the hermeneutical issues involved in the clash between romanticist and classicist approaches to Greek culture.

Much of Hegel's interpretation of Greek religion derived from his own long-standing study of the classical authors.[11] Among the pre-Socratics, he was familiar with fragments from Anaxagoras, Parmenides, and Xenophanes. Of the later philosophers, he relied on several of Plato's dialogues—*Phaedo, Phaedrus, Apology, Timaeus,* and *Republic*—and alluded to Aristotle's discussion of the mysteries in the *Nicomachean Ethics* and of the teleological proof in the *Physics* and *Metaphysics.* Of the great poets, he drew on Homer's *Iliad* and *Odyssey,* Hesiod's *Theogony* and *Works and Days,* and Pindar's *Odes.* The tragedians were sources of particular importance for Hegel's understanding of Greek religion: Aeschylus, *Eumenides, Prometheus Bound;* Euripides, *Iphigenia in Aulis, Hippolytus* (in connection with the latter work Hegel also cited Racine's *Phèdre* and A. W. Schlegel's *Comparaison entre la Phèdre de Racine et celle d'Euripide* [1807]); Sophocles, *Antigone, Trachiniae, Oedipus Rex, Oedipus at Colonus.* Among the comic authors, he referred only to Aristophanes. The Greek historians provided crucial information not only on Greek culture but also on other ancient civilizations: Thucydides, *History of the Peloponnesian War;* Herodotus, *Histories;* Diodorus Siculus, *Bibliotheca historica;* Pausanias, *Description of Greece;* and Xenophon, *Apology of Socrates.* Finally, Hegel was familiar with the church father Clement of Alexandria, and derived information about Greek religion from two of his writings: *Exhortation to the Heathen, (Protrepticus)* and *Stromata.*

As for modern authors and secondary literature, by far the most important was Georg Friedrich Creuzer, a personal friend who gave Hegel a copy of the second edition of his *Symbolik und Mythologie*

11. In the footnotes, we cite classical authors in the abbreviated form customary today. The Bibliography of Sources gives the editions of these authors probably used by Hegel.

der alten Völker, besonders der Griechen (4 vols., 1819–1821). Despite the friendship, Hegel was critical of Creuzer on certain important points, such as the distinction between "symbolic" and "classical" art, and the question whether a higher wisdom and a purer religion were taught in the mysteries. On the first matter, Hegel's position was analogous to the one taken by Gottfried Herrmann against Creuzer in *Briefe über Homer und Hesiodus* (1818); on the second, he was also critical of Voltaire's views as expressed in *Dictionnaire philosophique.* Yet he agreed with Creuzer's interpretation of the origin of Apollo and other Greek deities in the older nature religion, against the position taken by K. O. Müller, *Geschichten hellenischer Stämme und Städte* (1824).[12]

Other important secondary sources included Gottfried Herrmann's *Die Feste von Hellas* (1803); Etienne Clavier's *Mémoire sur les oracles des anciens* (1818); C. F. Dupuis' *Origine de tous les cultes; ou, Religion universelle* (1795); and Baron de Sainte-Croix's *Recherches historiques et critiques sur les mystères du paganisme,* 2d ed. (1817), whose work supported Hegel's interpretation of the mysteries. On the pre-Socratics, Hegel referred to the work of C. A. Brandis, *Xenophanis Parmenidis et Melissi doctrina* (1813); and in the last lectures he added a reference to C. A. Lobeck's *Aglaophamus; sive, De theologiae mysticae Graecorum causis* (1829). Occasional allusions are also found to the views of Greece on the part of such authors as Schiller, Goethe, Voltaire, and d'Holbach.

9. Roman Religion. Hegel relied primarily on only one secondary source for his treatment of Roman religion, Karl Philipp Moritz's *Anthousa; oder, Roms Alterthümer* (1791). While he quotes at length from Moritz's account of Roman festivals and deities, Hegel's interpretation of Roman religion was diametrically opposed to that of Moritz.[13] He had long been familiar with Gibbon's *History of the*

---

12. See below, *Ms.,* n. 202, and 1824 lectures, nn. 675, 678. See also Leuze's discussion of Hegel's relationship to Creuzer, *Die ausserchristlichen Religionen,* pp. 204–208.

13. See below, *Loose Sheets,* n. 8. We discuss this matter in connection with the treatment of Roman religion in the *Ms.* See also Leuze, *Die ausserchristlichen Religionen,* pp. 225–232.

Decline and Fall of the Roman Empire, owning an edition published in Leipzig in 1821; and for a few details he also drew upon Creuzer's *Symbolik und Mythologie* and *Abriss der römischen Antiquitäten* (1824).

Hegel was thoroughly acquainted with the Roman authors. In the 1821 lecture *Ms.,* where he worked out his interpretation of Roman religion in great detail, never significantly changing it thereafter, we find references or allusions to Ammianus Marcellinus, *Res gestae*; Plutarch, *De fortuna Romanorum*; the tragedies of Seneca (of whom he was highly critical); Dio Cassius, *Historia Romana*; Suetonius, *Divus Claudius* and *Gaius Caligula*; Tacitus, *Annals*; Livy, *Ab urbe condita.* In the 1824 lectures, references were added to Cicero's *De natura deorum* and Virgil's *Aeneid.*

3. The Structure and Development of "Determinate Religion"

This edition makes possible for the first time a comprehensive comparison of the structure of the four series of lectures Hegel presented on the philosophy of religion, as well as an analysis of the development in his conceptualization and treatment of the subject. A clear understanding of the structure and development of Part II of the lectures is of special importance for two reasons. First, the earlier editions (both the *Werke* and Lasson) gave the mistaken impression that *Determinate Religion* was divided into only two main sections, "nature religion" and "the religions of spiritual individuality," whereas it is clear that Hegel intended to give Part II a *triadic* structure. The twofold structure reflects only the lectures of 1824, and our analysis of these lectures will show that Hegel began them with the threefold structure in mind, shifting to the twofold arrangement as he went along, even though Roman religion did not properly fit under the category of "spiritual individuality." In 1827 and 1831 Hegel restored the threefold arrangement, but with significant changes introduced in the last series.

In the second place, and of greater significance, is the fact that Hegel never did arrive at a satisfactory arrangement for *Determinate Religion.* For Part III (*The Consummate Religion*) he arrived at his mature conceptualization in 1824, while for Part I (*The Concept of Religion*) he achieved it in 1827. But in the case of Part II, he introduced significant structural changes in 1831, which offered a quite different context for interpreting the Oriental and Near Eastern religions (including Judaism). While we of course do not know whether Hegel would have reorganized *Determinate Religion* yet again upon a subsequent offering, it is evident that 1831 does not provide a fully satisfactory arrangement, especially with regard to Jewish and Roman religion. At the same time, one senses a growing fascination with the history of religions, and it would not be inappropriate to suggest that this topic, rather than the concept of religion or the Christian religion, was at the cutting edge of Hegel's interest when he died in the fall of 1831. His evident willingness to incorporate new data and experiment with new schemes underscores the fact that for him philosophy was a kind of "conceptual play" based on imaginative variation in order to arrive at new insights. The hermeneutical questions remained open and lively from the earliest to the latest texts contained in this volume, and it is hoped that the reader will sense and share in the excitement they convey.

For what follows, readers will be helped by referring to the table providing a comparative analysis of the structure of the text, found on pp. 88–89. Section numbers and headings in all of the documents except the *Ms.* are the work of the editors and are not attributable to Hegel himself, although frequently wording in the texts suggests the formulations used for the headings. Reference is made to the more detailed discussion of specific matters in the editorial annotations, so as to avoid repetition between the introduction and the notes.

a. Hegel's Lecture Manuscript

General Structure

In a canceled heading at the end of *The Concept of Religion* (Vol. 1: 255 n. 185), Hegel states that in Part II the concept of religion will be "grasped in its determinate aspects," and that these aspects constitute the "forms of consciousness of the absolute idea." This formulation suggests that the whole of Part II is intended as a phenomenology of religion, that is, of the various forms of consciousness assumed by the absolute idea as it emerges and advances

through the history of religions. This is a helpful way of understanding what Hegel is about in Part II: although data are drawn
from the history of religions (in increasing wealth as the lectures are
repeated), and although Hegel controlled a vast amount of information, what is offered is not a historical account but a philosophical
description of stages of religious consciousness—a description that
is at once phenomenological and speculative, phenomenological
because it attends to the concrete stages of consciousness, speculative
because the interpretative perspective is already that of the absolute
idea.

The description is carried out through the application of two sets
of analytic categories—one internal to the religions, the other relating
them externally. The internal set identifies three "moments" of a
religion: its abstract concept of divinity, the ways in which God is
known representationally in the texts and symbols of the religion,
and the practical relationship in which communion with the deity
is established; or, in brief, a religion's metaphysical concept, its
concrete representation, and its cultus. It should be noted that initially
Hegel envisioned only a twofold scheme, which did not distinguish
between representation and cultus (see *Ms.*, n. 5), and that the triple
division was apparently worked out only in the course of treating
the determinate religions. This sort of analysis was applied most
clearly in the *Ms.* and the 1824 lectures; the last two series of lectures
were not ordered by it so consistently.

The external analysis arranges *Determinate Religion* into a triad
corresponding to the fundamental moments of logic, namely, being,
essence, and concept (see n. 6). But in the case of the religions, these
categories are applied in the mode of determinateness and finitude;
hence the operative triad is one of prereflective immediacy or undifferentiated substance (the Oriental religions of nature), differentiation in the the form of particularity (Jewish religion) or necessity
(Greek), and external purposiveness (Roman religion). The latter,
Roman religion, represents the apotheosis of finitude and thus
prepares the transition from all the finite religions to the true, infinite,
consummate religion (the Christian religion). This is what justifies
treating Roman religion as a separate stage of religious consciousness;
it is not "higher" than what has gone before but gathers up and makes

explicit the limitations of determinate religion as such. This seems to have been suggested to Hegel in a strange way through Goethe's notion of a "philosophical" religion (see nn. 12, 13). On the one hand Roman religion is universal, related "to the whole human race," not "ethnic" or national like the preceding religions. But on the other hand it is finite, concerned with what is "around us," not above or beneath us; lacking transcendence and depth, it is utterly prosaic, preoccupied with "earthly circumstances and arrangements."

Immediate Religion

Sec. A is quite brief in the *Ms.* (a mere seven sheets) since, as we point out in n. 15, Hegel does not treat the religion of magic at all, nor does he discuss the Oriental religions separately; rather he constructs a phenomenology of religious immediacy, with brief allusions to Chinese, Hindu, Persian, and Egyptian religion (but not to Buddhism).[14]

The section begins with a consideration of the proof of God appropriate to immediate religion, namely, the cosmological proof. God is understood to be "simple, pure being [*Sein*]," which, according to Hegel's *Logic,* is the most indeterminate and immediate of categories.[15] The "thought of universal, pure being is implicit in the many particular beings" because the latter do not have being in and for themselves, they are limited, finite, determinate. In other words, the contingency and finitude of *Dasein*—determinate or existent being—drives it to its other, its ground, *Sein*. This is a very simple proof, but, in the form we encounter it here, deficient. Pure being and finite being are sundered, and thus "the concreteness of existence,

---

14. Of these religions, only Egyptian religion is clearly discussed in chap. VII.A of the *Phenomenology of Spirit* under the rubric of "the artificer" (*der Werkmeister*). Hegel's reference to "God as light" (lit., "the light-essence," *das Lichtwesen*) has generally been taken as an allusion to Persian religion, but W. Jaeschke has argued that this is not the case (see below, n. 19). What Hegel means by "plant and animal" (*die Pflanze und das Tier*) is not at all clear. It is probably not a reference to Hinduism, as J. N. Findlay suggests in his commentary (*Phenomenology,* p. 579), but to the religions of Mesopotamia, or perhaps more generally to higher forms of what Hegel later defines as the "religion of magic" (see below, 1824 lectures, p. 288, where he describes how living things—plants and animals—come to serve as the objectification of divine power).

15. Hegel, *Science of Logic,* p. 82 (*GW* 11:43–44).

the unity, the synthesis [of being and finitude] float away from us." This has adverse consequences for both the infinite and the finite. Being remains abstract, infinite, empty, *actus purus,* while finitude remains unsublated, unnegated, regarded as something positive or affirmative in its limitedness. By contrast, according to Hegel, *true* being posits an other over against itself, imparts itself, overreaches the difference between infinite and finite; while what is to be affirmed about finite being is precisely its self-negation, not its positivity.

When God is taken "concretely" rather than "abstractly" at this stage of consciousness, he is identified with "immediate being just as it is, finite nature"—nature intuited (*angeschaut*), represented (*vorgestellt*) as God. This is not, however, a "prosaic intuition of abstract understanding," which sees things as material objects, but rather an intuition of the all-encompassing universal, which inspires fear, awe, longing, devotion. Certain natural elements have traditionally offered themselves as prime representations of the universal: light, sun, heaven, water. These elements are not initially construed symbolically but are taken as "the immediately present God." The obvious incongruity between such specific natural objects and the universal is overcome when reflective thought is able to grasp the totality of what appears—"world" or "nature"—as one, as, for example, in Spinozistic pantheism. But religious consciousness advances less rapidly; the next step comes with the recognition that the infinite, universal power which grounds all that is, is not dead matter but animate and subjective. This brings us to the stage where both animals and human beings are worshiped, not as symbols but in actuality: the Egyptian bull (Apis) and cat, the Hindu elephant and cow, the Dalai Lama and the Brāhmans.[16] While this may seem degrading to us, it represents an advance in consciousness. At the same time, consciousness is aware of the limitation of worshiping God in singular, finite (albeit living) things, and thus casts itself about so as to employ *all* the beauty and wealth of nature in order to intuit the divine essence; common things are elevated, then reduced and dissolved. This occurs in the fanciful imagination of Hinduism and

16. While the Christian doctrine of incarnation may be superficially similar, in fact, according to Hegel, the Christian religion does not worship a man as God but rather the "actuality of God" *in* a man.

in the personification of nature as a whole found in the ancient Greek myths.

The section concludes with a discussion of the cultus of immediate religion, much of it still in outline form (see *Ms.* sheet 38a and nn. 45, 49). Since at this stage of immediacy the cleavage between finite and infinite has not yet come fully to consciousness, what we find is reconciliation without disunion, hence no real reconciliation or repentance, no inward evil to atone for. Cultus is not set apart but is a life lived continuously in "the kingdom of light and good"; the details of external life are habituated in accord with religious purposes; the aim of the unending labor of religious life is immersion in the universal, self-resignation, mortification, even suicide. Especially in this discussion of the cultus, Hegel has juxtaposed practices from a number of different religions, Hindu, Persian, Mesopotamian, Egyptian. Obviously this procedure was unsatisfactory, and in the next lectures, those of 1824, the entire section on immediate religion was recast and greatly expanded. But already in the *Ms.* an interpretative horizon has been established, elements of which may be glimpsed in all the later lectures.

The Religion of Sublimity and Beauty

By contrast with the brevity of Sec. A, Hegel devotes some twenty manuscript sheets and nearly a month of lecture time to the discussion of "the religion of sublimity and beauty." Yet a structural similarity with Sec. A is retained in the sense that the two religions considered under this rubric—Jewish and Greek—are subordinated to the internal analytic categories (metaphysical concept, concrete representation, cultus) rather than being taken up in separate sections (see n. 56). What this signifies is that Hegel views Jewish and Greek religion as representing different, indeed contrasting expressions of the same stage of religious consciousness, the stage of "essence."

Essence is a difficult category to grasp, and a detailed analysis would require attending to its treatment in the *Science of Logic*.[17] For our purposes it is enough to say that essence entails a transition from the immediacy of being to differentiation in the form of "reflec-

---

17. *Science of Logic,* pp. 389 ff. (*GW* 11:233 ff.).

tion," reflection-into-self by intuiting self in what is other-than-self. Essence thus involves the sphere of ideality, of intelligibility, of thought, and hence it has "crossed the threshold of the spiritual world," having left behind the world of sensible, natural immediacy. But the ideality of essence is *concrete:* it is not abstract being-for-self but is a "showing" (*Scheinen*), a "manifesting" (*Manifestieren*) for itself and from within itself, independently. Because of this independence, it is what is "essential" as distinguished from the inessential.

In terms of religious consciousness, essence is first posited (or shows itself) as *power*—the "negativity that differentiates itself," that possesses and sublates the other, the idea of the other, in thought ("whoever *thinks* what others merely *are* is their power"). Defined as absolute and as subject, this negative power is the Lord, the One, the ruler of all. Finite self-consciousness is merely a semblance, having its being, feeling, and focus solely in this one Lord; "to be sure, it knows itself as essential (it is not annihilated as in Brahman), but at the same time it is the inessential in the essential" (n. 66). This, then, is the religion of sublimity (*Erhabenheit*) or Jewish religion— not the sublimity of the boundless, which is immediately present in finite shapes as in Oriental pantheism, but of the one Lord who utterly transcends such shapes. Essence then develops as *necessity,* which is the reality concealed beneath the show of power. Differentiation is now no longer merely a show or semblance but an essential manifestation of essence; it is in fact spiritual, but still finite and only finitely free. This is the religion of beauty, or Greek religion: beauty gives essence a positive, spiritual form, but still in the sensuous element of portrayal.

Following this introduction, Hegel turns first to the metaphysical concept of these two religions (Sec. B.a), and at this point they are still completely integrated. The metaphysical or abstract concept found in them leads immediately to the question of proofs, since the proofs merely express the content of the various definitions of God. God is no longer defined simply as pure being but as "the One" and as "necessary essence" or "necessity." Relating to the first is the proof of the oneness of God, which is based on the dialectic of the one and the many, a theme that is also present in Plato and the Neoplatonic philosophers. The problem with this proof is that it sets up oneness in the form of a definition, whereas all we have in actual experience is the many. The second proof has to do with the argument from contingency to necessity, with respect to which Hegel adopts the Kantian critique: the argument from effect to cause is valid only in the sensible world, and it yields only finite causes. Infinite causes simply do not enter into experience. The proof, moreover, is able to provide at best only a necessary essence, not the supremely real God.

Under the second and third analytic categories, Concrete Representation and Cultus, the two religions are treated in separate subgroups, and we shall distinguish them in the subsequent analysis.

Jewish Religion

The "great thesis" of Jewish religion is that God is one God—the personal One (*der Eine*), not the neuter One (*das Eine*), not substance but subject, the infinite reflected into itself as singular and concrete universality. This God is all-powerful, and the sublimity of his power is such that it is expressed representationally (Sec. B.b.α) not by physical force but by the pure word, which is pure light: "God said, Let there be light, and there was light, . . . light that is only a breath." By contrast, the contingency and dependence of the world is expressed in the doctrines of creation, preservation, and passing away. God's power in relation to the world remains *undetermined:* it does not acquire a determinate content, end, or purpose, other than the exercise of power as such, and the difference between the goodness and the justice of God is annulled. God is "not yet inwardly concrete, not yet elaborated within himself," but is merely abstract power, the being-for-self of the One.

The paradigmatic portrayal of the God of abstract power is found, according to Hegel, in the Book of Job. Hegel had been attracted to Job since his student days, through the influence of his teacher Schnurrer as well as that of J. D. Michaelis, whose translation of the Old Testament into German was published in 1769, and who regarded Job as the oldest book of the Bible, possibly written by Moses to comfort the Israelites in Egypt.[18] This dating of the book, together with Job's reputation among Enlightenment thinkers as "the

18. See 1827 lectures, n. 487. See also Leuze, *Die ausserchristlichen Religionen bei Hegel,* p. 172.

philosopher of Mosaic antiquity," helps to account for the prominence Hegel accords it especially in the first two lecture series. Both Schnurrer and Michaelis stressed the portrayal of divine majesty in Job, and Hegel echoes the inverse of this theme, namely, that divine majesty and inscrutability demand absolute submission on the part of human beings, "fear of the Lord." To be sure, God acts to bring souls out from the pit of Sheol (Job 33:18), but this act of justice or mercy is also merely an expression of divine power. In the end, "submission [to the Lord] restores Job to his former happiness."

The Jewish cultus, in Hegel's view (see Sec. B.c.α), is a fundamental expression of the servile consciousness and of the master-servant relationship. When God is comprehended only under the abstract category of the One, and not as dialectically self-mediated, then "this human lack of freedom" is the result, and "humanity's relationship to God takes the form of a heavy yoke, of onerous service. True liberation is to be found in Christianity, in the Trinity." The condition of servitude is to have one's self-consciousness solely in the other and on behalf of the other. "Fear of the Lord is the absolute religious duty, to regard myself as nothing, to know myself only as absolutely dependent—the consciousness of the servant vis-à-vis the master." What God demands is that his people should have "the basic feeling of their dependence." Here we encounter the first of Hegel's several allusions in the Ms. to Schleiermacher's just-published Glaubenslehre (see nn. 138, 292), and it is noteworthy that he regards Schleiermacher's famous description of religious consciousness as an expression of Jewish (and later of Roman) rather than of Christian piety.

If one has one's self-consciousness only in and through absolute dependence on the Lord, then there is also a sense in which one is absolutely reestablished in relationship to the Lord—a relationship that is singular, unique, and exclusive. Hegel thinks this is the source of Jewish "obstinacy" and "particularity," the conviction that the Jewish people alone are God's people, and that he alone is their God. While in this sense Judaism is a national or ethnic religion, it is not the case that this people can lay claim to the land they inhabit; it is rather solely the gift of God, who can take it from them and restore it to them.

This portrayal of Judaism still shares the interpretative perspective of the *Early Theological Writings* and the *Phenomenology of Spirit*,[19] even though new categories and themes have appeared. As Leuze suggests, Hegel has placed a different valuation on essentially the same characterization of Judaism.[20] While the master-servant relationship was earlier viewed as a primary instance of human self-alienation (although necessary to the emergence of self-consciousness), it is now seen as implicit in the concept of God as abstract power (which also entails alienation). And a basis is laid for the quite different interpretation of Judaism that makes its appearance in the 1824 lectures (see 1824, especially nn. 510, 551). For already in the *Ms*. Hegel alludes to the fact that the power of the Lord is *wisdom,* and he recognizes that a *reconstitution* of the self in the One occurs through "fear of the Lord."

Greek Religion

The discussion of Greek religion opens with a very difficult section on the category of "necessity" (Sec. B.b.β), the comprehension of which is assisted by some familiarity with Hegel's treatment in the *Science of Logic*.[21] Necessity is power that is not merely abstractly related to itself but repels itself from itself, providing a mediation

19. The place of Judaism in the *Phenomenology of Spirit* has been much discussed but never satisfactorily resolved (see Leuze, *Die ausserchristlichen Religionen,* pp. 166–169). It is likely that brief allusions to it are found in the section on the "unhappy consciousness"—e.g., the reference to "the alien essence" that "condemns singularity" (*Phenomenology,* p. 128 [GW 9:123])—and in the view of most interpreters that that is the extent of it. But Walter Jaeschke has recently argued that Hegel's discussion of "the light-essence" (*das Lichtwesen*) as the first form of "natural religion" (*Phenomenology,* pp. 418–420 [GW 9:370–372]) is not a reference to Persian religion, as generally thought, but to the God of Israel. He attempts to establish this by identifying numerous similarities between this brief section of the *Phenomenology* and the treatment of the idea of God in Jewish religion in the 1821 *Ms.,* where, for example, the sublimity of God is also defined in terms of the metaphor of "light"—the God who creates by the word that is pure light ("God said, Let there be light, and there was light, . . . light that is only a breath"), and who covers himself "with light as with a garment" (Ps. 104:2) (see below, *Ms.,* p. 136). See Walter Jaeschke, *Die Vernunft in der Religion: Studien zur Grundlegung der spekulativen Religionsphilosophie* (Inaugural diss., Ruhr-Universität Bochum, 1985), pp. 288–295.

20. Leuze, *Die ausserchristlichen Religionen,* p. 170.

21. *Science of Logic,* pp. 541–553 (GW 11:380–392).

for the diversity of determinate being. As such it is inherently blind, having not yet attained to the level of concept, purpose, determinacy, freedom, and thus it is experienced as cold, abstract, fate and as Nemesis. But necessity also entails the appearing of essence itself in a positive relation to the natural; it appears *in* the natural but not *as* the natural, and thus it requires an act of religious intuition or a work of art to raise the natural to the essential. It first appears in the natural and ethical powers, inherited from the old Greek folk religions; these powers are divine powers and as such are distinct from necessity yet at the same time have their subsistence in it (they are not immediately divine as in the nature religions). But the proper shape in which necessity appears is the human, spiritual shape. Human being is imbued "with the imprint of universality or of the simplicity of necessity"; and conversely "the external shape [of necessity] should be conceived solely in the spirit and begotten solely from it." Human products are more excellent than natural products, and, as the natural element recedes, the spiritual gods evolve out of the natural gods (e.g., Helios was once a Titan, Athena came out of Neith, n. 132). The gods made in the image of human individuality are more adequate representations than the old nature deities of the necessity that rules all that is.

The section on the cultus of Greek religion (Sec. B.c.β) opens with a subsection (α) on the stage of religious self-consciousness that expresses itself in this religion, which is now characterized as "the religion of beauty" (how beauty can be regarded as a manifestation of necessity is not at all clear). This is the stage of freedom—abstract and finite, to be sure, but freedom nonetheless—a consciousness of the implicit identity of myself and the universal, of finite and infinite. Yet the "objective essentiality" is still distinguished into two moments: absolute necessity and the spiritual, human shape. In relation to the former, the latter threatens initially to be annihilated, having no self-subsistence or self-purpose. This is not a matter of "fate" in the ordinary sense but of an orientation of self-consciousness to that which transcends its immediate singularity and gives it its "substantive aspect," namely, the ethical, the universally rational and true. Because the individual spirit is taken up into "universal substantiality," into "absolute essentiality," its eternal character emerges for the first time in the form of the idea of the immortality of the soul. At the same time self-consciousness recovers from this immersion in the universal through its own generative relationship to the gods, who are created, so to speak, out of its own passions (see n. 150). Because of their "scattered plurality," the divinity of the gods "cannot quite be taken in earnest," and as a result self-consciousness is freed from its gods and at the same time freed *by* the gods from *abstract* necessity; hence it is both serious and not serious about the gods (see n. 165). This is what constitutes the "absolute serenity" of the religion of art—no longer tied to nature, it also advances "to the point of doing away with God or gods and looking to itself for its own security."

Finally, in the subsection on "the cultus itself" (β), Hegel deals for the first time with the concrete forms of Greek religion, alluding to specific sources. Cultus in general consists of the actions whereby one gains the consciousness of unity with the gods, the universal powers, elevating them from the level of mere enjoyment or use, as in ordinary life, to that of "theoretical objectivity," such that they may be worshiped. The powers that are worshiped are "the distinctive powers of self-consciousness itself. Athena, whom the Athenians worship, is their very own city, their spirit, their technical and artistic talent; the muse that Homer invokes is at the same time his genius." Yet the powers that are thus elevated withdraw once again from the individual, resist manipulation, so that the cultus consists in these powers being recognized and emphasized for their own sake. Thought grasps the essential element in concrete life, and is also present to itself in what it recognizes and celebrates. Sacrifice is therefore not a giving up of self but self-fulfillment, an enjoyment of the universal power. In fact, it is the singular, external, natural form of the power that is sacrificed—which is an anticipation of the artistic transfiguration of the whole of life.

The divine essences or powers are combined into a universal element or nature, which is not yet grasped as infinite subjectivity or as spirit, and which is initially expressed in the symbolic forms inherited from the earlier religions. It is present in what is raw, primitive, unbeautiful, opaque, and mysterious, as distinct from the clarity and light of higher thought and ethical life. This leads Hegel into a discussion of the Greek mysteries and Orphic religion. Against the prevalent opinion of his time (Voltaire, Creuzer, see n. 202), Hegel argues that this more primitive form of religious consciousness did not contain higher truth or special wisdom. After all, "Socrates and Aristotle,[22] the wisest of the Greeks, were not initiated." The transition from savagery to ethical life was not yet completed in Orphism. This tension is clearly present in the Delphic oracles. It is a tension between justice and beauty, between power and purpose, between inner and outer, between the old gods and the new. In this situation, great stress is placed on natural signs, including especially the hearing of the divine voice at Delphi.

Poetry and drama are later and higher expressions of the Greek cultus. Poetry, which is "thinking phantasy," intuits, brings to life the universal essences that are present everywhere in nature but especially in human shape. Homer established the divine for phantasy; but at the same time a decline in religious vitality set in. Drama, tragic and comic, portrays the actual operations and effects of the essential powers in concrete instances. It is "the highest point" of Greek religious life, and Hegel draws upon the writings of Aeschylus, Euripides, and Sophocles, as well as of the Greek philosophers and historians, for his portrayal. While an antithesis remains between the particular gods, as particularized divine powers, and human beings, it is resolved amicably; no infinite estrangement has yet been experienced, nor universal reconciliation brought about.

This portrayal of Greek religion by no means simply repeats Hegel's presentation in the *Phenomenology of Spirit* under the rubric of "the religion of art."[23] The context and problematic have shifted, and the organization is different. The context in the *Phenomenology* is the role of religion in relation to Greek society and in particular the tension between social cohesion and individuality, whereas for the *Ms.* it is the role of religion in giving representational expres-

22. Hegel may be confusing Aristotle and Aeschylus; see n. 201.

23. See *Phenomenology of Spirit*, chap. VII.B. I am indebted at this point to the work of Daniel B. Jamros, S.J., *Religion in Hegel's Phenomenology of Spirit: A Study of the Text* (Ph.D. diss., Vanderbilt University, 1986). Christianity and Greek religion are the only religions to be treated at length in the *Phenomenology*, although, as Jamros shows, there are many allusions to other religions and stages of religious consciousness.

sion to essence in the form of *necessity* (a category lacking in the earlier treatment). The problematic of the *Phenomenology* is how art arrives at a form adequate to the expression of universal essence in individual spiritual shape, and Hegel traces this through the stages of the abstract work of art (the statue, hymn, oracle, and cultic sacrifice), the living work of art (the mysteries and athletic celebrations), and the spiritual work of art (epic poetry, tragedy, and comedy). The concern of the *Ms.* to distinguish between natural and spiritual-ethical phases of Greek religious consciousness (and to argue against Creuzer's romanticization of the earlier phase) is not present in the *Phenomenology;* and the organization of the *Ms.*'s treatment is determined by application of the analytic categories of metaphysical concept, concrete representation, and cultus. Art is no longer the central interpretative category, and in particular the *Ms.* does not repeat the extended discussion of Greek poetry and drama, which constitutes the focus of the *Phenomenology*'s presentation. Finally, whereas in the *Phenomenology* Greek religion provides the transition from "natural religion" (culminating in Egyptian religion) to Christianity, for the *Ms.* the relationships of Jewish, Greek, and Roman religion are the primary concern, and the many comparisons of Greek and Christian religious consciousness are lacking. All this is not to suggest that Hegel's basic interpretation of Greek religion has changed; it has not, although a shift is discernible away from the romantic image of Greece to a position between romanticism and classicism.[24] The philosophy-of-religion lectures demanded a different approach to Greek religion; the hermeneutical frame of reference was different, and new issues had arisen that needed to be addressed.

The Religion of Expediency: Roman Religion

Hegel devotes more attention to Roman religion in the *Ms.* than he does on any subsequent occasion—some fourteen manuscript sheets, or nearly half the number used for the whole of Part III, on the Christian religion. The preparatory materials for this part of the

24. See Leuze, *Die ausserchristlichen Religionen*, pp. 204–207, 215. Leuze has a detailed analysis of the treatment of Greek religion in the early writings and the *Phenomenology;* see pp. 181–203.

Ms. have been preserved and are printed in the Appendix (see below, *Loose Sheets*, esp. n. 1). Hegel seems to have been preoccupied in 1821 with the decadence of the Roman religion and empire, to which he compares his own age in rather apocalyptic tones at the end of the lectures (Vol. 3:159–160). More importantly, however, he was working out for the first time his own interpretation of this religion, and especially of fundamental differences between Greek and Roman religion, as opposed to the prevailing view that the two were essentially similar. This view was expressed by Hegel's major source, Karl Philipp Moritz's *Anthousa; oder, Roms Alterthümer* (1791), and Hegel used the detailed information on the Roman gods and festivals provided by Moritz to refute Moritz (see nn. 254, 257, and *Loose Sheets*, n. 8). Finally, Hegel was at pains to understand the transition from Roman religion, which "closes the cycle of the finite religions," to the Christian religion. Such "paradigm shifts"[25] were of great importance to him, and he devoted considerable attention to them.

The section opens with an analysis of the penultimate transition— the transition from Greek (and Jewish) religion to Roman religion. Logically, this is the transition from essence to concept, and more specifically, from necessity to purpose.[26] Necessity, according to Hegel, has no *inner* purpose, but only the formal requirement that there be *some* content, outcome, or activity. The concept "is the truth of necessity." When we conceive, we comprehend something as one moment in a coherent pattern, a coherence that involves both differentiation and inward connectedness. We grasp or hold together (*be-greifen*) the totality. The coherence of necessity is merely that of an external cause-effect relationship, whereas the coherence of the concept is that of internal purposiveness or intentionality. With

25. This term, borrowed from Thomas Kuhn, *The Structure of Scientific Revolutions,* 2d ed. (Chicago, 1970), p. 150, seems to be an apt way of characterizing Hegel's understanding of "passage" or "transition" (*Übergang*), especially the basic ones. We are, however, using the term "paradigm shift" in a sense somewhat different from that in which Kuhn uses it, since in this context we mean by "paradigm" a fundamental, exemplary construal of reality, not a scientific model of interpretation.

26. See the discussion of teleology and purpose (*Zweck*) in the *Science of Logic,* pp. 734–754 (*GW* 12:154–172). On the translation of *Zweckmässigkeit* as both "expediency" and "purposiveness," see n. 229, and 1824 lectures, n. 466.

inwardly purposive action "nothing is produced that is not already there beforehand," implicitly; hence purposive action is free action, action in which consciousness is at home with itself, action based on the "self-sustaining unity of the concept." Such action presupposes a distinction between purpose and reality—that is, between end and means—but also an inner connection or coherence. In Hegel's view, this distinction did not fully emerge in Greek religion (the gods are the powers of reality, not a purpose); in Roman religion purpose and reality stood in unresolved contradiction; while in the Christian religion the distinction has been overcome, sublated.

In other words, the purposiveness that is found in Roman religion is *finite* or *external* in character.[27] The purpose is realized or carried out through something that is alien to it; a means is utilized that has no intrinsic connection with the end, with the intentional act. This is the sort of relationship that is grasped by the "understanding" (*Verstand*) as opposed to the concept.

External purposiveness is at the heart of the teleological proof of the existence of God, in Hegel's view (Sec. C.a). As Kant points out in the *Critique of Pure Reason* (see nn. 241 ff.), this is a proof based on the wise, purposive, harmonious arrangement of the natural world, an arrangement so marvelous that we are compelled to seek an explanation for it outside the realm of contingency. However, the purposes and arrangements in question—such as the fact that rose bushes have thorns and cats claws, or that wood from trees is useful to shelter and warm human beings—are found in the natural world, not in the nature of God himself. For this reason they are extrinsic to God, and "God is [merely] seen as an understanding [*Verstand*], operating in nature, that orders and regulates them." Hegel shares Kant's critique of this proof and adds a few points of his own. The primary difficulty is that an argument from finite, contingent arrangements and purposes to a *supreme* wisdom and an *absolute* power entails a "leap" from the finite to the infinite that cannot be sustained logically and that must finally fall back on the ontological proof, which starts with the dialectics of the infinite rather

27. Hegel's distinction between internal and external purposiveness is based primarily on Kant's *Critique of Judgment;* see n. 237.

than with the finite. This is a leap or inference, moreover, which is based on a metaphysics of nature that understands only external, quasi-mechanical relations, as distinct from inner, vital, organic purposiveness (see n. 250). Finally, to bring in God as the explanation for such finite, contingent arrangements is to reduce the divine purpose to something extremely petty, such as providing bushes with thorns and animals with protective weaponry.

But of course this is just what the Romans have done (Sec. C.b). Their gods—and they have a veritable throng of them—are expedients that oversee, regulate, and protect the full range of human activities and purposes, especially those of a political and commercial character. This is the utterly utilitarian, practical, prosaic religion; specific human needs, such as happiness, satisfaction, self-seeking, define the content of the Roman gods. In this respect Roman religion is fundamentally different from Greek, which exists in "the realm of free beauty, joyous festival, and the enjoyment of divinity." The Greeks worship the gods for the sake of the gods, the Romans for the sake of humanity; they have no "free intuition of objectivity," only a practical assessment of their own subjective needs. "Their cultus consists in positing a power to help them in their need. Thus these gods have . . . a subjective root and origin, and have an existence so to speak only in worship, in the festivals." In the case of plague, for example, the Romans invent new gods, whereas the Greeks did not use their religion in this way.

Only thinly veiled in this analysis is the suggestion that *we* are very much like the Romans. The Roman religious practices are perhaps the most uninhibited instance of the "rotten point"[28] of religious belief wherever it is found, the belief in the gods of accusation and protection, of punishment and reward. Such belief is incipiently atheistic since it perverts religion into an instrument of human needs and purposes rather than constituting an act of genuine worship whereby the ground of being is glorified and enjoyed.

Hegel elaborates this critique in an unusually detailed examination of the Roman cultus (Sec. C.c). The purpose of this cultus is, first and foremost, political: it serves the interests of the Roman

28. See Paul Ricoeur, "Religion, Atheism, and Faith," in Alasdair MacIntyre and Paul Ricoeur, *The Religious Significance of Atheism* (New York, 1969), p. 60.

Empire. The Roman deity above all others is the goddess Fortuna—not necessity, not chance, not providence, but the universal prosperity of the Imperium Romanum. Beyond this are the general human requirements and activities: harvest, fertility, crafts, trade, travel. And beneath all of this is a fundamental fear of harm and disaster. This is why Hegel asserts—in a strained allusion to Schleiermacher (see n. 292)—that Roman religion is based on a "feeling of dependence," which, in developed form, leads to veneration of the power of evil and worship of the devil. He notes that the Romans dedicated altars to plague, fever, hunger, crop destruction, and the like, and wonders how such things could be worshiped as divine: "it is only the feeling of dependence and fear that can turn them into something objective." Other religions (Persian, Hindu, Greek) are *free* in the presence of their God, and it is only outside religion that they are dependent. The Romans have made of religion a thing of enslavement.

Enslavement to what? To finitude and death, in the final analysis. This is evident from the Roman festivals and spectacles, which consisted of the large-scale slaughter of beasts and human beings, a slaughter that was purposeless, staged merely for the entertainment of the spectators. "For the Romans, this prosaic pattern of spiritless butchery, cold and arid, constituted the supreme event of history." The gods warded off death as long as possible, but ultimately death prevails, and death is the one true divinity for the Romans, the final mark of finitude for the religion that venerates "unbounded finitude," "spuriously infinite" finitude.

It is just for this reason that Roman religion constitutes the final step before the transition to the Christian religion. It is a negative step, not a positive step; finite religion cycles back upon itself, it does not evolve progressively into infinite religion. The "necessity" of Roman religion is that the *highest* form of finitude is the *worst,* issuing in the absolute *un*happiness and grief of spirit, despite the Romans' constant preoccupation with happiness, gratification, success. It is only when finitude has played itself out to the end, only when the Sophist slogan "man is the measure of all things" has been elevated to a world standard, that finitude can be taken up into "the infinite universality of thought" and thereby purified—only then that God and world can be reconciled through the appearance of God in the shape of a single human being. God acquires present actuality, and the world is transfigured in its finitude. Yet the religion in which this occurred could not arise in the Greco-Roman world, since that world lacked a pure intuition of the one God, especially as a "community principle"; that is, while there may have been isolated philosophical intuitions of the One, they were incapable of taking on the concrete life of a religious community and cultus. Thus Christianity arose among the Jewish people when that people encountered the "finitude of the West" and the "age-old grief of the world."

b. The Lectures of 1824

The three moments of *Determinate Religion,* according to the introduction to the second lecture series, are immediate, natural religion (God intuited in the *natural* unity of the spiritual and the natural), the religions of spiritual individuality (the reflection of spirit into itself out of nature, God represented as an individual subject or subjects), and the religion of finite purposiveness. While this division is not based explicitly on the dialectic of being, essence, and concept, as in the *Ms.*, it is, according to Hegel, a "necessary classification that follows objectively from the nature of spirit"—but not so necessary, one may be permitted to observe, as to prevent Hegel from altering it in the process of developing the lectures (see 1824 lectures, n. 2).

Immediate Religion, or Nature Religion

Sec. A opens with a lengthy introduction in which primarily three matters are discussed. The first of these is whether immediate religion is not only the oldest but also the truest form of religion—a religion in which spirit exists in untroubled unity with nature. This is related to certain hypotheses concerning the original condition of humanity advanced according to Hegel by Schlegel, Schelling,[29] and other

---

29. Whether Schelling ever seriously held such views, at least after 1804, is subject to question. Hegel does allude to passages that seem to support them in *On University Studies* (1803) and *The Deities of Samothrace* (1815) (see 1824 n. 27). To be sure, in the latter work, Schelling declared that the religions of Greece, Phoenicia, etc., derived from a more ancient Pelasgian religion—a primordial revelation, perhaps, but not an original monotheism in which humanity possessed and later lost an explicit, complete, and true conception of God. And in the same work he criticized the advocates of an original Hebraic monotheism.

representatives of post-Enlightenment romanticism: they supposed a condition of original perfection and attempted to demonstrate historically that the human race actually began in a state of innocence; this belief sometimes led, or was supposed to lead, to the idea that in such a golden age humanity possessed all artistic and scientific knowledge and an immediate vision of God. Hegel is sharply critical of such views. Not only are they historically naive, but also they overlook the fact that nature and spirit originally exist in a state of conflict and that any unity must be *achieved,* brought about by working through the consciousness of *rupture.* He attributes these views, which postulate a past or future paradise, to the difficulty of living in the historical present and of recognizing "the ideal in actuality." At this point, according to the Hotho transcript, Hegel introduced a famous metaphor also used in the preface to the *Philosophy of Right:* "in order to pluck reason, the rose in the cross of the present, one must take up the cross itself" (n. 45). Reason is the rose in the cross of the present because it discloses the ideal and the rational in the midst of the actual and seemingly irrational; but to "pluck" reason involves the "hard labor" of attending to what is presently given rather than looking away to past or future.

The second major topic concerns the "metaphysical concept" of God that is implicit in nature religion. Hegel opens with some observations on the concept of the "metaphysical" in general. Properly understood, it concerns the logical, rational basis for all concrete historical developments, but in natural theology it took the form of proofs for the existence of God. At the basis of all religious proofs is the fundamental religious activity of human being, which is that of "rising" from finite to infinite, from singular to universal, to being-in-and-for-self. This "elevation" or "transition" occurs when finitude becomes aware of its own nothingness, negation, and limit; in fact, the limit of the finite is precisely the infinite, and in this sense the finite already belongs to and "is" its other, the infinite. However, just because what constitutes the transition is the self-*negation* of the finite, a proof cannot be based on it. To posit the infinite from the finite is to assume that the finite *is* something, but it is in fact nothing in itself. The only genuine proof of the infinite is its self-proof. As Hegel puts it, the finite does not posit or pose (*setzen*) the infinite but rather presupposes it (*voraussetzen*); that is, "it posits it in such a way that the *infinite* is rather the first, essential element." "What is meant in religion is not that the infinite *is* by virtue of the affirmative nature of the finite, its immediacy; on the contrary, religion is rather that the infinite is the finite being sublated and sublating itself." That which sublates it, the true infinite, is not an abstract "beyond," but a process of mediation that takes the finite into itself, includes being within itself. This criticism of the cosmological proof, which is considerably more developed than in the *Ms.*, reflects the distinctive way that the "speculative concept of religion" is articulated in the first part of the 1824 lectures.[30] It also provides the basis for a brief critical reference to pantheism, which in Hegel's view follows from universalizing the *finite* in its affirmative, positive qualities and regarding God as the universal being in all existent, determinate being. Such pantheism is found neither in nature religion nor in Spinoza, but it is characteristic of certain modern "enlightened" critics of Spinoza (see nn. 76, 80).

The last main topic to be addressed in this section is a survey of the forms of nature religion,[31] of which there are three. Spirit initially exists in the immediate, empirical form of singular self-consciousness, which knows nothing higher than itself and exercises power over nature; but at the same time there are the beginnings of a process of the objectification of the divine object over against consciousness. This is the religion of magic, including as its highest expression the religion of ancient China (n. 99). In the second place, objectified spirit possesses being and truth within itself, becoming inwardly self-determining and self-unfolding, but at the same time the differentiated moments (finite subject, infinite object) are simply juxtaposed and separated. The first historical expression of this stage of religious

30. See Vol. 1:314–324.

31. It is preceded by a brief section on "the representation of God," which seems to be a carryover from Sec. A.b of the *Ms.* Hegel seems to have started out with the analytic categories applied generally to immediate religion in the *Ms.*—metaphysical concept, concrete representation, cultus—but soon outstripped them. In this section on representation he makes the point that although God is represented in natural objects, these are raised by phantasy to spiritual significance and are not viewed as merely natural powers. In other words, spirit is already present in nature religion; there is no such thing as *purely* natural religion.

consciousness is Buddhism, the religion of being-within-self, although in terms of the organization of the 1824 lectures Buddhism appears as the last moment of the religion of magic; in any case, the pre-eminent exemplification of this stage is Hinduism, the religion of phantasy (see nn. 99, 102). Finally, a transition occurs out of undialectical objectification to the subjectivity of spirit, and God is imagined for the first time as a free subject but still in wholly natural images, so that a "monstrous contradiction" develops between the spiritual and the natural. This is the stage of Persian and Egyptian religion (the religions of light and of the enigma, n. 104), which in the 1824 lectures are treated in two separate sections, so that the religion of magic has four subdivisions rather than three. Hegel concludes this summary by observing that, while it may be difficult for us to grasp the spiritual aspect of nature religion, we can in fact "understand it from within" or "understand our way into it" (*hineinverstehen*), since it is after all a human product, even if we cannot sense, feel, or live in it from within (see n. 107). Reason transcends the barriers that delimit sensation and feeling, and such *Hineinverstehen* is precisely Hegel's agenda throughout *Determinate Religion*.

The Religion of Magic

This section (Sec. A.1) is entirely new in 1824, and Hegel provides a more detailed treatment than in any of the subsequent lectures. He is primarily concerned with the religious practices of Africans and Eskimos, although he makes brief references to Mongols, Chinese, and American Indians; his identifiable sources are a few missionary and travel reports (see n. 108). He distinguishes two basic stages of primitive religious consciousness.

In the first of these (Sec. A.1.a), empirical, singular human self-consciousness knows nothing higher than itself; it is a consciousness that takes the form of power over nature, but it is also confronted by power, the power of the spiritual, in nature. What Hegel calls the religion of magic *exercises* this power, not as an act of fear but out of the freedom (the "unfree freedom") that knows itself as higher than natural things. This knowledge is initially unmediated; that is, it exercises *direct* mastery over nature without the use of any means or media, and it is unaware of any object or power over against itself. Hegel thinks this most primitive kind of religion is found among the Eskimos, who, according to his sources, have no sense of a supernatural power, do not worship the sun, moon, stars, and so on, but who do have magicians ("angekoks") who exercise power over nature by means of words and gestures. Hegel also refers briefly here to certain forms of African religion, but the latter is found mainly at the second stage of religious consciousness.

In this second stage (Sec. A.1.b) a gradual process begins whereby the divine object is "objectified" over against human self-consciousness. Hegel distinguishes between two types of objectification, formal and absolute or actual (see n. 124). In the first of these, which is the subject of the present subsection, the divine power is represented in various ways as independently active over against consciousness. In the second, the divine attains an objectivity that exists in and for itself—a level that is fully realized only with the religion of being-within-self (Buddhism).

Hegel analyzes formal objectification at considerable length, offering a finely nuanced phenomenology of distinguishable stages within it. Initially he says there is a "threefold relationship between the divine object and consciousness," but in the course of exposition another stage is added that mediates between the second and third original stages. In the first stage, consciousness retains power over the object. This is very close to the most primitive form of magic ("singular self-consciousness as power over nature"), but the relationship is now mediated, and the magic is *indirect,* making use of means or media, since there now is an inchoate consciousness of a power over against the self (see n. 138). This type of magic or sorcery is found in "infinite variety," and it opens the floodgates of superstition since the basic principle of magic is that the connection between the means and the outcome cannot be known or understood. In the second stage the object becomes independent, exercising its own power, upon which human beings now find themselves dependent. It first appears as "great elemental objects" of nature, such as sun, moon, sky, sea, river, but these are not actually worshiped as divine until human beings arrive at an intuition of universality. There is little need to pay attention to them as long as they are functioning normally, but when something disruptive or threatening occurs—earthquake, flood, drought, eclipse—it is necessary to petition them. Hence the veneration of these powers is mixed in with magic.

In the next stage, the object or independent power is found in *living* things—plants and various forms of organic life, but especially animals. While it may seem to us degrading to worship animals as gods, this is actually a higher form of religious consciousness: animal cults are found wherever humanity has risen above the purely natural but has not yet grasped *itself* in its spiritual essence. The animal is alive, but because there is something secretive, impenetrable, wondrous about its behavior, it is not surprising that human beings should have regarded animal vitality as higher than their own. But at the same time animals, like other fetishes, can be more or less arbitrarily selected or replaced depending on human needs and temperament.

The fourth stage, finally, is the one at which self-consciousness recognizes its *own* essence in the religious object, but only in the form of single human beings rather than as a universal spiritual principle. Such individuals are usually priests, shamans, or rulers, and at this stage there is as yet no distinction between individuals as such and divinity: this contingent, particular, individual *is* the god. But spirit is believed to be present in humanity, and human self-consciousness is regarded as essentially the presence of spirit. This view "is also present in the Christian religion, but in a more exalted fashion and transfigured." The religions of spirit are found at both the lowest and the highest levels. At the lowest level, this belief often takes the form of veneration of the dead or ancestor worship. Death strips away the ephemeral element, leaving dead spirits that are able to exercise considerable power on the living. Hegel provides a detailed, gory description of how African sorcerers get the dead spirits to pass into their own bodies or exorcise them, by means of frenzied dancing and shouting, sexual orgies, human sacrifice, cannibalism, and the like—he was not one to mince the details of such practices. Cultic activities of this sort are still an attempt to exercise control over nature rather than being a "free, unforced veneration of the essentially spiritual element," which is what cultus properly is.

Chinese Religion

In the 1824 lectures, Chinese religion is treated as part of the religion of magic (Sec. A.1.c), exemplifying the fourth and final stage of formal objectification. What leads into it is the reference at the end of the preceding subsection to the role of dead spirits as rulers over the natural realms; this context accounts for the peculiar focus Hegel brings to bear on the ancient religion of the Zhou dynasty (see n. 172). In this religion, he says, existent singular self-consciousness is still the divine power, in this case the emperor of China, who governs by means of dead spirits known as Shen. Most of this brief section is devoted to a description of the installation ceremonies for a new dynasty, in which the Shen play an important role. Hegel scarcely refers to the Zhou concept of Tian (Heaven), understood as an impersonal power that rules the world by moral force, and he does not recognize that the Chinese clearly distinguished between Tian and the emperors. On Hegel's own terms, Zhou religion is properly an instance of actual rather than formal objectification of the divine essence. For subsequent lectures this subsection is considerably revised.

The Religion of Being-Within-Self: Buddhism

In 1824 this is the last subsection of the religion of magic (Sec. A.1.d); it is really a transitional section, since here we have clearly arrived at actual objectification of the divine object, which has its being precisely *within* itself. Buddhism occupies a key stage in Hegel's phenomenology of religious consciousness, since it constitutes the transition from magic to religion in the proper sense (see n. 183). Unfortunately, Hegel's knowledge of Buddhism was both limited and inaccurate. This was his first attempt to treat the subject, and he relied upon reports primarily by English travelers to the Far East, together with de Mailla's *Histoire générale de la Chine*. His sources were most explicit about Burmese and Tibetan Lamaism, but he did not understand the difference between it and Buddhism, nor was he familiar with the three main schools of Buddhism (Hīnayāna, Mahāyāna, and Vajrayāna) (see n. 190). The view prevalent in Hegel's day placed the life of Buddha around 1000 B.C., and this early dating probably led Hegel to assume that Buddhism was an older religion than Hinduism. Moreover, he seems to have confused the dates of Siddhartha Gautama with the introduction of Buddhism into China, which Hegel calls the religion of Fo after the Chinese name for Buddha (see n. 193). He assumes, therefore, that Buddhism/Lamaism existed well before the life of Gautama, who was one of several Buddhas.

As to the content of this religion, "genuinely objective universality" begins when consciousness comprehends essence as independent, having being-within-self (*Insichsein*); here "the place of divinity . . . emerges for the first time." The essential character of this being-within-self is "nothing else but *thought* itself," and thus human being can know it, have an affirmative relationship to it, find repose in it, allow itself to be absorbed into it. With the recognition that "essence is the eternal rest of inner contemplation," free worship is able to begin, a worship that is able to assume a "theoretical" rather than a "practical" attitude. This is a religion of tranquillity, repose, and contemplation, with "numerous monasteries and great priesthoods."

Hegel discusses only two Buddhist doctrines in any detail. The first is what he takes to be immortality of the soul, based on knowing essential being at rest with itself; but because the outward shape of the soul is a matter of indifference, and because "the inner element is not yet defined as spirit," we find a belief in the transmigration of souls, which applies to the eternal as well as to the human: Buddha and Lama exist in several shapes.[32] The second doctrine is that "'nothing' is the principle, the beginning and the end of everything existing." This "is not nothing in the sense of not being, but it is what is purely identical with itself, undetermined, a substantive being; it is thus completely pure, wholly simple and undifferentiated, eternally at rest; it has neither virtue nor power nor intelligence." Whether or not this nothing is understood to be simply identical with being-within-self, which Hegel earlier describes as "nothing else but thought itself," it does seem clear that he is attempting to interpret

---

32. It is now generally recognized that the Western categories of "immortality of the soul" and "transmigration of the soul" are a misrepresentation of the Buddhist doctrine of "rebirth."

nirvana in Western substance categories. He also seems to confuse two ways of understanding what it means to "attain" nirvana—on the one hand the Hīnayāna stress upon freedom from all worldy miseries, as suggested by one of his sources; and on the other hand, the Mahāyanā stress upon stripping away all desire and activity in a state of union with the Buddha, as suggested by another source (see n. 216).

The Religion of Phantasy: Hinduism

Being-within-self in the mode of indeterminacy is what the Buddhists call nothingness; it is not yet truly God, because only the unity of infinite and finite is genuinely divine. The next step, therefore, is for determination to come into play, for a progressive development of the divine as content to occur, but initially only in the realm of nature, where the different aspects remain held asunder as mutually independent. This independence is intuited at a prereflective stage in a colorful variety of animal and human shapes, between which there are no essential connections, only the fleeting ones provided by phantasy. "Thus we have before us an infinitely varied world of imagination—without objective coherence, an unrestrained revel encompassing all [the divine] content." This, says Hegel, is the Hindu religion (see n. 222); while its principal characteristics "are baroque and have often a wild and repulsive shape," the key thing is to grasp the concept that shows itself here.

This concept is the universal substance, which appears in three elements: first, as having being within itself, reflected into self, simple power locked into itself; second, as manifestation, objectivity, fixed independence; and third, as change, becoming, passing away, not-being (the third element is not yet defined as *spirit,* which would entail return into self). Hindu mythology expresses this concept in the form of the Trimurti—the one, absolute unity of Brahman, which appears in three figures: Brahmā (the active, generative father), Vishnu (manifestation, appearance, incarnation), and Shiva (mutability, creation and destruction). Hegel follows his sources in overestimating the importance of this triadic structure for Hindu thought (see n. 238), and he is not hesitant to find in it anticipations of the Christian Trinity, although of course at a pre-spiritual level. The fluidity in relationship between the principal figures, the introduction of other names such as Rudra, Krishna, and Mahadeva, and the multitude of Hindu sects relating to various deities, show that the conceptualization is still unrefined and unstable.

Hegel turns next to the cultus of Hinduism, which appears in three sorts of relationships between self-consciousness and Brahman. In the first place, every individual Hindu is momentarily Brahman. The implication of this is that "Brahman itself is not worshiped, and has no temple; the one God is not worshiped, no services are held in his honor, no prayers are addressed to him." It is impossible to have a relationship with Brahman because Brahman is the neuter One, not the personal One, the in-itself (*das Ansich*), not the for-itself; it is abstract and achieves subjective existence only in human self-consciousnesses. Brahman is thus to be contrasted with the personal God of Judaism and compared with the "supreme being" of the Enlightenment, which is similarly abstract, empty, unknown (see n. 271). Second, in an effort to give an endurance to Brahman that goes beyond its momentary existence in human awareness, attempts are made to become permanently one with Brahman through rigorously "austere" practices, which have the effect of achieving immobility and lifelessness. Finally there is a caste of Hindus, the Brāhmans, every member of which is immediately one with Brahman; this is a relationship stemming from birth, a natural relationship, not one based on thought, free will, or ethical life. This says a lot, in Hegel's view, about the sort of divinity represented by Brahman.

Hegel concludes that Hinduism is a religion devoid of spirit. Generally, where consciousness of the universal shines through into the particular, as it does in Hinduism, freedom of spirit also comes into being in some form, legal and ethical systems develop, and particularity is delimited by the substantive unity. The unity of Brahman is not genuinely related to the real, to living, active self-consciousness; the particular remains irrational and unfree; Brahman appears only to a few, and for the most part a multitude of particular natural objects are worshiped. Since Brahman itself is not worshiped, the cultus becomes infinite in scope, everything falls within it, the content is both insignificant and unintelligible. Rather than providing satisfaction, enjoyment, freedom, the cultus constrains and constricts, offering at one extreme "the escape offered by abstraction," in the middle a "crude numbing of the senses," and at the other extreme "wild debauchery," the "sorriest depravity."

What accounts for this severely negative assessment? In the first place, although Hegel also drew on less prejudiced articles published in *Asiatic Researches* and had apparently studied fairly carefully the Code of Manu available in the *Institutes of Hindu Law* (1794), most of the sources available to him were prejudiced or ill informed, as indicated in Sec. 2.4 above. In the second place, we know that Hegel was suspicious of the romantic attachment to India that had been prevalent in Germany during his own formative years, as expressed especially by Friedrich Schlegel's *Ueber die Sprache and Weisheit der Indier* (1808). It is evident that his general assessment of Hinduism, which he found confirmed in the English reports, was intended as a deliberate corrective to what he took to be uncritical enthusiasm in German intellectual circles.[33]

As the conclusion to this section, Hegel offers a summary of the structure of nature religion (see n. 296) that differs from that given at the end of the introduction to Sec. A, summarized above. According to this later version, the religion of magic is merely prolegomenon, not yet properly religion. Religion properly so called begins with Buddhism (the self-*containment* of absolute being), continues with Hinduism (the self-*differentiation* of absolute being), and terminates in its natural phase with Persian religion (the *reflection back* into itself of the absolute). Egyptian religion provides the transition from natural to spiritual religion. Thus nature religion is structured into a triad, although five distinct stages are examined.

The Religion of the Good or of Light: Persian Religion

Hegel's knowledge of the religion of ancient Persia (Zoroastrianism) was based primarily on his own study of the Zend-Avesta in the translation by Kleuker from the French edition of Anquetil du Perron, and a few secondary sources (see nn. 302, 308). Here the universal is known as "the good," a category that signifies an *affirmative* coherence between the universal and concrete life. The

33. See Leuze, *Die ausserchristlichen Religionen bei Hegel,* pp. 77–81, and our n. 295 to the 1824 lectures.

good is determined within itself, but it is also the substance present within things. But since the process of its self-determination is still incomplete, the good remains abstract, it has only an unmediated presence in things, and it encounters an *antithesis* that remains external to it and with which it struggles, namely, the realm of evil. Good is destined to overcome evil, "but only *destined* because the struggle has no end." Both good and evil have natural shapes in which they appear in their universality, namely, light and darkness. Light is not simply a symbol of the substantive, ideal element but *is* this element itself; light is the essentiality of all particular things. Thus light is not merely the sun, which is just a particular natural entity; rather, light has the root of subjectivity within itself because it is the universal medium of reflection and reflexivity—but only the root, since this is still a natural medium.

"We all know," says Hegel, "that the worship of light itself has actually existed as the Persian religion, the religion of the Parsees to this day. They revere light, not in the form of the sun—strictly and properly speaking, this is no nature worship—but light as denoting the good; and the good exists as an object, it has the sensible shape of light, a shape that corresponds to the content, which is itself still abstract." Light (or "primal fire" as distinguished from "material fire") assumes human shape in the figure of Ormazd, whose kingdom is the kingdom of light. This universal light is the "ideal" that is present in all things—human spirits both living and departed, animals, rivers, mountains, trees (see nn. 309–312). For Parsees who live in the kingdom of the light, life as a whole is their cultus: their religious law is to do good, live purely, be and act like light. Unlike Hinduism, this is a life-affirming, life-enhancing religion.

The Religion of the Enigma: Egyptian Religion

Hegel's discussion of the religion of "the enigma" (see n. 314) in the 1824 lectures makes few specific references to Egyptian religion; the focus rather is on the conceptual dynamics involved in the transition from natural to spiritual religion. Hegel's information about Egyptian religion was based primarily on reports of classical historians who had visited Egypt, notably Herodotus and Plutarch, as well as modern interpreters of these sources. During the 1820s new information became available as a result of the decipherment of the hieroglyphic system in 1824 and archaeological expeditions, but Hegel made little use of it.

We have already encountered the category of subjectivity in the preceding religions, says Hegel, but only as individual self-determination, not as constitutive of the nature of God. Subjectivity in general is a being-within-self that both differentiates itself in relationship to an other and negates this differentiation, maintaining itself in what it has distinguished, maintaining the other as a moment of itself. In Egyptian religion we begin to see this happening: the negative moment no longer falls outside the good, as in Persian religion, nor does it simply disappear into the One, as in Hinduism. But the divine subjectivity is still affected by nature, it is not free and purely spiritual. We have, after all, "only just embarked on the transition from substantiality to subjectivity"; subjectivity is still mixed up with substantive unity and with the multiplicity of independent configurations. This stage, therefore, is "shot through with inconsistencies"; it is an "enigmatic, confused mixture" of heterogeneous elements.

Hegel attempts to establish three dimensions of the Egyptian representation of God, although it is often difficult to know precisely what he is referring to—whether to ideal distinctions or to actual aspects of Egyptian belief. First, God is "the indwelling nature, the implicit power," for which the outward shape is contingent and arbitrary; it can be either animal or human, and many forms of animal worship are found in this religion, as in Hinduism, although at a certain stage a transition is discernible from the animal shape of God to the human shape.[34] Second, the divine subject relates negatively to itself vis-à-vis an other, which it does not simply absorb. It acts purposively, though still finitely, in relation to the other, which includes evil as well as good—evil objectified in the figure of Typhon (n. 336). A "death" of God appears to be necessary for the concrete realization and representation of God. The moment of negation takes

34. Hegel seems to say that this transition occurs as a "third moment" (of Egyptian religion?), but the third moment in the representation of God is the one in which the evil principle is vanquished and God "reestablishes himself." Hegel refers to two different "third moments," and the structure of the argument is not clear at this point.

on the shape of death, and this is not an accidental mortality as in the case of the Lama or Buddha, but comprises an element of God's essence. Finally, God reestablishes himself, rises from the dead, and thus becomes implicitly spirit, for spirit is what "eternally reverts back into itself." But at this stage the continued mingling of nature and spirit is evidenced by the fact that "the reborn god is simultaneously represented as deceased, as the god of the under-world"; the history of the divine subject coincides with the universal history of natural objects. This history of the dying and rising God is symbolically portrayed in the Egyptian god Osiris, but it is also the history of the sun, the Nile, the waxing and waning of the year; it is the natural cycle of birth, growth, death, and rebirth.

But the natural cycle itself and natural objects are not worshiped. They become symbols of something higher through artistic representation. Art is not needed when the deity merely has a natural shape; it comes into play, and must finally work only with human shapes, when God is defined as genuinely subject. Genuine art is religious art, and Egyptian civilization was the first to achieve genuine art in the service of religion; its cultus has "the form of art." The defect in art, says Hegel, is the fact that the artifact, the god, is fashioned by human hands; hence the need felt by the Egyptians to consecrate the images, to invest divine spirit in the images by incantation. Presumably this would not be necessary when the artistic form perfectly corresponds to the divine content, *is* the content. Greek art approximates this goal more fully than any other; but when the goal itself is reached, we are beyond art and have arrived at the religion of incarnation in which God, as spirit in-and-for-self, pro-duces *himself,* is not produced by human hands, presents himself as being for others in human shape. But Egyptian religion stands at the beginning of art, not at the end of art. It is only halfway to being spirit; in it we can witness the fascinating inversion of creative roles between nature and self-consciousness—we see the artistic shape forcing its way out of the animal and into the human in the image of the sphinx. Because of its continued intermingling of subjectivity and substantiality, because it continues both to imitate and to distort, this art does not yet have the shape of *beauty*—it is not yet fine art (*schöne Kunst*).

Hegel concludes this section with a summary of what is now designated as *four* stages of nature religion, and with a foretaste of what is entailed in completing the transition to the religions of spiritual individuality. The freedom resulting from God's free self-determination as subject becomes the basis of human ethical life; we are leaving the kingdom of nature and entering the kingdom of freedom.

The Religions of Spiritual Individuality

The basic characteristic of the new sphere (Sec. B) is spiritual subjectivity or individuality. Subjectivity is "the wholly free power of self-determination." When the power that is active in self-consciousness is *universal,* then it is what we call *wisdom;* and because it is a question of *self*-determination, this wisdom is *purposive* or intentional: it is a wise purpose and a purposive wisdom, not simply blind, purposeless power. The category of purpose is immediately involved in the concept of free subjectivity; and insofar as purposive action is determined through freedom or by the act of the subject, it "has no outcome save what is already there" within the subject implicitly. "Purposive action is wise action inasmuch as wisdom consists in acting in conformity with universal purposes that are valid in and of themselves." It is in such terms that God is now to be understood. But God is not a mere thought, idea, volition, or intention; rather he is one who appears, is a subject who acts, crosses over into existence or actuality. There must, accordingly, be a "soil" in which the divine purposes become actual and determinate. For the stage at which we have arrived, this soil is no longer nature but self-consciousness or finite spirit, that is, humanity. At this stage, however, the divine purpose is still contingent, finite, external, not truly determined by the divine concept. Therefore we have to do with religions of *finite* spirituality as distinguished from the infinite spirituality of the consummate religion.

This summary indicates that the conceptual framework for Sec. B of the 1824 lectures is quite different from that found in the *Ms.*, where the central categories are essence, power, and necessity. For the *Ms.*, the power of Jewish religion is not yet understood as wisdom (although there are hints in this direction); the necessity of Greek religion is not purposive but cold and blind (although the gods act purposively); and the category of purpose does not emerge until the third stage of determinate religion, that of Roman expediency. This shift has an obvious impact on Hegel's assessment of Jewish and Greek religion (especially the former), but it also occasions a reorganization of the whole of the latter part of determinate religion: the second and third stages of the *Ms.* (which are still distinguished in the Introduction to Part II of 1824) are combined into a single stage, the moments of which are determined by the different ways in which divine purpose actualizes itself in relation to finite spirit. Roman religion goes from being "transitional" to being fully incorporated into the religions of spiritual individuality.

Hegel's "division of the subject" summarizes the three religions of Sec. B as follows: (1) The religion of sublimity (Jewish religion). Here we have the infinitely self-contained power of the One, who exists solely for thought, who negates whatever is natural and immediate, and who tolerates no other gods beside him. The purpose of this God is unitary and infinite, but at the same time limited to a particular people. (2) The religion of beauty (Greek religion). Here we find not one but many purposes, which no longer are exclusive but serene, tolerant, friendly. This plurality of purposes allows the means to subsist alongside it, deigns to appear in the soil of nature and finite spirit, thus gives rise to the category of beauty, since the beautiful is "a purpose in itself that is amicably disposed to immediate existence." The price that is paid for this is the disappearance of the One, the absolute subject; and the universal hovers above what is beautiful as cold necessity that is neither subject nor wise. (3) The religion of expediency (Roman religion). Here the particularity and singularity of purpose have been enlarged to universal scope, but this is merely an "empirically external" universality, not a universality of the concept. It encompasses the whole world, having as its goal cold, absolute, abstract power—world domination, world mastery.

Hegel ends the division of the subject with the intriguing proposal that these religions correspond to three of the religions of nature "in inverse order." Jewish religion corresponds to Persian: in both we find a single, particular, inward purpose, the one expressed in the natural image of light, the other in the spiritual shape of the one absolute subject. Greek religion corresponds to Hindu: both have a plurality of purposes and subjectivities, with one abstract power over them (Brahman, necessity). And Roman religion corresponds to the religion of ancient China: the formal objectification of the divine in the singular self-consciousness of the Chinese emperor corresponds to the empirically universal purpose of Roman religion, which is the advancement of the Roman state. Whereas in the natural religions we have a gradual "withdrawal" of the natural manifold into the simple naturalness of light, in the spiritual religions we have an "unfolding" of the singular divine subject into empirical universality—but in such a way that it becomes destructive and meaningless, the power of death rather than of life. This is Hegel's way of suggesting in 1824, as he did also in the *Ms.*, that determinate or finite religion cycles back upon itself. Determinate religion is no longer composed of an inner triad (religions of nature, finite spirit, and expediency), but forms the first two parts of a larger triad (nature religion, religion of spiritual individuality, consummate religion) that culminates in Christianity. This "culmination," however, does not occur as a progressive advance, since finite religion ends in degeneracy and death, in a return to the primitive at a more developed stage of culture. The whole dialectical structure resists any monolithic, linear theory of progress. Whatever the reasons for this structural experiment, Hegel did not stick with it in the later lectures; he restored the inner triad to determinate religion—but with interesting surprises still in store.

The greater part of the introduction to the religions of spiritual individuality is taken up by a lengthy discussion of the proofs of the existence of God related to the metaphysical concepts of God found in these religions. The metaphysical concept of God in Judaism is that of unity; in Greek religion it is necessity; and in Roman religion it is purposiveness. Each of these yields a different sort of proof; the first two are versions of the cosmological proof, while the last is the teleological proof. At this point Hegel brings together and greatly expands upon his discussion in the *Ms.* of the cosmological proof as it relates to the religions of sublimity and beauty (*Ms.* Sec. B.a), and of the teleological proof as it relates to the religion of expediency (*Ms.* Sec. C.a) (see n. 409).

The proof based on divine unity utilizes the "quite impoverished categories of one and many. It is an ancient dictum, which we find already in Greek sources, that only the One is, and not the many" (see n. 421). While this may be logically correct, the question is whether the One *is God*. The concept of God is not exhausted by the category of oneness, which is an undialectical category, lacking mediation.

The proof related to the concept of necessity is based on the well-known argument from contingency to necessity. Hegel asks whether there is any essential difference between this form of the cosmological proof and the form based on the argument from finite to infinite, which we have already encountered in the religions of nature (see n. 428). While the logical form of these proofs is quite similar, the "contingent" is a richer, more concrete category than the "finite," since it contains its own negation within itself; it is precisely what is only possible, it may exist or not exist, and therefore the *truth* of contingent existence is necessity. The necessity in question must be *inner* necessity, since external necessity is itself contingent. The argument is typically set forth in the form of a syllogism: "Contingent things presuppose an absolute, necessary cause; contingent things do exist—I am, the world is; therefore an absolutely necessary cause exists." While the major premise is logically correct (without it we would have an infinite regress), the proof is defective in that it sets up contingent things on one side and necessity on the other, and then expresses the relation between them as one of "presupposing," "entailing," and so forth. Thus it appears that contingent things condition absolute necessity: *their* existence (the minor premise) is the condition for concluding that absolute necessity also exists. But absolute necessity cannot be conditioned by or dependent on anything outside itself. The authentic form of this proof would be to start with the process of mediation intrinsic to absolute necessity, and to comprehend contingent things as moments or stages in the process, posited by the absolute precisely as contingent, as negative, as not having being in and for themselves. But this is the ontological proof, not the cosmological proof. The only genuine proof must start with the infinite rather than attempt to *establish* the infinite from the empirical existence of the finite world. This critique is quite similar to the one advanced earlier regarding the argument from finite to infinite.

The proof based on purposiveness is the teleological proof. The purposiveness in question must be external rather than internal, since, while we do encounter internal purposiveness in organic life, such life is also dependent on external relations and means (on the distinction between external and internal purposiveness, see n. 466). Given the apparent, indeed marvelous harmony between externally related things in the world, a harmony that cannot be accounted for in terms of the things themselves, we must posit a "third thing," a third rational, ordering, principle, which enables externally related things to serve purposively as means for each other—hence the necessity of a supreme ordering being, a supremely wise, powerful, purposive being. This is the "physicotheological proof" (n. 484), and Kant has provided the classic refutation of it in *The Critique of Pure Reason* (see nn. 487 ff.). Hegel does not simply accept the Kantian critique but reworks and expands it. His key point again is that we cannot argue from empirically observed worldly circumstances, which are necessarily relative and finite, to the absolute and infinite. We cannot argue from power to *omni*potence, from wisdom to *omni*science. At best, what this proof affords is a concept of *great* wisdom, power, unity, and so on. But what we want in God is *absolute* wisdom, power, unity. "From 'great' to 'absolute' we make the leap." Moreover, observes Hegel, the worldly, human purposes in view are not only finite and contingent but also quite petty. If the aim is to stir the heart, that can be achieved by this proof—"there is nothing upon which piety cannot feed"—but to achieve cognition of *God* by means of it is another matter. Nor can a proof be based on the assumed predominance of good over evil in ethical matters, for the evidence is quite ambiguous. Finally, even if the proof should succeed, it could yield only a "power" that operates in conformity with purposes, not a personal, spiritual God. We arrive, therefore, once again at the conclusion that, while all these proofs contain valid elements, the only adequate proof is the ontological proof.

The Religion of Sublimity: Jewish Religion

Hegel's interpretation of Judaism undergoes a striking metamorphosis in 1824. The fundamentally negative cast of the treatment just three years earlier—the *Ms.*'s stress on the abstract power of God, the indeterminacy of God's relation to the world, the contingency and dependence of the world, the servile consciousness expressed in "fear of the Lord" and in the "feeling of dependence"—is replaced by a more balanced and fully developed assessment. The introduction of the categories of wisdom and purpose, mandated by the general reconception of the religions of spiritual individuality in the 1824 lectures, has something to do with this reinterpretation, but basically it seems to be the result of a deeper and more appreciative evaluation of the literature of the Old Testament on Hegel's part.

After a brief reference to the metaphysical concept of God in Judaism—the "infinitely important" recognition that God is simply and solely One, which is the ground of the absolute spirituality of God, "the path to truth" (Sec. B.1.a)—Hegel turns to the "divine self-determination" as expressed representationally, discovering much that he had overlooked before (Sec. B.1.b). The fundamental self-determination of God is not yet internal (for then he would be spirit) but external, the act of creation and preservation. God is not the result of the creative process—this is no theogony, an issuing-forth of the gods—but the starting point; and, as distinct from human production, this is an absolute creation, *ex nihilo*, an inner, "intuitive," eternal activity on God's part. God's creation and preservation of the world show forth his goodness and justice, indicating that what is at work here is infinite, purposive wisdom, not just abstract power. Created things are regarded as prosaic, stripped of divinity, devoid of autonomy, and the externality of nature is clearly recognized. This de-divinization of nature is a necessary step toward a valid understanding of the relationship of God and world. In Jewish religion this relationship is understood essentially in terms of God's *sublimity*. Sublimity means that God is exalted above the reality in which he appears, and that the reality itself is negated or totally subjected to God's power. For example, God creates by means of a word, which immediately passes away; or natural media such as wind, lightning, and thunder are totally obedient to God's bidding.

The representation of God's purpose is both "theoretical" and "practical." God's theoretical purpose is that he and he alone should be recognized (not yet cognized) and glorified. His practical, worldly purpose is now an ethical (no longer a natural) purpose, having its soil in human self-consciousness and freedom. But we are still at the stage of immediate, natural ethical life, and hence the family is the ethical form in which the divine purpose is realized—this one family, the Jewish people, to the exclusion of all others. Here we encounter the striking, "infinitely difficult" contradiction that is present in Jewish religion: on the one hand God is universal, the God of all humanity ("all peoples are called upon to recognize him and glorify his name," Ps. 117:1–2), but on the other hand his purposes and operations are so limited as to be confined to just this one people, defined by birth and race. For this reason, in Hegel's view, the universal content of the story of the creation and fall of humanity in Genesis 1–3 became disconnected from subsequent Jewish piety. Jewish particularity, however, is not polemical, because there is no obligation to convert other peoples to the God of Israel. While others are called upon to glorify the Lord, this is not a goal, as in Islam, which is pursued with fanaticism. Judaism has become fanatical only when attacked, only when its existence has been threatened.

The cultus of Jewish religion (Sec. B.1.c) has two closely related moments, one negative, the other affirmative. The negative aspect is fear, fear of the Lord. But—and this is where 1824 departs decisively from the *Ms.*—this is no earthly lord that is feared. It is rather fear of the absolute, in which everything ephemeral and contingent is given up and through which one is elevated to the level of pure thought. Hence fear of the Lord *is the beginning of wisdom.* "Wisdom" means not taking anything particular to be absolute and substantive; it means recognizing the relativity of all that is finite. Hence *this* fear of the Lord entails a fundamental liberation from all earthly forms of bondage, a letting everything go, an immersion in the Lord, "having this unity as one's object and essence." It is a far cry from what is termed a "feeling of dependence." Whereas in the *Ms.* Judaism is viewed as an embodiment of Schleiermacher's definition of religious piety, now it is just the reverse: Judaism is the first of the religions of freedom, and Schleiermacher's version of religion as dependence is reserved solely for the Romans (this matter is discussed at length in n. 551).

The affirmative side of Jewish worship arises directly from what has just been said. The fear of the Lord that is the beginning of wisdom yields an absolute trust, an infinite faith, which passes over into a distinctive kind of existence. This trust "is preserved through so many great victories, which are emphasized also in Christianity. It is this trust, this faith of Abraham's, that causes the history of this people to carry on." Such an assessment undoubtedly represents an important shift from the portrayal of Abraham and his people in *The Spirit of Christianity and Its Fate.* But Hegel himself does not take into account the history of this people; his treatment is limited to what he regards as the oldest biblical expressions of Israelite faith. Judaism is not viewed as a living religion; for that matter, no other religions are, either, except for Christianity.

Infinite faith is also the theme of the Book of Job. Rather than interpreting Job as the portrayal of abstract divine power, as in the *Ms.*, Hegel now stresses the divine wisdom. As over against the juridical morality of Job and his comforters, which presumes that the righteous will be rewarded and the wicked punished, the wisdom of God is revealed (by the voice from the whirlwind) to be infinitely higher and incalculable. Only when Job submits to this wisdom is he restored. Thus a reconstitution of human being occurs in this absolute relation to the absolute, a theme already sounded in the *Ms.* God's *covenant* with his people is a symbol of this reconstitution. Positively the covenant gives possession (not ownership) of the land; negatively it entails service to the Lord through obedience to the law and commandments. Hegel considers only the legal, not the prophetic understanding of the covenant; in this and other respects his approach is skewed by the narrow range of biblical literature that he consults.

The Religion of Beauty: Greek Religion

The form of Hegel's treatment of Greek religion in 1824 differs as greatly from the *Ms.* as the *Ms.* itself differs from *The Phenomenology of Spirit.* The material has been thoroughly reorganized, and the presentation is much clearer. The sources, however, as well as Hegel's basic interpretative perspective, remain largely unchanged (see n. 573).

The discussion of the metaphysical concept of God in Greek religion (Sec. B.2.a) is quite brief and entirely different from that in the *Ms*. No mention is made of necessity in this connection, as would have been expected not only from the *Ms*. but also from the introductory discussion of the metaphysical concept of God at the beginning of Sec. B of 1824. Rather the basic concept is that of subjectivity or self-determining power. In Judaism this power was universal but abstract, withdrawn, and singular in purpose; now, says Hegel, it *particularizes* itself in a "circle" of gods—"the divine penetrates into the determinate relationships of the actual spirit," providing a basis for real freedom of subjectivity and a scope for real ethical life. This process involves a "downgrading" of the transcendent universality of God but an elevation of purpose in the direction of the universal.

The lengthy second section (Sec. B.2.b) discusses both the content and the shape of the representation of God in Greek religion. Under *content*, three themes are elaborated. The first is that of "particularization" (*Besonderung*), which has already been mentioned. In Greek religion, divinity determines itself, "opens itself up," makes itself available to and infuses the finite world in the form of independent deities. The materials for the representation of the gods are drawn from both natural and spiritual realms; these are the universal elements, so to speak, of physical and natural life. In the old Greek nature religion, the gods were represented as natural powers; here Hegel alludes to the theogonic myth as presented by Hesiod (see n. 589). In the classical period of Greece, however, the spiritual principle vanquished the nature religions; the old gods of nature were subjugated by the new gods of the free spirit led by Zeus. But the natural element was sublimated, not eliminated; the new gods have physical ancestors and are "intrinsically dual" in nature. The second point with regard to content is that the universal power of necessity hovers above the gods. This power is devoid of purpose and subjectivity, it is incomprehensible and abstract; and these two sides of divinity remain unmediated. Finally, says Hegel, there is a purely contingent singularization of the divine content, based not on the principle of particularization but on contingent natural aspects (such as the procreative, generative element in nature) or on the involvement of the gods in human affairs.

With regard to the configuration or *shape* of God in human consciousness, Hegel distinguishes two aspects: on the one hand, the appearance of God is represented as something God does, on the other hand as something that consciousness does. "On the speculative level, this doubled activity must appear as one activity in which the two sides coalesce; but here two activities are apparent, the one coming from one side, the other as a process of production through the activity of the other side, namely self-consciousness." While the distinction remains because the standpoint is still finite, Greek religion in its more developed phase stresses the latter, this being its unique contribution to the history of religious consciousness. The "productive activity of the finite self-consciousness" is "the aspect under which human beings make or shape their God for themselves. Herodotus states categorically: "Homer and Hesiod made the Greeks' gods for them" [see n. 621]. . . . This is where art has principally its actuality."

But a natural element remains in this shaping and appearing of God. We are not yet in the sphere where absolute spirit exists for spirit, where God is worshiped in spirit and in truth. God does not yet appear as "the presence of a singular self-consciousness, i.e., a human being." To be sure, the sensible shape in which the divine appears is the *human* shape. But it is not the figure of an empirical human being, not one that expresses "implicit actuality immediately"; rather it is an *ideal,* essentially *beautiful* shape, an artistic representation of the spiritual in the natural. In other words, the natural or sensible is "molded to fit the content it is to express," to *resemble* the divinity in outward form or action. The sensible is still "soft enough" to be so molded. It is only when God appears in and as the subjectivity of spirit qua spirit that the sensible nature shows itself to be unsuited to his shape. "Sensible nature, immediate singularity is nailed to the cross. Spirit as universal, the community, is the soil for God's appearance. The appearance is absolute, its element spirit itself" (see n. 627).[35]

35. This has implications as well for Hegel's christology. See our discussion of the transition from the sensible to the spiritual presence of God in Christ, as portrayed by the 1824 lectures, in the editorial introduction to Vol. 3. In the 1831 lectures,

The *cultus* (Sec. B.2.c) "is the relationship through which the externality of the represented deity, its objectivity over against subjective consciousness, is sublated." Hegel considers three aspects: the disposition of the worshipers, the character of worship, and the process of reconciliation. Regarding the first, while the divine content is recognized and honored as objective, as valid in and for itself, it is also known to be objective in the subject as well. The divine powers for the Greeks are the people's own customs, ethical life, rights, spirit, and substance (Athena is the city and also the goddess), not an external substantiality. Thus worshipers are able to be free and serene, at home with themselves in the act of worship. But there is also a recognition that necessity has its own sphere over against humanity, encountered especially by heroes who raise themselves above custom and convention. Necessity evokes a disposition of sorrow rather than serenity—not discontent but sorrowful resignation, since there is no absolute or essential purpose in the cosmos. Regarding the aspect of worship, Hegel considers the role of sacrifice, games and festivals, and oracles. Finally, something like "reconciliation" occurs in Greek religion—an inward realization of the divine in the soul whereby its independence and estrangement are overcome. There must, first of all, be a sublation of the natural will and appetite through education and cultural formation, through a spiritual "conversion." This is essentially the function of the Eleusinian mysteries, which represent a mythic, prerational form of enlightenment. Hegel believes that the mysteries are a carryover from the old nature religion, no longer necessary with the artistic transfiguration of experience accomplished in classical Greece. Here Hegel touches upon his disagreement with Creuzer, which is more in evidence in the *Ms.* (see nn. 675, 678). Reconciliation is also necessary with reference to misfortunes and actual human crimes. However, sacrifices to propitiate the gods or avert a natural calamity are a relic

---

Hegel remarks that the problem with Greek religion is not that God is represented as *too* human, but rather that God is *insufficiently* human: the human shape of God does not penetrate to the spiritual core of humanity but remains fixed in the outward sensible shape (see below, n. 43). For Christianity, Jesus as an empirical individual does not outwardly resemble God; he is no Greek god. God appears in the spiritual, ethical shape of his life rather than in his physical shape.

from the past; and in the highest form of Greek consciousness, as expressed by the tragedians, crimes are atoned for not simply through punishment, revenge, or outward purification, but through an inward cleansing. Here we find a "foreshadowing" of the Christian conception of grace.

Throughout, Hegel's interpretation can be seen as pressing Greek religion to its limits as well as insisting upon the essential change that occurs with the artistic intuition of the divine in the shape of free though still finite spirit.

The Religion of Expediency: Roman Religion

Whereas for the most part the 1824 lectures expand and revise the corresponding *Ms.* sections considerably, in the case of Roman religion the 1824 version is much briefer and follows the *Ms.* in essential details (see n. 701). Having worked out his interpretation earlier, Hegel could now condense, focusing on the key issues and not according Roman religion undue attention. The category of purposiveness and the teleological proof had already been examined in detail at the beginning of Sec. B. It is also possible that Hegel found himself short of time, having introduced a great deal of new material on natural religion at the beginning of Part II.

What is primarily different in 1824 is the treatment of the transitions. The movement from Jewish to Greek to Roman religion is now viewed as a movement from exclusive (or singular) to plural to universal (though finite and external) purposiveness, rather than as a transition from power to necessity to purpose. Or, more precisely, the necessity that is essentially purposeless in Greek religion (although the gods express a multitude of purposes) is now identified with a purpose—a purpose that is as universal as necessity itself but at the same time empirical, external, and political in character, namely, world dominion on the part of the Roman Empire. Islamic religion, we are told, also has world dominion as its purpose, but of a spiritual rather than a political character.

Hegel's discussion of the "configuration of the gods" and the cultus in the second and third subsections is taken from the *Ms.* but compressed. He refutes the general notion that the Greek and Roman deities are essentially similar; the latter are "serious" and functional rather than serene and free. The two basic functions they serve are world dominion and the needs of everyday life. A description of the Roman deities and festivals, drawn from Moritz's *Anthousa,* leads us to wonder "how such things can be venerated as gods." New gods are introduced whenever particular needs arise—relief from plague, public sanitation, victory in battle, and so on—and thus Roman worship is "a theogony in progress." The Romans plundered the Mediterranean world, "carrying off whole shiploads of gods to Rome," where they made a pantheon in which "all the gods of all the peoples are set up side by side, so that they extinguish one another." Rather than serving as a liberation from worldly concerns, an elevation to the infinite and substantial, this religion is one of dependence, unfreedom, superstition (see n. 723). It is a religion that finally venerates above all else "death devoid of spirit," as evidenced by the Roman games and spectacles—a "murder game willed by irrational caprice."

The transition to the next stage is nuanced somewhat differently in 1824. What we find in Roman religion is an infinitization and universalization of the finite, indeed of the finite subject ("I am the absolute, self-sustaining atom"). Thus there appears in this religion for the first time an "infinitude of subjectivity"—but only in an empirical, immediate, untrue sense, which cannot be sustained. Infinite subjectivity must now be taken in a higher sense, as pertaining to the *idea,* to *absolute spirit* as it mediates itself with itself. This is the true infinite as opposed to the spurious deification of the finite ego, the most blatant form of which is worship of the Roman emperors. The stage has been set for the confrontation between Christ and Caesar.

c. The Lectures of 1827

The substance of Hegel's interpretation of the religions was established in 1824; hence it will not be necessary to provide an equally detailed synopsis of the remaining lectures. We shall focus, instead, on the shifts in emphasis, organization, and argument, and on the introduction of new materials. It should be noted, first, that our text of the 1827 lectures is only slightly more than half the length of the 1824 text, which is based on Griesheim. This can be explained by several factors. In 1827 the summer semester was shorter by nearly four weeks than the 1824 semester,[36] and at least half the reduction must have been accomplished in Part II of the lectures since Parts I and III are only moderately shorter. Furthermore, in 1827 Hegel transferred the proofs of the existence of God, which made up nearly a fifth of Part II in 1824, to Part I. Finally our text for 1827 is based on Lasson, who fragmented the materials and avoided duplication between 1824 and 1827 in his editing of *Determinate Religion*. We know, therefore, that Lasson's text is incomplete, and it can be only partially supplemented by the presently available transcripts.

Hegel did not simply repeat the earlier lectures, although he was working from an edited copy of Griesheim; as always, he was seeking new formulations and experimenting with new interpretative proposals. In many respects, the argument of the 1827 lectures is presented with greater clarity and simplicity, and with more concrete references to religious practices. It builds upon and refines the speculative attainments of 1824.

The introductory summary of the three stages of determinate religion is inherited from 1824, which, as we have pointed out, initially projected a threefold division as well. Already the summary anticipates certain changes that are more fully developed in 1831 (see 1827 lectures, n. 2), but it does not anticipate the reversal in the order in which Greek and Jewish religion are actually treated in 1827 (see nn. 18, 347). The three stages are: religion as the unity of the spiritual and the natural (nature religion), the elevation of the spiritual above the natural (Jewish and Greek religion), and the religion in which purposiveness is not yet spiritual (the religion of expediency, which can also be called the religion of fate or destiny because it is devoid of spirit).

Immediate Religion, or Nature Religion

From the introduction to Sec. A in 1824, the 1827 lectures retain only the discussion of the "original condition" of humanity and the summary of the forms of nature religion.

The discussion of the first matter expands the 1824 version by introducing an exegesis of the biblical story of the fall of humanity.

36. See Vol. 1:4.

In order to support his argument that the original condition was not a state of innocence and innate wisdom, but rather one of barbarism and savagery, Hegel appeals to the "profound" story in Genesis, which shows that the cleavage or rupture of consciousness occurred at the very beginning of human history. It is by means of this cleavage that the knowledge of both good and evil first arose, a knowledge that is the condition of possibility for human freedom and maturation. "That is the genuine idea in contrast with the mere image of paradise, or this stupified innocence devoid of consciousness and will." Hegel repeats this interpretation of the fall in Part III, which is the only context in which it is found in the *Ms.* and 1824. Since such repetition is unusual for him, he may initially not have intended to do so. In 1831 the discussion of the fall was transferred from Part III to Part II, but there it was treated in relation to Jewish religion rather than the so-called original condition.

Nature religion, says Hegel, is not religion in which natural, physical objects are taken to be God and revered as God. Rather it is the spiritual that is the object of nature religion as well, but "the spiritual [recognized] first in its immediate and natural mode," which is the sensibly existing human being. Thus the several stages of nature religion are distinguished on the basis of how human beings represent and relate to God as infinite and essential spirit. This leads to a somewhat different phenomenology of the initial stages of religious consciousness from that found in 1824. The primary difference, at least according to this introductory summary, is that objectification of the divine object appears to occur much later, at the point of the Persian religion of light rather than the Buddhist religion of being-within-self. Yet Buddhism is now clearly recognized to be a distinct stage and not simply the highest form of the religion of magic.

The Religion of Magic

In 1824 Hegel combined a phenomenology of stages of primitive religious consciousness with specific examples of the religion of magic in the first two subsections of "The Religion of Magic." In 1827 he separated these two elements, placing the phenomenology in the subsection we have titled "The Concept of Magic" and the discussion of specific historical practices in the subsection titled "Less Developed Religions of Magic." The analysis presented in the first subsection differs considerably in content from that found in 1824. Magic involves a more or less *direct* power over nature, and is to be distinguished from the kind of *indirect* power exercised by higher culture on the basis of stepping back from an immediate relationship to the natural world, understanding it scientifically in terms of physical laws, and measuring and controlling it through technical instruments. Gone from the 1827 treatment is the phenomenology of stages of the "formal objectification of the divine object," which discovered in 1824 the beginnings of an indirect relationship to nature already at an early stage. Rather, according to 1827, all the "less developed" forms of magic involve a direct use of power in one form or another. From this is distinguished only a "more developed" form of magic—the religion of ancient China, which in 1824 was identified with the fourth and final phase of formal objectification; yet the examples of the religion of magic presented in the second subsection are identical with the 1824 materials and drawn from the same sources.

The State Religion of the Chinese Empire and the Dao

This religion is still magic, according to 1827, but it is a *developed* religion of magic. Despite this classification, Hegel's treatment in 1827 has advanced considerably beyond that found in 1824—has advanced, in fact, to the point where it is difficult to argue that we really are still at the stage of magic (see n. 96). At the outset, Hegel distinguishes among three phases of Chinese religion: the oldest is the state religion of the Chinese empire, which is the religion of heaven; the second is the religion of the Dao, or of reason; the third is Chinese Buddhism, introduced in the first century A.D. The present subsection is concerned with the first two of these religions.

As to the first, Hegel now recognizes that what we find is not simply emperor worship but a higher religious symbol, that of heaven or Tian, which represents the power of nature but as displaying also moral characteristics. It designates "wholly indeterminate and abstract universality." Because of the abstractness of Tian, it is still

59

the emperor who is sovereign on earth. Only the emperor is connected with Tian, and only he rules over everything earthly, including the natural powers and the departed spirits. Tian itself is empty; everything concrete derives from the emperor and his direct control: hence in Hegel's view this is still a religion of magic. Following these references to Tian, Hegel, on the basis of closer study of the Jesuit *Mémoires concernant les Chinois* as well as volume 6 of the *Allgemeine Historie der Reisen,* returns to the rites surrounding the establishment of a new dynasty, including the role of the Shen, to which he devoted exclusive attention in 1824.

Hegel's discussion of the religion of the Dao ("reason" or "the way") is based on the *Mémoires concernant les Chinois,* Gaubil's French translation of the Shu-jing, and Abel-Rémusat's *Mémoire sur la vie et les opinions de Lao-Tseu.* According to these sources, the Daoist sect arose in the twelfth century, a view not supported by modern scholarship (see n. 115). Hegel believes that it is a sect of masters and teachers, withdrawn from the state religion, who lived in the mountains, devoted to the study of the way and to religious exercises. Because it represents a return of consciousness to itself and the demand for the inward mediation of substantial power, Daoism constitutes a transition to the next stage of nature religion, that of being-within-self. In Daoism itself, however, the symbols remain abstractly rational ciphers—exhibiting a triadic structure, to be sure—so that vitality, consciousness, and spirituality remain attached to the immediate human being, the emperor. In this respect we are still at the stage of magic, despite the reforms introduced by Lao-zi and Confucius.

The Religion of Being-Within-Self: Buddhism

Buddhism is now considered as a distinct phase of nature religion, not as the highest form of the religion of magic, and Hegel's portrayal is more fully developed, although it is not based on new sources; rather the sources available in 1824 are utilized more fully. Scant attention is paid to historical matters, which is just as well, considering the lack of reliable information.

Hegel focuses the 1827 treatment more specifically on the Buddhist conception of ultimate reality as "nothing" or "not-being."[37] This, he says, is "the absolute foundation, the indeterminate, the negated being of everything particular"; "only the nothing has genuine autonomy, for in contrast all other actuality has none." The goal of human existence is the state of negation in this nothing, which the Buddhists call nirvana—a state of eternal tranquility, of cessation, of indifference, of purity, of freedom from worldly miseries. It may seem strange to think of God as nothing, but in fact an important dimension of the truth about God is thereby expressed. For it means that God is nothing determinate; just this absence of determinacy constitutes his infinity. When we say that God is infinite, we mean that he is the negation of everything particular. Thus to say that God is nothing does not mean that he is not, but rather that God is "the empty," and that "this emptiness is God."

This sympathetic attempt to grasp the meaning of Buddhist nirvana—although couched in Western ontological categories—brings Hegel to a defense of Oriental pantheism over against the attacks on pantheism to which the 1827 lectures respond at a number of points (see n. 138). For Oriental consciousness the main theme is the independence and unity of the universal, whereas for Western consciousness it is the individuality of things, especially of human beings. But there is an essential truth in the Oriental intuition of the universal—not the spurious claim that "all is God" (which would be an apotheosis of finite things) but rather the truth that "the All is God," "the All that remains utterly one" and thus is the *negativity* of finite things (see n. 167). The "pan" of pantheism is to be taken as universality, not as totality. This is the essential truth that was grasped by Spinoza, despite the "babblers" who accuse him of atheism.

The limitation in the Oriental (and presumably also in the Spinozistic) view is that God is not merely substance, the absolutely one substance; he is also subject, the one infinite subject. Oriental

37. See n. 145. He also expands the 1824 discussion of the transmigration of souls, which is a sensible form of immortality.

consciousness recognized this only indirectly and imperfectly, by claiming that the one substance also exists in immediate sensible presence in empirical human beings. Hence we find the—to us "shocking"—view that a particular Buddha or Dalai Lama simply *is* God, indeed that the subjectivity and shapes of the one substance are multiple, since there are several lamas and many Buddhas. The "rational aspect" of such a view is that precisely thereby subjectivity and substance are mediated, though in a defective shape. The defectiveness is heightened for Hegel by the accounts of the Tibetan lamas provided by English travelers, especially Turner's version (see n. 188) of how a new lama was discovered in a still-nursing child when the previous one suddenly died of smallpox.

The Hindu Religion

The substance of Hegel's treatment of Hinduism in 1827 is quite similar to the 1824 version, even though he no longer employs the designation "the religion of phantasy" (see n. 192). The sources are also similar, though supplemented by Wilhelm von Humboldt's paper on the Bhagavad-Gītā (1826), of which Hegel wrote a lengthy review in 1827 (see n. 204), as well as A. W. Schlegel's edition of the Bhagavad-Gītā (1823) and H. T. Colebrooke's essay "On the Philosophy of the Hindus" (1824).

Hegel stresses once again the contrast between the one universal substance (Brahman) and its particularization in a multiplicity of finite personified powers, which are not images of a "beautiful imagination" (*schöne Phantasie*) but are merely "fanciful" or "fantastic" (*phantastisch*). In fact, the 1827 lectures are characterized by several comparisons between Hindu and Greek religion (always unfavorable to the former), which may reflect the fact that in 1824 Hegel argued that they represent corresponding stages of natural and spiritual religion, respectively. Perhaps he dropped the designation "phantasy" for Hinduism partly with the view in mind that Greek religion represents the true, the higher *Phantasie*. Hegel also provides in 1827, as he did in 1824, a detailed account of the three figures of the Trimurti—a triad that really remains external to the undifferentiated substance of Brahman; he describes the austere practices or yogi discipline through which union with Brahman is achieved, as well as the privileged caste of Brāhmans, and the elements of immolation, superstition, lack of ethical life, unruliness, and formlessness, which he found unattractive. On the whole, however, the presentation lacks the sharply negative polemic of 1824, even though in substance it is not much changed.

The section ends with a "Transition to the Next Stage," which is new in 1827. In the next stage, which is that of Persian and Egyptian religion, the Buddhist-Hindu distinction between the abstract universal and immediate subjects reverts to a concrete, implicitly spiritual unity; and there occurs a separation of empirical self-consciousness from absolute self-consciousness, "so that here God attains proper objectivity for the first time." God no longer subsists "in an empirically human mode" but becomes "truly and intrinsically objective," is "essentially object," "altogether in opposition to human beings." These strong claims suggest that Hegel is beginning to perceive a sharper distinction between the Far Eastern and Near Eastern religions; and, as a matter of fact, in the 1831 lectures they are treated in separate stages. Persian and Egyptian religion, together with Judaism, are viewed as the first of the religions of freedom, by contrast with the cleavage of consciousness (between substance and subject) present in the religions of China and India. Anticipations of the 1831 reorganization are clearly evident in the 1827 discussion of "the religions of transition."

The Religion of Light: Persian Religion

This section is similar to the corresponding section of the 1824 lectures in content and in the sources utilized, but the organization differs slightly. In 1827 Hegel distinguished more systematically between the philosophical concept of a religion and its historical instances, presenting the two topics in this sequence. While this is similar to the abstract concept-concrete representation distinction found in the *Ms.* and 1824, the principle is modified; we see this clearly in the present section.

The next stage after the Hindu dichotomization of unitary substance and multiple powers is the "resumption" of being-in-and-for-self into itself; just because the true content has independence and objectivity, it is "the good," from which all things proceed.

63

Negativity, however, is not included within the good; it remains external to it. Hegel attends more specifically to this "Oriental dualism" in 1827 than in 1824, comparing it with recent philosophical trends of which he is critical. The endless conflict between good and evil suggests the Kantian-Fichtean notion that the good can be realized only in an infinite progression (n. 277); and the dualism between good and evil anticipates the contemporary reemphasis of the gulf between finite and infinite: the separated, autonomous finitude of modern rationalism is precisely what is evil (see n. 278). The reason for the dualism is that the good, the ultimate, is still conceived in naturalistic terms. In nature, relationships remain external and sensible; hence, if good is symbolized as light, its opposite is darkness, which remains external to it. But if spirit is the basis of the relationships, they are mediated internally.

As to the historical aspects of this religion, the 1827 lectures include a discussion of the Mithra cult (nn. 287, 288) and of the organization of the Persian state as compared with the kingdom of light (n. 286); otherwise the presentation is quite similar to that of 1824.

Yet another "Transition to the Next Stage" is included at this point. The transition in question is that of the resumption of the multiple into concrete unity, a unity that includes subjectivity within itself. In Persian religion this resumption remains truncated because it is external and natural; and the two sides, the substantive and the subjective, are still unmediated. The next step is that subjectivity should unify within itself the opposed elements; indeed, subjectivity is precisely a process of such unification. The negative moment, construed as natural, is death; and if there is to be a true reconciliation, death is something that God himself must undergo. Thus we come upon a religion in which God dies and rises again to life. The negation of death is really posited in God, which is fundamentally different from the many transient incarnations of Hindu mythology; yet it remains a natural negation, not a spiritually self-imposed negation, as found in the Christian Trinity. In 1827 this transition is set forth as a theoretical moment in the process of religious cognition; in 1831 Hegel finds a historical instance of it in the so-called religion of anguish, a religion in which "for the first time we have the dying of God as internal to God himself."

Egyptian Religion

As compared with 1824, the 1827 lectures provide a much more extensive discussion of the actual materials of Egyptian religion, even though Hegel is still relying primarily on classical sources and modern studies of these sources—Creuzer's *Symbolik und Mythologie,* Dupuis's *Origine de tous les cultes,* and Hirt's *Aegyptische Gottheiten.* The recent archaeological discoveries have not yet made much of an impact.

Curiously, in 1827 Hegel almost entirely omits the conceptual elaboration (the "transition to the next stage" at the end of Persian religion may be intended to serve this role) and turns directly to the symbolic figure of Osiris. He first notes, as he did in 1824, that the negation and opposition represented by Typhon is taken into Osiris, who dies but is perpetually restored, serving as lord of the dead as well as of the living. Behind the Osiris myth is a grasping of the universal substance as subjectivity for the first time. But subjectivity is still known only in the mode of representation, and it is represented in both natural and human form. What we find in Egyptian religion is a curious passing back and forth between these forms in terms of the relationship between signifier and signified. Clearly, natural objects are now regarded as representational symbols of the universal, subjective essence; they refer not to themselves but to something other than themselves. Thus we have the sun, the Nile, the change of seasons: these all represent a cycle reverting back into itself, which is what subjectivity essentially is. On the one hand, Osiris signifies the sun; but on the other hand, the sun signifies Osiris. One is the inner element, the other the signifier by which the inner discloses itself outwardly. As we have said, the roles can reverse. "But what is in fact the inner is Osiris, subjectivity as such"; this is the direction in which Egyptian religion is moving.

Eygptian culture exhibited a tremendous impulse to express and construct outwardly this inner element. This is what gave rise to art for the first time. The testimony of the ancient historians is confirmed by the archaeological remains: the Egyptians engaged in an immense artistic labor from which there was no cessation; "the toiling spirit did not rest from making its representation visible to itself." What they produced, however, was not pure and fine art (*schöne Kunst*) but only the craving for fine art. This craving "involves the struggle of meaning with material," the striving "to place the stamp of inner spirit on outer configuration." But in Egyptian art the two remain separate and to some degree opposed. The artistic figure (*Gestalt*) "is not yet spiritualized to clarity; what is sensible and natural has not yet been completely transfigured into the spiritual." In fact, the tendency is for the spiritual to remain *buried* within the sensible. In a striking image, Hegel says that "the pyramid is a self-sufficient crystal, in which a dead man is preserved; but in the work of art, which is reaching out for beauty, the externality of the configuration is imbued with the inner soul, with the beauty of what is within" (n. 340).

This, finally, accounts for the *enigmatic* character of Egyptian religion. The inner, spiritual meaning has not yet achieved outward clarity of expression. This is how Hegel interprets the inscription related to the goddess Neith in Sais: "No mortal has yet lifted my veil" (see n. 345). The Greeks, however, lifted the veil.

The Elevation of the Spiritual above the Natural

If the religion of nature involves the natural unity of the spiritual and the natural, then the next stage of determinate religion entails the elevation of the spiritual above the natural; this is the religion of the Greeks and the Jews (see n. 347). The universal characteristic of this second stage, says Hegel, is that of "free subjectivity." Subjectivity has now attained mastery over nature and finitude. The subject now is *spirit,* and spirit is subjective; that is, it is free spirit, spirit that is for itself. The natural and the finite are only a *sign* of spirit, only instrumental to its manifestation.

What accounts for the reversal in the order in which the two religions dealt with in this section are treated, so that now Greek religion is considered first and Jewish religion second?[38] It seems to be based primarily on the different ways in which the "elevation" occurs in the two religions. For Greek religion, the natural element

---

38. A correlative advantage of the new arrangement is that it permits a transition directly from Egyptian to Greek religion, which suits Hegel's interpretation quite conveniently. This advantage is preserved in 1831 by placing Jewish religion ahead of Egyptian rather than after Greek. This may have been a contributory factor to the reorganization.

is taken up and transfigured in free subjectivity, but it is not purified of its externality and sensibility, so that this religion is still tinged by finitude: the gods are represented by the sensibly beautiful human shape, and they are many. For Jewish religion, the sensible element is left behind; it is ruled and negated by the one God who is infinite subjectivity and subsists without shape, only for thought, the God who is sublimely free spirit in relation to the natural world. Judaism, then, is the more purely spiritual religion. In this distinction, concludes Hegel at the beginning of the section on Jewish religion, lies "the necessity of the elevation of the religion of beauty into the religion of sublimity," namely, "that the particular spiritual powers, the ethical powers, should be embraced in a spiritual unity."

In the two earlier lectures, those of 1821 and 1824, the relationship between Jewish and Greek religion was considered as mutually complementary rather than as progressive; Hegel never referred to the "elevation" of one into the other. This is evident from the organization of the *Ms.*, in which the representational and cultic forms of the two religions are subordinated to an inclusive scheme, even though the portrayal of Jewish religion is considerably less attractive there than the portayal of Greek. The dialectical structure of the 1824 lectures resists, as previously mentioned, a linear or progressive development among the determinate religions. That Hegel should now speak of the "elevation" of the religion of beauty into the religion of sublimity seems to follow in part from his continuing and increasingly favorable reassessment of Judaism, but it may also be related to the polemical context of the 1827 lectures, namely, Hegel's defense against the charge of pantheism and atheism. Here he clearly aligns himself with Jewish monotheism.

But this "advance" from Greek to Jewish religion is not undialectical even in 1827. Judaism may not be tinged by finitude, but neither is finitude transfigured and overreached by infinitude in it. Moreover, the one universal God of Judaism is believed to be the God of a particular people. At the beginning of the section on Roman religion, Hegel refers to the "one-sidedness" of both Greek and Jewish religion, and this in fact seems closer to his actual view. It is only from particular perspectives that one appears as "higher" than the other. From the point of view of the idea of God, monotheism, and spiritual unity and subjectivity, Judaism is higher. But from the point of view of the idea of the mediation of divinity and humanity (i.e., the incarnation), as well as of free ethical institutions, Greek religion is higher. Their respective one-sidednesses are finally overcome, not in Roman religion, which proves to be an abortive and retrograde, arbitrary and expedient, unification of the religions, but in the Christian religion (although Roman religion plays a necessary transitional role). Perhaps one element in Hegel's 1827 "reversal" is his conviction that the unity and spirituality of the God of Israel is the necessary foundation of true and consummate religion: therefore Christianity must arise among the Jewish people. Hegel knew this already in 1821, but his assessment of Judaism in the earlier lectures did not bear it out.

The Religion of Beauty, or Greek Religion

In 1827 the presentation of Greek religion is oriented to a different central question, and as a consequence the organization of the material differs somewhat; but the actual content of the treatment is quite similar to that of 1824, and no additional sources are utilized. Whereas in 1824 Hegel was concerned to show how in Greek religion divinity determines or "particularizes" itself, making itself available to and infusing the world of human spirit, in 1827 the central concern is with the "elevation" of the spiritual above the natural.

The substantial foundation of Greek religion is that of the rationality and freedom of spirit, which results in the formation of an "ethical life" (*Sittlichkeit*). Consequently the Greek divinities must be essentially ethical/spiritual powers. At the same time, these divinities have been shaped out of the old gods of the primitive Greek nature religion. Thus the "war with the Titans" is the essence of Greek religion. Hegel elaborates on this at some length, showing how the natural element is subordinated but not totally vanquished, and what we continue to find is a "mingling" of the natural with the spiritual in the Greek gods; thus Zeus is the natural firmament generally, but also the father of gods and humans and especially the political god, the god of the state. Both the oracles and the mysteries are carryovers from the old religion. The first mode of giving oracles is by mere natural sounds; later the oracle is given in human tones but not in clear speech.

Two other aspects of the divine content—the relationship of the gods to necessity above and contingent singularization below—are taken over directly from the 1824 lectures. However, the discussion of the "shape" or configuration in which the gods appear differs somewhat in 1827. Because we are still only at the initial stage of freedom and rationality, the ethical gods must appear in an external, sensible shape. "Phantasy" (*Phantasie*) is the means of giving representational status to the divine. Phantasy, says Hegel, is the activity of shaping external or immediate being in such a way that "the external being is no longer independent but is downgraded into being just a sign of the indwelling spirit." We have seen phantasy at work in more primitive forms in Hindu and Egyptian religion. What distinguishes the Greeks is their recognition that the human figure is the only way in which spirit can be adequately represented in natural, sensible shape. "That is why the Greeks represented the gods as human beings." They were right in doing so, and they did so with consummate artistry, both plastic and poetic. The only problem is that the gods thus made are still finite. "This finitude of content is why they originate in a finite manner as human products. At this stage the divine is grasped neither by pure thinking nor in pure spirit." Hegel does not go on to compare the human shape of the gods in Greek religion with the Christian idea of incarnation, as he does in 1824 and more specifically in 1831.

The treatment of the Greek cultus in 1827 is almost identical with the 1824 version and need not be summarized again.

The Religion of Sublimity, or Jewish Religion

Quite apart from the reversal of the order in which Greek and Jewish religion are treated, and the argument for the necessity of "the elevation of the religion of beauty into the religion of sublimity," the 1827 lectures continue the trajectory of a favorable reassessment of Judaism established in 1824 and carry it further. Gone are all references to the "fear of the Lord" that is "the beginning of wisdom," and to the "execrations" of Leviticus; Job is mentioned only briefly, and the critique of Judaism is muted. Almost the entire section is given over to a careful analysis of the Jewish idea of God and to various aspects of the relationship of God and world. This material is already present in 1824, but it is reworked, expanded, and presented more clearly.

The great contribution of Israel to the history of religion is its comprehension of the "spiritually subjective unity" of God. This subjective unity is not mere substance but is absolute power, wisdom, and purpose, for which reason it is "holy," it merits the name "God" for the first time. It is in fact "infinite subjectivity," which is the highest philosophical concept; as such, God subsists without sensible shape, only for thought ("thinking is the essential soil for this object").

But this one God does not remain in self-enclosed, abstract identity with himself. Rather God's wisdom contains the process of "divine particularization" (a description reserved to Greek religion in 1824), that is, divine self-determining, judging, creating. This process is not yet posited *within* God concretely but remains abstract and external; it is not yet an immanent Trinity. But the act of creation is a highly important, in fact definitive, determination of the Jewish God. God *is* the creator of the world. This has implications both for the world and for God. First, the world does not emanate from God, as in Hindu and Greek cosmogonies, but is created *ex nihilo*. This means that the subjectivity of the One remains what is absolutely first and is not superseded by what has gone forth. Second, God's relations to the world—the more specific moments of divine wisdom, which are goodness and justice—are definitive of God's own being, so that we do in fact *know* God in knowing his relations. The categories of goodness and justice are now defined more fully. As good, God releases and sets free from himself the created world; only what is genuinely free can do this, can let its determinations go as free, can release them to "go their separate ways," which is the totality of the finite world. As just, God maintains the world in relation to himself, does not abandon it to radical autonomy, specifies its purpose. Third, the world is rendered profane, prosaic; nature is divested of divinity, and there is no cheap identity of finite and infinite. The manifestation of God in the world takes on the character of sublimity, which is its genuine form, or of miracle, which is specious. Finally, God's purpose is made manifest in the natural and human worlds. This purpose is simply that the whole earth and all peoples should proclaim the glory of God. This glorification of God is the "inner aspect" of all human ethical activity. Without it, moral righteousness counts as nothing; with it, one may be confident of the fulfillment of one's worldly existence. This is what underlies the "remarkable" faith of the Jewish people; it is the theme of the Old Testament as a whole but especially of the Book of Job. It is not finally a human quality but a dimension of the holiness of God.

At the end of this notably sympathetic phenomenology of the Jewish representation of God, Hegel mentions briefly certain "limitations." These are principally three: the self-determining wisdom of God is not yet an inward self-development (the idea of God as "what is eternally self-developing within itself" is found only in the manifest or revelatory religion); despite the implicit universalism, the God of Judaism remains a national God, the God of a limited national family rather than of the whole human family; and the divine purposes are abstract because they are simply commandments given by God as something prescribed and immutable, rather than purposes worked out in the conflict and dialectic of historical/ethical life. These limitations appear in the Jewish cultus, about which there is virtually no discussion in the 1827 lectures—whether because Hegel did not wish to emphasize the limitations, or because he was short of time, or because Lasson's text and the available transcripts are incomplete at this point, we do not know.

The Religion of Expediency, or Roman Religion

The treatment of Roman religion in 1827 is quite similar to that of 1824 and of comparable length; only the transitions are different.

What is still lacking is a divine purposiveness that is at once holy, universal, and concrete. The Greeks achieved concreteness in the ethical content of their gods, but lacked holiness and sacrificed universality to multiplicity. The God of Israel was one and holy, but was claimed as the God of a particular people, whose laws were abstract. Roman religion, says Hegel, is a *relative* totality, in which the Greek and Jewish religions "indeed lose their one-sidedness, but both of the principles perish conjointly, each by means of assimilation into its opposite; still, it is this very homogeneity that interests us in them. The religion of beauty loses the concrete individuality of its gods and hence also their ethical, independent content; the gods are reduced to means. The religion of sublimity loses the orientation to the One, the eternal, the transcendent." The universal purposiveness of the Romans is flawed because it is external, empirical, finite, utilitarian. Religion, when reduced to a means to extrinsic, worldly ends, is finally destroyed. Roman religion is the religion to end all religion—a fact symbolized by collecting the gods of all the religions into a single pantheon, where they are subjected to Jupiter Capitolinus and destroy one another, a veritable *Götterdämmerung*.

The transition from this state of affairs to Christianity is difficult to reconstruct from the conclusion of the 1827 *Determinate Religion* in the form in which we have it. The 1831 variant contained in n. 544 suggests that this destruction of the sublimity and beauty, the holiness and ethical quality, the faithfulness and serene happiness of religion "produced the monstrous misery and a universal sorrow, a sorrow that served to prepare the birth pangs of the religion of truth." Hegel may have had something like that in mind in 1827. Our text says only that, when the moments which subsist in contradiction and in a spiritless way in Roman religion are unified, then we shall have advanced to the "next and final stage of religion." Presumably these moments are the authentic moments of the religions of beauty and sublimity, as well as the heritage of the religions of nature—moments that have been "homogenized" in Roman religion, not truly unified.

d. The Lectures of 1831

For the lectures of 1831, Hegel undertook a major reorganization of *Determinate Religion*. The Oriental and Near Eastern religions are no longer considered under the general category of "nature religion" but in terms of distinctive phases of the dialectics of consciousness. While this is an important gain, new and unresolved problems are created for the appropriate treatment of Jewish and Roman religion. Thus we cannot assume that the 1831 schema represents Hegel's final position; he was still in process of refining and expanding his interpretation of the history of religions when he died.

Fortunately, Strauss's excerpted version can be supplemented by a number of extensive passages from no-longer-extant transcripts of the 1831 lectures included by the original editors in the *Werke*. These are juxtaposed to 1824 as well as to 1827 text since there are a number of places in Part II where the 1831 lectures parallel 1824 more closely than 1827 (e.g., the cosmological and teleological proofs). We have footnoted these passages in relation to 1824 and 1827 text (depending on the original *Werke* context) and have provided cross-references to them at appropriate points in the Strauss excerpts (see 1831 excerpts, n. 1). Some of them will be referred to in the following analysis. These *Werke* passages not only substantiate the accuracy of Strauss's version but also demonstrate that Hegel drew upon additional sources for his treatment of the Oriental and Near Eastern religions.

Determinate religion is still divided into three main stages (for this division see not only the excerpts but especially 1827 lectures, n. 5). In the first stage, that of natural religion, we find a relationship of immediacy between consciousness and its object, both of which are represented in natural, sensible terms. This is not a matter of sheer immediacy but rather of the *natural* unity of the spiritual and natural, a unity in which spirit knows itself as a power over nature. This is magic, which is not yet properly religious. Religion emerges with the inward cleavage or rupture (*Entzweiung*) of consciousness, such that "consciousness distinguishes its sensuous nature from what is essential, so that the natural is known only as mediated through those aspects that are essential." Consciousness knows a distinction between itself "as transitory accident" and "God as absolute power." This cleavage permits an "elevation" or exaltation of the spiritual above the natural, and Hegel now locates the beginning of this process at a much earlier point than he did in 1827; in fact, it corresponds to the "objectification of the divine object" that he identified as already occurring in the religion of magic in 1824. The second stage has its historical existence in what are now described as "the three Oriental religions of substance," namely, Chinese religion, Hinduism, and Buddhism/Lamaism (see 1827 n. 49).

The third stage entails the overcoming of the cleavage through a reconciliation of consciousness and its object at a higher, mediated level, where freedom becomes actual for the first time (both divine and human freedom). This occurs in three phases. The first phase is a transitional one in which, in reaction against the confusion of the natural and the spiritual in the preceding stage, subjectivity seeks to establish itself in its unity and universality. This struggle had its historical existence in three transitional religions: the religion of the good (Persian and Jewish), the religion of anguish (Phoenician), and the religion of ferment (Egyptian) (see 1827 n. 266). In the second phase, the subject knows itself to be free in relation to the divine object. This is the religion of freedom proper, or Greek religion. But since the subject has not yet passed through the infinite antithesis of good and evil, and since the gods are not yet infinite spirit, the reconciliation that occurs at this stage is not complete (see 1827 n. 18). Nor is the reconciliation completed by Roman religion, which issues instead in the infinite unhappiness and anguish that serve as the birth pangs of the religion of truth. Hence the third phase of the religion of reconciliation and freedom is one in which the relative reconciliation and freedom gained through the struggle of the preceding religions is undone, and the stage is set for the transition to the consummate religion.

It is noteworthy that this schema reestablishes a more clearly logical basis for the division of *Determinate Religion*. Over against the interplay of nature and spirit, to which Roman religion was appended in one fashion or another by the lectures of 1824 and 1827, the 1831 lectures in this respect approximate the structure of the *Ms.* However, it is not the dialectic of being, essence, and concept, but rather that of immediacy, rupture, and reconciliation, that is at work here; and the third moment is no longer simply identified with Roman religion, which was clearly inadequate, but with a plurality of "religions of freedom." These are not so much strictly logical categories as they are descriptive of the general life of the concept and of the dialectic of consciousness—a dialectic that is taken into the divine life and becomes genuinely trinitarian in the Christian religion. This is in line with one of the central theological motifs of the 1831 lectures.

Natural Religion

The discussion of nature religion (Sec. A) is much reduced in scope as compared with 1827 and 1824, being limited essentially to the religion of magic in the strict sense, that is, the belief in the direct power over nature on the part of self-consciousness. It appears that primitive religion has been given short shrift in order to accommodate the new focus of attention on the Oriental religions. In any case, the carefully nuanced phenomenology of stages of primitive religious consciousness found in 1824 is lacking. The section begins with a look at two senses of "natural religion" that Hegel intends to reject: the religion of reason (deism) and the notion of an ideal golden age of the past (primitive religion as *true* religion). The first of these matters was hinted at in 1827 but introduced into the discussion of natural religion only in 1831, while the second has been carried over from both 1824 and 1827. The actual treatment of magic follows closely the pattern established in 1827, in terms of both concept and historical examples.

The Internal Rupture of Religious Consciousness

In the second stage of determinate religion (Sec. B), "consciousness ruptures internally, splitting into two and setting up a substantive power over against itself as the natural and contingent; as singular it relates itself to this power merely as an accident that is of no account." This power, in which everything has its subsistence, is an object of thought but is not yet known as inwardly spiritual or self-differentiated. This is the form of religion called "pantheism." A detailed summary of its moments is provided in n. 49 to the 1827 lectures.

Two topics are identified for discussion in the introduction to the section. The first is the elevation of consciousness from finite to infinite, which is the quintessential movement of spirit, and which is expressed in the various forms of the cosmological proof: the argument from finite to infinite, from the many to the One, and from contingency to necessity. In the popular form of these proofs, the negative moment is lacking; that is, the attempt is made to argue affirmatively from the finite as a positive starting point to the infinite as result. Hegel here combines the analysis and critique found in two different sections in 1824 (the introductions to Secs. A and B). The second topic is that of pantheism, which follows from the way in which substance and accidents are related in these Oriental religions. In 1824 this topic is also connected with the cosmological proof, but in 1827 it is elaborated more fully in relation to the religion of being-within-self. Hegel makes the same point once again, namely that Oriental and Spinozistic pantheism, far from treating every finite thing as God, rather annihilates the finite in the infinite substance.

1. Chinese Religion: The Religion of Measure. Substance returned into itself from its accidents is known as "measure" (see 1831 n. 22). All of the "Oriental religions of substance" are really religions of measure, since here we do not find undialectical substance but substance mediated with itself through its accidents. Substance as measure is on the way to becoming essence and necessity. Hegel thought he had discovered a primary instance of "measure" in the categories or laws of the Dao and their signs, the Gua, based on the simple distinction between being and nonbeing, one and two, yes and no, yang and yin (see 1831 n. 24 and, for a more detailed elaboration, 1827 n. 106). Daoism and Confucianism have their roots in the ancient Chinese state religion; thus Hegel's treatment of the latter is now removed from the category of magic and reoriented to the theme of measure. The maintenance of the measures is the responsibility of the emperor, the son of heaven (Tian), and heaven is the power over the measures. Only at the end of this section does Hegel summarize the story about the installation of a new dynasty, which, in the picture of the Shen, gives a fanciful, superstitious version of the substantial powers. This reassessment of Chinese religion is based on sources already available in 1824 and 1827 but not fully utilized then.

2. Hindu Religion: The Religion of Abstract Unity. In the lectures of 1831, the treatment of Hinduism precedes that of Buddhism for the first time—whether for historical or for schematic reasons is not certain (see 1831 n. 30). In any case, Hinduism now provides the conceptual advance to unitary substance instead of Buddhism, and it receives a much more detailed analysis in these lectures than Buddhism does. In Hinduism the multiplicity of the Chinese measures is resumed into unity, into a One that determines itself by means of thought (Brahman). But its thinking remains locked in self-containment, so that the actual elaboration of difference falls outside it in a "wild infinity" where phantasy is given free rein. Finally

the unity is taken back into itself, but in a "spiritless" fashion. Thus the unity of Brahman is "abstract."

These three moments—the inward self-containment, the outward multiplicity, and the spiritless resumption—correspond to the three figures of the Hindu Trimurti (Brahmā, Vishnu, and Shiva), and the bulk of the 1831 presentation is organized according to this triad. Hegel attends in greater detail to the Hindu cosmogonies, to epics contained in the Mahābhārata, and especially to the Rāmāyana (see 1827 n. 244); but despite this attentiveness, and the more significant religiohistorical role accorded Hinduism, the interpretation is really no more favorable than in the earlier lectures. The "mismatch between content and form" accounts for the "ugliness of the mythological figures." There is no fixed shape or determinacy in the Hindu's infinite world of deities, powers, phenomena, incarnations. Phantasy passes back and forth between external existence and divinity; here "everything is a miracle, everything is crazy, and is not determined by a rational nexus of thought categories" (see especially 1827 n. 234).

3. Buddhism and Lamaism: The Religion of Annihilation. Whether Strauss's very brief summary reflects the actual discussion of Buddhism/Lamaism in 1831 is impossible to say, but some confirmation is provided by the paucity of *Werke* materials on this topic attributable to 1831. The chief of these (1827 n. 139) elaborates Strauss's cryptic remark that "these religions are very much akin to Hinduism." The "religion of being-within-self is the concentration and tranquilization of spirit as it returns, out of the destructive disarray of Hindu religion, into itself and into essential unity." While in Hinduism the relationship between unity and differences was one of constant alternation and progression, here "the essence is self-contained essentiality, the reflection of negativity into itself, and thus it is what rests and persists within itself."

In Lamaism, the "universal presence of substance already gives way to the concrete presence of the individual," that is, the individual lamas. But in Buddhism the object is a dead teacher, Buddha, and the goal is to be united with Buddha; "this annihilation is termed nirvana." It is hard to believe that this is all Hegel had to say about nirvana in 1831, in light of his sympathetic philosophical elaboration of it in 1827. A *Werke* fragment from 1831 may belong here (1827 n. 151), but it is not helpful. We must conclude that our sources do not permit a reconstruction of Hegel's presentation at this point.

The Religion of Freedom: Transitional Forms

In 1831 the transitional religions (Persian and Egyptian) have been transferred to the beginning of the third section (Sec. C) and have been supplemented by the inclusion of Jewish and "Phoenician" religions under the category of "transitional" as well (see 1831 n. 57). The transition in question is not only a transition from nature to spirit but also an inward self-determination and development of substance in such a way that the finite is released to exist independently but then taken back into the infinite and reconciled with it. Because substance at the same time preserves the unity it has achieved, it is defined as the good, but a good which, because exclusive and abstract, enters into conflict with evil, issuing in dualism (1827 n. 266). This dualism purportedly characterizes the first of the transitional stages, the religion of the good (Sec. C.1.a), but it properly applies to only one of the religions treated under this head, namely the Persian.

1. Persian Religion. The One as self-determining is the good, whereas sheer power is neither good nor wise. But at this transitional stage the good is still abstract, which accounts for the fact that it is represented in the physical form of light and is confronted externally by its antithesis, evil. In other words, its determination occurs solely in terms of external relations. This can be seen from the physical quality of light: in order for its manifestation to be real, it must strike upon a dark object, a solid body; nothing is made manifest by pure light. Thus this religion issues in a cosmic dualism (see 1827 n. 281). The discussion then moves to the historical religion, Parseeism, in which this form of religious consciousness emerges (see esp. 1827 n. 284). Some new details are introduced as compared with 1827 and 1824: the fact that light is not a *symbol* for the good but is wholly identical with it, the fact that the Parsees do not worship fire as such but the light that it gives forth, the connection between Ormazd, the stars, and the Amshaspands, the role

of the Amshaspands generally, and the cosmic struggle between Ormazd and Ahriman.

2. Jewish Religion.[39] Judaism is introduced into the discussion at this point through the category of the good—a connection that is not wholly convincing. Here, we are told, the good is "for itself" in such a way as to belong to the essence of the substance, to constitute the substance as free, personal, and subjective for the first time. The analysis then proceeds along the lines of the 1827 lectures, attending to the absolute subjectivity and unity of God, God as creator, and the relationship of creation in general and humanity in particular to the One. With reference to the second topic, 1831 draws a clear distinction between creation *ex nihilo* and a theogony of emanation. Only a free and infinite subject is able to create out of the nothing that constitutes its "negative relation to self" or "absence of all difference" by an act of "primal division" (*Urteil*). In other words, God creates out of God's own being, rather than out of primordial matter, but not by means of emanation or issuing forth. This is what constitutes God's eternal goodness.

It is only when the discussion arrives at the third point that the distinctive character of the 1831 treatment of Judaism emerges. The purpose of the creation, which is stripped of divinity itself, is to mirror divinity. Human beings do so in quite a different way than nature, since evil, the cleavage, is not something external—a cosmic force or enemy—but enters into the unity of spirit itself. The antithesis of good and evil is grounded neither in a cosmic dualism (the theogonic myth, exemplified for Hegel by Persian religion) nor in absolute substance (the tragic myth, as represented by the Greek theology of necessity or fate) but in the free fall of finite spirit (the Adamic myth).[40] This is the "profoundly speculative" feature of the

39. Strauss's excerpted version of Jewish religion is the most detailed of any of the "transitional" religions, which could reflect either Strauss's interest or the apportionment of material in the notebook he was excerpting. A number of important *Werke* passages on Judaism attributable to 1831 support and supplement Stauss's version. We draw upon these especially in the following analysis: 1824 nn. 541, 572; 1827 nn. 457, 492.

40. We have appropriated Paul Ricoeur's categories here (*The Symbolism of Evil*, trans. Emerson Buchanan [Boston, 1967], pp. 306–346), but they fit Hegel's analysis quite nicely.

story of the fall, which in 1831 has been transferred from Part III of the lectures, where it was earlier discussed in relation to Christianity, to Part II (see 1831 n. 64). Humanity "falls" through the acquisition of knowledge, which has within it the ambiguity both of being necessary to the emergence of consciousness and of giving rise to the cleavage between finite and infinite, creation and creator. This analysis is essentially similar to the interpretation of the fall in Part III of the 1821 *Ms.* (see Vol. 3:101–108).

What is more interesting for our purposes is why Hegel now attaches his exegesis of Genesis 3 to the discussion of Judaism rather than of Christianity. The external reason is the altered context for the treatment of Jewish religion, a context that raises the question of the origin of evil, its relationship to the good, and the overcoming of estrangement. But there seems also to be a deeper reason, which is related to Hegel's general interpretation and critique of Judaism in the last lectures. Hegel argues that the "story of the fall lay fallow in Jewish religion and attained its true meaning only in the Christian religion." To be sure, the struggle between good and evil does constitute an essential feature of Jewish religion; this is especially striking in the Psalms of David, where "anguish cries aloud from the innermost depths of the soul in the consciousness of its sinfulness, followed by the most anguished plea for forgiveness and reconciliation." But this depth of anguish is known only as pertaining to the single individual in contingent fashion rather than as an eternal moment of spirit, and it finally remains unresolved in Judaism. A similar tension is found between the intrinsic universalism of the Jewish idea of God, as expressed especially by the later prophets (see 1831 n. 67), and the belief that Israel alone is the chosen people of God since only they recognize and worship him.

These tensions or limitations point to the fact, or perhaps are explained by the fact, that the laws of God as revealed to the Jewish people are not laws of freedom. They are not given by reason but prescribed by God—all of them, ranging from the most petty cultic regulations to the universal ethical foundations of human existence. "All law is given by the Lord, and hence it is positive commandment throughout. There is in it a formal, absolute authority. The particular aspects of the political constitution [of Israel] are not developed out of the universal purpose at all, nor are they left to human beings to determine." The vocation of the Jewish people is to give itself up wholly to the service of the Lord, which accounts for their "admirable steadfastness," but which also means that "there is no freedom vis-à-vis this firm bond." The Lord finally does not enter into the human combat with evil but punishes evil. The finite subject engages in an unresolved struggle between good and evil, resulting in contrition and anguish, from which there is no liberation. There can be a liberation only if the struggle and anguish are taken into the divine life itself.

Hegel thus returns to critical themes first adumbrated in the 1821 *Ms.* but muted in later lectures. The reason for this seems in part to be the hermeneutical and political context of the 1831 lectures. We know that, as a result of recent events, in 1830–1831 Hegel had become deeply concerned once again with the question of the relationship between religion and state and especially with the task of creating and preserving free political institutions.[41] Only a free religion can serve as the foundation of a free state. In this respect Judaism is found wanting. It is on the way to freedom but has not arrived at its ethical actualization. Hegel has now taken up the other perspective to which we referred in analyzing the advance from Greek to Jewish religion in 1827. From the point of view of monotheism and spiritual subjectivity, Judaism is higher; but from the point of view of divine-human mediation and free ethical institutions, Greek religion is higher. This latter perspective pervades the 1831 lectures, as the summary at the beginning of the discussion of Greek religion makes clear.

The 1831 lectures combine an emancipatory, world-transforming motif with a dialectically related one, namely, the self-mediation of the triune God, a mediation that is both internal and external, both within the divine life and at the same time constitutive of worldly

41. See Walter Jaeschke, "Hegel's Last Year in Berlin," in *Hegel's Philosophy of Action*, ed. Lawrence S. Stepelevich and David Lamb (Atlantic Highlands, N.J., 1983), pp. 31–48. See also Hegel's discussion of the relationship of religion to the state at the end of Part I of the 1831 lectures (Vol. 1:451–460).

activity. In this respect, too, Judaism is found wanting. The God of Israel is not an "inwardly developing" God; God does not take the anguish of the world into and upon himself, nor is he engaged in the human sociopolitical and cultural struggle for freedom. This requires another step in religious consciousness. Just as we saw Hegel pressing Greek religion to its limits in 1824, so now we find him doing the same with Jewish religion. He does so not from an anti-Judaic perspective but for the sake of humanity. He has by now clearly established the fundamental truth and validity of the Hebraic idea of God, and thus has earned the right to press critical questions. Yet it is fair to say that he has not grasped the possibilities within Judaism on precisely these questions.

3. The Religion of Anguish. This is not "Phoenician" religion in any historical sense but a construct derived from classical mythology relating to the figure of Adonis (see 1831 n. 71). The *Werke* provides a complete text for this brief section (1824 n. 572) but faces insuperable difficulties in locating it in relation to its own structure. The symbolic representation of a god who dies and rises, who takes the struggle between good and evil into the divine process, constitutes a dialectical advance in religious consciousness, despite the purely mythological form in which it is presented.

4. Egyptian Religion: The Religion of Ferment. The term "ferment" is new in 1831—suggesting the emergence of spirit out of the fermentation of natural symbols (see 1831 n. 73)—but the description and interpretation of Egyptian religion is quite similar to what is found in 1827. Hegel does make the point that Egyptian religion and art furnish the specific transition to Greek religion, which explains why it is helpful to pass directly from one to the other without the intervention of other religions. He also refers to recent archaeological finds and the decipherment of hieroglyphic script (1827 nn. 339, 341), but these have little bearing on his interpretation. "No written documents were yet in existence among the Egyptians because spirit had not yet clarified itself," and hence the hieroglyphs, even deciphered, "will always be hieroglyphs." "Everything in Egypt denotes symbolically something unexpressed. The spirit of this people is the enigma. . . . It is the Greeks who make the transition from this enigma to the clear consciousness of spirit."

The Religion of Freedom: Greek Religion and Its Fate

The summary of "the religion of freedom" at the beginning of Sec. C.2 provides a valuable insight into the leitmotiv of the 1831 lectures as a whole—the emergence of freedom out of nature, first through the cleavage of consciousness, then through the idea of God as free subject who releases the created world to exist independently of God as God's image, then through the process of divine self-divestment and self-return, so that finitude is taken up into infinitude and reconciled with it, finally through the constitution of free ethical and political institutions based on free religion (see 1831 n. 89, 1824 n. 574).

Since free activity is activity in accordance with purposes, the foundation of free religion is the purposive activity or wisdom of God. The category of purposiveness introduces the teleological proof of the existence of God. Why the proof should be considered at just this point is not immediately clear, since purposiveness characterizes the Jewish concept of God as much as the Greek (see 1831 n. 91). Indeed, in 1824 Hegel had introduced the proof at the beginning of Sec. B, while at the same time acknowledging that the metaphysical concepts of Jewish and Greek religion (namely unity and necessity) lent themselves more to the cosmological proof, but without excluding the concept of purpose. In any case, Hegel does now tie the teleological proof specifically to the "free Hellenic spirit." His exposition of the proof in the 1831 lectures follows the line of argument earlier developed in the *Ms.* and 1824.[42] He starts with a summary of the classic version of the proof: "Since . . . things imply relations that they do not themselves posit, there must be an activity that posits these characteristics or purposes, which is the power of the things." Following a rehearsal of the Kantian critique, Hegel proceeds with his own two central criticisms. (1) At best the proof arrives at a God who functions as a life principle or world soul. (2) It succeeds in demonstrating only finite purposes, not a universal or absolute purpose, which scarcely can be inferred from

---

42. Strauss gives a detailed summary; in addition the complete *Werke* text, appended to the *Lectures on the Proofs of the Existence of God,* is printed in the Appendix (see *Teleological Proof,* n. 1).

the prosaic and ambiguous character of the finite nexus. Precisely these defects of the teleological proof are seen in the corresponding form of religion, the Greek.

Hegel's treatment of Greek religion in the last lectures (Sec. C.2.c) again varies in subtle ways from the earlier versions. The ethical category of freedom has become the more fundamental attribute; Greek art is beautiful to the extent that it matches the shape of free spirituality to which the Greeks attained (see 1831 n. 103). This shape is still finite; the Greeks attained "only to the first level of freedom," a freedom "infected" with natural being. For this reason their concept of God shares the defects of the teleological proof. God "is not yet raised to absolute infinitude" but is still finite spirit. He is made by human agency and in terms of content is anthropopathic. Accordingly, this is a "religion of humanity," of the serene enjoyment of freedom. The "human quality of the gods is what is defective, but at the same time what is attractive in Greek religion" (1827 n. 420).

Following the by now familiar argument that Greek mythology expresses the transition from natural to spiritual gods, a transition in which the natural is both left behind and contained within the new deities, Hegel returns to the theme of the finitude of the gods. They are finite not only because of their naturalness but also because "they are not yet thought, only pictured representationally, and are therefore not yet fused into a single God but are still many gods." This pictorial representation is a human activity, the gods are brought into being through the exercise of *Phantasie,* poetic imagination. In this sense, the Greek gods are "made" or "poetically created" (*gedichtet*), but they are not fictitious (*erdichtet*), because they emerge from phantasy as *essential* shapes; that is, they correspond to, they give expression to what is essential, what is necessary (see 1827 nn. 409, 412). And the Greeks found the appropriate shape by means of which to express this essence, namely the human shape. For this reason their art attained the quality of beauty, a beauty consisting in the congruence between spiritual content and sensuous form. In Hegel's view, this "ideal" beauty contrasts with the "symbolic" character of earlier art, where the outward symbol does not correspond to what is within.

If the gods are represented in human shape, then it can be said that they are "anthropopathic." "The main defect is not that there is too much of the anthropopathic in these gods, but that there is too little" (see 1827 n. 412 for the elaboration of this point). By this Hegel means that the Greeks represented the divine in idealized, sensuous human configurations; they did not penetrate to the spiritual core of an actual, concretely existing human being. "Humanity must be grasped in the divine or in God as *this* human being"—but this human being as at the same time sublated, taken up into the infinite. Nothing of God is sensibly visible in this human being, yet God appears in the actual historical course of his life, teaching, destiny, that is to say, in the spiritual-ethical quality of his life. The Jewish prohibition against making visible images of God (since God *is* essentially only for thought) must be combined with the Greek emphasis on the externalization and manifestation of God in human shape. We find this combination, says Hegel, in the Christian idea of the incarnation of God in Christ. The sensible presence of God in this single, actually existing human being, while necessary, is also sublated in the spiritual presence of God in the community. The communal shape of spirit is the true and final *Gestalt* of God in history.[43]

Above the array of finite gods hovers a single power, an abstract universality, which is fate, devoid of concept and purpose. When confronted by fate, human beings save their freedom only by a self-denying submission, so that fate conquers them externally, not internally. "The Greek spirit had still no absolute content to oppose to this external necessity." This is reflected in the character of Greek political life. Only tragedy is able to grasp the connection between destiny and ethical justice. Destiny is revealed as true justice in the collision of ethical powers, whereby their one-sidedness is destroyed. Only Zeus is the true, but what this truth is remains incomprehensible. Hence the need for oracles and mysteries.

After a discussion of the Greek cultus, which is similar to the discussion in the earlier lectures, Hegel makes the transition from

43. Similar implications for the Christian idea of incarnation are drawn from the analysis of the Greek representation of the gods in human shape in the 1824 lectures; see above, n. 35.

Greek to Roman religion as follows. Free spirit must come to recognize that "its value no longer consists in its being merely the free spirit of the Greeks, of the citizens of this or that state, but humanity must be known freely as humanity, and God is the God of all humanity, the comprehensive, universal spirit" (1824 n. 700). This happens when *one* of the limited folk-spirits "raises itself to become the fate of all the others." It does so through pretensions of universality, through the politics of world mastery and of oppression, so that other peoples become conscious of the weakness of their gods. "The fate that overthrew the world of the Greeks was the world of Rome."

But this fate was in fact an advance. The way to the cleansing of spirit of its finitude was through the absolutization of finitude, with the result that the whole world of the finite gods finally collapsed. The Romans orchestrated this *Götterdämmerung,* and this was their service to the history of religion. Much that was good also perished in this collapse—the happiness, serenity, and beauty of Greek religion, the transcendence, sublimity, and holiness of the God of Israel, the vitality and diversity of the religions of other peoples. The "monstrous misery," the "universal sorrow" thus produced by the Romans was to serve as "the birth pangs of the religion of truth" (1827 n. 544).[44]

Concluding Note. The only study to date of Part II of the *Philosophy of Religion* that takes into account the separation of the lectures and the development of Hegel's thought is Walter Jaeschke's essay, "Zur Logik der Bestimmten Religion."[45] Jaeschke points out that Hegel gave a rigorously logical structure only to the first lectures, those of 1821, which arranged *Determinate Religion* into a triad corresponding to the three basic categories of logic, namely, being, essence, and concept. He never provided a convincing justification for this arrangement and did not repeat it. While retaining the triadic

44. Aside from these transitional nuances, the 1831 treatment of Roman religion is virtually identical with that of the earlier lectures and need not be summarized again.

45. In *Hegels Logik der Philosophie: Religion und Philosophie in der Theorie des absoluten Geistes,* ed. Dieter Henrich and Rolf-Peter Horstmann (Stuttgart, 1984), pp. 172–188.

division (with one exception), in the later lectures he experimented with a variety of quasi-logical structures, applied quite flexibly and openly. Hegel has frequently been criticized for imposing a dialectical, ideal-genetic method on the history of religion. But according to Jaeschke, Hegel's method was neither initially dialectical nor in any way genetic; rather it was typifying, in part typologizing. On the basis of his typification and typology of the religions, Hegel attempted a systematic, to be sure dialectical, arrangement of the types through the application of a variety of conceptual schemas. But far from imposing an abstract, preconceived, a priori structure on the history of religion, he approached this subject matter as an experimental field in which virtually nothing should not be tried, at least once. What he in fact offered, in Jaeschke's view, was less a *history* of religion than a *geography* of religion. To be sure, religion is fundamentally historical, but its historicity follows from the historicity of human spirit. Contra Hegel, argues Jaeschke, we must recognize that there is no single history of human spirit and therefore no single, unified history of religion. At best, what we can attain is a history of religion*s*, or better, histories of religions—a diversity of histories that cannot be organized under a single, encompassing philosophical conceptuality, namely, the logic of the concept of religion itself. Hegel's claim to be able to do this was falsified by his actual achievement in the successive lectures, which should have made it clear, according to Jaeschke, that the objective of a logical construction of the history of religion could not be attained.[46] Hegel's geography of religion was in fact closer to the truth than the chimera of a universal history of religions, such as has been attempted again recently by certain theologians in the name of Hegel.

With this interpretation we are in substantial agreement. We should want to add that the relationships and points of contact among the religions remain important questions for theology and philosophy of religion, together with a clear recognition of their differences and of the relativity of perspectives. A unitary history of

46. Reinhard Heede makes a similar point, namely, that Hegel's attempt to work out a correspondence between the history of religions and the moments of logic ran into insuperable difficulties. *Die göttliche Idee und ihre Erscheinung in der Religion,* p. 177 (see above, n. 2).

COMPARATIVE ANALYSIS OF
THE STRUCTURE OF "DETERMINATE RELIGION"

Manuscript	*1824 Lectures*
Introduction (31a)	Introduction
A. Immediate Religion (32a) ⟶	A. Immediate Religion, or ⟶
	Nature Religion
	Introduction
	a. The Original Condition
	b. Immediate Religion in General
a. The Metaphysical Concept of God	(α) The Metaphysical Concept of God:
(32b) [The Cosmological Proof] ⟶	The Cosmological Proof ⟶
b. Concrete Representation (34a)	(β) The Representation of God
c. The Side of Self-Consciousness:	(γ) The Forms of Nature Religion
Subjectivity, Cultus (37a)	1. The Religion of Magic
Brief Reflection on the State,	a. Singular Self-Consciousness as
Freedom, Reason (39a)	Power over Nature
	b. Formal Objectification of the
	Divine Object
	c. The Religion of Ancient China
	d. The Religion of Being-Within-
	Self (Buddhism, Lamaism)
	2. The Religion of Phantasy (Hinduism)
	a. The Representation of God
	b. The Cultus
	3. The Religion of the Good or of
	Light (Persian Religion)
	4. Transition from Nature Religion to
	Spiritual Religion: The Religion
	of the Enigma (Egyptian Religion)
	a. The Representation of God
	b. Cultus in the Form of Art
B. The Religion of Sublimity and Beauty ⟶	B. The Religions of Spiritual ⟶
(39a)	Individuality
	Introduction
	a. Division of the Subject
a. Metaphysical Concept (41a)	b. The Metaphysical Concept of God:
[The Cosmological Proof] ⟶	Cosmological & Teleological Proofs ⟶
	c. The More Concrete Definition of
	God
b. Concrete Representation,	1. The Religion of Sublimity
Form of the Idea (43a)	(Jewish Religion)
α. The Religion of Sublimity (43a)	a. God as the One
β. The Religion of Necessity (44b)	b. The Form of Divine Self-
c. Cultus (47a)	Determination
α. The Religion of Sublimity (47a) ⟶	c. The Cultus
β. The Religion of Beauty (49a)	2. The Religion of Beauty
α. Spirit of the Cultus; Religious	(Greek Religion)
Self-Consciousness (49a)	a. The Concept in General
β. The Cultus Itself (51a)	b. The Content and Shape of
	Divine Representation
	c. The Cultus
C. The Religion of Expediency or ⟶	3. The Religion of Expediency ⟶
Understanding (59a)	(Roman Religion)
a. Abstract Concept (61a)	a. The Concept of Necessity and
The Teleological Proof (62b)	External Purpose
b. Configuration or Representation of	b. The Configuration of the Gods
the Divine Essence (64b)	c. The Cultus
c. The More Specific Nature of these	
Powers and Deities in General (66b)	

1827 Lectures	*1831 Lectures*

Introduction

A. Immediate Religion, or Nature
    Religion
    Introduction
      a. The Original Condition
      b. The Forms of Nature Religion

Introduction
    Division of the Subject
A. Natural Religion
    1. Rational Religion: Deism
    2. Primitive Religion

1. The Religion of Magic
    a. The Concept of Magic
    b. Less Developed Religions of
       Magic
    c. The State Religion of the
       Chinese Empire and the Dao
2. The Religion of Being-Within-
    Self (Buddhism, Lamaism)
3. The Hindu Religion
    a. The One Substance
    b. The Multiplicity of Powers
    c. The Cultus
    d. Transition to the Next Stage
4. The Religions of Transition
    a. The Religion of Light
       (Persian Religion)
       Transition to the Next Stage
    b. Egyptian Religion
B. The Elevation of the Spiritual Above
    the Natural: The Religion of the
    Greeks and the Jews

3. The Religion of Magic
B. The Internal Rupture of
    Religious Consciousness
    Introduction
    [Cosmological Proof, Pantheism]
    1. Chinese Religion: The
       Religion of Measure
    2. Hindu Religion: The Religion
       of Abstract Unity
    3. Buddhism and Lamaism: The
       Religion of Annihilation

C. The Religion of Freedom
    1. Transitional Forms
      a. The Religion of the Good
        (1) Persian Religion
        (2) Jewish Religion
      b. The Religion of Anguish
      c. Egyptian Religion: The
        Religion of Ferment

1. The Religion of Beauty, or Greek
    Religion
    a. The Divine Content
    b. The Cultus

2. The Religion of Sublimity, or
    Jewish Religion
    a. The Unity of God
    b. Divine Self-Determination and
       Representation
    c. The Cultus
C. The Religion of Expediency:
    Roman Religion
    1. The Concept of Purposiveness
    2. The Configuration of the Gods
    3. The Cultus

2. Greek Religion
    a. Summary
    b. The Teleological Proof
    c. The Religion of Freedom
      and Beauty
3. Roman Religion: The
    Religion of Expediency

religion, especially one that culminates in a single highest religion, is no longer acceptable. But structural analogies and fundamental thematic similarities certainly exist, which make possible an encounter and dialogue among the religions, and perhaps even mutual transformations.[47] For the sake of the future of humanity, such a dialogue, including mutual criticism and enrichment, is essential; and for the sake of such dialogue, Hegel's detailed interpretations and experiments in arrangement continue to be of singular interest. Few interpreters of religion have pressed so rigorously to uncover fundamental presuppositions and principles, similarities and differences, possibilities and limits. Hegel himself provides the clue to the deconstruction of his own logical construction of the history of religion. By following this clue, we may yet discover what hermeneutical treasures are hidden in these lectures.

47. See John B. Cobb, Jr., *Beyond Dialogue: Toward a Mutual Transformation of Christianity and Buddhism* (Philadelphia, 1982).

PART II
DETERMINATE RELIGION

HEGEL'S LECTURE MANUSCRIPT

[31a]

[Introduction]

First[2] the concept of religion [has been considered], and an account [has been] given of its moments as developed, [though still only] in a preliminary way, for it is really in the consummate religion[3] that the concept of religion is objective and thereby also assumes its developed [form]. In the religions that have not yet [developed] to that point, those that are still finite, the moments occur only in preliminary form. ⟨"Consummate religion" *means* that the substance of religion [is its] concept, what it truly is—the true religion. "True" [means that] it corresponds to its concept, i.e., not [just] for us, but here within self-consciousness—it corresponds to self-consciousness.⟩

[4][We must] now begin to consider the *development* of the concept, that is, the determinate forms in which it posits itself and

1. *Ms. adds in margin:* ⟨Finite Religion⟩
2. [*Ed.*] See Vol. 1:185–256.
3. [*Ed.*] See Vol. 3:61–162.
4. *Ms. margin:* ⟨Arrangement [of the religions] – not in the subjective sense but in the objective. Concept, nature of spirit:

Child (α) Immediate natural state, naive faith, unity [with the divine] – lacks freedom or a distinctive personality of its own.

Adolescent (β) Individuality, spiritual vitality without particular purpose. [Purposes here are] the beautiful, the great, the good universally. Whatever there is

Adult (γ) [Acts] for particular purposes
(δ) Old person

Nature of spirit in general⟩

through which it passes. They are nothing other than the general moments and forms of the concept itself in which the whole of the concept is displayed, and this whole appears in this determinateness, this ⟨tone of⟩ limitedness. In this element we have then to consider how the moments of religion are related to each other and how they are determined: (α) the determinateness of God, the metaphysical concept of God; (β) the subjectivity of self-consciousness, its religious disposition, and connected with this disposition, the meaning of its cultus by which it gives itself the certainty of identity with its essence.[5] |

Religion has to pass through these determinacies in order to attain from them the nature of its concept or to objectify its concept in the form of representation. For these determinacies are the moments, the becoming of the concept, and their resolution and the return [to itself] are what constitute the concept itself. Those who [are] already familiar with the nature of the concept will understand this more precisely; those who are not will see in it an example of the absolute, immanent method of science, and will gather from it the nature of the process, the movement of the concept. It belongs to the nature of the concept, its vitality and becoming, in fact its spirituality, that it does not exist at the beginning, full-grown on its own account; [it is] not immediate. Truth is not [there] for consciousness at the beginning.

5. [Ed.] This division is incomplete since it makes no mention of what actually occurs in the text as Sec. (β), "Concrete Representation," and therefore designates "The Aspect of Self-Consciousness, Subjectivity, Cultus" as the second section (β). It is possible that Hegel initially envisioned a twofold division of religion into "the metaphysical concept" and "the aspect of self-consciousness," arriving at the triple division only in the course of actually composing the lecture manuscript. In support of this is the fact that *The Concept of Religion* in the *Ms.* does not yet articulate the distinction between representation and cultus as an architectonic principle. The triple division was first worked out in the treatment of the determinate religions, and was subsequently introduced into the concept of religion in the 1824 and 1827 lectures. The three moments designate the abstract concept of God (including proofs of the existence of God), the representational relationship to and knowledge of God, and the practical relationship in which communion with the deity is accomplished. These analytic categories are grounded in the logical dialectic of unity, differentiation, and return (reconciliation, reintegration), and are applied to each of the historical religions (including Christianity in 1821).

This second part [of the philosophy of religion] contains the path to the concept. [It considers] religion only in terms of the stages of this path, the limited forms—in other words, *finite* religion. Only the third [part] is the true religion. ⟨[The second part] contains the main aspects of the history of religions.⟩ [31b]

First a preliminary indication of the parts.[6]

[7](a) Religion in the determinateness of immediacy or of *being* [is] religion that merely maintains itself in its substantiality. Being, abstract being, [is here] related to the finite, to determinate being. Actuality [is here] only what is vanishing and without measure. [It is] not [a matter of] abstract determinacies but [of] being in its *concrete* determination, related to what appears still as finitude over against it: Spinozistic unity,[8] Oriental—finitude not posited as a semblance.

---

6. [*Ed.*] The following summary shows clearly that Hegel intended to structure *Determinate Religion* into a triad corresponding to the fundamental moments of *The Science of Logic,* namely, being, essence, and concept. Here, however, we are not concerned with the logic of these categories but with their *determinateness.* Hence religion in the determinateness of being, or immediacy, is the religion of nature; religion in the determinateness of essence, or necessity, is the religion of sublimity and beauty (Jewish and Greek); and religion in the determinateness of concept—i.e., the *finite* concept or *external* purposiveness—is Roman religion. Hegel played variations on this triad in the later lecture series but never fundamentally abandoned it. For example, in the 1824 lectures the transition from Jewish and Greek to Roman religion is no longer simply an advance from necessity (essence) to purpose (concept) since now purpose is a category that applies also to Jewish and Greek religion; the transition is rather from an exclusive to a plural to a universal (although still finite) purpose. In 1827, because the order of treating Jewish and Greek religion is reversed, the transition is from abstract to particular to universal purpose. In 1831 the basic triad is reconceived as unity (immediacy), rupture, and reconciliation (freedom), and the ordering of specific religions under these categories is revised. Although Roman religion appears to be the highest of the determinate religions on the basis of this triad, it is in fact in many respects the lowest. It is the *decadent* manifestation of finite religion as a whole because of its apotheosis of utterly finite and expedient ends, namely those of the Roman state, and thus it prepares for the transition from the finite to the infinite concept of religion, which appears in the Christian religion in consummate form.

7. *Ms. margin:* ⟨(a) Immediate religion or nature religion – immediate nature – where the natural mode is, generally speaking, the predominant meaning of each – and self-consciousness [is] in service⟩

8. [*Ed.*] Hegel sees here as elsewhere a connection between a general Oriental principle of unity and Spinoza's concept of substance. See Spinoza, *Ethics* (1677), part I, esp. prop. 15: "Whatsoever is, is in God, and without God nothing can be,

⁹(b) Religion in the determinateness of *essence*. [Here there is] difference, determinate differentiation, the return of self-consciousness into itself over against its object, but still as an essen-
3 tial, inward | coherence. (α) Essence [is still] abstract, but essentially in relation to development and difference. (β) Hence this [is] only a semblance of objective essence; but at the same time self-consciousness still [remains] in identity with its object—[this is,] however, an immediately limited determinateness—the Jewish national God ⟨⟨determinateness submerging itself within itself—absolute finitude of actuality, not free from determinacy⟩⟩. [(γ)] The developed concept of the essence, however, the essence in its totality, is *necessity*—a higher determination in which [is found] freedom from finitude and serenity in finitude.

¹⁰(c) Religion in the determinateness of the *concept*—but the
4 concept that is still | *finite,* conceived in terms of antitheses; ⟨not yet [developed] as idea, as the concept *for* the concept, the infinite

---

or be conceived" (*Chief Works* 2:54). In the 1827 *Concept of Religion* Hegel treats this connection in a more nuanced fashion (see Vol. 1:375 ff.).

9. *Ms. margin:* ⟨(b) The religion of sublimity and beauty. Separation – spirituality in general. Nature as determined – posited. On the one hand, God [as] abstract essence vis-à-vis nature, on the other hand [as] a shape or moment – spiritual subject. As subject – spiritual – but as a particular individual.

(b) Spiritual individuality, particularity, freedom. The natural state [is] posited as semblance, as accident, [which] when contrasted with thought, with essence, is only the material of subjective substance, is only relative—mere corporeality, which has its meaning, its significance in the spiritual, in thought alone, as the *appearance* of spirit.

(α) Nature becomes semblance

(β) Spirit appearing only in a foreign element, not the way [it is] in and for self

   (αα) Separation of the two – the natural state, external being, as opposed to a correspondingly abstract spirituality, pure thought – sublimity; nature abstract, created

   (ββ) The inner unification of the two [comes] to expression as self-conscious individuality of the corporeal. God [has] manifold content in contrast with the concept; [he has] a particular character, free individuality, but [he is] not [purified] into absolute freedom, not to the absolutely free content, [he is not] purified spiritually. The [divine] content [has] limited characters and natural powers⟩

10. *Ms. margin:* ⟨(c) Transition [to] expediency. [Its] content [consists in] a universal, self-determined, independent purpose and fulfilled content, of which the gods and humanity alike are servants. The gods [are] powers subservient to ends or purposes, not powers in their own right (Venus does not take offense at Hippolytusᵃ

concept—but [found] instead [in the form of] objectivity, externality⟩. Therefore [it is] immediately (α) abstract within itself, or (β) determined within itself, [as] independence, yet an independence of the limited concept, which in its finite relation to externality should at the same time be objective. [This is] the totality of [its] development, the determination of purpose, the stage of external purposiveness or expediency.[11]

[Thus the arrangement of the religions follows] from the initial determinations [of the logical idea]: being, essence, concept. [It follows] from these determinations in their totality [but] without measure.

[The determinate forms include immediacy,] necessity, and external purposiveness.

[These are the so-called] "pagan religions"; Goethe called them "ethnic."[12] The Jewish [religion belongs] among them.

⟨[If we want] to name [the religions] historically, [they are] (α) the Oriental, (β) the Jewish and Greek, and (γ) [the religion that] inaugurates philosophical [religion],[13] the Roman, [with its] wholly

---

– the Romans appear not to have appealed to any particular gods such as Neptune when [consulting] auspices).

A purpose is a *concrete* determination; the gods are determinate, particular powers. What was previously an empty, indeterminate necessity above the gods [is now this concrete aim] – [previously there was] an accidental concurrence [between them] or one [of them] acts – in the Trojan War each [acts] contingently for himself, unconcerned about the whole⟩

[*Ed.*] [a]See below, nn. 173, 174.

11. [*Ed.*] On the translation of *äusserliche Zweckmässigkeit* as "expediency," see below, n. 229, and 1824 lectures, n. 466.

12. [*Ed.*] J. W. von Goethe, *Wilhelm Meister's Travels; or, The Renunciants: A Novel,* vol. 2 of Thomas Carlyle's translation of *Wilhelm Meister* (New York, 1901), chap. 10, p. 267: "The religion which depends on reverence for what is above us, we denominate the ethnic; it is the religion of the nations [*Völker*], and the first happy deliverance from a degrading fear: all heathen religions, as we call them, are of this sort, whatsoever names they may bear." *Wilhelm Meisters Wanderjahre* first appeared in German in 1821 (Stuttgart and Tübingen).

13. [*Ed.*] This reference is also clarified by the passage from *Wilhelm Meister,* p. 267. Goethe continues: "The second religion, which founds itself on reverence for what is around us, we denominate the philosophical," while Christianity is "the third religion, grounded on reverence for what is beneath us." Although Goethe does not have Roman religion in mind by this description, and although Hegel does not

abstract divinities—of fever, of the oven[14]—and infinite singularization.⟩ [32a]

A. IMMEDIATE RELIGION[15]

⁻Initially religion, the concept of religion, is still *our* thought; it
exists in this medium. But if this form of thought does not exist *for
itself* in reality, religion remains undeveloped and does not advance
to thought, to inward reflection. The mode of its existence [in this
externally reflective way] is immediacy,⁻[16] but this is not the total
5 concept itself. The truth of religion | is that it is as the idea, its con-
cept [is] duplicated by reflection and consciousness, [so that it is]
for itself as it is in itself. But initially the concept is [not] yet *mediated*

---

elsewhere refer to Roman religion as "inaugurating philosophical religion," nonetheless
the Goethean typology of three religions (ethnic, philosophical, and Christian) may
help to explain Hegel's decision to treat Roman religion as a distinctive form of religion,
in some sense intermediary between the preceding religions and Christianity. Roman
religion, in Hegel's view, is not an ethnic but a universal religion, although earthly
and finite. In that sense it may be "philosophical," and indeed Goethe says that the
philosopher surveys his relation "to the whole human race" and "to all other earthly
circumstances and arrangements."

    14. [*Ed.*] See below, pp. 217, 219.

    15. [*Ed.*] The discussion of immediate religion in the *Ms.* is both brief and elusive.
The brevity is due partly to the fact that "the religion of magic," or primitive religion,
is not discussed at all, and partly to the fact that Hegel was entering upon new territory,
for which there was no preparation in the *Phenomenology* or the *Encyclopedia*. The
elusiveness is attributable to Hegel's decision to draw together materials from several
quite different "Oriental" religions—Chinese, Buddhist, Hindu, Persian, Egyptian—and
treat them under the common categories of "concrete representation" and "self-
consciousness, subjectivity, cultus," rather than separately, as he did in the later lectures.
The basic interpretative scheme is present in the *Ms.*, but the content required extensive
revision and expansion prior to the 1824 lectures. Parts of the *Ms.* for Secs. b
and c (see especially sheets 37a–38a) are in the form of outlines, indicating that Hegel
had not yet worked up these materials thoroughly.

    16. W₂ *reads:* When we considered the concept of religion, this was *our* thought;
it existed in the medium of our thought. It is *we* who thought the concept, and it
had its reality in our thinking. Religion, however, is not only this subjective reality
but is objective in and for itself. It has a mode of existence on its own account, and
the first form it takes is that of immediacy, in which religion has not yet advanced
inwardly to thought, to reflection. But this immediacy itself presses on to mediation
because it is thought implicitly,

for itself ⟨([as opposed to] developed life, [where] everything [is] mediated, [e.g.,] a leaf, tree, lungs, stomach, blood, nerves, etc.)⟩. It is not there per se or as its own condition and ground but is only there immediately. Immediacy is a relation to self that is wholly unmediated, undeveloped, inwardly undifferentiated. This is only *one* moment, *one* determinacy of the concept, as that peculiarly characterizing it—or, more precisely, universality—in a word, religion in the form of *being*.

But since religion itself is only [inasmuch] as it is simultaneously *idea,* the relationship of self-consciousness to God, this differentiation [of self-consciousness and God] indeed emerges in it, but the fundamental character of this relationship is the absolute, undivided unity of both sides; and in all [of its] determinate forms this substantial, enduring unity is the essential, chief matter.

In general it is [in] the Orient [that we find this] undivided intuition, this intuition of God *in* all things without distinction; God *is* all things, ἕν καὶ πᾶν.[17] The heavens, the stars, the earth, plants, animals, human beings—[all] are one heavenly kingdom, one divine life—[but] not one love [since] love [entails] differentiated entities uniting in one consciousness. [Here] God [is] not separated from the earthly and temporal, he is not actually Creator and Lord, but is himself immediately all that is—[see the] *Shāh-nāma.*[18] [32b]

[We shall now consider] the moments [of immediate religion] more closely.[19]

---

17. [*Ed.*] Hegel alludes to the alleged deathbed confession of Lessing, as reported by Jacobi, which was taken at the time as simply a formula for pantheism: "The orthodox conceptions of the deity are no longer for me; I cannot take pleasure in them. Ἕν καὶ πᾶν [One and All]! I know no other" (F. H. Jacobi, *Briefe über Spinoza,* 2d ed. [Breslau, 1787], pp. 22, 23, 62 [*Werke* 4/1:54, 55, 89]).

18. [*Ed.*] Hegel erroneously writes *Schahinschahnahme,* but this must be a reference to the *Shāh-nāma,* the "Book of the Kings," by the pre-Islamic poet Firdawsī. See Joseph Görres, *Das Heldenbuch von Iran aus dem Schah Nameh des Firdussi,* 2 vols. (Berlin, 1820). The context of this reference indicates that Hegel apparently thought the *Shāh-nāma* contained a pure expression of Oriental pantheism—a view that does not take into account the undeniably dualistic mythology that envelops this work.

19. *Ms. adds:* (α) the metaphysical concept of God. *Ms. canceled:* (β) the relationship of self-consciousness.

a. [The Metaphysical Concept of God][20]

The abstract, metaphysical concept of God is extremely simple, indeed simplicity itself; [it is] nothing else but simple, pure | *being.* Our more profound representation of God cannot find this designation adequate.

6

Being—this first, pure category of thought[21]—becomes sublime[22] because it is taken in its concrete determination as that in which everything finite and determinate is negated: as soon as [being] originates, it becomes, as [mentioned] above, everything. "This" and "that" are all just *one,* [there is] only one "being." Parmenides expressed it—emphasized metaphysically on its own account—as the pure thought of being.[23] [The expression] "one" already reflects a higher level of determinacy in that "the many" is sublated,[24] but not in such a way as to be opposed to the many; rather the many is negated in the One, only the One exists.

[25]This thought, this sublimity, this elevation itself brought into thought, into specific form, results from the proof, in reflective form,

20. [*Ed.*] This section is primarily concerned with the cosmological proof, which is further discussed in relation to the metaphysical concept of the religion of sublimity and beauty. Already in Part I of the *Ms.*, Hegel adumbrated the cosmological proof, in terms of a demonstration of the necessity of the religious standpoint from the constitution of the finite world (see Vol. 1:110 n. 72, 221 n. 99), but did not develop it there as such, since it was his intention to take up the proofs in relation to the "abstract" or "metaphysical" concept of God as found in the various religions (see Vol. 1:110 n. 73).

21. [*Ed.*] See Hegel, *Science of Logic,* pp. 82–83 (cf. *GW* 11:43–44).

22. *Ms. margin:* ⟨*Dschelaleddin Rumi,* III, V. Balch, Mecca, died 1262⟩

[*Ed.*] Hegel became acquainted with Jalāl-al-Dīn Rūmī through a collection of fifty-two freely rendered poems by Friedrich Rückert, *Mewlana Dschelaleddin Rumi,* in *Taschenbuch für Damen auf das Jahr 1821* (Tübingen, 1821), pp. 211–248. The reference here is to poems III and V. The Muslim mystic Jalāl-al-Dīn Rūmī was born 30 September 1207 in Balch and died 17 December 1273 in Konya in Anatolia. Hegel's incorrect information about the date of death derives from Joseph von Hammer-Purgstall, *Geschichte der schönen Redekünste* (Vienna, 1818), p. 16. Hegel's reference to Mecca is probably due to the fact that it was during his visit there that Jalāl obtained the Book of Mysteries from Sheik Attar.

23. [*Ed.*] See Parmenides, frag. 6 in G. S. Kirk, J. E. Raven, and M. Schofield, *The Presocratic Philosophers* 2d ed. (Cambridge, 1983), p. 247; also Hegel, *Science of Logic,* p. 83 (cf. *GW* 11:45).

24. [*Ed.*] See Hegel, *Science of Logic,* pp. 170 ff. (cf. *GW* 11:98–99).

25. *Ms. margin:* ⟨These proofs rejected [in modern times] on account of [their] form – to be reinstated. Nothing other than the elevation of the mind; God's activity

of the existence of God, of God in the sense of being, the One, the universal.

[26](αα) The reflective form [of this proof] is as follows: because ⟨there is⟩ this colorful world of multiplicity, multiformity, and manyness | —this infiniteness of determinate forms of being, ⟨of determinate being in its particularity⟩—so [also] pure being exists, the simple, the universal.

The thought of universal, pure being is implicit in the many particular beings. ⟨More exactly,⟩ the many, the particular necessarily has an other as its ground; it does not ground itself by itself, it is not independent. For the many is a manifold, a diversity of things separated from one another, and just for this reason it is finite and delimited. In determinate being, the limit is precisely its *negation*— either directly (in which case [it] is merely being as such), or else what is limited is through an other ⟨and is a reflective thought; [but] it does not limit itself, because to limit itself would be to posit its other⟩. [It is] not [through—i.e., caused by—] something else that is limited, for this would be the same [problem over again], an infinite progression,[27] i.e., a repetition of the same thought, which does not surpass what it wants to surpass but immediately [33a] falls back into what it wants to leave behind. This other, [which is] actually an other of the many, is the One. The positive, the ground, the autonomous in all existence, is *being*.

---

comprehended in specific thought; whether necessary and whether for that reason correct. – [People] always act this way, reason this way, believe this way, even if, inasmuch as they grasp their argument in thought,⟩

26. *Ms. margin:*
⟨(αα) The reflective form of logical connection:
The finite presupposes the infinite
Now the finite exists
Therefore the infinite exists also
The two are one being. This mediating unity is the presupposition of the infinite through the finite. "The being of the one is the being of the other" is the major term [of the syllogism]. Everything depends on this connection.
(ββ) The being of the finite is not *its* being but that of its other. The finite [is] the limited – [this involves] negation, and this [result] is the infinite, not the finite again – [for it] is always the same.
(γγ) Unity or separation of the two
The former [is] ancient, the latter modern (to hold fast to the negative)
27. [*Ed.*] See Hegel, *Science of Logic,* pp. 147 ff. (cf. GW 11:82 ff.).

(ββ)[28] This form of a proof—that determinate being, the many, presupposes and necessarily has an other[29]—is deficient in not advancing beyond mediation as merely a transition to an other. Hence: (α) Being itself is always defined as an other because in contrast with it the being of the many remains an independent ⟨being⟩. (⟨For this very reason⟩ the progression appears as subjective, and being, when it is thought of in this way, appears as conditioned not in itself but in the course of our thought.) [Since] at the least [it is] essentially other, [it appears] namely as what stands over against [us]. Being is admittedly something | other than determinate being; in general ⟨we must distinguish between [them]⟩. But our distinction must not have the sense that being is an other in and for itself and thus also something limited. (β) But this *implies* that the limited, the many, continues to subsist in this form, and that being, or subsistence, is attributed to what is null. There are many things, manifold and limited, but they do not [exist] in and for themselves; hence they presuppose an other, which is being. ⟨Being is the universal that is divided into two spheres: on the one side, abstract being; on the other side, being too, but with a limitation.⟩

(γγ) This procedure has the peculiarity [of being] a proof of the existence of God. Initially God exists subjectively, in our representation, and being is something added. But here, in this way [of arguing], we begin from finite being. Being is in this respect positive, and the other *is* only insofar as the other as finitude, as limitedness, is stripped away, or more exactly is only put at a distance, posed in opposition [to being]. It is [not] the character of being that is appended to God, but the reverse: [it is] being to which God, the character of universality, is added.

(δδ)⁻Apart from⁻[30] the fact that God has only an entirely abstract significance, the deficiency indicated by this result [33b] is that finite being is still left with its limitedness as something positive; it is the

---

28. *Ms. margin:* ⟨(γγ) See below⟩

29. *Ms. margin:* ⟨Reflection is holding on to the differentiated characteristics and letting them be

(α) The difference between being as abstract and finite being; the former also [is] limited⟩

30. *Ms. reads:* Without disregarding

not-being-in-and-for-self of this limitedness—i.e., the nonbeing of the limitation, of negativity—that drives [us] to an other. The actual advance is rather this: because the limitation on being is only negation, the truth of being is only being as such. But this being is the being of | finitude itself, its positive element. God is the being 9 in all determinate being—and thus he is the immanent being.[31] ⟨Considered more exactly: the being of determinate being, the positive, is God; hence [there remains] a distinction between the two abstractions—between the positive and abstract negativity.⟩

(εε) Accordingly, what has happened is that being and limitedness are sundered, separated. ⟨The concreteness of existence, the unity, the synthesis [of being and finitude] float away from us.⟩ ⟨The question [arises] how these severed elements coalesce in the concreteness of existence. They should be absolutely opposed to each other,⟩ with no further connection between them. We have: (α) being; (β) finitude, limitation; and if ⟨this second side⟩ [is] defined (γ) as finite being, there are two elements in it, finitude and being, and the question is then how they coalesce. ⟨The coalescence [is] external.⟩ Finitude exists neither from pure being (since the latter is *only* pure being) nor from itself; it is altogether the negative. Finite being is posited, made, created. (α) But the activity of being is pure activity, not the sort of activity that produces finitude, for finitude is just what has become separated from it. ⟨Abstract being [is] not true, not sundered; [it is] idea but immediate idea.⟩ (β) What is limited [does] not [exist] through itself—otherwise it would be eternal, eternal matter existing independently in and for itself. It is rather the opposite that has been assumed. So upon closer inspection there only [occurs] a disintegration into two abstractions. ⟨The mind does not intend and want such abstractions. The finite is something sublated: thus the negative is a semblance or show in regard to being itself and its activity. | It 10 is not because the finite exists that infinite being exists but because the finite does *not* exist; it is the negation [of it] that is absolute being.⟩

(ζζ) The true is the process of elevation. Finite being has its truth in being. But this being sets bounds to itself, posits an other over

31. [*Ed.*] See below, 1824 Lectures, n. 76.

against itself, imparts itself. Its imparting constitutes the positive of the other, but this other is also only a semblance. ⟨Finite being is sublated: (α) as finite being it does not endure on its own account; (β) it does not [endure] as abstract nothingness nor God [as] infinite, empty being.⟩ What is one-sided in this process, in this disintegration, is just the specification of the absolute only as being, i.e., abstraction.

Thus for intuition absolute being [takes the form of] concrete representation. [34a]

b. Concrete Representation[32]

[33]Concrete self-consciousness does not rest content with abstract being but rather takes being in its concrete determination, in its truth, i.e., in the truth that God is able to have on this level of being, the level of immediate unity. As the concrete, the idea generally, God is directly on that account the unity of infinite and finite being. The determinateness that being has, the reality within which it appears for self-consciousness, is immediate being just as it is, finite nature. Nature exists, is intuited, represented, as God: Spinozism.[34] |

[35]However, the intuition of nature, the consciousness of this temporal, fleeting world (for the world is fleeting, albeit also essential, for this level of consciousness) is at the same time not that prosaic intuition of abstract understanding connoted for us by the term "world," an intuition fixated on things, aware of them only in their determinacy and finitude, but rather an intuition of the sun, ⟨stars, river, sea, of universal objects everywhere⟩—a reverence for the sun, a feeling of devotion for it, consciousness of it as a universal [object],

---

32. *Ms. reads:* (β)   *to which is added partially in the margin:* Concrete Representation   *followed by:* ⟨How [being] exists for an other—[whether] as determined for an other or as its absolute primal division—is an open question.⟩

33. *Ms. margin:* ⟨The more proximate mode of connection between the two [abstract being and concrete representation]:

(α) [On the] side of finitude – in immediate fashion
  Inner intuition, which has the meaning of the universal, of God⟩

34. *Ms. margin:* ⟨(α) Intuition marked by greater singularity⟩
[*Ed.*] See Spinoza, *Ethics*, part 4, Preface: "For the eternal and infinite being, which we call God or nature, . . . " (*Chief Works* 2:188).

35. *Ms. margin:* ⟨Meaning: natural power – spiritual power – abstractly good⟩

104

an indeterminate consciousness of a mighty being, a mighty, beneficent spirit, which we no longer have and scarcely are able to represent. For the sun [is for us] a globe of light or some form of matter, [and it has] laws of revolution, [which] make it rigidly determined, spatially confined to a particular path, etc.

The elevation of the mind is the expansion of individual consciousness to a universal, to something all-encompassing—devotion. In this elevation the determinate object in which consciousness glimpses the determinate mode of reality is expanded to a universal, encompassing all in *power*. For power is precisely the universal insofar as it is negative vis-à-vis otherness, and, as negative, exists in the form of something subjective that appears in a limited form. Power is the mediation of the all-inclusive universality with singularity—with the singular both as differentiated from and external to the universal, and as identical with the universal. So the object [34b] becomes something having power over nature, a natural subject generally. The indeterminacy or abstraction of this power fills the mind with fear, awe, and longing, and the spirit with the sort of ties that are to be found in this representational darkness—i.e., with links that are contingent and arbitrary. But the mind that once entertains such links, such presentiments and anxieties, is already caught up in setting its own inner [world] in motion and filling it, and in seeking to combine singularities of this kind.

It is not the creative fanciful imagination that unites finite | existence and infinite meaning into one configuration and a higher individual unity, [giving the finite] a higher justification. (α)[36] The justification for this unification is a manifestation of far-reaching and especially of abstractly pure effect; it is light, the sun, heaven generally (among the Chinese), water, the elements, which offer themselves to devotion as the universally operative element, as the representation of the universal. But what is immediately prominent here is

(β)[37] Precisely the incongruence between all such immediately natural objects and the universal that is represented and intended.

12

36. *Ms. reads:* ⟨αα⟩
37. *Ms. margin:* ⟨See below⟩

Just as when Thales, for example, as a philosopher of nature, designated water as the absolute essence or principle,[38] self-comprehending thought cannot recognize itself in such a limited entity and transcends it.

But it is not necessary that consciousness should be confined to such a limited existence and should confine its intuition to what merely subsists in opposition to its thought. Rather [35a] thought is able to equate intuition with itself, perceiving and venerating the whole world, physical and spiritual nature in its immediate subsistence, as the *One*. This expansion does not belong to the standpoint of immediate devotion, however, but to that of a later reflection, which, having retreated from immediate intuition, no longer intuits but reflects; it no longer adheres to the immediacy and singularity of the sensible, which it represents inwardly in its totality as a world, or as nature. For what we call "world" or "nature" is not immediately intuited; it is the totality of what appears—its modes of activity and relationships—grasped as one. That is what Spinoza's nature [is, or] the matter and nature of the materialists and naturalists: a natural totality, which in its actual, intuited existence, however, is just this infinite multiplicity of changing things; and even if in its extension it is boundless, this extension is precisely the form 13   that belongs only to representation. |

(γ) The immediate, more proximate intermixture of reflection.[39] [35b]

⟨(α)⟩ Consciousness in the determination of immediacy has the awareness of the idea in an immediate intuition of nature. The idea is itself concrete; the aspect of apparency (which is only separate from its absolute unity qua finitude) is its being for an other. A natural object of this kind is not a symbol whose signification of the infinite is distinguished from its immediate existence by thought and representation; rather the sun and similar objects are [for] self-consciousness the immediately present God.

---

38. [*Ed.*] See Aristotle, *Metaphysics* 983b. On the designation of water as the absolute principle, see Hegel, *Lectures on the History of Philosophy* 1:174–178 (cf. *Werke* 13:197–200).

39. [*Ed.*] The following bottom third of sheet 35a is blank, suggesting that Hegel may have intended to complete this point later.

⟨(β) Positive:⟩ The natural objects, the elements, are, by virtue of their general abstract nature, the existences that present themselves immediately as this aspect of being for other. ⟨(β) Negative:⟩ But this essence is essential power—the inward negativity of the other, maintaining and animating it. Thus it is *subjectivity*, and it is necessary that consciousness should advance to natural forms that are subjective, such as animals and *a fortiori* the power of human beings, [which are] more intensive existences. ⟨The sun and natural objects [are] not present [to us] as subjects.⟩ Religious intuitions of this [animate] kind are to this extent an advance, a deepening of the idea. For the idea has only the content or determination that its configuration has. This is what constitutes its deteminacy, and this determinacy is here present in an immediate intuition. Egyptians [worship] Apis, Hindus the elephant [and other animals], especially the monkey and the cow; this bull, cat, or monkey [is worshiped] not as a symbol but as it is in actuality. Human [forms]: the Dalai Lama or the Hindu kings and Brāhmans simply amplified into God. In this connection the Christian religion might occur to us, which does not worship God under the image of a man, but rather worships *in* this man the *actuality* of God. (α) [It must] be mentioned in the first place that by virtue of his human nature the God who is worshiped is deceased: Christ did not allow himself to be worshiped as God during his lifetime. (β) [Thus the truth is] rather that, | just 14 as the Christian religion is the most spiritual, so a religion [that worships God in a living person] [36a] is the most spiritless, the most unspiritual, the most vulgar. To worship an animal is necessarily contemptible in our eyes, and [to worship] *this* presently extant human being is similarly degrading in the highest degree. We do not judge the sun worship of the Parsees, Medes, and Peruvians[40] to be as bad as the worship of animals or an extant human being as God. The reason why this apparent advance is a degradation, a further finitization of the absolute essence, is that, while indeed it is an advance to a determination of subjectivity, ⟨to concrete existence,⟩

40. [*Ed.*] This mention of the sun worship of the Peruvians, which is not otherwise found in Hegel, could be based on Friedrich Schlegel's *Ueber die Sprache und Weisheit der Indier* (Heidelberg, 1808), p. 175 (cf. *Kritische Friedrich-Schlegel-Ausgabe* 8:275).

to singularity, the singularity is merely an *immediate* or *spiritless* one. The animal is simply alive; it is a quite transitory individual, with instincts, desires, vitality, and as such it is an infinitely higher entity than the sun. Its instincts interest us—this secret, purposeful activity moving outward from within, this undividedly rational [activity] that is both independent and unbounded in its desires. ⟨This implicit potential is its idea. But the way it exists⟩—this immanence of soul in its actuality—is precisely the modality of absolute singularization and finitization. ⟨This submergence in itself, this subjectivity, is a submergence into finitude, into singularity—not a submergence that is an elevation, a return [to self], ideality, but rather determined from all sides, and in this determinateness a losing of self, a consummate sensuality, finitude as such.⟩ [It is] rather the starting point for an elevation, the demand for which resides directly in its present, but only momentarily present, finitude. It is not, therefore, what it is in itself; for just this implicit being is the universal, and what is at issue is a mode of existence that is appropriate to it: the sun [is] much more appropriate than an animal. It is the same with human being in its immediacy, the human as this immediate man—not the one who suffered, the crucified, buried, and risen one, ⟨the Son of God raised to heaven to the right hand of the Father, | not the one baptized, etc.—but in this singular, direct mode⟩; not, that is, the one who even in terms of his immediate existence gives the form and history of spirit—but rather humanity in its mere immediacy and finitude, abiding still in its physical nature and finitude, remaining now in the now. Consequently, it is the most enormous contrast and denigration of spirit, precisely its debasement, to view the absolute in this supremely finite way. For human finitude [is] the most obstinate [form of] being-for-self, and to the extent that it is only immediate, [it is] degraded in its antithesis to the universal. [36b] For [this is] precisely not just a naive or superficially innocent consciousness but rather a consciousness that, in its claim to be *absolute* elevation, a claim that is inherent in its intuition, remains turned against this elevation, i.e., remains in its immediacy. This is where the deepest humiliation of spirit essentially lies. This is the most abandoned of religions.

15

⟨(β)⟩ But reflection, thought generally, advances to the consciousness of this contradiction, and of the mutual incongruence of the moments of its idea. [It advances] to the point of their mutual separation and the exaltation of the universal, self-subsistent [moments], not indeed into spiritual thoughts but into abstractions, in such a way as to supplement its *necessity*—the determinacy for which nothing other than immediate natural objects is available— and the inadequacy of the singular moments by allowing the imagination free rein to play over all manner of configurations and employ all the beauty and ⟨wealth of⟩ nature in order to intuit the [divine] essence in it; it hurls itself about in all directions and seems capable of doing justice to the infinite only by this casting around. This dissatisfied casting about is the origin of the sublime, puffing up finite configurations, thoughts, and phenomena to the point where they overreach their limit, their measure, and hover between a particular form and its dissolution. The | Oriental, Hindu images of   16 imaginative power are precisely those that elevate the most common thing to the highest and then reduce it to the point where its direct significance disappears. It is given an infinite meaning, under which it succumbs and dissolves. Every configuration and natural human form [is] puffed up into something infinite: kings, anthropogeneses, incarnations—incarnations for ordinary, human finite being and acting. Human being [is elevated to the point where] all gods and powers, even those that appear to be autonomous on their own account, again serve it and are made subject to it.

⟨(γ)⟩ Nature as a whole [is] personified: Cybele and Bacchus, reveling—the Universal Mother, eternally bringing forth. [This] ushers in another sphere. [37a]

c. The Side of Self-Consciousness: Subjectivity, Cultus

In its entirety being-for-other is this difference, which consists in the reflectedness of the idea or the self-consciousness for which the idea is there.[41]

---

41. *Ms. margin:* ⟨[We must] distinguish two kinds of things: (α) being, (β) boundlessness⟩

[42]The way in which this immediate idea is defined for self-consciousness has been stated:[43] the relationship of self-consciousness itself, immediate, substantive being in unity with its object. The cultus in its specific concept is the movement of the individual out of its separation, positing itself in identity with the absolute, giving itself the certainty of unity with the absolute—the feeling of raising itself to the love of the absolute.

[44] ˜Here, however, at this first stage of the immediate unity of the finite and the infinite, the primal division between the two

42. Ms. margin: ⟨(α) Proper, immediate unity: the universal⟩

43. [Ed.] Probably a reference to the survey at the beginning of this part of the lectures, above, p. 94.

44. W_2 reads, parallel in main text follows (for the identification of this text see the appended editorial note): At the first stage of immediate unity between finite and infinite, self-consciousness has not yet evolved into a totality, and to this extent the distinction is not taken seriously. While there must be negativity in general, it has not been imagined by self-consciousness itself, so that the negative is excluded from the inner relationship of subjectivity, stands over against it, and has to be shut off from the immediate unity as a realm of evil and darkness. Conflict and struggle with such a negative can come about, but in such a way that it is represented rather as an external war, and the hostility and its cessation do not exist as an essential moment of self-consciousness. This stage accordingly constitutes no genuine reconciliation, which presupposes the absolute rupture of mind and soul.

The essential characteristic of the cultus here is then that it does not constitute something distinctive, set apart from the rest of life, but a life lived continually in the realms of goodness and light. The temporal life of need, this immediate life, is itself the cultus, and the subject has not yet distinguished its essential life from the maintenance of its temporal life and the steps it takes to ensure immediate, finite existence.

While the subject must at this level have an express consciousness of its God as such, must be raised up to the thought of absolute essence, and must worship and praise it, this is initially an abstract relationship on its own account, in which concrete life has no part. As soon as the cultic relationship assumes more concrete shape, it takes up within itself the individual's external actuality, and the whole span of ordinary everyday life, eating, drinking, sleeping, and all activities for the satisfaction of natural needs, are related to the cultus; and the course of all these deeds and actions forms a life of holiness.

These actions are at the same time characterized by need and externality, so that if they are elevated into that essential unity, particular attention must be paid to them and they must be carried out in a carefully considered, deliberate manner, to the exclusion of all arbitrariness. In this way the commonest of actions of life are imbued with solemnity and dignity. The concrete existence of finite life is not yet regarded as a matter of indifference, not yet degraded by freedom to the level of externality, since inner freedom has not yet endowed itself with an independent sphere. The actions

sides—the idea in itself and subjectivity—is still only formal, i.e., it is not | yet inwardly independent, not yet inwardly developed to   17 the totality of the distinction, not yet taken in earnest. Over against its substance, its immediate unity, consciousness must also, to be sure, be dimly aware of the absolutely negative—⟨the negative [that is] not self-consciousness's own imagining⟩—of the kingdom of darkness, of evil, but hovering before it as something that has implicitly broken away from immediate unity (for this intuition of evil is abstract). Hence the other, the negative, hovers before it, but

---

of ordinary everyday life are accordingly referred entirely to the religious domain and are regarded as substantive. In order that these actions that we regard as contingent may be suited to the form of substantiality, they must be performed with solemnity, calm, and due regularity and order. All this is accordingly determined by universally applicable regulations, and there is no semblance of contingency since finitization has not yet broken away on its own account and endowed itself with its own sphere of action. Orientals, who stand at this level, regard neither their bodies nor finite affairs and their execution as their own but as a service to be rendered to another, to the universal, essential will; in the most trivial actions they must therefore proceed with dignity and deliberation in order that they may perform them fittingly, as befits the universal will for whom they are performed.

Such solemnity, however, is only a *form;* the content still consists in the *doing and being of the finite,* and the antithesis is thus not raised to the level of truth. Since the order governing the affairs of daily life is thus only an external form imposed on this finite content, external life—and what, for consciousness, is the absolute object—is still marked by actual diversity. Subjective existence must therefore be expressly sublated, and the manner in which this here comes about has to do with reflection on finitude and its opposition to the infinite. However, the negativity of the finite can also only come about in finite fashion. Here we have come to what is generally called *sacrifice.*

The immediate content of sacrifice is the surrender of an immediate finitude, in the sense of my testifying that this finitude ought not to be my own possession and that I do not want to keep it for myself. From the standpoint of this religious self-consciousness, sacrifice is therefore sacrifice—offering up—in the proper sense. Because the depths of mind and heart are not yet present, negativity cannot here reveal itself in an inner process. Sacrifice does not consist in a turning about of heart, mind, soul, and natural inclinations, that these should be broken. Rather what the subject is for itself, it is in immediate possession, and since in the cultus it surrenders its finitude, this is only to surrender an immediate possession and a natural existence. In this sense sacrifice is no longer to be found in a spiritual religion, and what is there called sacrifice can only be so in a figurative sense.

More specifically, sacrifice can be mere offering up of adoration and praise, whereby I bear witness that I have nothing that belongs to me but give it up in that I think myself in relationship to the absolute. The one to whom the possession is to be given

because of the immediate unity it is *excluded,* it is over there—
something with which one can wage an external battle as an enemy,
but not an inwardly necessary battle that enters into the cultus as
a moment. This separation and hostility that is evil does not occur

---

up is not thereby enriched—such is not the purpose; rather the subject acquires the
consciousness of separation superseded, and to this extent the subject's action is utterly
joyful action. This is also the significance of gifts in the East in general; the kings'
subjects and conquered enemies bring him gifts, not so that he may become richer,
for everything is in any event ascribed to him and belongs to him.

A further character which sacrifice can assume is as sacrifice of purification in
regard to a specific contamination. A *sin,* properly speaking, is here not committed;
the specific sacrifices of purification pertain rather to the whole sphere of finite action.
They are also not repentance or punishment, nor is their purpose spiritual conversion;
and they do not in any way represent some loss or damage that was incurred. This
notion is not that one has done something evil and must suffer another evil in its
place. To define sacrifice in any of these ways would involve the representational
idea of the subject's justification, but this is a form of representation that is here still
completely excluded. According to *our* standpoint such sacrifices would be regarded
as a loss, in that through them some item of property is given up, but at the standpoint we are here considering this way of looking at the matter does not arise; here
sacrifice is rather essentially something *symbolic.* Contamination has occurred, and
must be done away with in no less immediate fashion; however, the subject cannot
undo what has been done, nor repent having done it. There must therefore be a
substitution; something must be given up other than what was, properly speaking,
involved. The value of what is sacrificed may be much less than the value of what
I keep, what I have acquired. For example, the harvest I have reaped, the beast I
have slaughtered—these I take into possession, and if I now have to show that I do
not take these possessions seriously, this is done in a symbolic manner. It is not as
if what I do ought not to happen, for these actions are necessary; all it means is that
through the sacrifice this being-for-me (which is simply a form of finitization) is again
sublated.

The general character of these activities relating to the service or worship of deity
is what we call *ceremonial.* These ceremonies consist in what we would regard as
ordinary, everyday actions, which at the same time are necessary actions, determined
by ordinance. We have the right to proceed in such matters as we will or blindly to
follow custom; in the same way we do not deem purification a necessity just because
such actions as harvesting and slaughtering animals are necessary. Moreover, since
such sacrifices and purifications involve a reference to the religious aspect, there is
no distinction in regard to them that is unimportant. Thus the various foods are viewed
not merely in regard to taste and health. The different ways the various elements
in sacrifice and purification are combined are also relevant; the action whereby the
purification of another action is effected may have no necessary relation to it, and
the combination may consequently be merely contingent and external. This is why
this kind of cultus makes a painful impression. Whatever significance lies, or has lain,
in these ceremonies and combinations is a trivial, superficial significance, and inasmuch

112

in the cultus, which is an original state of reconciliation without disunion, i.e., without eternal, absolute disunion. ([The struggle with evil is represented] as an external history—the age when Ahriman was mighty.) Thus, properly speaking, [there is] not a state of reconciliation since [there can be no reconciliation] without a preceding disunion, only an original life in this unity. [37b]

---

as they become a habit, such actions lose whatever little significance they may once have possessed.

At this standpoint we also encounter *punishment* in the specific sense, insofar as a deed that is opposed to a given regulation has to be annulled, and insofar as what is involved is a transgression. Punishment for such an injury is another injury, and something is relinquished—life, property, etc. But such punishment has here the sense of an utterly dry, formal punishment in the manner of civil punishment. This is not directly concerned with the amelioration of the criminal, whereas ecclesiastical repentance in our sense is a punishment whose essential purpose is to better and convert the one who is punished. At this standpoint punishment cannot have a moral or, more accurately, a religious sense. Civil laws and the laws of the state are here identical with religious laws. The law of the state is the law of freedom, presupposes human dignity and personality, and refers essentially to the will, leaving aside a sphere of free choice for decisions on contingent, indifferent matters. At this standpoint, however, this distinction is not made, and what obtains in general is a situation of sheer necessity.

From the finite mode of being and acting, which the cultus just described brings into relation to what has being in and for itself, is to be distinguished a more fully determinate mode of acting, which *conforms to a purpose*. While the performance of actions that refer immediately to our need does not occur according to a purpose but is regulated in immediate fashion, purposive or expedient action is not merely necessitous action according to habit but is determined according to *representations*. Admittedly it is still finite action insofar as it has a finite purpose; but since prominence is here given to the principle that the finite should be elevated to the infinite, the finite purposes have also to be expanded to an infinite purpose. In this way the *labor* of religion enters into play, bringing forth works of devotion that are not destined for a finite purpose but are designed to be something that is in and for itself. This labor is what the cultus itself here consists in. Its works and productions are not to be regarded as our church buildings, which are only undertaken because they are needed; rather, as a *pure bringing forth* and as *perennial,* labor here is purpose for its own sake and accordingly never comes to the end of its task.

This labor is of differing kind and differing degree—from the purely bodily movement of dance to enormous towering edifices, whose prime significance is that of monuments, the erection of which is never at an end since as soon as one generation has completed its work a start must always again be made from the beginning.

The characteristic feature of such works is not free phantasy; what is produced has rather the character of the monstrous and colossal. Production is still linked essentially to what is natural and given, and all that remains open for the builder's activity is for the dimensions to be exaggerated and the given shapes to be rendered monstrous.

Thus the *cultus*[45] [is] a life in the kingdom of light and good; the people are a permanent, universal priesthood, a holy people

---

All these works too still fall within the sphere of sacrifice. For, as with sacrifice, the purpose is the universal, vis-à-vis which the characteristic properties and interests of the subject must be surrendered in action. All activity involves a *giving up*—a giving up no longer of something merely external but of inner subjectivity. This giving up and sacrificing involved in activity is, as activity, at the same time objectifying—it brings something about, but not in such a way that what is produced stems solely from me; rather it comes about according to a purpose, a purpose imbued with content. Human labor, whereby the unity of finite and infinite only comes about to the extent that it is permeated by spirit and wrung out of the action of spirit, is, however, already a more profound sacrifice and an advance beyond the kind of sacrifice that originally appeared merely as the giving up of an immediate finitude. For the sacrifice involved in productive human labor is the *action of spirit*—the effort that, negating particular self-consciousness, holds fast the purpose that dwells within representationally, and brings it forth outwardly, for intuition.

[*Ed.*] This lengthy passage in W₂ clearly forms a parallel to *Ms.* sheets 37a–38a. It can belong to either *Hn* or *MiscP*. In favor of *Hn* as the source is the fact that elements from the main text and marginal additions of the *Ms.* could form the basis for an oral presentation of this sort in 1821. Favoring *MiscP* as the source is the fact that in this section the *Ms.* has not been as fully worked out as is normally the case. Not only are the left and right columns filled with marginal notes, but also the bottom half of sheet 38a contains notes in outline form. Thus it is plausible that Hegel reformulated the text on the basis of these notes, and that the new sheets were used for the treatment of the cultus in 1824. In the latter case, Hegel would have removed this theme from the treatment of the religion of nature in Part II and introduced it into the concept of the cultus in Part I, since in 1824 the various cultic forms of the nature religions were much more sharply differentiated. Hence what served in 1821 as the entire treatment of the cultus of the religion of nature would in 1824 have been used only to offer a historical preview of the various cultic forms of these religions. Because of the uncertainty in identifying the source, this passage of special material is also printed in Vol. 1:353–357, as n. 178 to the 1824 *Concept of Religion*.

45. *Ms. margin:*
⟨(β) *Cultus*
   (α) Universal consciousness – an uplifting, to pray to, call upon, consciously express one's own unity [with], one's praise of the most high in comparison with oneself
   (β) [(αα)] Abstract, but a relation to actual life, actual being
     (ββ) Actual life – actual cultus [is] a concrete consciousness into which the vitality of existence enters – not yet merely inward (see opposite). Attention paid to everyday routines – contempt for
   (γ) Sacrifices (α) To offer up the immediate things of natural existence, in order to sublate the actuality of the distinction – Praise-offerings
     (αα) In general

(Paradhāta).[46] | The cultus is only a festival, an act of praise, an   18
explicit consciousness of life in the light, life in consummation. The
temporal life of need, immediate life, is itself this cultus; but to this
extent consciousness of the cultus [consists in] temporal activities—
eating, drinking, sleeping, ⟨illness,⟩ all such routine doings or
activities. ⟨And since there is this need, this externality implicit in
them, the cultus in regard to these activities is just to pay attention
to them | and carry them out in a prudent, regulated, uniform way,   19
excluding capriciousness. Pious Orientals regard their bodies, their
finite concerns and the business involved, not as their own but as
a service directed toward an other; they have to exercise propriety
and circumspection that this service is carried out properly and in
accordance with the will of the Lord—a universal will. The haste
and restless activity of Europeans [is], on the whole, entirely foreign
to Orientals, who comport themselves as a universal essence, not
as a contingent, wholly indifferent free will. Hence [they have]
general, orderly procedures, prescriptions, ceremonies, as though
[they do] nothing ordinary, but the ordinary routine is something
higher than substantive action—not subjective free will or fancy.
[What is] important [is] their contingent, indifferent actions, [such
as] eating and spitting. But (ββ) despite this, the actual diversity of

---

(ββ) There is an actuality of the distinction also: an impure action – not reconciliation –
(γγ) Punishment
[*In the margin to the left of the above:*] Aspect of *offering up* – sacrifice the most
natural relationship – depth of soul, spirit, inwardness not yet attained – natural things
– heart not antithetical
(γ) (αα) Offering of praise, of veneration; the conviction that I have nothing belonging
exclusively to myself, but rather, since I view myself in my relationship with
the absolute, offer it up and thus make myself conscious of the sublated
separation
(ββ) [Sacrifice] of purification – [for] specific defilements)
46. [*Ed.*] This term, *Paradhāta* ("Peshdādian"), appears in Hegel's German as
Pischdadier. He understands it in the first of the senses distinguished by Kleuker in
his edition of the *Zend-Avesta*, 5 vols. (Riga, 1776–1783), 3:32, i.e., not as a specific
dynasty of the mythological Golden Age, but as a designation for all persons who
lived under the first law, the law of Jamshid. See also Kleuker, 2:381, and the English
translation in *Sacred Books of the East*, 3 vols. (Oxford, 1880–1887), 1:220.

finite life, of external existence, remains. This subjective consciousness, existence [must] be expressly surrendered, annulled. [But here] corporeality, external existence [is] not yet reduced to something | indifferent, something immediate in contrast with the infinite—it is either identical [with the absolute] or unholy. [There must be] reflection on finitude and its contrast with the infinite.⟩ Controversy and discord are only superficial impurities. The general duty [is] to keep oneself pure, and defilement is an offense. Punishment [exists] as such; it is not intended to bring about reconciliation or improvement and does not have a moral purpose. The cultus [consists in] bringing about an external purification of this sort of activity[47] based on finite need. (The prophet Zarathustra[48] restored religion to its purity, but did not make a continuous, eternal restoration through repentance and conversion a goal or duty.)

Sacrifice means the voluntary surrender of one's finite possessions, [thus] purifying oneself of finitude, a finite action, a fault; [but it does] not [mean] to repent [in order to] redeem evil through evil or forfeiture. Sacrifice is not a matter of forfeiture or damages, not a matter of reckoning, but rather getting rid of some lack, some deficiency. It [is], however, essentially symbolic. Something impure is done and [must then] be undone in a simple, ⟨direct⟩ fashion—not by repenting and being inwardly overwhelmed with remorse but [by giving up something else]. However, I cannot undo this thing itself, this defilement, so I must get rid of something else—make an exchange.

An essential characteristic of this cultus is the mass of ceremonies—superstition, as we rightly call it. External life, the whole range of ordinary, daily activities and needs—eating, drinking, sleeping, the going to and fro all this involves, family relationships, ⟨buying and selling⟩— | [these constitute] a great sphere of activity that becomes habitual, i.e., they are undertaken intentionally,

47. *Ms. margin:* ⟨N. Schweankommen [?] – but a gift⟩

48. [*Ed.*] Hegel here uses the rare term *Zerduscht,* a middle form between Parsee and Pahlavi, instead of the more common Greek term *Zoroaster* or the transliteration of the Zend name as *Zarathustra.* Cf. J. G. Rhode, *Die heilige Sage und das gesammte Religionssystem der alten Baktrer, Meder und Perser oder des Zendvolks* (Frankfurt am Main, 1820), p. 130. The view that Zarathustra restored religion to its purity is probably attributable to Rhode, p. 126.

circumspectly, and in conformity with a purpose, but without [38a] consciousness being any longer aware of the conformity with purpose, without any choice still occurring, and so forth—a sort of natural, instinctual activity, viewed in general as [conforming to] subordinate purposes, [subsisting on] their own account, divorced from a higher purpose. [Thus we have] two kinds of life, a religious life and an ordinary, everyday life. But in this religion the two sides [are] not present: [there is] an everyday, external common life in relation to religion, as religious activity. But the relationship [is a matter of] accidental connections, arbitrary combinations, ⟨relating things that are contingent in themselves. [Thus we find] painfully precise distinctions, [such as] which foods [are] permitted and which [are] forbidden.⟩ [These then] become habitual, and the little meaning [they may once have had] is completely lost.

⁴⁹*General Characteristic:* substantial unity

Particular Features:

(α) Abstract devotion – calling upon [God] only in thought, without committing the rest of life (and thought itself [is] immediately universal, infinite)

(β) Concrete devotion, cultus in the proper sense
The relationship of concrete subjectivity [is] absolutely essential, for I *am* finite; concrete existence [is] not yet indifferent, not yet degraded to externality by freedom. [This is] the actual, rigid antithesis between subsisting finitude and infinitude

(αα) Activities of daily life

(αα) [They transpire] according to prescription, but this [is] only an external form; the content is finite | 22

(ββ) Notwithstanding the prescription, a finite being and doing – defilement

(γγ) A finite production – as such, to that extent according to a purpose, not merely immediate need

(ββ) Sacrifice

(ααα) In general | 23

---

49. [*Ed.*] This outline is written across the entire width of the bottom half of sheet 38a.

(βββ) Purification – [occurs] everywhere and generally, whenever a prescription is infringed – as [if it were] voluntary; [the violation has happened] against the will, against something established; sacrifice [is] purification from what is from the natural standpoint necessary. Violating one's will [is] distasteful, [I give up] what I would like to keep. |

24

(γγγ) Punishment – [mere] ceremonies, not reconciliation, when sacrifice [occurs] as forfeiture or damages. [It is] barren, formal punishment in the fashion of civil punishment, and [does] not [have] the religious significance pertaining to inner life, an ecclesiastical penitence, a call to mend one's ways, a *moral* viewpoint, a conviction of wrongdoing.

Unity of civil and state law with religious law. The former is the sphere of freedom, personality, human dignity. Free reason, the rational condition of freedom and free will [prevails] over indifferent, contingent things. This sphere [does] not yet exist for its own sake; hence there is also no rational condition of freedom, only a condition of necessity ("[these things] must not be"). The annulment [of the offense] by punishment without interiority [is] not the religious side.

(γγ) Labor – my finite being is finite activity – building temples, erecting monuments – building temples is already a more specific labor – [e.g.,] the temple of

25

Bel.[50] |

---

50. [*Ed.*] The fact that Hegel here uses the term *Bel,* derived from the Greek Βῆλος, rather than *Baal,* and in the context of building temples, suggests that he is not referring to the Old Testament but to the reports of Greek historians concerning the building of the temple of the Bel Marduk (the Babylonian Zeus), which was attributed by myth to the Assyrian queen Semiramis. Cf. Diodorus Siculus, *Bibliotheca historica* 2.9; Josephus, *Antiquities* 10.224; Herodotus, *Histories* 1.181. On the restoration of the temple under Alexander, see Arrian, *Anabasis* 3.16.

Productive activity [is] a relationship to absolute being without genuine fanciful imagination; [it is] a concrete, not a theoretical expression, such as language. [It is] finite insofar as it is activity, labor, insofar as a self-subsistent purpose is assigned to the product, a purpose for which [it] is produced. When the idea is intuited as an animal, self-consciousness is defined as active; it intuits its essence with the characteristic of activity, but the activity is geared especially to animal desires, immediate need. [Sometimes it is] exacted labor – knowing Bel at night.[51] *Labor* itself [is the essential thing], not that whatever is being built or produced should exist; [it brings] no satisfaction for itself [as] when it is finished for a purpose. But this labor is never finished ([in] Egypt every king [built] pyramids, labyrinths, etc.). For I am perennially a finite activity and therefore [must] also perennially infinitize this activity, sacrifice it, not merely negatively, but since it is productive, sacrifice only its purpose for myself. [38b] | 26

In this kind of productive activity the fanciful imagination begins to be involved, since form and configuration belong to subjectivity at work. ⟨All activity is itself a sacrifice, the offering up of one's subjectivity. [One gives up] not an external thing but one's internal subjectivity.⟩ The aim [is] the universal, as with sacrifice: in doing something, to give up one's distinctiveness, one's interest ⟨[as with] dancing, wearying oneself, satisfaction [valued] for its own sake⟩. But as activity [labor is] at the same time an objectifying, serious, nonplayful activity. Something comes into being, the purpose is full of content, is produced by me, ⟨comes from me, not as bees or birds build nests but based on an image, [so that there is] a significant purpose⟩. [Such activity is] not indifferent [to] being, to outward effect, [it is] not a game. Orientals are serious, respect being; thus

---

51. [*Ed.*] See the preceding note. Hegel is possibly alluding here to the report of Herodotus, *Histories* 1.181–182: no one is allowed to spend the night in the temple of Bel except a woman from Babylon chosen by the god, and it is reported by the priest of Bel "that the god enters the temple in person and takes his rest upon the bed." Herodotus adds that "the report does not seem to me very likely."

their production should be permanent and enduring. Purpose, configuration [comes] from within; [it is] a spiritual activity, but still 27 unmeasured and monstrous. ˜ |

These [are the] main features, the basic characteristics, of the cultus of nature religion.

But in the form to which it first passes—that of *boundlessness*—there is found the abstract separation of the infinite, of pure being, from the finite, and in relation to the former the finite is merely the *disappearing*. Religious intuition [is thus] a wallowing in the configurations of finitude, which are puffed up so as to equate them with the infinite but perish in it [instead]. ⟨Here the negative relationship [is] also a major moment; the finite [appears] as evil, as negative, not on account of its will but [simply] because it exists—not because of its guilt but because it *is* so. Thus it does not lie within its will to change, to be otherwise, to mend its ways, forsaking the old. [It is] without inward totality, such as could comprehend itself as freedom, give itself inwardly concrete infinitude. Rather [it is] perplexed and unable to help itself.⟩

⟨[There is here an] *absolute inconsistency:*

(α) Brahmā [exists] *(β)* alongside countless other divine figures. [In terms of] his characteristics, Brahmā can of himself be taken [as] what Jehovah [is]. But Jehovah is the one and only [God], to whom alone all worship rightly belongs. [But] Brahmā and Parabrahmā are not worshiped at all in India.[52] Human beings have no relationship at all to Brahmā; and while they have a relationship to Parabrahmā, it is absolutely negative—they only perish in him.⟩

To posit identity for oneself with this abstract infinitude is absolute abstraction, mortification of the finite, which is comprehended only as immediate and thus only as the negative of the infinite—infinite self-torment and austerities, not repentance. Errors are turning back, falling out of unity. Therefore [one must] always begin again at the beginning; it is not a question of [undergoing] punishment and repentance but of renouncing knowledge and will, positing negatively something that holds interest for us and then giving it up. For from the beginning the principle [is] this resignation that I should want

52. [*Ed.*] See below, 1824 lectures, n. 263.

to give everything up. Whoever resigns everything cannot be punished. [One practices] mortification, becomes a hermit [so that one can only] see to the end of one's | nose, undertakes pilgrimages 28 on foot, or covers long distances on one's knees. In particular, [one] commits suicide, ⟨sacrifices oneself, not (as in human sacrifices) others⟩—like the countless wives [who] are nothing for themselves, [who kill themselves] near the temple or hurl themselves into the Ganges. [They] seek [death] especially in the Himalayas, in the abyss, or in the snow (Webb, also Moorcroft, the Englishman who was in the Nitee Pass before Webb—*Quart. Rev.*, no. xliv, pp. 415 ff.).[53] [39a]

⟨Brief Reflection on the State, Freedom, Reason⟩[54]

It is self-evident that a European civil life based on personality, on free and absolute rights, is not to be found in such a religion. Genuinely ethical relationships—those of family, human benevolence, the obligation to recognize infinite personality and human dignity—[become impossible] with savage fancy and abominable deeds. ̄To be sure, [this savagery] is combined with the gentleness and charm of sensuous, loving feeling and its display, with infinite resignation and its embellishment. ⟨Love [is] most tender, sensuous, and inexhaustible in its Oriental expression. [Here one

53. [*Ed.*] See the anonymous review of *Sur l'elevation des montagnes de l'Inde, par Alexandre de Humboldt,* in *The Quarterly Review* (London), 22, no. 44 (1820): 415–430. The purpose of the review is to show that the meteorological data and hypotheses of Alexander von Humboldt in the work under review, and of William Moorcroft in the *Asiatic Researches* (London, 1806–1812), have to be modified in the light of the more recent investigations of Captain Webb in the Nitee Pass. In this connection the reviewer refers to the report by Moorcroft and Webb of a legend concerning a black rock on the way to the Pass, at the temple of Kedar-nath. At this rock the sins of the body may be expiated and a union with the deity accomplished by the voluntary sacrifice of life. After making expiation, the penitent must leap naked into the abyss of a snowy defile from a high precipice. Webb reports that shortly before his arrival three women, unable to discover the precipice, sought death in vain by wandering in the snow without food for three days and nights.

54. [*Ed.*] This is not a heading in the text of the *Ms.* but a line written on the upper margin of sheet 39a, intended to introduce a concluding paragraph to the section on immediate religion. It is added because Hegel considered the relationship of religion to the state to be an aspect of cultic life. It is not found as such in the later lectures because this matter is included under the discussion of the cultus of specific religions.

finds] a natural feeling for unity with others. [Where] reason and thought [are coupled with] unity, legal right and ethical life [also] exist. [But here natural feeling prevails,] imbued with all the riches, all the infinity of the phantasy of spirit, [producing] the most glorious fruits.⟩ Under these circumstances the feeling of love, the renunciation and surrender of personality, must necessarily have the highest kind

29 of beauty. But (α) [it remains] cut off | from freedom, right, the rule of law; and a people [is] unhappy and miserable where it is only such feeling that is exclusively cultivated, that alone possesses beauty. (β) Precisely because it lacks a basis in law, this feeling alternates with the most severe harshness. The free personality, the being-for-self that is at the same time [treated as] essential is mere savagery, forgetfulness of every firm bond, of everything that is higher than contingent, transient sensibility—[it is lacking a bond that is] firmly rooted in the will, or precisely in being-for-self.⁻⁵⁵

B. THE RELIGION OF SUBLIMITY AND BEAUTY⁵⁶

The determinateness of immediacy passes over into essence, into universal thought, with a conscious sublatedness of the immediate, [which] is initially characterized as something inessential, having no independence within itself.

55. W₂ *reads:* In the circumstances that properly belong to this standpoint, the gentleness and charm of the tenderest feelings and the infinite surrender of the personality must necessarily attain to the highest level of beauty, because with an irrational foundation of this kind this feeling alone is cultivated into beauty, to the exclusion of all else. But because this feeling of surrender lacks a basis in law, precisely on that account it displays an alternation with the utmost harshness, and the moment of being-for-self of the personality thus passes over into savagery, forgetful of all fixed bonds and trampling love itself under foot.

56. *Ms. margin:* ⟨29 June 1821⟩

[*Ed.*] Sec. B is developed in much greater detail than Sec. A, especially those parts of it treating Greek religion, and in particular the cultus of Greek religion. (A comparison of this date with that given in n. 229 indicates that Hegel devotes nearly a month to the religion of sublimity and beauty.) Sec. B retains a structural similarity with Sec. A in the sense that the two religions discussed here—Jewish and Greek— are subordinated to the general analytic categories (metaphysical concept, concrete representation, cultus) rather than considered in autonomous units, as in the later lectures. In both, according to Hegel, "the determinateness of immediacy passes over

⁵⁷Nature religion, [which] worships the absolute in an immediate object of nature, passes, in the boundless, out of this immediate identity⁵⁸ between immediate being and essence. In the boundless all natural being ⟨comes [into being] and⟩ disappears;⁵⁹ puffed up to the boundless, its shape bursts. ⁻At the same time this shape is not its immanent character but its natural shape, used externally and inappropriately for this purpose.⁻⁶⁰ [39b] No matter how negatively the natural is posited in it, it is still positive in its finite being vis-à-vis the negative. Or just as everything melts away out of sight in the boundless, | so the boundless is devoid of strength—the contradiction of power and powerlessness.   30

The truth, however, is that in fact the absolute One is the truth, and finite being is what is sublated and ideal. The contradiction is sublated in the ideality of essence, in its *concrete* ideality, which

into essence." Essence is then posited as *power,* and power is *necessity* or *fate,* the development of essence; the former is the characteristic cognition of the absolute in Jewish religion, while the latter is its cognition in Greek. It is this connection that enables Hegel to think of Jewish and Greek religion as different expressions of the same stage of religious consciousness. They are not related genetically or hierarchically, and their difference can be construed or constructed in different ways, as the 1824 and 1827 lectures demonstrate. Only in 1831 did Hegel sever the categorial connection between them.

Hegel had studied and written about both these religions since his student days. In the case of Judaism, the *Ms.* is still close to the interpretation found in the *Early Theological Writings* and the *Phenomenology,* especially the use of the concept of lordship and servanthood. Yet this relationship is no longer seen as indicative of human self-alienation, as in the early writings; rather it is implicit in the concept of God as one and all-powerful, which is the "great thesis" of Jewish religion. And the central role played earlier by Abraham is replaced by Moses and especially Job. In the 1824 and subsequent lectures, this interpretation of Judaism is changed in quite dramatic ways. In the case of Greek religion, Hegel has moved, in the *Ms.,* well beyond his earlier romantic attachment to the gods of Greece, he sees clearly both the depths and the limits of this religion, and he works out a definition of the "classical" influenced (both positively and negatively) by C. F. Creuzer's important work, *Symbolik und Mythologie der alten Völker, besonders der Griechen,* 2d ed., 4 vols. (Leipzig and Darmstadt, 1819–1821). For further details see the Editorial Introduction.

57. *Precedes in* W₂: It is true that the inappropriateness of the immediately external for what is inward was already demonstrated in nature religion.

58. W₂ *adds:* between the natural and the absolute and

59. W₂ *adds:* and begins to become the universal on its own account;

60. W₂ *reads:* at the same time infinitude is not yet an immanent characteristic and is still exhibited in external, inappropriate fashion by natural forms.

means that essence is not abstract being-for-self but is a *showing* [*Scheinen*] on its own account.

⟨(a)⟩ In this way it is posited as *power*,[61] the absolute negativity that has implicit being, the negativity that differentiates itself.[62] The powerful is that which possesses the soul, the idea of the other; the other simply *is*, it is [there] in its immediacy. (Whoever *thinks* what others merely *are* is their power.)

Logically, the advance from being to essence [is as follows].[63] What being was at first [only] in itself, [or] for us, it is now for self-consciousness; self-consciousness does not intuit [just] one essence— *one* higher essence—but *essence* itself as the true, i.e., the universal as absolute power.[64] Essence finds satisfaction within itself: it is inward totality, but not yet totality for itself; in order to be, it does not have to test itself in natural objects but has its determinateness within itself; its reality is the totality of its show [*Schein*].

Essence is little enough. ⁻But those people who have attained the level of self-consciousness where they know and revere essence⁻[65] have thereby passed over into the sphere of ideality, the realm of the soul; [they have] crossed the threshold of the spiritual world, torn the bands of sentient intuition and unthinking error from their brow, begotten and laid hold on thought, the intelligible sphere; they have won a firm basis within themselves. [40a] They have given what they worship a foundation | so that it is now firmly anchored on its own account; it is something inward that *shows*, that manifests itself, but only *as manifesting*—it does not fall back to the level of sensory being and seek its own determinate being there. Manifestation is the *determinate being* of essence, but as of what is within, subsisting and abiding [as] the inward element.

Being necessarily defined as *subject*, as the negative relating to itself, this negative power is *the Lord*, the ruler of all. ⟨[This is a]

61. [*Ed.*] Essence posited as power is the religion of sublimity, or Jewish religion.
62. W₂ *adds:* but in such a way that the distinctions are sublated, and are only semblance.
63. [*Ed.*] See above, n. 6.
64. W₂ *adds:* since all other determining characteristics are sublated in it.
65. W₂ *reads:* Those peoples whose self-consciousness has attained the level of knowing subjectivity as the ideality of the natural

pictorial image; as form *finite* lordship [is] not substantive but external lordship,⟩ so that there is no independent side to it. The view of matter as abstract and eternal reduced this power to a purely external relation of form; but all that is implicit in the power itself is the abstract moment that appears as matter in opposition to form only in its externality, but which on its own account is just one moment of the totality of show.

˜But the religion of power contains even self-consciousness within itself only as *show*—it is admittedly self-consciousness for that for which it manifests itself, ⟨i.e., in such a way that [it] has a positive relationship to it: being reflected into self is repulsion without mediation, so that self-consciousness here begins to be on its own account, to be valid, but it [is] initially abstract reflection⟩. It *is* infinitely fragmented, unfree, without inward breadth or scope, a constricted heart and spirit; its feeling [is] just | to feel the Lord; its determinate being [is just] happiness within this narrow confinement. [It is] obstinacy—⟨abstract subjectivity, like essence [itself],⟩ [having] attained differentiation, but only in a captive manner, not unrestrainedly or freely. Self-consciousness is concentrated exclusively into this one [fixed] point, the One [Lord]. [Its aim is] not annihilation as with the Hindus. Essence is what shows, [but] self-consciousness is the inessential in the essential; reality [is] this externality.˜[66]   32

˜Necessity or fate [is] the development of essence, the shattering of its [outward] show or semblance [to reveal] the form of independent realities, ⟨although [such realities are] implicitly [identical]⟩.

66. *W₂ reads:* Since the absolute is thus defined as the One [Lord] and as power, self-consciousness is merely a semblance of self-consciousness. It is admittedly something for which the absolute manifests itself and to which it has a positive relationship; for the reflection of power into itself is repulsion without mediation, and this *is* self-consciousness. Thus personality, self-consciousness, begins here to be valid, but is still characterized only abstractly, so that according to its concrete content it knows itself only as semblance. It is unfree, without inner breadth or scope for action; heart and spirit are constricted, its sole feeling is to feel the Lord, its determinate being and happiness lie exclusively within these narrow confines. Even if difference emerges as a result, it is still in bondage; it has not really broken away, has not been given free rein. Self-consciousness is concentrated exclusively into this one [fixed] point; to be sure, it knows itself as essential (it is not annihilated as in Brahman), but at the same time it is the inessential in the essential.

125

[Here we find] serenity: [one is] released from bondage [and attains] individuality; ⟨spirit [can] spread itself inwardly, [can] develop in such a way as to raise itself from its inessential determinate being to the shape [of divinity]⟩.

⟨(b) Power is *necessity, fate*.[67] This is where the different configurations [of spirit], the differing shapes [in which spirit is represented], emerge as essential. [But the differing shapes are] implicitly identical, so the shape or configuration is at the same time not a serious matter vis-à-vis self-consciousness. There is serenity [side by side with] the notion of fate.⟩̆[68]

[69]The absolute as necessity[70] [is] not abstract unity or being. Nor [is] distinction only show or semblance, but essential manifestation—spirit in itself, yet as necessity on its own account, stemming from spirit. [40b] (αα) This configuration or mode of being corresponds to spirit, | expresses its reality, [is] spiritual in form. (ββ) Yet [it is] still finite, still something *made,* not the reality of spirit in and for itself. The spiritual does not [here] lie on the side of reality as such, even though [reality is] a portrayal of spirit, a show whose sole meaning resides in the spiritual but that still preserves for itself a side that is not spiritual, a side that is immediate; and this is accordingly only a *posited* spirituality. But it still contains this moment of finitude because the development still has the character

33

67. [*Ed.*] Power as necessity or fate is the religion of beauty or Greek religion.

68. *W₂ reads:* Necessity is, to be sure, that development of essence which lets its [outward] show or semblance be shattered [to reveal] the form of independent realities, and the moments of such show reveal themselves as different shapes. But these moments are implicitly identical, and are not therefore to be taken seriously. All that needs to be taken seriously is fate, the inner identity of the differences.

69. *Ms. canceled:* (α) Metaphysical concept
  Ms. margin: ⟨(β) Concrete representation – particularity – configuration
  (γ) Cultus⟩
[*Ed.*] The first line was written in the main text as a heading but then was canceled when an additional page of introductory comments was added prior to beginning the discussion of the "metaphysical concept" on sheet 41a. The canceled heading and the adjoining marginal points provide a brief outline of the whole of "The Religion of Sublimity and Beauty." Here the distinction between representation and cultus is articulated (cf. n. 5 above).

70. *Ms. margin:* ⟨Necessity: (α) Implicit distinction. – Inner [element] and appearance as its immanent appearance. – In this way *shape* – only as semblance or show. – (β) External medium. (γ) *Its* appearance. Contradiction: serenity – . . . [*illegible, on frayed lower margin*]

of necessity, i.e., [it is] implicitly the idea, [or] a unity of the differentiated elements, but at the same time the elements are still posited as distinct configurations, not yet in their universal, absolutely all-encompassing being-for-self, ⟨i.e., they are not yet posited in themselves, [with] the universal in them, but the universal is above and beyond, as fate⟩. In other words [this is] not yet the free concept, which achieves its reality only in its wholly and completely distinctive element.

These two religions, of *essence* and of *necessity,* have accordingly been designated the religions of *sublimity* and of *beauty.* ⁻The sublimity here is not that of the boundless, which in order to attain determinate shape can avail itself only of what is immediately present (individuals, animals, and so forth, and their grotesque distortions); rather it is the sublimity that has done with these existences and modes of existence, pronouncing them to be mere show,⁻⁷¹ the essence being their Lord and master, ⟨the sublimity that is not driven to distort these existences in order to make them more fitting to it— on the contrary [the transition from it to] beauty [is] the free birth of the concept⟩. The religion of beauty gives essence a *positive* form, yet one deriving from spirit—a form that has merely spiritual significance | but is at the same time still burdened with externality, 34 still stands in the sensuous element of portrayal, the element of the natural appetites and passions. It is not in itself absolute spiritual unity. [41a]

a. Metaphysical Concept⁷²

This [has] already [been] considered and needs no lengthy discussion. (αα) [We are dealing first with] *essence,* but [construed] as power, as subjective unity with itself, the One; and then (ββ) as purely

71. W₂ *reads:* The sublime is moreover not the boundless, which in order to attain determinate shape can only avail itself of what is immediately present and the grotesque distortions to which it is subjected in order to make it suited to what is within. On the contrary, sublimity has [here] done with immediate existence and its modes, and is no longer driven to have recourse to them in order to portray itself, but pronounces them to be [mere] show.

72. [*Ed.*] One of the peculiarities of the *Ms.* is that it considers the cosmological proof twice, in relation both to immediate religion and to Jewish and Greek religion. The proofs, says Hegel, merely express the content of the different definitions of God. God is no longer defined as simple, pure being but as the One (Jewish religion) and

self-determined, not immediate determinations as [is the case with] power, but where the concept of power is posited as determined in and for itself: *necessity.*[73]

Two principal characteristics pertain to this sphere.

35   (α)[74]The progression from being to essence has been noted: | (αα) essence, (ββ) *ens* reflected into self, thing, *individuum,* universal *ens,* [God] as the One [*der Eine*].

---

as necessary essence or necessity (Greek); hence we no longer have a proof based on the relationship of finite to infinite being, but on that of the many to the One, and of contingency to necessity. These are all seen as forms of the cosmological proof, whereas in the 1824 lectures Hegel regarded the proof associated with Jewish and Greek (as well as Roman) religion to be the teleological proof.

73. *Ms. margin:* ⟨(a) One [God]⟩

74. *Ms. margin:* ⟨(α) Meaning of the proposition "God is one." [Previously we had] "that which is one," τὸ ἕν, which [applies also] to the manifold variety of determinate finite being—[here] being [is] the One. In this way [we] abstract from the multitude of finite things, but this very negation [is] the determination of being itself. [In this way we arrive at] essence, relationship.

(β) Meaning [of the proposition] "God is one." "One" is the definition of [God's] essence. Its meaning is not [that of a] proof of the existence of God but of the fact that he is one.

[It is] not [a matter of] God's being because "one" [refers to] form, not content, not substrate as such. "God is only one" is quite different from "God exists." "One" [gives] what is already universal the character of singularity, [whereas] in "God exists" [we proceed] from the singular, and indeed from the finite, to the universal⟩

W_2 *adds:* Being passes over into essence, i.e.—as reflected into self—what has often been called an *ens,* an *individuum.* When we say "God is the One," this has not the same meaning as when was said in former times, "The absolute, being, is one, τὸ ἕν." For example, Parmenides said that only being is, or only the One is.[a] But this One is only the abstract infinite, not reflected into self, and is accordingly rather what is boundless and powerless. For it is the infinite only as compared with the infinite manifold of determinate being, and its subsistence necessarily depends on this relation. It is only when power is comprehended as "he who is one" that the universal is in fact posited as power. "That which is one" is the one side, and over against it stands the multiplicity of the real world [*Weltwesen*]. But "He who is one" is singularity, the universal that is reflected into itself, whose other side itself encompasses all being, in such a way that the totality of being has returned into its unity.

At this point, reflection grasps the categorial determination of God's unity or oneness and tries to prove it. But this does not yield the form of a proof of God's existence. "The One" is distinguished from the substrate, and one's sole concern is to exhibit what is meant by "being one." The reason why reflection fastens on this is that "one" in general is nothing else but reflectedness-into-self.

[*Ed.*] [a]See above, n. 23.

As already noted,[75] [it is] a great advance [when] self-consciousness enters the realm and crosses the threshold of the intellectual world. [It crosses] the threshold, but that is all. Cognition of the unity of God [is] of infinite importance. [God is] not [characterized] as "that which is one" [*das Eine*], τὸ ἕν, for that which is one is abstract, [existing] not in the sense of the infinite reflected into itself but [as] the boundless, the impotent. It is only in "him who is one" [*der Eine*][76] that we do not have merely impotent universality but also singularity, universality as the side of reality, as the other side of the idea, universality as the sublatedness of immediate being.

There is only one God. This way of characterizing God is initially directed only against polytheism in general, and to this extent also against the other form, which we ⌐regard as more concrete,⌐[77] ⌐at least within itself, in regard to the concept, in regard to [its level of] determination; but this other form is itself still abstract, as *necessity*. Being thus determined in and for self [is] a mere "ought" ⟨and therefore [gives rise to] a plurality [of gods]⟩. That "God is one" is not the case, just as "he who is one" only *ought* to be the One who is inwardly concrete. The One [that is] not inwardly determined, [that is] necessity, "that which is one," certainly [has] shape or configuration, [but] is not [yet] "he who is one."⌐[78] [41b]

There is only one God, and he is a jealous God who will have no other gods before him [cf. Exod. 20:3, 5]. [This is] the great thesis of Jewish and of Arab | religion generally ([the religion of] the Near East and Africa. These two parts of the Orient [constitute] quite different natures and worlds.[)][79]   36

75. [*Ed.*] See above, p. 124.

76. [*Ed.*] The contrast is between *das Eine* (neuter) and *der Eine* (masculine), and hence between God conceived as substance and as subject.

77. W_2 *reads:* shall regard as the second form at this stage or level. We are therefore here assuming the refutation of the ensuing determination.

78. W_2 *reads:* At least this second form is more concrete within itself, in defining the concept; but as necessity, its being determined in and for self is a mere "ought," and therefore it is plurality, it still lacks *absolute* reflectedness-into-self, the character of being *one*. Even the character of the One is, to be sure, still one-sided, since it is only abstract form for its own sake, not form developed as *content*.

79. [*Ed.*] Like the medieval thinkers, Hegel associated Islam with North Africa and with Oriental civilization. While he may be intending to contrast Judaism and

¯(α)⁸⁰ The development of the necessity of this categorial deter-
mination, the elevation [of consciousness] to this one subject as "the
One," the proof that there is only one God—how is this to be carried
out? [At the outset we have]⁸¹ the one and the many—Plato and the
Neoplatonists⁸²—an abstract opposition without the definition of
God as one [person] [*Einer*].⁸³

⟨[There are] two kinds of relationships involving the many. The
contradiction appears here immediately.⟩ (α) One against many, as
opposing elements, entering into contact, into conflict. Here [we see]
the appearance of the contradiction that is resolved in absolute
unity—the battles of the gods, the elements, etc. This finite in-
dependence does not constitute | their truth. ⟨Admittedly, in the
representation of finite things,⟩ representation seems to [impute]
validity to an independent, *abstract* foundation, which merely
commits its surface to the conflict, holding itself in reserve (like
"force"). There are in fact various forces, but force [is] a determinateness only in the form of self-contained being. [The gods are]
subjects, infinite form for itself, infinite being-for-self (not in itself);
what they are—their content or power—[they are] only in antithesis.
Being-reflected-into-self [is] just what is lacking in content, independence in form; ⟨[the view of] many as different⟩ [gives] finitude
in content, the content being subject to the same dialectic as finite
being. ⟨Confronted with a presupposition,⟩ the presupposition of
absolute power, of the universal negativity of all that [simply] is,
this plurality of formally independent [beings] directly disappears.¯⁸⁴

Islam in this sentence, his meaning more likely is that the Semitic-Arabic worlds are
different from all the rest.

80. [*Ed.*] This α designates the first of two main points to be considered in this
section, namely the elevation to the one personal God or the proof of the *oneness*
of God. The second point is designated by the β on sheet 42a (n. 87) and concerns
the proof of the *existence* of God.

81. *Ms. reads:* (α)

82. [*Ed.*] A reference to the dialectic of the one and the many in Plato, *Parmenides*
137c–166c, and in Proclus, *Elements of Theology* and *Platonic Theology* (both in
Proclus, *In Platonis theologiam libri sex,* ed. A. Portus [Hamburg, 1618]). See *Lectures
on the History of Philosophy* 2:435 ff. (*Werke* 15:76 ff.).

83. *Ms. margin:* ⟨God presupposed⟩

84. W₂ *reads:* The development of the necessity of this categorial determination
of the One, the elevation [of consciousness] to this one subject as "the One," proceeds

¯(β) [Second, there are] the many, [seen] as merely distinct, not entering into contact—for example, the plurality of worlds, [which] do not come into conflict, so there is no contradiction, no appearance of contradiction. Representation [clings] more resolutely to this; it cannot be so easily refuted, since the presupposition contains no contradiction. [It is] in and for [itself] lame to argue that it is [42a] possible to represent [what is] to oneself [in this way]. [This view of] the many, [as] a mere empty possibility of representing, | [is] nothing other than diversity, i.e., the abstract, mutually exclusive relation of the diverse [beings] to each other.   38

A question that necessarily arises is what the diversity [consists in]. If one is as powerful as another, this [is] no diversity, ⟨and [these are] completely empty representations or images⟩. If one has more power than another, [then we have] a determinate diversity.¯⁸⁵ In this case one term lacks, for our reflection, whatever [pertains] to the other—but *only* for our reflection. For our reflection a stone is not as perfect as a plant, [yet] a stone lacks nothing for itself; it

---

as follows: being one is taken as predicate, God is presupposed as subject, and it is demonstrated that the character of plurality is contrary to the presupposition of a subject of this kind. The relationship between the many can now be viewed as their being mutually related; therefore they enter into contact, and come into conflict. But this conflict is immediately the appearance of the contradiction itself; for the different gods are supposed to maintain themselves in accordance with their quality, and this brings their finitude plainly into view. When God is presupposed as the universal, as essence, the finitude that resides in plurality is not appropriate to such a presupposition.

In the sphere of finite things we do indeed take the view that substances can be in conflict without losing their independence. It seems in that case that they merely commit their surface to the conflict and hold *themselves* in reserve. So we draw a distinction between the inner being of the subject, the substance, and its relations to others, and we treat the substance as passive, without prejudice to its other activities. This distinction, however, is unfounded. What the many are in content and in power, they are only in antithesis; being-reflected-into-self is just what is lacking in content. So if, in form, they are independent, they are nonetheless finite in content, and their content is subject to the same dialectic as finite being. Confronted with the presupposition of absolute power, of the universal negativity of all that [simply] is, the plurality of such formally finite [powers] directly disappears.

85. W₂ *reads:* It is a direct consequence of the presupposition of the universal that form and content cannot be separated in such a way that a quality would accrue to the one but not to the other. By their qualities the gods therefore directly annul one another.

Plurality, however, is also taken in the sense of the mere diversity that does not involve contact. For instance, we speak of a plurality of worlds, which do not enter

neither feels nor knows any lack. This kind of diversity is an image arising from our reflection.

⁻Thus reflection is differentiated in regard to making *real* distinctions, is differentiated in diversity; [it is] also opposed to [its] presupposition.

(γ) In the same way [its] proof is opposed to [its] presupposition; [its] definition, however, is identical with [its] presupposition. The essence [is] all-powerful—absolute power belongs only to the One [God]. The defect in this kind of proof [is that] a presupposition [is] set up as a definition that is merely compared [with what shows up in experience].⁻⁸⁶

(β)⁸⁷ As a proof of the existence of God [the appropriate one is the proof] ⟨de contingentia mundi, i.e., [the one that depends on] external, finite necessity⟩. From contingent being [we prove] the absolutely necessary—[this is the] cosmological proof. The finite is contingent, it does not have its ground within itself. [We are dealing with] the contingent, proceeding from one finite cause to another. [What is necessary is to] break off this series, i.e., of the finite as such. [This is] what we have previously seen: [one] finite and another finite are the same because negative. The negative of the finite [is] the infinite; and more precisely, it is necessary as *absolute;* in other words it is not necessary through another, [this is] not external necessity. | It is against such external necessity that the proof is ⟨directed⟩. ⟨Infinite progression pertains to the finite sciences. To

39

into conflict or contradiction with one another. Representation clings resolutely to this, opining that such a presupposition cannot be refuted since it contains no contradiction. But this is in fact one of the most common mistakes of reflection, to argue that we can imagine something to be so. We can, to be sure, imagine *anything,* and grasp it as possible; but that is beside the point. Suppose we ask wherein the diversity lies and receive the reply that one is as powerful as the other, that neither is deemed to have qualities that the other has not also; then diversity is an empty expression. Diversity must of necessity advance at once into a determinate diversity.

86. W₂ *reads:* This is how reflection argues, and its reasoning is correct, yet at the same time no less inappropriate. Essence, the universal, is presupposed as power, and the question arises whether the predicate of "the One" pertains to it. However, the characterization or categorial determination of oneness coincides already with the presupposition, for absolute power is immediately implied in the determination of singularity or oneness. The proof is therefore quite correct, but superfluous, and involves disregarding the fact that absolute power itself is already present in the determination of "the One."

87. *Ms. reads:* (b)

break off this progression, to move by transcendence to the infinite lies within the finite itself, as that which is the negative of itself. This [true] infinite [is] universal. Infinite progression is not the positing of the negativity of the finite but the finite itself, or only the abstractly negative (and therefore ever anew the positive finite).) The presupposition [is] contingent being, i.e., not [a mode of being] that can just as well be one way as another (Epicurean chance) but that which is deemed to have a ground, i.e., is absolutely [42b] determined by something else, and does not have its ground within itself. But the other likewise [has its ground] in an other. The other that has its ground in itself and is the ground of an other [is the infinite]— ⟨here [we are] thinking more specifically of finitude, and [of contingent] being⟩.

This is a necessary, universal mode of thought. ·

As we remarked previously, all that [is] amiss [with this proof] is the form of reflection, concluding from one mode of being to another mode of being, as if both were being in like measure. On the one hand [there is] an external, subjective advance in our reflection, from one mode of being to another; but inasmuch as this is a subjective advance, what happens is rather that we annul the character of being we assigned to the contingent, we retract this our first viewpoint, that of superficial intuition, and we no longer envisage two modes of being, but a semblance or show, and its true being that is necessary in and for itself. But on the other hand this second mode of being appears to be conditioned by the first, which contradicts the content [of the proof] itself. It is necessary [that there should be] (α) cause or ground *and* what is grounded, consequent, posited; but (β) [there is] only one necessary [mode of being], i.e., this distinction, this relationship [is] likewise annulled. [We are here speaking of] necessity in the world, (α) not the necessity of the world, i.e., it is not the world as such that is necessary. But (β) the necessity is not the world itself, which [is] only the ideal [content]. The necessity is in and for itself; it is not another being, precisely because actuality does not pertain to the world. |

40

Kant[88] in particular has revealed a nest of dialectical subleties in

88. [*Ed.*] See Kant, *Critique of Pure Reason,* trans. N. Kemp Smith (London, 1930), esp. B 637, also B 632, B 633–634, B 638–639.

this proof, and has triumphed over it. [There are] two sides [to his attack]:

(α) It is only in the world of the senses that one can conclude from a contingent [event] to a cause, not in the transcendent, intelligible world. [He is] correct, [to the extent that cause is comprehended] as finite cause [and inference made] from [one] being to another, equally finite. Infinite cause, however, does not reside in appearance. [43a]

(β) [The proof yields] merely a necessary essence, not yet by any means the supremely real (which is what we are concerned with, viz., the concept of God). (αα) The "supremely real" essence [is just] the former metaphysical definition, which cannot in fact be so very relevant to our purposes. (ββ) Anyway [the objection is] justified; God is here characterized no further than as necessity or the necessary essence.

[As] indicated previously,[89] the various proofs of God's existence [are to be seen] solely as relating to the various ways of defining God; the proofs express the content of these different definitions.

When we reflect on the difference [between] "there is one God" and "God is the necessary essence, necessity," [which is] here this process itself, [we see that] becoming is *implicitly* reflection into self, subjectivity; but [it is] not *posited* as this reflection into self, as subjectivity, it is not *free* necessity. [His being] "the One" [is] subjectivity, reflection into self, the category of freedom, but without *inner* content, determination, or purpose. [It is] a *necessary* determination, but without freedom; necessity is a passing over, but a passing over that does not yet involve the explicit maintenance of self—it is not freedom.

b. Concrete Representation, Form of the Idea

α. [*The Religion of Sublimity*]

[Initial Version][90]

In the religion of sublimity the form, determinacy, reality of the idea is already contemplated, power as lordship of "the One." In

89. [*Ed.*] See above, pp. 100 ff.
90. [*Ed.*] Beginning here, several passages are given in both an "initial version" and a "later version." The initial versions are found on the inner halves of the sheets,

the same way that in being the determinacy of immediacy meant that the reality of being lay in an immediate object of nature,[91] | here   41 too the same determinacy of the concept applies, and this also constitutes the determinacy of reality, what prevents it from being other than what it is. But in "lordship" the whole picture is already given (lordship over all), for the determinacy is in fact abstract negativity; [43b] there is no distinction, [God is] plenitude, so the mode of reality is not differentiated [from the concept], [so that it has] a positive configuration of its own; this is the religion of *thought.* ⟨The configuration of power is merely the negative as directed against the other, against immediate being.⟩

The relation to the other—nature, the world—is for this very reason only the negative relationship of power and lordship. ⁻More specifically, lordship contains the moments of creation and preservation, and also the decay of worldly ⟨things⟩. For representation these moments exist as differentiated in time⁻[92]—a world in general, whose content arises from its intuition, for the world does not exist as a purpose; or it is to the representation—to the primary act of dividing on the part of the subject—that this differentiation belongs. For in the concept this One is the absolute power, the world's truth, the positive and negative sides, the separation of being and nonbeing. But[93] precisely herein lies the more determinate differentiation of the moments of thought, for power is distinct from coming to be and passing away; [it is] a property. The moments [are]: (α) that of the

---

front and back, and were obviously composed first, while the later versions are found on the outer halves or outer margins. These are, however, more than marginal notations or additions to the main text; they are alternative versions of it. Two of the three sets of parallels are found in the sections treating Jewish religion. One might hypothesize that they represent revisions to the *Ms.* in preparation for the 1824 lectures, but in fact they clearly reflect the distinctive interpretative emphases of the 1821 rather than the 1824 lectures. They must, then, represent revisions to the *Ms.* prior to lecturing in 1821, and we must assume that when Hegel presented the material he drew upon both versions. This is supported by the fact that passages in the *Werke,* which most likely come from Henning's transcript of the 1821 lectures, parallel both the initial and the later versions (see, e.g., nn. 94, 95 [initial version], 100, 101 [later version]).

91. [*Ed.*] See above, p. 104.

92. W_2 *reads:* In the representation [the moments of] creation, preservation, and decay break up into different temporal stages.

93. *Ms. adds between the lines:* Re (β) (ββ) new manuscript

being of finite things ([God's] goodness); (β) their *finitude,* the manifestation of their nothingness ([God's] justice). ⁻These determinations characterize the concept itself, ⟨they are moments of the process inherent in power, of power as process,⁻⁹⁴ of the process which it is as lordship⟩. ⁻The same world, as having being, is *only* goodness; it is not inherently justified but contingent. In | the goodness [there is] contained at the same time its negativity. [It has] determinate being [*Dasein*], which is however only a show or semblance. Its negativity lies in the fact that it disappears—that non-being *is* its determinate being, which is there [*da ist*] in the form of negativity.⁻⁹⁵

⁹⁶Sublimity is therefore portrayed and expressed in nature and the world in such a way that these [are] represented as becoming and passing away within divine power, [as its] *utterance.* ⟨Power—this mode of utterance that contains infinite power within itself—[is] sublime. [God's] utterance [is his] speaking, thundering, breathing.⟩ God *spake*—⟨his utterance, his speaking, is the simplest, lightest, easiest form of utterance—no sooner spoken than it is gone. [God said, Let there be light, and] there was light [Gen. 1:3]; [it needed] only a breath and there was light, light [that is] only a breath. To sublimity [belongs all] pomp: natural things are only attributes, accidentals, its adornment, its servants and messengers.⟩ From thy breath worlds are created; at thy rebuke they flee ⟨(Ps. 104:28).⁹⁷ See also the verse of Psalm 104: Thou coverest thyself with light as with a garment, thou makest the winds thine angels and thy ministers a flaming fire.⟩ The explicit force of utterance [is] slight, but the infinite power of thought gives it infinite elasticity. Sublimity [is] not the distortion of a natural shape but the shape of the God who [is] powerful in the weak. Utterance [is] itself reduced directly to something accidental, which is not a way of characterizing something

94. W₂ *reads:* But in the concept these are essentially only moments of a *single* process, namely, the process inherent in power,

95. W₂ *reads:* In [God's] *goodness* the world has being only as contingently upheld and maintained, not inwardly justified; and this at the same time involves its negativity, posited in [God's] *justice.*

96. *Ms. margin:* ⟨Re (γ) new manuscript⟩

97. [*Ed.*] The allusion is to Ps. 104:29–30, 7 (not 104:28), and, in the next sentence, to Ps. 104:2, 4.

for itself, not a reality of thought, but is there only as an external mode. (The Hindu cow,[98] on the other hand, [is] grotesque with its infinite power because [it is] itself represented as subject.) Here human beings, such as Moses, [are there] *only* as organs. [43a]

[Later Version]

⟨ˉ(α)[99] The configurations or shapes to which power gives rise are not such that the reality is its own; it is essentially a negative relatedness. And inasmuch as what is differentiated | —the negative as its other, or how it is reflected into self—appears and must appear as reality, power has also a positive relationship to it, so that the positivity of the real is not its own but only that of power, and only in this abstract perspective. Power is in fact lordship, the content being the given world or "nature"—not defined in terms of power, for power [is] the undefined. [43b]   43

Power and lordship [are first] spirit, [as] the presupposition [or in] representation. ˉˉBut what matters is [not] how much is attributed to this spirit—[for example,] it has spiritual predicates such as wisdom, will, goodness, justice, mercy—but what its activity and works are. And its activity is here solely the activity of power. [It is] difficult to avoid confusion as to whether the activity of spirit displays its nature, as to whether "subject equals spirit" denotes a predicate. What matters is what spirit does and is—what pertains to its categorial determination, to reality.ˉ100 ˉˉ101

[The first moment is] creation, coming to be out of nothing. Power determines itself; [it is] negative relation to itself, sublation of its

98. [*Ed.*] A reference not only to the veneration of the cow in general but probably also to the cow of Shubula in *Rāmāyana* 463–471; see below, 1827 lectures, n. 244 including annotation.

99. [*Ed.*] This α parallels the α at the beginning of the initial version, which we have incorporated into the subhead designating "the Religion of Sublimity."

100. W_2 *reads:* But the being of the world is only the being of power; in other words, the positive actuality and independence of the world is not its own independence but the independence of power. Consequently, in regard to power the world must be pictured as something inwardly broken: on the one hand there is the multiplicity of differences, the infinite richness of existence, while on the other hand there is the substantiality of the world; however, this does not pertain to the world itself, but is the identity of essence with itself. The world does not preserve itself on its own account; on the contrary, its being-for-self is the power that preserves itself in the

abstractness, identity with self. [It is] the eternal counsel of God, his absolute will. [How are we] to conceive of [absolute] will? [For us, will is] contingent; will is doing this [rather than that]; will [involves] purposes. [We must] take as the starting point [for our conception] abstraction, emptiness, power as self-contained. |

44

[The second moment is] preservation. Determinate being *exists,* positively. The positive element in this other mode of being, the world, is the positive being of power. In this way the independence of the created world is sublated, its inner side [revealed]; it is inwardly separated, into its essence and its reality.

[The third moment is] the passing away of worldly things. [For there is] equally a negative relationship of power to this its positive being. Both [preservation and destruction] are one, [there is] one process: a negative self-relating, a distinguishing, the annulling of the self-identity. ‾This identity [involves]: (α) emptiness or nothing, and the creation of an other; (β) the subsistence of the world, and its annulment.‾[102]

‾[Thus we have:] (α) The identity of power with itself—identity as the being of things, the affirmative determination—[God's] goodness; maintenance is the goal, as stemming from the subject— "These things *shall* abide." Similarly [God's] justice [says], "They *shall* perish." [Both are] properties of one subject, purely properties, not an independent totality. [The subject is] still unmediated, still motionless, unfulfilled in its subjectivity.

---

differences, inasmuch as it *remains* being-for-self and so constitutes the *being* of the world. Thus the world is inwardly divided: on the one hand it is difference, lacking selfhood, lacking independence; on the other hand it is its *being*.

101. W_2 *reads:* But initially only the roots. For what matters is not how many spiritual predicates, such as wisdom, goodness, and mercy, are attributed to the one [God] but what he does and really is; what matters is his actual categorial determination and reality. A distinction has therefore to be drawn as to whether what God does expresses the spiritual mode. If God's activity is not such as to develop the nature of spirit, then the subject may well count as spirit in our picture of it, but is not yet itself truly spirit. However, the basic characteristic of activity is here initially *power,* which does not take shape in such a way that reality is its own; on the contrary, its attitude [to reality] is still essentially negative.

102. W_2 *reads:* The identity of power with itself is, on the one hand, the nothing from which the world was created and, on the other, the subsistence of the world and its annulment.

(β) Identity of power with itself—as nonbeing of worldly things (justice).⁻¹⁰³

(γ) Justice (as with Shiva) [involves] coming to be and passing away—[it is] a negative process, not the motion of return within self, not spirit.⟩ [44a]

But goodness and justice, ⁻because they contain a difference, would [on this view] become determinations of power.⁻¹⁰⁴ However, power is itself the *undetermined;* in other words, power prevails against this difference itself—its goodness is transposed into justice and vice versa. Posited on their own account, each would exclude the other, and through the determinations that they represent power would acquire a determinate content, [it would become] power [operating] according to purposes. But the very nature of power as power is that it | simply sublates determinacy, and goodness and justice are merely the moments involved in its process.

This portrayal of God's power ⟨becomes determinately concrete, it has its reality in the determinate being of the world. Wisdom [is] purely indeterminate; when opposed to power, it vanishes away. Power is what gives meaning to the world's relationships.

[What counts] vis-à-vis nature in general is essentially power as such. Apart from the one purpose [of God there is] no right that stands in and for itself in the existent world, no absolute purpose or content. The story of Job, his misfortunes and plight, stands apart from [the fate of] the people of God, who are the essential purpose. So here the reference is to God's general, broader purposes, and especially to the purpose that can appear in regard to the single individual—namely, justice as the harmony¹⁰⁵ of happiness with the individual's behavior, virtue, and piety. Virtue or piety would be a purpose in and for itself, [whereas] in fact it is only fear of the Lord, only absolute submission [to his will] that is valid—submission itself is the goal, is what counts.⟩

45

---

103. W₂ *reads:* This identity of power, which is also preserved in the being of things, is both their being and their nonbeing.

104. W₂ *reads:* although they contain difference, are not comprehended as a permanent determination of the [divine] power.

105. *Ms. adds:* and form

[This portrayal of God's power] is offered in the Book of Job—precisely as abstract power. Job, from being a happy man, [becomes] wretched, [but this] main content [is presented] in a very incoherent, inconsequential manner, quite incompatible with consistency of thought. At the end of the book Job praises his innocence and the change that has taken place in his circumstances through no fault of his own. [In contrast we find in] 31:2: "What would be my portion from God above, and my heritage from the Almighty on high? Does not calamity befall the unrighteous, and disaster the workers of iniquity? . . . Let me be weighed in a just balance, and let God know my integrity!"[106] Elihu [answers], 33:12: "Behold, in this you are not right. I will answer you. God is greater than man. Why do you contend against him?"[107] God acts thus to bring [souls] out from the pit [33:18], once and again—[this is] justice, directed moreover to the well-being of the individual. But [this viewpoint is] | limited, for at the close God comes onto the stage and gives expression exclusively to his power. ⟨Providence [is] founded on power.⟩

Chapter 38: "Then the Lord answered Job out of the whirlwind: 'Who is this that darkens counsel by words without knowledge? Gird up your loins like a man, I will question you, and you shall declare to me. Where were you when I laid the foundation of the earth? Tell me, if you have understanding. Who determined its measurements—surely you know! Or who stretched the line upon it? On what were its bases sunk, or who laid its cornerstone, when the morning stars sang together, and all the sons of God shouted for joy? . . . Have you entered into the springs of the sea, or walked in the recesses of the deep? . . . Can you lift up your voice to the clouds, that a flood of waters may cover you? Can you send forth lightnings, that they may go and say to you, "Here we are"? . . . Who is so wise that he can number the clouds?'"[108] Then [comes] the excellency of the beasts, ⟨Behemoth, Leviathan⟩.[109] [44b] [But this is] merely brute power, and they that do not fear the Lord shall be counted godless. Finally Job makes answer (42:1 ff.): "I know that thou canst

106. [*Ed.*] Cf. Job 31:2–3, 6.
107. [*Ed.*] Cf. Job 33:12–13, 29–30.
108. [*Ed.*] Cf. Job 38:1–7, 16, 34–35, 37.
109. [*Ed.*] Cf. Job 40:15 ff., 41:1 ff.

do all things, and that no thought can be withheld from thee. Heedless is the man who believes to hide his counsel. Therefore I acknowledge that I have uttered what I did not understand, things too wonderful for me, which I did not know. . . . But now my eye sees thee; therefore I despise myself and repent in dust and ashes."[110] It is this submission that restores Job to his former happiness. And as for the others, who sought to understand, to justify the ways of God, [the Lord said]: "You have not spoken of me aright, as my servant Job has. . . . Offer up a burnt offering for yourselves, and let my servant Job pray for you. . . . And the Lord gave Job twice as much as he had before."[111]

It is accordingly this power, this one and only [Lord], that exists invisibly, [as] God of thought, because God [as] essence has only negative relationship to reality and positive relationship only to the abstract being of power, not yet to its concrete being, because God is not [yet] further determined within himself.

β.[112] [*The Religion of Necessity*]

[Initial Version]

It is otherwise in the religion of necessity, where the essential shape or configuration | imparted to the concept is that of the reality of 47 the idea. The religion of necessity becomes the religion of beauty; in this way it is more concretely self-determined, but it relapses into naturalness and plurality.

[The logical] connection between the category of necessity and the configuration or shaping [is as follows]:

⟨(α)⟩ Necessity is ⟨inwardly concrete, being determined in different shapes [and so] achieving differentiated reality⟩; it is essentially a process of *appearing* in regard to necessity; it is power that is not merely abstractly related to itself but repels itself from itself. This self-repulsion provides a mediation for the diversity of determinate being. However, terms that cohere necessarily rather than freely do

110. [*Ed.*] Cf. Job 42:2–3, 5b–6.
111. [*Ed.*] Cf. Job 42:7, 8, 10.
112. *Ms. reads:* (b) *Ms. margin canceled:* ⟨Nemesis [*inadvertently not canceled:* Δικη] – justice – in making equal⟩ *Ms. margin:* ⟨Different modes of determination – reality, representation [*canceled:* of necessity] of spirit⟩

not stand together in mutual confidence as identical for one another but are externally opposed in this absolute connectedness.

Necessity therefore contains (α) being for an other, as simple unmediated being—reality, determinate being [as] positive ([divine] goodness)—such and such a thing *is*.

(β) However, this being is not the being of unmediated nature, but is an appearing; in other words, there is implicit in it an inner [being] (necessity). [We have here] revelation, manifestation as the determinate being of essence: God reveals himself in nature, he is the act of creating, the power that creates. Thus we may conclude that according to its essence nature exists only in and through him, while [45a] he is and remains the abstract, all-powerful, self-sufficient essence. Concrete nature does not exist implicitly in him, he is not present in its determinate form, but has reality only in his negativity. The revelation of God in nature consists only in our recognizing his power and glory, but as the *thought* of how great and glorious [he is]; [we do] not [say], this particular splendor or glory belongs to him, but [he is] only the essence, the abstract substance of this nature (what is undetermined [in it]).

But necessity entails the appearing of essence itself in a positive relation to the natural, [i.e.,] (α) externally (the natural state, natural material); (β) nonexternally—showing and portraying essence, [essence] showing itself in it. In nature religion God, the essence, is there in an unmediated form as natural essence; natural essence, natural essences, are God. But here | [the being of] essence is its having its determinate being, its reality, in an external mode, the mode of nature, but not as an immediate object of nature. Rather it is something that is only posited by what is within, it is a habitation, a direct reflection of what is within, a mirror image that has no significance or actuality by virtue of its own immediate existence. The natural mode is show, the shining [through] of essence, not immediately there but made, posited, floating out from within, produced, not self-mediated and self-sustained.

(γ) Thus the determinate being of spirit is only a product of art, comprising, on the one hand, determinate external being, not in the proper sphere of spirit, not God worshiped in spirit, but in necessity

48

(namely, the *natural* mode); on the other hand, not a natural object, an immediate existent, but nonetheless a posited, *external* existent, [in fact] a natural object raised to the level of the nonnatural by caprice or chance, or else a product of art. [Spirit is] still in the realm of the senses, and because of externality [there is] not yet freedom; but [there is] naturalness in the mode of freedom.

(δ) [At this stage] the idea is, for representation, universal, absolute essence, spiritual as well as natural substance; but what matters is the categorial determination that has been born from within it. [44b]

[Later Version]

⟨˜Necessity, as having universal determinacy within itself, is[113] the plenitude or cornucopia of all determinations. They press forward within it, | but as a multitude, each going its own way, one beside   49
the other, not turned back into self to produce the freedom of the concept; in representation they fall apart because [there is] not yet the freedom of the concept and essence [is] not yet [present] as spirit; only as universal spirit [is essence] for the first time the free and absolute unity.

(a) Necessity, absolute necessity, abstract in and for itself, disdains, in its appearing, all community, all configuration; it reigns awesomely over all, and [is seen as] cold, abstract fate. For necessity as such is inherently blind. It has not yet developed into the concept of purpose or achieved specific determinations; it contains determinacy as such within itself, but not yet freedom—it is without concept. [This is] the fate of the ancients and [yet] not, because [it is] not *only* [that].

(b) Because determinacy [lies] outside it, [as] world, yet is at the same time implicit in it, [necessity] is related to the world. This abstract relation is purely external unity, and therefore equality in general. Since it is without concept, and not further determined within itself, [it is] Nemesis, [which means] making the high and

___

113. *Ms. adds above, in margin:* ⟨Determinacy is one's *own* determinacy, in a *positive* relation to⟩

143

mighty low, establishing equality, universal recompense. But it does not yet [mean] raising up what is lowly, for the lowly does not yet exist—in other words, what is lowly is in its proper state, for it is finite, has not itself any absolute, infinite value within itself. The finite is subject to chance and contingency, it is not inwardly determined as to whether it is more one way or another. But to transcend the common lot and measure of finitude is contrary to equality.⁻¹¹⁴

50 ¹¹⁵(c) In addition, however, [we find here] various kinds of general determinateness, universal | natural and spiritual powers, [such as] rights of the family, law and government, agriculture, the universal ties and institutions of custom, civic status, virtue and the like, just as [we find] the sun etc. But as a result these general kinds of determinateness split off from necessity; in their concrete form they are distinct from it. They also split off from each other, and to a greater or lesser extent go their own ways; for there is no return into self, and it is only their ⟨foundation⟩ that is one. [45a]

(d) Determinacy [is here] (α) separated from abstract necessity, and therefore external, an appearing; but (β) at the same time

---

114. W₂ *reads:* This unity, as absolute necessity, encompasses universal determinacy, it is the plenitude of all determinations, but it is not inwardly developed, for instead the content is distributed in a particular way among the many gods who stem from it. It is itself empty and without content, it disdains all community, all configuration; it reigns awesomely over all, as a blind power, past all understanding or concept. It is without concept because only the concrete can be conceived, while absolute necessity is still abstract, has not yet developed into the concept of purpose or achieved specific determinations.

At this stage necessity is related essentially to the world. For determinacy is a moment of necessity itself, and the concrete world is *developed* determinacy, the realm of finitude, of determinate existence in general. Necessity has at first an abstract relation to the concrete world, and this relation is the external unity of the world, equality in general, which without further inner determination is without concept, and is [just] Nemesis. It brings the high and mighty down low and so establishes equality. But this equalizing is not to be understood as meaning that when what puts itself forward and what is on high is brought low, what is lowly is also raised up. On the contrary, the lowly is in its proper state, it is the finite, which has no particular claims, and has not yet any infinite value within itself to which it could appeal. Consequently it is not *too* lowly; but it may transcend the common lot and measure of finitude, and if it goes against equality in this way, then Nemesis puts it back where it belongs.

115. *Ms. canceled, above the line:* (c) Natural intuitions – sun, sky, earth, time, etc. – [these are] likewise positive determinacies, configurations

retained within absolute necessity in accordance with the concept of necessity and power.

(α) [There are] a multitude of universal divine powers. They are many by virtue of being determinacies, and divine inasmuch as they remain in positive relation to necessity.

(β) Conversely, therefore, the divine exists for an other; it is intuited and represented in external existence [*Dasein*]. The natural universal powers and objects *are* this reality.

But this external existence, retained within the inner self of unity as *appearance* (though not in the form of natural objects or forces), exists in our thought, as something inward. [It is] not an image of the divine, not posited of God himself as appearance. [It is] in God himself as appearance, either as subsisting positively or, as appearance, simply vanishing away, or [again] as the thought of vanishing away. Thus it does not here exist as the shape of necessity.

But the shape of necessity as such is *posited* necessity, i.e., the form of freedom. As posited necessity, [it is] no longer merely this totality in itself, but [has been brought] forth, is for an other; inasmuch as necessity is the annulling of this reality or determinacy, its unity exists on its own account. Hence posited *necessity* [is] *freedom*—i.e., being at home with oneself in [the sphere of] otherness as such. Life [is] determinacy (α) in being, (β) [but only] as resolved in universality, and consequently spiritual. | Life is the *living* thing— 51 though still only as something immediate or natural as such; in other words, it is the necessity that exists for itself; as life, it is not the simple necessity that is complete on its own account. This [the living thing] is just the spiritual shaping [of necessity]; it is only its meaning that is the whole universal necessity, the divine. The living thing is implicitly genus, but it is not that in its determinate being. The universal becomes the characteristic of necessity just so far as it does not relapse into immediacy, into naturalness.

The explanation for why [things happen as they do] is to be sought in fate. But in providing the explanation, [fate] continues to be a mediation [in terms of] external necessity; the father [acted] thus— [there was] a transgression—the family is old—the inheritance has passed down—[these are] the causes, grounds, and [necessary] connection of things.) [45b]

145

(d) ˉThese forms of determinateness, the natural and ethical powers or elementary substantive natures, because they belong to what is implicitly universal, to necessity, (α) emerge outside [the sphere of] necessity, because it is not yet explicitly posited in freedom as the concept,ˉ¹¹⁶ˉ(β) [but] at the same time, as universal powers, remain held within its unity and power.ˉ¹¹⁷ (γ) Equally, and for the same reason (the lack of freedom), they emerge in opposition to one another and are [present as] a multitude of particular powers. [They are] determinateness [that is] not [yet] returned within itself, [that is] not determined determinateness.

At this point, therefore, they are divine powers in general. Necessity is of itself nothing divine, i.e., it is not the divine. One can admittedly say, God is necessity, in other words necessity is one of his characteristics, though it is as yet unconsummated; but one cannot say, necessity is God, for necessity does not exist as idea; it is [only] an abstract concept. |

52

But the divine character of Nemesis resides in the fact that it is related to subsistent reality, whereas ˉtheseˉ¹¹⁸ powers are divine inasmuch as they are in themselves *differently* determined by necessity; as a result—being both distinct from one another and held within the [grip of] necessity—they are [present] as a unity of the wholly universal and particular.

(e) However, these powers are now further determined, as follows. In their separateness from the one necessity, they are, on the one hand, external to it, and therefore unmediated objects (immediate in the bad sense), natural existents such as sun, sky, earth, sea, mountains, human beings, or kings, something that is intuited or represented; ˉon the other hand, while remaining positively related to necessity, as divine beings they are at the same time sublated in it—in other words, at the same time they do not subsist in themselves

116. W₂ *reads:* The particular divine powers belong to what is implicitly universal, to necessity, but they emerge outside the sphere of necessity because it is not yet explicitly posited as the concept and characterized as freedom.

117. W₂ *reads:* The concept is not yet unveiled, and the aspect of its determinate being does not yet contain the content of necessity. But this also means that the freedom of the particular is only the semblance of freedom and that the particular powers are held within the unity and power of necessity.

118. W₂ *reads:* to an even greater extent these particular

[as immediate objects]. ⟨[The natural existents] are only appearance—⟩ they are not divine, not God or the gods in their immediacy. [46a] *That*⁻¹¹⁹ would be a falling back into the first type of nature religion, where the inward [element], the universal, has not yet achieved the separation of the two [aspects—i.e., the natural and the divine] from each other in thought; it has not arrived at the moment of *relationship,* the moment where determinacy is what necessity essentially and simply contains within itself, the moment in which the immediate is only something posited and sublated.

But further, this immediate or external aspect, these natural objects, are not appearance in the sense that their essence, their being within necessity, [and their] positive relation to it, should only subsist as a thought in us, as when we speak of forces of nature and so forth that exist only in an immediate, external form, in single phenomena (as we call them). A phenomenon of this kind is on the one hand positive, and on the other hand either transitory or permanent— i.e., it disappears like light or abides like earth. These are natural essences, but in their universality they are present only as our thought (e.g., light [as] identity). Thus God reveals himself for us in nature, | but not for sense perception (the relation to phenomena of this kind   53 as natural), for reflection. We can, if we choose, stand pat upon their sensuous or reflected finitude and externality. Forces are *universal* powers but not divine powers (just as God is not a force). On the one hand forces, [according to] their content, as it exists for reflection, [are] finite; on the other hand their determinate being or immediacy [occurs] only in singular, dependent, contingent modes that are determined from somewhere else as well.

But the natural or external implicitly has to be posited as at the same time sublated in its externality; it has to be posited in itself as *appearance.* The inward element itself has as such to become apparent in it, the universal has to exist as posited, so that externality is there and has meaning wholly and simply as this kind of externalization; it is the organ of thought, of the universal, thought as

---

119. W₂ *reads:* On the other hand, they also remain held by necessity, so that the natural state is sublated in them. If these powers were not still the divine essentialities according to their natural, immediate mode of *existence,* this

such exists in it. It is necessity that must appear in divine fashion, i.e., it must be there in determinate being as necessity in immediate unity with it. ⟨[It must be] posited necessity, i.e., necessity that is there, existing as simple reflectedness-into-self.⟩

Posited necessity is freedom, for it is determinacy negated according to its reality, the negative present to consciousness as negative, not lost from sight (for then it *is* not); [46b] [it is] simple necessity present here in the world as something simple one can point to. ⟨Religion is the presence of essence for self-consciousness; simple necessity (universality) is to be there for the immediate, intuiting consciousness.⟩ In absolute necessity determinacy [is] reduced to no more than the unity of immediacy (it *is* so). ¯Determinacy [as specific] is jettisoned [in favor of] the fixity that¯[120] holds fast to the empty predicate of being. But necessity that exists as determinate being is for the immediate intuition a determinate natural being which in its very determinacy takes itself back into its simplicity, and portrays this return to simplicity itself [as] a mode of determinate being which, being only in this process, exists for that very reason in freedom. ⟨[It is] determined determinacy—determinacy as | negativity, as reflected into self, submerging itself in simple necessity; [it is] self-relating determinacy—subjectivity, the power of the one.⟩

¯A reality of this kind, however,¯[121] is the spiritual shape, the human shape. Only the human shape is the mode of determinate being that is free being. It is a[122] natural mode of determinate being, something for immediate perception to see and feel, to picture to itself in an image, in images that have this kind of sensuous content; and it is simple necessity, a simple relation to self ¯—it heralds thought. The eye, the face, ⟨features,⟩ speech—it is all just something natural, even as thinking activity. The process of transforming, dissolving, fusing each and every contact into simple identity [is] the reaction that gives notice of something determinate, which is there

120. W₂ *reads:* But in this way the determinacy, the content, is jettisoned, and the fixity and freedom of the mind that holds fast to this form of intuition consists solely in the fact that it

121. W₂ *reads:* Now the reality for this process of necessity that is there as determinate being

122. W₂ *adds:* sensuous,

in the world, and simultaneously is for that very reason‾[123] an utterance of spirit.[124]

(f) This configuration [of necessity] has still to be defined in more detail. ⟨I do not just come face to face with this simplicity or absolute reflection.⟩ Life is | essentially just this infinitude of free being-in-the-world, and as a living thing, this subjectivity is what reacts against unmediated determinacy and posits it as identical with itself in its sensibility. ‾But it does so in such a way that the sensation of the brute is present infinitely in a determinate content; in other words, the utterance, the determinate being of its infinitude has simply and solely a determinate content—the content is limited, ⟨is absolutely formal,⟩ [but] it is not the simple immediacy of necessity (thought) that comes into appearance. ⟨[The animal is] wholly transposed into a state characterized only by singularity, from which it does not emerge but remains sunk in simple necessity. To eat like a beast—even here human satisfaction [is] not being simply sunk in the satisfaction of physical needs; a spiritual aspect [is] to be seen even here, [humanity] rises above it; [and the same is] even more the case in an infinity of other modes of outward expression. [They must] rest upon thought, have its form upon them, [possess] formal independence. But further, if we consider an actual human being, whether now alive or remembered in thought, such a being is one who thinks, whose mode of expression is thought, though at the same time such a being, as immediate and natural, is something fallen away

55

123. W_2 *reads:* whereby it heralds thought. Every contact, every utterance, is directly transformed, dissolved, fused into simple identity, and is for that very reason essentially

124. W_2 *adds:* This [logical] connection is not easy to grasp, that the basic determination, the conceptual aspect, is absolute necessity while the aspect of reality whereby this concept becomes *idea* is the human shape. In general, it is essential to the concept to possess reality. This determination is more specifically involved in necessity itself, since it is not abstract being, but what is determined in and for itself. Now because the determinacy is at the same time natural, external reality, it is simultaneously taken back into simple necessity, so that what is displayed in this variegated sensuous content is simple. It is only when the divine is no longer constituted by necessity but by spirit that it is intuited wholly in the element of thought. But at this stage the moment of external visibility is still present, even though simple necessity displays itself therein. It can do this only in the case of the human shape, because this is the shape of what is spiritual and only in this shape can reality be taken back for consciousness into the simplicity of necessity.

56   from universality, | [immersed] in temporal and transient life, an infinitude of singular purposes, dependent circumstances, and so on. The disharmony⁻[125] between what humanity is in itself (implicitly) and what it is in actuality obscures its universality and freedom through a host of relationships based on need. [Human beings] lack the inner reflection of infinity; instead there is within them the showing (shining) of what is other [i.e., of nature]. [47a]

[126]But that their determinate being should be imbued in all its features ⟨or parts⟩ with the imprint of universality, or of the simplicity of necessity,[127] that is what constitutes necessity, that the external shape should be conceived solely in the spirit and begotten solely from it;[128] it should be an ideal, a work of art, an ennobling, an erasing of what is merely natural (needs ⟨that belong to our [natural] form⟩); and it should be made by human agency.

125. *W₂ reads:* But the organic life of the animal, i.e., the determinate being and utterance of its infinitude, has simply and solely a limited content, it is sunk wholly in singular states. The simplicity into which this determination is taken back is something limited and purely formal, and the content does not match this form that it has. In thinking human beings, however, the *spiritual* is expressed even in their singular states, thus showing that even in this or that limited state humans transcend their limits, they are free and at home with self. It is very easy to distinguish whether people behave in a human or an animal fashion in satisfying their needs. The human is a delicate fragrance that spreads over everything one does. Moreover the content of human life is not purely organic but includes an infinite range of higher expressions, activities, and purposes whose content itself is the infinite, the universal. Humanity is thus the absolute reflection-into-self that we have in the concept of necessity. . . .

Actual, single human beings, however, still implicitly have the aspect of immediate naturalness in their immediate mode of being; this aspect appears as something temporal and transient that has fallen away from universality. This aspect of finitude introduces a disharmony

126. *W₂ adds:* Not all features and parts of individual human beings bear the imprint of simple necessity. Empirical singularity and the expression of simple inwardness are mingled, and the freedom and universality [that constitute] the ideality of the natural are blurred by the conditions of merely natural life and by a host of relationships based on need. In regard to the aspect that an other shines through in human beings, the appearance does not correspond to the shape, i.e., to simple necessity.

127. *W₂ adds:* (what Goethe appositely termed *significance* as the character of classical works of art)

[*Ed.*] Possibly belongs to the 1824 lectures; see 1824 n. 630.

128. *W₂ adds:* brought forth under its mediation;

˘What is common or base [must be] (α) [worked on till it achieves] human shape, ⟨the shape or form of spirit;⟩ (β) made by human agency, [for this is] more excellent than being a natural product. ⟨[It is not] as though natural products are made by God, works of art by human agency, | and not by God. There too [i.e., 57 in the natural order, things are made] of seed, air, water, etc.˘[129] A plant is just the way it ought to be—there is no sundering of its [conceptual] being from its determinate being, as there is with human beings by virtue of their freedom and caprice, and in their infinite plasticity, even with respect to their natural life. Human beings look infinitely more dissimilar to one another than roses, for example. [Roses are] organic, like animals, but [there is] not in them the mediation that lies in necessity, not the determinacy that is at once specified, mutually external, and existing in the real order [*in dem Dasein*] as universality. Fine art [produces] ⟨a multitude of figures that are divine powers, godlike, blessed, but still definite individuals; the overwhelming elemental power of nature, the titanic element has receded to the fringes of the world⟩.

˘Real spiritual being [*geistiges Dasein*] speeds on ahead of the *consciousness* of the content—the content [is] not yet spirit. However, this real being [is] not superficial: it thinks, but it is not spirit ⟨in itself, not spirit in its universality.˘[130]

(α) Spirituality [has here] the nature of the objective or divine because necessity [issues] from it into determinacy and differentiation, and [the objective or divine is] identical with itself in this determinacy

129. W₂ *reads:* This is more excellent than being a natural product. It may, of course, be said that a natural product rather is more excellent, because it is made by God, and works of art only by human agency—as though natural objects did not also owe their existence to immediately natural, finite things such as seed, air, water, and light, and as though the power of God lived only in nature and not in human activity too, in the realm of the spiritual.

130. W₂ *reads:* At this stage, where the divine still needs the sensuous for its essential portrayal, it appears as a multiplicity of gods. It is, to be sure, in this multiplicity that necessity portrays itself as simple reflection-into-self; but this simplicity is only form, for that in which it is portrayed is still immediacy, the natural sphere, not the absolute stuff of spirit. So it is not spirit as spirit that is portrayed here. Instead, real spiritual being speeds on ahead of the consciousness of the content, for the content is not yet itself spirit.

as its own otherness.[131] This is not the necessity by which objects are necessary, or have necessity as their predicate, but the necessity that is itself the subject | (and the subject in its predicates is external reality). Necessity is the subject.

(β) The various gods [are at this stage still] many, because [this is] still the realm of nature, not necessity for its own sake; universals [are here] not an object for universals; [we do] not [have] the idea in the element of thought.

(γ) The meaning [is], more precisely, this differentiation. The natural element [has] retired into the background; the meaning [is] spiritual or ethical. Helios [is] a Titan, Apollo is more a knowing [God]. Zeus [is] the power of the state (Athena [comes] out of Neith[132]). [There are still] echoes of nature: Isis [is] Cybele, Bacchus [is] wine, but [they are at the same time] mystical emanations of spirit; Ceres [is] the fruit but also the lawgiver [who gives] ethical custom, legal right, and property. [It is] the spirits of the peoples, not just of natural elements, that are intuited in them.

(δ) [They are] still images, not at the same time living, spiritual, consciousness in themselves; [they are only] displayed physically in marble, paint, or metal. [Here we have] portrayal in corporeal form, not in the absolute stuff of spirit. The spiritual, inner element [is present] only as a determinate content that is itself limited.⟩

c. Cultus

α. *The Religion of Sublimity*

[The cultus is] more precisely the relationship of the individual, of self-consciousness [with the divine]. It is in the first place the knowledge of one's unity with thought. [God is known as] awesome might, as Lord, but as Lord he is without passion or the like. The

131. *W₂ adds:* While it tends to be the case that natural products only flourish given what are for them external, contingent circumstances, and under their influence, in a work of art it is necessity that appears as the inner soul and as the concept of the outer reality.

132. [*Ed.*] Hegel is here apparently alluding to the implicit identification of Neith, the goddess of Sais (an ancient city of the Nile delta), with Athena by Herodotus, *Histories* 2.28, 59. Relying on this and on an anecdote recounted by Plato in *Critias* 109–112, Creuzer developed this identification more fully, *Symbolik und Mythologie*

relationship of abstract identity [is] *exclusive:* [God is] inwardly universal power, but vis-à-vis the concrete he is only negative. [God's power is] identical with the concrete, but at the same time not. [The viewpoint is] blinkered.

‾[As] the relationship of self-consciousness, the cultus [is] the movement it undertakes in order to bring about identity. | 59

[Initial Version]

The basic character of this relationship is determined by the definition of God as Lord, the One, the essence, [47b] not yet inwardly concrete, not yet elaborated within himself, merely abstract power, abstract thought, the being-for-self of the One. In this relationship, therefore, self-consciousness begins to become being-for-self, though without breadth or extension, subjectivity for self without any concrete characteristics. No determinacy that in other respects appears as finite is treated as holy; God is inwardly undetermined, infinite power, Lord; there is no tertium quid, no determinate being, in which they [the individual worshipers and God?] might find themselves together. There is so far an immediate relation; but equally the absolute is simply and solely a beyond for self-consciousness, an absolute power.

The antitheses are united—a pure relation in pure thinking, the intuiting of "the One," pure thinking and an abstract | return into 60 self; [thus] being-for-self [is achieved], but in such a way that pure thinking stands over against it as absolute power.

Self-consciousness on its own account, distinct from its object which is pure thought and can only be grasped in thought, [is] an empty, formal self-consciousness, not inwardly determined. All real, fulfilled determining [lies] in an alien power; [apart from that there is] only this abstract being-for-self. As a result [we have] self-consciousness simultaneously in its absolute antithesis. [We have] self-consciousness, i.e., pure freedom, in absolute unfreedom, in other words the self-consciousness of the servant vis-à-vis the

2:642–643, 656, 658, suggesting that in order to understand the essential meaning of Minerva (Athena), it is necessary to go back to the Egyptian temples and the Saitic genealogy, in which Neith plays a central role. Hegel's point seems to be that the "spiritual" goddess Athena has evolved out of the nature-goddess Neith.

Lord.‾¹³³ ⟨The Stoics and Skeptics [have this viewpoint], but their thinking is self-contained—that is to say, all content [becomes] true in and through my thinking, by being taken up into this objectivity. The object is for me this universal, [this] ground, as the criterion for all content. [There is] freedom as the form of the objective. [There is] something, thinking—abstract freedom [is] pure thinking, which thinks *nothing,* and the subjectivity of self-consciousness [is] precisely singularity, immediate determinacy; all content is not *thought.*⟩

Freedom exists only in concrete self-consciousness, i.e., my existence or objectivity [is] at the same time determined, raised to universality; thus [it becomes] my spiritual property.

‾Servitude is self-consciousness, reflection-into-self, pure freedom, but without inner content. Hence the content or determinacy is my immediate, sentient self-consciousness, the ego as *this* one. I am the purpose and content for myself as "this one"—infinitely selfish in

133. W₂ *reads:* The relationship of self-consciousness is to the *One,* so that it is initially an intuiting, a pure thinking of pure essence as pure might and absolute being, beside whom there is no other of equal rank. Now as reflection-into-self, as self-consciousness, this pure thinking is self-consciousness determined as infinite being-for-self, or freedom—but freedom without any concrete content. Thus self-consciousness is still distinct from actual consciousness; none of all the concrete determinations of spiritual and natural life, nothing from the fulfilled consciousness with its drives and impulses, or from the rich diversity of spiritual relationships, has yet been taken up into the consciousness of freedom. The reality of life still falls outside the consciousness of freedom, and freedom is not yet rational; it is still abstract, and there is still no fulfilled, *divine* consciousness.

However, since self-consciousness exists only as consciousness, but there is still no corresponding object present as object for the simplicity of thought and the determinacy of consciousness is not yet taken up [into thought], the ego is object to itself only in its abstract oneness with self, as unmediated singularity. Self-consciousness is accordingly without breadth or extension, without any concrete characteristics; God as infinite power is also inwardly undetermined, and there is no tertium quid, no determinate being, in which they [the individual worshipers and God?] might find themselves together. There is so far an immediate relation, and the antitheses—relation to the One in pure thinking and intuiting, and abstract return into self, being-for-self—are immediately united. Now since self-consciousness, as distinct from its object (which is pure thought and can only be grasped in thought), is an empty, formal self-consciousness, naked and not inwardly determined, and since, furthermore, all real, fulfilled determining belongs only to the [divine] power, in this absolute antithesis the pure freedom of self-consciousness turns into absolute unfreedom, or the self-consciousness is that of the servant vis-à-vis the Lord. Fear of the Lord is the basic characteristic of the relationship.

my immediate singularity. In this way the whole concrete content
| in its empirical singularity [is] taken up into formal self-
consciousness, wholly devoid of reason but clinging to this
singularity—the immediate [self] as such.

[My] relation to the Lord [is] having my absolutely essential self-
consciousness implicit in him; everything in me becomes as naught
when it is set against him—only by him and through him [does it
count]. At the same time [I have] reestablished *myself* absolutely
[48a]; this content is for me, and I have taken it up into this intuition
as the concrete element, justifying it in absolute terms through the
relationship [to God]. ⟨[We are] God's people to the exclusion of
other peoples, set apart from them,‾¹³⁴ the *odium generis
humani*,¹³⁵ on which the others—the goyim—get their own back for
the heavy yoke they have to bear.⟩ [Here we see the full] harshness
of the antithesis: [on the one hand] fear of the Lord is the absolute
religious duty, to regard myself as nothing, to know myself only as
absolutely dependent—the consciousness of the servant vis-à-vis the
master; [on the other hand] it is this fear that gives me absolute
justification in my reestablishment. [47b]

[Later Version]

⟨(a) (α) [First,] as pure intuition self-consciousness is the pure
thinking of pure essence ⟨and of essence as pure might⟩, i.e., of the

---

134. W₂ *reads:* For servitude is self-consciousness, reflection-into-self or freedom,
but a freedom that lacks universal extension and rationality and has the immediate,
sentient self-consciousness for its determinacy, for its content. The ego as *this* being
in its immediate singularity is therefore purpose and content. In their relation to the
Lord, servants have their absolute, essential self-consciousness; everything in them
becomes as naught when it is set against him. But by so doing they are reestablished,
absolutely on their own account, and their singularity, because it is taken up into
this intuition as the concrete element, achieves absolute justification through this
relationship. The fear wherein servants regard themselves as nothing restores their
justification to them. But because the servile consciousness clings stubbornly to its
singularity, because its singularity is taken up immediately into unity, such
consciousness is exclusive,

135. [*Ed.*] Hegel is here alluding to the ancient accusation, first leveled against
the Christians following the burning of Rome, that they were guilty of hatred toward
the whole of the human race. See Tacitus, *Annals* 15.44. Elsewhere Tacitus directed
the charge of hatred toward other peoples against the Jews (*Histories* 5.5).

One as absolute being, beside whom there is no other of equal rank who *is,* but on the contrary [all *are not*].

(β) [Second,] as reflection-into-self, as self-consciousness, this pure thinking is self-consciousness characterized by infinite being-for-self, or freedom.

(γ) However, this freedom is without any concrete content. In other words, nothing from the fulfilled consciousness, with its drives and impulses, or from the rich diversity of spiritual relationships, has yet been taken up into the consciousness of this freedom—the reality of life falls outside it. This freedom is not yet rational, it is quite abstract; there is still no fulfilled, *divine* consciousness.

(δ) However, since self-consciousness exists only as consciousness, but there is still no corresponding object present as object for the simplicity of thought (the determinacy of consciousness is not yet 62 | taken up [into thought]), I am here the object for myself, i.e., I am taken up into pure self-consciousness only in my abstract oneness with self, and as having abstract objective being, or unmediated singularity.

(ε) But this taking up does not include all the reality and fulfillment of this singular consciousness (its outer and inner world). "I for myself" am completely empty and naked, and all this fulfillment belongs only to [the divine] power, i.e., my consciousness knows itself through and through as dependent, as unfree. The relationship [is that] of the servant to a Lord; the fear of the Lord is what defines it. In any religion, such as Judaism or Islam, where God is comprehended only under the abstract category of the One, this human lack of freedom is the real basis, and humanity's relationship to God takes the form of a heavy yoke, of onerous service. True liberation is to be found in Christianity, in the Trinity.

(ζ) Through the mediation of its onerous service the consciousness regains a concrete existence; its being is wholly the gift of [the divine] power. As service rendered to this power, its service is not a mode of action that is rational on its own account; for in it self-consciousness has no inner freedom or extension. [It is a matter of] commandments as such, of orders; laws and service alike [are just] the Lord's commands. But laws governing what is one's *own,* i.e., the laws of freedom, call for reason, for one's own insight and [a system of] right.

(η) Because there is no extension [of self-consciousness], no rationality, the servile consciousness [can] never escape from its singularity, i.e., it [remains] wayward, obdurate, stiff-necked. Also it is exclusive of others: only this single, unmediated [being, i.e., Abraham] is taken up [48a] into [the divine] unity; and just because it is unmediated, the singularity is exclusive—a singularity that is natural and gains its extension through nature as a family and a people.⟩

(b) Such is the disposition in the cultus [at this standpoint]—the determination of self-consciousness. ⟨[The latter is] now a consciousness or representation of its relationship [to God. This is] the mode of [its] mediation.⟩ The detailed characteristics [are as follows].

¯(α) The | self-consciousness is [that of] a people that is God's,   63
but a people accepted through a bond of covenant (a bond conditional on fear and service). In other words, the self-conscious community is no longer in original, immediate unity inwardly as in nature religion, and only outwardly having a natural object over against it as God—⟨a division that is quite without essence since the rind that separates the two is merely a natural representation.[136] Here, in contrast, the division enters into absolute, pure thought⟩—whereas [self-consciousness] ⟨begins from⟩ absolute reflection into itself as abstract being-for-self. ⟨Hence there enters here the mediation between self-consciousness and its absolute essence⟩—but at the same time not as humankind in the sense of universality; [there is no awareness] that human beings | stand in relationship to God as   64
human beings. The relationship is a particular character, ⟨indeed a singular character, this or that human being⟩; on its human side one can call it *accidental*. ⟨For the absolute power everything finite is external; the finite is not a positive determination within God

136. [*Ed.*] "The rind that separates the two," in the case of nature religion, is the idol that stands between the cultic community and God, whereas in the case of Judaism the division between the people and God enters into pure thought.

himself.) (As far as God is concerned, an eternal counsel [determines all].) [The people's] entrance into religious relation with God is therefore a particular mark, not one among others but an outstanding privilege of infinite significance.[137] God's people is the one that he has accepted on condition that they shall fear him, and have the basic feeling of their dependence,[138] i.e., of their servitude. [He is their] national god. [The scope of this servitude is] broadened in Islam (being cleansed of nationalism), and at a later date [there are] also Jewish proselytes [in Judaism]. In Islam it is only being a *believer* that matters. [This is] not obstinacy but *fanaticism*, because although nationality, ⟨natural associations,⟩ family connections, homeland, etc., remain (limited connections, stable relationships are permitted), the service of the One logically involves the unlimitedness and instability of all subsistence. ⟨God's acceptance has occurred once and for all, and what replaces reconciliation and redemption is something that has implicitly *happened,* a choice, an election by grace involving no freedom. [We have here a] view grounded on power, a blind election, not an election made from the viewpoint of freedom.⟩⌐ [139]

137. *Ms. margin:* ⟨(α) This particular [people]. (β) Not the original or implicit [unity which is a matter of] God's love for humanity, but this unity is posited externally. (γ) [On] condition [of dependence and service])

138. [*Ed.*] Hegel alludes here for the first time in the main text of the *Ms.* to the just-published first volume of Schleiermacher's *Der christliche Glaube nach den Grundsätzen der evangelischen Kirche im Zusammenhange dargestellt* (Berlin, 1821), § 9. See below, nn. 256 and esp. 292.

139. W_2 reads: God's people is one that has been accepted through bond and covenant, on condition of fear and service. The self-conscious community is no longer an original, immediate unity with essence, as was the case in nature religion. The external shape of essence in nature religion is merely a natural representation, a rind, that does not truly separate the two sides of the religious relationship, i.e., it is a division that is quite without essence, just a superficial difference. Our present standpoint, on the contrary, is based on absolute reflection-into-self as abstract being-for-self, and hence there enters here the mediation of the relationship between self-consciousness and its absolute essence. However, self-consciousness is not humanity as such, in the sense of universal humanity. The religious relationship is a particularity that on its human side can be called "accidental," for everything finite is external for the absolute power, and involves no positive determination within God himself. But this particular character of the religious relationship is not one characteristic among others, but an outstanding privilege of infinite significance. What the relationship consequently means is that this people is accepted on condition that they shall have

(β) As [divine] service the cultus takes many forms, first of praise in general, and secondly of sacrifice. ⟨The cultus [is] merely the effort to continue as well-pleasing to the Lord, in one's servitude.⟩ Sacrifice does not simply mean ⟨symbolically⟩ renouncing one's finite side, [48b] maintaining one's union with the Lord, but is more precisely the recognition | of him as Lord, bearing witness to him of one's   65 fear and, by so doing, liberating and redeeming everything else [for one's use]. ¯[The worshipers give] the tenth part of all their possessions: the firstborn of them all belongs to the Lord, or must be redeemed.¯¹⁴⁰ ⟨Blood and life's increase is the Lord's; blood [is] not eaten, [but] the altar [is] sprinkled with it.¹⁴¹ There is no human lordship over nature in and for itself.⟩ ⟨¯And what [the Lord's servants] receive is the temporal possession of the [promised] land, not everlasting felicity, nothing eternal (for servants have nothing of that kind), no intuition or consciousness of the unity of one's soul—of an inward [life]—with the absolute. For they¯¹⁴² still have no inner space or extension, no soul of [sufficient] scope, such as would aim to find satisfaction within itself; it is the temporal [world] that is their soul's fulfillment and reality. What the individual yearns for is not reconciliation with God, not that the *soul* should be spirit objectively, that it should be satisfied as such, that it should be self-contained as idea or as its own reality (resting virtuously upon itself).

---

the basic feeling of their dependence, i.e., of their servitude. This relationship between infinite power and what has being-for-self is therefore not the kind that is posited in itself originally, or only through God's love for humanity; on the contrary, this unity is posited in an external way, it is founded in the *covenant*. And this acceptance of the [Jewish] people has occurred once and for all, and replaces that which is redemption and reconciliation in the consummate form of the revelatory religion.

140. W₂ *reads:* Human beings cannot regard nature as something they can use as they please, so they cannot simply lay hold on it directly but must obtain their desires through the mediation of someone or something else. Everything is the Lord's and must be redeemed from him; thus the tenth part of their possessions is set aside, and the firstborn is delivered up for ransom.

[*Ed.*] Cf. Exod. 13:2, 13; 23:16, 19.

141. [*Ed.*] Cf. Lev. 1:5, 11; 3:2.

142. W₂ *reads:* The reward for service is temporal possessions, nothing eternal, not everlasting felicity. The intuition and consciousness of the soul's unity with the absolute or of the soul's being received into the bosom of the absolute is not yet aroused. Human beings

159

Here there is] no *immortality*. [The individual] does not demand [immortality] for the soul: the servant [is] only a temporal being, and the servant's rewards are in time—the [promised] land.

The land they dwell in they have received from the Lord, not like people who inhabit the earth [because they have] taken possession of it, but as an exclusive possession, which [nonetheless] can be taken from them by others, and which they do not claim to be theirs by right, as against others. Rather it is the land that the Lord has given them—[it is not theirs by right] any more than there is any question of others having a right (in the same way as the Turks [recognize] no treaty rights, truce guarantees, or property rights as belonging to those who have submitted). [They are] ⟨without rights⟩ and [must] redeem [the land] continually in order to retain their share of it. | [They] took the land by force from the inhabitants of Palestine because God promised it to them. [They might say, "It is] not mine by right, therefore it does not [belong] to the others either." "Right" [means that] the ego [enjoys] extension, objectivity in [its] existence, freedom.

Hence [there is] no legal right among them, but [only] inheritance [of the share received] when the land was divided out—also no proper selling of land, merely the leasing of it; for after forty-nine years everything reverted in the jubilee year to the original family.[143]

⁻Sacrifices [function] also as penance to expiate for transgressions and faults—and as punishment, not just for purification as such but to do hurt to an evil will, [with the] meaning of "damages." [All] sacrifice [is] external.⁻[144] [49a]

β. *The Religion of Beauty*

⟨α. Spirit of the Cultus; Religious Self-Consciousness⟩

The relationship of abstract freedom, of the merely self-willed being-for-self, [to the divine] has its proximate truth in the fulfillment of this freedom, so that the object may not be in and for itself

---

143. [*Ed.*] Cf. Lev. 25.

144. W₂ *reads:* This externality of sacrifice derives from the fact that expiation is thought of as punishment, not as purification as such, but as doing hurt to the evil will, with the meaning of "damages."

something strictly otherworldly for self-consciousness, or so that this abstract certitude may be raised to an objectivity [of its own], to truth. Abstract freedom first attains to truth when I acquire a positive character in [the sphere of] being (mere subjectivity, feeling, certitude constitute untruth, and however I picture them to myself they are not); to have positive being is to have the intuition of antithesis [of self and world] as implicitly sublated and to know the essence as what is in itself concrete,[145] or as what has determinate being, determinacy within itself, in such a way that the determinateness belongs to its nature (not [as] power or the God of Abraham, | where [deter-   67 minateness does] not [belong] to its nature as such). The determinateness is thus my determinateness, and determinacy in general is my reflection-into-self, and my distinctness is sublated by being intuited in the unity of the absolute. In this way I have a consciousness of truth in that my universal subjectivity, as particularity or differentiatedness, has come to fruition as objectivity, or subsistence within the absolute.

The realm which self-consciousness has now entered is that of *truth,* i.e., of *rationality,* for reason [is] the implicitly subsisting objectivity of my consciousness, the fact that such objectivity subsists for me; and [it is the realm] of *freedom,* for that which differentiates or particularizes me is now itself implicitly identical with the universal. I am conscious of the unity of infinity with finitude; in other words, finitude has implicitly vanished. For finitude, [subsisting] solely in antithesis, no longer [has] any meaning in its unity with the infinite. It is itself only infinite form, and this infinite form is knowing, self-consciousness itself—the absolute known, precisely therewith, as spirit. [49b]

But we have already seen this object distinguished into two moments: absolute necessity and the spiritual, human shape. These two moments are still distinct: although determinacy has been posited within the universal, it is on the one hand abstract determinacy and, on the other, a manifold diversity given free rein and not yet taken back into unity. For this to happen would involve determinateness to [the point of] infinite antithesis being simultaneously accentuated

---

145. *Ms. margin:* ⟨Spiritual religion [is] to worship God in spirit and as spirit⟩

ad infinitum (as in the religion of sublimity); for it is only when pushed to that extreme that the antithesis is at the same time capable of coming to unity with respect to itself. ⟨Determinacy in its fully developed state, in the objectivity and universality that is then [present] with respect to it as such⟩—the whole circle of divine configurations—would itself have to be taken up into necessity, ⟨[as] one God⟩ in one pantheon. But the circle of gods can do this, they are worthy to do this, only if their manifoldness or diversity is universalized into simple distinction. Only then is the circle of gods commensurate with the element of necessity | and directly identical in itself. The spirits must be comprehended as *the* spirit; *the* spirit is their universal nature, which is inwardly concrete consciousness and at the same time universal, simple essence—as necessity, and then as One.

68

(α) In relationship to necessity, consciousness seems initially to be annihilated, to be related purely and simply to something beyond, and to find nothing here that is friendly to itself. But necessity does not take the form of one God for consciousness, which accordingly does not [subsist] for itself in this necessity.[146] In its relationship to him who is One, consciousness subsists for itself, seeks to subsist for itself, is preoccupied with itself. The servant has selfish ends in view in his service, in his subjection and fear, in his submissiveness to his lord. In the relationship to necessity, however, the subject is determined as not subsisting on its own account or for itself; it has surrendered itself up, retains no purpose on its own account—in fact, the worship of necessity is just what is meant by this orientation of self-consciousness, lacking all determinacy and antithesis. What tragic dramatists have nowadays accustomed us [50a] to call fate is the direct opposite of this orientation of self-consciousness. We speak of just and unjust, or merited, fate. We appeal to fate as an explanation, in other words [we see] the reasons for a situation, for what befalls individuals, i.e., their situation and circumstances ⁻(e.g., in [Schiller's] *Braut von Messina* an ancient curse upon the house[147]), not in the actions of the | individuals themselves—on the

69

146. W₂ *adds:* —in other words, is not a unity possessing selfhood in its immediacy.

147. [*Ed.*] Cf. Friedrich Schiller, *Die Braut von Messina,* vv. 1695–1969 et passim.

contrary the reasons, the ground for such a situation is an external necessity of nature that runs counter to the law of freedom and responsibility; [it is] unfreedom, and it presupposes an otherworldly ground; the ground [can be] only something otherworldly. The intuition or consciousness of necessity is rather the very opposite, namely, the [direct] transition, ⟨mediation only as⟩ the sublation of mediation, ⟨argument and reflection being annulled⟩.¯¹⁴⁸ We cannot speak of a *belief* in necessity, as if necessity were a matter of a nexus of causes, effects, and circumstances, as if it were present to consciousness in an objective shape. Rather, to say "It is necessary, it is the will of God," as do the Turks, is to have abandoned arguments in terms of causes and purposes—and in so doing, to have abandoned causes and purposes themselves; it is to imprison spirit in this simple abstraction. ¯This present orientation of spirit presupposes an unconditional, abstract, and initially inward freedom, the voluntary surrender of what, as the saying goes, fate snatches away—or rather it is surrendered already. "Fate," here, is just a manner of speaking. This possibility imparts to noble, beautiful characters greatness and the peace of mind and unconstrained courage that forms a characteristic feature in the Oriental world.¯¹⁴⁹

(β) [Such are] the general characteristics of self-consciousness in this relationship. In the second place, however, the self-consciousness is related to God defined as a natural and ethical power, ⟨a particular power⟩ that is present in an external, sensibly visible spiritual shape. Just as in necessity self-consciousness surrenders its fulfillment or realization, its relation to an end, so here it recovers it: from thine

---

148. W₂ *reads:* Here we have an external connection between cause and effect, whereby a hereditary evil, an ancient curse that rests upon the house, etc., breaks out in the individual. In such cases the meaning of fate is that there is some ground, but at the same time it is an otherworldly one, and fate is then nothing but a nexus of causes and effects—causes which those on whom the fate falls must needs regard as finite although there is a hidden connection nonetheless between what those who suffer are on their own account and that which undeservedly befalls them.

The intuition and worship of necessity is rather the very opposite; all such mediation and all arguments about cause and effect are sublated in it.

149. W₂ *reads:* This orientation of spirit, which has [voluntarily] surrendered what, as the saying goes, fate snatches away, imparts to noble, beautiful characters greatness, peace of mind, and the unconstrained nobility that we also find in the ancients.

own passions, πάθεσι, O mortal, hast thou [50b] created the gods.[150]

70 It is not mere | powers of nature but the very powers and essential aspects that are proper to spirit[151] that are here directly intuited and known as in and for themselves, known in their universality, free from appearance and contingency, intuited in their ideality. ¨¨Self-consciousness is accordingly conscious of *its* essentiality, its essence, in them: in them it is free. But ⟨its own doing and being⟩ are essential to it too, its genus, what it possesses and is conscious of in them, ⟨its specific character, if you will, or particularity,⟩[152] not its singular individuality or subjectivity—as in the religion of the One, where just this immediate thereness, this natural existence of the subject, [is] the purpose or end, where individuals are not aware of their universality as essential, ¨⟨nor of their singularity [as essential either]⟩;¨[153] the servant has selfish ends.¨¨[154]

On the one hand self-consciousness is hereby elevated above the

150. [*Ed.*] See Clement of Alexandria, *Exhortation to the Heathen* 2: "And some even of the philosophers, after the poets, make idols of forms of your passions [παθῶν], such as fear, and love, and joy, and hope" (*Ante-Nicene Fathers* [New York, 1885], 2:178).

151. *Ms. margin:* ⟨Particular forms of essence: (αα) the particular essentiality of spirit, and hence its real, positive freedom⟩

152. [*Ed.*] The *Ms.* reads in the margin *Wohl s. Besonderheit,* which our text gives as *wohl seine Besonderheit* on the grounds that Hegel frequently began his marginal notations with capital letters. But it is also possible to read as *Wohl seiner Besonderheit* ("the well-being of its particularity"), as does the variant from W_2 given in n. 154 (changing *seiner* to *ihrer* to agree with the feminine antecedent *Subjektivität*). But since it appears that W_2 is here following the *Ms.* rather than *Hn,* it affords no additional information on the interpretation of the text.

153. *Ms. adds in margin:* ⟨(αα) raised above their *immediate* singularity, which is defined [as] essential consciousness – fulfillment with *objective* power of this *substantive* kind⟩

W_2 *reads:* are raised above the concern about universality, and have their essential satisfaction in a substantive, objective power;

154. W_2 *reads:* In these powers self-consciousness has its own essential aspects as its object, and it is conscious of itself as free *in them.* But it is not the particular subjectivity that has itself as object in these essential aspects and knows the well-being of its particularity to be grounded in them (as in the religion of the One, where it is just this immediate thereness, this natural existence of the subject, that is the purpose or end, and individuals, not their universality, are what is essential, so that the servant has his selfish ends); here, on the contrary, in the divine powers self-consciousness has its genus, its universality as its object.

absolute demand for its immediate singularity; it is only the ethical,[155] the universally rational, or the law, that counts as essential in and for itself. The freedom of self-consciousness consists in the essentiality of its true nature, its rationality; that is the basis of right or law, of the ethical realm, | of the state in general, ⟨of naive ethical 71 life in general,⟩ etc. On the other hand[156] the consciousness of infinite subjectivity is lacking (of humanity insofar as it is individual, or of individuals insofar as they are human beings), the consciousness that the ethical relationship and absolute right belong to humanity as such, that by virtue of being self-consciousness human beings have in this formal infinitude the right as well as the duty of the genus. Freedom or ethical life is the substantive aspect of humanity; and to know this to be so, and actually to posit their substantiality in freedom and ethical life, is what gives human beings value and dignity. But it is *formal* subjectivity, self-consciousness as such, the inwardly infinite (as opposed to merely natural, immediate) individuality which constitutes the possibility of such value, i.e., the real possibility, and which on account of this possibility itself is vested with infinite right, albeit [only] in the nature of formal right, [such as the right] of personal freedom, the right to property, etc.

The substantial ethical life [51a] does not simultaneously contain the infinite antithesis, the absolute, formal reflection of self-consciousness into itself; it does not involve morality, one's own conviction and insight.

155. *Ms. margin:* ⟨(ββ) Ideality – ethics⟩ [For (αα) see n. 153]

156. *Ms. margin:* ⟨(ββ) Not the infinitude of formal self-consciousness, therefore (α) not morality and universal, infinite right. But the infinite being-for-self of self-consciousness [is] lacking, [so that we have] (α) slavery, (β) not a form of morality, (γ) not immortality.⟩

W_2 *adds:* Because the infinitude of formal subjectivity is not recognized in the naive ethical life [of the natural state], human beings as such are not *absolutely* valid, do not count as human in and for themselves, regardless of their inner fulfillment, place of birth, riches, poverty, community affiliation. Human freedom and the ethical realm are still *particular,* and the right of humanity is involved in contingency, so that at this stage there is essentially room for slavery. It is still a matter of chance whether one is a citizen of a particular state, whether one is free or not. Moreover, since the infinite antithesis is not yet present, and the absolute reflection of self-consciousness into itself (this culmination of subjectivity) is lacking, morality—as one's *own* conviction and insight—is not yet developed either.

(¯Second,¯¹⁵⁷ inasmuch as the subject can acquire, in ethical life,
72 an infinite value, | or inasmuch as individuality in general is taken
up into universal substantiality, there emerges at this point¹⁵⁸ the
representational image of the eternal character of the subjective
individual spirit—the immortality of the soul. ¯In nature religion,
[which is an] unmediated unity of natural and spiritual, there is no
room for this way of viewing things, [because] spirit does not [exist]
on its own account. Nor [did we] encounter it in the religion of the
One,¹⁵⁹ because although spirit there [exists] on its own account,
its freedom [is] abstract and unfulfilled. Hence its being is a purely
natural one, not being as the determinate being of spirit within itself;
it does not find satisfaction within itself, in the spiritual. [Instead
we have] only the duration of the family, this natural extension and
universality [of life], not the inward universality of spirit.¯¹⁶⁰ But
here [we have] self-consciousness inwardly fulfilled, spiritual; subjectivity [is] taken up into absolute essentiality and therefore known
inwardly as idea, intuited; at this stage [we find] the representation
of immortality. ¯[It is] more clearly defined in Socrates and Plato,¹⁶¹
[at] the time when morality [emerges]. Before that [we find it] only
as a representational image that does not have absolute value in and
for itself but is merely a general image, still not cognitively interpreted
in the formal self-consciousness of infinitude [or as] inwardly sub-
73 sisting universality.¯¹⁶² |

157. *Ms. reads:* (β)
158. *W₂ adds:* even if initially only as a weak semblance and not yet as an absolute
postulate of spirit,
159. [*Ed.*] I.e., the religion of sublimity, or Jewish religion.
160. *W₂ reads:* At the stages we have considered previously, the postulate of the
immortality of the soul still cannot occur (neither in nature relation nor in the religion
of the One). In the former the unmediated unity of the natural and the spiritual is
still the basic characteristic, and spirit does not exist on its own account. In the religion
of the One, spirit exists on its own account of course, but it is still unfulfilled, its
freedom is still abstract, and its being is still a natural one—the possession of a
particular territory and its prosperity. But this is not being as the determinate being
of spirit within itself, and the satisfaction does not lie in the spiritual. Duration is
only duration of the tribe, of the family, of natural universality in general.
161. [*Ed.*] See Plato, *Phaedo,* and *Phaedrus* 245–251. On Hegel's interpretation,
see *Lectures on the History of Philosophy* 2:36–43 (*Werke* 14:206–215).
162. *W₂ reads:* However, this level of consciousness is more clearly defined when
morality emerges, when self-consciousness penetrates deep within itself and reaches

Third, ¯just as self-consciousness lacks this subjectivity for its part, so the objective essentiality lacks it too.⟩ Consequently the particularizations of divine power also do not have this lofty¯[163] justification ⟨or seriousness⟩ either; for they can be justified only as moments of absolute subjectivity, as moments of *necessity* itself, or as rooted in this absolute unity that is reflected into itself. They are many different gods, and although their nature is divine their scattered plurality is at the same time a limited character, so that their divinity cannot quite be taken in earnest; and over self-consciousness and its many substantive essential aspects hovers this ultimate unity of absolute form constituted by necessity. ¯As a result [self-consciousness is] freed, even in its objective behavior, from its[164] gods¯[165] ⟨—it is not confined to singular particularities—and at the same time from abstract necessity, in that abstract necessity unites the determinate with necessity⟩.

This [is] what constitutes the absolute *serenity* of the religion of art, ⟨not immediately [one] with nature⟩. The extremes [are]: stern necessity, inflexibility, the finitude of indeterminate being; on the one hand there is the absolute superstition attached to natural objects—dryads, a hare that crosses one's path, everything [is taken to mean] something higher or divine; on the other hand there is the absolute presumptuousness, the finite self-consciousness inwardly advancing to the point of doing away with God or gods and looking to itself for its own security against and above everything. | 74

---

the point where it recognizes as true, good, and right only what it finds congruent with itself and its thinking. That is why we find explicit discussion of the immortality of the soul in Socrates and Plato, whereas previously this representational image was regarded rather as merely a general one, such as did not have absolute value in and for itself.

163. W_2 reads: just as self-consciousness still lacks infinite subjectivity, the absolute point of unity of the concept, so its essentialities lack it too. This unity is part of what we have become familiar with as its necessity; but this necessity lies outside the range of the particular, substantive essentialities [the gods]. Like human beings as such, the particular essentialities have no absolute

164. [Ed.] Our reading assumes that the pronoun refers to "self-consciousness" (neuter) rather than "necessity" (feminine), as suggested by the Ms.

165. W_2 reads: And the result of this unity is at the same time to free self-consciousness from its gods (even in its relationship to them), so that it is serious about them, and again not serious.

β. The Cultus Itself

The spirit of this cultus should enable us to deduce its concrete actual form. But in this case what is characteristic [is] the diversity of its outward manifestations.

[(α)] The cultus [is] a serious playing and a playful seriousness, a gravity that is gay.

The focal point of this cultus is beauty. We have here entered the realm of spirit: spirit is sure of itself, it finds itself at home in all particular appearances, in all the particular powers and objects of nature and of spirit. The spiritual [is] embodied and immediately present, the corporeal is spiritualized. [51b]

(Abstract necessity will not tolerate any cultic relationship; it rejects the thought of positive, sustaining acceptance, such as sustains the individual self-consciousness in identity with itself. The intuiting or thinking of necessity is itself nothing but the orientation of spirit that submerges its particularity in the "It *is* so" of necessity.[166])

Self-consciousness has, however, a relationship to the wide circle of the gods, ⟨even though [there is] something else in the background⟩; [this relationship is] simply to pay homage to the gods, make them favorably inclined to it (τιμᾶν). ¯They are | the natural or ethical powers that rule our lives; we find them realized in our immediate consciousness,¯[167] or they freely offer themselves in outward life for us to help ourselves to them at will (bread, crops, wine).

75

---

166. *Ms. margin:* ⟨Relationship [to] the particular powers
(α) to the *gods,* meaning of this precise cultus –
(β) to their *universality* – their universal beyond – nature [as] a mystical essence – the antithesis a greater demand to render service – to put off the [old] self – on the [part of the] individual –
(γ) On the other hand – their contingency [and the] beyond – hence they [are] receivers. Three sides or parts. [There is] no providence; God determines, he reveals, and in so doing determines. Oracles –⟩
[*Above this marginal note:*] ⟨(β) to the universal essence, (γ) to the power of singularity. Consciousness [is] the intuition of a deeper essence in them and of a more serious relationship of individuality to them⟩
167. W_2 reads: 2. Worship or service too, as the attitude one adopts to the gods in their spiritual aspect, does not have the meaning of appropriating these powers for the first time to oneself, or for the first time becoming conscious of one's identity with them. For this identity is already present [to consciousness], and the worshipers find these powers already realized in their consciousness.

〈ˉWhat does it mean then to gain the consciousness of identity with them? [They are] (α) delivered up to consciousness (without hindrance, insofar as they are objective); (β) directly identical with it.

(α) The gifts of nature offer themselves in friendly fashion for use.ˉ168 This life, the trees, crops and springs, are there to be laid hold on, drawn upon, consumed (water yields to our touch); they fall into our lap, we eat and drink the wine; they nourish us and inspire our minds. [It is] this nourishment, of which they are an essential ingredient, [that is] their effect, not the action and reaction, the dreary, repetitious monotony of the mechanical sphere. Instead it is honored [as] something *spiritual* present in outward life, *spiritual* sustenance. We do honor to the natural powers as we eat and drink. What higher honor [can there be] for natural things than to become, to appear as, what gives strength for spiritual action? ˉThey inspire; [for instance, wine inspires, but]ˉ169 it is human beings who first raise it to the level of what inspires and gives strength. ˉOur sense of need leads us to thank the gods for relieving need in this way. (These natural objects exist without need, and therein lies their inferiority: in the absence of need they atrophy or dry up; as the gifts of nature they have us to thank for the fact that they come to something.) But in general | people do not stand in a relationship of need to the gifts of nature; need [arises] through ownership, the resolve of an infinite will,ˉ170 through being alien and holding others at arm's length. By helping ourselves directly to the gifts of nature [we] enter into identity with them.

(β) Determinate spirituality, however, be it legal right, ethical custom, law, science, wisdom, the spirit of the people, or a universal

168. W_2 *reads:* Now if the divine powers deliver themselves up as gifts of nature, and offer themselves in a friendly fashion for use, then the service [of the gods] by which the human worshipers gain the consciousness of unity with their powers has the following meaning.

169. W_2 *reads:* Wine inspires, but

170. W_2 *reads:* to this extent the relationship of need disappears. Our sense of need leads us to thank the gods for the receipt [of these gifts], and this sense presupposes a separation that it is not in human power to annul. Need proper first arises where something is owned by a will that will not give it up. But our relationship to the gifts of nature is not one of need understood in this way; on the contrary, the gifts of nature have us to thank for the fact that they come to something; without us they would atrophy, dry up, and pass uselessly away.

76

essence such as love (Aphrodite), is actualized in individuals (law-abiding citizens, scholars, lovers, etc.). What counts is *their* will, *their* inclination, passion, what they themselves will and do.

¯Now if cultus [consists in] the actions whereby one gains the consciousness [of one's unity with the gods], then its content—this identity—is already directly present both for and in consciousness, and all that is still required to arrive at one's own sense of the cultus is⟩ to make them favorable to one in a purely general way, by recognizing them.¯[171]

Religion [is] just this objectifying, just the form of consciousness. [It is] not the drawing of the [divine] thing to oneself, as something alien, such as would keep to itself and impose conditions of arduous service, requiring to be wooed from its inflexibility (the Lord, greatly to be feared). But the form it takes is the consciousness of this unity as a unity with universal powers, or the elevation of the powers from the level of enjoyment, taking enjoyment and use—one's own being, willing, and doing—back out of the immediate identity of feeling, volition, etc., imbuing them with theoretical objectivity (as compared with our representational image), and so recognizing and worshiping them as powers. This theoretical objectivity is the work of phantasy, not of abstract thought: that they have their own implicit being, embracing an abstract, universal being-in-self in opposition to humanity—for example, God as essence, and specifically as the power over nature, or natural objects in the relationship of effects, something inwardly dependent [upon him]. Theoretical objectivity, however, leaves them in their determinate | being; it raises the particular features in their determinate content from the level of dependence, and in making them independent figures on their own account it gives them at the same time universal sensibility, ideality. [52a]

As far as we are concerned, [this does] violence [to our thought]. We can, to be sure, join in the phantasy, the phantasy of ideal beauty, but we cannot take it seriously in this way. Trees, wine, springs, mountains, cities, artifacts, legal relationships, modes of life,

77

---

171. W₂ *reads:* All that therefore remains for the cultus is to recognize these powers, honor them, and so raise up identity into the form of consciousness and make it theoretical objectivity.

agriculture, or land-surveying—¯it is beyond us, not to raise such things to the level of an abstraction or thought, but to offer them incense, prayers, sacrifices for their own sake, to recognize them as independent powers on their own account, possessing a will of their own. We cannot attain to the full seriousness of this antithesis, which lies in the lack of absolute subjective unity: particular configurations fall outside the limits of necessity. ⟨This [is for us] the limit, [we can] not pass beyond it and endow them with personality over against us. Infinite subjectivity consumes them, reduces them to beautiful images of phantasy.⟩¯ 172

⟨Such veneration in the form of sacrifices, or however it may be, [is] something intermediate: the offerings are brought and consumed, and the worshiper enjoys the best share of them.⟩

Now the cultus of these gods cannot be called service in the proper sense of the term; it is not service to an alien, independent will the contingent resolves of which would constitute the goal to be pursued. The veneration itself provides already an anticipatory reward, or is itself the enjoyment [of the sacrifice]. It is therefore not a question of calling a power back to oneself from the other world where it resides, | and to this end putting away, in order to be acceptable to it, whatever on the subjective side of self-consciousness constitutes the separation. It is therefore not a question of doing without, of renouncing or putting away a subjective idiosyncrasy, not a matter of dread, self-torture, or self-torment. The cult of Bacchus and Ceres is the possession and enjoyment of bread and wine, the consumption of which [produces] immediate gratification. The spiritual powers are thus the distinctive powers of self-consciousness itself.

78

172. W₂ reads: If we compare this objectivity with our viewpoint, then we too raise the universal out of our immediate consciousness and think it. We can also go so far as to elevate these universal powers to the ideal and endow them with a spiritual shape. But to pray or sacrifice to such images, that is the point at which we part company with this intuition [of the divine]; we cannot go so far as to ascribe to these images (for all that they are not products of the imagination but essential powers) singular independence, personality over against ourselves. Our consciousness of the infinite subjectivity as a *universal* subjectivity consumes these *particular* powers and reduces them to the level of beautiful images of phantasy, whose content and meaning we do indeed know how to appreciate but which we cannot regard as genuinely independent.

Athena, whom the Athenians worship, is their very own city, their spirit, their technical and artistic talent; the muse that Homer invokes is at the same time his genius, his power of composition; Aphrodite, worshiped as goddess, is [also] the love of the individual worshiper. In Phaedra, Hippolytus comes to grief because he worships only Diana [52b] and spurns love, which takes its revenge on him. His pathos lies in hunting, and he is ignorant of love.[173] For Racine,[174] in the French reworking of the legend, to give Hippolytus another object of passion is stupidity. For it is then no punishment inflicted by love as pathos that he suffers but just the ill luck that he has fallen in love with one girl and therefore pays no heed to another woman— admittedly she is his father's wife, but this ethical impediment is obscured by his love for Aricia. The cause of his downfall is thus not the injury or disregard of a universal power as such, nothing ethical, but a detail of life, a mere contingency.

It is also true, however, that the universal powers withdraw again, and recede far from the individual. The spring lets us draw from it freely, the sea lets us travel across it; but then too it is whipped up into storms, and ⟨like the constellations⟩ it is not only complaisant to humanity but terrible and catastrophic. The muse too is not always complaisant to the poet; she withdraws and serves him ill (though the poet invokes her only when he is writing, and his invocation, like his prize, is itself poetry). Athena herself does not keep troth; spirit, God does not keep troth. | The inhabitants of Tyre bound their Hercules with chains so that he should not leave their city—his reality, his actual existence.[175] Tyre fell, Athens was made subject to the Spartans, and so on. ⁻Magic offered a possible means of circumventing such alienation of their essential aspect, which

79

173. [Ed.] See Euripides, *Hippolytus,* esp. the dialogue between Artemis and Hippolytus, vv. 1389–1400.
174. [Ed.] Racine, *Phèdre,* esp. act 4, sc. 2 (Hippolytus to Theseus) (cf. Racine, *Œuvres complètes* [Paris, 1950], 1:786). Hegel's view accords closely with the interpretation of A. W. Schlegel, with which he was familiar, *Comparaison entre la Phèdre de Racine et celle d'Euripide* (Paris, 1807).
175. [Ed.] See Diodorus Siculus, *Bibliotheca historica* 17.41, 46; also Plutarch, *Lives* 24 (Alexander). Hegel probably spoke mistakenly of a binding of Hercules because Hercules was the god of Tyre. Also the practice in Tyre of binding the statue of Hercules-Melkarth led Creuzer to assume a long-standing custom; see Creuzer, *Symbolik und Mythologie* 1:178–179, 2:215 ff.

would lead to absolute scission or internal rupture, a means of combating it, an expression of the will to draw [the powers back] to oneself, as it were by violence of the spirit and of the cultus. But all such particular powers, and with them particular purposes, tended ⟨to sink⟩ into necessity and were in this way themselves surrendered.‾176

The cultus accordingly consists in these universal powers being emphasized for their own sake and recognized [53a]—thought grasps the essential, substantive element in its concrete life. A meditative reflection underlines the universal powers, not remaining dully buried and distracted in the empirical singularity of life, or capable of rising out of it only to the abstract One, the infinite beyond; on the contrary, it is the sense that remains present to itself and at the same time underlines the true, the Platonic idea, in its manifold determinate being, becomes conscious of it, intuits and portrays it to itself, and in the course of recognizing and honoring this universal, is itself present in the enjoyment. This [is] the presence of spirit in its essential aspects, and spirit [is here] conscious of them; hence this is on the one hand the thinking theoretical relationship that is worthy of the name, and on the other hand it is the joyfulness, serenity, and freedom that is sure of itself, and at home with itself, in them.

‾This cultus is consequently itself in part *poetry*, thinking phantasy, | which thinks and highlights the universal essences, setting them before itself in an intuitable, portrayable form, breathing life into them, clothing them, and raising them to autonomy.‾177 On the one hand these powers split up *ad infinitum;* all the mountains, grottoes, springs, trees, and so on are spiritual powers that admittedly form a self-contained circle; but because they are particular, they tend toward the infinity of relations found in actuality. ‾(Every god is conceived in a broadly particularized relation: Pallas Athena as

80

176. W₂ *reads:* However, such alienation of their essential aspect, leading to absolute scission or rupture of inner life, would oblige worshipers to draw the powers back to themselves, as it were by the violence of the spirit in the cultus (with the associated risk of lapsing into magic). The individual cannot enter into infinite antithesis to these particular powers, for as particular purposes they are submerged in necessity and are themselves surrendered in it.

177. W₂ *reads:* In Greek life, however, poetry, thinking phantasy, is itself the essential form of divine service.

a power armed with lightning, skill, dexterity, [goddess] of wisdom and knowledge, of the Muses and the fine arts, of spinning and technical [skills], of particular states or sections of the populace; ⟨Hercules as abstract strength, the sun, labors, renown, and so on⟩.)⁻¹⁷⁸ On the other hand it is in the human, sentiently spiritual shape that the ideal is to be portrayed. For these reasons the portrayal is inexhaustible, [53b] each model being continually carried further and replenished by another. For religious life itself consists in this continuous passage from empirical existence to the ideal. There is no hard-and-fast, spiritually determined body of teaching or doctrine here, no truth as such in the form of thought, ⟨in other words, it is not faith⟩; but the divine [is present] in this immanent, immediate connection with actuality, so that it is always *in* actuality and arises *from* actuality (which is always there in its externality); the divine is constantly raising itself and bringing itself forth anew. ⁻⟨[Its] consummation [is] in art: Homer or the Jupiter of Phidias established [the divine] for phantasy. [Conversely this marks] a decline of religious vitality.)⁻ ¹⁷⁹ |

⟨Sacrifice involves giving up, offering, depriving oneself of something, but here [the God] as a particular power is sacrificed too.⟩ Hence sacrifice does not here have the sense of sacrificing ⁻one's inner life and its fulfillment;⁻¹⁸⁰ on the contrary, it is rather just this fulfillment that is confirmed and itself enjoyed. To perform a sacrifice¹⁸¹ can only mean on the one hand recognition of the universal power; [it is] the theoretical surrender of a part [only], i.e., a

178. W₂ *reads:* ⟨how many particular relations are comprehended, for instance, in Pallas!⟩.

179. W₂ *reads:* Once this active production has been consummated through art, once phantasy has achieved its final, enduring shape so that the ideal has been established, then the decline of religious vitality is in train.

But as long as this standpoint exerts a fresh and active productive force, the highest assimilation of the divine consists in the fact that the subject makes the god present through itself, brings him into appearance in itself. This means that the conscious subjectivity of the god remains at the same time on one side, as something beyond, so that the portrayal of the divine in this way is simultaneously the recognition and veneration of its substantive essentiality.

180. W₂ *reads:* the inner life or concrete fullfillment of spirit;

181. *Ms. margin:* ⟨[In regard to] human sacrifice [see] La Croix, *Myst.* I, p. 276 – [citing] Thucyd. I, chap. 126 – "jeune et beau Cratinus; lorsqu'Epimenide purifiait les habitants de'Attique après le massacre de Cylon et de ses partisans."⟩

surrender which confers no benefit ⟨[or] which serves no practical purpose, i.e., does not further one's ends or one's enjoyment⟩—a beaker or goblet of wine is poured out on the ground. But at the same time the sacrifice is itself enjoyment: the wine is drunk, the meat is eaten. ⟨It is the natural power itself whose singular external and determinate being is sacrificed and destroyed.⟩ Eating is sacrificing, and sacrificing is to eat [what is sacrificed] oneself. In this way a higher significance attaches to all activities of life, and [there is] this enjoyment in partaking of them, not denying oneself, not as it were asking for forgiveness for eating and drinking, but every activity, everything we enjoy in everyday life, is a sacrifice; it is not the offering up of a possession or property, but a theoretical, artistic enjoyment idealized by meaning, a form of freedom and spirituality in one's daily, immediate life, a continuous thread of poetry running through life. ⟨Such [is] this cultus in general: ideal, artistic enjoyment, artistic activities, pomp and circumstance for the God [on the one side], and on the part of the community different forms of service, ceremonies, dances, and adornment. (α) [As regards] the *subjects,* whatever artistic principles enter into them, these adornments, dances, and contrivances include external, contingent features (e.g., the number and choice of flowers, colors, etc.), so the symbolizing comes into its own (labyrinthine dances [symbolizing] the course of the planets); [the result is] that the contingent, since it is not in itself capable of taking on spiritual shape, is raised [to a spiritual status] by | its *meaning.* But (β) as regards the portrayal of the *objective* element . . .⟩   82

The recognition [of the gods] in the cultus, the elevation of the actual powers into phantasy, the way in which they are held fast and represented, assumes a multitude of degrees and configurations. The highest configuration, ⟨where these powers are portrayed in a

---

[*Ed.*] Baron de Sainte-Croix, *Recherches historiques et critiques sur les mystères du paganisme,* 2d ed., rev. Silvestre de Sacy (Paris, 1817), 1:276. Sainte-Croix refers to Thucydides, *History of the Peloponnesian War* 1.126, and indeed Hegel regards Thucydides as the source of information about the sacrifice of Cratinus. However, in his report of the insurrection of Cylon, Thucydides follows another tradition (see 1.126). The tradition that Cratinus and Ctesibius were sacrificed in order to absolve the inhabitants of Attica is found elsewhere, e.g., in Diogenes Laertius, *Lives* 1.110.

detailed, dynamic way,⟩ is as they are intuited in tragedy and comedy, which portrayed the actual operation and effect of these powers in concrete instances and showed how they collided and fought with one another. The end of it all [was] their absolutely unique and equal justification, where one-sided service to just one power, which alone is held of any account, brings only misfortune. ⟨[This is] the highest point [of Greek religious life], the drama of the life of the gods; this is the [genuinely] Greek spirit, that of later times is cultured.⟩ [54a]

[182](β) It is, however, very closely bound up with the veneration of this multiplicity of divine[183] essences that there should also be a transition to the universality of divine power—¬not the universality of abstract necessity, which as something independent, standing over against one, is nothing "objective"; on the contrary, they are combined in a single concrete intuition. This absolute unity would be the infinite subjectivity of the One—an abstraction that has no place here. ⟨[It is] not [a question of] a Lord and (negatively) the service rendered him, nor yet of any absolute, inwardly concrete subjectivity as spirit.⟩ Instead the divine essences are combined in¬[184] a single unity that is all-embracing in concrete fashion. This is universal nature in general or a totality of the divine beings, | of the gods, that has a universal significance; ⟨even in its material aspect, this content of the sensible-spiritual world [is] combined in a unity⟩.

This deeper element remains in the nebulous realm of the symbolic, the allegorical. Since it cannot advance to the infinite subjectivity that would be inwardly concrete as *the* spirit, ¬the form of substantive unity involved is one that was a feature of the earlier religions instead; and it is here retained from them.¬[185] For the earlier, primitive religions are the determinate religion of nature,

83

182. *Ms. margin:* ⟨23 July 1821⟩
183. W_2 *adds:* —but, because it is a multiplicity, limited—
184. W_2 *reads:* The limited nature of the gods itself leads directly to the attempt to rise above them and combine them in a single concrete intuition (i.e., not just in abstract necessity, for this is nothing objective). At this point the elevation into unity cannot yet be the absolute, inwardly concrete subjectivity of spirit; but equally it cannot be a relapse into the intuition of the power of the One and into negative service rendered to the Lord; the One that becomes object to self-consciousness at this standpoint is
185. W_2 *reads:* the intuition of substantive unity is something that is already present at this stage, something that has been retained from the earlier religions.

which we have already considered,[186] the form of Spinozism that is based on the immediate unity of the natural and the spiritual. But the earlier religions are also typified by their location; their mode of comprehension and portrayal is also limited, it is inwardly more indeterminate and general until such time as they develop; in the fixing of his location each local god has at the same time the significance of universality; and inasmuch as this universality is steadfastly maintained against the fragmentation and particularization into characters and individuals that develops in the religion of beauty, it is in the raw, the primitive, the unbeautiful, the undeveloped that the service of a deeper, inner, universal element is continued—a universal that at the same time is not abstract thought but rather preserves within itself that earlier external, contingent configuration. [54b]

[187]Because of its simplicity and substantive intensity this older element can be termed deeper, purer, ⟨more solid, more substantial, concrete, concentrated,⟩ truer in meaning. But its meaning is in part shrouded on its own account in opaqueness; it has not developed to the level of thought, it lacks precisely the clarity of the particular gods, who have won for themselves the character and shape of spirit, ⟨[where] the daylight of the spirit has already dawned⟩. However, the service of this deeper, more universal element involves the *antithesis* between this deeper, more universal element itself and the particular, | more limited, manifest powers. It is on the one hand a return from them to the deeper, inner, and to that extent higher, ⟨i.e., deeper truths,⟩ ⟨preserving the unity of nature as what is within, bringing the plurality of separate gods back into the unity of nature—Aeschylus: Proserpine, mother of Diana[188]⟩. But it involves also the antithesis that this deeper element is what is dull, unconscious, barbaric, and savage as opposed to clear self-

84

---

186. [*Ed.*] See above, pp. 98–122.

187. *Ms. margin:* ⟨Unity of God – immortality of the soul – torment of the damned – intuition of the purification of the soul⟩

188. [*Ed.*] The source of this report is Herodotus, *Histories* 2.156, who states that on the basis of an Egyptian legend Aeschylus (unlike any earlier Greek poet) made Artemis (Diana) the daughter of Demeter (Ceres, Isis) and Dionysus, not of Leto and Zeus, as tradition had it (Leto merely nursed and saved her); see also Pausanias, *Description of Greece* 8.37.6. J. F. Cotta also mentions a Diana as

consciousness, the serenity of the daylight, of rationality. [189]The intuition in this form of cultus, therefore, will be a symbolized, universal natural life and natural power, a return to the inner, solid intuition; but on the other hand it is equally the intuition of the process, of the transition from ⟨savagery⟩[190] to legality, from barbarism to ethical life, from unconscious dullness to the self-illuminating certainty of self-consciousness. It cannot be a fully formed god nor yet an abstract doctrine that is intuited here, but [the intuition resides] essentially in the conflict between this original, primitive element in its undeveloped form and the clarity and higher levels of thought and custom, which are not just material but have been exposed to the daylight vision and form of consciousness.[191] ⟨The benefits conferred by Ceres and Triptolemus [were] agriculture and property, and the mysteries made it possible to envisage the miserable

---

supposedly the daughter of Proserpine or Persephone (traditionally also a daughter of Demeter by Zeus) on the basis of a report by Cicero, *De natura deorum* 3.58, but here there is no reference to Aeschylus. Aeschylus's tragedy, not named by Herodotus and Pausanias, has not been preserved. Herodotus's purpose here is to expose the origin of Aeschylus's theogony in an Egyptian myth; but he is also implicitly criticizing Aeschylus for having betrayed a secret of the Eleusinian mysteries, a betrayal with which Aeschylus was charged in his own time. Hegel refers to this betrayal again in a passage from the 1831 lectures in *W* (1824 lectures, n. 673, including annotation b). From this passage we may assume that Hegel is here following the interpretation of C. A. Lobeck; this is confirmed by the fact that the marginal passage in the *Ms.*, which can only have been added for the last lecture series, contains a phrase ("bringing the plurality of separate gods back into the unity of nature") that clearly derives from Lobeck. Cf. Augustus Lobeck, *Aglaophamus,* 2 vols. (Königsberg, 1829), 1:76–85, esp. 78. By combining the reports of Herodotus and Cicero, Hegel has confused Proserpine and Demeter.
189. *Ms. margin:* (a) Objective content
(α) Intuition of the universal force of nature
(β) Intuition of spirit in general – and of the process of spirit – an inwardly concrete representation – transition from the immediacy of nature to ethical life, from the sphere of the Titans to that of spirit.
These mysteries do not [come] from elsewhere, [they are] not Pelasgian or Asiatic
190. *Ms. originally read:* barbarism
191. *W₂ adds:* This representation is present already in many esoteric intuitions of mythology. For instance, the combat of the gods and the defeat of the Titans itself is the divine emergence of the spiritual through overcoming the untamed powers of nature.

barbarism in which people lived before the introduction of agriculture
| —Clement of Alexandria.¹⁹²⟩   85
¹⁹³⁻However, in this cultus the action of the *subjective side* and
the processes that such action involves also acquire a more deeply
determinate aspect.⁻¹⁹⁴ ⟨⟨(αα)⟩⟩ The cultus here cannot be simply the
serene enjoyment of the immediately present unity with the particular
powers, πάθεσι; for inasmuch as the divine passes over from its
particularity into universality, and indeed inasmuch as [55a] self-
consciousness [is] ⁻free⁻¹⁹⁵ (this it is that gives rise to the antithesis),
the divine withdraws within itself and is posited as more alien, more
remote. ⟨⟨(ββ)⟩⟩ Greater separation¹⁹⁶ is the starting point for uniting
[*Einigung*]: ⟨"pure" [*rein*] means "again one" [*re-ein*], united [*einig*]
with oneself again⟩. The cultus is here the process whereby the soul
is inwardly laid hold of; it is introduced and initiated into an essential
realm that is more ⁻remote⁻¹⁹⁷ and alien to it, into secrets that are
not found in its ordinary life and the cultus that is rooted there. When
it enters this sphere, [it is] required to lay aside its natural being and
essence. So this cultus is both a purification of the soul—a series of
steps leading to such purification—and a reception into the high
mystical essence, or the achievement of an intuitive vision of its
secrets. ⟨⟨(γγ) The mysteries⟩ have ceased to be secrets for even the
new initiate; they can continue to be secret only in the sense that

192. [*Ed.*] Hegel here emphasizes the agrarian character of the Eleusinian
mysteries. Demeter (Ceres) is the goddess of grain, Triptolemus the hero of agriculture.
The mention of Clement of Alexandria may be connected with the fact that in his
Exhortation to the Heathen 2.20–21 he discusses the mysteries (see also below,
p. 490). In Clement, however, the agrarian character of the mysteries recedes into
the background by contrast with the myth of Demeter, which is connected with the
Orphic myth and is therefore adjudged immoral. The reference to Clement in this
context seems somewhat displaced and would make better sense in relation to the
renewed allusion in the next paragraph to the birth of the gods out of the passions
(πάθεσι) (see above, n. 150). However, the criterion for arranging the text requires
the present location.
193. *Ms. margin:* (b) [*Follows canceled:*] Subjective Side
194. W₂ *reads:* It is here then that the action of the subjective side and the processes that such action involves also acquire a deeper determination of their own.
195. W₂ *reads:* turned back into self
196. · W₂ *adds:* than is presupposed in the manifest cultus
197. W₂ *reads:* abstract

these intuitions and this content are not drawn into the sphere of ordinary existence and consciousness and the play that is made of it in reflection. All Athenian citizens [were] initiates. A secret is essentially something known but not by all, but here [we have] something known by all but | treated as secret, ⟨as the Jews do not name the name of Jehovah,⟩ i.e., it is not something to be made the subject of idle chatter or common knowledge, and bandied about in everyday consciousness, ⟨just as in everyday life, conversely, there are things and circumstances that are known between acquaintances or generally but that are not spoken about⟩.

⟨(δδ)⟩ However, this cultus too is based on serenity. The path of purification is one that is traveled [physically]. There is no infinite pain and doubt in which abstract self-consciousness isolates itself, [relying] on abstract knowledge of itself, so that in this empty, contentless form it does no more than inwardly bestir itself, pulsating and trembling inwardly, and cannot, in this abstract certainty of itself, attain absolutely to any firm truth or objectivity or to a feeling for them. Instead, [55b] that unity is always based, and regarded as based, on the physical traveling of the road as an actually accomplished purification of the soul, an absolution; and with that originally unconscious basis it remains generally more of an external process of the soul.[198] Even if images that frighten or terrify, terrifying figures, and the like are used to produce deeper effects upon the mind (as are conversely, and alternating with them and [such intuitions of] the night, bright intuitions and images of splendor that are full of meaning), it is by traveling on through these intuitions and experiences that move the mind that the initiate is purified. These mystical intuitions correspond directly to the intuitions of the divine life, which is made visible in tragedy and comedy, | ⟨wherein self-consciousness is caught up and carried along willy-nilly (performances at the Bacchic festivals or the Thesmophoria[199])⟩; and the fear, the participation, the mourning,

198. W_2 adds: as the soul does not descend into the innermost depths of negativity, as is the case where subjectivity is fully developed to its infinitude.

199. [Ed.] The source of Hegel's information about the festivals was, in addition to the ancient reports, the book by Martin Gottfried Herrmann, Die Feste von Hellas historisch-philosophisch bearbeitet und zum erstenmal nach ihrem Sinn und Zweck

these states that are experienced in tragedy are equally steps to purification that achieve and have achieved all that is supposed to be achieved, just as the intuition of comedy and the act of laying aside one's dignity, one's self-esteem and opinion of oneself, and even one's deeper powers—this general sacrifice of one's whole self—*is* the cultus in which, by this sacrifice of everything finite, the soul enjoys and maintains the indestructible certainty of itself.

⟨(εε)⟩ Lastly it is in this cultus that the soul itself is exalted into a purpose on its own account.[200] The soul that comes to consciousness here is the more abstract, more estranged, more self-sufficient one; ⟨it is in and for itself—its nature and vocation is to be this⟩. The representational image of *immortality* necessarily enters on the scene at this point; the purification that it has undergone raises the soul [56a] above its temporary, ephemeral existence, and since it is now understood [*fixiert*] as free, the representation of the individual (as naturally deceased) passing over into eternal life is also bound up with this cultus; the dead receive the rights of citizenship in the more essential, ideal realm of the underworld where temporal [actuality] is reduced to the level of the world of shadows.

As regards the content of the cultus of mysteries, the evidence is very conflicting. Curiosity has been stirred to unveil what is secret, either because it is secret or in the belief that it contained a special wisdom. Any such belief [is] in and for itself stupid, if ony [because] Socrates and Aristotle, the wisest of the Greeks, [were] not initiated.[201] | Socrates (is the one who propounded] a new doctrine, 88 a new, unknown wisdom. But the generally accepted opinion that

---

erläutert, 2 vols. (Berlin, 1803), as well as Creuzer, *Symbolik und Mythologie,* vol. 3 and esp. vol. 4.

200. *Ms. canceled:* (In general, public cultus is not concerned with honoring the gods but with enjoying the divine – not here – but)

201. [*Ed.*] The Delphic oracle declared that Socrates was the wisest of the Greeks; see Plato, *Apology* 20e–21a, and Xenophon, *Apology of Socrates* 14. That Socrates was not initiated into the Eleusinian mysteries was reported by Lucian of Samosata, *Demonax* 11. Although Hegel alludes in the other lectures to the fact that Socrates was not initiated into the mysteries, he says it only here of Aristotle. His source is not known. Possibly he is confusing Aristotle and Aeschylus; Aristotle alludes to the charge that Aeschylus was not initiated because of his having betrayed the mysteries (see *Nicomachean Ethics* 1111a8–10). On the latter point Clement of Alexandria gives a full report (*Stromata* 2.14).

the unity of God and a purer religion were taught in the mysteries (in the sense that the official religion was here known and shown to be in error) [is] absurd.[202] ⟨Everything combines in the manner portrayed above.⟩

As we have shown, the unity of God [is] in the shape of universal natural modes pictured in a darkly obscure way; the immortality of the soul [is] not a formal doctine or dogma. [There is] a process or transition from savagery to ethical life, from dispersion to (albeit somewhat confused) unity, from nature to spirit, from the immediate existence and consciousness of the individual to a purer conciousness and a purer state that subsists in and for itself, the state of absolute eternal life. [56b]

⟨[There is a] wholly subjective need that stems from this. Particular subjectivity [is] not rooted nor preserved in fate. In the absolute, objective purpose, subjective purposes (even if, as particular, they are brought to naught, not realized) achieve their absolute essentiality, objectivity—the good—and, subjectively, eternal happiness.

(αα) Singularity, particular subjectivity.

(ββ) Absolute objectivity—*implicit* subjectivity, felicity—eternal life, all finite purposes being subordinated and surrendered (though at the same time they can only be *means* to such felicity).

(γγ) However, this characterization [still lacks] the universal objectivity that subsists in and for itself, still lacks divine objectivity—(α) providence, wisdom, (β) Christ.

Neither the truly infinite subjectivity of the individual as vocation and purpose, nor (objectively) the characterization of God as the absolutely wise one, embracing all private powers in one purpose, one idea, holding them in subordination to the one idea and harness-

89 ing them to it, is present in this religion. |

What is present is thus only the subjective need to know that particular purposes and individual interests are realized. To judge

202. [*Ed.*] Hegel's criticism of the accepted opinion that a higher wisdom and a pure religion, and indeed the unity of God, were taught in the mysteries is directed against a number of widely differing authors, including Voltaire, *Dictionnaire philosophique*, vol. 2 (*Œuvres complètes*, vol. 38 [1784], p. 516), and his friend Creuzer, *Symbolik und Mythologie* 1:199–202, whom Hegel here criticizes in unusually sharp fashion ("stupid," "absurd"). See also below, 1824 lectures, nn. 675, 678.

from appearances, however, happiness and unhappiness depend on whether people do this or that, go here or there, etc.: ¬it is their decision, which they know to be a merely contingent, subjective one,¬²⁰³ [but they want] to make it *objective,* i.e., as a rightful decision that objectifies itself. Because it is the subjective decision that decides, *consciously* decides in this way, it is not a father-confessor relationship or a matter of awaiting orders in all one does, but only of asking oneself, Is it useful to *me* to do this or that?⟩

(γ) Finally the moment of this religion that was present in the *oracles* belongs to its totality as well. ¬In the official cultus the concrete subjects entered into a relationship with the particular divine powers in their general essentiality, ⟨and at the same time [these powers stood] in immediate identity with them,⟩ whereas in the mysteries their relationship was with the *universal* divine nature, and the subjective essence, the universal inner soul of the individual, achieved its satisfaction. But behind the individual there is still | its 90 wholly particular, individual mode of action, state, condition, and it continues to refer these to God in accordance with the *objective* category that we call divine providence insofar as it extends to individual cases—the category that is present for Christians in providence, or more precisely in the divine essence, that God became a human being, and moreover did so in the wholly actual, temporal fashion that encompasses all private singularity along with it.¬²⁰⁴ The beautiful shape in which the gods were depicted in images,

203. W₂ *reads:* it is their doing, their decision, although they also know it to be contingent

204. W₂ *reads:* 3. But however much the worshipers become aware of their immediate identity with the essential powers, appropriate divinity to themselves, and rejoice over its presence in them and theirs in it—even though they consume the natural deities and make the ethical deities visible in ethical or community life, even though they live the divine life in practice and in their festival celebrations produce the shape and appearance of divinity in their own subjectivity—however much they do all this, there is still something beyond all of it, that is (for consciousness) held back, that which is quite particular in the individual's actions, states, and conditions and the reference of these conditions to God. Our belief in [divine] providence, that it extends also to what is single, individual, finds its confirmation in the fact that God became a human being, and moreover did so in the actual, temporal fashion that encompasses all private singularity along with it; for in this way subjectivity received the absolute moral justification by virtue of which it is the subjectivity of *infinite* self-consciousness.

stories, and local representations does, it is true, comprise and express in an immediate way the moment of infinite singularity, of the most extreme particularity. But it is a particularity that, for one thing, constitutes a major ground of complaint against the mythology of Homer and Hesiod;[205] and for another thing, these stories are so completely peculiar to the particular gods depicted in them that they in no way concern the other gods, or human beings—just as among humans all individuals have their own particular circumstances, actions, states and histories, which are wholly private to them. The moment of subjectivity is not present as *infinite* subjectivity. ⟨In the first place, wisdom is lacking.⟩ It is not spirit as such that is intuited in the objective shapes; but it is wisdom that must constitute the basic character of the divine. The divine must be comprehended as operating for a purpose, [as encompassed] in one infinite wisdom—[i.e.,] the one subjectivity that is the concept. That human affairs are ruled by the gods certainly forms part of Greek religion, but in a [57a] more general, indeterminate sense. For it is precisely the gods who *are* the powers that hold sway in all human affairs; and, of course, the gods are just. Justice is an old, titanic power; as justice it is *one* power, so it belongs to the senior among them. The beautiful gods insist on their own particular validity,[206] and so fall into collisions, which can only be resolved in an | *equality* of honor; and just for that reason this offers no immanent solution, it does not invest wisdom with any systematic unity that Zeus [holds sway] in everything (Sophocles, *Antigone:* ⟨οὐδὲν ὅτι μὴ Ζεύς⟩[207]).

91

(β) The divine [is] characterized as spirit ⟨(and is gracious [to us] in sacrificing itself)⟩, but not yet as wisdom, i.e., it is spirituality

205. [*Ed.*] Xenophanes, in a fragment transmitted by Sextus Empiricus, *Adversus mathematicos* 9.193, advanced this criticism (Xenophanes, frag. 11 in Kirk, Raven, and Schofield, *The Presocratic Philosophers,* p. 168: the Homeric and Hesiodic gods steal, lie, commit adultery, etc.) See also Plato's criticism of Homer, *Republic* 386c–392c, 598d–607a, and Creuzer's criticism of the rambling and loquacious character of the Homeric sagas (*Symbolik und Mythologie* 1:199).

206. [*Ed.*] On the controversy between justice as "an old titanic power" and the new "beautiful" gods Apollo and Athena, Hegel elsewhere refers especially to Aeschylus's *Eumenides* (see below, 1824 lectures, n. 694); see also Sophocles, *Antigone* 451.

207. [*Ed.*] Hegel erroneously gives *Antigone* as the source of this reference; it is found, rather, at the end of Sophocles' *Trachiniae,* vv. 1277–1278 ("Yet nothing appeared that is not Zeus").

determined in and for itself, but [only] a formal willing and know-ing. All of this formal willing [of the gods], their acts and deeds, their power, [is determined] by particularity, by contingency. In the same way their knowing remains formal.

Humans could not expect these gods to be *absolutely* wise or *absolutely* true to purpose in regard to the fates of individuals; this absolute return-to-self is not posited in them. But the need to have an objective determination of their particular actions and states, of their singular fate, still remains. (α) They cannot get this from the thought of divine providence and wisdom, so as to be able to trust to it as a general rule and, for the rest, to rely on their formal knowing and willing, looking to its absolute consummation in and for itself, and finding in an eternal purpose some compensation for their unhap-piness, and for the sacrifice or failure of their particular interests or purposes. (β) For this very reason it did not fall to individuals themselves to take on their own initiative the *final* decision, make the *final* act of volition—to engage in combat today, to get married or start out on one's journey today. For each one is conscious [57b] that objectivity does not reside in this personal act of will, which is purely formal; ⟨[we are aware that there is no objective guarantee] that if carried out it would be good and right (not according to what we intended, [as the] Sophists [pointed out])⟩. In order to[208] supply this additional objective guarantee one would need to derive the determination [to act] from outside, from something higher than oneself—the decision would have to come from an external, deter-mining sign. ⟨But since the divinity that is objective in and for itself cannot be what determines [the act], | only external objectivity, the power of nature as a whole or some natural phenomenon, [can decide it[209]]. In such phenomena people find, even as they marvel, something referring to themselves, because they still ‾have no implicitly objective point of reference in a thought [such as] force or law, the connection of cause and effect, or the idea.‾[210] The rational ground of this, from a formal point of view, is the feeling of (or faith in) the identity of inner and outer—‾and here the inner

92

208. W_2 *adds:* meet the desire to fill this gap and
209. [*Ed.*] This addition is provided by W_2.
210. W_2 *reads:* see no implicitly objective meaning [in them] and do not see an implicitly complete system of laws in nature as a whole.

185

is simply human purpose and interest. ⁻²¹¹⁾ It is inner caprice which, in order not to exist as caprice, makes itself objective—what this means here is that it makes itself into something other than itself merely outwardly, it takes a contingency, i.e., external caprice, as higher than itself, and accepts some outside stimulus in order to determine itself (just as we can draw lots or throw dice). ⟨(αα)⟩ ²¹²The unexpected or sudden, some sensibly significant but inexplicable change—lightning from a clear sky, a bird that starts up against a wide, unbroken horizon, whatever breaks the indeterminacy that indecision is—is a summons to the inner [mind] to act on the instant, to be inwardly resolved in this contingent fashion, without any consciousness of the reason or ground. For it is just at this point that the grounds are broken off, or are missing altogether. (This wholly subjective need—the bubbling of springs, Mercury, to stop one's ears—the first sound.²¹³) ⟨Particular, personal purposes have validity, at a lower level than fate, as it were in a naive, innocent fashion. [One must] presuppose that the gods in their essentiality are kindly disposed to these purposes. [It is necessary to] assume a coherent plan [Zusammenhang], and because this plan cannot just be in external nature in and for itself | (since the autonomous powers of nature such as sun or sea are not harmoniously directed toward our happiness, and what is good and useful cannot be distinguished on its own account), [the Greeks were obliged] to seek it in a voice, to let it be told them.⟩

⟨(ββ)⟩ The externally immediate phenomenon that best serves the purpose of determining one's action is a sound, a note ringing out or a voice, ὄμφη (which may well be the correct derivation for Delphi's epithet ὀμφαλός rather than the latter term's other meaning, "navel of the earth").²¹⁴ The Greek oracles were primarily based

211. W₂ reads: but the inner aspect of nature, or the universal to which it stands in relation, is not the coherence of its laws but a human purpose, a human interest.

212. Precedes in W₂: So in willing something, people require an external, objective confirmation in order to grasp the resolve as actual; they require to know the resolve as one that is a unity of subjective and objective, one that is confirmed and attested as true. In this respect

213. [Ed.] See second paragraph below.

214. [Ed.] See Etienne Clavier, Mémoire sur les oracles des anciens (Paris, 1818), pp. 72–73. After citing a number of views, Clavier gives his own interpretation, which Hegel adopts: "This place is called Omphalos, navel, not because it is in the midst of the earth, but because of the divine voice, Omphē, which has been heard there."

on such sounds and rustlings (Clavier, p. 35[215]). In Dodona the future was manifested by three kinds of signs: the movement of the leaves of the sacred oak, the murmuring of the sacred spring, and a noise made by a sacred bronze cask suspended from a willow; when the wind blew, the cask was struck by a switch of bronze thongs held by the bronze figure of a child perched in an adjoining willow.[216]

In Delphi too a principal role was played by the wind that issued from a cavern [58a] and by the noise it set up in the iron tripod (see Clavier[217]). ⟨The notes [were] brought together into a connected pattern, and some meaning or other [was elicited from them]. The enthusiasm of the priestess [also played a role].⟩ [But] the inspiration the Pythia received through the cavern exhalation [was] a later arrangement and representation.[218] ⟨[These are] very naive oracles: Αἱ τῶν δαιμόνων φωναὶ ἄναρθροι εἰσίν ([this is] the motto in Goethe's *Zur Morphologie,* vol. 2; [he] indicates where he got it from[219]).⟩ Faces may [have been seen] in Trophonius's cave.[220] Clavier, p. 6:[221] At Pharos in Achaea, Pausanias [saw] ⟨in the market⟩ a statue of Mercury that was asked for advice as follows. Incense was burnt on the altar and lamps were lit, then one whispered one's question into the god's ear, then ran from the market, holding one's hands over one's ears;[222] once out of the marketplace one took them away, and the first word that one heard was the answer to one's | question. ⟨Consulting sacrificial animals or inspecting entrails[223]   94

215. [*Ed.*] Ibid., p. 35.

216. [*Ed.*] Ibid., p. 31.

217. [*Ed.*] Ibid., pp. 73–75.

218. [*Ed.*] Ibid., p. 75. Cf. also the report of Diodorus Siculus, *Bibliotheca historica* 16.26.

219. [*Ed.*] J. W. Goethe, *Zur Naturwissenschaft überhaupt, besonders zur Morphologie,* vol. 2 (Stuttgart and Tübingen, 1823), back of the title page. Goethe, however, did not give the source; Dorothea Kuhn has since identified it as Nonnos, *Ad S. Gregorii orationem contra Julianum* 2.22; see Hegel, *Religionsphilosophie,* ed. K.-H. Ilting (Naples, 1978), p. 720. The marginal note in which this reference occurs obviously postdates 1821.

220. [*Ed.*] See Clavier, *Mémoire,* pp. 140–160, and esp. his translation on pp. 143–144 of the report by Pausanias, *Description of Greece* 9.39.

221. [*Ed.*] Clavier, *Mémoire,* p. 6, referring to Pausanias, *Description of Greece* 7.22.

222. *Ms. margin:* ⟨[For instance] Procos held [hands over ears]⟩

223. [*Ed.*] See the exhaustive description of the practice of inspecting entrails in Karl Philipp Moritz, *Anthousa; oder, Roms Alterthümer* (Berlin, 1791), pp.

[involves] a more remote connection. [It would] take us too far afield to enter into this sort of detail. [For instance,] earth tremors [were oracular signs for] the Lacedaemonians [Spartans]. If the first sacrificial animals yielded unlucky omens, further animals [were slaughtered] until favorable omens occurred. In this way the future shrouded in darkness had ultimately to accommodate itself after all to the desires of mortals (Moritz, *Anthousa,* p. 353[224]). [What matters is] not this reasoning—[for] the repetition is highly inconsequential—but the sense, the subjective confirmation.⟩ In Egypt, [when consulting] Apis one offered him food in one's hand. If he took it, [that was] a good sign; from Germanicus ([Clavier,] p. 4[225]) he turned away, and Germanicus died soon after. On the other hand, eating birds and the like is primarily a feature of Roman superstition.

Such are the main features of the religion of beauty. All aspects of the totality are present and find satisfaction in it. But the central point is the particular, personified [*partikuläre*] form of divine power; ⟨the god has advanced beyond both the substantive unity of the natural and the spiritual, and the abstractness of the One;⟩ ⟨human beings [are] free,⟩ ⟨and [there is] therefore an antithesis. The main feature [is], of course, the consciousness inherent in spirituality, [but there is] an antithesis (though it is only theoretical)—(α) particular gods (β) over against human beings [who are also particular]. But this antithesis is resolved amicably; and Greek religion [is] the consciousness, certainty, and enjoyment of this amicable settlement. [We do] not yet [have] infinite estrangement and universal spirit.⟩ This [divine power] thus [appears] as human shape. It is overwhelmingly characterized by spirituality, but the universal spirit is still lacking—i.e., this spirituality taken back into the absolute unity of subjectivity.

The basic abstract category [is here] necessity. The next higher

---

350–353, as well as the brief history of the practice of divination or soothsaying in Etruria and Rome by Petrus Frandsen, *Haruspices* (Berlin, 1823).

224. [*Ed.*] Moritz, *Anthousa,* p. 353 (at the end of the description of inspecting entrails).

225. [*Ed.*] Clavier, *Mémoire,* p. 4, referring to Pliny, *Historia naturalis* 7.71. Germanicus Caesar was a Roman general and heir apparent of his uncle, the emperor Tiberius; he died suddenly in somewhat mysterious circumstances in A.D. 19.

determining category is freedom, the concept and infinite subjectivity, but the concept as still finite—purpose, power determined by the concept, but according to a finite concept, a finite purpose. [58b] | 95

[226]This category [the religion of expediency] is directly contiguous to the religion of beauty. The meaning or abstract definition of the God of beauty is a quality (a power and property that are also human, immanent in humanity) and a spiritual power, inwardly determined as such, and in such a way that this determinateness exists as subjective; it is distinguished from objectivity initially in such a way that objectivity is the first kind of determinacy that is to be realized, while subjectivity exists as the formal power to posit this reality of the particular content, to make it objective for itself.

[227]This content is still, to begin with, determinate and finite, the concept of *formal* subjectivity. Hence the content becomes a finite, human purpose. [In the] religion of beauty [we have] determinate but free powers, [which, however,] float away; their ideal beauty, the universal [is] higher than their particular character: Mars is also willing to agree to peace. [They are] gods of phantasy, for the passing moment, and have no consistency, within themselves or on their own account. Now they come forward—Pallas, wisdom [is here]—then she returns again to Olympus. (There is a circle of twelve gods, but without [logical sequence].)

[228]But insofar as the basic category is purpose, determinateness is conserved; and being taken back into the infinite form, into infinite subjectivity, it is fixed.

In and for itself, however, finitude is not firmly fixed in the pure concept, the universal [concept], but only in humanity, in the spirit as finite. [The finitude is] human purposes.

Hence religion falls to the level of serving determinate purposes and interests; it stems from them and depends on them. [59a] | 96

226. *Ms. adds as a heading:* C. Religion of Expediency, or Initially of Self-Seeking, Self-Advantage
Ms. margin adjacent to the heading: ⟨(a) [Immediate Religion] / (b) Religion of Sublimity and Beauty⟩
Ms. margin adjacent to this line: ⟨(α) The concept [of] expediency⟩
[*Ed.*] Hegel initially started Sec. C at the top of sheet 58b, but then wrote a transitional passage and started the section again at the top of sheet 59a. We give the heading only once, in the latter location.
227. *Ms. margin:* ⟨(β) Finite [purposes]⟩
228. *Ms. margin:* ⟨(γ) Human [purposes]⟩

C. THE RELIGION OF EXPEDIENCY
OR UNDERSTANDING[229]

Purposive action is a distinctive feature not just of spirit but of life in general. It is the idea in action, for it is a kind of production that is no longer a transition into something else (whether that other is determined implicitly as something else, or—as in the case of necessity—implicitly determined as the same, though it is other in shape and externally). In purpose a content is there first, not dependent on the form of the transition or change, but maintaining itself therein. ⌐[In the case of] living form, the seed [is] the plant nature, its driving power; the influence of air, water, etc., brings it forth, but what they bring forth is only its development, [and this bringing forth is only] an empty form, the transition from subjectivity to objectivity. The seed germ is the preformed shape that manifests itself. [That is] how it is in the spiritual realm too.⌐[230]

⟨(α)⟩ Of itself, purposive action stands very close to the kind of spiritual form or shape we have been considering. What matters,

229. *Ms. margin:* ⟨27 July 1821⟩

[*Ed.*] The term *Zweckmässigkeit* is translated as both "expediency" and "purposiveness." When used as a title for Roman religion, it is translated as "expediency," but in the textual exposition it is more commonly rendered as "purposiveness" (and *zweckmässig* as "purposive"), thus preserving the affinity with "purpose" (*Zweck*). Literally, *Zweckmässigkeit* means "conformity to an end or purpose." Hegel's use of the term is directly influenced by Kant's discussion of extrinsic purposiveness and natural teleology in *The Critique of Judgement,* trans. J. C. Meredith (Oxford, 1952), §§ 63, 66, 79–86. Since, in the context of Hegel's treatment of Roman religion, *Zweckmässigkeit* refers to extrinsic rather than intrinsic purposiveness, "expediency" is an appropriate translation for it. See below, 1824 lectures, n. 466.

In the *Ms.* (and only in the *Ms.*), Hegel also designates Roman religion as "the religion of the understanding" (*Verstand*). It is such because the purposes or ends in view are essentially finite (even though allegedly divine); and it is the understanding that holds fast to finite purposes, neither submerging them in necessity nor resolving them in reason. Roman religion is, therefore, a "prosaic" religion, not a religion of free phantasy, of free spirit, of beauty.

Hegel devotes more attention to the religion of expediency in the *Ms.* than he does on any subsequent occasion—fourteen manuscript sheets, or nearly half the number used for the Christian religion. The probable reasons for this are indicated in the Editorial Introduction.

230. W₂ *reads:* The driving power of this plant nature, which may express itself outwardly under the influence of a wide variety of conditions, is just the bringing forth of its own development, and is only the simple form of the transition from subjectivity to objectivity. It is the shape preformed in the seed germ that reveals itself in the result.

however, is the inner concept (and human beings are as well able [as other living things] to act instinctively according to habit and custom). This [instinctive, Greek] shape is the original, superficial way in which a [spiritual] nature and spiritual determinacy make their appearance, without this determinacy being yet present itself as such in the mode of the idea or of purpose—⟨[there is] still not an estrangement⟩.

⟨(β)⟩ The abstract categorial foundation of the religion of beauty was necessity and, outside necessity, the fullness of spiritual | and 97
physical nature. Being physical, this fullness decomposes into ⁻[a multitude of] characteristics and qualities⁻²³¹ and is not held within the unity of necessity, even as that unity is, by itself, devoid of content. ⟨So these characteristics and qualities take root in themselves, and it is only their spiritual form and ideality which gives them the serenity that both lifts them above their determinacy and makes them indifferent.⟩ In other words, necessity is only implicitly freedom; it is not yet wisdom, it has no inner purpose; in necessity we liberate ourselves only to the extent that we relinquish the content [of our purpose]. [59b] What is necessary, however, is *some* content—an encounter, a situation, an achievement, whatever it may be; provided it *exists,* its content as such can be a matter of contingency. ⟨In the freedom of necessity the content is *relinquished,* given up as formal; now it is going to be preserved.⟩ The content can be this purpose or another; what is necessary is the formal requirement that there should be a content; what the content is does not matter. The necessity [is] simply and solely the holding fast of this abstraction.

⟨(γ)⟩ However, necessity immerses itself in the concept. The concept, freedom, is the truth of necessity—this [is] logical. [By] conceiving in general we mean comprehending something as one moment in a coherent pattern, which as coherent [implies] differentiation and is determinate, is fulfilled or realized. Coherence in terms of cause and effect is just the coherence of necessity; it is external necessity, i.e., it is merely formal. What it lacks is that a content is posited as determined on its own account, *traversant ce changement de cause en effet sans changer,*²³² one that passes through the alternation of cause and effect without changing (not merely in itself, but as a con-

231. W₂ *reads:* determinate time and quality
232. [*Ed.*] This citation cannot be referenced.

tent that is posited [as unchanging]). More precisely, this comes about in that the external relationship, the variety of actual shapes [that the content assumes] is degraded to the level of medium or means. 98 ⟨It [is] *mediated* with itself.⟩ A purpose needs to have means, | i.e., an external mode of effectuation that is, however, defined as subjected to the movement of the purpose, the movement by which the purpose maintains itself and sublates the transition [from cause to effect]. At the level of mechanism, cause and effect are implicitly the same content, but are posited as independent actualities that interact with one another (objectivity).

As identity with self, in opposition to the phenomenal difference between the shapes (found in actuality), this is thus a *posited* identity. So with purposive action, nothing is produced that is not already there beforehand: what is there just maintains itself. Life is a continual process of production, of bringing forth; but nothing is brought forth that is not already there. [With] individual and species it is the same. In a mechanical chain [of causes], however, something other than what is already there does emerge. Freedom therefore [is found] in concepts; necessity [is] downgraded to the form, to the transition from the subjectivity of purpose to objectivity. [60a]

[233]This is just where the difference between purpose and reality lies in the [concept of] purpose. The purpose maintains itself, it is mediated only with itself, it coincides only with itself, and it brings about its own unity—as subjective—with reality. However, it does this only through *means,* or through a process of necessity. Purpose is the power to dispose of means, the power that has at the same time an initial content determined in and for itself, a content that is both starting point and goal, the mode of necessity that has taken the external, particular content into itself and holds it fast against reality, which is defined in a negative manner, and reduced to the rank of means.

In life there is this unity of content that continually conquers reality, and through this use of violence frees itself from violence, and maintains itself; but the content is not free on its own account, not elevated into the mode of its identity in the element of thought— [i.e.,] it is not spiritual. In the ideals that are spiritually formed, there

233. *Ms. adds:* (β)

is the same unity, but at the same time it is present and represented as free. As beauty, that unity is higher than what is living, and its quality [may] from that point of view also [be represented] as purpose, and what it produces [as] purposive action. But its qualities are not represented in the guise of purposes. For example, it is not the *purpose* of Apollo or Pallas to produce and disseminate artifacts, science, or poetry; and Ceres and the Bacchus of the mysteries do not aim | to teach or to produce laws. They are the guardians of those things, so to speak; it is their care— μεδόνται—[to protect] a town or locality—Delphi, the island of Delos, or, [in the case of] Bacchus, Thebes. The category of purpose is very close at hand, but the separation of purpose from reality (and consequent conquest of reality) is not present here. The divine natures are precisely these powers and activities; the muses themselves *are* poetry, Athena herself *is* the life of Athens, ˉand so on.ˉ²³⁴ [60b] [They] operate immanently in their reality, like the laws of motion in the planets (e.g., Pallas in Homer). ˉHuman beings are not means, nor do [the gods]ˉ²³⁵ stand over against one another but themselves vanish out of sight in necessity. Every so often one of them—Mars, Neptune, Pallas—steps forth under Jupiter, like honest rough yeomen under their commander; they strut about importantly, but they submit to discipline, are called to order, accept the decision, and go off home, [as] Mars [went back] to Thrace, etc.

99

⟨(α) Purpose [is] posited as the identity of different actualities, as a unity determined in and for itself, that maintains its own determinateness as opposed to other forms of determinateness; the law of necessity [is] the dependence of one determination on another; [but here] the extinction of determinacy in necessity is inhibited, annulled. The gods [are] the *powers;* they are not a *purpose.*⟩

⟨(β)⟩ But now that the concept is freely posited for itself, it is initially confronted by reality, which is determined as a negative opposed to it. [Later on,] in the absolute concept or the pure idea, this reality, this hostile element, melts into unity, into friendship with

234. W₂ *reads:* and the happiness and well-being of the city is not her purpose. Rather these powers

235. W₂ *reads:* Moreover, in the same way that the gods are not means at the stage [constituted by the religion] of beauty, so they do not

the concept; it takes its distinctive character back and is itself freed in that way from being only a means.

But, to begin with, the purpose itself is still immediate, formal. Its first categorial determination is that what is thus inwardly determinate should exist on its own account, initially in opposition to reality, and that it should realize itself in reality as something | that resists. In other words it is initially a finite purpose, and the relationship [of divine purpose to the world] is a relationship of the understanding, and the religion that has this kind of foundation is the *religion of the understanding.* ⟨The transition to the category of *purpose* is extremely important; for the first time [we have here] a genuinely independent ideality.⟩

We have already seen²³⁶ something very near, very similar to this kind of purpose and religion in the religion of the One. ⟨The worshipers, as God's people, are themselves only means; they are not taken up into his will, as his purpose generally or as its fulfillment, because they are human as such—i.e., [there is] nothing in any way determinate [in his will]. [This is] a religion of the understanding inasmuch as the one God is abstract, and this thought is set over against all reality; the Jewish religion [is] a religion of the most stubborn, lifeless understanding. So there [is] a purpose [in it]—the one God who maintains himself. But the purpose [is] entirely general. (α) [It is just] the glorification of God's name, ⟨the fact that God exalts his name.⟩ [It is] *formal,* [it possesses] no content, no idea, [it is] not determined in and for itself, [but is] only an abstract manifestation. There is also, to be sure, a determinate purpose, [but] only in the way that a servant is a purpose for his master, not a content of God himself, not *his* purpose, not a divine determinacy.⟩ (β) [As for] God's people, the singularity of this people [is that] they are only the content of a [divine] purpose on account of their worship, and this purpose is one that is completely incomprehensible. [61a]

a. Abstract Concept

God is the essence that acts in accordance with a purpose, so he has definite purposes in the world. What God purposes and wills are

236. [*Ed.*] See above, pp. 127–129, 134.

finite things and states. God is what is *wise,* but not yet absolute wisdom.

This offers us a *teleological* way of regarding the world ⟨([and a teleological] proof of God's existence)⟩. (In the world in general [there are] such wise orderings, such a harmony and concordance between one conditioned thing and another. | Qua finite, the living, 101 spiritual being [has] infinitely many needs, depends in infinitely many ways on other things that are independent of it. These forms of dependence, the most manifold diversity of the qualities, presupposes that there is an equally manifold diversity in the corresponding things.) It also affords us a way of recognizing God in the wise ordering of nature, a proof of God's existence from this purposive arrangement of nature.

Before we study this new departure, this new way of interpreting things more closely, [we should] first point out that we are later going to examine the more determinate form of religion based on finite purposiveness. But, as in the case of necessity, what has to be considered here first is this categorial determination generally, to the extent that it is a determination of the divine essence; and with respect to it we have to notice what its place is, namely, a subordinate position, under a higher concept.

The first question is, of what kind are these finite purposes? They are to be sought in the natural and spiritual world, not in the nature of God himself, because they are finite. And for this reason the definition of them lies outside God, and God is seen as an understanding, operating in nature, that orders and regulates them.

More precisely, the significance of this external purposiveness is as follows. [61b] ⟨As we have defined it, the realization of the purpose [consists in] something else.⟩ Purpose is the self-sustaining unity of the concept, but in finite purpose ⟨the purposive relationship⟩ is one of external purposiveness; the means [is] the something else in and through which the purpose is realized, something external, and unity is not immanent in it, but external.[237] The teleological view of the world exhibits organic living creatures realizing themselves in the

237. [*Ed.*] The distinction between internal (intrinsic) and external (extrinsic) purposiveness is based primarily on Kant's *Critique of Judgment,* §§ 82, 63, 66.

natural realm as *conditioned*. They carry on their life, their concept by means of an inorganic nature, which occurs quite independently and contingently as far as they are concerned; they realize themselves uniquely in an infinitely manifold diversity, which must be matched by a nature that is no less infinitely diverse in its qualities | ⟨—for they are needy, dependent in an infinitude of ways—⟩ but that has on its own account no relation to their diversity. The conditions [of life are] (α) contingent objects, of themselves unrelated [to the life they condition], (β) yet [they are] necessary for an other. Thus plants need air, water, soil, etc., animals need food, a form of habitation, they relate to the air etc. in different ways. Again, animals are in themselves a manifold of organs and members; as life that is poured out into multiplicity, their needs [assume] an infinite variety of specific forms, ⟨[and remain] in themselves contingent in regard to it. The more singularized, the more particularized the forms, species, and modes of life of animals, the more they are contingent; for the more something else is equally possible, so much the more does diversity become possible *ad infinitum,* especially of conditioned, dependent [forms].⟩ Their external conditions too assume an infinite variety of specific forms; and the more specific they are, the more contingent they appear. A creature's relationship to the air for purposes of respiration does not appear so contingent as, for example, that a particular animal or insect should feed on only one species of plant, and that this should be there for it to feed on, or conversely that a particular organic structure should be suited to the particular elements of air and water. ⟨The specific character of the needs themselves, e.g., the construction of cells by bees and ants, or the need to hibernate, appears as an instinct that is contingent for the physical form in which it is found—[indeed, it is] contingent in general.⟩

In regard to human beings the same kind of concordance can be exhibited for the infinitely detailed variety of their needs. Human intelligence has devised an infinite number of means, but these means themselves must have a specified basis—iron, a particular kind of timber, etc.—to allow of their being used as the specific means for such specific needs.

Even more infinitely manifold and contingent are the circumstances which | condition, promote, further, or develop the   103
particular purposes that [contribute to] human well-being. 〈[There is] the particular spiritual vocation that one acquires〉 and internalizes; and in his maturation, progress, and development, everyone encounters particular circumstances, lives through a distinctive series or sequence of circumstances, which contribute the objective, realizing moment—what each has become; and the more contingent these [62a] circumstances are, the more miraculous their coincidence appears.

Because these coincidences are contingent, 〈what brings them to pass〉 is a tertium quid, quite apart from them, that links them into a chain, in such a way that certain circumstances are means in relation to the purposes [of our lives].

But the question at hand is this: among this multiplicity of vocations 〈and [modes of] existence〉, which are the purposes? 〈In general terms, which among the manifold existents is the means and which is the end? Purposive relation [is] not just a linkage, but a linkage in which one term is essential and the other inessential.〉 Purposes are the independent ideas that form a totality within themselves; the first natural purposes are living creatures. [Their purpose is] that life should be, that it should sustain and enjoy itself; the natural elements such as air, light, and water are not purposes within themselves, nor is the nature that is still inorganic even though it is individualized—[it is life that] is this self-sustaining unity [of] the concept and its process of return back into itself.

To a still greater extent, however, human beings are purpose, first as living creatures, second as thought. For [it is] precisely thought, whatever lies in it and is rooted within it, [that is] inwardly infinite purpose unto itself. [Thought can be] formal or objective too, according to the content; but the *absolute purpose* of human subjectivity is the absolute objectivity | of self-consciousness 〈(the in-   104
finite, ultimate, self-contained final purpose)〉, be it characterized as ethical perfection, a religious life or eternal life, i.e., the divine life of blessedness.

This is no finite purpose but the purpose of absolute spirit, that

197

"you must be perfect as he [your heavenly Father] is perfect" [Matt. 5:48]—for perfection is life in God, likeness to God, the mode in which God himself as spirit is realized in his community, or in subjective self-consciousness.

But at the point where we now stand, this kind of purpose is excluded because it is not yet present. Here we have only the finite purposes of nature and of human arrangements and the destinies of peoples and individuals, and these are accordingly here the field in which divine wisdom and providence are initially recognized and from which the very existence of a God is inferred. [62b]

It is a simple, natural process of thought to feel, to surmise, to recognize in this ⟨infinitely manifold⟩ harmony of relationships—of inorganic to organic nature and of both to human purposes—a higher, deeper principle, that of wisdom working according to a purpose.

But this implies that the concept of purpose must have emerged into human self-consciousness. In the Book of Job or the Psalms, for example, it is only the power of God that is especially singled out and lauded in natural phenomena, elementary and organic alike. This more definite awareness of purposive relations we find especially in Socrates;[238] in him this concept has emerged essentially in opposition to the earlier mechanistic view. The principle that he sets against the primordial elements as causes is the *good,* i.e., what is self-appointed purpose and conforms thereto.

"What is obviously useful, does this seem to thee a work of chance, τύχης, or of an understanding, γνώμης?" ⟨(Xenophon, *Memorabilia,* end of book I (Latin translation, p. 310; Greek, Stephanus, p. 422).[239]⟩ "God has [given] human beings | eyes to see, ears to

105

238. [*Ed.*] Hegel here briefly summarizes an important theme in his portrayal of Socrates, which is much more fully developed elsewhere; see *Lectures on the History of Philosophy* 1:411 ff., 405 ff., 385 (*Werke* 14:75 ff., 69 ff., 43). But the conception of the good as "self-appointed purpose" can scarcely be supported adequately from the sources. On p. 387 (p. 46), Hegel himself distinguishes the higher view of the good of Plato and Aristotle from that of Socrates, who accepted the good only in the particular sense of the practical.

239. [*Ed.*] Xenophon, *Memorabilia* 1.4.4. This reference is not found at the "end of Book I," since the latter has seven chapters. The edition Hegel used did not distinguish chapters, hence the rather vague reference.

hear, and so on, eyelids to close to protect the eyes when danger threatens, eyebrows so that the sweat of their brow should not run into their eyes, and so forth."[240] (What is petty in the teleological way of looking at things is immediately apparent here too. Even in the most limited form of life there are an infinite number of consequences and logical connections that tend to its preservation. If we make these consequences into purposes, [a matter of] utility, we are struck by the pettiness of the purposes, purposes that at the same time we are making into an aim of God. A divine aim must have an appropriate content. Thus, rosebushes and sloetrees have thorns, [whose] purpose [is] to protect them against the beasts; and the beasts [too have] their weapons. But the weapons are of no avail. All of them that are purposes [are] a means as well. But in general the contemplation of nature as living and growing, the life of the animal realm with its infinitely manifold organization and the specific ways in which it is organized so as to maintain itself, fill us with the thought of something higher altogether, something inward, not a mechanical linkage with an external cause. It is another way of thinking [that leads] to miracle; [this is] to make nothing the causal link—i.e., a linkage of this kind is natural.

This transition of thought from the purposive ordering of nature to a *cause* that operates according to purposes, in such a way as to arrive at a particular form of the moments it comprises and the way in which they are differentiated, [constitutes]

The Teleological Proof of God's Existence

⟨Kant, p. 650:[241] "The present world opens up to us such an immeasurable spectacle of diversity, order, purposefulness, and beauty, whether we pursue these in the infinite extent of space or in its limitless subdivision, that even with the knowledge that our weak understanding has succeeded in gaining of it, language is already at a loss to convey so many and such incomprehensibly | 106 great wonders, numbers cannot measure them, and even our thoughts cannot circumscribe them, so that our judgment of the whole

240. [*Ed.*] Ibid., 1.4.5–6 (not an exact quotation).
241. [*Ed.*] Slightly altered quotation from Kant, *Critique of Pure Reason,* B 650. Translation ours.

necessarily dissolves into a speechless but all the more eloquent astonishment. On all sides we see a chain of effects and causes, of ends and means, a regular pattern of coming about and passing away; and since nothing has arrived by itself at the state in which it presently is, it always points back to something else as its cause; and this cause necessarily commits us to the same inquiry; so that the entire totality must inevitably sink into the abyss of nothingness unless we assume something outside of this sphere of infinite contingency, something that subsists on its own account, primitively and independently, which has upheld it and being the cause of its genesis has at the same time assured its permanence.") [63a]

Kant, p. 651:[242] "This proof deserves at all times to be mentioned with respect. It is the *oldest* (? ⟨No!⟩), the clearest, and the one best suited to the common reason of humanity. It brings the study of nature to life just as it gets its own being from that study, and continually derives new force from it." ⟨However, dry description does not of itself suffice. [The study of nature] derived principally from and has been stimulated by the teleological proof; natural history was not regarded as worth spending time on unless it revealed something deeper, a link with the concept. Natural history [has been] treated in a wholly teleological fashion: [there is] testaceo-theology, helmintho-theology, crustaceo-entomo-theology.⟩ "This proof adduces purposes and intentions where our observation would not have discovered them by itself, and extends our knowledge of nature through the guiding thread of a particular unity, the principle of which lies outside nature. But this knowledge reacts again upon its cause, viz., on the idea that has led to it, and strengthens the belief in a supreme originator to the level of irresistible conviction."

P. 653:[243] "The chief points of the so-called physicotheological proof are as follows:

107 "(1) On all sides there are clear signs in the world of an | order in accord with a determinate intention, carried out with great wisdom, and in a whole whose content is indescribably varied, and whose scope is limitless in extent.

242. [*Ed.*] Exact quotations from B 651–652 except for the marginal insertions. Translation ours.
243. [*Ed.*] Slightly altered quotation from B 653–654. Translation ours.

"(2) [244]This purposive ordering is quite alien to the things of the world and is attached to them only contingently; in other words, the nature of different things could not of itself coincide,[245] through means that unite together in so many ways, to form determinate end-goals had they not been quite specifically chosen and designed for the purpose, by an ordering rational principle, according to its underlying ideas.

"(3) There exists therefore a sublime and wise cause (or more than one) that must be the cause of the world not merely as an omnipotent nature working blindly, through its fecundity, but as intelligence, through freedom.

"(4) The unity of this cause may be inferred from the unity of the reciprocal relation between the different parts of the world, as members in one single edifice constructed by art—inferred with certainty as far as our observation extends, and beyond that with probability, in accordance with all the premises of analogy." [63b] | 108

Kant's critique[246] [takes the following form].

(α) [The proof concerns] "only the contingency of the form, but not of the matter, the substance in the world"—⟨[it] extends [as far as an] architect of the world. In any case [there is] some more metaphysics [here] in that it assumes a matter independent of its

244. *Ms. margin:* ⟨Thus [they are] independent, reciprocally indifferent existents. Their relation [to the order of nature] is not *their* mode of determinate being but an *other*—not *their* existence

[But] the ordering [itself] – sun, living creature, food

Psychological proof – see below⟩

[*Ed.*] See below, n. 251.

245. *Ms. margin:* ⟨In other words, the products of nature are independent.

(α) They have a specific mode of organization, yet they are not posited as *products* (as produced by human or some other agency; owing to their wholly specific, nonindependent particularity [they occur rather] immediately as posited).

(β) [They are] logically connected with, conditioned by something else. [For example, they need] food, but [that is] not brought about by themselves, and [is] indifferent to any such relation, [just as] the sunshine or rivers [are indifferent] to our employment of them. [This has] infinitely far-reaching consequences for a higher being that is a purpose in itself, [i.e., for] humanity; it is not the sun that appoints the purpose for this higher being, or that posits this logical connection, for the determination of human activity does not lie in it. But neither is it humanity that appoints the purpose for its own concerns, and brings forth these means⟩

246. [*Ed.*] Cf. Kant, *Critique of Pure Reason,* B 654–655.

qualities. Matter without form [is] a non-thing. Admittedly, abstracting from all form, [I] can think of [matter as] eternal, unalterable, devoid of all determinacy: [but it] is then a product of reflection and not something that subsists ([and the same is true of] finite, active form without matter); in any event the thought [is] false—this matter [is] itself a determination of form. What is form, what are its forms? Identity [falls] under this heading. [But form] itself [is] identity. We must get beyond the separating of form and matter from each other as independently real. Here, in any event, purposes and purposiveness are determined by the purposefully operating cause—*soul,* substantiality; matter is only something external, or rather simply a determination of the form, one moment implicit in the concept.⟩

(β) [247]"The argument proceeds from the order and purposiveness so universally observed in the world, as a purely contingent arrangement, to the existence of a cause proportionate to them. Expressions of 'very great,' 'astounding,' or 'immeasurable power and excellence' give no determinate concept at all, only a representation of relationship. Now I do not suppose that anyone would be bold enough to claim insight into the relationship between what he observes of the world's magnitude (in extent and in content alike) and *omnipotence,* between the world order and *supreme* wisdom, or between the unity of the world and the *absolute* unity of its author. Physicotheology is therefore unable to give any determinate concept of the supreme cause of the world." One starts from "amazement at the magnitude of the power, wisdom, etc., of the author of the world"[248] and then, getting no further, leaps over to *infinite* wisdom and absolute reality.

⟨[This critique is] justified. The content consists in a multitude of determinate purposes, and this does not lead to a single purpose that is determinate in and for itself, inwardly infinite, such as would not only (perhaps) contain them all within itself but to which they would be subordinate—absolute, infinite wisdom. Purposive relation 109 | [is] infinite in form but not in content; [infinite] content [is] determinate unity maintaining itself. But even if [the purposive relation

247. [*Ed.*] Abbreviated and slightly altered quotation from B 655–656. Translation ours.
248. [*Ed.*] Cf. B 657.

is infinite in] form,⟩ [the physicotheological proof must take] refuge elsewhere—[namely in] the ontological proof, [where] the starting point [is] the supremely real essence; [it is] the most universal content.[249]

This harmony of purposiveness (α) has nothing *true* in it, i.e., it is not the immediately sensible, external [truth], that which is external to itself—here there is only a manifold of independent, mutually indifferent purposes; (β) is not [true] for *reflection*, [i.e., not] necessity (the form of reflection is a nexus in which identity is not posited); (γ) here, however, [the harmony is] the rational nexus of the concept, or determinacy maintaining itself in being other than itself.

Here [we have been considering] the idea that subsists in and for itself, rationality, *inner purposiveness*.

⟨*External purposiveness* [is] the understanding in general, the identity of thought with itself, maintaining itself against reality, transforming reality and determining it in accordance with itself. Kant does not here attack this relationship as one of finitude, [involving] only a proportionate, not an infinite cause. Certainly, the purposes [are] finite, but for the purposefully working cause not to be a proportionate cause, all that is needed is to view the finite purposes as subordinate, i.e., in another frame of reference to regard them once again as means and to recognize the highest, absolute, final purpose in which everything is unified.

When we look more closely, this proof or inference is made up as follows: (α) that there is a purposive arrangement in nature is a fact; (β) it is not due to these things themselves; (γ) therefore it is due to an other.⟩

This cause then is something other than nature; this [inference] depends on the metaphysics of nature, as though the nature of the thing were not itself this concept, this vitality, or this spirituality, but all essential coupling of the concept and its external reality, the conditions [of its realization], lay outside the nature of the thing. ⟨It is not at all the concept of organic nature [that we have here].⟩

249. [*Ed.*] A probable reference to Kant's claim in the passage immediately following the preceding citation that the physicotheological proof, failing in its undertaking, falls back upon the cosmological proof and ultimately upon the ontological. See B 657.

Then admittedly this connectedness, this order [is] external—merely a third existent. [64a]

Kant[250] [defines] what is living as self-appointed purpose, *causa sui,* all | [its] purpose and means in itself, producing and sustaining itself. ⟨External, inorganic nature [is] independent, as are the meager structures [of] insects or the numerous species of willows, oaks, lilies, and so on. (In theory [these forms of nature] are to be esteemed as highly; but in practice who does not kill flies or eat chicken, lamb, or beef? [If they] esteem mere life so highly, human beings will necessarily die.) As if these living creatures, because they assume the form of self-relating independence, were [really] independent of one another, and as if their nature, [the nature] of the thing, emerged from the concept producing itself within them, rather than both emerging merely as moments [of the concept].⟩

In spirit too the ordinary consciousness is struck by the fact that this organic, living unity is the nature of the thing. I remember hearing a lecture in which a professor of natural theology[251] gave a psychological proof of the existence [of God], as follows. There is such a great variety of human properties and powers—sensibility, understanding, reason, will, desire, instincts, [human nature is] itself so manifold. For all this to be unified, [something external is required]; it does not [lie in] the nature of their thinghood [*die Natur ihrer Sache*] to be one. [They need] a third outside [themselves] that disposes them in such a way and at the same time attunes them—a

250. [*Ed.*] Hegel is here attempting to modify Kant's criticism of the physicotheological proof in the *Critique of Pure Reason* by means of introducing the concept of vitality as inner, organic purposiveness, thereby bringing to the surface the externality of the coordination consisting in well-ordered world, ordering creator, and the point of view of proportionality. On the concept of inner purposiveness, see the passages referred to above, n. 237. The mention of the *causa sui* in this connection is an apparent reference to Kant's *Critique of Judgment,* § 64. But Hegel does not refer to Kant's reservations about or further delimitation of the concept of a purpose of nature, § 65.

251. [*Ed.*] It cannot be established to whom Hegel is referring here. But the psychological proof that he describes resembles a proof found in Moses Mendelssohn's *Morgenstunden; oder, Vorlesungen über das Dasein Gottes,* Part I (Berlin, 1786), esp. pp. 284–305: "XVI. Elucidation of the concepts of necessity, contingency, independence and dependence. Attempt at a new proof of the existence of God based on the incompleteness of self-knowledge." See also Vol. 3:353.

multitude of specifically distinct elements—in such a way that they match together in a harmony such as might be made by the strings of a well-tuned piano. The harmonic concordance of so many forces [must lie] outside them, which proves the existence of a third, namely God.

Now what is striking is that spirit is implicitly one. To be one is its nature, however diverse its forces may appear, ⟨however ill one thinks of spirit, even if one represents [its] manifold forces and properties to oneself as independent⟩. It is also their nature, the nature of the thing, to constitute a unity—[this unity] is fundamental [to them all].

Again, as in the case of necessity, inference [would be]:

(α) From the independence of the configurations;

(β) From what we note of their mutual relationship, the fact that they are essentially conditioned by | one another ⟨⟨[there is] dependence everywhere [but] only because the understanding presupposes the independence of the related elements—[which is a] direct contradiction⟩⟩;

111

(γ) [To] this unity external to them, in and for itself.

Rather is it the case that the conditionedness referred to under (β) sublates the independence [asserted in] (α), and reduces it to the level of a mere semblance or show. ⟨But in any event [there is] a higher idea [of spirit] than this immediate perception and reflection of the understanding.⟩

As soon as purposiveness is [taken to be] inward, immanent, or the nature of the thing, these configurations are no longer absolutely independent. ⟨Purposiveness alone [is] the nature of the thing: [it is] not these configurations as objects of perception and reflection; it is something other than them, i.e., than the merely sensible world; it is an intelligible world, a world of reason, whereas the sensible world is merely the phenomenal world. What reigns in this intelligible world is the concept, which—being infinitely articulated and divided—also constitutes the purposive connection of the parts; but the parts are themselves aspects of an absolute purpose, [so that] the purposiveness in them is only formal.⟩ But formally [regarded] ⟨—as life, or spirit in its finitude—⟩ the configurations remain finite in content, notwithstanding their purposive character. ⟨⟨Who will

205

regard an insect, [let alone] human destiny, in such a way?)⟩ [What human beings] ask for is an absolute purpose in itself, not [a goal] within their own life and existence. ⟨But this [is] a broader, higher standpoint.⟩ [64b] |

b. Configuration or Representation of the Divine Essence[252]

[253]⟨The most general basic determination of what subsists in and for itself, of what is absolutely objective [*Objektive*], is for a self-consciousness, its determination as something singular, an object [*Gegenstand*]—[this is] the mode of objectivity.⟩

⟨⟨(α)⟩⟩ When *we* say God is the power that works according to the purposes of wisdom, this has another sense than the one in which this definition of God is initially to be taken at the stage of conceptual development we have presently reached. To be precise, these purposes are limited, finite purposes in our sense too; but they are also purposes of wisdom, of the *one* wisdom, of what is good in and for itself, i.e., purposes that refer to one supreme final purpose. As a result, these limited purposes are simply subsumed under one final purpose; they, and the divine wisdom in them, are subordinated.

In the religion of expediency, however, the limitedness of the purposes is their basic character, and there is no higher category to which it is subordinate. So this religion is in no sense a religion of unity but of plurality: there is no unity of power or unity of wisdom, no *one* idea, that constitutes the basic definition of the divine nature.

⟨⟨(β)⟩⟩ The basic metaphysical definition [of the divine essence] is not as object [*Gegenstand*] in the sense of what is objective [*Objektive*] in pure thought ([i.e., it is] not for pure thought itself and in *its* element—this [is how it is] in scientific knowledge) but for representation. ⟨Hence [we have] (α) the natural element for

---

252. [Ed.] *Gestaltung, Vorstellung des göttlichen Wesens.* A freer rendering of this heading might read: "Configuration of the Divine Essence, the Forms or Shapes in Which It Is Represented." *Gestaltung* is a difficult term to translate or grasp in English. It can be defined as the representation of something in the form of a *Gestalt*, a figure or shape. The connection between "configuration" and "representation" is made explicit by this heading, and it is clear on structural grounds that Hegel here intends to treat the "concrete representation" of Roman religion.

253. *Ms. adds in margin, next to the heading:* ⟨Concrete Representation, the Form of the Idea⟩

sensible, external intuition; (β) [a representation] of human shape, the shape [that is] still more essential for the appearance of purposive action.⟩ And because the basic category is that of *particularity,* the mode of reality, or the way in which the divine is objective for [65a] consciousness as subsisting in and for itself | in accordance with the   113
idea (i.e., the *particular* mode or way), also obtains, in line with the earlier development that we have observed, in sensory representation: [there is] a throng of gods, also portrayed as present in sensible form, so that these images of gods vacillate between being merely external images for fanciful imagination and being themselves, inwardly, the immediate presence of the divine power—a vacillation that necessarily occurs everywhere to a greater or lesser degree.

⟨⟨γ⟩⟩ Thus there are in the first place the powers, gods, and images of the religion of beauty; for the finiteness of their definition [of the divine] is something common to both religions. ⟨[There is], however, an essential difference; Greek and Roman religion [are treated] habitually as one and the same,[254] but in their genuinely spiritual character [they are] essentially different. [Greek religion is] the realm of free beauty, joyous festival, and the enjoyment of divinity. Here [we find] on the contrary a preoccupation with finite purposes, an earthbound religion of [finite purposes].⟩ And here beauty is not the defining characteristic of the form or shape in which the gods are represented; serene enjoyment is not the quintessence of their cultus, just as it is not ethical power that principally characterizes their significance.

(The powers inherent in the purposes are not unconstrained [though] determinate; they are universal elementary powers that are not free powers, and the relationship to them is not one of free theoretical intuition.)

The divine essences of this sphere are practical, not theoretical gods; they are prosaic, not poetical, although, as we shall see in a moment, this stage will be the richest in continually discovering and bringing forth new gods. In point of fact, it is then *determinate*

254. [*Ed.*] Hegel is referring to an interpretation set forth in the source he relied upon most heavily, Moritz's *Anthousa.* For Moritz, Roman religion, like Greek, was a religion of cheerful and fanciful imagination, whereas for Hegel it was a religion of insipid understanding.

purposes that constitute the content of these forms or shapes. These purposes are not to be sought in physical nature, nor are they of a subhuman kind; among the many forms of existence and relationship, human existence and human relationships are the essential ones. The sun and stars and animal life [are] not ends unto themselves, whereas what is human has thought within itself; and every human final end, | no matter how inwardly insignificant it may be (to feed oneself, make life more agreeable, etc.), gives one the right to sacrifice natural things or animal life as much as one will without ado; if one is annoyed by a fly, one kills it without further ado—[yet] it is life, an organism, and can be the object of scientific observation. [65b]

And even within the gods, the purposes are not to be looked for objectively (in and for themselves) either. A purpose that is in and for itself must needs be one infinite ultimate purpose. Here [the purposes are] finite, and in the finite [world]; the finite is the root. These are *human* purposes, human requirements, either human needs or else happy ⟨circumstances or states⟩. To the extent that it is determinate, this religion owes its origin to requirement or need.

[There is] a distinction here from the preceding stage, where it was free, universal natural and ethical powers that constituted the object of veneration. Limited though they are, these powers [are] in and for themselves an objective content. In their contemplation the purposes of individuality are dissolved, and the individual is released from his needs and requirements. The powers themselves are free, and individuals achieve freedom in them; for this very reason they celebrate their identity with them, [the enjoyment of] their favor. They deserve such favor, for they are of themselves without resources vis-à-vis the divine powers. Purpose does not lie in their particularity—their needs and requirements, their well-being. As to whether their particular purposes succeed, they can only turn to oracles for the answer, and it is inherent in necessity that they [must] surrender them. Singular purposes acquire here the meaning of something negative, not subsistent in and for itself.

⁻But at this present stage, the objective powers [are] practical deities. [It is] a practical religion, a religion of utility. It is⁻[255] the

255. W *reads:* But in this religion of happiness it is

self-seeking of the worshipers that intuits itself in them as power, and that seeks satisfaction in and from them ⟨for a subjective interest⟩. | Human self-seeking ⟨(α) is inwardly determined, human beings in their particularity being infinite purpose for themselves; (β)⟩ has the feeling of its dependence,[256] precisely because it is finite, and this feeling is peculiar to it. Orientals who live in the light, Hindus who submerge their consciousness and self-consciousness in Brahmā, the Greeks who surrender their particular purposes in necessity and intuit in the particular powers those that befriend, inspire, and invigorate them, those that are united with them—all live in their religion without this feeling of dependence. Instead they are free within it, they cast away—and have cast away—their dependence; ⟨[they are] free in the presence of their God—they are within him and within him alone; outside religion [they are] dependent, but here [they have] their freedom⟩. [66a]

But self-seeking—need, requirement, subjective happiness and well-being that wills itself, holds fast to itself—⟨(α) feels itself oppressed,⟩ takes as its starting point the feeling of the dependent character of its interests; ⟨(β) at the same time [it feels] the power [to meet its needs] as a [divine] other; for subjective need, inasmuch as it also maintains itself (or its selfishness) as an end on its own account, maintains this selfish power (not the power of the One)⟩. The power to satisfy (or deny) these interests has a positive significance: it is of interest to subjective need in that its role is to fulfill the self's purposes. To this extent its sole importance is as a means of actualizing the worshiper's purposes. (There is cheating and hypocrisy in this humility because the worshiper's purposes are and are supposed to be the content of the power, *its* purpose.) Hence the attitude of consciousness in the religion of expediency is not theoretical; i.e., it does not consist in the free intuition of objectivity, or free veneration of the divine powers, but in *practical* self-seeking, ⟨the quest for the fulfillment of the singularity of this life⟩. This religion is prosaic,[257] it is a religion of the *understanding*. For it is the understanding that holds fast to finite purposes, ⟨to something

256. [*Ed.*] See below, n. 292.

257. [*Ed.*] For the interpretation of Roman religion as prosaic, Hegel refers in the *Loose Sheets* to Moritz (see below, *Loose Sheets*, n. 8); but see n. 254 above.

116   posited unilaterally by it, | concerning it alone,⟩ and neither submerges these abstractions, these singular concerns, in necessity nor resolves them in reason. The shapes in which the divine is represented in this religion are not therefore works of free phantasy, of free spirit, of beauty; they are not configurations in which precisely the antithesis between a definition in terms of the understanding (in terms of [finite] purposes) and reality is wiped out.

⟨(δ)⟩ Consequently the configuration of these spirits [the forms and shapes in which they are represented] should not be considered here separately from the cultus either. For this distinction [of the divine shapes from the cultus] and the free cultus [that belongs to them as distinct] presuppose a truth that is in and for itself, a universally objective, truly divine essence, one that subsists on its own account through its content, ⟨above and beyond particular subjective need⟩; and the cultus [is] the process by which self-consciousness gives itself the certainty of the identity of the divine essence with itself, and enjoys and celebrates this. But here interest begins from the subjective; the worshipers' needs and requirements and the dependence that they create are what make them pious, and their cultus consists in positing a *power* to help them in their need. ⟨Thus these gods have on their own account a subjective root and origin, and have an existence so to speak only in worship, in the festivals—the goddess Fornax, Pales (ovens, cattle fodder), etc.[258] Even at the level of representation this hardly constitutes independent being. However,⟩ the attempt, the hope to overcome this need through the power of these deities, the hope of obtaining satisfaction for one's requirements through their power, is only the second part of the cultus; the other, formerly objective aspect pertains to the cultus itself. [66b]

To give an example, Thucydides[259] (B. μη: The Egyptian plague in Athens) says not a word of any particular religious institutions,

---

258. [*Ed.*] On the festival of Fornax (the Fornacalia) see Moritz, *Anthousa,* pp. 44–45; on the festival of Pales (the Palilia), pp. 103–107.

259. [*Ed.*] Thucydides, *History of the Peloponnesian War* 2.47. "Equally useless" against the plague "were prayers made in the temples, consultation of oracles, and so forth; indeed, in the end people were so overcome by their sufferings that they paid no further attention to such things."

feasts, or festivals [for it, whereas] in the event of plague the Romans
consistently [devised new] gods, new forms of worship, ceremonies,
sacrifices, lectisternia.[260] | 117

So this particular area of the cultus has no distinctive, more general
interest that deserves to be considered on its own account.

c. The More Specific Nature of These Powers and Deities in General[261]

⟨(α)⟩ [262]The [divine] purpose is a determinate content, but this does
not mean just any content whatever; although finite and present to
consciousness, the purpose must inwardly be universal in its nature
(a universal need, a universal actuality). Inwardly and on its own
account it must have a higher justification than just any purpose
whatever.

But in the first place this purpose is *the state* generally, wherein
the particular purposes of individuals are subsumed and surrendered;
and secondly it is this year's harvest, [67a] ⟨not the universal powers
of nature themselves, but the concrete manifestation,⟩ the prospering
of whatever goes to satisfy the physical requirements of human beings
and promote their progress and welfare (just as in the state they have
legal protection for their property, and also the honor that custom
allots to them).

[263]⟨In regard to the state, concrete cases, singular actual [fortunes

260. [*Ed.*] The lectisternia were sacrificial festivals at which a banquet was spread
before images of the gods placed on couches. See Moritz, *Anthousa,* pp. 305, 307–309.
The *Ms.* adds an illegible word at the end of this sentence.

261. *Ms. reads:* ⟨γ⟩ *and adds in margin:* ⟨Important link to the Christian religion⟩
[*Ed.*] This section treats in detail the cultus of the religion of expediency. The
German edition changes the γ to an ε and considers this the next point in the sequence
α to δ above. There may be some basis for this since the discussion of the cultus
already is anticipated in δ, and Hegel may not have clearly differentiated between
"representation" and "cultus" in the *Ms.* (see above, n. 5). However, this γ (or c)
inaugurates a new sequence of subsection markings, and we construe it as indicating
a new phase of the discussion.

262. [*Ed.*] The text beginning here is transposed to this position by reference
marks. In the *Ms.* it is preceded by the main text on sheet 66b that is given below:
"(αα) In the preceding . . . happily carried out."

263. [*Ed.*] The following three paragraphs, through "(a) *Fortuna,*" are transposed
from the end of sheet 67a, following "inner powers," to the present position by reference
marks.

play the same role] as a prosperous harvest in regard to nature.) So this religion contains within it the more specific aspects needed to become a *political* religion. The state is a principal goal of this religion; but it is not a political religion just in the sense that, as was precisely the case at all previous levels, the people had its highest consciousness of the state and its ethical life in religion (so that veneration was due to [the gods] as free universal powers because the general institutions of the state—such as agriculture, property, and marriage—were their gift). | Instead the worship of the gods and thanksgiving is prosaically attached partly to singular determinate situations (salvation in cases of need) and actual events; and partly the religious aura in general attaches itself to all public authority, all official and state transactions. In part, however, because the operation of religion for finite purposes is itself represented in such a finite way, it is the [community's] singular decisions, undertakings, etc., in which the gods must be consulted and associated in initiating action. Superstition brings them in, in a finite mode, [67b] to give advice about everything, and since this counsel can be mediated only through human agency, this aspect of political power lies in the hands of the priests. The Romans' practice of consulting the Sibylline books, examining the flight of birds, [taking] the auspices, examining the entrails, and so on has quite a different shape and meaning from the consultations of oracles by the Greeks. The Romans had no oracles—at times they did, it is true, also consult them, but [oracles were] not a characteristic, indigenous feature in the Roman cultus.

[Let us look] briefly [at this level of cultus] in greater detail.

(a) *Fortuna*[264] [66b]

(αα) In the preceding stage of religion the universal, hovering above the particular, [was] necessity. At the present stage, in contrast, this cannot be the case. For in necessity finite purposes are sublated, whereas here they are the determining, subsistent [factor]. However, the universal is here a consenting to particular purposes; this consent in general, i.e., as itself undetermined in principle (because it is the

---

264. *Ms. margin:* ⟨(a) Fortuna see above⟩

[*Ed.*] This refers to the following four paragraphs on sheet 66b, which are transferred to this position by this reference.

purposes of single individuals and their generality is therefore only abstract), *is* fortune [*Glück*], Fortuna.

This Fortuna is not so different from necessity as to be chance or contingency (for then it would be necessity itself, in which *finite* purposes are only contingent); nor is it providence, the purposive disposition of human affairs in | general, but Fortuna with a definite 119 content. Specifically it is the happiness of purpose achieved, purpose happily carried out. ⟨This Fortuna, Fortuna Publica, is the universal prosperity that is the destiny of the Roman Empire; [this destiny is] divine—a [self-conscious] unity—Fortuna Publica. ([It is] not [the case] as Moritz says (p. 126)[265] that out of modesty they did not attribute everything to their insuperable courage and bravery but also assigned some part to fortune—*this* modesty is religion in general. What is immodest, and impious, is that this supreme essence is not for them a universal idea but this actual concern [of theirs].) The Romans were in any event entitled to regard the extension of their hegemony, the monstrous extent of their empire, as a portent, a unique condition of the world, which transcends all measure, all individuality.

Later on [it was] a celebrated theme, and one frequently discussed, as we learn from Ammianus Marcellinus,[266] whether Rome's greatness was due more to Fortuna or to her valor and sagacity. But all parties [shared] both implicitly and explicitly a clear intuition of and belief in Fortuna, the greatness of the Roman Empire; no longer [was there] any other realm to stand beside it; the Persians, Parthians, Britons, Germanic tribes, Dacians did not, in the [Roman] view, stand on the same plane; disputes and wars [were] quite marginal affairs on the frontiers—just as a house stands firm on its foundations even if rain etc. [causes damage] to the tiles, [or] an extensive estate [even if] some damage is caused here and there by wolves, and so on. No power [stood] beside Rome as her equal; [no power] threatened her existence: [she was] alone and unconquerable.

265. [*Ed.*] Moritz, *Anthousa*, pp. 126–127. The goddess of fortune, Fortuna, was worshiped under innumerable forms by the Romans, including above all Fortuna Publica since theirs (says Moritz) was the most fortunate of states.

266. [*Ed.*] Ammianus Marcellinus, *Res gestae* 14.6.3. See also Plutarch, *De fortuna Romanorum* 9.1.

[The name] Fortuna Fortis is also [to be found] (p. 167).[267] Servius Tullius, a man of the lowest estate, the son of a slave girl, erected a temple to [the goddess] Fortune; as a result he was commemorated by the common people, servants, and serving maids, who continued to rejoice at the good fortune that had befallen one of their own, so to speak.⟩ [67a]

(ββ) Second, the realization of these concrete purposes is characteristically confronted directly with failure; and since the purposes are finite, this failure is something to be feared. Ill success, misfortune in the political or physical fields, ill growth, | sickness, and so on are just as possible as prosperity and good fortune ⟨(in concrete terms fortune may be good or bad)⟩. A new categorial determination enters on the scene, that of a hostile bringer of misfortune—in general, fear for one's finite purposes. In the serene religion of art this aspect is pushed into the background; the underworld powers, ⟨which could be seen as hostile or terrible,⟩ are the Eumenides, the kindly ones, benevolent inner powers. [67b]

[268]This essence of immediate, universal actuality is accompanied by foreshadowings—but very weakly and superficially—of the worship of a higher, inner essence, a worship[269] of mysterious essences, something dread and indeterminate. [The Romans

120

267. [Ed.] Moritz, Anthousa, p. 167. The Servius Tullius mentioned in the next sentence was, according to tradition, the founder of the cult of the goddess Fortuna; we have translated Hegel's *dem Glücke* as "to [the goddess] Fortune," since it echoes Moritz's term *Glücksgöttin*.

268. *Ms. margin:* ⟨Deities without any element of phantasy⟩

269. *Ms. margin:* ⟨Rome has a secret, mystical name—ἔρως, Amor, Roma – Valentia⟩

[Ed.] See Creuzer, *Symbolik und Mythologie* 2:1002–1003. According to Creuzer, Romulus gave his city three names: a secret, mystical name (Amor, ἔρως), a priestly name (Flora or Anthusa), and a political name (Roma). The priestly name was explained by a legend: because most of the former deities did not oppose extension of the city by Tarquin, even though it meant deconsecration of their altars, soothsayers of the time felt justified in concluding that the boundaries of the city would endure forever. Thus, writes Creuzer, this city "was Flora, the flowering or flourishing, it was Valentia-Roma, the strong or vigorous." (Anthusa derives from ἄνθος, "flower," and hence is equivalent to the Latin Flora, while Valentia derives from *valeo*, "I am well.") In another work, *Abriss der römischen Antiquitäten zum Gebrauch bei Vorlesungen* (Leipzig and Darmstadt, 1824), p. 13, Creuzer refers to a legend that Rome was first called Valentia.

recognized] the abstract inwardness, [e.g.,] of right. For example, [the festival] of Bona Dea ⟨(Moritz, p. 118)⟩[270] [was held] at night in the presence of two vestal virgins in the house of one of the patricians; in this way Ops herself [was] sometimes [celebrated], the universal force of nature; ⟨[this force is] Pelasgian, as in the mysteries. In other respects [the old gods are] deities of field and pasture, not elevated by the beauty of human fancy into a theoretical circle of gods.⟩[271] Then [there is the] *mundus patens,* lasting three days, the opening up of the underground world, whether in a cave or an underground temple [dedicated] to Pluto and Proserpine ⟨(p. 200)⟩;[272] [during this festival there were] no meetings, no popular assemblies, no recruitment for the army, no public affairs were conducted, no ships left harbor, no weddings were celebrated. ⟨Subsequently the ceremonies of Isis (which | were often proscribed), of   121 Cybele, of the Jews and then Christianity, forced their way in, all for the same reason—the need for a religion containing something deeper, removed from common actuality. The same need [gave rise to] the Cynic, Stoic, Epicurean, and Skeptic schools of philosophy, and later Alexandrine philosophy. So it represented a very widespread way of thinking.⟩

(b) In part, the particular [divine] powers [were] a common [heritage] with the Greeks, but their primary reference and significance was directly political. They were viewed not as universal powers but as having done something particular for Rome, something political for which [the Romans] had to thank them; [they had saved it] ⟨in an emergency] and from an emergency. For example, [there

---

270. [*Ed.*] Moritz, *Anthousa,* pp. 118–119. Bona Dea (the "good goddess") was the goddess of the fertility of fields and of the fruitfulness and chastity of women. Ops was a goddess of the harvest. The Pelasgians were one of a group of early peoples mentioned by classical writers as the pre-Hellenic inhabitants of Greece and the eastern islands of the Mediterranean.

271. *W₂ reads:* Thus the dread of something unknown, indeterminate, and unconscious was always there with the Romans—everywhere they saw something mysterious and felt a vague foreboding that impelled them to adduce something that they revered as a higher [power] without understanding it. The Greeks, in contrast, made everything clear and wove a beautiful web of inspired myth about all of their relationships.

272. [*Ed.*] Moritz, *Anthousa,* pp. 199–201.

is the account of] Jupiter Stator (p. 168);[273] [this tells of] an encounter between Romans and Sabines in which the Roman commander fell and the Romans took flight; thereupon Romulus swore to build a temple to Jupiter [if he caused] the Romans to stand fast, and thereafter he was called Jupiter Stator. ⟨Jupiter Invictus[274] is no arbitrary epithet for a deity, [but is used] in reference to the Roman state. Page 260[275] [cites] Jupiter Latialis, who protects Latium, Jupiter of the alliance between Romans and Latins.⟩ In the same way in an emergency, when the state faced destruction as a result of factional quarrels, the people sent for the original Ceres, from Enna in Sicily, and on another occasion Cybele from Pergamus.[276] ⟨There are more specific representations [of] other Roman [deities] too.⟩ Juno was worshiped as Juno Moneta, her temple being the mint ⟨⟨p. 129⟩⟩.[277] [68a] ⟨Saturn's temple [was] the treasury—the exact counterpart.[278]⟩ Minerva's festival [was inaugurated] because the flute-players and other musicians who were threatened with loss of part of their emoluments were leaving the city.[279]

By and large, [there were] a great number of such political festivities, and any emergency was the occasion for the state to institute a new religious ceremony. [These new ceremonies were] the mandatory consequence of need, not a matter of free spiritual intuition. ⟨[They honor] powers of mere utility or harmful powers, [reverenced] prosaically. | These are not (α) friendly ethical determinations [with] a spiritual basis [that is thereby] brought nearer to us in friendly fashion; they do not give food for thought, something to interest the spirit, heart, mind, and thought. (β) There is no beauty.⟩

[There were festivals of] Concordia and so on—a host of patriotic

---

273. [Ed.] Ibid., pp. 168–169.
274. [Ed.] Ibid., p. 162.
275. [Ed.] Ibid., p. 260. Latium was the name of the region around Rome.
276. [Ed.] Ibid., pp. 100, 71–72. The "original Ceres" was the Greek goddess Demeter, who already was worshiped in Sicily and lower Italy, and whose cult was introduced into Rome upon the advice of the Sibylline books in 495 B.C. The Romans imported Cybele, goddess of nature, from Asia Minor in 204 B.C.
277. [Ed.] Ibid., pp. 128–129.
278. [Ed.] Ibid., p. 227.
279. [Ed.] Ibid., pp. 162–165. The festival in question was the lesser Quinquatrus.

festivals that were directly oriented toward state purposes, circumstances, etc.

(β) The other divine essences, ceremonies, and forms of worship related primarily to general, ⟨physical,⟩ human requirements and purposes, [which are] abstractly [necessary] in regard to state purposes. Of this kind was the worship accorded to Ops ⟨Consiva (p. 203)⟩,²⁸⁰ the consort of Saturn, a mysterious goddess who stores within herself the seeds from which all plants come, and ripens them. ⟨[It is a matter of] utility, [of] prosaic powers⟩—a host of rural deities and festivals about which there is much that is ⟨naive⟩ and natural. The bounteous fruitfulness of nature in all its manifold aspects [gave rise to] a large number of fertility and craft festivals. Jupiter had a special altar on the Capitoline hill as Jupiter Pistor ("the baker").²⁸¹ ⟨[We also read in Moritz] (p. 146)²⁸² that mention should be made in this connection of the goddess Fornax, i.e., the goddess of the oven, who presided over the parching of the corn in the ovens. There were also festivals of Vesta, to ensure that the fire should serve for baking bread.⟩ Among the main festivals were the Ambarvalia, a procession round the fields, or the Suovetaurilia (festival of swine, sheep, and bulls).²⁸³ [The same source] (p. 101)²⁸⁴ [mentions] the Fordicidia, where each curia offered up a cow in calf, as if it were [returning] tithes to the earth. ⟨In the Palilia (p. 103)²⁸⁵ the worshipers sought to win the favor of Pales, the goddess of cattle fodder, who caused fodder for the beasts to flourish, and into whose care the herdsmen commended their beasts, that she might guard them from all harm.⟩²⁸⁶ The Lares and Manes were venerated as family spirits and genii of the individual respectively.²⁸⁷ | Mercury [was]   123

280. [*Ed.*] Ibid., p. 203. In virtue of the conserving and ripening function here described, Ops, goddess of the harvest, was also known as Ops Consiva, and her festival was the Opiconsivia.

281. [*Ed.*] Ibid., p. 147.

282. [*Ed.*] Ibid., pp. 146–147.

283. [*Ed.*] Ibid., pp. 264–270.

284. [*Ed.*] Ibid., pp. 101–103.

285. [*Ed.*] See above, n. 258.

286. [*Ed.*] This marginal notation originally occurred at the end of this paragraph, following "poor," but was transferred to this position by reference marks.

287. [*Ed.*] Moritz, *Anthousa*, pp. 115–118. The Lares were household gods or ancestral spirits; the Manes, spirits of the dead and gods of the lower world.

honored [at] a feast where the traders brought him sacrifices, that he might bring profit to their dealings.[288] [Lastly there was] the Saturnalia, a festival [marked by] an intuition and feeling of natural equality and the annulling of the difference in estate between rich and poor.[289]

(γ) But here especially the harmful entered into consciousness just as the useful did in the preceding stage. There are times of prosperity, but [68b] equally there are times of disaster. In this prosaic awareness of the antithesis and of finitude, the harmful just as much as the useful takes on a fixed shape (as we remarked above). It takes the form of something fearful (the powers of evil). Fear for what is finite goes hand in hand with the finite itself. Finite situations are concrete outcomes corresponding to the purpose; in other words, what comes to pass is a purpose. (We are not here talking about powers on their own account, but about outcomes and the associations formed by reflection.)

˜Such finite purposes as the [political] fortunes and situation of the state have to be realized; the purpose has its own realization as its purpose. It is a question of succeeding and being there [*Dasein*]; but this being there is an immediate actuality, and as such (as well as by virtue of its content) it is contingent.˜[290] The harmful, or disaster, takes on a fixed shape, in contrast with the useful, with prosperity. In regard to finite purposes and conditions, human beings are dependent: what they have, enjoy, possess, is a positive mode of being;[291] in the limitation or shortcoming consisting of the fact that this mode of being lies within the power of an other, in the negative of this positive being, therein lies *dependence*—and therein they *feel* it. The proper development of the feeling of dependence[292]

288. [*Ed.*] Ibid., p. 123.

289. [*Ed.*] Ibid., pp. 220–252, esp. pp. 223–224.

290. W₂ *reads:* But when such finite purposes as the situation and circumstances of the state, and the prospering of whatever contributes to the satisfaction of human physical requirements and to the promotion of our human progress and welfare are the supreme goal, and it is a question of the succeeding and being-there [*Dasein*] of an immediate actuality, which, as such, by virtue of its content, can only be a contingent actuality, then

291. *Ms. margin:* ⟨What I am or have, that I *am* or *possess* [positively—i.e., in law]⟩

292. [*Ed.*] This is the third and most substantial allusion to Schleiermacher's *Glaubenslehre* in the main text of the Ms. (see above, nn. 138, 256); later allusions

leads to the veneration of the power of ill or evil, to worship of the devil. At the present stage we do not reach this abstraction of the devil, of evil and the evil one in and for himself; for the | defining   124
mark of this stage is its concern with present and finite actualities of limited content. It is only particular kinds of harm that one is frightened of at this stage, particular evils to which one bows the knee. Inasmuch as it is a negative, this concrete outcome is a situation; it exists as a concrete negative without any inner substantive content, without inward universality. Political power, purpose, popular or scientific knowledge—and also sea or wine—are implicitly [69a] universal essences; what is finitely concrete, however, is an actuality that also passes away, a type or mode of being that can be grasped by reflection as something externally universal ⟨—universal states grasped as [divine] powers—⟩ such as peace, Pax, quiet, Tranquillitas, ⟨Salus, the goddess Vacuna, leisure (p. 145),⟩[293] which take on fixed shape because of the Romans' lack of phantasy.

Allegorical, prosaic essences of this kind, however, are primarily and essentially those which are basically characterized by a shortcoming, harm, or damage. For example, the Romans dedicated altars to the plague, and also to fever, Febris, ⟨and the goddess Angerona, care and woe (p. 253)⟩.[294] They venerated hunger, Fames, and Robigo, wheat rust ⟨(p. 109)⟩.[295] It is hard to grasp that things of this kind were worshiped as divine. In such images every proper aspect of divinity is lost; it is only the feeling of dependence and fear that can turn them into something objective. Only the total loss of all idea, the evaporation of all truth, can hit upon such ways of

on sheets 83a and 103a are found in the margins. The present passage is anticipated by an entry in the *Loose Sheets,* connecting worship of the devil with "the feeling of dependence." See below, *Loose Sheets,* n. 9. The *content* of Schleiermacher's theology is not engaged at this stage, only the slogan *Abhängigkeitsgefühl* (repeated several times in this and the next two paragraphs). The "proper development" of the feeling of dependence in the direction of the veneration of evil or worship of the devil could not have reference to Schleiermacher (since among other reasons his views on evil etc. could not have been known prior to the publication of the second volume of the *Glaubenslehre* in December 1821) but only to Roman religion.

293. [*Ed.*] Moritz, *Anthousa,* pp. 145–146. Vacuna, according to Moritz, is the goddess of leisure. He alludes, for his source, to Ovid; cf. the latter's *Fasti* 6.307–308.

294. [*Ed.*] Ibid., pp. 287–288 (on consul Valerius Publicola, who erected an altar to the plague), 253–254 (on the goddess Angerona).

295. [*Ed.*] Ibid., pp. 109–111.

representing divinity, and they can be comprehended only [through the recognition] that spirit has come to dwell entirely in [the realm of] the finite, ⟨of what is immediately useful⟩.²⁹⁶ ⟨It is conscious only of its finitude, | i.e., of its dependence,⟩ and has forgotten everything that is inward and more universal, [the whole realm of] thought. Its being is prosaic and circumstantial through and through; and its escape, its exaltation above circumstances is nothing but a purely formal understanding, which grasps them all, all the different modes and patterns of being, in a single image and knows no other mode of substantiality.

125

⁻I do not need to recall that this is where the roots of superstition are to be found.⁻²⁹⁷ Generally speaking, superstition consists in treating something finite and external, some ordinary actuality just as it stands, as a *power,* a substance. Superstition stems from the oppressed state of the spirit, from a feeling of dependence in its purposes; [69b] it cannot free itself from its purposes and ⟨as a logical consequence⟩ defines the negative upon which they are dependent as something that is as temporal and finite as they are. In the same way magic is closely bound up with superstition: it seeks to bring a power of this kind under superstition's subjective control; and it has the capacity to do this, for the power in question is limited and finite.

⟨(δ)⟩ At this point I would like to say something in passing about the theatrical performances of the Romans ⟨in their cultus⟩. What is distinctive about performances of this kind is that they make the process of the substantive powers, the divine life in its dynamic, active aspects, visibly present before us; ⟨they present the essence of the divine and the human in pictorial form, before our very eyes. In a religion that has no doctrine, that is not absolute spiritual content, plays [have] a significance quite different [from that which they have for us], since they are the highest form of doctrinal teaching.⟩ In venerating and adoring the image of the deity, we have the image

296. W₂ *adds:* in the way that the Romans even regard as deities the skills that are related to their most immediate needs and their satisfaction.

297. W₂ *reads:* This is essentially superstition because the purposes and objects in question are limited and finite; but these purposes and objects, which are limited in their content, are treated as absolute.

before us in its static being; its dynamic aspect is [presented] by telling a story (the *myth*). Later on, in the Christian religion, | this aspect   126 is [conveyed] mainly by doctrine; but this teaching provides only inner, subjective representations. We have already noted that just as the representation of the deity in its static being develops into the work of art (i.e., to the mode of immediate intuition), so the representation of divine action develops into its ⟨external⟩ presentation in the drama, as tragedy and comedy. But this intuition of divinity was not indigenous to the Romans, it did not grow on Roman soil; and in accepting this alien importation they seized—to judge from the material that has come down to us, [i.e.,] in tragic drama [from] Seneca[298]—on what is empty, ugly, and horrible, devoid of any ethical or godly idea, while in comedy they seized on the merely farcical, in the tradition of the Late Comedy ⁻given over entirely to private relationships,⁻[299] stories [of quarrels] between fathers and sons, and especially stories about prostitutes, slaves, and slave girls.

In this immersion in finite purposes there could be no lofty intuition of the ⟨deeper,⟩ ethical, divine action, no theoretical intuition of divine, substantive powers. [70a]

The actions they were interested in watching as spectators, to the extent that this was a theoretical interest (i.e., when it did not concern their own practical interests), could themselves only be ⁻actual⁻[300] events, and indeed, if they were to be moved, a loathsome actuality.

⁻We include here dances that were full of art as well as pantomimes, ⟨chariot races, and martial displays,⟩ in which there is nothing spiritual and no scope for the truthful expression of spirit.⁻[301] | ⟨[It is] a later, ultimate manifestation of human nature   127

298. [*Ed.*] The harshness of Hegel's judgment with regard to Seneca is noteworthy in view of the fact that he shared the disregard for Seneca on the part of German classicism, which can be traced back to Lessing in particular. We do not know which of Seneca's tragedies Hegel was familiar with; the two editions of Seneca that he owned contain only philosophical writings. See also 1831 excerpts at n. 129.

299. *W₂ (1831) reads:* —nothing but bawdy scenes and private relationships,

300. *W₂ reads:* external, raw

301. *W₂ (1831) reads:* In Greek drama the main thing was what was said, the actors maintained a quiet, statuesque posture, and no use was made of actual facial gestures; the effect was produced by the spiritual element in the representation. With the Romans, on the contrary, the main thing was mime, a mode of expression that is not on a par with what can be put into speech.

[to have] developed one's skill in honor of the gods, [so] that the gods may be honored for what their worshipers can do.⟩ What is especially notable at the present stage is the combats of beasts, or rather the slaughter of beasts and especially of human beings. The spilling of rivers of real blood and battles to the death were the spectacles that the Romans loved best. What mattered on the theoretical plane was that this bloodletting was purposeless; it took place merely to entertain the spectators. And the spectators wanted to see not a spiritual history but one that was actually happening—the very one indeed that constitutes the ultimate change of fortunes, or περιπέτεια, in the finite sphere, namely *death*. ⟨They wanted this external, simple story of death, without meaning, the quintessence of everything external, the arid process of a *natural* death by violence or natural means, not death produced by an ethical power.⟩ At the festivals the emperors mounted shows at which many hundreds of wild beasts and human beings killed one another, three or four hundred lions in a day, four or five hundred elephants and bears, hundreds of tigers; crocodiles and strange exotic animals of various kinds such as buffalo and elk were brought to Rome for the purpose.[302] But above all, human beings were compelled to fight with the wild beasts, to be torn to pieces by them or else slay one another. Under Caius Caligula [there was] a sea battle with two fleets that sailed past him and called out, "We who are about to die salute thee, O Caesar." No quarter was granted; first they fought without doing one another any serious harm, but then soldiers compelled them to

302. [*Ed.*] The numbers mentioned here by Hegel are probably too high. The reports of the games found, for example, in Suetonius give lower numbers. Gibbon's *Decline and Fall of the Roman Empire* mentions a hundred lions and elephants and a rhinoceros; Hegel had long been familiar with this work and owned an edition published in Leipzig in 1821. In the *Lectures on the Philosophy of World History*, Sibree ed., p. 294 (Lasson ed., p. 681), Hegel also says that "hundreds of bears, lions, tigers, elephants, crocodiles, and ostriches were produced, and slaughtered for mere amusement." Hegel is apparently relying on Dio Cassius, who reports in *Historia Romana* 54.26 that, upon the occasion of the dedication of the theater of Marcellus in 13 B.C., some six hundred Libyan animals were slaughtered; at 55.10 he states that thirty-six crocodiles were slaughtered at the dedication festival for the temple of Mars; and at 59.14 that five hundred bears and several hundred other animals were slaughtered during the two-day birthday celebration of Drusilla.

fight in earnest, stabbing or drowning one another till all were dead.[303] [70b]

For the Romans this prosaic pattern of spiritless butchery, cold and arid, constituted the supreme event of history,[304] the highest manifestation of the fate which for the Greeks [had been] essentially an *ethical* transformation. To die imperturbably, | ⟨through an   128 irrational caprice having the force of necessity, not a natural death [through] something arbitrary, not [through] unfortunate circumstances or ethical powers either, but [where] sheer caprice [is] the supreme power (the *abstract* representation of power),⟩ was the ultimate and unique virtue that Roman patricians could exercise, and they shared it with slaves and malefactors condemned to death.

⟨(ε)⟩[305] Lastly it is notable that the Romans worshiped their *emperors* virtually as gods, or in fact as gods. Inasmuch as the content of the divine purpose consisted for them in finite human purposes, and the power over such purposes and the directly actual external circumstances ⟨was what made up the good fortune of the Roman Empire⟩, the obvious next step was to worship the *present* power over such purposes, the *individual* presence of that good fortune, as a god ⟨in whose hands it rested⟩. ⟨Political power [was] brought near, Fortuna Publica [was] realized in the emperor.⟩ The emperor, this individual quite out of the ordinary, was this arbitrary power over the life and happiness of individuals and whole ˜cities;˜[306] his power reached much further than that of Robigo; famine and other public necessities awaited his summons—the goddess of hunger was at his call. Nor was this all. ⟨Status, birth, nobility, riches ([being matters] of understanding) were all his making, he had the power over them.⟩ The formal rights of property, inheritance, etc., ˜developed by Roman understanding—over all these straw houses

---

303. [*Ed.*] Suetonius, *Divus Claudius* 21.44–45. Tacitus, in his report of this sea battle in *Annals* 12.56, says that there were nineteen thousand combatants, but in other respects his account differs from Hegel's.

304. *Ms. margin:* ⟨Infinite personality and its opposite⟩

305. *Ms. margin:* ⟨Emperor – divine power: (α) Happiness (β) Political festivals – (αα) Finite and hence negative states (γ) Dynamic intuitions⟩

306. W_2 *reads:* cities and states;

of the understanding the emperor was the overriding power;⁻³⁰⁷ the private citizen had a pretended right, but the emperor was the reality

129 of the right—he was the power of the state in | its actual willing and doing, ⟨the Fortuna of the Roman Empire⟩. To swear by his name, to bring him incense, sacrifices, women, as to a god, [implied that he was] *inter divos relatus*. ⟨[For this to be so, it was at least] partly required that he [should be] dead.⟩ [This can be seen in the cases of] Trajan and Titus.³⁰⁸ The form of the state, the senate, and the magistracies [were] preserved; the emperor was merely *princeps iuventutis*,³⁰⁹ or at most consul. [But there were] twenty-five consuls in a year, and Caligula made his horse consul.³¹⁰ ⟨This made it plain what the Roman constitution [*Wesen*] had come to.⟩ [The emperor might be] censor, aedile, tribune of the people, for several years or just for one year. But he had his soldiers and he could have anyone's head cut off or plunder everyone, just as he liked. The imperial will and the imperial guard were the goddess Fortuna; the guard could auction the empire. [They were] the Fortuna or *fatum* hovering over the life and well-being of each and every citizen.

For the Romans, sunk as they were in finitude, there was nothing higher than this individual, this power over their finite purposes. [They were] utterly at a loss: there were no principles, no institutions of the state, nothing sacred ⟨they were prepared to set against him. The whole world from the outermost parts of Britain to the

---

307. W₂ *reads:* etc.—[over all this] to the development of which the Roman spirit had devoted so much energy, he was the overriding authority;

308. [*Ed.*] In the early Empire, deification of the emperor (elevation to *divus*) occurred only after death. See Tacitus, *Annals* 15.74. Hegel's qualification may stem from the fact that in the late second century the title was also applied to living emperors, e.g., Commodus. But he could also have in mind reports such as those concerning the self-deification of Caligula found in Suetonius, *Gaius Caligula* 22.

309. [*Ed.*] The title *princeps iuventutis* (the first among the youth or the knights) was originally a predicate of nobility; cf. Livy, *Ab urbe condita* 1.12.15; Cicero restricted it to particularly prominent persons. Later, in the age of the emperors, only members of the imperial household could be so designated; but the title was limited primarily to the prince or princes selected as successors to Caesar.

310. [*Ed.*] This is apparently based on a report contained in Suetonius, *Gaius Caligula* 55.555. Because of the ostentatious manner in which Caligula maintained his horse Incitatus (marble stall, private palace in which to receive invited guests, etc.), it was said that he had in mind making him consul.

Tigris and Euphrates knew of nothing and had nothing to set against him, either inwardly or outwardly, no religion or morals, no shame or awe, no help, no legal or constitutional provisions; no individual [had] rights infinitely and inwardly. If things really went too far, the emperor was murdered by conspirators, as a matter of contingency. But there was nothing to limit his evil will. [He was like] no despot of Christian times, even in Turkey, [for the despot has] something inviolable set against himself, which if he infringes he is lost.⟩ [71a]

Thus the finite determinate purpose, together with its power, is concentrated and determined in the present, actual will of one individual human being. ⟨[Since all] are in bondage to life, one person's will is in fact the power over finite purposes, over the world; the Roman emperor [is] lord of the world, as long as he has guards to be the tool of this individuality; [but he has only] to offend these guards, and he is lost. His violent power [is] the death of | individuality, [since] life [is] the sum of all its finite purposes.⟩ Divinity, the divine essence, the inward, universal element, has come forth and revealed itself in the singularity of this individual; in him it has determinate being. ⟨[This is] a descent of the idea into the present but in such a way that the descent is the loss of its self-contained universality, the loss of its truth, its being-in-and-for-self and hence of its divinity.⟩ Power is completely determined, as singularity, but the universal moment has escaped. What is present [is] the world of outward happiness and the power over it—a monstrous *un*happiness. What is lacking is that power should be completely determined in such a way as to make it determinately determinate, [in other words] that the individual should become subjectivity, actually present, should become something inward, something inwardly substantive.

⟨[We may here interpose] a general reflection in regard to the standpoint, the level of determinateness we are here considering. Universal power (the abstract concept) [is] really fulfilled, it contains its own content. [This is] a *determinate* content but completely *external*. Hence [divine] power [is] external, universal mastery of the world. The infinite [is] presented within the image of the finite, so that the finite is the subject of the proposition; it remains and stands fast, and is not posited negatively in the infinite—which alone maintains itself equally in the spiritual realm.⟩

Finite purposes [are] developed; and for that reason there is one lord [over all] finite purposes.

[311]The Roman world is the most important point of transition to the Christian religion, the indispensable ˉlink; itˉ[312] is the side of the *reality* of the idea, and therefore ⟨implicitly⟩ of its *determinateness,* the side of the reality of the *mode* of being of the universal. As it becomes determinate, this reality, initially held in immediate unity with the universal, cuts adrift from it and emerges | on its own account as consummate externality, concrete singularity, ⟨totality. The side of reality [is, in this way,] fully accomplished on its own account; what is necessary, this determinate determinateness, [is] utter externalization, [forming] a self-contained totality. The totality of the reality of externality [is] implicitly capable of being taken up into universality. Consummated subjectivity—i.e., the external, objective side of the idea—can be taken back into the universal, in such a way that it achieves its true character and strips off its externality. In this way the idea as such achieves its perfect determination within itself.⟩

This religion of external purposiveness thus closes the cycle of the finite religions. Finite religion [is] the absolute concept of God, as *concept;* [it is still requisite] that God should *be,* that the concept (the determinacy) of God should be *posited,* in other words that the concept should be what is true *for* self-consciousness, i.e., it should itself be realized *in* self-consciousness (which is its own *subjective* side, namely, reality).

[313]Finite religion [knows] God first (α) [as] the simple universal and hence as intuited in immediate being; (β) (αα) God, this universal, [is known] as power ⟨(the sloughing off of immediate being [gives rise to] infinite negativity)⟩, as absolute power, and as One,

131

311. *Ms. margin:* ⟨[As regards the] necessity of this moment see the following page⟩ [*i.e., Ms. sheet 71b, esp. n. 317*]

312. W_2 reads: link: what has developed at this stage of the religious spirit

313. *Ms. margin:* ⟨(α) Pantheism (β) A [universal] falling apart into inwardly concrete spiritual freedom, essential but limited purpose⟩

as abstract subjectivity; (ββ) this One [is known] as containing determinacy within itself, but in a vanishing fashion; [this gives rise to] necessity, and with it the subsisting determinacy as itself essential in unity with the essence. But (α) [since] the determinacy is immediate, [there is] a diversity of powers; and (β) [since] the determinateness, or reality, [is] taken up into essence, [we have] beauty. [71b] ⁻⟨⟨γ⟩⟩ In the final phase, | there is this finite determinateness   132 as concrete purpose, inwardly determined and having a definite content:⁻³¹⁴ the concrete and finite, singularity, what is inwardly manifold and external, the actual situation, determinate being, the empire—a present, far from beautiful objectivity—in other words, *ipso facto,* the consummated subjectivity [of the emperor].

It is through purpose that determinacy first comes to be, first returns back into self; now it is determinacy in subjectivity—a determinate determinacy but, to begin with, a finite one—and because of its subjectivity and return [to self], [it is] unbounded (spuriously infinite) finitude.

³¹⁵The two sides of this unbounded finitude must be clearly identified and recognized.³¹⁶

⁻⟨In itself⟩³¹⁷ [it is] (α) consummated determinacy, the concept in its determinateness returned into self, form raising itself to the level of absolute form. The concept is the universal; but then it is abstract, not posited the way it is in itself. In itself it is the universal that is restored to itself *through* particularity, | i.e., [it is universal]   133 through the *mediation* of particularity—the mediation of determinacy

314. W₂ *reads:* It is this positedness that must develop on its own account into a totality too, if it is to be taken up into universality. And it is this further development of determinacy into a totality that occurred in the Roman world, for here determinacy is

315. *Ms. margin:* ⟨Finite and infinite coupled from the start

Second stage: self-consciousness – a spiritual power is related to the subject (α) Jewish: *this* people (exclusively); (β) Greek: *many* peoples; (γ) Universal self-consciousness (self-contained person [i.e., emperor])

Spirit is only posited *as* spirit, undergoing diremption into the two sides: (α) as universality, in and for itself, (β) the side of reality or purpose (self-contained determinacy infinite on its own account))

316. W₂ *adds:* the in-itself and the empirical appearing.

317. *Ms. margin:* ⟨(α) The *necessity* of this moment⟩

227

and emergence—and through the *sublation* of this particularity. This⁻[318] is absolute form, truly infinite subjectivity; this is genuine reality, reality in its truth. Reality is determinate being, determinacy—reality in its infinitude is just this.

In the religion of expediency it is accordingly this infinite form that has come to the intuition of self-consciousness. What counts for self-consciousness is this [manifest] shape. Hence the shape carries this absolute moment within it, within it the absolute moment develops. This absolute form is the definition of self-consciousness itself. So it contains the determination of self-consciousness—or of spirit—for the [ultimate] definition of the idea.

Herein lies the infinite importance and necessity of Roman religion. ⁻However, (β)[319]⁻[320] when it is comprehended in a finite mode, the highest is the *worst*. The deeper the spirit (or [communal] genius) goes, the more monstrously it errs. When superficiality errs, its errors also are superficial, of little account. Only what is intrinsically deep can just for that reason be the most evil, the worst. [72a]

The infinite reflection, infinite form without content or substantiality, ⟨simple, abstract inwardness,⟩ is boundless, unlimited finitude, limitedness that is self-absolute in its finitude. This is the reality of the Greek Sophists—"Man is the measure of all things,"[321] i.e., the human being with his immediate wishes, desires, purposes, interests, and feelings. In Roman religion and the Roman world we see this thought of "self" ⟨—the "person"—⟩ elevated to the valid stan-

---

318. W₂ *reads:* If we consider consummated determinacy as it is *in itself,* it is the absolute form of the concept, namely, the concept which in its determinateness has returned into itself. Initially the concept is only universal and abstract, and hence not yet posited the way it is in itself. What is genuine is the universal that is restored to itself through particularity, i.e., returned to itself through the mediation of particularity—the mediation of determinacy and emergence—and through the sublation of this particularity. This negation of negation

319. *Ms. margin:* ⟨(β) Thus a *person.* But in the empirical sense, as this immediate person, [the highest is] the worst⟩

320. W₂ *reads:* However, this absolute form is here still empirical: it is *this* person, this immediate person, and

321. [*Ed.*] Both Plato (*Theaetetus* 152a) and Sextus Empiricus (*Pyrrhonian Hypotyposes* 1.32.216) report the statement of Protagoras that "man is the measure of all things."

dard, raised to the level of being and consciousness of the world. We behold the complete ⟨disappearance⟩ | of all beautiful, ethical organic life ⟨and the crumbling away into finitude of all desires, purposes, and interests—a crumbling into momentary enjoyment and pleasure, a human animal kingdom [from which] all higher[322] elements have been abstracted. Coupled with this is⟩ the housing of the understanding in a formal system of legal right. For in the infinitude of subjectivity is the beginning of formal right; and this self-intuition of the subject in its infinity [constitutes] a lofty starting point. But [it is] a form without substantiality, without inner universality; until the content is true, it remains the formal legal right of the understanding, without reality, i.e., without a content that matches the form and sublates its one-sidedness just by matching it—⟨this or that possession, this or that interest, is my property⟩. It is a crumbling away into mere finitudes—finite existences, wishes, and interests—which for that very reason are held together only by the inwardly boundless violence of the despot, the singular [will] whose instrument is the cold-blooded, spiritless death of individual citizens, the negative that is as immediate [as their wishes], brought to bear upon them and holding them in fear of him. He is the One, the actually present God—himself the singularity of the [divine] will as the power over all the other infinitely many singular [wills].

(γ) This consummation of finitude itself, ⟨like the happiness of the emancipated slave,⟩ is initially absolute *un*happiness, the absolute grief of the spirit, spirit's supreme internal conflict; and the contradiction is unresolved, the antithesis is not reconciled. Absolute reflection-into-self is here universal determinateness. Spirit is thinking inasmuch as it [has] completely lost itself as externality in this reflection-into-self.[323] [Even] as thinking, [it is] thus just this same determinateness of reflection-into-self; it withdraws back into itself, and | in its own depth, as infinite form, as thinking, universal subjectivity, it has thus set itself upon the peak as the immediate subjectivity of self-

134

135

322. W₂ *adds:* and all substantive
323. *Ms. margin:* ⟨Real, i.e., inward, being-for-self, [i.e.,] relegating all external reality to infinite negativity, everything being consumed inwardly but preserved in God, in heaven⟩

consciousness. ⟨In this abstract form it appears on the scene, as already mentioned,[324] as philosophy, but more generally as the sufferings of virtue.⟩[325] [72b]

The resolution and reconciliation of this antithesis is[326] that this external finitude, the finitude that is left to its own devices, is taken up into the infinite universality of thought and thereby purified. It becomes substantive. And conversely this infinite universality of thought, which has no external existence or validity, acquires present actuality; and self-consciousness thus attains to consciousness of the actuality of the universal,[327] it has the universal, the divine, as something that has come into the world [als daseiend, als weltlich], as present in the world—God and the world reconciled [cf. 2 Cor. 5:19].[328]

How the finitude that is left to its own devices is sublated in the world, passes away, is broken and resolved in universality—⟨this is the spectacle that⟩ history will exhibit. The finite gods and the peoples that worship them disappear [when] their service is united and resolved in a pantheon; the difference between free citizens and slaves evaporates ⟨into unity and equality⟩ through the omnipotence of the emperor; and | inwardly and outwardly everything that makes for stability is destroyed. ⁻Fortuna [is] reduced to ruins,⁻[329] ⟨all concern for the state, all bravery, [has] vanished—only mercenaries, barbarians, Germanic tribes are brave⟩. The one death of finitude comes upon [the empire], ⟨[despite] the immense number of attempts made [to preserve it] by philosophy, religious observance, superstition, etc.⟩.

136

324. [Ed.] See above, p. 97.

325. W₂ adds: as desiring and reaching out for help.

326. W₂ adds: what the whole world stands in need of, and is possible only by virtue of the fact

327. Ms. margin: ⟨The purpose of [divine] power – freedom and necessity⟩

328. Ms. margin:
⟨(α) Just one idea: this subjectivity [is] divine determinateness, within the divine nature
(β) The diremption of subjectivity itself:
  (α) God as this particular process, within himself
  (β) Subjectivity as the process, in regard to God, in his [singularity]⟩

329. W₂ reads: since the Fortuna of the one world-empire itself also goes down to defeat,

[What is] accomplished in the Christian religion [is] the incorporation of finitude within religion—⁻[this is its] absolute form.⁻³³⁰ The other side [of what history exhibits] could not develop the intuition of this unity directly within these religions themselves—it could not arise in the Greco-Roman world. ⁻For even if [it] found the principle of the unity of thought ⟨as a positive principle⟩ within itself, in isolated cases, in philosophy, [this principle is] ⟨⟨α⟩⟩ not a community principle; (β) not the pure intuition [of] the universal as an object of this kind (the Stoics [derived] the world from *fire*,³³¹ so that even among them⁻³³² there was still this linkage with ordinary externality, ⟨this friendly regard for external actuality⟩). Instead, this union [with God] had to emerge in *one people*—the one people that had (for itself) the wholly abstract intuition of the one God, ⟨involving the total casting aside of all finitude, in order that they might grasp the intuition purified within themselves⟩. The Oriental principle of pure abstraction [had to] be combined with the finitude³³³ of the West, [so this people is] geographically in between the two regions, | in the land of Israel. It was, [as we] have said, 137 in the Jewish people that God took this [Oriental] principle upon himself as the age-old grief of the world; for here we find the religion of abstract suffering, of the *one* Lord, against whom and despite whom the actuality of life stands its ground as the infinite willfulness of self-consciousness, and all that is abstract is bound together. The age-old curse is undone, ⟨it has been met by salvation,⟩ in that finitude has for its part ⁻validated its claim to be both positivity and *infinite finitude*.⁻³³⁴

330. W_2 *reads:* [this is] the universal [that is present in this religion].

331. [*Ed.*] On Hegel's understanding of this doctrine, see *Lectures on the History of Philosophy* 2:245 ff. (*Werke* 14:438 ff.). Hegel is relying especially on Ioannes Stobaeus, *Eclogarum physicarum et ethicarum libri duo,* ed. A. H. L. Heeren, vol. 1 (Göttingen, 1792), bk. 1, p. 312. He also cites Diogenes Laertius, *Lives* 7.136, 142, 156–157.

332. W_2 *reads:* Even if the principle of thought had already developed, the universal was not yet an object of consciousness in its purity, since even in philosophical thought the linkage with ordinary externality was evident when the Stoics derived the world from fire.

333. W_2 *adds:* and singularity

334. W_2 *reads:* raised itself to the level of positivity and *infinite finitude*, and so validated its claim in that respect.

THE LECTURES OF 1824

Introduction[2]

The first thing is to classify these determinate, ethnic religions;[3] however, the particular forms that have to be considered under this heading only need to be defined in a general way at first.[4]

---

1. *Thus G; the heading in P reads:* Ethnic Religion or Determinate Religion *The heading in D reads:* Determinate or Ethnic Religions

2. [*Ed.*] The Introduction to the 1824 lectures contains a division of the subject similar to that found in the *Ms.* The division makes it clear that in 1824, as in the other lectures series, Hegel initially envisioned a threefold structure for *Determinate Religion,* namely, immediate religion or nature religion (greatly expanded in content from the *Ms.*), the religion of spiritual individuality (Jewish and Greek religion), and the religion of expediency (Roman religion). In the actual execution, however, Roman religion is treated quite briefly and as the third stage of the religion of spiritual individuality. It is evident that Hegel changed his plan at the beginning of Sec. B. See below, n. 386.

3. [*Ed.*] J. W. von Goethe, *Wilhelm Meister's Travels; or, The Renunciants: A Novel,* vol. 2 of Thomas Carlyle's translation of *Wilhelm Meister* (New York, 1901), chap. 10, p. 267: "The religion which depends on reverence for what is above us, we denominate the ethnic; it is the religion of the nations [*Völker*], and the first happy deliverance from a degrading fear: all heathen religions, as we call them, are of this sort, whatsoever names they may bear." *Wilhelm Meisters Wanderjahre* first appeared in German in 1821 (Stuttgart and Tübingen).

4. *The introductory section in the Werke includes a passage that probably stems from the introductory section to the lectures of 1831.* W₁ *reads:* If we want to sum up what has been said so far, we can say that in Part I religion was considered only in its concept, as what it is in itself, implicitly. But what is implicit does not yet therewith *exist,* and to the extent that something is in itself, it is not yet actual in its truth. The *realization* of the concept also has to be considered. Religion exists as idea only when it also exists as consciousness of what is the concept. The reality of the concept now has the more specific meaning that the determinacies contained in the concept are now posited. However, this positing has a still more specific meaning, namely

1. The initial [form of] religion is *immediate religion, natural religion, nature religion;* it is the unity of the spiritual and the natural.
140 | God ⁻is [always] the content,⁻⁵ but at this stage it is God in the natural unity of the spiritual and the natural. The natural mode is what characterizes this form of religion generally; but it also has a great variety of shapes.⁶ All these shapes are together called *nature*

---

that religion is consciousness, knowing for knowing, spirit for spirit; the concept realizes itself, what is posited or differentiated is finite consciousness; human consciousness is the material in which the concept of God realizes itself; the concept is purpose, and the material for carrying out the purpose is human consciousness. The successive developmental stages are not yet adequate to the concept. The concept must also return to itself again through its development. Moments of the concept are evinced in the course of development itself. These moments *appear* in the finite religions. W_2 *reads:* Now in the course of development as such, inasmuch as they have not yet attained the goal, the moments of the concept are still falling apart, in such a way that the reality is not yet on a par with the concept, and these moments as they appear in history are the finite religions. $W_{1,2}$ *read:* In order to comprehend these in their truth, one must consider them from the two sides—on the one hand, how God is known, how he is defined; on the other hand, how the subject knows itself in the process. W_1 *reads:* Both sides, the objective and the subjective, are imbued with the same determinacy. Both sides progress together in the same determinacy. W_2 *reads:* For there is one single basis for the further determining of the two sides, the objective and the subjective, and both sides are imbued with one determinacy and one determinacy alone. $W_{1,2}$ *read:* The representation people have of God corresponds to the representation they have of themselves, of their freedom. Knowing themselves in God, they know their imperishable life in God, they know the truth of their being, so that the notion of the immortality of the soul comes on the scene at this stage W_2 *reads:* as an essential moment entering into the history of religion. $W_{1,2}$ *read:* The notions of God and immortality are mutually related in necessary fashion. When we have true knowledge of God, we also have true knowledge of ourselves. God is at first something quite indeterminate; but in the course of development the consciousness of what God is gradually fills out, progressively loses the initial indeterminacy, W_2 *reads:* and actual self-consciousness also develops *pari passu.* The proofs of the existence of God, whose purpose is to demonstrate the necessity of rising to [the recognition of] God, also pertain to this progressive development. For the diversity of characteristics that are ascribed to God in the course of rising to this level follow from the diversity of the starting point, which in turn is rooted in the nature of the historical stage that actual self-consciousness has reached in each case. The different forms this ascending process yields will in each case give us the metaphysical spirit of the stage in question, to which the actual representation of God and the sphere of the cultus correspond.

5. *Thus P; G reads:* is everywhere,

6. W_1 *(Ed) adds:* which can be reduced essentially to three, with which we shall become more closely acquainted in a moment.

religion; we say that at this stage spirit is still identical with nature, that consciousness remains one with nature; and to that extent natural religion is the religion of unfreedom.

2. The second stage is the religion of *spiritual individuality* or *subjectivity;* it is here that the subject's spiritual being-for-self begins. The principal, or first, or determining element is thought, and the natural state is reduced to a mere semblance, something accidental over against what is substantive, related to it; ⌐the natural becomes merely material,⌐[7] or ⌐corporeality for the subject,⌐[8] | or is simply what is determined by the subjective. Two forms of this religion need to be distinguished. 141

Inasmuch as spiritual being-for-self is emerging, it is that which is adhered to purely for ⌐itself.⌐[9] There is therefore just the one eternal God, who has his being only in thought; and natural life, being generally, is only something posited, something that as such stands opposed to God, but has no substantiality over against him and has being only through the essence of thought.[10]

In the second form [of the religion of spiritual individuality] the natural and the spiritual are united—not, however, in the way they were in their immediate union, not like that, but in the kind of union where it is simply subjectivity that determines and combines the corporeal in union with itself, so that in this union the corporeal is only its organ, its expression, and displays itself as the appearing of the subject.

This is therefore the religion of divine appearing, of divine corporeality, materiality, and naturalness, but in such a way that this materiality is the appearing of subjectivity—in other words, that

7. *Thus P; G reads:* it becomes merely natural life,
8. *Ho reads:* natural life is merely the body of God,
9. W_1 *(following Ho) reads:* itself, reflectedness-into-self, as negation of the natural unity. W_2 *(following Ho) reads:* itself as reflectedness-into-self and as negation of the natural unity. *Ho reads:* itself. And indeed here for the first time we find the reflectedness-into-self of the spiritual as negation of the natural unity.
10. *Ho adds (continuing from the preceding footnote), similar in W:* [We find] the spiritually one, inwardly unchanging God, Jehovah, over against whom the natural, the worldly, the finite in general, is posited as something inessential, lacking substantiality. But as it is only by positing the inessential that God is the essential, this God thereby *shows* that it is only through it that he has being, and this inessential, this semblance or show, becomes an *appearing* of God himself.

here in this corporeality the self-appearing of subjectivity is made manifest; it appears not only for other but for itself. Natural life is thus the organ of the subject, whereby it makes itself appear. This spiritual individuality is therefore not the unlimited individuality of pure thought; it has only spiritual character. Thus on the one hand, the natural is determined as the body in regard to the spiritual realm; on the other hand, the subject is determined as finite because it employs the body in this way.

142　　The first moment or form [of the religion of spiritual individuality] is the religion of sublimity, | or the Jewish religion, while the second is the religion of beauty, or the Greek religion.

3. Third, there is the religion in which the concept, or in general a content determined for itself, a concrete content, has its beginnings; this content is *purpose,* fulfilled content, it is subserved by the general powers of nature or the gods of the religion of beauty. Moreover, it is a concrete content that embraces such determinacies within itself; it is the determinant, so that the previously isolated powers are made subject to one purpose.[11] The mode in which the concept first appears is that of external, finite purpose, external conformity to purpose or *expediency.* Absolute conformity to purpose belongs to the idea of spirit, where the idea is its own purpose and there is no other purpose save the concept of spirit itself, namely, the infinite, absolute final purpose, the concept that realizes itself. At this stage the spiritual is indeed the purpose; this moment has within it the inwardly concrete determinations, but its inwardly concrete determination is still finite, having a particular content; it is a particular purpose, which for that very reason is not yet spirit's relatedness to itself.[12]

These [then] are the three forms [of determinate religion]:

1. Nature religion in general, to which the *Oriental* religions all belong, wholly consisting as they do in this unity of nature and spirit and the mingling of them both.

11. *Ho adds, similar in* W: But this single subject is still an other over against such divine powers; they constitute the divine content, while the singularized subject is human consciousness, finite purpose. Now the divine content serves this culminating point of subjectivity, which the subject lacked in the religion of beauty, as a means of fulfilling, of realizing, itself.

12. *Ho, W add:* What the single, individual spirit wills in the gods is only its own subjective purpose; it wills *itself,* not the absolute content.

2. The religion of the spiritual for itself, as subjectivity in general that has being abstractly on its own account, the religion of pure thought and of the spiritual corporeality that is set apart and determined in itself, namely, *Jewish* and *Greek* religion.

3. The religion of external conformity to purpose or expediency, namely, *Roman* religion, forming the transition to the absolute religion. |

143

This classification must not be taken in a merely subjective way; rather it is a necessary classification that follows objectively from the nature of spirit. In the mode of existence that it assumes in religion, spirit in its naturalness is initially natural religion; the next stage is where the reflection of spirit into itself comes on the scene. Spirit becomes inwardly free, and this is the beginning of being-for-self—the subjective generally, which, however, does not yet have its freedom within itself but first emerges from the unity of nature, to which it is still related: This is the conditioned becoming-free of spirit. The third stage, then, is where spirit inwardly gets hold of itself, has the will to achieve inward self-determination, and accordingly appears in such a way that there is purpose, something that is expedient on its own account, but what is inwardly expedient is also at first still finite and limited. The last stage, then, is the absolute, where the spirit is for itself. Such are the basic characteristics that constitute the moments in the development of the concept of spirit, and are at the same time moments of the concrete concept. Spirit accordingly *is* this process.

These stages can be compared to the stages of human life. The child is still in the first, immediate unity of will and nature (both its own nature and that which surrounds it). The second stage [is] youth, this individuality, this becoming-for-self, this spirituality blossoming into life, still setting no particular purpose for itself but questing, searching this way and that, paying heed to everything that comes its way, taking heart from it. The third stage, maturity, is that of work for a particular purpose, to which adults subject themselves, to which they devote their strength. Hovering above maturity, finally, the fourth stage is old age, the age of thought, having the universal before itself as infinite purpose, recognizing this purpose—the age that has turned back from particular forms of activity and work to the universal purpose.[13] These characteristics are those that are logically determined by the nature of the concept.

144 | Ultimately, in the concept, in the idea, it becomes evident that the first immediacy does not have being as immediacy but is itself only something posited: the child, for instance, is itself something produced.

A. IMMEDIATE RELIGION, OR NATURE RELIGION[14]

Introduction[15]

Insofar as we concentrate on the *thought* that lies within nature religion, it will be evident that what has recently been called "natural religion" is the same as [what we are calling] "nature religion."

Since we are beginning with immediate religion, we must first refer to a way of viewing the matter ¯which we at once encounter.¯[16] What I refer to is the view that immediate religion must on the one hand be the true, the most excellent, the specifically divine religion, and also that this true religion and no other must have been historically the first. According to our classification, nature religion is the lowest level, the most imperfect and thus the first, while according to this other way of viewing it, it is not only the first but the truest. As we have noted, nature religion is in fact defined as the spiritual still joined with the natural in their first undisturbed, untroubled unity. That spirit is in untroubled unity with nature—it is this deter-

---

13. W *(following Ho) adds:* to the absolute final end, and from the broad manifoldness of existence has drawn itself together to the infinite depth of being-within-self. *Ho reads:* Old age leaves all limitation beneath it, has before it the universal, infinite, ultimate, absolute final end. It has turned back from the particularity of the living, of [particular] purposes, has drawn itself together from the broad manifoldness of existence to the infinite depth of being-within-self.

14. [*Ed.*] The heading in G reads: "Immediate Religion, or Natural Religion, Nature Religion."

15. [*Ed.*] The Introduction to "Immediate Religion" in 1824 incorporates elements of the discussion of the original condition of humanity from Part III of the *Ms.*, sheets 83b–85a (see Vol. 3: 96–101), as well as of the brief general treatment of "Immediate" Religion from Part II of the *Ms.*, sheets 32a–39a, to which it adds for the first time detailed treatments of the specific forms of the nature religions in the ensuing sections.

16. W_2 *(Var) reads:* which, in the light of what it understands by natural religion, makes definite claims for our attention at this point.

mination that is asserted to be the absolute, true determination, and the religion that is so defined is therefore acclaimed as divine. ⌐Spirit, so it is said, in | this¬[17] union with nature, is not yet reflected 145 into itself, has not yet taken upon itself this separation into itself from nature; it still stands—practically speaking, or as far as the will is concerned—in the unsullied faith ⌐of innocence. For¬[18] guilt first arises with freedom of choice, and freedom of choice consists in the fact that ⌐the passions posit themselves in their own¬[19] freedom while the subject selects from within itself only those determinations that it has distinguished from the natural. The plant exists in this unity; its particularity, its soul lies in this unity with universal nature. The individual plant will not be untrue to its law or to its nature, but will be as it should be; its being and what it should be are not distinct. It is the case with innocence generally that the universal is not separated from what spirit is; and this separation between what [spirit] should be. and its nature as such arises only with free will, which first comes into its own in ⌐the reflection of individuality into itself.¬[20]

a. The Original Condition[21]

For this way of viewing the matter, the next step is to imagine what it is like for humanity to be in the state of innocence, [in] just this unity of the spiritual with nature; and the notion arrived at is that by this [standard of] unity in regard to the theoretical consciousness, humanity is *perfect* in this unity with nature. Human being seems here to determine itself as identical with the concept of things; it has

17. W₂ *(1831) reads:* Humanity, so it is said, had a truthful, original religion in the state of innocence, before there occurred the cleavage in its intelligence we call the fall. This is grounded a priori in the notion that God, as the absolutely good, created spirits in the likeness of himself and that this godlike creation stood in absolute harmony with him. In such harmony spirit also lived in

18. W₂ *(Var/1831?) reads:* of innocence and was absolutely good;

19. *Thus G; P reads:* the subject posits itself in its

20. W₂ *(1831) reads:* reflection; but it is precisely this reflection and separation that is originally not present, and freedom was no less identical with law and the rational will than the individual plant is identical with its nature.

21. [*Ed.*] In the *Ms.*, the idea of the "original condition" of humanity as a state of innocence was treated in Part III, at the beginning of the discussion of estrangement (sheets 83b–84a). See Vol. 3:96–97. In the present context, Hegel draws together the themes of primitive condition and primitive religion.

not yet separated its own being-for-self from that of things; it sees into the heart of things.[22] It is only when the two are separated, when I am for myself and things are outside me, that things become enveloped in the bark of sense that separates me from them, and nature erects a screen before me, as it were.[23]

In terms of this unity of the spiritual with nature, the following can therefore be said in regard to intelligence: that in such a relationship, spirit | is immediately in the concept, knowing the universal, true nature of things immediately, understanding them intuitively, precisely because its intuition is not an external one. It is a grasping of what is inward to the concept, a form of clairvoyance, comparable to the sleepwalking state, which is a return of the soul to this inner unity with its world, in such a way that ˉthis inner world lies open to its viewˉ[24] because in this clairvoyance it is liberated from the external conditions of space and time, freed from the restrictions that result when things are defined in the terms of the understanding. In this unity, spirit is therefore clairvoyant, it is a free phantasy that has nothing arbitrary about it but wherein spirit shapes for itself nature and things according to their concept, according to their truth. And inasmuch as the attitude of spirit is here one of intuition, the object of the intuition is directly determined by the ˉconcept; it appears in its eternal beauty and transcends the conditions by which appearance is [otherwise] affected.ˉ[25] [26] With this view of things

146

22. W_2 *(1831) adds:* Nature is not yet for it something negative, something obscured.

23. [*Ed.*] Hegel's reference to "the bark of sense" (*die sinnliche Rinde*) may be an echo of the criticisms he has elsewhere directed against the tendency of reflection to split the unity of the object into an inner nucleus or kernel and an outer bark or husk; see *Encyclopedia* (1817), § 89. In this passage he is alluding to Albrecht von Haller's poem, "Die Falschheit der menschlichen Tugenden," in *Versuch schweizerischer Gedichte,* 6th ed. (Göttingen, 1751), no. 6, p. 100. Even if Hegel misunderstood the text of this poem (cf. *Enzyklopädie der philosophischen Wissenschaften im Grundrisse,* ed. Friedhelm Nicolin and Otto Pöggeler [Hamburg, 1959], p. 478), his criticism of the separation of kernel and husk on the part of the philosophy of reflection is not affected by this misunderstanding.

24. W_2 *(Var/1831?) reads:* the nature of things lay open to view for this original, intuitive understanding,

25. *Thus G; P reads:* concept, and has before it an intuition of divine life.

26. W_2 *(1831) adds:* In short, spirit had present before it, and intuited, the universal-in-the-particular in its pure configuration or shape, and also the particular,

there goes the idea that by virtue of this unity, spirit was in possession of all artistic and scientific knowledge; it is even imagined,
moreover, that when humanity is in this state of general harmony,
it sees this harmonic substance, the subject of this harmony, God,
directly, as he is—it has before it the world *in God,* God as *concrete,* the divine life in God himself, in the totality of his organic life.[27]

This is how primitive religion is viewed, for all that it was the
unmediated form of religion, and historically the first. The attempt
has been made, as we know, to substantiate this view through one
aspect of the Christian religion. The Bible tells of a paradise; | and
many peoples have such a paradise in the back of their minds,

147

---

the individual, in its universality as a divine, godlike form of organic life. And since
human beings grasped nature in its innermost determinacy and recognized its authentic
relation to the corresponding sides of their own nature, the attitude they adopted
to it was as to a well-fitting garment such as did not destroy the overall arrangement.

27. [*Ed.*] The acceptance of a condition of original perfection, which Hegel here
criticizes, was a widely held conviction of his time. Upon advancing this criticism
in Part I (the Introduction) of his *Lectures on the Philosophy of World History,* Hegel
alludes specifically to F. W. J. Schelling and Friedrich Schlegel. See the reference to
Schelling and to Schlegel's *Sprache und Weisheit der Indier* found in one of the auditor's
transcripts (Nisbet ed., p. 132; Hoffmeister ed., p. 158), as well as the allusion to
Schlegel's *Philosophie der Geschichte* 1:44 found in Hegel's lecture manuscript of 1830
(Nisbet ed., p. 231 n. 46; Hoffmeister ed., p. 159 n. f). On Schelling's acceptance
of a condition of perfection, see *On University Studies* (1803), trans. E. S. Morgan
(Athens, Ohio, 1966), p. 83 (*Sämtliche Werke* 5:287): "I firmly believe that the earliest
condition of the human race was a civilized one and that the first states, sciences,
arts, and religions were founded simultaneously, or, more accurately, that they were
not separated but were perfectly fused, as they will again be one day in their final
form." Hegel may also have had in mind Schelling's treatise on *The Deities of
Samothrace* (1815), since Schelling's belief in an original condition lies at the basis
of his interpretation of the mysteries in this work. "What if already in Greek mythology
(not to mention Indian and other Oriental mythologies) there emerged the remains
of a knowledge, indeed even a scientific system, which goes far beyond the circle drawn
by the oldest revelation known through scriptural evidences?" (trans. Robert F. Brown
[Missoula, Mont., 1977], p. 25; *Sämtliche Werke* 8:362). Friedrich Creuzer agreed
expressly with Schelling's interpretation in *Symbolik und Mythologie der alten Völker,
besonders der Griechen,* 2d ed., 4 vols. (Leipzig and Darmstadt, 1819–1821),
2:363–377. Hegel's criticism is also directed, therefore, against Creuzer; see below,
n. 678. The reference to Schlegel is to the latter's *Ueber die Sprache und Weisheit
der Indier* (Heidelberg, 1808), esp. pp. 198, 205 (cf. *Kritische Friedrich-Schlegel-
Ausgabe* 8:295–297, 303). However, Hegel's more exact description of the condition of original perfection is not traceable to Schelling and Schlegel. See further below,
n. 46.

lamenting it as lost or imagining it as the goal to which they aspire and which they will eventually reach. Whether as past or as future, such a paradise is ⁻⁻pictured to a greater or lesser extent as having a ⁻sensuous or, alternatively, a spiritual content.⁻²⁸ ⁻⁻²⁹

If we are to subject this way of viewing the matter to criticism, we must first say that it is in general necessary, i.e., that its inward content is necessary. The universal element in this representation, its inner [meaning], is the divine unity in a human reflection; in other words, it is humanity that stands as subjective spirit in this unity, that is in this unity.³⁰ But there is something else here too: that this unity is represented as a state in time, a state which ought not to have been lost and which was lost only by chance—⁻this is something else.⁻³¹

This representation, then, has differed to a greater or lesser extent among different peoples. On the one hand we must give it due credit for its merits, in that it includes the necessary idea ⁻of divine self-consciousness,⁻³² the untroubled consciousness of the absolute, divine essence. But on the other hand this idea is represented as *existing,* as a state which has occurred in time and is now over; and this union of consciousness with the divine essence is defined in principle as a natural | mode of being. This is in fact the crux of the matter. It is imagined, then, that the oneness of humanity with nature, and then with God, is original in the sense that this original is what comes first in existence. "Original" means on the one hand what is in the concept, the substantive, and on the other hand it has

148

28. *Thus D; G reads:* sensuous content. *P reads:* ethical content in regard to reason. *Ho reads:* sensuous or, alternatively, ethical content.

29. *W (following Ho) reads:* filled with ethical or unethical content, depending on the cultural level of the peoples in question. *Ho reads:* The pictorial images themselves are then filled, to a greater or lesser extent, with sensuous or, alternatively, ethical content, depending on the cultural level of the peoples in question.

30. *W₂ (1831) adds:* People thus have the impression that being-in-and-for-self is a harmony that has not yet given way to cleavage, neither the cleavage of good and evil nor the subordinate cleavage into the plurality of needs, with the violence and passion that accompany them. This unity, this resolution of contradictions, contains at all events what is genuine and authentic and is wholly consonant with the concept.

31. *W (HgG) reads:* This is to confuse what came first as *concept* with the *reality* of consciousness, the extent to which such reality is congruent with the concept.

32. *Thus G.*

the concept of what comes first in time. The view with which we are presently concerned is that this natural union of humanity with God is the true relationship in religion. At the same time we cannot but be struck by the fact that this paradise, ˜this saturnian age,˜[33] is imagined as a lost paradise, or that what we call paradise is something already lost. This already points to the fact that, more strictly speaking, images of this kind do not contain what is truthful, for divine history is totally lacking in any past or any contingency. If the existent paradise has been lost, then, no matter how that happened, it would be a contingent, arbitrary, capricious element, something that had intruded into the divine life from the outside. ˜The loss of paradise is certainly important—it is an essential determination—but it˜[34] must rather be regarded as divine necessity, and when it is so treated as contained in divine necessity, this imagined paradise sinks down to the status of one single moment in the divine totality, and to a moment that is not absolute and truthful. To define the content, the thought that is contained in this representation, more precisely: the thought is that this unity of humanity with God is, or rather has been, a natural, unmediated unity, an intuition of untroubled human beings, an intuition in which the heart of nature, and the nature of God, was laid bare before them, namely that at the center of nature and at the divine center stood *humanity*.[35]

33. *Ho reads:* this saturnian, golden time,

[*Ed.*] See esp. Hesiod, *Works and Days* 108–119; Virgil, *Eclogues* 4, 6. The Romans' belief in a golden prehistoric age, presided over jointly by Saturn and Janus, is referred to by Karl Philipp Moritz, *Anthousa; oder, Roms Alterthümer* (Berlin, 1791), p. 222.

34. *W₂ (1831) reads:* That paradise has been lost shows us that it is not essential in absolute fashion as a state of affairs. What is genuinely divine, in accord with its [essential] determination, is never lost but is eternal and has permanent being in and for itself. The loss of paradise

35. [*Ed.*] This idea and the terms Hegel uses to express it recur repeatedly in the writings of Jacob Boehme, although he used them to express his own mystical experiences. See especially his work, *De signatura rerum*, in *Theosophia revelata* (1715) (see n. 38); see also his autobiographical account in *Theosophia revelata*, vol. 2, appendix 7. Hegel refers to both works in *Vorlesungen über die Geschichte der Philosophie*, part 4 (*Vorlesungen*, vol. 9, ed. P. Garniron and W. Jaeschke [Hamburg, 1986]), p. 79. In this passage, as well as in the third part of the philosophy-of-religion lectures of 1821 (see Vol. 3:97–98), the different conceptions of a unity of being with nature expressed by Boehme in these passages probably fuse together in Hegel's mind.

149 Humanity's unity with nature is a fine-sounding, cherished expression. Understood correctly, it means the unity | of human beings with their own nature, with the nature that is truly their nature, i.e., with freedom and spirituality; it is the reasoning knowledge of the universal in and for itself. This reasoning knowledge of human beings who are [at home] in their true nature, human freedom thus defined, is no natural, unmediated unity.

Plants are in this unbroken unity; singularity is here never anything more than this particular existing plant. The spiritual, on the other hand, is not in immediate unity with its nature, ˉbut on the contraryˉ[36] it has to make its way across the infinite gulf that sets it apart from the natural; [unity] first comes into being as a reconciliation that is brought about; ˉit is not a reconciledness that is there from the outset,ˉ[37] and this genuine unity is achieved only through movement, through a process, through first getting away from one's immediate existence and then returning to self. We speak of the innocence of children, and we may bewail the fact that the child loses its so-called innocence; we lament the loss of the child's loving goodness, its unity, what is called the innocence of the child. Or we speak of the innocence of simple peoples (who are, however, more uncommon than is supposed), but this innocence is not genuinely human existence. Free ethical life is not the same as the ethical life of the child, and is at a higher level than this form of innocence; it is self-conscious volition, a willing that determines its purpose for itself by thoughtful insight. In the ethical realm this is the first genuine relationship. Just by being a free will, human beings have passed beyond this state of innocence.

This way of viewing the matter raises more specifically the question what this unity precisely represents. Does it mean, for example, that according to this unity, human beings once found themselves at the center, the midpoint of nature, that they saw into its heart, that in their intuition, in their immediate consciousness,

150 the very concept of things was at the same time before | them, the substantive essence? That this conclusion is entailed by the unity of

---

36. *Ho reads, similar in W:* in order to effect the return to itself
37. *Thus G; P reads:* [it is] not from the outset a unity of spirit with its nature,

humanity with nature is another distorted impression of the same kind.

We can distinguish in things, on the one hand, their determinateness, their quality, their essential relationship to other things. This is their natural or finite aspect. Human beings who are in the natural state can be better acquainted with things in this aspect of their peculiarity; they can have a conscious feeling, a much more definite knowledge of their particular quality than they have in the cultivated state. This side of things was also expressed in medieval philosophy, which spoke of the *signatura rerum*,[38] i.e., of certain outer qualities by which the particular, peculiar nature is denoted, so that in these external qualities [of things] the particular qualities, the specific peculiarity of their nature can be delivered up and made present to sense. This can happen in human beings in the natural state; and in animals, too, this link between the external quality and their [essence] is much more marked than is the case with human beings in the cultivated state. Animals are impelled by instinct, for example, toward whatever serves for their nourishment,[39] and ignore everything else.[40] In the same way, when they feel sick they are drawn by instinct to specific types of herbs by which the sickness is healed. In the same way, the deadly appearance and smell of plants are a sign of their harmful character for human beings in the natural state; their natural sense is more readily attentive to poisonous plants— they are more strongly repelled by them than those who are civilized. Accordingly, the instinct of animals is, on the whole, more accurate than the natural consciousness of humans, because as consciousness evolves, this instinct is impaired. One | can say that animals or human beings in the natural state see into the heart of natural things and grasp their specific quality more correctly; this constitutes their specific mode of relation to the "other," both to other animals and to humans. But this fact, that for *me* this specific quality is present

151

38. [*Ed.*] Although Hegel refers to "medieval philosophy," we may assume that he has Boehme in view; see Boehme's *De signatura rerum* in *Theosophia revelata,* pp. 2178–2404, esp. pp. 2180–2181.

39. *Ho, W add:* they devour only specific things,

40. *Ho adds, similar in W:* They are themselves specific types of individuals, and maintain themselves only by setting up in antithesis to themselves their other—not an other in general—and sublating the antithesis.

in this way, occurs only in regard to specific qualities that are purely finite in character. ⁻In the same way we know that sleepers or sleepwalkers⁻⁴¹ have this kind of natural awareness. In this case the rational consciousness has been stilled, but an inner sense or intuition has been aroused, of which it can also be said that in it human being and human knowing are much more in unity or in identity with the world and with one's [external] circumstances than in the waking state. This is why this condition is regarded as something higher than the normal condition. Only in such a state, to be sure, can there be present an awareness of things that are happening a thousand leagues away from where I am. This kind of sense or knowledge is to be found in a much higher degree among savage peoples than among those that are civilized. Such knowledge, however, is essentially limited to single events and to the destinies of single individuals; the coherence between oneself and others, between oneself and particular circumstances that belong within one's consciousness, is set vibrating and comes clearly into consciousness, but the cohering is that of ⁻a single nature, a single subject.⁻⁴²

This is not yet the real heart of things, however, for we reach this heart only with the concept, ⁻with their universal nature.⁻⁴³ The heart of a planet is the relationship between its distance from the sun, its | revolution, and so on; this is what is truly rational. And this heart is accessible only to someone with a scientific education, who is no longer in the natural state, whose mind is liberated from immediate intuition, from the immediate sensation of seeing, hearing, and so on, to one who has withdrawn his senses within himself and whose relationship to these objects is one of unfettered thought. This rationality and this knowledge emerge only [as] the result of the infinite mediation of thought and only come on the scene with the

152

41. *Ho reads:* This instinct sees only into the heart of things in their singularity; its vision does not pierce into the source of life of things in general, into their divine heart. The same relationship occurs in sleepwalkers [*im Somnambulismus*], who W (*following Ho and G*) *reads:* This instinct . . . occurs in sleepers, in sleepwalkers, who

42. *Ho reads: this* individual with *specific* events.

43. *G reads:* the universal idea. *D reads:* its universal nature. *Ho reads:* This slumber of the spirit cannot reveal to us the true heart of the world. This heart is the concept, the eternal law of things. W (*following G and Ho*) *reads:* the universal idea. This slumber . . . world.

last stage of human existence; the first stage of human existence is as an animal.

As for the other aspect of this way of viewing things—[the claim] that in this natural unity of humanity, this unity not yet broken by reflection, there lay also the genuine consciousness of God, that it lies in consciousness—if unity is represented as a natural, immediate unity, what we have said already applies here too. Spirit is only spirit, spirit is only *for* spirit, spirit in its truth is only for the *free* spirit; and this free spirit is the one that has learned to look beyond immediate sense-perception, the one that also looks beyond understanding, beyond the reflection based on understanding and suchlike. Or in theological terms it is the spirit that has come to the full knowledge of sin, i.e., that has penetrated to the consciousness of the infinite gulf, the rupture of the inner being, of being-for-itself, and has emerged once more from this separation into unity and reconciliation. Hence natural, immediate unity is not the true existence of the idea but rather its lowest stage, the one that is furthest removed from the truth. Such is the verdict on this type of representation.

The other point in this connection is that this view defines its ideal as something that is past and also future. That it should set up an ideal of this kind is necessary, for by so doing it expresses what genuinely is, in and for itself; but the shortcoming is that it simultaneously defines the ideal as something that will happen and that has happened. Thereby it turns the ideal into something that is not present, and immediately imparts to it the character of something finite. ˉ[But] what is in and for itself is the infinite, while in the reflective consciousness we have before us a state of finitude.ˉ44 | Reflection quite rightly distinguishes the two, but the   153 shortcoming of representation is that it adheres in principle to an *abstract* attitude, yet insists that what is in and for itself should also *appear* and be present in the world of external contingency. Reason allows chance and arbitrariness their proper sphere but knows that in this—superficially, to outward appearance, highly confused—

---

44. *Ho reads, similar in* W_2: The empirical consciousness is knowing the finite; what is in and for itself is what lies within this outer shell.

world, truth is still present. Such is the case with other ideals as well; for example, the ideal of a state may be very true in itself, but one forgets that it is not realized, not present. What we represent to ourselves as the realization of an ideal is that the complex pattern of law, politics, and economics should all be in conformity with the idea; here, then, we have a field such as *cannot* in fact match the ideal but which is nonetheless present, and within which the substantive idea is nevertheless actual and present. One can grant all the evil there is in the world, but what is awry and confused in existence is a long way from constituting the entire present. This whole range of appearance is only one side and does not embrace the totality that belongs to the present as a whole. In regard to the idea of this unity, unity is defined in an abstract manner. But it is not yet recognized that the idea is present in fact because fact is regarded solely with reflective understanding. That is the difficulty that remains, to recognize the actual existence of what is substantive in the idea through this outer bark; ⁻and because it is difficult to find the ideal in actuality, it is transposed to the past or the future.⁻45

45. *Ho reads, similar in W:* and to enjoy it; to be sure, this also involves hard labor: in order to pluck reason, the rose in the cross of the present, one must take up the cross itself.

[Ed.] This famous metaphor also occurs in the Preface to Hegel's *Philosophy of Right* (1821), trans. T. M. Knox (London, 1952), p. 12. Apparently it was suggested to him both by Luther's coat of arms, which had a black cross in the midst of a heart surrounded by white roses, and by the Rosicrucians (cf. Hegel, *Werke* 17:227, 403), a seventeenth-century secret society, which used as its emblem a St. Andrew's cross and four roses. Reason is the rose in the cross of the present because it discloses the ideal and the rational in the midst of the actual and the seemingly irrational. To "pluck" reason one must take up the actual, attending to what is *presently* given in the world; but because of the difficulty and pain involved in so doing, it is tempting to transpose the ideal into the past or the future. The metaphor is thus congruent with the main text as found in G as well as with the argument of the paragraph as a whole. It is curious that G, P, and D missed the metaphor. Perhaps they did not understand it and simply omitted it; or possibly *Ho* inserted it on the basis of familiarity with the Preface to the *Philosophy of Right*. It is plausible, however, that Hegel's actual lecture included both the metaphor with its accompanying stress on the present, as transmitted by *Ho,* and the warning against transposing the ideal into the past or the future, as transmitted by G. On Hegel's use of this metaphor and its possible meanings, see Karl Löwith, *From Hegel to Nietzsche: The Revolution in Nineteenth-Century Thought* (1941), trans. David E. Green (New York, 1967), pp. 13–18; and Wolf-Dieter Marsch, *Gegenwart Christi in der Gesellschaft: Eine Studie zu Hegels Dialektik* (Munich, 1965), pp. 271–274.

Attempts have also been made to demonstrate historically the view that the human race began in this way, that the human race enjoyed a state of perfection.[46] | There are numerous peoples among whom   154
have been found relics of art, of phantasy, and sometimes also of scientific knowledge, which seem to be incompatible with their present state. From this evidence of a better mode of existence people have inferred an earlier state of perfection, a state of completely ethical life—just as, when medieval monks came up with Greek and Latin writings, one could infer that writings of this kind did not come out of their own heads but belonged to another age. Among the Hindus a wisdom and knowledge has been found which is so great that it is not consistent with their present educational and cultural level. This and many other similar circumstances have been seen[47] as traces of a better past.[48] However, this wisdom of the Hindus, of the Egyptians, and of antiquity generally, has grown steadily smaller the more we have become acquainted with it; it is still diminishing as each day passes, and the facets of which cognizance *can* be taken either can be attributed to other sources or else are of ⁻no account in themselves.⁻[49]

b. Immediate Religion in General[50]

Let us begin now to consider nature religion, or immediate religion, in general. Its determining characteristic is the unity of the natural

46. [*Ed.*] See above, n. 27, and Friedrich Schlegel, *Über die neuere Geschichte: Vorlesungen gehalten zu Wien im Jahre 1810* (Vienna, 1811), p. 47 (*Kritische Friedrich-Schlegel-Ausgabe* 1:7:148)—a passage to which Hegel probably also alludes in his *Lectures on the Philosophy of World History,* Nisbet ed., p. 132 (Hoffmeister ed., p. 159).

47. [*Ed.*] See above, nn. 27, 46. In the philosophy-of-history lectures, Hegel refers critically in this connection to the Abbé Lamennais, Baron Ferdinand von Eckstein's journal *Le Catholique,* and the Congregation for the Propagation of the Faith; see *Philosophy of World History,* Nisbet ed., pp. 231–232 n. 47 (Hoffmeister ed., pp. 159–160 n. g).

48. W_2 *(1831) adds:* The writings of medieval monks, for instance, often did not, to be sure, come out of their own heads, but were the relics of a better past.

49. W_2 *(1831) reads:* very little significance. But this whole notion of an original paradise has thus shown itself to be a poetic figment, which has as its basis the concept, but the concept taken as immediate existence instead of being primarily mediation.

50. [*Ed.*] This "general" discussion is based on the *Ms.*, sheets 32b–39b, but the third of the topics in the latter, the cultus of immediate religion, is replaced by a brief

and spiritual, so that on the objective side God is posited as this unity, while the subjective side, self-consciousness, is entangled in natural determinacy. This natural element is to begin with a singular existence, not nature in general as a whole or an organic totality— these are all general conceptions not yet posited here at this initial stage; the natural is to be taken in its singularity. (Natural classes and genera belong to a higher stage of reflection and to the mediating work of thought.) It is this singular aspect of nature | (this visible sky, this sun or moon, a river, a tree, this beast or human being, and so forth), an immediate natural existence of this kind, that is apprised as God in general. What content this representation of God possesses is something we can for the time being leave undetermined here—at this initial stage there is something indeterminate, an indeterminate power generally, a presence of the spirit in phantasy and representation, which is capable of still further fulfillment. But since it is not yet the spirit in its truthfulness, this power, the categorial determinations of this spirit, are fortuitous; they become true only when ˉthe true God is in consciousness.ˉ⁵¹ This is therefore the first beginning.

155

In the sphere of natural religion, therefore, we shall first consider the metaphysical concept, secondly the form or shape of God, the way he is represented, and thirdly the cultus. But here the cultus will not be viewed abstractly; it is on the contrary more interesting to present the different forms of nature religion.⁵²

(α) The Metaphysical Concept of God⁵³

Under this heading there belongs the form of thought that is familiar to us as proof of the existence of God. To begin with, we

survey of the forms of immediate religion, since the 1824 lectures have incorporated the materials on the cultus into the description of the "practical relationshp" at the end of Part I (see Vol. 1, 1824 *Concept,* pp. 350–364, esp. n. 178).

51. W_2 *reads:* the true God is in consciousness and posits them. *Ho reads:* they are posited by the true God, the God who is in consciousness.

52. W_1 *(Ed?) adds:* itself and spend some time considering them.

[*Ed.*] It is "more interesting" because the abstract summary of the cultus of nature religion has already been presented at the end of Part I of the 1824 lectures (see above, n. 50).

53. [*Ed.*] In this section Hegel analyzes the cosmological proof of God, based on the rise of consciousness from finite to infinite, from determinate being to ab-

must discuss the *concept* of this "metaphysical" concept and explain what is meant by it.

At this point we have [before us] a completely concrete content, and whatever might be called a metaphysico-logical concept consequently seems to lie far behind us, just because we are in the realm of the absolutely concrete. We must be more specific. The content is certainly *spirit* in general; the elaboration of what spirit is forms the entire content of the philosophy of religion. The different levels at which spirit is intellectualized give rise to the different religions. This diversity of determinacy comes about as the different levels are constituted; | it appears as the external form grounded in spirit, the differences being posited within it in a determinate form that is at the same time an altogether simple universal, logical form. The form is consequently what is abstract. But this form is not only the external shell of this determinate spirit but also, as the logical element, its innermost kernel as the determinacy of what is inward. It combines both within itself—being the innermost kernel, the determinacy of what is most inward, and at the same time the outward form: this is the nature of the concept, to be the essential and at the same time the mode of appearance, the mode of difference or of form. On the one hand this logical determinacy is concrete as spirit, and this entirety is the simple substantiality of spirit; on the other hand it is its external form, by which it is distinguished from the "other."[54] It may seem that if another natural object is considered, it has the logical element as its inner kernel; and in the case of a concrete shape such as the finite spirit, this is in fact so. In the philosophy of nature and the philosophy of spirit, this logical form does not merit particular attention, for when we are dealing with something like nature or spirit, it is present in a finite way, and the exposition of

156

---

solute being, as is characteristic of nature religion in general. Into it he inserts an extended discussion of pantheism in which he shows that the concept of pantheism has been widely misunderstood in the recent controversies: neither nature religion nor Spinozism is pantheistic in any meaningful sense. In the 1827 lectures the discussion of pantheism is given greater prominence by being taken into the *Concept of Religion* (see Vol. 1:346 ff., 374 ff.).

54. *Ho, W add:* That inmost determinacy, the content of each successive level according to its substantive nature, is thus at the same time the external form.

the logical element can be displayed as a system of syllogisms or mediations.[55] But in the field in which we are now operating, it is the logical element that has resumed its former simple shape and can therefore be more easily considered, "that strikes the attention"[56] [in such a way] that it can be the special | object of consideration. It could be presupposed in this case too; but because of the simplicity to which it has reverted, what happens is that the simple, substantive logical element is considered here on its own account, just as it is in theology, the science of God. Hence we can in the first place *presuppose* this logical element, but secondly *treat* it—by virtue of its simplicity—because it is of interest in that it was formerly discussed in natural theology and is in general a topic of theology, the intellectual science of God [*die Verstandeswissenschaft von Gott*]. Since the advent of Kantian philosophy, this metaphysical topic has been cast aside as a poor, shoddy thing, unworthy of any notice, and it accordingly deserves to have justice done to it here.

These determinations should be considered, then, as they occur in the form of proofs for God's existence. As regards the relationship between these forms, these conceptual determinacies as such, these logical, substantive determinacies of the idea, and the forms of proof for the existence of God, the following should be borne in mind. A conceptual determination, indeed any concept, is not of itself something in repose but something that moves itself; it is essentially activity, and for that reason it is mediation within self, just as thinking in general is a form of activity or inward self-mediation, so that a particular thought also involves inward self-mediation.

55. *W (HgG/1831?) adds:* Without this comprehensive discussion, conducted solely in accord with the purpose [in hand], it would be insufficient to adduce and consider the simple determinacy of concept. *W continues, following Ho:* But because in these spheres the logical categories, as substantive foundation, are obscured and do not exist as simple, intelligible entities, it is not so necessary to single them out for attention on their own account, whereas in religion, spirit accords logical elements a more prominent place. *Ho reads:* Logical categories also provide the substantive foundation for nature and finite spirit, but since at these levels they are obscured and do not exist as simple, intelligible entities, it is not so necessary to single them out for attention on their own account; whereas in religion, spirit—breaking free from its finite shapes—reverts again to its inward simplicity and in the process accords logical elements a more prominent place.

56. *P reads:* [such] that it strikes the attention *G reads:* and this furnishes an excuse if it should strike the attention

Thus, when we consider the determination of the concept, we have before us nothing but mediations; and the proofs of God are likewise nothing else but mediations; their aim is to present him by using a mediation. It is thus the same in both cases. In the proofs of God's existence, however, the shape of the mediation is as if the recourse to it were for the sake of cognition, in order that a sure insight should develop for cognition; the aim is to prove it to me, and the mediation is only a subjective interest, that of my cognizing. From what has been said previously regarding the nature of the concept, however, it is clear that the mediation is not to be understood in this subjective way—to conceive it thus is to misconceive it from the very outset—but that the mediation is equally an objective mediation of God within himself, an internal mediation of his own logic. The mediation is contained in the divine idea itself, and it is only when it is understood in this way that it becomes a necessary determination, a necessary moment. In the proofs for God's existence, therefore, we must discard the form of understanding; | they must 158 show themselves to be a necessary moment of the concept itself, a *going forth* of mediation, an *activity* on the part of the concept itself.

It is characteristic of the next form that we are here still completely at the first stage (what we have called the unmediated stage, the stage of the unmediated unity of the spiritual and the formal), that the spiritual is involved with a certain [degree of] immediacy. From this characteristic of immediacy it follows that we are here dealing with entirely abstract determinations, for immediate (or unmediated) and abstract mean the same. When we say "immediate," we picture to ourselves [simple] being; but in thought, too, the abstract is the immediate category, the form of thinking which has not yet deepened itself inwardly and has not thereby fulfilled itself, enriched itself, made itself concrete through further reflecting. If we have this concrete spirit as our object, but only generally, and the natural state [as] the mode of its reality, and if we divest both of them of their concrete content and keep only the abstract determination, then what we have is an abstract determination of God and the finite. These two sides now stand over against each other as infinite and finite, the one as existence [*Dasein*], the other as being [*Sein*], the one as substantial and the other as accidental, as universal and as singular. Admittedly these determinations are in some measure distinct: for example, the singular is much more concrete than the accidental; the universal is, or is supposed to be, much more concrete than substance. However, we can here take them undeveloped, and it makes no difference in that case which form we take in order to consider them more closely; what is essential in these determinations or categories is their relationship to one another when they [are] submerged in religion.

159   [57]Humanity rises from the finite to the infinite, ˉrises | above the singular and raises itself to the universal, to being-in-and-for-self.ˉ[58] Thus religion consists in this, that human beings have before them in their consciousness the nothingness of the finite, are aware of their dependence, and seek the ground of this nothingness, of this dependence—in a word, that they find no peace of mind until they set up the infinite before themselves. Even when we speak of religion in these abstract terms, we already have here the relationship of *transition* from finite to infinite. This transition, however, is not simply a factual one but is grounded in the nature of these determinations as well; that is to say, it is grounded in the concept, and it may be noted here that there is no need for us to advance beyond this definition of the transition. Considering it in more detail, it is possible to grasp it in two ways: first as a transition from the finite to the infinite as a beyond—this is a more modern relationship. But secondly it can be taken in such a way that the unity of both is maintained and the finite is preserved in the infinite. This is how it is in nature religion. ˉThe consciousness in finite existence [*Existenz*] itself here becomes the infinite.ˉ[59] In this singular existence, God,

---

57. *Precedes in W (1831):* This relationship into which they are placed with one another is to be found in their nature as much as in religion, and must first be taken up from this side.

58. W_2 *(1831) reads:* Having the world before themselves, human beings feel in it what is inadequate (feeling also feels what is thought or what has to be thought). It does not suffice them as something ultimate, and they find the world to be an aggregate of finite things. They also know themselves to be something contingent, ephemeral; and in this feeling they rise above the singular and raise themselves to the universal, to the One that is in and for itself, an essence that is not affected by this contingency and conditionality but is simply *substance* as opposed to these accidents and the *power* by virtue of which these contingent things exist or do not exist.

59. *W (1831) reads:* In it some singular, unmediated existence, natural or spiritual, something finite, is extended infinitely beyond this its scope, and the limited intuiting of such an object constitutes at the same time knowledge of infinite being, free

he who is infinite, is present to ⁻existence⁻[60] in such a way that this natural existence does not thereby vanish but is rather the mode of God's being, so that natural existence is preserved in unmediated unity with the substantive. But to define this relationship more precisely, whether the infinite is separated from the finite, or whether there is a transition from the finite | to the infinite (the equality of   160 the two being retained, each being held fast in the other), this does not concern us.

As regards the fact that consciousness progresses in religion from the finite to the infinite, this progress from finite to infinite is not just a factual episode in the history of religion, but is necessitated by the concept,[61] and lies in the very nature of this determination. This transition is a mediation, is in fact naught but the transition of thought itself, and thought connotes nothing else but to know the infinite in the finite, the universal in the particular and singular.[62] When we think an object, we have before our eyes its law, its essence, its universal order. It is only thinking human beings who have religion; animals have none because they do not think. The next step is to show with regard to this definition of the finite, the singular, and the accidental that it is the finite *itself* which translates or transforms itself into its other—the infinite, the universal, and so on. It cannot abide as finite, but makes itself into the infinite; in virtue of its substance it *must* revert to the infinite. To demonstrate this transition, to show that they [the determinations of the finite] are themselves this transition, this passing-over implicitly, falls wholly within the logical consideration [of the finite].[63] | 161

substantiality. In a word, infinitude is simultaneously intuited in the finite thing—the sun, an animal, or whatever it may be—and inner, infinite unity or divine substantiality in the outward multiplicity of finite things.

60. *Thus P; G reads:* consciousness

61. [Ed.] See Hegel, *Science of Logic*, pp. 137–154 (cf. GW 11:78–85).

62. *W (1831) adds:* Consciousness of the universal, of the infinite, *is* thought, i.e., inner mediation, going outside oneself, in general sublating the external, the singular. This is the nature of thought as such.

63. *W₂ (1831) adds:* The contingency of the world does not provide the sole starting point for the process of elevation, in order to arrive at the necessity of the essence that is in and for itself; we can define the world in still another fashion. Necessity is the final category in being and essence, and is therefore preceded by many other categories. The world can be a many, a manifold, in which case its truth is the One. In the same way as a transition can be made from the many to the One,

Putting the matter as concisely as possible, the finite can be defined as follows. We say, "The finite is, it *is* something, and at the same time it is something *finite*." What it is, it is through its negation, through its limit.[64] "Finite" is a qualitative determination, a *quality*, and the finite has being in such a way that [its] quality is simply a determinacy that is immediately identical with *its* being. The "something" has a quality, and [this] is immediately one with what has being, so that if the quality passes away, this "something" passes away too. We say "something red"; here red is the quality, and if this ceases to be, then it is no longer this, and if it were not a substance that can tolerate this, then the "something" would be lost too.[65] It is no different with the spirit: there are men and women of quite determinate character, and if this is lost, they cease to be. Thus the fundamental quality of Cato was to be a Roman republican; when this ceased, he ceased to be. This quality is so bound up with him that he cannot subsist without it. The firm determinateness of quality here is character. This is the general nature of the qualitative. Now the qualitative is essentially finite. The determinateness is *this,* and is not something else; it is essentially | a limit, a negation. Cato's limit was that he was a Roman republican, and his spirit, his idea

162

---

from the finite to the infinite, *being* can provide the starting point for passing over to *essence*.

W *(1831) continues:* The transition from finite to infinite, from accidental to substantive, etc., belongs to the effective operation of thought in consciousness and is the very nature of these determinations themselves, what they in truth are. The finite is not the absolute, but it consists only in passing away and becoming the infinite; the singular consists only in reverting to the universal, the accidental only in reverting to substance. This transition is mediation to the extent that it is the movement from the initial, unmediated determinacy into its other, into the infinite, the universal; and substance as such is not something immediate but what becomes, what posits itself, through this passing over. That this is the genuine nature of these determinations themselves is demonstrated in logic, and it is essential to hold this fast in its proper sense—that it is not *we,* in merely external reflection, who pass over from one such determination to its other, but rather that they in themselves *consist* in passing over in this way. Let me say a little more about this dialectical element in regard to the determination we are here considering, namely, the finite.

64. W *(following Ho) adds:* through the beginning . . . itself. *Ho reads:* The finite *is,* but its being is finitude. In other words, what it is it is through its *end,* through the beginning, within it, of an other, which is not itself, i.e., its negative, its limits.

65. *Thus G.*

could go no further than this. This quality therefore constitutes the limit of the "something," and this we call a finite as such; its essence lies in its limit, in its negation, and this particularity, this negation, is accordingly essential only in relation to its "other." Now this "other" is not another finite, but the infinite. It is through its essence that the finite is what it is, what it should be, in such a way that its essence rather lies in its negation. Fully developed, the finite is an "other," namely, the infinite; the finite ¯is simply this, to be the infinite.¯[66]

The main thought is this, that the finite is something that is defined as finite, it does not have its being in itself but in an "other," and this "other" is the infinite.[67]

Now this progress is necessary, it is contained in the concept: the finite is finite within itself, that is its nature. The process of elevation to God is just what we have already seen: this finite self-consciousness does not remain bound to the finite; it relinquishes the nature of the finite, jettisons it, and pictures to itself the infinite; this is what happens, so to speak, in the process of elevation to God, and this is the rational element in that process. This progression is the innermost or purely logical element. To define God in terms of infinity does not exhaust his nature, for his content is concrete. This progression, however, expresses only one side of the totality. For the finite disappears in the infinite; this is its nature, to sublate itself and to posit the infinite as its truth. This progression is only one side of the whole | movement, and the infinite that has come to be   163
in this way is itself still only the ¯abstract infinite.¯[68] As this abstraction the infinite too is, on the one hand, essentially determined at

66. *Thus D; G reads:* is essentially the being of the infinite. *P reads:* has its truth in the infinite.
67. *W adds:* The finite consists indeed in having the infinite for its truth; what it is is not itself, but its opposite, the infinite. *Cf. Ho:* Of itself it therefore passes over into the infinite; it sublates itself, for the finite consists solely in sublating, and it posits the infinite as its truth. . . . But because of this negative side it needs, already for its being, an other, namely the finite; but in this way it is not itself the infinite but its opposite, the finite.
68. *W (following G or Ho) reads:* abstract infinite, determined in merely negative fashion as the nonfinite. *Ho reads:* abstract, what is determined in merely negative fashion as the nonfinite.

first in merely negative fashion; it has to sublate itself and determine itself *generally,* to annul its negativity and posit itself as affirmation. On the other hand it has to sublate its *abstractness,* particularizing itself and positing within itself the moment of the finite.

First the moment of the finite disappears in the infinite, and we then have only the infinite; but the finite does not have being, its being is mere show; so we have the infinite before us in merely abstract form within its own sphere, and its determination consists in sublating its own abstractness. This results from the concept of the infinite; the infinite is the negation of the negative, negation that relates to itself, i.e., it is affirmation, absolute affirmation, and at the same time being—simple relation to self is what is meant by being. In this way the second moment, the infinite, is also not merely negative, a beyond, but also affirmative, a being [i.e., God]. This also means that the infinite consists in inwardly determining itself, or validating the moment of finitude within itself (but as ideal). Hence it is the negation of negation and comprises what distinguishes the first negation from the other negation; consequently there is limit in it, and, with limit, there is the finite. If we are to define these two negations more precisely, the first is the finite and the second the infinite. This, however, is still the "bad" infinite; the infinite that is "over there" is the logical abstraction, and the genuinely infinite must be understood as the unity of both these negations. ¯What is noteworthy is that the infinite, being this affirmative, therefore includes being; this is here posited as result, as the simple relation to self to which the negation of negation reverts.¯⁶⁹ All this makes up the concept of the infinite. This infinite needs to be essentially distinguished from the form that we discussed ¯previously; | the infinite in immediate knowledge or as thing-in-itself in Kantian philosophy is at a low[er] level.¯⁷⁰ In immediate knowledge I know God, that he is beyond, above me; here [the infinite] is no longer something otherworldly, but has its determinacy within itself.

164

69. W (1831) reads: It is only the two moments together that make up the nature of the infinite and its genuine identity.

70. W (1831, with G) reads: previously, the infinite in immediate knowledge or as thing-in-itself, which is the negative, indeterminate infinite, merely the nonfinite in Kantian philosophy.

In nature religion too, the infinite is not meant in this way at all, as something "over there," with the implication that a transition is made from the finite to the infinite and that the finite vanishes in the infinite. On the contrary, ¯natural religion¯[71] already contains a consciousness of the divine in general as what is universally substantive but at the same time determinate. This determinateness has the form of a natural existence. What is intuited as God in natural religion is the genuine content, the infinite, this divine substance in natural form. In natural religion the content ¯is thus more concretely, and hence more perfectly, genuine¯[72] than the content that is obtained in the views of immediate knowledge, ¯i.e., that the infinite [God] is over there, formless, simply the indeterminate.¯[73] Natural religion stands already at a higher level than this view.[74]

¯Another point to be noted is that in this form of thought we have spoken of the finite generally. When we | speak in this way, 165 we take the finite as universal: the finite is everything finite. Speaking in this universal way, we say that nature religion is just this, to have the infinite before one in a finite-as-such; and if by this finitude we understand everything finite,¯[75] then we should have what is called pantheism. If we imagine that the infinite is immediately contained in everything finite, that it exists as unmediated determinate being [Dasein], but that this determinate being does not exist in a chance manner (it is not a singular existence [Existenz], such as a river and so forth, but universal finitude)—if finitude in general is expressed in such a way that the divine is immediately universal in

71. W (1831) reads: nature religion, though the way in which it defines the finite and the infinite yields a highly imperfect unity of the two,

72. Thus P; W (1831) reads: is thus more concrete, and hence more perfect, contains more truth,

73. Thus P; D reads: It is only the utterly formless, the indeterminate, that we are unable to cognize. G reads: which is unwilling to cognize God because he is indeterminate.

74. W (1831) adds: held by moderns, who in holding it still profess belief in revelatory religion.

75. W₁ (1831) reads: It can also be noted that the natural is to be taken in immediate fashion, as this or that singular (the sun, this river, etc., as contingency dictates), as it is first taken in nature religion. But if what is taken is the finite generally (everything singular, and thus in it, as it is, at the same time the universal generally), if the divine is known in each and every such present existence,

it, then we have pantheism. This pantheism is summed up in Jacobi's phrase: ˉ"God is the being (the universal) in all existent, i.e., determinate, being."ˉ⁷⁶ This determinate being contains being within itself, and this being within determinate being is God. When we speak of God in this way, that he is the being in all determinate being, this is the most inadequate of all definitions of God, the least satisfactory if he is to be spirit. If God is defined thus as being and it is said he is the being of determinate being in the singularized, finite world of the real, this denotes pantheism: Jacobi was very far from being a pantheist, but this phrase of his sums it up. There is, of course, a difference between what someone means and what he says; but science is not concerned with what someone means in his head, but with what he says.

Or again, according to Parmenides, "Being is all; only being is."⁷⁷ This appears at first to be the same as Jacobi's expression and so to be pantheism also; but it can be argued that Parmenides' thought is purer than Jacobi's expression, that the being of Parmenides is not pantheism. For he says expressly "There is only being," and all barriers, all so-called reality, all the modes of existence fall under nonbeing; nonbeing *is* not, and Parmenides is left solely with being.⁷⁸ 166 | On the contrary, if one says "the being in all determinate being," then being counts as affirmative, and the being in this determinate being is the affirmation in finite existence. In this sense one cannot

76. [*Ed.*] *Gott ist das Sein (das Allgemeine) in allem Da(= Bestimmt)sein.* Hegel is referring to Jacobi's description of Spinoza's teaching; see Jacobi, *Briefe,* p. 61: "Spinoza's God is the unadulterated principle of actuality in everything actual, of being in all existent being [*des Seins in allem Dasein*], wholly without individuality, and absolutely infinite" (F. H. Jacobi, *Werke* 4/1:87; cf. 56). His criticism of Jacobi is misplaced since the phrase he cites does not represent Jacobi's viewpoint but Spinoza's, which Jacobi himself criticizes (see below, n. 80). As regards the equivalence of "existent" and "determinate" as qualifying "being" (*Dasein = Bestimmtsein*), see *Wissenschaft der Logik* (*GW* 11:59): "Dasein ist bestimmtes Sein." (This distinction is not found in the English translation, which is based on the 2d ed. of the German, and which in any case translates *Dasein* as "determinate being.")
    W (1831) reads: "God is the being in all determinate being [*Dasein*]," and this also at all events yields spiritually rich definitions of God.
    77. [*Ed.*] See Parmenides, frag. 6 in G. S. Kirk, J. E. Raven, and M. Schofield, *The Presocratic Philosophers,* 2d ed. (Cambridge, 1983), p. 247; also Hegel, *Science of Logic,* p. 83 (cf. *GW* 11:45).
    78. *W (1831) adds:* In his case what is called determinate being is completely absent.

say Spinozism is pantheism, for Spinoza says, "What is, is the absolute substance"; all else are only modes to which he ascribes no affirmativeness or reality.[79] [80]

If we take the finite as thought, we mean by that everything finite, and this is pantheism. But a distinction must be drawn depending on whether, in speaking simply of the finite, we are speaking of this or that finite object or of everything. If the finite is taken as everything, this is already a movement of reflection, which passes beyond singulars; this complexifying of the finite belongs already to reflection. This is a [more] modern form of pantheism: to say "God is the being in all determinate being" is a modern way of viewing pantheism; it is a philosophical reflection. One can also say it is the pantheism of the contemporary Orient, of modern Muslims,[81] who say, "Everything, just the way it is, is a whole and is God," and the finite has being in this determinate being as universal finitude.[82] Where | we have spoken of the finite in thought forms, this is not to be taken in the universal sense in regard to nature religion; it is not to be taken reflectively but only as referring to an unmediatedly

167

79. *W (1831) adds:* So perhaps it cannot be said even of Spinoza's substance that it is as precisely pantheistic as the expression quoted above, for with him singulars remain as little an affirmative as does determinate being with Parmenides; with Spinoza determinate being, distinguished from being, is only nonbeing and "is" in such a way that this nonbeing has no being at all.

80. [*Ed.*] Hegel erroneously regards the phrase, "the being in all determinate being," as representing Jacobi's position, whereas Jacobi intended it only as a description of Spinozism (see n. 76). Hegel's error is probably related to the fact that he would not regard this formulation as an authentic statement of Spinoza's position, since it included in his view the very affirmation of finitude that Spinoza rejected. For Hegel's own presentation of a pantheistic affirmation of the finite, which did not, however, entail a pure equivalence of God and finite things but rather distinguished the divine in the finite, see Part I of the 1827 philosophy-of-religion lectures, Vol. 1:375–376—where, to be sure, Hegel does designate this view of the relationship of the divine and the finite as "Oriental pantheism or genuine Spinozism." On Spinoza's definition of "mode," see *Ethics* (1677), pt. I, def. V: "By *mode,* I mean the modifications of substance, or that which exists in, and is conceived through, something other than itself" (*Chief Works* 2:45).

81. *W (1831) adds:* especially Jalāl-al-Din Rūmī,
[*Ed.*] Hegel was acquainted with the Muslim mystic Jalāl-al-Din Rūmī (1207–1273) through a collection of poems freely translated by Friedrich Rückert, *Mewlana Dschelaleddin Rumi,* in *Taschenbuch für Damen auf das Jahr 1821* (Tübingen, 1821), pp. 211–248.

82. *W (1831) adds:* This pantheism is the product of reflective thinking, which extends the scope of natural things to embrace each and every thing, and in so doing

singular existence; and to this extent nature religion[83] is by no means pantheistic.

To revert to our consideration of this transition from the finite to the infinite, in the form in which it appears in the proofs of the existence of God, we find that it is here presented in the form of a syllogism. Among the proofs that are offered, the first is the *cosmological.* The shape in which we want to consider it here is not the same as what is called the cosmological proof in natural theology. But we then have [to] abandon considering the detailed course of this transition. By and large, the transition is the same in all of these proofs. In regard to its ˉcategorial contentˉ[84] the starting point of the cosmological proof is a contingent—or, as is sometimes said, "accidental"—being. It starts from the contingency of worldly things; and the subsequent determination is then in terms not merely of infinity but of necessity, of something that is in and for itself necessary. This is a much more concrete determination than that of the infinite, as we have it here; in regard to the content of the proof, in regard to its determinateness, what we are here speaking of is consequently something different.[85] |

168

---

pictures to itself the existence of God not as genuine universality of thought but as an "allness," i.e., in all singular natural existences.

W_2 *(1831) continues:* One further remark in passing. Recent philosophy's definition of spirit as unity with self, the world being grasped inwardly as something ideal, is also called pantheism or, more precisely, spiritualistic pantheism. But here "unity" is comprehended in a merely one-sided way, as opposed to "creation," where God is cause and the separation occurs in such a way that the creation is autonomous over against him. But this is precisely the basic characteristic of spirit, to be this differentiating and positing of the difference. This is the creation they are so keen on retaining. Then of course there is the further aspect that the separation does not endure but is sublated, for otherwise we are in the realm of dualism and Manichaeism.

We now revert to the categorial determination that substance as universal power is singled out by thought on its own account.

However, to raise up substance in this way, to know substance as being for self, is not yet religion, since it still lacks the moment that must not be lacking in religion as the consummate idea—the moment of spirit. What gives rise to the moment of spirit being established is that substance is not yet inwardly determined as spirit, nor spirit as substance. Spirit is thus outside substance, in fact is distinct from it.

83. W_1 *(1831) adds:* as the religion of the beginning
84. *W (1831) reads:* metaphysical content
85. *Ho adds, similar in* W_1: What we have in view here cannot be the cosmological proof, which is much more concrete, if only because the one side is the contingently

If we now put the transition into the form of a syllogism, our syllogism runs as follows: "The finite presupposes the infinite; but the finite is, this particular entity exists; therefore the infinite also is."[86] If we are asked to weigh the merits of a syllogism of this kind, we must say it leaves us cold. It belongs to the understanding. ¨When we are discussing the religious relationship, we require something quite different from syllogisms.¨[87] On the one hand, this is justified, but on the other hand the rejection of syllogisms implies quite generally that we are belittling thought, as if feeling and recourse to a mental image are needed in order to convince. But the true nerve of every argument is that the thought should be truthful; only when the thought is true are one's feelings truthful too.

What is striking in this syllogism is that a finite mode of being is assumed, and this finite being is seen as that through which the infinite mode of being is grounded. A contingent, finite mode of being, which *is,* is assumed; this provides the starting point and is seen as that from which the infinite is inferred or as ground of the infinite. In general terms, this is what is unsatisfactory. The mediation is established in such a way that the consciousness of the infinite derives from the finite, so that finite being is the ground of the infinite. More specifically, it is the case that the finite is expressed as having only a positive relation to the infinite. The proposition runs: "The being of the finite is the being of the infinite." There is posited only a positive relation between finite and infinite being. This is at once seen to be disproportionate, as when we say that the finite presupposes the infinite. But the finite is what posits. It remains the affirmative; this means, however, that there is a positive relation of the finite to the infinite, and the being of the finite is what comes first, the ground of | inference, and what remains. It should also be noted that when we say the being of the finite is the being of the

169

accidental and the other what is necessary in and for itself, even though the logical form of the transition is the same. W_2 *(Var) adds:* but only the logical nature of the transition enters into consideration.

86. [*Ed.*] On the logical basis for the relationship between finite and infinite as presented in this and the next three paragraphs, see Hegel, *Science of Logic,* pp. 137–154 (cf. GW 11:78–85).

87. *Thus P; G reads:* From matters of religion we require something else. *Ho reads:* In the case of religion we require more. *W reads:* In religion we require something else, something more.

infinite, then it is the being of the finite, which is itself the being of the infinite, that forms the major premise. But only the major premise is thus posited; the mediation between it and the being of the infinite is not indicated: the proposition is not mediated, and that is the very opposite of what is required.

If we consider this mediation, we see that true mediation includes a further characteristic, namely that the being of the finite is not its own being but that of the "other," the infinite; in other words, what gives rise to the infinite is not the being of the finite but the nonbeing of the finite; the nonbeing of the finite is the being of the infinite. The mediation takes the form that the finite stands before us as affirmation. Looked at more closely, ¯the finite is what it is as negation;¯88 thus we do not have the finite as a [mode of] being, but the nonbeing of the finite. The mediation between finite and infinite thus resides rather in the negative nature of the finite. Thus the genuine moment of mediation is not expressed in the major premise as given; on the contrary, it is the nonbeing of the finite that is the being of the infinite. ¯But because this transition is dialectical—because the speculative cannot be expressed in the form of a proposition,¯89 namely that the being of the infinite is the negation of the finite, the whole nature of the finite is to pass over into the infinite—for this reason the other propositions which belong to a syllogism cannot be added. For if one says that the nature of the finite is not to be, then one cannot, in the minor premise, any longer characterize the finite as being. What is amiss in the syllogism is that the finite is expressed as affirmative and its relation to the infinite is expressed as positive, whereas it is essentially a negative relation, and this dialectical element in the finite cannot be confined within the form of a syllogism of the understanding.

170

88. *Ho reads:* The finite is to be τὸ τί εἶναι through negation.
[*Ed.*] On Hegel's understanding of the Aristotelian τὸ τί ἦν εἶναι, see *Lectures on the History of Philosophy* 2:141–142, 151 (*Werke* 14:323, 334). Since this concept is only marginal to Hegel's understanding of Aristotle, the variant transmitted by *Ho* is unlikely to be correct.
89. *Thus P; D reads:* The speculative also cannot be expressed in the form of a proposition *G reads:* The deficiency of the syllogistic form is that this genuine content, what belongs to the concept, cannot be expressed in the form of a syllogism
[*Ed.*] See Hegel, *Science of Logic,* p. 90 (cf. *GW* 11:49).

"The finite presupposes the infinite"; this expression also implies the following, though it is not expressly stated. The finite presupposes the infinite; so the finite posits or poses, but its posing [*Setzen*] is rather a *pre*supposing [*Voraussetzen*], i.e., it posits in such a way that the *infinite* rather is the first, essential element. On closer analysis, the expression reveals the negative element of the finite and its relation to the infinite. What is meant in religion is not that the infinite *is* by virtue of the affirmative nature of the finite, its immediacy; on the contrary, religion is rather that the infinite is the finite being sublated and sublating itself. This then is the nature of this syllogism. The proof, the manner in which the finite is related to the infinite—the [entire] thought is distorted by the form of the syllogism. Religion, however, encompasses a way of thinking, a way of making this transition from finite to infinite, that is not contingent but necessary and that is conveyed by the concept of the nature of the infinite itself. What we have here *is* this way of thinking which constitutes the substance of religion; this way of thinking is not completely comprehended in the form of a syllogism.[90] |

171

90. W₂ *(1831) adds:* The defect in regard to the mediation offered by this proof is that the unconditioned is expressed as conditioned by another [mode of] being. The simple determination of negation is relinquished. In genuine mediation too, a transition is made from the many to the One, and again in such a way that the One is expressed as mediated. But this defect is remedied in the genuine elevation of spirit, by saying that it is not the many that has being but the One. This negation sublates the mediating, conditional aspect, and what is in and for itself necessary is now mediated by the negation of mediation. God *creates:* here we have a relationship between two, and mediation. But what is involved is a primary division: God is no longer the opaque essence wrapped up within itself, but manifests himself, reveals himself, posits a distinction and is for an other. In its highest expression this distinction is the Son. The Son exists through the mediation of the Father and vice versa; God is only revelatory in the Son. But in this other, God is present to self, is related to self; and since this is no longer a relatedness to other, the mediation is sublated.

Thus God is what is necessary in and for itself, and this determination is the absolute foundation. If this too does not yet suffice, God must be grasped as substance.

The next point is the converse, the relationship of substance to the finite. The elevation of the finite to substance involves a mediation that was annulled, posited as null, in the result. As substance turns against the many, the finite, etc., this annulled mediation has to be taken up again, but in such a way that it is posited as null in the [further] movement of the result. In other words, it is not merely the result that has to be comprehended but the entirety involved in it and the process in which it is engaged. Now if the whole is comprehended in this fashion, what we say is that

265

In considering the abstract concept of nature religion we have seen that making distinctions does not give any more profound a definition of this religion, which is the unity of the infinite and finite, in such a way that it [nature religion] is itself the infinite: the finite sublates itself to the infinite ˉand the infinite to the finite.ˉ91 Both finite and infinite are qualitative levels of determinateness, and there is no further determinateness within them. |

172

(β) The Representation of God92

If we now proceed to consider how God is represented at this stage, let us take this in the concrete sense that this concept [of God] is *spirit,* and therefore it is the unity of the spiritual and the natural, but in such a way that these two elements—i.e., the spiritual and the natural or, more precisely, the universal spirit and the singular natural spirit—are in more concrete fashion the natural world-essence in general. Thus both sides are very concrete, but their thought content, that of spirit in particular, is still nothing else than the

---

the substance has accidents, the infinite multiplicity that is in regard to this substance as [modes of] being that pass away. What is, passes away. But death is no less the recommencement of life, passing away is the beginning of coming about, there is naught but passing from being into nonbeing and vice versa. This is the alternating process of accidentality, and substance is the unity of this process itself. What endures is this alternation, and this, as unity, is the substantive, necessity, which is what causes coming-about to pass over into passing away and vice versa. Substance is the absolute power of being. Being accrues to it, but it is equally the unity of the alternating process whereby being passes over into nonbeing; again, however, it is the power over passing away, in such a way that passing away itself passes away.

The deficiency in regard to substance in Eastern religions, as in regard to substance as viewed by Spinoza, resides in the categories of coming about and passing away. Substance is not grasped as what is inwardly active, as subject and as purposeful activity, is not grasped as wisdom but solely as power. It is something devoid of content; the determinate element, purpose, is not contained in it; the determinate element that brings itself forth in this coming about and passing away is not grasped. It is merely the reeling, inwardly purposeless, empty power. This is the system called pantheism. In it God is absolute power, the being in all determinate being,[a] the purification of himself from determinacy and negation. That things *are,* is substance; that they are *not,* is likewise the power of substance, and this power is immanent in them in immediate fashion.

[Ed.] [a]See n. 80.

91. *Thus G.*

92. [Ed.] This section corresponds to Sec. A, "Concrete Representation," in the *Ms.* The naming of it is reminiscent of the 1824 *Concept,* Sec. 3.a, "The Theoretical Relationship: The Representation of God."

abstract determinateness of the unqualified infinite; it is called spirit, it is spirit, and it has the appearance of spirit, but it is still the spirit that is spiritless, that does not yet [have spiritual content]. However richly appareled it may be, it does not yet have spiritual content as spirit within itself; rather its genuine content is at this point still the same ⁻unqualified abstract infinitude.⁻⁹³

Now then, since it is the *representation* of God we are talking about, since we are discussing God as objective, ⁻the God that has being in consciousness,⁻⁹⁴ there are two aspects to be considered: (1) his *determinateness;* (2) his [representational] *shape.*

(1) In regard to the determinateness we have already said that this determinateness is still nothing else but *abstract* determinateness, which we have just rejected on that account.

(2) The second aspect is the shape [or way in which God is represented]; here in this field [of natural religion] generally the divine shape is defined as natural, belonging to the order of nature or immediacy. It may also be called spiritual, [God] may have a spiritual shape; or else the natural object, the immediate object, which is its configuration, the way in which God is manifested, may be raised by phantasy to the level of spiritual action or behavior, a spiritual mode and manner of manifestation, but the content does not correspond to this spiritual way of presenting it. If, for example, one | says, "The sea is a god," by this is meant something spiritual; actions can be ascribed to Oceanus; but these actions are *contingent,* still without spiritual content, inasmuch as the god is not yet further defined as spirit. His actions are not yet a content that is worthy of spirit, but are either natural events, natural effects, or, because they are represented as actions of spirit, they constitute purposes that belong to contingent spirit.

First, then, we must consider the shape [of God], its modes, the ways in which God is represented. The inner content is in fact still spiritless. In regard to the shape, it should be noted that we have to treat it simply as a shape—that if natural objects as such, the sky, the sun, this river, the sea, are viewed as God, they are not being

173

---

93. W₁ *(following Ho) reads:* abstract infinitude, the immediate unity of the spiritual and the natural. *Ho reads:* The spirit that is here represented is still the abstract, spiritless spirit, the immediate unity of the spiritual and the natural.

94. *Thus G; P reads:* as the consciousness we shall encounter in the cultus,

regarded as if they were merely natural powers. A natural power is what is powerful vis-à-vis human beings; in their existence they are related to it only as to power; so a prime factor in the relationship is that this god allows itself to be used by human beings, or alternatively, they are afraid of it. Human beings may be afraid of the sun, of thunder and lightning, and so on, but the fear of these natural powers is not the religious aspect [of the human relation to them]. For the abode of religion is essentially in the realm of freedom, and nowhere else, and to fear God is something different from being afraid of [natural] powers or violence. ⌐The fear that is the beginning of wisdom[95] cannot arise in nature religion; it is the fear of human beings who have shaken inwardly in their own singularity and have as it were shaken themselves off, worked through this abstraction, | in order to *think,* as free spiritual essence. At this point, not only does the natural life begin to quake, but the spirit that rises above it forsakes it, having established itself at a higher level than that of the natural unity—this it has left behind it. Fear in this higher sense, therefore, is not to be found in nature religion, any more than it is the fear of natural powers or violence that constitutes the beginning of nature religion. This beginning occurs rather in the opposite of all that can appear as fear.⌐[96] Hence this god, which is the unity of the spiritual and finite, is itself spirituality.

174

(γ) The Forms of Nature Religion[97]

The first characteristic or starting-point of nature religion is that spirit initially has being in immediately singular form, and what is interesting about the ensuing process is what may be termed the

95. [Ed.] See Ps. 111:10; cf. Prov. 1:7; 9:10; Job 28:28.

96. W₂ (MiscP) reads ("to the extent . . . sorcery" probably Ed): We are told that fear is the beginning of wisdom; this fear cannot arise in immediate religion. It first enters human beings when they know themselves powerless in their singularity, when their singularity shakes within them and they have accomplished the necessary abstraction in regard to themselves in order to have being as free spirit. Once the natural element quakes in this way in human beings, they rise above it and forsake it, having attained to a higher level, and pass over to thinking, to knowing. But it is not only fear in this higher sense that is not to be found here; even the fear of natural powers, to the extent that it does occur here, is transformed, in this initial stage of nature religion, into its opposite and becomes magic, sorcery.

97. [Ed.] This heading is not in G, but it is evident that Hegel here presents the brief survey of "the different forms of nature religion" promised earlier (see above, n. 52), replacing the discussion of the cultus found in the Ms.

objectifying [*Objektivierung*] of spirit; it is partly because of this that spirit becomes objective to me, steps out over against me; it is by stepping out over against me in this way that it becomes *object* [*Objekt*] for me, and so acquires the significance of a universal spirit, of something universally substantive in general. The universality ˉbelongs initially to [the sphere of] representation, not thought,ˉ⁹⁸ and is therefore still superficial. Spirit in the wholly immediate mode is this singular spirit; and the interesting point, as I have said, is that spirit acquires objective character, that it steps out over against the first syllogistic conclusion.⁹⁹

The second characteristic of its objectifying is that for the objectivity to be genuine, for the spirit that is an object to me to possess truth *within itself*, it would have to have being for me as inwardly self-determining, self-differentiating, *self-unfolding*. ˉAnd this unfolding, encompassed in its negativity,ˉ¹⁰⁰ would be the means by which spirit in its subjectivity came before me; it would appear not only to me but to itself, and it is this subjectivity of spirit that first imparts to the determinations of spirit a content worthy of spirit, a content that is itself spiritual in its nature. In nature | religion, however, this second characteristic of its objectivity does not extend thus far, but only to the point of differentiating and unfolding, and it is the determining characteristic of natural life that the two moments that differentiate themselves should stand separately next to each other. This unfolding is, on the one hand, a moment of the concept; hence it is necessary in order that the spirit may have being as spirit. But when thus juxtaposed, separate from

175

98. *Ho reads, similar in* W₁: still belongs, however, to the immediate sensuousness of representation, not to [the sphere of] thought,

99. [*Ed.*] The first form of nature religion is the "religion of magic," which, in 1824 at least, includes not only primitive religion, where spirit, i.e., the divine spirits, have being in immediate, singular form, but also ancient Chinese religion and Buddhism, where we see the process of objectification beginning to work itself out. In the later lectures, Buddhism is distinguished from the religion of magic and associated with the second stage, where objectified spirit possesses truth and being within itself (see the beginning of the next paragraph). In fact, Buddhism is already considered as manifesting this characteristic in the 1824 lectures, which indicates a tension between Hegel's organization and his conception.

100. W₁ *(following Ho) reads:* And this unfolding, negating the encompassment of its differences, *Ho reads:* If the represented spirit were genuinely infinite, it would, as object, be determined as being inwardly differentiated and negating the encompassment of its differences.

each other, the moments are themselves spiritless. In nature religion it is accordingly at times confusing to find spirit unfolded; one will find moments that belong to spirit but ˉare at the same time spiritless, because they are juxtaposed externally in this way.ˉ[101] For example, what in the Christian religion is called God's becoming a human being occurs in Hindu religion in the form of incarnation[102] —similarly the Trinity, but however much this conjures up the cept of spirit, it is at once in this case something quite different, for the very reason that these determinations are found only disjoined, separate from each other.[103] These are the two aspects to which interest is directed.

Third, then, we have the attempt to bring these isolated moments together, and this is in fact what constitutes the transition to the religion where subjectivity of spirit begins.[104] In this respect the [mode of] representation found in nature religion encounters serious difficulties. It is in every way inconsistent, or a contradiction in terms—there being posited on the one hand the spiritual, what is essentially free, while on the other hand it is represented in natural determinacy, in terms of a single [natural phenomenon], with a content of fixed particularity, which is therefore entirely incongruous with spirit, since spirit is essentially free. Hence arises the monstrous ˉcontradictionˉ[105] in nature religion. Admittedly mention has been

101. W₁ (1831) reads: at the same time do not belong to it, externally juxtaposed in this way.

102. [Ed.] The contrast is between *Menschwerdung Gottes* and *Inkarnation*. The former involves God's appearing or self-unfolding in a specific human being, while the latter involves the appearance of the divine in a multiplicity of finite, natural (fleshly) forms. Because Hinduism contains the notion of divine incarnations as well as the idea of the triadic self-unfolding of God (the Trimurti), it fully exemplifies the second form of nature religion.

103. *Ho adds, similar in* W₁: Thus we may find incarnations, even a triad, but not the Trinity [in Hinduism], for only absolute spirit is the power that transcends its [separate] moments.

104. [Ed.] The transitional religions are the religion of light (Parseeism or Persian religion, Zoroastrianism) and the religion of the enigma (Egyptian religion). In these religions, on the one hand God is conceived as free subject, but on the other hand he continues to be represented in essentially natural images. Hence the contradiction or inconsistency, which generates the need for transition, is at its peak in these religions.

105. W₁ *reads:* inconsistency *Cf. Ho:* Owing to its inconsistency it is extremely difficult to portray nature religion.

made of pantheism, but that was the pantheism of reflection, which gathers this finite together, encompasses it; this all-inclusive univer- sality, however, is a spurious form of reflection; in nature religion | there remains always the incongruity of the [divine] shape in 176 contrast with what ought to be the foundation, namely the spiritual.

It is therefore difficult for us to grasp the spiritual aspect of nature religion. We are used to the distinction between the spiritual and the natural. In this connection we are wont to employ nowadays the categories of cause and effect, ground, dominion, and so on, but these are not valid here. Here the spiritual is posited in a singular mode, and its immediate unity [with the natural] is [also] posited. In speculative unity what stands over against us becomes for us the self-posited, which [in turn] perishes for us in the unity with infini- tude. ˜Certainly we can *understand* nature religion therefore,˜[106] but we cannot *represent* it *from within,* we cannot have the *sense* or *feel- ing* of it *from within,* just as we can understand a dog without being able to share its sensations. [Its] representation [of the world] would necessarily be a mode of simple sensation, of simple feeling; but our feelings and sensations [are] spiritual, rational, and therefore quite different from those of a dog. Even hunger, thirst, and so on are not the same in us and in dogs, precisely because we are spirit. Only spirit fully comprehends spirit, and here, where we are not dealing with free spirit, we may be able to *understand* it *from within,*[107] but for this reason we cannot make the content of this religion entirely our own.

---

106. *W₂ reads (G with Var/1831?):* Certainly we can understand or think this form of religion, since after all we still have it before us as object of our thoughts,

107. [*Ed.*] Hegel here establishes a significant distinction between "understand- ing from within" or "understanding one's way into" (*hineinverstehen*), which is possible even in the case of spiritual manifestations quite foreign to our own, and "representing," "sensing," and "feeling" "from within" or "into" (*hineinvorstellen, hineinempfinden, hineinfühlen*), which are not possible in the case of wholly alien cultures and religions. In other words, we are able to enter *rationally* or *cognitively* into radically different forms of existence (even those of animals), although we are unable to *exist* at a sensing or feeling level in these other forms. This exercise of a rational entry into quite different forms of religious consciousness is precisely what Hegel undertakes in *Determinate Religion.* The category of *Hineinverstehen* proved later to be of significance for Wilhelm Dilthey.

1. The Religion of Magic[108]

a. Singular Self-Consciousness as Power over Nature

The first religion, the first form of nature religion, is the crudest and simplest. The question is, where should we look for the primitive locus of the presupposed spiritual element, i.e., what is the form of its existence? It must be a natural form: we must not think in this connection of natural objects, but of the first natural locus of spirituality, the one that precedes any unfolding, any type or mode of objectifying. This locus is the singular | self-consciousness itself, the empirical, contingent singular. This is to be cognized and apprehended in the way in which it is present too in the history, the determinate being, the existence, of religion. Thus it is the case that the empirical, singular self-consciousness—the human being—at first knows nothing higher than itself in its self-consciousness; and posited thus in its self-consciousness it has a relationship to nature which is as follows: because they are differentiated in this way, this singular self-consciousness takes the form of power over nature. But being natural itself, the natural singular self-consciousness is confronted by power. It is the *spiritual* that is power over nature. This is what we can call the religion of magic, the oldest, rawest, crudest form of religion. It follows from what has been said that God is necessarily spiritual, this is God's basic determination, spirituality. Spirituality is *for* self-consciousness; to the extent that it is an *object* for self-consciousness, we have a further advance, a distinction in regard to universal spirituality as such, spirituality [as such] having already

---

108. [*Ed.*] This section is new in 1824, and Hegel devotes considerable attention to it. His treatment is based on reports of missionaries and travelers, and focuses on the religion of the Eskimos, Africans, Mongols, Chinese, and American Indians. Given the unscientific character of the data with which Hegel had to work, together with his general developmental scheme (from lower to higher forms), the treatment is, by present-day standards, inadequate. But the reader should keep in mind that Hegel's objective, as he states it in the preceding paragraph, is to *understand* these religions *from within,* even if we cannot make their content entirely our own. Hegel's passion is to comprehend, to penetrate, seemingly alien materials, and his treatment evidences genuine phenomenological rigor. Any tendencies that *we* might detect to trivialize or ridicule these religions are traceable not so much to Hegel as to his sources, which he quotes at length, often verbatim. Hegel is not free of the prejudices of his time toward peoples of color, but there is also reflected in his work an obvious fascination with Oriental and African religion and culture.

been separated, within universal spirituality, from the contingent, singular spirituality of self-consciousness. But initially this separation has not yet occurred.

The very first religion, if we are willing to call it that, is when the singular self-consciousness knows itself as power over nature, and it is the exercise of this power that is called magic. This is no religion of fear, and does not begin in fear, but stems from freedom, from the unfree freedom that consists in the singular self-consciousness knowing itself as power, as higher than natural things, and this knowledge is initially *unmediated*.

This religion that is simply magic—religion in its crudest shape, in which, although it is without any mediation, there is already a beginning of empirical spirit, the spirit of the substantial (but the substantial is still completely unmediated)—this religion has been found by recent travelers, namely ˉCaptains Ross and Parry,ˉ[109] among the Eskimos (1819); with other peoples mediation has already taken place. |

178

According to Captain Parry's account,[110] the Eskimos have no idea that any other kind of world exists; they live on the seashore among rocks, ice, and snow, off seal meat and principally birds and

109. *Ho, W read:* Captain Parry [*Ho adds:* in 1818 and 1819] and, at an earlier date, Captain Ross,

[*Ed.*] See William Edward Parry, *Journal of a Voyage for the Discovery of a North-West Passage from the Atlantic to the Pacific* (London, 1821). Although a German translation was published in Jena in 1821, there is no evidence that Hegel read it; his reference to Parry could be based on the report by Captain Ross (see the next note).

110. [*Ed.*] This report is not written by Parry but by Captain Ross; Parry was an officer on the expedition of 1818. (It is possible that Hegel was also familiar with Parry's account of a further expedition in 1819–20, on which he was captain; see the preceding note.) See John Ross, *A Voyage of Discovery, Made under the Orders of the Admiralty, in His Majesty's Ships Isabella and Alexander, for the Purpose of Exploring Baffin's Bay, and Enquiring into the Probability of a North-West Passage,* 2d ed., 2 vols. (London, 1819), 1:168–169, 175–178, 179–180. We know that Hegel made excerpts from this report; see Hegel, *Berliner Schriften,* p. 710. Ross concludes (p. 178): "Although we could thus obtain no proof that this people had any notions of a Supreme Being, or of a spirit, good or bad, the circumstance of their having conjurers, and the tale of their going to the moon after death, render it probable that they possess some religious ideas, however barbarous, and that the unsatisfactory information which we obtained on this head, arose chiefly from our ignorance of their language, and from the very imperfect and limited communication which we had with them."

fish, and they do not know that nature offers anything else. These English travelers had with them an Eskimo who had spent a considerable time in England, was better educated, and acted as their interpreter. Through him they discovered that the Eskimos have not the slightest representation of spirit or of higher beings, of an invisible higher being above them, or of an essential substance as opposed to their empirical existence in general. Nor do they have any representation of the immortality of the soul or the eternal nature of spirit, or of the being-in-and-for-itself of the single spirit, nor yet of any evil spirit. And although they have a high regard for sun, moon, stars, and so on, they do not worship them—they also do not worship any image, man, beast, or the like. On the other hand, they have among them individuals whom they call "angekoks," who are magicians or sorcerers. They fetched one of them, ˉwho said of himself⁻¹¹¹ that it was within their power to raise or still the tempest, to attract whales, and so on, and that they learned this art from old angekoks. People are afraid of them, but there is at least one in every family. So there they were in the presence of one of these angekoks, who claimed to be able to make the wind get up and to attract whales. He said it was done through words and gestures. But the words (which they got him to repeat for them) were meaningless, and were not directed at any being [*Wesen*] that was supposed to act as intermediary, but directly at the natural object over which he wished to exert his power; ˉhe asked for no assistance from any being.⁻¹¹²
He was told that there is an omnipresent, all-providing, invisible being who has made everything. He was very surprised, and when

179 he asked where it lived and was | told everywhere, he was frightened and wanted to run away. When he was asked where people went to when they died, he replied they were buried: a very long time ago an old man had once said they ended up in the moon, but it was a long time since any sensible Eskimo had believed that.

These people can be regarded as standing on the lowest rung of

111. *Ho reads:* He was an old man who said
112. *Ho reads:* The sorcerer maintained he had the power through himself alone, through his magic formulas. They knew nothing of the power of some higher being, and were not able to understand what were "good" or "evil" spirits.

spiritual consciousness, but they do believe that self-consciousness is something that has power over nature.[113]

The Englishmen persuaded an angekok to cast a spell. This took the form of a dance in which he threw himself about wildly until he went into a trance and fell down exhausted, and ⁻in this state⁻[114] uttered strange words and noises.[115]

We find this religion of magic also, most notably, in Africa and among the Mongols and Chinese, but there we no longer have the completely raw, primitive shape of magic. Mediations are already coming into play, arising from the fact that the spiritual is beginning to assume an objective shape for self-consciousness.

This religion is more magic than religion. In it the relationship of the spiritual to the natural is such that the spiritual exists as the power of nature and accordingly appears in this first form as immediate self-consciousness; this is the first shape in which nature religion appears.

This religion of magic is most widespread in Africa among the Negroes; it is already referred to by Herodotus[116] and it has also been found in recent times. At the same time there are only a few cases in which these peoples invoke their power over nature, for they need but little, their needs are few, and in assessing their situation we must leave out of account the manifold need in which we | stand, 180 the tangled skein of means by which we seek to achieve our purposes. Their objects are, for example, that they need rain for their harvests and for their crops generally; the cultivation of their soil amounts to very little. There are illnesses they wish to avert, and in time of

113. W *(following Ho) adds:* without mediation . . . divine. *Ho reads:* So this is then the lowest stage of the religious spirit, where there is no representation of any higher universality, since self-consciousness in its singularity knows itself as power over the natural realm, without mediation, without its being opposed to what is divine.

114. *Ho, W read:* rolling his eyes

115. [*Ed.*] The dance to which Hegel refers is not that of an angekok but is rather an account of entertainment among the Eskimos; see Ross, *A Voyage of Discovery,* pp. 147–149.

116. [*Ed.*] Herodotus, *Histories* 2.33. In the preceding passage Herodotus relates a report concerning a Libyan expedition to the hinterland, and he adds here that according to the report as he heard it the peoples with whom the expedition had made contact were all sorcerers.

war they also need—or think they need—power of this kind. Our information on the state of these peoples comes mainly from missionaries of bygone days, and recent reports are few and far between; one must accordingly be on one's guard against much of the earlier information, especially since the missionaries are natural enemies of the sorcerers. All the same, the general picture is amply confirmed by a multitude of reports.

Here as with other religions, the complaint about the avarice of the priests is more or less beside the point. The sacrifices and presents that are offered to the gods do for the most part go to the priests, but we can speak of priestly avarice—and commiserate with the peoples involved about this useless loss of their property—only when property itself is held of high account. The peoples of whom we are here speaking, however, set little store by their possessions, and know no better use to make of them than to give them away.

For instance, they need rain, and if there is a long period without rain, it is for the magician to summon it up. Or they are plagued by hurricanes, which the magicians have to drive away. ⁻Other peoples have other particular needs. With one tribe in the Congo this power is attributed to the king,⁻[117] and he then transfers it to one of his ministers, and casts spells himself only in exceptional cases.

More light is thrown on the character of this magic by the way in which it is performed. The magician, a prince, or minister or priest, mounts a hill, inscribes all kinds of circles or figures | in the sand and utters all kinds of incomprehensible magic words, makes signs in the direction of the sky, blows against the wind, and draws in and holds his breath. A missionary who was with the advance guard of a Portuguese army recounts[118] that the Negroes who were their

181

117. *Ho reads:* This stage again assumes different forms from one people to another. Among the Eskimos there was a sorcerer in each family. In the Congo this is concentrated on the single individual as universal singularity, on the prince, who is the one and only sorcerer.

118. [*Ed.*] Joannes Antonius Cavazzi, *Historische Beschreibung der in dem unteren occidentalischen Mohrenland ligenden drey Königreichen Congo, Matamba, und Angola* (Munich, 1694), pp. 250–251. Cavazzi was a Capuchin friar on an apostolic mission to central Africa. It is not certain whether Hegel used the German translation or the Italian original, *Istorica descrizione de' tre regni Congo, Matamba, et Angola situati nell'Etiopia inferiore occidentale* (Bologna, 1687). On the one hand, there is

allies had brought along with them a magician of this kind. A hurricane made his spell-casting necessary, and despite the missionary's vehement protests the ceremony was put in hand. The sorcerer appeared in special, fantastic attire, bedecked with animal skins and birds, weapons and horns, and accompanied by a large escort. He inspected the sky and the clouds. Then he chewed a few roots, roots of tabs, murmured some barbaric words, let out a fearsome howl, and spat the tab-roots up into the sky. When the clouds came nearer all the same, he waved his arms and conjured the storm to go somewhere else. And when it stayed where it was, he flew into a rage, fired arrows at the sky, threatened that he would give it a hard time, and brandished a knife in the air. All of this has, then, the character of *determinate* consciousness of power over nature.

This magic is practically universal among Negro tribes. Very similar to these sorcerers are the Mongolian shamans, who wear fantastic clothing, hung with metal and wooden figures, make themselves besotted with intoxicating drinks, and in this state proclaim what is to happen and prophesy the future.

The main feature of this sphere of magic is direct mastery over nature through the will, the self-conscious awareness that spirit is something higher than nature. However bad such descriptions may look from one point of view, we are in any case dealing with something that is in a certain sense higher than when human beings are dependent on nature and fear it.

It should be noted here that there are Negro tribes ˉ(including some who since the end of the sixteenth century have appeared to be the most uncivilized)ˉ[119] who | believe that no one dies a natural 182 death. In the strength of their consciousness they believe that human beings are on too high a level to be killed by something unknown like the power of nature. Often, as a result, sick persons on whom

---

a reference to the German edition in n. 161 below (whether by Hegel or by the editors of *W* is not certain), and it was more widely available in Germany. On the other hand, Hegel may also have had recourse to the Italian edition (here at p. 215), since his reference to "tabs-roots" (*Tabswurzeln*) in the following passage is not confirmed by the German version, which refers simply to "a certain root" (*eine gewisse Wurzel*). The Italian pagination is given in parentheses following the German.

119. *Thus D, similarly P; G reads:* (namely, the Giaki, Jaga, or Agag, as they call themselves, conquerors of the wildest, most uncivilized kind, who since 1542

magic has been used in vain are put to death by their friends. ⁻The North American savages also had this practice of putting their parents to death when they became infirm, which clearly means that human beings should not perish through nature but that the honor should be done to them by others like themselves.⁻¹²⁰ ⁻Another people⁻¹²¹ cherish the belief that there will be general ruin if the high priest dies a natural death, so that as soon as he is sick and weak he is done to death. If nonetheless one dies through sickness, they believe another must have killed him by magic, and sorcerers have to find out who the murderer is; the sorcerer denounces someone, who is then put to death. Especially when a king dies, many people are killed, as we are told by an old-time missionary.¹²² The king's devil, so it is said, [must] be put to death, meaning, no doubt, whoever has been apportioned the blame for the king's death.¹²³

b. Formal Objectification of the Divine Object¹²⁴

This, then, is the first form, which cannot yet be properly called religion: for to religion belongs essentially the moment of objectivity [*Objektivität*]—that the spiritual power appears for the individual,

---

have descended several times on the coasts, carrying everything in their way) W₂ *reads:* (namely, the Galla and Gaga hordes, conquerors . . . way)

[*Ed.*] Hegel is apparently referring to the Jaga, leaders of one of the fiercest of the Bantu tribes of the Congo basin, the Bangala of Kwango, who were cannibals. See Cavazzi, *Historische Beschreibung,* pp. 212–214. In the Italian original (pp. 182–184), the name is given as *Giaghi* or *Giaki;* in the German version, as *Jagen;* in more common German transliteration, as *(D)schagga* = Jaga. With regard to their supposed belief that no one dies a natural death, see p. 255 (pp. 219–220). See also the 1827 lectures at n. 82.

120. *Thus G*

121. *Thus G; D reads:* In particular they

122. [*Ed.*] This account is based on Cavazzi's description of certain tribes in the Congo, *Historische Beschreibung,* pp. 92–94 (pp. 76–78).

123. [*Ed.*] Cavazzi, *Historische Beschreibung,* pp. 144–146 (pp. 121–123). See also Hegel's account in the *Lectures on the Philosophy of World History,* Nisbet ed., pp. 188–189 (Hoffmeister ed., pp. 232–233).

124. [*Ed.*] This section carries the discussion of primitive religion into a new phase. Hegel intends to distinguish formal objectification from absolute, actual, or genuine objectification, where the divine attains an objectivity that exists in and for itself. The latter is the religion of being-within-self (Buddhism, Lamaism), and it is where religion, properly speaking, begins. Formal objectification still falls within the sphere of magic; Hegel includes among its higher expressions the religion of ancient China.

for the single empirical consciousness, as something essentially universal in opposition to empirical self-consciousness, as an other, independent of it; this objectifying is an essential precondition of religion. ⸢However inadequate the representation of God may be, it means that the starting point is an *other* over against this empirical self-consciousness, an other in general.⸣[125] |

In regard to this objectifying, the mode of it that is merely formal must be distinguished from absolute objectivity. Formal objectification is where the unqualified spiritual power (God) ⸢is represented as independently active.⸣[126] Absolute objectification is where God is and is known to be in and for himself according to the categorial determinations that apply to spirit in and for itself.

What we have to consider here and now is only the formal mode of objectifying. It is with this mode, with the consciousness of subjective self-consciousness, with this distinction [between the single and the universal], that a relationship between the divine object and consciousness begins. This relationship is threefold in kind:

(1) The first moment is that the subjective self-consciousness, subjective spirituality, still remains the lord and master—this living power, this self-conscious might. This ideality of self-consciousness is still effectively in *command,* it retains power and authority over against the weakness of the merely formal object.

(2) The second moment, or opposite relationship, is when the subjective self-consciousness of human beings is represented as

125. *Thus P; G, W read:* Only with it does religion begin, only with it is there a God; and even with the lowest level or relationship there is at least a starting point for such objectifying. *Ho continues, similar in W:* A mountain or river is not the divine in its character of a heap of earth or body of water, but as a [mode of] the existence of God, of something essential and universal. But we do not yet find this with magic as such. What is powerful here is the singular consciousness as singular consciousness, and thus the very negation of what is universal. It is not a god in the sorcerer but the sorcerer himself who conjures and conquers nature. This is the religion of desire that is infinite for itself, and therefore of sensuous singularity that is certain of itself. But this religion already includes fear, reverence, sacrifice, and consequently the distinguishing of the single empirical consciousness from the magic-working consciousness, the empirical consciousness being the immediately singular, and the magic-working consciousness the universal. It is by this means that the religion of magic develops out of magic. And it is the distinguishing of the singular and the universal that first introduces a relationship of self-consciousness to the object.

126. *Thus P; G reads:* is made objective over against consciousness.

dependent upon this object. In this regard it should be noted that, if they are assumed to be immediate consciousness generally, human beings can only imagine themselves to be dependent in a contingent manner; only through some deviation from their ordinary existence can they come to be dependent. This is the case especially, therefore, with simple, primitive tribes or savages. Among them this dependence

184 is somewhat less | important since what they use is naturally available, they find it in nature; what they need exists and grows for them, so they do not see themselves as being in any dependent relationship; necessity is merely contingent.[127] It is only when human beings are represented as essence that dependence comes into play; as opposed to the other, nature, they become essentially a negative and no more.

(3) [128]The next step then is that spirituality as empirical, as merely natural will, should recognize—that humanity should recognize—its own essence in religion, and that in such a way that its basic characteristic ˉis notˉ[129] that it is dependent on nature but on the contrary that in religion spirit knows itself as *free*. Although at the lowest level it is only a formal freedom that spirit knows itself to have (nature shows itself to be what is dependent on spirit), ˉhuman beings can nonetheless despise this dependence and remain content with self.ˉ[130] It is another stage where God is said[131] to "thunder with his thunderous voice and yet we know him not" [cf. Job 37:5]. God can do better than just thunder; God can reveal himself; and spirit is not to be defined in terms of natural phenomena.

This third determination of the relationship of the object to

---

127. *Ho adds, similar in W:* It is only when consciousness is further developed, only when human being and nature, losing their immediate validity and positivity, are represented as something evil, as something negative, that the dependence of consciousness emerges, since consciousness demonstrates itself as negative in relation to its other.

128. *Ho reads, precedes in W:* But this negativity—the fact of being negative according to its very concept—sublates itself and shows itself to be only a transitional point of consciousness.

129. *Thus G; P, D read:* is

130. *Thus G with P, D; G, W read:* human beings despise this dependence, remain content with self, abandon the natural connection. *Ho, W add:* and subject nature to their power.

131. *Ho, W add:* as in a later religion

consciousness is free veneration, the relationship in which human beings revere the power they revere as free and recognize it as essence but not as something alien. |

185

If we consider objectification more closely, we are struck by two essential relationships. On the one hand, self-consciousness still maintains itself as power over the natural realm; on the other hand, in this object self-consciousness is faced not merely with natural phenomena but with the beginnings of something independent that has its own essence. Toward such an object, then, self-consciousness has the relationship of free, unforced veneration.

[1.] The first kind of objectification is formal objectification. This still falls within the sphere of magic: in it there is only the beginning of a consciousness of independent, genuinely essential objectivity—which is, however, still closed in on itself; in it there begins also the consciousness of an essential, universal power.[132] The two [magic and religion] are in part mixed together; and it is only when free, unforced veneration or the consciousness of a free power emerges that we leave the realm of magic, though we are still in the sphere of nature religion. For magic is something that has been present among all peoples and in all periods, and religion too is seated in the representations of each people, in the popular view of things, which contains the most inconsistent notions side by side. Notions of this kind are [also] to be found in religion, but in such a manner that the higher spirit still imbues them. But once there is objectification, it is to be noted that in the higher religions some sort of mediation comes into play along with it in such a way that spirit, being the higher concept, constitutes the power over the magic or what provides mediation with it.

Self-consciousness is for itself no longer what is unmediated, what is inwardly satisfied with itself; it is essentially what seeks and has its satisfaction in an other, through the mediation of an other, by passing through an other.[133] In free veneration human consciousness

---

132. *Ho, W add:* Magic is therefore retained, but it is joined by the intuition of an independent, essential objectivity; the magic-working consciousness knows that the ultimate is not *itself* but the universal power in *things.*

133. *Ho, W add:* The infinity of desire proves a finite infinity, constricted as it is by being reflected into a higher power.

186 also closes with itself, | but there is a mediation present such that objects have being for it, its own essence, universal power, has being for it (and it is distinct from such power). It is only by sublating its particularity that it brings forth its own satisfaction in its essence, closes with itself as essence, and attains to itself in its essence ˉwhen it surrenders its particularity; and for it to come to itself essentially in this way, it must achieve mediation through negating itself.ˉ134

As it initially appears to us, however, mediation occurs as [if] through some other, permanently external agent. In the way that this objectification occurs in the field of magic, ˉit remains the power of humanity over nature, and this is the power of a tertium quid.ˉ135 Humanity does not exert power directly but indirectly, through the medium of a magical tertium quid. We must now consider the various elements in this mediation.

The first immediate relationship in this regard is for self-consciousness as the spiritual element to be conscious of itself as the power over natural things. These things are again themselves a power over one another. But this is already a further reflection, ˉand we need not go beyond the first, immediate relationship.ˉ136 The first universal generalization arrived at by reflection is that ˉnatural thingsˉ137 cohere with one another, that one can be cognized by means of the other, that one is the effect of the other, that they are essentially coherent or interrelated. This coherency of things is already a form of objectivity or a form of universality, for when taken in this way, the thing is no longer singular but goes beyond itself, makes its influence felt in an other, or vice versa; in this way the

187 thing is amplified, | through its relation to its other. In the first relationship I am the ideality of the thing, the power over it. But now, as soon as they are posited objectively, things are power over against each other; one is what *the other* posits as something ideal. If this

---

134. *Thus D with P; G reads:* through its own negation.

135. *G reads:* it remains the power of humanity over nature. *P reads:* it remains the power of another, and this other is the power of a tertium quid.

136. *G reads:* and no longer an immediate relationship. W_2 *(Var) reads:* and no longer an immediate relationship, where the ego as singular stands over against natural things.

137. *Thus G; W (following G and Ho) reads:* natural things illuminate each other, *Ho reads:* one thing illuminates the other,

relationship is included in magic, then this is the second sphere of magic, indirect magic or magic using means or media, whereas the first sphere was direct magic.[138]

˜This is a mode of objectification that is merely a connection between external things, such that the subject does not assume direct power over nature, but only over the means.˜[139] This mediated type of magic or sorcery is found in infinite variety, at all times and among all peoples. It includes what we call "sympathetic magic," i.e., the doing of something in order to produce an effect in something quite different; the subject has the means to hand, and conjoins with the means the aim or purpose of producing a particular effect.[140] This change that is to be produced may of course be implicit in the nature of the means or medium, but what principally matters is the will of the subject. This relationship, this mediated magic, is extremely widespread, and it is difficult to define its limits and determine what, properly speaking, lies beyond them.

The principle of magic is that the connection between means and outcome should not be known. ˜For example, the practice of medicine | is not taken to be magic, nor is it; but it does also frequently happen [in medical practice] that the connection between means and result is unknown,˜[141] and all one can do is rely on

188

138. [Ed.] In the 1827 lectures, Hegel distinguishes between the two phases of the religion of magic—singular self-consciousness as power over nature, and formal objectification of the divine object—in terms of the distinction between direct and indirect magic.

139. Thus G.

140. Ho adds, similar in W: The ego is what works magic, but it is through the thing itself that I achieve mastery over the thing. And this necessarily follows from magic or sorcery as such. For in it things show themselves as ideal. Ideality is thus a characteristic that adheres to them as things; it is an objective quality, and it is through magic-working or sorcery that it comes to consciousness and is itself posited, used. Desire seizes directly on the things in question. But now consciousness reflects back into itself and interposes between itself and the thing the thing itself as something destructive; in so doing it at the same time reveals itself as the cunning or stratagem not to interject itself into things and the conflict between them.

141. W (following Ho and G) reads: Magic is wherever this connection is merely there, without being understood. This is also the case a hundred times over with medicaments, G reads: This is also the case a hundred times over with medicaments, Ho reads: But magic is wherever between means and result a connection is merely there, without being understood.

experience. The use of a certain means is associated with a certain change of condition. The rational situation on the other hand would be where one knows the nature of the means and infers from that the change it will bring about. But as for this perfect rationality, we know that physicans themselves do not claim to be able to deduce the result from the nature of the means employed. There is, they say, this connection, though we don't know what it is; it is merely a matter of experience. Experience itself, however, is infinitely self-contradictory. ⌐For example, Brown[142] used opium, naphtha, spirits, and so on to cure illnesses that had previously been cured by means of an entirely opposite nature.⌐[143] There is no saying where the boundary is, exactly, between what is a known and what an unknown connection. In any event, insofar as organic life is involved and living matter affects living matter (and to an even greater extent the spiritual affects the corporeal), there are connections here that cannot be denied but that must be regarded as inexplicable until such time as the deeper concept underlying this relationship is known. Already in magnetism [hypnotism], whatever would otherwise be termed a rational connection has ceased to exist; as matters are regarded in other spheres, the connection is unintelligible.

Once magic is thrown open to mediation in this way, the whole monstrous tide of what we call superstition can come flooding in. Every possibility, every single detail of existence, becomes significant; for every circumstance, each and every outcome and purpose—everything is mediated and at the same time mediating. Everything governs and is governed by everything else; what people do depends for its outcome on circumstances; and what they are, and what they

---

142. [*Ed.*] A reference to John Brown, the Edinburgh physician whose methods of treatment were much disputed at the time. Brown divided all illnesses into "sthenic" and "asthenic" (abnormally vigorous or abnormally weak vital processes), and for the treatment of the latter relied almost exclusively on the use of opium, spirits, and camphor as stimulants. See John Brown, *Elementa medicinae* (Hildburghausen, 1794), §§ 290, 298, 301, etc. (German translation, Frankfurt am Main, 1806). The reference to "naphtha"(*Naphta*), which occurs only in *G*'s transcript, may be due to a mishearing of "camphor" (*Kampfer*). Cf. also Christoph Girtanner, *Ausführliche Darstellung des Brownischen Systems der praktischen Heilkunde,* 2 vols. (Göttingen, 1797–1798), esp. 2:370–385.

143. *Thus G*

purpose, depends on a multiplicity of circumstances. By the very fact of existing, they have being in an external world, and this is what links this infinite multiplicity of random events and circumstances together; and individuals are a power over the whole nexus only to the extent that they are a power over the singular powers | that cohere   189 in it. Where general awareness of these connections is present in still indeterminate fashion, but the specific mode, the determinate nature of the things connected, is still unfamiliar, one is surrounded by[144] contingency. When, therefore, reflection enters this field of relationships, it proceeds in the belief that things act reciprocally on one another. And this is quite right, but the weakness of it is that this formulation is still abstract, and consequently it does not yet comprise the characteristic peculiarity of the things involved, their specific mode of operation, the way in which each particular thing coheres with the others. What the power is that transcends their mode of coherence or peculiarities is still unknown; and inasmuch as there is an established nexus, but its determinate character is still unknown, there is this contingency and arbitrariness in regard to the means. ¯In one respect most people stand in this relationship [with the world]; the attitude of whole peoples is such that this way of looking at things forms their basic viewpoint, governs their aspirations, their condition, their [whole] existence.¯[145]

Thus the premise of this mediated magic is correct; ¯but the determinate aspect [of the world nexus] is unknown.¯[146] Since one's actions are based on the abstract premise, the determinate aspect is left free. This explains the infinite number of magical means. Countless peoples use magic in whatever they undertake. Some of them cast a spell when the foundations of a house are laid, so that it may be kept safe from all danger; the orientation of the house and zodiac-region of the sky are significant in this connection. Or a spell is cast when sowing to ensure a good harvest. Similarly, relationships to other people, love, hate, peace, war, battles, journeys—whatever is to be brought about is brought about by some *means,*

144. *Ho, W add:* absolute
145. *Thus G*
146. *Thus G; P reads:* things stand in mutual coherence. *D reads:* things are finite single ends—that they are attained stands in the power of another.

285

190 and since the link between means and effect is unknown, | any one means is as good as any other. Much understanding is not to be met with in this sphere, which is why no more can be said of it.

Ancient peoples are often said to have possessed great insight into the use of herbs, plants, and so on for treating illnesses etc. There may be a genuine connection here, but it may just as well be pure chance and caprice. The understanding becomes aware that there is a connection but the more precise definition remains hidden from it; it becomes absorbed in the means, and phantasy provides a substitute for what is lacking in the abstract premise, introducing the determinacy which as such, properly speaking, is not yet found in the things themselves.

2. The content of the first, unmediated type of magic concerned objects that have a power over singular things, and over which human beings can exert power directly. What comes next is a relationship to objects that seem to be capable rather of being viewed as independent, so that power here appears to human beings as something other, something that is no longer under their control, a power that is not free power, empirical self-consciousness. Examples of such independent, natural things are the sun, moon, sky, sea—great elemental objects that are powers which appear to confront humanity purely as independent and autonomous. Insofar as the natural consciousness is confined to this sphere, limited to the standpoint of singular desires, it does not really have any relationship to these objects as universal nature, has not yet any intuition of their universality.[147] [With] such things as the sun and moon, for example, their course and their effects are uniform, their mode of working is unchanging; but the attitude that the consciousness which is still at the standpoint of natural unity, for which the unchanging is of no interest, takes to such natural objects is governed solely by its contingent wishes, needs, and interests, or [it is related] to them

191 only to the extent that their | mode of operation appears as singular, as contingent. People at this standpoint are interested by sun and moon only when they are eclipsed, by the earth only when there is an earthquake; the universal does not exist for them, does not excite

147. Ho, W add: and is concerned solely and exclusively with what is singular.

286

their desire, is of no interest to them. A river interests them only if they want to cross it. There is no theoretical interest at this stage, but only practical behavior relative to contingent needs.

People do not venerate these objects when they become thinkers either,[148] because they have a higher, *spiritual* universality in view, which alone is for them what is essential, while those who are still at this initial standpoint do not venerate them because they have not yet attained consciousness of the universality that is in these objects.[149] In the event of exceptional phenomena such as an earthquake, an eclipse, or the flooding of a river, then they may be afraid of them and address petitions to them; only at such times do they appear to them as power. When they are behaving normally, as when the sun shines, there is no need to petition them. But these petitions also have the sense of conjuring or casting a spell; we speak of "conjuring" someone to do something. A petition is an acknowledgment that one is in the power of the other. For this reason it often goes against the grain, because it means that I acknowledge the authority of another's arbitrary decision in regard to me. Begging in this way is therefore also a form of conjuring; one stipulates that the petition should have an effect, it is intended as the power to be exercised over the other, so that the two are intermingled—on the one hand, acknowledgment of the supremacy of the object and, on the other, consciousness of my power, by virtue of which I strive to exert supremacy over the object. Among peoples at this level we find, for example, cases where they make sacrifices to a river | if they wish   192
to cross it; they are imperiled by it and so offer sacrifices to it; similarly to the sun if it goes into eclipse. They occupy themselves with a host of means to propitiate this power; but on the other hand, these sacrifices are magical means, powers superior to the other expressions [of the natural power], deemed capable of constraining the natural powers and bringing about what the [conjuring] subject

148. *Ho, W add:* even when they are on a higher cultural level,
149. *Ho adds, similar in W:* At the first standpoint they have not yet attained the universality of existence, while at the second, natural existence generally is no longer of any account for them. But midway between the two relationships is the point where the natural powers come on the scene as something universal and accordingly having power vis-à-vis singular, empirical consciousness.

desires. The veneration of natural objects is thus highly ambiguous at this standpoint: it is not pure veneration, but the veneration is mixed with and subjected to magic.

This attitude can be coupled (to a greater or lesser extent) with a more universal, more essential way of representing these natural objects. What then happens is that the genie or spirit of the sun (i.e., the sun as genie), the genie of the river, of the mountain, or the like [is venerated], that veneration is accorded to this. This is a mode of veneration in which the singular aspect of the object is left behind; one grasps the object, represents it to oneself, in universal fashion and venerates it thus. But even if these genii are thus represented in universal fashion, and more precisely as a [type of] power, human beings can still harbor the consciousness of their own power over them. Their content is still only that of a natural essence; it is just the river, the mountain, the sun; it is still only a natural content, and self-consciousness can thus be aware of itself as power over this natural representation.

3. The next [mode of] objectification is where people recognize or find an independent entity, an independent power outside themselves in the living thing. Life, organic life or vitality as such, even in a tree but still more in an animal, is a higher principle than the mere nature of the sun, the river, and suchlike. Hence it has come to pass among countless peoples that animals have been worshiped. In our eyes there can be nothing more degrading than to worship animals as gods, and so in its way it is. But the fact that the beast is something living makes it a higher principle than that of the sun. The animal is a more excellent, more genuine [mode of] existence than a natural existence like the sun, and to this extent it is less degrading to worship animals as gods than the sun, rivers, stars, or suchlike. The fact that animals are living organisms | ⌐points to⌐[150] an active independence of subjectivity, which is what concerns us here. [151]Organic life is in any event the form or mode of existence that is most closely related to the spiritual. Animals are still worshiped by many peoples, especially in India and Africa, and have

193

150. *Thus G; P reads:* involves the recognition of
151. *Ho reads, precedes in W:* It is their self-consciousness that human beings make objective for themselves, and

been worshiped in all countries. The animal has this vitality, this passive independence, this quiet organic life which as it were holds to its course, makes its own choices; it moves as it wills, unpredictably, and there is no understanding it. There is something secret in its behavior and habits; it is alive but is not intelligible as one human being is intelligible to another. This secretness easily gives rise to wonder in human beings, so that they are all the quicker to regard this living vitality of animals as higher than their own. Even the Greeks venerated snakes, concerning which there has been this preconception from ancient times.[152] On the west coast of Africa there is a snake in every house; it is left alone, and for anyone to kill it is looked upon as the greatest of crimes. On the one hand, therefore, animals are venerated; but at the same time they may remain subject to highly arbitrary decisions in regard to their veneration. Negroes make the first animal that takes their fancy into their talisman; then if things don't turn out as they wish they reject it and take another—as it were, punish it.

What is of interest, then, is to secure some [kind of] objectivity. And living things generally do furnish such an object, in which one has before oneself a [kind of] independence. This then constitutes the essence of animal cults. In organic life, free independence at least makes its appearance. Animal cults are found wherever humanity, the spiritual element, has not yet grasped | itself in its genuine   194
essentiality; thus the vitality of humanity is only free independence.

It is to be noted, however, that in this realm of desire, where the particular self-consciousness exists for itself as the highest, where free, universal ˉindependenceˉ[153] is not yet recognized, either within

152. W (following Ho) adds: that they are accounted a good omen. Ho reads: Indeed, even the Greeks still venerate snakes, or at least they are accounted a good omen. When Hector purposes to storm the walls [of Troy] (Iliad, bk. XII, vv. 200–210), an eagle flies over the army with a snake that it lets fall, and Homer calls the snake a "sign from aegis-brandishing Jove."
[Ed.] Homer, Iliad 12.195–209. If Hegel supposed that the Trojans regarded this as a good omen, as Hotho would have us believe, he was mistaken; on the contrary, they regarded it as an evil omen. Hector himself makes no attempt to deny that the incident has a threatening significance, but believes himself justified in disregarding the flight of the broad-winged birds (v. 237) owing to the counsel he had already received from Zeus.
153. Ho reads: spirituality W_2 (Var) reads: objective spirituality

or outside itself, the living [organism]—to the extent that it is recognized—is not yet given the significance that it later acquires in the image of the so-called transmigration of souls. This image is grounded on the fact that the human spirit is something that endures, something immortal, something that abides in principle. But in order to exist through time it needs some [sort of] corporeality, and inasmuch as this is no longer human existence, it needs another shape; the one that is most akin to it is the living shape, the animal. In the kind of animal cult that is coupled with the transmigration of souls, it is an important and essential moment that not merely does this [animal] possess organic life, but the idea of an indwelling spiritual element merges with this organic life so that it is properly the spiritual subject in the living animal element that becomes the object of worship. But here, in the sphere where the the immediate self-consciousness is the basic determining characteristic, it is only organic life itself that is worshiped, which is why this veneration or worship of a living thing is contingent, being directed now to one animal, now to another kind, almost every unfulfilled wish bringing a change. This is what happens among the Negroes and the Chinese: they get on well enough with what they venerate until something occurs that displeases them; then they just as readily give up what they have been venerating. At that point one thing is as good as another for the purpose, an idol one has made oneself, a mountain, a tree, and so on. What one feels the need for is to have an independent power standing objectively over against one. In the same way as children have the impulse to play and adults to adorn themselves, so here there is the impulse to be confronted by something objective;[154] | here too there is conscious awareness of an arbitrary bond, which can just as easily be annulled again.[155]

195

This is what is meant more especially by fetishism. A fetish can be anything, a carving, piece of wood, ˜animal,˜[156] river, tree, and so on, even a grasshopper or locust one has shut in a box; and there

154. W (following Ho) adds: as something independent and powerful; Ho reads: to be confronted by an independent power as something objective;

155. Ho adds, similar in W: so that the more precise determinacy of the object appears initially as of no consequence.

156. W (Var) reads: lion, tiger,

are fetishes for whole tribes, ethnic fetishes, and also fetishes for individuals. (Fetish and idol are the same, the word "fetish" being the corrupt form of a Portuguese word signifying an idol.) And fetishism is the arbitrary selection of this or that as an idol, followed by its no less arbitrary replacement by something else.[157] Negroes switch from one fetish to another at will while other peoples have permanent fetishes. [158]For the Egyptians, for example, once the Nile has become for them the universal, the divine, it forms their substantive power, wherein their entire existence lies. But this is somewhat different from those fetishes that have their origin in the subject's need to worship or need to engage in magic. [The idol] is at once the object of worship and the means; it is supposed to do such and such, and if that does not happen, the idol is done away with. Honor is consequently meted out according to what happens to the subject.

4. The fourth stage, that in which independent spirituality is intuited, is essentially humanity itself. In humanity something independent is intuited, something that is also spiritual. Worship accordingly has here its more essential object; and in regard to the definition of objectivity a new characteristic enters into play, namely that it is not each and every contingent consciousness that has power over nature, but that there are exclusively a few (or exclusively just this one) who are intuited and venerated as essentially spiritual independence—there is a singling out to the exclusion of the others. In this existent [existierenden] self-consciousness is to be found what has more character, more authority than others, [what is] in com-

157. [Ed.] Hegel may be referring to the Journal by Professor Smith appended to Narrative of an Expedition to Explore the River Zaire, Usually Called the Congo, in South Africa, in 1816, under the Direction of Captain J. K. Tuckey, R.N. (London, 1818), p. 375: "The word [fetish] is Portuguese, feitico, and signifies a charm, witchcraft, magic, etc." Smith goes on to say that almost anything can serve as a fetish, and that in the case of misfortune the fetish is not blamed, though he does mention a case of misfortune where a fetish that had proved impotent was replaced. We know from his correspondence (Hegel: The Letters, trans. Clark Butler and Christiane Seiler [Bloomington, 1984], p. 496 [no. 473]) that Hegel endeavored to secure a copy of this book from the Royal Library on 26 May 1824, presumably for the lectures on the philosophy of religion.

158. Precedes in W (following Ho): The fetish . . . individual. Ho reads: The fetish on the contrary can be changed and becomes merely a means to procure something for the individual, so that if it fails in this, it is rejected.

parison with them essential *will,* essential *knowing*—the *command-* 196 *ing* power, | as that which appears to be essentially necessary in comparison with the others, whose will and knowing are contingent and subordinate, a focal point among the many. Inasmuch as it is a *self*-consciousness, a spiritual power, that is to be intuited or recognized as *objective,* there emerges the determination that it can only be one or a few, to the exclusion of others. Therefore it is necessarily one or a few individuals who are the magicians, who constitute this power; a few only are venerated as the highest power there is. Usually they are princes, for example the emperor of China. These are the ones who have authority over human beings and also over nature, over natural things. In that it is a self-conscious being that is venerated here, a distinction is immediately made between what such an individual is as inner spirituality and what he is according to his outward existence. In the latter regard, such an individual is a human being like others, whereas the essential moment is *spirituality,* being spiritual on one's own account, in contrast with the outward, contingent mode of existence.

At this point a distinction begins to emerge; at a higher level the distinction is that which is present in those whom we call lamas. Initially the distinction is just this, that a distinction is made between, on the one hand, individuals as such and, on the other, individuals as universal powers. Where this universal, spiritual power is represented on its own account, it yields the representation of a genie or of a deity that can itself be represented in sensuous form for intuition; and the actual living individual is then the priest of such an idol. At this present stage the power of the priest often coincides with that of the god. His inwardness can be hypostatized, but as yet the power of the spiritual over existence has not been separated out, so that the spiritual power on its own account is only a superficial representation. The priest or sorcerer is the principal person, so that on the one hand both aspects [priest and god] are represented separately, but when the deity gives utterance, becomes forceful, decides, etc., he does so only as this actual human being; the actual human being is the power that attains this actuality. At times these priests also have the secular ruler set over them, in cases where priest and prince are separate persons; the human individual is on the one

292

hand venerated as | God, on the other obliged to do what others 197
command. The Negroes who have magicians of this kind, who are
not at the same time rulers, tie them up and beat them until they
obey if they do not want to perform magic, are not in the mood for it.

Thus it is a *self*-consciousness that is venerated. The determination that *spirit* is present in humanity, and that human self-
consciousness is essentially the presence of spirit—this is a conjunction we shall trace through various religions; it belongs necessarily
to the first and oldest determinate religions, and we shall see that
it is also present in the Christian religion, but in a more exalted
fashion and transfigured.[159]

In this—human—shape [of consciousness], there are two ways
in which human beings attain objectivity. In the first they shut out
or exclude what is other. The second, natural way is for them to
be stripped of what is temporary and contingent; this natural way
is death. Death takes from people what is temporal and ephemeral
in them, but has no power over what is in and for itself. But the
fact that human beings have within themselves a region that is in
and for self still cannot, at the present stage, enter into consciousness;
self-consciousness still does not here possess the genuine, eternal
significance of its spirit. The process of stripping away involves only
sensuous existence. In all other respects humanity retains here its
contingent particularity, its sensuous presence; it is indeed removed
to the [sphere of] representation, but that wherein it is retained is
not its genuine [element]; on the contrary, what it retains in this way
is the whole contingent, sensuous mode of its existence. Consequently, veneration of the dead is still something utterly weak, with
contingent content; the dead are represented as a power that demands
to be served, but only as a very weak power.

What is enduring in the dead, what still impinges on the senses,
the immortal aspect that is at the same time still present in sensuous
form, is their bones. The various peoples accordingly venerate the

159. *Ho, W add:* The Christian religion interprets and transfigures it for the first
time.
    [*Ed.*] Hegel here establishes an interesting connection between primitive religion
and consummate religion: they are both religions of spirit, corresponding to the third
moment in the dialectic of the divine life.

bones of the dead and use them for casting spells. This may remind
198   one of sacred relics, and it is somewhat naive | of the Capuchins
on the one hand to inveigh against this heathen magic and on the
other hand to ascribe great power to their own relics. For example,
a Capuchin friar tells how the Negroes have this superstition, that
they procure bands for themselves and that whoever is bound with
such bands is supposed to enjoy immunity from wild beasts. The
preparation of these bands is something very complicated and
magical. He had often spoken against them—in vain. Now, says this
Capuchin, he was in the neighborhood of natives draped in such
bands, and he often saw them torn to pieces by animals, whereas
those to whom he had given relics had always remained unharmed.[160]

The dead, then, demand veneration, and this consists simply in
ensuring that they are cared for, e.g., given food and drink. Most
peoples of antiquity used to put food in the graves of the dead. What
is true, lasting, enduring, in the dead consequently plays a very minor
part in the way death is pictured. We find also the view portrayed
that the dead can reenter or be brought back into the present,
sometimes freely, in the shape of a power that seeks to avenge the
neglect it has suffered, sometimes conjured up by the power of the
sorcerer, of actual self-consciousness, and so subject to him.

The type of cultus found in this sphere will be more clearly
pictured from examples. The Capuchin friar Cavazzi,[161] who spent
a considerable time in the Congo, writes (among other things) a great
deal about these sorcerers, who are called Singhili. According to him,
they are highly respected and call the people, men and women,
together whenever the fancy takes them. They do this from time to
time, always making out that one or other of the dead drives them
to it and demands it. The following also illustrates the type of cultus
here involved. When the Singhili calls the inhabitants together, they
must assemble, each carrying a knife, while the sorcerer himself

160. [Ed.] Cavazzi, *Historische Beschreibung,* pp. 258–259 (p. 223).

161. *W (HgG/Ed?) adds: (Histor. Beschreibung d. drei Königr. Congo,* Munich,
1694),

[Ed.] Cavazzi, *Historische Beschreibung,* pp. 259–264 (pp. 223–227). Cavazzi
distinguishes between several different types of sorcerers with distinct functions,
whereas Hegel uses "Singhili" to cover them all.

appears carried in a net, decked fantastically with flowers, gems, feathers, and so on, and with a | crowd around him engaged in 199 singing, dancing, and rejoicing. Principally they make a fearful, barbaric, stupefying din, banging instruments and singing, which is supposed to make the dead spirit pass into the body of such a Singhili. He himself entreats the spirit to enter him; and when this happens, he slowly raises himself up and now appears like someone possessed; he tears his clothes, rolls his eyes, bites and scratches himself, mouthing what the dead man tells him and speaking in his person. Many of those standing round then ask him about their affairs. The dead man, who is thus represented as speaking, may threaten them with starvation and misery or call down tribulations on them; or he may abuse his blood relations for their ingratitude and complain of their neglect, especially in regard to food and drink, because they have not given him any human blood. The assembled company falls at the Singhili's feet. According to Cavazzi, the workings of hellish fury can be seen in him: he foams at the mouth and sets up a frightful howling; he runs about and himself calls for the blood that is still not being offered to him. Seeking blood, he runs about among the gathering with a knife, plunges it into one bystander's breast, strikes off another's head, splits open another's belly, and drinks the blood that flows out; he tears the dead bodies apart and divides up the flesh among the voracious bystanders, who eat it regardless, even though it may be that of their parents, brothers, or sisters—all is devoured. They know in advance this is how it will end, but go to the assembly nonetheless, with the greatest exultation.

Another way that the dead are operative is the following. The ˉGiaghi, or Jagga,ˉ¹⁶² imagine that the dead wander the earth and feel hunger and thirst. If, for example, anyone is ill, or especially if he has visions or dreams, he has a sorcerer brought to him and seeks his advice. The sorcerer asks about all the circumstances, and the upshot, the answer may be that the illness and dreams are visions of one of the sick person's dead relatives who | is actually present 200

162. *Thus G; W₂ (Ed) reads:* Gagas *P reads:* Zacka *Ho reads:* Jagen
[*Ed.*] Cavazzi, *Historische Beschreibung,* pp. 257–58 (pp. 221–223). On the terminology, see above, n. 119.

here and by whom he is being persecuted, and that the sick person must go to a particular Singhili to have the dead spirit driven away. For each Singhili has his own particular business. Once agreement has been reached with the Singhili, he takes the sick person to the grave of whoever it was that appeared, or is causing the illness. Here the Singhili calls forth the dead spirit with all his might, lights incense, and addresses it; if, however, the dead spirit refuses to come forth, he abuses it, flies into a rage, and finally declares that it has passed into the Singhili's body and has revealed to him what it demands and what must happen in order to reconcile it. This is what happens if the death occurred a long time ago; for someone buried recently, the corpse is taken from the grave, its head is cut off and opened up, and some of the liquids that flow from it are then mixed with dishes which the sick person has to eat, while the remainder is made into plaster casts that are attached to the body.

Things are most difficult when the dead person has had no burial, has been eaten by a friend, foe, or wild beast. Here, again, the dead spirit is conjured up, and the Singhili then declares that it has passed into the body of a monkey, bird, rat, etc., which as a result of the Singhili's incantations is caught. Its neck is then wrung and the sick person is given it to eat, whereupon the dead spirit has lost any right to exist in any form.[163]

It is evident from this that, as far as enduring existence is concerned, the spirit is assigned no absolute, free, independent power.

Death is portrayed as the stripping off of the empirical, outward existence; but the dead retain their whole contingent nature. Objectification still relates wholly to the external mode, is still wholly formal; the mode of objectifying is not yet the essential, ˉwhat is accounted as having being,ˉ[164] and what survives is still the contingent nature. Even the duration thus vouchsafed to the dead is a superficial characteristic:[165] they remain as contingent existences in the might and power of the sorcerer's living | self-consciousness, so that he can even let them die again, for a second time.

201

163. [Ed.] Cavazzi, Historische Beschreibung, p. 258 (pp. 222–223).
164. Thus G; D reads what comes before consciousness,
165. W₂ (Var) adds: and does not transfigure them

The image of immortality ˉis intimately bound up with that of God.ˉ[166] The higher the plane on which human nature is affirmed, and the more the power of spirituality is comprehended according to its genuine content, in eternal fashion, the worthier is the image of God and that of spirit, of the human individual.[167]

Human weakness and infirmity appear no greater here than they do in Greek mythology and in Homer. In the scene where Odysseus is on the Styx,[168] the scene of Odysseus's necromancy, when he summons forth the dead, they come because they cannot do otherwise. He slaughters a black ram; they then thirst for its blood in order that vitality may enter them. Odysseus allows some of them to drink but holds the others back with his sword.

The sensuous view of human spirit is matched by an equally sensuous view of what power is in and for itself.

These examples also show how little value human beings as individuals have from this standpoint. That they should be struck down and eaten, this contempt or scant regard in which some humans are held by others, is also to be found among Negroes in the state of slavery, which is very widespread among them. ˉIt is not only their prisoners but also their fellow citizens who are killed in the hundreds and thousands.ˉ[169] As the image of immortality grows in intensity, so the value of life too is enhanced—one might suppose that it would be the other way round. If one believes one is immortal, life should necessarily be all the more a matter of indifference. | On the one hand, this is partly so; but on the other hand, the value of the living becomes that much the greater, and the individual's right to life is recognized and acknowledged only when humanity appears as inwardly free, as in and for itself. ˉThe two determinations,ˉ[170] that

202

166. *Ho reads, similar in W:* depends invariably on the stage reached in regard to the metaphysical concept of God.

167. *W (following Ho) adds:* and of the immortality of spirit. *Ho reads:* the purer is the picture of immortality.

168. [*Ed.*] Homer, *Odyssey* 11.34–50.

169. *Thus P; G reads:* Captives are either enslaved or slaughtered.

[*Ed.*] See above, n. 123, although Cavazzi says only that the number of victims may be "as high as a hundred."

170. *Thus G; P reads:* The two determinations are representations in the spirit

of subjective, finite being-for-self and that of absolute power, what will subsequently emerge as absolute spirit, are intimately bound up together.[171]

In this immediate form of magic, where the singular self-consciousness is the universal power, where spirituality is only intuited as in the sphere of the singular self-consciousness, there can, properly speaking, be no question of cultus, as free, unforced veneration of the essentially spiritual element. At this stage, the cultus-relationship is rather the exercise of lordship over nature, the lordship exerted by a few endowed with self-consciousness over others endowed with self-consciousness; and the common cultus of those with authority and power [is the exercise of lordship] over the others who are noninitiates. The common cultus is then precisely a condition of being beside oneself, even being out of one's senses, a deadening of the senses, in which the particular consciousness, the particular will is forgotten, extinguished, and the abstract, sensuous consciousness is exalted as high as it can be. The means whereby this deadening of the senses is brought about are dance, music, shouting, eating voraciously, even sexual orgies. This is represented [as] the highest state and is the highest mode [of] what can be called cultus. [It has] abstract significance, and therefore sensuous

203 significance too. |

This sphere of magic is present in representation as a highly extensive, organized realm, the intuition of which is not without its grandeur and majesty. All moments are present in it, but one variant that is particularly striking is where the dead, being no longer among the living, are no longer within the realm of conscious will, yet, as dead, have authority over the natural realms and particular branches

171. W_2 (1831) adds: For this reason too, one might suppose that because human beings, as this power, are of so great account, they should here be greatly honored and have the feeling of their worth. But on the contrary, they are here completely devoid of value, for they do not possess worth by virtue of what they are as immediate will but only inasmuch as they have knowledge of something that has being in and for itself, something substantive, and subject and conform their natural will to it. It is only by sublating their natural unruliness, and knowing that something universal, having being in and for itself, is what is true, that they achieve worth—and life itself also becomes something of value.

of the latter. It could be said that they are raised to be lords of nature, but in fact they are demoted to being merely unconscious genii of the natural.

c. The Religion of Ancient China[172]

This way of viewing the matter can, or *could,* be found at its most fully developed in [ancient] China, being overlaid at a later stage by subsequent accretions. Let me therefore sum up the form that it took.

The content of the principle is that the existent singular self-consciousness is still the divine power. This time it is the emperor of China, the source of all laws in the present world, but also the lord of nature. He governs by means of genii, namely such of the dead as he appoints for the purpose. This emerges more clearly in

172. [*Ed.*] Hegel's sole source for this section consists of the memoirs written by seventeenth- and eighteenth-century Jesuit missionaries in Beijing: *Mémoires concernant l'histoire, les sciences, les moeurs, les usages, etc. des Chinois par les missionaires de Pekin,* 16 vols. (Paris, 1776–1814), 15:228–241. Because of the chaotic romanization of Chinese characters in the lecture transcripts made by Hegel's students, we have used the Pinyin system, officially adopted in 1958 and now the accepted scholarly norm. The first recognizable state in China, the Shang dynasty (dating from about 1600 B.C.), was overthrown by the Western Zhou in 1122 B.C. While the Zhou assimilated many Shang ideas and customs, including their ancestor veneration and agricultural rites, they brought with them a high god, Tian (Heaven), understood as an impersonal power that ruled the world by a moral force known as Dao (the Way). They also clearly distinguished Tian and the emperor, who was the "Son of Heaven" in the sense of relationship rather than of descent: the emperor reigned because he had received the "Mandate of Heaven" as a reward for his virtue, not because he had been born into the position. (See Niels Nielsen, Norvin Hein, Frank Reynolds, et al., *Religions of the World* [New York, 1983], pp. 261–64.) Although the *Mémoires* discussed at some length the relationship of the emperor to heaven ("le Ciel"), Hegel missed the significance of it, possibly because the Chinese name was not used, possibly also because the discussion occurred in the midst of an elaborate description of the installation ceremonies for a new dynasty. Hegel merely states that the imperial constitution had to be "agreed between him [the emperor] and heaven," and he places much greater stress on the manner in which the emperor governed the world and nature through the intermediary of dead spirits known as Shen. Thus in Hegel's version, divine power was localized in the person of the emperor, who ruled by essentially magical means, and we are halfway between a formal and an actual objectification of the divine object. Interpreted in this way, the religion of the Zhou fits Hegel's schema.

connection with the installation of a new dynasty, about which the following may be said.

The Zhou dynasty seized power in 1122 B.C., a period that is already clearly defined in Chinese history. The first Zhou emperor was Wu-wang. The last emperor of the preceding dynasty, Zhou-sin, like his predecessors, had ruled badly, so that the Chinese imagined it was ˉthe evil geniiˉ[173] who had ruled [in his stead]. When a new dynasty comes to the throne, everything in heaven and on earth has to be renewed:[174] there are new laws, new music, new ceremonies, new officials, and so on; and it is not only the | officials of the actual world who have to be renewed but also those who are dead.

The emperor is lord over nature, and sets all this in train. One of the main things to be seen to is that the tombs of the previous dynasty are destroyed, ˉand its officials dishonored.ˉ[175] Another factor is that the new empire includes families that supported the old dynasty, members of which had an honorable standing, held high office, especially military posts, and fought against the new dynasty, but that to injure such people would be impolitic; so a means must be found to avoid dishonoring their dead relatives. The new monarch Wu-wang did this in the following way. Once the flames in the capital (which was not yet Beijing) had been extinguished—flames which the previous ruler had caused to be lit in order to reduce to ashes the royal palace he had inhabited, with all the treasures, women, and so on that it contained—the realm and its sovereignty was made subject to the new dynasty, and the time was come for Wu-wang to enter the imperial city as emperor, present himself to the people, and issue laws to the people. He let it be known, however, that he could not do this until everything had been properly regulated between him and heaven. The imperial constitution, agreed between him and heaven, was reputedly contained in two books that had been

---

173. *Thus D, similarly P; G reads:* the evil genius that inhabited his body

174. W_2 *(1831) adds:* this was accomplished by the new emperor with the help of the generalissimo of his army—

175. *Thus G, W_1; W_2 (Var/MiscP?) reads:* i.e., destruction of the cultus directed at the ancestors who previously had power over families and over nature. *Ho reads:* But if there are still families that supported the former dynasty, it is necessary to avoid dishonoring it, in order not to injure them.

deposited on a mountain with a venerable sage. One was said to contain the new laws that were to be promulgated, and the other the names and offices of the genii, known as Shen, who were to be the new administrators of the empire in the natural world, the invisible officials over the natural world, as the mandarins are in the world of consciousness. Wu-wang sent his general off to fetch these books from the mountain; this general was already himself a | Shen, an actual genie, having attained this level while still alive 205 as the result of over forty years of study and exercises. Well, he came with the books, and there was a ceremony for the promulgation of the books. The emperor purified himself, fasted three days, and at sunrise on the fourth day emerged in his imperial attire, holding the book of the new laws in his hand. The book was placed on the altar and sacrifices were offered. The emperor gave thanks to heaven for imparting this book. Thereupon the laws were promulgated, being in all cases just the old ones with slight alterations.[176] The important thing was the second book; it was not opened, but the general was sent with it onto another mountain (there were four mountains) in order to make it known to the Shen, the genii, and inform them of the emperor's commands.[177]

The old man [the sage?] called the Shen together on the mountain and summoned them to appear there—this mountain lay in the region from which the house of the new dynasty had come. The account goes on to relate what then happened. The dead had assembled,[178] taking their place higher or lower on the mountain side according to rank, and the general, representing the emperor, sat himself ¨in their midst¨[179] on a throne that had been erected for this purpose and that was gorgeously adorned. An altar stood before this throne, which had been decorated with the eight Gua (signs of the Fo) and three kinds of sacred signs. On the table in front of it

176. W₂ (MiscP/Var?) reads: and to the people's utmost surprise and satisfaction it was found that they were all the same as before. In general, when there was a change of dynasty the old laws remained in force with slight alterations.

177. W (following Ho) adds: It included their appointment and dismissal. Ho reads: in order to inform them of the book of laws, which included their appointment and dismissal.

178. W (Ed) adds: on the mountain

179. Thus G; P reads: at the center of this empire

lay the imperial banners of the new dynasty and the scepter, the staff of authority over the Shen. Similarly, on the middle of the altar [was] the scroll of the venerable sage, giving the general authority to make the new commandments known to the Shen. The general first offered a sacrifice, | then read the scroll, which was then passed to the Shen. Those who had formerly held power were rebuked for their neglect,[180] declared unworthy to rule any longer, and dismissed from their office. They were told they could go wherever they chose, and even reenter human life in order to atone in this way for their errors. After their dismissal the general called on the new Shen who were to be promoted, and gave them instructions concerning their duties. He seated himself on his throne and called out those to be promoted. The first he appointed administrator over the mountain, a general of an earlier emperor, then others to be administrators of the other four mountains (which, properly speaking, are the four parts of the earth, for in the eyes of the Chinese China is the world); and these Shen are also administrators of the four seasons. A fifth genie was placed over the central mountain. A prince was then called out who had played a leading role under the last ruler of the previous dynasty; in peacetime he had been renowned for his fair dealing and in time of war he had been a great and valiant general and had done more than anyone else to prevent the new dynasty from overthrowing the old until he had finally been slain in battle. His name was called "next,"[181] and he was given the task of inspecting all Shen assigned authority over rain, wind, thunder, and clouds. He was to be appointed to this office, and the one who was appointing him was the general of the new dynasty who had waged war on him. This prince was therefore called before the new general. He did not approach the foot of the altar until his name had been called twice and he had been shown the staff of authority, and then he advanced with a haughty bearing and remained proudly standing. The general of the new dynasty, when he saw this, addressed him as follows: "You are no longer what you were in the body among men, you are nothing but a common Shen with as yet no office; I have here a commission

180. W₂ (Var) adds: as being the cause of the misfortune that had occurred,
181. Thus P; G reads: fifth,

for you from yon venerable | sage. Honor this command, as behooves 207 thee." At these words, the Shen fell on his knees before the altar; he was then harangued at length; after devoting himself for a long time to studies, then to weapons, and so forth, he was finally, as we have said, designated chief of all those Shen who command the rain, clouds, wind, and thunder. The general charged him to make rain in due season, to disperse the clouds when they threatened to cause flooding, to prevent the wind from becoming a tempest, and to make the thunder roll only in order to frighten the wicked and cause them to withdraw within themselves. He was given twenty-four adjutants,[182] each of whom received a particular [task of] inspection that changed every fortnight, while others were given other departments. Thus we get the picture of how all these offices were distributed one after another. The Chinese have five elements; one is fire, and one Shen was made responsible for it, in relation to conflagrations; six others were placed in charge of epidemics and were given the task of ameliorating human society by purging it from time to time of an excess of population. After the general had returned to the army, he gave the book back to the emperor. It still constitutes the astrological portion of the almanac. Two almanacs or directories appear in China every year, one concerning the mandarins, the other concerning the invisible officials, the Shen; the almanac shows then which Shen is in charge on each occasion. In the event of misfortune in some locality—crop failure, conflagrations, flooding, or the like—the relevant Shen are summoned and dismissed, the images wherein they had been venerated are torn down, and new Shen are designated. Thus in China the emperor's lordship over nature is a fully organized monarchy.

d. The Religion of Being-Within-Self (Buddhism, Lamaism)[183]

Up to this point we have seen objectivity consisting solely in formal universality; the content is still the sensuous world of a consciousness

182. *Ho adds:* (famous officers)
183. [*Ed.*] On Hegel's own terms, Buddhism should not be considered under the general category of "the religion of magic," since we are no longer dealing with formal but with actual objectification of the divine object, and have arrived for the first time at religion in the proper sense as distinguished from magic. In the 1827 and 1831

that is completely raw, the purpose is desire and whatever the
satisfaction of the desires requires from nature. | This formal objec-
tivity is not yet an objectivity that exists in and for itself: it is still
not a content that we can recognize as genuine, but only the power
of humanity over what is natural. Religion is the unity of the finite
and infinite, of concept and reality. It is these two moments we have
essentially to consider in the idea, in order to see how God defines
or determines himself. The finite is the immediate self-consciousness,
just this human being or these human beings; with the finite we are
concerned with the determinacy of the content. The other aspect,
the infinite, is the general power of the spirit over the contingent,
the sensuously external. Thus power is here the basic characteristic;
it is power that is the infinite aspect, the essential aspect generally,
power over the inessential. But the content of this power is still not
essential, it is not objective in and for itself, for sensuous desires and
suchlike are the content, the purpose, over which power is the master.
Power as such is negativity, essentiality, but only in relation to an
other, which it negates; it is negativity of the other. It is not inwardly
free, it is not power over itself, but essentially power over something,
so that the relation to an other is always present.

We now have to consider the next advance. *Prima facie* the
advance is that the infinite aspect, the essential aspect, is comprehended in a deeper, more genuine way than heretofore—or that
another spiritual moment becomes objective for consciousness, for
subjective spirit, [at this stage] as compared with what we have been
considering up to this point. This new determination can only mean
that consciousness comprehends itself, comprehends the essence as
independent, as essentiality having being within itself and relating
to itself, as this reflection of negativity within itself. And it is at this
point that true objective universality begins—universality that is
objective in itself according to the content. Thus genuinely objec-

208

lectures, Buddhism is in fact distinguished from magic and given an autonomous place
in the schema of nature religions. Hegel's information about Buddhism was both limited
and inaccurate. On his sources and general characterization of Buddhism and Lamaism,
or "the religon of Fo," see the Editorial Introduction and subsequent footnotes. Fo
is the Chinese name of Buddha.

tive universality begins with being-within-self [*Insichsein*] in general; it pertains thereto that self-consciousness reflects itself into itself, or sinks itself in itself, that thought comes to itself. Thought as power exists only in relation to an other; thought must therefore grasp essentiality, which is not tied to the determinacy of volition and knowing; essentiality must be constituted as what is genuine. Here lies the distinction between the | naturally, contingently determined self-consciousness—the raw, untamed character of whatever desire comes to power—and what rests and abides within itself, namely *spirit;* and here in this being-within-self the place of divinity in general emerges for the first time.

209

The sphere we have previously termed magic should not, properly speaking, be termed religion. Religion begins here, for it is only at this point that the consciousness of what has being-within-self, what is at rest and abides firmly, eternally within itself, begins; for the first time we have a genuinely divine characteristic—to be free on one's own account, to be the substantive, to be the universal. Initially this characteristic or determination is still abstract,[184] much more is [of course] needed in order for spirit to be defined in its truth, to be cognized and known. However unsatisfactory the other characteristics may be, we have here a solid base; [it is] a genuine determination of God that constitutes the foundation. And this religion, however base and lowly it appears, is nonetheless at a higher level than the form of religion which says that we know nothing of God, for in that religion there can be no worship at all, since we can only worship what is something "for us."[185] With this advance, therefore, a firm basis or determination has been won, and self-consciousness has here an affirmative relationship to this object, for the essential character [*Wesenheit*], this being-within-self, is nothing

184. *Ho adds, similar in* W$_1$: This characteristic or determination is, to be sure, still abstract, and the concept of spirit is still immensely far from being exhausted by it.

185. *Follows in* W *(HgG/1831?):* a common example used in Latin grammar is *Is colit Deum, qui eum novit.*

[*Ed.*] The grammar to which Hegel is referring has not been identified. But the idea is expressed by Seneca, *Ad Lucilium epistulae morales* 95.47: *Deum colit, qui novit.*

else but *thought* itself, and this is the distinctive essentiality [*Wesentlichkeit*] of self-consciousness. Hence there is nothing unknown or otherworldly in it. It has its own essence [*Wesen*] before it,[186] and has an affirmative relationship to it; but it also represents this essential [*Wesenhaftigkeit*] to itself as standing over against it, for it distinguishes this being-within-self, this pure freedom, from itself, from this particular self-consciousness, which is a contingent, empirical, | manifoldly determined self-consciousness. This then is the basic determination that we have at this point.

210

˜The second consideration is that the infinite, being at first the sinking-within-self, the self-absorption, of thought, is therefore only abstract to begin with, but it must also be essentially determinate, for what is true is concrete. There must be determinacy, and the only question is how there can still be determinacy here.˜[187] Here we are still at the standpoint of nature religion in general, and more specifically at the stage where the form or determinateness of the spiritual is still its immediate shape, or still has the form of *this* [singular] self-consciousness.[188] This is still the initial or proximate form for what is objective in itself. This infinite is *self*-referring, no longer determined merely as power, the unrest of power, which operates only outward. This is the first aspect; the second is that the side of existence, the shape [assumed by spirit], is raised up to infinite form too, but this comes later and separately from the first aspect. The raising of existence to the infinite of form is spiritual knowing, free intelligence as such: this is a later stage, here the form is still immediate, consisting initially in the fact that it is a singular

186. *W adds:* inasmuch as it knows this essential character to be at the same time its own essentiality, *Cf. Ho:* This determination or characteristic can be none other than that the consciousness has inwardly grasped itself as universal essentiality in its relation to itself.

187. W_2 *(1831) reads:* Substance is universal presence, but as inwardly subsisting essentiality, it must also become known concretely in an individual concentration.

188. W_2 *(1831) adds:* By comparison with the preceding stage, therefore, the advance is from the fantastic mode of personifying, which fragments into countless hosts [of shapes], to one that is determinately circumscribed and present. A human being is worshiped, and as such is the god, who assumes individual shape and in such shape offers himself for worship. In this individual entity the substance is power, lordship, the creation and preservation of the world, of nature and all things, *absolute* power.

self-consciousness. Since the two—on the one side, the determination of the infinite, and on the other side, reality—are, as has been said, separate, here again it is necessary that this form too should thus constitute a distinctive religion, and spirit make a halt at this stage. ˉFrom this standpointˉ[189] we have emerged from the sphere of magic, | of power, but the two things can very well continue to   211 subsist side by side—the secular power (the emperor) and the spiritual.

To turn to the overt historical aspect, we have now defined the religion of Fo in China; this is the religion of the Chinese, Mongols, and Tibetans, also of the Burmese and Ceylonese, except that what is in China called Fo they call Buddha. However, the two terms mean the same, and this is the religion we know under the form of Lamaism. The slight difference between the Fo religion and Lamaism is only superficial.[190] In the latter the side of reality or the shape [assumed by spirit] is a particular self-consciousness, an actual, living human being. There are several such chief lamas, in particular three, the Dalai Lama in northern Tibet, the Lama in southern Tibet, and then another leader of this kind out in Russian Mongolia, or Siberia, who are worshiped as gods. In contrast, Fo and Buddha are also human individuals, but they are represented as dead. Since, however, the lamas are living human individuals, it remains a matter of contingency that there may be several other lamas. Thus it is said

189. *Thus P, D; G reads:* If this standpoint is a resting-within-self,
190. [*Ed.*] This erroneous view derives from several of Hegel's sources. For example, the *Allgemeine Historie der Reisen zu Wasser und zu Lande; oder, Sammlung aller Reisebeschreibungen* (Leipzig, 1750), 6:381, asserts that in matters of religion the lamas and Chinese "are identical, and differ only in a few superstitious practices." See also Samuel Turner, in Wilhelm Harnisch, *Die wichtigsten neuern Land- und Seereisen,* 16 vols. (Leipzig, 1821–1832), vol. 6 (1824), p. 355: "The Tibetan worship of God is related to the same high God Buddha, or Fo, or Gautama, that is worshiped in Japan, China, Burma, and Indochina." Likewise Amherst's "Gesandtschaftsreise nach und durch China," in Harnisch, *Die wichtigsten Reisen,* vol. 5 (1824), p. 82: "Actually the Lama-worshipers are only a special kind of Fo-worshipers. They are related to other Fo-worshipers as Catholics are related to Protestants among Christians." Hegel was unfamiliar with the basic differences between the three main schools of Buddhism: Hīnayāna (or Theravāda), Mahāyāna, and Vajrayāna (including Lamaism).

of the Buddha that he has now to be venerated in Burma as Gautama.[191] There are, therefore, several lamas.[192] Gautama is supposed to have lived some forty years before Christ.[193] He is called the redeemer of souls, so that in this religion emphasis is already falling on the soul, on the spiritual. He is represented as coming after Buddha, as an incarnation of Buddha (so that several Buddhas have also followed one another), and is now venerated accordingly.

What we have still to consider is the relationship of the other, inessential forms of self-consciousness to these, in other words the relationship involving the subjective religion of the community. This is where free worship begins; for the community has recognized that the essence is ˉthe eternal rest of inner contemplation.ˉ[194] This is

191. W₁ (HgG/Ed?) adds: (Godama, savior of souls)

192. [Ed.] I.e., Buddhas. Hegel's point here seems to be that just as there can be several lamas at one time, so there can be several Buddhas at different times. The major source for Hegel's information about Buddhism is Francis Buchanan, "On the Religion and Literature of the Burmas," in Asiatic Researches, 11 vols. (London, 1806–1812), 6:249 ff. Buchanan discusses the question of the existence of several Buddhas; on this matter see also William Jones, "On the Chronology of the Hindus," in Asiatic Researches 2:121 ff., and Creuzer, Symbolik und Mythologie 1:579.

193. [Ed.] The source of this date, which is given by G and confirmed by Ho (50 B.C.), cannot be determined. The view prevalent in Hegel's day placed the life of Buddha around 1000 B.C. See, e.g., Allgemeine Historie 6:382; and Friedrich Schlegel, Ueber die Sprache und Weisheit der Indier, p. 140 (Kritische Friedrich-Schlegel-Ausgabe 8:243). William Jones, "On the Chronology of the Hindus," in Asiatic Researches 2:121 ff. works with a series of fanciful numbers, none of which is later than 1000 B.C. Francis Buchanan, "On the Religion and Literature of the Burmas," Asiatic Researches 6:262, questions the year 1000 as too early, but without suggesting a later date. It is not inconceivable that Hegel confused Gautama's dates with the time of the introduction of Buddhism into China, which however occurred in A.D. 67. The dates A.D. 63–65 were given in the sources available to Hegel, e.g., Allgemeine Historie 6:358. In the 1827 lectures Hegel dates the introduction of Buddhism as fifty years after Christ, and conceivably he confused the "before" and the "after" when dating Gautama in 1824 (especially if we follow Ho in reading "fifty years before Christ"). The generally accepted dates today for Gautama Siddhartha are ca. 563–483 B.C. In any event, Hegel assumed that Buddhism/Lamaism (the religion of being-within-self) existed well before the life of Gautama, who was one of several Buddhas, and the early dating of "Buddha"—and presumably Buddhism—prevalent at the time may have led Hegel to assume that it was an older religion than Hinduism and thus to treat it first, as he does in the 1824 and 1827 lectures (in 1831 the order is reversed). In Hegel's view the religion of Fo came later, with the introduction of Buddhism into China (see below, n 202), and he may or may not have thought that Gautama was associated with this event.

194. Thus P; G reads: substantial identity with self.

where the theoretical attitude begins; no longer is practical power the first moment, being in opposition to otherness, this negativity against others; and no longer the practical [need] either, whose content [is] | desire—craving and being satisfied. Here consciousness   212 is defined by peaceful being-within-self, barbarity is softened, desire [becomes] the transcending of desire, a renunciation that entails no sacrifice. The community is characterized by a tone of quietness and repose, tranquillity and obedience, of being without desires or being above them, and the life of its members is regulated by this ˉstill, gentle mode of being.ˉ195 But this cultus (for it is cultus we are here considering) is also open to the individual, who is at liberty to forgo outward, worldly life, permanently embrace this silence, and sink himself in self-contemplation, having no part in existence; and this union with theoretical substantiality is then regarded as the highest fulfillment. Tranquillity and repose are the keynote of the character of the community, and this gives rise to the establishment of numerous monasteries and great priesthoods, which pass their time in silent contemplation of the eternal, taking no part in worldly interests and concerns.196

There is a second characteristic we should notice in regard to subjective self-consciousness, which is that it is chiefly here that the doctrine of the transmigration of souls is to be found. 197Those who have made the transition to the theoretical know that there is a being that is at rest within itself, something truly essential; having arrived at this intuition, they know themselves as thinking beings, they know themselves too to be *theoretical* beings—fixed, enduring, substantive; and what is termed immortality of the soul (in the broadest sense) is what now for the first time emerges. As thinking beings they have consciousness of their eternity, of their unaltering, unchanging inner being, which is thought, the consciousness of thought.

195. *Thus P; D reads:* still mode of being. *G reads:* quietude of the senses.

196. [*Ed.*] Hegel's picture of Buddhist monastic communities is based on Francis Buchanan, "On the Religion and Literature of the Burmas," *Asiatic Researches* 6:273–280. The corresponding passages in *Allgemeine Historie* 6:358 ff. are distinctly pejorative in tone.

197. *Ho reads, precedes in* W₁: Magic-working, as the relationship of power, is essentially practical, for power occurs only as manifestation of the nullity of what it has posited as inessential.

But secondly, the shape of this eternal being, this eternal subjectivity is still an immediate one, because their thinking has not yet attained to the freedom of spirit and the representation of spirit. Spirit is in general that which frees itself. Here the eternal is still undetermined within itself: it is not yet spiritual, its determination is the determina-tion of | immediacy, i.e., a bodily, sensuous shape. Moreover, this bodily shape is contingent; it may be human or animal,[198] for it is already a long step forward, a much higher level of determination, [to say] that the shape or configuration should also match the deter-minacy of the content. [Here] being-within-self, eternal being has still no content, and so affords no criterion for the shape, and there cannot therefore be any question as yet of the shape's matching the inner determinacy. There is as yet no inner determinacy. Conse-quently there is bound up with this level the doctrine of transmigra-tion of souls, in other words *indifference* with regard to shape. Where the spiritual assumes a shape befitting it as a living, sensuous exter-nal existence, it can have only one shape, namely, the human, the sensuous appearance of spirit. But if the inner element is not yet defined as spirit, the shape is a matter of contingency and indif-ference.[199]

Indifference with regard to the shape here extends also to the objective element, to the eternal, to God. Buddha exists in several shapes, as does Lama; as soon as one lama dies, another takes his place, so that the essence is the same in both, and death brings no interruption in regard to the substantive essence. The rest is con-tingent and is of infinite diversity; the [essential] determination goes no further. Thus, among the people, [be they] Mongols, Burmese, [or] Chinese, it is [a matter of] sheer caprice, adventure, etc.

It may be noted that this religion is the most widespread and that which has most adherents. Its worshipers are more numerous than those of Islam, which itself has more adherents than Christianity. As in Islam, it is an undifferentiated eternal that constitutes the basic

198. *Ho, W₁ add:* The whole world of organic life, human and animal, becomes the variegated apparel of this colorless inwardness.
199. *Ho, W add:* The eternal life of Christians is the spirit of God himself, and the spirit of God is to be self-consciousness of himself as divine spirit. But at this stage being-within-self is still lacking determinacy, is not yet spirit. It is immediate being-within-self.

intuition and determination of the inner element, and | this ⁻deter-   214
minateness is more especially that of human shape, in part living
and present, in part represented as having existed previously.⁻²⁰⁰

⁻We get a more precise view if we survey what is known of the
essence of the religion of Fo and Buddha.⁻²⁰¹ The Fo religion as
such comes from China, and in historical fact it is somewhat later
than the form in which power is the dominant element. The French
missionaries cite a decree of Emperor Xian-zong²⁰² dissolving a large
number of monasteries and forcing their inmates to return to the
world, because these monasteries, these priests, did not cultivate the
soil and paid no taxes. The emperor's decree begins as follows:
"Under our three famous dynasties the Fo sect was never heard of,
it has emerged only since the Han dynasty." Here we have the
necessary historical progression. ⁻We must go into this more fully
in order to recognize the features of the concept in it.⁻²⁰³

⁻The principal doctrine of the Fo religion is the dogma of
metempsychosis, or transmigration of souls.⁻²⁰⁴ This is the source
and origin of the innumerable masses of idols and images that are

200. W₂ *(1831) reads:* simplicity of the principle is by itself capable of subjecting
various nationalities to itself.

201. *Thus G*

202. [*Ed.*] The name of the emperor is given only by G, where it reads "Hia-King."
Lasson gives it as "Hia-ring" and contends in a footnote (without referring to a source)
that the dynastic name of this emperor was "Wu-tsung" (Wu-zong), and that the decree
dated from 845, the year of one of the great persecutions of the Buddhists. However,
the wording of the text as well as Hegel's reference to "the French missionaries" makes
it likely that Hegel is not referring to a decree but to a petition of the Confucian scholar
Han-yu in 819. The petition was concerned with the religious fanaticism shown by
the Buddhists on the occasion of the ceremonial transfer of a relic (one of the Buddha's
knuckles) from a pagoda to the imperial palace; the emperor, whose name was Xian-
zong, was in fact well disposed toward the Buddhists, so Han-yu's action resulted
only in his banishment. The incident is referred to in Joseph-Anne-Marie de Moyriac
de Mailla, *Histoire générale de la Chine; ou, Annales de cet empire, traduits du texte
Chinois,* 13 vols. (Paris, 1777–1785), 6:423–424, where Han-yu is said to have pointed
out that a succession of earlier emperors had been long-lived and that under them
the people had enjoyed unbroken peace, adding, "but at that time there was no such
thing as God, and it is only under the Emperor Han-ming-ti that the doctrine of Fo
spread through the empire."

203. *Thus G*

204. W₂ *(Var/1831?) reads:* The dogma of the transmigration of souls is also
the point at which the simple cultus of being-within-self turns into the most manifold
idolatry.

worshiped wherever the veneration of Fo holds sway. Four-footed beasts, birds, insects, and reptiles, in a word the lowliest forms of animal life, have temples and are venerated because God in his reincarnations can dwell in individuals of all kinds, and each animal body can be inhabited by the human soul.

The principle of the Fo religion is that "nothing" is the principle, the beginning and the end of everything existing. Our first ancestors came from nothing and to nothing | they have returned. Everything that exists differs only through form, through quality. In the same way it can be said that I, a human being, an animal, etc., can be formed from the same metal; the basic determination is one mode, and all that is needed is for it to be overlaid by various qualities. However varied people and things may be, there is thus only one principle from which they stem, in which they are, through which they subsist, and to which they revert—this one principle is the nothing, completely unqualified, simple and pure. It is not nothing in the sense of not being, but it is what is purely identical with itself, undetermined, a substantive being; it is thus completely pure, wholly simple and undifferentiated, eternally at rest; it has neither virtue nor power nor intelligence; it lacks these determinate distinctions, being quite free of determination. As for the relationship of human beings to this principle, the rule is that in order to be happy they must endeavor, by dint of continuous speculation, continuous meditation and ⁻continuous self-conquest,⁻[205] to resemble this principle, to resolve or wish for nothing, to do nothing, have no passions, no inclinations or activities. With the attainment of this state of perfect impartiality or absence of concern, there is no longer any question of virtue and vice, reward and punishment, atonement, immortality of the soul, worship, and so on. All this has passed away, and human sanctity consists in ⁻finding union, in this silence, with God.⁻[206] In this cessation of all bodily movement or animation, all movement of the soul,[207] therein consists happiness, and once human beings have reached this level of perfection, there is no longer any

215

205. *Thus P, D; G reads:* self-contemplation,

206. *Thus G; P reads:* uniting oneself with this nothing, with this silence. *Ho, W add:* The clamorous voices of worldly life must be hushed; the silence of the grave is the element of sanctity and eternity.

207. *W₂ (1831) adds:* in this annihilation of self,

change, their souls have no further wanderings to fear, for they become completely identical | with the God Fo.[208] This is to-be-within-self: this purely theoretical moment is here expressed, and has come to intuition thus among this people. This is their basic intuition, their basic consciousness. 216

Bound up with this is the image of the transmigration of souls. Human beings who have not attained to ˜this [ultimate] happiness˜[209] in their lifetime through renunciation and self-absorption ˜still have this happiness *within* them, inasmuch as their spirit is this being-in-itself; but they still need *duration*—they are not [fundamentally] subject to change, but they [still] need the corporeal, and this is how the image of the transmigration of souls arises.˜[210] (It is said of the God Fo himself that he has changed his shape thousands and thousands of times, assuming human or animal shape.) Those who have attained this absolute repose are implicitly freed from change by death, but in order to achieve that happiness they have to migrate through a sequence of shapes. ˜Here magic again enters on the scene, the mediation of the human priests˜[211] who belong to the higher realm of the supersensible and yet at the same time have power over the configurations that humans assume; in this way the aspect of power and magic comes to be associated once more with this theoretical image. Adherents of the Fo religion are in this respect extremely superstitious. They represent to themselves that our human shape passes over into every possible shape, that of a cat, a snake, a mule.[212] A missionary[213] tells the story of a | man on his deathbed who had heard of the Christian religion who summoned him and 217

208. W₂ *(1831) adds:* The soul has ascended to the region of nothingness and is thus redeemed from being tied to the outward, sensuous configuration.

209. *Thus G; D reads:* this impassivity

210. *Thus G*

211. W₂ *(1831) reads:* 3. Now it is here that the side of power and magic-working links up again with this image and the religion of being-within-self ends in the wildest superstition. Because it is in fact inwardly empty, the theoretical relationship turns into the practical relationship of magic-working. The mediation of the priests enters on the scene, *G reads:* The mediation of the priests enters on the scene,

212. *Ho adds, similar in W:* So the priests, as living in the supersensible [realm], are the authorities who decree what shape or configuration the soul is to assume and can therefore save human beings from shapes that bring more misfortune.

213. [*Ed.*] See the account of the missionary le Conte in *Allgemeine Historie der Reisen zu Wasser und zu Lande* 6:362.

complained that a Bonze—that is, one of the priests or wise men who know what goes on in the other world—had told him that as he was currently in the emperor's service, he would remain in it after his death, his soul migrating into one of the emperor's post-horses, and that he was then to do his duty loyally, not kicking, neighing, biting, or stumbling, and being content with little fodder.

The transmigration of souls is based on the image of the being-within-self of spirit, which is raised up above change; and associated with it is magic.

The Buddhists come principally from the Kingdom of Burma, India, and Ceylon. Their God Buddha is venerated as Gautama. Here, as with Fo, what has being-within-self has a human shape, but it is that of a dead person. (This Gautama is also represented as the ninth incarnation of Vishnu by the Hindu Brāhmans, but not venerated by them.[214]) Buddha is again the universal, the good; according to his present, existing shape he is Gautama, and in this shape he must now be venerated. He is depicted in the attitude of self-absorption, with head bent and arms folded over his breast. His priests are the Rahāns[215] and are described by the English as the calmest and noblest of men. They live together, but in silence, and are described as free from particular desires. The state that is represented as the human goal the Buddhists call nirvana,[216] and in describing it they explain that when we are no longer subject to the

214. [Ed.] This is apparently based on a poem by Jayadeva, cited by William Jones, "On the Chronology of the Hindus," in *Asiatic Researches* 2:121. The fact that the Buddha is on the one hand judged very unfavorably by the Brāhmans, but on the other hand is regarded as an incarnation of Vishnu, is explained by Jones on the assumption that there were two Buddhas. On Buddha as an incarnation of Vishnu, see an Iranian source cited by Creuzer, *Symbolik und Mythologie* 1:578. Creuzer refers to *Ayeen Akbery; or, The Institutes of the Emperor Akbar*, translated from the original Persian by Francis Gladwin (London, 1800). See also Creuzer, 1:577, 602, 619.

215. [Ed.] This is probably based on Francis Buchanan, "On the Religion and Literature of the Burmas," *Asiatic Researches* 6:273–280.

216. [Ed.] See ibid., p. 266: "In saying that Godama obtained Nieban [nirvana], what is understood by that word? When a person is no longer subject to any of the following miseries, namely, to weight, old age, disease, and death, then he is said to have obtained Nieban. No thing, no place, can give us an adequate idea of Nieban: we can only say, that to be free from the four above-mentioned miseries, and to obtain salvation, is Nieban." In contrast with this source, which describes nirvana in accord with Hīnayāna Buddhism, Hegel generally understands it as a state of union with

ills of obesity, old age, sickness, and death, we have reached nirvana; we are then identical with God; and regarded as identical with God, we have become Buddha.

They also give a roughly similar description of the lama. Every abbot of a monastery is called lama; all the same, there are only three principal lamas in Lesser and ˉGreater Tibet.ˉ²¹⁷ They are honored by the Mongols | and Tibetans; the Chinese too respect the lamas.   218
ˉˉEnglishmen who have come to know the Dalai Lama—the envoy²¹⁸ saw him frequently—have the greatest respect for him.²¹⁹ His principal trait is quiet and gentleness, coupled with insight and a thoroughly noble being. The peoples likewise venerate him, ˉbecause they see him in the beautiful light of a life of pure contemplation;ˉ²²⁰ and this is the *substantive* element, what they venerate as eternal, possessing absolute eternity. When a lama is called upon to direct his attention to human affairs, then he is solely concerned with well-doing, with dispensing comfort and help by his blessing and exercising the first of all attributes, namely, forgiveness and pity.ˉˉ²²¹

This is the necessary content of the first mode of nature religion. It displays the same two moments that we have seen when we were

---

the Lord Buddha. This is based on a depiction oriented to Mahāyāna Buddhism, as found in another of Hegel's sources, the *Allgemeine Historie* 6:368–369, which stresses in particular the stripping away of all desire and mental and physical activity through which it is to be attained. Instead of "Nieban," which is based on the Pali form "Nibbana," we use the more familiar form of the term, "nirvana."

217. *Ho reads:* Upper Tibet and outer Siberia.

[*Ed.*] In Hegel's day the terms Greater Tibet (*Gross-Tibet*) and Lesser Tibet (*Klein-Tibet*) were used with a variety of meanings as together embracing the area we know as Tibet and Bhutan.

218. [*Ed.*] See Samuel Turner, "Copy of an Account Given by Mr. Turner, of His Interview with Teeshoo Lama," *Asiatic Researches* 1:197–205. However, the account relates to a journey to the lama of Tashilumpo, the Panchen Lama. Probably here as elsewhere (e.g., in the corresponding passage in the 1827 lectures) Hegel erroneously calls all the principal lamas Dalai Lamas.

219. *W₂ (1831) adds:* But above all the Dalai Lama is the appearance of consummate, satisfied being-within-self.

220. *Thus G; P reads:* because they say that they are immersed only in pure contemplation; *D reads:* in that they are always in a state of pure contemplation; *W₂ (1831) adds:* and the absolutely eternal is present in him;

221. *Ho reads:* The English envoy, from whom we have a description of his travels, was filled with awe in the presence of the Lama: "These peoples rest sunk in the

identifying the abstract categories. The first is constituted by power—that the spiritual self-consciousness as immediately one *is* this power—and the second is constituted by reflection into self, being-within-self. This being-within-self is the general basis of any idea of divinity. Identity with self is the basic category or determination; here for the first time we have a genuine foundation for religion, and so it is that by bringing together these two categorial determinations we make our transition to the second form of nature

219 religion. |

2. The Religion of Phantasy (Hinduism)[222]

The second form of nature religion can be called the nature religion of phantasy or fanciful imagination. The problem here is how to define it in more detail. First we have to consider [how] God [is represented] in it; the second point is the cultus, all that pertains to the relationship of the subjective, of the subject, the existent self-consciousness, to this God.

a. The Representation of God

The definition that we have arrived at is the first moment of truth,[223] the basic determination, self-communion, this remaining eternally

---

beautiful light of pure contemplation," he writes, and [continues]: "and if the Lama should ever direct his attention to human affairs (he rules through viziers), all that concerns him is well-doing, dispensing comfort and blessing. Thus forgiveness and pity are also his attributes."

222. [*Ed.*] We have translated the German *Phantasie* by using the variant English spelling "phantasy" in order to convey the sense of visionary, fanciful imagination, as distinguished from that of an unreal mental image or illusion. "Fancy" in the sense used by S. T. Coleridge is precisely what Hegel means by *Phantasie* in this context (see Vol. 1:56), but in ordinary usage has certain connotations which make it unsuitable for our purpose; we do, however, use "fanciful imagination" as an alternative rendering of *Phantasie* in some passages. Hinduism is the "religion of phantasy" because of the way in which ultimate reality, Brahman, is fancifully represented as present in and the substantial ground of all finite, natural, worldly things. In accord with modern English usage, we translate Hegel's *die indische Religion* as "Hinduism" or "Hindu religion." While "the religion of India" would be possible (though cumbersome and somewhat quaint), "Indian religion" could well be confusing. Since "Hindu" and "India(n)" derive from the same root, referring to the land on the river Indus, "Hinduism" simply means "the religion of India." On the sources and characteristics of Hegel's treatment of Hinduism, see the Editorial Introduction and the ensuing footnotes.

223. G *adds:* in all that is termed God,

---

self-contained, this infinity or the absolute reflection into self that resolves all negation and differentiation, a purely theoretical attitude in which differences, relationship to other, power—all distinctions pertaining to the practical sphere—are defined as resolved in the theoretical. This being-within-self, this self-communion, is initially the undetermined, and in the same way as the god Fo is represented, it too is therefore called *nothing,* the indeterminate generally. What must now happen is that at this stage determination comes into play and develops within the form; and, as *divine* form, this form is no longer determined as power, as immediate self-consciousness, but as grounded on this *theoretical* attitude, grounded in self-containment, in the unfolding of the essence, in the emergence of a divine world generally. At this stage the essence is not yet truly God. Though its principle is being-within-self, it is still undetermined, not yet genuine; only unity with the form, this unity of infinite and finite, is what is genuinely divine. Being-within-self must develop progressively according to the concept; life must emerge, must achieve fulfillment, and there must be fulfillment to yield a *concrete* divine life. Being-within-self is the first determination, while the second is the progressive development of the divine as concrete; and this second determination, this development, still belongs in the first place to the religion of nature. For the first, immediate mode of development consists in the different moments or aspects being inwardly negated by the concept; they fall asunder, and remain held asunder as mutually independent—this is, so to | speak, the curse   220 of nature. In this development we shall be confronted everywhere with echoes of the concept, of what is true; but these echoes, on the whole, are all the more horrifying to us because they are trapped in the mutual exclusion that is the characteristic quality of the natural state, and never escape from it.

This then is the second determination. Divinity is objective with all its plenitude of content. We have first considered contingent objectivity as empty form, and then the objectivity of being-within-self. The determination of being-within-self, of absolute identity with self, is now complemented by that of concreteness. At this second stage, [however,] the different moments continue to be held asunder, whereas the third stage—the spiritual—is where the concrete recapitulates itself within itself, being simultaneously—according to

317

the concept—*posited* and *known* as something ideal. At the present stage the moments are indeed present, but as far as their necessity is concerned, they are all separate, so that the moments are viewed independently, theoretically, are removed from [the sphere of] desire and exist as independent and objective in their particularity.

Thirdly the question arises, what are the forms of this independence, the shapes that it assumes. This is the kind of world we are in too, a world of things external to each other, a world of sense; hence our external sensuous consciousness has to deal with a world of varied multiplicity, which is present [to it] and bound up [with it]. Taken altogether, there are just *these* things—this is the basic determination—we call them "things" to characterize more precisely what objectively *is*.[224] We are also confronted inwardly by a multitude of powers, mental distinctions, and sensations, which the understanding again isolates from each other in the same way. Nature has set in our hearts this or that inclination or passion, this force of memory, that of judgment, and so forth. Similarly, if we pass on to characterize thinking, there too we find a host of determinations of this kind, each of which exists on its own: positive, negative, being, not-being. This is how our sensuously perceiving consciousness intuits independence, and this is the mode and pattern of independence for our understanding. After this pattern we have

221 | an intuition, a view of the world that is prosaic, however, because independence has this form of "thinghood"—of mental and other forces—and consequently *abstract* form. Inasmuch as it is present in this form, thought is here not reason but understanding.

The problem, then, is as follows. The manifold, concrete world here possesses independence. This is known theoretically here, and the question concerns the form of this independence. It cannot yet be the form of independence that *we* possess, for our prosaic mode of understanding involves more than is yet present: it involves a further advance of the cultural process through which these abstractions have become fixed. The objectivity of our consciousness is the objectivity of understanding. For us to view the world in this way is a *reflection* of the understanding and comes much later; in that

224. W₂ (Var/1831?) *adds:* and so distinguish it from spirit.

later guise the understanding cannot therefore occur at this stage either.

First we say that things [simply] are; second, that they are related to one another in a variety of ways, they are causally connected and depend on one another. This second moment, the moment of understanding, cannot be present at this stage. ‾This prosaic dependence, this objective coherence, where objectivity has the sense of abstract independence, [comes later].‾225 In other words, independence does not yet have this form. What then are we to take as the form of independence at this stage? The only form of independence that is found here is none other than that which is ‾for human beings the form of a concrete independent entity,‾226 and this first way in which independence appears is therefore the human way, and also an animal way; thus the two hang directly together. This is how | fulfillment is present; the concrete is for the first time intuited as [actively] having being, no longer as the [passive] object of power; from the point of view of power, all this is posited as negative, or as subject to power. Only the practical has being objectively in power, not the theoretical, whereas here the theoretical is given free rein.

‾‾The first concrete mode of freedom is human being or the organic life of animals. Here being has the form of human configuration, and the realm of phantasy arises, where objects are represented in wholly contingent fashion as human or animal shapes, the representation being carried out in a highly extravagant manner. |

‾We have now reached the stage of the theoretical element. All

225. W *(following Ho) reads:* [W₁: But since it is phantasy that determines the configuration, all intelligible determinate differentiation of the moments must necessarily be at once extinguished.] It is only the understanding as pure self-conformity that comprehends objects in these categories. Because the one is, it argues, so is the other, and it pursues this chain of connection relentlessly into false infinity. *Ho reads:* But since it is phantasy that determines the configuration, all intelligible determinate differentiation of the moments must necessarily be at once extinguished. For it is only the understanding as pure self-conformity that comprehends objects in this category and by this means differentiates [their] determinacies; and since they possess their determinacy, their self-conformity, only through the relationship to an other, it proceeds to portray their nexus as a necessary nexus. Because the one is, it argues, so is the other, and it pursues this chain of connection relentlessly into false infinity.

226. *Thus P; G reads:* the form of concrete self-consciousness itself,

the characteristics or determinations that are absolutely necessary constituents of the concept, and further have being as sense-objects, are here endowed with independence; because the theoretical is the basic determination, every content is represented independently.[227] But this independence or objectivity is not yet a stable category, not yet a determination in terms of forces and causes, or of the kind of objectivity to which we are accustomed as thinkers, as the result of our training in thought. Instead, independence is endowed here with the form of what is the independent element in and for representation, i.e., it has principally the human form, but also that of animals, the form of life generally. Animals have life, they have souls, and so do human beings—*a fortiori*—since they constitute the independent element vis-à-vis what is dependent. When we represent something independent to ourselves, we content ourselves with an image; and an image, an object, a basic characteristic must contain nothing heterogeneous. That is how it seems. We have an image of some sense-object, a tree, river, etc.; or else we make an image for ourselves; and for this to serve us as object we need merely to express and represent to ourselves that it *is;* it needs no other characteristics for us to characterize it as independent. But since it is then an *image* for us, ˉwe confer independence on it by presenting it as a force.ˉ[228] No matter what the content is, its independence always has for us the form of a category of the understanding. But the point is that at this stage there are no categories, and the elements that are independent as far as representation is concerned have to assume the role of categories vis-à-vis one another instead. So if the river is to be accepted as independent on its own account, or the image of the river (its sensuous intuition), the tree or the image of the tree, they must assume the form by which representation distinguishes the independent as such from other existents.ˉˉ[229] The sun, the sea, the tree, and so forth do in fact lack independence compared with

227. *Thus G*

228. *Thus P; G reads:* we say of it that we confer independence on it, we have its force in us, as caprice.

229. *W (1831) reads:* Since it is theoretical, spirit is two-sided: it inwardly relates itself to itself, and it relates itself to things, which are for it what is universally independent. In this way things themselves break into two for it—into their immediate, external, colorful mode, and into their free, self-subsistent essence. Because this is

what is living and free, so these | forms[230] are what in this sphere 224
of theoretical independence provide the supporting basis of ¯a given
content or take the place of the categories in regard to it. Free human
consciousness and life are what is in fact independent in the realm
of things, and to that extent poetry is rational, because where a
thought content is to be represented as independent, the human or
animal shape represents this independence. These categories (all the
moments posited by the concept, as well as the concrete things of
nature generally, sun, sky, land, mountains, and so forth) obtain
in this way this shape of free independence; and a second consequence
of this is that all intelligible connection in this content is dissolved
and destroyed. For the necessary is what is intelligible: the universal
relationships of necessity constitute intelligibility—where one is
posited, the other is posited also; the interdependence of things
according to their quality, their essential determinacy, is what in fact
constitutes intelligible coherence generally. But here everything is free
and independent, so what holds sway is caprice, or whatever interests
the imagination: this is the basic thought. Historical events and circumstances are in no way bound or circumscribed, every content

---

not yet a thing, nor the categories of the understanding, generally speaking, because
it is not the kind of abstract independence that is thought, what we have is independence
that has been imagined [vorgestellt], that is free—the imagination of human beings
or at least of living beings, which can accordingly be termed the objectivity of phantasy.
In order to represent to ourselves sun, sky, or tree as having being, as independent,
all we need is its sensuous intuition or image, to which nothing that seems
heterogeneous has to accrue. But this seeming or semblance is an illusion; if the image
is represented as independent, as having being, if we accept it as such, then it has
for us the determination of being, of a force, [it is] something caused, something
effected, by a soul, and its independence lies in these categories. But inasmuch as
independence has not yet advanced to the prose of the understanding, for which the
category of force or cause is in principle what characterizes objectivity, to grasp and
express that kind of independence is the poetry that makes the representation of human
nature and shape—or possibly animal nature and shape, or again the human in
association with the animal—the supporting basis and essence of the external world.
This poetry is what is in fact rational in fanciful imagination, for it must be held
firmly in mind that [even] if, as we have indicated, consciousness has not yet advanced
to the category, what is independent has to be taken from the existing world, and
indeed in antithesis to what is dependent, to what is represented as external; and
[W₁ reads: this alone is W₂ reads: here animal and human essence alone is] the shape,
mode, and nature of the free in the realm of things.
    230. W₂ (Var) adds: of what is independent

is at the disposal of the imagination; it can put whatever it likes in association, | can adorn and embellish as it fancies, in whatever shape takes its interest, since there is no objectivity; and it is equally unrestricted in its further advance, for it can take any course it pleases.

What we call necessity rests on the intelligible coherence of the manifold content; and this coherence is what, as we have put it, transmits the particular content of particular things; it constitutes the genuine objectivity of whatever is and appears. At this stage, this objectivity is not present; the intelligible coherence is dissolved, and because this objectivity of connectedness is not present, the independence we are dealing with here is not actual; it is not the mode of objective actuality but has the character of perfect contingency, and the world and all that it contains are thereby placed in the service of the imagination. God's world is in the suzerainty of the imagination (which is an infinite manifold that keeps growing in the measure that human beings cultivate their feelings and capabilities). It is typical of this cultural or educational process that all distinctions are particularly noted and preserved, and this aspect of culture is found here in the theoretical range. Desire‾[231] has a narrower range of purpose, of interest (and what is of interest to it, it negates); what is outside its range of interest it pays no heed to, ‾and consequently it remains unschooled.

Because of the form that independence takes, the independent categories | take on the character of contingency; and as a result, they are at once posited rather in the opposite way, as dependent instead. The content is determined, it is a particular content, and

231. W (1831) reads: the content. [W₂: The material is thus given a subjective soul, which is not, however, a category but concrete spirituality and organic life.]

The next consequence is that in the same way that objects in general and the universal categories of thought have free independence of this kind, the world's intelligible coherence is dissolved; this coherence is formed by the categories denoting [W₁: relationships, which, W₂: relationships of necessity, or by the mutual dependence of things according to their quality, their essential determinacy; all these categories,] however, are not present [at this stage], and representation is thus confronted by nature wild and unrestrained. Any flight of imagination, any interest in what happens and ensues [evokes an image]; relationships can shift free of all ties and limitations. All the splendor of nature and the imagination is at one's disposal to adorn the content, and the caprice of the imagination has entirely free rein to let itself go this way or that, passing whichever way it pleases. [W₂: Unschooled] appetite

it acquires the form of independence in a false, one-sided fashion; but because this determinate content is not rooted in genuine particular objectivity, it acquires the character of contingency and so loses its independence of action. It is delivered up to the imagination and stands in its service. Such is the basic characteristic of this sphere in abstract terms.

Thus we have before us an infinitely varied world of imagination—without objective coherence, an unrestrained revel encompassing all this content.[232] ¯The only thing that brings some stability into this jumble | of accidents is the universal basic categories 227

232. W_2 *(MiscP) reads:* At this standpoint of the imagination, however, all distinctions are especially heeded and borne firmly in mind, and whatever is of interest to the imagination becomes free and independent and is raised to the level of a basic thought.

W *(MiscP) continues:* Yet it is through this imagined independence itself that, conversely, the content and configurations are no longer firmly based. Since the configurations are of determinate, finite content, their only objective basis, [their only possibility of] recall and lasting renewal, would lie in the intelligible coherence that has now disappeared, as a result of which their independence, instead of being an actuality, becomes rather perfect contingency. The world as it appears is thus placed in the service of the imagination. The divine world is a kingdom of the imagination, the infinite multiplicity of which is increased by the fact that it pertains to the sphere of a luxuriant nature, and that this principle of free imagining, divorced from appetite, of theoretically based phantasy, has indeed enriched the mind and its emotions—emotions that, incubating in this gentle warmth, are permeated in a preeminent degree by a strain of pleasant, sweet tenderness but also of feeble softness.

W_2 *(1831) continues, following an insertion from the 1827 lectures:* For this reason too, the form of beauty cannot yet be created at this stage, because the content, these particularizations of substance, are not yet the genuine content of spirit. Now since the limited content is the foundation and is known as spiritual, the subject, this spiritual element, is an empty form. In the religion of beauty the spiritual as such constitutes the foundation, so that the content too is spiritual content. Then the images, as sensuous material, are only an expression of the spiritual. But here the content is not of a spiritual kind.

Thus art is symbolic art, expressing characteristics to be sure, but not characteristics of the spiritual. This is the reason for the unbeautiful, demented, fantastic aspects of art that emerge here. The symbol is not pure beauty, for it involves a content other than spiritual individuality. Free subjectivity does not permeate it, nor is it essentially expressed by the shape [of the symbol]. In this fanciful imagination there is nothing firm, nothing assumes the shape of beauty, which is given only by the consciousness of freedom. What is present here is the complete dissolution of shape, the singular casting this way and that, stretching out [in all directions]. The inward element, having no stability, passes over into external existence, and the way in which the absolute is displayed in this world of the imagination is merely an infinite dissolution of the One in the many and an unrestrained revel encompassing all content.

of the concept, which are the absolute powers into which everything returns. It is these basic categories that merit our consideration.

On the one hand these categories can be recognized in the perverted, sensuous mode produced by the whims of the imagination—and when we see them thus, the imagination gets its due. But on the other hand we must grasp the way in which these basic categories have been degraded, owing to their assuming the show of indifference inherent in mutual externality and so vitiating, by their form, the externally sensuous shape. It is this form that degrades them, and because of it these essential, basic categories emerge in a way that is perfectly devoid of spirit.[233]

In the way we have described them, these characteristics of the divine essence, of the divine world, have their [empirical] existence in the Hindu religion. However, we must here leave aside ⌐its innumerable, multifarious mythological events⌐[234] and confine ourselves to the principal chracteristics. ⌐It is of interest to consider these, | because they pertain to the concept; they are baroque and have often a wild and repulsive shape, having been dragged down to the level of everyday life, but it is the concept that here shows itself and exhibits its development on this theoretical soil. The first point is the *substantive* character of this process of reflection into

233. W *(1831) reads:* It is the system of universal basic categories as absolute powers to which everything returns and which permeates everything that alone brings thorough stability into this region of caprice, confusion, and feebleness, into this boundless splendor and softness; and it is this system—determined by the concept in and for itself—that [has] to be considered. What is of most essential interest is on the one hand to recognize these categories in the perverted, sensuous mode of arbitrary, externally determined shaping, and give its due to the essentiality underlying them, and on the other hand to note the degradation they experience, partly through their mutual indifference, partly through arbitrary human and local external sensuality, as a result of which they are relegated to the sphere of the most everyday. All passions, local features, features of individual memory, are attached to them; there is no judgment, no shame—no trace of a higher correspondence between content and form. Everyday existence as such has not disappeared but has been promoted to constitute beauty. W_2 *(1831) adds:* The lack of correspondence between content and form consists more precisely in the fact that the basic categories are depreciated because they seem to be on a par with mutual externality, and because they again vitiate, by their form, the externally sensuous shape.

234. G *reads:* this unending, multifarious mythology W *(1831) reads:* its multifarious, characteristically endless mythology and mythological forms

self; the second is the form, the determinations of the absolute: these are the moments that come to the fore in this religion, and because they display this character of *form* they recall the highest plane of the idea.⁻²³⁵ It is therefore appropriate to consider them more closely.

The first element in the concept, the element of genuineness, is this universal substance, as we have seen—the eternal rest of self-containment, this essence that has its being within itself, which is the universal substance. As the universal, ⁻this substance⁻²³⁶ is likewise the power that has being in itself. But it is not turned against something else, like appetite, but is still and invisible, being reflected into itself—and for that reason determined simply as power. This power that remains locked within itself in the form of universality must be distinguished from its manifestation, from what it posits; and it is [also] distinct from the elements that compose it. Power is the ideal element, the negative for which everything else has being only as annulled, negated. To power belongs already this self-determining, this production, the moments that come forth, but insofar as it is characterized as implicitly subsisting universal power, universal power that has being *in* itself, it is distinct from its constituent moments; and these moments accordingly appear on the one hand as independent essences and on the other hand as essences that also disappear in the One. They belong to the One of which they are only moments or elements; but as differentiated they appear on the scene independently, as perfectly independent persons, persons of the godhead, | yet at the same time persons who are the whole 229 itself, so that the first element [i.e., universal substance] disappears in these particular shapes as [shapes of] a totality [that] needs nothing

235. W *(1831) reads:* which are on the one hand baroque, wild, and horrible, repulsive, disgusting distortions, but at the same time show themselves to have as their inner source the concept, and (owing to the way in which the concept can develop in this theoretical soil) call to mind the summum of the idea, but simultaneously express the definite obscuration the idea undergoes when these basic categories are not brought back again to spiritual nature. The principal point of interest is the development, the explication of the form, as against an abstractly monotheistic religion as well as against the Greek religion—i.e., against a religion that has spiritual individuality as its principle. [*W₁ adds:* but through the concrete element of the individuality principle].
236. W₂ *(Var) reads:* this simple substance, which the Hindus call Brahman,

above it; but on the other hand they in their turn disappear in the one power. These alternations, with sometimes the One, sometimes the differentia as the complete totality—ˉthis is what constitutes the inconsistency of this sphere; but it is also the inconsistency of reason vis-à-vis the understanding.ˉ[237]

If we consider this further in an abstract manner, we have first the One, the universal, the absolute concept; the absolute concept is *this,* to manifest itself. Its manifestation can be called determinate being, *objectivity* in general, fixed independence, or what we call conservation in the relative sense that what now is appears as having come about previously. This is what can be termed the eternal goodness [of God], that the determinate, although it is only posited, only a semblance, still manages to *be,* is vouchsafed momentary being; it is, however, absorbed in power. It is only power that, out of its goodness, enables the determinate to subsist, although it is only something particular and finite. This manifestation, determinate being or existence in general as divine manifestation, becomes thereby itself the whole God, the totality, and finds itself opposed by that first unity, the power that has being in itself; or else the latter steps down to the level of a particular moment, so that above this absolute One another higher One (which may also be called God) must straightway be set in place. The third element then is *change* in general, becoming, justice generally—coming into being and passing away, being created and being brought to naught, the [mode of] being that consists in *not* being. These are the three basic determinations of the concept. The fact that spirit is totally lacking from this way of defining the form of the differentiae (even to the extent that it is the pure definition of the concept) is due to the third element being defined at once as becoming or change, whereas with the absolute idea the third element is defined as *spirit,* i.e., not as a transition or return into self, where | the differentiae are determined in

230

237. W *(following Ho and G) reads:* this is the inconsistent nature of this sphere that confuses the consistent understanding but is at the same time what constitutes the conceptually consistent nature of reason as opposed to the consistency of the understanding, abstractly identical with itself. *Ho reads:* And this inconsistency that confuses the consistent understanding is the conceptually consistent nature of reason as opposed to the consistency of the understanding, abstractly identical with itself.

this immediate way as being and nonbeing. These are the three basic forms.

We must now recognize in regard to Hindu mythology that it does in fact contain these basic determinations of the concept, the development of the concept. This trinity is the basic form, the abstract basic form of spirit; this is what the Hindus represent as Trimurti.[238] "Murti" means soul in general, every emanation of the absolute, [its] particular manifestations. So "Trimurti" means the three essences. The first One appears itself as one of three; it is then deposed, and the One that is the unity of the three is in turn represented as different from this initial One.

What comes first is Brahman, the absolute unity as neuter principle. As father, as active, as what is a particular moment among these three, the name chiefly given is Brahmā, but it also has other names, such as Parabrahmā, expressing the universal soul. Here we have then this inconsistency, grounded in reason; as soon as the One is expressed as one of three, it is particularized and something higher is needed, namely Brahman.[239]

The second essence is determinate being, conservation, manifestation, appearance on earth, which is then elaborated in its full entirety—the incarnation of Vishnu and so forth, whatever appears [on earth], humanity therefore in the form of particular human beings. Incarnations seemingly include princes or mighty kings who have made great conquests, but the principal intuitions of incarnation are afforded by human ideals in general—on the one hand conquests and [on the other] countless romances. Stories that for us are novels are for Hinduism incarnations. All that can be grasped as human

238. [Ed.] Hegel could draw on numerous sources of information about the Trimurti; he is also in agreement with them in overestimating its importance. The Trimurti belongs to a later, passing phase of the development of Brahmanism, represented by the second stratum of Mahābhārata, a number of Upanishads, and the Purānas. The relationships between Brahmā, Vishnu, Shiva, and the unity of the three are also more involved than Hegel suggests here and in the following three paragraphs. Much of his analysis is based on James Mill, The History of British India, 3 vols. (London, 1817), 1:215, 230 ff. Hegel's euhemeristic interpretation of the incarnations also reflects Mill's account (p. 241). It is to be noted, however, that Mill explicitly dissociated himself from the view that the Trimurti is analogous to the Christian Trinity (p. 244).

239. Thus G

passions is presented as incarnate in this fashion; we find there the noblest, the most beautiful, the most manifold in existence generally, but no judgment.

Third, there is the mutable, what creates and destroys. This third essence, which is implicitly according to the genuine concept the return to unity (i.e., when determined in all its concreteness it is spirit), is comprehended at this stage merely in the mode of being, as its becoming, arising, and passing away; this is Shiva, destroyer

231 | and creator. It is these three forms therefore that stand at the apex.

˜These are determinations that derive from the concept. What we still have to illustrate is how they are represented more concretely, and also how consciousness relates to this objectivity—in other words, the nature of the cultus.˜[240]

The basic determination of the theoretical consciousness is, as has been said, the category of unity, of what is called Brahmā, Bruhmā, and suchlike. I have pointed out that this unity lapses into the ambiguity that Brahmā is sometimes the universal, the all, at other times one particularity set against another; thus Brahmā makes his appearance as creator, but then he is placed in a subordinate position again, he himself speaks of something higher than himself, a universal soul. This confusion marking the Hindu presentation is notable in that this inconsistency has its ground in the very content of these determinations, in their necessary dialectic; all-ordering spirit is not yet present, so that the determinations appear first in one form, then that form must be annulled again as one-sided so that another form enters on the scene. Thus the necessity of the concept becomes apparent initially only as deviation or confusion, as something that has no internal stability within itself, and it is [only] the nature of the concept that brings a solid foundation into this confusion.

The first basic category is thus the purely and simply One, Brahman. This One appears as fixed on its own account, as the eternal in and with itself. But because this One must proceed to determination, even though its determinacy remains devoid of spirit, all of its determinations are in turn called Brahman themselves; and they *are* Brahman, they are themselves this self-contained One, One-

240. *Thus G; P reads:* There are a number of noteworthy moments or aspects.

within-itself. So they acquire the epithet of the One-in-itself; all that are posited as particular gods take it on themselves to *be* Brahman, with the result that an Englishman who has investigated most carefully the various ways in which Brahman is presented in order to determine what the term means arrives at the conclusion that it is an empty epithet of praise, because Brahman is not explicitly regarded as "this" One, but everything | applies the term Brahman to itself. 232 ⁻(I am referring to Mill's *History of India*.[241]) On the basis of a great number of Hindu texts he shows that Brahmā is in general a meaningless epithet of praise, which is applied to a variety of gods and in no way expresses the more refined concepts of perfection and unity that we represent to ourselves,⁻[242] and which do appear in other Hindu prayers. [243]According to Mill, Vishnu is also called the supreme Brahman, while Krishna [too] is referred to as the great Brahman: "That is my uterus, my womb, in which I place my progeny and from which I then cause nature to issue forth in all directions." Just for this reason the great Brahman is the procreative link in all natural configurations: "I am the father of all germination, of all that has in it an impulse to become."[244] Hence water is called Brahman, and the sun is Brahman. In the old Hindu Vedas, for example, the sun is especially exalted; and if one considers the prayers addressed to it in isolation, one may come to believe that the early Hindus saw Brahman merely in the form of the sun, and that their religion was thus different from that of their successors. But the air too, any movement in the atmosphere, is Brahman; the breath,

241. [*Ed.*] Mill, *History of British India* 1:230–231. Hegel goes on to say that, although the term "Brahmā" in no way expresses the more refined conceptions of perfection and unity, these do appear in other Hindu prayers; however, the latter point appears to be based on a misreading of Mill, who says that Brahmā is "no more indicative of refined notions of the unity, or any perfection of the Divine Nature, than other parts of their panegyrical devotions."

242. *Ho reads:* Mill (three quarto volumes on Indian history) writes: "The Hindu text that I have before me shows that Brahman applies to all gods, not to the image of one God."

243. *Ho reads, precedes in W:* This is illusion, for Brahman is on the one hand the One, the unchanging—which, however, because it itself implies change, is also applied to the plenitude of different shapes, since this is its *own* plenitude.

244. [*Ed.*] For this and the preceding quotation, see Mill, *History of British India*, p. 232. The quotations are not exact.

understanding, happiness—all these are called Brahman.[245] And it is more especially Shiva (or Mohadeva or Rudra) who also says of himself that he is Brahman. Shiva says of himself in the Oupnek'hat:[246] "I am what is and what is not, I am all that has been, I am now and ever shall be. What is, that I am; what is not, that I am also. I am Brahmā and also Brahman, I am the first cause, the truth, I am the ox and every living thing; ˉbefore anything was, I am; I am[247] | past, present, and future. I am Rudra, I am all worlds,"ˉ[248] and so on.

233

Thus Brahman is the One; and again, whatever exists independently and is represented as God is itself also Brahman. Hence it is said that consciousness also says to itself, "I am Brahman."[249] There is, for example, also a prayer to speech wherein speech says of itself, "I am Brahman, the universal supreme soul."[250] So Brahman is the One, but cannot be held fast exclusively as the One; Brahman does not have being in the way in which we say of one God, "This One is universal unity." This One here is *every* unity; here everything that is independent, identical with self, says "I am Brahman." But in the second place Brahman is chiefly represented as the creator; and we shall see the significance of Brahman more clearly (as also

245. [*Ed.*] The sources of these references are translations by H. T. Colebrooke contained in his articles "On the Religious Ceremonies of the Hindus" and "On the Vedas, or Sacred Writings of the Hindus," *Asiatic Researches* 5:349 ff.; 8:417, 456. However, Hegel's arrangement of the material shows that he is again following Mill, *History of British India,* p. 232. In regard to the special place accorded to the sun in the Vedas, Colebrooke (*Asiatic Researches* 8:396) cites the Rig-Veda to the effect that "the great soul" is called the sun, "for he is the soul of all beings."

246. [*Ed.*] Hegel does, to be sure, refer here to the *Oupnek'hat,* a collection of Upanishads in Persian translation, which was translated into Latin by Abraham Hyacinthe Anquetil du Perron under the title *Theologia et philosophia Indica: Oupnek'hat,* 2 vols. (Paris, 1801–1802), 2:12 ff. Since, however, there is no conclusive evidence that Hegel used this translation and his argumentation is very similar to Mill's, it may be assumed that he is using Mill's translation of the Upanishad in question, *History of British India* 1:227, although again the text as given diverges considerably from that reproduced by Mill.

247. *Ho adds:* life and death,

248. *Thus G; D reads:* Rudra is living and dead, what is and what will be, the whole world.

249. [*Ed.*] See Francis Wilford, "An Essay on the Sacred Isles in the West," *Asiatic Researches* 11:126.

250. [*Ed.*] See Colebrooke, "On the Vedas," *Asiatic Researches* 8:402–403.

the relationship between Brahman and the other gods, Vishnu and Shiva) if we examine how the creation of the world is pictured.

The creation of the world is not pictured as a definite story, the way we have it in the sacred books of Judaism. Among the Hindus everyone makes his own picture by contemplative speculation, with the result that there is no fixed pattern to be found and there are as many views of it as there are people.

[251]In a "dissertation" prefaced to his translation of a history of India in Persian, Colonel Dow[252] offers us a translation from the Vedas containing the following account of the creation of the world. Brahmā existed from all eternity, in a form of infinite dimensions. When it pleased him to create the world, he said, "Rise up, O Brahmā!" (Thus the starting point was desire or appetite, inner will; in speaking thus, he was speaking to himself.) Immediately a spirit of the color of flame issued from his navel, having four heads and four hands.[253] (This fire is again himself, ¯¯and has only itself, as immeasurable, for its object.) | Brahmā gazing round, and seeing nothing but the immeasurable image out of which he had proceeded (self-relatedness, and the creation of self-relatedness, is a fundamental category that occurs very frequently; elsewhere it is said that the world is produced by mediation, by this reposeful thought or self-relatedness), he traveled a thousand years, to endeavor to comprehend its dimensions. But after all his toil he found himself as much at a loss as before. Lost in amazement, Brahmā gave up his journey. He fell prostrate and considered what he had seen in these four quarters. The almighty, something distinct from Brahmā, so the account continues, then spoke thus to him: "Thou hast done well,

234

251. *Precedes in* W₂ *(1831):* Let me finally add the following illustration, in which are expressed together all those moments we have considered so far, in both their severance and their dialectic.

252. [*Ed.*] See Alexander Dow, *This History of Hindostan, from the Earliest Accounts to the Death of Akbar,* 2 vols. (London, 1768), 1:xlvi–xlix. Although a German translation of Dow's work was published in Leipzig in 1772–1774, Hegel appears to have used the English edition, which he gives in a reasonably accurate translation of his own until nearly the end of this paragraph. Our translation of Hegel's translation follows the English original as closely as possible. The parenthetical insertions represent Hegel's comments.

253. *Ho adds:* (also regions of the sky)

235 O Brahmā, for thou | canst not comprehend me. Go Brahmā, create the world, thou canst not comprehend thyself, make something comprehensible." Brahmā asked, "How am I to make a world?" The almighty answered and said, "Ask of me and power shall be given unto thee." Thereupon fire came again out of the figure of Brahmā and in his imagination he perceived the ideas of all things, as if floating before his eyes. He said, "Let all that I see become real, but how shall I preserve these things, that they be not annihilated?" In the instant a spirit of blue color issued from Brahmā's mouth, and ⁻this is himself again, Vishnu, Krishna, the preserving principle.⁻²⁵⁴ And Brahmā commanded the spirit to create all animals, with vegetables for their subsistence. But human beings were still lacking to rule the whole. Vishnu set to work on Brahmā's command, but the human beings that he made were idiots with great bellies and no knowledge, like the beasts in the field; ⁻they had no passions and no will but to satisfy their carnal appetites.⁻²⁵⁵ Brahmā, offended at the human beings, destroyed them, and produced four persons from his own breath. These four persons were ordered by Brahmā to rule over the creatures, but they did not want to rule over the world. They refused to do anything but to praise God, because they were created from Brahmā's breath alone, and had none of the mutable, destructible quality in them, no transient nature. Now Brahmā was angry, and his anger was a brown spirit that started from between his eyes, and sat down before him with crossed legs and arms and began to weep, asking: "Who am I and where shall be the place of my abode?" Brahmā said: "Thy name shall be Rudra (Shiva), and all nature shall be the place of thine abode; go now,

236 and make human beings." And he did so, | but the human beings he made were fiercer than tigers, having nothing but the destructive quality in their compositions; so they soon destroyed one another, for rage and anger were their only passion. In this story we see the three gods at work in isolation from one another, and what they

254. *Thus G; P reads:* This spirit received the name Krishna. *D reads:* this he named Vishnu. *Ho reads:* it was Vishnu, Krishna, he who sustains.
255. *Thus P; G reads:* with neither passions nor will but only carnal appetite. *D reads:* with neither passions nor will.

create is merely one-sided, devoid of truth. At last Brahmā, Vishnu, and Rudra joined their different powers and in this way created human beings—ten of them.⁻⁻²⁵⁶ In this account all the moments are necessarily expressed, with the mode of their appearance too. In the Laws [Code] of Manu a different picture of the creation of the world is given;²⁵⁷ in other words, every account gives its own particular view.

We can now let the matter rest regarding Brahmā generally, and we have also seen his connection with Rudra and Vishnu. Vishnu is, as has been said, that which incarnates itself, the essence that appears in human form, in the form of ruling princes, especially those who made revolutions, and great conquerors or lovers.

Thirdly, there is Mahadeva or Shiva, which ought, properly

256. *Ho reads:* he becomes for himself his own object and what is determinate over against his own immeasurable indeterminacy. Consequently it is also stated elsewhere that it was by meditating on himself that Brahmā created the world. Now Brahmā, the fiery spirit, looked around him and saw only the immeasurable image out of which he had proceeded. He needed a thousand years to encompass it, but after this long journey he knew as little as before. Then he fell down before the almighty, who cried, "Thou hast done well to prostrate thyself, for thou canst not comprehend me." "Speak comprehensibly," said Brahmā, "how am I to create the world?" "Ask of me," replied the almighty, "and power shall be given unto thee." And fire came out of the figure of Brahmā, whereupon [his] spirit perceived the ideas of all things as if floating before his eyes, and said, "Almighty one, let all that I see take firm shape. For how could I preserve all these images, that they be not annihilated?" A spirit of blue color issued from Brahmā's mouth; it was Vishnu, Krishna, he who preserves, and he was to cause all living things to subsist by giving them nourishment. In this way natural things were created, but there were still no human beings to rule over them. Human beings were created by Vishnu, but they were idiots, with no interest beyond the natural and wrapped up in their bellies. As such they offended Brahmā, who now caused four persons to issue from his breath; but inasmuch as these were created solely by the One, the universal being, and lacked the destructive quality, they only wished to praise him. Now Brahmā raged within himself, and the brown spirit that was his rage, springing forth from him, wept and asked, "Who am I, who am I to remain?" "Thy name shall be Rudra [*Ho reads:* Budar]," called Brahmā, "the whole world is thine, create human beings." Rudra obeyed, but his humans were like tigers, they could only destroy, and rage was their only passion. So the beings created by Vishnu merely wanted to exist; Brahmā's were pure spirits; and in contrast with this natural and spiritual positivity, Rudra's creatures could only negate, destroy. Then Brahmā joined all these qualities together and so made human beings.

257. [*Ed.*] See *Institutes of Hindu Law* (Calcutta, 1794), 1:5–12.

speaking, to be spirit returning into itself, but since the different moments or elements are here distinct, it is only becoming, change in general and, more precisely, life, the creative force.

In the Vedas there is no mention of Vishnu and Shiva. These are determinations that came on the scene only later.[258] It may further be noted that the Hindus are divided into a multitude of sects under the various deities; some worship Vishnu, others Shiva, and bloody wars have been fought on this account. Even nowadays, on the occasion of the great yearly festivals where millions of people are often assembled, disputes and fighting break out over the primacy accorded to one deity or the other.[259] The cult of Mahadeva in particular is very extensive, the cult of the vital force, this obscene ˉcult whose symbol stands erectˉ[260] in most Hindu temples. The image here is that Brahmā in his first desire, his first act of volition, split into male and female, the male being Mahadeva and the female Yoni; this primal desire of Brahmā produced all the characteristics
237   that make up the | male and the female generally.[261] This cult of the power of procreation and its symbol is the phallus cult, which has persisted in India, Egypt, and Greece. The remaining army of gods—Indra, the god of heaven, of fire, of created life, etc., including

258. [Ed.] Hegel is probably here summarizing the impression he gained from Colebrooke's "On the Vedas," *Asiatic Researches* 8:377–497, esp. pp. 494–495, where Colebrooke argues that although the three principal manifestations of the one deity are mentioned in the Vedas, the fact that worship of the different incarnations of Vishnu is a comparatively new development supports the view that the passages in question are later accretions.

259. [Ed.] See Mill, *History of British India* 1:226. Mill's statements in regard to the disputes between the different sects are based on several other authors, in particular J. D. Paterson, "On the Origin of the Hindu Religion," *Asiatic Researches* 8:46. Hegel may also have been familiar with W. C. Seybold's *Ideen zur Theologie und Staatsverfassung des höhern Alterthums* (Tübingen, 1820), where a footnote to p. 45 states specifically that the contention for preeminence between Vishnu and Shiva "was often the cause of bloody disputes between the Hindus."

260. *Ho reads:* cult of procreation whose symbols, the male and female pudenda (Shiva and Geroni) [*sic*], are erected.

261. [Ed.] It is not known to which of his sources Hegel is specifically indebted for his knowledge of the cult of the *lingam* (phallic emblem) and *yoni* (female organ); several of them refer to it, always in disparaging terms. The myth of Brahmā's division into male and female is to be found in the Code of Manu; see *Institutes of Hindu Law* 5:32.

the worship of the cow, the elephant, the horse, and so on—all belong to the sphere of mere imagination and confusion, where nothing determinate can be cognized further through or on the basis of the concept, but where such living things as apes and cows are taken and raised into universal essences, raised to gods; all this typically belongs to the category of the imagination.

b. The Cultus

We have to consider, secondly, the relationship of self-consciousness to its [divine] object, i.e., the cultus. This relationship has the same basic characteristics as we have observed in the world of its gods, namely the falling apart of the different aspects or moments.[262] | 238

1. Self-consciousness is to be considered in relation to Brahmā himself, to this basic category. In regard to this relationship there are three forms to be distinguished. First, every individual Hindu is momentarily Brahmā. Brahman is this One, the abstraction of thought, of the universal, and to the extent that people make the

262. W_2 (1831) adds: What corresponds to the character of the divine world is subjective religion, the self-comprehending of self-consciousness in the relationship to the world of its gods.

W (1831) continues: As the idea has developed in this world to the point where its basic categories emerge, but these are still external to one another—and the empirical world too is still external and unintelligible vis-à-the world of the gods and vis-à-vis itself, and so abandoned to the caprice of the imagination—consciousness too, trained to reach out in all directions, is incapable of rising to genuine subjectivity. What presides over this sphere is the pure homogeneity [Gleichheit] of thought, which is at the same time defined as self-contained, creative power. But this basic foundation is purely theoretical; it is still the kind of substantiality from which, to be sure, everything implicitly proceeds and in which everything is implicitly contained, but outside which all content has emerged independently and been made objective and universal, not according to its determinate existence and relatedness but by virtue of the unity [of thought]. Merely theoretical, formal thinking gets the content as it appears as contingently determined; while it can abstract from it, it cannot elevate it to form the connecting link in a system, i.e., to a regulated coexistence. In this way thought remains entirely bereft of practical significance; in other words, its categories do not acquire a universal character from effectiveness and will, and though the form develops implicitly in accord with the nature of the concept, it does not emerge as posited by the concept, contained in its unity. Hence the effectiveness of will does not attain to freedom of will, does not attain to a content determined by the unity of the concept, and so more rational, more objective, more regulated, or conforming to law. On the contrary, this unity remains power that is merely implicit, substantial, withdrawn

239 effort to attain this level, | to collect themselves inwardly, they *are* Brahman. This is a particularly noteworthy characteristic. Brahman itself is not worshiped, and has no temple; the one God is not worshiped, no services are held in his honor, no prayers are addressed

from existence—it is Brahmā, who has dismissed actuality as contingency and now leaves it to fend for itself, leaves it to its own uncontrolled caprice.

The cultus is in the first place a relationship of the self-consciousness to Brahmā, but then to the rest of this world of the gods that subsists outside him.

As regards the first relationship, that to Brahmā, this is excellent and distinctive on its own account in proportion as it keeps itself isolated from everything else that goes to make up life on the concrete, religious, and temporal planes.

Brahman is thought, human beings think, so Brahman has an existence essentially in human self-consciousness. But humanity is at this stage defined in principle as thinking; in other words, thinking as such—and in the first place as pure theory—here has universal existence, because thinking itself is defined as such, as inward power, and so includes form (form in general, i.e., abstractly) or the specification of determinate being [*Dasein*] in general.

Human beings as such are not merely thinking beings; rather at this stage they are *of and for themselves* thought [*für sich Denken*], they are conscious of themselves as pure thinking. For, as we have just said, thought here comes to existence as such, and human beings have the representation of it within them. They are of and for themselves thought, for thinking is in itself power; but power itself is the infinite, self-relating negativity that being-for-self [*Fürsichsein*] is. But being-for-self, wrapped in the universality of thought in general, raised in such universality to free homogeneity with self, is merely the *soul* of a living being. It is not self-consciousness, possessed of power, caught up in the singularity of appetite, but the *self* of consciousness, knowing itself in its universality, which—as thinking itself, inwardly representing itself—knows itself as Brahman.

W_2 *continues:* Or if we take as our starting point the notion that Brahman is essence or abstract unity, self-absorption, then even as this self-absorption it has its existence in the finite subject, in the particular spirit. To the idea of the true belongs the universal—substantive unity and homogeneity with self—but in such a way that this unity is not simply indeterminate, not solely substantive unity, but is determined inwardly. The determinacy of Brahman, however, is external. Thus its highest determinacy, namely consciousness, knowledge of its real existence, this subjectivity of unity, can only be the subjective consciousness as such.

W continues: This relationship should not be termed a cultus, for it does not constitute a relation to thinking substantiality as to something objective, but rather is known immediately as *my* subjectivity, as I myself. In fact it is *I* who am this pure thought, and the ego itself is indeed its expression, for the ego as such is this abstract, indeterminate self-identity within me; qua ego, I am simply thought as what is posited along with the character of subjective existence reflected into self, thought as what thinks. Likewise the converse must also be granted, that thought, as this abstract thinking, has as its existence this subjectivity immediately expressed by the ego. For genuine thinking—which is God—is not this abstract thinking or this simple sub-to him. The English author[263] of a treatise on Hindu idolatry has a great deal to say about this, for instance: If we ask a Hindu ˉwhether he reveres, prays, and sacrifices to Brahman as supreme being,ˉ[264] he will say, "Never! We bring him no sacrifices." If we then ask him what is this silent veneration and meditation that is enjoined on you and practiced so widely, he will reply: "When I ˉdirect my prayer to any of the gods, when Iˉ[265] seat myself on the ground, tuck in and cross my legs, fold my arms, look up to heaven, and collect my spirit and my thoughts without moving my tongue, I say within myself, I *am* Brahman, or the supreme being." |

[266]ˉˉIf we compare this with other configurations, for example

240

stantiality and universality, but thinking only as the concrete, absolutely fulfilled *idea*. The thinking that is merely the in-itself [*Ansich*] of the idea is none other than abstract thinking, which has merely this finite existence, i.e., existence in the subjective self-consciousness, over against which it lacks the objectivity of concrete being-in-and-for-self; therefore it is rightly not revered by self-consciousness.

263. [*Ed.*] See Francis Wilford, "An Essay on the Sacred Isles in the West," *Asiatic Researches* 11:125–126.

264. *W (1831) reads:* whether he worships idols, he will reply without a moment's hesitation, "Yes, I worship idols." If on the other hand we ask a Hindu (learned or unlearned doesn't matter) whether he worships the supreme being, Paramisvara, *G adds:* whether he prays and sacrifices to it,

265. *Ho reads:* pray, when I sacrifice, then I worship a specific God. But when I

266. *W (MiscP) reads (parallel in main text follows):* These characteristics of Brahman seem to have so much in common with the God of other religions, with the true God himself, that it seems not without importance, on the one hand, to point out the difference that does exist, and on the other to indicate why the way of characterizing subjective existence in terms of self-consciousness that is consistent with the pure essence of Hinduism does not occur in these other ways of viewing the matter. The God of Judaism is the same, nonsensuous, one substantiality and power that *is* only for thought: he is himself objective thought, but not yet the inwardly concrete One that God is as spirit. The highest Hindu deity, however, is only the neuter One, not the personal One. [*W₂:* It has being only in itself, not for itself.] It is Brahman, the neuter element or the universal category: Brahmā as subject, on the other hand, is from the outset one of the three persons, if one can so call them [*W₁:* or figures of the Trimurti. *W₂:* —which in truth one cannot, as they lack spiritual subjectivity as an essential basic characteristic.] It does not suffice that the Trimurti proceeds from and also returns into the neuter One; in this way Brahman is nonetheless represented only as substance, not as subject. One the other hand, the God of Judaism is the personal and exclusive One, who will have no other gods beside him. This is why he is defined not merely as the in-itself but as what has being for itself, a consuming [fire]. He is defined as a subject, posited in undeveloped form, yet genuine. To this extent his goodness and justice also remain only properties, or, as the Hebrews were

241

242

with the Jewish God, he too is the One, the universal, a completely nonsensible substantiality, which has being solely for thought, not for sensuous representation but | for representation only to the extent it partakes of thought. Here too, objectivity is defined in terms of objective thought, but this pure, self-identical substantiality is not yet the inwardly concrete, | which is spirit. Thus Brahman and the Jewish God are ⁻defined in the same way, but they also differ in that

---

more inclined to express themselves, "names," of God. These properties or names do not become particular configurations, although they also do not yet become the content by virtue of which the Christian unity of God is the only spiritual one. Consequently, the Jewish God cannot acquire the character of a subjective existence within self-consciousness, because he is rather a subject *in himself* and therefore does not need an other for [his own] subjectivity—an other in which he would for the first time acquire this character, but in so doing, because the subjectivity resided in an other, would also have only a subjective existence.

As opposed to this, what the Hindu says in and to himself, namely, "I am Brahman," must essentially be recognized as identical with the subjective and objective vanity of the present day, with what the ego is made through the oft-mentioned assertion that we know nothing of God. For to say that the ego has no affirmative relation to God, that he is for the ego something beyond, a nothing devoid of content, means that only the ego of and for itself is what is affirmative for the I. It is of no help to say, "I recognize God as above me, outside me"—for God is a notion devoid of content, whose sole categorial determination, all that can be cognized or known of it, all that it is supposed to be for me, is limited wholly and simply to the fact that this utterly indeterminate being *is* and that it is the negative of me. Admittedly it is not posited as the negative of me in the Hindu "I am Brahman"—quite the contrary. But the seemingly affirmative definition of God, that he is, is of itself on the one hand only the perfectly empty abstraction of being, and thus only a subjective definition, one that exists only in my self-consciousness, and, because it does so, pertains also to Brahman. On the other hand, inasmuch as it was also supposed to have an objective meaning, this in itself—leaving aside more concrete definitions, such as that God is a subject in and for himself—would suffice to make it something that is known of God, a category of the divine. And this is already too much: being is thus *ipso facto* reduced to the mere "outside me," yet is also expressly supposed to mean only the negative of me, a negation in which all that in fact remains to me is I myself. We are flogging a dead horse if we seek to pass off this negative of me, what is outside or above me, as an objectivity that is professed or at least supposed or recognized. For this is merely to express a negative, and to do so explicitly, through me; but neither this abstract negation nor the fact that it is posited by me and that I know this negation (and it alone) *as* negation constitutes objectivity. Nor is it objectivity at least of form, even if not of content, for the form of objectivity that is devoid of content, without content, is an empty form, something intended in merely subjective manner. (In Christendom, what had merely the categorial determination of the negative used to

---

the Hindu God, being God from the standpoint of consciousness, is just the One, just neuter, not a personal One.[267] Brahmā, defined as personal subject, is determined as one of the three persons of the Trimurti, or trinity, whereas Brahman as such—of whom the Hindu says, "I am Brahman"—is not yet defined as subject. On the other hand the God of Judaism is defined as the personal One, exclusive [of others], as subject, who will have no other gods beside him. This

be called the devil.) In this way the only affirmative element that remains is this subjectively intending ego. With a one-sided dialectic, it has in skeptical fashion emptied all content from the sensible and supersensible world and defined it as something negative for it. Since all objectivity has become vain for it, the only thing left is this positive vanity itself—the objective ego, which alone is power and essence, in which everything [W_1: has disappeared. W_2: has disappeared and all content is absorbed as finite, so that the ego is what is universal, the lord of all categories and the exclusive, affirmative point.]

The Hindu "I am Brahman" and the so-called religion, the I, of modern reflective belief, differ from each other only in the external circumstance that the former expresses the first, naive mode of comprehension, in which the pure substantiality of its thought comes about for self-consciousness in such a way that alongside its thought it also accords validity to all other content and recognizes it as objective truth. In contrast with this, the reflective belief that denies any objectivity to truth holds fast to and recognizes only solipsistic subjectivity. [W_2: In this fully developed type of reflection, not only all content but also the divine world is only something posited by me.]

This first relationship of the Hindu to Brahman is posited only in the single prayer, and since it is itself the *existence* of Brahman, the ephemeral aspect of this existence can immediately be seen as inadequate to the content, [W_1: in order to meet the demand W_2: which gives rise to the demand] that this existence should itself be made universal and lasting, as its content is. It is only the ephemeral aspect of time that appears as the proximate defect in that existence, for it is only that which stands in relation to that abstract universality, compares itself to it, and appears as inadequate to it. For in other respects its subjective existence, the abstract ego, is on a par with it. But to raise the single glimpse to a lasting vision means nothing other than breaking off the transition from the moment of quiet solitude to the fulfilled present of life, of one's needs, interests, and occupations, and remaining continually in this motionless, abstract self-consciousness. And this is what many Hindus who are not Brāhmans (about whom I shall be speaking later) accomplish in themselves. They devote themselves with the most persistent assiduity to years or decades of monotonous inactivity, in which they renounce all interests and concerns of everyday life and couple with this the constraint exerted by some unnatural attitude or posture of the body— sitting continuously, walking or standing with their arms above their heads, never lying down, even to go to sleep, etc.

267. [*Ed.*] The German makes this distinction by means of changing the gender of *Eine—das Eine* (the neuter One) and *der Eine* (the personal One).

is a quite essential difference,⁻²⁶⁸ residing solely in the free, pure, differentiating power of thought. Brahman is only the in-itself [*das Ansich*]; it does not exist as being-for-self [*das Fürsichsein*]. We have

243 noted goodness and justice, in relation to Brahman; with a *valid* | concept, in the personal One, who is *subject,* these determinations are mere properties, or "names," to use the expression of Jewish scholars.²⁶⁹ They do not become independent shapes on their own account ⁻vis-à-vis⁻²⁷⁰ the subjectivity of the One. In contrast with this subjectivity, Brahman is what is abstract (not subjectivity), which achieves subjective existence only in self-consciousness, in the human self-consciousness. He who is One, on the other hand, being already subject in and for himself, does not need for his own existence the subjective consciousness of another; he has being for himself, and in such a way as to exclude any other (including self-consciousness).

Second, we are now in a position to compare these characteristics with what is contained in contemporary reflective belief.²⁷¹ This present-day type of reflection holds fast to immediate knowledge, and it is characteristic of this that God is for me an unknown,

268. *Ho, W₁ read:* the same, as far as being what is substantial [*Substantialität zu sein*] is concerned; but the difference between them is also essential,

269. [*Ed.*] In the *Lectures on the History of Philosophy* 2:398–399 (*Werke* 15:31), and probably also in Part III of the *Lectures on the Philosophy of Religion* 3:277 (see n. 73), Hegel refers to a passage in August Neander, *Genetische Entwicklung der vornehmsten gnostischen Systeme* (Berlin, 1818), p. 12, where Neander describes how Philo came to regard the Logos both as the name of God and as having many names. Here and in the passage from Part III of the *Philosophy of Religion* Hegel equates properties and names of God. Philo, however, stresses on more than one occasion that while goodness and omnipotence, for instance, may be supreme forces and qualities, they are not actual names of God, who has no specific names. See Philo Judaeus, *De Cherubim* §§ 27–30; *De somniis I* §§ 228–231; *De mutatione nominum* §§ 11 ff. (*Opera omnia graece et latine* [Erlangen, 1820], 2:16–18; 5:102–104; 4:324–326). Though Hegel uses the relationship of subjectivity between the One and its properties as an argument against Hinduism, he fails to take into account that Dow (*The History of Hindostan,* p. lxxi–lxxii) and his other sources make similar statements with regard to Brahman.

270. *Thus G; P reads:* because of

271. *Ho adds, similar in W₁:* More closely related to Brahmā, on the other hand, is the God of the Enlightenment, the *être suprême*. God is the unknown, empty One, the abstraction of inwardly unmoved negativity consisting in the dissolution of all determinacy [*die Abstraktion der in sich unbewegten Negativität des Aufgelöstseins aller Bestimmtheit*].

something not known, i.e., that he has for me the character of a negative, a beyond. It may, of course, be acknowledged that he lies outside and above me, but this expresses only a negative relationship, whereby the other has being for me as a negative. Abstract being is itself the negative—for example, the *abstractum* that is Brahman; in other words, an abstract being of this kind has its existence in⁻[272] self-consciousness, only in my abstracting understanding. We are flogging a dead horse if we believe we have said anything objective about God in saying God is outside and above us. [273]This abstraction of the understanding is only posited by me; I am the only affirmative element that is present in such a statement, so this way of defining God coincides with the contemporary view, that I *am* the universal, the lord of all categories, since they are first posited by me, and obtain their validity through me.⁻[274] | This contemporary reflective stage is more sophisticated and freer than that of the Hindu, who in his silent contemplation says, "I am Brahman." This is the naive stage of abstraction, beside which all else in this divine world is still objective, whereas in present-day reflection the world, like everything else, is only posited by me. This position or standpoint of recent philosophy has emptied the sensible and supersensible world of all content, through reflection. For Hinduism this [reflective] moment exists on its own account, and other contents exist apart from it; in the form of present-day reflection, however, all content, sensible and supersensible, is, qua finite, submerged in the One, so that it is just this one exclusive point of affirmation in which everything else affirmative has being.

[2.] There are still two other aspects of cultus, i.e., of the relationship of self-consciousness to the One. In the cultus as described, the first relationship is posited only in the moment of individual prayer and reverence, so that Brahman exists only momentarily, and this existence does not measure up to the universality of the content. The

244

272. *Thus P; G reads:* existence, its

273. *Precedes in* W₁ *(following Ho):* This worthless residue, *Ho reads:* For it *is* flogging a dead horse to seek to assign to this worthless residue an objectivity outside what can be found in abstract thinking.

274. *Thus G; P reads:* and can [also] cause it to disappear. *D reads:* and that is posited only in self-consciousness.

demand immediately arises that this existence shall be made into a universal, just as the content is universal—it must be made to last. The momentariness is what is unsatisfactory. For the abstract ego as such is the universal, except that the ego itself is only a moment in this existence of the abstraction. So the next demand is that this *abstractum*, this ego, shall match the content, that the single glimpse shall be elevated to a lasting vision, an enduring contemplation. To achieve this, however, necessarily means breaking off the transition from the moment of quiet solitude to life, to the concrete present, to concrete self-consciousness; thus it means renouncing all that is living and all concrete relationships, both the religious relationship and the relationships between the remainder of concrete actual life and the One.[275] |

245

This is what we see among the Hindus, namely that such of them as are not Brāhmans undertake to make themselves the perfectly abstract ego—and in principle they succeed. Here [belong] the countless tales of how men settle themselves on the ground and refrain from all movement, renouncing every interest and every inclination, letting every family concern and every human contact go, and giving themselves up to silent abstraction; others come to venerate and feed them, but they remain speechless in stubborn inaction, their eyes closed or turned to the sun, so that the light blinds them. Some of them remain like this for their whole lives, others for twenty or thirty years, or for some other period with sacred significance.[276] One of these Hindus is said by an Englishman[277] to

275. *Ho adds, similar in W:* All concrete presence, whether it be of natural life or of spiritual life—family, state, art, and religion—is dissolved into the pure negativity of abstract selflessness.

276. [*Ed.*] See Mill, *History of British India* 1:271.

277. [*Ed.*] See Samuel Turner, *An Account of an Embassy to the Court of the Teshoo Lama in Tibet, Containing a Narrative of a Journey through Bootan, and Part of Tibet* (London, 1800), pp. 270–272. Turner's account was known to Hegel in the form in which it was included in Harnisch, *Die wichtigsten Reisen*, vol. 6 (Leipzig, 1824), pp. 287–362; see pp. 350–352. In referring to other such austere practices that had been devised, Hegel may have been thinking of Mill, *History of British India*, pp. 269–273, and the hero Vishvamitra's repeated "austerities" (see the W variant, n. 279, where the English word is misspelled) and self-mortification following his defeat and humiliation by Vashishta and other gods. See also Hegel's comments on this anecdote as recounted in the *Ramayana* in his review of Wilhelm

have traveled around for ten years without ever lying down, but slept standing up,⁻⁻ then to have spent the next ten years with his hands above his head, then to have planned to swing upside down above a fire, suspended by one foot, so that his body could rotate, for three and three-quarter hours, finally to have had himself buried for three and three-quarters hours. Emerging alive from all this, he had attained the highest level—this being only one of the austere practices of this kind that have been devised. In the Hindus' view, he who achieves this sort of immobility and lifelessness is immersed in the inner [element] and enjoys continued existence as Brahman.

It should be noted that such austerities must not be regarded as penances for offenses committed; nothing is made good by them.[278] The offender is one who has set his or her particular will up against the universal, and must then negate it. It is not penance in this sense that we have here, but austerities [*Strengigkeiten*][279] in order to attain the state of Brahman.[280] |

246

---

von Humboldt's *Ueber die unter dem Namen Bhagavad-Gītā bekannte Episode des Mahābhārata* (Berlin, 1826), in *Jahrbücher für wissenschaftliche Kritik,* 1827, pp. 1455–1456, 1468 (cf. *Berliner Schriften,* pp. 115, 127).

278. W_2 *(1831) adds:* This renunciation or abstinence does not presuppose the consciousness of sin.

279. *W (Ed?) adds: (austereties)* [*sic*]

280. *W (1831) adds:* It is not a question of doing penance with the intention that thereby some crime, sin, or blasphemy should be atoned for. Such an intention presupposes a relationship between the work of human beings, their concrete being and actions, and the one God—an idea rich in content, providing human beings with a yardstick and maxim for their character and behavior, and a model to which to conform their will and their life. But the relationship to Brahman does not yet contain anything concrete, because it itself is only the abstraction of the substantive soul; all further determination and content falls outside Brahman. So a cultus, as a relationship possessing content and directing and actuating concrete human beings, does not occur in the relation to Brahman; and even if such a relationship were present, it would have to be sought in the worship of other gods. But since Brahman is represented as the solitary essence, closed in upon itself, the elevation of the singular self-consciousness, which through the above-mentioned austerities strives to perpetuate its own abstraction, is rather a flight from the concrete actuality of heart and mind and the actuality of life. In the consciousness that "I am Brahman," all virtues and vices vanish, all gods, and finally the Trimurti itself. The concrete consciousness of oneself and of the objective content that is yielded in the Christian notion of penitence, and of the conversion of the ordinary life of the senses, is not defined as something sinful and negative (as in the penitential life of Christians and Christian monks and

Associated with this is the notion that people who in this way have achieved a permanent state of Brahman have thereby obtained, and henceforth are, the absolute power over nature.[281] It is supposed that such a one inspired fear and anxiety in the heart of Indra, God of heaven and earth, and that he ran to the great Brahman and 247 complained | that he was threatened with destruction. In one passage of Bopp's *Chrestomathie*[282] the story of two giants is referred to, who beg the almighty to grant them immortality, but as they have only engaged in such exercises in order to achieve power over nature, he grants their wish only insofar as they are only to die at each other's hands. So they now exercise all power over nature. Having achieved this, they give themselves over to every imaginable pleasure. Indra takes fright at them and resorts to the usual means to divert someone from such exercises: he conjures up a beautiful woman, each of the giants wants her for his wife, and in quarreling over her they kill each other, and so nature is preserved by this expedient.

[3.] Third, a quite distinctive characteristic in respect to self-consciousness is that every member of the Brāhman caste is deemed

---

in the idea of conversion), but encompasses, on the other hand, as we have just indicated, the very content that is in other respects deemed holy. On the other hand, precisely the character of the religious standpoint we are considering is that all its moments or aspects fall apart, and the supreme unity is not mirrored in what makes up the content of mind and heart, the content of life.

W_2 *continues:* If the absolute is grasped as what is spiritually free and inwardly concrete, then self-consciousness occurs as something essential in religious consciousness only to the extent that it becomes capable of moving in inwardly concrete fashion and is represented and experienced as possessing content. But if the absolute is an abstraction such as the beyond or the supreme being, so too is self-consciousness, because it is naturally thoughtful, naturally good, what it ought to be.

281. *Ho adds:* for this abstraction is the negation of all natural life and all finitude. In Hindu poetry ten years spent in this way becomes 10,000.

[*Ed.*] Here again Hegel is referring to the account of Vishvamitra's self-mortification, which he commented on in the Humboldt review (n. 277, cf. *Berliner Schriften*, pp. 119–123), and apparently also at length in the 1831 lectures (see n. 280).

282. [*Ed.*] By "Bopp's *Chrestomathie*" Hegel here denotes an edition of various episodes in the Mahābhārata recently published (with translation and commentary) by Franz Bopp under the title *Ardschuna's Reise zu Indra's Himmel, nebst anderen Episoden des Mahā-Bhārata* (Berlin, 1824), pp. 36–45. His account, and especially the reference to "two giants," is not entirely accurate, possibly because he also has in mind another episode narrated in an earlier work by Bopp, which did deal with a giant.

to be Brahman and for all other Hindus is God. However, this particular way of seeing things is consistent with the two characteristics we have already discussed. These two aspects make up, as it were, an abstract or detached relationship of the self-consciousness to Brahman, the first being purely momentary, the second merely the escape from life, ˉlooking away from self-consciousness, a renunciation.ˉ²⁸³ The third demand, therefore, is that the relationship to Brahman should not be merely escape, renunciation of the life principle, but that it should also be posited affirmatively. The question then is, what form must the affirmative mode of this relationship take? The only possible form is that of immediate existence. This transition is a difficult one to picture. What is merely internal, only implicit, that is what is merely external; the merely abstract assumes immediately a merely sensuous guise, it is merely sensuous externality. And since the relationship here described is the wholly abstract relationship to this wholly abstract substance, the affirmative relationship involved is likewise wholly abstract, but at the same time it is immediate. This is what secures the transition and maintains the necessity of the | determination in question; what is involved is therefore the *abstract transition.* ˉThe relationship of the self-consciousness to Brahman appears in concrete form simply by beingˉ²⁸⁴ an immediate, natural relationship; and hence, being a natural relationship, it is an *innate* relationship, one that stems from birth.

248

Human beings are always *thinking* beings, and if we stick to this we can say it is human nature to think; thinking is a natural human quality. But that human beings are thinkers in principle is still different from the characteristic that we are here discussing, namely, the consciousness of *natural* thinking in principle as what has absolute being. What we have quite generally in this form is the consciousness of thought. I am this consciousness, I think, and thinking is here posited as absolute being. This consciousness of thought, and of my being a thinker—this it is that is here posited as existing

283. *Ho, W read:* The second is everlasting life in Brahman as the everlasting death of all individuality.

284. *Thus G; D reads:* In concrete form the transition occurs in the priest, so that the relationship of the self-consciousness to Brahman is

naturally or is asserted to be innate, and that it appears in this form rests on the ˉconjoining of pure abstraction with the determinate immediacy of natural being.ˉ²⁸⁵

Inasmuch as human beings are *thinking* beings in principle, and a distinction is made between this and the *consciousness* of thought as of what is universal or has being in itself, and both thinking in principle and conscious thought are [regarded as] innate, it follows that there are in principle two classes of human beings. On the one side there are those who *merely* think, or the generality of humanity; on the other side there are those who are the *consciousness* of thinking, the *consciousness* of absolute being. These latter are the caste of Brāhmans, the born-again, those who are twice-born,²⁸⁶ once by a natural birth, and the second time as thinkers,ˉso that they can be treated and addressed accordingly, as born-again. The inward [element], knowledge, is for human beingsˉ²⁸⁷ | the source of their second life, the root of their genuine existence, the existence that they confer upon themselves through thought, through freedom.

249

Hence all Brāhmans are considered to be twice-born from the outset, and are held in the utmost veneration, compared with all other humans, who are worthless.²⁸⁸ If anyone of lower caste touches a Brāhman, he has incurred death. The Code of Manu²⁸⁹ prescribes a great variety of punishments for offenses against Brāhmans. If, for example, a Sudra (from the fourth caste) says something insulting to a Brāhman, a glowing iron rod ten inches long is forced into his mouth; and if he makes so bold as to want to instruct a Brāhman, hot oil is poured into his mouth and ears, and so forth. Brāhmans are supposed to have a secret power; it is said in the Code of Manu, "Let no king incur the wrath of a Brāhman, for if he is in a rage

285. *G reads:* entire relationship. W₂ *(1831/MiscP?) reads:* entire relationship; for even though it is a form of knowing, this consciousness must be immediate.
286. [*Ed.*] For the idea that Brāhmans are twice-born, see, e.g., *Institutes of Hindu Law*, pp. 39-39.
287. *Ho reads, similar in W:* This goes deep. For thought is here regarded as
288. W₂ *(1831) adds:* The whole life of Brāhmans expresses the existence of Brahman; their action consists in bringing Brahman forth; indeed, they have through birth the privilege of being the existence of Brahman.
289. [*Ed.*] See *Institutes of Hindu Law*, pp. 224, 285.

he can immediately destroy king and kingdom, with its army, strongholds, chariots, and elephants."

The third or concrete relationship of consciousness to Brahman assumes another, distinctive shape. This Brahman, this highest consciousness of the absoluteness of thought, has being on its own account; it is cut off, does not exist as a concrete, active spirit. And hence the subject has not any living connection with this unity either; the concrete element in self-consciousness has departed from this region, the connection is broken off. In fact, this is just what constitutes the character of this religious view, wherein, it is true, the different moments or aspects are developed, but in such a way that they remain external to one another. Now inasmuch as in the subjective self-consciousness this region of the One is thus cut off, it is devoid of spirit, i.e., it exists naturally, as something innate. This innate self-consciousness is thus something natural, something particular, and distinct from universal self-consciousness; consequently, it belongs only to a few, who find themselves at this standpoint through the accident of birth. |

⌐We must grasp quite definitely that this region is something devoid of spirit. This becomes clearer if we compare the Hindu religion with others where this is not the case.⌐[290] Where consciousness of the universal in general, of what is essential, shines through into the particular, is active in it and delimits it, there freedom of spirit comes into being in some form; and the legal and ethical realms depend upon the particular being delimited [in this way] by the universal. In private law, for instance, the freedom of the individual is his externalization in regard to the possession of things; and this is what gives rise to private law. In this particular realm of existence I am free, the article counts as mine in particular, ⌐[it belongs] to a free subject, and in this way particular existence is delimited by the universal; my particular existence is coherent with this universality. It is the same with family relationships. Ethical life

---

290. *Ho reads, similar in W:* The single individual is directly the universal, the divine. Spirit exists in this fashion, but the merely subsisting spirit is devoid of spirit. Thus the life of the individual *as* this single individual, and his life within universality, fall irremediably apart. *W continues:* In religions where this is not the case,

exists only where unity is what delimits the particular, and all particularity is delimited by the substantive unity.⁻²⁹¹ To the extent that this [delimitation] is not posited, consciousness of the universal is essentially cut off, ineffective, unfree, devoid of spirit. ⁻And through this isolation [of the universal], what is highest is turned into something unfree, only born naturally.⁻²⁹² With this third characteristic we have come closer to cultus properly speaking, where the relationship is not just posited as a flight from concrete life.

Properly speaking, cultus is the relationship of the self-consciousness to what belongs to the essence, what is in and for itself, consciousness of the One in this essence, and of one's unity with it. The second element is the relationship of the *manifold* consciousness to the—themselves manifold—[essential] objects, in other words to the numerous divinities. |

251   Abstract universality, Brahman, is not worshiped, it has no temples, religious services, or altars; the unity of Brahman is not related to the real, to the self-consciousness that is living, active. Regarding the more precise relation of cultus to nature, it follows from what has been said about consciousness of the One being isolated in this way that, ⁻in the relationship to the divine,⁻²⁹³ nothing is at this stage determined by reason; for that would mean that the particular actions, symbols, etc., are delimited by *unity*. But here the region of the particular is not defined by this unity; it has therefore the character of *irrationality* and *unfreedom* quite generally. The cultus is not a cultus of Brahman; there is only a relatedness to particular divinities—and they, being forsaken by the unity, are unrestrictedly natural beings; the most abstract elements are implicitly determined by the concept, to be sure, but ⁻the unity is only a formal, not a spiritual one,⁻²⁹⁴ and so their significance is only in the mode of a particular material. The defining characteristic is the life force in general, that which generates and perishes, the becoming

291. *Thus G*
292. *Thus G*
293. *Thus G, P; D reads:* in regard to concrete consciousness,
294. *Thus D; G reads:* not taken back into unity in such a way that the Trimurti would become spirit,

and changing of living matter; natural objects, animals and so on, then become attached to this as objects of worship.

The cultus at this stage is a relationship to these particular entities; and because *they* are cut off in a one-sided manner, it too is a relatedness to something that is only *implicitly* essential, to what is posited merely in a natural form or mode. Religious activity generally—i.e., activity concerned with the essence, with the universal, essential aspect of life—is pictured and performed in this way; this is how it is known and done, this is the religious way to act. It has from the outset a content that is *inessential,* devoid of reason. Because these materials in general are objectively (on the one hand) the intuition of God, and subjectively (on the other hand) what it is essential to *do,* because what is of prime concern becomes inessential, the cultus becomes infinite in scope, everything falls within it, the content is of no significance. There is no rhyme or reason to it, and because | the content is natural, external, there is no internal limit to its scope. Religious actions generally—inasmuch as [they] are inwardly devoid of reason—are also determined in a manner devoid of reason, determined solely by external factors. Religious duty, i.e., what is properly essential, is something steadfast, unchanging in its form, quite removed from subjective opinion and caprice. But what it enjoins at this stage is this senseless contingency; and religious practice is merely a fact, a customary usage that cannot be understood because there is no understanding in it.

On the contrary, what is in it is the dead hand of constraint whichever way one turns. To the extent that this is transcended, because religious practice must also necessarily bring satisfaction or enjoyment, over and above this constraint, the enjoyment happens only through a crude numbing of the senses. At one extreme there is the escape offered by abstraction, in the middle there is enslavement to sensuous activity, and at the other extreme there is wild debauchery; these are the elements of this religiosity, the sorriest depravity. To the extent that escape forms part of the cultus, the present practice is confined to execution of a purely external activity. The cultus consists of merely doing something, and this includes the most barbaric distractions, drunken orgies, sexual promiscuity, and all kinds of ugliness. This is the necessary character of this type of cultus, which derives from the fact that consciousness of the One is *isolated* from the unity of universality, the linkage with all other concrete [realities] being interrupted, so that everything falls apart. Caprice and freedom are released in the imagination, and it is in the imagination that *poetry* has its field. Among the Hindus we find the most beautiful poetry, but always with an underlying element of utter irrationality: we are attracted by its grace and at the same time repelled by the sheer confusion and nonsense of it.[295]

If we now consider how far we have come in regard to the nature of God,[296] God is now ˉthe trueˉ[297] as opposed to multiplicity, the peaceful *being-within-self* or *self-containment* of thought, this ground of universality. In part this self-containment includes power; in part

---

295. [*Ed.*] Hegel's very negative assessment of Hinduism is partly due to his direct and indirect sources, whose reports of contemporary India were often tendentious or ingenuous. See esp. Mill, *History of British India* 1:263–282; the report by Turner mentioned in n. 277; Jean Antoine Dubois, *Moeurs, institutions et cérémonies des peuples de l'Inde,* 2 vols. (Paris, 1825; for the lectures of 1824 Hegel may have been familiar with the English translation of this work already published in 1817); and W. Ward, *A View of the History, Literature and Religion of the Hindoos; Including a Minute Description of Their Manners and Customs, and Translations from Their Principal Works,* 2 vols. (London, 1817; Hegel would have been familiar with this work at least through the excerpts from it in E. F. K. Rosenmüller, *Das alte und neue Morgenland,* 6 vols. [Leipzig, 1817–1820]). These reports, however, in all probability merely confirmed the impression Hegel had gained from studying the texts available to him, in particular the Code of Manu (in the *Institutes of Hindu Law*). His general evaluation of Hinduism must in fact be regarded as a deliberate corrective to the uncritical enthusiasm for India generally prevalent in Germany at the time, especially in romantic circles.

296. [*Ed.*] Hegel summarizes the discussion of nature religion up to this point and prepares the ground for the next stage. The first stage, as described here, is the religion of *being*-within-self (Buddhism); the second is the religion of phantasy (Hinduism)—the self-*differentiation* of absolute being, which previously had been self-*contained;* while the third stage, the next to come, is the religion of the good (Persian religion)—the *reflection back* into itself of what at first had merely been at rest within itself and then differentiated itself into richly variegated forms. Thus it is evident that Hegel discovers a threefold dialectic—a triad of basic forms—in the development of nature religion. Magic and the formal objectification of the divine object merely anticipate the first basic form of religion, while the religion of the enigma is transitional. The triadic structure is more clearly presented in the 1827 lectures.

297. W_1 *(1831) reads:* substance

power lies outside it. The second stage is the emergence out of this first abstract unity, | the unfolding of the moments making up the 253 idea, for essence must unfold, there must be *self-differentiation* in the thinking of the absolute substance. But the shape achieved here does not get beyond this differentiation, and it is only in flight that unity is achieved. In other words, the differences, being accidental, are themselves swallowed up once more in this unity, but only in such a way as to disappear in it. The third stage, finally, is that of ¯*reflection-into-self,*¯[298] where thought contains self-determination; it does not merely contain determination within itself but *is* the process of determining itself, and the process of determining has worth and validity only to the extent that it is reflected into this unity. At this point the concept of freedom[299] is posited generally. This self-containment, this self-determining ¯that does not allow its determinations to escape into separated particular configurations but takes¯[300] them back into itself—this is the principle of *freedom,* of the *good.* In this way God is determined as the good; "good" is not here used merely predicatively, but God *is* the good. (This is a genuine definition; the proof, i.e., the logical development, is presupposed here.)

The concept of the divine is still the *unity* of the finite and infinite at this [present] stage too. Thought that is contained within itself, pure substance, is the infinite, while the multiplicity of gods are, in accordance with the categories of thought, the finite; unity here is negative unity, the abstraction that submerges the many in this One, but the One has not achieved anything by this means, and is no more

298. W₁ *(1831) reads:* the reflection of multiplicity into itself,

299. W₁ *(1831) adds:* objectivity

300. W₁ *(1831?) reads, similar in* G: can also allow its determinations to escape into particular configurations, but remains inwardly determined and can take *Cf.* Ho: In this way is expressed the concept of freedom, being-within-self, which does not shut itself off abstractly, in self-communion, from all determinacy, and by the very fact of insisting on its universality makes itself something determinate—which determinacy is then for it not itself but is rather for it an other. On the contrary, it opens itself up and posits the determinacy that is implicit in it—not leaving it to subsist as an independent distinction outside itself, but taking it back into unity with itself, since it is its own.

fully determined than before. In other words, the finite is affirmative only in this way, outside the infinite, not within it;[301] insofar as it is affirmative, it is something irrational, a finite that is no longer held within the unity. Here we have the finite, the determinate in general, taken up | into infinitude; form matches substance; infinite form is posited as identical with internally self-determining substance. We have substantive form, not merely the form of abstract power. This mode of determination, then, is the *nature religion of the good*.

254

3. The Religion of the Good or of Light (Persian Religion)[302]

The good is that wherein concrete life also intuits its affirmative roots, can become aware of itself in genuine fashion, for this unity we call the good *is* the process of self-determination. It is this determinacy that yields the coherence with concrete life; moreover, the coherence is affirmative, it is not a flight.[303]

This more intimate coherence *can* be grasped in such a way that one says things are "good by nature." "Good" is here used in its proper sense, not by the standard of some external purpose or some external comparison. We do use "good" for what is appropriate, what is good for some end, so that the end or purpose lies outside the object in question. But what we mean by "good" here, on the contrary, is the universal, that which is directly determined within itself. In this sense the good can be predicated of particular things,

---

301. [*Ed.*] The distinction between negative and affirmative forms of finitude and infinitude is one that Hegel makes a good deal of in Part I of the 1824 lectures (see Vol. 1:278–288, 294–310).

302. [*Ed.*] The religion of the good or of light (*Die Religion des Guten, die Lichtreligion*) was the religion of the ancient Persians, prior to their conversion to Islam. Hegel customarily refers to it as Persian religion or Parseeism (Parsee, or Parsi, derives from the word for Persia, *Pars*), while today it is known as Zoroastrianism, after the traditional founder, Zoroaster (also known as Zarathustra). Hegel's primary source is J. F. Kleuker's edition of the Zend-Avesta: *Zend-Avesta, Zoroasters lebendiges Wort, worin die Lehren und Meinungen dieses Gesetzgebers von Gott, Welt, Natur, Menschen; ingleichen Ceremonien des heiligen Dienstes der Parsen usf. aufbehalten sind*, translated from the French edition of Anquetil du Perron, 5 vols. (Riga, 1776–1783). Where possible we also cite the English edition in Sacred Books of the East (SBE), *The Zend-Avesta*, 3 vols. (Oxford, 1880–1887).

303. W_1 *(1831?) adds:* Its determinacy is taken up into universality. Cf. Ho: For the good is what determines itself in such a way that that the determinacy is as if permeated by its universality, something singular [but] conforming to the universality.

and these particular things are then good, the purpose they serve lies in themselves, they are suited not to an other but to themselves, to this purpose; they are good on their own account. The good is thus a substance that is present in them, not something otherworldly like the unity we have named Brahman; it is not merely over against them, nor merely negative in opposition to particular existence. This, then, is the general determinacy, the foundation of this religion of good.

The second point to be recognized is that the good itself is still initially abstract in principle. More exactly, it is the good in general, in other words the good is substantive unity with self, | the inward 255 process of self-determining; but this process of determining is still undeveloped, it is itself still a universal form, still lacks the definition of the "how." The determinateness, the particular, *is* this universality; inasmuch as it is *only* the particular that is posited, what we have is again utterly universal particularity. To the extent that we do not here move beyond immediate determinacy, all that we have is the good in general. One can say that the good does not yet have within itself the independence of existence. In order to *manifest* itself, the good would have to have being for [its] other, it would have to be internally differentiated or, as in Hinduism, it would have to undergo the separating of its constituent elements or moments, which would, however, continue to subsist in the unity, yet would nonetheless be distinct within this unity.

The first consequence is that the good has *unmediated* being in things, is their unmediated substance; and because its determinacy is still abstract, the true positing of the determinacy is its particularization, in other words merely the natural diversity of things in general.

To put the second point another way, because the good is still inwardly the substantive unity with its own determination, and the distinctions are not yet posited, the good has an *antithesis*. It is present in the particular nature of things as their substance in general, and it has its more exact determinacy in the particular substance of things. But then, second, it has at once a universal antithesis, whose particularity is opposed to it and not taken back within it. It has in [its] determinacy only the principle of reflection into self. Since the principle is still abstract, however, the good has the development of the negative outside it. Opposed to the realm of the good there stands the realm of evil, which is engaged in struggle with it. Two principles appear: the good is the true; the evil element is then defined as evil, not as a multiplicity of gods but as essentially other, not just as distinct but as opposite, as a definite antithesis, i.e., outside the good. ⁻Good is engaged in a struggle with evil, which it is destined to overcome, but *destined* only because the struggle knows no end.⁻³⁰⁴ |

256

Third, the good in its universality has a natural shape—the pure manifestation [of it] that is present in natural things, namely, *light*. The second point was that the substantive unity coheres with determinately existing things—the genus of determinacies. The third point [now] is that since the good itself is still abstract subjectivity, its singularity is the [external] moment of singularity—the moment or way in which it exists for others; and this moment itself still lies in [the realm of] sentient intuition, it is an external presence, which can now match the content, inasmuch as determinacy as such is taken up into the universal. As this more precise determinacy, as the intuitive mode, the mode of immediacy, its determinacy can here appear as matching the content. Brahman, for example, is merely abstract thought: intuited in a sensuous manner, perhaps only the intuition of space would correspond to it, i.e., a sensuous universality of intuition that is itself merely abstract. But at this stage the substantive element corresponds to the form, namely, the physically universal light, whose antithesis is darkness. Air, breath, spirit— these make up the category of invisibility, and are also physical properties; but this does not make them the ideal element itself, as it were universal individuality or subjectivity—this does not make them light, which manifests itself. That is what the *self*-determining moment of individuality or subjectivity consists in. Light appears as universal light in general and then as a particular, distinctive nature—the nature of particular objects, reflected into itself; it appears as the essentiality of particular things.

304. *Thus G*

Light is not to be understood here as meaning merely the sun. One can say that the sun is the most excellent light, but it is up there as a particular entity, a particular individual. The good, or light [as such], by contrast, has the root of subjectivity within itself, but still only the root; ˉaccordingly it is not posited as set apart in this individual way,ˉ[305] and hence it is to be taken as subjectivity, as the soul of things. Sun worship goes back a very long way, and many ascribe | the proliferation of Hindu gods to the sun. But the sun is   257 not to be confused with Brahman; it belongs to the natural world, to Indra, and in Hinduism this natural world has the form of independence. The prayers and notions of the Hindus took shape several thousand years ago; they derive from the most varied individuals, who are by no means all equally speculative, so that considerable vagueness arises. In the Vedas, for instance, there is no mention of Vishnu, but constant references are made to the sun, though in very general terms. One of the principal prayers that is encountered everywhere is addressed to the sun.[306]

We all know that the worship of light itself has actually existed as the Persian religion, the religion of the Parsees to this day. They revere light, not in the form of the sun—strictly and properly speaking, this is no nature worship—but light as denoting the good; and the good exists as an object, it has the sensible shape of light, a shape that corresponds to the content, which is itself still abstract. Light has essentially the meaning of the good, of what is right in general; it is also called Ormazd. As Ormazd it is a human shape, but this is still something superficial—Ormazd is the universal that is imbued with subjectivity, in its external form; he is the just one, the universal light, and his kingdom *is* the kingdom of light. The sun and the planets are the first and principal spirits of God, a great and shining company of heaven, each protecting, doing good, and blessing us; they take turns in ruling over the world of light. Light in general is Ormazd; the whole world is Ormazd, in all its different

305. *Thus G; P reads:* light generally, where light is, *D reads:* where light is,
306. [*Ed.*] Hegel is referring to Colebrooke's translation of the prayer of Gayatri in "On the Vedas," *Asiatic Researches* 8:399–400. The prayer is quoted in a slightly different form in Mill's *History of British India* 1:240.

levels and varieties, and in this kingdom of light everything is good, and what is good is light. Everything pertains to the light; the organic life of animal nature, all that enlivens, all essence, all spirituality, all activity, the growth of finite things—all of this *is* light, it is all Ormazd. Ormazd is not merely the everyday world of sense but all good, all love, all power, spirit, soul, happiness, and blessing: all is included in him. A human being, a tree or animal that lives, rejoices in existing, is affirmative in nature, and constitutes something noble, healthy; thereby it shines forth, it emits light, and this light is the quintessence of the substantive nature of each and every thing.[307] |

258 The universal light, and the light in all things, is venerated: the sun and stars are venerated as spirit. Ormazd is the universal and the first, the genius or spirit of the sun (this genius is distinct from its existence, though it is also present therein). And the other [stars] are genii who stand around his throne.[308] So, then, this world of light, these appearances of light are venerated, and in this connection the Parsees are well served by the regions in which they live, in particular by the light that can be [obtained] from the fountains of oil found there. This light is burned on their altars; it is not so much a symbol but rather the very presence of what is excellent and good. Everything good, noble, and excellent in the world is honored, loved, prayed to in this way; for it is counted as the Son, as the begotten one of Ormazd, in whom he loves himself, in whom he is well pleased. In the same way songs of praise are addressed to all pure human spirits. These spirits are called *fravashi,* and they include embodied, still existing beings as well as departed spirits; for example,

307. [*Ed.*] What Hegel says of light in this and the following paragraph can also be said of the primal fire, the two being equated in the Zend-Avesta (whereas "material fire" is merely an image, a product of the "primal fire"). See *Zend-Avesta,* ed. Kleuker, 1:44–45.

308. [*Ed.*] Hegel's turn of phrase echoes A. H. L. Heeren, *Ideen über die Politik, den Verkehr und den Handel der vornehmsten Völker der alten Welt,* 2 vols. (Göttingen, 1804–1805), 1:509: "Around Ormazd's throne stand the seven Amshaspands, the princes of light, among whom he himself is the first." In regard to Ormazd as one of the Amshaspands see also J. G. Rhode, *Die heilige Sage und das gesammte Religionssystem der alten Baktrer* (Frankfurt am Main, 1820), pp. 316–317, 365.

the Parsees pray especially to Zoroaster's spirit to watch over them.[309]
Animals are venerated too because they are imbued with life, light,
and vitality. In this connection the genii or spirits, the affirmative
elements in living nature, are singled out and revered, as are the ideals
of particular species or types of thing, as universal subjectivities that
represent divinity in finite form. As we have said, animals are
venerated, but the ideal of animal life is the heavenly bull[310] (as with
the Hindus a symbol of creation, standing alongside Shiva). Among
the fiery elements the sun is particularly revered; and among the
waters too there is an ideal of this kind,[311] the stream of streams,
the river from which all rivers flow, which rises on the Elburz. Elburz
is the ideal among mountains, the first kernel of the whole earth,
standing in a blaze of light from which proceeds all the beneficence
of heaven. There is also an ideal among the trees, the *haoma,* from
which flows the sap of life, or the water of immortality.[312] Thus

309. [*Ed.*] The concept of the *fravashi* was known to Hegel through Kleuker's
edition of the Zend-Avesta, and especially the editorial notes to vol. 1, pp. 12–15,
although it is noteworthy that they are there described as "the first, pure copies of
all future beings and creatures"; once embodied in existing beings, they act as their
protective spirit, keeping soul and body from contamination and error. Prayers
invoking the help of the *fravashi* and praising those of various named beings and
creatures (including Zoroaster) are to be found in vol. 2, esp. pp. 246, 258 (SBE
2:180, 201).

310. [*Ed.*] Hegel's mention of the "heavenly bull" makes it probable that he has
in mind here too the prayers of praise referred to in the previous note (*Zend-Avesta,*
ed. Kleuker, 2:257–258; SBE 2:200), where the creatures named include "the heavenly
word, pure essences, water, earth, trees, hearths, the bull."

311. W_1 reads: waters too there is an ideal of this kind, Elburz, W_2 reads: mountains too there is an ideal of this kind, Elburz, the mountain of mountains, *Cf. Ho:*
the river of rivers flows from the Elburz; there too is the mountain of mountains.

[*Ed.*] Hegel's reference to worship of the sun is based on Kleuker's edition of the
Zend-Avesta (2:104–108; cf. SBE 2:349–353), although the sun must not be equated
(as the text as we have it seems to suggest) with the ideal of fire, the primary fire;
see above, n. 307. The ideal of water is the river Arduisur (Ardvicura) (2:112), while
Elburz (Hara berezaiti) as the mountain of mountains is stated elsewhere (3:67–73)
to be the source from which it flows. The Elburz (given in Kleuker as Albordj or
Albordi) is a chain of mountains south of the Caspian Sea, the highest of which is
Demavend. W_1's confusion of the mountain and the river is corrected by W_2.

312. [*Ed.*] On the *haoma* tree, see *Zend-Avesta,* ed. Kleuker, 3:105: "Among
these trees is the white, wholesome, fruitbearing *haoma* [*Hom*]; it grows at the source

259 the Parsees have present before them for their intuition a world of the good, a world of ideals that are not, however, otherworldly abstractions | but are evident and present in the actual things that exist.

All of this involves the cultus. As far as the cultic observance of those Parsees who live their lives in the kingdom of light is concerned, their life as a whole is the cultus; living is what the cultus consists in; it is not something cut off and isolated from the rest of life, as it is with the Hindus. The religious law governing the Parsees is that they should do good, be pure in thought, word, and deed, spare life and promote it, make it invigorating, fruitful, and joyful. Inwardly and outwardly they are to be like light, to act like light. As a means of promoting life, for instance, they are enjoined to plant trees and engage in agriculture, to ensure that light and fruitfulness prosper everywhere, to care for the sick, to feed the hungry, give hospitality to travelers, plant deserts and irrigate the earth, which is a subject or genius (spirit). These are the general features of their religion, and we do not need to go into it any further.[313]

4. Transition from Nature Religion to Spiritual Religion: The Religion of the Enigma (Egyptian Religion)[314]

˜This is the fourth determinate phase of nature religion, the stage where the transition from unmediated nature religion to the religion

of the Arduisur. Whoever drinks of its water (sap) becomes immortal." For further information on the significance of this tree, see our Vol. 3:106 n. 117.

313. [Ed.] The source for Hegel's description of the Parsees' cultic observances is Kleuker's edition of the Zend-Avesta, although individual references are difficult to trace because of their general character; cf. 2:114, 118 (SBE 3:390).

314. [Ed.] Initially Hegel appears to have intended only three phases or stages for nature religion (see above, nn. 99, 102, 104, 296). Since this fourth phase is a transitional one, it could be regarded as not actually destroying the triadic structure. In 1827 Hegel solved this problem by linking Persian and Egyptian religion under a common heading, but he created a new one by not subsuming Buddhism under the religion of magic. Thus in 1827 he still had four stages of nature religion. Egyptian religion was the "religion of the enigma or riddle" [Rätsel] in Hegel's view because everything in it symbolically denoted something that remained unexpressed, and it did so in ways that were enigmatic and obscure. The paradigmatic instance of this was the representation of divinity by that mysterious artwork known as the sphinx,

of subjectivity takes place.¯³¹⁵ If we consider the previous stage, the good may well be implicitly concrete. It is what is primary and self-contained; this breaks apart inwardly, and there is then the resumption of its determinations back into the self-contained unity that the good is defined as. The good is implicitly concrete, but *only* implicitly so; | its determinacy is inwardly simple, not yet existing, manifested [as] the determinate; in other words, it is still abstract subjectivity and not yet real subjectivity. The next moment, in which we can see this [reality] foreshadowed, is the fact that evil, the negative, has been taken note of outside this realm of good. This determinacy [of goodness] is posited as simple and undeveloped,³¹⁶ and the development, the distinction, consequently is not yet present in it *as* distinct. The result is that one side still lies outside the good; evil is not yet perfectly concrete internally; it is not yet real subjectivity. ³¹⁷By the standard of the concept, we are now getting closer to the realm of subjectivity—i.e., to real, actual subjectivity. But first we must define the concept more precisely.

260

---

which was half human and half animal, and which, according to Greek mythology at least, strangled passersby who could not answer its riddles. The enigma of Egyptian religion was also evident, in Hegel's view, in its transitional character, its curious intermingling of subjectivity and substantiality. In the image of the sphinx, he says, we see the artistic shape forcing its way out of the animal form into the human; it had not yet arrived at the shape of beauty, which was the stage of Greek religion. It remained enigmatic; it had not yet entered into Greek "clarity." Hegel's source of information on Egyptian religion was primarily the classical authors who had visited Egypt, notably Herodotus and Plutarch. Modern explorations and excavations were just beginning in Hegel's time, and the hieroglyphic system was not deciphered until 1824. Hegel was familiar with G. B. Belzoni's *Narrative of the Operations and Recent Discoveries within the Pyramids, Temples, Tombs, and Excavations, in Egypt and Nubia*, 3d ed., 2 vols. (London, 1822), but this work was limited and unscientific.

315. W₂ *(1831) reads:* The form of the spirit's mediation with itself in which the natural is still predominant, the form of passing over where the starting point is the other as such, i.e., nature in general, and the passing over does not yet appear as spirit's coming to itself—this is the form peculiar to the religions of the Near East. The next thing is for this passing over to appear as spirit's coming to itself, but not yet in such a way as to constitute a reconciliation; rather, the struggle and striving *is* the object, but as a moment in the deity itself.

316. *Ho, W add:* it is not valid as determinacy, but only as universality,

317. *Ho reads, precedes in W:* Things are only good as illuminated, only from their positive side, but not also from the side of their particularity.

359

a. The Representation of God

We have already encountered subjectivity elsewhere, in all shapes, as self-consciousness concretely determined at each level. It is a source of particular difficulty when we are dealing with religion that we do not have a concept or a [clearly] defined idea before us, but along with each determinate form we have at the same time the whole totality; all the determinations [of the concept] are there at once. For the content is God, the absolute totality. The matter of the determinations is never lacking, therefore, but it is presented in this concrete field. The only difference [between different stages] is whether the moments that make up the totality are superficially[318] present, or whether they already subsist in what is inward and known to be essential;[319] this is what makes the enormous difference, whether the characteristics are merely external or in the essential content. Hence we find the mode of self-consciousness in all religions to a greater or lesser degree, and further that predicates such as almighty, 261 | all-knowing, and so forth are applied to God. In regard to such content we can read very lofty and profound portrayals of God in Hindu and Chinese sources, so that religions standing on a higher level are no more advanced in this respect, ¨even in regard to the shape in which self-consciousness occurs in them.¨[320] This is what

318. *W (1831/HgG?) adds:* externally
319. *W (1831/MiscP?) adds:* i.e., whether they occur only as superficial form and shape or are posited as categorial determination of the content, and thought accordingly;
320. *W (1831/MiscP?) reads:* There are so-called pure representations of God (e.g., in the case of Friedrich von Schlegel's *Weisheit der Indier*),ª which are regarded as what remains over from the perfect, original religion. *Ho reads, continues in W:* But in the inward element, in the concept, we get closer to actual subjectivity, for in the cultus of the religion of light we saw the singular evil [moment] already everywhere sublated. We already had subjectivity everywhere, directly as self-consciousness concretely determined. Already magic-working was the power of self-consciousness over nature. It is, to be sure, a source of particular difficulty when we are considering religion that here we are not dealing with pure thought-categories as in logic, or with categories of existence as in nature, but with such as already contain the moment of self-consciousness, of finite spirit as such, by virtue of having already passed through the [categories of] subjective and objective spirit. For religion is spirit's self-consciousness of itself, and it makes the various stages of this self-consciousness in which spirit is developed the object of consciousness. The content of this object is God, the absolute totality, so that the multiplicity of the material is never lacking.
[*Ed.*] ªSee above, n. 27.

prompts people to look more closely here for the specific categories that constitute the differentia of a religion. ⁻The tendency is to locate this differentia in the creating essence,⁻[321] which is everywhere and also nowhere, and also in whether there is one God or not. But this differentia is unreliable too, for the one God is even to be found in Hinduism, and the difference therefore resides solely in the way in which the many figures join together to make a unity. Many English authors[322] who have had experiential contact with the Hindu religion declare that the core of Hindu religion, the original Hinduism, recognized one God, whether as the sun or as Brahman, the universal soul. Predicates of the understanding, such as this, furnish no solution. Distinctions | and determinations of this kind are to be found more or less in all religions.   262

If I say of God, "He is wise or all-powerful," that is wholly correct. But these are only determinations of reflection; I do not in this way get to know his nature. Moreover, these are predicates that apply to finite natures, which are also just, powerful, wise, knowing; but when they are applied to God, they must be extended beyond all finite content through the "all"—as "power" becomes "all-powerful." And in this way they lose their specific meaning, which vanishes away out of sight, just as the Hindu gods disappear in Brahman. What is essential is the free substantive element, which is grasped and known in him as his immanent essential determinacy; and this is neither the predicates of reflection nor the external shape.[323]

Thus we have already encountered the category of *subjectivity,* or self-determination, but only in a superficial form; we have not yet encountered it as constitutive of the nature of God. [324]Subjectivity in general is abstract identity with self, the being-within-self that differentiates itself, the process of this differentiation, and at the same

321. *Thus P; D reads:* They locate the differentia [in] what distinguishes the creator from the creatures, *G reads:* They look for the differentia more especially in the creative activity or essence, *Ho reads:* For example, they may be sought in what differentiates creator and creature,

322. [*Ed.*] See above, nn. 245, 306.

323. *W (1831/HgG?) adds:* but idea.

324. *Precedes in W (1831):* In the religion of light this category was abstract, universal personification, because the person contains the absolute moments in undeveloped form.

361

time what negates the self-differentiation and maintains itself in what it has thus distinguished. At the same time it maintains this other as a moment, it does not let the other escape from it but remains the power informing it. It has being in the other, but it has it on its own account, having the difference as a moment of itself.

If we consider this in relation to the next form [of religion], we find that subjectivity is in fact this self-relating negativity; and it is to be noted that the negative [moment], evil, can no longer fall outside the good but must be contained and posited within the affirmative relation to self—and to that extent it is, to be sure, no longer 263 evil.[325] This subjectivity, | therefore, is no longer what Brahman is; in Brahman these differences just disappear; or, to the extent that difference or determinacy is posited, they are independent gods, and fall outside Brahman. The main point, therefore, is that the negative, as self-affecting in this manner [*in dieser Affektion seiner selbst*], is now posited as the defining category.

It should be noted to begin with that subjectivity, and essentially universal subjectivity—that this first type of subjectivity is not perfectly free and purely spiritual subjectivity, but is affected [*affiziert*] by nature; this subjectivity is essential, universal power, but instead of being the merely implicit power that we encountered previously, it is *posited* power; and it is posited when it becomes posited as an exclusive subjectivity.

This is the difference—the difference between power in itself and power inasmuch as it is subjectivity. The latter is posited power, posited as power that exists explicitly. ˉPower we have already met with in all of the previous shapes. As the initial basic category, it is crude power over what merely has being.ˉ[326] In that case the power is also the inward element exclusively, and its differentiations

---

325. *Ho adds, similar in W:* So the negative [moment], evil, can now no longer fall outside the good, but the good in itself is precisely what implies evil. As a result, to be sure, evil does not remain evil, but, as evil relating to itself as evil, it sublates its evilness and constitutes itself as good. Good is the negative relation to oneself, [i.e.,] to posit evil as one's other, in the same way that evil consists in positing—i.e., sublating—the movement, one's negativeness, as the negative. The double movement is subjectivity.

326. *Thus* G

appear as independent existences outside it; they have indeed emerged from it, but insofar as they have emerged, they are independently external to it. If they were to be comprehended within it, they would be lost to sight, just as the differentiations disappear in Brahman, in this abstraction, inasmuch as the self-consciousness says, "I am Brahman." Everything that is divine or good is lost to sight in Brahman in this way. This pure abstraction cannot contain or maintain any immanent content within itself; and to the extent that the content lies outside it, it is a law unto itself, a free revelry. In relation to these particularized existences power is the operative element, the ground of their existence, but it remains merely inward, and operates merely in a universal fashion. What the universal power brings forth—to the extent that it is only implicit—is also universal; it is what we call the laws of nature. These pertain | to the implicit 264 power, the power whose being lies in itself. This power is an implicit one, and its operation is likewise implicit; it operates unconsciously, and sun, stars, oceans, trees, rivers, human beings, animals, and so on appear as independent existences; only their inward life is determined by the power. To the extent that the power appears in this sphere, it can do so only as a power opposed to the laws of nature, so that this is the locus of miracles. There are no miracles in Hinduism, however, for in Hinduism there is in general no rational, intelligible nature; nature has no intelligible connective tissue, so that in Hinduism everything is miraculous, and therefore there can be no miracles. There can be miracles only where God is defined as a subject and operates as implicit power in the mode of subjectivity.

This is the definition of the power whose being is in itself generally; and it is clear that it makes no difference what shape is given to it, so that it has been located in animals etc. That living matter operates as immediate power is in fact indisputable, since power as implicit, power that has its being in itself, operates only invisibly and without any show.

Real power must be distinguished from this implicit power. Real power is in the first place subjectivity, in which two principal moments should be noted.

1. First, the subject is identical with itself and at the same time posits within itself specific differing characteristics, particular deter-

minations.[327] The good is the universal self-determination, so completely universal that it has the same undifferentiated scope as the universal essence; the determination is in fact not posited as a determination. Subjectivity therefore includes self-determination in such a way that the determined characteristics appear as a plurality; they have this reality vis-à-vis the concept, vis-à-vis the simple self-containment of inner subjectivity. But these characteristics are initially still included within subjectivity, they are inward determinations. |

265

2. The second moment is that the subject is exclusive, it relates negatively to itself, like power, but vis-à-vis an other; this other may also appear independently, but it is posited that its independence is mere show. Its being is such that its existence, its configuration, is merely a negative in relation to ˉpower,ˉ[328] which is consequently the dominant element. Absolute power does not dominate the other; in domination the other is merely submerged, substance is brought to naught. It is the subject that first dominates, and the particular subsists, but as posited, or as placed under law—it is obedient, it serves as a means. It is posited in this existent configuration with the character of the negative, of what is not truly independent. These are the two principal moments of this form of subjectivity.

Just how these two moments develop we have to consider further. They develop in such a way as to remain necessarily within certain limits, more especially because we have only just embarked on the transition from substantiality to subjectivity; subjectivity does not yet emerge in its freedom and truth; it is still mixed up with substantive unity—and, to an even greater extent, with the multiplicity of independent configurations. It is true on the one hand that subjectivity combines everything; but on the other hand it ˉhas the other [within itself] in this way as a result, insofar as it unites these manifold determinations with subjectivity,ˉ[329] and the mixture consequently still has the deficiencies of what it is still mixed up with, namely nature religion.[330] This stage is therefore shot through with in-

327. W (1831/HgG?) adds: [There is] one subject of these differences, [and they are] moments of one subject.
328. W (1831/HgG?) reads: the power of subjectivity,
329. Thus P; G reads: still lets the other subsist, because it is still immature,
330. Ho adds, similar in W: As regards the concrete representation of this stage, or the mode and nature of the shape in which spirit has its self-consciousness of self

consistencies, and the problem for it is to purify itself into subjectivity. This is the stage of the *enigma* [*Rätsel*], the Egyptian moment, the moment of *Egyptian religion.* |

266

[331]There is a special interest in the consideration of this standpoint because both ˉmodesˉ[332] occur here in their principal moments; they are not yet separated, so that there is merely ˉconfusion,ˉ[333] and it is only through the concept that one can discern how such a heterogeneous mixture coalesces, and which of the two [sides] the principal moments belong to.

1. At this stage, God is still the indwelling nature, the implicit power, for which the shape is therefore something contingent and arbitrary. This merely implicit power can be clothed in human or animal shape at will. Power is unconsciously active intelligence, intelligence that is not spiritual, but only concept, only idea—and not subjective idea but unconscious idea, unconscious vitality, life in general. This, however, is not subjectivity, is not *self* at all; but if life in general is also to be pictured as a shape, the easiest thing is to take something living. ˉAnimals [are] organic life;ˉ[334] and it does not matter, it is contingent, which living thing, which animal, which man, is selected. Hence we find animal worship in Egypt in a wide variety of forms, with different animals venerated in different localities.[335]

2. What is more important is the second characteristic—the fact that, as has already been generally indicated, the subject is determined immanently, within itself, it has being in its reflection onto self, and

---

as the object of its consciousness, this stage shows itself to be the transition from the earlier shapes to the higher stage of religion. Subjectivity is not yet a subjectivity that is self-subsisting and therefore free, but is rather the midpoint between substance and free subjectivity.

331. *Precedes in W (1831):* In this ferment all moments come into view.

332. W_2 *(following Ho) reads:* stages, the preceding stage of nature religion and the succeeding stage of free subjectivity, *Ho reads:* This standpoint can therefore afford particular interest, because both stages, the preceding one as well as the succeeding one, occur here in intermingling contact.

333. *W reads:* an enigmatic mixture and confusion, *Ho reads:* an enigmatic, confused mixture,

334. *Thus P; G reads:* Within life in general there are living things;

335. [*Ed.*] See Herodotus, *Histories* 2.65–76. Belzoni, in his *Narrative of the Operations and Recent Discoveries* 1:261 ff., 425 ff., describes finds of buried bones and mummies of bulls, cows, and various other animals.

this determination is no longer just the universal good. It *is* the universal good, to be sure, but it moves beyond this—it has evil beside and set against it, in the form of Typhon.[336] Moreover, real subjectivity posits differences essentially in its determinations, so that good is now posited in different forms; there is an inner | content that has specific determinations, not just a single universal definition. These different characteristics of the good ˉdo not yet, however, make up a totality of configurations.ˉ[337] The subject is for the first time a real subject—i.e., freedom first begins—where there can be for me several different things that are defined as good, so that there is the possibility of choice. Only then does the subject rise above particular purpose; and similarly the subject becomes free from particularity when particularity is not coextensive with subjectivity itself, when [this subject] no longer *is* the universal good, [but] merely *wills* the universal good. That the good is at the same time determined and elevated to infinite wisdom is a different view. That is something else.[338] At this point a plurality of goods is determined, so that subjectivity stands above them all, and whether to will one or the other good appears to be the choice of the subject. We are dealing now with the *subject* that has being only insofar as it is self-determining; it is the subject, but as such it is already posited as *resolving,* and we see appearing the category of *purpose,* or of practical action. As the substantive unity God does not engage in practical action; he creates[339] or he destroys, but he does not *act,* ˉjust as Brahman too does not act at all [insofar as Brahman is] first [cause]. Only the incarnations act.ˉ[340] However, it is still only limited purposes that can enter into play here at first; this is only

336. [*Ed.*] See Plutarch, *De Iside et Osiride,* esp. chap. 13, where he recounts the trick employed by Typhon, with the help of seventy-two conspirators and Aso, an Ethiopian queen who was on a visit to Egypt, to foment trouble against King Osiris and Isis, his sister and consort.

337. *Thus G with D; P reads:* have been called differentiated goods.

338. [*Ed.*] Probably a reference to Jewish religion.

339. W_2 *(following Ho) adds:* is the ground of things, *Ho reads:* God as substance, on the other hand, is only the ground of things, not action.

340. W_2 *(following G and Ho) reads:* Brahman for instance does not act; independent action is either only imagined or pertains to the changing incarnations. *Ho reads:* We do not see Brahman acting. In other instances acting is imagined, or human subjects are incarnations, whose purposes are at the same time confined to a definite people, a definite locality.

the first [mode of] subjectivity, whose content cannot yet be infinite wisdom and justice, since [it] belongs to one people, one locality exclusively.

3. The third moment is that the human shape or figure here makes its appearance more clearly, so that there is a transition from the animal shape of God to the human shape.

The animal shape of God may still occur, but where real, free subjectivity enters in, it is only the human shape that corresponds to such a concept. | It is no longer merely life but free determination   268 according to this or that purpose, so that the human shape characterizing the concept may be a particular [embodiment of] subjectivity, such as a hero, a particular king from ancient times [in] the locality of his realm or activity, or an indeterminate human figure. Ormazd, even Jamshid,[341] still have a wholly abstract figure and mode of action, that of the abstract principle of good. Here, where particular purposes enter into play as in primitive subjectivity, there is also a marked particularity attaching to the shape (which has its specific purposes, its specific places, and so forth). In this way the principal moments coalesce. In other words, the development of the determinate aspect must appear more specifically in the subject; to this extent the determinacy is *limited,* it is not determinacy in its totality. But determinacy must also appear as totality in regard to its subject; [fully] developed subjectivity must be intuited in it. However, these developed moments of subjectivity[342] first present themselves as a sequence, as the subject's course of life or successive states. ⁻It is only at a later stage that the subject, as absolute spirit, succeeds in having its moments as totality itself.⁻[343] At this stage the subject is still formal, limited in its concept, and hence in its deter-

341. [*Ed.*] Jamshid was the legendary ancestral king of the Parsees, identical with Yima, to whom—before Zarathustra—the law was first orally revealed. He was revered especially as the founder of culture (not just Iranian culture), but toward the end of his reign he transgressed the law. Hegel's knowledge of Jamshid was derived from Kleuker's edition of the Zend-Avesta (1:92, 3:304–309; cf. SBE 1:10-21, 3:230–239), as well as from Joseph Görres's translation of the pre-Islamic poet Firdawsī's *Shāh-nāma* (*Das Heldenbuch von Iran aus dem Schah Nameh des Firdussi,* 2 vols. [Berlin, 1820], 1:12–15).

342. W₂ *(Var) adds:* are not yet the totality of the shape, but *Cf. Ho:* Even if the entire form is there, it is not present in such a way that the moments are themselves totalities, or the totality [is] subordinated to a definition of its moments.

343. *Thus G*

minate character; and although totality does appear in it, there is still this limitation in its [mode of] appearance, that the moments have not developed beyond the level of states—i.e., determinations and the totality of these determinations, states; they are not each developed as a totality on its own account. What is intuited in the subject ˉis not the eternal history that constitutes its nature˗³⁴⁴ but only the limited history of successive states. The first moment is the affirmation as such that it is *this* subject; the second is its negation, and the third is the return of its negation into self. What is of particular relevance here is the second moment. | Inasmuch as negation appears as a state in regard to the natural subject as having being, [i.e., as negation] of its outward shape, the subject's externalization is *death,* and the third moment is *resurrection,* the return to a particular [mode of] lordship. The proximate mode in which negation appears in regard to a subject qua existing ˉin humanˉ³⁴⁵ shape, is death. Moreover, death as this negation has at this stage a further characteristic: because we are not yet dealing with eternal history, or with the subject in its totality, this death or negation directed against the singular existence appears to stem from without, it comes about through something else, through the evil principle, Typhon.

Third, negation is posited along with negation, so that death is slain and the evil principle vanquished. ˉIn the Persian religion it is not vanquished, for the good, Ormazd, remains standing opposite the evil one, Ahriman, and has not yet returned to self in this way. Here for the first time the vanquished state of the evil principle is posited.˗³⁴⁶ Inasmuch as God has human shape, wherever it may come from, or inasmuch as infinite form is first posited only as an external shape—ˉinfiniteˉ³⁴⁷ form is for the first time posited in infinite spirit, and is then for the first time equal to the substance, [while] here [the form] is still the natural mode of existence—ˉthe moment of negation shows itself in regard to this outward

344. W (1831/Ed?) *reads:* in such a way as to constitute its nature is not the eternal history
345. W (1831) *reads:* merely in natural shape in general, and also human
346. *Thus G*
347. W₁ (1831) *reads:* the genuinely infinite

shape;⁻³⁴⁸ since the moment of negation is part of the *concept* of spirit, it also manifests itself now in its *existence*. God is here figured principally in the human shape. This human shape does also occur in the highest religion, but there it is only a moment of the form. The death of God is a historical feature of many religions: in the Syrian religion there is the death of Adonis, and similarly in Egyptian religion the death of Osiris.

This death seems at first sight to be something unworthy of the divinity. In our representational picture it is the lot of the finite | 270 to pass away, and so far as the term "death" is used of God, it is applied to him only as a characteristic taken over from the sphere of the finite that does not befit him—God is not truthfully known in this way, and is demeaned by being defined in terms of negation. As against this assertion the first thing to be said is that God must be comprehended as the supreme being, as what is identical only with itself, and this representation of him is deemed to be the highest and most excellent one, so that spirit attains this true image of God only at the very end. If God is grasped in this way, as the essence without determinations, or as self-identical, then he is devoid of content; it is often remarked that this is the poorest way of defining God, and is in fact a very old way of representing him, only the first step towards an objective attitude. Brahman is just this abstraction without content; so is the good that is [defined as] light, which has the negative, evil, only outside itself, as darkness. But the main point is that now we have already gone beyond this abstraction, to the *concrete* representation of God; hence the moment of negation makes its entrance, in the specific form of negation, in the shape in which it means "death," insofar as God is intuited in human shape; thus death is seen as highly estimable, not as a determination of the finite as such, but as a content of God himself, immanent in his essence itself.[349] This is a sign that we have progressed to conscious

348. *Thus G; P, D read:* and it is in regard to this outward shape that the moment of negation presents itself;

349. *Ho adds, similar in W:* For self-determination involves the moment of inward, not outward negativity, as is already implicit in the word "self-determination." The death that appears here is therefore also not like the death of the Lama, of Buddha. For these are the pure substance of abstract being-within-self, to whom negativity is external, impinging on them as external power.

spirituality, to knowledge of the freedom that is in God. This moment of negation is an absolutely truthful aspect of God; ˉso natural death is the distinctive, specific form in which negation appears in regard to his shape. | For the sake of the divine totality of the higher religions this moment must also be represented, be known, in regard toˉ³⁵⁰ the divine idea, since the idea must not lack any of the moments.

271

Thus it is the moment of negation immanent in the essential process of manifestation of the concept of God that we here encounter. It is not a mortality like that of the Lama or Buddha. In these religions we have seen that God's essence is for the first time defined as abstract being-within-self or self-containment, as his own absolute substantiality; the Lama's moment of death is not a moment immanent in the substance but counts merely as an accidental, external form in which the deity shows itself. That this is something that happens to the deity itself, not simply to the individual entity in which it exhibits itself, does not emerge at that stage. This moment must accordingly comprise God's essence.

Linked with this is the third moment, that God reestablishes himself, he rises from the dead. Unmediated God is not God. Spirit is only what exists as inwardly free, by its own action, what posits itself. This self-contained and self-generated being involves the moment of negation. The negation of negation is the return into self, and spirit *is* what eternally reverts back into itself. For at this stage ˉmarked by the mingling [of spirit and nature]ˉ³⁵¹ the negative is represented as a manner of being that is outside the essence, as death, as evil—but an evil that is vanquished as Typhon. Spirit is what sublates negation, overcomes the death that appears as negation and the sphere of negation; by this victory the god is reestablished and, returning back constantly into himself in this way, he is spirit. A more exact definition is that the reborn god is simultaneously represented as deceased, as the god of the underworld; but it must

350. *Thus G with P; D reads:* natural death, this distinctive, specific form, must be represented, be known, in G, W read: so natural death is the distinctive, special form in which negation appears in regard to his shape. For the sake of the divine totality [W₁: and the higher religions, this moment must also W₂: the moment of his unmediated shape must also in the higher religions] be represented, be known, in regard to

351. *Thus P; G reads:* we encounter reconciliation, in such a way that

be noted that he is not only lord in the realm of Amenti[352] but also lord of the living, and in the former capacity he judges the dead by the standards of justice and morality. It is only in the category of subjective freedom that the *ethical* determination enters for the first time in any way; neither of them is to be found in the God of substantiality. Thus lordship here entails justice | and punishment; and the 272 *worth* of those individuals who determine their own lives by the standards of custom and right becomes evident. That is all that need be said in this regard.

We have now had the category of the subject that determines itself, that has rights and purposes, and further [noted] that with this objective realm the *development* of subjectivity also becomes apparent. Inasmuch as the characteristics that appear in subjectivity have now been posited as such, subjectivity is in the first instance distinct from nature, from the natural world, from individual human beings, and so on. To this extent a relationship of lordship has been grounded, but in this mingling [of nature and spirit] the subject is simultaneously represented as substance, and so has still the significance of substantiality. It is not distinguished from natural objects, but what pertains to the subject is at the same time the history of the substance. In the first instance, it is the history both of the subject and of the substance insofar as the substance is particularized. In other words, the subject is initially particular; the universal history (which is within one subject) is enacted in it, and what happens is at the same time the history of what is substantive and therefore the history of the substance. Inasmuch as substance is particularized, that subject also connotes the particularized objects, and its history is their history. Thus the history of the [divine] subject—his life, his battle against evil, his valiant deeds, his being momentarily conquered by evil—is also the universal history of natural objects.

352. [*Ed.*] See Plutarch, *De Iside et Osiride* 29, where Plutarch says that the Egyptians gave this name to the underworld where souls go after death. The Greek word Ἀμένθης (*Amenthēs*) is a Hellenized form of *Hnty-imntyer (Chonti-amentiu)*, meaning "the first of those in the West," i.e., lord of the dead, since "the West" was represented as the place of the dead. On the belief that Osiris (with Isis) was ruler of the underworld, see Plutarch, *De Iside et Osiride* 27. See also Herodotus, *Histories* 2.123: "According to the Egyptians, Demeter and Dionysus are rulers of the underworld" (Herodotus equates Dionysus with Osiris [2.144]).

Thus the history of God expressed in this stage, the stage that manifests itself in Egyptian religion, is, as we all know, the history of Osiris; it simultaneously connotes the history of the sun, of the Nile, and of the waxing and waning of the year. The Nile flows, then is dried up by the heat, or by Typhon; the sun, in its hostile phase, dries it up.[353] The sun goes far off, its force declines, and then it is born again after its going away; this is connected with the seasons. The story of the god similarly connotes the life of plants and sowing. What is sown in the earth dies and rots, but also rises again. Thus the history of the subject is also that of the substance in nature, and so it is the history of the natural objects that concern [humanity] and vice versa. | This subjective history expressly connotes natural ˉthings.ˉ[354] Each feature of the story here can be its meaning, or it may be the telling of the story itself. It can be said that the history of the sun or of the Nile forms the basis of the saga of the deity; but also conversely, what has been taken as [manifest] shape can also be taken as the inner [meaning], and we can say that the meaning is [either] nature [or] what is free, what is spiritual. All of these categories are here ˉunited into oneˉ[355] because there is no mediation between subject and substance—the one *is* the other. Because being-for-self and being-in-self are united in this way, the object, God, is all-encompassing, and what happens to him is the universal history. To this extent all moments are united in him. But conversely, in this intermingling, where subjectivity does not yet present itself freely, the opposite is the case too: these united moments are also presented in a fragmented form as figures of a particular kind and are represented separately as independent gods on their own account. So it is with the Egyptians. Osiris is only the principal god; in later days the other gods give way to him, though in earlier days they were his peers; as soon as thought becomes involved, he emerges as the principal figure. But the moments of intelligence united in him

273

---

353. [*Ed.*] Here, as in the other lecture series, Hegel refers less to the dualistic, astronomical significance of the Osiris myth than to its physical connotations, with Osiris symbolizing the irrigating, fructifying principle, while Typhon represents what dries up or consumes. See Plutarch, *De Iside et Osiride* 33.

354. *Thus D; P reads:* religion.

355. *Thus P; G reads:* entangled

are still to be found alongside him as diverse gods. And so we get a polytheism whose precise character is determined by a wide variety of circumstances—there are nature gods on the one hand, and local gods, which are totalities in themselves, on the other.

This one final point is needed to complete the subjective aspect of God. The divine shape is regarded as a totality, but the different moments also receive particular shapes of their own, and so become separate divinities. But for the totality to be complete, the principal god must be completely determined in his wholly external aspect. Hence he is outwardly a specific existence, determined in all directions. The particular god of a people or country exhibits in this external aspect his local origin and territorially limited concern. These are the principal points in this connection.

b. Cultus in the Form of Art[356]

But there is one other relationship to be mentioned, one of the most important. | At this stage God is first implicit power, ˉand secondly   274
a nature deity.ˉ[357] A third relationship still to be noted is that to self-consciousness, a relationship [that] embraces the cultus generally, ˉsince the cultus emerges only when God is characterized as subjective.ˉ[358] The distinctively novel relationship, however, is the standpoint of *art,* i.e., of *fine art.* This is the precise point where art must emerge in religion, and where it has a necessary role. Art, it is true, can also be mimetic, but not just mimetic. It *can* remain at that level, but then it is not *fine* art, not truly divine, not what is truly needed for religion; where it *is* that, where it *emerges* as it essentially *is,* it pertains to the very concept of God. We should

---

356. [*Ed.*] In Egytian religion, religious art appears for the first time, according to Hegel, and cultic activity assumes an artistic form. This is because God or the gods are represented as present in and as the work of art (the statue, icon, image, sacred figure, etc.). When the artwork has been consecrated, it becomes the bearer of divine spirit. This is a half-way spiritualization of religion, says Hegel, because the artifact has been produced by human being (subjective spirit) but is not yet the self-presentation of absolute or divine spirit. The religion of art reaches its consummation in Greek religion.

357. *Thus P; G reads:* possesses subjectivity.

358. *Thus P with D; G reads:* which has, in this mingling of the two spheres, the same content as the deity itself.

consider this connection more closely. Genuine art is religious art. This is not needed when the deity has a natural shape (for example, that of the sun, light, or a river); it is still not needed where the reality of God has human shape or the shape of a living animal; nor is it needed when the mode of manifestation is light, ˉnor when, as with Buddha, theˉ359 human shape has fallen away [i.e., he is dead] but still persists in the imagination, and hence ˉin the way that the divine shape is imagined.ˉ360 ˉIn the case of Buddha, the shape is only an imaginary one.ˉ361 The human shape, precisely in its aspect as the [actual] appearing of subjectivity, truly needs to be pictured for the first time only when God is defined as genuinely subject. The need to make the subject visible through art can arise only when | the moment of natural immediacy is overcome in the concept by the moment of freedom—or when the essence of God begins to be essentially free and self-determining, i.e., at the standpoint at which we now are. Since the mode of existent being is now determined by the inward [life], neither a purely natural shape nor a mere imitation of it will suffice any longer. Leaving aside the Jews and Islam, all nations have idols, but these do not belong to fine art; they are only362 signs of the subjectivity that is merely pictured or imagined, as long as subjectivity still has no being as an immanent characteristic of the essence itself. Religious representation has an external form, and it is essential to distinguish what is merely represented from what is known as pertaining to the essence of God. That God has become man occurs in the Hindu religion too; and all the moments or aspects that are present in the ultimate, truthful religion also occur in Hinduism. In the spirit[ual sphere] the totality is always present, but the difference lies in whether the different moments or aspects are regarded as pertaining to the essence or not.

As has been said, the need to portray God through fine art arises

275

359. *W (Var/HgG?) reads:* it begins when, as with Buddha, the present *Cf. Ho:* it is not needed where [religion] has God in natural shape—be it sun or light or river or unmediated human shape—any more than it enters on the scene where God is represented directly as shape, as with Buddha.

360. *Thus G; P reads:* in imagining in objective form.

361. *W (Var/HgG?) reads:* e.g., in images of Buddha, [W_1: and in the teachings of his followers. W_2: but also in the teachers, his followers.]

362. *W (1831) adds:* the personification of the representational picture,

only when the sphere of natural life is left behind, and when God is deemed to have being as free subjectivity by virtue of his spiritual self-determination, so that the way in which he manifests himself and becomes apparent in his determinate being is determined from within, by the spirit, and exhibits in itself the character of a spiritual production. It is not a mere natural appearance, not a mere sign.[363]

In regard to the emergence of art, two points in particular should be noted: first, that God is represented in art as something that can be intuited by the senses; second, that as a work of art the deity is something produced by human hands. Everyone knows that according to our own representational picture there are two ways [of being] that do not correspond to our idea of God. | The sensible manifestation, that which can be intuited, does not correspond to our idea of God—not, at least, where it is represented as though it were the only mode; for we well know, and we should take note, that God was once sensibly visible too; but that was only for a fleeting moment.[364] In the present case his sensible visibility is the universal mode, the only way in which God has being and is manifest for self-consciousness. The second point, that as a work of art God is produced by human agency, also does not fit our idea of God. We must now consider more fully how far both aspects are defective.

Here, then, art emerges, and this is bound up with the fact that God is comprehended as spiritual subjectivity. The nature of spirit is to produce itself, to posit itself, to give itself the form of determinate being; and this *is* quite generally what we have in art—not just universal representation but the fact that spirit appears, manifests itself, determines itself. Moreover, the mode of its existence is posited by spirit, it is an utterance that is posited by spirit itself, not by virtue of any contingent, natural aspect but a mode that corresponds wholly to thought. That the subject posits itself, manifests itself, determines itself, that its mode of existence is one posited by spirit—this is what is present in art generally.

363. *Ho adds, similar in W:* It is accordingly only when God himself is so characterized as to posit the distinctions under which he appears out of his own inwardness that art comes on the scene as necessary for the configuration of God.

364. *Ho, W add:* Art is also not the ultimate mode of our [own] cultus. But for the stage of subjectivity that is not yet spiritualized, and that therefore is still immediate, a directly visible existence [of God] is appropriate and necessary.

Thus the sensible [mode of] determinate being, in which the deity is intuited, corresponds to the concept of the deity; it is not a sign but gives expression at every point to the fact that it is produced from within, and corresponds fully to the thought or inner concept. But the essential ˉpointˉ[365] is that this determinate being is still a mode of sensible visibility. The determination that the universal should be defined in a differentiated manner is posited simply by the concept; but that this mode in which the subject posits itself is sensory—herein lies | the defect. And this defect arises from the fact that this is primitive subjectivity, the very first mode of the free spirit; it is still at the first level of defining, so that in this freedom there is still a natural, unmediated, primitive character, i.e., the moment of naturalness, of sensibility in general—it is born of spirit, to be sure, but it is still something sensory.

The second point is that the work of art is produced by human hands. ˉIn other words, the subject produces itself,ˉ[366] ˉbut what it produces is its own definition and at the same time has differentiated being—the abstract product is only "I equals I." What is posited must also haveˉ[367] the character of being differentiated, but in such a way that this is only posited, i.e., it is determined by subjectivity, or in such a way that the essence of subjectivity makes its appearance only in what is initially still something external. As we have seen, this is the first level of freedom; the next step is that the configuration produced in this way by the subject is taken back into subjectivity. The first stage is the creation of the world, the second is reconciliation, that this world is reconciled in itself with what is truly first. ˉIt is not yet the case that this [divine] shape itself transforms itself, returns to the first.ˉ[368] The shape of being for an other *is* produced,

365. *W (Ed/HgG?) reads:* deficiency

366. *W (Var/HgG?) reads:* This also does not fit our idea of God. *W continues (following G and Ho):* For the subjectivity that is infinite, genuinely spiritual, that has being for itself as such [*Ho:* as subjectivity]—this subjectivity produces itself, posits itself as other, as its shape,

367. *W₂ (Var) reads:* and it [the shape] is free only when self-posited and self-produced. But the configuration imparted to it, which is initially still reflected back into self as "I equals I," must also have expressly

368. *W (following G and Ho) reads:* But this return does not yet occur with the subjectivity we have at this stage; as its mode of being is still implicit, the fact that

but the idea is not yet present, for that involves the other's implicitly reflecting itself back to the initial unity, it implies that determinate being is not just implicitly something ideal, but that it raises itself to ideality, that ˉthe first unityˉ[369] | is sublated, precisely *in* what   278 is externalized.

This second part of the process involved in the divine idea is not yet posited here. From another angle it seems to be the first determination, which we consider both as purpose and as existent fact. When we consider it as purpose, then the first activity of subjectivity is admittedly purposive in general, but its purpose is a limited one; [for the subject is the god of] this people, [he is] this particular purpose. For the purpose to become a universal, truly absolute purpose, there must be a return; and in like manner the naturalness in regard to the shape must be sublated, in order for the purpose to be freed from its limitation, from this moment of immediacy. Only when this second stage in the process is added on, and the naturalness, the restrictedness of the purpose is sublated, is the idea properly satisfied; only thus does the purpose become for the first time universal. Thus what is posited here is in general that spirit is still, in respect of its purpose, only halfway to being spirit; and on that account it is still one-sided, it is still a finite spirit, i.e., it is in principle just subjective spirit, subjective self-consciousness, in other words just the *shape* of God, the mode of his being-for-other. The work of art is no more than something accomplished, something posited by the one-sided, subjective spirit. That is why the work of art must be produced by human means, for this process of spirit belongs to subjective consciousness; and it is why the artistic manifestation of the divine is at this stage necessarily a *human* artifact.[370]

According to his *true* idea, as self-consciousness that is in and for itself, God himself is spirit; he produces himself also, he presents

---

it is a subject falls outside itself into being-for-otherness. *Ho reads:* Because the mode of being of the subjectivity we have [at this stage] is implicit, the fact that it is subjectivity falls outside itself into being-for-otherness.

369. *P reads:* the first freedom *D reads:* externalization

370. *Ho, W add:* In the religion of absolute spirit, the shape of God is not made by human spirit.

himself as being for other—this is what we call his "Son," the configuration [he assumes]. In his own shape-taking, the other side of the process is at last present, when he distinguishes himself from the Son and *loves* the Son, positing himself as identical with him, but at the same time as distinct. The configuration—the aspect of determinate being—then appears as totality on its own account too, but as a configuration that is kept alive in love—here for the first time *spirit* is in and for itself.[371] | ⌐With art, spirit is still stuck at the halfway mark.⌐[372] This defect in art, the fact that the artifact, the god, is fashioned by human hands, is also recognized in these religions where this is the highest mode of manifestation; and an effort is made to offset the deficiency—but not objectively, only in a subjective way. It is recognized that the images of the gods must be consecrated. Everywhere from the Negroes to the Greeks[373] they were and are consecrated. In other words, the divine spirit is invested in the images by incantation. The ceremony comes from the consciousness or feeling of this deficiency, but the means by which it is offset is not objective, it is not contained in the idea itself, but ⌐is entirely subjective.⌐[374] ⌐The same is true of Catholic images; it is not, of course, the images that are themselves venerated; but ceremonies of reverence are carried out before them.⌐[375]

It is for these reasons that art necessarily emerges at this point; and the moments that we have pointed out are those by virtue of which God has being for others, by virtue of which he exists as work

279

---

371. *Ho adds, similar in W:* The Son's self-consciousness of himself is at the same time the knowledge of the Father, and in the Father the Son has knowledge of himself. But at the stage we are now considering, the determinate being [*Dasein*] of God as God is not a determinate being through him [the Son] but through what is other [*durch Anderes*].

372. *Thus G*

373. *Ho adds:* and right down to Proclus

[*Ed.*] If Hotho's version is correct, Hegel may have been referring to the report that Proclus was comprehensively initiated into the manifold ancient mysteries. See Marinus, *De vita Procli*, in Proclus, *In Platonis theologiam libri sex* (Frankfurt am Main, 1618), b2v–c5.

374. *W (HgG/1831?) reads:* impinges on it from outside.

375. *G, W read:* Even among Catholics this kind of consecration is to be found. *W continues:* e.g., of images, relics, etc. Cf. *Ho:* The same thing also happens in the case of Catholic images.

of art. ˉBut art does not yet emerge purely and freely as fine art.ˉ376 In this inversion it does make its entrance,377 but configurations that pertain to immediate nature and are not the creation of spirit retain just as much validity for self-consciousness—the sun, animals, and so forth remain valid shapes of God. What happens is rather that the artistic shape forces its way out of the animal, as we see in the image of the sphinx: ˉits body is animal, its countenance | 280 human,ˉ378 [so that it is] a mixture of the artistic and the animal shapes.379 The artistic shape is accordingly not yet in and for itself the shape of *beauty,* but involves a greater or lesser degree of imitation and distortion. What is universal in this sphere is the inter- mingling of subjectivity and substantiality.

The next advance consists in the emergence of the free form of subjectivity, consciousness of the divine as characterized by free subjectivity, in unadulterated form on its own account, inasmuch as such emergence is possible, that is, at the first level of free spirituality. But that this first level is known solely on its own account, that the divine is defined on its own account as subjectivity—this purification of the subject from the merely natural sphere and from mere substantiality is already expressed in the stage we have been considering. The subject is exclusive; the principle of freedom or of infinite negativity inheres in the subject generally; the natural, by contrast, is [just] the contingent form. In its content the principle of subjectivity is in and for itself universal; it lets nothing subsist alongside it that is merely natural, devoid of spirit, nor yet anything that is purely substantive, inwardly devoid of form. ˉThe principle of subjectivity will not tolerate empty, massive, indeter- minate substantiality beside it, norˉ380 the form that is not free, i.e., the form of the external natural state. This is the point of transition.

376. *G reads:* But here art is not yet free and pure. *Ho, W continue:* and is still in process of passing over to fine art.

377. [*Ed.*] *Sie tritt in dieser Verkehrung auf.* Hegel probably means the inversion of creative roles between nature and self-consciousness.

378. *Thus P; D reads:* approximating to art, to idealization

379. *Ho, W add:* A human countenance confronts us from an animal body; subjectivity is not yet translucent to itself.

380. *W2 (Var) reads:* Subjectivity is infinite form, and as such will not tolerate beside it, any more than empty, massive, indeterminate substantiality,

The basic characteristic therefore is that God is known as *freely self-determining,* still, it is true, in formal fashion only at this level, but nonetheless already inwardly free. And we can recognize this emergence[381] [of free subjectivity] in particular religions, and in the peoples among whom they are found, mainly by whether the peoples in question have *universal* laws, laws of *freedom,* and whether legal right and ethical custom are the fundamental controlling categories of their way of life. For when we say that God is known as subjectivity, i.e., that he is what is self-determining, and that | the modes of his self-determination constitute the laws of freedom, in other words the categories of self-determination, or that this form of free self-determining is made the content, which ⁻in turn means⁻[382] that the laws have freedom as their content—when this occurs, the natural state retires into the background and we see purposes emerging that are inwardly universal, even though they may still appear outwardly to be quite insignificant. ⁻Insofar as practical activity is ethical, it has as its principle universality, self-determination, freedom.⁻[383]

With this we advance out of [the sphere of] nature religion to gods who are essentially the founders of states, of marriage, of peaceful society, the progenitors of the arts, the gods who[384] bring forth and safeguard legal right and ethical life.[385]

Our progress to this point has been as follows. We began in the religion of magic with desire or appetite, and with the lordship and power of desire over nature, according to merely singular volition that is not determined by thought. The second stage was the theoretical definition of the independence of objectivity, in which all the different moments or aspects were left free and unconstrained,

---

381. W₂ *(Var) adds:* of free subjectivity

382. W₂ *(Var) reads:* then is necessarily connected with the fact

383. W₂ *(MiscP/Var?) reads:* or are not yet universal in scope, in the same way as ethical human beings may, in terms of the content of their actions generally, encompass an exceedingly small scope, and yet at the same time be inwardly ethical. W *continues, following Ho:* The brighter sun of the spirit causes the natural light to pale.

384. W *(1831) adds:* govern oracles and states, and

385. [*Ed.*] That is, the gods of Greek religion. The text contained in this paragraph and the preceding one is transposed by the *Werke* to the beginning of the next section, forming part of the "transition" to the religion of spiritual individuality.

so that they acquired independent status. The third stage is where this theoretical, independent element, this independence, is wholly abstract, and gathers up the free-ranging moments within itself again, so that conversely the practical is made theoretical; here we have the good, or self-determination in general. The fourth stage is then the intermingling of substantiality and subjectivity. | 282

B. THE RELIGIONS OF SPIRITUAL INDIVIDUALITY[386]

Introduction

a. Division of the Subject

Here in the second sphere of determinate religion we have the religion of sublimity, that of beauty, and then, as the transitional stage, the religion of singularized expediency.

If we consider this more closely in relation to how the idea of God has determined itself (i.e., to what we know of God), [we see that] the general idea of God is contained in what has gone before. [If we now ask] on the basis of what has gone before what God is, what cognitive knowledge we have of him, then the answer, according to the abstract form of the metaphysical concept, is as follows:

---

386. [*Ed.*] This heading is found in *G*; *D* reads "subjectivity" instead of "individuality." The religions of "spiritual individuality" properly include only Jewish and Greek religion, since the Roman gods are in fact not spiritual individualities or subjectivities. An inner tension occurs at this point in the organization of the 1824 lectures. At the beginning of Part II, Hegel makes it clear that the "religion of expediency" is a third, distinctive form of determinate religion; at the beginning of Sec. B, he refers to it as "transitional" between the religions of spiritual individuality and the religion of absolute spirit (Christianity); but then, when he sets forth the "division of the subject," he incorporates it as the third form of spiritual individuality. This permits him to argue that the religions of spiritual individuality correspond to three forms of nature religion "in inverse order," Jewish religion corresponding to Persian, Greek religion to Hinduism, and Roman religion to the religion of China. While an intriguing proposal, this obscures the basic threefold schema internal to *Determinate Religion*—a schema with which Hegel appears to have *begun* in 1824, modifying it, however, as he went along. In the modified version, Christianity (Part III of the lectures) becomes the third moment in the dialectic of the religions.

We have seen according to the abstract, relative way of defining him that God is the unity of the infinite and the finite, and the sole point of concern is to see how ˉdeterminacy, or finitude,ˉ[387] has been taken up into the infinite. Well then, what has happened in this regard so far? Following our definition, we say that God *is* the infinite generally; he is what is substantive, what is identical with self, the substantive power; and when we say this, we do not, to begin with, posit finitude as contained within it. Finitude is initially the wholly unmediated existence of the infinite, i.e., self-consciousness. The consciousness that this is what God is—infinity, the substantive power—springs from and is based upon the very fact that the truth of all finite things consists in their returning to the substantive unity, and the substantive power alone is their truth. To begin with, therefore, God is this substantive power—a definition whose utter abstractness makes it highly imperfect. The finite is a category that has to be incorporated into the infinite. So the second definition is that God is the self-contained substantive power, having being strictly on its own account as distinct from the multiplicity of the finite; this is substantiality reflected-into-itself—the fact that God is not merely substantiality in general but self-contained substantiality, which distinguishes itself from the finite. This affords a higher plane to build on; but the category of the finite | still does not have here its genuine relationship to the substantive power, such that the substantive power itself would be the infinite. This self-contained substantiality is now Brahman, and the subsistent finite is the multitude of gods. In the third stage, the finite is posited as identical with substantiality in such a way as to be equal in scope, while the pure, universal form exists as substantiality itself; this then is God as the good.

The basic characteristic of the new sphere is *subjectivity* in general. Initially this too is still formal. We have now to see more precisely what moments it contains. Spiritual subjectivity is the wholly free power of self-determination, i.e., the self-definition that is nothing, has no content other than the concept; it contains nothing but itself.

283

---

387. G *reads:* the particularity of the finite W₂ (*Var*) *reads:* particularity and determinacy, i.e., the finite,

This self-determining, this content, can be just as universal or as infinite as is power as such. And if we ask what we call it when universal power is active in the self-consciousness, it is what we call *wisdom*. Inasmuch as we are now at the level of spiritual subjectivity, we are at the level of self-determination, or of *purpose;* and these purposes or modes of self-determination are as universal as power. Hence a purpose of this kind is a wise purpose. The category of purpose is immediately involved in the concept of free subjectivity. Action for a purpose, expedient action, is an inner self-determination, i.e., it is determination through freedom or by the act of the subject; for there *is* nothing within it except the subject itself. Moreover, this self-determination is ˥infinite˥[388] power, and consequently it is achieved in external existence. Natural being is no longer valid in its immediacy. It belongs to power, and is for power something merely transparent, not valid. Insofar as the power externalizes itself—and it must do so, it must pass over into existence, subjectivity must endow itself with reality—this existence is no longer something independent, but is only the free self-determination of power, achieved in the process of realization, in this external existence, or in what appears as the natural state. Hence purposive action has no outcome save what is already there. The inner determination | is achieved, since what it is achieved in is natural, immediate existence. Such existence, however, is powerless against the purpose, being just the form or mode in which purpose is present outwardly, while the purpose is the inner aspect of all such immediate existence.   284

At this point, therefore, we are in the sphere of subjectivity, the sphere of purpose in general; and purposive action is wise action inasmuch as wisdom consists in acting in conformity with universal purposes that are valid in and of themselves. Nor does there seem to be any other kind of purpose yet in view, for what we have here is free, self-determining subjectivity. This wisdom, however, is initially still too indeterminate.

In fact, the *general* concept here is that of subjectivity, and hence of the power that simultaneously acts in accord with purposes,

388. *Thus P; D reads:* unmediated

operates, presents itself. Subjectivity is active; and what is needed is that the purpose should be wise, i.e., identical with the unlimited power that determines it.

The first point to be considered, then, is the relationship of this subjectivity to what appears as nature, to natural things, or, more precisely, to what we have previously called substantiality, the power that has being only implicitly. Merely implicit power remains something natural, but subjectivity is explicit power, as distinct from implicit power and its mode of reality. This implicit power is nature, the natural world, which is now demoted for explicit power to the rank of something dependent, more precisely to that of a means. ˉProperˉ[389] self-subsistence is taken away from natural things: [previously] they participated directly, so to speak, in substance, but now, at the level of ˉsubjective power,ˉ[390] they are downgraded to dependence, they have lost their substantive being, their being-in-themselves, and at the same time they are posited solely as negative. In this way the unity of subjective power is distinct from them, external to them, and we therefore have to comprehend them as means in relation to a purpose, or as modes that no longer have being but serve only for appearing; even if they are not defined as means, they are the soil in which things appear and are subordinated to what

285 *does* so appear. Their role is no longer | to exhibit themselves immediately but to display something higher that is implicit in them, namely free subjectivity. This is the definition we must have in mind in regard to what is differentiated from subjectivity.

The second point to be noted concerns a more specific definition of wisdom. As regards its purpose, wisdom is initially indeterminate. We do not yet know in what it consists, what the purposes of this power are, and have not yet got beyond this vague talk about the wisdom of God. God is wise, but what are his ways, his purposes? That is something wholly indeterminate. For us to be able to say what wisdom consists in, his purposes would have to be plain to us already in his determinacy, i.e., in his development into a pattern of distinct moments. Initially, however, we have here only purposive determination in general, i.e., indeterminate wisdom.

---

389. *Thus G; P reads:* Distinctive [*Canceled:* Proper]
390. *Thus G; P reads:* self-subsisting power,

Third, because God is real without qualification, we cannot rest content with this indeterminacy of his wisdom; on the contrary, his purposes also must be determinate. He is in principle one who appears, he is a subject who acts, i.e., he crosses over into existence, into actuality. Previously ⁻reality was merely immediate, for instance sun, mountain, river, etc.⁻[391] But at this stage it is also necessary that God should *be there,* i.e., that his purpose should be ⁻an actual⁻[392] purpose, and for that very reason a determinate purpose.

In regard to the reality of the purpose, two kinds of questions arise. First, on what soil can this purpose be accomplished, where can it be present? As an inward purpose, it would be a mere thought or representation, but as ⁻absolute⁻[393] power God is not mere thought, mere volition, intention, etc. On the contrary, he is action without any mediation. The soil on which the purpose is made real or actualized is none other than self-consciousness, | or what we call   286 finite spirit. Purpose *is* determination; but at this stage we have only abstract modes of determination, not developed ones.

Thus the soil of the divine purpose is self-consciousness or finite spirit. The second problem is that since we have only just embarked on the process of defining or characterizing wisdom, we still have no specific content for what it means to be wise; purpose is still posited in the concept of God in an ill-defined, indeterminate fashion. This is the first stage; the next stage is that the purpose must be actualized or realized. But as actual purpose it must be determinate; its determinate character, however, is not yet developed, the process of determination as such or the development has itself not yet been posited in the divine essence. The determinate character is therefore finite and external; it is a particular, contingent purpose. As an existent purpose it is not determined by the divine concept, but is determinate only so that it may be actual—i.e., it is merely contingent, a wholly limited purpose; in other words, the content of the purpose is not defined by the divine concept, it is a purpose

391. *Thus G;* W₂ *(following G and Ho) reads:* the unity of finitude and infinitude was merely immediate; thus it was the first and best finite—sun, mountain, river, etc.—and reality was immediate. *Ho reads:* we had an immediate unity of finitude and infinitude; thus the actuality of God was the first and best immediate natural being.
392. *Thus P; G reads:* a natural
393. *Thus P; G reads:* subjective

that differs from the divine concept itself, it is not the purpose that is in and of itself divine, the purpose that, once developed, would stand on its own and would in its determinacy express the divine concept. It is accordingly a contingent purpose.

In the nature religion of Persia we encountered the good, but there the good still had the meaning of substantive, immediate identity with essence, so that all things were good and filled with light. Here, on the contrary, we are characterizing the subject, the power that stands on its own, that has being on its own account. Here purpose is distinct from concept, the determinations [of the concept] are diverse; and this diversity of the purpose is for that very reason devoid of concept, its determinacy is merely contingent, because diversity is not yet taken back into the divine concept, not yet equated with it. So here we have only purposes that are finite in content. The soil of the divine purpose is thus essentially self-consciousness, but it is finite spirit as such, in its finitude; [hence] it is contaminated with the abstract, the finite, and thus with the contingent. For the purpose is initially contingent, it does not yet match the divine concept, and finite self-consciousness is initially the plane on which it is realized.

287 Such are in general the basic characteristics of the standpoint | we are presently considering, and we must now indicate how it is to be divided for more precise consideration.

On the one side we have self-contained power and abstract wisdom, and on the other, as we have shown, contingent, finite purposes. [Then] the two are joined together; wisdom is unlimited, but for that reason indeterminate, and consequently purpose, as realized, is contingent and finite. ⁻The division[394] that we have to make concerns the determinate character of purpose. In other words,⁻[395] the main question is, what is wisdom, what is purpose ([since it is] a purpose that is not equal to the power)?

394. [Ed.] In the preceding two sentences Hegel summarizes the three religions of spiritual individuality: Jewish religion (as here described) is the religion of self-contained power and abstract wisdom; Greek religion is the religion of finite purposes; while Roman religion combines indeterminate wisdom and contingent purpose. These three are epitomized more fully in the next three paragraphs.

395. Ho, W read: The mediation of the two sides to form a concrete unity, in such a way that the concept of wisdom is itself the concept of its purpose, is what constitutes the transition to the higher stage.

1. ¯First, then, we have a subjectivity of power. This pure subjectivity¯³⁹⁶ is not accessible to the senses. The natural, the immediate, is negated in it; it cannot be sensed, but is solely for spirit, for thought. This power that has being on its own account, is essentially One. ¯What we have termed "reality"¯³⁹⁷ is purely something posited and negated; it coincides with being-for-self, there is in it no plurality, no one and the other. Thus [God] is One, simply and exclusively; he has no other beside him, he will not tolerate anything that possesses autonomy. This One it is then who is wise, and his wisdom is universal wisdom. By him is everything posited, but for him it is merely something external, accidental: this is the *sublimity* of the One, of this power and this wisdom. The second thing is that just as this power is infinitely self-contained, actualizes itself, takes on existence, infinitely, and is self-consciousness as being for an other infinitely, so its purpose too is only one. But it is³⁹⁸ a limited purpose, one that is not yet determined by wisdom and is therefore an infinitely limited purpose. The two [moments] correspond, the infinity of the power and the limitedness of the actual purpose: on the one side sublimity and | on the other side its contrary, the sublimity of the negative,³⁹⁹ ¯which has just as much alongside it as ever, but harbors the pretension of being the one and only [God].¯⁴⁰⁰ This is the first form to be considered in regard to purpose.

2. The second form is that this purpose is not just one but raises itself up above this limitedness of the one purpose. Thus there are many purposes, the infinitely limited purpose being raised up to many. Here the real purpose is the purpose that is full of content. It is no longer exclusive, but is serene and tolerant; it recognizes a multiplicity [of gods or peoples] as valid alongside it. These purposes

288

396. *Thus G with P and D; G reads:* We have subjectivity, we have power, and this W₁ *(Ed) reads:* The subjectivity that can have power W₂ *(Var) reads:* The subjectivity that is inwardly power

397. *Thus G; D reads:* What we have termed the natural P *reads:* What we have seen appearing W₂ *(Var) reads:* What we have termed reality, namely, nature,

398. W₂ *(Var) adds:* the very opposite of sublime, it is

399. *D adds:* sublimity and hate, *Cf. Ho:* For sublimity is only the unity of the negative, of being hated.

400. *Thus P; G reads:* infinite limitation, constraint. *Ho, W read:* The One has infinite [existence] alongside it, but harbors the pretension of being the One.

are spiritually defined; they are self-determined. There are many of these subjectivities that are valid alongside one another, many of these unities ˉto which the manifold variety of existence in the finite world and its resources are relevant.ˉ[401] It is precisely thus that the friendliness of the subject with existence is established, by seeing that there are many particular purposes. This plurality of the particular does not scorn to present itself in immediate existence. Plurality, the particular subtype, simultaneously has universality within it. It is not simply exclusive like the One. Inasmuch as the purpose lets [other] particular subtypes subsist validly alongside it, it is in principle amicably disposed to particularity; the purpose itself appears in its means—as a particular purpose it lets the means subsist validly alongside itself and deigns to appear in it. This is where the category of *beauty* comes in. The beautiful is something particular; it is a purpose in itself that is amicably disposed to immediate existence; it asserts only its own validity, to be sure, but it also allows validity to the affirmation of immediate existence and makes this determinate [form] of existence into its own appearance. This signals the disappearance of the One. Power is selfless subjectivity, and subjectivity is no longer absolute power. The universal hovers above particularity in lonely state as a power that is neither subject nor wise | but intrinsically indeterminate; this then is *fate,* the cold necessity lacking all determinateness that hovers above what is beautiful.

289

3. Third, we have a finite, particular purpose once more,[402] but one that has been enlarged to universal scope.[403] Initially, however, the universality is empirically external; it is not the genuine universality of the concept, ˉbut a purposeˉ[404] that encompasses the world and all who dwell in it and that, being expanded to universality,

---

401. *Thus G with P and D; G reads:* to which the world of existence and its resources are relevant. W_2 *reads:* from which existence derives its resources. *Ho reads:* through which existence is what it is.

402. *W (following Ho) adds:* which in its particularity aspires to universality, *Ho reads:* Now the third [form], as opposed to the abstract unity and the abstract particularity of purpose, is where the particularity aspires to abstract unity, and the unity, on its side, fills itself out with particularity.

403. W_1 *(following Ho, as given in preceding note) adds:* and so fills itself out with particularity.

404. *Thus W (Ed/HgG?)*

promptly loses all determinacy and has for its goal cold, absolute, abstract power, with the result that it has on its own account no purpose at all.

In external existence these three moments are the Jewish, the Greek, and the Roman religions. Power as subjectivity defines itself as wisdom with a purpose; initially the purpose is still indeterminate; then particular purposes come into being, and the unity is distinct from them; finally, the purpose is at the same time empirically universal.

These religions correspond in inverse order to those we have already considered. The Jewish religion corresponds to the Persian, the distinguishing factor in both being that at this standpoint determinacy ˉlies within; the essence is intrinsically, universally concrete. The determinacy is a purpose that exists on its own account.ˉ405 In the preceding religions the mode of determinacy was a natural one. In the Persian religion it was light, something that is itself universal, simple, and physical: as we left the realm of the natural behind, this was the last thing to be encompassed in a unity like that of thought; here particularity is simple—an abstract purpose or power that is just wisdom and that is all. At the second standpoint we have many particular purposes, many subjectivities, and one power over them; this corresponds to the many natural realities that we had in Hinduism, | with Brahman above them, as the thought   290 that thinks itself. At the third standpoint we have an empirically universal purpose, which is really self-contained. It isˉfate,ˉ406 not true subjectivity; corresponding to this we had power as the singular natural self-consciousness, ˉan empirically universal purpose.ˉ407 The first mode of natural [spirit] is the single self-consciousness, in the natural state; the natural as single is what is present and defined [i.e., defines itself] as self-consciousness. Here, therefore, the order

---

405. *Thus P with G, similar in D; G reads:* lies within; the essence itself is the goal of self-determination W_2 *(Var) reads:* of essence, which is the goal of self-determination, lies within. Previously, however,

406. *Ho, W read:* selfless, [W: all-]destroying fate,

407. *Ho reads, similar in W:* Similarly, at the Chinese [standpoint] an individual presents himself to us as the unqualifiedly universal, as what determines everything, as God.

is the reverse of that found in natural religion: here the first thing is the subject, the thought that is inwardly concrete—a simple ⁻determinacy, which we then unfold; previously the first thing was the natural, manifold existence, which [gradually] withdrew into the simple naturalness of light.⁻⁴⁰⁸

b. The Metaphysical Concept of God: Cosmological and Teleological Proofs[409]

Next we have to consider the metaphysical concept of this sphere, the pure abstract thought-category upon which it is based; in doing so, however, we must abstract ⁻from representation. What we want to consider, therefore, is what is purely abstract, and the connection in which we have to deal with it is precisely the form in which this metaphysical concept has occurred as a proof for the existence of God.⁻⁴¹⁰ That is how the metaphysical concept determines itself

408. W₂ (Var) reads: subjectivity, which then proceeds to determination within itself, whereas in nature religion the starting point was the natural, immediate self-consciousness, unity being finally achieved in the intuition of light.

409. [Ed.] This lengthy discussion of the proofs of the existence of God, as related to the metaphysical concepts of God found in Jewish, Greek, and Roman religion, draws together and greatly expands the Ms. treatment of the cosmological proofs as related to the religions of sublimity and beauty (Ms. Sec. B.a), and of the teleological proof as related to the religion of expediency (Ms. Sec. C.a). Hegel does this because Jewish, Greek, and Roman religion are now considered in a single section, and because the metaphysical concepts associated with these religions—unity, necessity, and purposiveness—are in fact interrelated. Thus these proofs cannot simply be identified with one or another of these religions. Hegel seems to distinguish three forms of the cosmological proof: the argument from finite to infinite (associated with the religions of nature [Sec. A Intro. b.], the argument from the many to the one, and the argument from contingency to necessity. But he considers only one form of the teleological proof, the "physicotheological proof" (see n. 484); he does not examine the argument based on *moral* teleology, i.e., the argument that God is a necessary postulate of practical reason, which Kant regarded as the only genuine proof. The reason perhaps is that Hegel did not find this proof concretely represented in any of the religions, and was in any case unpersuaded by Kant's reduction of religion to a category of morality. In Hegel's view, the only genuine proof is the ontological proof, which is implicit in the Christian concept of God as absolute, self-mediating spirit. But the cosmological and teleological proofs are not simply false; they contain both valid and defective elements, which Hegel's account is designed to elicit.

410. *Thus P; G reads:* from the representation of spirit, of universal spirit, and also from the necessity of realizing the concept, the kind of essential realization that does not pertain to representation but is necessitated by the concept. What we have here is the metaphysical concept in relation to the form of proofs of God's existence.

now in contrast with the metaphysical concept for the foregoing sphere (which was the unity of finite and | infinite).[411] At that stage 291 infinity was absolute negativity, implicit power, and the thought that was the essence of the first sphere limited itself to this category of the infinity of implicit power. In that sphere the concept was for us, to be sure, the unity of the finite and infinite. But[412] the essence was defined solely as the infinite; the infinite is the basis, and the finite merely accrues to it. It is for this reason, as we have seen, that the sphere was characterized in natural terms; it was the sphere of natural religion, because the form needed some natural existence for its own determinate being. For us the infinite is itself the unity of the finite and the infinite; but in religion it is only the infinite that is defined, and the finite merely accrues to it, as the natural realm. Now, however, essence is itself characterized as unity of the finite and infinite, or as *real* power, as genuine, absolute negativity. The divine essence is inwardly concrete infinity, i.e., [it subsists] as the unity of the finite and infinite.

This, then, is what we have observed in the category of wisdom;[413] wisdom is inwardly self-determining power, and this process of determining is the finite side. In this way, therefore, the divine is known not as mere infinitude but as inwardly determining [itself] as wise; it is inwardly concrete, internally infinite form; this form is the side of the implicitly finite, but in this unity of the infinite it is itself posited here as infinitude. Because the categorization in terms of pure thought accordingly belongs to the definition of the essence itself, it follows that any advance in definition no longer falls merely on the natural side but is within the essence itself. The three stages of religion we have here adduced constitute an advance within the metaphysical concept itself; they are moments in the essence, distinct shapes that the concept assumes for religious self-consciousness at this standpoint. Previously there was progress only in the outward shape; here the progress is an elaboration of the concept itself.[414] In consequence

411. [*Ed.*] See above, pp. 250–266.
412. W_2 *(Var) adds:* for this stage itself
413. [*Ed.*] See above, p. 386.
414. *Ho adds, similar in W:* It is now essence on its own account, and the distinctions are accordingly its own reflection-into-itself.

292   we have here not just one metaphysical concept | but three: the first is unity, or the One; the second is necessity; and the third is purposiveness, finite, external purposiveness.

1. First, then, there is unity, absolute power, absolute negativity, negativity that is posited as reflected into self, that has being absolutely on its own account, absolute subjectivity, in such a way that the sensible is utterly and immediately wiped out in this essence; it is power that subsists on its own, infinite negativity; it tolerates nothing sensible, for what pertains to the senses is the finite, not yet taken up and sublated in the infinite—whereas here it is sublated. This subjectivity that subsists on its own account is what we have expressed as "the One."

2. The second concept is that of necessity. The One is just this absolute power; everything is posited in him, but negatively. This is the concept of the One. But when we speak in this way, no development is posited. The One is just the form of simplicity of that which we have observed; necessity is merely the process of the One itself, it is unity as inward motion. Therefore, it is no longer the One, but is self-contained oneness. The movement that constitutes the concept is oneness, absolute necessity.

3. The third [moment] is then purposiveness. For absolute necessity there is posited the movement that the One implicitly is, its process, and this process is the process of contingent things. If we consider what is posited and negated, they are contingent things. In necessity there is only[415] the coming and going of these contingent things, but it must also be posited that they have being and make their appearance quite distinct from necessity itself, distinct from this their unity, their process of necessity itself; they must[416] appear as subsisting, yet at the same time as belonging to the power whose control they never leave. Hence they are *means,* and unity consists in self-maintenance within this process of contingent things, self-production in these means. Unity is necessity itself, but it is posited

293   as distinct from what is in | motion within it, and at the same time

415. W₂ (*Var*) *adds:* the passing,
416. W₂ (*Var*) *adds:* at least momentarily

maintains itself therein; it has these subsisting things merely as a negative; in this way it becomes purpose in general.[417]

When we say that these are the three metaphysical concepts pertaining to the three religions, it must not be supposed that each of them pertains only to one religion.[418] Each of them pertains rather to all three religions; the sole difference is ˜which of these characteristics of the object [of religion]˜[419] counts as the essence, whether it be the One or necessity or power with its purposes, power conforming to a purpose, i.e., with a real purpose. The difference is then which of the three counts as essential, as the basic characteristic of the essence, in defining the religion in question.

What we now have to consider more closely is the form in which these defining marks have taken on the shape of proofs of God's existence, in other words [how they appear] in the mode of mediation.

1. As regards the concept of *the One,* it must be noted that we are not dealing here with the proposition that God is only One. In that proposition "One" is only a predicate of God, or one of his characteristics; we have "God" as subject and "One" as predicate, but he may also have other predicates. It is in fact a simple matter to show | that he has this one predicate, a purely logical matter turning solely on the quite impoverished categories of one and

294

417. *W adds:* These three moments are accordingly related as follows. *W continues, following Ho, which reads:* Since the essence is absolute negativity, it is pure identity with self, the One. Second, it is the negativity of this unity, which is, however, related to the unity and through this mutual interpenetration reveals itself as necessity. Third, the One turns back from its differentiated development as something involving relation in order to close [again] with itself; but this [regained] unity, as the collapse of form into itself, has a finite content, and as it develops this content into distinctions of form (as a totality), it yields the concept of purposiveness, but *finite* purposiveness [or expediency].

418. *W₂ (MiscP?) adds:* Where One is the essence, there is also necessity, but only implicitly, not in the determination of the One. Similarly the One determines himself according to purposes because he is wise. Necessity is also One, and expediency is also present here, though it falls outside necessity. If expediency is the basic category, then the purposes are also imbued with power, and the purpose itself is fate (*Fatum*).

419. *Thus G; P reads:* which in regard to which of these characteristics of what is objective *D reads:* in regard to which characteristic subjectivity

many.[420] It is an ancient dictum, which we find already in Greek sources, that only the One is, and not the many;[421] and if it has to be said that where one is, there is also many, nonetheless the One is what maintains itself, what has power over the many. [422]That there is only one God does not belong here, for that mode of procedure does not fit into the pure speculative form. God is the subject; to demonstrate predicates of God is the concern of reflection, not of the concept; there is no philosophical cognition of God along that path. Anyway that is not the sense of this concept; the true sense— inasmuch as we are here discussing the One—is that the One *is God,* in such a way that the One exhausts the whole essence of God. It is not [just] one characteristic alongside [any] other, but properly characterizes God's essence itself. Thus it is a characteristic that fulfills the essence in the sense of absolute power as subjectivity, or as reflected into self.[423] As for the form in which this concept could be portrayed as mediation, or in which it would appear as a proof of the existence of God, the situation is that this concept is not suited for the purpose. For the basis from which we are starting here in order to arrive at the characteristic "oneness" is the infinite as we have so far seen it, absolute power, absolute negativity. "The One" is only the added characteristic that this is the subject reflected into self, that which has being on its own account, in which everything sensible is sublated. It is only, as it were, within implicit being that there is movement in respect of the infinite; thus there is no media- tion in the [divine] shape, as we still have to consider it here. Certainly we can say that there is a progress from the infinite to self-determined

420. [*Ed.*] See Hegel, *Science of Logic,* pp. 164–169 (cf. *GW* 11:92-97).

421. [*Ed.*] Hegel is referring to Plato, *Parmenides* 159b–d, where Socrates dis- cusses the relationship between "the One" and "the others," and finally leads his interlocutor to agree that the others are not many. "For if they were many, the One would be each of them as part of the whole. So the others, as one, are neither one nor many, neither a whole nor parts, since they in no way have anything of the One in them."

422. *Precedes in* W_1 (*Ed*): To prove

423. *Ho adds, similar in W:* But speculatively "the One" is not a predicate of God as something subjective that has been [merely] hit upon; rather God is himself this movement of the subject out from itself and back to itself, its self-determination as the One, in such a way that subject and predicate are the same, each moving into the other, and that nothing remains interposed between them.

subjectivity; but the terminus a quo that is first in | this process is 295
the infinite, and this infinite ˉis a thought, it is absolute negativ-
ity.ˉ⁴²⁴ If we wished to consider the mediation in more detail, we
would begin from a thought, namely, the concept in and for itself
grasped as a thought, from which we proceeded to the other term.⁴²⁵
But at this point it is not yet the case that we have to start from the
concept, for the form of mediation in which the concept is taken
as starting point yields another proof of the existence of God, one
proper to Christianity, not to this religion.⁴²⁶ "The One" is not yet
posited as concept, does not occur for us as concept; the true or what
is concretely posited within itself, as [we find it] in the Christian
religion, is not yet present at this stage.

2. The second characteristic is that of *necessity*. Necessity is what
is itself posited as mediation; consequently there is here a mediation
for self-consciousness. Necessity is movement, or implicit process,
it is the fact that the things of the world are contingent, and that
this contingency implicitly sublates itself to necessity. Now, therefore,
inasmuch as the absolute essence is ˉposited and reveredˉ⁴²⁷ in a
religion as necessity, this same process is present here by which
necessity is constituted. It might seem as though we had already
witnessed this transition in the advance from finite to infinite⁴²⁸—the
truth of the finite was the infinite, [i.e., it was] the sublation of the
finite in itself to the infinite; it might seem that the contingent is that
same starting point and that the contingent reverts to necessity. ⁴²⁹It
seems to make no essential difference whether we define the advance
as from finite to infinite or from contingent to necessary. And in
fact both are defined basically in the same way, ˉbut here the content is at leastˉ⁴³⁰ more concrete than it was with the earlier form

424. W_2 *(Var) reads:* as absolute negativity is the subject reflecting-into-self, in
which every manifold is sublated.
425. W_2 *(Var) adds:* to being.
426. [*Ed.*] That is, the ontological proof; see Vol. 3:65–73, 173–184, 351–357,
360–361.
427. *Thus P; G reads:* intuited, known, and revered *D reads:* posited
428. [*Ed.*] See above, pp. 254–266.
429. *Precedes in* W_2 *(Var):* In regard to the advance
430. W_2 *(Var) reads:* so this is on the one hand correct; on the other hand the
difference is

296   of the process. The difference is as follows. | If we start from the finite, we may call it the finite, but the initial point of departure is that it is valid, that we let the finite count as subsisting. It exists, it is valid. In other words, we take the finite initially in an affirmative, positive form. Admittedly its end lies within it, but it is initially posited in the form of the affirmative, or of unmediated being. The contingent, on the other hand, is already more concrete; it may exist or it may not; the contingent is the actual that is just as well possibility, whose being has the value of nonbeing. Thus in the contingent its own negation is posited, and as the contingent both is and is nothing, it is a transition from being to nothing; ⁻like the infinite it is intrinsically negative,⁻⁴³¹ but since it is also nonbeing it is also the transition from nonbeing to being. So the category of contingency is much richer and more concrete than that of the finite. When it is developed, the subjectivity of the One becomes necessity. The contingent is, it has existence, but its existence has at the same time the value of possibility. The truth of the contingent existence is necessity; this is a determinate being that is mediated with itself through its nonexistence. Actuality is this sort of determinate being, where the process is wholly self-contained and closed, a determinate being that coincides with itself through itself.⁴³²

We have to distinguish the inner form of necessity from the external form.

External necessity is properly a contingent necessity. If an effect is dependent on causes, it is necessary; when these or those particular circumstances coincide, then this or that particular outcome must follow. But in this instance the circumstances under which the outcome follows obtain immediately; and since at this standpoint immediate being counts as having only the value of possibility, the conditioning causes are indeterminate, they are such as may equally well obtain or not. Hence the necessity is relative, it relates to the initiating circumstances, which just happen to be so, immediately and contingently. This is purely external necessity, whose value is no greater than that of contingency. One can, it is true, prove that

431. *Thus G; D reads:* like the finite into the infinite,
432. [*Ed.*] See *Science of Logic,* pp. 541 ff. (*GW* 11:380 ff.).

under certain circumstances something necessarily occurs, but these
| circumstances are always contingent, they may or may not obtain.   297
¯A tile falls off the roof and kills someone; the fact that the tile falls
and someone is underneath may be the case or not, it is contingent.¯433 In this external necessity it is only the result that is
necessary; the circumstances, on the other hand, are contingent. The
conditioning causes and the result are accordingly distinct from one
another. The one is categorized as contingent, the other as necessary;
this is the distinction in abstract terms, but it is also a concrete distinction; the outcome is something other than what was posited
initially.⁴³⁴ Since the forms vary, the content of the two is also distinct
one from the other. The tile falls in contingent fashion; the one who
is hit, in all his concrete subjectivity, the death of such a one, and
the falling tile are utterly heterogeneous, they differ completely in
content; what occurs is something quite other than the posited result.
If we treat living nature—animals, human beings, plants—in this
way, under the conditions of external necessity, or as the result of
earth, warmth, light, air, moisture, etc., as the product of these circumstances, we are speaking according to the relationship of external
necessity. This then is external necessity, which we must distinguish
from genuine or inner necessity.⁴³⁵

Inner necessity, on the contrary, means that everything ¯(causes,
stimuli, occasions, and the result) belongs to one thing alone, to
necessity;¯436 together they constitute a unity. What happens under
this necessity does not happen in such a way that from assumptions
made in advance something else results. All that happens is | that   298
what is assumed in advance itself comes about in the result, it merely
coincides with itself, or finds itself; in other words the two
moments—immediate existence and being posited—are posited as

433. *Thus G; P reads:* If a tile falls from the roof, it is a matter of necessity that
if someone is passing at the same time he will be hit by it. He had to pass that way,
and the tile necessarily had to fall.

434. *P adds:* Inner and outer are here no longer distinct from each other.

435. [*Ed.*] See Hegel, *Science of Logic,* pp. 546–553 (*GW* 11:385-392).

436. *Thus D; G reads:* that is posited in advance as cause, stimulus, or occasion
is distinct, while the result belongs to one thing alone, to necessity; *P reads:* that we
distinguish as circumstances, causes, stimuli [is posited in advance], and the result
alone belongs to necessity;

one moment. In external necessity there is contingency, and otherness has the character of having been posited. That which [immediately] is, is not posited, ¨it does not belong to this unity, it is¨[437] unmediated; ¨¨if it belonged to the unity, it ¨would¨[438] be posited by it.¨¨[439] The effect is what is posited, the cause what is original. In true necessity, cause and effect form a unity: the conditions and circumstances obtain, but they do not just obtain; they are also posited through this single unity (in themselves they are in fact contingent so that they sublate themselves). The negation of their being is the unity of necessity, the unity of their process, so that their being is something implicitly negated. The result is ¨not merely an effect but obtains equally.¨[440] Necessity thus consists in the conditions being posited in such a way that the circumstances that seem just to happen are actually posited by the unity; the result is also something posited, but at the same time it [is], and it is so by virtue of reflection, i.e., through the process, through the unity's being reflected within itself; this then is the *being* of the result. Thus in necessity what happens only coincides with itself. The unity dissipates itself, disperses itself in conditions and circumstances that seem to be contingent; it throws its conditions themselves carelessly about like so many insignificant pebbles, which then lie around and make their appearance directly, without arousing any suspicion. But | they are also posited, ¨being thus¨[441] inwardly broken. The result is only posited; its manifestation consists in their sublating themselves, bringing forth an other, the result, which, however, only seems an other in opposition to their fragmented existence. But the content is one and the same; what they are in themselves is the result. Nothing is changed but the manner and mode of appearing. The result is the

299

437. W₂ *(Var) reads:* the conditions do not belong to the unity, they are
438. *G reads:* would not
439. *Ho reads, similar in* W₂: the result is only posited, but not at the same time being.
440. W₂ *reads:* then not merely a result or merely something posited; rather being equally accrues to it. *Cf. Ho:* In the same way the result is not merely something posited by its circumstances, but *is* its circumstances themselves, so that it likewise retains the moment of immediacy.
441. *Ho reads, similar in* W: they do not belong to themselves but to an other, to their result. W₂ *adds:* Thus they are

gathering in of what the circumstances contain. ˉInorganic nature constitutes the conditions, and subjective form is then the result.ˉ442 It is life that in this way throws its conditions[443] and impulses overboard, ˉwhereupon they no longer look like life; rather the inner element, the in-itself, appears for the first time in the result.ˉ444 Thus necessity is the process, and it involves only a distinction of form between the result and what is posited in advance.

If we now consider how, in this form, necessity has acquired the shape of proofs of the existence of God, we see, to begin with, that ˉnecessity is a genuine concept:ˉ445 necessity is the truth of the contingent world generally. The more detailed development [of this thesis] belongs to logic. God, the absolute, is absolute necessity; this is an essential and necessary standpoint, not yet the highest, the authentic standpoint, but a necessary stage from which the higher standpoint emerges, which is itself a condition of the higher concept;[446] therefore the absolute is necessity. This form is defective. The concept of absolute necessity does not yet correspond to the idea we must have of God, which we may not, however, presuppose as a representation. The higher concept must conceive itself. So this is something subordinate, not what is authentic. This is a defect | in this proof of the existence of God. As regards the form 300 of proof that involves absolute necessity, this is the celebrated cosmological proof, and it runs simply as follows: "Contingent things presuppose an absolute, necessary cause"; "Now contingent things do exist—I am, the world is"; the conclusion is: "Therefore an absolutely necessary cause exists."

What is defective in this proof has already been mentioned. The major premise runs, "Contingent things presuppose an absolutely necessary cause." This proposition is in principle quite correct, and it expresses the coherence between contingency and necessity. In

442. *Thus D with P; G reads:* and its manifestation as shape.
443. *Ho, W add:* stimuli,
444. *Thus G; D reads:* but at the same time holds them fast within itself.
445. *Thus D; G reads:* the concept is a genuine one: W_2 *(Var) reads:* the content is the true concept:
446. W_2 *adds:* which presupposes this higher standpoint; *Cf. Ho:* This is an essential standpoint, but not yet the authentic one, which emerges from it only because it presupposes this earlier standpoint.

order to remove ⁻all blemishes⁻[447] from the proof it is not necessary
to say, "Contingent things presuppose an absolutely necessary cause";
⁻thus one can say that it is a relationship of the coherence of finite
things⁻[448] that they presuppose the absolutely necessary.[449] Then
the proposition contains more specifically a contradiction directed
against external necessity. Contingent things have causes, they are
necessary; and what makes them externally necessary can itself only
be something contingent; thus the conditions that make them
necessary lead us into an infinite regress. The proposition cuts this
short, and it is entirely right in that. Something that was necessary
in a merely contingent fashion would not be a necessity in principle;
real necessity is opposed to this proposition. The coherence[450] is
rightly claimed too; contingent things do presuppose absolute
necessity, but the mode of coherence is incomplete: the bond is expressed as one of presupposing, entailing, and the like; this is the
coherence of naive reflection. Expressed in this way, the coherence
involves—upon closer scrutiny—the placing of the contingent things
on one side and of necessity on the other side. | The two sides are
viewed in such a way that the understanding separates them, there
is a transition from one side to the other, and they are fixed, antithetical to one another.[451] In the minor premise this is even more
clearly expressed: "Contingent things exist; therefore an absolutely
necessary cause exists." Inasmuch as the coherence [of things] is so
constituted that the one subsisting being conditions the other, the
peculiar feature [of the argument] consequently lies in [reasoning]
as though contingent things conditioned absolute necessity, and as
if they were the condition for absolute necessity to exist. One thing
conditions the other, and absolute necessity thus appears as presupposed, i.e., as conditioned by contingent things. This is where the
proof goes astray, and this is brought into the open in the minor

301

447. *sonstigen Makel.* W₂ *reads:* all fault-finding [*sonstige Mäkeleien*]. *Cf. Ho:*
all "blemishings" [*sonstigen Macklungen* (an invented term)].
448. W₂ *(Var/Ed?) reads:* for it is a relationship of finite things, one can say,
449. W₂ *(Var) adds:* in such a way that this is represented as subject.
450. W₂ *(Var) adds:* in general
451. *Ho adds, similar in* W: and herein lies what is false, for the fixity of being
makes the contingent things a condition of the being of necessity, which consequently
appears as something merely posited.

premise: "Now contingent things exist." Absolute necessity is thus made dependent, in such a way that contingent things remain outside it.

The genuinely coherent pattern is as follows: contingent things certainly are, but their being has the value of possibility only; for equally they pass away, they are only posited. They are only posited in advance by the process of unity. In other words, unity *is* the process. Their first moment is to be posited with the semblance of unmediated existence; the second moment is that these merely posited things are negated. These implicitly negative things are *posited* as negative, so that they are comprehended essentially as appearances, as no more than moments in the process. In this sense it can fairly be said that they are an essential condition of absolute necessity. All there is is the process, and it only *is* by virtue of having this characteristic—to presuppose [them]. In the finite world we do take unmediated entities of this kind as our starting point, but in the world of truth external necessity is merely this appearance, and the unmediated is merely posited. This, then, is the defect in that type of mediation, that contingent things are nonetheless posited | as   302 having being, and are not comprehended as moments or stages in the process. At all events the thought,⌐452 the content, is the genuine one that the absolute must be cognized as absolute necessity.

The third point to be noted about absolute necessity is that necessity implicitly contains freedom, since necessity too consists in coinciding with itself; it exists simply on its own account, does not depend on anything else. The way it operates is free, consisting merely in coinciding with itself in the semblance of this reciprocal indifference; its process is simply that of finding itself, coming to itself, and this is what freedom is. Implicitly necessity is free, and it is only semblance that makes the difference. We see this in the case of punishment. Someone who merits punishment can regard this punishment as an evil, or as an act of force, or an alien power, in which he does not find himself—as external necessity, something external that has its way with him, and the outcome is something

452. *Thus P with D; G reads:* the type of mediations that are regarded as proofs of the existence of God. At all events

other than what he did; the punishment of his action is a consequence, but this is something other than what he willed. If, however, he recognizes the punishment as just, then it is the consequence of his own will, and its rightness lies in his action itself. His action is the action of a rational being; it is only the rationality of his action that comes to him with the semblance of something else. Thus someone who recognizes his punishment as just suffers no force. He is responsible for his own act, he feels himself free in it. What comes to him is properly his, his right, the rationality of his action; no violence is done to him. Thus it is only implicitly that necessity contains freedom: this is an essential point—it is only formal freedom, subjective freedom; and this implies that necessity still has no inward content.

Inasmuch as necessity is simple coincidence with self in the process [of the whole], it *is* freedom. We require that necessity should involve movement, circumstances, etc.—this is its aspect of mediation; but when we say, "This is necessary," "this" is a unity. What is necessary, *is*. "This" is the simple expression, the result, into which the process has coalesced. It is simple self-relation, the finding of self; necessity is what is most free, what is determined or limited by nothing, all kinds of mediation are once again sublated in it. Thus 303 necessity is ˉthe | form of mediation that surrenders itself.ˉ[453] To put it another way, freedom is implicitly involved in it. We might note here that the disposition to ˉhearkenˉ[454] to necessity that once marked the Greeks and still marks Muslims contains the disposition of freedom within itself, within the disposition of the subject, even though this does not appear to be the case; but this is only[455] formal freedom, as we shall see in more detail later on.

ˉSo far as we are concerned (since we are dealing with the concept), necessity is implicit freedom, or freedom in a formal sense. Nothing is of any account for it, it has no content; all content, everything hard and fast, vanishes before it, and the very fact that there is no content is the defect or the formal aspect in this defini-

453. *Thus G; P reads:* mediation, finding oneself, coming to oneself.
454. *Ho, W read:* submit
455. *Ho, W add:* implicit,

tion of God.⁻⁴⁵⁶ Real necessity is freedom, necessity according to its higher concept; it *is* freedom as such, the concept as such, or, more precisely, purpose. For necessity is devoid of content, or, in other words, although a difference is contained in it, that difference is not posited. Necessity is the process that we have considered; the mere process is becoming, and this has to contain differentiations, but these distinctions are not yet posited. Thus, what is contained in necessity *is* distinction, to be sure, but the defect is that it is not yet posited. Only through mediation does necessity become the process of coalescing with self, and mediation involves the positing of differentiation generally. To begin with, necessity is still abstract self-determination, ˉbut it must be as such; and that involves determinateness, particularization | generally. Now in the coalescence with 304 self, this determinacy is *ipso facto* posited as coalescing with itself or as sustaining itself in the process, against the passing over of the particular into necessity.⁻⁴⁵⁷ Determinateness has to be posited; this determinateness is the content that coincides with itself in the process of necessity, i.e., it is the self-sustaining content. The coalescence, thus defined as the content that sustains itself, is what we call purpose in general.

Regarding the determinateness in the process of coalescence, there are two forms of it that need to be noted: (1) The ˉform of the content as self-sustaining, the form thatˉ⁴⁵⁸ persists unchanged throughout the process and in the transition remains equivalent to itself; (2) The determinateness of the form, which here takes the more specific shape of the distinction between subjectivity and objectivity. Initially the content is subjectivity, and the process consists in this content's realizing itself in the form of objectivity. This realized

456. *Ho, W read:* No content, no intention, no determinateness is valid for necessity, and that is where it is still defective.

457. *Thus D with P; G reads:* but it must be determinateness, particularization generally; and in the coalescence with self this determinateness is *ipso facto* posited as maintaining itself against passing over in the process, it is self-sustaining in necessity. W₂ *(Var) reads:* determinateness, particularization must simply *be* generally; in order for the determinateness to be actual, the particularization and the distinction must be posited in the coalescence with self as maintaining itself against passing over in the process, as self-sustaining in necessity.

458. W₂ *(Var) reads:* determinateness exists as self-sustaining content, which

purpose is just as much purpose as it was before, ˉbut what was posited in the subjectˉ[459] is at the same time objective too. These are the principal moments.

3. With this we have arrived at the category of *purposiveness*. It is in "purpose" that the determinate being of the concept as such begins—the being of the free, of what exists as free. What exists as free, i.e., what is at home with itself, what comes back to itself, what maintains itself, is the subject. The subject defines itself inwardly; ˉon the one hand, it is the content, and in this its self-definition it is alsoˉ[460] free *in* the content; but at the same time, being at home with itself, it is free *from* the content. ˉThe contentˉ[461] is valid only to the extent that the subject allows it to be so. This is the concept in general.

Second, the subject also realizes the concept. Determinacy is initially simple, held within the concept, | ˉhaving being in the form of being at home with self, or being self-contained.ˉ[462] Thus this subjectivity is totality, but at the same time it is one-sided, merely subjective, just one moment of the form as a whole. This is the definition [we have reached], that the content is posited only in the form of equivalence or coincidence with itself. This form of coincidence with self is the one-sided form of abstract reflection, the simple form of identity with self, and the subject is the totality of being at home with itself. In that it posits itself to be merely subjective, this contradicts the totality, and the subject is driven to sublate this form and to realize the purpose; but even when it is realized, the purpose still belongs to the subject, the subject still possesses itself in it. It is itself that it has objectified: it has released itself from simplicity, yet has maintained itself in manifoldness. This is the concept of purposiveness in general.

The second [point about purposiveness] is that the world as such is now to be regarded as conforming to purpose. We encountered

459. *Thus D; G reads:* the content remains what it was, *but* W₂ *(Var) reads:* the content remains what it was, it is subjective, but

460. W₂ *(Var) reads:* this definition is on the one hand content, and the subject is

461. *Thus P; G reads:* It W₂ *(Var) reads:* It is the subject's content, and

462. W₂ *(Var) reads:* in the form of being at home with self and having returned within self.

earlier the categorial determination of things as "contingent"; to view the world from a teleological standpoint ¬involves a higher category. We can readily agree that immediate consciousness leads us to the contingency of things, but we¬[463] may hesitate whether to go further and consider things as conforming to purpose—some of them being themselves purposes and others related to these as means. We *can* maintain that there is no such thing as purpose in the world, and that what appears as purpose has only been produced mechanically by external circumstances. Purpose is something fixedly determined, and it is with purpose that *fixed* determinateness begins. The purpose maintains itself in the process; it is what marks the beginning and end of the process; hence it is the final end. It is something fixed that is exempt from the process; it is not determined by anything else, but has its ground in the subject—it is determined by the free self-determining of the subject. The antithesis [before us] therefore is whether we should remain at the standpoint where things are determined by other things, the level of their contingency, of external necessity, ¬[of] | what does not exist by virtue of itself, and is not   306
fixed but only posited by something else, i.e., the standpoint of merely external necessity.¬[464] Both [contingency and external necessity] are alike; we have already noted earlier that external necessity is opposed to purpose, that it is being posited by something else—the concurrence of the circumstances is what brings about the result, the outcome is something that was not there before. In the case of purpose the outcome is not something other than what was already present; purpose is what perdures, what stimulates, what acts; it is the sublating of one's subjective form and the realizing of oneself; it pertains to the subject. So these two ways of considering things, in terms of external necessity and in terms of conformity to purpose, stand opposed to each other.

There is nothing else that properly needs to be said about this point. We have seen that external necessity reverts to absolute necessity, which is the truth of it; but absolute necessity is implicitly

463. *Thus D, P; G reads:* and in terms of its purposiveness, involves a higher category. We W₂ *(Var) reads:* and the thought of its purposiveness, involves a higher category. We may agree to the previous determination, but
464. *Thus P; W₂ (Var) reads:* or [should place ourselves] at the level of purpose.

freedom, and what is implicit must be posited. If it is posited, it becomes determinate, and its determinacy appears as ¯purposiveness; the genuine or higher concept [of it] is the concept of purposiveness as such.¯465 It must therefore be said in general that to the extent that things exist for us in the immediate consciousness (i.e., the reflected consciousness), they have to be characterized as conforming to purpose, as having purposes within themselves—in other words, the teleological is an essential way of viewing things.

But this way of viewing things at once introduces a distinction, namely that between external and internal purposiveness.466 And even an internal purpose may once more be finite in content, in which case it falls back into the relational system formed by external purposiveness or expediency.

1. External purposiveness is as follows. One way or another, a purpose is posited; this purpose is to be realized; for this to happen, inasmuch as the subject is a finite, determinate being existing immediately with its purposes, there is apart from the subject initially the other determinant of the realization [of the goal]. On the one hand there is immediacy; thus the subject with its purposes is an immediate existence, and the side of objectification is at the same time present as something external—i.e., the realization is posited

307

---

465. *Thus P; G reads:* subjectivity and objectivity, and so we have purpose.

[*Ed.*] On the concept of purposiveness, see Hegel, *Science of Logic,* pp. 734–754 (*GW* 12:154–172).

466. [*Ed.*] External purposiveness (*äussere Zweckmässigkeit*) may be regarded as expedient purposiveness because the material used for the realization of the purpose is a mere, contingent means, external to the purpose, having "no soul of its own." It is appropriated, exploited for the sake of the purpose. When *Zweckmässigkeit* is intended in this sense, we often translate as "expediency." Roman religion, for example, is the religion of external purposiveness, hence of expediency.

In explaining the distinction between external and internal purposiveness, Hegel refers in Part I of the 1827 lectures to Kant and Aristotle (see Vol. 1:428–429). He mentions the discussion in Kant's *Critique of Judgment,* Part II, Critique of Teleological Judgment (see esp. §§ 63, 66, 82), which centers on the unique purposive structure characterizing in organic beings the relation between the parts and the whole. He affirms that this also corresponds to Aristotle's view of nature (see *Physics* 2.8–9), according to which every living thing is a *telos* or purpose that has its means implicit within it. As for external purposiveness, by contrast, he states in Part II of the *Ms.* that the means whereby the purpose is realized is something external, and the unity between whole and parts is no longer immanent in the purpose as it is in the case of organic living creatures.

as a material, as what is⁻posited from outside⁻[467] in order that the purpose may be realized. As against the purpose this material is, to be sure, only a means. It is in the purpose that we have what stands independently on its own account, what has coalesced with itself, what sustains itself and is fixed; while that which can be otherwise— the side of reality, the material for the realization of the purpose—is what does not stand on its own, does not exist independently in opposition to the fixed purpose, and is therefore only a means, with no soul of its own and no purpose of its own within it; the purpose lies outside it and is incorporated in it only through the activity of the subject, which realizes itself in the material. Thus external purposiveness has only an external, dependent objectivity outside it, in contrast with which the subject with its purposes is what is fixed. External purposiveness consequently begins with the separation [of the objective world] from the subject. The material can offer no resistance to the subject, since it has no purpose or power of its own; [it] is only the means for the purpose that is realized in it. But by the same token the purpose that is realized in this way is itself only an outward form for this material, for the material is something immediately found there beforehand; so it is something that is not independent, yet also it is independent because it is found there beforehand. Thus the two of them, the means and the end, remain externally opposed to each other [even] when they are combined. The purpose is only the form for this material. What people bring forth in this way they call purpose; the stone and timber are means, and the realized purpose is also stone, timber, or whatever it may be, that has acquired a certain form; but in this combination the material is still something external to the purpose.

2. Inner purposiveness is that which has its means implicit in it. Thus whatever is alive is an end for itself, it maintains itself in [its own life-]process; it makes itself the end, and what | is end is here   308
also means. What is alive is[468] an articulated organism—its end is equally its means too. Inasmuch as the living subject produces itself

467. W₂ *reads:* found there beforehand from outside and serves *Cf. Ho:* This [realization of the purpose] is accordingly found there beforehand as the external material, as what, to be sure, has no fixed validity vis-à-vis the subject (since subjectivity is at the same time totality of form), but does serve it as means.
468. *Ho, W add:* the simple inwardness that realizes itself in its members, it is

inwardly, it has the aim of containing its own means in itself. Each organ, each member or joint in the human body is an end, it exists on its own account, maintains itself; and at the same time it is the means of producing and maintaining the other organs; it consumes and is consumed, and the other parts are maintained at its expense; there is no part of the body that is not continually being consumed. It is not the material particles but the form or organ in question that remains the same, that maintains itself constantly through the process of their change. In this way what is alive is an end in itself.

3. But this end-for-itself is also involved in the relationship of external purposiveness as well. Organic life is also related to inorganic nature, it finds therein the means whereby it maintains its existence, and these means exist independently over against it. In this way inner purposiveness also has the relationship of external purposiveness. Life can assimilate the means to itself, but they are found there [in the world] beforehand, they are not posited by life itself. Life can produce its own organs but not the means.

At this point we are in the sphere of finite purposiveness; absolute purposiveness we shall encounter later.

The teleological worldview contains all these varied forms of relationship and of purpose. There are fixed ends and means, yet even that which is an end for itself is only a finite end, one that needs and depends on the availability of its means. Hence the purposiveness we are discussing is to that extent a finite one, and its finitude consists primarily in this relationship of externality. The purposes that are ends in themselves cannot be realized unless the external means are present, and then only if the means are powerless against what is purpose. The primitive truth about this relationship between end and means is universal power generally, by virtue of which things are present, can be seen, as ends-for-themselves or as means. From the standpoint of purposiveness | ˉthoseˉ⁴⁶⁹ that are ends have the power to realize themselves in the material, though they do not have the power to ˉpositˉˉthe means or material;ˉ⁴⁷⁰ but theyˉˉ⁴⁷¹ appear

309

469. W₂ reads: the things Cf. Ho: things as ends
470. Thus G; D reads: posit themselves as ends for themselves;
471. W₂ (Var) reads: the means; the purpose and [from G: the material, both]

to be mutually indifferent, the purpose and the materials both exist in unmediated form, the means being there beforehand, ready for the purpose.

⌐In dealing with purposes we distinguished external purposiveness or expediency in general. As a human being I have purposes, and these purposes [are] mediated through material means. Secondly we considered inner purposiveness, which has its material in itself. What has now to be added in the third place to this relationship in order to sublate the finitude that still marks the second form is for the universal, the whole, to be defined in the terms that we established for it earlier, and which we have called inner independence. Power is what posits the end-for-itself in unity with the means.⌐472 What is alive has internal purposes, and means and material for its existence; it exists as the power over such means and material. Initially all this is present only in the living individual. Its organs are the means whereby it realizes itself, and it is itself the material and the means. They are permeated by the purpose, do not exist independently on their own account. A bodily organ cannot exist without the soul, without the living unity of the body to which it belongs. What appears in this way has now to be posited as universal; in other words, the means and materials that appear to be independent, to exist in a contingent fashion, vis-à-vis what is an end in itself, are [posited as being] in fact subordinated to its free power, in that they are not in themselves in relation to the purpose, while their nature *is* | to be related to it. In spite of their seemingly indifferent subsistence, they are related to their life-principle [*Seele*] in the purpose alone. Thus the universal idea is the purpose-oriented power, and it is the *universal* power that realizes itself according to purpose; in other words, insofar as there is a purpose, an end for itself, and inorganic nature outside it, this inorganic realm in fact belongs to the purpose-oriented power, so that the existent beings that appear immediately exist only for purpose. We might say that there are two

310

472. *Thus D with P and G; W₂ (Var) reads:* Now their implicit potential is necessarily the power that posits the end, the end-for-itself, in a single unity with the means; and, in order to sublate the finitude in the relationship that we have observed up to this point, what needs to be added now is for the totality of the process to become apparent in inner purposiveness.

kinds of things in the world, those that are ends in themselves and those that appear as means; but this categorization will not hold good, for the ends in themselves can in their turn be the means in a given relation while the means can hold their ground firmly against the ends. But what conforms to purpose does not exist as power. So the second class, the class of things that seem to subsist independently, is implicitly posited, not by the power of the [finite] purpose but by a higher power that has being in itself; ⌐and for that reason it is subordinated to the particular power of the [finite] purpose.⌐[473]

Such is the concept of the purpose-oriented power. The truth of the world *is* this purposive power; and this idea of wisdom, or of the power that is wisdom, is the truth of this world. To put it differently, the world viewed in teleological terms, or that shows itself to be⌐effective in terms of purposes, requires a power that operates according to purposes. In other words, the absolutely universal power operates according to purposes, and since the world as such is its manifestation, the truth of the world is ⌐the being-in-and-for-self of the manifestation of a wise power.⌐[474]

In the third place, if we consider this in the form of mediation, [i.e., if we consider] how the understanding comprehends the mediation and proves the existence of God, then there are two definite aspects that call for our attention. For in that perspective it is the

311 *wisdom,* the wise power, | that constitutes the absolute process, ⌐and the process itself consists in⌐[475] operating, effecting, being active. There is, first of all, this wise power; its concept is the positing of a world, an inwardly purposive world, one that has purposes within itself. Wise power is power that manifests itself, that passes over into determinate being, and what we mean by determinate being is that the diversity, the manifold character of external existence is posited. This is another point that we have already encountered;

---

473. *Thus G with D, P; G, W₁ read:* and for that reason they are subordinate to the [*G:* weaker *W₁:* higher] power of the purpose. *W₂ (Var) reads:* and that brings them into conformity with the purpose.

474. *Thus G; P reads:* that this truth, the category of a wise power, should be in and for itself.

475. *Thus P; G reads:* it is power, *W₂ (Var) reads:* within itself, it is power

but at this stage the distinction involves a more important, more essential level of determination. [Here] power brings forth as wisdom; and what is brought forth is the distinction between that which is an end in itself and that which is merely a means, that which only conforms to purpose, is contingent, is not purpose within itself. These two [kinds of things] exist determinately in the manifold, i.e., in the world. This is the distinction, that one is a means for the other. This is the first point about mediation; the other aspect of mediation at this standpoint is precisely that there is this distinguishing power which distinguishes purposes that are contingent and exist solely as means—that this power is what relates these two sides to each other. It maintains the purposes in precisely the sense that it determines one category to be ends and ˉthe other means.ˉ476 [It is] *power* inasmuch as it maintains these [particular] ends and the others as their means. As regards the first aspect of the mediation of what has been thus distinguished, it is what we call "creation"; creation begins from the concept. This wise power operates and distinguishes—and this is the concept of creation.

1. The first point to be noted is that this aspect of mediation does not belong to the proof of the existence of God, for it starts from the concept of wise power—from the fact that it is diremptive or, more concretely, that it is creation. However, we have not yet reached the point where the proof starts from the concept;477 [the teleological proof starts] from determinate being. The category of creation does not occur in the earlier religions. Here [in the religions of spiritual individuality] for the first time the proper concept of creation gets its place; | creation as such is not involved in the previous definitions 312 of the divine nature. The concept was first defined as the infinite, then as power in general. In the infinite we have only the negative of the finite; similarly, in necessity finite existence simply slips away, things vanish in it, as its accidental aspect. ˉIt is said that what is, is necessary, but it is necessary here only as a result, and to the extent

476. W₂ *(Var) reads:* determines the other as means [*G:* power] and is thus what maintains the purposes.
477. [*Ed.*] The proof that starts from the concept is the ontological proof. The teleological proof, like the cosmological, starts from determinate being (*Dasein*), but views it as having been purposively created.

that it is. With [simple] being, all that counts is being, that a particular thing is as it is,⁻⁴⁷⁸ though it could also be otherwise; all that really then counts in regard to it is that it is. Right or wrong, fortunate or unfortunate, are all one; things are as they are, no purpose [makes them] this way or that. All that counts is this abstract, formal being-found-to-be-so, not what *is,* not the content. Thus in [simple] necessity there occurs only the formal ⁻affirmation that this is the situation. Nothing holds out against this necessity,⁻⁴⁷⁹ there is nothing determinate as such, ⁻nothing that could be an absolute purpose.⁻⁴⁸⁰ But at this point, when we speak of "creation," this involves the positing and being-posited of affirmative existences; this is not just the abstract affirmation that they *are,* but that their *content* is too.

It is for this reason that creation first comes upon the scene at this point. Creation is not the operation of power simply as such, but of wise power, of power as wisdom; for it is only power as wisdom that is self-determining, [so that] what appears as finite is already involved in the power itself. Because it is wise, i.e., affirmative, the determinations [of power] belong to it; in other words, the finite existences, the creatures, are genuinely affirmed. Thereby they are posited as valid—as purposes or ends, and necessity is demoted to being just a moment as against the ends. The purpose is what subsists in the power, it is what subsists against the power and by means of it; it is what holds out, that in which the process of power runs its course. ⁻Power⁻⁴⁸¹ is at the call of | purpose; its process is to maintain and realize the purpose; the purpose stands above it, and it is posited merely as one aspect, so that only part of what is created is subject to power and appears therefore as contingent. This, then, is the concept of creation. Previously what was determinate merely came forth, it was not posited as self-determination. Power is demoted to being a moment; and one part

313

---

478. W₂ *(Var) reads:* What is, is only as result. To the extent that it is, all that counts in regard to it is *that* it is, not *how* it is—it can be this way

479. W₂ *(Var) reads:* affirmation, not the content; here there is nothing that holds out,

480. *Thus G; D reads:* and purpose requires determinateness.

481. W₂ *(Var) reads:* Necessity

of creation is thus only contingent and subject to power. Thus we have shown that this distinction itself emerges from the concept of the wise power.

2. We began with the simple concept and have progressed to this distinction. Through the concept we have in the second stage two sides, purposes on the one side, and contingent things on the other. This second stage is the mediation between them. They are the living [on one side] and the nonliving, the inorganic, on the other side. The two sides are distinct, each existing immediately on its own account, with an equal right to be there; they [simply] are, and the being of the one is no more[482] than the being of the other. These are living ends, and hence they are individuals—unmediatedly singular, rigid points, each opposed by an other, which exists on its own account and offers resistance to it. The mediation between the two sides consists in the fact that they do not both subsist for themselves in the same way: one is subjective being-for-self, while the other is only an abstract, material being-for-self, with no higher significance.[483]

This second determination, this mediation, is what is now grasped in the form of the *physicotheological proof*[484] of God's existence.

Living things are in fact power, but in the first instance they are power only in regard to themselves; within its organs the living soul constitutes power, but not yet over the inorganic, which also exists. The living thing becomes on the one hand the sphere of power, but on the other hand also has [over against it] an inorganic nature; nature remains as an infinite manifold beside it. So ˉthe content is on the one hand what is still contingent; | qualitatively, living souls   314

482. W_2 *(Var) adds:* justified
483. W_2 *(Var) adds:* even if they are alive.
484. [*Ed.*] In the *Critique of Judgment,* § 85, Kant defines "physicotheology" as "the attempt on the part of reason to infer the supreme cause of nature and its attributes from the *ends* of nature—ends which can only be known empirically." The physicotheological proof can at best arrive only at a first cause but can make no judgments as to its goodness or wisdom. Thus in Kant's view it must be supplanted by the proof based on moral teleology or "ethicotheology," which is "the attempt to infer that cause and its attributes from the moral end of rational beings in nature—an end which can be known *a priori.*" The latter is the program that Kant carries out in the *Critique of Practical Reason.*

are initially (or immediately)⁻⁴⁸⁵ mutually indifferent, but they need their material, and the material has the same determinate particularity as they themselves have. And the other point is first that living things are the power over their material; this is the point upon which the understanding bases its construction of the so-called physicotheological proof.

According to this argument there are two kinds of determinate being, and they are mutually indifferent; what is needed [to overcome this indifference] is a third kind of thing. The harmony through which the purpose is realized is not one that is there in fact—what is immediately there is rather just the mutually indifferent existence of these two kinds set against each other; ˉhere this harmonyˉ⁴⁸⁶ is not a fact of immediate existence. This tertium quid, the implicit existence of the harmony, the concept of the wise power, is this inner element, and it is this to which the proof points after its manner. Kant examined and criticized the teleological proof with particular care, and regarded it as quite disposed of—even though he did not deal with it in a formal fashion. As he presents it, it has the following moments:⁴⁸⁷ we find in the world clear traces of wisdom, indications of a wise dispensation according to purposes. This is what a preliminary reflection on the world [shows]. The world is full of life, both spiritual life and natural vitality. These living things are organized in themselves, they are the power in regard to themselves; but already in respect of these organs the different parts can be regarded as mutually indifferent. Of course, life is the harmony of the parts, but the fact that they exist determined in this way, for this harmony, does not seem to be grounded in their determinate being. ˉEach plant and blossom, each species of animal, has its own particular

---

485. *Thus P with D; G, W_1 read:* on the one hand [G: there are still (these) qualities, W_1: there is still (this) quality,] this initially immediate being, [as] W_2 *(G with Var) reads:* on the one hand there are still [this] quality, this initially immediate being, and living souls [as]

486. *Thus P; G, W read:* [*precedes in* W_2: there reigns here] goodness—that each kind of thing, being self-related, is indifferent to other things, that they are distinct, *W (Var) adds:* that they are opposed—[this]

487. [*Ed.*] Kant, *Critique of Pure Reason,* B 650–657.

nature;⁻⁴⁸⁸ plants | need a particular climate and soil, animals   315
belong to a particular genus, and so on—their natures are particular.
To these particular natures belong particular means, a particular kind
of material, in order that it may exist in this process, and its
maintenance, its determinateness is the production of itself [from
these resources]. Life only produces; but it does not pass over into
the other with which it forms a process, but remains itself, continually
changing and reconstructing the process. This spectacle of vitality,
this concordance of the world, and of the organic and the inorganic
moments in it, the conformity of existence with human purposes
generally, this is what amazes human beings who begin to reflect,
for what offers itself initially to their perception is independent
existences, existences that exist completely on their own account but
that harmonize with *their* existence. The wonderful thing is that even
phenomena that appear at first sight to be completely indifferent to
one another turn out to be essential to one another; and what is
wonderful is the very contrary of this indifference, viz., conformity
to purpose. Thus we have here a principle completely different from
the principle of their immediate determinate being.

⁻This teleological ordering is [not] grounded in the world, and
attaches to it only in contingent fashion.⁻⁴⁸⁹ The nature of different
things could not spontaneously concur through so many [separate]
existences toward just one final end; and that is why a third principle
is needed, a rational, ordering principle such as the existing things
themselves are not.

Things show themselves to be ends [*Zwecke*] and also means for
each other [*zweckmässig für einander*]. That they are means to ends
is not posited by the things themselves. Admittedly life acts in such
a way as to use inorganic nature; it maintains itself by assimilating
natural things, negates them and posits itself as identical with them

488. W₂ *reads:* And living things also have a relationship to the exterior, each
being related to its own inorganic nature; *Ho reads:* Moreover, every living thing
is oriented to the exterior, has a relationship to a specific inorganic nature peculiar
to it;
489. *Thus P; G reads:* This first principle applies to them only in contingent
fashion.

while maintaining itself in them. Life is, to be sure, the activity of the subjects, who make themselves the focal point, and everything else the means. But this second determination⁻—that there | are things they can use—is something that lies outside them.⁻⁴⁹⁰ That they are externally indifferent to one another in their mode of existence, this—like their existence itself—is not posited by the [subjective] purpose. So then, in the third place, this mutual indifference of things is not the genuine relationship [between them] but only a semblance. The category that defines them genuinely is the teleological one of conformity to purpose. And this implies that they are not mutually indifferent; the teleological relationship is the essential one, the one that is valid and genuine. The proof demonstrates the necessity of a supreme ordering being.⁴⁹¹

There consequently exists a wise cause which, as freedom and intelligence, is the cause of the world; and so on. Against this proof Kant argues⁴⁹² that it only shows God to be the architect of the world, not its creator. The proof concerns only the contingency of form, not the substance. For what is requisite is just this relation between objects, this quality of conformity to purpose; if the conformity is posited by a power, what is required is just this, that the objects shall be posited purposefully. This quality, says Kant, is only form, and the positing power would merely be actualizing forms, not creating the substance.⁴⁹³ As regards this criticism, the distinction is an empty one.⁴⁹⁴ If we are at the standpoint of the concept, then we must long since have left behind the distinction of form and matter,⁴⁹⁵ and ⁻with it any conception of a formative action of absolute power in which the form could be thought without positing

490. *Ho, W read:* lies outside them. For human beings certainly use things, assimilate them to themselves, but that there *are* such things that they can use—this is not something posited by them.

491. *Ho, W add:* But that the cause is one can be inferred from the unity of the world.

492. [*Ed.*] Kant, *Critique of Pure Reason,* B 655.

493. [*Ed.*] Ibid., B 654–655.

494. *Ho, W₂ add:* For the power cannot posit the form without positing the matter.

495. [*Ed.*] On Hegel's definition of the relation between the two, see *Science of Logic,* pp. 450–456 (cf. *GW* 11:297-302).

the matter.⁻⁴⁹⁶ If we speak of form here, the form appears as a particular quality, but that is only a mode of form that is present here. The essence of form as it is present here, however, is the concept of the purpose that realizes itself. Form in this sense, that of being the concept, is what is genuinely substantive; it is the soul. What can then | be distinguished as matter is something formal, wholly subsidiary; ⁻here the form is the concept itself.⁻⁴⁹⁷ 317

Kant goes on to say⁴⁹⁸ that the conclusion is based on the order and purposiveness that subsists in the world at the moment and is merely observed; this is just a contingent existence. ⁻My being is contingent, and so is that of the plants; they are not posited by me as subject. The contingent⁻⁴⁹⁹ is observed, and in this way we are cognizant of the order and know that it is there. From this subsistent purposiveness, says Kant, the argument infers ⁻the existence of a proportionate⁻⁵⁰⁰ cause. This is the other moment [of Kant's critique], and it contains a categorial determination that is quite correct; but it has to be pressed further.

We say that the purposive arrangement that we observe cannot simply come about [of itself]; it requires a power that operates in conformity with purposes. So the content *is* this cause: the wisdom of the postulated cause extends only as far as we have insight into its purposes. Observation always gives us only a relationship, and no one can argue from power to omnipotence, from wisdom and unity to omniscience and absolute unity; so the physicotheological proof affords us only a concept of great wisdom, great power, great unity, and so forth. But the content that we want is God, absolute power, absolute unity and wisdom; this does not lie within the con-

496. *Thus P, D; G reads:* one must know that absolute form is something real, that form therefore is something, [but] without matter is nothing.

497. *Thus G; P reads:* If the [opposition of] form and matter has no truth, it has [absolutely no] place here, where the form is the concept itself. W_2 *(Var) reads:* or merely a formal category in regard to the concept. *Cf. Ho:* As determinate, the qualities are merely a formal aspect, in themselves a determinateness of form.

498. [*Ed.*] Kant, *Critique of Pure Reason*, B 655–656.

499. *Thus P; G reads:* Existence, to be sure, is contingent; what is, W_2 *(Var) reads:* This is, to be sure, correct in existence; the contingent

500. W_2 *reads:* a proportionate, purposive *Ho reads:* a proportionately purposive

tent of observation, however. From "great" to "absolute" we make the leap. We begin with the sense of wonder at the power before us and we never get any further. This is a wholly justified comment; the content from which we start is not the divine concept.[501]

To get any further we must now consider this more precisely. The starting point is the category of conformity to purpose, taken in its empirical aspect; there are finite, contingent things, and they | also serve purposes. Well, what kind of purposiveness is this? It is *finite*. The purposes it serves are finite, particular purposes, and the purposiveness appears as contingent because the purposes themselves are contingent. This is what is wrong with this physicotheological proof, the fault we are from the outset dimly aware of, and what makes us suspicious about the whole argument. What are the purposes or ends? For instance, human beings. Human beings need food and drink; so here the ends are animals, light, air, water, edible plants, that these should be maintained. It emerges at this point that these are completely limited ends; edible plants and animals are both ends and means, for one animal is eaten by another, and that one in turn by others. The physicotheological view is apt to pass over into such petty singular details as this; for there is nothing upon which piety cannot feed. So if the aim is to stir the heart, [that] can be achieved by this view. But to achieve cognition of God by it[502] is another matter. When we speak of absolute wisdom, or of the power that operates according to its purposes, the question arises—What are those purposes? And the content of the divine activity is then constituted by the finite purposes to which we have referred, and these are only such purposes as are to be found in existence. Absolute (or higher) purposes would be ethical life, or freedom. So one has to show that the ethically good is a purpose on its own account, and further that an absolute purpose of this kind is achieved in the world.

318

501. [*Ed.*] The proof that starts with the divine concept (a concept that includes within itself being or reality) is the ontological proof. In Hegel's view it is the only adequate proof, since the "leap" of which he speaks can never be required or demonstrated rationally.

502. W_2 *adds:* and speak of absolute wisdom *Cf. Ho:* But to speak of absolute wisdom and power, which [operate] according to purposes that themselves are absolute, would be another matter.

But at present we are nowhere near the stage where we can talk of the absolute purpose; here we are only in the sphere of purposive action generally, and what is present for our observation at this point are ⁻simply *finite* purposes.⁻⁵⁰³ If we nevertheless say that the absolute purpose is good, then we must still ask, for example, What does this "good" consist in? The answer may be [that it consists in] the ethical life of individuals, | that happiness should be meted out   319 to them according to the measure of their ethical life. But if one hazards the observation that the [absolute] purpose is that the good should be happy and the evil unhappy, then one sees that this is brutally gainsaid in the world, and one finds that there are about as many inducements to an ethical way of life as there are reasons for going astray. The good person fares ill, and the evil person prospers. In a word, as far as mere perception and observation are concerned, there is evidence of conformity to purpose, of purposive arrangement, but there is just as much evidence of the contrary, and ultimately one would have to count whether the examples of one or the other are more numerous. And it is this kind of finite content that is supposed to make up the content of the divine wisdom!

So the defect in this proof lies in the fact that purposiveness and wisdom are defined only in general terms, and we have to turn to the observations or perceptions ⁻in which such relative purposes exhibit themselves.⁻⁵⁰⁴

It follows that even if the divine nature is comprehended as a power that operates in conformity with purposes, we still do not arrive at what we want when we speak of God, i.e., we do not have what we call the personality of God, or spirit. For spirit is not the only power that operates in conformity with purposes; natural vitality is also such a power. The concept of vitality is [that of] an end-for-itself, an existing purpose, involving effectual action to realize it. So there is nothing more before us here, in respect of content, than is involved in living nature and its concept.

As for the formal aspect of this transition, the form here is in general that of the syllogism of the understanding. That is to say,

503. *Ho, W read:* finite, limited purposes. The power that operates according to purpose [*W:* purposes] is only vitality, it is not yet the spirit, the personality of God.
504. *Thus G; D reads:* which evince arguments for and against it.

there are existences that are teleologically defined, in other words purposive relationships generally; and the determinate being of the objects having the character of means and that of the ones in which the purposes lie is [reciprocally] contingent. The second point, however, is that at the same time they are not contingent in this relationship, but rather it is inherent in the concept of the purposively active power, or in the concept of vitality, that not only are the purposes posited but also the objects | that are used as means for them. That is all quite correct. But the matter can also be presented as follows: Things in the world that are purposefully ordered have for their inner essence, their implicit potential, a power that relates, posits, creates the two sides in such a way that they match each other. This is the major premise. Next it is said, "Such things exist"; here again the being of the things in question is the affirmative moment, the starting point, but the transition [to the conclusion] involves rather the moment of their nonbeing just as much [as their being]. Things that are used as means are *not* [because they are consumed]; they *are* only inasmuch as they are posited as negative in their [simple] existence; they are only contingently [there] for purpose; what is therefore required, however, is that they are not indifferent existences for [their] purpose. When we say that there are such things, the [logical] moment has to be added that their being is not their own, but is a being that has been demoted to the level of means. Similarly in regard to the purposes that stand in need of the means, when we say there are objects of this kind, objects that have a goal before them, then it is true that these objects are [there]; but inasmuch as the conclusion to be reached is the power that so disposes them, the existing purposes are posited together with the existence of their means. It is not *their* being that, as positive being, can ground the mediation or transition effected at this stage; rather it is the case that precisely in this transition their being is turned into a being-posited. ˉThe minor premise always turns being into the mediating term.ˉ505

This then is the form of this proof in [all] its manifoldness.

The general content of this form is as follows: The world is to

---

505. *Thus D; Ho, W read:* But the minor premise remains fixed upon the being of things, instead of also taking into account their nonbeing.

be comprehended as a purposive world generally, a pattern of purposive relationships—about the detailed nature of the purposes we say no more. Conformity to purpose is the concept—not merely the concept that exists in finite things but the concept defined in absolute terms, the concept in its divinity, an absolute advance, a necessary [stage in the] definition of God. God's being is to be power and self-determination, and this involves self-determination according to purposes. The main defect in this teleological | proof is that it starts from perception and appearances; these give us only finite conformity to purpose, not the concept of purpose as such; but the pure purpose is just the universal and absolute purpose as such.

321

c. The More Concrete Definition of God[506]

Let us now turn to the concrete, the more specific form of this religion, the concrete definition of God. The concept is that of the universal power that is purpose-oriented. But in the sphere of religion we stand immediately at a different viewpoint. The standpoint of religion is that of the consciousness—or self-consciousness—of spirit. In religious consciousness we have this concept, not as mere vitality, but as it determines itself in consciousness. So we now have religion as the consciousness of the spirit that is the universal power operating according to purposes. The object of religion includes the representation of spirit as such, but everything depends on what moment of thought or of the spirit is operative. The inner essence of this spirit is not yet spirit in-and-for-itself; the content of this representation, the way its object is defined, does not yet express the content of spirit; instead this content is here a power that operates according to purposes. The second point is that while we have characterized religion as the consciousness of spirit in general, it has here the specific character of self-consciousness; we have here divine self-consciousness in general, both objectively as a characteristic of the object and subjectively as characteristic of the finite spirit.

506. [*Ed.*] In this concluding introductory section, Hegel summarizes what he normally considers under the category of "concrete representation," namely the specific representational and cultic forms of a religion. He returns from the lengthy excursus on the teleological proof to the specific religions in view at this stage, namely, the Greek, Jewish, and Roman.

We have noted that the consciousness of spirit here determines itself as self-consciousness. This follows from what precedes; let us consider briefly how it does so. We have seen that in the concept of purpose, or in the power that is wisdom, the defining character belongs to the concept itself, i.e., determinateness is posited in its ideality. But this means that determinacy is what appears as determinate being, as being for an other. Along with consciousness there is posited distinction, initially vis-à-vis the self; determinacy is here posited as the distinction that properly belongs to the self, in other words it is the self's relationship to | itself, i.e., it is self-consciousness. Thus God is posited as self-consciousness insofar as consciousness ˉofˉ[507] the object has its being essentially as self-consciousness. ˉThe determinate being of God for the other consciousness is therebyˉ[508] something ideal, it is spiritual, being as subjective; to put it another way, God is now essentially *for* spirit, for thought in general, for the supersensual, and the fact that he exists as spirit for spirit is at least one side of the relationship. That God is worshiped in spirit and in truth [John 4:24] *may* constitute the whole relationship, but at the very least it is to be posited as an essential character of it.

322

The second point to be noted in this regard [is as follows]. As we have seen, the concept must be characterized as purpose. This purpose, however, must not maintain the form of being self-contained, it must not keep to itself; instead, the shape must attain a [distinct] reality. The question now is, if wisdom is to become operative, if the purpose is to be realized, what is the soil as such in which this can occur? This soil cannot be anything save spirit itself, or more precisely humanity. Humanity is the object of purpose, of the power that defines itself and acts accordingly, the power that is wisdom. Human being—or finite self-consciousness in general—is spirit in the determinate category of finitude. To realize the purpose is to posit the concept in a manner distinct from its mode of being as absolute concept subsisting in and for itself; it is to posit it in the

---

507. G *reads:* [in relation] to W₂ *(Var) reads:* and its relation to
508. *Thus P, D; G reads:* The other—God as object for what stands over against him—is W₂ *(following Ho) reads:* The determinate being of God, his objectivity, the other, is Ho *reads:* So God's objectivity, or the manner in which he has being for consciousness, is

mode of finitude generally, but a mode that is at the same time spiritual. Essentially, spirit only is *for* spirit. Spirit is here defined as self-consciousness; hence the other in which it realizes itself is finite spirit; and in finite spirit it is at the same time self-consciousness. So the soil in which it realizes itself, or the universal medium of reality generally, is itself something spiritual; it must be a soil in which spirit at the same time exists for itself. Humanity, the human world, is thus posited as essential purpose, as the soil of the divine wisdom and the divine power. |

323

What follows, thirdly, [is] that human beings obtain in this way an affirmative relationship to their God, for the basic determining character here is that he is self-consciousness. ¯Thus humanity, as one side of reality, has self-consciousness, it exists affirmatively vis-à-vis God,¯[509] it is consciousness of the absolute essence as its own essence; in other words, the *freedom* of consciousness is hereby posited as such within God—in him humanity is at home with itself. This moment of self-consciousness is an essential moment of freedom; it is a basic characteristic, even though it is not yet the whole content of the relationship. By virtue of it human beings exist for themselves as ends in themselves; in God their consciousness is free, it is justified in God, it exists freely on its own account, essentially for itself; and inasmuch as it directs itself toward God, human consciousness produces *itself*.

This is the general picture. The more specific forms of this standpoint are the religions of sublimity, of beauty, and of expediency, each of which we now have to consider more closely.

1. The Religion of Sublimity (Jewish Religion)[510]

First we have the religion of sublimity, that of the One. The moments of this religion are as follows. First, God is defined as the absolute

509. *Thus G; D reads:* For as regards the relationship, this is self-consciousness.
510. [*Ed.*] Judaism is the religion of sublimity [*Erhabenheit*] because of its high, exalted conception of the one God. Here for the first time the idea of God is truly attained in the history of religions. Hegel's treatment of Judaism in 1824 differs in significant respects from the interpretation offered in the *Ms.* The primary difference is that the category of "wisdom," though mentioned in 1821, is now elevated to a position of prominence. The absolute power of the Lord is wisdom, wise power, a power that acts in accord with purposes or ends, which on the one hand are abstract

power that is wisdom; and power as wisdom is, to begin with, reflected into self as subjectivity, and exists initially within itself. This self-determination of power is the completely abstract, universal self-determination that has not yet inwardly sundered itself but is merely reflection-into-self as such. Its determinacy is just determinacy as such. Because of this utterly undifferentiated self-reflectedness God is defined simply as One. In this unity all particularization, all distinction disappears. Second, natural things, the finite in general, the particular, no longer have independent validity in their immediacy; there is just the one power that can stand on its own; | everything else is posited, held in check by the One, for it is abstract subjectivity. It is itself shapeless; configuration counts only as something posited; against the One there is nothing that can stand on its own. The third moment is the defining of its purpose. On the one hand it is itself the purpose—it is wisdom; in addition, its wisdom must be equal to its power. But the One is only universal purpose for itself, i.e., its wisdom is merely abstract, it is only called wisdom. But this wisdom must be realized, and the mode of particularity must accordingly be implicit in it too. This is the first, immediate particularization, whose content is therefore completely limited and entirely singular.

324

We are dealing with the determining of the concept. [But] this determinacy must not just remain within the concept; it must also

---

and universal, but on the other are oriented exclusively to one people, the Jewish people. The fear of the Lord is the beginning of wisdom, but Hegel now stresses, against Schleiermacher (see below, n. 551), that this fear does not issue in a "feeling of dependence" but in a liberation from dependence on all earthly, particular things. It is thus the basis of human freedom, which in Judaism takes the form of absolute trust or infinite faith in the Lord, as exemplified by Abraham and Job. This contrasts sharply with the *Early Theological Writings,* where Abraham is portrayed as epitomizing the alienated and servile consciousness, as well as with the *Ms.,* where the stress is on the *fear* rather than on the wisdom that issues from it. Hegel had long been attracted to the Book of Job ("Job's situation," he says in these lectures, "is a universal one"), and already in the *Ms.* he quotes extensively from Job 31, 33, 38, 40, 42. These quotations are repeated in somewhat briefer form in the 1824 lectures. It is conceivable that the interpretation offered in 1824 reflects the influence of F. W. C. Umbreit's *Das Buch Hiob; Uebersetzung und Auslegung,* published in Heidelberg 11 April 1824. Whereas earlier interpreters had stressed the portrayal of divine majesty in Job, Umbreit stressed the divine wisdom. See Reinhard Leuze, *Die ausserchristlichen Religionen bei Hegel* (Göttingen, 1975), pp. 169–180, esp. 172.

acquire the form of reality. This *form* of reality, however, is the initially immediate reality, an immediate reality. The purpose of God, therefore, is just this primitive reality, and hence it is a quite specific single purpose. The next stage is for this determinate purpose on its side to be raised into[511] universality. In this way we do have here on the one side pure subjectivity, but the determinacy [of its purpose] does not yet correspond to this subjectivity. Its initial purpose is a completely limited one; but, as we have said,[512] humanity is the purpose, self-consciousness is its soil, and as the divine purpose it must at the same time be an inwardly and implicitly universal purpose, universality must be contained within it. The universality it contains, however, is still primitive, it is a natural universality. The purpose is something human as such, and ˉmore exactlyˉ[513] it is the family. What we have here, then, is a patriarchal religion. Then the family expands into a people. It is this nation, then—a nation is a people as constituted by nature—that is the limited purpose. This family, this people, is the divine purpose to the exclusion of all else.

Such are the basic characteristics of the religion of sublimity or of the One. We now have to consider it in its concrete essence. | 325

a. God as the One[514]

The absolute essence is he who is One, and we have indicated what this definition means. It is subjectivity, which is infinite power, so this subjectivity is simply and solely One. That God is solely One is infinitely important, trivial as it may seem to us, since we are accustomed to think of God as One. As a definition it is formal, too, but it is nonetheless infinitely important, and it is not surprising that the Jewish people regarded it as so important that they worshiped God *as* the One. That God is One is ˉthe ground of absolute spirituality,ˉ[515] the path to truth. The definition of absolute truth is involved in it; it is not yet the truth as truth, for that involves

511. *W (HgG) adds:* concrete
512. [*Ed.*] See above, p. 422–423.
513. *Thus P; G reads:* so *W (HgG) reads:* also naturally
514. *G reads:* 1
515. *Thus P; G reads:* the root of subjectivity, *Ho reads, similar in W:* the absolute root of subjectivity, of the intelligible world,

development, but it is ˉthe principle, truth's absolute harmony with itself, which in concrete terms *is* truth.ˉ516

This one God is therefore without shape or form, for he is pure power; everything particular is posited in him as negative, i.e., as not belonging to him, not befitting him, not yet worthy of him. In nature religion we have seen the aspect of [divine] determinacy as a natural existence, as light, and so forth. We have seen [God's] self-consciousness determined in this manifold fashion; in the infinite power, on the contrary, all this externality is annihilated. Here there is the essence that has no shape and image, that does not have being externally in any natural way for the other, but *is* only for thought, for spirit. This first, formal, simple way of defining the One provides the ground for grasping God as spirit ˉor as self-consciousness; it isˉ517 the root from which his spirituality as such derives, the root of his concrete, genuine content.

b. The Form of Divine Self-Determination[518]

The second point is the form of the divine self-determination generally, the manner of God's particularization. This cannot be absent, ˉfor it isˉ519 | necessarily contained in the idea. Initially it is not a matter of God's being particularized internally, for then God would be known as spirit. ˉThis is only one side, that of defining God, not his inner self-determining.ˉ520 This particularization is initially the divine process of determining in general, and that is what we call *creation,* to which we have already referred. It should be noted that the particular form of creation does not consist in a going forth of the particular from any sort of One, as in the case of Brahman. What is expressed by "going forth" is that what has gone forth is independent; to put it another way, the alteration involved

326

---

516. *Thus P; G reads:* the beginning of truth. *W₂ (following G, Ho) reads:* the beginning of truth and the formal principle of absolute harmony with itself. *Ho reads:* only its formal principle, absolute harmony with itself.

517. *Thus G; W₂ (Var/Ed?) reads:* and for self-consciousness it is

518. *G reads:* 2

519. *Thus D; G reads:* it is *W (HgG) reads:* wisdom is

520. *Thus G, P; W₂ reads:* Because God is One, particularization falls on the other side. *Cf. Ho:* But as God is One, this moment of particularization does not fall within him but outside him.

in arising is only something transitory, and what has arisen thus loses the character of having arisen ˉand becomes an enduring, independent deity.ˉ521 But what we have here is not this mode of going forth; the positing is not something transitory, and everything that has gone forth continues to have the character of being a posited *creature*. Hence all things are stamped with the mark that shows they are *not* truly independent. That all things created are just posited beings remains basic to their definition, since it is God who, as subject, is the infinite power. This power is the One, and what is particular is defined merely as something negative, merely a posited being in contrast with the subject.

The second inherent characteristic of creation is that God is a presupposed subject, just as he is an enduring subject as power. ˉHe also goes forth on this account [into particularization] in Greek mythology and cosmogony,ˉ522 but there the spiritually present deities are the last to be begotten. But this is not the case with the one God, the subject that is presupposed and endures; here whatever has gone forth is only a creature. This accordingly lies in the very concept of creation; otherwise | creation is simply a vague notion all too evocative of mechanical, technical, *human* production; and that is a notion that must be eschewed. God is what is [logically] first; his creation is an *eternal* creation, in which he is not the result but the starting point. The higher mode of creation is that in which spirit generates itself, without stepping forth outside itself, at once the beginning and the result; then it is posited as spirit. But here it is not posited [as] achieving its return-to-self through its process of particularization. And since God is simply what comes first, we must not think of the human mode of production. Human, technical production is external; the subject is what comes first, then it begins to be active, steps outside itself, and so enters into an external relationship with the material, which is worked on and molded, resists, and has to be bent to one's wishes; maker and material exist

327

521. *Thus P; G reads:* and endure independently, is God. *D reads:* according to which God remains simply something independent.

522. *Thus D; G reads:* He is also a presupposed subject among the Greeks, Ho *reads:* The Greeks also [have] a theogony, an issuing-forth of the gods; Uranus and Cronus come first; Jupiter [Zeus], the spiritual deity, is the last.

as objects, each already there over against the other. ¯God, however, creates absolutely, out of nothing; here we do not have one object over against another, but a mode of production in which God is the subject, is simply intuitive, infinite activity. Human production can

328 be represented as follows: here I am, with my | purpose and my consciousness, and I also have a material, about which I know, so that I am in the relationship of a conscious being inasmuch as I am in relationship with something else. Intuitive production, on the contrary, is not conscious production so far as it is intuitive. Instead it is the eternal production of nature, which falls under the concept of vitality. It is an inward act, an inner activity, not directed against something already present to hand—the falling asleep of the intelligence, as the saying went;¯[523] it is vitality, nature being

523. Ho reads, similar in W: But here too, creation is not something done externally on a material that has to be subdued by the subject; for God creates absolutely, out of nothing. Only he is being, what is positive. But he is also the positing of his power. In himself he is the same [power?] as the immediate that sublates itself. Hence the positing of his power is the positing of the immediate as sublated, as posited. This immediate does not lie within God himself, for he is the sublated immediate. So the immediate posited as sublated falls outside him, as the creature. The creature has within itself both moments—to be immediate and to be posited. The fact that God is necessarily the positing of his power is the birthplace of creation and of everything that is created. This necessity is the material out of which God creates; this material is God himself, hence he creates out of nothing material, for he is the *self*, not what is immediate or material. He is not merely One over against something else, already there, but he himself is the something else as determinacy. Because, however, he is *only* One, this determinacy falls outside him as his negative movement. Creation is the infinitely intuitive activity of positing oneself as power. In their productive role human beings are consciously related to something else, but this is not divine creation. The positing of nature necessarily falls under the concept of spiritual life, of the self, and is the falling asleep, for instance, of the intelligence.

[*Ed.*] The source of the expression, "falling asleep of the intelligence," has not been traced. In the *Lectures on the History of Philosophy* 3:517 (*Werke* 15:652), Hegel refers in a comparable context to Friedrich Schelling's *System des transcendentalen Idealismus* (Tübingen, 1800), p. 4, where Schelling says that so-called dead nature is merely an "immature intelligence" (*eine unreife Intelligenz*), which can be seen at work, although still unconsciously, in its phenomena. Hegel comments that by "immature intelligence" Schelling means "torpid, fossilized intelligence" (*erstarrte, versteinerte Intelligenz*), so the phrase "falling asleep of the intelligence" may be an allusion to Schelling. Hegel uses a similar metaphor in his lectures on the philosophy of right; see Hegel, *Vorlesungen über Rechtsphilosophie 1818–1831*, ed. K.-H. Ilting, vol. 4 (Stuttgart-Bad Canstatt, 1974), p. 632 (Griesheim's transcript of § 258): "Spirit also realizes itself in nature, but only as the other of spirit, as sleeping spirit."

produced continually anew. As opposed, therefore, to the definition of the One as the subject, there is the particular that comes forth in this productive activity in nature and externality, the sphere of intuition; in general it is something posited, something created.

The second characteristic that accrues to God in respect of creation is his goodness and his justice. As infinite wisdom, power is no longer mere necessity: created things are in any case, and they are only posited, necessarily determined as being or not being. But here another characteristic is added; as a moment of the divine, the being of finite things must be characterized as [a work of] *goodness;* their nullity and its manifestation is then [the work of] divine *justice.*

Thus the defining and production [of created things] is in the first place an outgoing process. Goodness and justice are moments of power; because the One is presupposed as the subject, they appear as properties, as subjective moments. In consequence, the being of things˞has the form of purpose: that they shall be is [the work of] goodness; that they shall perish is [the work of] justice˞[524]—and in both cases it is the subject who decides. At this point, therefore, there is room for properties, which can be regarded as determining characteristics of the concept itself. But the thing that possesses the properties does not have its nature in them as such; its basic determining characteristics are the One and the power. Its properties do define the subject, but in such a way that the concept, the most inward nature of the subject is still posited independently of them. For if the properties did in fact belong to the subject, these determining characteristics would | themselves be totalities, for the concept is absolute goodness, and its characteristics are self-imparted. Only when they form a totality is the concept posited as idea, and no longer as abstract subject. For them to be posited in the concept they themselves would therefore have to constitute the entire concept, which would thus for the first time become truly real; the concept would then be posited as idea and the subject as spirit, its goodness and justice being totalities, not just an abstract determinacy. It follows that the negative moment is justice, to the end that the nullity

329

524. *Thus G; D reads:* is defined in the terms that it shall be, in the same way as their disappearance, that it shall not be

of existent things may be made manifest, as we have seen in the coming into being and passing away of Shiva; it is only the aspect of process as such, of the contingent, whose nullity is manifested. So this negativity is not the infinite return-to-self that would characterize spirit; it is just the negativity of justice.

The third point to be noted is what sort of determinateness things that are real receive quite generally. The definition of things is just that they are created, that they have entered into the categories of the external and nonautonomous. In other words, the nature of natural things is here prosaic: they are stripped of divinity and are within themselves devoid of independence—˜for all independence is concentrated in the One.˜525 Now it may seem to be a commonplace to complain that in a religion nature has been stripped of divinity; what is then prized on the other hand is the unity of the ideal and the real, of nature with God, in which natural things—sun, animals, trees—are regarded as independent and divine, as subsisting freely. This is what is called the identity of ideality and reality. And indeed the idea does have to be viewed in terms of this unity, but this does not amount to much. This definition of the identity is completely formal, even cheap. There is this identity of the ideal and the real anyway; but what matters most is how it is further defined. There is a genuine identity of the real and the ideal only in the spiritual [realm], in the God who determines himself as
330 real, which means that the | different moments or aspects of the concept of God have their own being at the same time as moments or aspects of the totality. Natural things, however, according to their singularity, are in fact implicitly, in their concept, external and opposed to spirit, set against the concept; so finite spirit itself, and its vitality as such, is something external and opposed to the concept also. Vitality is essentially something inward; but insofar as it is only life, the identity of the ideal and real is something external as against the absolute internality of spirit. So it is too with the consciousness of ˜spirit.˜526 Abstract self-consciousness, whatever we call natural, ˜the world, natural being, living being,˜527 is, by its nature,

525. Ho reads, similar in W₂: for divinity is only in One.
526. Thus P; D reads: the finite.
527. Thus P; G reads: the whole array of finite things, abstract being itself,

something implicitly external, and it is just this character of externality that things are first endowed with at this stage. They are posited according to the concept, in their truth. One may lament this externalization of nature, but one must in any case admit that the beautiful union of nature with the gods is valid only for the fancy—the picture is very beguiling, but it is not one that will do for reason. For those who inveigh against the loss of divinity and extol the identity of the real and the ideal, it nevertheless surely remains very hard (if not impossible) to believe in ¯a "ganga,"[528] a cow, a monkey, a sea, and so forth.¯[529] No, the truthful attitude is the one that we have indicated; here the basis is laid for understanding things as cohering together. ¯For on account of its externality just this intelligible coherence of things is [the subject matter of the sciences]. But scientific understanding does not belong to this stage.¯[530]

Once things have been defined in this prosaic manner, | God's   331 relatedness to the world as [an assemblage of] these prosaic, external things is thereby determined too. Even if God's relation to the world is comprehended as his appearing immediately in these things, any such appearance is a singular, individual event, for a definite purpose, in a particular sphere; so it is here that miracles can enter on the scene. There are no miracles in Hindu religion, because there are not as yet any [properly] natural things, there is no determinate being or process amenable to the understanding; therefore there are no miracles.

A miracle is a singular appearance of God in or upon one of these natural and understandable things. His appearing in or upon such

528. [Ed.] African term, originally derived from the Bantu languages, for a practitioner of white magic. The word is used by Cavazzi, *Historische Beschreibung,* pp. 89–90 (p. 74), though in a very derogatory sense, to apply to sorcerers and others who did all they could to counter the teaching of the missionaries and so retain their privileged position in the tribe.

529. *Thus G; P reads:* a Greek or Hindu god.

530. W₂ *(MiscP) reads:* But the theoretical elaboration of this consciousness to the level of science does not yet occur here. For that would call for a concrete interest in things, and the essence would also have to be grasped not merely as a universal concept but as determinate concept too. The notion of abstract wisdom and one single, limited purpose cannot yet give rise to a determinate sort of theoretical intuition.

a thing is contrary both to the character of the thing and to the concept of God himself. The need for miracles and for belief in miracles manifests itself ⁻when the existing [world of] understandable things is not grasped in such a way that God's appearances in or upon them occur merely as the eternal laws of nature. Belief in miracles disappears when natural things are grasped in such a way that God manifests himself as essence; [then he] implicitly exists according to his concept, essentially in a universal and inwardly necessary way, a way that expresses the concept. This is the system of what we call natural laws. The way that God works is then grasped as a universal and essential effectiveness, and the coherence of things then becomes objectively understandable. The singular things are then known as at any rate subsisting only in coherence, and this coherence, which displays their divine element, is a wholly universal, for all time inwardly necessary, pattern.⁻531 Belief in miracles has its place [only] in a representational scheme of this kind, defined in this way.

332   The second way in which God is related absolutely to things in the world | generally is that they are made by him and upheld by him, and that he manifests himself in them as the power over them. This is the intuition of his sublimity, expressing his relationship to natural things.

Sublimity is the idea that expresses or manifests itself, but in such a way that in thus appearing in or upon reality it at the same time shows itself as sublime, exalted above this appearance and reality, so that the reality is simultaneously posited as negated, and the emerging idea is exalted above that in or upon which it appears, so that its appearance is an inappropriate expression.532

To express sublimity it is not enough that what is substantive is in and for itself higher than the shape in which it is represented; even

531. W_2 (MiscP) reads: as long as the coherence of things is not grasped as their objective nature, i.e., as long as God's appearance in or upon them is not thought of as the eternal, universal laws of nature, and his effectiveness is not thought of essentially as universal effectiveness. The understandable coherence that is for the first time grasped at this stage is merely the objective coherence that in finitude the singular thing as such is for itself and thus is in an external relationship.

532. Thus G; W_1 (HgG) adds: and indeed expressly so, not unconsciously.

if the shape is accentuated, even if it is raised beyond its normal measure, this does not amount to positing sublimity; for sublimity it must also be posited that what manifests itself is at the same time the power over the shape. In Hindu religion the images are grotesque, lacking all measure, but not sublime—they are distortions; or else they are not distortions—for example, the cow and the monkey, which express the whole power of nature—but the meaning and the form do not match, there is nothing sublime, and this absence of correspondence is the greatest deficiency. For the sublime to appear, the negated state of the appearance—the power over this shape— must therefore be posited simultaneously.

In their natural consciousness human beings may have very trivial things in view, but their spirit is not like that. There is no correspondence between it and the objects. There is nothing sublime in simply looking around, but in looking up to heaven and transcending what is before one. This sublimity epitomizes the relation of God to natural things in general. For example, the scriptures and literature of the Jews, the Psalms, the prophets, etc., are famous for their sublimity. The Greek author Longinus[533] quotes from the very beginning of the [first] Book of Moses: "God said, 'Let there be light'; and there was light." This is one of the most sublime passages. "God said"—the text tells us how he works. | Outwardly displayed, in an image, his working is speech. But there is nothing that costs as little effort as a word; as soon as it is spoken, it is gone. Yet this breath [of God] is here light as well, the world of light, the infinite outpouring of light, so that light here becomes merely a word, something as transient as a mere word. God is also pictured [in Psalm 104] as using wind and lightning for his servants and messengers. "Thou makest the winds thine angels," and so on. What God needs is realized, but in such a way that it is merely an instrument; thus nature

333

533. [Ed.] See Dionysius Longinus, De sublimitate (Leipzig, 1769) 9.9; the biblical reference is to Gen. 1:3. According to Karl Rosenkranz, Georg Wilhelm Friedrich Hegel's Leben (Berlin, 1844), p. 10, Hegel made a complete translation of De sublimitate at the age of sixteen, between the winter of 1786 and September 1787, which was still preserved when he died. When he lectured in 1824 he apparently was unaware of the recent discovery that the treatise had been wrongly attributed to Longinus.

is obedient to him. We read: "Thou girdest thyself with lightning as with a garment," and again: "Thou sendest forth thy breath, worlds are created; at the voice of thy thunder they haste away. Thou openest thy hand, they are filled with good; thou hidest thy face, they are troubled; thou withholdest thy breath, they return to the dust; thou sendest forth thy Spirit, they are recreated."[534] ⌐This is what sublimity is—that nature is represented in this wholly negated, subordinate, transitory fashion.⌐[535]

The third point we have to speak about here is God's purpose—what can be represented as God's purpose at this level. Initially sublimity is only the representation of power, not yet of a purpose. The purpose, not merely of the One but of God in general, can be nothing else than God himself: that his concept should become objective for him and then return within him, that he should possess himself in what is realized. This would be the universal purpose as such. But if at this point we want to regard the world and nature in general as the purpose of God, it is only because his power is manifested in them. In the world his power becomes objective to him, and his wisdom is still wholly abstract. But if we speak of purpose, then it cannot be mere power; it must be somehow determined as well. The soil in which this purpose is to be found cannot be anything else but spirit as such. And since in spirit as consciousness God is purpose in the spirit set over against him (i.e., here in the finite spirit as such), therefore | his being represented, his being recognized in finite spirit, *is* his purpose. God is here confronted by finite spirit; other-being is not yet posited as having absolutely returned into itself. This finite spirit is essentially consciousness; God must therefore be the object of consciousness as [his own] essence. In consciousness he *is* his own purpose—the purpose being that he should be recognized and venerated. The glory of God is his prime purpose, and this purpose is just what is [achieved] in the world. So the reflection [*Reflex*] of God, the determinacy of God, is in the

334

534. [*Ed.*] This and the preceding two quotations are drawn loosely from Ps. 104; cf. vss. 4, 2, 7, 28, 29, 30.

535. *Thus G; P reads:* This notion of sublimity, too, characterizes God's relationship to the world generally; there can be no sublimity other than that through which he expressly manifests himself.

awareness that he is recognized; he is not yet cognized but only recognized. For him to be cognized, he would, as spirit, already have had to posit distinctions within himself, whereas at this stage he still has only the abstract characteristics that we have so far considered.

It is an essential characteristic at this stage that religion as such is the purpose—that God shall be known in the self-consciousness, that in it he is object [for himself, and hence] affirmatively related to it. ¯God is self-contained;¯[536] but secondly he appears, and essentially in another spirit, which qua finite is initially set against him. Thus defined, the purpose can be termed the theoretical purpose; for God to be recognized, venerated, honored, means that the finite self-consciousness represents God to itself, knows him as its purpose. But the purpose can also be defined in practical terms, as purpose realized, authentically real, God's purpose in and in regard to the world as actualized (though always on the spiritual plane). This realized purpose that we are here considering is now God's prime or first purpose. As God's purpose it has its being in the actual spirit; therefore it must have inward universality and be the genuinely divine purpose within itself; it must be the purpose that is substantive, that has substantive universality. A substantive purpose internal to spirit is one such that the existing spiritual individuals know themselves as one, behave as one, are united. It is essentially an inwardly universal, infinite purpose, an ethical purpose, for its soil is in self-consciousness, in freedom, in freedom realized. This is where the practical side first emerges, [God's] purpose in actual consciousness. Second, because it is the first purpose, | this ethical character is   335 directly still the unmediated, natural ethical life, and the existence of this immediate ethical life is therefore the family—the natural ethical realm of family solidarity. Thus the purpose is the family, and this family is one family to the exclusion of all others.

The real, directly prime purpose of the divine wisdom is still wholly limited and singular because it is the *first* purpose. One may wonder how this character of most limited singularity can cohere with the fact that God is absolute power and wisdom. He is absolute wisdom, but still in the sense of a wholly abstract wisdom; the

536. *Thus P, D; G reads:* He is God as infinite power and inward subjectivity;

purpose inherent in the divine concept is still a wholly universal purpose, and consequently devoid of content; in its determinate being, this indeterminate purpose that lacks all content turns into unmediated singularity, the utmost limitedness.[537]

The fact that God's real purpose is inwardly universal therefore determines that it is the family, this single family; [for it to be] many single families would already involve extending the purpose by reflection. This is the striking contrast, infinitely difficult, the most difficult of all. On the one hand God is universal, the God of heaven and earth, the God of all humanity, absolute wisdom and universal power; on the other hand, his purpose and operation in the spiritual world are so limited as to be confined to just this one family, just this one people. All peoples are called upon to recognize him and glorify his name [Ps. 117:1–2], but the actual work that is really brought about is a limited one—just this people, in its conditioned existence, its inner, outer, political, and ethical determinacy. God operates within one single family. Thus he is just "the God of Abraham, Isaac, and Jacob," and subsequently "the God who led us out of Egypt."[538] Abraham, Isaac, and Jacob are the families as families; those that are led out of Egypt are the nation—it is the heads of the families who here constitute the determinate content of the purpose.[539] |

336

The five Books of Moses begin with the creation of the world. The famous story of the fall [Gen. 3] conveys the intrinsic nature of humanity. But this universal content, [this story] of the creation of the world, the story of Adam and the fall of Adam, representing humanity, has no connection with what the Jewish religion subsequently became. It is merely a piece of wisdom whose universal content did not become truth for the people of Israel. But this

---

537. W₂ (Var) adds: In other words, the implicit potential in which wisdom still holds itself is itself immediacy, the natural realm.

538. Ho adds, similar in W: Because God is only One, he is only in one universal spirit, in one people, one family.

539. W (1831) adds: Universality is thus still natural universality. So the purpose is solely human, and thus the family. Religion is accordingly patriarchal. The family then extends in scope to become the people. A people is called nation because it has being primarily through nature; this is the limited goal or purpose, and the divine purpose is exclusive vis-à-vis other.

absolute determinateness, and the one God, then entered on the scene in such a way that God is just the God of this people, not of all humanity or of many peoples.

In regard to this connection between God's inwardly universal wisdom and the utterly limited character of the real purpose, a further point can be made in order to clarify the notion. When human beings will the universal good as such, have the universal good as their purpose, they have already thereby made the capriciousness of their will into the principle of what they resolve and undertake. For this general good, this wholly universal purpose does not yet contain any specification within it; and since there has to be action, the real purpose must be somehow determinate. This determinacy can only be found outside the concept, as the concept itself is still indeterminate, abstract; specification is not yet posited precisely because it has not yet been taken up into the universal purpose of the good. In politics—even though the law itself is supposed to be sovereign—still the governing authority is the pure caprice of the individual. The law becomes real only insofar as it is inwardly organized, i.e., insofar as the particular is determined by the universal. It is only through being particularized that the universal becomes alive. So this is the relationship of the real purpose [to universal wisdom].

A more specific way in which the other peoples | are excluded   337 from this single, real purpose is that the people in question possesses its own nationality, it consists of certain families, so that to belong to God's people, to be a member of his folk, to stand in this relationship to God, is a matter of birth. This naturally calls for a particular constitution, laws, ceremonies, and public worship.

This singleness further includes in its developed form the possession of a particular territory, and of it alone, in such a way, moreover, that each single part of it belongs to particular families or tribes. [It] is something inalienable, with the result that the [divine] exclusiveness acquires this wholly empirical, external presence. There is initially nothing polemical about it, the reality being the particular possession, the enjoyment uniquely confined to this one people, and the relationship of this one people to the all-powerful, omniscient God. It is not polemical in this sense, that there is no obligation to bring other peoples to this form of worship or religion. The others are called upon to glorify the Lord, but that they should come to do so is only a wish, not a real purpose or goal; ¯as a goal we first find it in Islam. Here it is only a singular purpose that all peoples should be brought to glorify the Lord. So it is not fanatical; only in Islam does it become so.¯540 Fanaticism is found among the Jews, but only where their possessions or their religion come under attack, and only then because this single purpose of theirs is utterly exclusive and admits of no mediation, no sharing, no fusion with anything 338 else.541 |

540. *Thus G, P; W₂ (Var) reads:* they are merely called upon to do so, in a lazy way, not to any practical effect. A real purpose of this kind first appeared in Islam, where the singular purpose is raised to universal purpose, and so becomes fanatical.

541. *Follows in W (1831):* ªThird characteristic. What is primarily sublime in all creation is humanity; it is human beings that know, that cognize, that think. Thus humanity is the image of God in quite another sense than this is true of the world. What is experienced in religion is God who is thought; only in thought is God venerated.

We have had dualism in Persian religion. We also have this antithesis in the Jewish religion, but it does not pertain to God but to the other [viz., to finite] spirit—God is spirit, and his product, the world, is also spirit; it is in respect of the world that he is implicitly the other of his essence. Finitude implies difference as scission. In the world God is present to self; the world is good, [W₂: for the world's nullity, out of which it was made, is the absolute itself;] [W₁: this primal division of God W₂: however, the world as this first primal division of God] does not proceed to the absolute antithesis—only spirit is capable of this absolute antithesis, and this is [the measure of] its depth. The antithesis pertains to the other spirit, which is consequently finite spirit. This is the place of the struggle between good and evil, the place where this struggle must also be fought to an issue. All these categories follow from the nature of the concept. This antithesis is a difficult point, for it constitutes the contradiction; good is not contradictory by virtue of itself, it is only through evil that the contradiction enters in, it pertains solely to evil.

But the question arises, How did evil come into the world? This question has meaning and interest at this point. In Persian religion this question cannot give rise to any difficulty, for there evil exists in the same way as good exists. Both have issued forth from the wholly indeterminate. Here, on the other hand, where God is power and the One is subject, where everything is posited solely by him, here evil is contradictory, for God is indeed only the absolutely good. In this regard the Bible has handed down to us an ancient image, that of the fall. This well-known portrayal of how evil came into the world is clothed in the form of a myth—a parable, as it were. Now if what is speculative and authentic is thus portrayed in sensuous configuration, in the manner of something that has happened, unsuitable features inevitably occur in it. The same happens with Plato, when he speaks of the ideas in figurative fashion, that an inappropriate relationship becomes evident. We are told then that after Adam and Eve had been created in Paradise God forbade these first two human beings to eat of a certain tree [Gen. 2:17], but the serpent induced them to do so, saying "You shall become like God" [Gen. 3:5]. God then imposes a heavy punishment on them, yet says, "Behold, Adam has become like one of us, knowing good and evil" [Gen. 3:22]. Thus on the one hand humanity has, as God expresses it, become God; on the other hand it is said that God barred the way to humanity, driving it out of Paradise.

This simple story can no doubt be taken in the first place as follows. God made a commandment, and Adam, impelled by an infinite presumption to become like God (a thought that came to him from outside), transgressed this commandment, and was then severely punished for his pitiful, one-sided pride. God made the commandment in merely formal fashion, in order to enable Adam to prove his obedience.

Thus according to this interpretation everything proceeds in everyday, finite consequentiality. At any rate God forbids evil. This is something quite different from forbidding to eat of a mere tree; what God wills and does not will must be of an authentic, eternal nature. Moreover, such a prohibition must be directed solely at a single individual. Human beings are rightly indignant at being punished for another's guilt; they are prepared to stand accountable only for what they themselves have done. [But] there is rather in the whole story a deeply speculative meaning. It is Adam or humanity as such who appears in this story; what is related here concerns the nature of humanity itself. And it is not a childish, formal commandment that God lays upon him; the tree from which Adam is forbidden to eat is the tree of the knowledge of good and evil [Gen. 2:17]. And this being so, the externality and form of a tree falls away. Adam eats of it and attains knowledge of good and evil. The difficult point, however, is that we are told that God forbade humanity to acquire this knowledge. For this knowledge is precisely what constitutes the character of spirit. Spirit is spirit only through consciousness, and the highest consciousness lies precisely in such knowledge. How then can this have been forbidden? Cognition or knowledge is this two-sided, dangerous gift; spirit is free, and this freedom embraces good and evil. It can also involve acting capriciously, doing evil. This is the negative counterpart to the affirmative side of freedom. Humanity, we are told, was in the state of innocence. This is, as such, the state of natural consciousness, and it must be sublated as soon as the consciousness of spirit enters in any way on the scene. This is the eternal history and nature of humanity. At first, humanity is natural and innocent and so cannot be held responsible—in the child there is no freedom; yet it is the vocation of humanity to attain to innocence once again. What is its final vocation is here represented as its primitive state—the harmony of humanity with the good. That is what is defective in this figurative representation, that this unity is portrayed as an immediately obtaining state. This original natural state must be the starting point, but the separation that then occurs must also in turn be reconciled. And this is here represented as meaning that that first state ought not to have been relinquished. In the whole figurative portrayal what is inward is expressed as outward, what is necessary as contingent. The serpent says that Adam will become like God, and God confirms that it actually is so, that this knowledge constitutes likeness to God. This deep idea underlies the narrative.

But then Adam is also punished; he is driven from Paradise, and God says: "Cursed is the ground because of you; in toil you shall eat of it all the days of your life; thorns and thistles it shall bring forth to you; and you shall eat the plants of the field. In the sweat of your face you shall eat bread till you return to the ground, for out of it you were taken; you are dust, and to dust you shall return" [Gen. 3:17–19].

We have to acknowledge that these are the consequences of finitude, but on the other hand the nobility of humanity is precisely to eat [bread] in the sweat of its brow and gain its sustenance for itself by its own activity, labor, and understanding. Animals have this happy lot (if it can so be termed), that nature provides them with what they need. Human beings, on the other hand, raise even what is naturally needful to them to [W_2: something pertaining to] their freedom. This is in fact the use they make of their freedom, even if it is not their highest point, which consists rather in knowing and willing the good. That human beings are free in regard to their natural side too is inherent in their nature and is not in itself to be regarded as punishment. [W_1: Even for those W_2: The mourning implicit in the natural state is in any case linked with the nobility of the human vocation. For those] who do not yet know the higher vocation of spirit, it is a mournful thought that human beings must die, and for them this natural mourning is, as it were, the last word. But the lofty vocation of spirit is that it is eternal and immortal. However, this human nobility, this nobility of consciousness, is not yet contained in this story, for there we read that God said, "And now, lest he put forth his hand and take also of the tree of life, and eat, and live for ever" (Gen. 3:22). And also (v. 19), "till you return to the ground, for out of it you were taken." Consciousness of the immortality of spirit is not yet present in this [W_1: religion, but first awakens with the Egyptians. W_2: religion.]

Throughout the story of the fall these main features occur in a seemingly inconsistent manner, owing to the figurative way in which the whole is represented. The noble element, which God himself here expresses, is the emergence from the natural state, the necessity that consciousness of good and evil should enter on the scene. What is defective is that death is portrayed as something irremediable. The basic determination of the portrayal is that humanity is called upon to be something other than natural. Implicit in this is the genuinely theological affirmation that human beings are naturally evil; evil is to remain standing in this natural condition, out of which human beings must emerge with freedom, with their will. The next stage is for spirit to regain absolute unity within itself, to achieve [W_1: reconciliation. As regards the Jewish religion, it W_2: reconciliation, and it is in fact freedom that entails this return of spirit into itself, this reconciliation with itself, but at this stage spirit has not yet turned about in this way, differentiation has not yet been taken up within God, i.e., reconciled. Evil still has its abstract character. It] has still to be noted that this story remained dormant among the Jewish people and was not developed [to its true dimension] in the Hebraic writings; [W_1: there is no mention of it in them (as may be the case in later books). W_2: apart from some references in the later apocryphal books,[b] there is no mention of it in them.] For a long time it remained fallow, and for the first time attained its true [W_1: valuation W_2: meaning] in Christianity. This is not by any means to say that humanity's internal combat found no place among the Jewish people; on the contrary, this combat is an essential category of the religious spirit among the Hebrews. But it was not grasped in the speculative sense that it derives from human nature itself. [W_1: If they sought to depict a just man, they did not view this combat as an essential moment, W_2: but only as something contingent, represented as occurring in single individuals. Over against sinners and those engaged in combat

Such are the main aspects of the religion of the One, ¯as they are immediately entailed in the concept.¯⁵⁴² | 339

c. The Cultus⁵⁴³

The third point is the cultus. The first was the metaphysical concept, the second the representation of God, the third is the relationship of self-consciousness to this its essence, or spirit to the extent that it is determined as an "other" over against absolute spirit.⁵⁴⁴ God is | essentially related to self-consciousness; ¯he is purposive action,   340 wisdom and power combined; for this absolute spirit, self-consciousness is the first "other."¯⁵⁴⁵ What we have to consider first here | is the religious disposition within this self-consciousness, and   341 mediation to the extent that it is a disposition. To mediate is to posit [explicitly] the identity that is implicitly posited and is a mediating

---

they sought to depict the just man, in whom evil and the inner combat is not viewed as an essential moment,] but justice is said to consist in doing the will of God and continuing in Jehovah's service by observing the ethical commandments as well as [W₁: through the cultus. W₂: ritual and civic prescriptions.] Even so, humanity's inner conflict is everywhere apparent, especially in the Psalms of David; anguish cries aloud from the innermost depths of the soul in the consciousness of its sinfulness, followed by the [W₁: most urgent W₂: most anguished] plea for [W₂: forgiveness and] reconciliation. This depth of anguish is, to be sure, present in this way, but rather as pertaining to the single individual than as known as an eternal moment of spirit.

[Ed.] ªThe 1831 lectures transfer this discussion of the "fall" of humanity from the section on "differentiation" in the Christian religion (Part III), where it occurs in the earlier lectures (see Vol. 3:101–108, 207–211, 300–304), to the section on Jewish religion in Part II. ᵇHegel's statement that the story of the fall was not mentioned in the other books of the Old Testament "apart from some references in the later apocryphal books" probably relates to Ecclesiasticus 25:24 ("From a woman sin had its beginning, and because of her we all die"); see Vol. 3:107 n. 119. Although the pseudepigraphic Apocalypse of Moses or Life of Adam and Eve carries on the story from the time of the expulsion from Eden, Hegel cannot have had any direct knowledge of it.

542. W₂ (Var) reads: insofar as they concern the [inner] sundering and purposive character of the One. This latter characteristic, that of purpose, leads us to the cultus.

543. G reads: 3.

544. [Ed.] This summary shows that Hegel has applied his standard analytic categories here as elsewhere: abstract or metaphysical concept of God, concrete representation, and cultus. In the 1824 lectures, the second and third are understood as the theoretical and practical relationships to God.

545. W₂ (Var) reads: because the soil upon which his purpose appears is finite spirit.

441

342 movement. The disposition represents the innermost moments or aspects of this mediating movement within | self-consciousness; the first moment is negativity, and the second is the affirmative attitude.

The first moment, that of negativity, is fear, fear of the Lord, the inmost aspect of the religious disposition. ‾Fear is what comes over me when I imagine that a possession or interest may be harmed or alienated, and I am without fear when‾[546] I care nothing for the force that threatens me with this, the negating of my own force— when I know myself as a countervailing power so that that force has no power over me—but also when I care nothing for the possession or interest ‾that is to be wrested from me. For then the violence cannot touch me, I give it no chance, because I give the possession up. This power can lay hold on me only through something determinate, some interest or means of satisfying an interest.‾[547] Fear involves, quite generally, a prejudice against oneself, more especially in that I who am afraid do not know myself as power, have not the will to present myself as power; ‾‾the fearful are not prepared to

343 push this presentation | of themselves as power to the uttermost, to lay hold on the impregnability they can acquire by staking their whole range of interests; in this way they show that the power of their will extends so far and no further. Those who will without qualification, stick to their resolve and seek to make their will prevail, gather up all their strength and all their interests, and sacrifice them voluntarily, the main concern being just to display this energy.

Now as far as the fear of the Lord is concerned, it is no earthly lord that is feared; the earthly lord is a contingent power, such that, even if I do not fear it, I am only relatively independent in my opposition to it—‾this or that possession or interest could be taken from me by another.‾[548] The fear of the Lord is rather fear of the

344 invisible, i.e., of the absolute | power. This fear of the Lord is the

546. *Ho reads, similar in W:* Fear in general is what comes over me as the result of imagining a power above me that [negates] me in what is valid for me, whether this appears inwardly or outwardly, as possessions etc.; and I am without fear when, conscious of invulnerable independence,

547. *Ho, W_1 read:* and so stand there in the last resort, stand there invulnerable. *W_2 (Ed) reads:* and so stand there invulnerable, even when injured.

548. *Thus P; G reads:* it is open to question whether another is not stronger than I, to become lord over me.

contrary of the consciousness of my power, the contrary of consciousness; the consciousness of $^{-549}$ all one's own strength disappears in it, all particular interests vanish in it. In this fear of the Lord everything that belongs to our earthly nature, everything ephemeral and contingent, is given up. Hence it is the absolute negativity, it elevates us to the level of pure thought, which surrenders all else and has before itself nothing but this pure thought, remains this free element, wills only this. This fear of the Lord, we are then told, is the beginning of wisdom.^{550} For wisdom is not the taking of something particular—be it interest, inclination, or what you will—to be absolute and substantive, but taking it only as a moment or aspect of the one idea. The fear of the Lord is this absolute negativity that is the one essential aspect of freedom; it is not the bad kind of fear that is afraid of something, but the fear that lets everything go, gives everything up. It is the intuition of pure, absolute power, surrendering everything particular, abstracting absolutely from everything particular. Consequently it is not at all what is termed a "feeling of dependence"^{551} etc. On the contrary, this fear of the Lord sublates

549. *Thus P; G reads:* with consciousness
550. [*Ed.*] See Ps. 111:10; cf. Prov. 1:7; 9:10; Job 28:28.
551. [*Ed.*] See Friedrich Schleiermacher, *Der christliche Glaube nach den Grundsätzen der evangelischen Kirche im Zusammenhange dargestellt* (Berlin, 1821), § 9. Hegel refers to Schleiermacher in the same context in the 1821 Ms. (see *Ms.*, n. 138), but there the interpretation is just the reverse: "God's people is the one that he has accepted on conditon that they shall fear him, and have the basic feeling of their dependence, i.e., of their servitude." In the *Ms.* Judaism is interpreted as the antithesis of the religion of freedom, but now it is viewed as the first of the religions of freedom precisely because the "fear of the Lord sublates all dependence," "sets us free" from all finite lords, negates our own negativity, issues affirmatively in "absolute trust" or "infinite faith," which is found also in Christianity. Not only does this interpretation reflect a reinterpretation of Judaism; it also fits in with the dominant emphasis of the 1824 lectures, which provide a sustained critique of any attempt to ground religion in feeling, and an insistence that the relationship of the finite to the infinite must be understood affirmatively rather than merely negatively (for the latter, God remains totally other and beyond, unknowable). (See Vol. 1:71–72, 288–310; on Hegel's assessment of Schleiermacher in the 1824 lectures, p. 279, n. 37.) In Hegel's view as we now find it, Judaism did grasp the affirmative aspect of the divine-human relationship in the concepts of radical faith and covenant; the problem is that the covenant was exclusive, limited to a particular people; in other words, Judaism remained a provincial religion, not actualizing its own potential universality. Furthermore, lacking a trinitarian conception of God, it was unable to grasp the true

all dependence. Human beings depend on the particular; but the free human is free of all dependence; the fear of the Lord sets us free from all particular interests. When we say that the goal of individuals is blessedness, this is positing individuals themselves as ends, so it is not dependence but liberation, being free from all dependence. The fear of the Lord is this ¯negation of one's own negativity, the sublation of all dependence.¯552 The affirmative then arises from and within this fear of the Lord; pure affirmation is nothing else but this infinite negativity, this negativity that goes back into itself.

The affirmative aspect is then what we call absolute trust, or infinite faith. This infinite trust consists in having given up what is particular and one's own, and immersing oneself in the Lord, having this unity as one's object and essence. | At a later stage, this trust can take the form of self-consciousness immersing itself in itself, resting upon itself, relying on its own strength of soul and fortitude, being completely reduced to this abstraction—Stoic freedom.¯¯553

345

---

infinite as that which "overreaches" the finite, which in Hegel's view is the ultimate cognitive basis for understanding the relationship as "affirmative." In sum, as Hegel's criticism of Schleiermacher's interpretation of religion sharpened and became more stringent, his assessment of Judaism became more favorable: no more than Christianity could it be regarded as exemplifying a "feeling of dependence"; that opprobrium is now reserved solely for Roman religion (see below, n. 723), with its superstitious dependence on a multitude of finite deities that control every facet of life. It is another question whether Schleiermacher has been rightly interpreted. In the variant from *Ho* contained in n. 553, Hegel writes: "So absolute fear is not a feeling of dependence, but casting off all dependence and purely abandoning oneself in the absolute self." But is not the latter precisely what Schleiermacher means by the "feeling of *absolute* [*schlechthinig*] dependence"? For Schleiermacher as well as for Hegel, *absolute* dependence entails a liberation from dependence on all finite things, a "pure self-immersion in the Lord" (*Ho* variant). Both reflect at this point the profound influence of the—Jewish—philosopher Spinoza. Hegel's affirmation of Spinoza against the superficial critics of his own time, e.g., Jacobi (see Vol. 1:376–380), may have helped him to reinterpret Judaism. But he never properly understood what Schleiermacher meant by the feeling of absolute dependence. It is true that the adjectival qualifier *schlechthinig* was not used in the first edition of the *Glaubenslehre*, to which alone Hegel had access (see Vol. 1:279 n. 37), but even without it, it is clear that Schleiermacher intended to distinguish *religious* feeling from all forms of worldly dependence.

552. *Thus P; G reads:* absolute negation of everything particular, all being-for-self.

553. *Ho reads, similar in W:* But here fear is not the finite's fear of finite violence. For what is finite is contingent power, which can impinge on me and cause me injury even when I am not afraid. Here fear is rather fear of the inevitable, the absolute;

But at this stage, freedom does not yet have inwardly the form of the subjectivity of self-consciousness; instead ¨¨this trustingness is the affirmation that I am identical with the One, that I am the substantive unity; but this One with which I am identical is at the same time represented as "the other," who is my Lord, the absolute power of God. So within the unity there is this repulsion, but at the same time there is ¨the unity¨[554] too.¨¨[555] In the Jewish cultus this is the first moment of the religious disposition.

The second aspect of the cultus is the concrete mediation, which is the first consequence of this trustfulness. Trust has a consequence; to begin with, it is wholly abstract, it has surrendered everything, it is itself only the purpose, i.e., what simply ought to be in and for

---

it is the contrary of my consciousness of myself; it is the consciousness of the infinite self in opposition to me as the finite self. Through the consciousness of this absolute as the only and simply negative power, all force of my own disappears, everything that belongs to earthly nature is simply eradicated. As this absolute negativity of oneself, this fear raises one to the pure thought of the absolute power of the One. And this fear of the Lord is the beginning of wisdom, which consists in not allowing what is particular and finite on its own account to have validity as something independent and ultimate. What is valid can be valid only as a moment in the organization of the One, and this One exists only as the manifestation of his sublimity, i.e., as the sublation of everything finite. This wise fear [W_2 adds: is the essential single moment of freedom and] consists therefore in freeing oneself from everything particular, in breaking away from every contingent interest [W_2 adds: in general, in feeling the negativity of everything particular]. Thus it is not a particular fear of the particular but just the positing of this particular fear as null, emancipating oneself from fear. So absolute fear is not a feeling of dependence, but casting off all dependence and purely abandoning oneself in the absolute self, vis-à-vis which and in which one's own self evaporates and dissolves.

But in this way the subject exists only in the infinite One, while absolute negativity is relation to oneself, or affirmation. Through absolute fear the self, in its self-surrender, thus rests in what is absolutely positive. In this way fear turns into absolute trust, infinite faith. This is the self's pure self-immersion in the Lord—this One alone is essence and object. At other stages trust can have the form of the subjective self's resting upon itself. This is, for example, Stoic freedom in chains. Ho, W_1 continue: At this stage where we now are, however, trust has not this form of subjectivity, but precisely the converse form. The self is absorbed in the One, but the One is equally again represented for me as "other," and trust comes about only through the eternal mediation of fear.

554. Thus P, D; G reads: infinite trust
555. W_2 (Var) reads: self-consciousness has here to immerse itself in the One, though the One, represented as "the other," is again the principle of repulsion, in which self-consciousness recovers its self-certainty.

itself—faith; but it also has consequences, it passes over into its opposite. Here we have the same turning around of the abstract, infinite power and wisdom into particularized reality that we noted previously: trust passes over immediately into what is determinate, into the obtaining, maintaining, and positedness of a particular kind of existence.

This trust is what strikes us as remarkable in the writings of the Jewish people; it is preserved through so many great victories, which are emphasized also in Christianity. It is this trust, this faith of Abraham's, that causes the history of this people to carry on; it also constitutes the turning point in the Book of Job. Properly speaking, Job's situation is a universal one, the whole story is external to God's people, it does not happen within the [exclusive] territory of this religion. Job becomes unfortunate in this [material] way; it gets to the point where, proclaiming his innocence and the fact that his

346　change of fortune is undeserved, [he] finds | it unjust that this should happen to him. Thus it is here implied that what ought to be God's purpose is that the good, the just and the God-fearing should prosper. Justice for humanity should be the implicit purpose of God, and it ought to be realized by his might; in other words, human beings ought to be happy. In chapter 31 Job speaks: "What would be my portion from God above, and my heritage from the Almighty on high? Does not calamity befall the unrighteous, and disaster the workers of iniquity? Does not he see my ways, and number all my steps?" [Job 31:2–4]. ⁻And the others, who dispute with him, adopt the same principle: "Behold,⁻⁵⁵⁶ it is from this we find against you that you are not just; for God is greater than man. For God acts thus, that he may turn man aside from his deed and hide him from pride" [Job 33:12, 17]. Then God himself answers Job out of the whirlwind, giving voice exclusively to his might: "Who is this that darkens counsel by words without knowledge? Gird up your loins like a man, I will question you, and you shall declare to me. Where were you when I laid the foundation of the earth? ⁻Tell me, if you have understanding. Who determined its measurements?" [Job

---

556. W (1831) reads: His friends answer in the same sense, except that they turn it around: "Because you are unfortunate,

38:2–5]. "Who is so wise that he can number the clouds?" [Job 38:36]. Here God's might is preached.⁻⁵⁵⁷ Finally Job makes answer: "I know that thou hast made everything, and that no thought is hidden from thee. Heedless is the man who thinks to hide his counsel. Therefore I acknowledge that I have uttered what I did not understand, things too wonderful for me, which I did not know" [Job 42:2–3]. "And the Lord turned the captivity of Job, and gave him twice as much as he had before" [Job 42:10].

Thus it is his submission and renunciation that justifies Job, in that he recognizes the boundless power of God, and the others are rebuked. It is only in consequence of this pure trustfulness, this pure intuition of [God's] power that he has before him, that Job is restored to his former happiness.

The point we had reached was that the intuition of absolute | 347 power turns in a flash into absolute trust. This trust is what comes first, but temporal happiness is what follows from it. The next step then is that the abstract mediation, trust, gains a concrete shape. Trust is trust on the part of self-consciousness that is now essentially an inwardly self-determined self-consciousness. ⁻The concept is here the concept of the subjectivity⁻⁵⁵⁸ that has its purpose within itself and is inwardly determined. An individual having this kind of trust is at the same time inwardly determined simply and concretely, and this concrete determinateness enters into trust and is inseparable from it. It is not as it was with Brahman, where inner devotion, setting itself apart, jettisons all vitality, all worth, the entire range of determinate being; here trust is this pure moment of consciousness at home with itself, determined essentially in such a way that its essential determinateness enters into the divine relationship, into the idea, into the holy of holies, so to speak, of this actuality. And the result is that the determinateness acquires absolute, essential worth within itself; it is installed in the sanctum of the divine inwardness.

As we have already seen, this determinateness is the family, the empirical existence of the people and the survival of the family, and

557. *W (1831) reads:* There follows a very fine and beautiful description of God's might, and

558. *Thus P, similarly G; D reads:* What is basic in this sphere is nothing else but subjectivity

the existence of the family involves property—a land. So the possession of a land, the continuance and subsistence of the family, are what this self-consciousness obtains from its God. So trust in him is *ipso facto* the same as the absolutely limited content of individual family existence.[559] This possession and the worship [of God] are identical, indissociable. This is what was also expressed as God's covenant with his people. His people possesses the land of Canaan. God made a covenant with Abraham [Gen. 15:18], and this is one side of the covenant—the affirmative side in this sphere of empirical particularity. Thus the two sides are *ipso facto* indissociable—on the one side possession and on the other trust, piety, | worship. [The fact of] possession thus acquires an infinite, absolute justification, a divine justification, though at the same time this does not take the shape of a[560] right or of ownership—"ownership" is distinct from possession and is not applicable here. Ownership stems from personality, it has its origin in the freedom of the single individual; human beings are essentially owners in virtue of being persons. Possession as such, on the other hand, this empirical aspect of possession, is completely free, and at the mercy of chance: what I possess is a matter of chance, of contingency, of indifference. It is only when I am recognized as the owner that I am free subjectivity. Possession is the external mode, the free mode—I can give the item in question to another, sell it, and so on. In the present case, by contrast, this possession as such is indissolubly identical with trust, and it is this possession that has such absolute preeminence. The category of ownership does not intervene between the two.[561] God (the absolute idea), free spirit, and lastly ownership and possession are three different stages; here ownership, the intermediate link, falls away and possession is taken up directly into the divine will. It is this empirical, singular [fact of] possession that is willed by God, and

348

559. *Ho adds, similar in W (in Ho a transition to the story of Job, corresponding to the third paragraph above):* Precisely because human beings, in this absolute negativity of self-surrender, exist in what is utterly positive and are thus restored to immediacy, trust—as surrendered finite interest—turns into the surrender of this surrender [and thus] into the realized finite individual, into his happiness.

560. *W (1831/HgG?) adds:* juridical

561. *W (1831/HgG?) adds:* nor does the category of free will in this respect come into play.

that is to be valid as such.[562] Arbitrary free will [*Willkür*] is made infinite, made into something divine.

The second side of the covenant corresponds to the affirmative side, by virtue of which this particular family, just as it empirically is, is represented as taken directly up [into God's will]. To this affirmation of its empirical existence there corresponds the negation of this relationship. The recognition of [God's] might must also be characterized as the negative side empirically and outwardly, as a singular fact. Particular actions and real behavior must have their negative side, equally with recognition | of the Lord; action must be the Lord's service, not ⁻simply this [feeling of] fear⁻[563] but a mode of ⁻serving.⁻[564] That is the other side of the covenant, that on the one hand the people should have the possession, but on the other they should also furnish the service. Just as the servants in this land are bond servants under this people, so the people are likewise bound under the service of the law. Now this law [does have] an ethical content in the shape of family laws and relationships on the one hand; but the main point about it on the other hand is that what is inwardly ethical is observed as a purely positive law (to which naturally a host of external, contingent circumstances are adjoined that have to be adhered to without question). The irrationality of the service corresponds to the irrationality of the possession; the service is an abstract obedience that does not need to have any inwardness in respect of its determinacy, just as the possession is only abstractly justified.[565] The keeping of these commandments, obedience in this duty, obedience to God, is directly bound up with the maintenance of the people's present state and existence. To observe these commandements is the condition for its preservation—this is the other side of the covenant. Because of human free will, departure from the laws is possible; ⁻any such disobedience incurs a punishment,

349

---

562. W₂ (1831/HgG?) adds: and as thus something justified, *then continues (1831/MiscP?):* and is withdrawn from the free determination of the single individual, who cannot sell the possession but can only lease it for a period, and never beyond the jubilee year.

563. *Thus P; G reads:* the surrender of fear

564. W₂ (*Var*) *reads:* surrendering in the particular.

565. W₂ (1831/MiscP?) adds: Because God is absolute might, the actions in themselves are indeterminate and consequently quite external and arbitrary in character.

which is likewise a⁻⁵⁶⁶ loss of the external possession, or else its diminution or wastage. The punishments that are threatened are external and sensible in nature; they concern undisturbed possession of the land. Just as the obedience is not spiritually ethical but is only a determinate, blind obedience, not that of ethically free persons, so too the punishments are | determined externally. The laws and commandments are merely to be carried out and executed as by servants.

If one contemplates these punishments with which the people of Israel are threatened in dread execration, it is noteworthy how this people became real masters at execration; but the curses affect only external fortunes, not what is within, the ethical realm. In chapter 26 of the Third Book of Moses we read:

> But if you will not hearken to me, and will not do all these commandments, if you spurn my statutes, and if your soul abhor my ordinances, so that you will not do all my commandments, but break my covenant, I will do this to you: I will appoint over you sudden terror, consumption, and fever that waste the eyes and cause life to pine away. And you shall sow your seed in vain, for your enemies shall eat it. . . . Those who hate you shall rule over you, and you shall flee when none pursues you. And if in spite of this you will not hearken to me, then I will chastise you again sevenfold for your sins, . . . and I will make your heavens like iron and your earth like brass; and your strength shall be spent in vain, for your land shall not yield its increase, and the trees of the land shall not yield their fruit.
>
> Then if you walk contrary to me, and will not hearken to me, I will bring more plagues upon you, sevenfold as many as your sins. And I will let loose the wild beasts among you, which shall rob you of your children, and destroy your cattle, and make you few in number, so that your ways shall become desolate.
>
> And if by this discipline you are not turned to me, but walk contrary to me, then . . . I myself will smite you sevenfold for your sins. And I will bring a sword upon you, that shall execute vengeance for the covenant; and if you gather within your cities I will send pestilence among you, and you shall be delivered into the hand of the enemy. When I break your staff of bread, ten women shall bake your bread in one oven, and

566. W₂ (1831/MiscP?) reads: but this is only a departure from the commandments and the ceremonial service, not from what is original, for this is valid as such, as it must be. Consequently the punishment attaching to disobedience is also not absolute punishment but only an external misfortune, in other words

shall deliver your bread again by weight; and you shall eat, and not be satisfied.

And if in spite of this you will not hearken to me, but walk contrary to me, then I will walk contrary to you in fury, and chastise you myself sevenfold for your sins. You shall eat the flesh of your sons, and you shall eat the flesh of your daughters. And I will destroy your high places, and cut down your incense altars, and cast your dead bodies upon the dead bodies of your idols; and my soul will abhor you. And I will lay your cities waste, and | will make your sanctuaries desolate, and I will   351 not smell your pleasing odors. And I will devastate the land, so that your enemies who settle in it shall be astonished at it. And I will scatter you among the nations, and I will unsheathe the sword after you. . . . [Lev. 26:14–33]

And so on and on. "I will take you to my bosom again only if you acknowledge that I am God."[567] Thus there is an indissoluble bond in this abstraction of self-consciousness; and the absence of division is no less indissoluble at the level of empirical fact.

The third aspect of cultus is reconciliation. Properly speaking, this can only concern particular transgressions of single individuals, and reconciliation is effected through sacrifice. We have already noted that in sacrifices something is consumed, individuals sacrifice something they own, something that belongs to [their] real existence; in this way they demonstrate in the very deed that they recognize another before whom ownership is regarded as null and void.[568] This sacrifice is here bound up in particular with [the view] that the punishment deserved—the manifestation that is deserved of the nullity of the one who has asserted himself in the sin—can, as it were, be transferred to this part [of the sinner's existence] that is sacrificed.[569] [570]‒‒In this connection it was more especially blood that was offered up on the altar of the | Lord, vitality ‾[was sur-   352

567. [Ed.] This is not an exact quotation but appears to be a summary of Lev. 26:40–45 ("But if they confess their iniquity . . . I will for their sake remember the covenant with their forefathers, whom I brought forth out of the land of Egypt in the sight of nations, that I might be their God")—an important basis for Hegel's recognition that an "indissoluble bond" remains despite the punishments and the execration.

568. Ho adds, similar in W_2: This is sin. It must be expiated.

569. Ho adds, similar in W: This is sacrifice. The individual manifests the nullity of what it sets store by. In this way God is reconciled, and the intuition enters in

rendered];⁻⁵⁷¹ what is vital or alive is also given up in this way, dispatched into the wilderness as that which bears the sin of the people. Blood plays a principal role [cf. Lev. 1:5, 11; 3:2] since it was regarded as that which human beings may not consume, containing as it does, in the Jewish view, the life of the animal; this soul or life-principle, therefore, may not be consumed or destroyed, but

353   must be respected.⁻⁻ ⁵⁷² |

that the manifestation that is deserved of the nullity of the sinner is transferred to the sacrifice, inasmuch as God recognizes the sacrifice and thereby again establishes the self in a positive manner or [as] having its being in him.

570. *W₂ (MiscP) reads (parallel in main text follows):* With this is also connected the fact that it is more especially blood that is offered up and sprinkled on the altar. For if vitality is to be surrendered as the highest type of possession, then something actually vital or living must be given up, and the blood wherein the animal's life resides is given back to the Lord. In the case of the Hindus it was the whole animal that was venerated; here this veneration is no longer the case, but the blood is still deemed something untouchable, something divine, is still held in respect and may not be consumed by human beings. The latter still do not have the feeling of their concrete freedom, which makes mere life as life something subordinate.

571. *W₁ (following Ho) reads:* was surrendered as the highest type of possession; *Ho reads:* because what is vital or alive is the highest type of possession;

572. *There follows in W₁ at this point, corresponding to the order of the 1831 lectures, a section on the "religion of anguish," which in W₂ is located in the religion of nature (see the attached editorial note). W (1831) reads:* We have already seen that in Judaism evil pertains to the subjective spirit, and the Lord is not in combat with evil but punishes it. Evil consequently appears as something externally contingent; thus in the portrayal of the fall it stems from outside, inasmuch as humanity is led astray by the serpent.

God punishes evil as what should not be; all that should be is the good which the Lord commands. There is no freedom up to this point, not even the freedom to investigate what is divine and eternal law. The categories of good, which are, to be sure, also categories of reason, are deemed to be prescriptions of the Lord, any infringements of which he punishes; this is the wrath of God. This attitude of the Lord involves only a "should": what he commands, "should" be, is law. Punitive justice belongs to the Lord; what pertains to the subject as finite is the struggle between good and evil. Thus there is in the subject a contradiction, and this introduces the contrition and anguish that the good is only what "should" be.

W₂ reads: We have just been considering the character of the struggle and of the victory [of good] over evil; as the next moment we now have to consider this struggle as anguish. Though the struggle as anguish is seemingly a superficial expression, it implies that it is no longer merely an outward confrontation but occurs in one subject and its inner experience.

W reads: [W₁: The advance is W₂: The struggle is then] the objectification of anguish. But anguish is in general the course of [W₁: finitude. We have considered the character of the struggle and of the victory (of good) over evil, but must not forget that this is a moment in the nature of spirit, and must enter into the further determination of spirituality. W_2: finitude and, subjectively, the contrition of heart and mind. This course of finitude, of anguish, of struggle, and of victory is a moment in the nature of spirit, and must enter into this sphere, where power determines itself further as spiritual freedom.] The loss of oneself, the contradiction consisting in being at home with oneself in the other, a contradiction that is sublated in the infinite unity [of the two] (the reference here can only be to genuine infinity), the sublation of the antithesis, these are essential characteristics in the idea of spirit that now enter on the scene. Now we are, to be sure, aware of how the idea develops, of its trajectory as well as of its moments, the totality of which constitute spirit. But this totality is not yet constituted [as such], but allowed to subsist as [separate] moments that successively present themselves in this sphere. [W_1: From the relationship between master and servant we go on to the anguish of the servant on becoming aware of his lack of freedom.]

[W_1: Further in regard to the form of this moment, as this moment W_2: As the content] is not yet posited as entering into free spirit, since the moments are not yet taken back up into subjective unity, [W_1: this moment W_2: the content] exists in immediate fashion and is relegated to the form of natural life; it is presented in a natural course, which is, however, known essentially as symbolical and is accordingly not merely a course of external nature but a universal course. [W_1: We do not yet have spirit but abstract power, which merely rules, whereas subjective spirit merely serves. And the next moment in the idea is that of conflict. W_2: As opposed to the standpoint which has been ours so far, where the ruling element is not spirit but abstract power, the next moment in the idea is that of conflict.] Spirit consists essentially in coming to itself from its other-being—and from the vanquishing of this other-being—through the negation of negation. Spirit brings *itself* forth. It experiences its own estrangement, [W_1: but the return from estrangement is W_2: but as it is not yet *posited* as spirit, this course of estrangement and return is not yet ideal, not yet posited as a moment of spirit, but] immediate and therefore in the form of the natural realm.

The characteristic we have seen here took representational shape in the Phoenician religion and the religions of the Near East generally. The process referred to is to be found in [all] these religions; more especially in the Phoenician religion, emphasis is placed on the defeat and estrangement of God and his resurrection. The image of the phoenix is well known; it is a bird that immolates itself in the flames, and from its ashes a young phoenix issues forth in renewed vigor.

This estrangement, this other-being defined as natural negation, is death, but the death that is likewise sublated, in that a rejuvenated new life arises from it. The eternal nature of spirit is to die to itself, to make itself finite in natural life, but through the annihilation of its natural state it comes to itself. The phoenix is this well-known symbol; it is not the struggle between good and evil but a divine process, pertaining to the nature of God himself [W_2: and proceeding in one individual]. More specifically, the form in which this process is posited is Adonis, a form or shape that also passed over into Egypt and Greece, and is also mentioned in the Bible, under the name of Tammuz (Ezekiel 8:14): "and behold, there sat women weeping for Tammuz." In springtime a principal festival of Adonis was celebrated; it was a festival of the dead, of lamentation, which lasted for several days. For two days the mourners went about seeking Adonis; the third day was the festival of joy, when the god had risen again. The whole celebration has the character of a festival of nature, which dies in winter and in spring reawakes. [W_1: But this process must be taken symbolically; it is not just by way of being a reflection regarding the way nature operates, but it is known as a moment of the absolute, of God. This transition has also been a noteworthy feature in the cultus of the Egyptians; in addition, traces of it are to be found more especially in the Greek myth of Adonis. According to this W_2: On the one hand, then, this is a natural process, but on the other hand it is to be taken symbolically as denoting a moment of God, as denoting the absolute generally. The myth of Adonis is itself bound up with Greek mythology. According to Greek mythology] Aphrodite was the mother of Adonis; when he was still a tender child, she kept him hidden in a box which she brought to Ais; and when its mother asked for the child back, Persephone was unwilling to give it up. Zeus resolved the dispute as follows, that each of the two goddesses could keep Adonis for a third of the year, while the last third was left to his own choice; and his preference was to spend this time too with Aphrodite, the universal mother who was at the same time his own mother. It is true that according to its [W_2: most obvious] interpretation this myth refers to the seed lying hidden beneath the earth and then awakening. The myth of Castor and Pollux, who alternate between the underworld and the surface of the earth, relates to the same phenomenon. [W_1: Its significance is W_2: But its true significance is] not merely the changing pattern of nature but the transition, generally speaking, from vitality, from affirmative being, to death, to negation, and again the process of rising out of this negation—the absolute mediation that belongs essentially to the concept of spirit.

W_2 reads: Thus this moment of spirit has here become religion.

[Ed.] Hegel's brief treatment of "the religion of anguish" (Schmerz) is found only in the 1831 lectures, where it follows Jewish religion and precedes Egyptian religion. In the last lecture series, all of the Near Eastern religions (Persian, Jewish, Phoenician, Egyptian) are considered as "transitional" forms of the religion of freedom, which is the third and final moment of Determinate Religion. Since the 1831 structure differed quite radically from that of 1824, which forms the basis of both editions of the Werke in Part II, the editors faced irresolvable difficulties in locating the religion of anguish. W_1 attached it to the discussion of the cultus of Jewish religion, thus obscuring the fact that it was treated as an independent religion by Hegel, while W_2 placed it between Persian religion and Egyptian religion in the final, transitional moment of the religion of nature. Furthermore, both editions locate the first two paragraphs, which in 1831 point forward from the religion of sublimity to the religion of anguish, immediately after the quotation from Lev. 26 and before the paragraph treating the third aspect of Jewish cultus (reconciliation). The Strauss excerpts confirm that Hegel did in fact discuss the religion of anguish in 1831, and that this section in the Werke was not inserted from the Lectures on the Philosophy of World History by the original editors, as suspected by Lasson.

The "religion of anguish" was not Phoenician religion in any historical sense, but a construct that Hegel seems to have derived from classical mythology relating to the figure of Adonis. Following ancient tradition, Hegel implicitly equates the cult of Adonis with that of Attis. This is also shown by the fact that he explicitly equates "the universal mother," i.e., Magna Mater, with Aphrodite. He departs from the usual form of the myth in that, according to him, Adonis could choose where to spend the last third of the year, whereas in other accounts the choice lay with Zeus, who then delegated it to Aphrodite. For the interpretation of the myth in terms of the growth

2. The Religion of Beauty (Greek Religion)[573]

[574]In [historical] existence the religion of beauty is that of the Greeks. On its external side, this religion is itself an infinite, inexhaustible

---

of the seed, an interpretation clearly influenced by the Eleusinian mysteries, see in particular Firmicus Maternus, *De errore profanarum religionum* 3. It is only here that there is reference to the rebirth of Attis. It is also probable that the "true significance" of the Adonis myth, as portrayed by Hegel, is not original but stems from a fusion with the cult of Osiris. Hegel's treatment is largely based on Creuzer, *Symbolik und Mythologie*, vol. 2, chap. 4. It is noteworthy, however, that whereas Creuzer, following C. F. Dupuis, *Origine de tous les cultes; ou, Religion universelle*, 4 vols. (Paris, 1795), 3:476–477, also interprets the myths in astronomical terms, the only trace of such an interpretation in Hegel—his reference to the myth of Castor and Pollux—does not derive from Creuzer. See also E. F. K. Rosenmüller, *Das alte und neue Morgenland* 4:318 ff.

573. [*Ed.*] Hegel's interpretation of Greek religion in the 1824 lectures is essentially in line with that found in the *Ms.*, reflecting both his deep and long-standing appreciation for Greek culture and his mature recognition of the limits of Greek religion. The influence of Creuzer's *Symbolik und Mythologie der alten Völker, besonders der Griechen* continues to be felt, although Hegel is critical of it at many points. In 1824 Hegel is especially interested in the way in which theogonic tradition and poetic creativity merge to produce the Greek gods. By arguing that the Homeric gods are the result of a poetic transformation of the old nature religion, Hegel mediates between the approaches of classicism (Winckelmann) and romanticism (Creuzer, who already hints at the mediation). (See Leuze, *Die ausserchristlichen Religionen bei Hegel*, pp. 204 ff.) "Beauty" is only one of the attributes of Greek religion; Hegel also designates it as the religion of art, of freedom, of humanity, and (as in the *Ms.*) of necessity. The classical ideal is to find the true form for the true content, and the result is beauty. The beauty of the human shape and spirit is expressed in plastic form by Greek art and poetically by the Greek gods and myths, but the expression remains finite and external; the gods stand under the necessity of destiny (*Anankē*), and their collapse is inevitable. The true infinite remains beyond the grasp of the Greeks, and the happiness of their religion masks an underlying unhappiness.

574. *Precedes in W (1831):*[a] [W$_1$: The point we are now coming to is the definition of God as free spirit. At first, God was defined as substantive power purely on his own account; then we saw this power as creative; God was here W$_2$: Here, to be sure, we are in principle in the sphere of free subjectivity, but in the religion of sublimity this category does not yet permeate the totality of the religious consciousness. God has been defined as the substantive power for thought and as the creator, but as creator he is to begin with only] the Lord and master of his creatures. Thus the [divine] power is the cause that divides itself [W$_1$: absolutely, but what is posited by it is only mastered, and W$_2$: but only masters that into which it divides. And] further progress consists in this other being something free, [W$_2$: given free rein] and God becoming the God of free beings, who are [W$_2$: of themselves] free even in their obedience to him.

If we consider this standpoint abstractly, it contains the following moments; God is of himself free spirit and manifests himself in positing his other over against himself. This other posited by him is his image, for the subject only creates itself, and that as which it determines itself is again only itself. But for it to be actually determined as spirit, it must negate this other and revert to itself, for it is not free until, in the other, it knows itself. But if God knows himself in the other, then the other too has being for self and knows itself to be free [W_1: of itself. Here again we have an other given free rein, but this other is free. God remains then the same, the power that creates. W_2: The other is given free rein as something free and autonomous. Then freedom adheres to the subject, and God is still defined as the power that is for itself, on its own account, and gives the subject free rein.] The difference or further determination we have added seems accordingly to consist solely in the fact that the creatures are no longer merely serving, but in service itself have their freedom [W_1: and are thus free]. This moment of the freedom of the subjects for whom God is, [W_1: is something we have already encountered abstractly in the notion W_2: which is not found at the present standpoint, that of the religion of sublimity, is something we have already encountered at a lower stage, in the sphere of nature religion, namely in Syrian religion; and at the higher stage to which we are now passing over, what was there still envisaged in natural, immediate fashion has to be transposed into the pure soil of spirit, with its inward mediation. There, in the religion of anguish, we encountered the notion] that God loses himself, that he dies and only *is* through the negation of himself. This mediation is the moment that has to be taken up again here: the god dies, and from this death he rises again. This is his negation, which we grasp on the one hand as his *other,* as the world, and he dies *to himself,* which has the meaning that in his death he comes to himself. But as a result the other is posited as of itself free, so that the mediation and the resurrection accrue to the other side, the side of what has been created.

Hence the concept of God does not itself seem to change, but only the side of the other. [W_1: Here freedom comes on the scene. God dies in his other-being, in the finite, but then the divine issues forth again from the finite. W_2: That this is where freedom comes on the scene, that the side of the other becomes free, is implied in the fact that in the finite this other-being of God dies and so the divine issues forth again on its own account in the finite.] Consequently the worldly is known to be what has the divine implicit in it, and other-being, which initially has only the character of negation, is in turn negated and implies the negating of negation. This is the mediation that pertains to freedom; freedom is not mere negation, an act of flight and surrender that is not yet true affirmative freedom [W_2: but only negative freedom]. [W_1: What is natural negates itself, and so the affirmative category of freedom issues forth. The world, or finite consciousness, is the other, other-being; its servitude, its accidentality is negated—this mediation we have just seen. W_2: The affirmative category of freedom first arises with the negation of the natural state, inasmuch as this state itself already occurs as the negative. Since the other, i.e., the world, finite consciousness and its servitude and accidentality, is negated, this mediation comprises the category of freedom.] Now what spirit does in raising or elevating itself is to raise itself in this way above the natural state; but this elevation, if it is to be freedom, must be such that in it the subjective spirit too is free on its own account. So this appears, to begin with, only in regard to the [W_1: subject, but likewise accrues also W_2: subject: "God is the God of free beings." But in the process of further definition it also comes to accrue equally] to the nature of [W_1: spirit. W_2: God.] God is spirit, but he is so essentially only in that he is known to be in himself his own diremption, eternally creating, in such a way that this very creation of the other is a return to himself, into knowledge of himself. It is in this way that God is a god of free beings.

[W_1: The human in general is the other. Since God is present to self in this other, since this human element is a determination of God himself, human beings know that the human element in God is one moment of the divine itself W_2: Since it is part of the definition of God himself that he is implicitly the other of himself, and that this other is a determination in regard to him (in such a way that in it he reverts to himself and this human element is reconciled with him), then the determination is thereby posited that humanity is inherent in God himself; and human beings thus know the human element to be one moment of the divine itself] and are as a result free in their attitude to God. For that to which they relate themselves as to their essence is contained within the category of humanity itself. In this frame of reference, human beings relate themselves on the one hand to the negation of their natural state, and on the other to a God in whom the human element is itself affirmative, an essential determination. In this relationship to God, human beings are therefore free. [W_2: What is comprised in concrete human beings is represented as something divine, substantive, and human beings are present in the divine according to all their characteristics, according to whatever has value for them. It was, according to one of the ancients,[b] from their passions, i.e., from their spiritual powers, that human beings made their gods.] . . .

[W_2: This is the whole of this relationship, which has now become part of the religious spirit:] God is in himself the mediation that is [W_1: spirit W_2: humanity], humanity knows itself in God, and God and humanity say of one another: That is spirit of my spirit, [W_1: both are spirit,] humanity is spirit like God; to be sure, it has in it also finitude and separation, but in religion it sublates its finitude, as it is the knowledge of itself in God. [W_1: This is the religion of humanity, of freedom. The next point to consider is the universal aspect of this stage, but W_2: So we now come to the religion of humanity and freedom. But] the first form of this religion is itself infected with immediacy and naturalness, so that we shall still see the human element in God himself in natural fashion. The inner aspect, the idea, is admittedly in itself what is genuine, but it is not yet raised up out of the first, immediate shape of naturalness. The human element in God constitutes only his finitude, so this religion still belongs, according to its foundation, to the finite religions. It is, however, a religion of spirituality, because the mediation [W_1: here breaks down into its moments and constitutes its foundation. W_2: which, as separated and broken down into its moments, formed the preceding transitional stages, being grasped now as a totality, constitutes its foundation.]

[*Ed.*] [a]This passage shows evidence of editorial revision in order to make it serve as a transition from Jewish to Greek religion. For in the context of the 1831 lectures, Phoenician (Syrian) and Egyptian religion intervene between Jewish and Greek religion, and the transition in question is one from all of the Near Eastern religions (Persian, Jewish, Phoenician, Egyptian) to the religion of humanity and freedom. This passage shows in particular how in 1831 Hegel viewed Phoenician or Syrian religion as an advance toward the humanization of God found in Greek religion. The frequent variations between W_1 and W_2 may reflect editorial work, or they may simply be attributable to the additional auditors' transcripts used by W_2. [b]See Clement of Alexandria, *Exhortation to the Heathen* 2: "And some even of the philosophers, after the poets, make idols of forms of your passions [παθῶν], such as fear, and love, and joy, and hope" (*Ante-Nicene Fathers* [New York, 1885], 2:178).

457

material whose friendliness, charm, and beauty tempt us to linger.

354 But we cannot here | go into the details; instead we must confine

355 ourselves strictly to defining the concept.[575] |

a. The Concept in General

With regard to the concept in general, our basic concept is the category of subjectivity or self-determining power. We have already encountered this subjectivity, this wise, self-determining power, as

356 the One who is simply | indeterminate within himself, but ¯who¯[576] by very reason of this abstractness is transformed, on the plane of reality, into the most singular and most limited goal of all. The next

357 stage is where this subjectivity, this wise | power of mighty wisdom, *particularizes* itself. This stage thus involves on the one hand the downgrading of universality, of abstract unity and infinite power, its demotion into a state of limitedness, a "circle" of particularity;

358 | but on the other hand it also involves raising the limited singularity of the purpose realized, and its development in the direction of universality. Both aspects are present in the particular, which emerges at this point. This then is the general definition of the next stage. But then we have to consider first that the determinate concept, the content of the self-determining power (which is a particular content, for it exists in the element of subjectivity)—that this particular content subjectivizes itself inwardly: it has particular purposes, and these particular purposes, these elements of subjectivity, are subjectivized on their own account to begin with, thus producing a "circle" for a host of distinctive divine subjects.[577] Thus there is scope for real

---

575. *W (Ed?) adds:* So we have A. to describe the concept of this sphere, [W_1: then to consider B. the mode and manner [of the representation] of God and C. the cultus as the finite subject's relationship to this its essential, absolute subject. W_2: then to consider B. the shape of God and C. the cultus as the movement of self-consciousness in the relationship to its essential powers.]

576. W_2 *reads:* whose goal *Cf. Ho:* the wise power whose goal

577. *Ho adds, similar in W:* For subjectivity as purpose is self-determination. Hence it implies particularization, and indeed particularization as particularization, as a world of existing differences that are, however, the divine itself, subjectivities as divine configurations. For subjectivity in sublimity has already a determinate purpose—family or people. But this purpose is fulfilled only to the extent that the Lord's service is not neglected. By reason of this requirement that the subjective spirit for which the determinate purpose exists be sublated, the determinate purpose becomes

ethical life as such; for as the divine penetrates into the determinate
| relationships of the actual spirit and determines itself, in accord   359
with [its] substantive unity, the ethical *is* these determinate
relationships.

On the one hand, then, particularization concerns the content.
The divine posits particular content within itself, which becomes
ethical. But the second determinacy is that of the form, of the
antithesis between the essential self-consciousness and finite self-
consciousness, between the essential spirit and this finite realm. Here,
in this determinacy of the form, the appearance of the divine in the
natural shape of subjectivity comes into the picture. Subjectivity
assumes a natural guise, and the finite self-consciousness imagines
this natural figure as divinity, but standing over against itself, as it
were. This is where the real freedom of subjectivity enters for the
first time. The determinate content is common to the finite subject
and its God; its God ceases to be something otherworldly and has
determinate content. On his determinate side God is raised to
essentiality, ˉnot mere singularity but singularity diversified, the
diverse aspects going their separate ways.ˉ[578] So much for the
concept of this sphere.

b. The Content and Shape of Divine Representation

The second point is how the content is represented, the mode and
manner of divinity in this sphere, and the third point is the cultus,
the finite subject's relationship to God as its essential, absolute
subject.

In regard to how God is represented, we have two aspects to
consider: (a) the determinate *content* itself, determinacy and particu-

---

universal. If, then, on the [one] side subjectivity is downgraded to particularity as
the result of the one subjectivity's being fragmented into a plurality of purposes, on
the other side particularity is conversely raised to universality, and these differences
thereby become divine, universal differences. This particularity of purposes is therefore
the convergence of the abstract universality and singularity of purpose, their golden
mean. This particularity constitutes the content of universal subjectivity; and to the
extent that the content is posited in the element of subjectivity, it subjectifies itself
as subject.

578. *Thus P; G reads:* by the annulling of unmediated singularity becomes an
essential content.

larization as the content of God, as what he is, as his quality in general; (b) determinacy insofar as it is the object of the singular self-consciousness, i.e., the *shape* of God.

(a) The *content* of God. What strikes us at once is the diversity of this content among the Greeks and Romans, as against what we found in earlier religions. We express this by saying that their religion is a religion of humanity, in that concrete human beings are present to themselves in their gods according to what they are, according to their needs, inclinations, passions, and habits, according to | their spirit, their ethical and political characteristics, with everything that is valid and essential therein, also in their rights and duties. In other words we say that their gods have the very same content as is also the content of concrete human beings. This humanity of the gods is what appears in one respect (i.e., in its most external aspect) to be what is inadequate in this religion; but at the same time it is what is attractive in it, because there is here nothing unintelligible, nothing incomprehensible; there is in God no content that is not familiar to human beings, nothing they do not find, do not know within themselves. Here again there are several characteristics for us to distinguish: first, there is the particular content, that in which intrinsic quality properly lies, the particularity of content; but second, above this particular content, above this circle of the gods there remains the One, hovering over their particularization; it is this One that makes them limited. What hovers over them is simple necessity, the fate that is necessity devoid of concept because it lacks all determinacy—ineluctable, unapproachable necessity. Even as in their God human beings possess themselves, so too this same necessity lies above both alike. Third, there is purely contingent singulariza- tion, the opposite of the second characteristic—the figure of God degraded to a content that appears in purely contingent, external, arbitrary fashion.

˜First, then, there is the way God is represented in this sphere. Initially the content is particular; he who is the One, this power and wisdom, must constitute himself, must open himself up, determine himself. This is the essential moment at which we now stand—the inward determinacy of this One.˜[579] This particularization must

579. *Thus* G

then also itself acquire the mode of subjectivity: the determinations must become independent deities, for the particularizing of the concept, i.e., subjectivity, is the particularizing of reality, in which the moments become subjective wholes. This is not the particularizing that consists in properties or a multitude of determinacies; these are not the proper content [of particularization]. [For] on the one hand they express relations to others; and on the other hand they belong to the stage of external reflection. Particularization, as the realizing of subjectivity, | is here the totality; being thus reflected into self, it becomes independent deities.   361

The next question is where this content comes from, what kind of content it should or can be. It cannot be anything else than what is present to consciousness, the material of the natural and spiritual world; but it is this content in its essential aspect, and not the wholly contingent, momentary, merely empirical content [of consciousness]. It has to be the content in its conceptual aspect, and although it is particularized, it must therefore be grasped in its essentiality. It is composed, therefore, of the universal powers, the elements of physical and spiritual life. Every power makes its entrance as this essential content—heaven and earth, rivers, mountains, day and night, the divisions of time, and also the ethical realm: justice, giving of oaths, family, marriage, bravery, science, art, agriculture, civic and political life. Bravery consists especially in the eradication of wild beasts. Thus Diana does not have most notably the meaning of hunting in general but essentially that of hunting for beasts of prey. These beasts, which in other spheres—for example, with the Hindus, Egyptians, and so on—are respected as having absolute validity, are here, by the bravery of spiritual subjectivity, laid low and slaughtered for use. In the words of a sage of antiquity, "From ˉhuman passions⁻[580] didst thou derive thy gods."[581] The content here is derived from spirit, from whatever [enters consciousness] powerfully as passion, as essential interest or as right.

ˉˉThus we have initially two kinds of content, natural and spiritual. | [582]But the basic determination here is *spiritual* subjectivity; and to this extent it is not the natural element or power that   362

580. *Ho reads:* thine own passions, O man,
581. [*Ed.*] See editorial annotation b to n. 574 above.
582. *Precedes in* W₁ *(HgG/Ed?):* On the one hand, to be sure, [they] fall apart

can be accounted essential on its own account, but only spiritual subjectivity, spiritual resolve. Even if the natural element or power is also represented as a subject, as the gods of nature, still the shape of this natural content, its subjectivity, is only something borrowed,

363 fantastic, not something true. ⁻⁻⁻Subjectivity⁵⁸³ as such, which | is here the basic determination, cannot have a merely natural content. So it is not the case that Greek phantasy peopled nature with gods, in the way that for the Hindus the figure of God derives from all natural shapes or figures—from just this bird, mountain, or river.

364 | No, the principle of Greek religion is rather the subjective freedom of the spiritual: the natural is no longer worthy to constitute by itself the inner quality or content of any such God. But, in the second place, this free subjectivity is not yet absolutely free. It is not the idea that ⁻has genuinely realized itself inwardly as spirit.⁻⁵⁸⁴ We have not yet attained that level; the⁵⁸⁵ content provided by free subjectivity exists as particular content as such, but⁵⁸⁶ spiritual. But because, as spirit, it is particular content, its particularity ⁻is⁻⁵⁸⁷ at the same time a natural side.⁻⁻⁵⁸⁸ Thus there are two characteristics present in the God of particular subjectivity: the essential, basic characteristic is

583. *Precedes* Subjectivity *in* W₁ *(HgG/Var?):* Insofar as it is full of content, [*cf. n. 588, 3d sentence*]

584. *G reads:* genuinely preserves itself inwardly as spirit. W₁ *(HgG?) adds:* universal, infinite subjectivity.

585. W₁ *(HgG?) adds:* spiritual, ethical

586. W₁ *(HgG/Ed?) adds:* remains

587. W₁ *(Ed/HgG?) reads:* has

588. W₂ *(MiscP) reads:* But the new gods too are themselves dual in content, combining within themselves the natural and the spiritual. The natural element or natural power was not in any event what is generally independent for the essential intuition of the Greeks, but only spiritual subjectivity. Insofar as it is full of content, subjectivity as such, which determines itself according to purposes, cannot bear within itself a merely natural inner quality. For this reason Greek phantasy also did not people nature with gods in the way that, for the Hindus, the shape of a god springs forth out of all natural shapes. The Greek principle is rather subjective freedom; and in that case the natural is at all events no longer worthy to constitute the content of the divine. But on the other hand this free subjectivity is not yet absolutely free. It is not the idea that has truly realized itself as spirit, i.e., it is not yet universal, infinite subjectivity. We have not yet attained that level. The content of free subjectivity is still particular; it is spiritual, to be sure, but since spirit has not made itself the object, the particularity is still a natural particularity and is itself still present as one characteristic of the spiritual deities.

that he is of a spiritual kind; but the other characteristic, stemming from the particularity of spirituality, is that of naturalness. The subject is thus the union of a spiritual and a natural power, it has a spiritual but also a natural content—united in such a way that the spiritual principle is dominant, having subjugated the natural principle. Such then are the basic characteristics of God at this stage.

Well, then, there are two relationships that occur in regard to this principle. On the one hand we find the natural and the spiritual quite distinct from each other, and on the other we find them genuinely unified.⁻⁻⁻⁵⁸⁹⁻Spiritual subjectivity exists only as the triumph over what is natural, as self-produced result, as dominating the

589. Ho reads, similar in W: inasmuch as the basic determination is spiritual subjectivity, the natural power cannot of itself count as what is essential. It is, however, one of the particularities and, as the immediate, the first, which must be sublated before the other spiritual powers arise. For we saw that the power of the One and his sublimity on its own account first resulted from creation. This one foundation, as the self of the absolute, is lacking here. So the starting point here is from the sphere of immediate naturalness, which cannot here appear as created by the One, but appears as immediate. In other words, the unity in which these particularities, the natural powers, still rest is not spiritual, but is itself a natural unity, or chaos. "But first of all," sings Hesiod, "was chaos." Hence chaos is itself something posited. But what posits it we are not told: all we are told is that it was or became. For the foundation is not the self but the selfless, necessity, of which it can only be said that it is. Chaos is the unity that sets the immediate in motion, but itself is not yet subject or particularity. So it is not said of it that it creates; on the contrary, as it itself only "becomes," so too this necessity only "becomes" out of it—the "far-flung earth," "the shades of Tartarus," Erebus and Night, and Eros "adorned with beauty before all the immortals."

We see arising the totality of particularity: the earth, the positive element, the universal foundation; Tartarus, Erebus, the night, the negative element; and Eros, the uniting, active element. The particularities themselves *give birth:* the earth brings forth the sky and the mountains, and, without fructifying love, the deserted Pontus; but, united with the sky, it brings forth Oceanus and its rulers. It also gives birth to the Cyclopes, the natural powers as such, whereas the earlier progeny are natural things themselves as subjects. Thus earth and sky are the abstract powers that, fructifying themselves, give rise to the spheres of natural particularity. The last of the progeny is inscrutable Cronus. Night, the second moment, brings forth whatever, from the natural side, has within itself the moment of negation. Third, these particularities couple mutually together and produce positive and negative. Subsequently these are all vanquished by the gods of spiritual subjectivity; Hecate alone remains, as destiny from the natural side.

To consider next the power that rules over this sphere of natural forces: this is the unqualified abstraction out of which they arose, viz., Uranus; and since he is only power as the positing of his abstraction as what is valid, he suppresses all his natural.‾590 For this reason two kinds of deities now make their appearance: the natural too appears as independent, as distinct from the spiritual, even if it is only a subordinate aspect. ‾This is the most important point in Greek mythology.‾591

With the Greeks we have the old deities, the Titans Coeus, Crius, Hyperion, Iapetus, Oceanus, Cronus, Uranus, Helios, Selene, and 365 so on:592 these are natural beings, not spiritual beings, | a purely natural content without any spiritual determination. The essential point is that these Titans are subjugated, that the spiritual principle has vanquished nature religion. They are dethroned, driven out to the margins of the earth, the margins of the world of self-consciousness, driven into the twilight, or right out to the limits of

---

progeny. But the result of the sky is inscrutable Time, the last to be born. And Time vanquished Uranus thanks to the cunning of the earth. For everything here is in the shape of subjective purpose, and cunning is the negative of force or violence. But since these particular forces now make themselves free and valid [on their own account], Uranus gives them the "punitive name of Titans, whose iniquity is sooner or later chastised."

Now the first moment in this natural sphere is therefore chaos with its moments, posited by abstract necessity; the second is the period of creation under Uranus's rule, when these abstract moments issued from chaos are what give birth; the third is the rule of Cronus, when the particular natural powers (who have themselves been born) give birth in turn. In this way what has been posited itself becomes what posits, and the transition is made to spirit. This transition can be more clearly seen in regard to Cronus, in that he gives birth to what in turn destroys him. It is by sublating the immediate shapes that he is ruler. But he himself is immediate and therefore the contradiction, in that, in himself immediate, he is [at the same time] the sublation of immediacy. He produces the spiritual deities out of himself; but insofar as they are, to begin with, only natural, he sublates them, does away with them. But his sublation of the spiritual deities must itself be sublated; and this again happens through cunning in opposition to the natural force or violence of Cronus. Zeus, the god of spiritual subjectivity, lives. Thus Cronus is opposed by his other, and there occurs the battle—for battle it is—between the natural powers or offspring of Uranus and Gaia and the offspring of Cronus and Rhea or the deities of spirit.

[Ed.] The whole of the theogonic myth presented in this variant, which is transmitted only by Ho (and followed by W), is taken from Hesiod's Theogony, vv. 116–735. It is highly probable that it represents a subsequent interpolation by Hotho.

590. Thus G

591. Thus G

592. [Ed.] See Hesiod, Theogony 133–134, 168 ff., 371. The Titans Coeus, Crius, Hyperion, Iapetus, Oceanus, and Cronus are offspring of Uranus and Gaia, while Helios and Selene are offspring of Hyperion and Thea.

the night. They have been overcome by the new gods, led by Zeus. These new gods are now in command; they are the gods of the free spirit, but they are individually characterized by particularity, so they are not yet the gods of the spirit that knows itself according to its absolute freedom. Still they must be distinguished from the Titans. The struggle between the Titans and the new gods is a principal moment in Greek mythology; the victory over the Titans is in such a way that they preserve their honor, even though they lose command. They are natural powers but are not the supreme powers—which are ethical, spiritual, and true. There are still two points to be noted and distinguished in regard to them. Some, such as Helios, Uranus, Coeus, and so on, are mere power; others, the wholly self-contained powers, are also spiritual, but because their content is merely self-contained spirituality, raw, abstract spirituality, they are reckoned among the old deities—for example, ˉthe oath, Styx,ˉ⁵⁹³ the Eumenides, Dike, whose judgments are purely internal, belong to the old gods. In the kingdom of the new gods, that of Zeus, what counts is civic life, laws that have been promulgated and a system of right based on them, not a law of conscience, which is where the giving of oaths belongs, not the hidden justice of Nemesis and Dike—for this is only the superficial justice of humbling the proud, it lays low him who is exalted though his only crime consists in being raised up, which is not an *ethical* wrong. So this distinction between the old and the new gods is a very important and necessary point in Greek mythology.

This progressive sequence of gods is to be found for instance in Aeschylus's *Eumenides,* where at the beginning of the play the Pythia says: "Worship with your prayers Gaia, vouchsafer of oracles";⁵⁹⁴ the Pythia is then followed by Themis, who is the second after Mother Earth to have her seat in this μαντεῖον [shrine]; | thus she 366 is Dike, a spiritual entity, a right but still an indeterminate right. The third possessor of the oracle is a female Titan, Phoebe, who finally delivers the oracle to Phoebus, the new god, who now has his seat here. Pindar too speaks of this succession of gods who

593. *Ho reads:* oaths [belong] to Styx or Orcus,
594. [*Ed.*] Aeschylus, *Eumenides* 1–8. *Ho* uses the Greek term πρωτόμαντιν (first prophet or seer) instead of "vouchsafer of oracles" (*Orakelgeberin*).

vouchsafed oracles. He makes Night the first, followed by Themis and then Phoebus.[595] This is the general pattern of the transition from the natural shapes to the new gods.

Now the new gods are intrinsically dual in content, inasmuch as the natural principle is to be found in them. Phoebus is on the one hand the one who knows, and on the other hand he is Helios, the sun, which illuminates everything. In the same way Zeus is the firmament, what is meant by Uranus, principally the force of atmospheric variation, force in the meteorological realm, the Thunderer, the atmosphere in its changeableness—[as when the Romans said] *sub Jove frigido;*[596] but apart from being this natural principle, he is also the father of gods and men. He it is to whom civic life essentially belongs; he is the [guardian] power of friendship and hospitality, a many-sided ethical power generally. So it is with other deities too. Poseidon is the sea, Oceanus, but essentially keeping to himself control of the raging sea; ¯[at the same time,] however, he is essentially represented as a spiritual subject.¯[597] In these deities there is still this echo of natural elements, but it is refined because what is dominant is their spiritual determinacy. All the same, no perfect consistency is to be looked for in this respect: sometimes one element emerges more strongly, sometimes the other.

Prometheus[598] is also numbered among the Titans. He gave human beings fire and taught them to offer sacrifices; but he taught them to do so in such a way as to gain something from the sacrifice

---

595. [*Ed.*] The succession Night-Themis-Phoebus does not occur in Pindar himself but in a general scholium to the Pythian hymns. See Pindar, *Carmina,* ed. C. G. Heyne, 3 vols. (Göttingen, 1798–1799), vol. 2, *Scholia in Pindari carmina,* part 2, *Scholia in Pythia Nemea et Isthmia,* pp. 483–484.

596. [*Ed.*] See Horace, *Carmina* 1.1.25: "Manet sub Jove frigido / Venator, tenerae conjugis immemor" ("Unmindful of his tender spouse, / The hunter tarries beneath chill Jove").

597. *W (Ed/HgG?) reads:* however, he is also taken up among the new gods.

598. [*Ed.*] On Prometheus see esp. Hesiod, *Theogony* 510–615, and *Works and Days* 48–58. Hegel's account does not bring out the connection that exists between Prometheus's two deeds. After he has tricked Zeus out of the meat on the occasion of the sacrifice, Zeus hides the fire, but Prometheus steals it from him and gives it to the human race. On the new gods' opposition to Prometheus as the offspring of Titans (he was the son of Iapetus and Clymene), see Aeschylus, *Prometheus Bound* 928–931, 955–960.

too: Zeus is tricked in that he is given only the bones, covered over with the skin, while the worshipers keep the meat for their own use. So it was Prometheus who taught the human race to eat meat, as well as endowing it with other arts. But these arts, and the discoveries and inventions too that belong to the cultural development of humanity, are all of them just the arts of life; there are no ethical authorities, no social laws, etc., involved. These fall | partly within 367 the domain of Zeus, partly within that of Demeter (agriculture, the institution of marriage). The ethical is not Titanic but pertains essentially to the new gods.[599]

~There is one other god who can be particularly singled out, namely Hercules.[600] Hercules is principally represented as having lived and died as a human being who was then raised up among the gods.~[601] He possesses human individuality, and he worked like a slave; ~he was in service, and | by dint of this human toil he earned 368 himself a place in heaven. In Hercules, for instance, there is this purely spiritual natural element. There is no longer any echo of power over nature in him as there is in Apollo; as a human being he has purely spiritual individuality as such for his principle. This spiritual individuality of human beings is on a higher level than that of Zeus and Apollo, for human spirituality is a singular, free, pure, abstract subjectivity, undetermined by nature. Hercules too is a singular subject, with his own natural life, within which his labors and his virtues lie. But this natural life, this conditionedness, this dependence upon natural life is precisely finitude. At the same time it is [only]

599. *Ho adds:* But precisely because Prometheus is still a Titan and what he teaches is Titanic, he is punished by Zeus.

600. [*Ed.*] Heracles. While normally we follow modern conventions for classical names and figures, including the use of Greek names for Greek gods and heroes, in this instance we give the Latin form Hercules, since it was evidently used by Hegel himself, both in lecturing and in the written *Ms*.

601. *Ho reads, similar in W:* But even if the gods are spiritual particularity in regard to the substance that fragments into them, on the other hand we see humanity through human service raising itself in advance to God and bringing itself into conformity with the divine purpose. [W_2: on the other hand the limitation of the particular is thereby conversely eliminated from substantive universality.] In this way we obtain the unity of the two sides, the divine purpose made human and human purposes raised to the divine. This yields the heroes and demigods. Of particular note in this respect is the figure of Hercules.

abstract finitude, the point of singularity, that has comprehended all natural content within itself, but which, as a spiritual subject, both *can* break free from it and *has* done so. The other gods are not free in this way; they still have in their essence a natural content from which they cannot purify themselves.‾⁶⁰² Zeus is duration, the firmament, etc. There is much evidence to show that the Greeks saw this distinction and were quite aware of it. For instance, they assign to Hercules a very high place indeed. Aeschylus⁶⁰³ makes Prometheus say that what comforts him in his defiance is the fact that Zeus will have a son who will cast him down off his throne; by this he means Hercules. ‾The same view occurs in Aristophanes⁶⁰⁴ too, but in his own joking fashion, in that he makes Bacchus praise Hercules as the heir of Zeus, supposing Zeus dies.‾⁶⁰⁵

602. *Ho reads, similar in* W: by his virtue he earned himself a place in heaven. So the heroes are not immediately gods, but are of implicitly divine origin and must first inwardly posit the divine for themselves by labor. For the gods of spiritual individuality, though now at rest, have being only through the struggle with the Titans. This their implicit being is posited in the heroes. So the spiritual individuality of the heroes is on a higher level than that of the gods themselves; they are *actually* what the gods are *implicitly*, the activation of this implicit being; and even if they have to labor in order to succeed, in so doing they discard the naturalness that the gods still have in them. The gods derive from the power over nature, but the heroes from the gods.

W *(1831) continues:* So inasmuch as the spiritual gods are what results from over-coming the power over nature, but first exist only through this power, they have their becoming in themselves and show themselves as concrete unity. The powers over nature are contained in them as their foundation, even if this implicit potential is, in them, transfigured. Accordingly this echo of the natural elements is still present in the gods, [W₁: but the main thing is their spiritual determinacy. W₂: an echo that is not present in Hercules. And there are various pointers to the fact that the Greeks themselves were conscious of this distinction.]

603. [*Ed.*] Aeschylus, *Prometheus Bound* 755–768 (dialogue of Zeus and Prometheus).

604. *Ho adds:* in the *Frogs,*
[*Ed.*] Aristophanes, *Birds* 1641–1645. Hegel erroneously attributes these lines to the *Frogs,* as is evident not only from *Ho* but also from the fact that Hegel places the words in the mouth of Bacchus, who in the opening scene of the *Frogs* asks Hercules for the way into Hades.

605. W₂ *(MiscP) reads:* The same prophecy as to the downfall of Zeus's lord-ship, and that this will come about through the posited unity of the divine and the human that resides in the heroes, is expressed in Aristophanes, who makes Bacchus say to Hercules: If Zeus dies, you shall be his heir.

The second point is that above all these deities there hovers the universal power. Inasmuch as there are so many particular deities, their determinate aspects must be brought under a unity. Initially this is the unity that reigns among themselves, and in which they remain independent. It is Zeus who provides this paternal or patriarchal kind of rule, in which the ruler always ends by doing what the others[606] also want—they have their say about everything | that happens. But this kind of lordship is not serious; so the unity   369
is something much more serious. The true lordship consists in their being subordinate to an absolute power—this is the absolute unity.

This power is not yet *fulfilled:* its content or fulfillment is essentially shared out among this multitude of gods—allotted to each of them in his particular way. For this reason the unity that stands over them is a unity devoid of purpose, of subjectivity, a principle without purpose, for the subject is here characterized only as something particular with a particular content. Thus the higher power, above all these gods in their beauty, is abstract necessity, a necessity without purpose and incomprehensible, a necessity that has no concept because it does not contain its own determining within itself; there is [only] a separation into mutually external particulars. Above this divine world of beauty there stands the necessity that spells the disappearance of the particular powers or authorities for whom justification is here afforded—and that mourns for their disappearance. This [abstract necessity] represents one extreme as opposed to this midpoint [of beauty], and in it they [the gods] possess one extreme. The midpoint is not yet absolute unification. Unity lies outside them, because it is not yet the unity that is simply filled with content in and for itself. The other extreme is the extreme of singularity, which is not yet taken up into the midpoint either. That is why it is an extreme; it lies outside the concept. But what is outside the scope of unification is contingent being in general, external contingency. This external contingency is not moderated by the idea, not yet taken up within it. Necessity has no inherent criterion of wisdom, does not yet have its determining or content for itself. Hence it is unsecured on one side, given over to chance and to fancy. These gods therefore

606. W₂ *(Var) adds:* by and large

present a multitude of external aspects, a mass of purely contingent content, which plays upon them from outside, adding the finishing touches that make them just these [singular] divinities. This [singular aspect] is not yet identical with the unity of the concept.

It is to be noted that among the Greeks the twelve principal gods of Olympus are not ordered according to the concept. They are differentiated into particular shapes, and it is a waste of effort to try to systematize them. One or another essential moment or aspect of the idea is displayed to a greater or lesser extent in [each of] them, but it is not to be seen as fully implemented in them; | apart from it, there is a contingent, particular content in each of them. Regarding the contingency of the content it should be borne in mind that each figure is an absolutely individual one; hence it does not have merely an abstract content or an abstract activity—on the contrary, as subjects they also draw on the rich treasury of subjective properties. If only one property were dominant in a particular deity so that it could be comprehended thereby, it would be an abstraction, a universal, like justice, the oath, and suchlike; these are abstract properties, which then become formal deities—inasmuch as they are further vested with subjective configuration—and are therefore only universal. In this [formal vesting] divinity is a form to which the content—justice etc.—does not correspond. Thus Pallas is wisdom, but there is war in her also, technical skill, measure, and other qualities too; for subjectivity is no longer merely an external form, but every deity is made up of a wide range of qualities. They are distinct from one another, but the distinctions are by no means abstractly definite in character.

Particularization comes about in another way too. ˜˜There is a natural element in these gods, which has a large number of determinately particular aspects on its own account; for example, the sun rises, sets, becomes bright, obscured, and so on. The divisions into years, months, days, and hours are so many ways of determinately qualifying the abstraction of time. The natural element that is involved here can be characterized in many ways. But since the main characteristic here | is individuality, subjectivity, the modes of determinacy in which the echo of nature is present are transformed into determinate modes of self-conscious subjectivity; thus transformed,

370

371

they lose their former significance and meaning and appear as contingent content. ˉDupuis⁶⁰⁷ made the Greek gods into calendrical deities, definite divisions of the calendar. Such divisions pertain to time, to the extent that time is involved in physical change. When they are vested with the shape of self-conscious individuals, they no longer have this determinate aspect but appear to be contingent [in their ordering] and must be ennobled; they are not entitled to any respect and can be made into anything at all.ˉ⁶⁰⁸ This is (for one thing) the main justification for seeking among these gods for the so-called philosophemes.ˉˉ⁶⁰⁹ Zeus spent twelve days carousing with the gods among the Ethiopians, he suspended Juno between earth and sky, and so on⁶¹⁰—all this is merely contingent. [But] these representations ˉrelate to or derive from some abstract representation or other, denoting something regular and essential, but in prosaic fashion; and we have the right to investigate what that something is. Traces of this kind can still be found in these forms of subjectivity; but they have been degraded into contingent figures, and we are under no commandment to reflect these representational images. Self-consciousness has no use for determinate aspects of nature such as these.ˉ⁶¹¹

607. [Ed.] C. F. Dupuis, *Origine de tous les cultes; ou, Religion universelle,* 4 vols. (Paris, 1795). It was Hercules in particular whom Dupuis identified as a calendrical deity; see 1:317 ff., where he equates Heracles with the sun and, following Porphyry, his labors with the divisions of the zodiac. See also below, n. 678.

608. *Thus G*

609. *W₂ (MiscP) reads:* But even if sublated, the natural element is still a determinacy of the particular powers, and by being taken up into the figure of self-conscious individuals it has become a copious source of contingent determinations. The specification of time, division of the month and the year, all this is still so intertwined with the concrete gods that attempts have even been made, for instance by Dupuis, to make them calendrical deities. Intuition of the creative action of nature, the process of arising and passing away, also gave rise to numerous other connotations in the sphere of the spiritual gods. But once raised to the level of self-consciousness involved in the shape of these gods, these natural determinations appear as contingent and are transformed into determinations of self-conscious subjectivity, which is to deprive them of their significance. There is no gainsaying the major justification for seeking in the actions of these gods for so-called philosophemes.

610. [Ed.] See Homer, *Iliad* 1.423–425, 15.18–21.

611. *W₂ (MiscP) reads:* have at any rate their first source in an abstract representation relating to natural circumstances, natural forces, and what is regular and essential in them; and we therefore have the right to investigate what they are. But these natural

The plastic figures of the gods etc. are the figures of the gods in their purity. Represented, by extension, in poetry, taken up into the field of representation, they give rise to a great variety of stories. These have their original source in particular natural relationships—which are not in the pure state, however, but have been changed into forms that are appropriate to the subjective mode. This is the source of the [stories recounting] Zeus's countless | amorous adventures; the procreative, generative element in nature here has its [representational] form. A second source[612] is the spiritual realm itself, spiritual individuality.[613] The god is manifested to human beings in their own destinies, in the destinies of a state, in this or that event that is seen as the god's doing, and as [evidence of] his benevolence or his enmity. In this way ⁻an infinitely diverse content arises.⁻[614] Just as the God of Abraham, Isaac, and Jacob gave his people the land of Israel, and led them out of Egypt, so a Greek god has done this or that which befalls a people and is envisaged by it as divine.[615] These divine acts or utterances have a local, temporal point of reference. The priests declare the event, whether fortunate or disastrous, to be the act of the god; and this provides the material for a more precise, external definition of the god's actions. This then is the particular material for the infinite mass of what is contingent, indeterminate; it is not inherently contradictory to the facts, but is *poetizing*. Poetizing is not the same thing as inventing or lying. The starting point for poetizing, the prosaic event that the prophets declare to be an act of the god, yields a great many contingent characterizations of God's activity and being. This, then, is the other extreme. Inasmuch as it enters into particularity, the universal lets these characterizations stand separately side by side; and as a result,

372

---

relations are at the same time demoted to contingencies, since they have not preserved their purity but are changed into forms appropriate to the subjective, human mode. The free self-consciousness has no more use for such natural determinations.

612. W_2 *(MiscP) adds:* of contingent determinations

613. W_2 *(MiscP) adds:* and its historical development.

614. W_2 *(MiscP) reads:* arises an infinitely diverse but also contingent content when an event, whether fortunate or disastrous, is raised to be the act of a god and serves to define the god's actions more precisely and in detail.

615. W_2 *(MiscP) adds:* or as self-determination of the divine.

contingency enters in. This is the essential determinant in regard to the content of the objective god.

(b) The second aspect pertaining to the representation of the god is his *shape*. The first is that subjectivity determines itself inwardly, has content, the second is that this objective content turns toward what we call finite self-consciousness. Here [the principle of] the division into particulars is not the inward element in content, through which a whole heaven full of gods | is produced, but is that through which divinity forms one side, and the finite self-consciousness for which it exists forms the other side. This is a spiritual form—the diremption of the infinite concept, the fact that spirit divides itself: since it is for itself, it is for an other also; this other is itself, and that is how it first comes to be for itself. But here this other is the finite world; this other—the fact that spirit exists for itself as external and finite—this is the mode of its configuration or shaping, of its appearing. 373

God appears therefore, i.e., he has a shape, and what we now have to determine is the type and mode of this shape. There are two sides to this appearing or shaping. God appears, he is for an other, he enters into externality. This gives rise to a division, a differentiation which is so determined that there are two modes of appearing. One mode is that which is appropriate to the god as such, the other, to consciousness or to the finite spirit that stands over against him. Appearing is being turned outward, toward an other: it thus comprises two moments—one being what God is represented as doing, the other what consciousness does, for which his action exists.

The side of appearing that is represented as pertaining to God in himself is his revealing himself, showing himself, the activity of appearing attributed to God as such. From this angle self-consciousness merely has the sense of taking something in that shows itself to it, something that is given to it. This mode of showing occurs principally for thought; what is eternally in and for itself shows itself; it is taught, is ˉreceived, it appears as something merely given.ˉ616

616. W₂ *(MiscP) reads:* given, and is not posited by the caprice of the singular [self-consciousness].

Thus here too [i.e., in Greek religion] there is one side that is [just] God's appearance; he shows himself in dreams, and there is traditional teaching about him. And self-consciousness accepts this as given by the gods. ˉIn the case of oracles, too, what shows itself is attributed to the god himself.ˉ⁶¹⁷ In this regard the Greeks had

374 all possible forms | ˉincluding that of a divine image that was a stone fallen from the sky, a meteorite.ˉ⁶¹⁸

The other side, which is just as essential, is that the appearance is a product of the self-consciousness to which the god appears. It is the shared limit that separates and relates them, ˉˉin which both are present, and in which the activity belongs to both; and that is just what causes serious difficulty. Later on, in Christianity, this appears as the grace of God, as God's indwelling spirit. At the one extreme human beings are purely passive, just standing there like stones while the spirit works in them; at the other extreme the activity is theirs. Here on the one side there is the appearing that is the work of God; on the other side there is the fact that it is the activity of self-consciousness. It is essential that here at the level of representation, these two sides appear as distinct. On the speculative level, this doubled activity must appear as one activity in which the two sides coalesce; but here two activities are apparent, the one coming from one side, the other as a process of production through the activity of the other side, namely self-consciousness. This standpoint still contains distinction, or the standpoint of particularity. There are both sides of the human [experience] in the divine; human beings

375 intuit | themselves in God, ˉprimordially as content. This is the action of God in them, the essential powers of their spirit.ˉ⁶¹⁹ The other side is the form opposed to this content—activity, production. The two sides are still distinct because the standpoint here is still that of the finite. Similarly it is one aspect of the appearing of God,

617. *Ho reads, similar in* W₂: Dreams and oracles are modes of appearing of this kind.

618. W₂ *reads:* for instance, a divine image fallen from the sky, or a meteor or thunder or lightning, is regarded as an appearance of the divine. *Cf. Ho and the 1827 lectures; Ho reads:* a divine image has fallen from the sky; Demeter taught agriculture and the laws, Apollo wandered about among the shepherds.

619. *Thus P; G reads:* in him they have their authentic essentiality, their essential power.

one aspect of his shape, that the appearance is attributed to God himself; the other aspect is the productive activity of the finite self-consciousness. This is the aspect under which human beings make or shape their God for themselves.⁻⁻⁶²⁰ Herodotus⁶²¹ states categorically: "Homer and Hesiod made the Greeks' gods for them." And it has always been the artists who have been responsible for shaping the gods. ⁻Their shape is one that is posited subjectively, by finite spirit.⁻⁶²² The appearing [of God] is essentially the product of conscious willing; what brings forth the [divine] shape—the posited [god] with the consciousness that it *is*—is the finite side. So this is where art has principally its actuality.

⁻[Second,]⁶²³ there is a natural moment in the appearing [of God], because the shape has a sensible aspect. We have not yet reached the sphere where | pure, absolute spirit exists for spirit, where God   376 is worshiped in spirit and in truth [John 4:24], [as] pure thought for pure thought. So it is not the case that appearing—the aspect of determinate being—reaches the point of being immediate actuality, the presence of a singular consciousness, i.e., a human being. The shape that is most genuine and proper [for God] is necessarily that the spirit that exists absolutely for itself goes forth to show itself as a single, empirical self-consciousness. Here we have not yet reached this destination: there is a natural moment in the appearance; [it] has a sensible aspect—but this aspect does not reach the extreme of a particular sensible human being [*die aber nicht bis zum sinnlichen*

620. W₂ *(MiscP) reads:* Basically, however, the activity belongs to both sides, though it is very difficult to grasp this genuinely. The same difficulty arises later in connection with the notion of God's grace. Grace illuminates the human heart, it is the spirit of God within human beings, so that they can be represented as passive when it is at work within them and the activity is not their own. In the concept, however, this doubled activity must be grasped as one. At the stage where we now are, this unity of the concept is not yet posited, and the side of productive activity, which also belongs to the subject, appears as independent on its own account, in the sense that the subject brings about the appearance of the divine consciously, as its own work.

621. [*Ed.*] Herodotus, *Histories* 2.53. What Herodotus actually said was that Homer and Hesiod "established the genealogy of the gods in Greece and gave them their eponyms, apportioned offices and honors among them, and revealed their form."

622. *Thus P; D reads:* In this sphere the absolute is known as something posited by self-consciousness.

623. *P reads:* (2)

Diesen fortgeht]. This aspect is therefore something made by human agency in such a way that what is thus made—wherein the divinity appears—has a sensible aspect. This sensible aspect is necessarily made to match the concept, the content of divinity, which is to be expressed by it. The role of the shape is to represent the divine: the natural or sensible is, as it were, still soft enough to be molded to fit the content it is to express.[624] It is only when the process of particularization within God reaches the absolute limit, [when God] emerges in human shape as unmediated consciousness, that this externality is let go, so to speak, and sensibility is given free rein as sensibility—in other words, God makes manifest the contingency and conditionedness of externality.[625] At the present stage sensible matter does not yet have this distinctive feature but remains true to its content.[626] [627] |

377

624. W_2 *(Var) adds:* as it appears.

625. W_2 *(Var) adds:* and its unfitness for the concept.

626. *Ho reads:* Now third, as regards the work of art, it is the positedness of the doubled activity of God's self-revealing and human shaping. It is therefore a product. But at this stage of differentiation as such, a work of art is something other as opposed to the god who has implicit being and as opposed to human spirit. The god who has implicit being does not return out of his particularity into himself (as we saw when considering the concept for this stage). The unity does not involve self, the process is only the process of necessity. So the work of art is not itself spirit, not God who has being for himself, but only itself the implicit being of being-for-self, being-for-other as such. This includes both explicit and implicit being but without mediation, as an abstract result to which mediation is extraneous. So the side of determinate being does not go so far as to make the god (as work of art) self-knowledge; knowledge is extraneous to him and pertains to the human, subjective spirit.

627. *Ho adds, similar in W_1, abridged in W_2:* Now in regard to the shape of the work of art, it would have to be said that it must be the shape of the self, for the god is the divine particular self, a spiritual, universal power. But this power derives from the naturalness it possesses as posited, so it must still have the natural for its element of configuration, and it must become apparent that precisely the natural is the mode of expression of the divine. The god appears in the stone, the sensible still deems itself to be what is appropriate for the expression of the god as god. It is only when the god himself appears revealingly as this singular being that spirit, the subjective knowledge of spirit as spirit, is the genuine appearance of the god. It is only then that sensible nature for the first time becomes free; that is to say, it is no longer wedded to the god, but shows itself to be unsuited to his shape. Sensible nature, immediate singularity is nailed to the cross. Spirit as universal, the community, is the soil for God's appearance. The appearance is absolute, its element spirit itself.

Now the shape in which the sensible expresses the divine is the *human* shape only, for there is no other bodily shape that would be an embodiment of the spiritual; but it is not the figure of an empirical human being, not a shape that could belong at the same time to the sphere of contingent existence, not one that expresses implicit actuality immediately.[628] Instead it is an ideal, an essentially beautiful shape; and this essentially beautiful shape is the essential expression of the spiritual character, the determinate representation of the spiritual that an artist has and expresses.[629] As Goethe[630] says, it is *significance* that constitutes the character of classical works of art, i.e., in every feature the figure expresses the defined character. The figure of an empirical human being does not yet evince this significance of the spiritual [as such], but also contingency, the influence of the natural and contingent; this gives us forms and figures that are not just significant in their reference to spirit and do not just express the substantive spirituality that is the foundation of the concept of God.

This is the law of appearance. This beautiful shape is the universal law, and the beautiful configuration or shaping is, as it were, the organon for understanding the world. | 378

We explain human and natural events by adducing their ground or cause, possibly in terms of some inner force or abstract reflection. Here we do not have an abstraction of that kind. The shape of that from which explanations are derived is not something as prosaic and intellectual as that; instead it is the shape of the beautiful. Among

628. *Ho, W₁ add:* Poetry, to be sure, is also a spiritualized appearance; even so, it still has as its material the tone. Admittedly this is a form of materiality that sublates itself; even so, the existence of the god consists in tone, gesture, mask, etc.—something sensible in general, not the spirit that knows itself.

629. *Ho, W₁ add:* The shape in this sensible material is the human shape. For the god is posited by human beings. But this positedness is mediated by the sublation of the singular self, so that the shape is not that of the single human being as such, but the universal, essentially beautiful shape, and so an expression of spiritual character.

630. [*Ed.*] This does not appear to be an exact quotation but a reference to Goethe's discussion of "significance" [*Bedeutsamkeit*] in various writings on art (especially classical art) and art theory. See esp. J. W. von Goethe, *Werke* (Weimar, 1887 ff.), div. 1, vol. 47, p. 17; div. 1, vol. 48, p. 102; also *Goethe-Wörterbuch* (Stuttgart, Berlin, Cologne, Mainz, 1980), s.v. *Bedeutsamkeit*.

the Greeks everything is molded to this shape. That is how the vast number of delightful stories that supposedly establish the ground of this and that, the infinite number of fables the Greeks had, originated. They are figures of phantasy, explaining events. In Homer, for instance, Achilles makes to draw his sword but manages to get hold of himself. Nestor, Calchas the priest, or the poet himself explains that Athena held him back.[631] What motivates the action is always something beautiful or charming of this kind.

Such are the basic determinations in the objective aspect of God and of the gods, first according to its own content, and second regarding the way that that content turns outward toward finite self-consciousness.[632]

c. The Cultus[633]

The cultus is the relationship through which the externality of the represented deity, its objectivity over against subjective consciousness, is sublated; through the cultus the identity of the two is brought about, and self-consciousness becomes conscious of the indwelling of the divine.

1. As regards the *disposition* [*Gesinnung*] of the worshipers in this cultus, the first moment is that the gods are recognized and honored; they are the substantive powers, the essential fulcrum of the natural and | spiritual universe, the universal. Humanity recognizes ˉthisˉ[634] because it is thinking consciousness, and hence

379

631. [*Ed.*] See Homer, *Iliad* 1.188–219, where, however, the episode is interpreted without mention of Nestor or Calchas.

632. *Ho adds, similar in W:* If the work of art is the self-revealing of the god and of human productivity as the positing of this revelation by the sublation of human beings' particular knowing and willing, then it also involves on the other hand the sublatedness of humanity and of God as alien to each other. And the positing of this implicit being of the work of art [*W₂*: of what is implicit in the work of art] *is* the cultus. It is therefore the relationship whereby the external objectivity of the god vis-à-vis subjective knowledge is sublated and the two are represented as identical. In this way, then, the external existence of the deity as being separate from existence in the subjective spirit is [also] sublated, and the god is integrated within subjectivity itself.

633. *G reads:* 3.

634. *W₂ (Var) reads:* these universal powers, as they are removed from contingency,

the world is no longer present for it in a merely external, contingent manner, but in truth—we *recognize* these universal powers. For example, we honor duties, justice, scientific knowledge, civic and political life, family relationships; these essentialities are what is true, they are the bonds that hold the world together; what is more, they are the substantive [frame] in which all else subsists.

This content has accordingly to be recognized and venerated as what is essential, what is valid, the only thing that stands out against the contingency and the independence that acts against it.

In the second place, this content is the objective, and it is objective in the genuine sense, namely it is what is *true,* what is valid in and for itself—i.e., it is the objective in the subject as well. For example, these divine powers are people's own customs, their ethical life, the rights they have and exercise, their own spirit, their own substantiality and essentiality, not an external essentiality and substantiality. Thus Athena is the city and also the goddess. The deity is the spirit of the people, not ˉtheirˉ[635] guardian spirit or suchlike, but ˉtheir living, actual, present spirit represented in its essentiality, its universality.ˉ[636] The Erinyes are not the Furies, as the representation of something externally objective, but are one's own deeds with their consequences.[637] They are what we call conscience; ˉfor example, Oedipus's Erinys is the father's curse upon the son.ˉ[638] ˉEros | is the objective element, but he is also love as sensation, the pathos experienced by the subject.

380

In this recognition and worship of the essentially substantial, the worshipers are therefore free, are immediately at home. They have their real life in it, and they know it as their own real life. So it is

---

635. *W (1831) reads:* an external

636. *W (1831) reads:* the living, present spirit, actually living in the people, immanent in the individual; this spirit is represented as Pallas, according to its essential [content].

637. *W adds in the context of the 1827 lectures a sentence from Ho:* The Erinys is not merely the external Fury that pursues the matricide Orestes but is his own deed; the spirit of matricide brandishes its torch over his head.

638. *W (1831) reads:* In *Oedipus at Colonus* Oedipus says to his son: Your father's Eumenes [Erinys] will pursue you.

[*Ed.*] See Sophocles, *Oedipus at Colonus* 1383–1392, although Hegel is here paraphrasing, not quoting. The Erinyes were avenging spirits; in milder form they were known to the Athenians euphemistically as Eumenides ("the kindly ones").

not a case of their being conscious of something that is beyond their reality or actuality; on the contrary, their religious consciousness is that their own concrete subjectivity is still the essential principle of their real life. In recognizing their essential substance they are free, so the recognition is a serenely free recognition, a veneration of powers that are dear to them because they dwell within them. The universal powers are actualized in deed through subjectivity. This character of freedom in the religious consciousness⌐639 is what constitutes the basic characteristic of this disposition. It is the disposition of freedom, of serenity, of immediate satisfaction in making this recognition.

But over and above this disposition of freedom there is another one related to necessity, and the serenity of the former is counterbalanced by the sorrow of the latter. Necessity has its own sphere; it refers only to the particular element in⌐640 individuality (insofar as a collision [between it and] the spiritual | power is possible, or insofar as ⌐it is subject to contingency and circumstance in its external, present determinate being⌐641). In their contingent aspect events are affected by necessity and are subject to it. The individuals who raise themselves above the ethical state and seek to carry out something

381

639. *Ho reads, similar in W:* Eros is thus not merely what is objective, the god, but also inward sensibility. Anacreon describes a contest with Eros: "I also," [he] says, "will now love; for a long time now it was offered me by Eros, but I would not follow. Then Eros attacked me. Armed with breastplate and lance I defended myself. Eros shot all his arrows but then leapt right into my very heart. What use," he concludes, "are bow and arrow to me then? The combat is right within me."[a] So in this recognition and worship the subject is simply at home, the gods are the subject's own πάθος. Knowledge of the gods is not knowing them as abstractions beyond actuality, but rather is knowing one's own concrete objective subjectivity, for the gods are also within one. In this way the recognition shows itself to be free. The [divine] powers are well disposed and friendly [toward] human beings, dwell within their breast; and human beings actualize them and know their actuality to be at the same time their *own* actuality. This breath of serene freedom wafts through the whole world, and

[*Ed.*] [a]See *Anakreon und Sapphos Lieder nebst anderen lyrischen Gedichten,* ed. and trans. J. F. Degen, 2d ed. (Leipzig, 1821), poem 14 ("Auf den Eros"), pp. 36–39. The reference to Eros having "shot all his arrows" (*verschoss sich*) reads "paid no heed" (*verschloss sich*) in *Ho* and W_1. We follow W_2 since Degen's translation reads, "Already his quiver was empty."

640. *Thus G, D; P adds:* divine

641. *Thus P; G reads:* its particular, circumstantial aspects are subject to contingency

particular on their own account are particularly subject to necessity, and preeminently tragic. The principal personages in Greek tragedies are like this—and for this reason they are also called heroes. They distinguish themselves from their fellow humans by virtue of their own willing. They have an interest transcending the peaceful state represented by the divine authority and government. The others, the chorus, are exempted from this fate; they remain confined within the normal, ethical sphere of life and do not stir up any of the powers in enmity to themselves. Those that belong to the chorus, to the people, are liable to the common lot of mortals, to experience misfortune and the like, to die. They may die in this way or in that, but this is the common lot of mortals, and this universal course that we all run is itself justified. That the individual has his chance misfortunes, that he dies, is part of the order of things.

In Homer[642] we find Achilles weeping over his early death, and his horses weeping at it too. It was possible for Homer to impute this sort of consciousness to Achilles.[643] Nowadays it would be stupid for a writer to do so. It can indeed make a classical Greek, an Achilles, sad, but only momentarily. It is a valid truth for him, it is a fact, but that it is so does not affect the rest of his conduct; he may be sad, but he is not discontented about it. Discontent is a contemporary feeling: it presupposes a purpose that demands something more; and this is a demand that our contemporary caprice holds itself empowered, entitled to make. Where this further purpose is not fulfilled, we tend to be easily discouraged nowadays in regard to all the rest, and have no will to follow our vocation in the other ways | that we could in any case set as our goal; we give up all the rest of our vocation, and set no goal for ourselves at all; in order to have our revenge [for the loss of our destiny in the beyond] we willfully destroy our own vocation and our own courage and energy—we deny the purpose of destiny that we could otherwise still achieve. This then is discontent. But discontent does not enter into

382

642. [Ed.] Hegel is probably referring to Iliad 19.404–424, where Achilles' horse Xanthus foretells his death, bowing its head to the ground and then falling dumb in its distress.

643. W_2 (Var) adds: for the reason that it can alter nothing in what he is or does; the situation is what it is for him, and he too is what he is.

the character of the ancient Greeks; instead there is just sorrow in regard to necessity. The Greeks did not presuppose any purpose as absolute or essential, such that it must be vouchsafed, so their sorrow is a resigned sorrow. It is grief pure and simple, and therefore it has this serenity within it; no absolute purpose is lost to the individual subjects; even in their grief they remain at home, and what has not been fulfilled can be renounced. Things are as they are, so they withdraw into abstraction and do not set their being up against this. What sets the heart at rest about it is nothing other than this abstract unity of the subjective will with what is; the subject is free, though only in an abstract fashion. Such is the character of the religious disposition.

2. The second aspect of the cultus can be described as [*divine*] *service* or *worship* [*Dienst, Gottesdienst*]. ⌐This is concerned with the attitude of concrete consciousness to its determinate concrete object; the two are represented as standing or being set against each other, so that⌐⁶⁴⁴ divine service consists in the reciprocity of giving and receiving. ⌐The divine gives, and the finite receives, the religious disposition being the form of inner mediation, of inner relatedness. The externals of worship are what mediates the external relatedness. There are several points that can be distinguished in this connection.

383   (a) First it is clear that if the divine and human | stand over against each other and are to be united, they must come nearer to each other and must both let go some of their mutual independence. It is not just the giving on the one side that is posited, but the finite self-consciousness must also let go, surrender part of its particularity. It is precisely this independence, the form of being parted from each other, that separates them, and they must accordingly modify their

644. W₂ (*Misc P*) *reads:* If subjectivity has consciously to make itself identical with the divine that stands over against it, then both sides must give up some of their determinateness: God descends from his heavenly throne and offers himself up, while humanity, receiving the gift, must negate the subjective self-consciousness, i.e., recognize the deity, or receive the gift with recognition of the essentiality that is in it.

[*Ed.*] The reference to "God descending from his heavenly throne" is an echo of Schiller's poem "Das Reich der Schatten" in *Die Horen,* vol. 1, no. 9 (Tübingen, 1795), where it is in fact presented as a consequence rather than, as here, the counterpart of humanity's free and unreserved recognition of divinity. Cf. Friedrich Schiller, *Werke: Nationalausgabe,* vol. 1 (Weimar, 1943), p. 250.

mode of existence.‾⁶⁴⁵ Their original external relationship is that the god, as we here have him, has a natural element within himself, and inasmuch as he stands over against the subjective consciousness as independent, his determinate being is some external, natural appearance. The cultus is not the stage where the representation of the god is *produced;* on the contrary, in cultus the immediate self-consciousness [of the community] is that the members come and go, just as they are, and over against them there appears this god. He has a natural element within himself, and he appears to them just as they immediately are, appearing in a natural way, in the naturally determinate mode—one god appearing more often, another less. This first relationship can thus be comprehended as one between human beings and the gods of nature. So in this relationship divine service is on the one hand the recognition that these natural things have an inherent essence, that they are an essential idea of nature or natural determination that does not depend on human subjects; and hence it is the recognition of their essentiality as distinctive, abiding powers. On the other hand, ‾in that they appear, these natural powers‾⁶⁴⁶ offer themselves up, sacrifice themselves. The god is this sacrifice of himself, delivering himself up to finite consciousness and allowing it to take possession of him; he sacrifices himself, and what the human worshipers have to do then is to take possession of this sacrifice, while at the same time recognizing the essentiality that is in it.

At the extreme of externality we have sacrifice in general, where the sacrifice is not yet propitiatory. Among the Greeks eating, drinking, and feasting were called sacrifice, and a sacrifice meant nothing more. They ate and drank bread and wine as Ceres and Bacchus; | this Ceres is a spiritual as well as a natural power. These   384
natural powers are recognized, but here Ceres and Bacchus offer themselves up to be consumed by humans. They sacrifice themselves, and their essentiality is recognized as they do so. This recognition of their universality finds expression in the fact that the worshipers

645. W₂ *(MiscP) reads:* Each side lets go some of the particularity that separates them from each other.

646. *Thus D; P reads:* these natural powers appear, *G reads:* [is] this natural power in which the gods appear,

do not consume everything but pour a few drops of wine from the beaker or a little meal out onto the ground, and burn what they cannot use—the front hairs, the entrails, the fat. They wrap the meat with fat and burn it away, just as cooks do nowadays when they pour fat over a roast.

(b) ⌐In this way the gods offer themselves up, and the cultus consists in the enjoyment of assimilating them while at the same time recognizing their power, for the gods still maintain their power.¬[647] Next there is the subject's attitude to the gods on their spiritual side. Here again the subject's attitude is one of assimilating on the one hand, of making the god present within and through oneself, causing him to appear in oneself, i.e., in the subject. On the other hand the god, as the conscious subjectivity of the divine, also remains something otherworldly, and the attitude of the human consciousness is that of a mere recipient who has come to the god [for help]. So there is this second aspect, the attitude to the gods as the spiritual and ethical powers generally. Admittedly "service" is not the right word in this context; for at this level in particular there is no service, no servitude. As addressed to these substantive, essentially ethical, spiritual powers, cultus once more consists in recognizing these essentialities of the spiritual and natural world and making them accessible to representation in eulogies, festivals, triumphs, plays, dramas, songs, and so forth—which is how *art* comes in. In this way these deities are properly worshiped—especially in the games and festivals named after them. That is how they are honored. For to have a lofty image or notion of someone and make this notion visible, make it apparent through the way one behaves, *is* to honor that person. |

385 What ⌐the community¬[648] has to bear witness to, therefore, is the pictorial representation and recognition of the gods in such a way as to make it appear in the community itself. The subjective consciousness causes this representation of the divine to appear in itself by honoring the divine in[649] festivals, odes, and so on; it has the cultus in itself. In other words, in its [religious] festivals humanity shows its excellence, displays its best side, the best that it can make

647. *Thus G*
648. *W (HgG/Ed?) reads:* the people
649. *W (HgG/Ed?) adds:* artistic productions, in

of itself. This includes self-adornment: costly jewels and ornaments, apparel and adornment, dancing, singing, and combats, all have a part to play in showing honor to the gods. ˉFor this we exhibit our mental and physical agility and our riches; to honor God humanity displays itself, and derives enjoyment from the way God thus appears in the individual.ˉ[650] This is still the case today, when people on feast days let their wealth, their fine clothes, and their talents be seen. ˉIn a word, the people cause their representation of the gods to appear in them through their own acts by presenting themselves in their outstanding achievements and thus declaring their recognition of the gods.ˉ[651] Reference can here be made to the high honors paid to the victors in the Olympic Games; they were the most honored of the people, and at the great festivals they sat beside the archons, and it even happened that in their lifetime they were honored as gods, because through the ability they had shown they had brought the divine into appearance in themselves. In this way individuals make the divine appear in themselves. In their practical activity they honor the gods, act as ethical beings; for the will of the gods consists in the ethical commandments. In practical life they *actualize* the divine. ˉWhen they held her pageant on the feast of Pallas, the people of Athens were the presence of Athena, the spirit of the people; the people of Athens are the living spirit, displaying in itself all the skill and dexterity, all the deeds of Athena (Minerva).ˉ[652] But while | individuals thus honor God in themselves on the practical plane, it is a different matter on the theoretical plane, or in regard to consciousness.

In this way human beings can make this divinity their own; the presence of the divine may ˉcause them joy,ˉ[653] but behind this there remains an otherworldly aspect of divinity. This lies in the sphere of contingency, within the bounds of what limits them, what befalls them, what they can resolve or decide; here they are incapable of attaining for themselves substantive knowledge. On a practical level they are capable of bringing forth the god in themselves, but

650. *Thus* G
651. *Thus* G
652. *Thus* G
653. W₁ *(Ed) reads:* inspire them,

485

knowledge as divine stands over against them. [654]Inside this [human] sphere, knowledge is contingent: this contingent knowledge does not relate to the ethical, the truly substantive, to our duties in respect of fatherland, state, and suchlike—such things the people *know,* they know what the laws of their state or fatherland are—but they do not and cannot know the contingent facts.[655] There is, however, a need to know such matters, and this need is involved in the level of self-consciousness that we are here considering. It is a common experience that people would very much like to know how this or that undertaking will turn out. At this level of self-consciousness ⁻this is definitely an essential need,⁻[656] for self-consciousness is still free individuality here—it is not yet the inwardly infinite subjectivity that trusts itself to take the final decision in regard to what is external; it is not yet the kind of subjectivity that knows an absolute, moral justification within itself; it is only the free subjectivity of infinite

387 | self-consciousness. So it takes this or that decision, acts, and leaves the rest to God. At a deeper level, self-consciousness has the inward force and authority to take the decision by itself. But at this stage the objectivity of self-consciousness is not this infinite inner certainty; for self-consciousness to attain such certainty a higher justification is required, one that is more full of content, namely the belief in providence, or in the absolute wisdom and goodness [of God], for which even the individual self-consciousness as such is a purpose. Inasmuch as the individual has not yet inwardly grasped at this stage that its freedom is infinite, this subjectivity, this final moment of decision, is for it something that lies outside the subject.

(c) This is the third aspect of cultus, namely oracles; [these are] altogether essential in this sphere. The final choice, the final resolve,

654. *Precedes in* W₂ *(MiscP):* I can, to be sure, decide in the light of the circumstances I know; but apart from these ones I know, there may also be other circumstances, through which the realization of my purpose is brought to naught. So with these actions I am in the world of contingency.

655. W₂ *(MiscP) adds:* To this extent the decision can accordingly be nothing firm, nothing inwardly grounded; on the contrary, in deciding, I know at the same time that I depend on something else, something unknown. But since the moment of infinite subjectivity is not present either in the divine or in the individual,

656. *Thus P; G reads:* this need has an essential place, W₁ *(Ed) reads:* this need exerts an essential influence,

today to fight a battle, to set off on a journey or to marry, is something that self-consciousness at this level does not yet muster up from within itself; for deciding is just this arbitrary willing and resolving on the part of the individual. But as this individual it does not yet have the [higher] value or justification we have just mentioned; it is not yet posited in itself as infinite subjectivity. This is a point that it is essentially necessary to bear in mind about the freedom of the Greeks. An individual who wishes to marry or engage in some undertaking consults the oracle for advice; but even a general or the state itself as a whole gets the ultimate decision from outside himself or itself, so that some external phenomenon is required to determine his or its course of action. This external phenomenon is a sound, a note ringing out or a voice; but the oracles gave no articulate answer. There was an ancient saying that the voices of the demons (αἱ φωναὶ τῶν δαιμόνων) are inarticulate.[657] And the oracles too were an indeterminate tone or something of the sort, especially the rustling of leaves, springs, and so on. In Dodona it took three forms: the sound produced by the movement of the leaves of the sacred oak; the murmuring of a spring; and the noise made by a bronze cask ˉunder the action of the wind; opposite the cask hung a switch that struck | against it when the wind blew.ˉ[658] ˉIn Delphi, too,ˉ[659] it was the wind that issued from a ravine, and the noise it set up on the bronze tripod played a principal role. It was only later that vapors had to be used as a means of inspiring the Pythia; and then in her ravings she uttered disconnected, inarticulate words, which then had to be interpreted by the prophet. The prophet also interpreted dreams. In this way the attitude of consciousness was purely receptive. In [Trophonius's cave]

388

657. [Ed.] Nonnos, Ad S. Gregorii orationem contra Julianum 2.22, quoted by Goethe on the back of the title page to vol. 2 of Zur Naturwissenschaft überhaupt, besonders zur Morphologie (Stuttgart and Tübingen, 1823).

658. W₂ (Var) reads: against which the wind blew bronze switches. Ho reads: when the wind set in motion a switch in which was held a bronze statue.
[Ed.] See Etienne Clavier, Mémoire sur les oracles des anciens (Paris, 1818), pp. 31, 35.

659. Ho, W read: In Delos, too, the laurel tree rustled, while in Delphi
[Ed.] Clavier, Mémoire, pp. 73–75.

it was faces that the questioner saw.[660] In Achaea, according to Pausanias,[661] there was a statue of [Mercury] set up in the market; one burnt incense and whispered a question into the god's ear, then ran from the market clapping one's hands over one's ears; the first word one heard after taking one's hands away was the answer, which was then made to cohere intelligibly with the question through an interpretation. Among the other merely external methods of this kind we can include inspecting the entrails of sacrificial animals, interpreting the flight of birds, and so on. Sacrificial animals were slaughtered until one had external, objective justification[662]—a decision for something external, this external [phenomenon], some utterance or other. ⁻⁻With oracles ⁻there were two things that counted; on the one hand the decision was through the external phenomenon, and on the other it was through⁻[663] the interpretation. From this point of view the attitude of consciousness is purely receptive,[664] in the same way that in the phase discussed previously it caused the gods to appear in itself.⁻⁻[665] [666] |

389

660. W (following Ho) adds: and that were interpreted to him. Ho reads: faces that were interpreted.
[Ed.] Clavier, Mémoire, pp. 143–144.

661. [Ed.] Clavier, Mémoire, p. 6.

662. [Ed.] See Karl Philipp Moritz, Anthousa; oder, Roms Alterthümer (Berlin, 1791), p. 353.

663. W (Ed) reads: two moments yielded the decision—the external phenomenon and

664. W₂ (Var) adds: while on the other side, as interpreting, it is inherently active, for the external phenomenon in itself is indeterminate.

665. Thus G

666. Ho adds, similar in W: But as a concrete expression of the god, these oracles are ambiguous. Human beings act according to them in extracting for themselves [just] one side. Then the other side comes on the scene in opposition. Those who consult them thus have a collision [with the oracle] and are now accountable to themselves. In consulting oracles human beings posit themselves as unknowing, but the god as knowing. Unknowing, they wait on what the knowing god has to say. Thus they are not knowledge, but ignorance, of the manifest. They do not act knowingly in accord with the revelation of the god, who, as universal, does not [have] determinacy within himself and so must be ambiguous in [regard to] to the determinate possibility of the two sides. If the oracle says, "Go there, and the enemy will be conquered,"ᵃ then both opposing sides are "the enemy" [for each other]. This revelation, as divine, is universal, and must be universal; human beings, as unknowing, interpret it and act according to it. What they do is their own deed, hence they know themselves to be accountable. A flight of birds or rustling of leaves in oak trees is

3. The third defining characteristic of the service of God or worship is something much more serious. The first was the disposition [of the worshipers], the second was the cultus [⌐as service⌐667], the concrete relationship, into which, however, negativity as such, an independent relationship of the two sides, has not yet entered. The third aspect is the earnest inward service of God, more precisely the service that involves *reconciliation.* Here the aim is that the divine should be realized inwardly, in the soul, in the subject. The presupposition is that the soul is independent vis-à-vis the divine, negatively determined in contrast with it, and [hence] estranged from it. Their union cannot come about in an immediate way, as it did in the previous phase. It requires a mediation in which something essential must be given up—something which in other contexts counts as settled and independent. This negative element that has to be sacrificed in order to overcome the estrangement, the gulf between the two sides, can be regarded in two ways. First, the soul, in its virgin naturalness, is already something negative as opposed to spirit. The second negative is then something positively negative, some misfortune—and especially a moral misfortune or a transgression, for a transgression or crime [is] the highest misfortune, the ultimate estrangement of the subjective self-consciousness from the divine.

As regards the first negative, the natural soul is not the way that it ought to be, for it ought to be free spirit; the soul becomes spirit only by sublating the natural will and appetite in general. This sublating, this subjecting of oneself to the | ethical and, what is more, becoming habituated to so doing, so that the ethical or spiritual becomes the individual's second nature, all this is the task of education and of cultural formation. But this elevation or reconstruction of human nature must enter consciousness at this level, so as to be recognized as a necessary change of direction; for our present stand-

390

---

a universal sign. To a specific question the god, as universal, gives a universal answer, for only the universal, not the individual as such, is the divine purpose. But the universal is [W: indeterminate and] ambiguous, for it contains both sides.

[Ed.] ªHegel is probably alluding to the Delphic oracle's utterance to the effect that if Croesus attacked the Persians he would "destroy a great kingdom." See Herodotus, *Histories* 1.53.

667. *Thus* W *(Ed)*

point is that of self-conscious freedom generally. If this process of cultural formation and this change of direction are represented as essential aspects and as essentially living, then we have the pictorial image of a path that the soul has to travel—and in consequence it is an instituted ˉnecessity that the soul must travel this path, both concretely, substantively, in [outer] life, and abstractly in its own inwardness. This involves, for one thing, the intuiting of the path.ˉ668 The soul must traverse the path by intuition, it must be seized by this intuition, renounce its natural state, and rise out of this negation. This then is what the mysteries ˉof ancient times were about. Their content was that this path, this reorientation, this death [of nature] is something spiritual, something necessary.ˉ669 In the words of Clement of Alexandria, ˉthese mysteries are full of battles of the gods, the deeds of the gods, their being buried but also their rising again,ˉ670 ˉOut of them the soul grew into the certainty of its

391 unity with the deity.ˉ671 |

As a natural soul a human being is not spirit, is not what he ought to be, any more than God, viewed as Father, is as he ought to be. It is only through the conversion [of life] that natural humanity becomes spirit; the intuition of such conversion was, of course, the object of the mysteries; and in personally experiencing this intuition, surrendering to it, the subject ˉpassed through the terror, the fear

668. W_2 (1831/MiscP?) reads: arrangement in which the intuition of this path is given to it. But if this process of turning about, negating oneself, and dying away is to be set forth for intuition as absolute and essential, it must be envisaged in the divine objects themselves. And help in this direction is in fact afforded by a process that has operated as follows in regard to the way the world of the gods was envisaged.

669. Ho, W read: were about—[they were] portrayals of the necessity of this process of spirit.

670. Thus P with G; G reads: the mysteries are a people of living gods, the gods die, are buried, and rise again. Ho reads: "the death, burial, and resurrection of the gods was presented in the mysteries."

[Ed.] Hegel is probably referring here to Clement's Protrepticus 2.19.2: "And this, let it be said once and for all, is what all mysteries are concerned with, with death and burial." It should, however, be noted that Clement does not speak here of "rising again"; above all, the sentence quoted occurs in the context of his sharp criticism of the mysteries, not of their interpretation as an intuition of the soul's unity with God.

671. Ho reads, similar in W_1: What is displayed is what spirit is as such, and in this way the soul, in purifying itself as spirit, grew into unity with God.

from which its natural essence retreated,⁻⁶⁷² and through which the freedom of spirit itself comes about.

These mysteries were secret but nonetheless familiar; all citizens of Athens were initiated into the Eleusinian mysteries. ¯They were secret and mystical in another sense—just as the public teachings of Christianity have been called mysteries even though they revealed the Godhead. The mystical is the speculative, what lies within. So these teachings were secret, but as we have said, this meant no more than that they could not be made the object of idle chatter, of reflection, or of arbitrary phantasy; they were not to be interpreted in terms of contingency or change.[673] [They had to] be something

672. G reads: passed through the terror, the fear into which its natural essence retreated, P reads: thus [the soul] passed through these terrors [from which] in [its] natural essence it retreated,

673. Ho, W₁ add: The Greek spirit as such comes from the Orient, and represents to itself in the mysteries the path it has had to traverse. In them it posits to itself its becoming.

W₁ (1831) continues: We must not believe that behind the mysteries deep secrets lay hidden, implying that the priests were cheats and themselves knew something better—this was an opinion for which Voltaire and other French writers[a] have been particularly responsible. But in the first place, a people cannot be lied to and cheated in its religious faith, for the religious, eternal truth resides in the spirit; moreover, the priests themselves are not in advance of the spirit of the people. In one of his tragedies Aeschylus is supposed to have betrayed something of the mysteries, namely that Ceres is the daughter of Diana,[b] but no particular weight is to be attached to a mystery of this kind. The little that has come down to us about the mysteries is best contained in the compilations of the French writers Sainte-Croix and Silvestre de Sacy.[c] In any event it seems that ancient notions were preserved in the mysteries, and human beings are often most reverential toward what they do not understand. These notions, however, do not belong to the higher sphere of Greek clarity, but are images of phantasy that have not yet developed to perfection.

In the Eleusinian mysteries it was mainly figurative portrayals that were presented, such as the soul's introduction to an essentiality that lies more remote from it, or the representation of a path that the soul has to traverse—portrayals based on the call to discard the natural state, the presentation of the purification of the soul and its acceptance into a high mystical essence. This seems to have been the main content of the mysteries, to which also attaches the notion of the immortality of the soul. Socrates was said by the oracle to be the wisest of all the Greeks;[d] to him can be traced the complete reorientation [W₂: what was in fact a complete reorientation] of self-consciousness among the Greeks. Yet this pivotal figure [in the development] of self-conscousness was not himself initiated into the mysteries, which were at a much lower level than what he brought to the consciousness of the thinking world. [The

392   unchanging, untouchable. | If the Greeks had spoken of them, they would have done so only in myths.⁻⁶⁷⁴ But the content is precisely not a matter for reflection, for the understanding, and so not for phantasy either. Another point that is logically connected with this one is that the content of these mysteries evidently consisted in representations and traditions derived from the old nature religions, whether Pelasgian, Hindu, Egyptian, or other. Representations of this kind are symbolic; that is to say, their meaning is not the same as what they portray externally. The Greek gods are not symbolic: they have no meaning other than what they show; they are what they portray, in the same way as the concept of a work of art is to express what is meant, not that what lies within should differ from the exterior.

    Even if the Greek gods originated from ancient symbolic elements

---

last two sentences also in W₂, *preceded by:* This was also the reason why the mysteries could not endow the self-consciousness of the Greeks with genuine reconciliation.]

    [*Ed.*] ªVoltaire's criticism of priests is directed primarily against their worldly power, although on occasion he also accuses them of deceiving the people; see, e.g., *Dictionnaire philosophique*, vol. 6, s.v. "Pierre, Saint," "Prêtres," "Superstition." By "other French writers" Hegel probably has in mind especially Paul Henri Thiry d'Holbach, *Le christianisme dévoilé* (London, 1756), esp. chap. 15; and *Théologie portative; ou, Dictionnaire abrégé de la religion chrétienne* (London, 1768), s.v. "Sacerdoce," "Sacrilège." See also Vol. 1:383 n. 47.

    ᵇHegel is probably following the interpretation of C. A. Lobeck, *Aglaophamus; sive, De theologiae mysticae Graecorum causis libri tres*, 2 vols. (Königsberg, 1829), 1:76–85, who suggested that what Aeschylus discloses is that Diana, daughter of Proserpine, is really the mother of Ceres (Demeter); but the terms in which Hegel presents it involve a confusion of Proserpine and Demeter, resulting from the combination of reports by Herodotus and Cicero.

    ᶜHegel was probably acquainted only with the second, enlarged edition of the work of Baron de Sainte-Croix, *Recherches historiques et critiques sur les mystères du Paganisme*, rev. Silvestre de Sacy (Paris, 1817).

    ᵈThe Delphic oracle declared that Socrates was the wisest of the Greeks; see Plato, *Apology* 20e–21a, and Xenophon, *Apology of Socrates* 14. That Socrates was not initiated into the Eleusinian mysteries was reported by Lucian of Samosata, *Demonax* 11.

    674. W₂ *(MiscP) reads:* But these intuitions were not mystical in the sense that the public teachings of Christianity have been called mysteries. For in the latter case the mystical is the speculative, what lies within. The main reason why the intuitions afforded by the Greek mysteries had to remain secret was that the Greeks would not have been able to speak of them except in myths, i.e., without altering what was old.

of this kind, what the poets and other artists made of them was the work of art, which perfectly expresses what it is meant to be. There have been many investigations—that of Creuzer particularly—into the historic origin of the Greek gods and their underlying significance.[675] | But where the god is the object of art, only a good work of art portrays him.[676] In Egyptian religion this is secret; there is an inner element, a symbol.[677] Osiris is a symbol of the sun, just as Hercules is (his twelve labors relate to the months).[678] To the extent that Hercules is a symbol of the sun, [like] Osiris, he exists in another way, a symbolic way. He is a calendrical deity and not what he is as a work of art, i.e., no longer the Greek god of classical times. Thus the content of the mysteries was essentially symbolic in nature, primarily Ceres (Demeter), Bacchus, and the secrets attaching to them; in the same way as Ceres,[679] who goes in search of her lost daughter, [is] the harvest corn delivered over to the underworld—or, in prosaic terms, the seed that must die in order to preserve and bring to life what lies implicit in it—so the process of the seed [being buried] into the earth and then sprouting is itself something symbolic, for this process also has the higher meaning of resurrection, as it does in the Christian religion. In other words,

393

675. [Ed.] See Creuzer, *Symbolik und Mythologie*. Hegel accepted in particular Creuzer's interpretation of the origin of Apollo. In 1827 he was to take issue with K. O. Müller, who, in his *Geschichten hellenischer Stämme und Städte* (Breslau, 1824), vol. 2, pt. 1, pp. 284, 287–288, argued against any original identity of Apollo and the sun. See also below, n. 678.

676. *W₂ (Var) adds:* as what he is.

677. *W (following Ho) adds:* because the shape does not reveal the indwelling significance but is only *supposed* to reveal it. *Ho reads:* The Egyptian gods, nevertheless, have a secret element, precisely because their shape . . . it.

678. [Ed.] In equating the labors of Heracles with the months of the year, Hegel is again following Creuzer, *Symbolik und Mythologie* 2:248–249, although the same interpretation had also been advanced by Dupuis (see above, n. 607). It should be noted that Hegel distinguishes this—symbolic—deity from "the Greek god of classical times," and in so doing diverges from Creuzer's view. His divergence from Creuzer is summed up in his assertion at the end of the previous paragraph that "the Greek gods are not symbolic." On the problem of the symbolic, see also Gottfried Herrmann and Friedrich Creuzer, *Briefe über Homer und Hesiodus* (Heidelberg, 1818). Hegel's position is analogous to the one taken by Herrmann against Creuzer; it is also closer to the position of Johann Heinrich Voss than to that of Creuzer.

679. *Thus W₂; G reads:* Ceres

we can take it ˉin the spiritual sense.ˉ680 The sense of the symbol alternates: sometimes the content denotes a notion or process, at other times what is denoted itself symbolizes another meaning. For example, Osiris is the Nile, which is dried up by the sun and the scorching wind (Typhon) but then is created anew; but he also symbolizes the sun, a natural power that gives life to all. Lastly, however, Osiris is also a spiritual figure, and then the Nile itself and the daily rebirth of the sun in turn symbolize the spiritual realm. The content of the mysteries is symbolic portrayals of this kind, where old natural powers were represented [in] a process to which the necessary movement of the spirit also corresponds. Such symbols | are naturally secret: the inward [meaning] is still unclear—it is there at first as a sense or significance that has not yet achieved a genuine portrayal.681 This is the first form of reconciliation.

394

The second form of reconciliation, the other negative, can be defined as misfortune in general, as sickness, famine, and other adversities. This negative is what was explained by the prophets and put in the context of a relationship of guilt: some offense had been committed. A negative of this kind first becomes apparent on the physical plane, in external events such as sickness or famine. Agamemnon682 was held back by unfavorable winds, and this physical state was viewed and explained as something having a spiritual connection, i.e., as involving a misfortune—the gods' anger or obduracy toward humanity—resulting from some offense. Thunder and lightning, earthquakes, the appearance of snakes, and so forth were explained as a negative factor of this kind, implicitly [ethical] and pertaining to a higher, spiritual, ethical power. In this case the offense that had occurred was to be sublated by a sacrifice, [the belief being] that any transgression can be made good in this way. Whoever, by transgressing, has acted presumptuously accepts a personal loss; for every offense is an act of presumption, an offense against a higher spiritual power to which humility then has to

680. W₂ (Var) reads: in the sense that it applies to spirit, whose implicit potential can first bear fruit through the sublation of the natural will.
681. Ho, W add: The shape does not fully express the content, so that it remains lying partly unexpressed without emerging into existence.
682. [Ed.] See Euripides, Iphigenia in Aulis 87–92.

sacrifice something in order to propitiate it.[683] Among the Greeks it seems to have been rather a relic from the past ⁻that Agamemnon performs a rite of human sacrifice in order to obtain a favorable wind when he sacrifices his daughter.⁻[684] | ⁻A human sacrifice also occurs 395 in Sophocles,⁻[685] but later this sort of thing no longer seems to occur. Thucydides says nothing of sacrifices or ceremonies to propitiate the gods during the famous plague in Athens at the time of the Peloponnesian War. He speaks[686] only of a prediction that the plague will cease—⁻a prediction that⁻[687] in fact implies the obsolete character of such sacrifices ⁻and of all such ways of winning the gods to one's side.⁻[688] Thus the outcome of the plague was regarded as something that *had* to happen, as a matter of necessity or fate, where there could be no more question of reconciliation. It was regarded as something inevitable.

The third form of reconciliation is that the negative is an actual crime, and is regarded and spoken of as such, not as something which one first uncovers by having an external misfortune explained. So an individual, or else the state and its people, has committed a crime;

683. W₂ *(following Ho) adds:* and restore symmetry. Ho *reads:* In order to restore symmetry, an act of presumption must be followed by the humility of giving up [something].

684. Ho, W *read:* When the Greeks wanted to set sail from Aulis and were held back by unfavorable winds, Calchas declared the storm to be the wrath of Poseidon, who was demanding Agamemnon's daughter as sacrifice. Agamemnon is prepared to give her up to the god, but she is saved by Diana.

[Ed.] See n. 682.

685. Ho *reads:* We find them [human sacrifices] in the case of Oedipus and in that of Agamemnon, W₂ *(1831) reads:* In the *Oedipus Rex* of Sophocles a sickness is inflicted through which the patricide's deed is laid bare.

[Ed.] As there are no other references to human sacrifice in Sophocles, the text as given by W₂ probably affords the key to the cryptic references in the main text and that transmitted by Ho. However, this interpretation could have been provided by one of the sources or by the editor. On the sickness in Thebes, see Sophocles, *Oedipus Rex*, esp. 1–77.

686. [Ed.] See Thucydides, *Peloponnesian War* 2.54. Neither here nor in 2.47, where Thucydides speaks of the outbreak of the plague, does he in fact refer to its cessation; the prediction was only that it would inevitably follow the outbreak of war between Athens and Sparta.

687. Ho, W *read:* and this recourse to oracles

688. Ho *reads, similar in W:* If in fact advice is sought from the oracles, this means that the outcome of the plague is regarded as determined by God himself, as necessary.

in human terms punishment is atonement for the crime, in the form of[689] revenge. But here free spirit has the self-consciousness of its majesty, [i.e., its power] to undo *inwardly* what has happened. The external [form of] pardon and so on is something different. But that free spirit should be able to undo in itself what has happened, this is the higher prerogative of free self-consciousness. Where evil as such has its abode—not merely as a deed but as a fixture—is actually in the sinful soul. But the free soul is capable of cleansing itself inwardly from such evil. These pointers to a complete inward reorientation are to be found in the Greek portrayal [of reconciliation], though the character of reconciliation here is more that of external purification. But among the Greeks this external form also appears to be something handed down from the past. From Athens a few such purifications are known to us. | ⌐One of Minos's sons came freely to Athens⌐[690] and was there murdered; and because of this crime, purification was undertaken.[691] Later an⌐ambassador⌐[692] of Epimenides by the name of Chilon was also murdered, whereupon a youth called Cratinus offered himself for sacrifice in order to purify the city.[693] Aeschylus recounts how Orestes was pursued by the Furies, and then absolved by the Areopagus, thanks to the voting

396

689. W₂ *(following Ho) adds:* punishment or, more brutally, *Ho reads:* The human way of atonement for crime is punishment or, more brutally, revenge.

690. *Ho reads:* When Theseus came to Athens with Androgeos

691. [*Ed.*] See Diodorus Siculus, *Bibliotheca historica* 4.60–61. The "purification"—whereby the drought and famine inflicted on Athens as punishment for the crime were to be lifted—consisted in doing whatever Minos demanded; and this was of course that seven youths and seven maidens should be sent to his court every nine years for the Minotaur to feed upon.

692. *Thus G; P reads:* δοκήτες
[*Ed.*] This word, which occurs in comparatively clear script in *P*, is not given even in the *Thesaurus Graecae Linguae;* it could be a mishearing for δοκιμαστής, "investigator," which might possibly fit the context.

693. [*Ed.*] This sentence, based essentially on G and confirmed by P, confuses the story of Minos's son Androgeos (see preceding sentence) and the story of the treacherous massacre of Cylon and his followers after their unsuccessful revolt and surrender. In the latter connection, following Sainte-Croix, *Recherches historiques et critiques sur les mystères du paganisme* 1:276, Hegel merges two different accounts of the purification of Athens—by Epimenides and by the sacrifice of Cratinus and Ctesebius. Neither account corresponds to that given by Thucydides in *Peloponnesian War* 1.126.

pebble of Athena.[694] Here the reconciliation appears as an external event, not as an inner conversion. But the kind of complete inward reorientation that foreshadows the Christian conception is represented in *Oedipus at Colonus*,[695] where the aged Oedipus, after killing his father, marrying his mother and having children by her, and then being driven from the city by his sons, ¯has a clear inner vision and hears a voice from the gods calling him to come.¯[696] This sounds more like a pure reconciliation of spirit, like a reception into grace so to speak, as in the Christian religion.[697]

Other sacrifices belong even more to the external mode, such as the sacrifices Achilles performs on the grave of Patroclus; he slays a number of Trojans so as to propitiate the Manes of Patroclus through the blood of his enemies.[698] ¯What is involved is to reestablish the equality of fate on the two sides.¯[699]

Such are the main characteristics of the religion of beauty.[700] | 397

694. [*Ed.*] See Aeschylus, *Eumenides*, esp. 734–741.

695. [*Ed.*] See Sophocles, *Oedipus at Colonus*, esp. 1623–1628, 1658–1664.

696. *Thus P; G reads:* achieves honor among the gods, who call him to them. *Ho reads:* His inner vision becomes clear, as does his eye, and he hears a voice from the gods calling him to the place of his death.

697. *Ho adds:* But Oedipus still retains his character. He rejects Creon's request, and lays his curse on his son.

[*Ed.*] Sophocles, *Oedipus at Colonus* 761–799, 1348–1392.

698. [*Ed.*] See Homer, *Iliad* 1.26–28, 23.173–176.

699. *Ho reads:* Crime as such is injury to the gods; to establish this [reconciliation] involves recognizing the injury and extinguishing it through purification.

700. *As a transition from the religion of expediency to the Christian religion, W contains the following passage, which in the 1831 lectures formed the transition from the religion of beauty to the religion of expediency:* [W_1: We have considered Olympus, this heaven of the gods, a circle of the fairest figures ever to have been conceived by phantasy. The circle composed of these fair essences has W_2: Olympus, this heaven of the fairest figures ever to have been conceived by phantasy, had] shown itself to us at the same time as free ethical life, as free but still limited folk-spirit. Greek life is fragmented into numerous small [city] states, [W_1: ethical life is limited to W_2: into] these stars that are themselves only limited points of light. [W_1: Free spirituality can be attained only if this limitedness is sublated and the fate that hovers remotely over the Greek world of gods makes its influence felt on Greek civil life, so that W_2: In order for free spirituality to be attained, this limitedness must be sublated and the fate that hovers remotely over the Greek world of gods and folk life must make its influence felt on them, so that the spirits of] these free people collapse. Free spirit must grasp itself as pure spirit in and for itself; its value no longer consists in

3. The Religion of Expediency (Roman Religion)[701]
In the religion of beauty we have observed two aspects: abstract, empty necessity and, quite apart from this, the particular powers in the realm of right and of ethical life, ˉthe universal substantialities.ˉ[702] Furthermore, these particular powers are not abstractions but individual spirits or deities; and as individual deities they are particular folk-spirits such as Athena for Athens or Bacchus for Thebes; and also family deities. At the same time they are communicable, they have within them at the same time the character

---

its being merely the free spirit of the Greeks, of the citizens of this or that state, but humanity must be known freely as humanity, and God is the God of all humanity, the comprehensive, universal spirit. Now this fate [W_1: is what holds particular freedom in check. By this means it is brought about that one of the folk-spirits attains the level of a universal power, the fate (that hangs) over the others. W_2: which is what holds particular freedoms in check,] and suppresses the limited folk-spirits, so that [W_1: they W_2: the peoples become disloyal to the gods and] become conscious of their weakness and powerlessness, in that their political life is destroyed by [W_1: a higher W_2: the one, universal] power. This fate was the Roman world and Roman religion.

701. [Ed.] In the 1824 lectures, the section on Roman religion, as the religion of expediency or external purposiveness (aüsserliche Zweckmässigkeit), is much reduced in size as compared with the lecture Ms., becoming in effect a mere appendage to Sec. B. The lengthy discussion of the teleological proof found at this point in the Ms. is moved to the beginning of Sec. B since now Jewish and Greek religion are also considered under the category of purposiveness. In the brief introduction to Roman religion that follows, Hegel argues that the movement is from exclusive purposiveness (the Jewish God is one and almighty but limited to a particular people) to a plurality of purposes (the Greek gods) to a universal purpose, which, in Roman religion, because of its finitude and externality, becomes necessity or fate (Fatum). The transcendence and holiness of Jewish religion are lost, as well as the freedom and beauty of Greek religion. Roman religion is the religion of "unfreedom" because human beings become dependent on a host of finite deities that control every facet of life. These deities are abstractions, not spiritual individualities; hence Roman religion does not fit readily under the general category of "The Religions of Spiritual Individuality." In fact, as we have pointed out, in the 1821 and 1827 lectures it is treated as a separate, third moment of Determinate Religion. But in 1824, as Hegel's treatment evolved in the course of the lectures, Determinate Religion is composed of only two moments, and the triad is completed by Consummate Religion. Of course, in 1824 as elsewhere, Roman religion provides a transition to Christian religion by depicting the collapse, as it were, of finite religion in upon itself. For Hegel's major source, see below, n. 719.

702. Thus P, D; G reads: and natural powers, the universal, spiritual, ethical substantiality.

of a broader universality, and are thus capable of being communicated, worshiped by other peoples as well. | Accordingly the objects   398
of these gods are particular cities too, particular states, particular
purposes, of which there are any number.

The next demand of thought, or necessary development in the
concept, is that the abstract necessity should be united with the
particularity of the purposes. As fate, necessity is devoid of purpose;
[but now] purpose, wisdom, providence, self-determining individuality are to be equated with this power of universal necessity; in
other words, the power of universal necessity is to be what wills.

In the first religion of this sphere, the religion of sublimity, ˉwe
had abstract wisdom, the universal power and wisdom, where the
actual content takes the form of a completely single purpose, a quite
singular people, one family to the exclusion of others.ˉ⁷⁰³ In the second religion of this sphere, the religion of beauty, the multitude
of particular powers rest in the lap of the gods and the multitude
of particular realities participate in divinity itself. Within divinity
the multitude of real folk-spirits find fulfillment and are purposes;
there is, so to speak, a divine aristocracy. The third stage is for it
to be a *real* purpose that is carried out by the divine power. First,
then, there is an exclusive purpose, then many purposes, and these
many are now to be extended into a universal purpose; and this one
real purpose must itself become necessity, that which is highest. Such
is the concept of this third type of religion.

a. The Concept of Necessity and External Purpose⁷⁰⁴

What reigns is necessity, fate [*Fatum*], power, and what is initially
posited to be identical with it is itself a purpose that is in the first
place an empirical, indeed an external purpose (as in the religion
of sublimity)—but a purpose that is here raised to the level of an

703. *Ho reads:* the one and only content of the unity was *itself,* so that its real
purpose was the absolutely singular purpose (the third purpose is the prophecy of
reconciliation, that the head of the serpent shall be trodden under foot [Gen. 3:15]—the
proclamation of the Messiah).

704. [*Ed.*] Since the teleological proofs have been considered in detail in the
introduction to Sec. B, the present section is quite brief and focuses on the distinctive
conceptuality of imperial Roman religion.

all-encompassing reality. What makes it empirical is its content; and this next mode of universality—incomplete, abstract universality—is where the empirical purpose is extended to embrace [the whole of] external reality. This purpose thus becomes a universal condition of the world, world dominion, | universal monarchy. ¨This must be clearly¨[705] distinguished from the purpose that can also be observed in the Islamic religion; there, too, world dominion is the purpose, but what is to have dominion is the One of thought.[706] Just as in Christianity it is said that God wills that all should come to ¨a knowledge¨[707] of the truth, so too in Islam the purpose is universal actualization, but of a spiritual nature, and individuals have their place in it as thinking, spiritual, free individuals; they are present in it, and the whole purpose is focused on them—it is not an external purpose. In this way they take the whole scope of the purpose into themselves. At the present stage, on the other hand, the purpose is still an external, empirical purpose, an all-encompassing purpose but on the plane of empirical reality—i.e., the purpose is a *world dominion*. The inherent purpose is one that is external to the individual, and it becomes ever more so the more that it is realized and externalized, so that the individual is merely subordinated to the purpose, merely *serves* it.

This directly implies the absolute unification of universal power and ¨singularity in all being,¨[708] but it is, so to speak, a raw unification, one that is devoid of spirit. The power is not wisdom, its reality is not implicitly and explicitly a divine purpose. It is not the one God, whole fulfillment is himself. It is not in the realm of thought that this fulfillment is posited; it is worldly power, mere lordship, worldliness merely as lordship. The power in it [i.e., in the universal empire] is in itself irrational. ¨At the same time the power

705. W_2 *(Ed/MiscP?) reads:* Just as this category of external purposiveness is distinct from the ethical spirituality of Greek life and from the identity of the divine powers and their external existence, in the same way the purpose comprised by this universal monarchy or dominion must be

706. *W (Ed) adds:* [as] derived from the Jewish religion.

707. W_2 *reads:* consciousness

708. W_1 *(Ed) reads:* universal singularity in all being, W_2 *(Ed) reads:* universal singularity,

of the particular [i.e., of the folk communities] crumbles away⁻⁷⁰⁹ because the particular is not | taken up into it [the universal]   400 rationally. It lies outside the posited unity, it is a content that lacks divinity—it is the egoism of the individual, seeking satisfaction apart from God, ⁻in particular interests.⁻⁷¹⁰ It lies outside reason; lordship stands cold and egoistic on one side, and the individual equally so on the other.

Such is the universal concept of this religion. In it is implicitly posited the demand for the highest—the unification of what is purely self-contained with the purpose pertaining to particularity in its determinacy, but at this stage the unification is just this raw ungodly one [imperial authority].

b. The Configuration of the Gods

The second point to be considered is the configuration of this god [imperial authority] and of the gods. What we have here is a religion of expediency, of a purpose that is not in and for itself the divine, spiritual purpose, so that "purposiveness" here designates conformity to an external purpose generally. In the intuition of the essential, *seriousness* becomes a basic feature as opposed to the cheerful serenity of Greek religion; for what characterizes the content here is an essential purpose. ⁻In the case of the Greek gods (absolute necessity and the array of particular beautiful divine individuals), the basic characteristic is freedom, and this is what is meant by "serenity" or felicity. The gods are not tied to a singular existence; they are essential powers and are at the same time the expression of irony in regard to what they seek to do. For they attach no importance to the singular, empirical outcome.⁻⁷¹¹ The seriousness that arises from the purpose is a basic feature in regard to Roman religion. Dionysius of Halicarnassus (Creuzer, *Symbolik,* volume 2⁷¹²) compares Greek and Roman religion, praising the religious

709. *Thus P; G reads:* The reason why the particular crumbles away in opposition to this power is
710. *Thus G; P reads:* externally singularized purposes.
711. *Thus G*
712. [*Ed.*] Creuzer, *Symbolik und Mythologie* 2:992. Creuzer here cites Dionysius of Halicarnassus (*Roman Antiquities* 2.18 ff.) in terms very similar to those employed in this and the next sentence.

institutions of Rome and showing what a great advance the Roman religion made over the Greek. The Romans had temples, altars, ceremonies, sacrifices, religious truces, festivals, symbols, and so forth, ¯just as the Greeks did; but they threw out the myths that depicted the gods with blasphemous features, their mutilations, imprisonments, wars, bargaining, and so on. Yet these features belong to the serene configuration of the gods; they let us take advantage of them, and make fun of them in comedy, but throughout all this they retain their determinate being and their untroubled security. In the serious view of them | the shape or figure, the actions, and the events must all match the principle;¯[713] in free individuality, on the other hand, there are as yet no such fixed purposes or categories of the understanding; the gods contain the ethical, but they are not a one-sided, ethical category of the understanding. Instead they exist at the same time in their determinateness; they do have *one* principal feature in their character, [but] they are many-sided individualities, they are concrete. In this many-sided individuality, what we call seriousness of character is not a necessary constituent; rather, such individuality is free in the singularity of its utterance, it can light-mindedly spin around in all directions, yet remain what it is. ¯These unworthy-seeming tales hint at general views regarding the nature of things, the creation of the world, and so on, and originate in old traditions and abstract views concerning the action and interaction of the elements. The universal import is obscured but hinted at, and in this disorderly externality one's attention is awakened to the universal or intelligible.¯[714] On the other hand, in a religion where the determinate purpose is power [i.e., imperial dominion], there is no longer room to attend to all these theoretical viewpoints of the intelligence. ¯Theogonies and so on of this kind and what they have given rise to,¯[715] along with all such universal concerns, are not to be found in the religion of expediency.

401

713. *Thus G*
714. *Thus G*
715. *Thus P; G reads:* Theories, *Ho reads:* This theogony also disappears at this stage.

The second point [after seriousness] is that the deity now has a determinate content, which is declared to be the lordship of the world. This is an empirical universality, not ethical or spiritual but a *real*[716] universality that is not spiritual as in the Christian and Islamic religions. The god is here the ruling power, the world-dominating power, and it has its reality in this people, which is inspired and filled by this god. Its dominion is only an abstract one, a cold dominion that is just power as such. This then is the Roman religion, and its characteristics are evident to us in its spirit. This dominion, this dominating authority, is none other than the city of Rome itself, and the lordship consists in | necessity or fortune. There 402 was in Rome a temple dedicated to Fortuna Publica. This divine ruler also takes the shape of Jupiter, but with a different meaning than Zeus—he is essentially Jupiter Capitolinus. Zeus is lord of all the gods and of mortals generally, but this Jupiter Capitolinus is the real lord of existing human beings; i.e., he is the ruler in a real sense. This is the general basic characteristic, to which all else is subordinate.

In the second place [we should notice] that the particular powers also emerge. As we have already seen, it is the *abstract* lordship of the Roman state that is divine necessity. The particular or the concrete accordingly lies outside it. The particular aspect is manifest partly in the way the Greek gods appear [in Roman religion], but we do not here meet them in the beauty of their free individuality, not in this unconstrained, serene mode, but all gray as it were, because one either knows not where they come from or else knows that they have arisen in definite situations. They have here no proper sense, and we must carefully distinguish the way in which later writers such as Virgil and Horace took them up in their poetic compositions [from their appearance in Greek poetry]. Virgil seems to have copied the Greek models completely, imitating them slavishly and lifelessly, and so they appear as plagiarisms, more or less devoid

716. [*Ed.*] The German adjective *real* has the sense of "material" or "empirical" by contrast with *ideal/ideell,* which is "ideal," "ethical," "spiritual." Both the ideal and the real are "actual" (*wirklich*).

of spirit.[717] They give the impression of stage machinery, just as they appear in the second-rate works of modern French dramatists as stuffed figures and mechanical devices.[718] This is why the Roman figures of the gods have appealed more to recent times than the Greek gods, because they come before us more as empty deities of the understanding, they belong to a phantasy that has been degraded and is no longer free, no longer alive. Another kind of particularity, the second type, has a content that belongs wholly to the everyday requirements of life. Apart from, and at a more mundane level than, the universal purpose that we have already considered, lie the particular purposes of individuality, of domesticity, and the requirements of family life; when all this is pictured as something essential, it appears as a god, and as a god who is more concerned with matters of practical utility. Thus everyday requirements, the arts of the understanding, were viewed as something essential, as gods, even though they are concerned with wholly subordinate matters, relating to everyday | life, in which the only religious aspect is the formal one that these purposes have now achieved the empty shape of essentialities. Somewhat better in this sphere are the Lares and Penates, as the spirits of the family. Otherwise it is everyday requirements in general that are what the gods are here concerned with.

403

We must bear in mind that the state, as the world dominion, is one side; this is the abstract power that presses and weighs upon individuals, consuming and sacrificing them. On the other side, where individuals attain to their subjectivity, to a free consciousness that enjoys itself, we have a simply uncultured state of nature. On the one hand we have the state in all its rigor, on the other an

717. [Ed.] Hegel had already made a similar criticism of Virgil in *The Difference between Fichte's and Schelling's System of Philosophy*, trans. H. S. Harris and W. Cerf (Albany, 1977), p. 89 (*GW* 4:12). To judge from the context, on that occasion he had Virgil's *Aeneid* in mind. See also *Aesthetics*, trans. T. M. Knox (Oxford, 1975), 2:1073–1075 (*Werke* 10/3:369–372); and *Lectures on the Philosophy of World History*, Sibree ed., p. 293; Lasson ed., p. 680.

718. [Ed.] Hegel criticizes French dramatists in almost identical terms in the *Lectures on Aesthetics*, without however citing the names of authors or works there either. In the *Ms.* he does specifically criticize Racine's *Phèdre* for making Hippolytus fall in love with Aricia, thus robbing the drama of ethical content.

uncultured condition. For example, there are in this religion constant references to the age of Saturn and to forms of activity that pertain to such a condition, that relate to such a state of nature. The age of Saturn is a natural life of bliss and happiness. A great many Roman festivals[719] relate to this—the Saturnalia, Lupercalia, rustic, country-side life—and the requirements, arts, and so forth that have a place in this state or condition are therefore essential states, essential purposes that have been exalted to divine status. For instance, the Romans had a large number of fertility and craft festivals and deities, e.g., Jupiter Pistor. Jupiter is, generally speaking, a *nomen appellativum,* and there are three or four hundred uses of the name— Jupiter Stator, Capitolinus, and so on. And the same is true of Juno. Jupiter Pistor is the god of the bakers, for the art of baking was a gift of the god. So they had a goddess Fornax, the goddess of the oven, [identical with] the art of roasting corn in the oven, and a goddess Vesta, who was the particular kind of flame needed for baking bread. ¬They had festivals devoted to pigs, sheep, and cattle as well as¬[720] the Palilia, the festival of the goddess of cattle fodder. In regard to the Roman state also, utilities of this kind were venerated as essential—for example, Juno Moneta, the art of minting being an essential one. Mercury too was qualified in special ways. The political deity was Jupiter Capitolinus, and there was Jupiter Latialis, the protector of Latium, and Jupiter Stator, who stayed the Romans' steps when they were put to flight. The representation of the age of Saturn was particularly | celebrated in the Saturnalia, the festival in which the distinction between rich and poor was done away with.

There are other deities that form part of this pattern, both harmful

404

719. [*Ed.*] The source for most of Hegel's knowledge of Roman festivals and the different appellations of gods and goddesses, as presented in this and the following paragraph, was Karl Philipp Moritz, *Anthousa; oder, Roms Alterthümer* (Berlin, 1791). See, for example, on the festivals of Fornax (the Fornicalia) and Pales (the Palilia), pp. 44–45, 103–107; on the Saturnalia, pp. 223–224; on Jupiter Pistor, p. 147; on Jupiter Stator, p. 168; on Jupiter Latialis (Latium was the name of the region around Rome), p. 260; on Juno Moneta, p. 129; on Pax (or Tranquillitas) and on Vacuna, p. 145; on Robigo, p. 109; and on Plague, Febris (Fever), and Angerona (Care and Sorrow), p. 253. Hegel has here greatly condensed his description of the Roman festivals and deities from that found in the lecture *Ms.,* where it continues for several sheets.

720. *Ho reads:* The Ambarvalia and Suovetaurilia are also festivals, as are

powers and also useful powers (or rather situations generally that were grasped in the form of independent gods and goddesses and venerated accordingly). Prosaic contents of this kind, quite devoid of phantasy, are the goddess Pax or Tranquillitas, the goddess ˉVacuna or Leisure,ˉ[721] and also harmful powers like Febris or Fever, Robigo or wheat rust, Plague, and Care and Sorrow. It is hard for us to grasp how such things can be venerated as gods. The content can be anything, provided it appears essential for the common needs; it can be any situation, which is [then] comprehended without phantasy and on its own, all idealization and all living phantasy being excluded. It is consistent with this prosaic situation in regard to power that the Romans later came to worship their emperors too as gods. The emperor was an individual who indubitably constituted a power set over them, weighty and with more actual effects than Febris, Robigo, and so on, capable of bringing about a worse state of affairs than *those* powers.

This is how the divine is given shape [at this stage]. But it should be added that all these configurations are subordinated to the universal, real power; they all give way when they come up against the universal, strictly essential power of domination, the greatness of Rome that extends over the whole known civilized world. Within this universal power the destiny of these particular specializations exalted to divine status is necessarily to be dismissed in this abstract universality, to perish just like the living individual divine spirits; their destiny is to succumb to the yoke of this one abstract lordship. Rome becomes the pantheon in which all the gods of all the peoples are set up side by side, so that they extinguish one another; and they are all subject to the one Jupiter Capitolinus, the one necessity, or to the one Rome and her Fortuna. This shows up in single details of a more empirical nature—for example, in Cicero,[722] where we

721. *Ho reads:* Paounia [*sic*] (having nothing to occupy one),
722. *Ho adds:* (*De natura deorum* 3)
[*Ed.*] According to *Ho,* Hegel is here referring to book 3 of Cicero's *De natura deorum,* i.e., to the speech of Cotta, presenting the New Academy's criticism of the traditional representation of the gods and especially the use made of it by Stoic theology, but not to the presentation of Epicurean doctrine by Velleius or of Stoic doctrine by Lucilius Balbus. Cicero's lists of numerous Vulcans, Apollos, and Jupiters, referred to below, are found in various chapters of book 3 of this work.

find this type of cold reflection upon the gods. In Cicero, cold reflection is the subjective | authority over all of them. He makes a coherent   405
pattern of their genealogy, of what befalls them, of their doings, and
so forth; he lists large numbers of Vulcans, Apollos, and Jupiters
and puts them side by side; this is the reflection which, by making
comparisons, renders doubtful and imprecise what otherwise has a
sharp outline. The information he gives in his treatise *De natura
deorum* is exceedingly important in other respects, e.g., in regard
to the genesis of myths, but all the same the gods are degraded by
this reflection on them, their determinate aspects no longer feature
in their portrayal, and disbelief and distrust are aroused. We see the
Romans conquering Magna Graecia, Sicily, plundering and destroying the temples and carrying off whole shiploads of gods to Rome.
In Rome there is toleration; all the religions come together there and
are commingled: the Syrian, Egyptian, Jewish, Christian, Greek,
Persian religions, Mithraism—the Romans seize on all of them, and
precisely in this fusion what gives each religion its shape, the
particularity that pertains to art and phantasy, is lost. And as a
further result the search is set under way for something more solid.

c. The Cultus

We now have to consider in more detail the different moments of
the cultus. The first moment here is the religious disposition. What
we have in this religion is *empirical* purposes, the one main purpose
being dominion over the world. On the subjective side the pathos
here is what has been called Roman virtue, or the Roman disposition. This dominion is all that matters. Everything must be sacrificed
to it; all living things, all the distinctive variety of ethical life, must
give way to this necessity. The subjective consciousness has value
only insofar as it devotes itself and all that it is or has to this, insofar
as it concentrates on the salvation of the state. This is the so-called
Roman virtue. In it the citizens are free; this it is that constitutes
their true will, wherein they find themselves as subjects—that is, quite
simply, their disposition. But this disposition is, so to speak, a
political one; it is not an immediately religious disposition as such
(the highest mode of our disposition in regard to actuality). The
religious disposition as such means [in Rome] that lordship or the

universal in general is owed to the gods; it belongs to Fortuna, to Juno or Jupiter, to a power that is in and for itself, and which is recognized and venerated in Rome's dominion.

The second aspect of the Roman disposition is that apart from this one goal of the lordship of Rome, human beings, as concrete, 406 | have many other purposes, interests, and wishes and, in the case in point, that imagination equates the real worldly purpose with the infinite. The [divine] power is represented as operating purposively, as willing real purposes. So the human disposition is imbued with purposes—empirical purposes, conditional, finite, worldly, external purposes, not purposes that exist in and for themselves. These conditional, external purposes have behind, within them a power that can grant them to this or that person in this or that situation. So we get prayers and invocations addressed to the gods, and expressions of thanks when the purposes are vouchsafed. This religion is consequently one of dependence; the prevailing feeling is one of dependence, of unfreedom.[723] Within the lordship of Rome human beings know themselves to be free, but ˉthe purpose is oneˉ[724] that remains external to the individual; Roman virtue too is an external purpose, not one they can realize concretely within their spirit. This is still more true of the particular purposes, and it is in regard to them that the feeling of dependence essentially arises.

According to Cicero[725] the Romans are the most pious of all nations, always thinking of the gods, always turning to them, giving them thanks for everything, etc. This is the beginning of the kind

723. [Ed.] As indicated above, n. 551, in the 1824 lectures Hegel associates Schleiermacher's concept of the "feeling of dependence" (Glaubenslehre, 1st ed., § 9) only with Roman religion, not with both Jewish and Roman religion, as in the Ms. In the next paragraph he says that for the Romans the feeling of dependence was essentially superstitious because oriented to finite powers and purposes that regulate every facet of life; hence Roman religion is the religion of unfreedom. This argument is also found in the Ms., but in 1824 Hegel does not go on to suggest, as he did earlier, that the "proper development" of the feeling of dependence leads to the veneration of evil and worship of the devil (see Ms., n. 292). That unfair charge, made even before the second volume of Schleiermacher's work had appeared, could not be sustained.

724. W₂ (Var) reads: that in which they possess themselves is a purpose

725. [Ed.] Although this does not appear to be an actual citation from Cicero, he did express himself more or less to this effect on several occasions, e.g., in De natura deorum 2.8.

of piety that calls on the immortal gods, is thankful to them, and so on, but which is not free in this relationship because the content of what it calls upon is a finite, limited content. This is the soil of superstition, of unfreedom. When the content is limited and finite, then self-consciousness, that which seeks to embrace the content, that which makes it its essential subject matter, is in the sphere of dependence, on the soil of unfreedom. Religion as such is essentially intuition, consciousness of the infinite essence that is inwardly unbounded; in the intuition of this essence human beings become conscious of themselves only insofar as they abandon their limited, finite interests, wishes, and hopes. Their religion is a dependent one only to the extent that they do not have as their object in a purely theoretical sense the *idea*—i.e., that which is substantive and unlimited. Hence in this Roman religion the feeling of dependence is essentially superstition, because | the purposes here are limited and   407
finite; objects that are limited in their content are treated as absolute purposes. This is therefore a religion of unfreedom.

The second moment (the cultus proper) falls partly into the form that we have already observed. One of its principal distinguishing features is that the gods are recognized and reverenced in regard to purposes that the worshipers want to achieve. The Romans worship the gods because they *need* them, in other words primarily at times of stress and anxiety, i.e., because they wish to have their own narrow interests maintained as essential. So not only do we see them call upon their gods in distress, but we see also the introduction of new gods in particular moments of need, with an oath to dedicate to the new god a new temple. From this point of view the cultus is a theogony in progress—the universal necessity of the gods realized in singular events (victories, triumphs, situations, incidents, and so on). The divine is not the genuine, eternal, implicitly and explicitly ethical power. Fortune is indeterminate; the lordship of power exists only through particular victories or as a consequence of other events, i.e., as the successful accomplishment of particular purposes. It is particular needs, as it were, that call for particular gods and bring them into being. Theogony is the genesis of the particular offspring of necessity. ¯And that is why other divine [power] too is in the service of this realized purpose of lordship; the Romans made use of auspices, and the oracles, the Sibylline books, and so on were in the custody of the state, of the magistrates.⁻⁷²⁶

Mention should also be made of the particular games and festivals. With a religion that has no doctrine it is particularly through the deity's portrayal in festivals and spectacles that his essentiality is presented in visible form to the community. In a religion of this kind, stage spectacles have a completely different importance from what they have for us. | The Romans took over not only Greek gods but also Greek games and spectacles. [But] one thing was distinctive in their case: the spectacles that consisted in nothing but the slaughter of animals and humans, the rivers of blood, mortal combats. Such spectacles mark the acme, so to speak, of what could be brought before their eyes. [Yet] they are totally devoid of ethical interest, there is not in them the tragic reversal whose content is an intrinsically ethical ill, but only the totally arid reversal effected by death. The Romans built up these spectacles to such a monstrous degree that hundreds of human beings, four or five hundred lions, tigers, elephants, and crocodiles, were slain by gladiators who had to fight with them and who also slew one another. What is brought before the spectators' eyes here is essentially the process of a death devoid of spirit, a murder game, willed by irrational caprice, serving only to give them something to feast their eyes on. This is a necessity that is mere caprice, murder without content, or having only itself for content. This and the envisagement of fate are the acme of experience, to die imperturbably through an empty caprice, not from natural causes, nor through the external force of circumstances, nor in consequence of offending against something ethical. Thus dying is the only virtue a Roman patrician could exercise, and it is one that he has in common with slaves and with condemned criminals. These two extremes here stand opposite each other, the finite or temporal as such—that the particular person is an absolute end—and again that the particular person is of no account, a plaything in the hand of sheer caprice. Over against both stands the present

726. *Ho reads, similar in W:* In this way necessity is transformed by imagination into empirical singularity; empirical singularity is divine, and there arises in identical manner, along with superstition in the form of [religious] disposition, a whole sphere of oracles, auspices, Sibylline books, which on the one hand serve the purpose of the state and on the other private purposes.

power over this finitude: the emperor, an individual, whose willful caprice is inevitably devoid of right and of ethical life. The Romans fared no better under the best emperors than under the worst; under Domitian the peoples of the empire were better off than under the noblest emperors. So on the one side there is Fortuna, death, cold and empty death, and on the other the individual who had the power, the individuality of the emperor.

Such are the main aspects of the religion of expediency.

If we may now add one further general reflection about the standpoint that we have been discussing, the stage we have reached is as follows. Infinite power, the absolute negativity of the concept, | determines itself, it has a purpose; and this purpose is not a limited purpose but a universal one. Yet it is a universal purpose that is still a finite one; indeed, when comprehended in its objectivity, it is just this [universal] dominion. Its particular content is just this or that finite situation. ‾Thus the finite is posited as the absolute purpose, as what has being on its own account—it is not idealized, not posited as sublated in the infinite ideality, but is valid on its own account.‾[727] This is what characterizes this standpoint, and it is essentially necessary. As we have said, it is finitude that is here made into infinitude; the finite is abstract; more precisely, it is subjective self-consciousness in general, finite spirit. It is this subjective self-consciousness that is now regarded as what is strictly the essential— world dominion, the finite purpose as such. This is present for us, it achieves its real significance, only insofar as it is the existence and execution of the purposes of self-consciousness. In this aspect, therefore, it is the releasing of subjectivity as such from all bounds. This infinitude of subjectivity as such can be expressed more precisely as personality, the category into which a human being enters as a person in the realm of right. As a person a human being owns property, has the right of possession.[728] It is the person who enjoys recognition as such, but only the abstract person, the abstractly

409

727. *Thus G; P reads:* Thus it is the finite, and the infinite is transformed into the finite by imagination; the finite is what abides, what is valid on its own account as finite.

728. [*Ed.*] *Recht des Besitzes.* Here as in his lectures on the philosophy of right, Hegel is probably alluding to the title of a work by Friedrich Carl von Savigny, *Das Recht des Besitzes* (Giessen, 1806; the 1st ed., which appeared in 1803, was titled *Abhandlung der Lehre vom Besitz*).

juridical person capable of ownership. It goes no further than that, and I count as infinite in this sphere [only]; as the infinite reference of myself to myself, I am the absolute, self-sustaining atom. Such is the more precise meaning of the definition given in the proposition that the finite is within the infinite. But when the finite is grasped in this way as subject, it is still taken in its immediacy, it is absolute being-for-self but abstract, and this is as far as we have here developed the aspect of personality.

This personality, however, or infinitude of the subject, must also be taken in a higher sense, where the personality of the subject pertains to the idea rather than merely being a person immediately. Implicitly, this category is infinite form, and nothing else—not subjectivity as this | immediate person, but subjectivity as such, the absolutely infinite form, the form of self-knowledge and of what knows itself generally, the form of what distinguishes itself both inwardly and in opposition to an other. This infinite subjectivity that is infinite form is the[729] moment that is here won for substance and for power; it is what power or the god of substantiality still lacked— his inner self-determination as infinite subjectivity. In power we have had subjectivity in principle, but this power has only one or more singular purposes; its purpose is still not infinite. Only infinite subjectivity has an infinite purpose, i.e., it is the purpose for itself, and its purpose *is* just inwardness, this subjectivity as such. ⌐So, abstractly, this category constitutes what spirit is.⌐[730] Spirit has being only insofar as it is posited as spirit, dirempts itself inwardly, makes itself its own purpose; but in doing so it initially distinguishes itself from itself, and what it distinguishes from itself is spirit; it is the side of reality, the aspect of determinateness that is inwardly infinite for itself. ⌐It is defined as the other, but since this existence is also defined as self-containedly absolute, this is at the same time to posit that spirit is for spirit.⌐[731]

This is the abstract definition to which we have now come and through which we now pass over to the Christian religion.

729. W_2 *(Var) adds:* great

730. W_2 *(Var/Ed?) reads:* This determination of spirit is consequently achieved in the Roman world.

731. *Thus* G

THE LECTURES OF 1827

Introduction^2

^{3}Here belong the particular religions or determinate religions, religion
in its determinateness; for there are determinate, particular, | and   412

1. *B, Hu, An read:* Religion in its Determinacy
2. *[Ed.]* The introduction to the 1827 lectures reestablishes the threefold division of *Determinate Religion* inherited from the *Ms.* but modified in 1824 into a
twofold structure. The summary provided in the introduction is similar to that found
in 1824, which is not surprising since Hegel made use of Griesheim's transcript of
the 1824 lectures when lecturing in 1827. In fact, the introduction to the 1824 lectures
also anticipated a threefold structure. The 1827 introduction anticipates certain changes
that are more fully developed in 1831, e.g., the two senses of "natural religion" as
meaning both primitive religion (the religion of immediacy) and rational religion (see
n. 8), and the recognition that in the higher of the so-called nature religions (Buddhism,
Hinduism, Persian and Egyptian religion) there is already an elevation of thought
above merely natural powers, hence an implicit cleavage of consciousness (in 1831
this leads to the treatment of these religions under entirely different categories from
that of "nature religion"). With respect to the second main stage, the elevation of
the spiritual above the natural, the introduction does not anticipate the reversal of
order in which Greek and Jewish religion are in fact treated in 1827 (see below,
nn. 18, 347). It suggests, in line with 1824, that the sequence is from particular (Jewish)
to plural (Greek) to universal (Roman). Thus it is evident that, just as in 1824, so
also in 1827 the initial plan was altered as Hegel proceeded with the detailed treatment. Finally, the distinctiveness of Roman religion from Greek and Jewish is
reaffirmed: it cannot be subsumed under the general category of the "religions of
spiritual individuality." While providing a transition to Christianity, it does so only
in a negative sense: it is universal and purposive but also utterly finite, external, and
utilitarian. It is scarcely a religion of freedom and spirit.
    3. *W contains the following introduction to the 1831 lectures:* When we speak
of determinate religion, it is implied, in the first place, that religion generally is taken
as genus and the determinate religions as species. From one point of view this
relationship of genus to species is quite legitimate, as when we pass over from the

universal to the particular in other sciences. But in that case the particular is understood only in an empirical manner; it is a matter of experience that this or that animal, this or that right exists. In philosophical science it is not permissible to proceed in this fashion: the particular cannot just be added to the universal; on the contrary, the universal itself definitely resolves itself into the particular. The concept divides itself; it produces an original determination from out of itself. In all cases of determinateness, determinate being and connectedness with an other are directly posited. What is determinate is for an other, and what is indeterminate is not there at all. That for which religion is, its determinate being, is consciousness. Religion has its reality as consciousness. What is to be understood by the realization of the concept is this: that the content is determined by its being for consciousness and being in a certain way. Our procedure is as follows: We began by considering the concept of religion, what religion implicitly is; that is what it is for us, as we have seen it; it is quite another matter [W_1: how it comes to consciousness. W_2: for it to bring itself to consciousness.] . . . Only in the true religion does what it is in and for itself, what its concept is, become known; for actual religion is concordant with the concept. We now have to consider the course by which genuine religion comes about. Religion is still not *a* religion in its concept either—for it is essentially present as such only in consciousness. This is the sense of what we are here considering, the self-realizing of the concept. How realization occurs has already been indicated in a general way: the concept is, as it were, a potentiality within spirit, it constitutes the innermost truth, but spirit must attain to the knowledge of this truth. Only then does genuine religion become actual. It can be said of all religions that they are religions, [W_1: but if they are still limited W_2: and correspond to the concept of religion; but at the same time, in that they are still limited,] they do not correspond to the concept. And yet they must contain it, or else they would not be religions. But the concept is present in them in different ways. At first they contain it only implicitly. These [W_2: determinate] religions are only particular moments of the concept, and for this very reason they do not correspond to the concept, for it is not actual within them. Thus, while humanity is, of course, implicitly free, Africans and Asiatics are not, because they have not the consciousness of what constitutes the concept of humanity. Religion is now to be considered in its determinacy. The highest that is or can be attained is for the determinacy itself to be the concept; for in that case the barrier is sublated and religious consciousness is not distinguished from the concept—this is the idea, the perfectly realized concept, but we can discuss that only when we reach the concluding division of our subject.

To educe the concept of religion and make it the object of consciousness has been the labor of spirit over thousands of years. The way this labor has been performed is that immediacy or the natural state formed the starting point; and this had then to be overcome. Immediacy is what is natural, but consciousness is elevation above nature. Natural consciousness is sensuous consciousness, just as the natural will is desire, the individual that wills itself in accordance with its natural state and particularity—sensuous knowing and sensuous willing. Religion, however, is the relationship of spirit to spirit, spirit's knowledge of [W_2: spirit in] its truth, not in its immediacy or its natural state. Religion becomes determinate as it advances from the natural state to the concept. Initially the concept is only the inward element, the implicit potential of consciousness, not its expression. Regarding this ambiguity, that the concept originally *is* but that its first existence is not its authentic originality, we shall have something more to say later.

hence finite religions, the *ethnic religions* generally.[4] Up to this point we have spoken generally of God, of consciousness of God and connection with God, of our human knowledge of the divine spirit within ourselves and of ourselves within the divine spirit. [These connections] have been referred to only as indefinite representations, but we want to have them [as definite] in our consciousness. (The third division is the absolute religion, the fulfilled concept of religion, religion worked out in its fullness.) It is in determinate religion that determinations first enter into that universal essence; this is where cognition of God begins. By means of | thoroughgoing determination, the thought of God first comes to be the concept.

413

Even as the content, God, determines itself, so on the other side the subjective human spirit that has this knowledge determines itself too. The principle by which God is defined for human beings is also the principle for how humanity defines itself inwardly, or for humanity in its own spirit. An inferior god or a nature god has inferior, natural and unfree human beings as its correlates; the pure concept of God or the spiritual God has as its correlate spirit that is free and spiritual, that actually knows God. In determinate religion, spirit is determinate both as absolute spirit or object and as the subjective spirit that has its essence or absoluteness as its object. Here both sides first achieve their determinateness.

[5]In determinate religion as such, in finite religion, | we have before us only subordinate determinations of spirit or of religion;

414

---

4. *L (1827?) adds:* (The third division is the absolute religion, the fulfilled concept of religion, religion educed in its fullness.)

5. *W₂ (1831) reads (parallel in main text follows):* Hence the sphere we have to deal with first contains the determinate religion that does not yet emerge from determinacy so far as its content is concerned. A fully achieved freedom is not involved in the activity of emerging from immediacy, but only a process of breaking free, which is still entangled in that from which it is freeing itself.

The first step here is to consider the form of natural, immediate religion. In this first, natural religion, consciousness is still natural, i.e., sensuously desirous consciousness. Hence it is immediate. As yet there is here no inward cleavage of consciousness, for a cleavage of that kind has the characteristic that consciousness distinguishes its sensuous nature from what is essential, so that the natural is known only as mediated through those aspects that are essential. This is where religion can first originate.

In connection with this exaltation to the essential, we have to consider the concept of this exaltation generally. Here the object is defined with certainty, and this *true* object, from which consciousness distinguishes itself, is God. This exaltation is the

we do not yet have the religion of absolute truth. But the progression [of finite religions] is a condition for the arrival of religion at its absolute truth, for spirit's coming to be for spirit, for the relationship of spirit to spirit, a condition for the attainment by spirit itself 415 of its truly infinite determinateness. | These determinate religions

---

same one that occurs in a more abstract way in the proofs of the existence of God. In all of these proofs there is the very same exaltation; it is only the starting point and the nature of this essence that differ. But this elevation to God, however it may be defined, is only the one side. The other is the converse: God, defined thus and so, enters into relation with the subject that has thus elevated itself. At this point then arises the question of how the subject is defined; but this is known just in the way that God is defined.

It is also necessary to adduce the subject's conscious turning toward this essence, and this brings in the aspect of the cultus, the subject's uniting with its essence.

The division [of the subject matter] is therefore as follows.

1. Natural religion is unity of the spiritual and natural, and God is here comprehended in this unity that is still natural. Humanity in its immediacy is just sensuous, natural knowing and natural willing. Insofar as the moment of religion is involved in this, and the moment of elevation is still shut up within the natural state, there is something there that has nonetheless to be regarded as higher than anything merely immediate. This is magic.

2. Second, there is the cleavage of consciousness within itself, so that it knows itself as merely natural and distinguishes the genuine or the essential from this. Within the essential [being] this natural state, this finitude, is of no value and is known to be such. In natural religion spirit still lives in neutrality with nature, but God is now defined as the absolute power and substance, within which the natural will, the subject, is only something transient, an accident, something lacking selfhood, devoid of freedom. The highest merit of humanity here is to know itself as something null.

But initially this elevation of spirit above the natural realm is not yet carried through in a consistent manner. On the contrary, there is still present a fearful inconsistency, as a result of which the different spiritual and natural powers are all mixed up with one another. This still inwardly inconsistent elevation has its historical existence in the three Oriental religions of substance.[a]

3. But the confusion of the natural and the spiritual leads to the struggle of subjectivity, which seeks to establish itself in its unity and universality. This struggle has also had its historical existence in three religions, which form the religions of the transition to the stage of free subjectivity.[b] But since spirit has not yet completely subjected the natural to itself in these stages, any more than in the preceding ones, they constitute, together with the preceding ones, the sphere of

A. Nature Religion.

Set against this is the second stage of determinate religion, at which the elevation of spirit is carried through consistently vis-à-vis the natural realm, i.e.,

B. The Religion of Spiritual Individuality, or Free Subjectivity.[c]

[Ed.] [a]By the "three Oriental religions of substance" Hegel means in the 1831 lectures Chinese religion, Hinduism, and Buddhism/Lamaism. Cf. the 1831 passage

are definite stages[6] of the consciousness and knowledge of spirit. They are necessary conditions for the emergence of the true religion, for the authentic consciousness of spirit. For this reason too, they are extant historically, and I will even draw attention to the historical mode in which they have existed, for we come to know them in these particular forms as historical religions. In the true science, in a science of spirit, in a science whose object is human being, the development of the concept of this concrete object is also its outward history and has existed in actuality. Thus these shapes of religion have also existed successively in time and coexisted in space. We shall now discuss their general classification.⁻

Of necessity the *first* form of religion is immediate religion, what we can also call *nature religion*. In the modern period this term "nature religion" or "natural religion" has for some time had a different sense; we have understood it to mean what human beings⁻are supposed to be able to cognize⁻[7] through their reason, through the natural light of their reason.[8]

---

transmitted by W_2 in n. 49 below. The W_2 and Strauss texts corroborate each other. bBy the "three religions of transition" Hegel means in the 1831 lectures the religion of the good (Persian and Jewish), the religion of anguish (Phoenician), and the religion of ferment (Egyptian). Here again the materials in W_2 (n. 266) and the Strauss text confirm each other. cThe concluding outline, beginning with the words "But since spirit," has been editorially revised. It confuses the design of the 1831 lectures with that of 1824. According to Strauss, the "religions of transition" are not included under nature religion, which is confined to magic, but follow the "three Oriental religions of substance," forming the beginning of the third stage of *Determinate Religion,* the "religion of freedom." The only lectures in which Hegel refers to the "religions of spiritual individuality" are those of 1824.

6. *In B's margin:* 15 June 1827

7. *W (Var) reads:* can educe and cognize of God

8. [*Ed.*] The concept of the natural light of reason can be traced back through the Enlightenment, Descartes, Francis Bacon, and Thomas Aquinas to Cicero; see his *Tusculanae disputationes* 3.1. The concept of "natural religion" was widespread among thinkers of the Enlightenment, e.g., Leibniz, *Theodicy* (1734), ed. A. Farrar, trans. E. M. Huggard (New Haven, 1952), p. 51 (*Philosophische Schriften,* ed. C. J. Gerhardt, 7 vols. [Berlin, 1875–1890], 6:26–27); and Christian Wolff, *Theologia naturalis,* Pars posterior, 2d ed. (Frankfurt and Leipzig, 1741), p. 497 (§ 512), and *Philosophia moralis,* Pars tertia (Halle, 1751), chap. 9, pp. 731 ff. While Leibniz made natural religion clearly subordinate to revealed religion, Wolff already placed the two on an equal level. Hegel's criticism of the concept of natural religion could have been prompted by Hume's *Dialogues Concerning Natural Religion* (London, 1779), with which he was probably familiar, although this cannot be confirmed.

From that point of view natural religion has been opposed to revealed religion, ˉas the religion delivered by reason.ˉ9 "Natural reason" is an erroneous expression. We do indeed speak of the nature of reason, i.e., its concept; but on the whole "the natural" is understood to mean "the immediate," the sensible generally, the uncultivated. Reason then, by contrast, is the not being [of something, and specifically of human nature] in the way that it immediately is to begin with; spirit is precisely this self-elevation above nature, this self-extrication from the natural; not only is it liberation vis-à-vis the natural but the subjection of the natural to itself, making it fit the measure of, and be obedient to, itself. Because of this ambiguity we should avoid the expression "natural | reason" in this modern meaning. The genuine sense of natural reason is "spirit or reason according to the concept." When reason is taken in this sense, however, as what reason or spirit truly is within itself, then there is no antithesis between it and revealed religion. The latter is revelation of God, revelation of the Spirit. We should nevertheless remark here that spirit according to its concept can indeed be set in opposition to revealed religion; but on the other handˉrevealed religion is valid onlyˉ10 for spirit, and spirit can reveal itself only to spirit. What spirit is in its essence, or according to its genuine meaning, cannot be revealed to what is devoid of spirit or devoid of reason; on the contrary, for reception through the Spirit to be possible, the receiver must itself be spirit. "Spirit must bear witness to the Spirit,"ˉˉas it is traditionally expressed in religious terms.ˉ11 All religion is natural in the sense that spirit has to bear witness, i.e., it is in conformity with the concept and addresses spirit.

"Natural religion," as the term has been employed in more recent times, has also referred to mere metaphysical religion, where "metaphysics" has had the sense of ˉˉ"understandable thought."ˉ12

416

9. W₂ (Var) reads: and maintains that only what human beings have in their reason can be authentic for them.

10. Hu reads: only revealed religion is valid

11. Thus Hu; L (1827?) reads: The witness that spirit bears to spirit is the highest witness; all other kinds of attestation or authorization serve merely as a stimulus for the standpoint of consciousness that we have to consider here. Once spirit has attained to its consciousness of self, it has risen above external attestations of the kind that are directed to its phantasy etc.

12. W (Var) reads: understandable thoughts, representations of the understanding.

That is the modern religion of the understanding—or what is called "deism," a result of the Enlightenment, the knowledge of God as an abstraction, ‾the knowledge that God is the father of all humanity.‾[13]

The first [stage] for us is nature religion, i.e., religion defined as the unity of the spiritual and the natural, | where the spirit still is in unity with nature. In being this way, spirit is not yet free, is not yet actual as spirit.[14] This placid unity, this neutrality with nature or mingling of the spiritual with the natural, spirit in its wholly immediate mode, is first of all the human individual. Religion begins in the situation where the human being as singular counts as the highest or absolute power; one takes oneself to be an absolute power and is so regarded by others.

417

The *second* stage of religion is the *elevation of the spiritual above the natural.* This can occur in two ways: on the one hand *in thought,* namely that God is for thought and only for thought, i.e., "God" can be regarded abstractly; on the other hand, that God is present as a *concrete individuality.* But this individuality does not exist in an immediate or natural manner only, and is not a natural essence at all; for on the contrary, the spiritual is the ruling or dominant aspect, although it still has the natural as its reality or outward shape. It is not yet present as pure spirit[15]—as spiritual individuality. In consequence the natural is subordinated to spirit, and at the same time the individuality is this particularized one. It follows at once that there is a multitude of such particularized individualities, which

13. W₂ *reads:* to which all definitions of God—all belief—are reduced. *L, W (1827?) continue:* This cannot, properly speaking, be called natural religion; it is the final, extreme position of the abstract understanding that results from the Kantian critique.

[*Ed.*] A reference to Kant's criticism of all speculative theology in the *Critique of Pure Reason,* trans. N. Kemp Smith (London, 1930), B 659–732, esp. 703.

14. *L (1827?) adds:* God is everywhere the content; but here it is God in the natural unity of the spiritual and the natural. It is the natural mode that characterizes this form of religion in general. It assumes many different shapes, all of which are called nature religion. In nature religion, so we are told, spirit is still identical with nature, consciousness stands united with nature, and to that extent this religion is the religion of unfreedom.

15. *L (1827?) adds:* That first moment, that first form, is the religion of sublimity, the Jewish religion. The other moment is where the spiritual appears as concretely spiritual

519

are still burdened with natural existence and a natural config-uration.[16]

˜The *third* form is the *religion of expediency or purposiveness,*˜[17] where there is posited in God a purpose, or purposes generally, albeit a rather external purpose and not yet a purpose that is purely spiritual, not yet the absolute purpose. This can also be called the

418 religion of fate or destiny, | because the purpose is not yet a free and purely spiritual purpose. One particular purpose is posited in God, and this purpose is then something without any [absolute] reason as compared with other private purposes, because those purposes might be no less justified than this one, which is only another particular purpose too.

So far as the historical development is concerned, nature religion is the religion of the East. The second form of religion, namely that in which the spiritual elevates itself above the natural, is in one aspect the religion of sublimity (that of the Jews) and in the other aspect the religion of beauty (that of the Greeks).[18]

If we speak here of "the elevation of spirit," this must be defined more precisely, for even within nature religion we will find an elevating of thought above mere natural powers, above the dominion of the natural. But this elevation is carried out inconsistently, and it is just this monstrous and terrible inconsistency, in which the

16. L *(1827?) adds:* —this is the religion of beauty, or Greek religion.

17. L *(1827?) reads:* In its gods, singular spirit wills only its own subjective purpose; it wills itself, not the absolute content. So the religion of expediency is that

18. W_2 *(1831) adds:* In the religion of sublimity, the one God is the lord, and the singular subjects behave as his servants. In the religion of beauty too, the subject has purified itself from its merely immediate knowing and willing; but it has also retained its will and knows itself as *free.* It knows itself as free, moreover, because it has completed the negation of its natural will and, as an ethical, free being, has an affirmative relation to God. But the subject has not yet passed through the consciousness and the antithesis of good and evil. Hence it is still contaminated with naturalness. So even if the religion of beauty forms the stage of reconciliation as contrasted with the sphere of sublimity, this reconciliation is still an unmediated one, because it is not yet mediated through consciousness of the antithesis.

[*Ed.*] In the 1827 lectures Hegel actually treats Greek religion (the religion of beauty) first and Jewish religion (the religion of sublimity) second. See below, n. 347. In 1831 the order of 1821 and 1824 is restored, but Jewish and Greek religion are treated under different categories—consciousness of good and evil, and consciousness of reconciliation and freedom, respectively.

differentiated powers, the natural and the spiritual, are blended together, just this mixture of the spiritual and the natural, that is the content of this stage. The second stage is therefore the consistent elevation into self as against the natural, so that the natural is subordinated: on the one hand, as something entirely mastered (in the religion of sublimity); on the other hand, so that it serves only as the outward shape, appearance, ¯or manifestation of subjectivity.¯[19]

The third form, the religion of external purposiveness or expediency, is Roman religion, which we certainly have to distinguish from Greek religion | and which constitutes the transition to absolute religion.[20] It is the religion of external purposiveness—external in that although the purpose is essentially posited, the only extant purposes are limited ones, themselves finite and external. These are the three forms of the determinate religions.

A. IMMEDIATE RELIGION, OR NATURE RELIGION

Introduction[21]

a. The Original Condition

Before we consider religion in its characteristic shape, we need to pay attention to a representation that is customary, which our imagination depicts for us, and which moreover is affirmed and treated as valid. It was the view that the first religion was also the true and excellent one, and that all subsequent religions present only

419

19. *Thus L; Hu reads:* manifestation, or beauty.
20. *In B's margin:* 18 June 1827
21. [*Ed.*] The introduction to Sec. A of the 1827 lectures retains only the discussion of the "original condition" of humanity as represented in religious mythology. The lengthy treatment of the cosmological proof, which occurs here in 1824, is gone, having been assimilated along with the other proofs into the section on "Religious Knowledge as Elevation to God" in Part I. The generic representation of God in nature religion is also removed from the introduction, which concludes with an outline of the four main forms of nature religion. The four differ from 1824 in that the religion of being-within-self (Buddhism, Lamaism) is no longer considered a subcategory of the religion of magic, and the Persian and Egyptian religions are combined under the category of "the religions of transition."

a degenerate state of this religion. Remains, fragments, and indications have survived from the decline of this religion, and these are the foundation of the subsequent religions; these remains are recognizable, and historical cognition of them holds particular interest for us.[22]

This view is believed to be justified partly in and for itself or a priori, and partly in a historical way, a posteriori. If we pursue the history of religion, science, and cognition right back to its origin, we find there traces of truths and cognitions that indicate a yet higher origin and that have preserved themselves in the later states of religion—traces that we are unable to understand in connection with the determinate religions themselves or even with the scientific culture and information of the nations concerned.

The a priori aspect is just the view that we have already mentioned: that human beings were originally created by God and in God's image [Gen. 1:26–27]; that the first human beings were in conformity with their concept; that in the purity of their concept they were good without evil; and, more specifically, that [they lived] knowingly in this unity with God and nature, so that in this original 420 purity they knew God | as God is; that they behaved in accordance with God's essence and with their own proper essence; that they had not yet stepped forth into duality and were still uncorrupted. And so, because spirit's gaze was not yet clouded and darkened, because humanity had not yet sunk down into the prose of reflection and understanding, which is just what constitutes the divorce between the subject and nature; because they had not yet found themselves thus sundered from nature, or from external things, and did not yet have particular interests that could make them view [nature] practically as a complex of useful things—because of this they beheld the inner being of nature itself, they knew the inner being of nature

22. [Ed.] Hegel is alluding especially to the views of F. W. J. Schelling and Friedrich Schlegel. See Schelling's On University Studies (1803), trans. E. S. Morgan (Athens, Ohio, 1966), p. 83 (Sämmtliche Werke 5:287); Schelling's Treatise on "The Deities of Samothrace," trans. R. F. Brown (Missoula, Mont., 1977), p. 25 (Sämmtliche Werke 8:362); and Schlegel's Ueber die Sprache und Weisheit der Indier (Heidelberg, 1808), pp. 198, 205 (Kritische Friedrich-Schlegel-Ausgabe 8:295–297, 303). See also below, n. 42, and 1824 lectures, n. 27.

and cognized nature truly.²³ ⁻Just as they related themselves to the pure God according to their own purity, | so also they related to nature not as to an external thing; instead they saw into the heart of nature as it is; thus they possessed absolute knowledge just as they did the true religion.⁻²⁴ We can form this representation readily for ourselves just by thinking; but, as we have already said, it is also found in the religions of diverse peoples. Most religions begin with a sojourn in paradise, and hence with an original state of human innocence—thus the Greeks have the golden age and the Romans the Saturnian age.²⁵ This is very much a universal representation

421

23. [Ed.] Expressions of a mystical unity with nature are found in Albrecht von Haller's poem, "Die Falschheit der menschlichen Tugenden," in Versuch schweizerischer Gedichte, 6th ed. (Göttingen, 1751), no. 6, p. 100; and in Jacob Boehme's De signatura rerum, in Theosophia revelata (1715), pp. 2178–2404, esp. pp. 2180–2181. See 1824 lectures, n. 35.

24. W (1831) reads: Cognition of nature of the former [i.e., pre-rational] kind is explained as intuiting, which is nothing else but immediate consciousness. If we ask, "What has been intuited?" it is not sensuous nature superficially considered (a kind of intuition that can also be attributed to animals) but the essence of nature. But the essence of nature, as the system of its laws, is nothing but the universal. Nature in its universality, the system of developing organic life, and this development in its authentic form, [W₁: this W₂: not nature in its singularity, in which it exists for sensuous perception or for intuition, but the form of the natural,] is nature as permeated by thought. Thinking, however, is not something immediate; it starts with the given, but rises above [W₁: it W₂: the sensuous manifoldness of what is given]. It negates the form of singularity, forgets what has happened in sensuous form, and produces the universal, the genuine. This is not action of an immediate kind but is the labor of mediation, the emergence from finitude. [W₂: It is of no avail to contemplate the heavens no matter with what pious and innocent faith; what is essential can only be thought.] Hence the assertion that one has a direct sight or vision of things [ein Schauen], an immediate consciousness, proves itself to be worthless as soon as we ask what is to be seen in this way. The knowledge of nature in its truth is a mediated form of knowing, not immediate knowing. And it is the same with willing. The will is good insofar as it wills the good, what is right and ethical. But this is something quite different from the immediate will. The immediate will is the will that does not advance beyond singularity and finitude, that wills the singular as such. The good on the contrary is the universal; in order for the will to attain to the point of willing the good, a mediation is necessary through which it has purified itself from that sort of finite willing. This purification is the education and labor of the mediation, and the mediation cannot be something immediate and primary. The same applies to the cognition of God; God is the center of all truth, the pure truth without any boundary, and in order to attain to him it is even more imperative that human beings should have labored to free themselves from their natural particularity of knowing and willing.

25. [Ed.] See Hesiod, Works and Days 108–119, and Virgil, Eclogues 4, 6.

which even in modern times thought has sought to justify once more by argument alone.

This, then, is what[26] has been understood by "nature religion"—an initial or original revelation, a revelation first impaired by human beings, lost or corrupted by them as they passed over to the evil side through sin, passion, and evil generally. Of course it is easy to recognize that evil, ignorance, passion, selfish inclination, private pursuits, and the will that wishes to determine itself for itself obscure the moment of insight into truth as the knowing and willing of the good. So the question is whether this character [of innocence] is to be viewed as a state, and in fact as the initial, original, and authentic state.

So far as the basic determination in that representation is concerned, it must be acknowledged not only to be correct but also, as a true representation, to be foundational. But we must distinguish the form, i.e., whether in fact this true representation should be characterized as an initial, original, natural, and authentic *state*. The basic determination is nothing else but this, that the human being is no natural essence as such, is no animal, but rather spirit. Insofar as humanity is spirit, it has this universality in itself quite generally, the universality of rationality, the activity of concrete thought | and reason; and it is partly the instinct of reason, and partly its development, to know that reason is universal and that nature is therefore rational. Of course nature is not conscious reason, but it has determination according to purpose within it. Nature is rationally ordered, it was made by a wise creator—and wisdom is purpose, concept, free rationality itself. Thus spirit also knows that God is rational, absolute reason, absolute rational activity, and it has this belief instinctively, it knows that it cognizes God as well as nature, that it must find in God something quite distinct [from itself] but also its own essence too, when it relates itself to these objects in its rational investigation. Spirit believes that in its rational inquiry into God and nature it will recognize itself, the rational.

This is undoubtedly the basic determination [of the story]; but now the question is whether it describes the initial state. As far as

422

26. *L (1827?) adds:* apart from the metaphysical meaning discussed earlier,

the representation of the lost paradise is concerned, however, we should declare here that the very fact that it is a *lost* paradise shows already that it is not an essential state. The true or the divine does not get lost; it is eternal, and abides in and for itself. So if this unity of humanity with God and nature is represented as the true, then the higher concept shows that this [lost paradise] is not the state of the true.⁻[27] This unity of humanity with itself, with God, and with nature is, in the universal sense or as in-itself, in fact the substantial, essential determination. Humanity is reason, is spirit; in virtue of the capacity of reason, of the fact that humanity is spirit, it is implicitly what is true. But that is only the concept or the in-itself, and when we arrive at the *representation* of what the concept is, or what is in itself, we are quite accustomed to represent it to ourselves as something past or future, not as something inward that is in and of itself. We picture it instead in the mode of immediate, external existence, as an [actual] state.[28] |

So, of course, the concept must realize itself; but the realization of the concept, the activities through which it actualizes itself, and the present shapes and appearances of this actualization and of the actuality, have a different look to them than does that which is the simple concept within itself. The unity of which we speak is in fact the concept, or the in-itself, and not an actual state or existence; only the realization of the concept constitutes actual states or existence, and this realization must be quite different from the way that the state of paradise and innocence is depicted.

The human being is essentially spirit, and spirit[29] is essentially this: to be for oneself, to be free, setting oneself over against the

423

---

27. *Thus An with B and Hu; L (Var) reads:* But as we have said, it is not to be represented as a state, as it is pictured among most peoples that what was original in point of time is the true human state and the one we long for, the loss of which was a misfortune and an occasion for mourning.

28. *W₂ (1831) adds:* So what is involved here is only the form of existence or how the state occurs. The concept is what is inward, the implicit potential, but it has not yet come into existence. So the question arises what stands against our believing that the implicit potential was present in advance as actual existence. And what does stand against it is the nature of spirit. Spirit is only what it makes itself. This bringing forth of what is implicit is the positing of the concept of existence.

29. *W₂ (Var) adds:* is not in immediate fashion, but

natural, withdrawing oneself from immersion in nature, severing oneself from nature and only reconciling oneself with nature for the first time through this severance and on the basis of it; and not only with nature but with one's own essence too, or with one's truth. We make this truth objective to ourselves, set it over against us, sever ourselves from it, and through this severance we reconcile ourselves with it. This oneness brought forth by way of severance is the first spiritual or true oneness, that which comes forth out of reconciliation; it is not the unity of nature. The stone or the plant is immediately in this unity, but in a oneness that is not a unity worthy of spirit, is not spiritual oneness. Spiritual oneness comes forth out of severed being.

A misunderstanding can arise when we call that initial state the state of *innocence*. Then it can seem objectionable to say that human beings must depart from the state of innocence and become guilty. But the state of innocence consists in the fact that nothing is good and nothing | is evil for human beings; it is the state of the animal; ¯paradise (παράδεισος) is in fact initially a zoological garden [*Tiergarten*];[30] it is the state where there is no accountability. An ethical state of humanity begins only with a state of accountability or of capacity for guilt,¯[31] and this is now the human state. "Guilt" means in general "holding to account."[32] But guilt in the universal sense means that for which human beings are accountable; to have guilt means to be accountable, that this is one's knowledge and one's will, that one does it as what is right.

424

---

30. [*Ed.*] See Xenophon, *Anabasis* 1.2.7, where Cyrus is said to have kept wild animals in a large park for hunting. The Hebrew word for "garden" was translated in the Septuagint as παράδεισος, which stems from the Old Persian *pairi daēza*, meaning a park enclosed by a wall. See also Diodorus Siculus, *Bibliotheca historica* 2.10, and Josephus, *Antiquities* 10.226.

31. *Thus An with B and Hu; L (Var) reads, similar in W:* —(paradise = zoological garden)—or of unconsciousness, where humanity is totally ignorant both of good and of evil, and what is willed is not determined either as good or as evil. If there is no knowledge of evil, then there is no knowledge of good either. But the state of guilt, in contrast with this, is the state of accountability,

32. *L (1827?) adds, similar in W:* "Guilt" is usually taken in a pejorative sense. It is usually understood to mean that someone has done something evil. What this says is that humanity *must* become evil.

As a state of existence, that initial natural oneness is in actuality not a state of innocence but the state of savagery, an animal state, a state of [natural] desire or general wildness. The animal in such a state is neither good nor evil; but human beings in the animal state are wild, are evil, are not as they ought to be. Humanity as it is by nature is not what it ought to be; human beings ought to be what they are through spirit, to which end they mold themselves by inner illumination, by knowing and willing what is right and proper. This point, that human beings as they are according to nature are not as they ought to be, has been expressed in the thesis that human beings are by nature evil. When it is represented as original sin [Erb-sünde], then inheritance [Erblichkeit] is a form that exists for representation, a form of popular guise.[33] In this way the primordial state according to the concept hovers before the imagination of [all] peoples, and this primordial state is oneness. But they express this primordiality as either a past or a future state. What is primordial as a state, however, is | savagery, while on the other hand what is   425
primordial in thought is the concept, which realizes itself by releasing itself from the form of its naturalness.

We find in the Bible a well-known story [Vorstellung] abstractly termed *the fall*. This representation is very profound and is not just a contingent history but the eternal and necessary history of humanity—though it is indeed expressed here in an external and mythical mode. For this reason there are bound to be inconsistencies in this representation. In its vitality the idea can be grasped only by thought and can be presented only by thought; when it is expressed in sensible imagery, then, of necessity, elements that will not fit together must emerge. Therefore the story is not without inconsistencies. But the essential or basic features of the idea are contained in it: namely that, although human beings are implicitly this unity, they depart from this in-itself or leave the natural state behind because they are spirit, so that they must come into distinction, into (primal) division, must come to judgment between what is theirs and what

33. L (1827?) adds, similar in W: What this implies is that human beings, insofar as they live only according to nature and follow their heart, i.e., what merely springs up spontaneously, their inclinations, ought to regard themselves as not being as they ought to be.

is natural. Only thus do they first know God and the good. When one knows this, one has it as the object of consciousness; and when one has it as the object of consciousness, then, as an individual, one distinguishes oneself from it. So if the idea, that which is in and for itself, is portrayed mythically in the mode of a temporal process, then inconsistency is unavoidable.

The basic features of this representation are as follows [cf. Gen. 3]. The tree of the knowledge of good and evil portrayed in it belongs to the sensible mode; we see that straightaway. Then the story says that human beings let themselves be led astray and ate this fruit, and in this way they came to the knowledge of good and evil. This is called the fall, as if they had come only to the knowledge of evil, and had become only evil; but they came equally to the knowledge of good. The story says that this should not have happened. ˉBut on the one hand it is involved in the concept of spirit that human beings must come to the knowledge of good and evil.ˉ34

426   As for what the story | says—that they ought not to have come to this knowledge—this too is involved in the idea, inasmuch as ˉreflection, or the rupture of consciousness, is contained in this knowledge of good and evil. In other words, there is posited here the cleavage that is freedom, the abstraction of freedom. Insofar as human beings exist for themselves (i.e., they are free), good and evil exist for them and they have the choice between the two. This standpoint of formal freedom in which human beings are face-to-face with good and evil and stand above both, are lords of both, isˉ35 a standpoint that ought not to be—ˉthough not, of course, in the sense that it should not be at all or should not arise. On the contrary, it is necessary for the sake of freedom, else humanity is not free, and is not spirit; rather it is a standpoint that must be sublated, that must

34. W_2 (Var) reads: But it is involved in the concept of humanity that it should come to knowledge; in other words, spirit consists in becoming cognitive consciousness. L (1827?) adds: However, as already noted, humans know nothing of good if they know nothing of evil. And yet this knowledge is also essential; humans are human and rational only to the extent that they have this consciousness, this knowledge, of good and evil.

35. W_2 (Var) reads: the cleavage and reflection constitute freedom, implying that the human being has a choice between the two sides of the antithesis and stands before us as lord over good and evil; so we have

come to an end with reconciliation, in the union with the good.⁻³⁶ Consciousness grasps the double aspect within itself: on the one hand this cleavage, namely that together with reflection and freedom it contains within itself the bad or evil, that which ought not to be; on the other hand, however, it is likewise the principle or source of healing, of freedom, i.e., it is spirit. It is also clear that both aspects are contained in the story. The one aspect, that the standpoint of cleavage ought not to persist, is implied by the statement that a crime has been committed, something that ought not to be, ought not to endure. ⌐It was the serpent who said: "You will be like God."⁻³⁷ The arrogance of freedom is the standpoint that ought not to persist. The other aspect, that the cleavage ought to persist, insofar as it contains the source of its healing, is expressed in the speech of God: "Behold, Adam has become like one of us, knowing good and evil." So what the serpent said was no lie; | on the contrary, even God himself   427 corroborated it. But this verse is usually overlooked, or else nothing is said about it.

So we can say that it is the eternal story of human freedom that we do go forth out of this stupor, in which we are in our earliest years, and come to the light of consciousness, or, speaking more precisely altogether, that there is good for us and also evil.³⁸ So far as we apprehend what is actually there in this portrayal, it is the same as what ⌐appeared again later in the Christian religion,⁻³⁹ namely that human beings, as spirit, must come to reconciliation.⁴⁰ That is the genuine idea in contrast with the mere image of paradise, or this stupefied innocence devoid of consciousness and will.

36. W₂ (Var) reads: that must be sublated. It is not, however, one that should not make its appearance at all, the truth rather being that this standpoint of cleavage terminates, according to its own nature, in reconciliation.

37. W₂ (Var) reads: Thus it is said that the serpent beguiled humanity with its lies.

38. L (1827?) adds: On the one hand this standpoint also involves cleavage, formal freedom, evil, pride; here human beings have the choice between good and evil, so that it is also necessary for them to emerge from this standpoint, to the extent that it is a standpoint of cleavage.

39. Thus Hu; L, W (Var) read: is in the idea,

40. L (1827?) adds, similar in W: or, to put it superficially, that they must become good, must fulfill their vocation. In order for this to come about, this standpoint of reflective consciousness, or cleavage, is [L, W₁: no less necessary. W₂: no less necessary than the abandonment of it.]

That in that initial state human beings ⌐had the most perfect acquaintance with the good and with nature has certainly been an accepted notion, but it is quite absurd.⌐⁴¹ ⌐I have this brief comment

428 about it. The laws | of nature and the like are discovered only through meditative thinking, and it is only the maturest meditation that arrives at the knowledge that these things are in accord with the idea; this thinking is in utter contrast with immediate knowledge.

As for the historical data that have been appealed to [in support of the claim] that the oldest religions and sciences still contain remains of earlier sciences, it is partly untrue and partly based upon the earlier erroneous historical accounts of the lofty knowledge of the Indians and the Chinese. Since we in Europe have become acquainted with the sources, such notions have shown to be invalid. Thus, for example, Delambre has exposed the false assertions of Bailly[42] regarding Indian astronomical records.⌐⁴³

41. *W (Var) reads:* had the highest knowledge of nature and of God, occupied the highest standpoint of science, is a foolish view, and one which, moreover, [has] been shown to be quite unfounded historically.

42. [*Ed.*] The view that the earliest tangible evidences of scientific knowledge are simply the remains of the science of an earlier, forgotten period was fairly widespread at the end of the eighteenth century. See, e.g., Jean-Sylvain Bailly, *Histoire de l'astronomie ancienne depuis son origine jusqu'à l'établissement de l'école d'Alexandrie*, 2d ed. (Paris, 1781), pp. 106–107. Hegel believed that Bailly's view of the matter—which was shared by Schelling, *Treatise on "The Deities of Samothrace,"* pp. 25, 37 (cf. *Sämmtliche Werke* 8:362, 416–417), although Schelling was here referring to Greek mythology and the Kabbala rather than Chinese and Indian mythology— had been refuted by Jean-Joseph Delambre in his *Histoire de l'astronomie ancienne,* 2 vols. (Paris, 1817), esp. pp. vi, xix, 400.

43. *W (1831) reads:* When Indian literature was first discovered, it was said that the huge chronological numbers point to a very great age of the culture and appear to yield quite new information. Recently, however, we have been compelled to abandon this [implausible] Indian chronology, [W_1: for in a few places the numbers express ratios or orders of magnitude, but are otherwise quite meaningless. W_2: for the numbers express no prosaic conditions whatever as regards years or recollection of the past.] The Indians are also said to possess great astronomical knowledge; they have formulae for calculating the eclipses of the sun and the moon, but they use them in a quite mechanical way, without knowing what is presupposed in them or how to derive the formulae. More recently, however, the astronomical and mathematical knowledge of these peoples has been more closely investigated.[a] A distinctive cultural tradition is acknowledged to be undoubtedly present here, but in these branches of knowledge the level that they reached was still far below that of the Greeks. The astronomical formulae are so needlessly involved that they are far behind the methods of the Greeks,

b. The Forms of Nature Religion

Let us sum up as briefly as possible our discussion of this initial form of religion, or nature religion; knowledge of God in the universal sense belongs to religion generally, and we can assume at least this much, that God is spirit. Hence nature religion contains the spiritual moment directly,[44] so that the spiritual is the highest reality for human beings.

This rules out the view that nature religion is one in which human beings revere natural objects as God. Reverence for natural objects does indeed play a part in it, but in a secondary way. Even in the basest religion the spiritual is, for human beings as such, always nobler than the natural; for instance, the sun is not | nobler than   429
a spiritual being for them. ¨Hence nature religion is not a religion in which external, physical objects are taken to be God and are revered as God; instead it is a religion in which the noblest element for human beings is what is spiritual, but the spiritual [recognized] first in its immediate and natural mode. The initial and natural mode is the human being, this existing human being. Inasmuch as it is natural, therefore, nature religion has the natural within it, but not sheer external or physical naturalness; it has a spiritual side at the same time, but what is *naturally* spiritual, this human being here present and sensibly facing us.¨[45] The spiritual element is not the idea of humanity, Adam Kadmon, the primordial human being,[46]

---

let alone our own; genuine science is precisely that which seeks to reduce its problems to the simplest elements. These complicated formulae point, no doubt, to a praiseworthy diligence, to painstaking effort, but more than that is not to be found in them; what they rest on is long-continued observations.

[Ed.] ªIn addition to the work by Delambre cited in the preceding note, Hegel could be referring to a number of works on Indian astronomy. See, e.g., *Asiatic Researches,* vols. 8 (J. Bentley), 5 (F. Wilford), 2 (W. Jones).

44. W *(Var)* adds: and therefore essentially,

45. W_2 *(MiscP/Var?) reads:* In its beginnings, or as immediate religion, the religion of nature means this: the spiritual, a human being, even in its natural mode, ranks as what is highest. This religion does not have the merely externally and physically natural element as its object, but the *spiritually* natural, this human being as the one actually facing us.

46. [Ed.] The idea of Adam Kadmon as receiving and transmitting the divine primal energy is referred to by August Neander in his *Genetische Entwicklung der vornehmsten gnostischen Systeme* (Berlin, 1818), pp. 88 ff., 102. Hegel drew heavily from this work.

or the Son of God—those are more developed images only present through thinking and for thought. Therefore it is not the thought-image of human beings in their universal essentiality, but rather this particular and natural human being. It is the religion of the spiritual in its externality, naturalness, and immediacy, that is to say, this human being here present, immediately and sensibly facing us. This is another reason why it concerns us to become acquainted with nature religion, in order to make us conscious that God is always a present reality for human beings from time immemorial, and in order to bring us back in this way from the abstract otherworldliness of God.

The way forward from this initial, abstract determination is for spirit to be purified of this externality and naturalness, this sensible immediacy, and to be known as spirit in thought, i.e., that human beings should attain to the representation of spirit as spirit in both their imagination and their thought.[47]

The *first* religion is this, that consciousness of the highest is consciousness of a human being as dominion, power, and lordship over nature. This first religion, if we can call it that, is the religion of 430   *magic.* |

[48] [49] ˜The *second* form, which contains the higher element, is no longer the human being in the immediate, natural state, in immediate

---

47. *L (1827?) adds:* Such is the definition of the field of nature religion, of which we see different forms; for the sphere of the natural is always the mutual externality of distinct elements.

48. *In B's margin:* 19 June 1827

49. *W₂ (1831) reads (parallel in main text follows):* The way forward from this first form of religion is for spirit to be purified from externality, from sensible immediacy, and attain to the representation of spirit as spirit in both imagination and thought.

The interesting feature in this advance is just the objectifying of spirit, i.e., that spirit becomes purely objective and comes to have the meaning of universal spirit.

II.

The Inward Rupture of Consciousness within Itself

The first step forward is for the consciousness of a substantive power, and the powerlessness of the immediate will, to enter on the scene. Since God is here known as the absolute power, this is not yet the religion of freedom. For although the entry of a substantive power upon the scene of consciousness means that humanity does rise above itself, and although the essential differentiation of spirit is accomplished, still, since this power on high is known *as* power and is not yet further determined, the particular is something merely accidental, merely negative and of no account. Everything subsists by means of this power; in other words, it is itself the subsistence of everything, so that the freedom of subsisting-for-self is not yet recognized. This is pantheism.

This power, which is something thought, is not yet known as a thought product or as inwardly spiritual. Since it must now have a spiritual mode of existence but does not yet have the moment of being free on its own account within itself, it once more has the moment of spirituality only in one human being, who is known as this power.

In the elevation of spirit with which we are here concerned, the point of departure is the finite, the contingent, this being defined as the negative, and the universal, self-subsistent essence as that in which and through which this finite is something negative, something posited. Substance, on the contrary, is what is not posited, the self-subsistent, the power in relation to the finite.

Now the consciousness that elevates itself does so as thought, but without having a consciousness regarding this universal thought, without expressing it in the form of thought. And to begin with, the elevation is an upward movement only. The other movement is the converse one, namely, that this necessary element has returned to the finite. In the first movement the finite forgets itself. The second is the relationship of substance to the finite. Since God is determined here only as the substance of the finite and the power over it, he himself is still undetermined. He is not yet known to be inwardly determined on his own account; he is not yet known as spirit.

On this general basis several forms take shape, progressive attempts to grasp substance as self-determining.

1. To begin with (in the religion of China), substance is known as the simple foundation, and so is immediately present in the finite or contingent.

The progress made by consciousness comes from the fact that even though substance is not yet grasped as spirit, spirit is nonetheless the truth implicitly underlying all the phenomena of consciousness and that therefore even at this stage nothing can be lacking of what pertains to the concept of spirit. So here too, substance will determine itself as subject, but the question is how it does this. At this point the determinations of spirit, which are present implicitly, come on the scene in an external mode. Complete determinateness, the culminating point of the shape of being-for-self, of the unity of being-for-self, is now posited externally, in the sense that an actually present human being [*ein präsenter Mensch*] is known as the universal power.

This consciousness is already apparent in the Chinese religion, where the emperor is at all events what wields or actuates the power.

2. In Hinduism substance is no longer known merely as foundation, but as abstract unity, and this abstract unity is also more nearly akin to spirit, since spirit is itself this abstract unity as ego. In raising itself to its inner abstract unity, humanity raises itself here to the unity of substance, identifies itself with it, and thus gives it existence. Some by nature partake in the existence of this unity, while others are capable of rising to it.

Of course, the unity that is here the dominant element does also attempt to unfold itself. The true unfolding, and the negativity that grasps all differences at once, would be spirit, which determines itself inwardly and becomes apparent to itself in its subjectivity. This subjectivity of spirit would give it a content worthy of it, and this

self-consciousness, or in subjective desires, but instead the human being as entering into self and concentrating self internally, so that
431 this inwardness | is the essential, higher, powerful and ruling factor. This second form is the human being as *being within self* or *self-contained [in sich seiend]*.

The *third* form is then this, that human consciousness (albeit self-
432 contained and withdrawn into itself) is at the same time outside | this abstraction of being-within-self, that the concrete is not situated in the self-containment as such but is instead a disintegration into endlessly many powers, configurations, and universal moments, which stand in connection with the self-contained essentiality, and which are more or less *imaginative forms of this essentiality.* ̄

The *fourth* form is the incipient separation from the immediate individual, *incipient severance or objectification of* what is known as *the highest.* This has two shapes. In the first, the simple is set against the concrete in this objectification; but this simple aspect is

---

content would itself have a spiritual nature too. But in the present case the characteristic of naturalness still remains, inasmuch as an advance is made to differentiation and unfolding *only,* and the moments occur in an isolated fashion alongside one another. Thus the unfolding that is necessary in the concept of spirit is here itself devoid of spirit. Hence one is sometimes at a loss to find the spirit unfolded in nature religion. This is the case, for instance, with the image of the incarnation and the triad in Hindu religion. Moments will be found that pertain to spirit, but they are interpreted in such a way that at the same time they do not pertain to it. The characteristics occur in isolated fashion and present themselves as falling to pieces. Thus the triad in Hinduism does not become the Trinity since only absolute spirit has the power over its own moments.

The representation of nature religion evinces major difficulties in this respect; it is everywhere inconsistent, and inwardly contradictory. Thus on the one hand the spiritual, which is essentially free, is posited, while on the other hand it is represented in natural determinacy, in a [state of] singularity, with a content that has hard-and-fast particularity, and that is therefore wholly inappropriate to spirit, since it is only as free spirit that spirit is genuine.

3. In the last form that belongs to this stage, that of the cleavage of consciousness, the concrete embodiment and presence of substance subsists and lives in *one* individual, and the unstable unfolding of the unity that was peculiar to the previous form is sublated at least to the extent that it is nullified and evaporated. This is Lamaism or Buddhism.

Before proceeding to consider more closely the historical existence of this religion, we have [to discuss] the general determinacy of this whole stage and its metaphysical concept. More precisely, we have here to define the concept of elevation and the relationship of substance to the finite.

still abstract, and in a natural mode, though it equally contains the spiritual determination within it. Accordingly ⁻the⁻[50] second shape of the objectification of the substantial consists in the fact that the concept of subjectivity or of the concrete, the development of the concrete and this development as totality, come to consciousness explicitly in the subject.

These are the four forms of the religion of nature. As noted, these configurations or determinations are existing configurations of | 433 religion; so the course of these forms or determinations of spirit is at the same time the foundation of the history of religion.[51]

1. The Religion of Magic[52]

a. The Concept of Magic

[53]We shall discuss now the first stage of nature religion, the religion of magic, which we may deem unworthy of the name "religion." In order to grasp this standpoint of religion we must forget all the representations and thoughts that we are perhaps so familiar with and that themselves belong to the most superficial habits of our culture.[54] We must consider human beings all by themselves | upon   434

50. *L (Var) reads:* this
51. *L (1827?) adds:* Beyond nature religion and in the religion of beauty and sublimity God for the first time emerges—partly in thought, partly in phantasy—in distinctive independence as free vis-à-vis the immediate individual.
52. *[Ed.]* The treatment of the religion of magic is briefer in 1827 than in 1824 since Buddhism/Lamaism is no longer considered under this category. The section is also organized differently since now the phenomenology of primitive religious consciousness is concentrated in subsection a and examples of the religion of magic are in subsection b. While the latter are taken almost verbatim from 1824, the former differs considerably from the earlier lectures. Now all the "less developed" forms of magic involve a direct exercise of power over nature, from which is distinguished only a "more developed" form of magic—the religion of ancient China, the treatment of which is also revised considerably (see below, n. 96).
53. W_1 *(Ed) adds:* It has to be regarded from both sides, as the religion of magical power and as that of being-within-self.
    1. The Religion of Magical Power.
54. W_2 *(1831) adds:* For natural consciousness, which is what we here have before us, the prosaic categories such as cause and effect are not yet valid, and natural things are not yet degraded into external things.
    Religion has its soil only in spirit. The spiritual knows itself as the power over the natural, it knows that nature is not what has being in and for itself. This

the earth, the tent of the heavens above them and nature round about them, and so, to begin with, without any reflective thought,[55] altogether devoid of consciousness of anything universal; only on this basis do more worthy concepts of God emerge.

It is difficult to get the sense of an alien religion from within. ¯To put oneself in the place of a dog requires the sensibilities of a dog.¯[56] We are cognizant of the nature of such living objects, but we cannot possibly know what it would mean to transpose ourselves into their place, so that we could sense their determinate limits; for that would mean filling the totality of one's subjectivity wholly with ¯¯these characteristics. They remain always objects of our thought, not of our subjectivity, of our feeling; we can grasp such religions, but we cannot get the sense of them from within. We ¯can grasp the Greek divinities, but we cannot get the inner sense of genuine adoration toward a divine image of that kind.¯[57]

But the first nature religion is much more remote from the totality of our consciousness than this.¯¯[58] Human beings in that situation

---

[knowledge] constitutes the categories of the understanding, in which nature is grasped as the other of spirit and spirit is grasped as what is genuine. This basic determination is the starting point for religion.

Immediate religion, in contrast, is that in which spirit is still natural, and where the distinction between spirit as absolute power and spirit as what is single, contingent, transient, and accidental has not yet been drawn. This distinction, the antithesis between universal spirit (as universal power and essence) and subjective existence (with its contingency), has not yet entered into play. It forms the second stage within nature religion.

In the primal, immediate religion, here in this immediacy, humanity still knows no higher power than itself. There is, to be sure, a power over contingent life, over its purposes and interests, but this is still no essential power, as a universal in and for itself, but falls within the compass of humanity itself. The spiritual subsists in a singular, immediate mode.

55. W (Var) adds: or elevation to thinking,

56. An reads: We have the representational image of the elephant, but to think ourselves completely into its nature is beyond our capability; to do so we would have to have an elephant's nature.

57. An reads: have a representation of the Greek religion of beauty. We can understand it, and its gods, and grasp them in thought, but we cannot bend the knee to them.

58. W_2 (Var) reads: a singular determination of this kind, so that it would become our determinateness. We cannot enter experientially in this way even into religions that approach more nearly to our [own] consciousness; they cannot for a single moment become our determinateness to the point that we would, for example, worship the

still exist in a state of immediate desire, force, and action, behaving in accord with their immediate will. They do not yet pose any theoretical questions such as: "Where does this come from?" "Who made it?" and "Must it have a cause?" This inward divorce of objects into a contingent and an essential | aspect, into a causative aspect and the aspect of something merely posited, or of an effect, does not yet occur for them. Similarly, even the will in them is not yet theoretical; there is not yet this rupture in them, nor any inhibition toward themselves. The theoretical element in willing is what we call the universal, right, duty—i.e., laws, firm specifications, limits for the subjective will. These are thoughts, universal forms that belong to the thought of freedom. They are distinct from subjective arbitrariness, desire, and inclination; all of the latter are restrained and controlled by the universal, or are conformed to this universal; the natural willing of desire is transformed into willing and acting in accord with such universal viewpoints.

435

But here human beings are still undivided with regard to willing; desire[59] is the governing factor here. Similarly in their representations, in the imagination of these human beings, they ˉcarry onˉ[60] in this undivided state, this benighted condition, a stupor in the theoretical domain and a wildness of will. This is just spirit's primitive and wild reliance upon itself. There is indeed a fear present here, a consciousness of negation, though not yet the fear of the Lord; it is instead the fear of contingency, of the forces of nature, which display themselves as mighty powers over against humanity.[61] The fear of the Lord, which is the beginning of wisdom,[62] is fear before a spiritually self-sufficient being opposed to arbitrariness. This fear

---

Greek statue of a god, however beautiful it might be. And the stage of immediate religion is still further off—as remote from us as it can be. *L (Var) adds:* In this case one must forget just those views that are most commonly accepted. *W₂ (Var) continues:* since in order to make it intelligible to ourselves we have to forget all the forms current in our culture.

59. *W₂ (Var) adds:* and wildness of will

60. *Thus W; L reads:* maintain themselves *An reads:* hold themselves *Hu reads:* relate themselves

61. *W₁ (Ed) adds:* We have here to deal (a) with magic in general, (b) with the characteristics of the religion of magic, and (c) with the cultus.

62. *[Ed.]* See Ps. 111:10; Prov. 1:7; Job 28:28.

first enters human experience when in one's singularity one knows oneself to be powerless, when one's singularity is inwardly shaken. The beginning of wisdom is when singular privateness and subjectivity senses itself as not being what is true, and, in the consciousness of its singularization and impotence, by way of negation, it passes over to knowledge, to universal being-in-and-for-self.

This earliest form of religion—although one may well refuse to call it religion—is that for which we have the name "magic." To be precise, it is the claim that the spiritual aspect is the power over nature; | but this spiritual aspect is not yet present as spirit, is not yet present in its universality. Instead the spiritual is at first just the singular and contingent human self-consciousness which, in spite of being only sheer desire, self-consciously knows itself to be nobler than nature, and knows that self-consciousness is a power transcending nature.[63]

436

Two different points are to be noted here. First, insofar as immediate self-consciousness knows that this power lies within it, that it is the locus of this power, in the state where it is such a power it certainly distinguishes itself altogether from its ordinary state. When human beings do ordinary things, such as eating, drinking, sleeping, and the like, when they go about their simple occupations, they are concerned with particular objects; in these pursuits they know that they are dealing just with these things, for instance in fishing or hunting.[64] Consciousness of this ordinary existence ¯with its instincts¯[65] and its activity is one thing, whereas the consciousness of oneself as having power over the general ¯vicissitude¯[66] of nature is another matter altogether. In the latter case individuals do not know themselves [to be engaged] in ordinary activities and instincts; rather one knows that, insofar as one is a higher power,

63. L (1827?) adds: So the main characteristic of this sphere is the direct mastery of nature by the will, by self-consciousness, the fact that spirit is something higher than nature. However bad this appears in one perspective, it is nonetheless higher than the situation where humanity is dependent on nature, and afraid of it.

64. W_2 (Var) adds: and they confine their energy to that activity alone.

65. W (Var) reads: and instincts Cf. An: where human beings are only conscious of the existence of nature and make use of natural objects, in pursuit of their desires

66. W_2 (Var) reads: power of nature, and over the vicissitudes

one must transport oneself into a higher state, distinct from ordinary consciousness. This higher state is the state and gift of particular human beings—ˉand these are the magiciansˉ[67]—who transport themselves into it in order to be this power.[68] |

The second point is that this power is a direct power over nature generally, one not to be compared with the indirect power that we exercise upon natural objects in their singularity. Such power of trained persons over single natural and perceptible things presupposes that they have already stepped back from the world, that the world has acquired externality in their eyes, that they have accorded to it over against them an autonomy, specific qualitative characteristics and laws, that these perceptible things are also relative to one another in their qualitative determinacy and stand in a web of connections with one another. ˉThe specially trained person exercises a powerˉ[69] through familiarity with the qualities of perceptible things, i.e., ˉofˉ[70] things as they are relative to other things; that is where something else has an impact upon them and their vulnerability is manifest. One learns to know this susceptibility, and through it acts upon things by equipping oneself with a means through which one lays hold of[71] this weakness. One brings external things into such a connection that they act upon one another according to one's purpose. Thus it is the one trained [in traditional lore] who freely releases [the power of] the world in its quality and qualitative connections. This really entails that human beings are free—inwardly free. For only free persons can allow the external world, other human beings, and natural things to confront them freely. But for the one who is not free, others are not free either. Only from the standpoint where human beings are inwardly free, and set the world free to confront them, does *indirect influence* upon natural things, a mediating dominion over nature, fall within their

67. *Thus Hu, similar in B; An reads:* not of races and strict castes
68. *L (1827?) adds, similar in W:* and who have to learn by tradition the ways of utilizing this state. There is a select group of individuals who go to the elders for instruction, and who sense within themselves this obscure inwardness.
69. *W (Var) reads:* This power, which freely releases [the power of] the world in its qualitative aspect, is exercised by the specially trained person
70. *W (Var) reads:* with
71. *W (Var) adds:* and capitalizes on

power and range of vision. In contrast, a *direct efficacy* of human beings by means of representation and will presupposes a corresponding absence of freedom, in which power over external things is indeed vested in human beings as the spiritual factor, but not as a power that behaves in a free manner. For this reason it does not behave in a mediating fashion, over against what is free; instead the power over nature has in this case a direct relationship—and | that is magic. ¯Now, in the self-consciousness of these peoples this is the noblest feature;¯[72] and it continues to insinuate itself deeply into other, higher religions in a secondary way, for instance the practice of witchcraft in Christendom, and of invoking devils. But, on the one hand, it is there known to be unavailing, and on the other hand it is regarded as something unfitting and godless.

Prayer has been regarded (even in the Kantian philosophy, for example) as if it were a kind of magic, because human beings want to effect and bring forth something not by means of natural mediation but directly from the spirit.[73] But the distinction is that, in turning to God in prayer, one is turning to an absolute will for which even the single individual is the object of care, which can grant the petition or not, and which in so doing is altogether determined by the furtherance of the good. ¯But it is black magic when, at their own subjective caprice, human beings have the spirits or the devil under their control and compel them to do whatever they wish.¯[74] There is a mediation in this case, too, but one where the human will conjures and commands them, and those powers of nature obey it. From the standpoint of magic the human will is the authority and the higher powers are at its disposal.

This is the general characterization of this first and wholly immediate standpoint, i.e., that ¯human¯[75] consciousness, this

72. *W (Var) reads:* As far as the outward existence of this view is concerned, it is found in a form that implies that this magic is what is highest in the self-consciousness of [these] peoples;

73. [*Ed.*] See Kant, *Religion within the Limits of Reason Alone,* trans. T. M. Greene and H. H. Hudson (New York, 1960), pp. 182–183 (on prayer as an illusion), 165–166 (on the illusion of thinking one can conjure up divine assistance by magic).

74. *Thus An; L (Var) reads, similar in W:* But magic consists precisely in the fact that, in their own natural state of desire, human beings have [*L:* nature *W:* it] in their power.

75. *Thus W; Hu reads:* the first human *L reads:* natural

human being in his own will, is known as power over the natural. But what is meant by "natural" here has by no means any wider scope; ˉthe natural objects [controlled] are the things that immediately surround one. The | universal form that nature possesses   439 for the will is: "That is just how it is"—without the application of any meditative thought. Human beings are at first insensible toward the environment, toward the stirring of nature. The sun rises and sets, and they observe it daily but remain unmoved; it becomes for them something they are used to. What is on the whole stable—day and night, the seasons—is just what *is;* that is what they are accustomed to. What touches or awakens interest in them is a disruption of the stable, i.e., such unstable conditions as earthquakes, thunderstorms, protracted drought, flood, rapacious beasts or enemies.ˉ[76]

b. Less Developed Religions of Magic

[77]Now we are going to cite more detailed descriptions of how these types of magic have developed in human societies. The religion of magic is still found today among wholly crude and barbarous peoples such as the Eskimos. Thus Captain Ross—and others, such as Parry[78]—discovered Eskimos who knew no other world than their icy rocks. When interviewed, these people said that they had no representation of God, or of immortality and the like. They do hold the sun and moon in awe. But they have only magicians or conjurers, who claim the authority to produce rain and gales, or to cause a whale to approach them. They say that they have learned their art

---

76. W_2 *(MiscP/Var?) reads:* as in our view of it. For at this stage the greater part of nature is still indifferent to humans, or is just as they are accustomed to see it. Everything is stable. Earthquakes, thunderstorms, floods, menacing beasts, enemies, etc., are another matter. To defend themselves against these they have recourse to magic.

77. *In B's margin:* 21 June 1827

78. [*Ed.*] John Ross, *A Voyage of Discovery, Made under the Orders of the Admirality, in His Majesty's Ships Isabella and Alexander, for the Purpose of Exploring Baffin's Bay, and Enquiring into the Probability of a North-West Passage,* 2d ed., 2 vols. (London, 1819), 1:168–169, 175–178, 179–180; William Edward Parry, *Journal of a Voyage for the Discovery of a North-West Passage from the Atlantic to the Pacific* (London, 1821). We know that Hegel was familiar with Ross's account, but not necessarily Parry's. See 1824 lectures, nn. 109, 110.

from ancient magicians ("angekoks"). These magicians put themselves into a wild state; their gestures make no sense. One could hear them invoke the ocean, but their words were not directed to a higher essence; they only have to do with natural objects. They have no representation of a universal essence. For example, someone asked one of them where the Eskimos believed they go after death. He replied that they were buried. In ages past an old man had indeed said they might go into the moon, but no rational Eskimo believes that any longer.

We still find this form widespread in Africa, and it is developed more fully among the Mongols and the Chinese. Long ago Herodotus said that the Africans are all magicians.[79] In whatever historical period people became acquainted with them, they were invariably characterized in this way. So in Africa, too, there are particular individuals whom we would term priests, and who are called Singhili.

440 As do the shamans among the Mongols, | these people also transport themselves into a state of ecstasy, a wild state of stupefaction. This state is the higher standpoint that they attain in contrast with ordinary consciousness and ordinary action. Among the populace there are particular individuals who dedicate themselves to this ecstatic state and are esteemed for that reason; or else there is a particular family that is highly respected alongside the king and that exercises particular power over the tribe.

Where their condition is more developed, so that they form a kind of state, an aristocracy or monarchy, these magicians do not constitute a particular priestly caste, but instead the king himself is at the head of these Singhili; he both participates in such activities himself and also delegates them to his ministers; he makes these individuals into persons whose task is to exercise such authority. In contrast, among tribes where this type of organization is not prevalent, the clan or tribe always retains power even over these magicians. But these magicians do not possess a secure worldly power. When the people need their help, they bring them gifts; if the magicians refuse, then even violence is used against them [and they are] terribly ill-treated. The special occasions for their recourse

79. [Ed.] Herodotus, *Histories* 2.33.

to the magicians are in storms that last a long time and against which they cannot protect themselves, during sickness, and when they are of a mind to wage war.[80] Here therefore we have "immediate" human beings, who ascribe to themselves this [direct] dominion over nature, or to whom it is ascribed.

Regarding the Africans, who still stand essentially at the stage of direct magic, we can indeed say that they also progress a small step further through their veneration of the dead, in that they ascribe power over nature to the deceased, to their departed relatives. A dead person is already no longer a wholly sensible | immediacy and   441 singularity, but is elevated into the form of representation and is not in the immediate present. If the representation is stressed, then the deceased has lost sensible singularity and already partakes in the character of something more universal, something elevated to thought. At this stage the dead, the departed ancestors or relatives, do not receive veneration in the strict sense; there is here no cult of the dead, but instead present [ill] effects are to some extent attributed to them, and a remedy for these ills is sought from them. The onset of this trouble is attributed to them, but people turn to them for averting it as well. What we call "natural" these people still do not yet know to be natural; they know nothing of natural causality. So they attribute sickness, for example, not just to a living enemy but more especially to a dead one who has projected hatred upon the diseased person. For they represent the departed not as transfigured, but as wholly subject to sensible passions and necessities like those that the living themselves have. In the same way, too, a calamity of a different kind, such as crop failure and the like, is attributed to them.

Some of the bones of the dead are carefully preserved, and when one wishes to make use of them or they are supposed to render a service, then service or reverence is shown to them, a procession is made to them, an adoration or ablution performed. People even carry

---

80. *Thus B, An, Hu; L (Var) reads:* For example, if there is no rain or persistent drought, the priest must help them and must undertake the requisite ceremony; if he does not come willingly, he is dragged along forcibly and is ill-treated. Thus it is the will of the king or of the ordinary people, the will of the tribe; they have in their hands someone to whom they ascribe direct power [over nature].

them along with them in valuable coffers, especially the skulls of slain enemies through which, they believe, they have at their disposal might against the tribes to which those enemies belonged.

[81]A missionary (Cavazzi)[82] tells of terrible phenomena concerning the Jaga—a tribe from the south of Africa, from the Congo, with which the Portuguese had extensive dealings. They had a queen who had given laws to them. All the wilder types of magic were present among them to the highest degree, and the queen is supposed to have introduced the veneration of the dead, or at least made it into the sole cultus. If their Singhili want to produce rain, then sacrifices are brought to the dead; | they make gestures toward the sky, they address, entreat, command, scold, and threaten the sky, they take rods in their hands and strike out against the sky and spit at it; and when a cloud makes an appearance they redouble their entreaties, and when the rain will not come they utter the greatest abuse at the sky, shoot arrows toward it, and swear that they will treat it badly.[83]

The missionaries describe in detail different scenes that they observed. When it is a matter of making the sick well, one goes to the magician, who then declares the reason for the sickness; it is some enmity, and the enemies, in particular those who are deceased, must be compelled to desist from their vengeance. The precise way of accomplishing this is frightful, and usually it is accompanied by murder. The Singhili and all about begin a fearsome shrieking that lasts for several hours. One of their views about this is that the magician compels a dead person to enter into him and to disclose what must occur in order to have power or in order to conciliate another dead person—murder, gruesome practices, or bloody sacrifices. Also, the Singhili then states that he needs two human beings who must be sacrificed, and designates them from the

81. *Precedes in L (1827?):* So the dead play here an especially large role.

82. [*Ed.*] J. A. Cavazzi, *Historische Beschreibung der in dem unteren occidentalischen Mohrenland ligenden drey Königreichen Congo, Matamba, und Angola* (Munich, 1694), p. 233 (*Istorica descrizione de' tre regni Congo, Matamba, et Angola situati nell'Etiopia inferiore occidentale* [Bologna, 1687], pp. 198–199). Since it is not certain whether Hegel used the German or the Italian edition, we give the Italian page references in parentheses. The Jaga were leaders of one of the fiercest of the Bantu tribes of the Congo basin, the Bangala of Kwango, who were cannibals.

83. [*Ed.*] Cavazzi, *Historische Beschreibung,* pp. 250–251 (p. 215).

bystanders, takes a knife, stabs them, drinks their blood, distributes their pieces among the bystanders, and the whole company devours their flesh. Such bloody sacrifices are very common.[84] It is recounted of that queen of the Jaga that, in order to be strong in war, she pounded her own son in a mortar and, in company with her female companions, devoured his flesh and drank his blood.[85] What is evident here is precisely the frightful means through which [natural] human beings seek to raise themselves above ordinary consciousness, to make themselves aware of something higher—an elevation that manifests itself here in that horrible expedient of murdering human persons according to chance.

It is told of another king that when war was imminent, he consulted with the Singhili and received from them the | instruction   443 that during the night he should sound his horn and so give his bodyguards the sign[86] to murder all of those they might encounter on the street. Thirty years ago an English ambassador found himself in this capital and, together with his entourage, he escaped destruction only because that secret was made public and he was warned. The resolution was actually carried out, and although not very many succumbed, this nightly havoc nevertheless continued for seventeen days.[87]

In all these cases we see a uniquely special elevation above immediate consciousness, and one that involves representations of the deceased, who on the one hand are regarded as powers[88] and yet on the other are compelled to do whatever those still alive want them to do. This goes so far that the Negroes, who with their still wild sense have not yet attained to a universal rationality, encounter the deceased in dreams and are tormented by these dead persons;

84. [*Ed.*] Ibid., pp. 259–264 (pp. 223–227).
85. [*Ed.*] Ibid., pp. 218–219 (pp. 187–188).
86. *Thus An; Hu reads:* there was a great procession to the grave of the enemy king, and there they prayed; then a command was issued, on behalf of the king,
87. [*Ed.*] See T. E. Bowdich, *Mission from Cape Coast Castle to Ashantee* (London, 1819), pp. 419–421. Bowdich does not actually refer to the Singhili but only to "the officers whose duty it is to attend at sacrifices"; and according to him the sign was given by drum rather than horn. In other respects Hegel's account is accurate but condensed.
88. *In B's margin:* 22 June 1827

various magical means are adopted against this. When their bodies still exist they are disinterred, the head is struck off, and the fluid from it is given to the tormented persons to drink, in order to cause the deceased pain and to take power from them.[89] In this way the empirical self-consciousness remains very much the master and has no other dominion over against it.

On this account every illness is supposed to be the consequence of an enmity, and in this connection they think the same thing about death too. Therefore they do not want human beings to appear to die of natural causes. Sick people, especially kings, are killed by them. If a king grows ill or old, then they do not let things get to the point where he would be killed by a hostile nature, but instead they slay him themselves. Dissatisfied chiefs seek by that means to get rid of the king themselves. If a king rules too harshly, then they inform him that he must die—he is allowed to determine the ceremonies himself.[90] In other words, they find it fitting that a human being should die through human will. Natural causation or connection is not yet present to the spirit of this | people; they attribute everything evil to the ill will of human beings, living as well as dead, or to other nonnatural forces; everything is explained in an unnatural manner and attributed to something else. This representation further intensifies into what we call "the devil." Belzoni,[91] an Italian who brought great treasures with him from Egypt, also transported a colossal head of Memnon to England, a stupendous work. The Egyptians had always seen this head lying on the bank of the Nile; but when they were motivated by monetary payment to carry this great head into the ship, and had indeed handled it themselves, they were very frightened and—despite the fact that they had done it—attributed the movement to the power of the devil.

The Negroes have an endless multitude of ˉdivine imagesˉ[92]

444

89. [Ed.] Cavazzi, Historische Beschreibung, pp. 257–258 (pp. 221–223).

90. [Ed.] Hegel is possibly referring to the same report which he gives at much greater length in his philosophy-of-history lectures. See Lectures on the Philosophy of World History, Nisbet ed., p. 187; Hoffmeister ed., p. 230. The source of the report has not been identified.

91. [Ed.] G. B. Belzoni, Narrative of the Operations and Recent Discoveries in Egypt and Nubia, 3d ed. (London, 1822), 1:68–69.

92. W (Var) reads: idols, natural objects

which they make into their gods or their "fetishes" (a corrupted Portuguese term).[93] The nearest stone or butterfly, a grasshopper, a beetle, and the like—these are their Lares[94]—indeterminate, unknown powers that they have made themselves; and if something does not work out or some unhappiness befalls them, then they throw this fetish away and get themselves another.[95]

The use of charms and fetishes among these peoples does, of course, lead to the representation of a power outside of empirical consciousness, or of the will and passion of the living and the dead; but this power is set forth only as something external and sensible, and remains completely within the caprice of those who have raised things of this sort to such power.

We have yet to mention a more developed form of this religion whose character we have outlined, where humanity has not yet emerged from its subjective particularity, not yet gone out into the separation of something universal in and for itself, as opposed to its own isolated being and to nature. | This more developed form is the religion of the Chinese empire.

445

c. The State Religion of the Chinese Empire and the Dao[96]

This religion still stands within the scope of this principle; it is a developed religion of magic.

93. [Ed.] Hegel may be referring to the Journal by Professor Smith appended to *Narrative of an Expedition to Explore the River Zaire, Usually Called the Congo, in South Africa, in 1816, under the Direction of Captain J. K. Tuckey, R.N.* (London, 1818), p. 375. See 1824 lectures, n. 157.

94. W (Var) adds: from whom they expect to derive good fortune

95. W (Var) reads: and, accordingly, if anything unpleasant befalls them, [W₂: and they do not find the fetish serivceable,] they do away with it [W₂: and choose another].

96. [Ed.] Hegel's treatment of ancient Chinese religion is considerably revised in 1827 as compared with the 1824 version (see 1824 lectures, n. 172). He recognizes more clearly that Tian symbolizes heaven, although in his view it represents physical power rather than a spiritual deity. He discusses at greater length the relationship between Tian and the emperor, although he continues to view them as more closely identified than they were in fact. And he introduces for the first time references to the Dao and Daoism, which have their roots in the Zhou traditions (see below, n. 115). Hegel's basic source remains the Jesuit *Mémoires concernant les Chinois,* 16 vols. (Paris, 1776–1814), and he draws upon them more fully although he makes use of other sources as well. See the subsequent annotations for details. In place of

In the Chinese empire there is a religion of Fo or Buddha, which was introduced in A.D. 50[97] Then there is the ancient Chinese religion 446 of Dao—this is a distinctive god, | reason. But the state religion, the religion of the Chinese empire, is the religion of heaven, where heaven or Tian is acknowledged as the highest ruling power. What is called "heaven" here is not merely the power of nature, but the power of nature bound up together with moral characteristics, through which this power of nature dispenses or withholds its blessings according to moral deserts and conduct.[98]

We seem, therefore, to have entered a quite different and higher sphere. For us "heaven" signifies "God"—without the admixture of anything physical. With this Tian, which is first of all physical power, we seem, insofar as it also determines itself morally, to have left the sphere of nature religion and magic behind. But if we consider it more closely, we find that we are still standing wholly within this sphere where the single human being, the empirical consciousness, the will of the individual, is what is highest.

Tian means "heaven." There were many controversies over this, especially among the Catholic orders that had been sent to China as missionaries.[99] They were most welcome at the court; they were

_____

the chaotic romanization of Chinese characters in the sources available to L and W, we have used the Pinyin system, officially adopted in 1958 and now the accepted scholarly norm.

97. [Ed.] The *Allgemeine Historie der Reisen* (Leipzig, 1750), 6:358 gives a date "some sixty-five years after the birth of our Lord," while the *Mémoires concernant les Chinois* 5:51, 58 give A.D. 63 or 64. See also Francis Buchanan, "On the Religion and Literature of the Burmas," *Asiatic Researches* 6:262. Present estimates are between A.D. 65 and 67.

98. *L (1827?) adds:* Consequently this physical power also determines itself in a moral way.

99. [Ed.] The controversies among the different Catholic orders began with the missions to China on the part of the Franciscans, Dominicans, and Augustinians, beginning in 1633. The Papal bull *Ex quo singulari* condemned the Jesuit mission in 1742. Reference to the Capuchins is found only in *An,* and could be due to an error in the source or a misunderstanding on Hegel's part. The controversy did not center principally on the designation of God but on the permissibility of combining Chinese rituals, especially those of Confucianism and the ancestor cult, with Christianity. Hegel, however, represents it as focusing on the question how the designation of God as "heaven" is to be properly understood. This may be regarded as an indication that his treatment is based primarily on the account in the *Allgemeine Historie* 6:386, where it is presented in this light.

occupied with the preparation of the calendar, which the Chinese were at one time unable to do. The Jesuit missionaries propagated the Christian religion there, but they allowed the Chinese to use the name "Tian" for God; for this they were harshly indicted before the Pope by other orders (the Capuchins and Franciscans), because "Tian" designates the physical power and not a spiritual deity.^{‾100} Tian is the highest, though not only in the spiritual and moral sense. This Tian designates wholly indeterminate and abstract universality; it is the wholly indeterminate sum of the physical and moral nexus as a whole. In this context it is the emperor and not heaven who is sovereign on earth; it is not heaven that has given or gives the ‾laws‾¹⁰¹ of religion and ethical life, which human beings respect. It is not Tian that rules nature, for the emperor rules everything and only he is connected with this Tian. Only he brings offerings to Tian at the four main festivals of the year; | it is only the emperor who   447

100. W₂ *(1831) reads:* We have now to consider the more specific forms in which pantheism has defined itself as a religion.
1. The Chinese Religion, or the Religion of Measure
a. Its General Determinacy
    In the first place, substance continues to be thought of under that aspect of being which does indeed come nearest to essence, yet still pertains to the immediacy of being; and spirit, which is distinct from substance, is a particular, finite spirit, i.e., it is a human being. This spirit is on the one hand the wielder of authority, the one who carries the power into effect; while on the other hand, as subject to the power, it is something accidental. If a human being [such as the Chinese emperor] is represented as this power, so that it is regarded as operative in him or that it comes, through the cultus, to the point of positing itself as identical with him, then the power has the shape of spirit, but of finite, human spirit; and with this we have the [element of] separation from others, over whom the power is exercised.
b. The Historical Existence of this Religion
    It is true that we have gone beyond the immediate religion constituted by the standpoint of magic, inasmuch as the particular spirit now distinguishes itself from the substance and its relationship to the substance in that it regards it as the universal power. In the Chinese religion, which is the closest approximation, in historical form, to this relationship to substance, substance is known as the entire sphere of essential being, as measure; measure is regarded as what has being in and for itself, the unchangeable, and Tian, heaven, is the objective intuition of this sphere of being-in-and-for-self. However, the characteristic of magic-working also still intrudes into this sphere, insofar as in actuality the singular human being, with its will and empirical consciousness, is what is highest. The standpoint of magic has here broadened to yield an organized monarchy, whose intuition has something grandiose and majestic.
    101. W *(Var) reads:* divine laws, laws

converses with Tian, who directs his prayers to Tian. He alone stands in connection with Tian, and thus it is the emperor who rules the whole earth. Among us the prince rules, but God does, too; the prince is bound by the divine commandments. But here [it] is the emperor who has dominion even over nature and rules the powers themselves, and that is why all things on earth are the way they are.

We distinguish the world or worldly phenomena in such a way that God rules beyond this world too.[102] That is where heaven is, which is perhaps populated by the souls of the dead. The heaven of the Chinese or Tian, by contrast, is something totally empty.[103] The souls of the dead do indeed exist and survive their departure from the body, but they, too, belong to the world,[104] and the emperor rules over them as well, putting them in their appointed places and removing them from them.[105] It is this single self-consciousness that consciously carries out the perfect governance.[106] |

448

102. *W₂ (Var) adds:* But here it is only the emperor that rules.

103. *In Hu's margin:* It has no sway over higher spirits or the bodies of the deceased, as is sometimes imagined to be the case in other religions.

104. *W₂ (Var) adds:* since they are thought of as lords over the natural spheres,

105. *W₂ (MiscP/Var?) adds (cf. n. 103):* If the dead are represented as directors of the natural realms, it might be said that in this way they are exalted; but in fact they are demoted into genii of the natural world, and therefore it is right that the self-conscious will should direct them.

Hence the heaven of the Chinese is not a world that forms an independent realm above the earth (as we picture it with angels and the souls of the departed, or in the way the Greek Olympus is distinct from life on earth). On the contrary, everything is upon earth, and everything that has power is subject to the emperor.

106. *W (1831) adds:* [W₁: In this connection, what is noteworthy is how what has being in and for itself is known as order and determinate existence. In this form, substance is conceived as measure. But there is also the power over these measures, over this substance—this power is the emperor. Measure itself is an established categorial determination; it is called Dao, or reason. W₂: As regards measure, there are established categorial determinations which are called reason (Dao).] The laws of Dao, or the measures, are categorial determinations or figurations, [W₁: not of abstract being or of abstract substance, but established, universal determinations. These figurations can in turn be viewed more abstractly, in which case they characterize nature and human spirit, they are laws of human will and human reason. W₂: not abstract being or abstract substance but figurations of substance, which can be viewed in more abstract fashion but also characterize nature and human spirit, are laws of human will and human reason.] The detailed exposition and development of these measures would comprise the entire philosophy and science of the Chinese. Here we merely need to draw attention to the principal points.

The measures[a] in their abstract universality are quite simple categories: being and not-being, one and two (which is equivalent in general to the many). These universal categories were denoted by the Chinese with straight lines. The basic figure is the line; a simple line (–) signifies the one, an affirmation or "yes"; the broken line (– –) denotes two, cleavage, and negation or "no." These signs are called Gua, and the Chinese story is that they appeared upon the shell of the tortoise. There are many different combinations of these signs, which in turn give more concrete meanings of the original categorial determinations. In particular, these more concrete meanings include the four quarters of the world and the center; four mountains corresponding to these regions of the world, and one in the center; and five elements, earth, fire, water, wood, and metal. There are likewise five basic colors, each of which belongs to [W_1: one region of the world. W_2: one element.] Each ruling dynasty in China has a particular color, element, etc. There are also five key notes in music, and five basic ways of characterizing human actions in relation to others. The first and highest is the behavior of children toward their parents, the second is reverence for deceased ancestors and the dead, the third is obedience to the emperor, the fourth is the behavior of brothers and sisters toward one another, and the fifth is how one behaves toward other people.

These determinations of measure constitute the basis—reason. Human beings have to conform to them; and as regards the natural elements, their genii are to be venerated.

There are those who devote themselves exclusively to the study of this reason, who hold aloof from all practical life and live in solitude. Yet what is always the important thing is that these laws should be applied in practical life. If they are observed, if human beings perform their duties, then everything is in order in nature as well as in the empire; both the empire and the [dutiful] individuals prosper. There is a moral coherence here between human action and what happens in nature. If misfortune overtakes the empire, whether owing to floods or to earthquakes, conflagrations, drought, or the like, this arises entirely from the human failure to follow the laws of reason, from the fact that the determinations of measure have not been properly maintained in the kingdom. Because of this omission the universal measure is destroyed, and this kind of misfortune strikes. This measure is known here as what has being in and for itself. This is the general foundation.

The next step concerns the implementation of measure. Maintenance of the laws is the prerogative of the emperor, of the emperor as the son of heaven, which is the whole, the totality of measures. The sky [W_1: is on the one hand the visible firmament, but it is also W_2: as the visible firmament is at the same time] the power over the measures. The emperor is directly the son of heaven (Tian-zi); he has to honor the laws and secure recognition for them. By means of a careful education, the heir to the throne is made acquainted with all the sciences and with the laws. The emperor alone renders honor to the law; his subjects have only to give [W_1: honor to him, as the one who administers the laws. W_2: him the honor that he renders to the law.] The emperor brings offerings. This means nothing else than that the emperor prostrates himself and reverences the law. Among the few Chinese festivals one of the main ones is that of agriculture. The emperor presides over it; on the day of the festival he himself plows the field; the corn that grows upon this field is used as offerings. The empress has under her direction the production of silk; this supplies the material for clothing, just as agriculture is the source of all nourishment. When floods, plague, and the like lay waste and scourge the country, the emperor alone must deal with

From the Jesuit memoirs and from ancient history books there has come to us a quite unusual representation that has something magnificent about it, a representation of the events antecedent to a change of dynasty | —how the Zhou dynasty came to rule and

449

the situation; [W_2: he acknowledges his officials, and especially himself, to be the cause of the misfortune—] if he and his magistrates had maintained the law properly, the misfortune would not have occurred. The emperor therefore commands the officials to examine themselves and to see how they have failed in their duty; and he in like manner [W_1: spends time in W_2: devotes himself to] meditation and penitence because he has not acted rightly. Thus the prosperity of the empire and the individual depends on the fulfillment of duty. In this way the entire service of God reduces to a moral life for the subjects, and nothing more. So the Chinese religion can be termed a moral religion (and this is the sense in which it has been possible to ascribe atheism to the Chinese). For the most part these determinations of measure and specific rules of duty derive from Confucius; his works are principally concerned with moral questions of this kind.

This might of the laws and of the determinations of measure is an aggregate of many particular determinations and laws. These particular determinations must now be known as activities too; as something particular they are subject to the universal activity, namely the emperor, who has power over the whole range of activities. But the particular powers are also represented as human beings, and especially as the departed ancestors of existing persons. For people are especially known as power when they are [W_1: dead. But they are also equally this power when they segregate themselves from the world, i.e., when W_2: departed, in other words no longer entangled in the interests of everyday life. But people can also be regarded as departed if they segregate themselves from the world, in that] they sink deeper within themselves, direct their whole activity to the universal or to the cognition of these powers; when they renounce the associations of everyday life and hold themselves aloof from all enjoyments; in this way too they have departed from concrete human life, and consequently they also come to be known as particular powers. In addition to them, there are also creatures of phantasy that possess this power. Thus the realm of these particular powers is very extensive. They are all subject to the [W_1: power W_2: universal power, namely that] of the emperor, who installs them and gives them commands. The best way to gain a knowledge of this wide realm of representation is to study a section of Chinese history as we have it in the information given by the Jesuits in the learned work *Mémoires sur les Chinois.*[b]

[Ed.] [a]Hegel's references to the categories of measure (*das Mass,* the measures *die Masse*), and their signs, the Gua, as found in the 1831 lectures, are derived from Fr. Gaubil's annotated translation of the Shu-jing published in Paris in 1770 under the title *Le Chou-King, un des livres sacrés des Chinois,* as well as from other sources, such as the *Mémoires sur les Chinois.* For the specific information contained in this paragraph, see *Le Chou-King,* pp. 165, 169–170; and *Mémoires* 2:35–36, 167, 181, 186. The Gua are discussed primarily in the Yi-jing, but Hegel does not seem to have been familiar with it. The two universal categories are more commonly known as yang (one line) and yin (two lines). [b]See *Mémoires* 15:228–241.

expelled its predecessor.[107] The establishment of this dynasty is fully narrated there, how the new prince Wu-wang decreed the laws of his | dynasty and organized the realm. This dynasty came to rule   450 in 1122 B.C. ¯Chinese history contains documents from 2300 B.C.¯[108] Since this description is very characteristic, I will present an excerpt from it. This new prince came to the throne. The [imperial] residence was not yet Beijing. The last prince of the preceding dynasty had consumed himself in flames, together with all his wealth, his mandarins, etc., in his palace in the capital—a palace that was itself a city. When the flames were extinguished, the new prince made his entrance, but had it proclaimed that he would not solemnly take possession of the throne until everything was regulated between him and heaven, i.e., until the laws and the administration of the empire were brought into order. This regulation consisted of the emperor's publication of the two books that had been preserved up to that time by an old man on an ancient mountain. One book contained the new | laws, ¯though they were almost the same as the old ones;¯[109]   451 and they were promulgated. The other book contained the titles of officials of the realms; the mandarins constituted [one of] the two classes of officials; the other kind of official consisted of the dead, the Shen. These Shen were appointed by the emperor just as were the living officials of the new administration. From that day on the emperor still rules the genii of his realm, who are the dead, and the state calendar today still consists of these two divisions. Then the narrative tells how the emperor's general undertook the filling of the offices according to the emperor's will. The general, who obtained the books and was commissioned with the nomination of the Shen,

---

107. [Ed.] For the information contained in this and the next paragraph, see *Mémoires concernant les Chinois* 15:228–241.

108. *Thus Hu, who reads:* 23,000

[Ed.] It is now known that this computation is not based on historical evidence but on later cosmological speculation. Hegel disregards the statement in the *Allgemeine Historie* 6:408–409 that Chinese chronology can only be reliably extended back to 400 B.C., and instead follows Gaubil's translation of the Shu-jing, which begins its dating of events from 2357 B.C.; see *Le Chou-King*, pp. 1 ff.

109. *Thus Hu; in An's margin:* the content of which, however, was nothing new; they are entirely those that had been introduced previously;

then tells of his expedition on the occasion of his investiture of the genii[110] in their offices, which is the main point.

"The recognition of the dead, the nobility of the [earlier] empire, simultaneously honored their [surviving] families and linked them to the new dynasty."[111] The general was sent to one of the holy mountains; there he built an altar, set himself upon a throne, laid his scepter of command [before him], and bade all the dead to come into his presence. After the sacrificial offering, the general made known the emperor's command:[112] they should respectfully accept the decrees of heaven that were to be proclaimed to them by the emperor and announced by the general. He made known what sort of offices these spirits were given by the emperor. He continued by reproaching in the strongest terms the assembled genii because of their negligence. The Shen, especially the more recently dead, were rebuked for the poor administration of the realm, | as a result of which the empire fell into ruin. Then he said, to those who were the cause of the state's disorder, that they were dismissed by heaven and could go wherever they wished—even to enter upon a new life in order to rectify their errors. Then the whole company of the Shen drew back; the general donned his cuirass and took the yellow flag in his left hand. "Thereupon, from the throne, he ordered a certain Bo-qian to read aloud the register of the imperial promotions. First stood the name of Bo-qian; he had therefore become the first Shen. The general congratulated him, who had averted so much misfortune from the state by his victories. The fallen ones from the preceding dynasty were brought forward."[113] Among these stood Wen-zong, the name of the uncle and field marshal of the previous

452

110. *An adds:* (in the register)

111. *L (1827?) reads:* The Shen are not immediate natural powers or natural phenomena, but are rather the form of powers, or of forces, that [are] not merely represented for the imagination but are deemed to belong to human beings who are deceased. What was interesting here was, first, that no power was independent of the emperor, and, second, that those men who had been esteemed in the previous dynasty were also honored, and a bond (therefore, a political tie) was established between their families and the new emperor.

112. *In B's margin:* 25 June 1827

113. *W₂ (Var) reads:* The delegated commander in chief named the new Shen and ordered one of those present to take the register and read it aloud. He obeyed, and found his name to be the first on the list. The commander in chief congratulated him that his virtues had been recognized in this way. He was an old general. Then

ruler; he was at first unwilling to appear; then he came, but was unwilling to kneel; he alone remained standing. The general spoke to him, saying: you are no longer the one you were during your lifetime; now you are nothing; you should therefore heed the commands of heaven with complete deference. Then this Wen-zong did fall to his knees, and he was appointed the chief inspector over clouds, storms, and rain. Then twenty-four other genii were appointed over fire, epidemic diseases, etc.—in short, over everything of which natural humanity stands in need.

That is the imperial organization with respect to the invisible powers. The emperor is lord over the visible world of the mandarins just as he is over the invisible Shen. The Shen of rain, of rivers, and the like, are the general overseers who have the particular local genii under them, those who watch over the rain, rivers, etc., in smaller regions. Almost every particular mountain, shrub, or village has its particular Shen. The Shen were indeed worshiped; but one did not hold them in particular esteem. They were subordinate to the mandarins, to whom the emperor gave his commands directly. The mandarins | must take care to rule well; if they do not, then both they and the Shen are removed from office. This is the form of this nature religion: the emperor alone knows the mandates of heaven, he alone stands in communication with heaven, and his lordship extends over both the visible and the invisible.

We have yet to mention a particular circumstance concerning the reported constitution of Wu-wang.[114] After the emperor had made known to his people the official charter that had previously been disclosed to the Shen, the emperor held his own grand inauguration, performed a sacrifice to Tian, and elevated his entire deceased family to imperial dignity, whereby they enjoyed particular honor. Then he rewarded all his generals and officers. He showered them all with benefits—only one class remained excluded from his rewards, namely those who professed the particular faith of the Dao, the followers of the sect of the Dao.

453

the others were summoned, some having been killed in the interests of the new dynasty, others having fought and sacrificed themselves on behalf of the former dynasty.

114. [*Ed.*] Hegel's source for the account in this and the following paragraph is *Mémoires concernant les Chinois* 15:249–252.

Dao generally means "the way," the right way of spirit, i.e., it means "reason." The sect of the Dao occurs already (as we see) in the twelfth century B.C.[115] It was a noteworthy event that the emperor passed over esteemed officers with his rewards; ˉhis intention was in a subtle way to put them to one side,ˉ[116] to separate them from his other retainers. These gallant officers included masters of the teaching as well as some who were only initiates at a lower level. Seven noble officers had distinguished themselves by particular deeds of valor; in the eyes of the mass of soldiers they were regarded as Shen who had only assumed human bodies, and they presented themselves in that light as well. On a ceremonial day the emperor addressed them, saying he had not forgotten them, that he recognized very well the value of their merits. "Even though you have bodies," he continued, "you are Shen, of that there is no doubt. The outstanding actions that you have performed under my eyes are sufficient proof of that to me. The intention, for the sake of which you returned to the earth, can only be to acquire for yourselves new merits, to disclose new virtues. I can do no better than to put you

454 in a position | to practice these virtues, by safeguarding you against the corruption of the times." He therefore determined the mountains to be their residence, where they could spend their remaining time in intimate association with the Shen who no longer have human shape. They were supposed to take with them all who belonged to

115. [Ed.] A similar date is given in Hegel's sources. While the idea of the Dao (the "way," the ultimate ordering principle of the world as evident in the regular patterns of nature) goes back to the Western Zhou period (1122–771 B.C.), Daoism as a movement did not appear until toward the end of the Eastern Zhou dynasty. According to legend, its founder was Lao-zi, an elder contemporary of Confucius (551–479 B.C.), to whom is attributed the *Dao De Jing* (Classic of the Way and Its Power), which scholars today believe was probably compiled in the third century B.C. The doctrines of Confucius and Lao-zi were opposed in fundamental respects—the one being ordered to social ritualization and the other to natural conformity. However, they both represent appropriations of the ancient concept of the Dao. See N. Nielsen, N. Hein, F. Reynolds, et al., *Religions of the World* (New York, 1983), pp. 264, 266–276. While Hegel's reference to "the sect of the Dao" seems to suggest Daoism as a movement, he may have the older, generic concept in mind here, since he identifies it with reason rather than with mystical experience (as was characteristic of Daoism), and since he refers below to a later "renewal or improvement of the Dao teaching, attributed especially to Lao-zi" (see n. 120).

116. *An reads:* he wanted to purge his state of these men without deeds of violence,

their sect, all who strove solely to attain immortal life. He made these seven into chiefs over all the mountains of the realm and gave them all rights of dominion over the initiates. Thus they were to apply themselves to the study of the Dao and to the effort to make themselves immortal; together with the other Shen, they were also supposed to acquire information about the secrets of nature that are impenetrable to other human beings. Thus they were separated from actual society.

From this account we see that at that time there was already a class of people who occupied themselves with the inner life, who did not belong to this universal state religion but built up a sect that devoted itself to thinking, withdrew within itself and in its thinking sought to bring to consciousness what the true might be.[117]

Therefore, the next stage of this initial configuration of nature religion—which was this very knowing by immediate self-consciousness of itself as the highest, as the ruling element, i.e., this immediacy of taking immediate willing to be what is highest—is the return of consciousness into itself, the demand that consciousness should be inwardly meditative—and that is the sect of the Dao. Linked with this, in any case, is the fact that human beings who recede into thought or into the inner domain, who ¯applied themselves to the abstraction of thought,¯[118] have at the same time the intention ¯of being immortal, of being pure sages,¯[119] of whom some are newly initiated while others have attained the mastery or the goal and | already regard themselves as higher essences also with respect to their existence and actuality.   455

Therefore we already find among the Chinese in antiquity this orientation toward the inner, to the Dao, an orientation to abstractly pure thinking, which orientation constitutes the transition to the

---

117. [Ed.] See *Mémoires concernant les Chinois* 15:209–210, although the stress in this passage is on acquiring knowledge "of all the operations of nature," in its entirety and as a whole.

118. *W (Var) reads:* apply themselves to the abstraction of thought, *B reads:* applied themselves to thought, *L reads:* live in the abstraction of thought,

119. *Thus Hu; B reads:* of becoming immortal, *L (Var) reads:* of becoming in essence immortal on their own account, *W reads:* of becoming immortal essences, pure on their own account,

[Ed.] Where *Hu* reads *Weise* (sage), *L* and *W* read *Wesen* (essence).

second form of nature religion. There occurred in later times a renewal or improvement of the Dao teaching, attributed especially to Lao-zi,[120] a sage who was somewhat older than Confucius but who lived contemporaneously with Confucius and Pythagoras.[121] Confucius is thoroughly moralistic and no speculative philosopher. Tian, this universal power of nature, which by the emperor's authority is an actuality, is linked to the moral nexus, and Confucius chiefly developed this moral aspect. His teaching coalesced with the state religion. All the mandarins had to have studied Confucius. But the sect of the Dao based itself solely on abstract thinking.

[122]Dao is the universal. It is quite noteworthy that the determination "three" immediately comes into play[123] to the extent that Dao is something rational and concrete. Reason has produced one, one has produced two, two produced three, and three the universe—the same doctrine that we see in Pythagoras. The universe rests upon the dark principle and is at the same time embraced by the bright principle, by light. A spirit or breath unites them, and brings about their harmony and maintains it.[124] The initial determination of the triad is the One, and is called J; the second determination is the Chi or light breathing; the third is Wei, what is sent, the messenger. These three symbols are perhaps not Chinese; one sees in them the three letters J, H, W, and correlates this with the Hebraic tetragram Jehovah, and with the trigram Yao of the Gnostics.[125] [126]The One

120. [Ed.] This is probably based on Abel-Rémusat, *Mémoire sur la vie et les opinions de Lao-Tseu* (Paris, 1823), who states, p. 2, that Lao-zi "flourished at the beginning of the sixth century B.C." and "is still considered to be the patriarch and reformer of the sect of the Dao."

121. [Ed.] See ibid., pp. 36 ff. Hegel makes no mention of the later, legendary report of a visit of Confucius to Lao-zi (ibid., p. 4).

122. *In B's margin:* 26 June 1827

123. W₂ (*Var*) adds: in Dao—in the totality—

124. [Ed.] Hegel's source for the three preceding sentences is again Abel-Rémusat, *Mémoire,* p. 31, although Abel-Rémusat does not at this point draw a parallel with Pythagoras or refer to the "dark principle" and the "bright principle," but only to "matter" and "aether."

125. [Ed.] The preceding two sentences are drawn from a much longer passage in Abel-Rémusat, *Mémoire,* pp. 40–49. The identification of J with the life-giving energy of the One, of Chi with a light breath, and of Wei with the messenger is not accepted by Abel-Rémusat, who attributes it to Montucci and says that the three characters in fact have no meaning but are used simply to denote sounds that do not

is the indeterminate, that without characteristics, the impoverished initial abstraction, what is wholly empty. ⌐If it is to be internally concrete, | to be living, then it must be determinate, and thus it is the Two, and the Third is the totality, the consummation of determinateness. Thus, even in the first efforts of humanity to think in the form of triunity or trinity, we can observe this necessity.⌐[127] Unless three determinations are recognized in God, "God" is an empty word. Right at the beginning of thinking we find the very simplest and most abstract determinations of thought. If, from this assertion that the absolute power is, there occurs the progression to the universal, then thinking begins, though the thinking itself is originally quite empty and abstract. Further developments of this relationship are found in Chinese literature. The symbol of the Dao is on the one hand a triangle, and on the other hand three horizontal lines one above the other, the middle one of which is shortest, with a vertical stroke through all three as a sign that these three are to be grasped essentially as one.[128] In China these symbols are called Gua.[129] The [eight] Gua embody the elements of the higher Chinese reflection.

456

Thus in the sect of the Dao the beginning consists in passing over

---

occur in Chinese. And his lengthy discussion of whether the Hebraic tetragram (JHWH) came to be expressed in three Chinese characters, and if so how, is not at all reflected in Hegel's flat statement that they were correlated. This view was reinforced by H. J. Klaproth in his review of G. Pauthier, *Mémoire sur l'origine et la propagation de la doctrine du Tao, fondée par Lao-tseu* (Paris, 1831), in *Nouveau Journal Asiatique* 7 (1831): 491–493— a view no longer regarded as correct. Hegel also quotes from this passage of Abel-Rémusat in the *Lectures on the History of Philosophy* 1:124–135 (cf. *Werke* 13:444), but adds: "If philosophizing has got no further than such expressions, it is still at the first stage."

126. *Precedes in L (1827?), similar in* W₂: As soon as we arrive at the element of thinking, the determination "three" makes its appearance at once.

127. W₂ *(Var) reads:* If it is to have the principle of organic life and spirituality, an advance must be made to determination. Unity is actual only insofar as it contains two within itself, and this yields the triad.

128. [*Ed.*] Hegel's source for this assertion has not been identified. In any case it seems to be erroneous. The Gua (see the following note) include neither a triangle nor the sign described by Hegel consisting of three horizontal lines intersected by a vertical stroke. The latter suggests the sign 王 (*wang*² = king, prince); the character for the Dao is much more complex: 道 (*dao*⁴ = way, truth, reason).

129. [*Ed.*] In regard to the eight Gua, see above, n. 106, annotation a.

into thought, the pure element; but one should not believe that a higher, spiritual religion has established itself in this case. The determinations of the Dao remain complete abstractions, and vitality, consciousness, what is spiritual, do not, so to speak, fall within the Dao itself, but are still completely within the immediate human being. Thus Lao-zi is also a Shen, or he has appeared as Buddha.[130] [131]The actuality and vitality of the Dao is still the actual, immediate consciousness; in fact, it is even a deceased individual such as Lao-zi, although it transforms itself into other shapes, into another human being, and it is vitally and actually present in its priests. Just as Tian, this One, is the ruling element, though as this abstract foundation, whereas the emperor is the actuality of this foundation, the one who in fact rules; so the same is the case with the Dao, with the represen-

457   tation of reason. Reason is likewise the abstract foundation that | has its actuality for the first time in existing human beings. [132]Since the universal, the higher, is only the abstract foundation, the human being thus abides in it without any properly immanent, fulfilled inner element; one has no inner hold on oneself. One has for the first time a footing within oneself when freedom and rationality emerge, when one has the consciousness of being free and when this freedom elaborates itself as reason. This developed reason provides absolute principles and duties; and people who are themselves conscious of these principles in their freedom and within their conscience—people in whom they are immanent characteristics—have for the first time a footing within themselves, in their conscience. ˉBut insofar as human beings find themselves in that preceding relationship, where

130. [Ed.] See *Mémoires concernant les Chinois* 15:255, 258, where, however, it is not claimed that Lao-zi had appeared as Buddha, only that he had himself claimed to have been a Shen.

131. *Precedes in L (1827?), similar in W:* God is for us the universal, but inwardly determined. God is spirit, his existence is spirituality. But here

132. *Precedes in W₂ (1831):* Cultus is, properly speaking, the whole existence of the religion of measure, the power of substance having not yet inwardly assumed the shape of firm objectivity; and even the realm of representation, to the extent that it has developed in the realm of the Shen, is subject to the power of the emperor, who is himself merely the one who implements the substantive in actuality.

If, then, we inquire into cultus in the narrower sense, there is only the relationship of the general determinateness of this religion to inner life and to self-consciousness left for us to investigate.

the absolute is only an abstract foundation, they⁻[133] have no footing within themselves, no immanent, determinate inwardness. For that reason everything external is for them something inward; everything external has significance for them, it has a relation to them, and indeed a practical relation. This relationship is in general the constitution of the state, the circumstances of being ruled from without.

No inherent morality is bound up with the Chinese religion, no immanent rationality through which human beings might have internal value and dignity[134]; instead everything is external, everything that is connected with them is a power for them, because in their rationality and morality they have no power within themselves. The consequence is an indeterminable dependence on everything external, the highest | and most contingent kind of superstition.[135] The Chinese are the most superstitious people of the world;[136] they have a ceaseless fear and anxiety of everything, because everything external has a significance for them, is a power over them, is something that exerts authority over them, something that can affect them. Divination in particular makes its home there; anxiety in the face of every contingent situation impels them to it. In every locale there are many who occupy themselves with prophesying; the correct place for one's dwelling, for one's grave (both the

458

133. *Thus An, Hu; L (1827?) reads, similar in W:* Only insofar as human beings have knowledge of God as spirit and of the determinations of spirit—only then have these determinations of the divine become essential, absolute determinations, or, in a word, rationality; what is duty within them, what, as far as they are concerned, is immanent within them. But where the universal is merely this abstract foundation as such, they

134. *W₂ (Var) adds:* and protection against what is external

135. *W₂ (1831) adds:* Speaking generally, what lies at the foundation of this external dependence is the fact that nothing that is particular can be placed in an inner relationship with the universal that remains merely abstract. The interests of individuals lie outside the universal determinations put into effect by the emperor. With regard to particular interests, what we find is rather the representation of a power that exists on its own account. It is not the universal power of providence, which extends its sway even over particular destinies. Instead, the particular is made subject to a particular power. This power is that of the Shen, and with this an enormous realm of superstition comes into play.

136. [*Ed.*] Hegel's examples of Chinese superstition are taken from *Allgemeine Historie* 6:389–390.

locality and the spatial arrangement)—the Chinese engage in such things throughout their entire lives. In the building of a house, if another house flanks one's own, or if the front has an angle facing it, then ⌐all possible ceremonies are performed with respect to it, and so on.⌐[137]

2. The Religion of Being-Within-Self (Buddhism, Lamaism)[138]

[139]Thus the second form of nature religion, the more determinate and intensive being-within-self, which is coherent with the mode of

137. *Hu reads:* they have first to consider the location carefully and to think whether it might not give rise to some misfortune. W_2 *(1831) omits:* and so on *and adds:* and the particular powers are rendered propitious by means of gifts. The individual is wholly without the power of personal decision and without subjective freedom.

138. [*Ed.*] In the 1827 lectures, Buddhism/Lamaism is no longer considered under the category of magic, as in 1824, but as the second form of nature religion, in which the absolute is grasped as substance, as being-within-self. In this connection, Hegel introduces another discussion of pantheism, arguing (as he does characteristically in the 1827 lectures) that no true religion is pantheistic in the sense of claiming that "everything is God," and comparing Oriental consciousness with Spinozism. See Vol. 1:375–378. In the 1824 lectures, the question of pantheism is considered more briefly in the introductory discussion of the metaphysical concept of God. On the whole, the 1827 treatment of Buddhism is more fully developed and balanced than in 1824, evidencing a better mastery of the available sources. Hegel sometimes refers to Buddhism as "the religion of Fo"; Fo is the Chinese name of Buddha. See 1824 lectures, n. 183.

139. *Precedes in W_2 (1831), following the treatment of Hinduism, as in the order of the 1831 lectures:* Since there has been no rational determination such as could achieve solidity, the condition of this people as a whole could never become one that is founded in right and inwardly justified; it was always merely a condition of sufferance, a contingent and confused one.
3. The Religion of Being-Within-Self
a. Its Concept
   The general foundation here is still the same as that which is peculiar to the Hindu religion; what advance there is consists merely in the necessity of the categorial determinations of Hindu religion being brought together again out of their wild, unrestrained falling-apart into separateness; it consists in their being brought out of their natural segregation, and into an inner relationship with one another, so that their unchecked reveling is stilled. This religion of being-within-self is the concentration and tranquilization of spirit as it returns, out of the destructive disarray of Hindu religion, into itself and into essential unity.
   The essential unity and the differences have so far been mutually exclusive to the point where the latter stood independently by themselves, and vanished in the unity only in order to emerge again at once in all their independence. The relationship between the unity and the differences was an infinite progression, a constantly

going-into-self that we have just considered—a going-into-self in the Dao, which is still wholly abstract and does not separate itself from the immediate personality—is as follows. | The highest power or the 459 absolute is grasped not in this immediacy of self-consciousness but as substance, as an essence which, however, at the same time still retains this immediacy, so that it exists in one or more individuals. This substance, with its existence in these individuals, is power or dominion; it is the creation and maintenance of the world, of nature and of all things—the absolute power over the world.

This form has a multitude of more detailed configurations whose distinctions we do not want to go into. ˉThe religion of Fo—or of Buddha in India—belongs here; this Buddha is also called | Gautama. 460 The religion of the Lamas belongs in the same context. In India Buddha is a historical person. These deceased persons are revered, but at the same time they are represented as being present in their images just as they are in their priests. In the religion of Lamaism the view is that definite individuals are God, that they are the divine substance as living, as sensibly present here.ˉ[140] This sensible presence in a human being is the abiding, principal feature [of this religion]. It is the most widespread religion on earth—in Burma and

---

alternating disappearance of differences in unity and their [reemergence] in self-subsistent independence. Now this alternation is cut short, because what is implicitly contained in it is actually posited, namely the coming together of the differences in the category of unity.

As this being-within-self for which all other-connectedness is now precluded, the essence is self-contained essentiality, the reflection of negativity into itself, and thus it is what rests and persists within itself.

Defective as this determination may be, since the being-within-self is not yet concrete and is only the disappearance of the independent differences—

140. W_1 (Var) reads: With the Hindus, too, Buddha is a divine incarnation, and also a historical person, as is Fo. These are deceased historical persons; [as such] they are venerated, but they are also represented as present and operative in their images as well as in their priests.

Lamaism holds that some of these human beings are the deity itself, that they are the [divine] substance as living, as here present. There is in itself nothing contradictory in the fact that an individual—in this case, the Dalai Lama—is known as the absolute power of substance; he is, of course, mortal, like the rest of us, but even so the deity is present within him. Beyond this no extraordinary power attaches to him, but the power of substance is within him, an immediate, unconscious power that is utterly permeating and directly present. This view coheres very closely with what we were considering previously.

China, in Mongolia, etc. The peoples adhering to this religion are more numerous than the Muslims, as the Muslims in turn are more numerous than the Christians.

Here we find the form of substantiality in which the absolute is a being-within-self, the one substance; but it is not grasped just as a substance for thought and in thought (as it is in Spinoza); instead it has at the same time existence in sensible presence, i.e., in singular human beings. ¯With reference to the character of the people who adhere to this religion, this substantiality involves an elevation above the immediate, singular consciousness as it presents itself in magic, where it is just the singular consciousness that is the power, [natural] desire, or a yet untamed savagery.¯141 At the stage to be considered here, on the other hand, the highest is known as the One, the substantial, and it involves an elevation above desire and singular will; it involves the limitation of untamed desire and immersion | in this inwardness, [i.e., it involves] unity. The image of Buddha is in the thinking posture, with feet and arms intertwined so that a toe extends into the mouth—this [is] the withdrawal into self, this absorption in oneself.142 Hence the character of the peoples who adhere to this religion is one of tranquillity, gentleness, and obedience, a character that stands above the wildness of desire and is the cessation of desire. Great religious orders have been founded among these peoples; they share a common life in tranquillity of spirit, in quiet, ¯tranquil occupation of the spirit,¯143 as do the Bonze in China and ¯the shamans in Mongolia.¯144 Attainment of this

461

141. W_2 *(1831/Var?) reads:* This religion of substantiality has particularly influenced the character of the peoples who adhere to it inasmuch as it has made the immediate, singular consciousness an omnipresent requirement.

142. [*Ed.*] The image is not a representation of the Buddha. Hegel is probably referring to fig. 2 in plate xxi of the volume of illustrations accompanying Friedrich Creuzer's *Symbolik und Mythologie der alten Völker* (Leipzig and Darmstadt, 1819). Creuzer identifies (p. 9) the subject as Brahmā Nārāyaṇa, a Hindu figure from the cosmogony of the Code of Manu whom he elsewhere (1:597) associates explicitly with the posture described. See also below, annotation a to n. 217.

143. W_2 *(1831) reads:* contemplation of the eternal, without taking part in worldly interests and occupations,

144. *Thus An; L (Var) reads:* the Rabane in Burma.

[*Ed.*] "Rabane" is probably a misreading for "Rahāns" or "Rahāne." See Francis Buchanan, "On the Religion and Literature of the Burmas," *Asiatic Researches* 6:273–280.

pure, inward stillness is expressly declared to be the goal for human beings, to be the highest state.

ˉSo far as this stillness is also expressed as a principle, especially in the religion of Fo, the ultimate or highest [reality] is therefore nothing or not-being. They say that everything emerges from nothing, everything returns into nothing.[145] That is the absolute foundation, the indeterminate, the negated being of everything particular, so that all particular existences or actualities are only forms, and only the nothing has genuine independence, while in contrast all other actuality has none; it counts only as something accidental, an indifferent form.ˉ[146] | For a human being, ˉthis state of negation is the highest state: one must immerse oneself in this nothing, in the eternal tranquillity of the nothing generally, in the substantial in which all determinations cease, where there is no virtue or intelligence, where all movement annuls itself. All characteristics of both natural life and spiritual life have vanished.ˉ[147] ˉTo be blissful, human beings

462

145. [Ed.] The remainder of this paragraph follows fairly closely a passage in the *Allgemeine Historie* 6:368–369, which describes the concept of "the empty" or "nothing" found in the "religion of Fo" as the source from which everything emerges and to which everything returns. In other words, it is described in Western ontological categories as the ground of being, and it is in these terms that Hegel attempts to make sense of it. Union with the nothing, or the state of nirvana, is achieved by stripping away all desire and all mental and physical activity. One thereby becomes "perfect as the God Fo." The depiction of nirvana found here—although the term is not used in this passage from the *Allgemeine Historie*—is oriented to Mahāyāna Buddhism.

146. W_2 *(MiscP) reads:* 1. The absolute foundation is the stillness of being-within-self, in which all differences cease, and all determinations characterizing the [merely] natural state of spirit, all particular powers, have disappeared. Hence the absolute, as being-within-self, is the undetermined, the annihilation of everything particular, so that all particular existences, all actual things, are only something accidental, or are merely indifferent form.

2. Since reflection into itself as the undetermined (according to the standpoint of nature religion, do not forget) is merely immediate reflection, it is expressed as a principle in this form: nothing and not-being is what is ultimate and supreme. It is nothing that alone has true independence; every other actuality and every particular thing has no independence at all. Everything has emerged out of nothing, and into nothing everything returns. The nothing is the One, the beginning and the end of everything. However diverse human beings and things may be, there is only the one principle, nothingness, from which they proceed, and it is form alone that constitutes quality and diversity.

147. W *(Var) reads:* [W_1: this state of negation is the highest: W_2: inasmuch as the stillness of being-within-self is the extinction of everything particular, is nothingness, this state of negation is also the highest human state, and one's vocation is] to im-

themselves must strive, through ceaseless internal mindfulness, to will nothing, to want [nothing], and to do nothing. When one attains this, there is no longer any question of something higher, of virtue and immortality. Human holiness consists in uniting oneself, by this negation, with nothingness, and so with God, with the absolute. A human being who has reached this holiness, this highest level, is indistinguishable from God, is eternally identical with God; and thus all change ceases. The soul no longer has to fear [trans]migration. Thus the theoretical moment finds expression here: that this pure nothing, this stillness and emptiness, is the absolutely highest state; that the individual is [something] formal.⁻¹⁴⁸ In the practical do-

463 main | human beings will ⁻and act where they [suppose that they] are the power.⁻¹⁴⁹ ¹⁵⁰[But here] one has to make nothingness of

464 oneself.¹⁵¹ ⁻Within one's being one has to behave in this negative |

---

merse oneself in this nothing, in the eternal tranquillity, the nothing as such—or in the substantial in which all determinations cease, and there is [W_1: no virtue,] no will, no intelligence [W_1: where all characteristics of the natural state and of spirit have vanished].

148. *W (Var) reads:* By persistent immersion and inward mindfulness every human should become like this principle, should be without passion, without inclination, without action, and should arrive at a condition of willing nothing and doing nothing.

There is no question here of virtue or vice, of reconciliation or immortality. Human holiness consists, in this negation and silence, of uniting oneself with God, with the nothing, the absolute. The highest state consists in the cessation of all bodily motion, all movement of the soul. Once this stage has been attained, [W_2: there is no descent to a lower stage, no further change, and] one does not have to fear [trans]migration after death, for then one is identical with God. Here the theoretical moment finds expression: that a human being is something substantive and self-subsistent.

149. *W (1831) reads:* and when they will, what is is an object for them, which they alter and upon which they imprint their form. The practical value of religious sensibility is determined in accordance with the content of what is regarded as the true. But in this religion [W_1: there is at least this value W_2: there is, however, first of all this theoretical element still] present: that this unity, this purity, this nothingness is absolutely independent vis-à-vis consciousness, i.e., that its characteristic is not to act in opposition to what is objective, to mold it, but [$W1$: that this stillness may be preserved and produced in it. W_2: to let it be preserved so that this stillness is produced in it.]

150. *Precedes in L (Var):* This stillness, or emptiness, is the absolute. *Precedes in W (Var):* This is the absolute.

151. *W (1831) adds:* The value of a human being consists in this, that one's self-consciousness is affirmatively related to that theoretical substantiality. This is the opposite of the [Buddhist] relationship which, since the object has no determination

way, to resist not what is external but only oneself. The state that is represented as a human being's goal, this state of unity and purity, the Buddhists call nirvana, and it is described in the following way. When one is no longer subjected to the burdens of stress, old age, sickness, and death, nirvana has been attained; one is then identical with God,⁻¹⁵² is regarded as God himself, has become Buddha.

¹⁵³At first glance it must astonish us that humans think of God as nothing; that must be extremely strange. More closely considered, however, this characterization means nothing other than that God

---

for it, is of a merely negative nature, and which for that very reason is affirmative only as a relation of the subject to its own inwardness (which is the power to change all objectivity into a negative)—or in other words, it is affirmative in its vanity alone. In the first place, that still, gentle state of mind has, momentarily in the cultus, the consciousness of such eternal tranquillity as essential, divine being, and this gives the tone and character for the rest of life. But it is also open to self-consciousness to make its entire life a continuous state of that stillness and of that contemplation devoid of existence; and this actual withdrawal from the externality of needs and the actuality of life into the quiet inner region, and the consequent attainment of union with this theoretical substantiality, must be considered the supreme consummation.

W_1 continues: A more detailed view of these general determinations is offered by the reports available to us about the characteristics that the worshipers of Fo or Buddha—or perhaps rather of Fo and Buddha, both being in equal measure the supreme head of the religion of Lamaism—adduce as the essence of this God of theirs.

There are still two other determinations to be mentioned, which derive from what has been demonstrated; one of them relates to the shape of God, the other to the external nature of the subjective self-consciousness. But we must confine ourselves to the general basic determinations of both, since they follow quite simply from the definition of the divine nature that has been given. For the divine nature itself has not got beyond the undeveloped abstraction of tranquil being-within-itself that lacks all determinacy. Consequently any further shaping or representation [of it] is surrendered, partly to the contingency of empirical historical events, and partly to that of the imagination; these less structured details belong to a description of the countless, confused products of the imagination concerning the adventures and destinies of these deities, and of their friends and disciples, as well as the other ceremonies and practices of the external cultus—a mass of material which has but little interest or value of any other kind as far as its inner content is concerned, and which (as we have already indicated) has not the interest of the concept.
[Ed.] Cf. n. 186.

152. Similar in W_1; W_2 (MiscP) reads: If one assumes this negative mental attitude and resists not what is external but only oneself, and if one unites oneself with nothingness, rids oneself of all consciousness, of all passion, one is raised to the state that the Buddhists call nirvana. One is then unburdened, no longer subject to stress, to sickness, old age, or death; one

153. In B's margin: 28 June 1827

purely and simply is nothing determinate, is the indeterminate; there is no determinacy of any sort whatsoever that is applicable to God; God is the infinite. For when we say that God is the infinite, that means that God is the negation of everything particular. When we adopt the forms that are commonplace today, i.e., "God is the infinite, the essence, the pure and simple essence, the essence of essences and only the essence," then this sort of talk is necessarily either totally or tolerably synonymous with the claim that God is nothing. That does not mean, however, that God is not, but rather that God is the empty, and that this emptiness is God. ˉWhen we say, "We can know nothing of God, can have no cognition, no representation of God," then this isˉ[154] a milder | expression for the fact that for us God is the nothing, that for us God is what is empty; that means that we must abstract from every determination of whatever sort. What remains left over then is the nothing and the essence; and the essence only, without any further determination, is surely the empty, the indeterminate. That is a definite and necessary stage of religious representation: God as the indeterminate, as indeterminacy, as this total void in which ˉthe initial mode of immediacyˉ[155] is superseded, has disappeared.

465

The principal cultus for human beings [in this religion] is the uniting of oneself with this nothing, divesting oneself of all consciousness, of all passions. This cultus consists of transposing oneself into this abstraction, into this complete solitude, this total emptiness, this renunciation, into the nothing. When one has attained this, one is then indistinguishable from God, eternally identical with God.

In the doctrine of Fo we findˉthe dogma ofˉ[156] the transmigration of souls. This standpoint is [higher than] that according to which the followers of the Dao wish to make themselves Shen, wish to make themselves immortal. While Daoism presents the attaining of immortality through meditation and withdrawal into oneself as the highest destination of human beings, it does not in that connection declare that the soul persists intrinsically as such and essentially, that

154. W (Var/Ed?) reads: That modern way is therefore only
155. W₂ (Var) reads: immediate being and its seeming independence
156. W (Var) reads: the representation of [W₂ adds: immortality and]

the spirit is immortal, but only that human beings can make themselves immortal through the process of abstraction[157] and that they should do so. The thought of immortality lies precisely in the fact that, in thinking, human beings are present to themselves in their freedom. In thinking, one is utterly independent; nothing else can intrude upon one's freedom—one relates only to oneself, and nothing else can have a claim upon one. ˉThis equivalence with myself, the I, this subsisting with self,ˉ[158] is what is genuinely immortal | and subject to no alteration; it is itself the unchangeable, what has actual being only within itself and moves only within itself. The I is not *lifeless* tranquillity but movement, though a movement that is not change; instead it is *eternal* tranquillity, eternal clarity within itself. Inasmuch as it is first at this stage that God is known as the essential and is thought in his essentiality—that being-within-self or presence-to-self is the authentic determination—this being-within-self or this essentiality is therefore known in connection with the subject, is known as the nature of the subject, and the spiritual is self-contained. This essential character also pertains [directly] to the subject or the soul; it is known that the soul is immortal, that it has within itself this [power of] existing purely, or being purely inward, though not yet of existing properly as this purity, i.e., not yet as spirituality. But still bound up with this essentiality is the fact that the mode of existence is yet a sensible immediacy, though only an accidental one. This is immortality, that the soul subsisting in presence to self is both essential and existing at the same time. Essence without existence is a mere abstraction; essentiality or the concept *must* be thought as existing. Therefore realization also belongs to essentiality. But here the form of this realization is still sensible existence, sensible immediacy.

So there is therefore the representation that the soul is immortal and still persists after death; but it is always known in another sensible mode, and this is the transmigration of souls. Because it is grasped abstractly as a being-within-self similar to God, it is thus

466

157. W *(Var) adds:* and elevation
158. *An reads:* Freedom is the genuinely infinite, *Hu reads:* This universal I—I am free—is the infinite, W_1 *(Var) adds:* the genuinely infinite, W_2 *(Var) adds:* the genuinely infinite—this, it is then affirmed at this standpoint,

a matter of indifference into what sensible form the soul passes over after death, whether into a human or an animal form; spirit is not known as something concrete. Only the abstract essence is known, and the determinate being or the appearance is just the immediate, sensible shape.[159] But a human being who attains this self-negation, this abstraction, is thus exempted from transmigration of souls, is relieved from resumption of this [mode of] existence, i.e., from being tied to this external, sensible configuration.

467 God is grasped as nothing, as essence generally; this has to be explained more precisely, | and in particular the fact that this essential God is nevertheless known as a specific, immediate human being, as Fo, Buddha, or Dalai Lama. This may appear to us as the most repugnant, shocking, and unbelievable tenet, that a human being with all his deficiencies could be regarded by other human beings as God, as the one who eternally creates, preserves, and produces the world. ¯A Dalai Lama has this image of himself and is revered as such by others.¯[160] We must learn to understand this view, and in understanding it we shall see its justification. We shall show how it has its ground, its rational aspect, a place in [the evolution of] reason. But it is also pertinent for us to have insight into its defective and absurd aspect. ¯It is easy to say that such a religion is just senseless and irrational. What is not easy is to recognize the necessity and truth of such religious forms,¯[161] their connection with reason; and seeing that is a more difficult task than declaring something to be senseless.

159. *L adds, similar in W (1827?):* The fact that a human being passes over into this [new sensible] shape is now combined with [the thought of] morality, or of merit.

160. *W₂ (1831) reads:* When God is worshiped in human shape in the Christian religion, that is something altogether different; for the divine essence is there envisaged in the man who has suffered, died, risen again, and ascended to heaven. This is not humanity in its sensuous, immediate existence but a humanity that bears upon its face the shape of spirit. But it appears as the most monstrous contrast when the absolute has to be worshiped in the immediate finitude of human being; the latter is an even more inflexible singularization than is [the finitude of] the animal. For the human shape embodies the further demand of self-transcendence [*Erhebung*], and hence it seems repugnant that this demand should be debased into a sheer persistence in ordinary finitude.

161. *W (Var) reads:* We must learn to see in [all] religions that our object is not merely something senseless and irrational, that what matters more is to recognize what is true [in them],

Being-within-self is the essential stage, consisting in the progression from immediate, empirical singularity to the determination of essence, of essentiality; or to the representation or consciousness of substance, i.e., of a substantial power that governs the world, that causes everything to come about and be produced according to a rationally coherent pattern. About this substantial power we know only that it is something operating unconsciously; but just for that reason it is undivided efficacy, it has in it the characteristic of universality, it is the universal | power. For this to be made clear   468 to us, we need to recall at this point the efficacy, spirit, and soul of nature; in speaking this way we do not mean that the spirit of nature is a conscious spirit; we are not thereby thinking of anything conscious. The natural laws of plants and animals, of their organization and activity, are something devoid of consciousness. These laws are the substantial aspect of living organisms; they are their nature and their concept. This is what they are implicitly, the reason immanent in them, the living soul; but it is unconscious.

The human being is spirit, and one's vitality consists in spirit determining itself as soul, as the unity of what is living—a vitality which, in the unfolding of [a person's] organization, is simply one, permeating and supporting everything. This efficacy is present in the person so long as one lives, without one's knowing it or willing it, and yet one's living soul is the cause, i.e., the original thing [*Sache*]¹⁶² that makes it actual. The human being who is this very living soul knows nothing of this, does not will the circulation of the blood nor prescribe it, and yet one does it and the doing is one's own deed: the human being is the motive power that actualizes what takes place within its organization. This unconsciously operative rationality or unconsciously rational efficacy, the efficacy of nature, the ancients called νοῦς. Anaxagoras says that νοῦς rules the world.¹⁶³ But this

---

162. *W (Var) adds:* the substance

163. [*Ed.*] In the *Lectures on the History of Philosophy,* Hegel relies principally on the accounts of the pre-Socratics found in Aristotle. In one passage of the *Metaphysics* (984b15–22), Aristotle does attribute to Anaxagoras the view that "reason is present in nature, as in animals, as the cause of order," although he also asserts (985a18–21) that Anaxagoras only drags "reason" in to explain the creation of the world in a mechanical manner, when he does not know why something is "necessarily" so. See Aristotle, *Metaphysics,* ed. W. D. Ross (Oxford, 1924), 1:125–126. See also Aristotle, *De anima* A 2, and Plato, *Phaedo* 97b–99d.

rationality [is] not conscious. In more recent philosophy this rational efficacy has even been called intuiting; Schelling in particular designated God as intuiting intelligence.[164] ˜God is intelligence,˜[165] and reason, as intuiting, is the eternal creating of Nature—what is called preservation of nature, for creating and preserving are not to be separated. In finite intuition we are immersed in things; they occupy us fully. This immersion in objects prior to any representing, reflecting, and judging, is the lower level of consciousness. Reflecting upon them, arriving at representations, producing points of view from oneself and applying these to objects, judging—these things are no longer intuiting as such.

This, therefore, is the standpoint of substantiality or of intuiting—the very one that we presently have before us; it is just the one | that should be understood as the standpoint of "pantheism" in its proper sense—this Oriental knowing, consciousness, or thinking of this absolute unity, of the absolute substance and its internal efficacy, an efficacy in which everything particular or singular is only something transitory or ephemeral, and not genuine independence. This Oriental way of viewing things is opposed to that of the Occident: just as the sun sets in the west, so it is in the West that human being descends into itself, into its own subjectivity. In the West singularity is the main determination, so that the singular [consciousness] is what is independent. Whereas in Oriental consciousness the main determination is that the universal is what is genuinely independent, in Western consciousness the singularity of things and of human beings stands higher for us. The Occidental viewpoint can indeed go so far as to maintain that the finite and finite things are autonomous, i.e., absolute. The expression "pantheism" has the ambiguity that universality alway has. ῀Εν καὶ πᾶν means the one

469

164. [Ed.] Hegel is probably referring to Schelling's concept of intellectual intuition; further evidence to this effect is provided by the *Lectures on the History of Philosophy* 3:520–521 (cf. *Werke* 15:655). See F. W. J. Schelling, *System of Transcendental Idealism* (1800), trans. Peter Heath (Charlottesville, 1978), pp. 27–28; and *On University Studies*, trans. E. S. Morgan (Athens, Ohio, 1966), p. 49 (cf. Schelling, *Werke* 3:369–370, 5:255–256)—although God is not explicitly designated in these works as intuitive intelligence.

165. W *(Var)* reads: God, intelligence,

All, the All that remains utterly one; but πᾶν also means "every-thing," and hence the phrase passes over into a thoughtless, shoddy, unphilosophical view. Then one understands "pantheism" to mean that everything is God—the doctrine that "everything is God" [*Allesgötterei*], not the doctrine that "the All is God" [*Allgötterei*]. For in the doctrine that "the All is God," if God were the All there would be only one God; in the All the singular things are absorbed, they are merely accidental, or are only shadows or phantoms.[166] But philosophy is presumed to be "pantheism" in that first sense.[167] That is precisely the ambiguity of universality. If one takes it in the sense of a universality of reflection, then it is "allness" [*Allheit*], and allness is initially represented in such a way that the singular things remain independent. But the universality of thinking, substantial universality, is a unity with itself in which everything singular or particular is only something ideal, and has no true being.

On the one hand, this substantiality begins here. It is the basic determination, but *only* the basic determination, of our knowledge of God. The basis or ground, however, is not yet what is true. We say, "God is the absolute power, all actual being is only ideal within the absolute | power of God." Everything that ventures to say of   470
itself that it is, that it has actuality, is[168] only a moment in the absolute power of the absolute God. Only God is, only God is the one, genuine actuality. Even though it is not yet idea, this represen-tation of substantiality underlies the representation of God in our

166. W *(Var/1831?) adds:* They come and go, their being consists precisely in this, that it disappears.

167. [*Ed.*] It is not entirely clear to what "in that first sense" refers. In regard to the two senses of πᾶν, the first would in fact be the philosophical sense, namely, that the All "remains utterly one." But this conception is not for Hegel something which philosophy is "presumed" to hold; rather it is a necessary philosophical conclusion—even if not the highest conclusion. Consequently he would seem to be referring to the second of the two senses he distinguishes, the doctrine that "everything is God." It is doubtful that "more recent philosophy" could be accused of a literal deification of everything that is. Yet a consistent philosophy of the understanding (Enlightenment rationalism) is commonly reproached for identifying the cosmos—as the totality of nonsublated but subsisting finite things—with God; whereas for Hegel the quintessence of the concept of the All was just the *negativity* of the finite. On the charge of "cosmotheism," see below, nn. 172, 177.

168. W₂ *(Var) adds:* sublated, is

religion, too.[169] The "omnipresence of God" (to the extent that this is not an empty phrase) is just the way that this substantiality is expressed; substantiality is its ground. But these[170] expressions are babbled away senselessly or in mere rote memory; there is no seriousness about them, ⁻for one is serious only about what is in thought. When Spinoza grasped the omnipresence of God in thought, as substantiality, he was reproached with pantheism,[171] for one forgets straightway that when God is grasped as substance, as all-effective, i.e., as operative in everything, then precisely by this comprehension all things are annihilated inasmuch as God is verily what is operative in them.⁻[172] As soon as one ascribes true being to the finite, as soon as things are independent and God is excluded from them, then God is by no means omnipresent; for when one says God is omnipresent, then one is at the same time saying that God is actual.[173] But God is not alongside things, in the interstices, like the God of Epicurus;[174] instead God is actual in the things; but then the things are not actual. This is the ideality of things. But in

---

169. L (1827?) adds: But it is difficult to grasp this. Although the finite is said to have no authentic being, opponents of this way of thinking forget this and say, "Well then, everything is God"; the finite that has just been sublated they straightway take as authentic being.

170. W (Var) adds: profound

171. [Ed.] Hegel sees here as elsewhere a connection between the general Oriental principle of unity and Spinoza's concept of substance. See Spinoza, Ethics (1677), part I, esp. prop. 15.

172. Thus An; L and W (Var) read, one page previously: This is how theologians in particular speak; indeed they even censure Spinozism on these grounds, inasmuch as what is singular or particular has disappeared in the Spinozistic substance and no truth, no actuality, no being is attributed to it.

[Ed.] Hegel is probably referring especially to F. A. G. Tholuck, Die Lehre von der Sünde und vom Versöhner; oder, Die wahre Weihe des Zweiflers, 2d ed. (Hamburg, 1825), p. 231, where Hegel's name was linked with those of Spinoza, Fichte, and the Eleatics as exponents of "pantheism of the concept," as distinct from "pantheism of the imagination" (Schelling) and "pantheism of feeling" (the mystics). The problem of interpreting Spinoza to which Hegel refers is more clearly dealt with by Jacobi than by Tholuck. Jacobi regards the argument—advanced by Hegel among others— that Spinoza is not an atheist but an acosmist (because he does not deny the existence of God but of the world) to be a mere play on words, and himself terms Spinoza a cosmotheist. On Spinoza's acosmism see Vol. 1:377, n. 27.

173. W₂ (Var) adds: and things are not.

174. [Ed.] Hegel is referring to the Epicurean doctrine that the gods live in the intermundia, the spaces between the different worlds. See Cicero, De divinatione 2.17, and De natura deorum 1.18.

this feeble thinking, one concludes that therefore the things are God, i.e., they are and remain insurmountably preserved, as an insurmountable actuality. So if we are serious when we say "God is omnipresent," | then God must have a truth for spirit, for the mind, for thought, and spirit must have an interest in this issue.[175]   471

Jacobi said of Spinozism that it is atheism,[176] he attacked it most violently, and yet this very Jacobi himself said: "God is the being in all determinate being."[177] This being, however, is nothing else but substance. But by the very fact that God is the affirmative, the singular thing is not the affirmative but is only what is ideal, what is sublated. Spinozistic philosophy was the philosophy of substantiality, not of pantheism; "pantheism" is a poor expression, because in it there is the possible misunderstanding that πᾶν be taken as a collective totality [Allesheit], not as universality [Allgemeinheit].

In all higher religions, but particularly in the Christian religion, God is the one and absolute substance; but at the same time God is also subject, and that is something more. Just as the human being has personality, there enters into God the character of subjectivity, personality, spirit, absolute spirit. That is a higher determination, although spirit remains nevertheless substance, the one substance. This abstract substance, the ultimate element of Spinoza's philosophy, this substance that is thought, that only is for thinking, cannot be the content of a folk religion; it cannot be the belief of a concrete spirit.[178] Concrete spirit supplies what is lacking, and the deficiency is that subjectivity, i.e., spirituality, is lacking. But at this point, at the level of nature religion which we are now dealing with, this spirituality is not yet spirituality as such, it is not yet a spirituality that is thought or universal; instead it is sensible and immediate spirituality. Here it is a human being as a sensible, external, immediate spirituality: a [particular] human being.

175. L, W (Var/1831?) add: God is the persisting of all things.

176. [Ed.] See Jacobi, Werke 4/1:216, also his Preface to Vol. 4 (pp. xxxvi–vii), where he says cosmotheism is just the same thing as atheism, which he defines (pp. 216–219) as the belief in a supreme being but one that acts only according to necessity. Thus Hegel's and Jacobi's concepts of atheism are different.

177. [Ed.] Jacobi, Briefe, p. 61 (Werke 4/1:87). Jacobi, however, is not representing his own view here but that of Spinoza, which he criticizes. See 1824 lectures, n. 76.

178. L (1827?) adds, similar in W: Spirit is concrete. It is only abstract thinking that sticks to this one-sided determinateness of substance.

472 This substantiality known in its truth is subjectivity inwardly, and thereby this pure substantiality includes spirituality; at the standpoint of immediacy, however, there is not yet self-knowing spirituality, but instead spirituality in an immediate | mode, though in the shape of a particular human being.[179] [180]And if this human being abides within itself (in contrast with this substance, the universal substance), then when the question arises how a human individual can be represented as universal substance, we must recall what was stated above:[181] that as living substantiality the human being is after all this inwardly substantial actuality, an actuality determined by one's corporeality. It must be possible to think that in this vitality life is substantially effective within one.

This standpoint contains the universal substantiality in an actual shape. Here therefore is found the view that it is in mediation, in preoccupation with self or deep absorption within self, that a person is the universal substance, not just (let us say) in terms of his vitality; ¯instead,¯[182] the νοῦς [is] then posited as center, but in such a way that the νοῦς within does not become conscious of itself in that person's character or development. This substantiality of the νοῦς, this deep absorption represented in one individual, is not the meditation of a king who has before him in his consciousness the administration of his realm; it is to be represented in such a way that this absorption within the self, this abstract thinking in itself, *is* the effective substantiality, is the creating and preserving of the world. This is the standpoint of the Buddhist and Lamaist religion.

There are three Dalai Lamas: in Lesser Tibet, in Greater Tibet, and in southeastern Siberia, in the mountain valleys of the Asian plateau from which Genghis Khan set out.[183] It makes no difference that there are multiple high lamas, and that they are also the superiors of religious orders that dedicate themselves to a life of withdrawal, and that others are held in honor comparable to that of the Dalai

179. W₂ (Var) adds: of an empirical, single consciousness.
180. In B's margin: 29 June 1827
181. [Ed.] See above, pp. 531–532.
182. W (Var) reads: but rather in the immersion within self or in the center of νοῦς;
183. [Ed.] Hegel here erroneously calls all the high lamas Dalai Lamas. By this he means the Dalai Lama from Lhasa (an incarnation of Avalokiteshvara), the Panchen Lama (an incarnation of Buddha Amitabha) in Tashilumpo and, presumably, the chief

Lama. Here the subjective shape is not yet exclusive; only with the penetration of spirituality, of subjectivity and of substance, is God essentially One. Thus here the substance is indeed one, but the subjectivity and the shapes are multiple, and | it is immediately 473 implicit in them that they are multiple. For in its relationship to substantiality this configuration itself is, to be sure, represented as something essential, but also at the same time as something accidental. Antithesis or contradiction first emerges in consciousness and volition, in particular insight; hence there cannot be multiple worldly sovereigns in one land, but there can well be multiple Dalai Lamas. But although this spiritual efficacy does indeed have a spiritual form for its existence and its shape, it is still only efficacy of substance, and not a conscious efficacy, a conscious will.

There is a distinction between Buddhism and Lamaism; but this account is common to both.[184] It is said of Fo[185] that eight thousand times he has incarnated himself ⌐in existence as a human being.⌐[186] ⌐Europeans have hardly ever come to where the great

---

of the Khutuktus. For Hegel's knowledge of the Panchen Lama, see below, n. 188; the report by Samuel Turner referred to there also mentions a visit by the Dalai Lama to the Panchen Lama. On the chief of the Khutuktus (legates of the Dalai Lama) see *Allgemeine Historie* 7:219–220. In Hegel's day the terms Greater Tibet (*Gross-Tibet*) and Lesser Tibet (*Klein-Tibet*) were used with a variety of meanings; by "Greater Tibet" Hegel also understands the area surrounding Lhasa, whereas in the *Allgemeine Historie* the term "Greater Tibet" is equated with Bhutan.

184. *W (1831) adds:* and those who worship Fo and Buddha worship the Dalai Lama also. The latter is worshiped, however, more under the form of someone deceased, but one who is also present under [the form of] his successors.

185. [*Ed.*] According to the *Allgemeine Historie* 6:360, the disciples of Fo claimed that their teacher had been born eight thousand times, but in animal as well as in human form. Cf. *Mémoires concernant les Chinois* 5:59.

186. *W (Var) reads:* and been present in the actual existence of a human being.
W_2 *(1831) continues:* Such are the basic determinations that follow from what is here the divine nature, and which are all that follow from it, since the divine nature itself has not got beyond the undeveloped abstraction of the tranquil being-within-self that lacks all determinacy. Consequently any further shaping or representation [of it] is surrendered, partly to the contingency of empirical historical events and partly to that of the imagination; the details belong to a description of the countless, confused products of the imagination concerning the adventures and destinies of these deities, and of their friends and disciples, and yield material that has but little interest or value so far as its inner substance is concerned, and which (as we have already indicated) has not the interest of the concept.[a]

In regard to the cultus too, we are not concerned here with outward ceremonies

474   lama in China lives, | whereas (about 1770) Englishmen visited the one in Lesser Tibet.[187] From the English emissary, Turner, we have an account[188] of the lama in Lesser Tibet; the lama was a child two or three years of age whose predecessor had died of smallpox on a journey to Beijing, where he had been summoned by the Chinese emperor; the lama was rediscovered in a two-year-old child. Acting on this child's behalf in matters of governance, there was a regent, the minister of the previous Dalai Lama, known as his cupbearer.[189] That child was indeed still nursing, but was a lively spirited child who conducted himself with all possible dignity and propriety, and seemed already to have a consciousness of his high office.[190] And the emissaries could not adequately praise the regent—and his associates—for the noble disposition, insight, dignity, and dispas-

---

and customs. All we have to describe is the essential element, namely, how being-within-self, the principle of this stage, appears in the actual self-consciousness [of the worshipers].

[Ed.] [a]Cf. n. 151.

187. *An reads (in place of first clause):* The Chinese keep Europeans away from their sovereign domain, and so from Greater Tibet. *W₁ (1831) reads, similar in W₂:* There are three principal lamas. The first, or Dalai Lama, is to be found in Lhasa, to the north of the Himalayas, where Europeans have not yet come, since this city is indeed within Chinese territory. Then there is another lama in Lesser Tibet, in Tashilumpo, in the neighborhood of Nepal. *L (1827?) adds:* From reports about the Dalai Lama, he could be regarded as in the main a charlatan, who takes advantage of these peoples. The English, however, found matters quite otherwise.

[Ed.] On the principal lamas and the geographical terms, see above, n. 183. The *Allgemeine Historie* 7:222 speaks of a Capuchin friar, Brother Horace, as having paid a number of visits to the Dalai Lama, but this seems to have escaped Hegel's attention.

188. [Ed.] See Samuel Turner, "Copy of an Account Given by Mr. Turner, of His Interview with Teeshoo Lama," *Asiatic Researches* 1:197–205. The "cupbearer" is referred to in another narrative by Turner, "An Account of a Journey to Tibet," *Asiatic Researches* 1:207–220, in which he describes a journey by Poorungeer to Tashilumpo, although it is clear that the cupbearer and the regent are two different persons. The information that the young lama's predecessor had died of smallpox on a journey to Beijing and that the young lama was still nursing cannot have come from these accounts, but rather from an edited version of Turner's accounts in Harnisch, *Die wichtigsten Reisen* 6:343–345, 358–359. Hegel may also have been familiar with Turner's monograph on his journeys published in London in 1800.

189. *W₁ (1831) adds:* Lastly there is yet a third lama living in Mongolia.

190. *In An's margin:* It is absurd to think that this is a case of priestly deception and to regard the Dalai Lamas as charlatans. As soon as a Dalai Lama dies, the world spirit passes into another human individual, and the only difficulty then is to locate

sionate tranquillity that the child possessed. The previous lama had also been an insightful, dignified, and noble man.[191]

We have indicated the relevance of the fact that the substance is, as it were, present in particular in one individual, that it has concentrated itself in him in order to show itself outwardly. This substantial efficacy is what is universally effective in the world, this substance is the universal νοῦς; and it is not such a very different matter to suppose that the latter has its existence in one human being | in particular, that it is present to and for other people in a sensible, external manner. Here we will let these determinations stand. We are still at the standpoint of the substantiality that is indeed necessarily bound up with subjectivity, with spirituality; but here what is spiritual is still in immediate, sensible existence, and this subjectivity is still an immediate subjectivity. The standpoint of substantiality also constitutes the foundation of what is to follow, and we are not yet ready to abandon it; but we can now pass over to the third form.

475

3. The Hindu Religion[192]

⌐This is the third form of religion.⌐[193] It is defined in such a way that here the substantiality is found in the totality of its externality; it

---

and identify him; a few external traits serve this purpose.[a] Cf. W_1 (Var): For when a Dalai Lama dies, the god has for a moment withdrawn his personal presence from humanity; but then he immediately appears in another human shape, and he has only to be sought out again, as he can be known by certain signs.

[Ed.] [a]This reference was probably drawn from the *Allgemeine Historie* 7:217. In any event, the information transmitted by Strauss that the Lama is recognized by facial lines shows that Hegel was acquainted with other regulations governing the succession. See 1831 *Excerpts*, n. 54.

191. L, W_2 (1827/1831?) add: There is, however, an inner consistency in the fact that an individual in whom the [divine] substance has become concentrated should outwardly display this worthy, noble demeanor.

192. [Ed.] In 1827 Hegel does not appear to have provided a philosophical designation for Hinduism; he simply refers to it as *die indische Religion,* rather than as *die Religion der Phantasie* as in 1824. This may be because he now views Hinduism as having two primary characteristics: the unity of substance and the multiplicity of powers—and it is only with reference to the latter that Hindu phantasy comes into play. In 1831 primary emphasis is placed on the first characteristic since Hinduism is defined as "the religion of abstract unity"; thus 1827 plays a transitional role between 1824 and 1831. However, 1827 follows 1824 in treating Hinduism after Buddhism, whereas in 1831 the sequence is reversed. The decisive advance of religious con-

sciousness to substantiality is still accredited to Buddhism. The German term *Phantasie* is translated by the English variant spelling "phantasy" in order to convey the sense of visionary, fanciful imagination, as distinguished from that of an unreal mental image or illusion. Hegel's *die indische Religion* is rendered as "Hinduism" or "Hindu religion." Whereas in the preceding section, on Buddhism, we have consistently translated *Insichsein* as "being-within-self," in the present section we have alternated between this rendering and "self-containment," which is more appropriate when the reference is to the Hindu concept of Brahman as impersonal metaphysical substance.

193. *W₂ (1831) reads:* The second main form of pantheism, when this latter actually appears as religion, is still within the sphere of this same principle of the one substantive power, in which all that we see around us, and even human freedom itself, is only something negative or accidental. We saw that the substantive power, in its first form, is known as the multitude and range of essential determinations, and not known as what is in its own self spiritual. The question immediately arises, therefore, how this power is determined in its own self, and what its content is. Self-consciousness cannot, like the abstractly thinking understanding, confine itself in religion to the representational image of the power that is known only as an aggregate of determinations that merely *are*. For then the power is not yet known as real unity, subsisting by itself, it is not yet known as principle. The opposite of this way of defining it is for the manifold determinateness to be taken back into the unity of self-determination. This concentration of self-determining contains the beginning of spirituality.

1. As self-determining, and not merely as a multitude of rules, the universal is thought, and exists as thought. It is in our thinking alone that nature, the power that brings forth everything, exists as the universal, as this one essence, as this one power that is for itself. What we have before us in nature is this universal, but not *as* universal. What is true in nature is brought into prominence on its own account in our thinking as idea or, more abstractly, as universal. In its own self, however, universality is thought; and, as self-determining, it is the source of all determining. But at the stage where we now are, the stage where the universal emerges for the first time as what is determinative (or as principle), the universal is not yet spirit but abstract universality generally. Being known as thought in this way, the universal remains as such shut up within itself. It is the source of all power, but it does not externalize or express itself as such.

2. The act of differentiating and fully developing the difference belongs to spirit. The system of this full development includes both the concrete unfolding of thought on its own account and the unfolding which, as appearance, is both nature and the spiritual world. But since the principle that comes on the scene at this stage has not yet reached the point where this unfolding could occur within the principle itself—since, on the contrary, it is held fast in a simple, abstract concentration—the unfolding and the richness of the actual idea falls outside the principle, and consequently differentiation and manifoldness are abandoned to the wildest externality of phantasy. The particularization of the universal appears in a plurality of independent powers.

3. This multiplicity or wild dispersal of powers is [finally] taken back again into the initial unity. In terms of the idea, this retrieval, this concentration of thought, would consummate the moment of spirituality if the initial, universal mode of thinking were to make itself inwardly accessible to differentiation and were known inwardly as the act of retrieval. On the foundation of abstract thought, however, the retrieval

is represented and known in and by this externality, by the totality of the world. The first thing that we find here, therefore, is this same substantiality in which everything | else, the determinate and 476 particular, the subject, is only something accidental, is even mortal. But the second thing, the additional aspect, is the concrete, the richness of the world, the particularizing of that universal substance which, with reference to the substance | or the universal power, also 477 represents itself for consciousness; i.e., it is both spiritual power and natural power. The result is that those distinctions are also known as belonging to the absolute, those powers appearing in one aspect as particular and independent, but at the same time vanishing, being consumed, and standing under that initial unity, under the universal being-within-self of the initial substantiality.

⁻Here, therefore, the horizon is enlarged; we have here the totality. The viewpoint is concrete; that is the necessary progress. | We still have substance as this one essential power; but the other 478 aspect is the concrete, what previously was, in this way or that, nothing but a contingent element. What is more determinately concrete is in the first place this, that the idea is one, it is immediate and identical with self. But just as the One is God, the absolute power, so also in the second place the idea differentiates itself internally; it particularizes itself, and these particularizations yield distinct, particular configurations or powers. The third aspect is that these particular configurations, these spiritual powers of nature, are represented as returned into and contained by the One. We have here an intelligible realm that particularizes itself, arrives at subsistence,

---

itself remains devoid of spirit. Nothing is lacking here as far as the moments of the idea of spirit are concerned; the idea of rationality is present in this advance. But these moments do not constitute spirit; the unfolding is not so consummated as to yield spirit, because the determinations remain merely universal. There is merely a perpetual return to that universality which is self-active but which is held fast in the abstraction of self-determining. Thus we have the abstract One and the wildness of unrestrained phantasy, which is, of course, known to remain identical with the first [principle] but which does not expand into the concrete unity of the spiritual. The unity of the intelligible realm achieves its specific permanence; but this last does not become absolutely free, for it remains confined within the universal substance.

But just because the unfolding does not yet truly return to the concept and is not yet inwardly taken back by the concept, it still retains its immediacy along with its return into the substance.

but does not become absolutely free on its own account, being instead contained by the universal substance. The foundation for rational development is present here, but only in its most general characteristics.

a. The One Substance

A more precise cognition of this standpoint specifies it as the standpoint of the Hindu religion.⁻¹⁹⁴ In Hinduism there is just this one

194. *W (1831) reads:* Subjectivity is inward power, as the connection of infinite negativity with itself; it is not merely implicit power—on the contrary, in subjectivity God is for the first time posited as power. Of course, these ways of characterizing it have to be distinguished from one another, and are of particular importance in relation both to the ensuing concepts of God and also to an understanding of the preceding ones. We must therefore consider them more closely.

Both in religion generally and in the wholly immediate and crudest religion of nature, power in general is the fundamental determination, as the infinitude which the finite, as sublated, posits within itself. And insofar as this is represented as outside the finite, is represented as *existing,* it nevertheless comes to be posited only as something that has emerged from the finite as from its ground. The determination that is all-important here is that the power is posited to begin with simply as the ground of the particular configurations or existences, and the relationship of the self-contained essence to these existences is that of substantiality [to what is accidental]. Thus it is merely implicit power or power lying within the existences; and as self-contained essence or as substance, it is posited solely as the simple and abstract, so that the determinations or differentiae are represented as being configurations existing in their own right outside it. This self-contained essence may indeed also be represented as self-sufficient, in the way that Brahman is self-thinking. Brahman is the universal soul; in creating, it goes forth out of itself as a breath, it contemplates itself, and from then on it is for itself. But this does not at the same time eliminate its abstract simplicity, for the moments, i.e., the universality of Brahman as such and the "I" for which that universality is, are not reciprocally determined, and their relation itself is therefore simple. Thus, as having being abstractly for itself, Brahman is, of course, the power and the ground of existences, and everything has emerged from it, just as—in saying to themselves, "I am Brahman"—they are all returned to it and have disappeared in it. They are either outside it (exist independently) or within it (have disappeared); there is only the relationship of these two extremes. But being posited as differentiated determinations, they appear as independent entities outside Brahman, because it is at first abstract, not inwardly concrete.

Posited only implicitly in this way, power acts inwardly without appearing as [external] efficacy. I appear as power insofar as I am cause, and more specifically insofar as I am subject—whenever I throw a stone, etc. But power that has being implicitly operates in a universal manner, without this universality being a subject on its own account. The laws of nature, for instance, are this universal mode of operation, grasped in its true character.

W₁ (Ed) continues: We have already indicated how this standpoint is manifest, how it appears in its existence.

substantiality, and it is, of course, present as pure thinking, pure being-within-self, and this self-containment is distinguished from the multiplicity of things; it is external to particularization, so that it does not have its existence or its reality as such in the particular powers. This is not the way God has his existence or determinate being in the Son, for this being-within-self instead remains abstractly inward, purely by itself, as abstract power; but at the same time it is power over everything, and the particularization or distinction falls outside of this being-within-self. But because it is abstract in this way, the self-containment must in turn have an existence, and insofar as this existence itself is still immediate, still outside the distinction, it is not authentically divine existence, but is once more an immediate existence in the concretely existing, immediate human spirit. | 479

b. The Multiplicity of Powers

That is the first aspect; the second then is the distinction into many powers, and these many powers [depicted] as a plurality of deities— an unbridled polytheism that has not yet progressed to the beauty of figure. These are not yet the beautiful deities of Greek religion; ⁻⁻nor is the prose of our understanding present here to any great extent. In part the powers are objects such as sun, moon, mountains, or rivers; or they are greater abstractions such as generation, perishing, ˉchange of shape.⁻¹⁹⁵ These are the particular powers that maintain themselves externally to self-contained being, so that they are not yet taken up into spirit, are not yet posited as truly ideal, but also are not yet distinct from spirit. The substance is not yet spiritual,⁻⁻¹⁹⁶ for the powers are not yet posited outside of spirit. They are not yet considered by understanding, but neither are they

195. W (Var) reads: change, taking shape.
196. W₂ (MiscP) reads: Only when the prose of thinking has permeated all relationships, so that we humans behave everywhere in an abstractly thoughtful fashion, do we speak of external things. At this stage, on the contrary, thinking is only this substance, only this presence to self; it is not yet applied and has not yet permeated humanity as a whole. The particular powers, which are partly objects such as sun, mountains, rivers, or else are greater abstractions such as generation, perishing, change, taking shape, etc., are not yet taken up into spirit, not yet genuinely posited as ideal. But they are also not yet distinguished from spirit by the understanding, for pure being is still concentrated in that self-containment of substance which is not yet spiritual substance,

images of a beautiful imagination [*schöne Phantasie*]; they are merely fanciful [*phantastisch*]. They are particular powers, although it is a wild particularity in which there is no system but only intimations of what is understandable and necessary, echoes of understood moments but still no understandable totality or systematization, much less a rational one; instead only a multiplicity in a colorful throng. The specification that the particular is grasped with understanding is not yet present.

⌐We say of natural objects that they are things that have external being, such as sun, moon, ocean, and the like.⌐[197] But here pure | being is not concentrated in that self-contained being. At this stage thinking has not yet permeated ⌐thought as a whole,⌐[198] spirit as a whole. ⌐Only the prose in which thinking is universal speaks of universal things. When we consider the world, we think it; we say that the objects are; that is their category, that they are external things; hence they are grasped prosaically. But at this stage thinking is the substance, the in-itself. Thinking is not yet applied; the natural powers are not yet grasped in categories;⌐[199] categories such as "independence" and "thing" are not yet in command.[200]

Furthermore, the objective content is not grasped in the mode of beauty either; i.e., these powers, universal natural objects or the powers of the soul such as love, are not yet grasped as beautiful figures. Moreover, there belongs to beauty of figure that free sub-

480

---

197. *W₁ (Var) reads:* We say of a universal natural entity (and likewise of universal natural powers) that such a thing *is;* for example, the sun is. These are externally existent beings, are "things": to say something is a "thing" is to predicate this reflected being of it.

198. *Thus B; W₁ (Var) reads:* humanity as a whole

199. *W₁ (Var) reads:* The understanding says that they are, that we think them and we think them as distinct from ourselves; this is their predicate, their category, this is how they are comprehended in prosaic terms. Not until prose or thinking has permeated all relationships, so that human beings everywhere behave in an abstractly thinking fashion, do they speak of external things. Here, on the contrary, thinking is only this substance, this presence to self; thinking is not yet applied; objects are not yet regarded in the form of this category, as external, as cohering, as cause and effect;

200. *L (1827?) adds, similar in W₁:* Independence of the natural powers is spiritual personality; although spirit has not yet advanced to [the level of] the understanding, they are nonetheless independent, inasmuch as they are personified.

jectivity which, even in the sensible, in determinate being, both is free and knows itself freely. For the beautiful is essentially the spiritual that expresses itself sensibly, that shows itself in a sensible mode of determinate being, but in such a way that this being is thoroughly and totally permeated by the spiritual, in such a way that the sensible does not have being on its own account, but only has complete significance within the spiritual and through the spiritual, and is the *sign* of the spiritual. This is genuine beauty—that the sensible does not have being on its own account, does not exhibit its own self but rather directly represents as itself something other than it itself is. In the living human being, in the human countenance, there are many external influences that inhibit pure idealization, this subsumption of the corporeal and sensible under the spiritual. | This relationship [i.e., the mode of beauty] is not yet present here, and so, because the spiritual is at first still present only in this abstract characteristic of substantiality, the relationship has also not developed into these particularizations or particular powers; for the substantiality is still by itself, and has not yet permeated or overcome this particularization, these its particularities, and the sensible, natural mode of being. The substance is, as it were, a universal space that has not yet organized what fills it, namely, the particularization that has proceeded from it, has not yet idealized this and subordinated it to itself. Because these powers are not at the same time represented in a universal way, because they are present as independent only for representation but are not thought, the independence attributed to them is one that human beings have in principle. The highest determination that has been grasped is spiritual determination; those powers are personified, but in a fanciful mode, not in a beautiful mode.

481

The substance is the foundation, so that the distinctions emerge or appear from the One as independent deities, as universal powers, but in such a way that, besides being independent, these deities also resolve themselves again into the unity. This shocking inconsistency is present here and permeates the entire world of images. On the one hand, the independence of the deities is represented; on the other it is shown that they are the One, through which their particular shape and nature, their particularity, once again vanishes. At the same time this One or this substance is not just objectively known, and does not yet have this [abstract] objectivity for thinking; instead the One has essential existence[201] as the human being who elevates himself to this abstraction, i.e., it has existence as human consciousness.

[202]The next feature is the representation of the objective content of this standpoint. The basic content is the one, simple, absolute substance; this is what the Hindus call "Brahman" and "Brahmā"; "Brahman" [Brahm, Brahman] is neuter or is, as we say, "the divinity"; "Brahmā" [Brahma] expresses the universal essence more as a person or subject. Incidentally, this is a distinction that is not consistently observed, and indeed in the different grammatical cases it disappears | of its own accord, for masculine and neuter have many cases the same.[203] [204]

The distinctions also emerge with respect to this simple substance, and ˉthese distinctions occur in such a wayˉ[205] that they are determined according to the instinct of the concept, that precisely the basic determination and development of the concept is present. The first is the totality in general as One, taken quite abstractly; it emerges here as one of three, it is downgraded, and what embraces the three is represented as distinct from this initial One. The second is determinacy or distinction in general, and the third is in accord with genuine determination, so that the distinctions are led back into the unity, the concrete unity. ˉThis formless unity is Brahman;

482

---

201. W₁ (Var) adds: in human consciousness

202. In B's margin: 2 July 1827

203. L (1827?) adds, similar in W: Moreover, no great stress should be laid on the distinction in this regard either, since Brahmā is only superficially personified, and the content of Brahman remains, as we said, this simple substance.

204. [Ed.] Wilhelm von Humboldt drew attention to the distinction, and the fact that it is often obscured in Sanskrit grammar, in a paper read to the Berlin Academy of Sciences on 30 June 1825 and again on 15 June 1826. See Über die unter dem Namen Bhagavad-Gītā bekannte Episode des Mahā-Bhārata (Berlin, 1826), pp. 22, 40–41. The problem was also discussed by A. W. Schlegel in a letter reproduced in his journal Indische Bibliothek 2, no. 4 (Bonn, 1827): 420–424. See also Hegel's review of Humboldt's paper in Jahrbücher für wissenschaftliche Kritik, 1827, p. 1476 (Berliner Schriften, pp. 136 ff.).

205. W (Var) reads: it is noteworthy that the way in which these distinctions occur is

according to its determinacy it is three in unity.⁻²⁰⁶ ⁻When we express it more precisely, the second moment is one of distinct powers. This triad is only a unity; distinction has no | right as against the absolute unity, and so it can be called the eternal goodness; rightness or justice [*Gerechtigkeit*] accrues to the distinction from the fact that [though] what subsists [initially] is not, it attains its right, it becomes changed, it becomes a particular determinacy.⁻²⁰⁷ ⁻The triad as totality, which is a whole and a unity, the Hindus call Trimurti. "Murti" means "soul," or in general every emanation, everything spiritual; the Trimurti is the three essences.⁻²⁰⁸

483

The first, which is ⁻the simple substance,⁻²⁰⁹ is what is called Brahmā or Brahman; but we also meet with Parabrahmā, that which

206. L *(Var) reads (at the end of this paragraph), similar in W (at this point):* This threefold nature of the absolute, grasped according to its abstract form or when it is merely formal, is sheer Brahman, the empty essence; in its determinateness it is three, but only within a unity, so that this triad is only a unity.

207. W *(Var) reads:* If we define this more closely and speak of it under another form, the second [point] means that there are distinctions, different powers; but the distinct power has no right as against the one substance, the absolute unity; and since it has no right, we can call it eternal goodness that what is determinate [is allowed to] exist, too—it is a manifestation of the divine that even what has been distinguished [i.e., set apart] should attain the state that it *is*. This is the goodness by virtue of which what the power posits as show or semblance obtains momentary being. It is absorbed in the power, but goodness allows it to subsist.

Upon this second [point] follows the third, namely the rightness or justice through which—[though] the subsistent determinate [initially] is not—the finite attains to its end, its destiny, its right, which is to be changed, to be transformed always into another determinateness; this is justice in general. Becoming, perishing, and generation all belong to it in abstract fashion; even nonbeing has no right, for it is an abstract determination over against being and is itself the passing over into unity.

208. W *(1831) reads:* This totality, which is unity or a whole, is what the Hindus call Trimurti (*murti* = shape, and all emanations of the absolute are called *murti*). This highest being [is] inwardly differentiated in such a way that it has these three determinations within it.

This trinity in unity is indisputably the most striking and greatest feature in Hindu mythology. We cannot call them persons, for they lack spiritual subjectivity as a fundamental determination. But to Europeans it must have been in the highest degree astonishing to encounter this lofty principle of the Christian religion here; we shall become acquainted with it in its truth later on, and we shall see that spirit as concrete must necessarily be grasped as triune.

[*Ed.*] The 1831 lectures give the correct definition of the Sanskrit term *murti*. Hegel's source or sources are not known.

209. W *(Var) reads:* the One, the one substance,

is above Brahmā—a complicated business! All sorts of stories are told of Brahmā insofar as he is subject; but thought or reflection once again goes beyond such a characterization as Brahmā in which something determinate is grasped[210]; it goes beyond what is just determined as one of these three and makes for itself that higher aspect which is determined by its contrast with what is other. Insofar as Brahmā or Brahman is utterly substance and in turn appears only as one alongside another, it is the requirement of thought to have yet a higher, Parabrahmā—but then one cannot say in what determinate relation such forms stand to one another.

Brahmā is what is grasped as the substance from which everything proceeds or is begotten; this is the power that has brought forth or created everything. But inasmuch as the one substance (or the One) is thus the abstract power, | it also equally appears as what is inert, as formless, inactive matter. Here, then, we have in particular the formative activity, as we would express it. Because it is only the One, the one substance is the formless—and this is also one way in which it becomes apparent that substantiality is not satisfied—namely because form is not present. Thus Brahman, the One, the self-same essence, appears as something inert, indeed appears as begetter but at the same time behaves passively, as if it were the feminine principle. Vishnu says: Brahman is my uterus,[211] in which I sow my seed, so that everything is procreated. [212]Everything goes forth from Brahmā: gods, world, human beings; but it is at once apparent that this One is inactive, is what is inert.[213]

This distinction also carries over into the different cosmogonies or portrayals of the creation of the world. We should not suppose, by the way, that the Hindus have a definite story or a firmly established representation of creation such as we possess ˉfrom the Jewish books;ˉ[214] instead, everyone there—poet, seer, or prophet—

484

210. *W₂ (Var) adds:* as one of these three
211. *W (Var) adds:* the mere recipient
212. *Precedes in L (1827?), similar in W:* Even in the definition "God is essence," the principle of movement, of bringing forth, is not contained; it involves no activity.
213. [*Ed.*] See James Mill, *The History of British India,* 3 vols. (London, 1817), 1:232.
214. *W₁ (Var) reads:* in the Christian and Jewish religion;

constructs his own representation in personal fashion, by speculative immersion within himself. Hence there is nothing fixed, but instead everyone has a different viewpoint. This creation is [described] one way in the Code of Manu, but differently in the Vedas and other religious works[215]—each account has its own special version. In general, one cannot say that the Hindus maintain this or that about creation; for everything is always simply the view of one sage; the common element consists only in the basic features that we have presented. Thus in the Vedas a description of the world's creation is advanced in which Brahmā is alone in solitude, wholly by himself, and in which an essence that is then represented as something higher says to him that he should expand and beget himself. For a thousand years, however, Brahmā had been in no position to grasp his expansion; for he | had again receded into himself. Here Brahmā is indeed represented as world-creating, but because he is the One, because of being inactive and needing to be summoned by something other and higher, Brahmā is represented as what is formless.[216] Hence there is need for another. On the whole, Brahmā is this one, absolute substance.[217] | 486

Then the second [essence] is Vishnu or Krishna, i.e., the embodying of Brahman; this is the determinate being of preservation,

485

---

215. [Ed.] For the cosmogony of the Code of Manu and of the Vedas, see annotations a, e to n. 217; see also Alexander Dow, *The History of Hindostan, from the Earliest Accounts to the Death of Akbar*, 2 vols. (London, 1768), l:xlvi–xlix.

216. [Ed.] See Francis Buchanan, "On the Religion and Literature of the Burmas," *Asiatic Researches* 6:273–280.

217. *W (1831) adds:* As this simple activity, power is thought. In Hinduism this characteristic is the most prominent of all; it is the absolute foundation and is the One, Brahman. This form is in accordance with the logical development: first came the multiplicity of determinations, and the advance consists in the resumption of the determining into unity. That is the foundation. What still remains to be added is partly just historical, but partly it is the necessary development that follows from that principle.

As the active element, the simple power created the world. This creation is essentially a relating of thought to itself, a self-referring activity and not a finite one. This too is expressed in the Hindu ways of viewing the matter. They have a great number of cosmogonies, which are all more or less barbarous, and out of which nothing of a fixed character can be derived; [W_1: as was the case with the Jewish myths. W_2: there is not just one representation of the creation of the world, as in the Jewish and Christian religion.] In the Code of Manu, in the Vedas and Puranas, the cosmogonies are continually comprehended and presented differently; but there is always one feature essentially present in them, namely that this thinking, which is at home with itself, is the begetting of itself.

This infinitely profound and true feature constantly recurs in the various portrayals of the creation of the world. The Code of Manu begins as follows: "The Eternal with a single thought created the waters," and so on.[a] We also find that this pure activity is called "the Word," just as God is in the New Testament.[b] With the Jews of later times, e.g., Philo, σοφία is the first-created [being] that goes forth from the One.[c] The "Word" is held in very high esteem by the Hindus, it is the image of pure activity, something that has external, physical, finite being, but which does not abide. Instead it is only ideal, and disappears immediately in its externality. The Eternal created the waters, the record then says,[d] and deposited fructifying seed in them; this seed became a resplendent egg, and in it the eternal itself was born again as Brahmā. Brahmā is the progenitor of all spirits, of what exists and what does not exist. In this egg, the story goes, the great power remained inactive for a year; at the end of that time it divided the egg by thought, and created one part masculine and the other feminine. The masculine force is itself [W_2: begotten, and becomes again a begetter and] effective only when it has practiced strict meditation, i.e., when it has attained to the concentration of abstraction. Thought therefore is what brings forth, and what is brought forth is just that which brings forth, namely the unity of thinking with itself. The return of thinking to itself is found in other accounts too. In one of the Vedas (from which some fragments have for the first time been translated by Colebrooke[e]), a similar description of the first act of creation is to be found: "There was neither being nor nothing, neither above nor below, [W_2: neither death nor immortality,] but only the One enshrouded and dark. Outside of this One there existed nothing, and the One brooded by itself in solitude; through the energy of contemplation it brought forth a world out of itself; desire or impulse first formed itself in this thinking, and this was the original seed of all things."

Here again thinking is presented in its self-enclosed activity. The thinking is, however, further known as thinking in the self-conscious essence, in the human being who constitutes its actual existence. The Hindus could be reproached with having attributed a contingent existence to the One, since it is left to chance whether or not the individual raises itself to the abstract universal [W_2: to abstract self-consciousness]. But [this is unfair because] Brahman is immediately present in the caste of Brāhmans; it is their duty to read the Vedas and to withdraw into themselves. Reading the Vedas is the divine element (is God's very self), and so is prayer. The Vedas can even be read without taking in the sense, or in complete stupefaction; this stupefaction itself is the abstract unity of thought; the I and its pure intuitive activity is what is perfectly empty. Thus it is the Brāhmans in whom Brahman exists; through the reading of the Vedas Brahman is, [W_2: and human self-consciousness in the state of abstraction is Brahman itself].[f]

[Ed.] [a]See Institutes of Hindu Law (Calcutta, 1794), chap. 1, On the Creation, esp. pp. 1–2. [b]A probable reference to the cosmogony described by Alexander Dow (see above, n. 215). Hindu cosmogonies had already been compared with the creation by the Word, by William Jones, "On the Gods of Greece, Italy, and India," Asiatic Researches 1:244, although as Jones pointed out, in the case of the Code of Manu the creative activity is attributed to thought rather than word. [c]A probable reference to August Neander's treatment of Philo in Genetische Entwicklung der vornehmsten

the manifestation or appearance on earth that is quite completely developed, the appearing one, humanity, particular human beings. The Hindus enumerate many different instances of this incarnation. The general point is that here Brahmā appears as a human being. Nevertheless we still cannot say that it is Brahmā who appears as a human being; for this becoming-human is not posited as the bare form of Brahman. The vast poetic creations of the Hindus are relevant here.[218] The representations of these incarnations seem in part to contain resonances of historical events; it seems that there are princes and mighty kings among them, that they include great conquerors | who have given a new shape to the conditions of life, who are deities.[219] ⁻These deities are also the heroes of amorous tales.⁻[220]

487

The third [essence] is Shiva, i.e., Mahadeva[221]; this is [the moment of] change in general; the basic character is on the one hand the vast energy of life, and on the other the destroyer, the devastator, the wild energy of natural life. His principal symbol is therefore the bull

---

gnostischen Systeme (Berlin, 1818), p. 10. ᵈSee above, annotation a. ᵉSee H. T. Colebrooke, "On the Vedas," Asiatic Researches 8:404–405, where Colebrooke gives a translation of the Nāsadiya hymn from the eleventh chapter of the Rig Veda. In the part played by "darkness"and "desire," as portrayed in the hymn, Colebrooke sees an analogy to Hesiod, Theogony 116. ᶠOn the divinity of reading the Vedas, see esp. J. A. Dubois, Moeurs, institutions, et cérémonies des peuples de l'Inde (Paris, 1825) 1:186–187, a passage to which specific reference was made by P. von Bohlen, Das alte Indien (Königsberg, 1830), 2:13. The Brāhmans' duty to read the Vedas was supposedly assigned to them by the Supreme Being at the time they and the other castes were created (see Institutes of Hindu Law, p. 12). On reading them in a dull, thoughtless manner see H. T. Colebrooke, "On the Vēdas, or Sacred Writings of the Hindus," Asiatic Researches 8:390. On the immediate presence of Brahman in Brāhmans see Institutes of Hindu Law, p. 286.

218. W (Var/1831?) adds: Krishna is also Brahmā, Vishnu.

219. L (1827?) adds, similar in W: [W: and are thus described as deities.] The deeds of Krishna are conquests, and the way they happen is quite ungodlike.

220. W (Var) reads: Generally speaking, conquest and amours are the two aspects or the principal acts of the incarnations.

221. W (1831) adds: the great god, or Rudra, who ought to be the return into self. The first stage, Brahman, is the remote, self-enclosed unity. The second, Vishnu, is manifestation, life in human shape. (The moments of spirit are up to this point unmistakable.) The third stage ought to be the return to the first, in order that the unity should be posited as returning within itself. But it is just this third stage that is devoid of spirit; it is merely the category of becoming generally, or of generation and perishing.

on account of its strength, the image of natural virility but at the same time also the destroyer; the most general representation for it, however, is the lingam (something revered among the Greeks as the phallus), this symbol that most temples have—the innermost sanctum contains this image. Hence, as we said, the third aspect here is only change in general, procreation and destruction. [222]The authentic third aspect in the profound concept is spirit, the return of the One to itself, its coming-to-self; not just change, but change through which the [moment of] distinction is brought to reconciliation with the first [moment], and the duality is sublated.

In this religion, which still belongs to nature, this process of becoming is still grasped as sheer becoming, sheer change.[223] This distinction is essential and is grounded upon the whole standpoint. From the very standpoint of nature religion it is even necessary.

As we said, the distinctions presented are finally grasped as unity, as the Trimurti; and the Trimurti, not Brahmā itself, is grasped as the highest. But ⁻equality⁻[224] each person of the triad is also in turn taken alone, by itself, so that it is itself the totality, is the entire god.

It is noteworthy that the older portions of the Vedas do not speak of Vishnu, even less of Shiva; there Brahmā, the One, is God altogether alone. The distinctions of the Trimurti are determinations that are introduced only later.[225] ⁻There are also castes; one reveres

488

222. *Precedes in* W₂ *(1831), similar in* W₁ *(at the end of this paragraph):* Such are the three fundamental determinations. The whole is portrayed by a figure with three heads, again in a symbolical manner, and not beautifully.
   [*Ed.*] Again Hegel is probably referring to an illustration depicting the Trimurti, accompanying Creuzer's *Symbolik und Mythologie,* plate xxii, fig. 1. The Trimurti is also said to be represented by the image of three conjoined human heads, in the account of FitzClarence's journey in Harnisch, *Die wichtigsten Reisen,* vol. 7 (1825), pp. 60–61.
   223. *L (1827?) adds, similar in* W: It is not a change in the differentia, through which unity produces itself as the sublation of the difference into unity. Consciousness or spirit is also a change in the first or immediate unity. The other element is the primal division or judgment, the having of an other over against one. I know that I exist in such a way that, inasmuch as the other is for me, I have returned to myself in that other, I am within myself. But here, instead of being what reconciles, the third moment is only this wild play of begetting and destroying. W₂ *(1831) continues:* So the unfolding ends in a wild, delirious whirl.
   224. W *(Var) reads:* just as this is grasped as Trimurti, so
   225. [*Ed.*] This is probably derived from Colebrooke's "On the Vedas," *Asiatic Researches* 8:377–497, esp. pp. 494–495. See 1824 lectures, n. 258.

only Krishna, the other Shiva, and great strife arises from this.⁻²²⁶ ²²⁷The one called Vishnu says about himself in turn that he is everything, that he is the absolutely formative activity, that Brahman is the womb in which he engenders all. Indeed, he even goes on to state: "I am Brahman."²²⁸ Here the distinction is sublated. Likewise when Shiva ⁻avows that⁻²²⁹ he is the absolute totality, the fire in jewels, the luster in metal, the power in the male, the reason in the soul; he, too, is in turn Brahman.²³⁰

⁻Apart from these distinctions, the particular phenomena | and powers are further represented as both free and having being on their own account; but they are personified. Hence sun, moon, the Himalayas, the Ganges and the other rivers, are represented as persons; and similarly, particular subjective sentiments such as vengeance, or powers such as evil, are personified; everything is in confusion. Their being is a personification even if they are represented as animals; they are spoken of in human terms, and always as alive.²³¹ | The first bird to alight on the branch is the god of love; the cow and the ape enjoy great reverence. They do not have hospitals

489

490

226. *W (Var) reads:* The Hindus, moreover, are divided into many sects. Among many other differences the principal one is this, that some worship Vishnu and others Shiva. This is often the occasion of bloody conflicts; at festivals and fairs especially, disputes arise which cost thousands their lives.

[*Ed.*] This may be based on W. C. Seybold, *Ideen zur Theologie und Staatsverfassung des höhern Alterthums* (Tübingen, 1820), p. 45; see also Mill, *History of British India* 1:226.

227. *Precedes in W (Var):* Generally speaking these distinctions are to be understood as meaning that

228. [*Ed.*] See Mill, *History of British India* 1:232.

229. *W (Var) reads:* is brought on the scene speaking,

230. [*Ed.*] Hegel is obviously referring again here to the Atharvasira Upanishad; but most of the comparisons he lists in fact belong to the self-avowal of Krishna in the Bhagavad-Gita. He probably includes them here because he has already mentioned them in Part I (Vol. 1:376). On "the luster in metal" and "the reason in the soul" see *Bhagavad-Gita,* ed. A. Schlegel (Bonn, 1823), pp. 162 ff. (10.36, 22). The comparison to "the fire in jewels" is found elsewhere, serving as a reference to the Mahābhārata in the Mārkandēya-Purāna; it is not certain what Hegel's source is. See also 1824 lectures, n. 246.

L (1827?) adds, similar in W: In this way everything dissolves into one person, into one of these [three] distinctions, even the other two persons, along with the other powers, nature deities, and genii.

231. *L (1827?) adds, similar in W₁:* That the [divine] substance should also have animal form is a commonplace for the Hindus.

for sick people, but they do for sick cattle.[232] Even the god of heaven, Indra, stands far below Brahmā, Shiva, and Vishnu;[233] he in turn has many deities beneath him, even the stars. All of the particular powers in their peculiar natures attain this independence, although it is a vanishing independence.¯[234]

232. [Ed.] See Mill, History of British India 1:281, where a footnote refers to a report by Dr. Tennant to this effect, except that Tennant does not say there were no hospitals for the sick generally, but none "for the sick poor."

233. [Ed.] Hegel does not refer to the fact that this subordination of the old Vedic god of thunderstorm and of war, Indra, reflects the replacement of the old religion of the Vedas by Brahmanism, despite the fact that elsewhere he shows that he has a rudimentary knowledge of this development in the history of Hindu religion.

234. W (1831) reads: Apart from this main foundation and fundamental determination in the Hindu mythology, everything else is personified superficially through phantasy. Great natural objects, such as the Ganges, the sun, the Himalayas (which are in particular the dwelling place of Shiva), are identified with Brahman itself. Everything—love, deceit, theft, cunning, as well as the sensuous powers of nature in plants and animals, [W₂: so that substance has animal form]—is comprehended by phantasy [W₂: and represented as free on its own account]. Thus there arises an infinite world of deities of the particular powers and phenomena, which is known nonetheless to be subordinate to something above it. At the head of this world stands Indra, the god of the visible heavens. These gods are mutable and perishable, and subject to the supreme One; abstraction absorbs them. The power which humankind acquires by means of abstraction strikes them with terror; indeed, Vishvamitra even creates another Indra and other gods.[a]

W₂: Thus at one moment these particular spiritual and natural powers are regarded as gods subsisting independently, and at another moment [they are regarded] as vanishing [beings] whose nature it is to be submerged in the absolute unity, in substance, and again to arise out of it.

So the Hindus say that there have already been many thousand Indras, and there will be still more; in the same way the incarnations are posited as transient too.[b] Since the particular powers return into the substantive unity, the unity does not become concrete but remains abstract; and it also does not become concrete inasmuch as these determinacies emerge from it—rather they are phenomena defined as having their independence outside it.

W: To form an estimate of the number and value of these deities is out of the question here. There is nothing that partakes of a fixed shape, since the phantasy we are dealing with is totally lacking in determinacy. These configurations disappear again in the same way as they are created. Phantasy passes over from an ordinary external mode of existence to divinity, and this in turn reverts in like manner to what was its basis. It is impossible to speak of miracles here, for everything is a miracle, everything is crazy and is not determined by a rational nexus of thought categories. In any event much of it is symbolical.

[Ed.] [a]See below, n. 244. [b]See below, n. 255.

c. The Cultus

⁻Now we are going to speak of the cultus, of the relation of human beings to Brahman.⁻²³⁵ The absolute or highest cultus is that most complete emptying out of the human, the renunciation in which the Hindus relinquish all consciousness and willing, all passions and needs (nirvana), [or] this union with God in the mode of integral self-concentration (yoga). The sort of person who lives only in contemplation, who has renounced all worldly desires, is called a yogi. On the one hand the devotion of the Hindus, when concentrated within themselves, is a passing state like our devotion;⁻on the other hand, however, the Hindus make this abstraction into | the   491
character of their consciousness, and of their entire existence. [Their goal is] total indifference toward everything, and complete austerity. One essential determination is that, while it is the case for Hindus, as it is for us, that devotion is a momentary elevation after which one returns to one's former activity and interests, it is also the case that for them this abstraction also appears as something that persists for the whole of life, so that what prevails is total indifference toward everything ethical, toward all worthy human pursuits. In this state devoid of thought, in this pure egoism, the human being is Brahman itself. But when an Englishman²³⁶ asked such a person: "What is Brahman, this meditation? Do you have a temple for Brahman?" the reply was: "We revere one Brahmā. We have no temple for Brahmā, but only for Vishnu and Krishna, just as the Catholics have no church for God, but always just for a saint." (Canova pledged his great artistry to his native city, in order to build a magnificent church to the honor of God; but the clergy would not allow it, for it must belong to a saint.²³⁷) When one asks the Hindu what this absorption is called, however, the reply is: "When I direct

235. W_1 *(Var) reads:* The relationship of the subject to the absolute and especially to Brahman (which relationship is the cultus) will show more precisely what this Brahman properly is.
236. [*Ed.*] Francis Wilford, "An Essay on the Sacred Isles in the West," *Asiatic Researches* 11:125–126.
237. [*Ed.*] Hegel makes the same comparison in his Humboldt review, p. 1484 (*Berliner Schriften*, pp. 145–146; cf. pp. 708–709), citing official reports as his source. It has not been possible to identify them more precisely.

my devotion to the honor of some god, when I concentrate totally within myself, then I say inwardly to myself that I am Brahman itself, that I am the highest essence."[238] Pure being-with-myself is Brahman.[239]

[240]The highest point in this cultus is the state of being dead to the world, the making of this inward immobility of self into one's character or one's fixed principle. [241]Those who have attained this are | called yogis. There are distinct levels of yogis. An Englishman[242]

492

238. [Ed.] See above, n. 236.

239. W_1 (Var) reads: but on the other hand, the fact is that humans make this abstractness (which they initially attain only momentarily) into their character, the character of their entire consciousness, of their entire existence. Hence they do not just elevate themselves momentarily, but remain at this level, completely indifferent to ethical concerns, to the ties that bind us together as human, to society, to what merits their attention and involvement. One who remains at this abstract level, who renounces everything and is dead to the world in general, is a yogi.

One who inwardly concentrates oneself in this thoughtlessness, this emptiness, this pure selfhood, this pure presence to self, is Brahman. And the highest mode of the cultus for Hindus is to make this abstractness something completely habitual.

W_2 (1831 with 1827?) reads: The highest point to which one attains in the cultus is that union with God which consists in the annihilation and stupefaction of self-consciousness. This is not affirmative liberation and reconciliation, but is rather a wholly negative liberation, complete abstraction. It is the complete emptying that renounces all consciousness, will, passions, needs. In the Hindu view, persistence within one's own consciousness is ungodly. Human freedom consists not in emptiness, but precisely in being at home with oneself in one's willing, knowing, and acting. To the Hindu, on the contrary, the complete submergence and stupefaction of consciousness is what is highest, and one who remains at this abstract level and is dead to the world is called a yogi.

240. In B's margin: 3 July 1827

241. W_1 (Var) reads (parallel in main text follows): Even nowadays there are still individual Hindus who inflict such exercises and torments on themselves in order to attain to the power of the Brāhmans, a power that is itself above the gods; for example, they spend ten years with their arms above their heads, they have themselves buried alive, have themselves swung through fire, etc.

One who has reached the highest rung on the ladder of penances (in other words, he has had himself buried alive) has attained consummation and is the actual Brahmā who has power over all gods; Indra and all the gods of nature are subject to him, so that he is accounted to be what we saw previously in the sorcerer (namely that this singular subject exercises all power over the violent forces of nature). The Brāhman is born with this merit of the yogi; he is twice-born, and hence he has universal power over nature.

242. [Ed.] Samuel Turner, An Account of an Embassy to the Court of the Teshoo Lama in Tibet, Containing a Narrative of a Journey through Bootan, and Part of Tibet (London, 1800), pp. 270–272. See 1824 lectures, n. 277.

who had journeyed to the Dalai Lama reported that he had known one who was at the first stage and who had slept in a standing position for twelve years. The second stage was going to be when he would keep his hands folded over his head for another twelve years. After one had accomplished this, other trials then ensued, such as sitting in the midst of five fires for three and three-quarter hours. One yogi got to the point where he wanted to hang suspended by one foot over a fire, also for three and three-quarter hours, but he was unable to endure it. The greatest test is to allow oneself to be buried alive and to continue in this situation for three and three-quarter hours. Having endured all this, one is then perfect and has absolute power over the whole of nature, over all deities; one is Brahmā himself, and is accorded the status that we saw previously in the case of the sorcerer, of having power over the forces of nature.[243] ⌐From an epic we know that a certain Vishvamitra wanted to attain this status (cf. the poem "Rāmāyana").⌐[244] | 493

243. [*Ed.*] It is clear from his Humboldt review, p. 1459 (*Berliner Schriften,* p. 117), that Hegel is again referring here to Humboldt's paper on the Bhagavad-Gita (see above, n. 204).

244. *W (1831) reads:* There is an episode in the Rāmāyana[a] that transposes us completely to this standpoint. The story of the life of Vishvamitra, the companion of Rama (an incarnation of Vishnu), is related as follows: There was a mighty king, and being so mighty, he demanded a cow (which in India is worshiped as the generative force of the earth) from the Brāhman Vasishta, after he had got to know of its marvelous energy. Vasishta refused to give it; thereupon the king seized it violently, but the cow escaped back to Vasishta and reproached him for having allowed it to be taken from him, [*W₁:* and promised him, as a Brāhman, all power, which would be greater than that of a Kshatriya, which the king was. *W₂:* since the power of a Kshatriya (which the king was) did not exceed that of a Brāhman.] Vasishta then charged the cow to raise up for him a power wherewith to resist the king, who then confronted this power with his whole army, and both armies struck repeatedly at one another. Finally, however, Vishvamitra was conquered, after his hundred sons too had been destroyed by means of a wind that Vasishta had caused to issue from his navel. Full of despair, he handed over the government to his sole remaining son and betook himself with his consort to the Himalaya Mountains in order to obtain the favor of Mahadeva (Shiva). Moved by the severity of his exercises, Mahadeva is prepared to fulfill his wishes. Vishvamitra asks to have complete knowledge of the science of archery, and this is granted him. Armed with this, Vishvamitra intends to coerce Vasishta; with his arrows he lays waste his forest. But Vasishta seizes his staff, the Brahmā weapon, and lifts it up; thereupon all the gods are filled with apprehension, for this violence threatened the entire world with destruction. They entreat the Brāhman to desist. Vishvamitra acknowledges the Brāhman's power and

597

now resolves to subject himself to the severest disciplines in order to attain that power. He retires into solitude and lives a thousand years in abstraction, alone with his consort. Brahmā comes to him and addresses him thus: "I recognize thee now as the first royal sage." Not content with this, Vishvamitra begins his penances anew. Meanwhile a Hindu king had applied to Vasishta with the request that he would raise him up to heaven in his bodily shape. The request was refused, however, on account of his being a Kshatriya; but as he haughtily persisted in it, Vasishta degraded him to the chandala caste. He then betook himself to Vishvamitra with the same request. Vishvamitra prepares a sacrifice, to which he invites the gods; however, they refuse to come to a sacrifice offered for a chandala. But Vishvamitra, through his strength, raises the king to heaven. At the command [W_1: of the gods W_2: of Indra] he falls down, but Vishvamitra sustains him between heaven and earth, and thereupon creates another heaven, another Pleiades, another Indra, and another circle of gods. The gods were filled with astonishment, repaired in humility to Vishvamitra, and agreed with him about a place to be assigned to that king in heaven. After the lapse of a thousand years, Vishvamitra [W_1: was called W_2: was rewarded, and Brahmā called him] chief of the sages. [W_2: But he did not yet declare him to be a Brāhman. Then Vishvamitra begins his penances all over again.] The gods in heaven become apprehensive; Indra attempts to excite his passions (for a perfect sage and Brāhman should have subjugated his passions). He sends him a very beautiful girl, with whom Vishvamitra lives for twenty-five years; but then he removes himself from her, having overcome his love. In vain, too, do the gods try to provoke his anger. Finally, his Brahmā strength has to be conceded.

Precedes in W_1 (1831): It is only the Brāhmans who are privileged to read the Vedas, and this privilege belongs to them by right of birth. Their whole life expresses the existence of Brahman; they enter into all worldly affairs, to be sure, but they are regarded as already possessing the absolute power in themselves. All other castes stand far below the Brāhman caste. The highest point that can be attained in the cultus is stupefaction, the annihilation of self-consciousness; this is not affirmative liberation and reconciliation, but rather wholly negative liberation, complete abstraction. In the Hindu view, persistence within one's own consciousness is ungodly. But human freedom consists precisely in being free in willing, knowing, and acting. To the Hindu, on the contrary, the complete submergence and stupefaction of consciousness is what is highest.

The Brāhmans are the existence of Brahman.[b] According to the myth, they issued from its mouth. Those who are not Brāhmans can also raise themselves to this level, but only through ceaseless asceticism, by forcing themselves to mortify themselves for years at a time and so attaining what the Brāhman has immediately through birth. When the most ignorant Brāhman reads the Vedas, Brahman is within him. Other Hindus can raise themselves to this level, by bringing themselves to the point of being quite lifeless in the final stupefaction of consciousness. This is a basic trait in Hindu life. What the great epic poems of the Hindus principally express[c] is the Brāhman's loftiness, and they treat of the monstrous tasks and penances that the Kshatriyas have performed in order to attain this perfection of power. Hindu renunciation is the way of perfection that does not presuppose sin.[d]

[*Ed.*] [a]The account transmitted by W follows fairly closely *The Ramayuna of Valmeeki* in the translation by W. Carey and J. Marshman, vol. 1 (Serampore, 1806), secs. xli–lii, except that it is not Vasishta but Vishvamitra who terrifies the gods and

The Brāhmans enjoy from birth the status of the yogi; they are called twice-born⁻⁻ —first a natural birth, secondly one via the abstraction of spirit. This means that when a Brāhman is born, then a powerful god is born; the king should | beware of provoking such a person to anger, for he could destroy the king's entire power. No king can call them to account. The other castes have boundless reverence for these Brāhmans. According to the Hindu law books the Brāhman holds this elevated status even though he is only human like everyone else. Nowadays the life of the Brāhmans has changed very much; they are employed by the English as scribes and in other activities. In the last insurrection of the Burmese, Brāhmans also were among the captives; | they were shot just like the others—though according to the laws Brāhmans cannot be brought to justice by the king.²⁴⁵

494

495

---

worlds by use of "the Brahmā weapon." It is also not Vasishta himself but his sons who utter the curse whereby the king is made a chandala. The same error occurs in the extract Hegel made from the English translation in his Humboldt review, pp. 1460–1464 (*Berliner Schriften,* pp. 119–123), despite the fact that he was also familiar with a German translation of the same episode by Franz Bopp in *Über das Conjugationssystem der Sanskritsprache* (Frankfurt am Main, 1816), pp. 159–235. Thus we may assume that in lecturing, Hegel based himself on the text of his review or the materials he had assembled for it. The shifts between past and present tense occur in W_1 and W_2. ᵇFor the idea that Brāhmans are sprung from the mouth of Brahman, see *Institutes of Hindu Law,* p. 12. ᶜThis in fact applies only to the Rāmāyana. ᵈThis sentence indicates that the term "penances" (*Büssungen*) is an inappropriate expression for what the Hindus call "austerities" (Sanskrit *tapas*)—the term in fact used by Hegel's source, the Carey-Marshman translation. Without sin there can be no "penance." Hegel may have been unfamiliar with the English term "austerities." In the 1824 lectures, where his source was most likely Bopp's German translation, he uses the term *Strengigkeiten* instead of *Büssungen* and says specifically that such *Strengigkeiten* are not "penances" (*Bussübungen*) for offenses committed (see above, p. 343). The W text adds following *Strengigkeiten* the misspelled word "austereties" (see 1824 n. 279)—probably the hand of the editor.

245. [*Ed.*] On the concept of the twice-born, see *Institutes of Hindu Law,* p. 38. The statement that Brāhmans cannot be "brought to justice [*gerichtet*]" by the king probably refers to pp. 237–238; the German verb can mean either "sentenced" or, sometimes, "executed" (more properly, *hingerichtet*), and it is clear from the source that the latter is intended here. On the power and elevated social status of the Brāhmans, p. 224; on their divine dignity, pp. 13, 286. The source of Hegel's remark concerning changes in the status of Brāhmans has not been positively identified, although it is possible he is again referring to an incident in Mill's *History of British India* 2:129–130, 134, where the author describes how the French governor of

[246]Thus the highest point is this detached contemplation as Brahman wholly for itself, which comes into existence in this deep absorption in nothing, in this wholly empty consciousness and intuition. The remaining content of spirit and nature, however, is allowed to run wild in all directions. The [contemplative] unity that stands uppermost is, to be sure, the power from which everything proceeds and into which everything returns; but it does not become concrete as the bond of the manifold powers of nature, nor does it become concrete in spirit as the bond of the many and varied spiritual activities and sensibilities. In the first instance, when the unity becomes the bond of natural things we call it necessity; this is the bond of natural forces and phenomena. This is how we consider natural properties and things, as being in their independence essentially conjoined to one another. Laws and understanding are in nature, in the fact that phenomena cohere in this way. But the unity of Brahman remains solitary, by itself; hence its fulfillment is here a wild and unruly one. Similarly in the spiritual domain, we do not have the concrete here; the universal or thinking does not become something concrete in the spirit, something internally self-determining. When thinking determines itself internally and the determinate is sublated within this universality, when pure thinking is concrete, that is what we call reason. There is duty and right only in thinking. These determinations, posited in the form of universality, are rational with regard to conscious truth and insight, and likewise with regard to the will. But such concrete unity, reason, and rationality does not also become that One of Brahman, that solitary unity. On this account there is no right or duty present here either. For freedom of will and of spirit is precisely a being present to oneself

---

Pondicherry exacted forced labor from all the inhabitants, regardless of caste, and later had six Brāhmans shot from the muzzles of guns as spies. In his Humboldt review, p. 1490 (*Berliner Schriften*, pp. 152–153), Hegel also referred to FitzClarence's report that any Brāhman who held a subordinate post with the English was treated with scant respect.

246. *Precedes in L (1827?):* No reverence is shown to Brahman; it is not worshiped or venerated, has no temple or altars; its unity is not related to what is real, to actually effective self-consciousness. From the fact that consciousness of the One is isolated in this way, it follows that at this level nothing in the relationship to the divine is defined by reason.

in determinacy; but this presence to self or this unity is here abstract
and lacks determination. | 496

In one respect this is the source of the fanciful polytheism of the
Hindus. We have noted that there is here no category of being. They
have no category for what we call the independence of things, for
what we articulate by the phrase "there are" or "there is"; rather,
in the first instance, human beings know themselves alone as independent. For this reason an independent element in nature is represented
as endowed with our own human type of independence, the kind
we carry in our own being—in our human shape and consciousness.
Hence the imagination here makes everything into deities. This is
what we see in its own way among the Greeks, too, where every
tree is made into a dryad, every spring into a nymph. There we say
that the beautiful imagination of human beings animates everything,
ensouls everything, represents everything as inspirited; that human
beings walk among their own kind, anthropomorphize everything,
and through their beautiful fellow-feeling give to everything the
beautiful mode [of life] that they themselves have.[247] Among the
Hindus, on the contrary, it is a wild and unruly mode. We duly note
that they are so generous as to share their mode of being; but we
must state that this liberality has its ground in an impoverished image
of themselves and, to be precise, in the fact that their humanity does
not yet have in it the content of freedom, of the eternal, of actual
being truly in and for itself, and they do not yet know that their own
content or specification is nobler than the content of a spring or a
tree.[248] Among the Greeks there is more a play of imagination, while
among the Hindus there is no higher self-feeling or self-awareness
present. The view that they have of being is simply the one they have
of themselves; they set themselves on the same plane with all their
images of nature. This is the case because thinking has slipped back
so wholly into abstraction.

Furthermore the powers of nature, whose being is known and
represented anthropomorphically, transcend concrete human beings
who, as physical beings, are dependent on them and have not yet

247. W₂ (Var/1831?) adds: and so embrace everything as ensouled.
248. W₂ (Var/1831?) adds: Everything is squandered on the imagination, and
nothing is kept back for living.

distinguished their freedom from their natural aspect. Coherent with this is the fact that human life has no higher worth than the being 497 | of natural objects or the life of a natural being. Human life has worth only when humanity itself is inwardly nobler; but for the Hindus human life is something contemptible and despicable—it has no more value than a sip of water. Here one cannot ascribe worth to self in an affirmative way, but only negatively: life gains worth only through negation of self. Everything concrete is only negative when measured against this abstraction. Every aspect of the Hindu cultus follows from this, such as the fact that human beings sacrifice themselves and their parents and children; widow-burning after the death of the husband fits in here too.[249] This sacrifice [of self] has a higher value when it is done expressly with regard to Brahman or some god; for the god is also Brahman. It counts as a higher sacrifice when they climb up to the snowy crags of the Himalayas where the sources of the Ganges are, and cast themselves into these streams.[250] Those are not penances for transgressions, not offerings in recompense for some evil, but rather a sacrifice merely to gain worth for oneself. This worth is just what can only be attained in a negative manner.[251]

Bound up with the fact that the human being is in this way without freedom and has no inner self-worth, there is a concrete expansion of this unspeakable and endlessly variable superstition, these tremendous fetters and limitations. The relationship of dependence

249. [*Ed.*] See H. T. Colebrooke, "On the Duties of a Faithful Hindu Widow," *Asiatic Researches* 4:205–215.

250. [*Ed.*] Hegel is referring to an anonymous review of Alexander von Humboldt's *Sur l'élévation des montagnes de l'Inde,* in *The Quarterly Review* (London), 22, no. 44 (1820): 415–430. See also his reference to a report of Turner on the practices of a yogi, above, n. 242; and to the mortification of Vishvamitra, above, n. 244.

251. W_2 *(1831) adds:* The Hindu's animal-worship is also closely connected with the position that is here given to humanity. An animal is not a conscious spirit, but precisely in this concentration of unconsciousness, human being is not far removed from the beasts. Among the Hindus efficacy is not viewed as a specific activity but as simple force that operates through everything. Particular activity is held of little account; only stupefaction is valued, and all we are then left with is the organic life of the animal. When no freedom, no morality, no ethical life is present, then power is known only as internal, obscure power, such as pertains both to animals and to those people in the most complete torpor.

upon outward and natural things that is insignificant to the European is made into something fixed and abiding. For this is precisely where superstition has its ground: in the fact that human beings are not indifferent to external things—and they are not indifferent when they have no inward freedom, when they do not | have true independence of spirit.[252] Thus it is prescribed with what foot one should stand up, and how one should pass water, whether to the north or to the south. This is where the prescriptions that Brāhmans have to observe fit in (see also the tale of Nala in the Mahābhārata).[253] And just as the superstition arising from this lack of freedom is unbounded, so it also follows that there is no ethics to be found, no determinate form of rational freedom, no right, no duty. The Hindu people are utterly sunk in the depths of an unethical life.

498

[254]The essence is absolute unity, inward self-absorption of the subject. This self-absorption has its existence in the finite subject, in the particular spirit. To the idea of the true there belongs the universal, the substantial unity with self, and self-equivalence; but this belongs to the true in such a way that it is not only indeterminate, not only substantial unity, but is determinate within itself. What is called Brahman has determinacy external to it. The supreme determinacy of Brahman is, and can only be, the consciousness and knowledge of its real existence; and this determinacy or this subjectivity of the unity is here the subjective self-consciousness as such. In another form the determinacy is the particularization of the

252. W_2 (1831) adds: All that is indifferent is fixed, while all that is not indifferent, all that belongs to right and morality, is jettisoned and given over to caprice.

253. [Ed.] Hegel is referring to the extremely detailed prescriptions in the Institutes of Hindu Law, chap. 4 ("On Economics and Private Morals"). The prescription "with what foot one should stand up" is not, however, found in this chapter. The phrase "to the north or to the south" reads in Hu (our only source at this point) gegen Winter oder gegen Süden. Sec. 4.50 instructs a Brāhman to void feces or urine "to the north" by day and "to the south" by night; however, 4.48 instructs him never to do so "facing the wind." Hegel probably cited both passages, while Hube conflated them, mishearing Wind as Winter. For the tale of Nala, see Franz Bopp, ed. and trans., Nalus: Carmen Sanscritum e Mahābhārato (London, 1819).

254. [Ed.] The next thirteen paragraphs (ending on p. 612) are derived almost exclusively from L; they are not substantiated by B and only in a very fragmentary fashion by An and Hu. However, it is clear from the dates given by B that the text delivered was more or less of a length that would include them.

universal, the particular spiritual and natural powers. This particular aspect also steps outside the unity, and as a result there is only a fluctuation, so that the particular powers that have the value of deities are at one time independent and at another vanishing; they are what perishes in abstract unity or in substance, and then emerges from it once more. Thus the Hindus say: "There have indeed been many thousand Indras and there will be still more."[255] In the same vein, incarnations are posited as something transitory. Although the particular powers return into the substantial unity, it does not become concrete; rather it remains an abstractly substantial unity; and although these determinacies emerge out of it, | the unity does not become concrete even on that account, for they are outside it, they are phenomena posited with the characteristic of independence.

499

d. Transition to the Next Stage

[256] The transition at which we stand is this [state of] being distinct; this existence or subjectivity collapses into a category where we are

---

255. [Ed.] See H. T. Colebrooke, "On the Philosophy of the Hindus," *Transactions of the Royal Asiatic Society* 1 (1824): 27, although the statement was originally intended in a historical sense, meaning that the Vedic world of gods would give way to later philosophical conceptions, rather than in the futuristic sense that Hegel gives it.

256. W_2 *(MiscP) reads (parallel in main text follows):* In respect of its necessity, this transition is based upon the fact that the truth which in the preceding stages is present implicitly, as the foundation, is here actually drawn forth and posited. In the religion of phantasy, and [that] of being-within-self, this subject, this subjective self-consciousness, is identical, but immediately identical, with the substantive unity that is called Brahman or that is indeterminate nothingness. This One is now grasped as unity determined within itself, as implicitly subjective unity, and consequently this unity is grasped as implicit totality. If the unity is defined as implicitly subjective, it contains the principle of spirituality; and it is this principle that unfolds in the religions that stand at this transitional point.

In Hinduism, moreover, the One (or the unity of Brahman) and determinateness (or the many powers of the particular, and the emergence of differences) stood in the relationship that the differentiae were at one moment held to be independent while at another they had disappeared and were submerged in the unity. The dominant and universal feature was the alternation between origination and perishing, between the particular powers' being annulled in the unity and their emerging from it. It is true that in the religion of being-within-self this alternation was brought to rest insofar as the particular differentiae fell back into the unity of nothingness; but this unity was empty and abstract, while the truth, by contrast, is the inwardly concrete within the universal. Subjectivity is a determinate being, is being for another, manifestation, appearance. The transition is that this subject, this subjective self-consciousness, is posited as identical with the substantial unity that is called Brahman, that this One is now | grasped as determinate unity within itself, as subjective unity 500 intrinsically, and so this unity is grasped as totality in itself. In accord with the initial element in which this unity is implicitly determined, is grasped as subjective, the unity therefore has implicit in it what makes it into spiritual unity, what belongs to it because its being is spiritual; because it is subjectively determined implicitly, it has the principle of spirituality in itself. ⁻This unity is spiritual, although it is not yet absolute spirit. But since it is also concrete totality, it no longer requires the self-conscious subject. For the Hindus it is not separated, and is inseparable, from them; insofar as it is still what is incomplete—not being the subjective unity implicitly—the unity still has the subject outside it. As complete totality it no longer needs the subject. At this point, however, begins genuine independence, and with it this separation of consciousness from ob-

---

unity and totality. In this way even that abstract unity, together with diversity, enters into the genuine unity in which the differentiae are sublated, are ideal, are posited negatively as dependent but are at the same time preserved.

W₂ (1831) continues: Up to this point, therefore, the unfolding of the moments of the idea, the self-differentiation of the thought of absolute substance, was defective, because on the one hand the shapes lost themselves in rigid fixity, while on the other hand it was only the flight that achieved unity (or to put it another way, the unity was merely the disappearance of the differences). But now the reflection of manifoldness into itself comes into play—or the fact that thought itself contains determination within itself, in such a way that it is self-determining; and determining has worth and inner content only to the extent that it is reflected into this unity. With this the concept of freedom, of objectivity, is posited, and as a result the divine concept becomes a unity of the finite and the infinite. The infinite is the thought that is only self-contained, the pure substance; the finite (according to this thought-category) consists of the many gods; the unity is negative unity, the abstraction that submerges the many in this One. But the One has not gained anything through this submergence; it is as undetermined as before. The finite is affirmative only outside the infinite, not within it; and hence, as affirmative, it is finitude without any rationality. But at this next stage the finite, or the determinate in general, is taken up into infinitude, the form is commensurate with the substance, infinite form is identical with the substance that determines itself inwardly and is not merely abstract power.

ject or content, the objectivity of the absolute, consciousness of its self-made independence.⁻²⁵⁷

Up to this point we had this unseparated unity. Heretofore the highest aspect in this form of religion was still not separated from the subjective, empirical self-consciousness—it was just this unseparated unity. Now | the split occurs, and it does so precisely to the extent that this content becomes known in itself as concrete totality.

Implicit in this transition are two noteworthy definitions that have to be relegated to the science of logic for their development, and that emerge here more as subsidiary propositions to which we will appeal further.

²⁵⁸One of these lemmas is that this unity that we saw as Brahman, and then these determinacies—these many powers, the empirical subject, this emergence or emerged being of the distinctions which at one time count as independent but at another time have vanished and hence have perished—are not mutually external, that that unity and these distinctions revert to the concrete unity. Their truth is the internally concrete totality or unity, such that what is present is no longer an alternation between particular powers being annulled in the unity and their emerging from it—an alternation of origination and perishing as for the Hindus. Instead, the idea or the true is this, that the distinctions are sublated in the unity; they are ideally or negatively posited on the one hand as without independence, but equally on the other hand they are preserved. The fact that this concrete unity is what the true is gets developed in logic, and here we can only refer to it.⁻⁻

The other, equally essential definition is that at this point there occurs for the first time the separation of empirical self-consciousness from ⁻absolute self-consciousness,⁻²⁵⁹ from the content of the

---

257. W₂ (Ed?) reads, in a later passage: So substantive unity is still inseparable from the subject, and insofar as it is still what is incomplete, and is not yet in itself subjective unity, it still has the subject outside it. We do not yet have the objectivity of the absolute, the consciousness of its independence on its own account.

258. In B's margin: 5 July 1827

259. W (Var) reads: the absolute,

highest, so that here God attains proper objectivity for the first time. On the preceding levels it is the inwardly absorbed empirical self-consciousness that is Brahman, this inward abstraction; or the highest is present as a human being. Only now does the break between objectivity and subjectivity begin, and only here does the objectivity properly merit the name "God," even though this object is still incomplete. And we have this objectivity of God at this point, because this content has determined itself implicitly as being concrete totality in itself. This means that God is spirit, that God is spirit in all religions.

Nowadays when one says especially of religion that subjective consciousness belongs to it, that is a correct | view. This is the instinct that subjectivity belongs to religion. But we see what the [prevalent] view is, namely that the spiritual can occur as an empirical subject; ‾we see that people take a natural thing as their god,‾[260] with the result that spirituality is able to fall only within consciousness, and God, too, as natural essence, is able to be the object of this consciousness. Thus on the one side there is God as a natural essence. But God is essentially spirit—this is the absolute determination of religion and accordingly the fundamental determination, the substantial foundation in every form of religion. The natural thing is represented in a human guise, even as personality, or as spirit or consciousness; but the gods of the Hindus are only superficial personifications. Personification still does not produce the result that[261] God is known as spirit. There are these particular objects, such as sun and tree, that are personified (even in the incarnation [of God]); but the particular objects have no independence, because they are particular[262]; they have only an imputed independence. What is highest, however, is the spirit, whereas this ‾characterization derives‾[263] from empirical, subjective spirit, from subjective self-

502

260. W_2 (Var) reads: which can then as empirical consciousness have a natural thing for its God,
261. W_2 (Var) adds: the object or
262. W_2 (Var) adds: and natural objects
263. W_1 (Var) reads: spiritual characterization derives W_2 (Var) reads: spiritual characterization and independence derives in the first instance

consciousness, and applies to it either to the extent that it is developed, or because Brahman has its existence in and through absorption of the subject into itself.

But now it is no longer the case that the human being is simply God, and God simply the human being, that God is only in an empirically human mode; instead God is truly and intrinsically objective, God is [264] essentially object and is altogether in opposition to human beings. We will take up later their reconciliation and return, the fact that God even appears as a human being, as the God-man.[265] But it is from this point onward that God's objectivity begins. ⁻As this concrete totality, God is in a twofold way. That is the

503   fourth mode of this wild totality. |

This new form is the incipient separation from the immediate individual, the incipient severance and objectification of what is known as the highest.⁻[266] ⁻This resumption, differentiation, or

504   objectification has two forms. It is first portrayed in a pure | and

264. W₂ (Var) adds: in himself totality, concretely determined within himself, i.e., is known as being in himself subjective; as a result he is for the first time

265. [Ed.] See Hegel's portrayal of the Christian religion, Vol. 3:290 ff.

266. W₂ (1831) reads: But if the universal is grasped as inwardly self-determining, then it comes into opposition with what is other, and is in strife with this its other. In the religion of power there is no opposition, no strife, for the accidental has no value for substance.

Since it determines itself by its own act, power does not now, to be sure, have these characteristics as something finite. On the contrary, what is determined subsists in its implicit and explicit truth. Thereby God is defined as the good; and "good" is not here posited as a predicate—on the contrary, God is *the* good. In what is indeterminate there is neither good nor evil. Here, on the other hand, the good is the universal, but it has a purpose, a determinacy concordant with the universality in which it subsists.

To begin with, however, self-determining at this transitional stage is exclusive. Thus good comes into relation with what is other, with evil, and this relation is strife—a dualism. Reconciliation (here only as becoming or as what is to be) is not yet thought of as within and implicit to the good itself.

A necessary consequence of this is that the strife comes to be known as a characteristic of substance itself. The negative is posited in spirit itself, and this is compared with its affirmation, so that this comparison is present in sensation and constitutes pain and death. The strife that resolves itself at this stage is, in the last analysis, spirit's struggle to come to itself, to attain to freedom.

From these fundamental determinations there results the following division of this transitional stage.

1. The first determination is that of Persian religion. Here the being-for-self of

simple way, but then in a seething manner, as a unity that is at the same time struggle, the fermenting of these distinct elements into a unity—an impure subjectivity that is the striving toward pure unity itself. The first of these modes is for us the fourth form.⁻²⁶⁷

4. The Religions of Transition²⁶⁸

a. The Religion of Light (Persian Religion)²⁶⁹
The first form is thus the pure, simple totality, though for that very reason still the abstract totality. It is the form in which God is known as what truly has being in and for itself, and known truly as this;

---

the good is still superficial, so that the good has a natural shape, but as a natural being that is shapeless: light.

2. The form in which strife, pain, or death itself becomes part of the essence: the Syrian religion.

3. The struggling out of strife, the advance to the determination of free spirituality in the proper sense, the overcoming of evil, the consummated transition to the religion of free spirituality: the Egyptian religion.

Generally speaking, however, what is common to these three forms of religion is the resumption of the wild, unrestrained totality into concrete unity. That giddy whirl [*Taumel*] in which the determinations of unity are precipitated into externality and contingency, where this wild world of gods, without any concept, proceeds out of unity, as it did out of Brahman, and where development breaks up into confusion because it is not concordant with the unity—this state devoid of anything to give it steadfastness has now passed away.

267. W₂ (*Var, possibly with editorial additions) reads:* This resumption into the substantive unity, which is in itself subjective, has two forms, however. The first resumption is that seen in Parseeism; here it occurs in a pure, simple fashion. The second is that which ferments in the Syrian and Egyptian religions, where the fermentation of totality mediates itself into unity, and unity comes into being in the strife of its elements.

268. [*Ed.*] In the 1824 lectures, the transition from nature religion to spiritual religion is provided by Egyptian religion; in 1827 Persian religion is also included among the transitional forms. God is now known as that which is self-determining within itself, and hence as good, but this goodness is still represented in natural images such as light. The interpretation of Persian religion is essentially similar to what is already found in 1824, but its reclassification reflects a general upgrading of the Near Eastern religions, a process that is carried even further in 1831.

269. [*Ed.*] The historical name used by Hegel is *die Religion der Parsen,* "the religion of the Parsees" or "Parseeism." Today Parseeism usually refers to the Zoroastrian sect in India descended from a group of Persian refugees who fled from the Muslim persecutions of the seventh and eighth centuries A.D. However, Hegel intends by this term the religion of ancient Persia, whose classic text was the Zend-

so God is in truth what is independent, what is inwardly determinate, and hence God is the good. But for that reason God is the good that itself still has its existence in a natural mode. In general, this form is what is called the religion of light; and in it the concept of subjectivity, or of what is concrete, the development of the concrete and its demonstration as totality, come directly to consciousness for the subject. We have to consider the determinations in it more closely, and to exhibit their necessity, which is a necessity arising from the concept or from thought. We shall on the one hand presuppose the logical element, but on the other hand only hint at the sort of necessity this is.

The first point is that the resumption is what is true. It is a substantial unity that is inwardly subjective, and hence it is altogether self-determining; in other words, this unity determines itself, but not in such a way that its determinations once more attain externality or contingency. That wild, nonconceptual world of deities emerges from Brahmā; the development is not compatible with the unity, but falls outside it and is fragmented. But here, in contrast, the unity 505 is inwardly self-determining. So the determinateness is not an | empirical or manifold determinateness, but is itself what is pure, universal, and self-identical; it is a determining of substance whereby it ceases to be substance—the unity that defines itself as subject. It⁻²⁷⁰ has a content, and the fact that this content is what is determined by it and in conformity with it (or that it is the universal content) is what is called the good or the true. For goodness and truth are only forms that pertain to the subsequent distinctions of knowing and willing, though in the supreme subjectivity they are only one truth, i.e., they are particularizations of this one truth. The fact that this universal is through the self-determining of spirit, that

---

Avesta, and which today is known as Zoroastrianism. Hegel is aware that in modern times the old religion survives in India and in Iran only in small sects (see n. 284), and at one point he specifically distinguishes between "Parsees" (*Parsen,* the people of the religion) and "Persians" (*Persern,* the people of the land) (see n. 286). Since "Parsee" simply means "Persian," and since Zoroastrianism was the state religion of the ancient Persian Empire, we can refer to it as "Persian religion," which is the term used in the editorial section headings, but in the text we usually follow Hegel's practice and translate as "religion of the Parsees."

270. W₂ *(Var) reads:* and begins to be subject. This unity, as self-determining,

it is determined by spirit and for spirit, is the aspect according to which it is truth. It is the good inasmuch as it is posited through spirit, and is a self-determining in conformity with its unity; i.e., it is its own self-determining whereby in its universality it remains true to itself, and no other determinations than that unity itself emerge. It is therefore the true content that has objectivity, the good that is the same thing as the true; this good is at the same time the self-determining of the One, of the absolute substance, and hence it remains immediately the absolute power. The good as absolute power: that is the definition of the content.

The second point is that precisely in this determining of the absolute lies the connection with the concrete, with the world, with concretely empirical life in general. All things proceed from this power. This fact, that all things proceed from it, is only a subordinate moment of what we saw previously,[271] that this mode of self-determination has abstract significance as a mode of determination; it is not a self-determining that has gone back into self and remains identical, [as what is] universally true and good, but is just a general determining instead.[272] This moment is present here too, but as subordinate. It is[273] the world in its manifold | existence; but the important point is that the connection of the good with the concrete world is contained in the good, inasmuch as the good is self-determining and this absolute determination lies within the good itself.

506

There is subjectivity or particularity in general within this substance, within the One itself, the absolute subject. This element that pertains to particular life, this determinacy, is at the same time posited within the absolute itself and is, accordingly, an affirmative coherence of the absolute, the good and true, the infinite, with what is called the finite. In the previous forms of religion the affirmative

271. [Ed.] See the discussion of Hinduism, above, pp. 579 ff.
272. W₂ (1831) adds: Power as such is neither good nor wise; it has no purpose, but is determined merely as being and nonbeing; it is characterized by wildness, by a general disorderliness [Aussersichkommen] of action. For this reason power is intrinsically what lacks determination.
273. W₂ (Var) adds: therefore concrete life, cf. Ho: The good is that in which concrete life too can intuit its affirmation,

coherence is found in part only in that pure absorption in which the subject says, "I am Brahman"; but that is an absolute, abstract coherence, which subsists only through this obscuring or abandoning of all concrete actuality of spirit, that is, only through negation. This affirmative coherence is, as it were, a pure strand; moreover, it is the abstractly negative—those acts of sacrifice and self-mortification. In the affirmative coherence at this present stage, however, it is said that [finite] things are altogether good. Because of it, the stones, animals, and human beings are altogether good; the good is a present substance in them, and what is good is their life, their affirmative being. So far as they remain good, they belong to the realm of the good; they are received into grace from the outset: it is not the case that only a subset of them are twice-born, as in India, but rather the finite is created from the good and is good.

The third point to note is that although this good is, of course, internally subjective, although it is internally determined and determines itself as good, although it is in conformity with the substantial unity, with the universal itself, in this definition it is still abstract. The good is internally concrete, yet this determinateness of being concrete is itself still abstract.[274] The good [thing] can be employed this way or that, or the | human agent has good intentions; but the question is, "What is good?" A further development or determination of the good is required. Because we still have the good in such an abstract way, it is still one-sided for us, still burdened with an antithesis. It is the absolute antithesis to another, and this other or opposite is evil.

In this simplicity of the good the negative is not yet accorded its rightful place. Hence we have two principles, the realm of the good and that of evil, this Oriental dualism. It is this great antithesis that has here arrived at its universal abstraction.[275] The good is indeed

507

274. W_2 (1831) adds: For the good not to be abstract, the form must be developed, the moments making up the concept must be posited. In order to be the rational idea, in order to be known as spirit, its determinations, the negative element, the differentiae as constituting its powers, must be posited in it through thought, and so known.

275. L (1827?) adds, similar in W: There is manifoldness and differentiation, to be sure, in the multitude of previous gods; but for this duality to have become the universal principle, for the differentiated elements to stand confronting each other as this duality—that is another matter altogether.

the true and the powerful, but it is in conflict with evil, so that evil stands over against it and persists as an absolute principle. [276]Evil ought surely to be overcome, to be counterbalanced; but what ought to be is not. "Ought" is a force that cannot make itself effective, it is this weakness or impotence.[277]

Religion and philosophy as a whole turn upon this dualism. This is the concern of religion and of philosophy—the distinction grasped in its complete universality. In the mode of thought this antithesis attains the universality that is proper to it. Dualism is a form [of thought] even today; but when we speak of it today, it is in meager and delicate forms. Whenever we take the finite to be autonomous, so that the infinite and the finite stand opposed to one another, so that the infinite has no part in the finite and the latter cannot cross over to the infinite,[278] we have the same dualism as the antithesis of Ahriman and Ormazd, or that of Manichaeism—except that we lack the thought or the heart to represent these antitheses to ourselves [honestly]. The finite, in its broadest sense maintaining itself as finite and autonomous, over against and thereby in conflict with the infinite or the universal, is what is evil. But all the same, we stick with this thoughtlessness in which both are accorded value, finite as well as infinite. God, however, is only *one* | principle, *one* power, and therefore the finite, and evil as well, have no true independence.

508

276. *In B's margin:* 6 July 1827

277. [*Ed.*] Hegel implicitly relates Persian religion to the philosophy of Kant and Fichte, according to which, in Hegel's view, the good is to be realized only in a progression that extends to infinity, and thus is not recognized as something already present at all times. See Kant, *Critique of Practial Reason,* esp. pp. 126–127 (Kant, *Werke* 5:122); and Fichte, *Science of Knowledge,* p. 231 (Fichte, *Gesamtausgabe* 2:397).

278. [*Ed.*] Hegel is criticizing contemporary attempts, beginning with Jacobi, to reemphasize the gulf between finite and infinite in contrast to Spinoza's attempt to replace this type of transition from the one to the other by the principle of an immanent cause. In Hegel's view, the consequence of present-day criticism of the pantheistic concept of immanence is that the transition from finite to infinite becomes unintelligible, and this in turn has the result that the infinite, placed in isolation on the other side, likewise becomes something finite too. See in this connection Jacobi, *Briefe,* p. 24 (*Werke* 4/1:56); also Schelling, "Philosophische Briefe über Dogmatismus und Kriticismus," letters 6 and 7, in *Philosophisches Journal einer Gesellschaft teutscher Gelehrter* 3 (1795): 190–191, 196 ff.; and Schelling, *Abhandlungen zur Erläuterung des Idealismus der Wissenschaftslehre,* in *Sämmtliche Werke* 1:367–368.

˜The third determination is that the good in its universality has at the same time a natural mode, a pure manifestation, a natural being, the simple manifestation—light. Light is this abstract subjectivity within the sensible. Space and time is the abstract; the concrete, [not in particular] but in its physical universality, is light.˜279 ˜From this [naturalistic] viewpoint, Brahmā would only be space that does not yet have the inner strength to be represented as internally independent; Brahmā requires the empirical self-consciousness of the human being.˜280

281˜˜There is perhaps a difficulty, in that the good to which we have come is also still supposed to have in itself essentially the aspect of natural being, | although it is of course the pure natural being

509

279. W (Var) reads: But furthermore, good, [W₁: in its W₂: by virtue of its] universality, has at the same time a natural mode of existence, of being for other— [W₁: a form of W₂: light, which is] pure manifestation. In the same way that the good is what is self-identical or is subjectivity in its pure identity with [W₁: itself, so the manifestation is what is pure and simple, namely light. Light is this abstract subjectivity in the sensuous realm—pure physical intuition—as the good is in the realm of the spiritual. Space and time are the primary abstractions in the sphere of mutual exclusion, but the concrete physical element in its universality is light as the good. W₂: itself in the spiritual realm, so light is this abstract subjectivity in the sensuous realm; space and time are the primary abstractions in the sphere of mutual exclusion, but the concrete physical element in its universality is light.] W₂ (1831) continues: If therefore the inwardly good, because of its abstractness, comes to have the form of immediacy and therefore of naturalness (for immediacy is what is natural), then this immediate good, which has not yet purified itself and raised itself to the form of absolute spirituality, is light. For in the natural world light is pure manifestation, the act of self-determining, but in a wholly simple, universal manner.

280. W (Var) reads: If Brahman had to be represented in a sensuous fashion, it could only be represented as abstract space. But Brahman still does not have the inner strength to be represented independently; instead it has the empirical self-consciousness of the human being as its reality.

281. W₁ (1831) reads (parallel in main text follows): In the Hindu religion, Brahman was what is highest—the One as unconsciousness and indeterminateness; at this stage, substance is not yet determined in itself. What comes next is the self-determining One; and the inward determination of the One, in its highest form, is what is good. The true and the good are one and the same; the former [is expressed] in knowing, the latter in willing. That is what power advances to. Power is neither wise nor good; it has no purpose, but is determined merely as being and nonbeing. It is characterized by wildness, by a general disorderliness. For this reason power is intrinsically what lacks determination. (It is then a logical progression that the indeterminate passes over to the determinate, and we adopt this point as a lemma

of light. But nature cannot be altogether omitted from spirit; it belongs to spirit. Even when God is grasped as internally concrete and as pure spirit, God is at the same time essentially creator and lord of nature. Therefore the idea in its concept, God in his inward essence, must posit reality or this externality that we call nature. The moment of natural being cannot be lacking; but here it is abstract, it is still in immediate unity with | the spiritual, with the good, 510 because the good itself is still this abstraction. The good contains determinateness within itself, and in the determinateness is the root of all natural being. We say, "God creates the world." "Creating" is the subjectivity to which the determinateness in general belongs. The determination of nature lies within this activity or subjectivity, and indeed the more precise relation is that it is something created. But here this further precision is not yet present; what we have instead is abstract determinateness. This determinacy has essentially the form of nature generally, the form of light and of immediate unity

---

[to our argument]; but this progression must also be one accessible to the imagination.) What lacks determination passes over to a purpose, and to one that is concordant with universality too; it passes over to the absolutely final end (which is the good in general), and this is the final end that has to be realized. Brahman, we can say, is what is inwardly good; and this is itself still abstract to begin with; because of its abstractness this self-contained good is posited in the form of immediacy, but of pure immediacy. Immediacy, however, is what is natural, or the purely physical, which is light, the manifestation that is only determined in a quite simple and universal manner. It is not the good that has purified itself, but is to begin with the immediate good. There is a logical or conceptual linkage here, so it is not to be taken as contingent that light has been intuited as the good.

But in the next step, the good passes over directly into its antithesis, into evil and darkness. W: Light is an infinite expansion, it is as rapid as thought; but in order for its manifestation to be real, it must strike upon [W_1: a dark object, a solid body. W_2: something dark.] Nothing is made manifest by pure light [W_1: as such]; it is only by means of this other that determinate manifestation enters on the scene and good accordingly emerges in opposition to evil. This manifestation is a determining, but it is not yet the [W_2: concrete] development of the determining; hence the concreteness of the determining lies outside it; owing to its abstractness it [W_1: is related to an other. This antithesis belongs to the concept of spirit, and the question is what position it occupies vis-à-vis the unity. W_2: has its determination in the other. Without the antithesis there is no spirit, and it is only in the development of spirit that the question arises as to what stance the antithesis occupies toward the mediation and toward the original unity.]

with the good; for the immediate, just as it stands, is the ˉabsolute,ˉ²⁸² because the determinateness [we are dealing with] is only this universal, undeveloped one. Hence the light has darkness over against it. In nature these determinations are external to one another. This is the impotence of nature, that light and its negation are side by side, although light is the power of banishing darkness. Therefore the ˉidea ofˉ²⁸³ God that we have here is itself still something powerless. Because of its abstraction, it is unable to embrace the antithesis or contradiction within itself and to endure it, so it has evil alongside it instead. Light is the good and the good is light—this inseparable unity is the basic idea.ˉˉ

²⁸⁴ˉˉHistorically this is the religion of the Parsees. Ormazd and Ahriman are superficial personifications. When the content | is still

511

282. W (Var/Ed?) reads: abstract,
283. W (Var) reads: determination in
284. W (1831) reads (parallel in main text follows): [W₁: This W₂: This religion of light—or of what is immediately good—] is the religion of the ancient Parsees, founded by Zoroaster. There are still some communities that belong to this religion, in Bombay and on the shores of the Black Sea, in the neighborhood of Baku, where naphtha springs are particularly numerous; and some have imagined they could find an explanation for the fact that the Parsees have made fire the object of their worship in this accident of geography.ᵃ We get some information about this religion from Herodotus and other Greek writers,ᵇ but it is only in later times that a more accurate knowledge of it has been achieved, through the discovery of this people's principal and fundamental books (the Zend-Avesta) by the Frenchman Anquetil du Perron;ᶜ these books are written in the ancient Zend language, a sister language to Sanskrit.

The light that is worshiped in this religion is not like a symbol of the good, an image under which the good can be represented; on the contrary, it might just as well be said that the good is the symbol of light. Neither of them is the meaning or the symbol, but they are directly identical. [W₁: What is substantive here confronts the subject in its particularity; W₂: At this stage—among the Parsees—worship enters on the scene, and substantiality is here objectified for the subject in its particularity;] humanity as a particular kind of good confronts the universal good, [W₁: and also] light in its pure, as yet undisturbed, manifestation [W₂: i.e., the good as natural existence].

The Parsees have also been called fire-worshipers.ᵈ This is incorrect inasmuch as the Parsees do not direct their reverence toward consuming, material fire, but only to fire as [W₁: light. And this light is personified too, but only superficially, for substance is not yet known as subject. W₂: light, which comes into appearance as the truth of what is material.] . . .

[W₁: It has been claimed that the first syllable "Or-" has affinities with the Hebrew אוֹר.ᵉ] The stars are lights appearing singly. [W₂: Since what appears is something particular, natural,] there arises a distinction between what appears and

616

what is implicit; [W_1: the stars are W_2: and what has implicit being is then also something particular, a genius. Just as the universal light is personified, so too are the particular lights. Thus the stars are] personified as genii. On the one hand they are appearance, but on the other they are personified as well. They are not differentiated into light and good, however; instead it is the whole unity that is personified; the stars are spirits of Ormazd, i.e., of the universal light, and of what is good in and for itself.

These stars are called the Amshaspands,[f] and Ormazd, who is the universal light, is also one of the Amshaspands. The realm of Ormazd is the realm of light, and in it there are seven Amshaspands. One might think of the planets in this connection, but they are not more precisely characterized either in the Zend-Avesta or in any of the prayers, not even in those that are addressed to them individually. The lights are the companions of Ormazd, and reign with him. Like this realm of light, the Persian state is portrayed as the realm of righteousness and good. The king was surrounded by seven magnates, too, who formed his council, and were regarded as representatives of the Amshaspands, just as the king was thought of as the deputy of Ormazd. Taking turns day by day, the Amshaspands govern with Ormazd in the realm of light; so what is posited here is merely a superficial distinction of time.

To the good or to the realm of light belongs all that has life. What is good in all beings is Ormazd; by thought, word, and deed he is the life-giving element. So we still have pantheism here, to the extent that the good or light is the substance informing everything; all happiness, blessing, and felicity flow together in it; whatever exists as loving, happy, strong, etc., that is Ormazd. He bestows the radiance of light on all beings, upon trees as well as upon noble humans, upon beasts as well as upon the Amshaspands.

[Ed.] [a]Hegel is probably referring to J. G. Rhode, *Die heilige Sage und das gesammte Religionssystem der alten Baktrer, Meder und Perser oder des Zendvolks* (Frankfurt am Main, 1820), p. 111, where the author speaks of the continuous petroleum (naphtha) flares emitted from holes in the ground in the neighborhood of present-day Baku (which is on the Caspian Sea, not the Black Sea). In regard to Hegel's knowledge of the Parsees in Bombay, see Carsten Niebuhr, *Voyage de M. Niebuhr en Arabie et en d'autres pays de l'orient*, 2 vols. (Switzerland, 1780), 2:460–464. [b]See Herodotus, *Histories* 1.131–140. Of the other classical writers who gave an account of Zoroastrianism, Hegel was familiar in particular with Plutarch, *De Iside et Osiride* 46–47, and with those whose references to the subject were included in *Zend-Avesta, Zoroasters lebendiges Wort*, trans. and ed. J. F. Kleuker from the French ed. of Anquetil du Perron, 5 vols. (Riga, 1776–1783), supp., vol. 2, pt. 3. [c]Hegel was familiar with the Zend-Avesta through Kleuker's translation (see annotation b). It is uncertain whether or not he also knew the original French text of Anquetil du Perron (Paris, 1769–1771). [d]See *Zend-Avesta*, ed. Kleuker, 1:149–150 (cf. *Zend-Avesta* [SBE], 2:357–361). On how and why the Parsees first became known as "fire worshipers," see Joseph Görres, *Das Heldenbuch von Iran aus dem Schah Nameh des Firdussi*, 2 vols. (Berlin, 1820), 1:8. [e]It has not been possible to identify Hegel's source positively. He is probably referring to Kleuker's linguistic parallels in his edition of the *Zend-Avesta*, supp., vol. 2, pt. 2, p. 14; but similar parallels were to be found in several other authors of the period. For example, Friedrich Sickler drew a parallel between אור and the Greek ΩΡ, but only as an ending; see *Kadmus; oder, Forschungen in den Dialekten des semitischen Sprachstammes* (Hildburghausen, 1818),

not an inwardly developed subjectivity, the personification is only formal. The deities were represented as subjects or persons among the Hindus, too; but how the person is determined in its substance or its essence depends solely on the content. If the substance | is not yet determined as developed subjectivity, then the subjectivity, which appears as personality, is only a superficial mode; that is again the case here.

512

Everything belongs to the light, everything living, all essence, all spirituality. The entire world in all its levels and kinds is Ormazd, and in this realm of light everything is good. Distinction belongs to subjectivity. Everything hinges on the way in which the distinctions are brought to unity, whether they are mutually external or are posited in a truly ideal fashion. Thus even light differentiates itself, and sun, stars, and planets are also personified. The sun is the power of vitality, upon which the cycle of vitality depends and with which it therefore coheres. Hence the sun and the planets are represented as the first principal spirits, as deities presiding over the world of light by turns, a heavenly people pure and great, each protecting, benefiting, and blessing [the world]. By the same token the act, the growth of finite things, everything energetic, everything spiritual—all is light, is Ormazd. Light is not simply the universal, sensible life, but is the energy, spirit, soul, love and bliss therein; all this belongs

---

p. xxii. Schelling established a similar connection, to which he traces the name of the deity Chrysor, and with which he associates the meaning of the German prefix *Ur-*, the inner, essential fire; see *The Deities of Samothrace*, n. 64 (p. 34) (*Sämmtliche Werke* 8:388). ᶠEvidence for Ormazd himself being an Amshaspand (Amesha Spenta) could be found in the *Zend-Avesta*, ed. Kleuker, 1:81 (cf. *Zend-Avesta* [SBE], 3:196); see also A. H. L. Heeren, *Ideen über die Politik, den Verkehr und den Handel der vornehmsten Völker der alten Welt*, 2 vols. (Göttingen, 1804–1805), 1:509; and J. G. Rhode, *Die heilige Sage und das gesammte Religionssystem der alten Baktrer* (Frankfurt am Main, 1820), pp. 316–317, 365. Regarding the organizational similarity between the kingdom of light and the Persian state, see below, n. 286. It is in the 1831 lectures that Hegel first deals in any detail with the Amshaspands. They are not referred to in the Zoroaster Gāthās but only in the later parts of the Avesta. The Amesha Spentas are glorious immortal beings who possess saving powers. As their names indicate, they are personifications of certain qualities; the six usually mentioned in addition to Ormazd are Good Thinking, Truth, Mastery, Submissiveness, Wholeness, Not Dying. They are regarded as protective spirits for the realm of the ethical as well as for that of the natural.

to the realm of Ormazd. He is the substance, and all the particular things contain this substantial element; for that reason they are good, and belong to the realm of light, as good actions do also. In their particular existence, however, things are distinguished from the universal as well. Everything living—sun, star, tree—is revered as something good, but only the good or the light in it, not its particular shape, its finite, transitory mode.[285] |

513

The state, too, is represented in this way. The prince of the Parsees[286] is regarded as deputy of the highest light [i.e., the sun], but not of the pure Ormazd himself; his officials are regarded as deputies of the planets and stars, the ministers and aides of Ormazd.ˉˉ One among them is Mithra, whom Herodotus already knows, the μεσίτης or mediator.[287] It is peculiar that Herodotus already singles him out; for in the religion of the Parsees the determination of mediation or reconciliation seems not yet to have been dominant. The worship of Mithra was developed generally only later

285. L (1827?) adds (following a sentence from the 1824 lectures), similar in W: There is a separation between the substantial and what belongs to transience. But that is a minor difference; the absolute distinction is between good and evil.

286. L (1827?) adds, similar in W₁: —and it was reputedly the same with the Persians—

[Ed.] This organizational similarity between the kingdom of light and the Persian state is emphasized in the introduction to Zend-Avesta, ed. Kleuker, 1:57–72. Rhode, Heilige Sage, pp. 536 ff., is very reticent in this regard; but Heeren states categorically, Ideen über die Politik 1:513, that the form of government is modeled on the hierarchy in the kingdom of Ormazd, though subsequently, pp. 527 ff., he also mentions the differences and concludes from them that Zoroaster cannot have been a contemporary of the Persian state as we know it.

287. [Ed.] Hegel is referring to Herodotus, Histories 1.131, where, however, the reference is to Mitra, who seems to be a Persian love-goddess quite distinct from Mithra—Herodotus says that Mitra is the Persian name for Aphrodite. Moreover, it is not, as Hegel seems to think, Herodotus who calls Mithra the "mediator" but Plutarch, De Iside et Osiride 46. Creuzer also, though he distinguishes between the Mithra mentioned in Plutarch and the Mitra mentioned in Herodotus, proceeds to combine them as a single androgynous deity; see Symbolik und Mythologie 1:728–738. The situation is further confused by the fact that the Persian Mithra does correspond to an Indian god of light, Mitra, who is obviously distinct from Herodotus's love-goddess. In any event it is important to distinguish between the Persian Mithra and the later Roman cult of Mithra(s), which the Romans imported into northern and western Europe.

on, when the need for reconciliation became stronger and more conscious, more vital and determinate in the human spirit. Herr Rhode[288] in Breslau disagrees about this with Creuzer, who exalts Mithra a great deal; [Rhode] maintains that in the Zend writings Mithra does not yet have his complete development; that is quite true. He gained a particular development among the Romans in the Christian era (and even in the Middle Ages we still find a secret worship of Mithra, ostensibly connected with the Order of Knights Templar). One essential image belonging to the Mithra cult is that of Mithra thrusting the knife into the neck of the bull; it has been found frequently in Europe.

˹One kind of genii in this religion are the so-called Fravashis. Here we find the representation that the water of immortality springs from a tree—a striking agreement with the tree of knowledge.˺[289]

Light is the highest element in everything that the Parsees revere. The Parsee cultus follows immediately from this determination of their religion.[290] | The entire life of the Parsee should be this cultus, one should carry out the good in words, deeds ˹and thoughts,˺[291]

---

288. [*Ed.*] Rhode's repeated criticisms of Creuzer's *Symbolik und Mythologie* on this score relate to the first edition (1810–1812). In the second edition (1819–1821) Creuzer replied very sharply (1:783) to Rhode's criticisms, without really entering into their substance. The criticisms were directed not only against Creuzer's fusion of later, Hellenistic ideas with the Mithra of the Zend-Avesta but in general against Creuzer's tendency to interpret Oriental mythology in the light of Greek antiquity and then to readmit the ideas thus retrojected into earlier times, in other words to derive Greek mythology from the East.

289. W_1 *(Var) reads, similar in* W_2 *(at the end of next to last paragraph):* A distinction is posited in humanity too; something higher is distinguished from our immediate corporeality, naturalness, and temporality, from the insignificance of our external being or finite existence. This higher aspect is represented by the genii, the Fravashis. One among the trees is singled out; from the tree called Hom springs the water of immortality; Hom is to be compared with the tree of the knowledge of good and evil. These are parallels that should be noted, but no great weight should be attached to them.

290. W_2 *(1831) adds:* Its purpose is to glorify Ormazd in his creation, and the adoration of the good in everything is its beginning and end. The prayers are simple and uniform, without any distinctive nuances. The main characteristic of the cultus is that humans should keep themselves pure inwardly and outwardly and should maintain and disseminate this purity everywhere.

291. W *(Var) reads:* everywhere, should foster all that is good among humans, as well as human beings themselves, [W_1: should foster all life,]

should dig ˉwells,ˉ²⁹² plant trees, make life fruitful, be lively and cheerful, and promote all good, so that good and light may flourish everywhere.²⁹³ ²⁹⁴

Transition to the Next Stage²⁹⁵

The religion of light was the first form in this transition, this resumption of the manifold, the natural, into concrete unity; the second form, which contains concrete subjectivity within itself, is the abandonment to externality of that simple subjectivity; the subjectivity is developed, but in a way that is at the same time still wild and has not yet attained the composure of the spirituality that actually is inwardly free. Just as this development was fragmented for the Hindus—with alternating generation and perishing, but no return into itself—so here we have determinateness in its untrammeled state, but in such a way that these elementary powers of the spiritual and the natural are essentially tied to subjectivity, so that it is *one* subject that traverses these moments, ˉone subject that keeps distinction enclosed within itself and overpowers it.ˉ²⁹⁶

The onesidedness of this form consists in the fact that this pure unity of the good—this reversion to self and presence to self—is lacking; here freedom | merely arises, thrusts itself outward, and brings itself forth, but does not yet attain completion. It is not yet the beginning whereby the end or result is produced. So we have

515

---

292. W (Var) reads: canals,

293. W (1827?) adds, following a sentence from 1824: Such is this one-sidedness of abstraction.

294. [Ed.] On the Parsee cultus, see Zend-Avesta, ed. Kleuker, esp. 2:114, 118 (SBE 3:390).

295. [Ed.] This transitional section anticipates in certain respects the separate discussion in the 1831 lectures of "Phoenician" or "Syrian" religion as the "religion of anguish." See the reference in the concluding paragraph to the dying and rising of God, as well as the allusion to "other diverse configurations" of the type from which Egyptian religion has been singled out at the beginning of the next section (below, n. 317).

296. W (1831) reads: We had generation and perishing in Hinduism too, but not subjectivity or the return into the One, not a One that passes through these forms or these differences itself, and in and from them returns to itself. It is this higher power of subjectivity which, when it is developed, lets the distinction go out of itself, yet keeps it enclosed within itself, or rather overpowers it.

here subjectivity in its reality, though not yet in truly actual freedom but only seething in and out of this reality.

Here the dualism of light and darkness that we had before us at first begins to unify itself, so that the dark or negative aspect occurs within subjectivity itself, an aspect that in its intensification becomes evil. The unifying within self of opposed principles is what subjectivity is—it is the might to endure and resolve this contradiction within itself. Ormazd always has Ahriman opposed to him. To be sure, the representation that in the end Ahriman will be overcome and Ormazd alone will rule is maintained too, but it is not expressed as a present state, it is only something future. God, the essence or the spirit, must be present and contemporary, not relegated to the domain of imagination, into the past or the future.[297]

This standpoint is the unity, the drama of the subjectivity that itself traverses these different moments—it is the affirmation that itself passes through negation and reconciles negation with itself, concluding with the return into self, with reconciliation. But it does this in such a way that the deed of subjectivity is found only in its ferment, rather than its being the subjectivity that actually has fully attained and consummated itself. These are the moments of this stage.

A subject is this distinction, something inwardly concrete, a development in which subjectivity introduces itself into the developed powers and unites them in such a way that[298] this subject has a history, the history of life and of spirit. It is inner movement, in which it fragments into the distinction of these powers and inverts itself into something strange to itself. The light does not perish; but here it is a subject that estranges itself from itself and is held fast in its own negativity, yet within and out of this estrangement it restores 516   itself. | The result is the representation of free spirit, though at first only the drive to bring forth its emergence.[299]

297. W₂ (Var?) adds: The next requirement is that the good must also be posited in actual fact as real power within itself, and must be grasped not only as universal subjectivity but also as real subjectivity.

298. W (Var) adds: they are set free,

299. L (1827?) adds, similar in W: Here we have God as subjectivity generally, and the principal moment in it is that negation does not fall outside, but within, the

[300]It is this moment of negation that we have to make some further remarks about. ˉThe moment of negation,ˉ[301] insofar as it is posited as natural, and is a determinate aspect of natural being, is death. Hence the determination that makes its entry here is the death of God. The negative as an abstract expression has very many determinacies, it is change in general. Even change involves partial death. On the natural level negation appears as death; in this guise negation itself is still within natural being, is still not purely in spirit, or the spiritual subject as such. On the spiritual level negation appears within human life, within spirit itself, as the characteristic that one's natural will is something other for one, that essentially and spiritually one distinguishes oneself from one's natural will. Here this natural will is the negation, and the human being comes to itself and is free spirit in overcoming this naturalness; one has reconciled one's heart or natural individuality—which is other than rationality or the rational—with the rational, and so one is present to oneself. This being at home with self, this reconciling, is present only through the movement or through this process. The natural will appears as evil; thus negation (as natural will) appears as something already there. In raising themselves up to their truth, human beings find this natural determination already there in opposition to the rational.

We shall discuss negation in a still higher and more spiritual form later on.[302] For in another perspective, negation is something posited by spirit. Thus God is spirit in that God begets his Son or his own other, | posits what is other than himself; ˉbut in this other, God   517 is present to himself.ˉ[303] There the negation is something vanishing as well, and therefore negation in God is this determinate, essential moment.

---

subject itself; and the subject is essentially a return into itself, i.e., it is self-communion. This being at home with itself includes the difference that consists in positing or having an other than itself. It includes negation, but it also includes the return into itself, and being at home or identical with itself in this return—i.e., it includes affirmation.

300. *In B's margin:* 9 July 1827

301. *W (Var) reads:* There is *one* subject; the moment of the negative,

302. *[Ed.]* See Vol. 3:275–290.

303. *Thus also W; W (Var) adds:* [W₂: and beholds himself and is eternal love.] Here the negation is likewise the vanishing element. *In An's margin:* a negation that immediately vanishes again, however, since God beholds himself in the Son himself.

But here we have at first only the representation of subjectivity in general. The subject itself goes through these distinct conditions as its own, so that this negation is immanent in it. Insofar as this negation therefore appears as a natural determination, the determination of death makes its entrance too, and God with the characteristic of subjectivity appears here ‾as the eternal history,‾[304] as being the absolutely affirmative, which itself dies,[305] becoming estranged from itself and losing itself; but through this loss of self it rediscovers itself and returns to itself. It is[306] one and the same subject that traverses these[307] determinations. The negative that we had [in Persian religion] in the form of evil as Ahriman, so that the negation did not belong to the ‾being‾[308] of Ormazd, here belongs to the self of God.

[309]In Hindu mythology there are many incarnations; for instance, Vishnu is the history of the world and is now in the eleventh or twelfth incarnation;[310] similarly, in that religion it is the case that the Dalai Lama and Buddha, likewise Indra, the god of natural life, die, and other gods also die and come back again. But this dying is different from the negativity we are discussing here,[311] for the latter pertains especially to the subject. In making this distinction everything depends on logical determinations. Analogies and similitudes can be found in all religions, for example God's becoming human [in Christianity] and | the incarnations [in Hinduism]. Volney[312] even linked

518

304. W (Var) reads: in his eternal history, and shows himself
305. W (Var) adds: —the moment of negation—
306. W (Var) adds: in this religion, then,
307. W (Var) adds: different
308. W (Var) reads: self
309. Precedes in L (1827?), similar in W: We have already had negation in the form of death too.
310. [Ed.] It has not been possible to identify Hegel's source. Since reference to an "eleventh or twelfth" incarnation occurs only in L and W (11:433) and is not corroborated by An, Bo, or Hu, it is probable that we have here an erroneous transmission by the transcript upon which both L and W may have relied. Buddha is reckoned as the ninth incarnation of Vishnu (see Creuzer, Symbolik und Mythologie 1:578, citing an Iranian source); the tenth incarnation—Kalki—has not yet occurred.
311. W (Var) adds: namely death,
312. [Ed.] See C. F. C. de Volney, Les ruines; ou, Meditations sur les revolutions des empires, 2d ed. (Paris, 1798), pp. 275, 386.

Krishna and Christ by virtue of their names.[313] But correlations of this kind are extremely superficial even though they embody a common element, a similar characteristic. The essential thing, the thing that matters, is precisely a further determination that is overlooked. The thousandfold dying of Indra or the rising again of Krishna is of a different kind than the death of the subject: the substance remains one and the same. At the death of the lama the negation does not apply to the substance; the substance just vacates ⌐the¬[314] body of one lama, but has immediately selected another. The substance is not concerned with this dying, this negation; here the negation is not posited in the [divine] self or in the subject as such; it is not a proper, inner moment or immanent determination of the substance, and the latter has not the anguish of death. Thus it is only now that for the first time we have the dying of God as internal to God himself, the determination that the negation is immanent in God's essence[315]; and it is essentially through this that this God is verily characterized as subject. This is what the subject is—bringing itself forth by giving to itself inwardly this otherness, and returning to itself through the negation of itself. For this reason the third determination in regard to this anguish and death is rising again from the dead and being restored [to life].

b. Egyptian Religion[316]

⌐Religion exists in this mode of determinacy as the religion of the Egyptians. What I have stated is its soul or principal determination; it is on this account that Egyptian religion has been singled out from

313. *In An's margin:* in his *Ruins*
314. *W (Var) reads:* this individual
315. *W (Var) adds:* is within himself.
316. [*Ed.*] In 1827 as in 1824, Hegel describes Egyptian religion as the religion of the enigma or riddle (*Rätsel*) because everything in it symbolically denoted something that remained unexpressed, and it did so in ways that were enigmatic and obscure. The primary instance of this, he says, is the image of the sphinx, half human and half animal, in which we see the artistic shape forcing its way out of the animal form into the human; it has not yet arrived at the shape of beauty, which was the shape of Greek religion; it remains enigmatic, lacking Greek clarity. Hegel's source of information remained primarily the classical authors (Herodotus and Plutarch), but he was increasingly familiar with recent archaeological expeditions (see ensuing notes).

other diverse configurations[317] as the principal figure [of this type].[318] |

519

When we consider it in detail, the image of this standpoint is that the principal figure, called Osiris, has opposed to him (as his enemy) the negation as external or other, as Typhon.[319] But the negation does not remain thus external to him, so that he would only abide in struggle, as in the case of Ormazd; instead, the negation enters into the subject itself. The subject is killed, Osiris dies; but he is perpetually restored, and thus—posited as one born a second time, as a representation—he is not something natural but something set apart from the natural and the sensible. Thereby he is defined and posited as belonging not to the natural as such but to the realm of representing, to the soil of the spiritual, which endures beyond the finite. According to his own inner definition, Osiris is the god of representation, the represented god. The fact that he dies, but is also restored to life, expresses explicitly the point that he is present in the realm of representation as opposed to sheerly natural being. But he is not merely represented in this way, for he is also known as such; it is two different things, whether he simply is as a represented being, or is also known as a represented being.

In his role as a represented being, then, Osiris is the ruler in the

---

317. [Ed.] Hegel probably has in mind here the so-called Phoenician or Syrian religion, to which he devotes a separate section in the 1831 lectures.

318. W₂ (Var) reads: In this religion, as it actually exists in the religion of the Egyptians, we encounter an endless multiplicity of images. But the soul [or living principle] of the whole is what constitutes the chief characteristic, and it is emphasized in the principal figure.

W₁ (1831) has the following transition to the Eygptian religion at another place: If we express the idea as meaning that spirit is what coalesces with itself through the negation of the other, and stress this moment of negation of the other on its own account and in isolation, then we are beginning from the other of spirit, and not from spirit, not from the fact that spirit is the setting of something against itself; but the other of spirit as such is nature generally, so that the transition then appears as the moment that has been stressed. The next step, then, is where the passing-over is not yet grasped as reconciliation in love, but as strife and struggle. God is intuited in this struggle itself; what is to be attained by it is the elevation of spirit out of the natural state. We find this struggle most notably in the Egyptian religion; this is the religion of ferment, in which everything is mixed together.

319. [Ed.] On the opposition of Osiris and Typhon, see Plutarch, De Iside et Osiride, esp. chap. 13; also Diodorus Siculus, Bibliotheca historica 1.21.

realm of the dead, of Amenti;[320] just as he is lord of the living, so also he is lord of what no longer exists sensibly, of the soul that continues to exist divorced from the body, from the sensible and the transitory.[321] | Typhon, the evil one, is overcome, and pain with him, and Osiris is the judge over right and justice. Inasmuch as evil is overcome and condemned, judging enters for the first time at this point in such a way that this judging is the decisive thing, i.e., the good has the might to enforce its authority.[322]   520

If we say then that Osiris is a ruler of the dead, this means that the dead are precisely those who are not posited in the sensible or the natural realm, but endure by themselves on a higher plane. Linked to this is the fact that the singular subject is known as something that endures; it is withdrawn from the transitory and is secure by itself, is distinct from the sensible. For this reason it is a most important saying of Herodotus about immortality, that the Egyptians were the first to declare that the human soul is immortal.[323] We find survival and metamorphosis in China and India, but—like the perpetuation of the individual—in Hinduism immortality itself is only something subordinate and nonessential. The highest state there is not an affirmation or perpetuation, but rather nirvana, a state of annihilation of the affirmative, one that only seems to be affirmative, that of being ˉsimilarˉ[324] to Brahman. This identity with Brahman, however, is at the same time dissolution into that unity which does indeed seem to be affirmative but is totally devoid of determination or internal distinction. In Egyptian religion, then, the following is logically involved: the highest element of consciousness is subjectivity as such; this is totality and is capable of being inwardly

320. [Ed.] Plutarch, De Iside et Osiride 27, 29; also Herodotus, Histories 2.123. See 1824 lectures, n. 352.

321. W₁ (Var/1831?) adds: This involves the higher vocation of humanity. W₂ (Var/1831?) adds: The realm of the dead is the one where natural being is overcome; it is the realm of representation where precisely what does not have natural existence is preserved.

322. W (Var) adds: and to destroy what is null, what is evil.

323. [Ed.] Herodotus, Histories 2.123. Hegel also refers to this report by Herodotus on a separate sheet (Berliner Schriften, pp. 706–707), but there observes that belief in immortality rests on the feeling of the inner infinitude of spirit and that this was not yet present in Egyptian religion.

324. W (Var) reads: identical

independent—it is the representation of true independence. The independent is what is not in antithesis but overcomes it. It does not ˉsetˉ³²⁵ something finite over against itself but has the antitheses within itself and by the same token has overcome them. This characteristic of subjectivity, which is objective and befits the objective, befits God, is also the characteristic of subjective self-consciousness in the mode of immortality. It | knows itself as subject, as totality and true independence and thus as immortal.³²⁶

521

This is the universal. Around this universal plays an endless throng of representations and deities. Osiris is but one of them, and according to Herodotus³²⁷ he is even one of the later deities; but he has elevated himself above all the deities, most notably³²⁸ as ruler of the dead or as Serapis (which is the focus of greatest interest).³²⁹

325. *W (Var) reads:* retain

326. *W₂ (Var/1831?) adds:* With this knowledge the higher vocation of humanity has dawned upon consciousness.

327. [*Ed.*] Herodotus, *Histories* 2.144–145. Hegel's account is a condensation and to some extent an inference from Herodotus's actual words. Hegel also misrepresents the relationship between Osiris and Serapis: Serapis is not a particular incarnation of Osiris but a Hellenistic amalgam incorporating, it is true, many features of the earlier Osiris. Hegel probably has in mind Plutarch's statement, *De Iside et Osiride* 27, that Osiris received the name of Serapis "after he had changed his nature." Hegel's knowledge of the Serapis cult also came from J. D. Guigniaut, *Sérapis et son origine: Commentaire sur les chapitres 83–84 du livre IV des Histoires de Tacite* (Paris, 1828).

328. *W (Var) adds:* in the kingdom of Amenti,

329. *W (1831) adds:* [W₁: But the principal figure is Osiris.] Herodotus, following the statements of the priests, gives a sequence of the Egyptian gods, and Osiris is here to be found among the later ones. [W₂: But] the further development of the religious consciousness also takes place within a religion itself, and we have already seen in the case of the Hindu religion that the cultus of Vishnu and Shiva is of later date. In the sacred books of the Parsees, Mithra is listed among the other Amshaspands and stands on the same level with them; but Herodotus already gives prominence to Mithra,ᵃ and by Roman times, when all religions were brought to Rome, the worship of Mithra was one of the principal religions, [W₁: not the worship of Osiris. W₂: while the worship of Ormazd did not have the same importance.]

Among the Egyptians too, Osiris is said to be a deity of later date. We know that in the time of the Romans Serapis, a special shape of Osiris, was the main deity of the Egyptians; yet [W₂: even though he emerged for spirit at a later stage] Osiris is nonetheless the [Egyptian] deity in which [W₁: the higher consciousness W₂: the totality of consciousness] disclosed itself. [W₁: Just as the Parsees have the antithesis of light and darkness, so the Egyptians have that between Osiris, who portrays light or the sun, and Typhon or evil generally. But this antithesis W₂: The antithesis contained

628

As with | Mithra, so also here: the [logical] determination that lies   522
within him has been lifted out as the most interesting one, and just
as the Parsee religion became the worship of Mithra, so the Eygptian
religion became that of Osiris. Osiris, however, became the focus
not of the immediate world but of the spiritual, intellectual world.

From what we have said, we can see that here for the first time
we have subjectivity in the form of representation. We are dealing
with a subject, with something spiritual that is represented in a
human fashion. But it is not an immediate human being that is
revered by the Egyptians—its existence is not posited in immediacy,
in the realm of immediately determinate being, but in the realm of
representation. It is a content that in its movement is subjectivity,
one that has within it the moments and movement through which
it is subjectivity; but even in its form, on the soil of spirituality, it
is exalted above the natural. Thus the idea is posited on this soil
of representation, and its deficiency is that it is only the representation

---

in the Egyptian way of viewing the matter] for its part loses its profundity and becomes
a superficial one. Typhon is physical evil and Osiris is the vitalizing principle; the
barren desert belongs to the former, and he is represented as the burning wind, the
scorching heat of the sun. Another antithesis is the natural one between Osiris and
Isis, the sun and the earth, which is regarded as the principle of procreation generally.
Thus even Osiris dies, vanquished by Typhon, and Isis seeks everywhere for his bones;
the god dies, which is again this negation. The bones of Osiris are then buried, but
he himself has now become the ruler of the realm of the dead. Here we have the course
of living nature, a necessary cycle returning into itself. The same cycle also belongs
to the nature of spirit, and this is expressed in the fate of Osiris. Here again the one
signifies the other.

The other deities are [logically] tied to Osiris; [W_1: They are, as it were, only
singularized moments of Osiris, who unites the whole within him. One of the principal
deities is Amon (Jupiter Ammon), who especially represents the sun, W_2: for he is
their point of union, and they are only singularized moments of the totality that he
represents. Amon for instance is the moment of the sun,] a characteristic which also
pertains to Osiris. There are, in addition, a great number of deities who have been
called calendrical deities because they relate to the natural revolutions of the year.
Particular periods of the year, such as the spring equinox, the early summer, and
the like, are singled out and personified in the calendrical deities.

Osiris, however, signifies not only what is natural but what is spiritual. He is a
lawgiver, he instituted marriage, he taught agriculture and the arts. These figurative
accounts contain historical allusions to ancient kings; and thus Osiris contains historical
features too. In the same way the incarnations of Vishnu and the [legendary] conquest
of Ceylon [by Rama] seem to allude to the history of India.

[Ed.] [a]See above, n. 287.

of subjectivity, that subjectivity is only abstractly there in its foundation, that it is still present only in its abstract foundation. The depth of the universality of the antithesis is not yet in it, subjectivity is not yet present in its absolute universality, absolute spirituality. Because it is not yet known in the depth of universality, but only in representation, it is thus a contingent, superficial, external universality.

The content that is in the representation is not bound to time; ˉon the contrary, it is universality.ˉ[330] That something is in this time, in this space, that it is this sensible singularity, is stripped away. Through representation, in that it is on the soil of spirit, everything already has a universality even though but little of the sensible is stripped away (as, for instance, in the representation of a house). Thus the universality is only an external universality, what is common to many instances. [331]This coheres with the fact that the foundation, this representation of subjectivity, has not yet gone down absolutely into its inward depth, it is not yet the internally fulfilled foundation, so that the world would be posited in it ideally, and all natural things would be absorbed in it.

To the extent that this subjectivity is the essence, it is the universal foundation, and the history that the subject is, is known at the same time as the movement, life, and history of everything in the immediate world. As a result, we have the distinction that this universal subjectivity is also the foundation of the natural, that it is the inner universal, or that which is the substance of the natural. We have therefore two determinations here, the natural and the inner substance, and that gives us the definition of the symbolic. Another foundation is ascribed to natural being, the immediately sensible receives another substance: it is no longer immediately itself, for it represents something else that is its substance and its significance (and that is what a symbol is). The story of Osiris is[332] also the inner, essential story of the natural, of the order of nature in Egypt. To

330. W_1 *(Var) reads:* it is universality. W_2 *(Var) reads:* it is planted in the soil of universality.
331. *Precedes in* W_2 *(Var):* The fact that external universality is still the dominant feature here,
332. W_2 *(Var) adds:* in this abstract connection

this story belong the sun and its path, and the Nile with its fecundating and changing stages. |

524

The story of Osiris therefore is the story of the sun. The sun climbs to its zenith and then recedes. Its rays and its strength grow more feeble [up to] December 21; but after this period of growing feeble and weak, it begins again to rise higher in the sky; it is reborn with new strength. In this way Osiris signifies the sun and the sun Osiris.[333] The sun, the year, and the Nile are grasped as this cycle turning back upon itself.

The particular aspects in a cycle of this kind are momentarily represented as independent, as particular deities each of which designates a single aspect, a moment of this cycle. If we say the Nile is the inner, that the sun and the Nile are the significance of Osiris, that other deities are calendrical deities, all this is correct.[334] One is the inner element and the other is the portrayer, the sign or signifier by which the inner discloses itself outwardly; here there is changeableness, this being the case at one time, the reverse at another. The natural cycle of plants, of seeds, and of the Nile occurs in this manner, for its life is the same universal story. One can take them reciprocally, one as the inner, and the other as the form of its presentation or the form for grasping it. But what is in fact the inner is Osiris, subjectivity as such, this cycle going back into itself.

This is how the symbol is the ruling element, something inner and on its own account that has an outward mode of determinate being. The two are distinct from each other. It is the inner, the subject,

---

333. *L (1827?) adds, similar in W:* The sun is comprehended as this cycle, and the year regarded as the one subject that of its own accord traverses these various states. The natural realm is grasped in Osiris in the sense that it is a symbol of Osiris. Thus Osiris is the Nile, which rises, making everything fruitful, overflows its banks, and then becomes small and impotent during the hot season—here the evil principle comes into play—but eventually recovers its strength.

334. *[Ed.]* Hegel is probably referring to Creuzer, *Symbolik und Mythologie* 1:279, 289–290, where Creuzer argues that the Osiris myth as a whole and in its details is an allegorical portrayal of the solar and lunar years. Regarding the identification of Osiris and the Nile, see Plutarch, *De Iside et Osiride* 36, although he merely says that the Nile is an "emanation" of Osiris; and neither he nor Creuzer speaks in this connection of "the inner element" as opposed to a sign. See also C. F. Dupuis, *Origine de tous les cultes; ou, Religion universelle,* 4 vols. (Paris, 1795), esp. 1:366–395.

that has here become free and independent, so that the inner is the substance of the outer, not in a contradiction or dualism with it but as the significance, the representation on its own account, as against the sensible mode of determinate being. The final aspect in this sphere is that, inasmuch as the significance constitutes the focus over against
525 the sensible aspect, ˉthere lies in it the impulseˉ[335] | to bring the representation to an intuited state. [336]The representation as such must express itself, and it is human beings who must bring this significance forth from themselves to intuitable visibility. The immediate has disappeared. If it is to be brought to intuition, to the mode of immediacy—and representation has the need to complete itself in this manner—if the representation so integrates itself, then this immediacy must be ˉa mediating,ˉ[337] a human product. Previously we had the intuitable aspect—the immediacy as natural thing—in a natural mode that is quite unmediated. In India, for instance, Brahman has its existence, the mode of its immediacy, in thinking, in the sinking of the human being into self. Or in Persia, ˉlight isˉ[338] the form of immediacy, which is in an immediate way. But here, since representation is the starting point, it must bring itself to intuition, to immediacy; and therefore immediacy is here mediated and posited by human beings. It is the inner that has to be brought to immediacy. The Nile and the course of the year are immediate existences, but they are symbols of what is inner; their natural history is comprehended in representation as the subject. This comprehended being, both this process as a subject and the subject itself, is inwardly this returning movement; this cycle is the subject, it is this comprehended whole that is the representation, and as subject it should be made intuitable.

Generally speaking, this impulse toward intuition can be regarded as the cultus of the Egyptians, the infinite impulse to labor, to construct outwardly what is to begin with still inward, what is

335. W (Var) reads: [W₁: subjectivity in this determinacy, subjectivity as represented, W₂: the fact that subjectivity is represented in this determinacy as the focus] is closely connected with the impulse
336. In B's margin: 10 July 1827
337. W (Var) reads: something mediated,
338. W₂ (Var) reads: the good is light, and therefore in

contained in representation, and for that reason has not yet become clear to itself. The Egyptians toiled for millennia, above all to prepare and preserve their soil; their labor in its connection with their religion, however, is the most astonishing thing ever brought forth either upon the earth's surface or beneath it: works of art that are extant now only in dilapidated ruins | (as compared with what they once were) but which have amazed everyone on account of their beauty and of the effort involved in their construction. This was the occupation and the deed of this people, to keep on bringing forth such works. The entire people was involved in this endeavor, driving on beyond all measure. There was no pause in this production; the toiling spirit did not rest from making its representation visible to itself, from bringing to clarity and consciousness what it inwardly is. These works are grounded immediately in the definition that God has in this religion.[339] |

526

527

339. W (1831) adds: [W$_1$: Thus in Osiris we see spiritual moments also revered, W$_2$: First of all we may recall how, in Osiris, spiritual moments are also revered,] such as right, morality, the institution of marriage, art, and so forth. But Osiris is especially the lord of the realm of the dead, the judge of the dead. We find countless pictures in which Osiris is portrayed as the judge, with a scribe before him who is enumerating for him the deeds of the soul that has been brought into his presence.[a] This realm of the dead, the kingdom of Amenti, constitutes one of the main features in the religious representations of the Egyptians. Just as Osiris and Typhon were opposed as the life-giving and the destructive principles, and the sun was opposed to the earth, so here the antithesis of the living and the dead now comes on the scene. The realm of the dead is just as fixed a representational image as the realm of the living. It discloses itself when natural being is overcome; it is there, in the realm of the dead, that what no longer has natural existence persists.

The enormous works of the Egyptians, which have come down to us today, are almost entirely works that were destined for the dead. The famous labyrinth had as many chambers above as beneath the ground.[b] The palaces of the kings and priests have been transformed into heaps of rubble, while their graves have defied time. We have found deep grottoes extending for quite some distance that were hewn in the rock for the mummies, and all their walls are covered with hieroglyphics. But what excites the greatest admiration are in particular the pyramids, temples for the dead [that were built] not so much in their memory as in order to serve them as burial places and as dwellings. Herodotus says that the Egyptians were the first who taught that souls are immortal.[c] It may occasion surprise that, although the Egyptians believed in the immortality of the soul, they nonetheless devoted so much care to their dead; one might think that people who deem their souls immortal should no longer have particular regard for their bodily side. Yet it is precisely the peoples who do not believe in immortality who deem the body to be of little account after its death

This colossal diligence of an entire people was not yet in and for itself pure fine art; rather it was the impulsion toward fine art. Fine art involves the characteristic of free subjectivity; spirit must have

528   become free from desire, | free from natural life generally, from subjugation by inner and outer nature; it must have become inwardly

---

[W_2: and do not provide for its preservation]. The honor that is shown to the dead is in every way dependent upon the way immortality is represented. [W_1: Humans do not want nature to exert its power directly W_2: Even if the body must fall into the grip of a natural power that is no longer under the control of the soul, then at least we humans do not want nature as such to be what exerts its power and physical necessity] over the inanimate body, this noble casket of the soul. [W_2: It must be we humans, rather, who bring this about—at least in some degree.] So we seek to protect the body against nature as such or we return it (of its own free will, so to speak) to the earth or destroy it by fire. In the Egyptian mode of honoring the dead and preserving the body, there is no mistaking the fact that they knew human beings to be exalted above the power of nature, and hence they sought to preserve the human body from that natural power in order to exalt the body (as well as the soul) above nature. The ways that different peoples deal with the dead are altogether bound up with their religious principles, and the different burial customs always have significant connections [with those principles].

[W_2: Well then, in order to grasp the particular standpoint of art at this stage, we have to recollect that although subjectivity does, of course, emerge here, it only emerges in a basic way, and the picturing of it still passes over into that of substantiality. Consequently the essential differences have not yet mediated and spiritually permeated one another but are still only mixed together instead.] [W_1: There are a few other W_2: There are several] noteworthy features that can be listed to elucidate the way that what is present and living is intermixed and combined with the idea of the divine— so that on the one hand the divine is made into something present, or on the other hand human, and in fact even animal, figures are elevated into a divine and spiritual moment. Herodotus refers us to the Egyptian myth that the Egyptians had been ruled by a succession of kings who were gods.[d] Here we have the mixture already, in that the god is known as the king, and the king in turn as the god. There are also countless artistic portrayals representing the consecration of kings, in which the god appears as the consecrator and the king as the son of this god; and then, too, the king himself is represented as Amon. It is related of Alexander the Great that the oracle of Jupiter Ammon declared him to be the son of that god.[e] This is quite in accordance with the Egyptian character, for the Egyptians said the same thing about their own kings. And the priests too are regarded on the one hand as priests of the god, but also as the god himself. We have many monuments and inscriptions from the later Ptolemaic age, where King Ptolemy is always just called the son of God or God himself; and the Roman emperors are treated in the same way.

[W_1: Particularly astonishing in the case of the Egyptians W_2: Astonishing to be sure—although in the light of the intermingling of the representation of substantiality with that of subjectivity, no longer inexplicable—] is the animal worship that was practiced [W_2: by the Egyptians] with extreme crudity. The different districts of Egypt

free, it must have the need to know itself as free, and to be free, as the object of its own consciousness. Inasmuch as spirit has not yet arrived at the stage | of freely thinking itself, it must freely intuit itself, it must have itself before its eye intuitively as free spirit. The fact that it becomes an object for intuition in the mode of immediacy

529

---

worshiped particular animals, such as cats, dogs, monkeys, and so on, and even went to war with one another on their account. The life of these animals was held absolutely sacred, and their killing was severely punished. Dwellings and possessions were allotted to them, moreover; and provisions were collected for them. Yes, and even in time of famine, starving human beings were left to die, rather than their drawing upon these stores.[f] Apis was most revered, for they believed that this bull represented the soul of Osiris. In the coffins in some of the pyramids, Apis-bones have been found carefully preserved.[g] [W_1: It has been said that all forms of religion were to be found in Egypt, including animal worship; to be sure, W_2: All the forms and shapes of this religion were mingled in with animal worship. To be sure,] this worship of animals belongs to the most offensive and odious aspect of it. But we have already shown, in connection with the religion of the Hindus, how human beings could come to the point of worshiping animals. If God is known [W_2: not as spirit but] as power in general, then this power is an unconscious working—perhaps a universal life. Hence when this unconscious power emerges into outward shape, it is initially the shape of an animal. For the animal is itself something unconscious, it bears within it a dull, still life (as compared with human free will) such that it may seem as if it had within itself that unconscious power [W_2: which works in the whole]. One especially typical [W_2: and characteristic] configuration [W_2: however,] is that the priests or scribes frequently appear in sculptures and paintings wearing animal masks—as also do the embalmers of mummies. This duplication—an external mask concealing another figure beneath it—conveys the awareness that consciousness is not just submerged in dull, animal vitality, but knows itself also to be separated from that animal state, and recognizes a further meaning in this fact.

[W_1: Regarding the political state of Egypt, W_2: We find the struggle of spirit seeking to extricate itself from immediacy in the political state of Egypt too;] our histories often speak of the battles of the kings with the priestly class, and Herodotus mentions them as dating from the earliest times, saying that King Cheops caused the temples of the priests to be closed, while other kings reduced the priestly caste to complete subjection and wholly excluded them [from politics].[h] [W_2: This antithesis is no longer [typically] Oriental.] Here we see human free will rebelling against religion. This emergence from dependence is a trait which it is essential to take into account.

[W_1: There are some naive and highly intuitive portrayals of spirit's struggle to escape from the natural state. This emergence and struggle is expressed in many shapes. W_2: This struggle of the spirit to escape from the natural state and its emergence from it is, however, expressed in particular in naive and highly intuitive portrayals in the visual arts. We need only to remember the image of the Sphinx as one example.] In Egyptian works of art everything is symbolical; significance attaches even to their smallest detail; even the number of pillars and of steps is not calculated to serve ordinary external purposes, but instead signifies such things as the months [of the year]

(which is a product) implies that this, its determinate being or immediacy, is wholly determined by spirit, and has through and through the character of dwelling here as a free spirit. But this is just what we call the beautiful, where all externality is completely characteristic and significant, is determined from within as from what is free. It is a natural material such that its features are only witnesses to the spirit that is internally free. The natural moment must be mastered everywhere in such a way that it serves only for the expression and revelation of spirit. And since the content in the

---

or the number of feet that the Nile has to rise in order to overflow the land. The spirit of the Egyptian people is, in fact, an enigma. In Greek works of art everything is clear, everything is set forth; in Egyptian art we are everywhere presented with a problem—the work of art is an external object that hints at something [else] not yet expressed.

[W_2: But even though at this stage spirit is still in a state of fermentation and still entangled in obscurity, and even though the essential moments of the religious consciousness partly are just mixed together and partly are in a state of mutual strife in terms of, or rather because of, this mixing: in any case, what is emerging here is free subjectivity.]

[*Ed.*] [a]Hegel's knowledge of portrayals of this kind probably comes in particular from the collection of the Prussian general and Egyptologist J. H. C. von Minutoli, which he saw in Berlin in April 1823; see Hegel's letter to Creuzer, 6 May 1823, *Hegel: The Letters,* trans. Clark Butler and Christiane Seiler (Bloomington, 1984), p. 370 (no. 450a). See also the list of items in J. Passalacqua, *Catalogue raisonné et historique des antiquités découvertes en Égypte* (Paris, 1826). [b]See Herodotus, *Histories* 2.148. Herodotus says that the labyrinth, which he claims to have seen himself, was built slightly above the lake of Moirios, near the so-called "city of crocodiles"; he gives a detailed description of it and says it was even more grandiose than the pyramids. [c]See above, n. 323. [d]Herodotus, *Histories* 2.144. In the Temple of Zeus there were 345 statues representing 345 generations of high priests. Herodotus says he was told that before the line of high priests, Egypt had been ruled by gods, the last of whom was Horus, the son of Osiris, whom the Greeks called Apollo. [e]Hegel is referring to Alexander's visit to the oracle of Ammon in the Libyan oasis of Siwa; see Plutarch, *Life of Alexander* 27. The story recounted by Plutarch was that the prophet who gave utterance to the oracle intended to address Alexander as "my son" (*paidion*) but through unfamiliarity with Greek said *paidios* instead, which Alexander interpreted to mean "son of Zeus." [f]See Diodorus Siculus, *Bibliotheca historica* 1.84, though what Diodorus says is that many actually resorted to cannibalism but no one was ever accused of eating one of the sacred animals. [g]This is based on G. B. Belzoni, *Narrative of the Operations and Recent Discoveries within the Pyramids, Temples, Tombs, and Excavations, in Egypt and Nubia* (London, 1822), 1:425–426; see also Belzoni's description of the mummified remains of cattle, sheep, monkeys, foxes, cats, crocodiles, fish, and birds, pp. 261 ff. [h]See Herodotus, *Histories* 2.124, 127.

Egyptian determination is this subjectivity, there is present here that | impulsion or craving for fine art which operated especially in the 530 domain of architecture and at the same time sought to pass over to beauty of figure. Insofar as this was only craving, however, beauty itself has not yet emerged here as such.

This craving or impulsion involves the struggle of meaning with material, with external shape generally; it is only the attempt or the striving to place the stamp of inner spirit on outer configuration.[340] Here it is only craving because meaning and its portrayal, representation and determinate being, are still separated; as distinction they are in principle mutually opposed. The distinction subsists because the subjectivity is to begin with only general and abstract; it is not yet fulfilled and concrete.[341] ¬The figure has not yet risen to be a

340. *L (1827?) adds, similar in W:* The pyramid is a self-sufficient crystal [*ein Kristall für sich*], in which a dead person is preserved; but in the work of art, which is reaching out for beauty, the externality of the configuration is imbued with the inner soul, with the beauty of what is within.

341. *W (1831) adds:* Thus the Egyptian religion actually exists for us in the works of Egyptian art, in what they tell us when they are combined with the historical record that has been preserved for us by ancient historians. In recent times in particular, the ruins of Egypt have been examined by many investigators; the mute language of the statues has been studied, and the enigmatic hieroglyphs as well.

[W₁: Above all, therefore, we must W₂: We must] recognize the superiority of a people that has consigned its spirit to works of language over one that has only left mute works of art behind it for posterity. [W₂: But we must at the same time bear in mind that no written [religious] documents were yet in existence among the Egyptians because spirit had not yet clarified itself but had consumed all its energy[a] in what was indeed an external strife, as is apparent in the works of art.] By dint of prolonged study, progress has been made in deciphering the hieroglyphic language, to be sure; but in some ways the goal has still not quite been achieved, and the hieroglyphs will always be hieroglyphs.[b] Numerous rolls of papyri have been found alongside the mummies, and it was believed that these constituted a real treasure-trove that would yield important conclusions. They are nothing but a kind of archive, however, and for the most part they contain deeds of purchase regarding pieces of land or objects that the deceased had acquired. So it is therefore principally the extant works of art whose language we have to decipher, [W₁: and apart from that we can only hold fast to the information handed down by the Greeks. W₂: and from which a cognitive grasp of this religion is to be derived.]

Now if we contemplate these works of art, we find that everything in them is wonderful and fanciful, but always with a definite meaning, which was not the case among the Hindus. Thus we have here the immediacy of externality along with the meaning, or thought. We find both together in the monstrous conflict of the inner

531   free and beautiful one, | it is not yet spiritualized to clarity; what is sensible and natural has not yet been completely transfigured into the spiritual so that it would be only an expression of the spiritual; and this organization and its features are only signs, only signifiers of the spiritual.⁻³⁴²

The Egyptian principle therefore still lacks clarity and transparency on the part of the natural or external features of the configuration; what abides is just the task of becoming clear to itself. ⁻⁻⁻The stage this principle exhibits can be grasped quite generally as that of the *enigma:* the meaning is something inner that impels itself to make itself outwardly visible; but it has not yet arrived at the consummation of its portrayal in externality.⁻³⁴³ The inscription of the

---

with the outer; there is a monstrous urge on the part of what is inner to work itself free, and the outer aspect portrays this struggle of spirit for us.

[*Ed.*] ᵃ*sich abarbeiten.* This verb has the double meaning of "wearing oneself out" and "working oneself clear." The contrast between *sich noch nicht abgeklären* and *sich abarbeiten* in this sentence suggests the former meaning, but Hegel may have intended both, especially in light of what he says at the end of the variant about the "urge on the part of what is inner to work itself free." ᵇA reference to the success achieved over preceding years in deciphering hieroglyphic script thanks to the Rosetta Stone. See J. F. Champollion, *Lettre à M. Dacier relative à l'alphabet des hiéroglyphes phonétiques* (Paris, 1822); and *Précis du système hiéroglyphique* (Paris, 1824). Hegel speaks of numerous investigations of Egyptian ruins and writings, but we do not know to what extent he was informed of the attempts made by Silvestre de Sacy and Johann Akerblad to decipher the hieroglyphs. Hegel's daybook indicates that already in Jena he had become acquainted with earlier efforts through reports in the *Allgemeine Litteratur-Zeitung,* vol. 4 (October–December 1802). In the *Philosophy of World History,* Sibree ed., p. 200 (Lasson ed., p. 463), Hegel deals at greater length with the deciphering work of Thomas Young and J. F. Champollion. He also owned a copy of the French translation of Brown's *Aperçu sur les hiéroglyphes d'Égypte* (Paris, 1827), which discusses the problems in detail. Brown (p. 34), however, contests Champollion's claim to be the first to decipher the hieroglyphs and contends that the credit belongs to Young's article on Egypt in a supplementary volume to the *Encyclopaedia Britannica.*

342. *Similar in W; An reads:* The spiritual [content] and the form are not yet in free unity.

343. *W₁ (1831) reads:* Hence we can intuit the Egyptian spirit only as still caught up in a state of fermentation. This obscurity toils, so to speak, in the field of outward expression; in these works of art we find the moments mixed together, especially the moments of strife. We have already considered the antithesis of good and evil, or of light and darkness, in the religion of the Parsees; and we find these antitheses again here.

temple of the goddess Neith in Sais is given in full as follows: "I am what was, what is, and what will be; | no mortal has yet lifted my   532 veil."¯¯[344] The fruit of my body is Helios, etc."[345] This still hidden essence expresses clarity or the sun, that which is itself becoming clear or the spiritual sun, as the son who is born from it.

This clarity is what is attained in the forms of religion that we now have to consider, in the religion of beauty, or that of the Greeks, and in the religion of sublimity, or the Jewish religion.[346] In Greek religion the riddle is solved; according to one very significant and admirable myth the Sphinx is slain by a Greek and the riddle is resolved in this way: the content is the human being, the free, self-knowing spirit. So much, then, for the first form, the religion of nature, with which we have tarried so long because it is the more remote from us, and because nature is burdened precisely with the fragmentation [of the religions] into their proper independence.

We proceed now to the second stage of ethnic religion, which we have to consider next.

344. W_2 (MiscP) reads: It is now that the spiritual consciousness seeks for the first time—as what is inward—to struggle free from the natural state.

The most important presentation, the one in which the essence of this struggle is rendered completely visible to intuition, is to be found in the image of the goddess at Sais, who was portrayed as veiled. What is symbolized in this image, and is explicitly expressed in the superscription in her temple—"I am what was, what is, and what will be; no mortal has yet lifted my veil"—is that nature is something inwardly differentiated, namely, something other than the appearance that presents itself immediately—it is an enigma, it has an inner [content], something hidden.

But this inscription continues as follows.

345. [Ed.] Hegel quotes this inscription not in the form handed down by Plutarch, De Iside et Osiride 9, but in the form found in Proclus, In Platonis Timaeon 1.30 (except for the final sentence). Hegel's statement that the inscription stood in the temple of the goddess is a further reference to Proclus; according to Plutarch it was on the goddess's throne at Sais. Drawing on Schiller, "Das verschleierte Bild zu Sais," Die Horen, vol. 1, no. 9 (1795) (cf. Schiller, Nationalausgabe 1:254–256), Hegel understands the veil as a shroud for the statue of Neith, not as an allusion to the goddess's virginity. Elsewhere he criticizes the customary reference to a "veil" of the goddess, citing from Aloys Hirt, Ueber die Bildung der aegyptischen Gottheiten (Berlin, 1821), p. 7, the formula, "No one raised my tunic," noting that there was no mention of a veil in the description, nor was one to be seen in the pictorial representations. See "Hegel und die ägyptischen Götter: Ein Exzerpt," ed. Helmut Schneider, Hegel-Studien 16 (1981): 65.

346. W_2 (Var) adds: i.e., in art and in the beautiful human shape on the one hand, and in objective thought on the other.

B. THE ELEVATION OF THE SPIRITUAL
ABOVE THE NATURAL:
THE RELIGION OF THE GREEKS AND THE JEWS[347]

This is the stage where the spiritual elevates itself above the natural, to a freedom that is partly beyond natural life, and partly within it, so that the [simple] blending of the spiritual and the natural ceases. It is the second stage of the ethnic religions.

The first stage was the religion of nature. It comprises much within it. On the one hand it is the most difficult to grasp because it is the farthest removed from our imagination, and because it is the crudest and most incomplete stage. On the other hand the natural thus has diverse configurations within it because in this form of naturalness and immediacy [the moments of] the universal, absolute content fall apart from one another. What is higher is also deeper, for there these different moments are comprehended in the ideality of subjective

---

347. [Ed.] Our title for Sec. B is adopted from the heading found in the Königsberg anonymous transcript used as the basis for Lasson's edition. According to Lasson (2/1:249–250), the heading was quite lengthy and consisted of a phrase, "The Elevation of the Spiritual above Nature," followed by the words making up the first sentence of the preface to the section, and ending with a second heading, "Religion of the Greeks and the Jews." The first phrase corresponds to the language used in the summary of the whole of *Determinate Religion* at the beginning of Part II: "The second stage of religion is the elevation of the spiritual above the natural." The second phrase is supported by the Hube transcipt. Thus we have combined the two phrases. This is apropos because the problematic of "elevation" pervades Hegel's entire discussion of Greek and Jewish religion. It should be noted, however, that the German edition uses as a heading for Sec. B: "The Religion of Beauty and Sublimity: The Religion of the Greeks and the Jews."

The 1827 lectures restore the basic structural arrangement of the *Ms.* in the sense that Roman religion is considered under a third separate category, that of "expediency," which is not a subcategory of Sec. B as in 1824. Far from representing the "elevation of the spiritual above the natural," the purposiveness of Roman religion is not yet (or no longer) a free and purely spiritual purposiveness. It is rather an external, utilitarian, totalitarian purpose, although universal in a political sense. While it may combine elements from the religions of beauty and sublimity, it also destroys them; their true fulfillment is found only in the Christian religion.

The most significant organizational innovation of the 1827 lectures, however, is the reversal of the order in which the religions of sublimity and beauty were treated in the first two series, so that now Greek religion is considered first and Jewish religion second. The reasons for this change and its implications are discussed in the Editorial Introduction.

unity, and this fragmenting of immediacy | is sublated, is brought 533
back into subjective unity. That is the reason why whatever falls
under the determination of natural life exhibits such a multiplicity
of configurations, which present themselves as indifferently external
to one another, as properly independent.

The universal characteristic of this [second] stage is the free
subjectivity that has satisfied its [definitive] craving or impulse. It
is the free subjectivity that has attained lordship over the finite
generally, over the natural and finite aspects of consciousness, over
the finite whether it be physical or spiritual, so that now the subject
is spirit and the spirit is known as spiritual subject. [The subject is]
related to the natural and the finite in such a way that the natural
is ⁻only instrumental;⁻³⁴⁸ it has only the characteristic of glorifying,
manifesting, and revealing the spirit; [what it reveals is] that in this
freedom and power, in this reconciliation with itself within the
natural and the finite, the spirit is on its own account and is free.
It has come forth and is distinguished from this finite natural-spiritual
[world]; it is distinct from the situation of empirical, changeable
consciousness, as well as from that of external being. That is the
characteristic determination of this sphere. Because spirit is free and
the finite is only an ideal moment in it, spirit is posited as inwardly
concrete, and because we consider it as inwardly concrete (i.e.,
consider spirit's freedom as inwardly concrete), it is rational spirit;
the content constitutes the rational aspect of spirit. According to the
relationship of the content, this determinacy formally is just the one
that we stated above: that the natural and finite is only a ⁻sign⁻³⁴⁹
of spirit, and is only instrumental to its manifestation. Hence we
have here the religion within which rational spirit is the content.

This free subjectivity has at once a double determination, one we
have to distinguish. In the first place, the natural and finite is
transfigured in the spirit, in the freedom of spirit. Its transfiguration
consists in the fact that it is a sign of spirit, in which connection the
natural itself constitutes in its finitude the other side to that [spiritual]
substance; or, in this transfiguration of the physically or spiritually

---

348. W (Var) reads: partly just instrumental, but partly the garment of the spirit
[that is] present concretely within it, as representing that spirit;

349. W₂ (Var) reads: witness

natural element, it stands over against that essentiality, the substan-
534 tiality, or the god. The god is the free subjectivity of which the |
finite is posited only as a sign, ¯within which¯[350] the god, the spirit,
appears. That is the mode of present individuality, or of beauty—
Greek religion. The other form is the religion of sublimity, namely
that in which the sensible, the finite, the spiritually and physically
natural element, is not taken up and transfigured in free subjectivity.
For when it is transfigured in free subjectivity, the finite element still
has at the same time a natural and external aspect: although it is
elevated into a sign of spirit, it is nevertheless not purified of
externality and sensibility. The other determination, therefore, is that
free subjectivity is raised up into the purity of thinking, this other
extreme. We have this in the religion of sublimity—¯in the¯[351] form
that is more in keeping with the content than the sensible aspect is.
Here [however] the sensible is ruled by this free subjectivity, which
is in itself a power and within which the other is only an ideal element
and has no genuine subsistence as opposed to free subjectivity.[352]

In the first form the reconciliation of the spiritual and the natural
has occurred, so to speak, in such a way that the natural is only a
sign or moment of the spiritual. But the spiritual continues to be
afflicted with this externality. It is in the second form that the finite
is first ruled by spirit, with spirit elevating itself [so that it is] raised
up beyond naturalness and finitude, and is no longer afflicted with
and clouded by the external (as is still the case with the form of
beauty). The first form yields the religion of beauty, the second the
religion of sublimity.

1. The Religion of Beauty, or Greek Religion

We could directly call this the religion of the Greeks, which is an
infinite, inexhaustible theme. The content that especially interests
us is that this religion is a religion of humanity. Humanity comes
535 to its right, to its affirmation, | in which what the human being
concretely is, is portrayed as the divine. There is no content in the

350. *Thus also* W₂; W₁ *(Var) reads:* inasmuch as
351. W *(Var) reads:* a
352. W *(Var) adds:* Spirit is what raises itself, what is raised above the natural,
above finitude. This is the religion of sublimity.

Greek divinities that was not essentially familiar to humans. Here we have to consider first the objective, God in his objectivity; and secondly the cultus.

a. The Divine Content[353]

There are three aspects to distinguish in the content, namely (1) what is full of import as such, the divine in its essentiality, (2) what stands over this divine aspect as the higher [power], i.e., fate, and (3) what stands beneath this divine aspect as the subordinate [level], i.e., the external individualities.

As for the import as such or the pure content, the substantial foundation is, as we showed in the transitional remarks, rationality in general, the freedom of spirit or essential freedom. This freedom is not caprice; it must certainly be distinguished from that. It is essential freedom by definition, the freedom that determines itself. Because the freedom that determines itself is the foundation of this relationship, it is rationality or, more precisely, ethical life. The way this follows here is to be assumed as a lemma: freedom is the self-determining, what is formal; it first appears as something formal. That this formal element turns over into the content that we call ethical life is something we presuppose. Concrete rationality is essentially what we call ethical principles. The point that freedom is a willing of nothing else than itself, i.e., freedom, and that this is ethical life and that ethical determinations result from it, cannot be developed further here.

Because ethical life constitutes the essential foundation here, what we are dealing with is the initial [mode of] ethical life so to speak, ethical life in its immediacy. There [simply] is this [social] rationality, the rationality or ethical life being wholly universal, being therefore in its substantial form. The rationality does not yet subsist as a subject, it has not yet raised itself up out of this unalloyed unity in which it is ethical life, into the unity of the subject, nor has it deepened itself inwardly. For this reason | the spiritual and essentially   536
ethical characteristics appear as a mutually external [complex]. It is a content most full of import, but [its elements are] mutually external.

---

353. *Text reads:* 1. The Content. *In B's margin:* 12 July 1827

Ethical life has to be distinguished altogether from morality; the latter is the subjectivity of the ethical, what knows itself as inwardly accountable—having premeditation, intention, ethical purpose, and also knowing the substantial being that the ethical realm is. Ethical life is just the substantial being, the true being of the ethical, but it is not yet the knowing of this ethical domain. The ethical is an objective content such that a subjectivity or this internal reflection is not yet present.

Because it has this character, the ethical content fragments. Its foundation is constituted by the πάθη,[354] the essential spiritual powers, the universal powers of ethical life—especially political life, life in the state, and also justice, valor, family, oaths, agriculture, science, and the like. Bound up with the fact that the ethical fragments into these, its particular determinations, ˉis the factˉ[355] that the ˉcreaturelyˉ[356] domain also comes forward against these spiritual powers. The character of immediacy that has this fragmentation as its consequence involves the characteristic that natural powers [such as] heaven and earth, mountains and streams, day and night, emerge over against [the spiritual]. These are the general foundations.

But however much this fragmentation obtains, in which the natural powers appear as by themselves, as autonomous, the unity of the spiritual and the natural likewise emerges more and more, and this is the essential thing; it is not, however, the neutralization of the two, but instead the spiritual is not only the preponderant aspect in it but also the ruling and determining one; while the natural on the contrary is idealized and subjugated.

The relationship appears on the one hand in the fact that there are nature deities: Cronus, Time (in this mode, an abstraction), Uranus, Oceanus, Hyperion, Helios, Selene. In the cosmogonies, which are at the same time theogonies, we encounter these nature deities—universal powers of nature, formations and configurations

---

354. [Ed.] See Clement of Alexandria, *Exhortation to the Heathen* 2: "And some even of the philosophers, after the poets, make idols of forms of your passions [πάθη], such as fear, and love, and joy, and hope" (*Ante-Nicene Fathers* 2:178).

355. W_2 (*Var*) *reads:* is the other fragmentation, namely,

356. W (*Var*) *reads:* natural

of nature, which we number together among the Titans.[357] They, too, are personified; but in their case the personification is superficial; | it is only personification, for the content of Helios, for 537 example, is something natural and not something spiritual, it is no spiritual power. That Helios is represented in a human fashion or is active in human fashion is an empty form of personification. Helios is not the god of the sun—the Greeks never express themselves this way; one nowhere finds ὁ θεὸς τοῦ ἡλίου; there is not a natural sun and then also a Helios as god of the sun, but rather Helios, the sun, is the god. ˉOceanus is likewise the god itself. These are theˉ[358] powers of nature.

The second point, therefore, is that these powers of nature are subordinated to the spiritual ones, and this is not merely our view of the Greek gods, for the Greeks have expressed it themselves; they are conscious of it themselves. About this aspect we need only say what the Greeks themselves have said about their gods; for the concept, the essential, is contained in what they said. A major point of their mythology is that the gods, with Zeus at their head, have gained the mastery for themselves by a war, by violence. The spiritual power has cast down the giants, the Titans, from the throne; the sheer power of nature has been overcome by the spiritual, the spiritual has elevated itself above it and now rules over the world. Thus this war with the Titans is not a mere fairy tale but is the essence of Greek religion. The entire concept of the Greek gods lies in this war of the gods.[359] ˉThat the spiritual principle elevated itself, that it subordinated the natural to itself, is the gods' own proper deed and history.ˉ[360] | The Greek gods have indeed done none other than 538

357. [Ed.] See Hesiod, Theogony 133–134, 168 ff., 371.

358. W_1 (Var) reads: Oceanus is not god of the sea and such like; he is the god [itself]. . . . What we have here are these W_2 (Var) reads: Oceanus is not god of the sea in such a way that the god and what he rules over are distinguished from each other; on the contrary, these powers are

359. L (1827?) adds, similar in W: When they take up the cause of an individual, of Troy, this is not something that gods do to one another. W_2 (Var) continues: So it is no longer their history and is not the historical development of their nature.

360. W_2 (Var/1831?) reads: But the fact that, as the spiritual principle, they have attained the mastery and have overcome the natural realm is what constitutes their essential act; and this is the essential consciousness that the Greeks have of them.

this. ⁻The Titans were banished to the edge of the earth; therefore they still exist. But, in their being posited as subordinate to the spiritual, not only are they external with respect to the spiritual, but they also constitute an intrinsic determination with respect to the spiritual gods. The victory over them is of the kind in which they nevertheless still retain their rights and their honor. They are powers of nature, but they are not the higher, ethical, and true power, the spiritually essential forces. Nevertheless there is still a natural moment contained in those forces themselves.⁻³⁶¹ But it is only a trace of the natural element, and hence it is only one aspect in them.

But there are still two varieties to be distinguished among the ancient gods themselves. For it is not only the nature powers, which are sheer power, that belong among them; Dike, the Eumenides, the Erinyes, the Oath, the Styx, νέμεσις, and φθόνος are counted among them too. Although they are of a spiritual type, these deities distinguish themselves from the newer ones in that they are the aspect of the spiritual as a power that has being only inwardly; they are the powers that merely subsist within themselves but that are also spiritual. Yet because the spirituality that subsists only inwardly is only an abstractly crude spirituality and is not yet true spirituality, they are for this reason counted among the ancient gods; they are the universals that are to be feared: the Erinyes are just the internal judges, the Oath is this certainty in my inmost self—whether or not I declare it externally, its truth resides within me; we can compare the Oath with conscience. In contrast, Zeus is the political god, the god of laws and of lordship, but of laws that are well known. What is valid here is not the laws of conscience but right according to public laws. In the state it is not conscience but rather the laws (what is established) that have the right. What conscience, if it is of the correct

361. W (1831) reads: Thus the natural gods are subdued, and driven from their throne; the spiritual principle is victorious over the religion of nature, and the natural forces are banished to the borders of the world, beyond the world of self-consciousness, though they have also retained their rights. Though they are the powers of nature, they are posited also as ideal, as subject to the spiritual; so that they constitute one determination with respect to what is spiritual or to the spiritual gods themselves, and the natural moment is still contained in the gods themselves.

sort, ought to know as the right must also | be objective.[362] Alongside   539
Dike, Nemesis is also an ancient deity; she is [found] together with
φθόνος [and] with love and consists in bringing down the stiff-
necked, the proud, the self-exalting ones whose wrong consists only
in being someone exalted, and is not an ethical wrong. It is a justice
that is of the superficial sort, consisting only in equalization and in
leveling; it is envy, a dragging down of what is superior so that it
stands on the same level with the rest. Only strict, abstract right is
contained in Dike. Orestes is pursued by the Eumenides, therefore
by gods of strict right; he is acquitted by Athena, by ethical right,
the visible, ethical power of the state.[363]

Here we want to give a few examples of how the natural is mingled
with the spiritual. Zeus is the firmament generally, atmospheric
change (*sub Jove frigido*);[364] he is the thunderer; but, apart from
this natural principle, he is not merely the father of gods and human
beings but also the political god, the god of the state, and the right
and ethical life of the state, the highest power on earth, [and also]
the power of hospitality.[365] Phoebus is sometimes the knowing god.
But obviously, according to the analogy of the substantial logical
determination, knowing corresponds to light and [Apollo] is the
aftereffect of the sun's power; he is Helios, the sun that shines upon
everything. Indeed, light and knowing correspond implicitly and
explicitly, and the logical determination is just that of making

362. *L (1827?) adds, similar in W:* What is genuine is not hidden but manifest.
If human beings appeal to their conscience, one may have one conscience and another
another; in order that one's conscience may be of the correct sort, what one knows
to be right must be in conformity with objective right, it must not merely dwell within
one. If conscience is right, then it is a conscience recognized by the state, once the
state is ethically constituted.

363. *L (1827?) adds, similar in W:* Ethical right is something other than merely
strict right; the new gods are the gods of ethical right.
[*Ed.*] See Aeschylus, *Eumenides*, esp. 734–741.

364. [*Ed.*] Horace, *Carmina* 1.1.25.

365. *Thus Hu; L (1827?) adds (after an insertion from 1824), similar in W:* with
reference to the old customs at a time when the relationship of the different [city-]
states was not yet defined, and hospitality was the essential sphere of the ethical
relationship of citizens belonging to different states. *Precedes in W:* He is, moreover,
a many-sided ethical power, the god of hospitality

540 manifest | whether in the natural or in the spiritual [realm]. So Phoebus is not only the knowing one, the revealing one, the oracle; he is also called the Lycian Apollo, and λύκειος has an immediate connection with light. That comes from Asia Minor; the natural aspect, the light, is more prominent to the East. In his work on the Dorians, to be sure, Müller[366] denied this affinity of Phoebus with the sun, but right at the beginning of the *Iliad* Phoebus sends pestilence over the Greek camp near Troy;[367] this connects directly with the sun, this effect of the hot summer, the sun's heat, and in a hundred other portrayals we find this same point echoed.[368]

Pindar and Aeschylus too (in the *Eumenides*) speak of a succession of oracles of the ancient gods right up to the new god Phoebus.[369] In the *Eumenides* of Aeschylus the initial scenes take place before the temple of Apollo. ¯There Pythia states that the first to be worshiped are Gaia and Themis, and then the other or new gods.[370]

---

366. [*Ed.*] See Karl Otfried Müller, *Geschichten hellenischer Stämme und Städte*, vol. 2 (Breslau, 1824), pp. 284, 287–288. Müller's conclusion was that the identification of Apollo and the sun was a late development, after the old gods had been turned into predicates of νοῦς or interpreted as material forces and objects. Müller himself also established a link between Apollo's epithet λύκειος and the adjective λευκός ("light"), without however attaching weight to it as an argument for identifying Apollo and the sun. In opposing Müller, Hegel also implicitly took up a position against J. H. Voss and in support of Friedrich Creuzer, according to whose interpretation, based ultimately on Herodotus, "two Egyptian sun-gods contributed to the genesis of a twofold Hellenic Apollo" (Creuzer, *Symbolik und Mythologie* 2:158; cf. also pp. 132 ff. for the interpretation of λύκειος). On other matters, such as the assessment of the symbolic character of the Greek gods, belief in the mysteries, and Mithra, Hegel is not so close to Creuzer's viewpoint (see above, n. 288).

367. [*Ed.*] Homer, *Iliad*, bk. 1, esp. vv. 9–10 concerning Apollo's anger against Agamemnon.

368. *L (1827?) adds, similar in W:* Even the pictures of Phoebus have attributes and symbols that are closely connected with the sun. *W (1831) continues:* The same divinities that were Titanic and natural in the earlier phase appear later with a spiritual basic character, and this is the predominant one; it has been disputed, indeed, that there was any natural element still in Apollo. In Homer at all events, Helios is the sun, but at the same time he is immediately brightness, the spiritual moment that shines upon and illuminates everything. But even at a later period Apollo still retained something of his natural element, for he was portrayed with a nimbus around his head.

369. [*Ed.*] This succession does not occur in Pindar himself but in a general scholium to the Pythian hymns.

Thus we see what follows: that the natural gods are the lowest and the spiritual gods are higher. This is not to be taken historically, but in a spiritual way.⁻³⁷¹ | 541

³⁷²Thus the first mode of giving oracles, the noise and rustling of leaves and suspended cymbals, as in Dodona, is by mere natural sounds. Only later appears [the figure of] the priestess who gives the oracle in human tones (although in keeping with the oracle's mode she does not do so in clear speech).³⁷³ Similarly, the Muses are at first nymphs, i.e., springs, the rippling, murmuring, and burbling of brooks; everywhere the beginning arises from the natural mode, from powers of nature that are transformed into a god of spiritual content.³⁷⁴

370. [Ed.] Aeschylus, Eumenides 1–8.

371. W (1831) reads: Here we have the summons to worship. The first to be worshiped is the giver of oracles (Γαῖα), the nature-principle, then Θέμις, who was already a spiritual power, though, like Dike, she belongs to the ancient gods; next comes night, and then Phoebus—the oracle has passed over to the new gods. Pindar also speaks of a similar succession [W₁: of the gods W₂: in connection with the oracle]. He makes night [W₁: first among the gods W₂: the first oracle-giver], then comes Themis and next Phoebus. Thus we have here the transition from natural figures to the new gods. In the sphere of poetry, where these doctrines originate, this [sequence] is not to be taken historically [W₂: is not so hard-and-fast as to preclude any deviation from it].

372. Precedes in L (1827?): This is the universal, even though it was not particularly noticeable in the gods taken one by one.

373. [Ed.] See Etienne Clavier, Mémoire sur les oracles des anciens (Paris, 1818), pp. 72–75.

374. W₂ (1831) adds: A similar transformation can be seen in Diana. The Diana of Ephesus is still Asiatic and is represented with many breasts and bedecked with images of animals. Her foundation is natural life in general, the procreative and sustaining force of nature. The Diana of the Greeks, on the other hand, is the huntress who slays animals; she has not the sense and meaning of hunting generally, but of the hunt directed at wild animals. And these animals are indeed subdued and killed through the bravery of spiritual subjectivity, whereas in the earlier spheres of the religious spirit they were regarded as absolutely inviolate.

[Ed.] This portrayal of Diana of Ephesus is found in Minucius Felix, Octavius 22.5 in terms similar to those used by Hegel. However, Hegel probably has in mind not this text but the illustration in Creuzer's Symbolik und Mythologie, plate 3, no. 4. In his Handbuch der Archäologie der Kunst (Breslau, 1830), pp. 472–478, K. O. Müller also discusses the difference between the modes of portrayal prevalent in Greece and those in Asia Minor.

[375]Prometheus gave fire to humanity and taught people to sacrifice.[376] This means that the animals had belonged not to humanity but to a spiritual power, i.e., human beings had [previously] eaten no meat. Then Prometheus took the entire offering to Zeus; he had made two constructs, one wholly of bones and entrails with the skin drawn over it, and the other entirely of meat; but Zeus seized the first one. So to sacrifice means to hold a feast, with the gods receiving the entrails and the bones. Zeus was deceived when the bones wrapped in fat were offered up to him while human beings themselves enjoyed the meat. This [Titan] Prometheus taught human beings to lay hold of animals | and make them their food.[377] [378]So it was Prometheus who taught human beings to eat meat, and imparted to them other skills as well; he is recalled with gratitude as the one who made human life easier. ˉBut notwithstanding the fact that human powers of understanding are displayed here, he still belongs among the Titans for the very reason that these skills are only to satisfy human needs—they have no ethical authority, they are not laws.ˉ[379] A passage in Plato,[380] where he speaks of Prometheus, contends that Prometheus indeed fetched fire from the

542

375. *Precedes in W (1831):* Prometheus, who is also reckoned among the Titans, is an important, interesting figure. Prometheus is a natural power; but he is also a benefactor of human beings, in that he taught them the first arts. He brought fire down from heaven for them; the power to kindle fire already presupposes a certain level of civilization; humanity has already emerged out of its primitive barbarism. The first beginnings of culture have thus been preserved in grateful remembrance in the myths.

376. [*Ed.*] Hesiod, *Theogony* 510–615, and *Works and Days* 48–58.

377. *L (1827?) adds, similar in W:* Among the Hindus and Egyptians, on the other hand, it is forbidden to slaughter animals.

378. *Precedes in L (1827?):* Artemis is the human power to hunt animals. In this connection there are various myths that refer to this new departure in the matter of the relationship of human beings to animals.

379. *W (1831) reads:* But Prometheus is a Titan. He is chained to the Caucasus and a vulture constantly gnaws at his liver, which always grows again—a pain that never ceases. What Prometheus taught human beings was only the skills that pertain to the satisfaction of natural needs. In the simple satisfaction of these needs there is never any [final] satiety; instead the need comes back again, and always has to be ministered to afresh. That is what is signified by this myth.

[*Ed.*] See in particular Hesiod, *Theogony* 520 ff., and Aeschylus, *Prometheus Bound.*

380. [*Ed.*] Plato, *Protagoras* 321c–d.

Acropolis but that he was unable to bring the πολιτεία or ethical life down to human beings; that was kept in the citadel of Zeus, ˉZeus withheld it for himself.ˉ[381] In Aeschylus[382] Prometheus says that in his defiance he takes solace and satisfaction in the fact that to Zeus will be born a son who will cast him down from his throne: Heracles, the only god who was first a human being and then was placed among the gods. What is asserted here is that Heracles will attain the lordship of Zeus; that can be viewed as a prophecy that has come to pass.

[383]ˉUp to this point we have considered concrete characteristics of the Greek gods; now we want to indicate the abstract ones.ˉ[384] The | gods are scattered; Zeus rules them as a family. The higher 543 power, absolute unity, stands above the gods as a pure power. This power is what is called destiny, fate, or simple necessity. It is without content, is empty necessity, an empty, unintelligible power that is devoid of the concept. It is not wise, for wisdom falls within the circle of the gods and includes concrete characteristics that belong in the sphere of the particular, and pertain to single gods. Destiny is devoid of purpose and wisdom, it is a blind necessity that stands above all, even above the gods, uncomprehended and desolate. The abstract cannot be comprehended. Comprehending means knowing something in its truth. What is debased and abstract is incomprehensible; what is rational is comprehensible because it is inwardly concrete.

As far as the disposition of finite self-consciousness [toward this

381. W (1831) reads: and this expresses the fact that it belonged to Zeus personally.

382. [Ed.] Aeschylus, Prometheus Bound 755–768.

383. In B's and Hu's margin: 13 July 1827

384. Thus Hu; L reads: The two moments that have still to be considered are the extremes. The midpoint of this religion is the thought of God in his concrete determination. . . . The other two moments are the abstract determinations as opposed to the concrete ones. . . . There is a plurality of gods; in and for itself, of course, the content is the genuine, spiritual, ethical substance; but it is still fragmented, it is still divided into many particularities. W₁ (Var) reads: 1. There is a plurality of gods—[though] the content is in and for itself the genuine, spiritual, ethical substance. But it is still fragmented, [there are] still many particularities, and together they make a unity. W₂ (1831/Var?) reads: The unity that binds the plurality of the particular gods together is still at first a superficial unity.

necessity] is concerned, and its relationship to it, this necessity [is viewed as] underlying everything, gods and human beings alike; on the one side there is an iron power, on the other a blind obedience without freedom. But there is still one form of freedom that is at least present, and that is on the side of [finite] disposition. In having this conviction regarding necessity, the Greek achieves inner peace in saying: It is this way and there is nothing to be done about it; I must be content with it. This implies that I *am* content with it and thus that freedom is present after all, in that it is my own state. This conviction implies that human beings are confronted by this simple necessity. In adopting this standpoint and saying, "It is this way," one has set aside everything particular, one has renounced it and abstracted from all particular goals and interests. Dissatisfaction occurs when human beings hold fast to a goal ¯and there is no harmony or agreement | between what they want and what is.¯385 But from this standpoint [of fate] all dissatisfaction and vexation are removed, because human beings have withdrawn into this pure rest, this pure being, this "it is." In that abstract freedom there is on the one hand in fact no solace for human beings.386 One needs solace [only] insofar as one demands a compensation for a loss; but here ¯no compensation is needed, for one has given up the inner root of what one lost. One has wholly surrendered what has been given up.¯387 That is the aspect of freedom, but it is abstract and not concrete freedom, the freedom that only stands above the concrete but is not posited in essential harmony with what is determinate,

544

385. *W (1831) reads:* and will not give this up; and if things do not match this end or are even in conflict with it, they are dissatisfied. There is no harmony then between what is actually present and what they want, because they have within themselves the ought: "That ought to be."

Thus discontent and inward cleavage are present; but from this standpoint one does not hold firmly to any purpose or interest in the face of actually existing circumstances. Misfortune, discontent, is nothing but the contradiction, [W_1: that there is opposition to what I want to be. W_2: the fact that something is contrary to my will.]

386. W_2 *(Var) adds:* but solace is also unnecessary.

387. W_2 *(Var) reads:* one has renounced the inner root of racking worry and discontent and has wholly surrendered what is lost, because one has the strength to look necessity in the face.

the freedom that is pure thinking and being, or being-within-self, the annulment of the particular.[388]

¯The opposite extreme to that universality is external singularity, and this likewise is not yet taken up into the middle term; it also stands on its own account, as does that abstraction of thinking, of retreat into self.¯[389] Both extremes emerge from the same ground, from the same general determinacy, viz., that rationality, the rational content and ethical import, is still immediately present, is still | in 545 the form of immediacy—¯¯this is the logical determination from which the further characteristics proceed. Singular selfhood is subjectivity, but only in an external way. It is still not the one infinite subjectivity that is posited; for in that the external singularity is superseded. ¯Here on the contrary¯[390] the singularity is an external one just because it is not yet infinite subjectivity;¯¯[391] and the manifold content that plays about the gods falls on the side of externality. ¯Hence contingency of content enters into this sphere.¯[392] ¯¯So we should not believe, for instance, that the twelve main gods of Olympus are ordered and arrayed in correspondence with the concept. ¯They are not sheer allegories but are | concrete 546 (though not infinite) spirituality instead. They are also individual figures, and as concrete essences they have diverse properties; [but]

388. W_2 *(MiscP/1831?) adds:* In contrast, there is in the higher forms of religion the consolation that the absolutely final end will be attained despite misfortune, so that the negative changes around into the affirmative. "The sufferings of this present time are the path to blessedness [*die Leiden dieser Zeit sind der Weg zur Seligkeit*]." [*Ed.*] The rhyming of the German suggests that the source may be a Lutheran hymn, but there is also an allusion to Rom. 8:18: "I consider that the sufferings of this present time are not worth comparing with the glory [*Herrlichkeit*] that is to be revealed to us."

389. *Precedes in* W_1 *(MiscP/Var?):* Necessity is the one extreme. W_2 *(MiscP/Var?) reads:* Abstract necessity as this abstraction of thought and of the retreat into self is the one extreme; the other extreme is the singularity of the particular divine powers.

390. W_1 *(Var) reads:* External singularity is one thing, while subjectivity as inwardly infinite is something different. Here

391. W_2 *(MiscP/Var?) reads:* in other words, subjectivity is not posited as infinite subjectivity, and hence singularity comes on the scene in its external guise;

392. W_2 *(MiscP/Var?) reads:* But since particularity is not yet tempered by the idea, and necessity is not a meaningful measure of wisdom, an unlimited contingency on the part of the content enters into the sphere of the particular gods.

they are only imagined as concrete in such a way that what is inward is only one property. They are, however, still no universals.⁻³⁹³ ⁻⁻³⁹⁴ The natural element is still a factor in these determinations of the concrete and constitutes one side of the contrast. For instance, the sun rises and sets; the year, the appearance of the months, plays a part here, and for that reason the Greek gods have been made into calendar gods.³⁹⁵

One moment that we have to hold on to [firmly] is the so-called philosophical meaning [*Philosopheme*]; this is a moment that has its seat originally in the mystery rites. The mysteries are related to the manifest religion of the Greeks in the way that natural elements are related to the spiritual import: ⁻They are the most ancient cultus, the crude, natural cultus.⁻³⁹⁶ Just as the ancient gods are in the main only natural elements, so the content of the mysteries is the sort of crude content that spirit has not yet permeated. This is the relationship that both is necessary in and for itself and also at the same time is historical. But just as it was believed that ⁻particular depths of

---

393. W₂ *(1831) reads:* Finally, the free individuality of the gods is the main source of the manifold contingent content that is ascribed to them. Even though they are not yet infinite, absolute spirituality, they are at least concrete, subjective spirituality. As such they do not have an abstract content, and there is not just one property in them, but they unite several characteristics within them. If they possessed only *one* property, it would be only an abstract inner [content], or one simple meaning, and they themselves would merely be allegories, i.e., only *imagined* to be concrete. But in the concrete richness of their individuality they are not tied to the limited direction and kind of efficacy of one single exclusive property. Instead they can let themselves go freely in any direction they choose, including arbitrary, contingent ones.

394. W₁ *(Var) reads:* The twelve principal gods of Olympus, for example, are not ordered by means of the concept, they do not constitute a system. Moreover, they are concrete spirituality but not yet absolute subjectivity, and hence they are individual figures.

As concrete spirituality they do not have abstract content; what they have in them is not one distinctive property but several (as concrete). Were there only one property they would be allegories, they would only be *imagined* as concrete, with the result that the inward [content] or the meaning would be just the one distinctive property. But here we have subjective spirituality, though not yet infinite subjectivity.

395. W₁ *(Var?) adds:* as Dupuis does.

[*Ed.*] Dupuis, *Origine de tous les cultes* 1:317 ff. Dupuis identified Heracles in particular as a calendrical deity.

396. W₁ *(Var) reads:* This is either ancient religion or a more recent, imported cult.

religion were at home in India,⁻³⁹⁷ so it is believed here.³⁹⁸ From ⁻all of this [the mystery rites],⁻³⁹⁹ some elements also find their way into the concrete representation of the spiritual gods who are raised above this level. Inasmuch as the representations of origination and perishing are carried over into the spiritual circle, there are echoes of that transference here too. This is the case when an endless number of amours is acribed to Zeus, occasioned by the sort | of myths re- 547 ferring to natural relationships and natural powers.⁴⁰⁰

The other aspect of the content is that of appearance or of its shape.⁴⁰¹ At this stage beauty is everywhere the dominant factor. The god appears. These powers, these absolutely ethical and spiritual determinations, are known, they exist for the empirical self-consciousness. Thus they exist for an other, and what must concern us now is the precise manner in which they exist for their other, for the [worshiper's] subjective self-consciousness.

The first point is therefore that this content reveals itself in the innermost [being], comes into prominence within the spirit; but this

397. *Thus L; An reads:* great and ancient wisdom belonged to the Hindus and Chinese,

[*Ed.*] Hegel is probably referring in particular to Friedrich Schlegel, *Ueber die Sprache und Weisheit der Indier* (Heidelberg, 1808), pp. 90, 103 (cf. *Kritische Friedrich-Schlegel-Ausgabe* 8:193, 205). See above, n. 22.

398. *L (1827?) adds, similar in W₁:* Origination and perishing was comprehended in Hinduism as a content and was known in particular as a universal power. The mysteries contain premonitions in which an attempt was made to see the natural forces grasped in a universal way.

399. *W₁ (Var) reads:* this epoch,

400. *L (1827?) adds, similar in W:* Another relevant feature is the locality in which the consciousness of a god first began; in this regard the cheerfulness of the Greeks, the element of production, gave rise to a number of delightful stories. To investigate these different aspects, to decide where this or that single detail originated, is the task of scholarship.

401. *L, W (1831) add:* So far we have considered the way that the configuration of the divine is grounded in the implicit potential of these divinities, i.e., in their individual natures, their subjective spirituality, their geographically and temporally contingent emergence, or as it occurs in the involuntary transformation of natural determinations into the expression of free subjectivity. The configuration that we have now to consider is the one that is accomplished with consciousness. This is the appearing of the divine powers that occurs for "another," i.e., for subjective self-consciousness, and is known and shaped within the latter's own comprehension.

ethical and true content can reveal itself only within a spirit that itself is in itself and has been elevated to this spiritual freedom. These universal determinations come to consciousness for it, they manifest and reveal themselves inwardly. Contrariwise the other aspect is that, inasmuch as this level is only one of initial freedom and rationality, that which is a power within the spirit appears as an outward mode [of intuition]. That is the natural aspect with which this standpoint is still afflicted.[402] This whole external aspect is the rustling of the trees at Dodona, the silence of the wood where Pan is, falling stones, thunder and lightning—in short, the external phenomena in nature

548 that are taken to be something higher. | These phenomena occasion only the initial manifestation, so to speak, for the consciousness for which these determinations exist.[403]

⁻So the other to that immediacy or being, whether internal or external, is the grasping of that initially abstract [freedom], and is the real stuff of self-consciousness. ⁻⁻But the organ by which self-consciousness grasps this subsisting thing, this substantial and essential [being], is phantasy, which images what is initially abstract, the inwardly or outwardly subsisting [essence], and produces it as

549 what is first deemed to be a god.⁻[404] | Explanation here consists in

402. W₂ (Var) adds (cf. the following footnote): If the authorities and laws that announce themselves to the inward [thought] are spiritual and ethical, still they are [such] initially just because they are, and it is not known whence they come.

[Ed.] Hegel is referring to Antigone's defense of her behavior vis-à-vis Creon; see Sophocles, Antigone, vv. 453–457.

403. L (1827?) adds, similar in W₁ (cf. the preceding footnote): These shapes [W₁: authorities] and these laws simply are, the ethical is, and no one knows whence it came; it is eternal, or it is something external, thunder and lightning.

404. W₂ (Var/1831?) reads: It is self-consciousness that grasps, clarifies, or images what was initially abstract (whether inwardly or outwardly so) and produces it as what is deemed to be God.

W₂ (1831) continues: Natural phenomena or this immediate, external [mode of appearing], however, are not appearance in the sense that the essence would be only a thought within us—as when we speak of the forces of nature and their expressions. Here it does not lie in the natural objects themselves, does not lie objectively in them as such, that they exist as appearances of what is inward; as natural objects they exist only for our sense perception, for which they are not an appearance of the universal. Thus it is not in light as such, for example, that thought, the universal, announces its presence; on the contrary, in the case of natural essence we must first break through the outer shell behind which thought, or the inwardness of things, is hidden.

making it representational, in enabling consciousness to represent to itself something divine. We have already seen what the definition of this phantasy is: because this content still has in it this finitude of being immediate rationality, so that it presents itself as a particular, as a content that is not yet within infinite subjectivity, it involves finitude as such and is afflicted with the natural aspect. Phantasy is the activity of giving shape either to what is inwardly abstract or to what is external, what is initially an immediate being (for example, thunder or the ocean's roar); it shapes both of these aspects and posits them as something concrete, one of which is the spiritual and the other the natural; the result is that the external being is no longer independent but is downgraded into being just a sign of the indwelling spirit, into serving just to make the implicit spirit apparent.‾‾405

Hence the gods of the Greeks are products of human imagination or sculptured [*plastisch*] deities formed by human hands. They originate therefore in a finite manner, one produced by poets, by the Muse. The gods have this finitude because they have finitude within them in accord with their own import; that is, they have particularity, or the falling asunder of the spiritual power and the natural

---

But the natural, the external, at the same time must be posited in itself, it must in its externality be posited as sublated and in itself be posited as appearance, with the result that it has meaning and significance only as the outward expression and organ of thought and of the universal. Thought must be for intuition; in other words, what is revealed is on the one hand the sensuous mode, while what is perceived is at the same time thought, the universal. It is the necessity that has to appear in a godlike way, i.e., it has to appear within [finite] being as necessity in immediate unity with finitude. This is posited necessity, i.e., the necessity that has being and exists as simple reflection into itself.

405. W₂ *(MiscP/1831?) reads:* Phantasy is now the organ with which self-consciousness gives shape either to what is inwardly abstract or to what is external, what is initially an immediate being, and posits it as concrete. In this process what is natural loses its independence and is downgraded into the sign of the indwelling spirit, so that it just lets the implicit spirit be apparent.

W₂ *(1831) continues:* The freedom of spirit here is not yet the infinite freedom of thought; the spiritual essentialities are not yet [subjected to] thought. If human beings were thoughtful in such a way that pure thinking constituted the foundation, there would be for them only one God. But here they do not come upon their essentialities as present and unmediated natural shapes; to the contrary, they bring them forth for the imagination. As the midpoint between pure thought and immediately natural intuition, this bringing forth is phantasy.

550   aspect. ¨¨This finitude of content is why they | originate in a finite manner as human products.[406] At this stage the divine is grasped neither by pure thinking nor in pure spirit. ¨God is not yet worshiped in spirit and in truth [John 4:24].¨[407] The divine is not yet [present] as absolute truth, it is not even grasped by the external understanding, in the abstract categories of the understanding; for these categories are what constitute prose. For this reason these gods are humanly made—not [with respect to] their rational content but [in their appearing] as gods. Every priest was, so to speak, such a maker of gods. Herodotus says that Homer and Hesiod made the Greeks' gods for them.[408 ¨¨409] [410]This interpretation of an external [phenomenon] just means shaping it, giving it the shape of the activity

551   of a god. ¨The explanation | here is not for the understanding but¨[411] is produced by phantasy for phantasy.

406. *L (1827?) adds:* The gods' shape is one that is posited by the subjective side and by finite spirit, and human beings themselves are conscious that they are the ones who have brought forth this shape.

407. *Thus An, similar in Hu; L (Var) reads, similar in* W_1: There is truth in this rationality, the truth that this is only something manifesting the spiritual.

408. W_1 *(Var/1831?) adds:* i.e., every priest or experienced old man.

[*Ed.*] Herodotus, *Histories* 2.53. What Herodotus actually said was that Homer and Hesiod "established the genealogy of the gods in Greece and gave them their eponyms, apportioned offices and honors among them, and revealed their form."

409. W_2 *(1831) reads:* They are discovered by the human spirit, not as they are in their implicitly and explicitly rational content, but in such a way that they are *gods*. They are made or poetically created [*gedichtet*], but they are not fictitious [*erdichtet*]. To be sure, they emerge from human phantasy in contrast with what is already at hand, but they emerge as *essential* shapes, and the product is at the same time known as what is essential.

It is in this sense that we have to understand Herodotus when he says that Homer and Hesiod made the Greeks' gods for them. The same could be said of every priest or experienced old graybeard who was capable of understanding and expounding the appearance of the divine and of the essential powers in the natural.

410. *Precedes in L (1827?), similar in W:* When the Greeks heard the roaring of the sea at the funeral of Achilles, Nestor came forward and said that Thetis was taking part in the mourning.[a] And during the plague Calchas said that it was sent by Apollo because he was angry with the Greeks.[b]

[*Ed.*] [a]Homer, *Odyssey* 24.47–56. [b]Homer, *Iliad* 1.92–96.

411. *Thus Hu; L (1827?) reads, in part similar in W:* In the same way they give a shape to the inward element. Achilles restrains his anger; the poet expresses this inner prudence, the restraining of anger, as the doing of Pallas: Achilles has been restrained by Pallas. We explain things quite differently in physics and psychology. Here explaining consists in making the matter visualizable by consciousness. It becomes

[412]Insofar as spirit has natural and sensible existence, the human figure is the only way in which it can be intuited. | That does not   552
mean, however, that spirit is something sensible or material, but rather that the mode of its immediacy and reality, its being for an other, is its being intuited in human shape. That is why the Greeks

---

so because it is given shape that is an image, W_2 *(1831) continues:* Those innumerable charming tales and the endless quantity of Greek myths originated in this kind of interpreting.

From whatever side we are able to consider the Greek principle, we see the sensuous and the natural permeating it. In the way that they issue from necessity, the gods are limited, and also for that reason they have the resonance of the natural in them, since they betray their own origin from the struggle with the powers of nature. The appearance with which they announce themselves to self-consciousness is still external, and even the phantasy that gives form and shape to this appearance still does not elevate their starting point into pure thought. We have now to see how this natural moment is wholly transfigured into beautiful shape.

412. *Precedes in* W_1 *(1831) (in* W_2 *partly shortened, partly MiscP?):* These gods are spiritual powers, but spirit is fragmented into its particularities, there are many of these spiritual powers, and hence we have polytheism here; this is the side of finitude. One side of this finitude is that freedom still bears the resonance of the natural state, while the other moment of it has just been noted.

The many powers are [there] for humanity. They are the absolute essentialities of human spirit, and in this way they are distinct from the changeable individuality of humans; but they are *represented;* and for that reason another form of finitude comes into play, one pertaining to the imaginative mode. What we have here is not yet the infinite freedom of thought, the spiritual essentialities are not yet [subjected to] thought; if these humans were thoughtful, there would be for them only one God. But divinity here falls entirely within [the range of] representation, which is not the foundation of pure thinking. It is only the religion of absolute truth that has thinking as its pure foundation. The Greek gods subsist for phantasy. Human beings do not come upon these essentialities as natural shapes ready to hand; they bring them forth for the imagination instead; and this bringing forth *is* phantasy. The shapes of the gods emerge from human phantasy in contrast with what is already there for the finding, but they emerge as *essential* shapes; there is a sensuous element involved in this, but it is raised through beauty into conformity with the spiritual. The Greek religion is the religion of beauty. There is a spiritual foundation in the Greek gods, but inasmuch as they are represented objectively, a natural element enters into them. They have the natural [side] in their manifestation: they are made or poetically created [*gedichtet*] (thinking and poetizing are linked), but they are not fictitious [*erdichtet*]. And this [poetic] product is known to be what is essential; it is something spiritual, not burdened by the natural. Instead, nature itself has only the meaning of the spiritual, because it is beautiful. [W_1: Manifestation here falls on the subjective side, it is finite. Thus God is something made by human beings. Poets, sculptors, and painters taught the Greeks what their gods were; they beheld their god in the Zeus of Phidias. What is manifested and exhibited for phantasy [however] is the representational shape of

659

a thought. For this reason the Greek religion is the religion of beauty. The consciousness of free spirituality pertains to beauty even though the content is limited and finite. But if it is to be manifested in sensous form, free spirituality can be manifested only in human shape. This is the shape of spirit that has existent being. W_2: If manifestation falls on the subjective side in this process, so that God appears as something made by human beings, that is only *one* moment. For this positedness of God is mediated rather by the sublation of the singular self; that is why it was possible for the Greeks to intuit their god in the Zeus of Phidias. The artist did not give them his own work (in some abstract sense); he gave them the proper appearance of the essential, the shape of necessity in existent being.]

W continues: Thus [W_1: this shape W_2: the shape of the god] is the ideal shape. Before the time of the Greeks there was no genuine ideality, [W_1: neither with the Hindus nor in the Near East nor with the Egyptians. Moreover, this Greek ideality could not W_2: nor could it] occur at any subsequent time. Certainly the art of the Christian religion is beautiful, but ideality is not its ultimate principle. [W_1: The Greek gods are anthropopathic, i.e., they involve the determinations of finitude generally, even as something immoral, which may perhaps originate in higher myths. But the main defect is not that there is too much of the anthropopathic in the Greek gods; not at all, for there is still too little humanity in them for one thing. There is still too little that is human in God. W_2: We cannot get at what is lacking in the Greek gods by saying that they are anthropopathic, a category of finitude to which we can then also impute the immoral element, for example the amours of Zeus, which may have their origin in older myths based on a [mode of] intuiting that is still natural. The main defect is not that there is too much of the anthropopathic in these gods, but that there is too little.] [W_1: Humanity must be grasped in the divine or in God as *this* human being; but only as a moment, as one of the persons of God, in such a way that this actually existing human being is posited in God, but as taken up into infinitude—and this only by means of a process, in that he, as this single, sensibly existing human being, is sublated. The Jewish commandment, "Thou shalt not make unto thyself any image of God,"[a] refers to the fact that God is essentially for thought; but the other moment of divine life is its externalization in human shape, so that this shape is involved in it as [its] manifestation. The manifestation, however, is only one side and is essentially taken back into the One, who thus is [present] for the first time as spirit for thought. Spiritual freedom has not yet come to consciousness in infinitude. W_2: In this inversion, however, it also becomes clear that the externalization of God in human shape is only one side of the divine life; for this externalization and manifestation is taken back again into the One, who thus for the first time is [present] as spirit for thought and for the community; the single, actually existing human is sublated and is posited in God as a moment, as one of the persons of God. In this way humanity, as this human being, is for the first time truly within God, the appearance of the divine is thus absolute, and its element is spirit itself. The Jewish view that God is essentially for thought alone, and the sensuousness of the Hellenic beauty of shape, are equally contained in this process of the divine life and, being sublated, they are freed from their limitedness.]

[*Ed.*] [a]See Deut. 27:15. This original form of the prohibition comes closest to Hegel's interpretation since here the stress lies on not worshiping God in an image made by human hands. The later, better-known formula of Exod. 20:4 relates rather to the ban on worshiping foreign gods.

represented the gods as human beings. | People have taken amiss   553
this practice of the Greeks as also that of [other] peoples. [413]It must
not be said that human beings do it because it is their own shape,
as if that were all it amounted to; but in fact they are right to do
it because this is the only shape in which spirit exists;[414] ˉthe
spiritual surely cannot come forth, for example, in the shape of a
lion.ˉ[415] [416]ˉThe organization of the human body is, however, only
the [phenomenal] shape of the | spiritual; the necessity of this linkage   554
belongs to the realm of physiology or of the philosophy of nature
and is a difficult point, in fact one still too little discussed.ˉ[417]

These are the principal moments on which the knowledge of God
in his determinacy depends.

413. *Precedes in L (1827?):* Xenophanes said that if lions had gods, they would
picture them as lions. But it is just this point that lions never get to. *Cf. W₁ (Var):*
A philosopher of ancient times says that if lions had gods, they would picture them
as lions.
  [*Ed.*] Hegel is referring to a fragment of Xenophanes contained in C. A. Brandis,
*Xenophanis Parmenidis et Melissi doctrina e propriis philosophorum reliquiis
veterumque auctorum testimoniis exposita* (Altona, 1813), p. 68. See Xenophanes,
frag. 15, in G. S. Kirk, J. E. Raven, and M. Schofield, *The Presocratic Philosophers,*
2d ed. (Cambridge, 1983), p. 169: "But if cattle and horses or lions had hands, or
were able to draw with their hands and do the works that men can do, horses would
draw the forms of the gods like horses, and cattle like cattle, and they would make
their bodies such as they each had themselves."
  414. *L (Var) adds:* That is not a matter of chance, but the physiological link with
the shape assumed by spirit. *W₁ (Var) adds:* That is not a matter of chance. On the
contrary, the linkage is a necessary one.
  415. *W₁ (Var) reads:* in animal shapes spirit does not give itself its *own* existence.
  416. *Precedes in L (1827?):* As Aristotle pointed out, in the transmigration of
souls it is assumed that the soul and the corporeal organization of a human being
are only accidentally connected. *W₁ (Var) reads:* As Aristotle noted, in the transmigration of souls it is assumed that the soul and the corporeal organization of a human
being are only contingently posited. The human organism is only the shape of the
spiritual. *W₂ (Var) reads:* That only the human organization can be the shape of the
spiritual was stated long ago by Aristotle, when he marked it as a defect of the [doc-
trine of the] transmigration of souls that on that view the corporeal organization of
a human being would be merely contingent.
  [*Ed.*] Aristotle, *De anima* 407b13–26.
  417. *W (Var) reads:* The proper task of physiology is to discern the human
organism, the human shape, as [W₁: the one authentic shape for spirit W₂: the only
one that is authentically adequate for spirit]; but it has so far done little in this respect.

b. The Cultus

Now we shall discuss the cultus. The cultus of the Greek religion covers a wide scope; we can draw attention only to the main points. [418]The character of [any] cultus is this, that empirical consciousness raises itself up, giving itself the consciousness or feeling of the indwelling of the divine within it, of its unity with the divine. The general character of this [Greek] cultus is that the subject has an essentially affirmative relationship to its god. Here the cultus involves the recognition and reverence of these ⌐absolute powers, of this essential inner substance that is removed from contingency.⌐[419] ⌐But at the same time these powers are the ethical aspect that is proper to humanity, the rational aspect of [human] freedom, the ethical vocations of human beings, their extant and valid | rights, their own spirit, not an external substantiality and essentiality. This implies that, with respect to the content, one has this affirmative relationship to one's gods; this substantial element that is revered as God is at the same time the proper essentiality of the human being.⌐[420] ⌐Thus, for example, Pallas Athena is not the goddess of the city.⌐[421] What is represented in Pallas Athena is the living, actual spirit of the Athenian people according to its essentiality. The Erinyes are

555

418. *In B's margin:* 16 July 1827
419. W_1 *(Var) reads:* substantial powers, of the essential inner substance of the natural and spiritual universe (which is removed from contingency), in the way that these essentially valid spiritual powers are present in the empirical consciousness.
420. *W (1831) reads:* [W_2: The Greeks are therefore the most *human* people. They affirmatively endorse and develop all that is human; for them the human is the norm.]
This religion is, in general, a religion of humanness. In other words, concrete humanity is present to itself in its gods—concrete humanity in its being, in all its needs, inclinations, passions, and habits, in its ethical and political determinations, or with respect to everything that is of value and essential in all this. The gods have this content of the noble and the true which is at the same time the content of concrete humanity. This human quality of the gods is what is defective, but at the same time what is attractive in Greek religion. There is nothing unintelligible, nothing incomprehensible, in it; the god has no content that is not known to us humans and which we do not find or do not know within ourselves. [W_2: Human confidence in the gods is at the same time human confidence in humanity itself.]
L (1827?) adds, similar in W: The Pallas who restrains the outbreak of Achilles' wrath is Achilles' own prudence.
421. *Thus Hu; An reads:* Athena is the city of Athens, the goddess [is] Athens.

the presentation of the [guilty] human's own deed, and the consciousness that plagues and torments one (insofar as one knows that deed as evil *within* one). They are the just ones, and for this very reason the well-disposed ones, the Eumenides.[422] Eros is the power, but precisely the subjective sensibility, of the human [lover]. In the recognition of this objective [power] the human [worshipers] are at the same time in communion with themselves, and for this reason in the cultus they are free. Here there is not only the negative relationship as with the Hindus, where the relationship of the subjects—even when of the highest sort—is only the sacrifice or negation of their consciousness.

⌐Freedom constitutes the cheerfulness or serenity of this cultus.⌐[423] In the cultus, honor is bestowed upon the god, but revering God turns into the reverence proper to humanity itself, the reverence that makes the consciousness of one's affirmative relationship and unity with the gods valid in one's own self. In this worship, human beings celebrate their own ⌐honor.⌐[424] But inasmuch as the god still has an external, natural aspect, this unification has further modifications. Bacchus and Demeter, wine and bread, are external [goods] for the human being. The way to make oneself identical | 556 with them is to consume them, to assimilate them into oneself. The singular [natural product], the gift of the gods, still remains external to the [divine] power of nature. But the natural forces or productive

422. *L (1827?) adds, similar in W:* This is not a euphemism; on the contrary, it is the Eumenides who desire right, and those who infringe it have the Eumenides within themselves.

423. *Thus B, similar in Hu, An; L, W₂ (1827/1831?) read:* Speaking generally, this religion has the character of absolute cheerfulness or serenity[a]; self-consciousness is free in its relationship to its own essentialities, because they *are* its own; and at the same time it is not fettered to them because absolute necessity floats above the essentialities themselves and they return into it too, just as consciousness with its particular ends and requirements sinks back into it.

[*Ed.*] [a]"Cheerfulness or serenity" renders *Heiterkeit*. If Hegel meant to depict the Greeks as serene, this may be an attitude toward them influenced by Schiller or Hölderlin. The typical Greek disposition, however, was more an active, energetic happiness than a calm, passive composure (especially by contrast with the meditative disciplines of the Oriental religions).

424. *W₁ (Var) reads:* subjectivity.

powers are spiritual essences as well; Bacchus and Demeter are the mystical divinities.[425]

In the festivals where the god is worshiped, it is humanity that shows itself forth; the worshipers let the divine be seen in themselves, in their joyfulness and cheerfulness, in the display of their bodily dexterity.[426] Their artistic productions have a place in these festivals too, ¯and human artists are honored in the festivals at the same time (in dramas etc.).¯[427] At the festival of Pallas there was a great procession. Pallas is the people or nation itself; but the nation is the god imbued with life, it is this Athena who delights in herself.

Besides the content of the gods we must recall the two previously mentioned relationships, i.e., those of necessity and contingency. The dispositon corresponding to necessity is the restfulness that holds itself in stillness, or in the freedom that is still an abstract freedom. To this extent it is a flight; but at the same time it is freedom insofar as the human being is not vanquished or bowed down by fate as something external. Whoever has this consciousness of independence, should he die, is indeed outwardly defeated but not conquered, not vanquished.

In addition to this relationship to simple necessity within the consciousness of the divine and its relation to human beings, there is also, conversely, another aspect to mention briefly, namely that the divine is also known to share in the lot of the finite and in the abstract necessity of the finite. To the abstract necessity of the finite there belongs death someday, the natural negation of the finite. But in the way it appears in the divine, finitude is the subordination of the ethical powers | themselves. Because they are particular, they have to experience transitoriness in themselves, one-sided being and the lot of one-sidedness. This is the consciousness that the ancients have represented and brought to view most notably in the tragedies— necessity as something that fulfills itself, something that has import

557

---

425. L (1827?) adds, similar in W₁: Demeter, or Ceres, is the founder of agriculture, of property, of marriage. In general, both [Bacchus and Demeter] are in charge of the mysteries.

426. W₁ (Var) adds: and beauty.

427. W₁ (Var/1831?) reads: so that they regard them as having divine content, but at the same time as [displaying] their own expertise and skill.

and content. The chorus is withdrawn from natural destiny, it abides in the peaceful course of the ethical order and arouses no hostile power. The heroes, however, stand above the chorus, above the peaceful, static, uncleft ethical process; they are the ones who properly will and act. They bring forth order, and because of their action, changes are effected; in further development a cleavage comes about. The higher cleavage, the cleavage that is properly of interest for spirit, is that in which the ethical powers themselves appear as severed and as coming into collision. The resolution of the collision is when the ethical powers that are in collision (due to their one-sidedness) themselves renounce the one-sidedness of independent validity; and the way that this renunciation of one-sidedness appears is that the individuals who have committed themselves to the real-ization of the singular, one-sided, ethical power perish. ˉFor example,ˉ428 in the *Antigone* the love of family, the holy, the inner, what is also called the law of the lower deities because it belongs to sentiment, comes into collision with the right of the state. Creon is not a tyrant, but rather the champion of something that is also an ethical power. Creon is not in the wrong; he maintains that the law of the state, the | authority of the government, must be preserved   558
and punishment meted out for its violation.429 Each of these two sides actualizes only one of the two, has only one side as its content. That is the one-sidedness, and the meaning of eternal justice is that both are in the wrong because they are one-sided, but both are also in the right. In the unclouded course of ethical life, both are acknowledged; here each has its validity, but one counterbalanced

428. *L reads:* I regard it as the absolute example of tragedy when *W (1831/Var?) reads:* Fate [*Fatum*] is what cannot be conceptualized; it is where justice and injustice disappear in abstraction; in contrast, in tragedy destiny [*Schicksal*] falls within the sphere of ethical justice. We find the most sublime [expressions] of this in the tragedies of Sophocles. Both destiny and necessity are spoken of in them; the destiny of the [tragic] individuals is portrayed as something incomprehensible, but the necessity is not blind; on the contrary, it is recognized as authentic justice. This is what makes these tragedies such immortal spiritual products of ethical understanding and com-prehension [*W₂*: or such eternal models of the ethical concept]. Blind destiny is an unsatisfying thing. In these tragedies, justice is *comprehended.* The collision between [*W₁*: ethical *W₂*: the two highest ethical] powers is portrayed in a plastic fashion in the absolute example furnished by tragedy when

429. [*Ed.*] See Sophocles, *Antigone,* esp. 480–485, 659–675.

by the other's validity.[430] In this way the conclusion of the tragedy is reconciliation, not blind necessity but rational necessity, the necessity that here begins to be [rationally] fulfilled.

[431]This is the clarity of insight and of artistic presentation that Greece reached at its highest stage of culture; but there still remains something unresolved, to be sure, in that the higher element does not emerge as the infinitely spiritual power; there remains an unhealed sorrow here because an individual perishes. The higher reconciliation would consist in the subject's disposition of one-sidedness being overcome, in its dawning consciousness that it is in the wrong, and its divesting itself of its unrighteousness in its own heart. But to recognize its guilt and one-sidedness, and to divest itself of it, does not come naturally in this domain. This higher [reconciliation] would make external punishment and natural death superfluous.

The first signs and anticipations of this reconciliation do indeed emerge here too; | but the inner conversion still appears more as an external purification.[432] In the *Eumenides* Orestes is acquitted by

559

430. W (Var/1831?) adds: It is only the one-sidedness [in their claims] that justice comes forward to oppose.

W₂ (1831) continues: We have another example of collision portrayed in Oedipus. He has slain his father, and is seemingly guilty, but he is guilty because his ethical power is one-sided; that is to say, he falls unconsciously into this horrible deed.[a] Yet he is the one who excels in knowing, the one who solved the riddle of the Sphinx.[b] Hence a counterweight is set up as [his] Nemesis. The one who knew so much stands in the power of the unconscious, so that he falls as deeply into guilt as the height on which he stood. Here, then, there is the antithesis of the two powers, that of consciousness and that of unconsciousness.

[Ed.] [a]See Sophocles, *Oedipus Rex,* esp. 800–819, 1183–1185. [b]A reference to the Theban sphinx legend, as distinguished from the Egyptian sphinx.

431. Precedes in L, W (1831): It is justice that is in this way satisfied with the maxim, "There is nothing that is not Zeus,"[a] i.e., eternal justice. Here we have an active necessity, but one which is completely ethical; the misfortune suffered is perfectly clear. There is nothing blind or unconscious here.

[Ed.] [a]See Sophocles, *Trachiniae* 1277–1278.

432. L (1827?) adds, similar in W: A son of Minos had been slain in Athens; for this reason a purification was carried out, and the deed was declared to be undone. It is spirit that wants to make what has been done undone.

[Ed.] See Diodorus Siculus, *Bibliotheca historica* 4.60–61. See 1824 lectures, n. 691.

666

the Areopagus.[433] In that instance, too, there is a collision. He has murdered his mother—on the one hand here is the greatest crime against piety; on the other hand he has gained justice for his father. He was head of the family and also of the state. In one and the same action he committed an outrage and at the same time carried out complete and essential necessity. ˜The acquittal is a uniting of these one-sided stances.˜[434] *Oedipus at Colonus* hints at reconciliation, and more precisely at the Christian representation of reconciliation: [Oedipus] comes to honor among the gods, the gods call him to them.[435] Today we require more, because for us the representation of reconciliation is higher: [we have] the consciousness that this reversal (whereby what has been done is made undone) can occur within the inner self. Human beings who turn over a new leaf, who surrender their one-sidedness, have purged it from within themselves, from within their wills where the enduring abode or place of the deed would be, i.e., they have negated the deed at its root. But this kind of reconciliation is not pervasive among the ancients. It is more in accord with our feelings that the tragedies have denouements that are reconciling.

This is the relationship of necessity.

The other is the relation to the other extreme, to the singularity that we see playing about these divine essences themselves, the singularity that is present in the human [agent] and comes in question here. This singular aspect is the contingent aspect, and at this level of religion human beings are not yet free, not yet universal self-consciousness; they are indeed the self-consciousness of ethical life, but [only] of its substance generally, and the ethical substance is not yet the subjectivity that is inwardly universal.

In the sphere of the contingent, therefore, what a human being has to do falls outside of ethical duty. Since God | is not yet deter-   560
mined as absolute subjectivity, this contingent element is not yet placed in the hands of a providence, but instead in those of destiny.

433. [*Ed.*] Aeschylus, *Eumenides,* esp. 734–741.
434. *Thus Hu; L, W (Var/1831?) read:* Acquittal [*Lossprechen*] means precisely this, making something undone.
435. [*Ed.*] Sophocles, *Oedipus at Colonus,* esp. 1623–1628, 1658–1664.

This means that human beings do not know themselves as free; they are not the decisive subjectivity. Connected with this is the fact that they allow the decision to be given from without; here occurs the aspect of religion that we call oracles. These oracles have a natural origin, for ˉhere no articulated answer was given.[436] Their manifestation is some sort of external transformation, metallic forms, the rustling of trees, the blowing of the wind, visions, examination of sacrificial animals, and contingencies of that sort. People needed such things in order to reach decisions. The Greeks are not free in the sense that we are free, i.e., in their self-consciousness; they let themselves be determined from without.ˉ[437]

These are the principal moments of the religion of beauty. Spirit or reason is the content, but reason is still substantial in its content, so that it falls asunder into its particular [shapes]. In its form, the spiritual shape, the human shape, has the natural in it, [but] as ideal,

436. [Ed.] In the Ms. Hegel refers to them as "very naive oracles," alluding to the Greek motto (Αἱ τῶν δαιμόνων φωναὶ ἄναρθροι εἰσίν) found on the back of the title page of Goethe's Zur Morphologie (1823), which is vol. 2 of his Zur Naturwissenschaft überhaupt.

437. W_1 (Var) reads: they are external in character for human beings, and the manifestation is some sort of external, natural change—sounds from the rustling of leaves or ringing tones.

No articulated answers are given by oracles. In Delphi it was the wind that blew out of the gorge and produced a rushing noise. Elsewhere it is visions, or the examination of sacrificial animals, chance externalities that have a natural origin or are externalities as such—these it is that humans use in order to make their resolve.

The free Greek is not free in self-consciousness as we are free. The commander who wishes to engage in battle, or the state that is about to establish a colony, consults the oracle;[a] this democracy still did not have the force or energy of self-consciousness that [enables] the people to determine itself, to form its own resolve.

Socrates was the first to recognize that one's own resolve is what counts. His δαιμόνιον is nothing else but this.[b] He says of it that it only told him what was good, and then only about completely external, contingent circumstances. It did not reveal any truths to him, but only gave him the decision in singular cases of action. Here fate [Fatum] is the subjective will, the resolve.

[Ed.] [a]The Lectures on the History of Philosophy 1:423 (cf. Werke 14:97) shows that Hegel is here thinking in particular of Xenophon, Anabasis, and Herodotus, Histories 9.33 ff. [b]In Xenophon, Memorabilia 1.1.1–9, esp. 1.1.4, Socrates is said to have spoken in such and such a way, or advised his friends to do thus and so, because his daimonion (divine sign) had so indicated. See also Plato, Apology, esp. 24b–c, 26b–e.

so that it is only an expression of the spiritual and is no longer something independent. The finitude of this religion has been made plain from every aspect. |

2. The Religion of Sublimity, or Jewish Religion[438]

What is common to the religions of this sphere is this ideality of the natural, the fact that it is subordinated to the spiritual, that God, who is spirit, is known as spirit. To begin with, then, God is known as spirit whose determinations are rational and ethical. But this God still has a particular content, i.e., is still only his ethical power. God's appearance is that of beauty; but this appearance is a natural material and a soil of sensible, external stuff or of sensible representation. The soil of that religion is not yet pure thought. The necessity of the elevation of the religion of beauty into the religion of sublimity lies in what we have discussed already, i.e., in the need that the particular spiritual powers, the ethical powers, should be embraced within a spiritual unity. The truth of the particular [moment] is the universal unity, ˉwhich is subjectivity and is inwardly concrete,ˉ[439] inasmuch as it has the particular within it but at the same time subsists essentially as subjectivity. But for this rationality that subsists as subjectivity—indeed, it even subsists as universal subjectivity with respect to its content and is free with respect to its form—for this pure subjectivity the soil is pure thought; it is withdrawn from the natural and so from the sensible [realm], withdrawn both from external sensibility and from sensible representation. It is the spiritually subjective unity—and for us this is what first merits the name of God.

438. [Ed.] As noted earlier (n. 347), in the 1827 lectures the treatment of the religion of sublimity follows that of the religion of beauty; the reasons for this reversal are discussed in the Editorial Introduction. The 1827 interpretation of Judaism carries further the favorable reassessment initiated in 1824. Almost the entire section is devoted to an analysis of the representation of God as creator and the implications of this for understanding the relationship between God and the world. While this material is already present in 1824, it is expanded and systematically ordered, becoming the focus of the whole section.

439. W_1 (Var) reads: and subjectivity is inwardly concrete W_2 (Var) reads: which is inwardly concrete

a. The Unity of God

This subjective unity is not substance, ˉfor it is subjective,ˉ⁴⁴⁰ but it is indeed absolute power; the natural is only something that is posited by it, is only ideal and not something that is independent. The unity does not appear or reveal [itself] in natural material, but instead does so essentially in thought: thought is the mode of its determinate being or appearing. Absolute power ˉwe have seen often enough already;ˉ⁴⁴¹ but the main point is that here it is concrete and inwardly determinate—hence it is absolute wisdom. |

562

Also, the rational determinations of freedom, the ethical determinations ˉunited in one purpose and one determination of this subjectivity, areˉ⁴⁴² holiness. In this way ˉdivinityˉ⁴⁴³ determines itself as holiness. The higher truth of God's subjectivity is not just a beautiful subjectivity where the import or the absolute content is still separated out into particularities⁴⁴⁴—a relationship like that of animals to human beings. Animals do in fact have particular characters; the character of universality belongs to humans. The ethical rationality of freedom and the explicitly self-subsistent unity of this rationality is what authentic, inwardly self-determining subjectivity is. This is wisdom and holiness. ⁴⁴⁵ˉThe contents of the Greek deities are the ethical powers; they are not holy, because they are still particular and limited.

Here the absolute, or God, subsists as the One, as subjectivity, as universal and pure subjectivity, or conversely this subjectivity that is the universal inwardly is precisely the one inwardly determined unity of God.⁴⁴⁶ It is not a matter of the unity being exhibited implicitly, of the unity of God being the underlying ground, being implicit: that is the case in the Hindu and Chinese religion. For there,

440. W (Var) reads: but rather subjective unity,
441. Thus Hu; L (Var) reads: is also in the earthly realm; W (Var) reads: is also in Hinduism;
442. W (Var) reads: are united in one determination, one purpose, and thus the defining characteristic of this subjectivity is
443. W (Var) reads: ethical life
444. W₂ (Var) adds: but is the characteristic of holiness; and the relationship between these two determinations is
445. In B's margin: 17 July 1827
446. W (Var/1831?) adds: so that there is a consciousness of God as One.

when God's unity is only implicit, God is not posited as infinite subjectivity and the unity is not known, it is not [present] as subjectivity for consciousness.[447]

Thus the unity of God contains one power within it, which is accordingly the absolute power. Every externality,[448] every sensible configuration | and sensible image, is sublated in it. For this reason God here subsists without shape[449]—he subsists not for sensible representation but only for thought. The inwardly infinite, pure subjectivity is the subjectivity that is essentially thinking. As thinking it subsists only for thinking, and therefore subsists in its [activity of] judgment. Thinking is the essential soil for this object. Here we must now mention the characteristic of divine particularization, of divine judgment.

563

b. Divine Self-Determination and Representation

God is wisdom; what this involves is God's self-determining, God's judging, and hence (more precisely) what is called God's creating.[450] God's wisdom consists in being purposive, or determinative. But this wisdom is at first still abstract, being still the initial subjectivity, ˉthe initial wisdom,ˉ[451] and therefore God's ˉjudgmentˉ[452] is not yet

447. W (1831) adds: God is now known as a personal One [Einer] rather than as a neuter One [Eines] as in pantheism. Thus the immediately natural mode [of representing God] disappears, for instance the mode that is still posited in the Parsee religion as light. Religion is posited as the religion of spirit, but only in its foundation, only upon the soil that is proper to it, the soil of thought.

448. W (Var/1831?) adds: and consequently all that belongs to sensible nature,

449. W (Var/1831?) adds: without any externally sensible shape; having no image,

450. W (1831) adds: Spirit is what is utterly self-mediating inwardly, or what is active. This activity is a distinguishing from self, a judging (or primal division). The world is what is posited by spirit; the world is made out of its nothing. But the negative of the world is the affirmative, the Creator, in whom the nothing is what is natural. Within its nothing, therefore, the world has arisen out of the absolute fullness of the power of the good. It has been created from its own "nothing," which (its other) is God.

451. W (Var) reads: and that is why it is abstract to begin with,

452. W (Var) reads: particularization

[Ed.] The interchange between "judgment" (Urteil) and "particularization" (Besonderung) is not surprising since etymologically the two terms have a similar sense, that of "sundering" (sondern), "division" or "parting" (teilen). Hegel intends to connect them through their root meanings: the divine particularization is a judging, a primal division (see n. 450 and the last sentence of the preceding paragraph of the main text).

posited as internal to itself. Instead what is assumed is that God decrees, and what is posited or determined by God subsists at once in the form of an unmediated other.[453] Were God's wisdom concrete, then God would be his own self-determining in such a way that God himself would produce within himself what is created and sustain it internally, so that it would be[454] known as sustained within him as his Son; God so defined would be known as ˜truly concrete˜[455] spirit. But since the wisdom is here abstract, the judgment or what is posited is thus something subsisting although only as a form: it is the subsisting world. |

564

Thus God is creator of the world. The world is something immediate, but in such a way that the immediacy is only something mediated: the world is only a created product.[456]   [457]God's creating is very different from procession, wherein the world goes forth from God. ˜˜For the Hindus, the ˜worlds go˜[458] forth from Brahmā.˜˜[459] In the Greek cosmogonies the highest or spiritual gods finally go

453. *W (1831) adds:* The higher view is certainly that of God's creation within himself, that he is in himself beginning and end, and hence he has the moment of movement (which still falls outside him at this present stage) within himself, in his inner nature.

454. *W (Var) adds:* created and

455. *W (Var) reads:* the concrete God, genuinely known as

456. *L (1827?) adds (cf. n. 461):* The creature is something that is not inwardly independent; it may *be* (or it has being), but it does not have independence. This distinction is essential.

457. *Precedes in* W_2 *(1831):* Since power is represented as absolute negativity, so its essence (i.e., what is identical with itself) is to begin with in a state of repose, of eternal calm and seclusion. But just this self-contained solitude is merely a moment of power, not the whole. Power is also negative relation to self, inner mediation, and since it refers negatively to itself, this sublation of abstract identity is the positing of difference, of determination, i.e., it is the creation of the world. But the nothing from which the world is created is the absence of all difference, the very category in which power or essence was first thought of. So if it is asked where God got matter from, the answer is, just that simple reference to self. Matter is what is formless, what is identical with itself; this is only one moment of the essence, and as such it is something other than absolute power, and hence it is what we call matter. The creation of the world, therefore, means the negative reference of power to itself, insofar as it is initially defined as what is only identical with itself.

458. *Thus B; An reads:* world goes *Hu, L, W read:* gods go

459. *W (1831) reads:* All peoples have theogonies or, what comes to the same thing, cosmogonies, in which the fundamental category is always going-forth, not being-created. *W (Var):* The gods go forth from Brahmā.

forth; they are the last to emerge. [460]What has gone forth is what exists, what is actual, so that the ground from which it has gone forth is posited as sublated, as nonessential, and what has gone forth ˉcounts as independent.ˉ[461] Here, in contrast, the subjectivity of the One is what is absolutely first, the initiating factor, and the conditioned state | is sublated. Over against this posited [being], over against the world, which is God's creation, over against the totality of its determinate being, of its negation, over against the totality of immediate being, God is what is presupposed; God is the absolute subject, which remains the absolutely first. Here the fundamental definition of God is this: subjectivity that relates itself to itself. As abiding subjectivity that has being within itself, it is what is first. But for the Greek gods—and precisely for the highest or spiritual gods—the status of having gone forth belongs directly to their finitude. It is the condition of their being, the presupposition upon which their nature rests, just as in the case of finite spirit [its] nature is presupposed.

565

Thus over against the determination of the One as the subject is the particular, what comes forth in this producing, in nature, externality and dependence; in general, what is created in the posited [world]. Only the divine subjectivity that is abiding within itself is self-relation and accordingly is the first.

But although subjectivity is here what makes the absolute beginning, it is the initiating factor only, and it is not the case that this subjectivity could be determined also as the result.[462] God is the first; God's creation is an eternal creation; but God is the initiator of creation, not the result. If the divine subjectivity were determined as result, as self-creating, then it would be grasped as concrete spirit.[463]

460. *Precedes in W (1831):* At this point the inadequate category of going-forth disappears, since the good, or the absolute power, is a subject. This going-forth is not the relationship of what is created [to its creator].

461. *W (Var/1831?) reads (cf. n. 456):* is posited not as a creature but as something independent, not as the sort of thing that lacks inward independence. W_1 *adds:* It may *be,* it has being, but not independence.

462. *W (Var) adds:* and as concrete spirit.

463. *L (1827?) adds:* For at the higher stage, when God is defined as spirit, he is the one who does not step outside himself, and so he is also the result, or that which is self-creating.

If what is created from the absolute subject were this subject itself, then in this distinction the distinction would likewise be superseded, the ⁻last subject would be⁻⁴⁶⁴ that which results from itself. We do not yet have that determination here, but only the one where the absolute subject is what is utterly initiating, is the first.⁴⁶⁵ |

566

The second aspect is God's relation to what is created. What we call God's attributes—these characteristics of God in relation to the world and to the creatures—are God's determinacies. Or in other words, since we already saw God's particularizing or self-determining, and saw this as the creation of the world, saw the determinate as a subsisting world, then the attributes of God are God's relation to the world. That is to say, the attributes are the determinate [result] itself but as known in the concept of God. One aspect [the world] is the determinate known as what has being, not as reverting into God or belonging to God, and the other [the attributes] is the state of determinateness as God's own determinacy. This is what is called God's relations to the world, and it is a misguided expression if it means that we only know about this relation of God to the world but know nothing about God. Instead that relation is God's very own determinateness, and hence God's own attributes.

⁴⁶⁶The way in which one human being is related to another—that is just what is human, that is human nature itself.⁴⁶⁷ When we are cognizant of how an object is related [to everything else], then we are cognizant of its very nature. To distinguish between the two [i.e., relation and nature] is to make misguided distinctions that collapse straightaway because they are the productions of an understanding that does not know what it is doing—an understand-

---

464. W_1 (Var) reads: last subject would be the first, W_2 (Var/Ed?) reads: first subject would be the last,

465. L (1827?) adds: God is not yet grasped here as spirit, as what first returns into itself through its particularization. But since God is what is utterly first, his creating must not be thought of under the guise of human producing.

466. Precedes in L (1827?), similar in W: Even from the sensual point of view something is, and that something is on its own account. Its properties, its relation to another, are distinct from it; yet these are what constitute its peculiar nature.

467. L (1827?) adds, similar in W: The acid is nothing else than the specific mode of its relation to the base—that is the nature of the acid itself.

ing unfamiliar with them, one that does not know what it is dealing with in these distinctions.

As something external and unmediated, [but] as the determinacy of God himself, this determinacy is God's absolute power; as we have seen, however, this power is wisdom.

The specific moments of wisdom are goodness and justice. Goodness consists in the fact that the world is. The world does not attain being [proper].[468] Being, the truly actual, *is* only in God. The being of what is | mutually external, outside of God—that being has no claims; it is only the self-externalization of God, the fact that God releases himself from himself, and sets his content (which is the determinacy of absolute subjectivity) free even from his absolute unity—that is God's goodness, and only here can God be the creator in the true sense as infinite subjectivity. In that role God is free, and so his determinateness or self-determining can be set free. Only what is free can have its determinations over against it as free, or can let them go as free. This release that lets them go their separate ways so as to yield the totality of finitude, or the world—this [mode of] being is goodness. Justice in turn is the manifestation of the nullity or ideality of this finite [being], it is the fact that this [finite] being is not genuine independence—this manifestation [of God] as power is what endows finite things with their right.

This goodness and justice must not be regarded merely as moments of substance but as moments of the one subject; in substance these determinations are found to be subsisting just as immediately as not subsisting but as coming into being. But here the One subsists not as substance but as the personal One, as subject. The being of things is posited herein as purpose; it is the specification of purpose, the proper determinacy of the concept. The world ought to be, and likewise it ought to transform itself and pass away. This is justice as the specification of purpose, justice as the subject

567

---

468. *W (1831) adds:* for being is here downgraded to a moment, and is only a createdness or positedness. This judgment or primary division [*Ur-teilen*] is the eternal goodness of God. What has been differentiated has no right to be, it is outside the One, it is a manifold and therefore a limited, finite [thing] whose destination is *not* to be; that it nonetheless *is,* is the goodness of God. But as something posited, it also passes away, it is only appearance.

that distinguishes itself from its own determinations, or from its world.

The third aspect is the form of the world, the character that things in general obtain, the reality that they receive. Or, the world is now prosaic, it confronts us essentially as a collection of things, it is rendered profane. Now nature is divested of divinity. In the Orient and especially with regard to the Greek god, people delight in friendliness and cheerfulness, and in the relationship to nature and to the divine, in the fact that inasmuch as human beings relate themselves to nature they relate themselves to the divine.[469] This unity of the divine | and the natural—we call it the identity of the ideal and the real—is an abstract and wholly formal determination, an identity that is cheaply obtained. In fact it is everywhere. What matters most would be the authentic specification of this identity; and the authentic identity is the one found within infinite subjectivity, that which is grasped not as neutralization or reciprocal blunting [of differences], but just as infinite subjectivity. Since infinite subjectivity determines itself as such, and lets its determinations go free as the world, these determinations are things without any independence as they truly are. They are not deities but merely natural objects. The particular ethical powers, which are in essence the supreme deities for the Greeks, have independence only according to their form, because the content as particular is dependent and finite. That is a false form. For the situation with dependent things that are immediate is this: we are only aware of their being as something formal, something without independence. The only being that pertains to them, therefore, is not absolute or divine but is an abstract, one-sided being. Since abstract being is their lot, they stand under the categories of being; and since finitude is their lot, they are subject to the categories of the understanding.

At this stage, therefore, there are prosaic things, just as the world contains prosaic things for us also, as understanding beings—external things in the manifold nexus of understanding, of ground and consequent, of quality and quantity, subject to all these categories of the understanding. Here then is what we call natural or necessary connection; and for that reason the category of "miracle" emerges

569. L (1827?) adds, similar in W: Their liberality spiritualizes what is natural, makes it something divine, gives it a soul.

here for the first time too, as opposed to the natural connection of things. In Hindu religion, for instance, there is no miracle; everything is jumbled together there from the outset. Only in contrast with order, with the lawfulness of nature, with natural laws—even though these laws are not recognized and one finds only a consciousness of a natural nexus—only in that context does the category of "miracle" arise; then miracle is represented as God being sporadically manifest in singular events.[470] The true miracle is the appearance | of spirit in nature, and the authentic appearance of spirit is, in its 569 fundamental aspect, the spirit of humanity and the human consciousness of the world.[471]

In this religion, therefore, the world appears as finite things that act upon one another in a natural way, things that stand within an intelligible nexus. The relationship therefore is: God, world, creation of the world, the fundamental categories of worldly things. Miracle is grasped as a contingent manifestation of God; the genuine manifestation of God in the world, however, is the absolute or eternal manifestation, and the mode or manner of this manifestation, its form, appears as what we call "sublimity," and for that reason we call this religion the religion of sublimity. The infinite subject in its self-containment one cannot call sublime; it is the absolute in and for itself, [i.e.,] it is holy. Sublimity emerges as the appearance or relation of this infinite subject to the world. The world is grasped as a manifestation of this subject, but as a manifestation that is not affirmative; or one that, to the extent that it is indeed affirmative, still has the primary character that the natural or worldly is negated as unbefitting ⌐the subjective,⌐[472] ⌐so that God's appearing is at once grasped as sublimity that is superior to appearance in [ordinary] reality.⌐[473]

---

470. W_2 (Var) adds: and at the same time in opposition to their [natural] outcomes.

471. L (1827?) adds, similar in W: For what we know of the world is that in all this confusion and manifold contingency it still maintains regularity and reason everywhere—relatively speaking, this is a miracle.

472. W (Var) reads: and is known as such,

473. W (Var) reads: [W_1: It is the appearance and manifestation of God in the world in such a way that this appearing W_2: Sublimity is therefore the mode of God's appearance and manifestation in the world, and it may be defined as follows: this appearing] does at the same time show itself as sublime, as superior to appearance within [ordinary] reality.

In the religion of beauty we have a reconciliation of the meaning with the material, with the sensible mode, with being for another; the spiritual reveals itself wholly in this outward manner. The outward mode is a sign of the inner, and this inner is completely recognized in the shape of its externality. ¨Sublimity, by contrast, simultaneously annihilates | the matter or the material in which the sublime appears. The material is directly and expressly known as inadequate; it is not an inadequacy that is unconsciously overlooked. For it does not suffice for sublimity that the substantial is in and for itself something higher than its shape; instead the primary point is that the inadequacy is directly posited in the shape. For the Hindus there is only wildness and grotesqueness, but no sublimity.

God is explicitly the One, the one power as inwardly determined. God is the wise one, i.e., he manifests himself in nature but in a sublime manner. The natural world is only something posited and limited, only a manifestation of the One in such a way that God is at the same time superior to this manifestation; God at once distinguishes himself from the manifestation even within it, and does not get his being-for-self, his essential presence [*Dasein*] from this externality, as in the religion of beauty.¨[474] Nature is submissive and manifests only God, but in such a way that God subsists at the same time outside this manifestation.

The ¨fourth aspect¨[475] is God's purpose. Here we are concerned with the category of *essential* purpose, namely that above all God is wise—wise in nature generally. Nature is God's creation and God makes his power recognized in it, though not only his power but also his wisdom. This is evident in its products, from their purposeful

570

474. W_2 *(Var/MiscP?)* reads: The sublimity of the appearance, by contrast, simultaneously annihilates its reality, its matter and material. In his appearance God also distinguishes himself from it, in such a way that it is expressly known as inadequate. The One does not therefore have his being-for-self and his essential presence [*Dasein*] in the externality of the appearance, as do the gods of the religion of beauty; and the inadequacy of the appearance is not something that is unconsciously overlooked, but is expressly and consciously posited as such.

475. *Hu reads, similar in An:* third aspect

[*Ed.*] The three preceding aspects are: (1) creation, (2) the attributes of God, (3) the form of the world. If this is an error of Hegel, it is explicable from the fact that he was using the Griesheim transcript of the 1824 lectures as the basis of the 1827 presentation, and in G the theme of purpose is the "third point."

orientation. But this purpose is only something undetermined and superficial, it is more ˉexternal.ˉ[476] The true purpose and its realization do not fall within nature as such, but essentially within consciousness instead. Purpose manifests itself in nature, but its essential appearance is its appearing within consciousness as in its reflection [*Widerschein*]; it appears reflectedly in self-consciousness in such a way that its purpose is to become known by consciousness, and for consciousness the purpose is to acknowledge it. Acknowledgment and | praise of God is the determination that emerges here: the whole world should proclaim the glory of God, and indeed God's universal glory. Not merely the Jewish people but the whole earth, all peoples, all the Gentiles should praise the Lord.[477] This purpose of becoming known by consciousness can above all be called God's theoretical purpose; the more determinate sort is the practical purpose that is realized in the spirit of the world as such.

571

So this essential purpose is in the first place ethical life or uprightness, namely, that all human beings should keep legality or right in mind in whatever they do; this legality or right is precisely what is divine, and insofar as it is something worldly within finite consciousness, it is something decreed by God. God is the universal; the human being, in determining itself or its own will,[478] is free and therefore universal will. It is not one's own particular ethical life or right conduct that is the basic determination here, but rather walking before God, a freedom from self-seeking aims, the righteousness that has value before God. The human being does what is right in relation to God, to the glory of God; so this righteousness has its seat principally in the will, in the inner self.

The natural state of existence, of human beings and their action, stands opposed therefore to this willing, to this inwardness with regard to God. This broken state is posited in humanity: God *is* on his own account, while nature has a sort of being [*ein Seiendes*], but

---

476. *Thus Hu; L (1827?) reads, similar in W:* an external purposiveness: "Thou givest to the beast its fodder" [Ps. 147:9].
In B's margin: 19 July 1827
477. [*Ed.*] See Ps. 117:1: "Praise the Lord all ye nations, praise him all ye peoples." See the quotation of this Psalm in the 1831 text contained in n. 492 below.
478. W_2 *(Var) adds:* in terms of this universal

under [the Lord's] dominion. This same distinction is found within the human spirit, namely, the distinction between right conduct as such and humanity's natural existence. But the latter is determined by the spiritual relationship of the will, just as nature in general is something posited by absolute spirit. Humanity's natural mode of being, our external, worldly existence, is posited in connection with the inner aspect. If one's will is an essential will and one's action is right conduct, then the outward existence of the human agent should also be in agreement with this inner aspect or right; a human being should ⌐prosper, but should prosper only according to his

572 works.⌐479 One should ⌐in general | not only behave ethically,⌐480 observe the laws of one's country, and sacrifice oneself for one's country, no matter how one fares as a consequence; but also there crops up the definite requirement that prosperity should come to the one who does right. We have here the relationship that real existence or outwardly determinate being is conformed and subordinated to the inner aspect, to the right, and is determined by it; and this relationship comes into play here in consequence of, and on the ground of, the fundamental relationship of God to the natural and finite world. Here there is a purpose, and this purpose shall be carried out—a distinction, however, that should at the same time be in harmony, so that natural existence shows itself to be ruled by the essential, by the spiritual. The natural existence of human beings is likewise supposed to be determined and ruled by the truly inward, by ⌐what is upright.⌐481 In this way human well-being is affirmatively and divinely legitimated; but it has this legitimation only to the extent that it is conformed to the divine, to the ethically divine law.

This is the bond of necessity, but it is no longer blind as in Greek religion, no longer just an empty, indeterminate necessity devoid of concept, so that the concrete is outside it.482 Now, on the contrary, the necessity is concrete; what is actual being in and for itself is what

479. W (Var) reads: prosper only according to his works.
480. W₂ (Var/Ed?) reads: not only behave ethically in general,
481. W₂ (Var) reads: right-doing.
482. L (1827?) adds, similar in W: Among the Greeks the gods, the ethical powers, stand apart from necessity and are under it; necessity does not have what is ethical and right in its definition.

gives the laws—it wills the right, the ˉlaw.ˉ[483] In consequence, this being has conformed to it a determinate mode of being that is affirmative, an existence that is well-being, prosperity. In this sphere, human beings know this unity and harmony. That prosperity is permitted or indeed owed to one, is something conditional; the human being taken as a whole is an end for God. But the human being as a whole is itself something inwardly differentiated, for it involves both will and external existence. Such a [divided] person knows then that God is the bond of this necessity, is this unity that produces well-being commensurate with the inner will, makes it correspond to right conduct; one knows that this connection ˉis the divine, universal | will (and the divine is the power), but moreover that it   573 is also the inwardly determined will of the finite spirit.ˉ[484]

The consciousness that this linkage obtains is the faith and confidence that is a fundamental feature of the Jewish people; and indeed it constitutes one of their remarkable features. The Old Testament scriptures are full of this confidence.[485] It is this pattern of events too that is presented in the Book of Job, ˉa book whose connection with the Jewish tradition is not precisely known.ˉ[486] [487] Job is guiltless; he finds his misfortune unjustifiable and so is dissatisfied. This means there is an antithesis within him, the con-

---

483. W (Var) reads: good.

484. W₁ (Var) reads: exists—the divine universal will (and the divine is the power to achieve this), but also this inwardly determined will. W₂ (Var) reads: exists, for the divine, universal will is at the same time the inwardly determined will, and hence it is the power to bring about this connection.

485. W (Var) adds: especially the Psalms.

486. Thus B; W (Var) reads: the only book whose connection with the soil of the Jewish people is not precisely known.

487. [Ed.] The origin and date of compilation of the Book of Job were at that time highly controversial matters. J. D. Michaelis, whose translation of the Old Testament into German was published in 1769, regarded it as the oldest book in the Bible, possibly written by Moses to comfort the Israelites in Egypt. This view is reflected in the prominence Hegel accords to it, especially in the first two lecture series. J. G. Herder, by contrast, in The Spirit of Hebrew Poetry (1787), trans. James Marsh, 2 vols. (Burlington, Vt., 1833), vol. 1, dialogue 5 (esp. pp. 103–111), expressed the view that the author was not an Israelite at all. In his translation and commentary, Das Buch Hiob (Heidelberg, 1824), F. W. C. Umbreit discussed the opposing standpoints and concluded that the book is purely Hebraic in origin, but of post-Mosaic date. See 1824 lectures, n. 510.

sciousness of the justice or righteousness that is absolute and of the incongruity between his fate and this righteousness. He is dissatisfied precisely because he does not regard necessity as blind fate; it is known to be God's purpose to bring about good things for those who are good. The critical point, then, occurs when this dissatisfaction and despondency has to submit to absolute, pure confidence. This submission is the end point. On the one side there stands the requirement that the righteous should prosper, and ¯on the other side is a submission, a renunciation, an acknowledgment of God's power; upon that submission there follows the restoration of good fortune by God, precisely as the consequence of this acknowledgment.¯488 This trust in God, this unity and the consciousness of this harmony of the power of God with the¯truth¯489 and righteousness of God, the consciousness that God is inwardly characterized as purpose and that God has purposes, is the first step, and God's blessings are what follow from it. That trust in God is none other than the consciousness of this harmony between power and wisdom. |

574

We have still to draw attention here to this inwardizing of spirit, its own movement within itself. A human being is supposed to do right; that is the absolute commandment, and this right conduct has its seat in one's will. As a result one is directed to one's inner being, and one must be occupied with consideration of one's inwardness, with whether it is in the right, whether one's will is good. The inner inquiry about this and the grief when it is not so, the crying of the soul for God, this descent into the depths of spirit, this longing of spirit for the right, for conformity to the will of God, is a particular characteristic that is dominant in the Psalms and the Prophets.

In addition, however, this [divine] purpose appears at the same time as a limited one. It is indeed the aim that human beings should know and acknowledge God, that they should do whatever they do for God's glory, that what they will should be conformed to God's

---

488. W (1827 with 1831?) reads: on the other side even this discontent must give way. This renunciation, this acknowledgment of God's power, restores Job to his property and his former happiness; this acknowledgment is followed by the restoration of his good fortune. At the same time this good fortune must not be expressed by the finite [creature] as a right vis-à-vis the power of God.

489. W (Var) reads: wisdom

will, that their will should be true will. [But] this aim has also a limitation, and we will now indicate to what extent this limitation lies in the definition of God, how far the concept or representation of God still contains a limitation. If the representation of God is limited, then these further realizations of the divine concept within human consciousness will also be limited.[490]

God is what is self-determining in its freedom and according to its freedom, ¯God is the spiritual, free being¯[491]—this is wisdom. But this wisdom, this purpose, is only an initial purpose, wisdom in general. The wisdom and self-determining of God does not yet include God's development. This development in the idea of God is first found in the religion where the nature of God is open and manifest. The defect of this idea at the present stage is that God is indeed the One, but yet is within himself only in the *determinacy* of this unity; he is not what is eternally self-developing within itself. This is still not a developed determination; | to this extent what we call wisdom is an abstraction, it is abstract universality.   575

[492] ¯Hence a limitation is present in [this] religion, insofar as it is consciousness of God, a limitation understood partly in terms of

490. *L (1827?) adds, similar in W:* This is always the essential but also the most difficult point, to recognize limitation in the One as also a limitation of the idea, so that the idea is not yet the absolute idea.

491. *W (Var) reads:* in such a way that the spiritual is the free

492. *W (1831) reads (parallel in main text follows):* (2) God is the exclusive Lord and God of the Jewish people. It need not surprise us that a [W_2: an Oriental] nation should limit religion to itself, and that its religion should appear as wholly tied to its nationality, for we see this in Eastern lands quite generally. The Greeks and the Romans were the first to adopt foreign forms of worship; all types of religion infiltrate Roman culture, but they do not have the status of a national religion there. But in the Eastern lands, religion is completely tied to nationality. The Chinese and the Persians both have their state religions, which are just for them. Among the Hindus, birth already indicates each individual's social status and relationship to Brahman; hence they do not in any way demand that others should adopt their religion. For the Hindus such a demand makes absolutely no sense because, on their view, all the peoples of the earth belong to their religion, and the foreign peoples are reckoned collectively as one particular caste. All the same, this exclusiveness rightly astonishes us more in the case of the Jewish people, for the binding of religion to nationality completely contradicts the view that God is grasped only in universal thought and not in a partial [*partikular*] definition. For the Persians God is the good; that too is a universal way of characterizing him, but it is itself still in the sphere of immediacy, so that God is identical with light, and that is a partial view. The Jewish God is only

576 the fact that the Jewish God is only a national God, has restricted himself to this nation. | Certainly this is the case, but such is true of other religions as well; the God of the Christians is restricted too. We may well be aware of a [universal] Christendom, but we also represent it as one [particular] family, one nation, or one people;

---

for thought, and that stands in contrast with his limitation to the nation. It is true that consciousness rises to universality among the Jewish people too, and this is expressed in several passages. Psalm 117:1[–2]: "Praise the Lord all ye nations, praise him all ye peoples. For his grace and truth are great toward us to all eternity." The glory of God is to be made manifest among all peoples; it is in the later prophets especially that this universality emerges as a higher demand. Isaiah makes God even say: "Of the heathen who shall honor Jehovah will I make priests and Levites,"[a] and a similar thought is expressed in the words, "In every nation anyone who fears God and does what is right is acceptable to him."[b] This, however, comes later. According to the dominant basic idea, the Jewish people is the chosen people, and universality is thus reduced to partiality [Partikularität]. [W₁: But this partiality derives from the subjective side. What is proper to the Jews is their worship and acknowledgment of Jehovah; W₂: But we have already seen above, in the development of the divine purpose, how its limitation is grounded in the limitation that is still involved in the definition of God, and we have shown that this limitation in turn stems from the nature of the servile consciousness; and we can now see also how this partiality derives from the subjective side too. What is proper to the Jews, as his servants, is this worship and acknowledgment of Jehovah;] and they are quite conscious that it is peculiar to them. It is also linked to the history of the Jewish people: the Jewish God is the God of Abraham, of Isaac, and of Jacob, the God who brought the Jews out of Egypt. [W₁: etc. W₂: and there is not the slightest reflection that God also may have done other things, that he also may have dealt affirmatively with other peoples.] So partiality here enters on the scene from the subjective side, [W₂: from the side of the cultus,] and in any case it can be said that God is the God of those who worship him, for God is the one who is known in the subjective spirit, and knows himself in it. This moment belongs essentially to the idea of God; and knowing and acknowledging belong essentially to this definition of him. It often appears in what is for us a distorted guise, as when, for instance, God is said to be mightier and stronger than the other gods, as if there were other gods in addition to him.[c] But for the Jews, these are the false gods. [W₁: This partiality pertains therefore to the side of subjective worship.]

It is this people that worships him, and so he is the God of this people, he is its Lord in fact. He it is who is known as the creator of heaven and earth, he has established for everything its purpose and measure, bestowed on everything its distinctive nature, and even given to humanity its measure, its goal, and its right. This is the definition under which he (as the Lord) gives his people their laws, laws of every kind, both the universal laws, the Ten Commandments, which are the universal basic ethical and rightful foundations of lawgiving and morality and are not regarded [by them] as rationally based but as [simply] prescribed by the Lord, and also all the other political ordinances and regulations. Moses is called the lawgiver of the Jews, but he was not to the Jews what Solon and Lycurgus were to the Greeks (for these two legislated

thus this consciousness of God is also consciousness of a national God. When we represent ourselves thus as a family, then God is | 577 restricted to this family. In the consciousness of the family that knows such a God there is, however, not only the element that God is the universal creator and lord of the world; in addition, God should also

---

simply as human beings). Moses just made known the laws of Jehovah; according to the story, it was Jehovah himself who engraved them on the stone.[d] Attached to the most trifling regulations, e.g., to those concerning the arrangement of the tabernacle, or to the usages in connection with sacrifices and all other ceremonial matters, we find in the Bible the formula "Jehovah says." All law is given by the Lord, and hence it is positive commandment throughout. There is in it a formal, absolute authority. The particular aspects of the political constitution are not developed out of the universal purpose at all, nor are they left to human beings to determine, for the unity [of the absolute] does not permit human caprice, human reason, to persist alongside it, and every political change is called a falling away from God. But as something given by God, the particular is [valid] as established forever. And the eternal laws of right and morality are here placed in the same rank and stated in equally positive form with the most trifling regulations. This forms a marked contrast with our concept of God. Their cultus is then the service of God; the good or righteous person is one who performs this service by keeping and observing both the moral commandments and the ceremonial laws. That is the service of the Lord.

That the Jewish people gave itself up wholly to this service is connected with their representation of God as the Lord. This explains also their admirable steadfastness, which was not a fanaticism of conversion, as exists in Islam, [W_2: a religion that is already purged of nationality and recognizes believers only,] but a fanaticism of stubbornness. It rests entirely on the abstraction of the one Lord. Vacillation of spirit occurs only when various interests and points of view come to stand beside one another; in a combat between them, one can take one side or the other, but in this concentration on the one Lord, the spirit is completely held fast. It follows that there is no freedom vis-à-vis this firm bond; thought is tied utterly to this unity, which is the absolute authority. Many consequences follow from this. Certain institutions were regarded as divine among the Greeks too, but these had been established by human beings; the Jews, however, drew no distinction between the divine and the human in this way. [W_1: And for this reason W_2: And on account of their lack of freedom] they did not believe in immortality either; for although one might, if one wished, point to a few traces of it, these passages always remain very general in character and do not exert the least influence on religious and moral points of view. The immortality of the soul is not yet recognized; hence there is no higher purpose than the service of Jehovah, and the purpose of humanity with reference to itself is to preserve life for oneself and one's family as long as possible. According to the law, each family received a plot of land, which could not be transferred to the ownership of someone else; and this was to provide for the family. The main purpose of life was consequently the preservation of it.

[*Ed.*] [a]See Isa. 66:21. [b]See Acts 10:35. Hegel seemingly regards this verse as an Old Testament text, somewhat similar to Ps. 146:18–20 or 147:11 and Isa. 56:6–7,

be universally honored, all peoples should attain a cognition [of him]
578 | such that they do not hold the knowledge of God to be something
particular just for themselves. In accord with the nature of this unity,
the proclaimed purpose is that all peoples should come to cognition
of the true God, that this knowledge should spread throughout the
whole earth. It is only a limitation in this respect and not a limitation
of the religion [as such].

But at this stage the limitation is present in yet another way.
Because the purpose is still in fact abstract, the consequence is that
the commandments, both those in force as properly religious and
those of the cultus, appear only as something given by God, as
something prescribed and immutable, something eternally and firmly
posited. The purpose is still abstract; and when we speak of "abstraction" in the purpose, we are referring to something immediate in its
determinate being or existence—something subsisting in just this one
way, something immutable.

c. The Cultus

The cultus is what is called ceremonial service, an action done
because it is so commanded, so prescribed, a carrying out of [a law]
that is abstract, wise indeed, and universal; but for the very reason
that what is done in this way is [also] the carrying out of something
particular, it therefore involves the requirement that these activities
be understood, that their wisdom be known; it demands the insight
that these activities are rational, that they have a connection with
the particularity of human life and sensibilities (indeed, with its
legitimate particularity). But here wisdom is not a developed wisdom.
Here there are particularities in which the wisdom is not recognized;
it is undeveloped and does not penetrate into feeling. To that extent
the divine commandment is only an abstract precept of wisdom; in

---

although he judges correctly that it cannot date from before the Exile or post-Exilic
period. ᶜSee, e.g., Jethro's avowal in Exod. 18:11: "Now I know that the Lord is
greater than all gods." Hegel is referring to the widespread evidence for a period of
Old Testament henotheism, to which one of the sources available to him, C. P. W.
Gramberg's *Kritische Geschichte der Religionsideen des Alten Testaments,* 2 vols.
(Berlin, 1829–1830), devoted an entire chapter (chap. 6). ᵈThis is in accord with
one tradition: Exod. 31:18, 32:16, 34:1; Deut. 4:13, 9:10, 10:1–4; but cf. Exod.
24:4, 34:27–28.

this mode it is not understood, it is done as something external. Because God is absolute power, the activities are intrinsically indeterminate, and for that reason they are external, being determined quite arbitrarily.

The same pattern holds for other commandments beyond the scope of the cultus itself. Details of the political constitution and other institutions are likewise given as something prescribed by God only abstractly, something simply to be obeyed and forever immutable. As worldly, the political domain and statutory institutions are inherently changeable; but here they are taken to be something that is immutable. Part of this same pattern is the fact that the territory that this people has in its possession likewise counts as an immutable possession. | 579

There is one family; the condition is wholly patriarchal, the political constitution imperfect. The people possesses a land; the particular family has its particular lot, share, and family goods. This is an inalienable possession which forever belongs to the family, and the individual cannot freely dispose of it. If it was sold or obligated for debts, it reverted to the family in the Jubilee Year.[493] This is not a rising above, not an indifference to, worldly existence or property. Property in the legal sense is not yet present. These features constitute the limitation in the idea and in the realization of the idea in self-consciousness.¯

C. THE RELIGION OF EXPEDIENCY: ROMAN RELIGION[494]

[495]The religion of nature was the first form. The second, that of spiritual being-for-self, comprised the religion of beauty and the religion of sublimity. The third form of the determinate religions is that of purposiveness, the totality in this domain [of determinate religion], being primarily the unification of the religions of beauty and of sublimity.

493. [Ed.] See Lev. 25.
494. [Ed.] The treatment of Roman religion in 1827 is quite similar to that of 1824 and is of comparable length. Only the transitions are different—the transitions from Greek and Jewish to Roman religion, and from Roman to Christian—and these are analyzed in the Editorial Introduction.
495. In B's margin: 20 July 1827

1. The Concept of Purposiveness

[496]It is the next requirement of thinking that abstract necessity should be filled by particularity, by inward purpose. We had that already in the religion of sublimity; but there the purpose partly is an abstract wisdom, and partly (in its reality) is only an isolated purpose expressed in a single family that is restricted to a natural territory. The higher stage now is that this purpose is enlarged to embrace ¯particularity in general. | This developed, extensive, ¯[497] manifold particularity we had in the religion of beauty; the fact that it is now also posited in unity cannot furnish that truly spiritual unity, the pure spirit of thinking as in the religion of sublimity.

580

¯First of all it [the religion of expediency] is the one relative totality, ¯[498] a totality in which those two religions do indeed lose their one-sidedness, but the two principles perish conjointly, each by means of assimilation into its opposite; still, it is this very homogeneity that interests us in them. The religion of beauty loses the concrete individuality of its gods and hence also their ethical, independent content; the gods are reduced to means. The religion of sublimity loses the orientation toward the One, the eternal, the transcendent. ¯In their combination the two religions turn into a primarily empirical universal purpose, into a fully developed, externally universal aim. In the religion of expediency the purpose is this comprehensive [universal], but one that is external and therefore falls within the human sphere. ¯[499] [500] This [human]

496. *Precedes in L (1827?), similar in W:* In the religion of beauty we have empty necessity, and in the religion of sublimity we have unity as subjective. To the former there pertains ethical substantiality, what is right, what is present and actual in empirical self-consciousness—outside of necessity. In it we have the ethical powers represented as individuals, as spiritual, concrete subjects (particular folk-spirits, living spirits). This particularity, when reduced to a single theme, is the next determinacy.

497. W_1 *(Var) reads:* particularity, and develops it. The extensive, W_2 *(Var/Ed?) reads:* power, and power itself is developed in consequence. The extensively developed,

498. W_2 *(Var) reads:* Instead the characteristics of the earlier stages are merely taken back into a relative totality, into

499. W_2 *(Var) reads:* But their union results in progress, in that the singular purpose and the particular purposes are broadened into one universal purpose.

500. W_1 *(Var?) adds:* Thus it is the religion of the understanding.

[Ed.] In the *Ms.*, Hegel describes Roman religion as, among other things, the religion of the "understanding" (*Verstand*), because it is the understanding that holds fast to finite, external purposes.

purpose is to be realized, and the deity is the power for realizing it.[501]

This is the relationship of purposiveness; it has this defect, that the purpose is one posited by human beings, it is an external and empirical purpose. But this defect has its ground in a yet higher defect—in the fact that God has *this* purpose. This purpose is to be realized. According to its content it is an external purpose; so its realization is external too—within the finite, out in the world. ¨The | true ¨realization¨[502] would be that the purpose or the concept is realized, and through this realization is posited the unity of the concept, God or the divine subject, with that in which it is realized, i.e., with objectivity.[503] This latter is then God's nature itself, it is the inner purposiveness in which the aspect of reality itself in the concept is identical with the concept; it is this process, this movement, in which the concept itself objectifies itself and posits this objective aspect as identical with itself¨¨[504]—in which it is the absolute purpose, the absolutely final purpose. But at the present stage the absolute idea is not yet present as this circle, as this self-relation; and for this reason the concept ¨that is to be realized¨[505] is something external, and the content that is to be realized is the sort that occurs within the world, in human consciousness, insofar as it is to be realized.

581

What the purpose here consists in is, more precisely, as follows. In the religion of sublimity the purpose, albeit a limited one, is an essential purpose as well, though one that is as yet undeveloped. Thus its inner [being] is the family, or natural ethical life as such. Now this purpose gets enlarged; the comprehensive, essential end is in general the state. This state is an external, worldly end, so that the ¨content¨[506] does not yet properly fall within God himself; it does

501. W₁ *(Var) adds:* There is an affirmative unity of God and humanity, and God is the power to realize that purpose.

502. *Thus B, Hu, similar in An;* W₁ *(Var) reads:* purposiveness

503. W₁ *(Var) adds:* with its realization.

504. W₂ *(MiscP/1831?) reads:* Genuine purposiveness is where the unity of the concept, the unity of God, the divine subject, with that in which the concept realizes itself, with objectivity and realization, is posited. It is the very nature of God that accomplishes itself in objectivity, so that it is identical with itself under the aspect of reality.

505. W₁ *(Var) reads:* the substantial, what is to be objectified,

506. W₁ *(Var) reads:* purpose

of course fall within God, but is not God's own proper nature. Also, this state is, to begin with, only the abstract state; it is the unification of human beings under one bond but in such a way that the unity is not yet a rational organization internally, and the state is not yet a rational organization internally because, so to speak, God is not yet rational organization within himself, God is not yet concrete spirit. The purposiveness is external; if it were grasped as internal, it would be God's own proper nature. Because God is not yet this 582 concrete idea, not yet his true fulfillment through himself, this | purpose or the state is not yet this rational organization or rational totality internally; hence also it does not merit the name "state." Instead it is dominion, the uniting of individuals and peoples within one bond, under one power. And since we have here the distinction between purpose and realization, this purpose is initially present as subjective only and not as developed, while the realization is conquest, acquisition of dominion, the realization of a purpose that is a priori, that takes priority over the peoples and simply fulfills itself. That is what the specification of the purpose involves; this distinction is quite essential.

We pointed out earlier that Athena is the spirit of the people. There [in Greek religion] the well-being of the city of Athens and its fortune is not the purpose of Athena; in that instance there is no relationship of a purpose that ought to be realized. On the contrary, Athena is the substantial unity, the spirit of the people, and Athens is the outward existence of this spirit, is immediately identical with it. ⁻Pallas is not the goddess of Athens, who has Athens for her purpose.⁻⁵⁰⁷ But now this category of external purposiveness is the main point upon which everything hinges.⁵⁰⁸

2. The Configuration of the Gods

Our second task is to describe the external appearance of this religion or the soil on which it came to be, and the type of configuration of its god or gods. As an external phenomenon, this religion is the religion of the Romans. We always introduce the external appearance

507. W₁ (Var) reads: This is not the relationship of purpose to the realization of purpose.
508. W₁ (Var) adds: That is the general characteristic of this sphere.

in order first to show that the religion accords with the determinacy of the concept; and this provides the opportunity to develop concretely the more detailed characteristics that are contained in the concept. On a superficial view, Roman religion is lumped together with Greek religion; but the spirit in the one is essentially quite different from that in the other. Even though they have configurations [of the gods] in common, these nevertheless have a quite different standing in Roman religion from what they had in Greece. The whole religion and the religious disposition is essentially distinct in each case, as is quite evident even from an external and superficial consideration. | For it is generally granted that the state or the 583 constitution and the political fate of a people depend upon its religion, that religion is the basis and susbstance of politics, its foundation. But the spirit, culture, and ˉhistoryˉ[509] of the Greeks and the Romans are essentially distinct from one another; ˉtherefore the two religions also must be distinct.ˉ[510]

Moreover, with regard to the abstract disposition or the orientation of spirit, the first thing to note is the seriousness of the Romans. Where there is a purpose that is to be realized, an essentially firm purpose, the understanding comes into play and with it the seriousness that holds firmly to this purpose as against the variety of other impulses in the mind or in the external environment.

The cheerfulness or serenity of Greek religion, its basic dispositional feature, has its ground in the fact that there is, to be sure, a purpose in Greek religion too, something revered and holy. But at the same time the freedom from purpose is immediately present in it, in that the Greek gods are many. Each Greek god has a more or less substantial trait of its own, an ethical essentiality; but just because there are so many particularities, the consciousness or spirit also simultaneously stands above this multiplicity or manifold and is withdrawn from its particularity. Consciousness lays aside what is determined as essential and can even be treated as an end; consciousness is itself this mode of treating things ironically. In contrast, wherever there is a highest principle or highest purpose,

509. W (Var) reads: character
510. W₂ (Var) reads: and this in itself must lead to the distinction in religious substance.

this cheerfulness cannot occur. Moreover, the Greek god is a concrete individuality; each of these many particular individuals in turn has within it many different characteristics: it is an opulent individuality which must necessarily have contradiction in it and must exhibit it simply because the antithesis [of one and many] is not yet absolutely reconciled. Because the gods have this abundance of outward characteristics in themselves, indifference toward these particularities is also present, and frivolity can have fun with them. The contingency that we observe in the divine stories about these gods falls under this heading. |

584

⁻The definite⁻⁵¹¹ purpose is precisely the purpose of dominion, and the god is the power of realizing this purpose, the highest or universal power, this dominion over the world. We can see this god in the figure of Fortuna Publica, for example. ⁻This Fortuna Publica is the inherent⁻⁵¹² necessity, the necessity that embodies the Roman purpose itself; it is just Rome itself. Rome is the dominant lord and, as such, is exalted as a holy, divine essence. This dominant Rome in the form of a ruling god is Jupiter Capitolinus.⁵¹³ He is the principal god who makes Rome dominant—the Jupiter who has the meaning of ruling and has a purpose within the world, and it is the Roman people through whom and for whom he accomplishes this purpose.⁵¹⁴

The second point is that this God of real [world] dominion is not the genuine One, the spiritual One; and just for that reason the particular falls outside this unity of dominion. The power is only

511. W_1 (Var) reads: The character of the Roman disposition is this seriousness on the part of the understanding, a seriousness that has a definite purpose; this

512. W (Var) reads: It is the necessity that is for others a cold, unsympathetic necessity; it is the inherent

513. W (Var?) adds: a particular Jupiter—for there are many Jupiters, maybe three hundred Joves in all.

[Ed.] Hegel is probably relying on a faulty recollection of a reference in Tertullian's Apology 14.9. Tertullian quotes the figure of three hundred Joves from a satire by Varro, no longer extant, in order to pour scorn on Roman religion. A similar criticism is found in Minucius Felix, Octavius 22.6.

514. W_2 (MiscP/1831?) adds: The Roman people is the universal family, whereas in the religion of beauty many families were the divine purpose, and in the religion of the One, by contrast, one family only.

692

abstract, it is only power; it is not a rational organization, or a self-contained totality. For that very reason the particular makes its appearance as something that falls outside the One, the ruler. And so we have here the appearances of gods of the sort that, as indicated, may also in fact be Greek gods or else ones equated with them—for one nation sometimes does equate its gods with those of other nations. Thus the Greeks [sometimes] find their gods in Persia, Syria, and Babylon, [a discovery] which was after all at the same time something different from the distinctive way in which their own gods were intuited and characterized; only at a level of superficial generality are they to be viewed as similar. ˉBut they [the Roman gods] have no free individuality | as in Greece. They ˉ515 appear to 585 be old and gray, so to speak; we know not where they came from, but only that they have been introduced from elsewhere. These Roman gods have then no true meaning; in the poets they are only a lifeless imitation of the Greek gods. There is not to be found in them that consciousness or feeling of humanity and subjectivity which is the substantial element in gods as it is in humans, and in humans as in gods. They show themselves to be derivative; they appear to be machinery devoid of sense. (Mechanical gods of this kind were introduced in France also.516) They show themselves to be really gods of the understanding who have no place in ˉa beautifulˉ517 imagination.

Apart from these particular gods that appear to be common to both Romans and Greeks, the Romans have many of their own typical gods and forms of worship. Dominion is the goal of the citizen; but the individual is not wholly taken up with that. The

515. W_1 (Var) reads: Generally speaking, these [Roman gods]—or many of them—are the same [as the Greek gods]. But these [Roman] gods, who do not have that beautiful, free individuality [of the Greek gods], W_2 (Var) reads: Generally speaking, the particular Roman deities—or many of them—are the same as the Greek gods. However, they do not have that beautiful, free individuality, for they

516. [Ed.] Hegel criticizes French dramatists in almost identical terms in the Lectures on Aesthetics, without however citing the names of authors or works there either. In the Ms. he does specifically criticize Racine's Phèdre for making Hippolytus fall in love with Aricia, thus robbing the drama of ethical content.

517. W (Var) reads: a beautiful, free spirit, within a beautiful, free

individual has also a particular purpose, and these private purposes fall outside of that abstract purpose.[518] But these particular purposes become wholly and prosaically private matters; what emerges here is the shared private concerns [*Partikularität*] of human beings according to the multiple aspects of their need, or of their ties with and dependence upon nature. The god is not the concrete individuality.[519] Private life [*Partikularität*] by itself in this way, forsaken by that universality, is just the wholly common and prosaic private

586   concerns | of human beings. But that is their human goal; one needs this thing and that, and whatever is a human goal then becomes in this sphere a determination of the divine. Thus human purposes count as divine purposes and accordingly as divine powers. Human purpose and divine purpose are one and the same; but the goal is one that is external to the idea. In this way the goal is first of all the universal goal; dominion over the world is one aspect. This is the abstract power that is oppressive and burdensome for individuals, the power that consumes and sacrifices them. The second aspect is the goal as private; for that reason private aims, needs, and powers also appear as gods, because [fulfillment in] the human sphere is the fulfillment of God.

This is the basic feature of Roman religion. It is the common needs that furnish the content for the gods here. So we have many highly prosaic deities. The content of these gods is practical utility; [520]they serve ordinary, practical functions. The Lares and Penates belong to the private citizen, to be sure, though they are connected with natural ethical life and piety, i.e., with the ethical unity of the family. But most [of the religion] has a content that pertains to merely private utility.

518. *L (1827?) adds, similar in W:* As against the universal of dominion there is something particular present, human purposes and interests, these private purposes, human life and human needs. Thus on one side we see this universal power that is sovereignty; in it individuals are sacrificed, having no value as such. The other side, the determinate element, falls outside the divine unity just because God is what is abstract, and the human element is essentially purpose. The filling of God with a content is the human aspect.

519. *W (Var) adds:* Jupiter is merely sovereignty, while the particular gods are dead, devoid of life and spirit, or, what is worse, they are borrowed.

520. *In B's margin:* 23 July 1827

Since this human life and activity also takes on a form that is at all events lacking the negative [moment] of evil, the satisfaction of these needs is thus a simple, peaceful, uncultured, natural state. The satisfaction of the needs appropriate to it appears as a host of gods. A state of innocence hovers before the Roman mind as the Age of Saturn. They have many festivals[521] connected with the benefit of the earth's fruitfulness and the human ability to utilize the gifts of nature. Furthermore, these are gods of the skills and types of activity that are wholly concerned with immediate needs and their satisfaction: for example, Jupiter Pistor, the baker or the skill of baking[522]; Fornax, the oven in which the grain was dried | ˉand the oven for baking, is the oven goddess.ˉ[523] Vesta [is at first] the fire for baking bread (ˉand later has a higher significanceˉ[524] relating to family piety); the festival of Pales, the goddess of livestock fodder; Juno Moneta [the mint]. ˉAnd [there are gods] for all sorts of human conditions [and concerns]: the goddesses Pax, Tranquillitas, Vacuna [leisure], Febris [fever], Pestis [plague], Robigo or wheat rust, and Aerumna, the goddess of trouble and care—all these relate to quite prosaic needs. Nothing could be so devoid of imagination as a circle of such gods!ˉ[525] [526]

587

ˉThis multitude of gods constitutes a very wide-ranging circle of divinities, to be sure; but it is the immediate character of the universality of Roman destiny, or of the ruling Jupiter—it lies in the very

521. *W (Var) adds:* and a host of gods

522. *W (Var) adds:* ranks as something divine, and the power to exercise it counts as something essential

523. *W (Var) reads:* is a goddess by herself.

524. *W (Var) reads:* for as Ἑστία she has acquired a higher significance

525. *W₁ (Var) reads:* Certain special human conditions [and concerns] are also regarded as divine power, insofar as they are injurious or useful, or insofar as they appear friendly or inimical: the goddesses Pax and Tranquillitas, Vacuna, the goddess of leisure, also Febris, Fames [famine], Robigo or wheat rust, Aerumna and Angerona (i.e:, care and woe), etc. They also dedicated altars to the plague.

Furthermore, these are gods of the skills and types of activity that are wholly concerned with immediate needs and their satisfaction—highly prosaic deities, devoid of phantasy: there is nothing more devoid of imagination than a circle of such gods. Here spirit is more perfectly at home in the finite and in what is immediately useful.

526. *[Ed.]* For this description of Roman festivals and divinities, Hegel is relying on the detailed account provided by K. P. Moritz, *Anthousa; oder, Roms Alterthümer* (Berlin, 1791).

definition of this foundation—that all these gods together, the individual gods, are gathered into one.[527] The extension of the Romans' worldly dominion consisted in this: that individuals and peoples were brought under one power and rule, and likewise their ethical powers, the divine national spirits, were ˉcompressed into one pantheon,[528] assembled under one destiny, subordinated to the one Jupiter Capitolinus. Whole cargoes of gods were hauled to Rome from | Egypt, Greece, Persia (the Mithra worship), etc. Rome ˉis a potpourri of all sorts of religions;[529] the total condition is one of confusion.[530]

588

3. The Cultus

Our third topic is the character of the cultus. Its specification lies in what has already been said: God is served for the sake of a purpose, and this is a human purpose. The content does not begin, so to speak, with God—it is not the content of God's nature—but instead it begins with humans, with what human purpose is. The Romans were praised by Cicero[531] for being the most pious nation, one that[532] associates religion with everything it does.[533] This, we can say, is in fact the case. What is present [in this piety] is precisely the abstract inwardness of the Roman principle, the universality of the purpose that is the destiny in which particular individuals with their ethical life and humanity are suppressed and not permitted to have concrete presence or self-development. This universality[534] is the foundation for the way that everything is connected with the universal, and because everything is connected with this inwardness, there is religion

527. W_2 (Var) reads: Viewed from another aspect, however, there was also a more general religious requirement (together with the oppressive power of Roman destiny) that assembled the individual gods into a unity.

528. W_1 (Var) reads: suppressed by one power and sovereignty,

529. W (Var) reads: thus became the assembly of all religions, of the Greek, Persian, Egyptian, and Christian religions, and of the worship of Mithra;

530. W (Var) adds: in which every kind of cultus is jumbled together.

531. [Ed.] Although this does not appear to be an actual citation from Cicero, he did express himself more or less to this effect on several occasions, e.g., in De natura deorum 2.8.

532. W (Var) adds: thinks on the gods in all aspects of life, one that

533. W (Var) adds: and thanks the gods for everything.

534. W (Var) adds: and inwardness

in everything.[535] But at the same time this inwardness, this higher or universal element, is only the form; the content or purpose of this power is human, it is given by human beings, and the gods as powers are supposed to carry it out. More specifically, we see that the Romans worship the gods because they need them and when they need them, especially in "times of particular exigency."[536] [537]For the Romans, such need is the | general theogony from which their gods 589 arise. The oracles and the Sibylline Books are the higher means for informing the people what "ought to be done."[538] But they are in the hands of the state, of the magistrates. Thus on the one hand the individual perishes in the universal, in the sovereign authority, in the Fortuna Publica; but on the other hand human purposes hold sway and the human subject has an independent, essential value. These extremes and their contradiction are the whirlpool in which Roman life tosses and turns.

Roman virtue or *virtus* is that cold patriotism [which dictates] that the individual must serve the interest of the state or the sovereign authority completely. The Romans themselves even made this negativity, this submergence of the individual in the universal, into a spectacle; it is what constitutes an essential feature in their religious plays. The religious dramas of the Romans consist of the shedding of torrents of blood. There is no ethical interest, no tragic reversal and upheaval that would have for its content an ethical interest or a misfortune that might be connected with ethical characteristics; instead the picture is that of the dry, cold conversion of death. Hundreds and thousands had to slay one another. This cold-blooded murder was a delight to their eyes; in it they beheld the nullity of

535. *W₂ (1831/MiscP?) adds:* Thus, in complete accord with the Roman spirit, Cicero derives religion from *religare,* for in fact religion in all its relationships was for the Roman spirit something that binds and commands.

[*Ed.*] This etymology of "religion" is not as unambiguous as Hegel makes out. The derivation from *religare,* which he accepts as correct, is in any event not to be found in Cicero but in Lactantius, *Divinae institutiones* 4.28.2, who there opposes Cicero's derivation from *relegendo (De natura deorum* 2.72).

536. *W (Var) reads:* the exigency of war.

537. *Precedes in W (Var):* The introduction of new gods happens at times of exigency and fear or because of vows.

538. *W (Var) reads:* is to be done or is to happen in order to obtain a benefit.

human individuality, the worthlessness of the individual (because individuality has no ethical life within it). It was the spectacle of the hollow, empty destiny that relates to human beings as a contingency, as blind caprice.

There is a further characteristic that can be linked to this, one that draws together all that we have said; despite the fact that it is not an integral part of religion, it can become caught up in it. ‾‾Since cold, irrational destiny or sheer dominion is in fact what predominates, in the viewpoint prevalent in the Roman | Empire there appears, transcending individuals, the all-pervasive power, the power of arbitrariness [that is vested in] the emperor—a power that can rage wildly and without restraint, beyond all legal or ethical bounds. It was in fact quite consistent for the emperor, this supreme power, to receive divine honors; for he is purely and simply this ungrounded power over individuals and their circumstances.

This, therefore, is one aspect, the perishing of ‾the individuals;‾539 and the other extreme stands opposed to it.‾‾540 Namely, a goal for the power is present at the same time too. In one respect it is blind, and spirit is not yet reconciled and brought into harmony; for that reason the two sides stand one-sidedly opposed to each other. This power is a purpose, and the purpose is the human, finite purpose. This [divine] purpose is dominion over the world, and its realization is the dominion of human beings—of the Romans. In the real sense this universal purpose has its ground or seat in self-consciousness. ‾So the independence of this self-consciousness is thereby posited.‾541 On the one side there stands an indifference to concrete life, on the other the reserve or inwardness that is equally the inwardness of the divine and that of the individual, though it is a wholly abstract inwardness on the part of the individual. This involves what constitutes for the Romans the basic feature, the fact that the abstract person as such has attained this visible status. The

590

539. W_1 *(Var) reads:* the individual in general;

540. W_2 *(MiscP/1831?) reads:* In contrast with this extreme of empty destiny in which the individual perishes, the destiny that finally found its personal portrayal in the power of the emperor, an arbitrary power that rages wildly regardless of ethical considerations, the other extreme is the worth of the pure singularity of subjectivity.

541. *W (Var) reads:* So this self-consciousness is independent, since the purpose pertains to it.

abstract person is the person with rights. Hence the elaboration of right[542] is an important feature of Roman culture; but right is restricted to juridical right, to the right of property. There are higher rights than this: human conscience has its right,[543] and a right much higher still is that of ethics, of morality. But these higher rights are no longer present here in their concrete and proper sense, for the abstract right of the person prevails here instead, a right that consists in the determination of property alone. It is personality, to be sure, that maintains this exalted position, but only abstract personality, only subjectivity in this abstract sense. |

591

These are the basic features of the religion of expediency.[544] Contained in it are the moments whose unification constitutes the definition of the next and final stage of religion. The moments that in the religion of expediency are individuated though they subsist in relationship and for that very reason in contradiction—when these moments (present here in a spiritless way) are united in accord with their *truth*, they give form to the determinate shape of spirit and of the religion of spirit.

542. W *(Var) adds:* or the category of property

543. W *(Var) adds:* (for it is equally a right)

544. W *(1831) adds:* [W₁: In this religion God was known as what is purposive too; but here the purpose W₂: In this religion of purposiveness the purpose] is none other than the Roman state, so that the Roman state is the abstract power over all other national spirits. In the Roman pantheon the gods of all the peoples are assembled and cancel out one another through the very fact of their union. The Roman spirit [W₁: brings to pass this misfortune of the destruction of the beautiful life and consciousness. It was fate [*Fatum*] as the Roman spirit that destroyed this happiness and serenity of the preceding religion. W₂: as this fate destroyed the happiness and serenity of the beautiful life and consciousness of the preceding religions, and compressed all their shapes into unity and uniformity.] This abstract power it was which produced this monstrous misery and a universal sorrow, a sorrow that served to prepare the birth pangs of the religion of truth. [W₁: By it the limitation and finitude in the religion of the beautiful spirit was negated too.] Repenting of the world, laying aside finitude, and [W₁: renouncing all hope of finding satisfaction in this world W₂: despairing of finding satisfaction in temporality and finitude, a despair that gained the upper hand in the spirit of the world]—all of this served to prepare the soil for the genuine, spiritual religion. This preparation had to be carried out on the part of humanity [W₁: —"When the time was fulfilled," we are told, "God sent his Son"; the time was fulfilled when this despair of finding satisfaction in temporality and finitude had gained the upper hand in the spirit. W₂: in order that "the time might be fulfilled."]

[*Ed.*] A reference to the New Testament concept of the fullness of time; cf. Mark 1:15; Gal. 4:4; Eph. 1:10.

APPENDIXES

THE TELEOLOGICAL PROOF
ACCORDING TO
THE LECTURES
OF 1831[1]

Kant has already criticized this proof too,[2] like the other proofs of God's existence; and he has in large measure destroyed their reputation, so that it is now hardly considered worthwhile to examine the proofs themselves at all carefully. Yet Kant himself says of this proof that it deserves at all times to be treated with respect;[3] when he adds that the teleological proof is the oldest, however, he is mistaken. The first definition of God is that he is *power;* it is only later that he is defined as wisdom. Moreover, this proof first occurs among the Greeks; it was formulated by Socrates (Xenophon, *Memor.,* end of book 1).[4] Socrates makes purposiveness—especially in the form of the good—the basic principle [of reason]. The reason for his imprisonment is, according to him, that the Athenians have deemed it good.[5] Even historically, therefore, this proof coincides with the development of freedom.

We have already considered the transition from the religion of power to the religion of spirituality in general. The same mediating

1. [*Ed.*] In the 1831 lectures Hegel treated the teleological proof in relation to Greek religion, whereas in the *Ms.* it was considered in relation to Roman religion, and in 1824 at the beginning of Sec. B, preceding the discussion of Jewish, Greek, and Roman religion. The *Werke* reproduced the 1831 version of the teleological proof in an appendix at the end of vol. 12 along with other materials (see our Vol. 3:351 n. 1). Our text for this section is based on W_2 12:517–535, and may be compared with Strauss's excerpted version of the same section (Sec. C.2.b) printed below.

2. [*Ed.*] Kant, *Critique of Pure Reason* (London, 1930), B 648–658.

3. [*Ed.*] Ibid., B 651. In relation to this and the following references, see *Ms.*, pp. 199–204 and relevant notes.

4. [*Ed.*] See *Ms.*, nn. 239, 240.

5. [*Ed.*] See Plato, *Phaedo* 98a–99a.

process that we were cognizant of in the religion of beauty we have also encountered already in the intermediate stages; but in these stages it is still interpreted in a manner devoid of spirit. Now that this transition to the religion of spirituality has introduced a further essential determination, we must first identify and demonstrate it in abstract fashion.

We have here the category of freedom as such, the definition of an activity as freedom—a creating in accord with freedom, no longer an unrestrained creation in accord with power, but in accord with purposes. Freedom is determining oneself; and what is active, to the extent that it determines itself inwardly, implicitly has self-determination as its purpose. Power is simply self-projection in such a way that | there is something unreconciled in what is projected; it is, to be sure, implicitly a mirror image, but it is not yet explicit in consciousness that, *in* its creature, what creates is merely preserving and bringing forth *itself,* so that in the creature the [essential] characteristics of the divine are themselves present. God is here grasped under the defining characteristic of wisdom, of purposive activity. [Divine] power is benevolent and just, but it is only purposive action that has this defining mark of rationality—[the certainty] that from [divine] action only what is already determined in advance emerges, i.e., this identity of the creator with itself.

What distinguishes (differentiates) the proofs of God's existence is just the diversity of their defining categories. [Each of] them has mediation, a starting point, and a point of arrival; in the teleological and physicotheological proof the defining category of purposiveness attaches both to the starting point and to the conclusion. The proof begins from a [mode of] being that is now defined as purposive, and what is thereby mediated is God as positing and activating his purpose. The being which, as immediate, is the starting point of the cosmological proof is, to begin with, a manifold, contingent being; God is then defined as necessity that has being in and for itself, the power over the contingent. The higher specification here is that purposiveness is present in [contingent] being. In this purpose rationality is already explicit, as a free self-determining and activating of this [contingent] content, to the end that (although, as purpose,

594

it is initially something inward) it should be realized and reality [should] correspond to the concept or to the purpose.

A thing is good insofar as it fulfills its definition, its purpose; this means that the reality matches the concept or the definition. We can perceive in the world a concordance of external things, things that are present without reference to one another and come into existence on their own account (quite accidentally as far as the others are concerned and having no essential connection with each other); yet, although these things are quite separate from one another, a unity shows itself, by virtue of which they are directly in conformity with one another. Kant describes this in detail as follows.[6] The world that we are in offers us an immense spectacle of multiplicity, order, purposiveness, etc. This purposive character is particularly apparent in living matter, both inwardly and in its connection with the external environment. | Both the human and the animal [organism] are 595 implicitly a manifold (with just these limbs, internal organs, etc.). Although they seem to subsist merely side by side, it is everywhere just the general purposive definition that maintains them; the one exists only through the other and for the other, and all human limbs and components are merely means for the self-preservation of the individual, which is here the purpose. The human [organism], or living matter in general, has a multitude of requirements. Air, nourishment, light, etc., are necessary for its preservation. All this is present on its own account, and the capacity to serve as purpose is something external to it; the animals, meat, air, etc., that human beings need do not in themselves have the express character of being purposes, yet the one is purely and simply a means for the other. There is here an inner coherence, which is necessary, but which does not exist as such. This inner coherence is not brought about by the objects themselves, but is produced by something other than the things themselves are; purposiveness does not come about by itself, the purposive activity is extraneous to the things, and this implicit and self-positing harmony is the power over these things, which determines that they shall stand in a purposive orientation to one

6. [Ed.] Kant, *Critique of Pure Reason*, B 650.

another. Thus the world is no longer an aggregate of contingent things but a mass of purposive connections—but the connections accrue to the things themselves from outside. This purposive connection must have a cause (and a cause that is full of power and wisdom).

This purposive activity and this cause is God.

According to Kant, this proof is the clearest and is intelligible to the ordinary man; through it, nature has, for the first time, a [moral] interest, it brings the study of nature to life (just as it is from that study that it derives).[7] This is, in general terms, the teleological proof.

Kant's critique, now, is as follows.[8] He argues that the first deficiency in this proof is that only the form of things enters into consideration here. The purposive relation concerns only the definition of the form: everything maintains itself, and hence it is not merely a means for something else but a purpose unto itself; and that by virtue of which a thing can be a means concerns only its form, not its matter. The sole conclusion to be drawn, therefore, would be that there is a form-giving cause, but this cause does not also bring

596 forth matter. Thus the proof, says Kant, does not fulfill | the idea of God (that he is the creator of the matter, and not merely of the form).

Form contains the determinations that relate to one another, whereas matter is supposedly what is formless and so devoid of connections. Accordingly, in Kant's view, this proof yields only a Demiurge, one who shapes the material; it does not yield the creator.[9] In respect of this criticism it can be said at least that *all* relation is form—this is how form is separated off from matter. We can see that God's activity would consequently be a finite one. For if we produce something technical, we must take the material for it from outside; in this way our activity is limited, finite, and matter is thus posited as subsisting on its own account, or as eternal.

That whereby things are turned against [their] other is their qualities, their form, not the subsistence of the things as such. Their subsistence is their matter. To begin with, this is right enough, to be sure, that the relations between things pertain to their form; but

7. [*Ed.*] Ibid., B 651–652.
8. [*Ed.*] Ibid., B 654–655.
9. [*Ed.*] Ibid., B 655. See *Ms.*, n. 246.

the question is whether this distinction, this separation between form and matter, is admissible, whether we can put everything on the [one] side [or on the other] in this particular way. On the contrary, we have shown in the Logic (*Encyclopedia*, § 129)[10] that matter without form is an absurdity, a pure abstraction of the understanding—one that we can indeed construct but that should not be given out to be something true. The matter that is set up against God as something unchangeable is merely a product of reflection; to put it another way, this identity of formlessness, this continuous unity of matter, is itself a formal determination; hence we have to recognize that the matter that is here put on one side does itself belong to the other side, the side of form. But in that case, form is identical with itself too. It relates to itself, and in so doing it has just the self-subsistence that is differentiated as matter. The activity of God itself (simple unity with itself, or form) *is* matter. Thus there is this subsistence, this abiding unity with self, with respect to the form—so that it relates to itself, and this is *its* subsistence, the very thing that "matter" is. So there is no form without matter or vice versa; rather they are both the same.

The starting point for the syllogism, Kant continues,[11] is the order and purposiveness that is observed in the world—there are purposive arrangements, and this connection between things, which they do not themselves imply, consequently serves as the starting point; by virtue of this | a tertium quid, a cause, is posited. From the purposive[ness that we observe] we infer the existence of the author who is responsible for the purposiveness of the connections. So we cannot [validly] infer anything more than what, as far as content is concerned, is given in what is present, and concordant with the starting point. Now the purposive arrangements show themselves to be astonishingly great, highly excellent and wise, but a very great, a properly marvelous wisdom is not yet absolute wisdom; we recognize an extraordinary power in it, but that is not yet omnipotence. The leap to omnipotence, says Kant,[12] is one that we are not entitled to take; so we have recourse to the ontological proof,

597

10. [*Ed.*] *Encyclopedia* (1830), § 129; cf. *Science of Logic*, pp. 450–456 (*GW* 11:297–302).
11. [*Ed.*] Kant, *Critique of Pure Reason*, B 655–657; see also above, *Ms.*, n. 247.
12. [*Ed.*] Ibid., B 657–658.

the one that starts from the concept of the most real essence. But mere perception, which provides the starting point in the teleological proof, does not extend to this totality.

We must in any case grant that the starting point has a lesser content than what is arrived at: in the world there is only relative wisdom, not absolute wisdom. This should be examined more closely, however. We have here a syllogism: from one thing something else is inferred; from the way the world is constituted, we infer an activity, something that binds together the mutually extraneous existences, an activity that is their inner [side], their implicit potential, and which does not already reside immediately within them. The form of the inference gives rise to a false semblance, as though God had a foundation, which provides our starting point; God appears as conditioned. The purposive ordering or arrangement is the condition, and the existence of God seems to be expressed as something mediated or conditioned. This is the particular objection that Jacobi[13] has underlined, that the proof aims to attain to the unconditioned through conditions. But, as we have already seen, this is only a false semblance, one that is sublated in the meaning of the conclusion itself. As far as this meaning is directly concerned, it will be granted that it [the proof] is only the process of subjective cognizing. The mediation in the proof does not attach to God himself. For he is, indeed, what is unconditioned, the infinite activity that determines itself according to [its] purposes, and orders the world purposively. The argument does not imply that the conditions that provide our starting point are prior to this infinite activity. On the contrary, the whole process is one of subjective cognizing, and the conclusion it arrives at is this, that it is God who posits these 598 purposive arrangements | and that these are therefore from the beginning what is posited by him, and not the abiding foundation. The ground [Grund] that we start from is itself undermined [geht zu Grunde] by what is defined as the authentic ground. This is the meaning of this syllogism, that what conditions can in its turn only be explained as what is conditioned. The conclusion expresses the fact that it was a defect to posit as foundation something that is itself

13. [Ed.] Jacobi, Briefe, Beilage VII, p. 424–426 (Werke 4/2:153–155).

conditioned. Thus this process is in fact and in its climax not just a subjective process, not something that is mired in thought; instead this defective aspect is itself eliminated by the conclusion. Thus what is objective expresses itself even in the cognition. It is not merely an affirmative passing over, but it involves a negative moment, although that is not posited in the form of the inference. In this way there is a mediation that is the negation of the first immediacy. The process of spirit is indeed a transition, a passing over to the activity that subsists in and for itself and posits purposes; but at the same time it is implied by the process that the determinate being of this purposive order is not to be taken for what is in and for itself (only reason, only the activity of eternal reason, is what is in and for itself). The being of the purposive order observed in the world is not something authentic but only the show or semblance of the eternal activity.

There is, moreover, a distinction that must be made, in the determination in terms of purpose, between form and content. If we consider the form in its purity, we have a purposive being that is finite; and as far as the form is concerned, the finitude consists in the fact that the purpose and the means are distinct—the means being the material in which the purpose is realized. This is its finitude. Thus, for our purposes we need a material; the activity is ours; and the material is something distinct from it. This is the finitude of purposive being, the finitude of form; but the truth of this relationship is not finite in this way. The truth is in the purposive activity that is at the same time means and material in itself, an activity that brings its purposes to fruition all by itself—that is the *infinite* activity of purpose. The purpose accomplishes itself, it realizes itself through its own activity, and thus it closes with itself in the course of its execution. As we have seen, the finitude of purpose lies in the separateness of the means and the material; where this obtains, the purpose is still a *technical* mode of operating. The *truth* of purposive determination [i.e., the genuine case] is where the purpose contains its own means in itself and the material in which it accomplishes itself as well; in this case | the purpose is authentic in regard to form, 599 for objective truth consists precisely in the correspondence of the concept to reality. The purpose is authentic only when the mediating [activity] and the means, equally with the reality, are [all] identical with the purpose. In that case the purpose is present as what has reality in itself; it is not something subjective, one-sided, for which the moments are extraneous. This is the authentic case of purpose, whereas the purposive connection in a finite situation is the inauthentic case.

We must remark at this point that purposive activity, the purposive connection as it has just been defined according to its truth, exists as something higher, even though at the same time it is present; we can no doubt say of it that it is the infinite—since it is a purposive activity that has its means and material in itself—but at the same time it is finite in another respect. This true case of purposive determination that we are seeking actually exists (even if only one-sidedly) in what is living or organic. Life as subject is the soul, and the soul is purpose, i.e., it posits itself, it brings itself to fruition. So the product is the same as the productive [activity]. But what is living is an organism, and organs are means. The living soul implies a body; and only with that body does it constitute a whole, something actual. The organs are the means of life, and these means—the organs—are also that in which life comes to fruition and preserves itself; they are also the material. This is what self-preservation is; what is alive preserves itself, it is the beginning and the end; the product is also what starts [the activity]. What is living is, as such, always in activity; need initiates activity and drives toward its satisfaction, but this is again the beginning of need. The living organism is [there] only to the extent that it is always a product. Here we have the truth of purpose in regard to form: the organs of what is living are means but also end; in their activity they bring forth nothing but themselves. Each organ maintains the other and thereby maintains itself. This activity constitutes *one* purpose, *one* soul [or living principle] that is present everywhere [in the organism]: every part of the body has sensation, the soul is present in it. This is purposive activity in its authenticity.

But the living subject is also something finite through and through; so purposive activity has here a formal truth, but one that is not complete. What is alive produces itself, it contains in itself the material for its own emergence; | every organ secretes the animal

600

710

lymph that is used by others to reproduce themselves. What is alive contains its material in itself, but this is only an abstract process; the finite aspect of it consists in the fact that while the organs are living off themselves, they need material from outside. Everything organic is in an active relation to inorganic nature, which is out there as something independent. In one respect the organism is infinite, since it forms a circuit of pure return into itself, but there is at the same time a tension between it and the external inorganic nature— it has *needs*. The means for meeting these needs come from outside; human beings need air, light, and water; and they also consume animals and other living things, which they thereby make into inorganic nature, into a means. It is this relationship in particular that leads us to assume a higher unity, i.e., the harmony in which the means correspond to the end. This harmony does not lie within the subject itself; yet, as we have seen, the harmony that constitutes organic life *is* within the subject. The whole structure of the organs— the circulatory and nervous system, the intestines, lungs, liver, stomach, etc.—is marvelously concordant. But does not this harmony itself require something else extraneous to the subject? We can leave this question aside; for if one grasps the concept of the organism as we have presented it, this development of the purposive determination itself necessarily follows from the mere fact of the subject's being alive, and if this concept were not grasped, what is living would no longer be the concrete unity that we have defined it to be. And then, in order to understand the unity, one has recourse to conceptions involving external mechanical processes (in the circulation of the blood) or chemical processes (for the decomposition of foodstuffs); but processes of this kind cannot render an exhaustive account of what life itself is, so that a tertium quid must be assumed which has established these processes. But in fact this unity, this harmony of the organism, is precisely the subject; this unity, however, also involves the active relation of the living subject to external nature, which has only a contingent, indifferent being vis-à-vis the subject.

The conditions involved in this relationship are not developed by the living thing itself; yet if it did not find them already present, it could not exist. The consideration of this immediately brings with

601 it the feeling of something higher, | something that has established this harmony; and this at once arouses human emotion and wonder too. Every animal has its own small range of foodstuffs; indeed, many animals are restricted to a single food (this is another respect in which human nature is the most general). The fact that this external, quite peculiar condition holds for every animal arouses humanity to an astonishment that passes over into a high veneration for that third being (in addition to nature and the subject) who has posited this unity. This reverent wonder is the elevation of humanity to the higher being that brings forth the necessary conditions for its own purpose. The subject is actively concerned with its own preservation; this active concern is present—though unconscious—in every living thing. It is what we call instinct in the animal; one animal secures its own maintenance by violence, another produces it by ingenuity. This is the wisdom of God in nature (in which this infinite multiplicity of activities and conditions necessary for all particular forms is encountered). When we consider the particular ways in which living beings are active, we see that they are something contingent. They are not posited by the subject itself, but require an external cause. In the life principle, only the general principle of self-preservation is posited; but living beings differ in an infinitude of particular ways, and this [particular variety] is posited by an *other*.

But the question is: how is inorganic nature adapted to the organic, how does it come to be capable of serving as the means for organic life? Here we encounter a view of the matter that grasps this coincidence in a distinctive fashion. Animals are inorganic vis-à-vis human beings, and plants are inorganic vis-à-vis animals. But the nature that is inorganic in itself, such as the sun, moon, and whatever appears as a means or as matter generally, has *immediate* being in the first place, i.e., it is already there before the organic. Consequently the relationship is so constituted that the inorganic is independent, while the organic by contrast is what is dependent; the inorganic, which is here termed the immediate, is the unconditioned. Inorganic nature appears as self-sufficient: plants, animals, and humans are added to it afterward from outside; the earth could subsist without vegetation, the vegetable kingdom without animals, and the animal kingdom without humans; hence these different aspects appear to be independent of one another. We appeal to experience in support of this too: there are mountains without any vegetation, and without animal | or human life; the moon has no   602 atmosphere, there is on it no meteorological process such as provides the necessary condition for vegetation, so it subsists without any vegetation; and there are other similar examples. Something inorganic of this kind appears to be self-subsistent; humanity is an extraneous addition to it. So we come to the view that nature is inwardly a productive power that produces blindly, from which issues forth vegetation; out of vegetation there springs the animal world; and last of all humanity with its thinking consciousness. In any case we can say that nature produces stages, among which each one is always the condition for the next one.

But if organic life and humanity are contingent accretions of this kind, the question that arises is whether human beings will or will not find what is necessary there ready for them. According to this view this will likewise be a matter of chance, since on this view there is no unity that is valid on its own account. Aristotle already suggests this same opinion:[14] nature produces living beings continually, and the question then is whether they can exist; whether one of them can maintain itself is wholly a matter of chance. Thus nature has already conducted an infinite number of experiments and has produced a whole host of monsters; many myriads of configurations have emerged from it, but they were not able to survive; their disappearance, however, was of no importance. As evidence to prove this assertion, we are referred especially to the remains of monsters that are still to be found here and there. These genera perished, so it is assumed, because the conditions necessary for their existence had ceased to obtain. In this way the concordance of the organic and the inorganic is established as contingent; there is no need to ask for a unity, and the very fact of purposiveness is explained as contingent.

The conceptual determinations involved here, therefore, are the

14. [Ed.] Aristotle, Physics 198b32–36. But Aristotle's argument in this passage seems to be that everything—or nearly everything—produced by nature occurs of necessity and nothing as a matter of chance.

following: speaking generally, what we call inorganic nature as such is represented on its own account as self-subsistent, while the organic is represented as an external accretion, so that it is a matter of chance whether it finds in what stands over against it the necessary conditions for its existence. We must take note here of the form of the conceptual determination; inorganic nature is what is first and immediate. (It also matches the childlike sense of the Mosaic age that heaven and earth, light, etc., were created first and the organic emerged later in time.[15]) The | question is whether this is the authentic way of defining the concept of the inorganic, and whether living beings and humanity are what is dependent. Against this view, philosophy exhibits the truth involved in the determination of the concept; but even without that, human beings are in no doubt that they are actively related to the rest of nature as [its] end or purpose, and that nature has only the role of a means vis-à-vis humanity—for this is the role of the inorganic generally vis-à-vis the organic. In formal terms, the organic is in itself what is purposive—it is both means *and* end, and so it is implicitly something infinite; it is purpose returning into itself, and even on the side of its external dependence it is defined as purpose. Therefore, it is what is genuinely first as against what has been termed the immediate, i.e., as against nature. This immediacy is only a one-sided determination, and must be downgraded to being only something posited. The genuine relationship is this: humanity is not an accidental accretion upon what comes first; on the contrary, what comes first is, for the organic, itself; and the inorganic has only the semblance of being in regard to it. This relationship is logically developed in science itself.[16]

But in this relationship we still have separation, the fact that the organic involves on one side an external relatedness to inorganic nature, instead of inorganic nature being posited implicitly in the

603

---

15. [*Ed.*] See the Priestly account of creation, Gen. 1:1–2:4a. The Yahwistic account, Gen. 2:4b–25, interposes the creation of Adam before that of plants and animals, and thus may be said to have more of a "childlike sense" than the Priestly account.

16. [*Ed.*] See Hegel, *Encyclopedia* (1830), part 2, *The Philosophy of Nature,* sec. 3, §§ 337–376.

organic itself. The living being develops from the seed, and development is the action of the members, the inner organs, etc.; the soul
is the unity that brings forth this action. Here too, however, the truth
of organic and inorganic nature is only the essential connection
between the two, their unity and inseparability. This unity is a third
term, which is neither the one nor the other; and the absolute
category that unites the organic and the inorganic is not to be found
in immediate existence. The subject is what is organic, and the other
term appears as object; but then it changes into the predicate of the
organic and becomes posited as belonging to it. This is the reciprocity
of this connection; the two terms are posited in one, within which
each of them is something dependent and conditioned. In general
terms we can call this third term to which consciousness raises itself
God; but a great deal is still lacking from the concept of God. God
is in this sense the activity of production, which is a primal division
[Urteil] through which the two sides are both produced together;
| in this one concept they fit together, they are for one another.   604

We are therefore quite right in emphasizing that the truth of the
purposive relation is this third term, as we have just defined it. But
this only defines the third term formally, on the basis of what it is
the truth of; it is itself living activity, but this is still not spirit or
rational action. The correspondence of the concept, as the organic,
to reality, as the inorganic, is nothing but the meaning of life itself.
More specifically, this is what the ancients called νοῦς:[17] the world
is a harmonic whole, an organic life that is determined according
to purposes—this was what the ancients understood by νοῦς.
Another way of defining it was as the world soul, or λόγος.[18] All
that is posited by this is vitality [the life principle]; it is not yet posited
that as spirit the world soul is distinct from its life principle. The
soul is the life principle in the organic, and no more; it is not
something sundered from the body, something material, but is the

17. [Ed.] Hegel is probably referring to Anaxagoras, Plato, and Aristotle. For
Anaxagoras, see 1827 lectures, n. 163; for Plato, esp. Timaeus 29d–36d; and for
Aristotle, esp. Metaphysics A 3–4.
18. [Ed.] See Plato, Timaeus 30b–36d, esp. 34a–b, where Plato says that the
universe consists of a body and a central, all-permeating soul.

life force that permeates the body. For this reason Plato called God an immortal ζῷον, i.e., an eternally living principle.[19] He did not get beyond this category of life principle.

When we grasp the life principle in its truth, we find that it is *one* principle, one organic life of the universe, one living system. Everything that is, constitutes the organs of the one subject; the planets that revolve around the sun are only giant members of this one system. Thus the universe is not an aggregate made up of many mutually indifferent accidents, but a system based on the principle of life. This account, however, still does not involve the positing of the category of spirit.

We have [now] considered the formal side of the purposive relation. The other side is that of content. Here the question is: what are the determinations of the [divine] purpose, or what is the content of the purpose that is realized, or how are these [determinate] purposes constituted with respect to what was called *wisdom?* As regards the content, the starting point is again what is found ready in experience; we start from immediate being. It is consideration of the purposes in this empirical light (as they are found in experience) that has been largely responsible for the teleological proof being set on one side, and indeed for its being looked down on with contempt. 605 We talk of the wise orderings of nature. | As determinate forms of organic life, the manifoldly various types of animal life are finite; and the external means to support all this life are present. The living forms are the goal; if we ask then what constitutes the inner substance of the goal, the answer is that it is nothing but the preservation of these insects, these animals, etc. We can, indeed, rejoice about their vitality, but the necessity of their being as they are is a very inadequate, or representational, type of necessity. It is a pious way of looking at it to say that God has arranged it all thus; it exalts the mind to God. But what is represented in regard to God is an absolute, infinite purpose; and these petty purposes contrast sharply with what is found in regard to God. When we survey the higher spheres and consider the human purposes that we can regard as being

19. [*Ed.*] Plato, *Timaeus* 30b–31a. In *Phaedrus* 246b–d, Plato describes the world as an immortal living entity (ζῷον), explaining that by living entity he means a whole in which soul and body are conjoined.

relatively the highest, we find that for the most part they are stultified and perish without issue. In nature millions of seeds perish in their seed phase, without germinating to develop into a living [organism]. For the most part everything alive lives basically upon the death or decay of other life. It is the same story with the higher purposes. If we traverse the field of ethical life to its highest stage, that of the life of the state, and observe whether the purposes are fulfilled or not, we shall, to be sure, find that many of them are fulfilled, but that still more (including the greatest and noblest) are stultified and brought to grief by human passions and vices. We see the earth covered with ruins, with the remains of the splendid buildings and monuments of the noblest peoples—those whose goals we recognize as essential. Great natural objects and human artifacts do indeed endure and defy time, but the glorious life of those peoples has perished irrevocably.

Thus on the one hand we see petty, subordinate, even despicable purposes fulfilled; on the other side, those which we recognize as essential come to grief. When we deplore the ill fortune and the perishing of so much that is excellent, we must in any event ascend to a higher category and a higher purpose. However much they interest us, we must regard all these purposes as finite and subordinate, and ascribe the destruction that has befallen them to their finitude. But the universal purpose we have to consider here is not to be found in experience, and this radically alters the character of the transition [in the argument]. | For we started our argument from 606 what is already present, we drew a conclusion from what we find in experience. But what we encounter in experience has a character of limitedness. The highest purpose is the good, the universal final goal of the world; and reason has to *regard* this as the absolute final goal of the world, the purpose that is directly grounded in the category of reason, the purpose beyond which spirit [itself] cannot go. And the source in which this purpose is recognized is thinking reason. This purpose, moreover, shows itself to be fulfilled in the world; but the good is what is determined in and for itself by reason, and nature stands over against it—physical nature, on the one hand, which goes its own way and has its own laws, but also the natural aspect of humanity, with all the private purposes that run counter

717

to the good. When we appeal to perception, we can see that there is much good in the world, but also an infinite amount of evil; and one would, of course, have to count the sum of the evil and of the good that does not come to its own fruition in order to learn which has the upper hand. However, it is of the very essence of the good to *be;* it pertains to it essentially that it should be realized. But it only *ought to* be actual, for (such is our premise) it does not demonstrate itself in experience. It remains a postulate and does not get beyond what "ought to be." And since the good has not of itself the power to realize itself, a tertium quid is postulated through which the final goal of the world *will be* actualized. This is an absolute postulate; what is morally good is the affair of human beings; but since their power is only finite, and the good in them is limited by their natural aspect, humanity is itself the enemy of the good and is therefore incapable of actualizing it. God's determinate being is represented in this [moral] argument merely as a postulate, an "ought," which *should* have subjective certainty for human beings, because the good is the ultimate category in their reason. But this certainty is only subjective; it remains just a faith, an "ought," and it cannot be demonstrated that it is actually the case.[20] In fact, if the good as such is to be an actually present *moral* good, it has got to be postulated and presupposed that the disharmony will be everlasting, for the morally good can only subsist, it only has its being, in the battle against evil; thus the everlasting activity of the enemy, or of what is opposed to the good, is a postulate too.[21]

20. [*Ed.*] Hegel is referring to the doctrine of postulates, in particular the postulate of the existence of God, in Kant, *Critique of Practical Reason* (New York, 1956), pp. 128–136 (cf. Kant, *Werke* 5:124–132). On the concept of "ought" and infinite progress, see also the following note.

21. [*Ed.*] See Hegel's reference to Kant and Fichte in the context of his interpretation of Persian religion in the 1827 lectures, above, p. 613. He is criticizing Kant and Fichte for tying the good to the moral activity of the individual subject and also for their view that the good is realized only in infinite progress. He has in mind on the one hand Kant's use of infinite progress in justifying the postulate of immortality (see Kant, *Critique of Practical Reason,* esp. pp. 126–127 [Kant, *Werke* 5:122]), and on the other hand Fichte's reference to the infinite self-directed striving of the ego as the condition for the possible existence of an object (see Fichte, *Science of Knowledge* [New York, 1970], p. 231 [Fichte, *Gesamtausgabe* 2:397]). It is clear that Hegel has the latter reference in mind from his *Lectures on the History of Philosophy* 3:498 (*Werke* 15:633).

When we turn to the content, therefore, we find that it is limited; and when we pass on to the | highest purpose, we find ourselves 607 in a different domain. Here the starting point is internal; we do not start from what is present in experience. If, on the contrary, the only starting point is experience, then the good, the final goal, is itself just something subjective, and the contradiction between the other side and the good has necessarily to last forever.

EXCERPTS

B Y D A V I D F R I E D R I C H S T R A U S S
F R O M A T R A N S C R I P T O F

THE LECTURES OF 1831[1]

PART II. DETERMINATE RELIGION

Introduction

~~ ~Religion is genus, and religions species. These species, however, are not to be taken empirically but must be deduced from the universal. We began with the concept of religion, i.e., what it is implicitly or for us; the next thing is to see how this concept of religion realizes itself in and for itself. It is only in the true religion that consciousness first matches the concept of religion; while the concept of religion is also present in lower religions, it is present only implicitly, and what it is in truth is not yet present in consciousness. These are therefore untrue religions, even if they have the concept of religion implicit within them; for in this connection everything

---

1. [Ed.] On the Strauss excerpts of the 1831 lectures, see the Editorial Introduction to Volume 1. The excerpts indicate that the conception and treatment of Determinate Religion differed quite radically in 1831 from that found in the earlier lectures. Evidence for the new treatment is found in the Werke, although the Werke itself follows the basic structure of the 1824 lectures. The original editors included a large number of passages from no-longer-extant transcripts of the 1831 lectures in Part II of the Werke editions; these are juxtaposed to passages of both 1824 and 1827 text (rather than just 1827, as in the case of Parts I and III). In accord with the principles of this edition, they are footnoted in relation to 1824 and 1827 text (depending on the original Werke context), and the more substantial passages (at least 15 lines in length) are cross-referenced to the Strauss excerpts at the appropriate points below (with parallel passages marked by tildes). For the sake of uniformity with the earlier lectures, we have altered the system by which headings are enumerated, but the headings themselves are for the most part those provided by Strauss.

depends on consciousness—it is of no help to Africans, for example, that humanity is implicitly free, because they do not have this in their consciousness.

Religion is the relationship of spirit to spirit; but this relationship, this concept, occurs initially in its immediacy and naturalness; and the action, the advance of spirit consists in sublating this immediacy.‾²‾Our first task, therefore, is to consider natural religion. In it consciousness is still sentient, it is not yet ruptured within itself.

The next step is for consciousness to raise itself above this naturalness—and here we have to note the various ways in which it does so, which then become various ways of characterizing the divine, corresponding to the various proofs of the existence of God.

This progressive definition of religion also has the historical aspect that these determinate forms of religion are the religions of the various peoples. These religions are not our religion, but they are all 612   contained within it as moments of it.‾‾³ |

Division of the Subject

A. Religion in its *immediacy,* or *natural* religion. Here humanity is no more than natural in both its knowing and its willing (i.e., animal willing). Properly speaking, therefore, this is not religion; what is called magic falls under this head.

B. Religion, properly speaking, is first introduced with the inward *rupture of consciousness* into God as absolute power, and the subject as transitory accident.‾⁴

‾C. The *reconciliation* effected within this sphere is the religion of *beauty.* The subject has purified itself from its naturalness into the ethical [subject], so that the divine is no longer related to it negatively but affirmatively. But on the one hand the subject has not yet passed through the infinite antithesis of good and evil, while on the other hand the gods are not infinite spirit but are still burdened with naturalness.‾⁵

2. [*Ed.*] See *Werke* text, 1827 lectures, n. 3.
3. [*Ed.*] See *Werke* text, 1824 lectures, n. 4.
4. [*Ed.*] See *Werke* text, 1827 lectures, n. 5.
5. [*Ed.*] See *Werke* text, 1827 lectures, n. 18.

A. NATURAL RELIGION[6]

1. The name of natural religion has also been given to what human beings are able to cognize of God through the light of their reason—deism. But this is not a religion of naturalness but of abstraction. 2. Another sense in which the term is used is that natural religion was the *primitive, true* religion of the human spirit. Fragments of this religion supposedly occur in all other religions (Friedrich von Schlegel).[7] However, the Hebrew and Greek traditions of a time of innocence and a golden age speak only of simplicity of needs and absence of passions, not of cognitive knowledge of the deity. In any case, these peoples were portraying what is in itself or the essence of humanity as a past or future state. Against the view that it was actually a temporal state, and in fact the first temporal state, stands the concept of spirit, which only *is* what it makes itself, so that it does not emerge | immediately as spirit but to begin with is spirit   613 only implicitly, i.e., as something to build on. ˉNeither willing nor knowing can be immediately perfect. Knowledge as knowing the universal arises only with the negation of perception, just as willing the good arises only with the negation of immediate, purely natural willing. Both are therefore something mediated. *A fortiori,* in order to attain to the cognition of God, human beings must have sloughed off their natural particularity.ˉ[8] As regards the supposedly historical

6. [*Ed.*] The scope of nature religion is drastically reduced in the 1831 lectures, being limited essentially to the religion of magic (par. 3 below). The section begins with a discussion of the meanings of the term "natural religion" (paras. 1 and 2). The first sense of the term alludes to the Enlightenment controversy over "natural" vs. "revealed" religion—the one being "rational" and the other "suprarational"—and is discussed fully for the first time in 1831, although anticipations of the theme are found in 1827 (see 1827 n. 8); the second sense, namely, that natural religion is "primitive" religion, picks up the earlier discussion of the "original condition" of humanity.

7. [*Ed.*] See Friedrich Schlegel, *Ueber die Sprache und Weisheit der Indier* (Heidelberg, 1808), esp. pp. 198, 205 (cf. *Kritische Friedrich-Schlegel-Ausgabe* 8:295–297, 303). Schlegel refers to the traditional Hindu belief that error arose when the human spirit forsook or lost the simplicity of divine knowledge, although "traces of such knowledge continued to shine forth in the midst of superstition and night."

8. [*Ed.*] See *Werke* text, 1827 lectures, n. 24.

evidence adduced for such an original religion, this does not stand up to examination.[9]

3. By natural religion as the most basic form of religion what is commonly understood is a religion in which natural objects—sun, moon, mountains, rivers, etc.—are worshiped. But this is false. ¯Even at the earliest stage of self-consciousness, human beings experience the spiritual (i.e., themselves) as something higher vis-à-vis nature; for religion has a place only in the realm of spirit. In immediate religion, however, the spirit is still immediately natural—it has not yet differentiated itself as universal power from itself as singular, contingent, and accidental. Human beings are entirely dependent on external things and impelled by equally finite purposes. They know spirit as power over these natural beings, but only as the power to avert this or that evil or procure this or that sensuous enjoyment. This power is still not an essential one, and so pertains immediately to human beings themselves.¯[10] The next step, however, is that, after all, human beings are not immediately this power, i.e., not *all* human beings and not without preparation—a mediation, through exaltation, is involved. Human beings in this external state are now known to be the power over this set of natural circumstances. This is the *religion of magic,* as we still find it among many peoples. It does on the one hand include the moment of freedom, though still very imperfectly because directed only to natural ends; on the other hand it is dominated by fear.

This is the only religion found among the Eskimos. They have magicians, known as angekoks, who can summon whales, arouse storms, etc., and also use dancing in their incantations.[11]

Very similar are the shamans of Mongolia and elsewhere. These are | individuals with a disposition to magnetic [hypnotic] sleepwalking, who intoxicate themselves through potions and leaping, etc., fall to the ground, and then in this state make wild utterances.

We already find Herodotus[12] telling us that all Negroes are magicians. And they still are. The village chief is supposed to bring

614

9. [*Ed.*] See 1824 lectures, pp. 242–249; and 1827 lectures, p. 530, incl. n. 42.
10. [*Ed.*] See *Werke* text, 1827 lectures, n. 54.
11. [*Ed.*] See 1824 lectures, nn. 109, 110, 115.
12. [*Ed.*] See 1824 lectures, n. 116.

rain—but for the purpose they tie him up and constrain him. Then they go up onto a hill, fantastically attired, talk, shout and spit against the sky.[13] Here again the main thing is ecstasy. In a state of ecstasy, individuals transcend their habitual limited state and so become power over nature.

But they do so even more when they are *dead*. For this reason Negroes assign to the dead power over the living. Evil and death are the doing of a dead enemy, or sometimes of a still living enemy, for they do not regard death as an act of nature but always solely as the doing of human hands.[14] The dead are constrained by spells; if they have not been buried for long, they are exhumed, their heads cut off, etc. Recourse is also had to sorcerers; they fly into a rage and then declare how the dead person is to be propitiated. Power lies especially in the blood and the bones, so the bones are preserved, painted with blood, etc. They also hang themselves about with bones as power over wild beasts.[15] At this stage, religious belief is magic.

The Negroes also make themselves gods, *fetishes*. They make anything, a tree, a beast, into their fetish, their demon. If anything happens to them, the fetish is destroyed.

This lowest form of religion is widespread, especially in Africa, the midpoint for the debasement of consciousness, a debasement that shows itself also in social life in the form of cannibalism and slavery. Dignity does not accrue to human beings as natural, immediate will but only inasmuch as they have knowledge at least in principle of something that exists substantively in and for itself, and go on from that to surrender the natural subject to it. | 615

B. ¯THE INTERNAL RUPTURE OF RELIGIOUS CONSCIOUSNESS

Introduction
Consciousness ruptures internally, splitting into two and setting up a substantive power over against itself as the natural and contingent; as singular it relates itself to this power merely as an accidental that

13. [*Ed.*] See 1824 lectures, n. 118.
14. [*Ed.*] See 1824 lectures, nn. 119, 123, 161, 162, 163.
15. [*Ed.*] See 1824 lectures, n. 160.

is of no account. This power is the subsistence of everything but at the same time its passing away; this is the form [of religion] that is called pantheism. This power is admittedly something thought, but it is not yet known as inwardly spiritual. There are different aspects to be considered in this regard.‾16

‾(1) The *elevation* of consciousness. This is not merely our thought, but it pertains to the consciousness of this form of religion itself, for consciousness here elevates itself to thinking, but without having any thought of what it is doing. Thoughtful consideration of this thinking elevation is what we add to the process.‾17

(2) However, we also have to consider the relationship of this power to the contingent. Since the contingent is nothing on its own account, the substance is present immediately, and this is the defining characteristic of *pantheism.*

(3) Since substance is not yet determined as spirit, it seeks to endow itself with this configuration [of spirit], but in such a way that this only accrues externally and is not known as determination of the essence. Here we encounter diverse flights of phantasy.

(4) The last point of determinacy is the *one,* or this single entity; determination as singular individuality pertains to the character of subjectivity. But this is here known externally in such a way that a sensibly present human being is known as the universal power.

(5) What human beings have to do in order to remain united with their essence is the *cultus.*

We shall consider the first two of these points—which are of a general nature—on their own account, while the others will be considered under the concrete forms of religion.

1. *The elevation of consciousness from the finite to the infinite.* This is the quintessential movement of spirit; it is what is expressed in the *cosmological proof.* [It is] not as though, | in thus raising themselves to the level of God, people made this formal inference, nor as though their conviction rested on this inference. Consciousness of the single steps of this inference pertains only to the cultured consciousness. Of course this elevation takes place in thinking, but it cannot be said often enough that thinking is one thing and the

616

16. [*Ed.*] See *Werke* text, 1827 lectures, n. 49.
17. [*Ed.*] See *Werke* text, 1824 lectures, n. 63.

consciousness of it another. Human beings are conscious of themselves and the world; but since they experience both themselves and the world as merely contingent, they are not satisfied by either and elevate themselves into something that has being in and for itself, something necessary, which is the power over this contingency. This can occur in the simplest form of feeling, as when one looks up to the heavens.

The purely formal description of this process is the cosmological proof as an inference: Everything contingent presupposes something necessary; but this world is something contingent, a mere aggregate; therefore it presupposes something necessary. This proof goes from the contingent to the necessary; but instead we can also posit the finite and infinite, or the one and many. The ordinary formulation of this inference is as follows: because there is the contingent, there must also be the necessary. But the truth is that the contingent, the many, etc., do not truly exist, but only the One. This can also be grasped abstractly as follows: The truth in all determinate being [*Dasein*] is being [*Sein*]. The singular finite being *is* the infinite inasmuch as it is essentially related to its negative (human beings to air, water, etc.) and so raises itself to the infinite. ¯In the common consciousness of these proofs the negative moment is lacking; the finite, the starting point is left standing, as it is, so that the infinite appears as something mediated, conditioned. But inasmuch as the many is posited rather as something that does not have being, the transition and mediation are also reduced to the level of semblance.

The other aspect is

2. *The relationship of substance to accidents.* The substance turns toward the accidents, which have been forgotten in the process of elevation. Spirit does not confine itself to the result of the process but | grasps it in its entirety. What is in and for itself necessary *is* 617 without qualification, but it also implies accidents, which are determined as a kind of being that is nothing, as a nullity. These accidents are constantly alternating and transmuting between being and nothing, etc.; birth is death and death birth. All that subsists is this change, and the latter thought of as unity is the substantive. This is the Oriental or Spinozist substance.¯18

18. [*Ed.*] See *Werke* text, 1824 lectures, n. 90.

What is now lacking is that we have only coming to be and passing away, not the self-activity of substance. Substance is not yet subject, it is still inwardly without determination. Shapes come and go, but without purpose. Everything enters into substance, but nothing comes back out of it,[19] i.e., nothing determinate, only a revel of confused images (as in the case of the Hindus). This system is usually called *pantheism*. Substance relates itself passively and negatively to things: on the one hand it is only through things that it subsists; on the other, substance is the purification of being from this limitation, i.e., the annihilation of the finite. To interpret pantheism as treating every [finite] thing as God is just for this reason absurd. Pantheism is to be found in the loftiest form among Oriental poets, especially the Persian Muslim poets, e.g., Jalal-ud-din Rumi [translated] by Rückert.[20]

ˉThe essential relationship of substance to the accidental is to be its power. The abstract thought of substance can perhaps confine itself to this one aspect, but religion, as the consummate idea, must also, even in its subordinate stages, include the moment of spirit, which is still absent from mere substance. Now as substance itself is not spirit, spirit is external to substance, in the form of finite spirit, a human being, as the executor of this power that pertains to substance.ˉ[21] But this is only one aspect of the matter, that humanity in this or that individual exercises authority; the other aspect is that human beings are of no account vis-à-vis substance; so it is only through subjection and renunciation that they achieve identity with this power. Thus substance for its part is actual as finite spirit, but over against it stand other [beings] that are not independent. |

618

Such [is] the general character of this form of religion. It has come into existence in determinate fashion in three forms of Oriental religions:

(1) *Chinese* religion. Here the substance is known, but as inwardly determined foundation, as *measure*.

---

19. [*Ed.*] Hegel's analysis at this point touches on his critique of Spinoza, as elaborated especially in his lectures on the history of philosophy.
20. [*Ed.*] See *Ms.*, n. 22.
21. [*Ed.*] See *Werke* text, 1824 lectures, n. 82.

(2) *Hindu* religion. Substance as abstract unity, akin to spirit; human beings raise themselves to the level of this *abstract* unity.

(3) *Lamaism* and *Buddhism* find in a particular individual substance made concrete in this way, a level to which other human beings then also raise themselves, this being *annihilation*.

1. ¯Chinese Religion: The Religion of Measure[22]

Fundamentally the Chinese state religion is likewise a pantheism of this kind.¯[23] ¯Substance is known as measure, and these hard-and-fast determinations are called reason. These laws and measures are initially figurations, then, grasped more abstractly, categories, e.g., – yes, – – no.[24] These categories have their concrete significance in regard to nature, in regions of the world or elements, and also in regard to human beings, in the five basic laws—relationship to one's parents, one's ancestors, the emperor, brothers and sisters, spouses,

22. [*Ed.*] We have added the subhead since it indicates the unique way that Hegel defined Chinese religion in 1831. It is noteworthy, of course, that ancient Chinese religion is no longer treated under the category of "nature religion" but is the first of the religions of rupture (*Entzweiung*). In the *Science of Logic*, pp. 327 ff. (cf. *GW* 11:189 ff.), "measure" (*Mass, Maass*) is the third category of the doctrine of being, in which the first two are united, namely quality and quantity (or determinateness and magnitude). It is *qualitatively* determined *quantity*. Hegel regards it as replacing the Kantian categories of relation and modality, and the Spinozistic category of mode, which is the third after substance and accidents, or substance returned to itself. In the 2d ed. of "The Doctrine of Being" (1832), on which the English translation is based, and which Hegel was preparing for publication while lecturing on philosophy of religion during the summer of 1831, he refers to "Indian pantheism" as an instance of measure (including both Hinduism and Buddhism) (pp. 328–329). Measure in its more developed, reflected form, as with the Greeks, is necessity or fate. Thus to conceive God as "measure" is an advance beyond an undialectical view of substance, and an approximation to an understanding of God as "essence," since essence is already implicit in measure. It would appear, then, that Hinduism and Buddhism are also religions of measure, but at a higher stage, the stage at which substance takes the accidents back into its abstractly determined unity.

23. [*Ed.*] See *Werke* text, 1827 lectures, n. 100.

24. [*Ed.*] A reference to the eight Gua, which are discussed first and foremost in the Yi-jing. One line signifies yang, two lines yin. Hegel also draws on the Yi-jing in his *Lectures on the Philosophy of World History*, Sibree ed., p. 117; Lasson ed., p. 280. However, he does not seem to have had any direct knowledge of the Yi-jing himself, and is probably relying on the account in the edition of the Shu-jing that was available to him, namely, *Le Chou-king*, trans. Gaubil, ed. de Guignes (Paris, 1770). p. 353, where the two lines are explained. See also 1827 lectures, annotation to n. 106.

and all one's fellow human beings.[25] Many devote their entire lives to the study of this reason, but the main point is that these laws are to be applied to everyday life in the empire, for otherwise misfortune befalls the state as a punishment. The maintenance of these measures is the responsibility of the emperor, the son of heaven, of Tian, i.e., of the visible heaven with its proportions. The emperor alone worships and sacrifices to the law, to heaven; the others worship the emperor. If public misfortune occurs in the form of wars, flooding, or cholera, the emperor does penance for not holding the reins of the kingdom as tight as he should have done, and he also calls on his officials to examine themselves.

In Chinese religion everything is reduced to a moral life, and it can therefore be termed a moral atheism.[26] These duties and categories of measure are, though | of more ancient origin, contained especially in the work of Confucius.[27]

These hard-and-fast categories, however, are an aggregate of many many particular determinations, which are also known as activities and powers, but as subject to the emperor. They are pictured more particularly as deceased ancestors, but also as fantastic images or genii.‾[28] A new dynasty installs a new circle of genii; on this occasion the graves of the ancestors who had previously been powers are destroyed and the new pattern of organization [is] read out to the genii by a general, those who have been deposed being roundly abused. This is what happened with the inauguration of the Zhou dynasty in 1142 B.C.[29] The particular vocations of the individual are also specified by particular powers, especially the Shen or genii. This

619

25. [Ed.] See *Mémoires concernant les Chinois,* 16 vols. (Paris, 1776–1814), 5:28. In his lectures on the philosophy of world history, Hegel refers in this regard to the Shu-jing (see *Le Chou-King,* pp. 12, 33, 154).

26. [Ed.] Contrary to the wording of the text, Hegel in all probability applied this epithet not to Chinese religion as a whole but to Confucianism. See *Le Chou-King,* p. iii.

27. [Ed.] Hegel's knowledge of the works of Confucius is derived partly from the earlier, influential work, *Confucius Sinarum philosophus* (Paris, 1687), and partly from the translation of the Lun-yu by J. Marshman, *The Works of Confucius* (Serampore, 1809), vol. 1. He could also have found a detailed if somewhat embellished account of Confucius's life in *Mémoires concernant les Chinois,* vol. 12.

28. [Ed.] See *Werke* text, 1827 lectures, n. 106.

29. [Ed.] See 1824 lectures, n. 172. The actual date was 1122 B.C.

opens the door to all manner of superstition; people find their freedom in imputing whatever runs counter to them not to themselves but to this or that genie. The Chinese also make fetishes for themselves and have soothsayers; prophecy takes the form of throwing little rods, which correspond to these universal lines.

2. Hindu Religion: The Religion of Abstract Unity[30]

¨¨Whereas in Chinese religion the [divine] power is known as an aggregate of basic characteristics—in other words, not as reason or as [first] principle, [i.e.,] as spirit—in Hindu religion this multiplicity is resumed into unity, and this concentration is the beginning of spirituality, is thinking, which is the One determining itself [*das Eine sich selbst Bestimmende*]. The starting point of Hindu pantheism is that substance is a kind of thinking, and exists in our thinking. But this still does not make spirit an absolute of this kind. Thinking remains locked in self-containment; it may be the source of all power, but it gets no further than this representational image. Second, thinking is in and for itself the elaboration of the difference to yield the system of appearance. Since, however, the principle of Hinduism has not yet matured to this level, this development [i.e., the elaboration of the difference] falls outside it and is at the mercy of a wild infinity. Third, the spirituality of the idea is completed as a result of the | differences being finally taken back into unity. This return does occur in Hinduism, but in a way that is devoid of spirit. All moments of spirituality are present, but they do not constitute spirit. 620

30. [*Ed.*] In 1831 Hegel reverses the order in which he treats Buddhism and Hinduism, taking up Hinduism as the older of the two religions and the source of Buddhism, which of course it is. In his time there was still scholarly uncertainty as to which of the two was older. Hegel's reversal may not reflect more precise historical information but rather a clearer articulation of his basic religio-geographical-historical schema, namely, the advance of *Geist* from China to India (and the India-born religions), then to the Near East (Persian, Jewish, "Phoenician," Egyptian religion), and finally to Greece and the West. In any case, since Hinduism now precedes Buddhism, it assumes the role of providing the conceptual advance to unitary substance that Buddhism held earlier, and consequently Buddhism receives only brief attention. Moreover, the defining characteristic of Hinduism is now "abstract unity" rather than "phantasy" (phantasy is rather the mythological form of the unity). Finally, in line with his 1831 highlighting of the Trinity and of triadic logical structures, it is not surprising that Hegel attends at greater length than before to the Hindu Trimurti.

We have now to consider in the first place this abstract One, ˉthen the wildness of phantasy given free rein,ˉ³¹ and finally the taking back [of everything] into the One.ˉˉ³² The cultus is bound up with this third stage.

1. ˉHere the principle is a determinate and self-determining universal, but it does not advance beyond this formal level of knowing.

This initial principle is called Brahman, about which we are told that we think this universal and that our thinking itself *is* this universal. Brahman enters into existence as this thinking. This principle, and our abstract thinking, is power.ˉ³³ ˉThis pure power has created the world; in Hindu presentations it is portrayed in very different ways, but always with the basic feature that the pure self-relating activity of thinking is self-production. This pure activity is also termed the "word." According to one presentation, Brahman created water and placed in it a seed from which was formed an egg; in the egg Brahmā was born; he divided it by the power of his thought, and by his word he brought into being the other forces.³⁴ According to another, there was initially only the One, who through the power of thought first created desire, etc.³⁵

This thinking, however, is known as thinking in self-conscious beings, in *human* beings; in other words, Brahman exists in the caste of Brāhmans, and their reading of the Vedas is God himself.ˉ³⁶ Since self-consciousness in its abstraction is Brahman itself, the cultus of Brahman coincides with Brahman itself, and it has no separate cultus. In cultus, human beings are filled with the content of the divine essence but are still capable of distinguishing it clearly from themselves. With Brahman this distinction, and with it cultus, disappears. The task of Brāhmans is to bring about this abstract self-consciousness. When a Hindu prays to the honor of some deity, with eyes closed, arms folded and mind devoid of thoughts, this *is*

31. [*Ed.*] See *Werke* text, 1824 lectures, n. 231.
32. [*Ed.*] See *Werke* text, 1827 lectures, n. 193.
33. [*Ed.*] See *Werke* texts, 1824 lectures, n. 262, and 1827 lectures, n. 194.
34. [*Ed.*] See 1827 lectures, annotation a to n. 217.
35. [*Ed.*] See 1824 lectures, n. 251.
36. [*Ed.*] See *Werke* text, 1827 lectures, n. 217. See also annotation f to this note.

Brahman.[37] ⌐The acme of cultus consists not in affirmative but in purely negative redemption from finitude, the dulling and annihilation of consciousness; instead of liberation it is only the shunning of particularity. |

621

The Brāhmans are born from Brahmā's mouth; they are this absolute power immediately. The other castes can rise to this only through the mediation of endless penances.⌐[38] ⌐But "penances" here is not to be taken in the Christian sense; they are here the path to perfection without the presupposition of sin. Hindu philosophy is equally abstract; its purpose is not concrete insight into God, the world, etc., as it is with us, but rather withdrawal from all concrete content.⌐[39]

The abstract self-consciousness, however, is known here as the absolute power. Whoever achieves it through such austerities is called a Yogi. A Yogi or Brāhman can control the weather, unmake kings, fly, etc.[40] But this self-consciousness is known generally as the power of *nature;* a Brāhman inherits the world—but unconsciously,[41] just as this absolute thinking is always unconscious thinking.

The Hindus also have animal worship; the cow in particular is greatly venerated. In the dulling of consciousness that is the divine, humanity is not far removed from the beast. Since any given human activity ranks as a nullity, there is also no freedom in India; for freedom implies that particular human purposes are regarded as essential.

2. Since unity is known only as abstract, multiplicity lies outside it. This is where mythology takes root. Just as unity is what is devoid of figure, multiplicity is a multiplicity of figures. The mythology has a twofold aspect: (1) this manifold content, which is not known as the inward unfolding of the first [the unity] but falls outside it. ⌐But (2) these manifold forms are not regarded prosaically according to their determinate categories, as things, but are invested through

37. [*Ed.*] See 1824 lectures, p. 337, including n. 263.
38. [*Ed.*] See *Werke* text, 1827 lectures, n. 244. See also the editorial annotations to this note.
39. [*Ed.*] See *Werke* text, 1824 lectures, n. 280.
40. [*Ed.*] See 1824 lectures, nn. 277, 289.
41. [*Ed.*] See 1827 lectures, annotation f to n. 217.

phantasy with spirituality, with soul.¯⁴² As the content is wholly limited, e.g., the Himalayas or Ganges, the subjective element attaching to it is empty form. ¯In the religion of beauty the spiritual form of the subject is always matched by a spiritual content, but in Hinduism by a natural. This mismatch between content and form lies at the root of what is the ugliness of the mythological figures—a deity with elephant's head, etc.¯⁴³ ⁴⁴ |

622

The most important element in Hindu mythology is the Trimurti: Brahmā, Vishnu, and Shiva.⁴⁵ Vishnu is here the main determining factor; he is active in this world below through his incarnations. His incarnations are described—how he comes as loving shepherd, etc., depicted with all the grace of Hindu arabesque. Shiva, or Mahadeva (*magnus deus*), [is the third moment]. This third moment, if it wanted to be spirit, and to have the dignity of the Christian Trinity, would have to be the return of the whole within itself. The first, abstract, only implicitly subsisting being of Brahman would thus have to become a concrete, posited unity. But instead, this third moment is only the spiritless determination of coming to be and passing away. Shiva is represented more particularly in the symbol of procreation, as male and female. The Trimurti is also portrayed with three heads.⁴⁶ Thus the way it is figured echoes the spiritual, but in spiritless fashion; in this being-outside-self there is only a wild spinning around, devoid of spirit. Krishna and Shiva are produced only later, as the fruits of phantasy impelled by reason and instinct; they are not to be found in the oldest books of the Vedas.⁴⁷ Some Hindus worship Krishna, others Shiva, and this often leads to religious wars.⁴⁸ In themselves both are Brahmā.

42. [*Ed.*] See *Werke* text, 1824 lectures, n. 229.
43. [*Ed.*] See *Werke* text, 1824 lectures, nn. 232, 233.
44. [*Ed.*] Hegel is referring to the Hindu god Ganesha, a companion of Shiva, with whose image he was probably familiar from G. F. Creuzer, *Symbolik und Mythologie der alten Völker, besonders der Griechen,* 2d ed., 4 vols. (Leipzig and Darmstadt, 1819–1821), plates xxvii, xxix. See also William Jones, "On the Gods of Greece, Italy, and India," *Asiatic Researches* 1:226 (the elephant head is a "symbol of sagacious discernment"), including the figure following this page; also 1:586.
45. [*Ed.*] See 1824 lectures, n. 238.
46. [*Ed.*] See 1827 lectures, annotation to n. 222.
47. [*Ed.*] See 1824 lectures, n. 258.
48. [*Ed.*] See 1824 lectures, n. 259.

ˉIn addition to these general foundations, everything possible is personified in the same superficial manner—the Ganges, the Himalayas, love, the cunning of a thief, etc. At the summit of the subordinate world of deities stands Indra, the god of the heavens. These gods are transitory and tremble before Vishvamitra.ˉ49

The cultus consists in particular usages and texts whose purpose is the blotting out [of consciousness]. For instance, there are various ways of reading the Vedas—backwards, by repeating every second word, etc.50 The acme is this annihilation—even in a bodily sense, by drowning in the Ganges, being crushed beneath the wheels of Shiva's chariot,51 also intoxication through sensual overindulgence. | 623

3. ˉBuddhism and Lamaism: the Religion of Annihilation

These religions are very much akin to Hinduism.ˉ52

Lamaism is also pantheism, but the universal presence of substance already gives way to the concrete presence of the individual, who is worshiped as absolute power. This individual eats and dies like any other, yet is at the same time the power of substance, which is something unconscious. There are three Lamas, chief among whom is the Dalai Lama in Lhasa under Chinese rule; the second was in Tashilūmpo when he was visited by the Englishmen, a child three years old; the third was in northern Tartary.53 If a Lama dies, a new one must be sought, for which purpose there are distinguishing marks in the folds of the face.54

49. [Ed.] For the parallel Werke text, see 1827 lectures, n. 234; for a Werke addition on the Ramayana account of Vishvamitra, see 1827 lectures, n. 244, including the editorial annotations.

50. [Ed.] See H. T. Colebrooke, "On the Vēdas, or Sacred Writings of the Hindus," Asiatic Researches 8:390. Colebrooke actually says, "repeating the words alternately, backwards and forwards," which is somewhat different; he adds that copies of the Rig-Veda and Yagush are especially prepared for these modes of recital.

51. [Ed.] For the source of Hegel's reference to the practice of drowning oneself in the Ganges or allowing oneself to be crushed beneath the wheels of one of the chariots used to carry images of certain gods (the source does not actually speak of Shiva) during solemn festivals, see James Mill, The History of British India, 3 vols. (London, 1817), 1:274–275. The term Rädernlassen, which we have translated "being crushed beneath the wheels," is uncertain in S's text but is confirmed by the source.

52. [Ed.] See Werke text, 1827 lectures, n. 139.

53. [Ed.] See 1827 lectures, n. 183.

54. [Ed.] The source of this assertion has not been identified. For other methods of regulating the succession see 1827 lectures, n. 190.

Unlike Hinduism and Lamaism, Buddhism does not have a living being but a dead teacher, Buddha, as its object, though Buddha is also worshiped by the Hindus as an incarnation of Vishnu. His physical presence, however, is preserved by religion. This religion is very widespread, in Ceylon, China, among the Burmese, etc. In this religion, as in Hinduism, the acme is to be united with Buddha, and this *annihilation* is termed nirvana.⁵⁵ Those who do not attain this nirvana during this life have to undergo the transmigration of souls.⁵⁶

C. THE RELIGION OF FREEDOM⁵⁷

ˉThe essence of this stage is that substance determines itself inwardly.ˉ⁵⁸ ˉThis determinateness, because [it is] *self*-determina-

55. [*Ed.*] See *Werke* addition, 1827 lectures, n. 151.

56. [*Ed.*] On Buddha as an incarnation of Vishnu see 1824 lectures, n. 214; on nirvana, 1824 lectures, p. 314 and n. 216, and 1827 lectures, pp. 565–568.

57. [*Ed.*] The third section of the 1831 lectures begins with the "transitional" religions, Persian and Egyptian, which in the earlier lectures were treated at the end of the first section. Judaism (earlier the first of the religions of spiritual individuality) is now included among these transitional religions, to which a brief section on the religion of anguish is also added. This arrangement has the advantage of linking together all of the Near Eastern religions in a single section and showing certain logical connections and progressions between them. It also shows the advance of spirit from China to India to the Near East to Greece, Rome, and the West. It has the disadvantage of seeming to reduce Judaism to the same level of significance as the other religions treated in this section. In fact, however, Hegel's discussion shows that he attributes far greater significance to Judaism than to the others. It is certainly misleading to categorize Judaism under the term "dualism," as Hegel does in the outline at the beginning of the section. If Judaism is dualistic, it is so in a quite different sense than Persian religion is: it is the duality or difference between Creator and creation, and the fact that the anguish of finitude does not seem to be taken into the divine substance itself, as it is in the religion of anguish, with its symbolic representation of the death of God. When Hegel actually discusses Judaism, it is as the "religion of the good," i.e., of the God who is good and wise as well as omnipotent. This shift indicates that the schema is still fluid in Hegel's mind. In fact, the "division of the subject" at the beginning of the 1831 lectures gives yet another picture, locating the transitional religions at the end of the second moment rather than at the beginning of the third (see Vol. 1:463). Finally, the new arrangement has the disadvantage of downplaying the difference between Greek religion and Roman. Can the latter be described as a religion of "freedom" and "reconciliation"? Again the actual treatment shows that it cannot.

58. [*Ed.*] See *Werke* text, 1827 lectures, n. 256.

tion, is not a finite determinateness but rather one that is appropriate to universality; therefore substance is defined right away as good. But good exists on its own account, self-containedly, and hence it enters into conflict with evil, which gives rise to dualism. But this is initially one of the

1. Transitional forms.
   a. Dualism [Persian and Jewish religion]. The next step then is | 624
   b. That this conflict is taken into substance itself as a constituent moment, in the form of anguish ["Phoenician religion"]—the god dies.
   c. This is then a self-dissolving conflict, a struggle to emerge from this conflict and come to oneself and to freedom [Egyptian religion].⁻⁵⁹ This ultimately gives rise to
2. Greek religion.
[3. Roman religion.]

1. Transitional Forms

a. The Religion of the Good
The religion of the good has been manifest in two forms, (1) as the *Persian* religion, where, however, personality was only superficial, confined to a natural configuration, and (2) as the *Jewish* religion, where the good exists on its own account, as creating nature.

(1) Persian Religion
ˉBrahman was unity devoid of determination and therefore devoid of consciousness. The next step is for the One to determine itself. But the highest level of the self-activity and [self-]determination of spirit is, on the side of knowledge, truth, and, on the side of volition, the good; and the true and the good are the same. Power is also determining, but only in general; [it is] something contingent because the determining [is] devoid of purpose. This is the point where the essential determination—definition in terms of the absolute purpose—enters into play, and this is the good. At the very outset, however, this good is only abstract, and consequently it is there in

59. [*Ed.*] See *Werke* text, 1827 lectures, n. 266.

737

the purely immediate form of the physical [being] that has not yet been particularized, the form of *light*.

Because this good and self-determining [power] is initially abstract, however, there is in addition something other than it; pure light is not manifest without darkness, nor abstract good without evil.⁻⁶⁰ This is *dualism*. ⁻Light is here wholly identical with good—it is not merely a symbol. Persians do not worship fire because it burns, | but only what gives light within it. Personified in a superficial manner, light is called Ormazd. Ormazd himself, like his manifestation, the light, is a particular [being], a genie; he is himself one of the "amshaspands," the spirits of the stars. The kingdom of light was mirrored in the Persian state, where the king stood at the apex and seven notables beside him. Ormazd is the life-giving element; everything that has life and shares it belongs to his kingdom.⁻⁶¹ The special role of the cultus is to glorify Ormazd in his creation, by promoting life, agriculture, etc. Alongside this kingdom of light, however, there is pictured the kingdom of darkness, of Ahriman, the two being locked in mutual struggle, and this struggle is also represented as that between Iran and Turan.⁶²

625 (in margin)

(2) Jewish Religion

Whereas the good as light only had personality attached to it as something superficial, in the Hebrew religion the good is *for itself* in such a way as to belong to the essence of the substance; the light of Persian religion on the other hand could as readily give free rein to the characteristic of personality. At the same time this absolute, free subjectivity now exists as an exclusive singularity—God essentially as the One. What we now have to consider is (a) this absolute

60. [*Ed.*] See *Werke* text, 1827 lectures, n. 281.
61. [*Ed.*] See *Werke* text, 1827 lectures, n. 284, including the editorial annotations.
62. [*Ed.*] On the struggle between Iran and Turan, see *Zend-Avesta*, ed. Kleuker, 2:200, 202, 251 et passim (cf. *Zend-Avesta* [SBE] 2:67, 71, 189). The mythical story of this struggle was, however, probably known to Hegel less from these isolated references than from J. Görres's translation of the *Book of Kings*, which centers on this struggle (*Das Heldenbuch von Iran aus dem Schah Nameh des Firdussi*, 2 vols. [Berlin, 1820]). See also above, *Ms.*, n. 18 (where, however, Hegel appears to regard this book as pantheistic rather than dualistic).

subject, then (b) what is posited separately from the One, namely, the world, and (c) the relationship of humanity to the One.

(a) In reference to God, every natural mode' of existence disappears, because he is posited to subsist merely for thought; hence this is where the religion of spirit begins. It is precisely this subjectivity that constitutes the progress as compared with Persian religion: the Persian power of light is an impersonal unity, that which is One, while the Jewish God is personal, he who is One. As subject, God is what is mediated with itself, and hence he is no longer the unmediated, the natural; no image may be made of him, he cannot be cognized in immediate, sensuous fashion, but only through the medium of thought.

(b) Here for the first time God is truly known as *creator* and lord of the world. For it is only as what mediates itself with itself that the [divine] subject is what effects primal division—and this is the creation of the world. | ˉCreating is not an immediate mode of being; instead the world is made from nothing, i.e., from *its* nothing, and this negative is itself the affirmative once more, the plenitude of power of the good.ˉ[63] In the earlier religions the [first] category is always theogony, and the basic characteristic is the mistaken category of issuing forth, of emanation; it is only with subjectivity that this disappears and the category of creation comes in, as that of primal division [*Urteil*]. This primal division is the eternal goodness of God, for as falling outside the One, what has been differentiated has, properly speaking, no right to exist. This negative character is also manifest in it; it passes away and so characterizes itself as appearance.

[64]ˉ(c) As regards the relationship of this creation to the One, the good, absolute subjectivity's bringing forth is not a wild release; on

626

---

63. [*Ed.*] See *Werke* text, 1827 lectures, n. 457.

64. [*Ed.*] Beginning here, and continuing for the next four paragraphs, Strauss's excerpts show that in 1831 Hegel introduced into his treatment of Judaism a discussion of the story of the fall, which in the earlier lectures had been taken up in relation to Christianity because the story of Adam and the fall had been appropriated by the Christian religion but neglected by the Jewish. Now, however, the problematic under which Hegel is treating Judaism is that of good and evil: it must be shown how and why evil enters into the unity of finite spirit but not of God as absolute spirit. Just this marks the profound difference between Jewish and Persian religion; the antithesis

the contrary, it is at home in what it brings forth, the creation is a likeness of the creator. In the process the world, as external, is demoted to the level of what we call prosaic things; it is stripped of divinity, it becomes no more than the manifestation of God. To be this mirror of divinity is the purpose of the world. Thus this religion is the religion of sublimity.

[But] human being, as active, mirrors God in quite a different way than does nature. The antithesis of good and evil also occurs in Persian religion; for it, however, evil is not found within the unity of spirit itself but outside God in another being. In the Jewish religion evil, as cleavage, enters into the unity of spirit itself—though, to be sure, not of spirit as *absolute* spirit, for even in its absolute and primal division, in the world, absolute spirit is at home; the world is good. But spirit as *finite* is the locus of good and evil and the struggle between them.

Here for the first time the question how evil has come into the world acquires a meaning. In Persian religion, good and evil *existed;* but here, where God is defined as subjectivity and everything is posited by him, evil contradicts this whole foundation. We are told about this in the form of a parable or myth, Genesis, chap. 3, where unsuitable features have also entered in because of the historical form. There is a profoundly speculative feature in this story. Adam is humanity in general, and what happens to him concerns human nature as such. It is forbidden to eat of the tree of knowledge of good

627 | and evil, though such knowledge constitutes the essence of spirit, the likeness of God. But knowledge has this two-sided aspect, the freedom to determine itself to caprice [*Willkür*] or to the good. Humanity's aim is to transcend this cleavage, to enter again into harmony with itself and with God, to regain the state of innocence; this is represented here as meaning that the cleavage should never

---

of good and evil is grounded neither in a cosmic dualism nor in absolute spirit but rather in the free fall of finite spirit. This is the insight conveyed by the Adamic myth, which accordingly is internal to the logic of Jewish religion (as well as Christian). Hegel's recognition of this reflects a deeper appreciation for Judaism, even if the structural framework in which he takes up Jewish religion in 1831 is in other respects unsatisfactory. A lengthy variant text from the *Werke* is found in the 1824 lectures, n. 541 (parallel in the excerpts follows).

have occurred. God's judgment [*Urteil*] is on the one hand that human beings have actually become like God, and on the other hand that they are, by way of punishment, driven out of Paradise, with death and toil as their lot in consequence. Here we can see what this consciousness lacks, for the fact that human beings by their own activity fashion themselves as a likeness[65] [of God] and so show their superiority over nature is one of their advantages; and death is fearful, a punishment only to those who have still no consciousness of spirit in its essentiality. The true tenor of this story accordingly consists in positing the necessity of humanity's transcending the natural state but positing also the task of spirit's return into absolute unity with itself.

This story of the fall lay fallow in Jewish religion and attained its true meaning only in the Christian religion. The struggle between good and evil does indeed appear as an essential characteristic of Judaism, but in such a way that evil is represented as occurring in a purely contingent fashion, in single individuals, over against whom stand the just, in whom such a struggle is wholly absent or at least does not exist as an essential moment. Justice is said to consist in worshiping God and fulfilling his commandments; the struggle and pain of evil is portrayed in an especially striking manner in the Psalms, but to a greater extent only as pertaining to the individual.¯

In Hebraic religion, God is known essentially as lord and doubtless also as love and justice; but in the Book of Job,[66] for example, the claim made on God's justice is resignedly subordinated to his power. ¯God is the Lord of the people of Israel, and *only* of them. The other Oriental religions are such that they cleave to nationality because with them God | is still known in a categorially particular way. With   628
the Hebrews, however, God is known in his full universality. Objectively speaking, therefore, God is universal lord, but viewed subjectively the Jewish people alone is his chosen property, because it alone recognizes and worships him. But the extension of this subjective relationship, meaning that the Gentiles also are to be worshipers of Jehovah, is expressed in many writers, particularly

65. [*Ed.*] *Ebenbild:* reading uncertain.
66. [*Ed.*] See Job 40:3–4; 42:1–6.

in the prophets.[67] We too can say that God is only the God of those who worship him, for his nature is to know himself in his image, in subjective spirit. Objectively God is creator of heaven and earth. To be sure, we also find here the distorted formulation that he is mightier than other gods.[68] God has imposed his measure and his aim on all, including humanity. The laws do not yet appear as laws of reason but as prescriptions of the Lord, and in that connection all manner of political prescriptions enter in, down to the smallest detail, in external categories, so that the eternal laws of right and ethics, which subsist in and for themselves, stand on a par with laws relating to blue or yellow curtains.[69] All this stems from the characterization of God as the lord whose worship is a form of service through which the subjective spirit does not attain freedom; thus there is no differentiation between divine and human laws. In this abstract direction toward the one Lord lies the ground for that formalism of constancy which we find in the Jewish spirit in reference to its religion, in the same way as in Islam we find the formalism of expansion. And because the subjective spirit achieves no freedom in it, there is also no immortality; rather the individual vanishes away in the goal of the service of Jehovah, preservation of the family, and long life in the land.⁻[70]

⁻Thus we have here at one and the same time both struggle and anguish in the finite subject. The next step is the objectification of this anguish; for if power and substance are to become spirit, this moment of antithesis and its resolution are indispensable. This anguish of unfreedom is to be found on its own account—not yet taken back into unity—in a number of religions, which we can designate the "religion of anguish." |

629

67. [Ed.] This inclusion of other peoples is found especially in the exilic prophets, e.g., Isaiah 40–55 (Deutero-Isaiah), and in the postexilic period, e.g., Haggai 2:6 ff. Although Hegel does not distinguish the different prophetic periods, he recognizes that this universalism occurs in later writings. Thus in the variant from the *Werke* contained in the 1827 lectures, n. 492 (see below, n. 70), he alludes to Ps. 117:1, Isa. 66:21, and other passages (see annotations to that note).

68. [Ed.] See 1827 lectures, n. 492, annotation c.

69. [Ed.] Hegel is probably referring to the furnishings, not of the temple, but of the tabernacle. See Exod. 35–38, 40, esp. 36:35, 37; and 38:9, 16, 18.

70. [Ed.] See *Werke* text, 1827 lectures, n. 492.

b. The Religion of Anguish[71]

[It is found] specifically in a few Near Eastern, and especially Phoenician, religions. In Hebraic religion we have spirit as lord and as servant, i.e., estranged from itself; in order to be actual spirit, it must turn away from this estrangement and return to itself. However, this still pertains to the element of natural life as a process with symbolic significance.

Here belongs the representation of the *phoenix,* a death that is the reentry into a rejuvenated life—and this is what spirit is. Here we no longer have the struggle between two distinct principles but the process in regard to a *subject* itself, and not a human but rather the divine subject.

A more proximate form of this process is Adonis. In spring there is a festival of mourning during which Adonis is sought with great lamentations, then on the third day a festival to commemorate his resurrection. On the one hand this has the character of a consciousness of the course of nature, but it is also to be taken symbolically as meaning that this transition is a universal characteristic, a moment of the absolute.⁻[72]

---

71. [*Ed.*] What Hegel describes as "the religion of anguish" is not Phoenician religion in any historical sense, but a construct that he seems to have derived from classical sources. Phoenician religion was in fact a form of Canaanite nature religion, lacking any association with the sacred bird known as the phoenix. It was the Greeks who called these Canaanite peoples "Phoenicians," probably because their sailors had reddened, sunburnt skin; "Phoenician" derives from φοῖνος, meaning "bloodred." A word deriving from the same root, "phoenix" (φοῖνιξ), was also used for the sacred bird of the Egyptians, in stories recounted by Herodotus, Pliny, and Tacitus. From an excerpt contained in the *Berliner Schriften,* p. 706, it appears that Hegel's source was Creuzer, *Symbolik und Mythologie* 1:438, where Creuzer gives Herodotus, *Histories* 2.73 as the chief source for the myth of the phoenix. However, Herodotus's account, in which the phoenix carries its father from Ethiopia to the sanctuary of the sun in an egg made of myrrh, does not support Hegel's interpretation, which derives from other sources cited by Creuzer, including Pliny, *Natural History* 10.2. Hegel was attracted to the image of the phoenix as a representation of the death of God, and it is around this image that he constructed his "religion of anguish," which is properly attached to Greek and Egyptian rather than Semitic, Syrian, or "Near Eastern" sources. As indicated below, n. 72, the *Werke* provides a complete text of this section; see 1824 lectures, n. 572 (including the annotation).

72. [*Ed.*] See *Werke* text, 1824 lectures, n. 572.

c. Egyptian Religion: The Religion of Ferment[73]

ˉProperly speaking, the transition to Greek religion is found in Egyptian religion, or rather in Egyptian works of art. Here too we find phantasy, as with the Hindus, but not empty phantasmagoria; everything is symbolic, and the externalia merely express spirit's struggle to understand itself,ˉ[74] ˉa struggle that is grasped as the activity of God himself. Egyptian religion is the religion of ferment.ˉ[75]

ˉThe main figure is Osiris, admittedly one of the four younger gods, from whom, according to Herodotus,[76] eight older gods are distinguished; but it was in fact later on that the higher consciousness emerged into view. Osiris as what fructifies is opposed by Typhon, the principle of the desert. Beside Osiris stands Isis as the female principle, i.e., as the earth where he is the sun. Here again we have a natural process involving the sun, the Nile, and annual fertility.

630 | Thus the sun and the Nile symbolize the higher thought constituted by Osiris, and conversely this personification of Osiris symbolizes the Nile and sun. Osiris is killed by Typhon, Isis seeks and buries his bones, but his death is not his end; he is lord of the kingdom

---

73. [Ed.] In 1831 the name for Egyptian religion shifts from "enigma" (although this term is also used at the end of the section) to "ferment"(Gärung). The idea seems to be that spirit is struggling to rise forth out of the ferment of natural symbols that characterize Egyptian religion. This image perhaps accords more closely with the central features of this religion—the Osiris cult, the belief in immortality, the role of animal symbolism. The sphinxes may be enigmatic figures, but Hegel of course knew that the story of the riddle of the sphinx and its solution by Oedipus was of Greek rather than Egyptian provenance. In fact it is just this point that furnishes the transition from Egyptian to Greek religion in 1831.

74. [Ed.] See Werke text, 1827 lectures, n. 341.

75. [Ed.] See Werke text, 1827 lectures, n. 318.

76. [Ed.] Hegel is probably referring, even if not quite correctly, to Herodotus, Histories 2.43. It was, according to Herodotus, not Osiris but Heracles who belonged to the circle of twelve gods—a middle group from whom the third, youngest group of gods stemmed, including Osiris, who was equated with Dionysus (see above, 1827 lectures, n. 327). Thus Hegel disregards the distinction between the second and third generations of gods. For the relationship of the first group of eight gods to the second group of twelve (four more being added to the original eight), Hegel was dependent on the interpretations of Aloys Hirt, Ueber die Bildung der aegyptischen Gottheiten (Berlin, 1821), and P. E. Jablonski, Pantheon Aegyptiorum, 3 vols. (Frankfurt am Oder, 1750–1752).

of the dead.[77] It is true that the natural aspect is here predominant, but inasmuch as this cycle also pertains to the concept, the natural symbolizes the spiritual, but also vice versa.

There are in addition other deities who express only individual aspects of this process. Osiris is also lawgiver, founder of marriage, etc.; thus his intrinsic quality is spiritual.⁻[78] ⁻Particular prominence, however, attaches to the kingdom of the dead, of Amenti.[79] According to Herodotus,[80] the Egyptians were the first to teach the immortality of the soul. It might seem surprising, therefore, that they took so much care to preserve the dead body. However, the regard paid to the soul is rigorously coherent with that paid to the body. When the body is dead and has paid its due to the power of nature, other peoples endeavor at least to prevent nature from exerting its power over it directly—they lay the body in the flames or the earth, and this then appears as a human deed, as the doing of spirit. In the same way the Egyptians knew human beings with their bodies to be on a higher plane than nature, and so honored the body.

In the Egyptian spirit the divine is on the one hand made [sensibly] present, while on the other hand consciousness has worked its way forward to the level of the spiritual. The tradition that the Egyptians were previously ruled by a race of robbers[81] furnishes the reference

77. [Ed.] See 1824 lectures, n. 353, and 1827 lectures, n. 334. On Isis as the earth principle and her search for the bones of Osiris, see Plutarch, De Iside et Osiride, chaps. 38, 18.

78. [Ed.] See Werke text, 1827 lectures, n. 329.

79. [Ed.] See 1824 lectures, n. 352.

80. [Ed.] See 1827 lectures, n. 323.

81. [Ed.] Räubergeschlecht. S reads Rbrgsch. According to Herodotus, prehistoric Egypt was ruled by a race of gods (Göttergeschlecht) (see 1827 lectures, n. 327); according to other interpretations, by a race of shepherds (Hirtengeschlecht) (but see Creuzer, Symbolik und Mythologie 1:299 ff.). The reading Räubergeschlecht is uncertain, but Königsgeschlecht (i.e., a race of kings who were gods) or Hirtengeschlecht would be inconsistent with the text. Since a source for Hegel's version of the legend cannot be found, it is possible that he has here confused legends concerning the early days of Rome and Egypt. In the Lectures on the Philosophy of World History, Sibree ed., pp. 283–288 (Lasson ed., pp. 665–673), he affirms on several occasions that the Roman state originated with a "band of robbers" or a "company of robbers" or "robber-herdsmen." But it is also possible that Hegel was comparing the Roman and Egyptian legends, and that the comparison was truncated by Strauss or his source.

to nature. The king of the Egyptians is known not merely as the favorite of the god, especially of Ammum or Ammon, the sun-god, but as this god himself. (Alexander the Great.[82]) In the same way the priests too are themselves in turn regarded as gods.

Peculiar to the Egyptians is the *worship of animals,* which is also found, as we have seen, in Hinduism, but assumed its severest form in Egypt. The different districts worshiped different | animals. To harm them brought murder and death in its train. Particular honor was paid to Apis, in whom the soul of the animal was thought [to be present].[83] Even if God is not yet cognized as spirit but only as unconscious power, as natural striving, still this power does come forth in animal shape. Animals' heads are often used as masks, e.g., for mummies, and this implies that the spiritual is cognized behind this animal mask and independently of it. In Egypt for the first time we see a struggle between the priestly caste and the warrior caste,[84] so that here we have human political will stepping forth in opposition to the cultus and its substantiality. The sanctuary of Neith bore the superscription: "No mortal has yet lifted my veil—I bear a son, Helios,"[85] [which means that] nature is something hidden but there issues from it something other, the manifest. Everything in Egypt denotes symbolically something unexpressed. The spirit of this people is the enigma. The transition from this enigma of the natural to the spiritual is the sphinx, with its animal body and human head.[86]

It is the Greeks who make the transition from this enigma to the

82. [*Ed.*] See 1827 lectures, annotation e to n. 339.

83. [*Ed.*] See Herodotus, *Histories* 2.65–76, esp. 69 (worship of crocodiles) and 71 (hippopotamuses); and, in regard to the sacred bull Apis, 3.28. Herodotus, however, says nothing about Apis representing "the soul of the animal," and Hegel probably got this idea from Plutarch, *De Iside et Osiride* 23, where Apis is described as a "soul-imbued image" of Osiris, which, however, is born only when a shaft of moonlight impregnates a cow already in calf.

84. [*Ed.*] As confirmed by the parallel *Werke* text (see n. 86), Hegel is referring to Herodotus's report that the Pharaohs Cheops and Khafre closed the temples and prevented the people from sacrificing throughout their reigns (*Histories* 2.124, 127). The ensuing rift between the priestly and warrior castes is referred to in 2.141, and was also described in detail in A. Heeren, *Ideen . . . der vornehmsten Völker der alten Welt,* 2 vols. (Göttingen, 1804–1805), 2:595–614.

85. [*Ed.*] See 1827 lectures, n. 345.

86. [*Ed.*] See *Werke* text, 1827 lectures, n. 339.

clear consciousness of spirit; and they express it in the most naive form in the story of the sphinx, whose riddle was solved by the Greek Oedipus when he pronounced the answer to be: man.[87] It is Greece that makes the transition to God being known as spirit inasmuch as it knows in him essentially the moment of humanity.

2. Greek Religion[88]

a. Summary[89]

¯The first moment was the [divine] power as substance, and then as creator and lord of created things. The next step is that this other of substance is something free, that human beings are not simply obedient to the commandment of God but that they are at the same time free on their own account in this obedience. To begin with, this determination seems to relate only to the subject, to human beings; but it relates no less to the nature of God: God is spirit only inasmuch as he eternally divests himself in the other and returns from this other into himself. As creator he posits over against himself | 632

87. [Ed.] Hegel does not here distinguish between the Egyptian sphinx and the Theban sphinx that was overcome by Oedipus. For the Theban sphinx legend, see *Encyclopaedia Britannica*, 15th ed., s.v. "sphinx."

88. [Ed.] The section on Greek religion is unusually long in Strauss's excerpts; while this may reflect his personal interest in the subject, much of his text is confirmed by parallel passages in the *Werke*. The section begins with a summary of the argument, continues with a detailed synopsis of the teleological proof, and then turns to a description of Greek religion as the religion of freedom, albeit still a freedom infected with natural being, hence the religion of beauty; we have added subheads to mark these points.

89. [Ed.] In this summary, which is both retrospective and prospective, the category of "freedom," or "religion of freedom," clearly transcends Greek religion as such. Freedom as it relates to God first appeared in the Persian idea of the good but more especially in the Hebraic understanding of God as the personal One and as wise, purposeful creator, advanced with the "death of God" in the image of the phoenix, and reached its consummation in the Christian Trinity. The freedom of humanity came to birth in Greek religion but remained tinged with finite and natural immediacy; the true basis of human freedom is when humanity knows itself to be a moment, an essential determination, in the life of the infinite God, as in the Christian idea of incarnation. Thus the religion of freedom began to emerge in Greece (and in Israel, Persia, and Egypt), but reached its consummation in the Christian West, after the setbacks it suffered in the political religion of imperial Rome had been overcome.

an other that is his likeness, and in so doing he sets himself up over against himself; but this is still not a divestment—for he continues to be defined as head, and what stands over against him is defined as subservient. The next step in the advance to the liberation of spirit is essentially this, that God loses himself, that he *dies,* and only has being through this negation of himself. This negation, this other-being of the divine, is created being; but since God also returns into himself from out of this negation, this other is a moment of the divine, and is essentially reconciled with it. Thus human beings know humanity as a moment of God; it is true on the one hand that in obedience to God they behave in a negative manner, but inasmuch as they obey a God in whom the human is an essential determination, they behave in such obedience as free. In the death of God, death itself dies again within the finite and the divine emerges from it; in this elevation above the natural state lies freedom.

The first form of this religion of art is still characterized by immediacy and naturalness. Humanity first possesses the divine in an immediate, and therefore also a finite, manifold form—this is the religion of beauty, the Greek religion, which, although its basis [is] true thought, nevertheless belongs to the finite religions because of this sensible aspect.¯[90]

As regards the abstract foundation of this religion of freedom in its primal shape, what first emerges here is the thought of *purpose,* of purposeful activity, of the wisdom of God. For free activity is activity in accordance with purposes. Power creates, but it is not known that what creates maintains itself in what is created, that it comes together with itself in it. Purposeful doing, by contrast, is that in which no other content emerges than what was posited in advance, a doing which is only the self-maintaining of what is active. This is free activity; free power is what determines itself, and its self-determinations are called purposes.

b. The Teleological Proof[91]

¯Once God is raised up into this category of purposeful, wise activity, the teleological proof of God's existence comes into being. In this

90. [*Ed.*] See *Werke* text, 1824 lectures, n. 574.

91. [*Ed.*] W₂ provides a secondary transmission of the full text of the teleological proof in 1831, which we have printed as an appendix preceding the excerpts (see

proof the two extremes, the world (as the point of departure) and God (as the point of termination[92]), are held together through the categorial determination of purpose. | This proof is essentially a 633 continuation of the cosmological proof: God is first known as power, and only on that basis as wisdom. This proof does first occur, properly speaking, in the free Hellenic spirit. In the words of Socrates, God has given human beings eyes to see, eyelids to cover their eyes, and eyebrows to hold back the sweat that runs from their forehead.[93] In the world we perceive a series of things that are mutually contingent, and yet a unity is evident to which they utterly conform. For example, human beings need light, air, water, and food; but these things come into being and exist independently on their own account, and their relation to human beings is for them an external one. Animals too are complete and self-contained; they do not express explicitly the fact that they are means for human beings, yet they are so. And since in this way things imply relations that they do not themselves posit, there must be an activity that posits these characteristics or purposes, which is the power of the things.

Kant's critique[94] of this proof is, first, that purposive relations concern merely the *form* of things, not their material—so that God, as he who posits purpose, is merely the fashioner of the world, or demiurge. What Kant is saying is that where things are portrayed in the relationship of purpose, their relation to an other does not already contain their relation to self, the latter being separated off, as matter, from the former, as form. The question now arises whether it is right to make this distinction. This relation to self, this quiet

---

Teleological Proof, n. 1). A disadvantage of the new arrangement is that, if purpose is central to the Jewish concept of the wisdom of God (as it surely is, although not emphasized as such by Hegel in 1831), then Jewish as well as Greek and Roman religion should be considered in relation to the teleological proof. In the *Ms.,* Hegel took up the teleological proof only in connection with Roman religion; in 1824, in relation to Jewish, Greek, and Roman religion; and in 1831, in relation to Greek and Roman. Here is another example of the fluidity of his conceptual schema.

92. [*Ed.*] Reading *Endpunkt* for S's abbreviated *End(?)t,* in parallel with *Ausgangspunkt* ("point of departure"). The abbreviation could also be deciphered as *Endlichkeit* ("finitude"), in which case Hegel may have intended a wordplay: the God of the teleological proof, the God who is the end or purpose of the world, who creates the world according to purposes, is still a finite God.

93. [*Ed.*] See *Ms.,* n. 240.

94. [*Ed.*] See *Ms.,* n. 242.

stability, this abiding unity with self that is matter, is itself one of the determinations of form; in other words, matter is nothing other than the quiet relation to self that also marks form in all of its activity. So if God creates the form of the world, he does not first need to get the matter for it from somewhere else.

Kant's second criticism[95] of this proof is that from the great and multifarious but only relative wisdom that we perceive in the world we infer an absolute wisdom; in other words, the conclusion of the inference does not match its starting point. This much must be granted, but spirit is entitled to *think* its perceptions, i.e., to raise them from their contingency to universality. |

634

A further deficiency in these proofs, which Jacobi[96] especially has underlined, is that in this form of inference the starting point, the world, appears as a foundation for God, who thus appears as something conditioned. But this is only a false appearance arising from the inference, which is only the process of subjective cognizing; and in the inference itself, what appeared as conditioning returns to being the conditioned. The result itself expresses the fact that the starting point was defective. The syllogism involves the negative moment that the determinate being of the finite purposive order is not vouchsafed for the subject that has being in and for itself, but that the eternal reason is what is true.

True purposiveness is not where purpose, material, and means are separated; on the contrary, it is the purpose that accomplishes itself in and through itself. This infinitude of the form of purpose exists in organic life; the living organism produces itself, it has itself for purpose. But its finite aspect is that it needs material from without. And, of course, every living organism needs its own peculiar nourishment as well as its inorganic nature. Since what is organic needs its inorganic material in this way, yet the inorganic is not posited by the organic, there must be a tertium quid that posits both. Moreover, the purposive activity of the organism, the instinct of animals, is something unconscious, not posited by them, and requires a cause [external[97]] to this subject. If nature is thought of as a power

95. [*Ed.*] See *Ms.*, nn. 247, 248.
96. [*Ed.*] See *Teleological Proof*, n. 13.
97. [*Ed.*] Replaces an illegible word.

that produces blindly, first the inorganic and then the organic realm, then it remains a matter of chance that the organic has found [in the inorganic] what makes its existence possible; it might just as easily not have found it, as the ancients used to say about monsters that had perished for that very reason. In recent times a so-called philosophy of nature has breathed new life into this ancient representational picture.[98] But, properly speaking, human beings know themselves essentially as purpose over against the rest of nature, and furthermore they know the organic as purpose over against the inorganic. But the organism is nonetheless always related to what is outside it; there are two [terms] that stand in opposition—their truth is their unity; and the unity is in a third term that | posits this primal division. This third we can in general call God, and spirit raises itself to him from out of this purposive relation. But in order to complete the concept of God much is here still lacking; God is initially posited as organic life, as νοῦς, which rules the world, as the world soul (but a soul that is not separated from its body).[99] Thus we arrive at the concept of the organic life of the universe, wherein the seemingly independent images are downgraded to the level of moments or aspects.

635

So far, however, we have been discussing only the form of the purposive relation; now we are discussing its content also. On this side there is in the first place a marked contrast between the finite tenor of the purposes and God, to whom they are related. For instance, this plant is ordained by God precisely to provide nourishment for this animalcule. But it also happens that many of these purposes are in no wise fulfilled: the goal of animals is a contented feeling of life, yet they are slaughtered; the goal of the seed is to unfold, yet it fails to develop and dies. In the spiritual realm, purposes of this kind are stultified to an even greater extent through human passions, through evil; whole peoples perish. So we see small purposes coming in part to fruition, and in part remaining essentially

98. [Ed.] In his history-of-philosophy lectures Hegel refers to the idea found in contemporary philosophy of nature of a mere "issuing forth" (Hervorgehen), which is not to be confused with purposive development. On the "ancient representational picture," see Teleological Proof, n. 14.

99. [Ed.] See 1827 lectures, n. 163, and Teleological Proof, nn. 17, 18.

unfulfilled. But this is what reveals these purposes to be limited, and we must ascend to a *universal* purpose, which, however, we no longer find in appearance but which we infer rationally. This supreme purpose Kant apprehends as the good, and the next thing would be that the world should correspond to it.[100] But nature, and *a fortiori* human passions, have laws and purposes of their own, and the question would be to inquire into whether the sum of good or of evil in this world is the greater. Kant merely insists that the good *ought* to be realized, and since it is not itself the power whereby it is actualized, a tertium quid is here postulated—and by this means Kant arrives at God.[101] These then are the defects of the physicotheological proof: (1) formally speaking, as regards the form of the purposive activity, it attains no further than life; (2) materially speaking, if determinate being is taken as the starting point, all that is demonstrated are finite purposes (and if the starting point is the concept of good, there is no advance beyond the level of "ought").⁻[102]

c. The Religion of Freedom and Beauty[103]

636 These defects of the physicotheological proof are also to be seen | in the corresponding form of religion, namely, the Greek. Through

100. [*Ed.*] Hegel is referring to the definition of the final end (*Endzweck*) in Kant's *Critique of Judgement* (Oxford, 1952), esp. p. 116 (Kant, *Werke* 5:448). That the world should correspond to it is probably an allusion to pp. 128–129 (*Werke* 5:458).

101. [*Ed.*] See *Teleological Proof,* nn. 20, 21.

102. [*Ed.*] See the *Werke* text of the 1831 version of the teleological proof, above, pp. 703–719. In the 1827 version, Hegel adds: "The genuine form [of the proof] is as follows: there are finite spirits. But the finite has no truth, for the truth of finite spirit and its actuality is instead just the absolute spirit. The finite is not genuine being; it is implicitly the dialectic of self-sublating or self-negating, and its negation is affirmation as the infinite, as the universal in and for itself. It is surprising that this transition was not specified in the proofs of God" (Vol. 1:431). In fact this deficiency characterizes Greek religion, to which Hegel now turns, for Greek religion thematizes *only* the finitude of humanity, not recognizing the lack of truth and the self-sublation of finitude.

103. [*Ed.*] In the 1831 lectures, Hegel uses several terms to characterize Greek religion: it is the religion of freedom, of humanity, of beauty, of art. The first two seem to form an ethical pair, the second two an aesthetic. Our subhead is intended to indicate this double focus. It is conceivable that in the last lectures Hegel emphasizes the ethical implications of Greek religion because of his heightened concern at this

the category of purpose, Greek religion attained to freedom, but only to the first level of freedom; it was infected therefore with natural being, a finite freedom. The natural is certainly posited as subordinate and God consequently as subject, but he is not yet raised to absolute infinitude; on the contrary, God is still finite spirit. ˜On the one hand he is made by human agency, on the other hand in terms of his content he is anthropopathic. And this is why this religion is a religion of humanity, or of the serene enjoyment of freedom. Everything that is humanly great is known as divine.˜[104]

˜As regards the natural then, it is on the one hand left behind; spirit has wrestled its way out of it. On the other hand it is still contained within spirit, though in a subordinate position.˜[105] Greek mythology clearly expresses the transition from natural to spiritual gods; the natural gods have a merely superficial personality, only a mask of spirituality—they are called the old gods or Titans, Uranus, etc. But this naturalism is a widespread feature of Greek mythology (as the elemental stuff of a figure like Phoebus, etc.). The old deities are gods of nature; admittedly they also touch upon the spiritual, but just as some are abstract externality, so others are abstract internality—e.g., the Erinyes with their wholly internal judgments. But these old gods or Titans are cast down by the new deities and banished to the borders of the earth, to outer darkness, while the new gods have established their hegemony in the clear light of human consciousness.

The new gods are spiritual, ethical, but still with an echo of the natural. Helios gives way to Apollo, he who gives light to him who knows, but Apollo still has the sun's rays around his head.[106] Cronus becomes Poseidon, founder of cities; but the principal god is Zeus,

---

time with the question of religion and state (see Vol. 1:451 n. 1). In any case Hegel attends in a special way to the connection between freedom and beauty on this occasion. Greek art is beautiful because and to the extent that it matches perfectly the concept of free spirituality (this is the mark of classical as distinguished from symbolic art). In this sense the ethical category of freedom has become the more fundamental attribute.

104. [Ed.] See Werke text, 1827 lectures, n. 420.

105. [Ed.] See Werke text, 1827 lectures, n. 404.

106. [Ed.] For the linking of Helios and Apollo, see 1824 lectures, n. 675, and 1827 lectures, n. 366.

the divinity of the state, and as far as his natural echoes are concerned the god of thunder and lightning.

As regards the beginnings of human consciousness and education, Prometheus is especially worthy of note. The Greeks often depict the natural state by saying that human beings used to live off plants and vegetables and were not allowed to eat the sacred oxen of Helios. It was Prometheus who taught humans to subdue the beasts and, more especially, to make fire. He then taught them to eat the | flesh themselves and sacrifice to Zeus only skin and bones. It might seem surprising that this teacher of the human race should be numbered among the Titans and chained to the Caucasus.[107] But the arts he taught relate only to the satisfaction of natural needs, and here we come up against the insatiability of appetite, which (like Prometheus's liver) continually grows again as often as it is satisfied. Plato says of Prometheus that he was unable to bring to humanity the art of politics as this lay hidden in Zeus's citadel.[108]

A similar transition from natural to spiritual is portrayed in Artemis. The Ephesian Artemis is bedecked with bosoms and animal figures as the generative and nourishing power of nature; the Greek Artemis on the other hand is the huntress.[109] Hercules too gloried in the slaying of wild beasts; in this transition the killing of beasts emerges as a major moment.[110]

Demeter is not only the teacher of agriculture; she also institutes the ethical bond of marriage and landed property. For nomads as for slaves, the ownership of land is the real beginning of divine, ethical freedom.

Pallas Athena is particularly noteworthy as the folk spirit of Athens, as the city's ethical, spiritual life. In all of these gods the basic characteristics of the rational, free will are honored. ¨But the spirit that is in them is still fragmented into its particular aspects—

107. [Ed.] See 1824 lectures, n. 598.
108. [Ed.] See 1827 lectures, n. 380.
109. [Ed.] See 1827 lectures, editorial annotation to n. 374.
110. [Ed.] Reading "major moment" (Hauptmoment) is uncertain. Hegel is referring to the labors of Hercules, in particular the overpowering of the Nemean lion, the Lernean hydra, the Arcadian doe, the Erymanthine boar, the Stymphalian birds, the Cretan bull, the Bistonian mares, the Geryonian cattle, the dragon Lado, and, last but not least, Cerberus.

hence polytheism. The finitude of these gods consisted on the one hand in their naturalness, while on the other it lay in the fact that they are not yet thought, only pictured representationally, and are therefore not yet fused into a single God but are still many gods. ⁻Human beings do not simply find these essences [*Wesenheiten*] outside them, but bring them into being through their representation, as phantasy.⁻¹¹¹ That is why the gods are given a sensuous configuration; but because at the same time they emerge as essences, the sensuous element is wholly matched to the spirit—the religion of beauty.

⁻Since, however, it is the representation of phantasy from which the gods proceed, they appear as "made": ποιηταί | means "makers." As Herodotus¹¹² says, Homer and Hesiod made their gods for the Greeks,⁻¹¹³ while Phidias's image [of Zeus] gave them their absolute representation of the father of the gods.

638

Greek religion is essentially religion of beauty. For if it is to be portrayed in sensible form, there is no other figure [*Gestalt*] for the free spirituality to which the Greeks had attained than the human figure, as the essential and necessary figure for spirit. At the same time the human figure [of Greek art] is ideal. Earlier art was symbolic—in other words, it sought to externalize some abstract representation; but then the external element could not correspond to what was within. It is only when the concept and spirit are concrete that their configuration can become adequate. In what is not beautiful there is a rupture between the eternal concept and what exists in externality; for instance, something else has contributed to the face of a Socrates¹¹⁴ than the inner concept. Where the corporeal is portrayed as begotten wholly from the spiritual soul, however, there we have beauty. But the spiritual is portrayed only through the facial features and the bodily attitude and gestures, and this can

111. [*Ed.*] See *Werke* text, 1827 lectures, n. 405.
112. [*Ed.*] See 1824 lectures, n. 621.
113. [*Ed.*] See *Werke* text, 1827 lectures, n. 409.
114. [*Ed.*] Hegel is probably referring to Alcibiades' speech in Plato's *Symposium* 215a–b. Alcibiades, addressing Socrates, declares that outwardly he resembles a statue of the satyr Marsyas (and thus is quite grotesque) but that whether the resemblance pertains in other respects is another matter.

also be presented in clothed figures; for the rest, the body is only a living organism, and its portrayal nude belongs only to [the sphere of] sensible beauty.

Although the Greek god certainly does have spiritual freedom as its foundation, it is still affected by the finitude of contingency. So there are a host of local and historical features, of natural and symbolic echoes, that enter into [the makeup of] the single deities. Subordinate categories come into play that do not belong to free spirituality—for example, the category of procreation and Zeus's countless marriage-beds. These legends obviously originate in another sphere.

The Greek gods are no longer abstracta but subjects and, as such, individual; they combine within themselves more than one [abstract] feature. It is the same with the heroes: Achilles is not merely the abstraction of bravery but is also love, etc. This is precisely why the Greek gods do not form a system. It is the anthropopathic side of the Greek gods. It must be said, however, that the Greek gods are marked by too small rather than too large an anthropopathic element. The God-man in Christianity is much more markedly anthropopathic; | he is an actually existing, sensible human being, but is sublated in divinity.⁻⁻¹¹⁵

Above this great array of finite gods there is a single power. Because the concrete is something finite and particular, this universality stands above it. But because the finite is the concrete, this universality is an abstract one. This is fate [*Fatum*], the power that is devoid alike of concept and purpose. When confronted by fate, it is only by self-denying submission that human beings can save their freedom—so that although fate conquers them externally, it does not do so inwardly. Because outward existence is not in harmony with *their* purpose, they abandon *all* purpose—this is an abstract freedom. The viewpoint of the absolute religion is that even misfortune yields an absolute content, so that the negative turns into the affirmative once more. But the Greek spirit had still no absolute content to oppose to this external necessity. Similarly, over against external contingency, the Greek people still did not possess in its

115. [*Ed.*] See *Werke* text, 1827 lectures, n. 412.

political life the infinitude of the subjective will, [i.e., the ability] to make one's decisions purely from oneself; being [only] the first level of freedom, its freedom was tinged with finitude, and this is what made oracles a necessity. In deciding whether to build a house, get married, or engage in battle, one relied on the rustling of leaves, the words of priests in a trance, etc. Deciding inwardly, from one's own resources, begins with Socrates' *daimonion,* which all people now have within themselves.[116]

¯However, destiny [*Schicksal*] in the form of ethical justice finds its truest and loftiest portrayal in Greek tragedy, especially the tragedies of Sophocles.[117] Here destiny is partly expressed as something incomprehensible [i.e., fate, *Fatum*], but on closer examination it is revealed as true justice. It is the collision of ethical powers, which [are] equally justified but also equally one-sided and, as they collide, perish.¯[118] The conclusion then is that only Zeus is the true.[119] Greece did not yet have this consciousness in its Homeric texts but only achieved it at the highest point of its culture. The colliding powers are family and state, conscious and unconscious.

As one of its moments the Greek cultus therefore involves enjoyment, because in cultus the Greek spirit is immediately at home with itself. More specifically it involves the recognition of these powers— all of these powers, | not simply this and that one in a one-sided   640 manner. Another aspect of the cultus is teaching. The rhapsodies taught the Greeks their Homer. During the festivals the tragedies provided profound teachings. In the mysteries representational images were communicated that are far removed from idle chatter or argumentation; in all its lucidity the Greek spirit had still the

116. [*Ed.*] On Socrates's *daimonion,* see Xenophon, *Memorabilia* 1.1.1–9, esp. 1.1.4, where Socrates is said to have spoken in such and such a way, or advised his friends to do thus and so, because his *daimonion* (divine sign) had so indicated. See also Plato, *Apology,* esp. 24b–c, 26b–e; and Hegel's interpretation in the *Lectures on the History of Philosophy* 1:421–425 (cf. *Werke* 14:94–101).

117. [*Ed.*] Elsewhere in these lectures Hegel refers on more than one occasion to Sophocles' tragedies, *Antigone, Oedipus Rex, Oedipus at Colonus,* and *Trachiniae.* See *Ms.,* p. 184; 1824 lectures, pp. 479, 497, nn. 638, 695, and annotation to n. 697; and below, *Loose Sheets,* n. 3.

118. [*Ed.*] See *Werke* text, 1827 lectures, n. 428.

119. [*Ed.*] See *Ms.,* n. 207.

premonition that there was something beyond its sphere—hence the altar to the unknown god.[120] ⁻The mysteries conveyed figurative portrayals of the purification of the soul and of its being taken up into the higher essence; the doctrine of immortality was particularly important here. But Socrates, the wisest of all the Greeks, refused to be initiated[121]—which shows that all this stood far beneath what Socrates had accomplished.⁻[122] Inasmuch as in the Greek cultus humanity knows itself to be identical with the essential powers, this cultus is stamped by serenity. Cultus itself is a game in which humanity manifests itself and human beings enjoy themselves at their highest pitch of beauty and dexterity. Here there is no longer a disharmony between humanity and God, but reconciliation from the start.

⁻The next step is for this free spirit to cleanse itself of its finitude⁻. The way this happens is that fate breaks in upon Greek life, these folk spirits in their particularity and naturalness perish; God is known as pure spirit, and all humanity (no longer merely a few citizens) is known as free in and for itself. One of these particular spirits raises itself to become the fate of all the others, which, being thus oppressed in their political existence, become conscious of the weakness of their gods. This fate that overthrew the world of the Greeks was the world of Rome.⁻[123]

3. Roman Religion: the Religion of Expediency[124]

Roman religion is not to be confused with Greek. Its principle is not beauty but external purposiveness or expediency. God is known as something that operates purposively, and the absolute purpose is the

120. [*Ed.*] See Acts 17:23.
121. [*Ed.*] See *Ms.*, n. 201.
122. [*Ed.*] See *Werke* text, 1824 lectures, n. 673.
123. [*Ed.*] See *Werke* text, 1824 lectures, n. 700.
124. [*Ed.*] The principle of Roman religion is not beauty, says Hegel; nor is it freedom, since this is a religion that binds and dominates. Roman religion does not fit the broad category ("freedom") under which it is treated in 1831 any more than in 1824. It is merely transitional: the way to the "cleansing" of spirit of its finitude is through the absolutization of finitude, with the result that the whole world of the gods collapses—a *Götterdämmerung*.

Roman state as the abstract power over all other states. The Roman spirit is the power of abstract universality, and was worshiped by them as Fortuna Publica or Jupiter Capitolinus. | 641
The Romans are said to be the most religious of all peoples:[125] but religion was for them something binding and dominating. Their *virtus* consists in unreservedly serving the state. The particular aspects of religion also serve this purpose: the auspices in the hands of the aristocrats, and the majority of the gods introduced superstitiously at a time of need. In a writer like Virgil, gods such as Minerva or Apollo are dead machinery;[126] on this alien soil they lack what is proper to them, their ethical freedom.

The Romans also have a whole host of powers of prosaic utility, devoid of any ethical character, [such as] Fornax (the art of baking bread), Pax, Pestis.[127] Likewise a rustic element with festivals like the Palilia. The Saturnalia [were] of similar character. This is the one side of Roman religion—that the gods are wholly limited, external powers of nature.

The other side, however, is an abstract inwardness, a dread of some unknown inward element—an inner fate, as it were. Under this heading falls Rome's secret name: Amor and Eros or Valentia.[128] Whereas the Greeks were able to fashion something beautiful, a myth etc., out of anything, the Romans stood fast in this sullen inwardness, which adhered to everything as a sense of awe. For this reason the Romans had a large number of specific regulations, as for example in the event of a monstrous birth. They themselves produced no fine works of art but stole them from the Greeks. In their tragedies— e.g., in Seneca—there is no ethical principle, only slaves, wretched servants, etc.[129] In Greek drama, speech and bodily attitude were what counted most, while mime was inhibited by the use of masks;

125. [*Ed.*] See 1824 lectures, n. 725.
126. [*Ed.*] See 1824 lectures, n. 718.
127. [*Ed.*] See *Ms.*, pp. 210–219; and *Loose Sheets*, pp. 765–766.
128. [*Ed.*] See *Ms.*, annotation to n. 269.
129. [*Ed.*] On Hegel's adverse view of Seneca's tragedies, see *Ms.*, p. 221 and n. 298. However, even the sharpness of the judgment pronounced there does not justify what is said here. Strauss is seemingly mingling Hegel's criticism of Seneca and of the Later Comedy.

with the Romans, pantomime came into its own,[130] only to be succeeded by the bloody combats of wild beasts. Here the spectacle was one of prosaic death; to die imperturbably was for the Romans the pinnacle of greatness, e.g., Seneca—abstract greatness.[131]

This abstract power of the Roman spirit was then personified in the emperor. The emperor was God, and rightly so to the extent that he was a totally different power from wheat rust, pestilence, etc. This brought to naught the serene happiness of the previous religion. ¯This abstract power brought into the world the monstrous unhappiness and anguish that were to be the birthpangs for the religion of truth. It was by renouncing satisfaction | in this world that the soil for the true religion was prepared. And in the fullness of time,[132] i.e., when this state of despair had been brought about in the spirit of the world, God sent his Son.¯[133]

642

130. [*Ed.*] Hegel is possibly referring to a report in K. A. Moritz, *Anthousa; oder, Roms Alterthümer* (Berlin, 1791), pp. 88–89, which speaks of mimes performed principally by troupes from Etruria.

131. [*Ed.*] See Tacitus, *Annals* 15.62–64.

132. [*Ed.*] A reference to the New Testament concept of the fullness of time; cf. Mark 1:15; Gal. 4:4; Eph. 1:10.

133. [*Ed.*] See *Werke* text, 1827 lectures, n. 544.

RELATING TO HEGEL'S
LECTURE MANUSCRIPT[1]

[156a]
Roman religion – of expediency
Necessity passes over into concept – [to the] subjective [concept] – particular
content
Oracles are not a [form of] cultus – they have particular subjectivity for
their content
God comprehended, grasped, as expediency according to specific finite
purposes – purposes of human beings
With the Romans this the main purpose – Etruria – *haruspex*, soothsayer,
Sibylline Books – Pontifex – popular assemblies – *fasti* and *nefasti dies*
On occasion of Thucydides' plague Greeks introduced no particular new
religion[2]
Oedipus of Sophocles[3] – plague – at that time pray to Apollo
Melampus introduced particular rite to Greece[4]
Roman gods created out of a need
Lectisternia – where the purpose is finite – [to resist] the enemy or what
restrains

1. [*Ed.*] These sheets are from the literary estate of Karl Rosenkranz, now deposited
in Houghton Library of Harvard University. For further information, see the Editorial
Introduction to Vol. 3, pp. 6–7. The sheets printed in this volume contain preparatory
materials for Hegel's discussion of Greek and especially Roman religion in the *Ms.;*
they are interspersed with sheets containing similar materials on the Christian religion,
which are printed as an appendix to Vol. 3.
2. [*Ed.*] See *Ms.*, n. 259, and 1824 lectures, n. 686.
3. [*Ed.*] Sophocles, *Oedipus Rex,* prologue, vv. 1–150.
4. [*Ed.*] Hegel is referring to Herodotus, *Histories* 2.49. The "particular rite" was
the festival of Dionysus, together with the accompanying procession bearing a phallic
image.

[Being] on one's own account [means] offering resistance
Hunger [is the god] Fames, [and there are gods called] Febris,
Cloacina
Sibylline books
Innumerable festivals [dedicated] to the emperors – to make them *divi*
Where there is consensus about expediency new gods and new [forms of]
worship [are] continually [introduced]
For finite purposes are of themselves mutable – they may be forwarded [or]
they may not
Gods for finite purposes prove themselves impotent, ineffective
Russians beat their saints, throw them into the fire and replace them by others[5]
Just as the Greeks created theoretical [gods] – works of art – so the Romans
[created] practical gods or gods for practical life [*Praxis*]
Compare Roman expediency with the People of God – [whose purpose was
the] dissemination of his name
   (α) Human purpose, requirement, need or happiness not natural
     – this [human concern is] the content and genesis of expediency
644   – not free power or beauty |
     [The divine] powers [are] free, not a particular purpose on its own
     account, surrender it in necessity
   (β) Negatively – [in] hostile [situation] – to get something or protect
     oneself against something – selfishness – fear
Cultus identical

[157a]
Mystical worship – universal intuition (and setting in motion) of what is
within
Many essentialities in one – presentiment
   (α) Not as purpose – with the [Greek] gods – [or with] oracles
For human beings their particular destiny is their purpose
Not a [divine] purpose, not wisdom – though it may be justice
Human beings could [believe] in these gods
Unveiling of what repels the individual
In other respects contains everything – revelatory – [shows it] forth
Out of all this:
   (α) Expediency of finite purposes – have to be sought in the world, in
     the natural and spiritual world

5. [*Ed.*] Hegel's source has not been identified, but there is a similar report in a
book from which he is known to have made extracts (cf. *Berliner Schriften*, pp.
717–718), namely, C.-F. P. Masson, *Mémoires secrets sur la Russie*, vol. 2 (Paris,
1800), pp. 98–100, where, following a description of the so-called "pocket deities,"
it is said that a princess heaped reproaches and insults upon her crucifix when things
went badly.

(β) In the spiritual world [there is] infinite purpose; all that remains for subjectivity are the natural, finite purposes – subjective too, but subordinate –
as finite purposes, subordinate [to] the purpose that is in and for itself

Thought (α) chance, not cause, external necessity
  (β) but a purposive connection – in opposition to [something] – an external connection
  (γ) [one that is] in itself, i.e., an inward [connection]

Categories for nature
  (α) External necessity, cause and effect
  (β) Contingent external connection, and yet unity

[What is] right or just is a formal purpose

Expediency in natural things – psychological proof of the existence of God[6]

Concordance of independent, [mutually] indifferent [forms of] determinate being – to the extent that one [such form] is used as means – utility

External purposiveness [is] a tertium quid – the understanding

Presupposition of their independent existence – only sides of a relationship

Foundation, manifoldness devoid of unity | 645

All bonding [seen] as external, as not the nature of the thing – on the contrary, plurality [is] the nature of the thing

Psychological forces – equally striking here – the nature of the thing is here the ego, the unity that I am

For admittedly unity is putting in order – externally

As if God were not needed for what is the nature of the thing

Mountains, sea – inorganic unities

Life, self-directed purpose the organization of a life –

Edifying considerations – theoretical

Disposed in a merely marginal, subordinate position, subordinated to an absolute purpose – felicity.

Finite purpose, so that the basic categorial determination of religion is the highest of finite human purposes – the state
  Cultus one with the objective category
  Need, requirement determines the object
  "From thy πάθεσι" – here [becomes] "From thy needs"[7]

[156b]
  Religion of the understanding
  (α) Hard-and-fast determinacy
  (α) Necessity – freedom, concept, expediency –

6. [Ed.] See Ms., n. 251.
7. [Ed.] See Ms., n. 150.

Without purpose, not wisdom – [here means] surrender of all
purposes
Necessity involves mediation in general, determinacy – but in pure
necessity as such [determinacy is present] only as disappearing – in other words it is so, this event has occurred – so even
in terms of its content it exists as a contingent [determinacy].
Formal process of necessity – to hold fast just to the abstract
alone
[There is here] a sense of depth, once the concept is a content that
maintains itself against the passing over
Form of the purposive category – not something lacking ground,
the coming forth of an other, but determined in advance
"Conceived" [means] to see something as [one] moment of a coherent
whole – formally – [in terms of] cause and effect, even external
necessity – but [the necessity] of a coherence whose inner substance

646   is something determinate in and for itself, something primary. |
What purpose still unspecified –
Necessity degraded to the level of form
(β) Character, determinacy of the gods
Justice, virtue in Hercules – passed over from humanity to Olympus
Human virtue not defined as purpose – [that] is a Christian way of
representing it – [it] is a universal purpose – [we are] not yet [at
that point]
(β) Separation of purpose and reality – purpose as power over reality –
negative definition
Spiritual shape – comes close to purpose – but not the understanding – beauty
[does] not [see] separation impending –
In life and the ideal – to build many definitions – this purposiveness [is]
unity of the concept and reality
(γ) Finite purpose – initially the purpose itself [is] formal but [it is] *one*
purpose – the Roman republic – the state
(Not the infinite purpose with individuals)
(α) However, human beings [are] not means – immanent forces – do it
themselves –
(β) Not in opposition to one another

[157b]
Prosaic religion. Moritz[8]
Boxers and wrestlers – p. 92 – no tragedies – behind the wings returns to
life – but [there is] a veritable life-and-death struggle

8. [*Ed.*] Hegel bases his interpretation of Roman religion as a prosaic religion on
detailed information provided by Karl Philipp Moritz, *Anthousa; oder, Roms
Alterthümer* (Berlin, 1791). Although in what follows he refers solely to this work
and uses virtually no other source for the 1821 lectures, his interpretation is directly

[In Greek religion] ethical drama – here only ugly [drama] and actuality
Singing songs of praise p. 93
Cereals in Greek religion – very many other peoples too
P. 100 they had the aged Ceres brought from Enna in an emergency
Similarly the aged mother of the gods from Pergamus
A succession of sacrificial animals
Jupiter Pistor p. 147 – Stator p. 168
Not produce beautiful images themselves – mainly statues of individuals
P. 101 cow in calf – reconciling the earth
P. 103 Palilia goddess of cattle fodder
[P.] 109 [festival] of Robigo, wheat rust, a terrifying being
Flora – Lares – Manes
P. 124 merchants, have their wares blessed | 647
Fortuna Publica p. 126
Juno Moneta 129 – muliebris 177, virilis, fortis 167 – Lares – Manius
Goddess Carna
Ara Tranquillitatis Ventorum
No oracles
Mundus patens 200
Patriotic festivals, one after another
Sibyls p. 276
Ops consiva 203 – the day after Mundus patens
Opalia p. 252
Sancus 136
Occasion [for festivals] in every case a completely prosaic Roman event
Abstracta – Saturn
(α) Patriotic festivals
(β) Trade and fertility festivals, Ambarvilia p. 164. – The thirty curias
    p. 101 celebrated the Fordicidia, each one separately – cow in calf
(γ) Festivals on the occasion of an emergency
(δ) Festivals of abasement
Temple of Saturn [was] the treasury
P. 229. The masters waited on the servants
Gifts a serious matter – Martial p. 235
Pliny removes himself 237 so as not to embarrass his slaves
Angerona p. 253 troubles and woes
Mania 255

---

opposed to that of Moritz, who indicates in his preface (p. vii) that he understands
the sacred practices and festivals of the Romans to be the expression of a "religion
of phantasy," and indeed of the "consecration of ordinary life." Virtually every line
of what follows can be referenced to passages in Moritz's work. The German edition
provides such references, but we have omitted them, referring the reader instead to
the corresponding materials in the *Ms.* (see above, pp. 206–219), where Hegel's
interpretation is set forth quite clearly and his use of Moritz is annotated.

Festival of Mens 137
– of Vacuna or leisure 145
– Jupiter Pistor 147
– Fornax 146
Pluto and Proserpine
[P.] 287 for being saved from the plague
Circumstances (α) Purpose; the state

[162a]
(β) The most finite religion
The human taken seriously; principle of immediate pr nce,
648   Emperor power for worldly purposes |

[163b]
Prose – negative states of affairs, for us – the negative or concrete is only
    a state of affairs – allegorical essences, pertaining to reflection – fever,
    plague, hunger – having no inner substantiality or universality – [mere]
    circumstances – is not easy to comprehend
Superstition, magic-working, miracles – their belief [was] in finite things
    taken in isolation – as absolute
Important link in the transition [to Christianity] – [God represented] con-
    cretely – [as] finite, immediate actuality
Revering the devil, from a feeling of dependence
Worshiping the emperor, an actual human being, as God – a cause of situa-
    tions far more malign than fever or pestilence – [he is] lord over hunger,
    [and] immediately over life – revered the devil – in this [we see] the feeling
    of dependence at its strongest[9]
The categories of the concretely finite – concrete purpose – developed into
    immediate actuality
Transition to Christian religion
Intermediate link (α) Purpose, a concrete categorial determination
                     (β) Immediate actuality and singularity – spirit driven
                         back into itself
Spectacles – murders

9. [Ed.] An allusion to Schleiermacher. On its significance, and especially Hegel's
attempt to link devil worship with "the feeling of dependence," see Ms., n. 292. See
also the excerpt found in Berliner Schriften, p. 708: "Febris [fever], Pestis [pestilence],
and Cloacina [purifier, from cloaca, sewer] were deities for them. – From this it is
a short step to the devil. – These are mere physical devilments – if we raise them
to the spiritual plane, then we have devils." Hegel's point seems to be that it is bad
enough to venerate malignant physical powers, but it is even worse to worship the
emperor. The latter is the strongest case of the feeling of dependence—but this is
a somewhat different point from the one made in the Ms.

TI ̃ ORIGINAL SOURCES
FOR THIS EDITION

HEGEL'S LECTURE MANUSCRIPT

The *Ms.* numbers ("a" = recto, "b" = verso) are given in the text in square brackets but are reproduced here for the sake of convenience.

THE LECTURES OF 1824

The pagination given here is that of the Griesheim transcript. While our basic text is *G*, it has been supplemented and corrected by *P* and *D*, which are not noted either in the text itself (except where there is an uncertainty about the reading) or in this listing.

THE LECTURES OF 1827

The pagination given here is that of the Lasson edition. When Lasson's text has been supplemented or replaced by two or more sentences from one of the extant sources (*An, B, Hu*), this is noted in the following list by the symbol "Q" (meaning *Quelle,* source). Commas indicate breaks in Lasson's text.

*THE TELEOLOGICAL PROOF ACCORDING TO
THE LECTURES OF 1831*

SPECIAL MATERIALS FROM THE WERKE

Page numbers of passages from the *Werke* are correlated with the numbers of the footnotes containing these passages. Footnotes are numbered consecutively through each lecture series. The first right-hand column lists W_1 volume and page numbers; the second column lists W_2 volume and page numbers.

Hegel's Lecture Manuscript

n. 16	11:255–256	n. 119	12:114
n. 44	11:226–233	n. 120	12:120
n. 55	11:380	n. 121	12:120–121
n. 57	12:11	n. 122	12:121
n. 58	12:11	n. 123	12:121
n. 59	12:11	n. 124	12:121
n. 60	12:11	n. 125	12:121–122
n. 62	12:12	n. 126	12:122–123
n. 64	12:12	n. 127	12:123
n. 65	12:5	n. 128	12:123
n. 66	12:19	n. 129	12:123
n. 68	12:44	n. 130	12:125–126
n. 71	12:43	n. 131	12:123
n. 74	12:15	n. 133	12:78–79
n. 77	12:15	n. 134	12:80–81
n. 78	12:15–16	n. 139	12:84–85
n. 84	12:16–17	n. 140	12:90
n. 85	12:17	n. 142	12:85–86
n. 86	12:17–18	n. 144	12:91
n. 92	12:56–57	n. 146	12:111
n. 94	12:57	n. 148	12:112
n. 95	12:57	n. 149	12:112
n. 100	12:56	n. 153	12:94–95
n. 101 ·	12:50	n. 154	12:94
n. 102	12:57	n. 156	12:129
n. 103	12:57	n. 158	12:129
n. 104	12:57	n. 160	12:129–130
n. 114	12:109–110	n. 162	12:130
n. 116	12:113	n. 163	12:130
n. 117	12:113	n. 165	12:130–131
n. 118	12:113	n. 167	12:139

n. 168	12:136	n. 318		12:183
n. 169	12:137	n. 320		12:184
n. 170	12:137	n. 322		12:184
n. 171	12:139–140	n. 325		12:185
n. 172	12:140	n. 326		12:185
n. 176	12:139	n. 329		12:187
n. 177	12:140	n. 330		12:187
n. 178	12:140	n. 332		12:187
n. 179	12:141	n. 333		12:188
n. 180	12:137	n. 334		12:188
n. 183	12:148			
n. 184	12:148	*The Lectures of 1824*		
n. 185	12:148–149	n. 4	11:42–43	11:78–80
n. 191	12:150	n. 6	11:185	
n. 194	12:150	n. 9	11:185	11:260
n. 195	12:150	n. 10	11:185–186	11:260
n. 196	12:150	n. 11	11:186–187	11:261
n. 197	12:150	n. 12	11:187	11:261
n. 198	12:152	n. 13	11:188	11:262
n. 203	12:144	n. 16		11:264
n. 204	12:142	n. 17		11:264
n. 208	12:144	n. 18		11:264
n. 209	12:145	n. 20		11:265
n. 210	12:145	n. 22		11:265
n. 211	12:145	n. 24		11:265
n. 212	12:145	n. 26		11:265–266
n. 230	12:158	n. 29	11:191	11:266
n. 231	12:158	n. 30		11:266–267
n. 234	12:160	n. 31	11:192	11:267
n. 235	12:160	n. 34		11:271–272
n. 255 12:137	12:170	n. 36	11:196	11:272
n. 271	12:176–177	n. 39	11:197	11:274
n. 290	12:172	n. 40	11:197	11:274
n. 296	12:173	n. 41	11:197–198	11:274
n. 297	12:176	n. 43	11:198	11:275
n. 299	12:179	n. 44		11:277
n. 300	12:179	n. 45	11:201	11:277
n. 301	12:179	n. 48		11:278
n. 306	12:174	n. 49		11:279
n. 307	12:174	n. 51		11:279
n. 312	12:182	n. 52	11:203	
n. 314	12:182	n. 54	11:203	11:312
n. 316	12:183	n. 55	11:204	11:312

n. 57	11:205–206	11:314	n. 136		11:293
n. 58		11:314	n. 137	11:230	11:293
n. 59	11:206	11:315	n. 140	11:231	11:294
n. 62	11:207	11:315	n. 141	11:231	11:294
n. 63	11:207–208	11:316–317	n. 144	11:232	11:295
n. 64	11:208	11:317	n. 147	11:234	11:297
n. 67	11:208	11:318	n. 148	11:234	11:297
n. 68	11:209	11:318	n. 149	11:234	11:297
n. 69	11:210	11:319	n. 151	11:236	11:299
n. 70	11:210	11:319	n. 152	11:236	11:299
n. 71	11:210	11:319	n. 153		11:300
n. 72	11:210	11:319	n. 154	11:237	11:300
n. 74	11:210	11:319	n. 155	11:237	11:300
n. 75	11:210		n. 156	11:237	11:301
n. 76	11:211	11:323–324	n. 158	11:237	11:301
n. 78	11:211	11:324	n. 159	11:239	11:303
n. 79	11:211	11:324	n. 161	11:241	11:304
n. 81	11:212	11:325	n. 162	11:241	11:305
n. 82	11:212	11:325–326	n. 165		11:306
n. 83	11:212		n. 166	11:243	11:306
n. 84	11:212	11:319	n. 167	11:243	11:306
n. 85	11:212	11:319	n. 171		11:307
n. 87	11:213	11:320	n. 174		11:332
n. 90		11:322–323	n. 175	11:249	11:332
n. 93	11:215		n. 176		11:333
n. 96		11:283	n. 177	11:250	11:333
n. 98	11:217		n. 178	11:250	11:333
n. 100	11:217–218		n. 180		11:333
n. 101	11:218		n. 184	11:254	
n. 103	11:218		n. 185	11:254	11:385
n. 105	11:218		n. 186	11:254	11:385
n. 106		11:281	n. 187		11:385
n. 109	11:223	11:286	n. 188		11:385–386
n. 113	11:224	11:287	n. 191	11:255	
n. 114	11:224	11:287	n. 197	11:271	
n. 119		11:289	n. 198	11:272	
n. 125	11:227	11:290	n. 199	11:272	11:394
n. 127	11:228	11:291	n. 200		11:386
n. 128	11:228	11:291	n. 204		11:401
n. 130	11:228	11:291–292	n. 206	11:273–274	11:400
n. 131	11:229	11:292	n. 207		11:400
n. 132	11:229	11:292	n. 208		11:400
n. 133	11:230	11:293	n. 211		11:400

n. 400	12:36	12:43	n. 464		12:28
n. 401		12:44	n. 467		12:29
n. 402	12:37	12:45	n. 468	12:23	12:30
n. 403	12:37		n. 469		12:30
n. 404	12:37	12:45	n. 471		12:31
n. 405		12:45	n. 472		12:31
n. 406	12:38	12:45	n. 473	12:25	12:31
n. 407	12:38	12:45–46	n. 475		12:32
n. 408		12:46	n. 476		12:32
n. 412		12:11	n. 478		12:33
n. 414	12:11	12:12	n. 479		12:33
n. 415		12:13	n. 481		12:33
n. 416		12:13	n. 482		12:33
n. 417	12:12	12:13–14	n. 483		12:34
n. 418		12:14	n. 485	12:27	12:34
n. 422	12:13		n. 486	12:28	12:34
n. 423	12:13	12:18	n. 488		12:35
n. 424		12:18	n. 490	12:29	12:36
n. 425		12:18	n. 491	12:29	12:36
n. 429		12:20	n. 494		12:36
n. 430		12:20	n. 497		12:36
n. 437		12:22	n. 499		12:37
n. 439		12:22	n. 500		12:37
n. 440		12:22	n. 502		12:38
n. 441	12:17	12:22	n. 503	12:31	12:38
n. 443	12:17	12:23	n. 505	12:33	12:39
n. 445		12:23	n. 507		12:41
n. 446		12:23	n. 508	12:41	
n. 447		12:23	n. 511	12:41	12:49
n. 448		12:23	n. 513	12:42	12:49
n. 449		12:23–24	n. 515	12:42	12:49
n. 450		12:24	n. 516		12:49
n. 451	12:18	12:24	n. 517		12:50
n. 454	12:20	12:26	n. 519	12:44	12:52
n. 455	12:20	12:26	n. 520		12:53
n. 456	12:20	12:26	n. 523	12:43	12:51
n. 457		12:26	n. 525		12:59
n. 458		12:27	n. 530		12:60
n. 459		12:27	n. 531		12:60–61
n. 460		12:27	n. 532	12:52	
n. 461		12:27	n. 537		12:69
n. 462		12:27	n. 538	12:60	12:70
n. 463		12:28	n. 539	12:60	12:70

n. 540		12:71	n. 613	12:115
n. 541	12:62–67	12:71–77	n. 614	12:115
n. 542		12:77	n. 615	12:115
n. 545		12:77	n. 616	12:117
n. 546	12:67	12:79	n. 617	12:117
n. 547	12:67	12:79	n. 618	12:117
n. 553	12:68–69	12:79–80	n. 620	12:117–118
n. 555		12:80	n. 624	12:124
n. 556	12:57	12:67	n. 625	12:124
n. 557	12:57	12:67	n. 627 12:104–105	12:125
n. 559	12:72	12:86	n. 628 12:105	
n. 560	12:73	12:86	n. 629 12:105	
n. 561	12:73	12:87	n. 632 12:107	12:126
n. 562		12:87	n. 634	12:126
n. 564		12:87	n. 635 12:109	12:127
n. 565		12:88	n. 636 12:109	12:127
n. 566		12:88	n. 637 12:109	12:127–128
n. 568	12:76		n. 638 12:109	12:128
n. 569	12:76	12:91	n. 639 12:109–110	12:128
n. 570		12:91	n. 643	12:132
n. 571	12:76		n. 644	12:136
n. 572	12:75–76,	12:89–90	n. 645	12:136
	77–79	11:418–421	n. 648 12:118	12:141
n. 574	12:79–82	12:91–95	n. 649 12:118	12:141
n. 575	12:82	12:96	n. 653 12:119	
n. 576		12:96	n. 654	12:144
n. 577	12:83	12:96–97	n. 655	12:144
n. 582	12:88		n. 656 12:120	
n. 583	12:88		n. 658	12:146
n. 584	12:88		n. 659 12:121	12:146
n. 585	12:88		n. 660 12:121	12:146
n. 586	12:88		n. 663 12:121	12:146
n. 587	12:88		n. 664	12:146
n. 588		12:104	n. 666 12:121–122	12:146–147
n. 589	12:86–88	12:99–102	n. 667 12:122	12:147
n. 597	12:91	12:105	n. 668	12:148
n. 601	12:94	12:108	n. 669 12:123	
n. 602	12:94–95	12:108–109	n. 671 12:123	
n. 605		12:109	n. 673 12:124–125	12:154
n. 606		12:109	n. 674	12:151
n. 609		12:114–115	n. 676	12:153
n. 611		12:115	n. 677 12:125	12:153
n. 612		12:115	n. 679	12:153

n. 680		12:153	n. 59		11:282
n. 681	12:126	12:154	n. 60	11:220	11:282
n. 683		12:155	n. 61	11:220	
n. 684	12:127	12:155	n. 64		11:284
n. 685		12:155	n. 65	11:221	11:284
n. 687	12:127	12:155	n. 66		11:284
n. 688	12:127	12:155	n. 69	11:221	11:284
n. 689		12:155	n. 70	11:221	11:284
n. 700	12:147–148	12:186	n. 71	11:222	11:284
n. 705		12:163–164	n. 72	11:222	11:285
n. 706	12:131	12:164	n. 74	11:222	11:285
n. 707		12:164	n. 75	11:222	11:285
n. 708	12:123	12:164	n. 76		11:285
n. 724		12:176	n. 92	11:237	11:300
n. 726		12:178	n. 94	11:237	11:301
n. 729		12:183	n. 95	11:237	11:301
n. 730		12:184	n. 100		11:326–327

The Lectures of 1827

			n. 101	11:245	11:327
n. 3	11:183–185	11:255–257	n. 102		11:327
n. 5		11:257–259	n. 104		11:327
n. 7	11:189	11:263	n. 105		11:327–328
n. 9		11:263	n. 106	11:245–249	11:328–331
n. 12	11:189	11:263	n. 113		11:333–334
n. 13	11:189	11:263–264	n. 118	11:256	11:335
n. 18		11:260–261	n. 123		11:336
n. 24	11:198–199	11:275–276	n. 127		11:336
n. 28		11:268	n. 132		11:337
n. 29		11:268	n. 134		11:338
n. 34		11:270	n. 135		11:338
n. 35		11:270	n. 137		11:338
n. 36		11:270	n. 139		11:384–385
n. 37		11:270	n. 140	11:259	
n. 40	11:195	11:271	n. 141		11:395
n. 41	11:195	11:271	n. 143		11:397
n. 43	11:201–202	11:278	n. 146		11:386–387
n. 44	11:216	11:279	n. 147	11:261	11:396
n. 45		11:280	n. 148	11:261	11:396–397
n. 49		11:308–311	n. 149	11:261	11:397
n. 53	11:219		n. 151	11:261–263	11:397
n. 54		11:280–281	n. 152	11:263	11:398
n. 55	11:219	11:282	n. 154	11:263	11:387
n. 58		11:281–282	n. 155		11:387
			n. 156	11:264	11:398

n. 157	11:264	11:398		n. 227	11:301	11:362
n. 158	11:264	11:398		n. 229	11:301	11:362
n. 160		11:388		n. 234	11:300–301	11:361–362
n. 161	11:266	11:388		n. 235	11:305	
n. 162	11:266	11:389		n. 239	11:306	11:370
n. 165	11:267	11:389		n. 241	11:309	
n. 166	11:268	11:390		n. 244	11:306–309	11:371–373
n. 168		11:391		n. 247		11:381
n. 170	11:268	11:391		n. 248		11:382
n. 173		11:391		n. 251		11:383
n. 175	11:269	11:391		n. 252		11:383
n. 179		11:392		n. 256		11:401–403
n. 182	11:270	11:393		n. 257		11:403
n. 184	11:271	11:394		n. 259	11:327	11:403
n. 186	11:271	11:394		n. 260		11:403
n. 187	11:259	11:393		n. 261	11:327	11:404
n. 189	11:260			n. 262		11:404
n. 190	11:259–260			n. 263	11:328	11:404
n. 191		11:396		n. 264		11:404
n. 193		11:339–341		n. 266		11:404–406
n. 194	11:285–286	11:349–350		n. 267		11:406
n. 195	11:287	11:342		n. 270		11:406
n. 196		11:342		n. 272		11:407
n. 197	11:287			n. 273		11:407
n. 198	11:287			n. 274		11:408–409
n. 199	11:288			n. 279	11:333–334	11:410
n. 201	11:289			n. 280	11:334	11:410
n. 205	11:290	11:350		n. 281	11:336–337	11:412
n. 207	11:290–291	11:351		n. 282	11:335	11:411
n. 208	11:291	11:351–352		n. 283	11:335	11:411
n. 209	11:291	11:352		n. 284	11:337–339	11:413–415
n. 210		11:352		n. 289	11:341	11:416–417
n. 211	11:292	11:352		n. 290		11:417
n. 214	11:292			n. 291	11:342	11:418
n. 217	11:293–295	11:353–355		n. 292	11:342	11:418
n. 218	11:298	11:359		n. 293	11:342	11:418
n. 219	11:299	11:359		n. 296	11:342	11:421
n. 220	11:299	11:359		n. 297		11:422
n. 221	11:299	11:359–360		n. 298	11:343	11:422–423
n. 222	11:299	11:360		n. 301	11:352	11:431
n. 223		11:361		n. 303	11:353	11:432
n. 224	11:300	11:361		n. 304	11:353	11:432–433
n. 226	11:301	11:362		n. 305	11:353	11:433

n. 306	11:353	11:433	n. 384	12:95	12:109
n. 307	11:353	11:433	n. 385	12:96	12:111
n. 308	11:353	11:433	n. 386		12:111
n. 311	11:354	11:433	n. 387		12:111
n. 314	11:354	11:433	n. 388		12:112–113
n. 315	11:354	11:434	n. 389	12:97	12:113
n. 318		11:435–436	n. 390	12:97	
n. 321	11:355	11:436	n. 391		12:113
n. 322	11:355	11:436	n. 392		12:113–114
n. 324	11:356	11:437	n. 393		12:116
n. 325	11:356	11:437	n. 394	12:97	
n. 326		11:437	n. 395	12:97	
n. 328	11:359	11:438	n. 396	12:99	
n. 329	11:359–360	11:438–440	n. 399	12:99	
n. 330	11:361	11:440	n. 401		12:116
n. 331		11:440–441	n. 402		12:117
n. 332		11:441	n. 403	12:100	
n. 335	11:363	11:442	n. 404		12:118
n. 337	11:363	11:442	n. 405		12:118–119
n. 338		11:443	n. 408	12:101	
n. 339	11:364–368	11:444–448	n. 409		12:119
n. 341	11:374–375	11:454–456	n. 411		12:120
n. 343	11:376		n. 412	12:102–106	12:123–125
n. 344		11:455–456	n. 413	12:103	
n. 346		11:456	n. 414	12:103	
n. 348	12:3	12:3–4	n. 415	12:103	
n. 349		12:4	n. 416	12:103	12:122
n. 350	12:37	12:44	n. 417	12:103	12:122
n. 351	12:36	12:43	n. 419	12:107–108	
n. 352	12:36	12:43	n. 420	12:108–109	12:127
n. 355		12:99	n. 423		12:131
n. 356	12:85	12:99	n. 424	12:110	
n. 358	12:89	12:101	n. 426	12:110	
n. 359		12:102	n. 427	12:110	
n. 360		12:102–103	n. 428	12:113	12:133
n. 361	12:90	12:103	n. 430	12:114	12:134
n. 365	12:91	12:105	n. 431		12:134–135
n. 368	12:91–92	12:105	n. 434	12:115	12:135
n. 371	12:92	12:106	n. 437	12:116	
n. 374		12:106	n. 439	12:39	12:46
n. 375	12:92–93	12:106–107	n. 440	12:39	12:47
n. 379	12:93	12:107	n. 441	12:39	12:47
n. 381	12:94	12:108	n. 442	12:39–40	12:47

n. 443	12:40	12:47	n. 501	12:130	
n. 444		12:47	n. 502		12:161
n. 446	12:40	12:48	n. 503	12:130	
n. 447	12:40	12:48	n. 504	12:130	
n. 448	12:40	12:48	n. 505	12:130	
n. 449	12:40–41	12:48	n. 506	12:130	
n. 450	12:42–43	12:50–51	n. 507	12:131	
n. 451	12:43	12:51	n. 508	12:131	
n. 452	12:43	12:51	n. 509	12:133	12:165
n. 453	12:43	12:51	n. 510		12:165
n. 454	12:43	12:51	n. 511	12:135	
n. 455	12:43	12:51	n. 512	12:135	12:168
n. 457		12:51–52	n. 513	12:135	12:168
n. 458	12:44	12:52	n. 514		12:168
n. 459	12:44	12:52	n. 515	12:136	12:168
n. 460	12:44	12:52	n. 517	12:136	12:169
n. 461	12:44	12:52	n. 519	12:137	12:169
n. 462	12:46	12:54	n. 521	12:139	12:172
n. 464	12:46	12:54	n. 522	12:139	12:172
n. 468	12:47	12:55	n. 523	12:139	12:172
n. 470		12:60	n. 524	12:139	12:172
n. 472	12:50	12:61	n. 525	12:139–140	
n. 473	12:50	12:61	n. 527		12:175
n. 474		12:61–62	n. 528	12:141	
n. 478		12:64	n. 529	12:141	12:175
n. 479	12:55	12:65	n. 530	12:141	12:175
n. 480		12:65	n. 531	12:142	12:177
n. 481		12:66	n. 533	12:142	12:177
n. 483	12:56	12:66	n. 534	12:142	12:177
n. 484	12:57	12:66	n. 535		12:177
n. 485	12:57	12:66	n. 536	12:142	12:177
n. 486	12:57	12:66	n. 537	12:142	12:177
n. 488	12:57–58	12:67	n. 538	12:142	12:177
n. 489	12:58	12:67	n. 539		12:180–181
n. 491	12:58	12:68	n. 540	12:144	
n. 492	12:69–72	12:81–86	n. 541	12:145	12:181
n. 497	12:129	12:157	n. 542	12:145	12:181
n. 498		12:157	n. 543	12:145	12:181
n. 499		12:157–158	n. 544	12:148	12:186–187
n. 500	12:129				

BIBLIOGRAPHY OF SOURCES
FOR HEGEL'S PHILOSOPHY
OF RELIGION

This bibliography includes all of the sources to which Hegel explicitly makes reference in the *Lectures on the Philosophy of Religion* or which can be inferred with reasonable certainty from his formulations. Works cited in the footnotes as evidence for ideas contained in the lectures, but which cannot be established as sources upon which Hegel himself drew, are not included in the bibliography.

In the footnotes, works are frequently cited in abbreviated form, without full bibliographical information. In cases where a short title is not immediately recognizable from this bibliography, it is so designated in parentheses following the full title. Frequently cited works by Hegel are listed at the beginning of this volume.

With respect to classical authors, the bibliography does not list specific works—e.g., individual tragedies of Aeschylus or dialogues of Plato—but rather editions with which Hegel is likely to have been familiar. In the footnotes, classical works are cited in the abbreviated short form customary today, followed by book, chapter, and section references, but without indicating the editions that Hegel himself used or modern editions. Works with both Greek and Latin titles are cited only with the Latin title.

The sources given in this bibliography fall into four groups:
- Works listed in the Auction Catalogue of Hegel's Library are designated by an asterisk (*).
- Works to which Hegel refers in these lectures or elsewhere, and which he almost certainly made use of, are designated by a dagger (†).

– Works probably used by Hegel, but for which there are no explicit references, are listed without a sign.

– Modern editions or English translations to which reference is made in the footnotes are indented following the original entries. Otherwise modern editions are not included.

Abel-Rémusat, Jean Pierre. *Mémoires sur la vie et les opinions de Lao-Tseu.* Paris, 1823.

* ———. *Observations sur quelques points de la doctrine samanéenne, et en particulier sur les noms de la triade suprême chez les différens peuples buddhistes.* Paris, 1831.

Aeschylus. *Tragoediae.* Edited in accordance with the Glasgow transcript. Leipzig, 1812.

Allgemeine Historie der Reisen zu Wasser und zu Lande; oder, Sammlung aller Reisebeschreibungen. Vols. 6 and 7. Leipzig, 1750.

Amherst. "Gesandschaftsreise nach und durch China." In Harnisch, *Die wichtigsten Reisen 5* (Leipzig, 1824). *See* Harnisch.

Ammianus Marcellinus. *Rerum gestarum qui de XXXI supersunt libri XVIII ad optimas editiones collati.* With introduction and appendixes prepared under the auspices of the Zweibrücken Society. Zweibrücken, 1786.

Anakreons und Sapphos Lieder nebst andern lyrischen Gedichten. Edited and translated by J. F. Degen. 2d ed. Leipzig, 1821.

Anselm of Canterbury. *Opera.* 2d ed. Paris, 1721.

———. *Proslogium; Monologium; An Appendix, In Behalf of the Fool, by Gaunilon; and Cur Deus Homo.* Translated by S. N. Deane. Chicago, 1903.

* Aristophanes. *Comoediae undecim.* Basel, 1532.

* Aristotle. *Opera quaecunque hactenus extiterunt omnia.* Edited by Desiderius Erasmus. 2 vols. in 1. Basel, 1550. (Hegel owned the edition of 1531.)

* ———. *Metaphysik.* Translated by E. W. Hengstenberg. Edited by C. A. Brandis. Vol. 1. Bonn, 1824.

* ———. *Physik.* Translated and edited by C. H. Weisse. Leipzig, 1829.

* ————. *Von der Seele und von der Welt.* Edited and translated by C. H. Weisse. Leipzig, 1829.

* Arrian. *Expeditio Alexandris.* Stereotype ed. Edited in accordance with the best manuscripts. Leipzig, 1818.

Asiatic Researches; or, Transactions of the Society Instituted in Bengal for Inquiring into the History and Antiquities, the Arts, Sciences, and Literature, of Asia. Vols. 1–11. London, 1806–1812. (Reprint of the Calcutta edition, 1788 ff.)

Bailly, Jean Sylvain. *Histoire de l'astronomie ancienne, depuis son origine jusqu'à l'établissement de l'école d'Alexandrie.* 2d ed. Paris, 1781.

* Baumgarten, Alexander Gottlieb. *Metaphysik.* 2d ed. Halle, 1783.

* Bekker, Georgius Josephus. *Specimen variarum lectionum et observationum in Philostrati vitae Apollonii librum primum.* Additional notes by F. Creuzer. Heidelberg, 1818.

Belzoni, Giovanni Battista. *Narrative of the Operations and Recent Discoveries within the Pyramids, Temples, Tombs, and Excavations, in Egypt and Nubia; and of a Journey to the Coast of the Red Sea, in Search of the Ancient Berenice; and Another to the Oasis of Jupiter Ammon.* 3d ed. 2 vols. London, 1822.

† *The Bhagavat-Geeta; or, Dialogues of Kreeshna and Arjoon, in Eighteen Lectures, with Notes: Translated from the Original, in the Sanskreet, or Ancient Language of the Brahmans.* London, 1785.

† *Bhagavad-Gita, id est* Θεσπέσιον Μέλος; *sive, Almi Krishnae et Arjunae colloquium de rebus divinis, Bharateae episodium.* Edited, with critical commentary and Latin translation, by A. W. von Schlegel. Bonn, 1823.

* Boehme, Jacob. *Theosophia revelata; Das ist, Alle göttliche Schriften des gottseligen and hocherleuchteten deutschen Theosophi.* 1715.

* Bohlen, P. von. *Das alte Indien mit besonderer Rücksicht auf Aegypten.* 2 vols. Königsberg, 1830.

† Bopp, Franz. *Ueber das Conjugationssystem der Sanskritsprache in Vergleichung mit jenem der griechischen, lateinischen, persischen und germanischen Sprache.* Together with episodes of the Rāmāyana and the Mahābhārata in exact metrical translations from the original text and selections from the Vedas. Edited by K. J. Windischmann. Frankfurt am Main, 1816.

* ———, ed. and trans. *Ardschuna's Reise zu Indra's Himmel, nebst anderen Episoden des Mahā-Bhārata.* Edited for the first time in the original language, translated metrically, and provided with critical notes. Berlin, 1824.

———, ed. and trans. *Nalus: Carmen Sanscritum e Mahābhārato.* With Latin translation and annotations. London, Paris, Strasbourg, 1819.

* ———, trans. *Die Sündflut nebst drei anderen der wichtigsten Episoden des Mahā-Bhārata.* Translated from the original. Berlin, 1829.

† Bouterwek, Friedrich. *Idee einer Apodiktik: Ein Beytrag zur menschlichen Selbstverständigung und zur Entscheidung des Streites über Metaphysik, kritische Philosophie und Skepticismus.* 2 vols. Halle, 1799.

Bowdich, T. Edward. *Mission from Cape Coast Castle to Ashantee, with a Statistical Account of That Kingdom, and Geographical Notices of Other Parts of the Interior of Africa.* London, 1819.

† Brandis, Christian August. *Xenophanis Parmenidis et Melissi doctrina e propriis philosophorum reliquiis veterumque auctorum testimoniis exposita.* Altona, 1813.

* Brown[e], [James]. *Aperçu sur les hiéroglyphes d'Égypte et les progrès faits jusqu'à présent dans leur déchiffrement.* Translated from English. With a plate illustrating the Egyptian alphabets. Paris, 1827.

Brown, John. *Elementa medicinae.* Preface by P. Moscati. Hildburghausen, 1794.

———. *Sämmtliche Werke.* Edited by Andreas Röschlaub. Vols. 1–2, *Anfangsgründe der Medizin.* Frankfurt am Main, 1806.

Bruce, James. *Reisen zur Entdeckung der Quellen des Nils in den Jahren 1768, 1769, 1770, 1771, 1772 und 1773.* Translated by J. J. Volkmann. Preface and notes by J. F. Blumenbach. Vol. 4. Leipzig, 1791.

Brucker, Jacob. *Historia critica philosophiae.* Vol. 3. Leipzig, 1743. Vol. 4, Part 2. Leipzig, 1744.

Buchanan, Francis. "On the Religion and Literature of the Burmas." *Asiatic Researches* 6:163–308.

Buhle, Johann Gottlieb. *Geschichte der neuern Philosophie seit der Epoche der Wiederherstellung der Wissenschaften.* 6 vols. Göttingen, 1800–1804.

* Buttman, Philipp. *Ueber den Mythos des Herakles.* A lecture presented 25 January 1810 at the commemoration of Frederick II in the Royal Academy of Sciences. Berlin, 1810.

Cavazzi, Joannes Antonius. *Historische Beschreibung der in dem unteren occidentalischen Mohrenland ligenden drey Königreichen Congo, Matamba, und Angola, und derjenigen Apostolischen Missionen so von denen P. P. Capucinern daselbst verrichtet worden.* Edited and translated by Fr. Fortunato Alamandini. Munich, 1694.

Cavazzi da Montecuccolo, Giovanni Antonio. *Istorica descrizione de' tre regni Congo, Matamba, et Angola situati nell'Etiopia inferiore occidentale e delle missioni apostoliche esercitatevi da religiosi Capuccini.* Bologna, 1687.

† *Le Chou-king, un des livres sacrés des Chinois, qui renferme les fondements de leur ancienne histoire, les principes de leur gouvernement & de leur morale: Ouvrage recueilli par Confucius.* Translated with notes by Fr. Antoine Gaubil. Revised by Joseph de Guignes. Paris, 1770.

* Cicero. *De natura deorum.* Based on the J. A. Ernesti edition, including the variorum notes from the J. Davis edition, with a critical apparatus and notes by G. H. Moser and additional notes by F. Creuzer. Leipzig, 1818.

———. *Opera.* 5 vols. Leipzig, 1737.

* Clavier, Etienne. *Mémoire sur les oracles des anciens.* Paris, 1818.

* Clement of Alexandria. *Opera omnia graece et latine quae extant.* Based on the edition by Daniel Heinsius. Cologne, 1688.

———. *Exhortation to the Heathen* and *The Stromata.* In *The Ante-Nicene Fathers,* edited by Alexander Roberts and James Donaldson, 2:163–206, 299–568. New York, 1885.

Colebrooke, Henry Thomas. "On the Duties of a Faithful Hindu Widow." *Asiatic Researches* 4:205–215.

———. "On the Philosophy of the Hindus." *Transactions of the Royal Asiatic Society* (London) 1 (1824): 19–43, 92–118, 439–466, 549–579.

———. "On the Religious Ceremonies of the Hindus, and of the Brāhmans Especially." *Asiatic Researches* 5:345–368; 7:232–287, 288–311.

———. "On the Vēdas, or Sacred Writings of the Hindus." *Asiatic Researches* 8:377–497.

† *Confucius Sinarum philosophus; sive, Scientia Sinensis, latine exposita.* Compiled by Frs. P. Intorcetta, C. Herdtrich, F. Rougemont, and P. Couplet, S.J. Paris, 1687.

† *The Works of Confucius, Containing the Original Text, with a Translation.* Vol. 1, *To Which is Prefixed a Dissertation on the Chinese Language and Character,* by Joshua Marshman. Serampore, 1809.

* Creuzer, Friedrich. *Abriss der römischen Antiquitäten zum Gebrauch bei Vorlesungen.* Leipzig and Darmstadt, 1824.

* ———. *Briefe über Homer. See* Herrmann, Martin Gottfried.

* ———. *Commentationes Herodoteae: Aegyptiaca et Hellenica.* Part I. With summaries, scholia, and variant readings of the Palatine Codex. Leipzig, 1819.

* ———. *Symbolik und Mythologie der alten Völker, besonders der Griechen.* 2d ed. 4 vols., plates. Leipzig and Darmstadt, 1819–1821.

† Delambre, Jean Joseph. *Histoire de l'astronomie ancienne.* 2 vols. Paris, 1817.

* Descartes, René. *Specimina philosophiae; seu, Dissertatio de methodo.* Translated from the French; complete text checked and in places emended by the author. New ed., carefully reviewed and corrected. Amsterdam, 1656.

————. *Meditationes de prima philosophia, in quibus Dei existentia, & animae humanae a corpore distinctio, demonstrantur: His adjunctae sunt variae objectiones doctorum virorum in istas de Deo & anima demonstrationes; cum responsionibus auctoris.* Latest ed., including additions and emendations. Amsterdam, 1663.

* ————. *Principia philosophiae.* New ed., carefully reviewed and corrected. Amsterdam, 1656.

————. *A Discourse on Method and Selected Writings.* Translated by John Veitch. New York and London, 1951. Contains: *Discourse on the Method of Rightly Conducting the Reason and Seeking Truth in the Sciences* (1637); *Meditations on the First Philosophy* (1641); *The Principles of Philosophy* (1644).

* Devīmāhātmyam. *Mārkandeyi Purāni sectio.* Edited by L. Poley, with Latin translation and annotations. Berlin, 1831.

* Dio Cassius. *Historiae Romanae quae supersunt.* Stereotype ed. Edited in accordance with the best manuscripts. 4 vols. Leipzig, 1818.

* Diodorus Siculus. *Bibliothecae historicae libri XVII.* Lyons, 1552.

* Diogenes Laertius. *De vitis, dogmatibus et apophthegmatibus clarorum philosophorum libri decem.* In Greek and Latin. Leipzig, 1759.

† Dow, Alexander. *The History of Hindostan, from the Earliest Account of Time to the Death of Akbar; Translated from the Persian of Mahummud Casim Ferishta of Delhi, Together with a Dissertation Concerning the Religion and Philosophy of the Brahmins; with an Appendix, Containing the History of the Mogul Empire, from Its Decline in the Reign of Mahummud Shaw, to the Present Times.* 2 vols. London, 1768.

Dubois, Abbé Jean Antoine. *Moeurs, institutions et cérémonies des peuples de l'Inde.* 2 vols. Paris, 1825.

Dupuis, Charles François. *Origine de tous les cultes; ou, Religion universelle.* 4 vols. Paris, 1795.

* Eichhorn, Johann Gottfried. *Einleitung in das Alte Testament.* 2d ed. Reutlingen, 1790.

* Euripides. *Hippolytus.* In Greek and Latin. Edited by G. H. Martin, from the text established by Brunk, with notes. Leipzig, 1788.

* ———. *Tragoediae octodecim.* Edited by J. Oporinus. Basel, 1544.

* Fichte, Johann Gottlieb. *Appellation an das Publikum über die durch ein Kurf. Sächs. Confiscationsrescript ihm beigemessenen atheistischen Aeusserungen: Eine Schrift, die man erst zu lesen bittet, ehe man sie konfiscirt.* Jena, Leipzig, Tübingen, 1799.

* ———. *Gerichtliche Verantwortungsschrift gegen die Anklage des Atheismus.* Jena, 1799.

* ———. *Grundlage der gesammten Wissenschaftslehre als Handschrift für seine Zuhörer.* Leipzig, 1794.

———. *Science of Knowledge (Wissenschaftslehre).* Translated by P. Heath and J. Lachs. New York, 1970.

* ———. *Das System der Sittenlehre nach den Principien der Wissenschaftslehre.* Jena and Leipzig, 1798.

* ———. "Ueber den Grund unsers Glaubens an eine göttliche Weltregierung." *Philosophisches Journal einer Gesellschaft teutscher Gelehrten* (Jena and Leipzig), edited by J. G. Fichte and I. Niethammer, vol. 8, no. 1 (1798).

———. "On the Foundation of Our Belief in a Divine Government of the Universe." In *Nineteenth-Century Philosophy,* edited by P. L. Gardiner, pp. 19–26. New York, 1969.

† ———. *Versuch einer Critik aller Offenbarung.* Königsberg, 1792.

———. *Attempt at a Critique of All Revelation.* Translated by Garrett Green. Cambridge, 1978.

————. *Gesamtausgabe.* Published by the Bavarian Academy of Sciences. Edited by R. Lauth, H. Jacob, and H. Gliwitzky. Division I. Stuttgart–Bad Cannstatt, 1964 ff.

† Forster, George. *Johann Reinhold Forster's Reise um die Welt, während den Jahren 1772 bis 1775 in dem von Seiner itztregierenden Grossbrittanischen Majestät auf Entdeckungen ausgeschickten und durch den Capitain Cook geführten Schiffe the Resolution unternommen.* Written and edited by his son and travel companion, George Forster. Translated from English by the author, with excerpts from Captain Cook's diary and other additions for the German reader, and illustrated with prints. Vol. 1. Berlin, 1778.

* Frandsen, Petrus. *Haruspices.* Berlin, 1823.

* Frank, Othmar. *De Persidis lingua et genio: Commentationes Phaosophico-Persicae.* Nuremburg, 1809.

† Fries, Jakob Friedrich. *Wissen, Glaube und Ahndung.* Jena, 1805.

* Gibbon, Edward. *The History of the Decline and Fall of the Roman Empire.* New ed. 12 vols. Leipzig, 1821.

* Görres, Joseph. *Das Heldenbuch von Iran aus dem Schah Nameh des Firdussi.* 2 vols. Berlin, 1820.

* Goethe, Johann Wolfgang von. *West-östlicher Divan.* Stuttgart, 1819.

† ————. *Wilhelm Meisters Wanderjahre; oder, Die Entsagenden: Ein Roman.* Part I. Stuttgart and Tübingen, 1821.

————. *Wilhelm Meister's Travels; or, The Renunciants: A Novel.* Translated by Thomas Carlyle. 2 vols. New York, 1901.

* ————. *Zur Farbenlehre: Des ersten Bandes erster, didaktischer Theil: Entwurf einer Farbenlehre.* Tübingen, 1810.

————. *Theory of Colours.* Translated by C. L. Eastlake. 1st ed. 1840. Reprint. Cambridge, Mass., 1970.

† ————. *Zur Naturwissenschaft überhaupt, besonders zur Morphologie: Erfahrung, Betrachtung, Folgerung, durch Lebensereignisse verbunden.* Vol. 2, Part 1, *Zur Morphologie.* Stuttgart and Tübingen, 1823.

————. *Werke.* Commissioned by Grand Duchess Sophie of Saxony. Divisions 1–2. Weimar, 1887 ff.

* Gramberg, C. P. W. *Kritische Geschichte der Religionsideen des Alten Testaments.* Preface by W. Gesenius. Vol. 1, *Hierarchie und Kultus.* Berlin, 1829. Vol. 2, *Theokratie und Prophetismus.* Berlin, 1830.

Grotius, Hugo. *De veritate religionis Christianae.* New ed. In *Operum theologicorum tomus tertius, continens opuscula diversa.* Amsterdam, 1679.

* Guigniaut, Joseph Daniel. *Sérapis et son origine: Commentaire sur les chapitres 83–84 du livre IV des Histoires de Tacite.* Paris, 1828.

* Guilhem de Clermont-Lodève, Guillaume-Emmanuel-Joseph, Baron de Saint-Croix. *Recherches historiques et critiques sur les mystères du paganisme.* 2d ed. Revised by Baron Silvestre de Sacy. 2 vols. Paris, 1817.

Haller, Albrecht von. *Versuch schweizerischer Gedichte.* 6th ed. Göttingen, 1751.

Hammer-Purgstall, Joseph von. *Geschichte der schönen Redekünste Persiens, mit einer Blüthenlese aus zweyhundert persischen Dichtern.* Vienna, 1818.

Harnisch, Wilhelm, comp. *Die wichtigsten neuern Land- und Seereisen: Für die Jugend und andere Leser bearbeitet.* 16 parts. Leipzig, 1821–1832. (= *Die wichtigsten Reisen*)

† Heeren, A. H. L. *Ideen über die Politik, den Verkehr und den Handel der vornehmsten Völker der alten Welt.* 2 vols. Göttingen, 1804–1805.

Herder, Johann Gottfried. *Aelteste Urkunde des Menschengeschlechts.* Vol. 2, containing Part 4. In Herder's *Sämmtliche Werke: Zur Religion und Theologie.* Vol. 6. Tübingen, 1806.

————. *Vom Geist der ebräischen Poesie: Eine Anleitung für die Liebhaber derselben und der ältesten Geschichte des menschlichen Geistes.* Vol. 1. Leipzig, 1787.

————. *The Spirit of Hebrew Poetry.* Translated by James Marsh. 2 vols. Burlington, Vt., 1833.

* ———. *Gott: Einige Gespräche*. Gotha, 1787. 2d ed.: *Gott: Einige Gespräche über Spinoza's System; nebst Shaftesburi's Naturhymnus*. Gotha, 1800
———. *God: Some Conversations*. Translated by F. H. Burkhardt. Indianapolis and New York, 1940.

* Herodotus. *Historiarum libri XI; Narratio de vita Homeri*. With Valla's Latin versions. Edited by H. Stephanus. Also contains Ctesias's *De rebus Persis et Indis*. 2d ed. Paris, 1592. Hegel's other edition of Herodotus lacks a Greek text: Herodotus. *Libri novem, Musarum nominibus inscripti*, trans. Lorenzo Valla. Cologne, 1562.

* Herrmann, Martin Gottfried. *Die Feste von Hellas historisch-philosophisch bearbeitet and zum erstenmal nach ihrem Sinn und Zweck erläutert*. 2 vols. Berlin, 1803.

* Herrmann, Martin Gottfried, and Friedrich Creuzer. *Briefe über Homer und Hesiodus vorzüglich über die Theogonie von Gottfried Herrmann und Friedrich Creuzer: Mit besonderer Hinsicht auf des Ersteren Dissertatio de Mythologia Graecorum antiquissima und auf des Letzteren Symbolik und Mythologie der Griechen*. Heidelberg, 1818.

* Hesiod. *Opera et dies, et Theogonia, et Clypeus. Theognidis sententiae. Sybillae carmina de Christo, quorum mentionem facit Eusebius & Augustinus. Musaei opusculum de Herone & Leandro. Orphei Argonautica, Hymni, & de Lapidibus. Phoclydis Paraenesis*. Venice, 1543.

† Hirt, Aloys. *Ueber die Bildung der aegyptischen Gottheiten*. 11 tables. Special edition published by the Royal Academy of Sciences. Berlin, 1821.

d'Holbach, Paul Henri Thiry [Boulanger, pseud.]. *Le christianisme dévoilé; ou, Examen des principes et des effets de la religion chrétienne*. London, 1756.

* ——— [Mirabaud, pseud.]. *Système de la nature ou des loix du monde physique & du monde moral*. 2d ed. 2 vols. London, 1771.

——— [Abbé Bernier, pseud.]. *Théologie portative; ou, Dictionnaire abrégé de la religion chrétienne*. London, 1768.

* Homer. *Ilias.* Stereotype ed. Edited in accordance with the best manuscripts. 2 vols. Leipzig, 1819–1821.

———. *Odyssea.* New ed. 2 vols. Leipzig and Leiden, 1820.

* Horace. *Eclogae.* Corrected and annotated by W. Baxter. Additional variant readings and notes by J. M. Gesner. 2d ed. Leipzig, 1772.

* [Hülsemann.] *Ueber die Hegelsche Lehre; oder, Absolutes Wissen und moderner Pantheismus.* Leipzig, 1829.

* Humboldt, Wilhelm. *Über die unter dem Namen Bhagavad-Gītā bekannte Episode des Mahā-Bhārata.* Paper read to the Academy of Sciences, 30 June 1825 and 15 June 1826. Berlin, 1826.

Hume, David. *Geschichte von Grossbritannien.* Translated from English. Vols. 18–20. Frankenthal, 1788.

† *Institutes of Hindu Law; or, The Ordinances of Menu, According to the Gloss of Cullūca, Comprising the Indian System of Duties, Religious and Civil, Verbally Translated from the Original Sanscrit.* Calcutta, 1794.

* Jacobi, Friedrich Heinrich. *Jacobi an Fichte.* Hamburg, 1799.

———. *Auserlesener Briefwechsel.* 2 vols. Edited by Friedrich Roth. Leipzig, 1827.

† ———. *David Hume über den Glauben; oder, Idealismus und Realismus: Ein Gespräch.* Breslau, 1787.

† ———. *Ueber die Lehre des Spinoza in Briefen an den Herrn Moses Mendelssohn.* New, enlarged ed. Breslau, 1789.

* ———. *Von den Göttlichen Dingen und ihrer Offenbarung.* Leipzig, 1811.

* ———. *Werke.* 6 vols. Leipzig, 1812–1825.

* Jäsche, Gottlob Benjamin. "Ansichten des Pantheismus nach seinen verschiedenen Hauptformen: Eine Parallele zwischen dem Alten und dem Neuen in der antidualistischen Philosophie des ῞Εν τὸ Πᾶν. *Dörptische Beyträge für Freunde der Philosophie, Litteratur und Kunst* (Dorpat and Leipzig), edited by Karl Morgenstern, 1814, no. 1 (published in 1815).

Jones, William. "On the Chronology of the Hindus." *Asiatic Researches* 2:111–147.

———. "On the Gods of Greece, Italy, and India." *Asiatic Researches* 1:221–275.

Josephus. *Des fürtrefflichen jüdischen Geschicht-Schreibers Flavii Josephi Sämmtliche Wercke.* Edited by J. F. Cotta. Tübingen, 1735.

* Kant, Immanuel. *Critik der practischen Vernunft.* Riga, 1788.

———. *Critique of Practical Reason.* Translated by L. W. Beck. New York, 1956.

† ———. *Critik der reinen Vernunft.* 2d ed. Riga, 1787.

———. *Critique of Pure Reason.* Translated from R. Schmidt's collation of the 1st (A) and 2d (B) editions by N. Kemp Smith. London, 1930.

* ———. *Critik der Urtheilskraft.* Berlin and Libau, 1790.

———. *Critique of Judgement.* Translated by J. C. Meredith. Oxford, 1952.

———. *Grundlegung zur Metaphysik der Sitten.* Riga, 1785.

———. *The Fundamental Principles of the Metaphysics of Ethics.* Translated by O. Manthey-Zorn. New York, 1938.

* ———. *Die Religion innerhalb der Grenzen der blossen Vernunft.* Königsberg, 1793.

———. *Religion within the Limits of Reason Alone.* Translated by T. M. Greene and H. H. Hudson. La Salle, Ill., 1934.

———. *Gesammelte Schriften.* Edited by the Royal Prussian Academy of Sciences. Berlin, 1900 ff.

* Klaproth, Heinrich Julius. Review of *Mémoire sur l'origine et la propagation de la doctrine du Tao, fondée par Lao-tseu,* by G. Pauthier. *Nouveau Journal Asiatique; ou, Recueil de mémoires, d'extraits et de notices relatifs à l'histoire, à la philosophie, aux langues et à la littérature des peuples orientaux* (Paris) 7 (1831): 465–493.

Köppen, Friedrich. *Ueber Offenbarung, in Beziehung auf Kantische und Fichtische Philosophie.* 2d ed. Lübeck and Leipzig, 1802.

* Lactantius. *Divinarum institutionum libri VII; De ira Dei, lib. I; De opificio Dei, lib. I; Epitome in libros suos, liber acephalos.* Edited by M. Thomasius, with notes, a comprehensive index, and Latin equivalents for Greek terms. Antwerp, 1570.

* LaPlace, Pierre Simon. *Darstellung des Weltsystems.* Translated from French by J. K. F. Hauff. 2 vols. Frankfurt am Main, 1797.

* Leibniz, Gottfried Wilhelm. *Essais de theodicée sur la bonté de Dieu, la liberté de l'homme, et l'origine du mal.* New ed., augmented by a history of the life and works of the author, by M. L. de Neufville. Amsterdam, 1734.

———. *Theodicy: Essays on the Goodness of God, the Freedom of Man, and the Origin of Evil.* Edited by Austin Farrer. Translated by E. M. Huggard from the Gerhardt edition. New Haven, 1952.

† ———. *Opera omnia.* Edited by L. Dutens. Geneva, 1768.

———. *Die philosophischen Schriften.* Edited by C. J. Gerhardt. 7 vols. Berlin, 1875–1890.

———. *Selections.* Edited by Philip P. Wiener. New York, 1951.

Lessing, Gotthold Ephraim. *Anti-Goeze; D. i. Nothgedrungene Beyträge zu den freywilligen Beyträgen des Hrn. Past. Goeze.* Braunschweig, 1778.

———. *Axiomata, wenn es deren in dergleichen Dingen gibt: Wider den Herrn Pastor Goeze, in Hamburg.* Braunschweig, 1778,

———. *Briefe, die neueste Litteratur betreffend: Geschrieben in den Jahren 1759 bis 1763.* 24 parts, index. Berlin and Stettin, 1776.

———. *Eine Duplik.* Braunschweig, 1778.

† ———. *Nathan der Weise.* Drama in five acts. 1779.

———, ed. *Zur Geschichte und Litteratur: Aus den Schätzen der Herzoglichen Bibliothek zu Wolfenbüttel.* Fourth contribution by G. E. Lessing. Braunschweig, 1777. (The author is Hermann Samuel Reimarus.)

———. *Sämtliche Schriften.* Edited by K. Lachmann. 3d ed. Revised by F. Muncker. Leipzig, 1886–1924.

* Lobeck, Christianus Augustus. *Aglaophamus; sive, De theologiae mysticae Graecorum causis libri tres.* With various fragments from the Orphic poets. 2 vols. Königsberg, 1829.

* Longinus, Dionysius. *De sublimitate.* Edited by S. F. N. More from the text established by Z. Pearce, with the editor's selection from previous commentaries and additional comments of his own. Leipzig, 1769.

* Lucian of Samosata. *Opera.* Greek and Latin. Edited in accordance with the edition of T. Hemsterhus and J. F. Reitz; with variant readings and annotations. 9 vols. Zweibrücken, 1789.

[Luther, Martin.] *Die gantze Heilige Schrift Deudsch.* Wittenberg, 1545.

† [Macartney.] *Reise der englischen Gesandtschaft an den Kaiser von China, in den Jahren 1792 und 1793: Aus den Papieren des Grafen von Macartney, des Ritters Gower and andrer Herren zusammengetragen von Sir George Staunton.* Translated from English by J. C. Hüttner. 2 vols. Zürich, 1798–1799.

† de Mailla, Joseph-Anne-Marie de Moyriac. *Histoire générale de la Chine; ou, Annales de cet empire, traduits du Tong-Kien-Kang-Mou.* 13 vols. Paris, 1777–1785.

* Maimon, Salomon. *Lebensgeschichte.* Edited by K. P. Moritz. 2 vols. Berlin, 1792.

† [Masson, Charles-François Philibert.] *Mémoires secrets sur la Russie, et particulièrement sur la fin du règne de Catherine II. et le commencement de celui de Paul I.: Formant un tableau des moeurs de St. Pétersburg à la fin du XVIIIe siècle.* 3 vols. Paris, 1800–1802.

† *Mémoires concernant l'histoire, les sciences, les moeurs, les usages, etc. des Chinois par les missionaires de Pekin.* 16 vols. Paris, 1776–1814.

* Mendelssohn, Moses. *Jerusalem; oder, Über religiöse Macht und Judentum.* Berlin, 1783.

* ———. *Morgenstunden; oder, Vorlesungen über das Daseyn Gottes.* Berlin, 1786.

† [Meyer, Johann Friedrich von.] *Die Heilige Schrift in berichtigter Uebersetzung mit kurzen Anmerkungen.* 3 vols. Frankfurt am Main, 1819.

Michaelis, Johann David. *Deutsche Uebersetzung des Alten Testaments, mit Anmerkungen für Ungelehrte.* 13 vols. 1769–1783. Part I, containing the Book of Job. Göttingen and Gotha, 1769. Part II, containing the Book of Genesis. Göttingen and Gotha, 1770.

Mill, James. *The History of British India.* 3 vols. London, 1817.

Milton, John. *Das Verlohrne Paradies.* Translated from English in free verse, with annotations, by F. W. Zacharias. 2 vols. Altona, 1760–1763.

Molière, Jean-Baptiste. *Le Bourgeois Gentil-Homme: Comédie-Ballet.* In *Les œuvres de Monsieur de Molière.* New ed. Vol. 4. Paris, 1733.

* Moritz, Karl Philipp. *Anthousa; oder, Roms Alterthümer. Ein Buch für die Menschheit. Die heiligen Gebräuche der Römer.* Berlin, 1791.

† Müller, Karl Otfried. *Geschichten hellenischer Stämme und Städte.* Vols. 2–3, *Die Dorier.* Breslau, 1824.

* ———. *Handbuch der Archäologie der Kunst.* Breslau, 1830.

† Neander, August. *Genetische Entwickelung der vornehmsten gnostischen Systeme.* Berlin, 1818.

Niebuhr, Carsten. *Voyage de M. Niebuhr en Arabie et en d'autres pays de l'orient: Avec l'extrait de sa description de l'Arabie & des observations de Mr. Forskal.* 2 vols. Switzerland, 1780. (In the Catalogue of the Hegel Library this work is cited as: Niebuhr. *Reisen durch Aegypten and Arabien, mit Karten.* 2 pts. Bern, 1779).

* Niethammer, Friedrich Immanuel. *Der Streit des Philanthropinismus und Humanismus in der Theorie des Erziehungs-Unterrichts unsrer Zeit.* Jena, 1808.

Parmenides. *See* Simplicius.

* Passalacqua, Joseph. *Catalogue raisonné et historique des antiquités découvertes en Égypte.* Paris, 1826.

Paterson, J. D. "Of the Origin of the Hindu Religion." *Asiatic Researches* 8:44–87.

* Pausanias. *Graeciae descriptio.* Edited in accordance with the best manuscripts. 3 vols. Leipzig, 1818.

† Philo. *Opera omnia graece et latine.* Edited by A. F. Pfeiffer from the text established by T. Mangey. 5 vols. 2d ed. Erlangen, 1820.

* Philostratus. *Historiae de vita Apollonii libri VIII.* Eusebius of Caesarea. *Adversus Hieroclem, qui ex Philostrati historia Apollonium Tyaneum salutori nostro Jesu Christo aequiparare contendebat, confutatio, sive apologia.* Latin translations carefully corrected against the Greek, and editorial annotations added by Gybertus Longolius [i.e., Gilbert de Longueil]. Cologne, 1532.

* Pindar. *Carmina.* Revised and edited by C. G. Heyne, with variant readings and annotations. 5 vols. Göttingen, 1798–1799. Vol 3. *Scholia in Pindari Carmina, Volumen II, Pars II: Scholia in Pythia Nemea et Isthmia.* Göttingen, 1798.

* Plato. *Opera quae extant omnia.* Latin translation by Joannes Serranus [i.e., Jean de Serres]. Edited by H. Stephanus. 3 vols. [Geneva], 1578.

* Plutarch. *Quae supersunt omnia.* Edited by J. G. Hutten, with annotations and variant readings. 14 vols. Tübingen, 1791–1804.

* Proclus. *In Platonis theologiam libri sex.* Edited by Aemilius Portus, with a short life of Proclus by Marinus Neapolitanus. Hamburg and Frankfurt am Main, 1618. Also contains *Institutio theologica.*

———. *In Platonis Timaeon commentariorum libri quinque, totius veteris philosophiae thesaurus. Et in eiusdem politices difficiliorum quaestionum omnium enarratio.* Cologne, 1534.

* Quatremère, Etienne. *Mémoires géographiques et historiques sur l'Egypte, et sur quelques contrées voisines, recueillis et extraits des manuscripts coptes, arabes, etc. de la Bibliothèque Impériale.* 2 vols. Paris, 1811.

* Racine, Jean. *Œuvres*. Vol. 3. Paris, 1817.

† *The Ramayuna of Valmeeki, in the Original Sungskrit*. Translated and annotated by William Carey and Joshua Marshman. Vol. 1. Serampore, 1806.

* *Ramayana; id est, Carmen epicum de Ramae rebus gestis*. A work of the ancient Hindu poet Valmiki. Edited by A. W. von Schlegel on the basis of a collation of manuscript codices, with a Latin translation and critical notes. Vol. 1, pt. 1. Bonn, 1829.

† Review of *Sur l'élévation des montagnes de l'Inde*, by Alexander von Humboldt. *The Quarterly Review* (London) 22, no. 44 (1820): 415–430.

† Rhode, J. G. *Die heilige Sage und das gesammte Religionssystem der alten Baktrer, Meder und Perser oder des Zendvolks*. Frankfurt am Main, 1820.

* ———. *Über Alter und Werth einiger morgenländischen Urkunden*. Breslau, 1817.

Rixner, Thaddae Anselm. *Handbuch der Geschichte der Philosophie zum Gebrauche seiner Vorlesungen*. 3 vols. Sulzbach, 1822–1823.

Robinet, Jean-Baptiste. *De la nature*. New ed. Amsterdam, 1763.

* Rosen, Fridericus. *Corporis radicum sanscritarum prolusio*. Berlin, 1826.

† ———. *Radices Sanscritae, illustratas edidit*. Berlin, 1827.

† Rosenmüller, Er. Fr. Karl. *Das alte und neue Morgenland; oder, Erläuterungen der heiligen Schrift aus der natürlichen Beschaffenheit, den Sagen, Sitten und Gebräuchen des Morgenlandes*. 6 vols. Leipzig, 1817–1820.

Ross, John. *A Voyage of Discovery, Made under the Order of the Admirality, in His Majesty's Ships Isabella and Alexander, for the Purpose of Exploring Baffin's Bay, and Enquiring into the Probability of a North-West Passage*. 2d ed. 2 vols. London, 1819.

Rousseau, Jean-Jacques. *Discours sur l'origine et les fondemens de l'inégalité parmi les hommes*. Amsterdam, 1755.

———. *Aemil; oder, Von der Erziehung*. Translated from French, with annotations. Berlin, Frankfurt am Main, Leipzig, 1762.

* Roy, Remmohon (Bramin). *Auflösung des Wedant; oder, Auflösung aller Wed's des berühmtesten Werkes braminischer Gottegelahrtheit, worin die Einheit des höchsten Wesens dargethan wird, so wie auch, dass Gott allein der Gegenstand der Versöhnung und Verehrung sein könne.* Jena, 1817.

† Rückert, Friedrich. "Mewlana Dschelaleddin Rumi." In *Taschenbuch für Damen auf das Jahr 1821,* pp. 211–248. Tübingen, 1821.

Sailer, Sebastian. *Schriften im schwäbischen Dialekte.* Edited by Sixt Bachmann. Buchau, 1819.

Saint-Croix, Baron de. *See* Guilhem de Clermont-Lodève, Guillaume-Emmanuel-Joseph, Baron de Saint-Croix.

* Schelling, Friedrich Wilhelm Joseph. "Darstellung meines Systems der Philosophie." *Zeitschrift für spekulative Physik* (Jena and Leipzig), edited by Schelling, vol. 2, no. 2 (1801).

* ———. "Philosophische Briefe über Dogmatismus und Kriticismus." *Philosophisches Journal einer Gesellschaft teutscher Gelehrter* (Neu-Strelitz), edited by F. I. Niethammer, 2, no. 3 (1795): 177–203; 3, no. 3 (1795): 173–239.

* ———. *System des transscendentalen Idealismus.* Stuttgart, 1800.

——— . *System of Transcendental Idealism* (1800). Translated by Peter Heath. Introduction by Michael Vater. Charlottesville, 1978.

* ——— . *Ueber die Gottheiten von Samothrace.* Lecture presented to the Bavarian Academy of Sciences, 12 October 1815, as a supplement to the *Weltalter.* Stuttgart and Tübingen, 1815.

——— . *Schelling's Treatise on "The Deities of Samothrace."* Translated by R. F. Brown. American Academy of Religion Studies in Religion, vol. 12. Missoula, Mont., 1977.

* ——— . *Von der Weltseele: Eine Hypothese der höhern Physik zur Erklärung des allgemeinen Organismus.* Hamburg, 1798.

† ———. *Vorlesungen über die Methode des academischen Studium.* Tübingen, 1803.

———. *On University Studies.* Translated by E. S. Morgan. Edited by Norbert Guterman. Athens, Ohio, 1966.

———. *Sämmtliche Werke.* Edited by K. F. A. Schelling. 1st Div. 10 vols. Stuttgart and Augsburg, 1856–1861.

* Schiller, Friedrich, ed. *Die Horen: Eine Monatsschrift.* Tübingen, 1795.

———. *Nationalausgabe.* Vols. 1 and 10. Weimar, 1943, 1980.

* Schlegel, August Wilhelm. *Comparaison entre la Phèdre de Racine et celle d'Euripide.* Paris, 1807.

* ———, ed. *Indische Bibliothek.* Vol. 2, no. 4. Bonn, 1827.

Schlegel, August Wilhelm, and Friedrich Schlegel, eds. *Athenäum: Eine Zeitschrift.* Vol. 1, no. 2. Berlin, 1798.

† Schlegel, Friedrich. *Über die neuere Geschichte.* Lectures presented in Vienna, 1810. Vienna, 1811.

* ———. *Ueber die Sprache und Weisheit der Indier: Ein Beitrag zur Begründung der Alterthumskunde: Nebst metrischen Uebersetzungen indischer Gedichte.* Heidelberg, 1808.

———. *Kritische Friedrich-Schlegel-Ausgabe.* Edited by Ernst Behler, with Jean-Jacques Anstett and Hans Eichner. Paderborn, Munich, Vienna, 1958 ff.

———, ed. *Lyceum der schönen Künste.* Vol. 1, pt. 2. Berlin, 1797.

† Schleiermacher, Friedrich Daniel Ernst. *Der christliche Glaube nach den Grundsätzen der evangelischen Kirche im Zusammenhange dargestellt.* 1st ed. 2 vols. Berlin, 1821–1822.

———. *Kritische Gesamtausgabe.* Div. 1, vol. 7/1-2, *Der christliche Glaube.* 1st ed. Edited by Hermann Peiter. Berlin and New York, 1980.

———. *The Christian Faith.* Translated from the 2d German ed. of 1830 by H. R. Mackintosh, J. S. Stewart, et al. Edinburgh, 1928. (= *The Christian Faith* or *Glaubenslehre*)

† [Schleiermacher, Friedrich.] *Über die Religion: Reden an die Gebildeten unter ihren Verächtern.* Berlin, 1799.

* Seneca. *Opera Philosophica.* Halle, 1762.

* ———. *Opera, quae extant omnia.* Lyons, 1555.

Sextus Empiricus. *Opera.* In Greek and Latin. *Pyrrhoniarum institutionum libri III.* Edited and translated into Latin by H. Stephanus. *Contra mathematicos, sive disciplinarum professores, libri VI. Contra philosophos libri V.* Translated by G. Hervetus. Greek texts checked against manuscript codices, Latin versions revised, and the whole annotated by J. A. Fabricius. Leipzig, 1718.

* Seybold, W. C. *Ideen zur Theologie und Staatsverfassung des höhern Alterthums.* Tübingen, 1820.

Shakespeare, William. *Schauspiele.* New ed. Translated by J. J. Eschenburg. Vol. 12. Strasbourg, 1779.

Simplicius. *Commentarii in octo Aristotelis physicae auscultationis libros cum ipso Aristotelis textu.* Venice, 1526.

* Sophocles. *Tragoediae septem.* Emended in accordance with the best available copies. Translated and annotated by R. F. P. Brunck. 2 vols. Strasbourg, 1786.

* Spinoza, Benedictus de. *Opera quae supersunt omnia.* New ed. Edited by H. E. G. Paulus, with a life of the author and some notes on the history of the writings. 2 vols. Jena, 1802–1803.

† ———. *Adnotationes ad Tractatum theologico-politicum.* Edited from the author's original manuscript by C. T. de Murr, with a preface and notes on Spinoza's writings. The Hague, 1802.

———. *Chief Works.* Translated by R. H. M. Elwes. London, 1883. Contains: *Theologico-Political Treatise* (1670); *The Ethics* (1677); *On the Improvement of the Understanding* (1677); *Correspondence.*

Stobaeus, Joannes. *Eclogarum physicarum et ethicarum libri duo.* Supplemented and corrected from manuscript codices and furnished with annotations and a Latin version by A. H. L. Heeren. Göttingen, 1792.

Suetonius. *Opera.* New edition with commentary and key to names referred to by the author, by D. K. W. Baumgarten-Crusius. 3 vols. Leipzig, 1816–1818.

* *Sybillae carmina. See* Hesiod.

Tacitus. *Opera.* New ed. by J. J. Oberlin, based on the text established by J. A. Ernesti. 2 vols. Leipzig, 1801.

* Tennemann, Wilhelm Gottlieb. *Geschichte der Philosophie.* 11 vols. Leipzig, 1798–1819.

* Terence. *Comoediae sex.* New annotated ed. by Christopherus Colerus. Frankfurt am Main, 1594.

† Tholuck, Friedrich August Gotttreu. *Blüthensammlung aus der morgenländischen Mystik nebst einer Einleitung über Mystik überhaupt und morgenländische insbesondere.* Berlin, 1825.

† [Tholuck, Friedrich August Gotttreu.] *Die Lehre von der Sünde und vom Versöhner; oder, Die wahre Weihe des Zweiflers.* Hamburg, 1823. 2d ed. 1825.

* Tholuck, Friedrich August Gotttreu. *Die speculative Trinitätslehre des späteren Orients: Eine religionsphilosophische Monographie aus handschriftlichen Quellen der Leydener, Oxforder und Berliner Bibliothek.* Berlin, 1826.

* Thucydides. *De bello Peloponnesiaco libri VIII.* Edited by H. Stephanus. Latin version based on the translation by Lorenzo Valla. Frankfurt am Main, 1594.

† Tiedemann, Dieterich. *Geist der spekulativen Philosophie.* 6 vols. Marburg, 1791–1797.

† Tuckey, J. K. *Narrative of an Expedition to Explore the River Zaire Usually Called the Congo, in South Africa, in 1816, under the Direction of Captain J. K. Tuckey, R.N.: To Which Is Added the Journal of Professor Smith.* London, 1818.

Turner, Samuel. "An Account of a Journey to Tibet." *Asiatic Researches* 1:207–220.

―――. "Copy of an Account Given by Mr. Turner, of His Interview with Teeshoo Lama at the Monastery of Terpaling, Enclosed in Mr. Turner's Letter to the Honourable the Governor General, Dated Patna, 2d March, 1784." *Asiatic Researches* 1:197–205.

―――. "Des Hauptmann Samuel Turner's Reise in Bhutan und Tibet." In Harnisch, *Die wichtigsten Reisen* 6 (Leipzig, 1824): 287–362. *See* Harnisch.

———. *An Account of an Embassy to the Court of the Teshoo Lama, in Tibet: Containing a Narrative of a Journey through Bootan, and Part of Tibet.* London, 1800.

* Volney, Constantin François de Chasseboeuf. *Les ruines; ou, Meditations sur les revolutions des empires.* 2d ed. Paris, 1798.

Voltaire. *La Bible enfin expliquée.* London, 1776.

———. *Dictionnaire philosophique.* 7 vols. In *Œuvres complètes* (1784), vols. 37–43.

———. *Examen important de Milord Bolingbroke.* In *Œuvres complètes* (1784).

* Weisse, Christian Hermann. *Darstellung der griechischen Mythologie.* Part I, *Ueber den Begriff, die Behandlung und die Quellen der Mythologie: Als Einleitung in die Darstellung der griechischen Mythologie.* Leipzig, 1828.

* ———. *Ueber das Studium des Homer und seine Bedeutung für unser Zeitalter: Nebst einem Anhange mythologischen Inhalts und einer Rede über das Verhältniss des Studiums der Geschichte zu der allgemeinen Nationalbildung.* Leipzig, 1826.

† Wilford, Francis. "An Essay on the Sacred Isles in the West, with Other Essays. III. Sweta Devi; or the White Goddess." *Asiatic Researches* 8:245–376; 9:32–243.

* Windischmann, Carl Joseph Hieronymus. *Die Philosophie im Fortgang der Weltgeschichte.* Part I: *Die Grundlagen der Philosophie im Morgenland.* Bonn, 1827–1829.

Wolff, Christian. *Philosophia moralis sive ethica, methodo scientifica pertractata.* Part 3. Halle, 1751.

———. *Philosophia prima sive ontologia methodo scientifica pertractata, qua omnis cognitionis humanae principia continentur.* New ed. Frankfurt am Main and Leipzig, 1736.

———. *Theologia naturalis methodo scientifica pertractata. Pars prior, integrum systema complectens qua existentia et attributa Dei a posteriori demonstrantur.* New ed. Frankfurt am Main and Leipzig, 1739. *Pars posterior, qua existentia et attributa Dei ex notionis entis perfectissimi et naturae animae demonstrantur.* 2d ed. Frankfurt am Main and Leipzig, 1741.

* Xenophon. *Quae extant opera.* Edited by H. Stephanus. 2d ed. [Geneva], 1581.

* ———. *Anabasis: De expeditione Cyri minoris: Feldzug nach Oberasien.* Edited by F. H. Bothe with a Greek-German index. 2d ed. Leipzig, 1818.

† *Zend-Avesta, Zoroasters lebendiges Wort, worin die Lehren und Meinungen dieses Gesetzgebers von Gott, Welt, Natur, Menschen; ingleichen Ceremonien des heiligen Dienstes der Parsen usf. aufbehalten sind.* [Translated and edited by J. F. Kleuker] from the French edition of Anquetil du Perron. 5 vols. Riga, 1776–1783. (= *Zend-Avesta,* ed. Kleuker)

The Zend-Avesta. Sacred Books of the East, 3 vols. Oxford, 1880, 1883, 1887. [= *Zend-Avesta* (SBE)]

INDEX

INDEX

NAMES AND SUBJECTS

Terms common to Hegel's philosophical vocabulary occur with great frequency in the text and are indexed on a selective basis only when a more sustained discussion of them occurs. Mythological names, and terms related to religious history and practices, are also indexed selectively. The German for key concepts is given in parentheses. The German edition contains, at the end of Part 2 (*Vorlesungen*, Vol. 4b, pp. 859–1024), a set of exhaustive indices for the complete work—biblical references, philosophical and theological concepts, mythological names, terms relating to religious practices, proper names, and personal names. These indices can be used in conjunction with the English translation by referring to the page numbers in the margins.

Immortality, 37, 166, 181,
297, 568–570, 627–628,
633n–634n
Incarnation: Buddhist/Lamaist,
570, 577, 579, 624; com-
pared in Greek and Christian
religion, 53, 85, 475–477,
756; compared in Lamaism
and Christianity, 570n; compared with worship of
human beings, 107, 108;
distinction between *Inkarnation* and *Menschwerdung*,
270, 270n; Hindu, 327,
604, 624
India, 316n
India, religion of. *See*
Hinduism
Indians. *See* Hindus
Indra, 594, 596n, 604, 624–
625, 735
Infinite (*Unendliche*), 257–259;
as abstract, 257–258; bad or
spurious (*schlechtes*), 258;
and finite, 31–32, 382;
genuine, 56, 258
Innocence (*Unschuld*), 244,
526–527
Intuition (*Anschauung*), 572
Isaiah, 9, 684n
Isis (Greek). *See* Demeter
Isis (Egyptian), 366n, 744,
745n
Islam, 4, 50, 55, 156, 158,
310, 438, 500, 564, 742

Jablonski, Paul Ernst, 744n
Jacobi, Friedrich Heinrich,
99n, 260, 261n, 574n, 575,
613n, 708, 750
Jaeschke, Walter, 1–3, 21n,
81n, 86–87
Jaga (African tribe), 277n–
278n, 295, 544–545
Jahāl-al-Dīn Rūmī, 100n,
261n, 728
Jamros, Daniel B., 24n
Jamshid, 367

Jesuit missionaries, *Mémoires*
of, 5, 299n, 547n, 548–549,
552n
Jesus Christ, 625
Jewish people: as chosen
people, 436–438, 684n;
exclusiveness of, 155, 157,
160; faith or trust of, 444–
447, 681–682; steadfastness
of, 685n
Jewish religion: anguish of,
682, 741–742; cosmological
proof in, 128–132; covenant
in, 448–451; cultus of,
152–160, 441–452, 686–
687; editorial analysis of,
18, 19–21, 48–51, 69–71,
79–82; God as creator in,
671–674, 739; Hegel's
assessment of, 443n–444n;
Hegel's early study of, 123n;
idea of God first attained in,
423n, 669; lack of freedom
in, 685n, 742; law in, 80–
81, 449–451, 684n–685n,
686–687, 742; location in
lectures of 1831, 736n;
liberating consciousness of,
443–444, 445n; oneness of
God in, 425–426, 670–671;
particularity and universality
of, 436–438, 679, 683–686,
741–742; as patriarchal
religion, 425, 687; purpose
of God in, 434–438, 678–
679; reconciliation and
sacrifice in, 451–452; relation of God and world in,
426–433, 739–740; relation
to Greek religion in, 66–68,
669; relation to the land in,
159–160, 448, 687; as
religion of the good, 738–
742; as religion of unity,
392; representation of God
in, 134–141, 153–155, 426–
438, 671–686, 739–740;
service of God in, 449–451,

ERRATA

To *Volume 1*:

Page 340, line 7, read: When Mendelssohn was urged by [the Abbot] Jerusalem to change over . . .

Page 340, note 157, lines 2–3, read: Hegel is not using "Jerusalem" as a reference to the Abbot Jerusalem but is . . .

To *Volume 3*:

Page 141, lines 20–21, read: . . . be it ever so vain—*nos prona natamus*;[210] not to have shared . . .

Page 141, note 210, read: "We swim lying on our stomachs." Possibly the meaning of this unidentified aphorism is that, no matter how vain, frivolous or conceited innocence may be, in fact, just as a swimmer looks downward and cannot see far ahead, so the innocent person does not share in the truth of spirit and in that sense is sinful. This aphorism may contain an allusion to Is. 25:11, an ambiguous text, which in medieval tradition was interpreted as equating the activity of swimming with the plight of the damned ("he [Moab?] will spread out his hands in the midst of it [a dung-pit?] as a swimmer spreads his hands out to swim; but the Lord will lay low his pride . . .").

Page 193, note 78, read: This is an allusion to Goethe's *Die Braut von Corinth*, vv. 120–123.